International Encyclopedia of the
SOCIAL
SCIENCES

International Encyclopedia of the

SOCIAL SCIENCES

DAVID L. SILLS EDITOR

VOLUME 2

The Macmillan Company & The Free Press

International Encyclopedia of the SOCIAL SCIENCES

B

[CONTINUED]

BANKING, CENTRAL

Central banking, the function of central banks, consists essentially of the exercise of the public duty of influencing—by regulation, persuasion, or market operation—the behavior of banks and other financial intermediaries in a country. Although they have antecedents as private institutions in the economic development of a few countries, central banks are now primarily public institutions for implementing economic policies of governments. They are appropriate to the Western-type economies; in the communist countries, where economic activity is more comprehensively organized by governments, there is little scope for central banking, although institutions described as central banks exist. In true central banking the public interest is universally paramount, although for historical and other reasons there is some clinging to vestigial private forms and some insistence on a peculiar independence from the central machinery of government.

The activity of central banking emerged gradually from attempts by bankers to protect themselves by organized action and attempts by governments to ensure that monetary conditions serve the purposes of financial policy (at first) and general economic policy (later); this twofold origin is reflected in the formal organization of central banks as banks and in their ultimate subjection to the sovereign power in the state. Before 1900, the development of central banking was almost entirely empirical. Ideas on the subject sprang largely from the efforts of the Bank of England to deal with practical problems; there were also important experiences in the United States before 1836 and in

Europe at times during the nineteenth century. Although some aspects were discussed in official inquiries, in English pamphlet literature (W. Bagehot's *Lombard Street*, 1873, being the classic example), and in European controversy on the issue of bank notes, systematic thought on central banking in recognizably modern form can be dated from the United States controversy and public inquiry from which the Federal Reserve System emerged in 1913.

The development of thought received further impetus from the problems of monetary reconstruction in the years immediately following World War I; it was in this phase that the central bank was seen as the independent controller of the supply of money, and therefore as the custodian of its value against the assaults of improvident ministers of finance. Incidental to the rehabilitation of the monetary systems of countries that had passed through extreme inflations, new central banks were established and older institutions were reconstructed and explicitly charged with the function of central banking.

Since 1945 there has been a further spate of new central banks, especially in countries emerging from the breakup of colonial empires. In this latest phase, in these and other underdeveloped economies, central banks have been seen as part of the administrative machinery for speeding economic growth. There has also been a disposition to regard a central bank as a symbol of economic independence in reaction against the tutelage of the colonial period. In the more highly developed economies, the emergence of more positive and more complex economic policies (such as "full employment") has tended to make the objectives of cen-

1

tral banks more complex and their operations more extensive.

Early philosophy.   Because central banking grew out of the attempts of practical men to deal with situations arising in the business world, the historical theories of central banking have had little logical relationship with each other, although all have left their mark on the broad body of ideas current among central bankers in various countries. Throughout the earliest phase the "stand-by" theory was predominant: the central bank was a large institution continuously but cautiously engaged in the ordinary business of banking, but having a public duty to prevent, by its occasional aid to other financial operators, the collapse of the structure of credit. In fulfillment of this duty—a duty that served alike the needs of government finance and of the banking community—the central bank emerged as the "lender of last resort." This function as lender of last resort remains a cardinal feature of central banking; from it much else has developed, including powers of control more continuous than anything envisaged in the pure stand-by theory.

Emergence of the central bank as lender of last resort and as a curb on the lending practices of commercial bankers was closely associated with, and sometimes preceded by, its emergence as "the bankers' bank," in the sense of allowing the commercial banks to keep their own banking accounts with itself. In London, this development arose primarily from the strength of the Bank of England as the government's banker, enjoying privileges won in return for its substantial help to a needy government in time of war. The prestige of this privileged body, combined with its business as banker to the government, gave bank notes issued by it a circulation displacing, in London, the notes of other bankers. Both because other banks had continuous business with it as the government's banker and because its notes were in such demand, other London banks soon found it advantageous, and eventually vital, to keep accounts at the Bank of England. The Bank had become the bankers' bank. The other banks found it convenient to settle clearing differences by transferring Bank of England debts (at first notes and later deposit balances), and the Bank gained further prestige.

There were analogous developments in some European financial centers, but slower development of the banking habit on the Continent, and particularly the absence of such extreme financial centralization as that of London in the English economy, made the process slower and more dependent on deliberate centralization of the note issue. In the United States and other countries with no effective central bank before 1900, there was no analogous evolutionary process; instead, there has been simple application, by legislative fiat, of the theory that the central bank must be the bankers' bank and lender of last resort. This twofold relationship with the commercial banks gives the central bank, incidentally, a twofold sanction: a recalcitrant bank would be unable to count upon help in time of trouble, and at any time its business could be drastically inconvenienced by enforced closure of its account at the central bank. This double sanction remains important: its existence, although not often mentioned, is as important as any legislative sanction in giving force to the moral suasion that has become such an important part of the central bank's practice in England and elsewhere.

Stand-by theory.   In its strictest form the stand-by theory of central banking leaves the central bank comparatively inactive at ordinary times: the central bank comes importantly into play only on rare crisis occasions, when it has to save the banking system from collapse. A more sophisticated form of this theory appeared in the controversies leading to the establishment of the Federal Reserve System. The pre-1913 banking system of the United States, lacking a central bank, was alleged —perhaps without adequate justification—to lack the "elasticity" desirable for seasonal and other variations in the "needs of trade." Coinciding with the traditional banking view that the safest lending is that which provides for the legitimate needs of trade, the demand for elasticity was responsible for the doctrine that the reserve banks should adopt the passive role of standing ready to rediscount good commercial paper when commercial banks, finding themselves unable to meet their customers' requirements for finance of current trade, brought paper to the reserve banks. On this view, although it was a stand-by theory of central banking, the central bank was expected to be operating continuously, and not only at periods of incipient crisis, to meet the continually varying needs of the economy.

Stand-by theories of central banking, of varying sophistication, continue to be held in some quarters, although rarely explicitly. The attitude is consistent with the central bank's taking continuous interest in the "quality" of credit granted by various financial institutions; this is a side of central banking more systematically developed since 1935. It has received added impetus from the policy, important in the underdeveloped countries, of promoting healthy financial institutions to facilitate the growth of the economy.

Regulator of credit. The second main strand of development in central banking has its roots in the Bank of England's preoccupation, over a long period, with the connection between the terms at which it lent to customers and its power to maintain convertibility of its notes into gold at a fixed rate. Into discussions of this practical problem the theoretical ideas of economists were woven early in the nineteenth century. Throughout this century development flowed, however, rather from efforts of practical men than from economic theorists; but in the twentieth century the economists have taken a leading part in the formulation of ideas on the duty of the central bank as the regulator of the price and quantity of credit. From the first, both theorists and practical central bankers have regarded the price (the rate of discount or interest) and the quantity as being interdependent: regulating the price has implied regulating the quantity, and regulating the quantity has implied regulating the price. In the two major countries in which central banking has been most consciously developed —Britain and the United States—the emphasis has been different. In Britain the emphasis has nearly always been on regulation of the rate of interest, whereas in the United States the emphasis has been rather on regulation of the quantity of credit.

British experience. The view that control of the quantity of money is the prime function of the central bank derives directly from the classic debate in Britain—the Bullionist controversy—during the Napoleonic wars. The Bank of England began to think of control of the volume of its own lending (with important influence on the total supply of credit) as the principal means of protecting its gold reserve and maintaining the gold standard. This policy (always liable to modification in crisis, when the Bank had, as lender of last resort, to *increase* its own lending to avert a collapse in the supply of credit) soon led to the device of manipulation of the discount rate (Bank Rate), which was destined to alter the whole complexion of English central banking.

The movement of the Bank of England's discount rate, or Bank Rate, was at first seen simply as a practical banker's method for protecting his cash reserve against the effects of unusual demands for credit. To raise Bank Rate was a less abrupt alternative to outright refusal of customers' requirements, and it was at first seen in this light of a more tolerable and less damaging way of rationing credit and so of limiting any demand for gold in exchange for notes. Theorists were quick to connect this practical view with quantity theory views [*see* MONEY, *article on* QUANTITY THEORY] of the determination

of price levels: a rise in Bank Rate, enforcing limitation of the volume of credit, caused prices to fall, thus both reducing the demand for gold for circulation and, by improving the balance of trade, eliminating the demand for gold for export. Correspondingly, when its gold reserve (the Bank's "cash" reserve) was unnecessarily large, Bank Rate could be reduced, encouraging expansion of credit and rising prices. This simple association of Bank Rate movements with the behavior of prices, and so with the maintenance of the gold standard, remained for more than a century the mainstream of orthodoxy on the working of monetary systems. From it flowed the view that central banks could and should regulate their monetary systems by manipulation of discount rates.

Whether the English—or any other—monetary system ever did work like this is unlikely, although doubtless there was always an element of truth in the theory. Certainly the English economy in the second quarter of the nineteenth century, with its immense dependence on a speculative export trade and a connected but equally speculative import trade, both largely dependent on mercantile credit, was an economy unusually sensitive to the price and quantity of credit. The association of rising discount rates with the imminence of an extreme liquidity crisis—always liable to occur in pre-Bagehot England—was another factor enhancing the responsiveness of the price level to the movement of Bank Rate. Both these circumstances were, however, fading as the nineteenth century went on, while the power of the Bank to maintain the gold standard by manipulating Bank Rate grew beyond question.

This extraordinary power of Bank Rate was based on the position of London as an international financial center. In the first decades of the use of Bank Rate, it had already been noticed that a rise of rates in London deterred the discounting of international bills in London and attracted some foreign money into the purchase of bills in London. This influence on international movement of short-term capital grew with London's importance as an international financial center, and after about 1870 this effect of Bank Rate changes was so much more obvious than any other that it came to be regarded as almost the whole mechanism. The Bank saw its central duty as the maintenance of the gold standard, which it could protect by raising Bank Rate to attract short-term money and to repel short-term borrowers whenever the gold reserve was running down. The success of this policy depended partly on the disposition, in that period, of some of the principal European central banks to maintain stable discount rates, so that the *absolute* movements in London implied relative international change.

Throughout the remaining decades before 1914, this manipulation of Bank Rate remained the Bank of England's principal function, such open-market operations as it engaged in being usually designed to ensure that the discount rates ruling in the market remained close to the official Bank Rate. Open-market operations were said "to make Bank Rate effective," a phrase that underlined the importance attached to short interest rates, to the exclusion of any repercussions of Bank Rate on the internal economy. Indeed, in such discussion of the system as there was in these decades, the possibility that a high Bank Rate would have effects on industry and trade was regarded rather as an incidental disadvantage than as an integral part of the mechanism of international economic adjustment. The importance attached to maintenance of the gold standard by differential movements in discount rates bit deeply into the philosophy of practical central bankers. This emerges in the correspondence between Montagu Norman of the Bank of England and Benjamin Strong of the Federal Reserve Bank of New York, where development of a short-money market in New York is seen as a prerequisite of an international gold standard in which gold reserves—and so internal credit conditions—are seen as protected from international exchange disequilibria by differential movements in short rates. This strand of thought, besides influencing the development of central banking in the United States, also lay behind the wish of Montagu Norman to see money markets develop as an essential framework for central banking in the British Dominions and elsewhere. Much of the recent fostering of new money markets has its roots in this notion of how an international gold standard should be managed by central banks on the pre-1914 Bank of England pattern.

U.S. experience.   The development of the Bank of England's functions in the pre-1914 period had some influence on the American discussions leading up to the establishment of the Federal Reserve System in 1913–1914; but a more powerful influence was the desire to provide directly for avoidance of the supposed (and perhaps real) disadvantages of the existing monetary system under the National Bank Acts. The new system was to operate as lender of last resort, and so save the United States from the periodic breakdowns that had characterized the banking history of previous decades; but it was to go further, and provide an elastic system responsive to "the needs of trade" as manifested in the supply of good commercial paper in the commercial banks. It was also—in further protection against periodic breakdown, and to reduce the need to adjust internally in the face of an international disequilibrium—to pool the reserves. In the light of subsequent developments, it is instructive to note that the possibilities and aims of open-market operations did not feature prominently either in the preliminary discussions or in the early history of the system itself.

The new system gradually got on its feet during World War I, especially in developing banking and in conducting foreign exchange business for the government. In the immediate postwar phase, it found itself confronted with an inflationary situation, and in dealing with this the Federal Reserve System relied mainly on a steep rise in discount rates. The use of this weapon—and the system had, at this juncture, no effective alternative—seemed appropriate not only in the light of the pre-1914 Bank of England practice but also in the light of economists' views, now focused on this aspect of economic policy and henceforward exercising more influence on central bank thought.

Development of theory.   Stemming directly from the quantity theory and the theory of the international price mechanism as formulated by the economists, and enlivened by controversies on the effects of changes in the production of the precious metals, monetary theory had in the first decades of the twentieth century attracted further interest from economists' attempts to penetrate the mysteries of the trade cycle. Fisher in the United States, Marshall in Cambridge, Wicksell and Cassell in Sweden, and Fanno in Italy were prominent in developing this theoretical background of the first postwar policies of central banks. The grafting of this theoretical work on to the notions of the central bankers themselves, deriving from the practices of the immediate prewar period, can be seen in the English Cunliffe Report, of 1918. This report, aimed at the elimination of inflation and restoration of the international gold standard, pinpointed the central bank's discount rate (Bank Rate) as the proper weapon. In advocating the use of Bank Rate, the Cunliffe Report concentrated not, as might have been supposed from prewar practice alone, on its influence on international capital movements, but on its influence in reducing the volume and use of credit internally, thus causing reductions in prices and employment.

The functions of central banks were now much under review; central banking became for the first time fully self-conscious; and the theory of the internal effects of Bank Rate changes quickly gained influence in many countries of the world. When, in the 1920s, new central banks were founded, or old ones were rechartered, discount rate was accorded the highest importance, even in countries where it could have little relevance to its traditional field of international capital movements.

In Britain, where the practical men found in its prewar success a reason for reliance on Bank Rate, and where it indeed still had some relevance to international capital movements, Bank Rate policy was given a new lease on life as the principal business of the central bank. Simultaneously, there was a great burst of interest among the theorists, especially Hawtrey and Keynes, in central banking in general and Bank Rate in particular. Hawtrey stressed the direct impact of Bank Rate on demand for working capital, while Keynes, along Wicksellian lines, stressed indirect influence on the demand for fixed capital goods. Whether they leaned to Hawtrey or to Keynes, all alike among the economists and practical men came to think of Bank Rate as having a pivotal place in the control of the internal situation of prices and employment; the conduct of the central banks was therefore of great interest in interpreting the difficulties of the restored international gold standard and in evolving national policies for stimulating revival after the breakdown of that standard.

Extension of powers.   In the United States there was a similar trend in thought, but the upshot in practical central banking took rather a different turn, largely as a result of the radically different situation in which the Federal Reserve System found itself. The early postwar inflation, which the system had fought by high discount rates and other hindrances to the expansion of credit, was soon over, and the international trading position brought to the United States an unnecessarily large gold reserve. In an effort to overcome the technically weak position in which the reserve banks found themselves, the system stumbled into a great extension (from about 1922–1923) in its open-market operations. The effect of these operations on the reserves of member banks was at once realized and arrangements were made within the system to coordinate the open-market operations. This was the beginning of the Open Market Committee, now the effective policy-making body in the system. Thanks to the strength of classical views on changes in the quantity of money, the open-market operations quickly came to be regarded as a fairly direct way of operating on the internal price and employment situation, and not, as analogous operations in London had traditionally been, as merely technical devices for enforcing the central bank's

discount rate. With its strong balance of payments and excessive gold reserve, the Federal Reserve System was then able to develop its open-market operations, *with discount rate policy in support,* for the purpose of stabilizing the price level, this being regarded as the most effective way of averting cyclical fluctuations in output and employment. From some points of view, this radical development of American monetary policy, dating from about 1923, can be considered the beginning of genuine central banking. In the sense of there being avowed recognition of a complex of public (noncommercial) objectives, and a final break from reliance on semiautomatic indicators within the central bank's asset structure, this is indeed the beginning of the self-conscious, discretionary central banking we know today.

The new turn in central banking in the United States was watched with great interest by authorities in other countries; along with the new British interest in the internal effects of Bank Rate, the American open-market operations became prominent in the literature of central banking. This literature included works by Keynes (*Treatise on Money*, 1930), Hawtrey, and leading United States economists both inside and outside the Federal Reserve System; there were important official inquiries in the United States (especially the "stabilization" inquiry), in Britain (the "Macmillan" Committee on Finance and Industry), and in the British Dominions. Much of this academic and official literature belongs to the restored gold standard period (1925–1931) and takes an international standard for granted.

Later, after the 1931 breakdown, central banks were also seen as advisers to governments on foreign exchange questions and as official operators in the foreign exchange markets. In the 1940s these functions were commonly extended to include administration of foreign exchange restrictions, and since 1945 the establishment of the International Monetary Fund and the elaboration of international cooperation generally have meant that frequent contacts with other central banks form an important function of a central bank.

In many countries, the disasters of the early 1930s prompted sharper assertion of the ultimate authority of political ministers for monetary policy and therefore, implicitly if not explicitly, for the activity of central banks. Another effect was extension of the technical powers of central banks, in the hope that a broader range of weapons would enable central banks more effectively to stem the contraction of bank credit in a slump. In the United States, where the system had proved a broken reed in the slump, no great change occurred in constitutional relationships, but the centripetal forces in the Federal Reserve System became stronger, changes were made in the power of the reserve banks to act as lenders of last resort, power to vary reserve ratios was introduced, and the system was given some control over stock market credit. Throughout the world, the crisis had the effect of shaking up thought on central banking, and it became normal to regard every country—or almost every country—as needing a central bank that would pursue a complex of aims with a wide range of technical weapons.

The central banks established since 1945—most of them in the emergent countries of Asia and Africa—have therefore been based on the view that the main business of a central bank is to control the monetary system in a way conducive to the broad economic policies of government (high levels of employment, economic growth, stable prices, foreign exchange stability, etc.) by exercising the following powers: (1) action as lender of last resort at an announced rate of interest (Bank Rate); (2) open-market operations; (3) fixing reserve requirements for commercial banks; (4) supervision of commercial banking; (5) banker to the government (generally involving important functions in relation to government debt); (6) adviser to the government on foreign exchange policy; (7) custodian of the country's international reserves; (8) administrator of foreign exchange restrictions; and (9) dealer in foreign currencies and gold.

The relative importance attached to these powers varies greatly from country to country, in reflection of the varying histories, institutions, and prevailing economic doctrines in the different countries.

Regulation of credit. Importance is universally attached to the power of the central bank to avert a breakdown of the system, acting as lender of last resort. In most countries, however, this is no mere safety valve for operation in rare emergencies; the central bank commonly lends considerable amounts to banks at penalty rates of interest, and bankers therefore take note of the rates announced by the central bank. An elaboration of this Bank Rate weapon is the use of a *scale* of interest rates, rates higher than the basic rate being charged for successive tranches of assistance; or higher rates may be related not to the amount of lending but to some recent increase in the assisted bank's lending to its customers.

Similar elaboration has been seen in reserve requirements, which are usually in the form of cash in hand and/or deposits at the central bank, but occasionally include also certain government securities. Normally these requirements are fixed as percentages of prescribed deposit liabilities. Until the 1930s such percentages were unvarying, but most central banks now have power to vary the percentages and other features of the requirements; in some European countries such variations have become frequent, especially where the central bank encounters technical difficulty in the use of open-market operations to vary the absolute levels of reserves available to the commercial banks. In addition to the basic percentage, a commercial bank may be required to make deposits (at the central bank) proportional to its "excess" lending to customers, or certain groups of customers; this elaboration of reserve requirements is particularly useful in action against an inflation that is being obviously fed by bank lending in particular directions.

Outside Britain and the United States, the scope for open-market operations (the immediate object of which is control of the absolute level of bank reserves) has been narrowly limited by the absence of active markets in the classes of securities (primarily government short-term bonds and first-class short-term commercial paper) in which central banks are willing to deal. The Bank of Canada, however, has been outstandingly successful in fostering a market and then operating in it to control bank reserves. The National Bank of Belgium has also advanced notably along this line; so, in narrower limits, has the Netherlands Bank, but the central bank of West Germany has been notably impeded by the difficulty of any large-scale operations. In some other European countries, and in the emergent countries of Africa and Asia, central banks have not been able to do anything at all with this traditional weapon.

Central banks universally act as bankers for their governments, although the extent of these duties varies from one country to another. In some European countries this banker–customer relationship has allowed the authorities to operate on the reserve position of the commercial banks, in that the retention of an unusually large balance in the government's account at the central bank has effectively prevented growth (from other origins such as influx of gold) in the reserves of the commercial banks, and vice versa.

As the government's banker, the central bank advises the government on debt operations; and it has become usual for the government in such operations to heed the central bank's view of the monetary repercussions of the debt operations. Usually the actual management of the debt is in the central bank's hands; even where, as in the United States, it is deliberately kept out of the bank's hands, there is cooperation between bank and Treasury.

Historically, some central banks established themselves largely by gaining from the government —in return for some financial support—privileges of note issue, which allowed them to become the principal, and sometimes the sole, issuers of bank notes in the country. Under nineteenth-century conditions, high importance came to be attached to control of the note issue, and the tendency in some countries has been to concentrate the note issue exclusively in the central bank. With the development of commercial banks and other credit institutions, the note issue has lost its former pivotal position, but management of the note issue remains one of the important routine functions of the central bank.

International functions. Under the gold standard conditions prevailing in the late nineteenth century and the early twentieth century, the notes issued by the central bank were freely convertible into gold (at fixed rates) and gold into notes, and the holding of a gold reserve—eventually the country's principal or only gold reserve—by the central bank was thus incidental to its function as issuer of notes. After the breakdown of the gold standard in 1931, foreign exchange rates became flexible and matters of great political interest, and central banks became more active in foreign exchange markets. Foreign exchange restrictions then and later were administered by, or in consultation with, central banks. Under the International Monetary Fund system ruling since 1946, central banks have been responsible for maintaining the foreign exchange rates within the agreed narrow limits, and in some countries (notably England) they have been active in futures markets in foreign currencies. With the development of international monetary cooperation throughout the postwar period, this side of central banking has been accepted as an essential part of management of a country's monetary system. It is significant that in the United States discussion of foreign exchange business has become, alongside domestic open-market operations and discount rates, the regular business of the Federal Open Market Committee.

In the 1920s, in the Sterling Area, contact with the new central banks in the British Dominions was cultivated by Montagu Norman, governor of the Bank of England; since 1939 the contacts and cooperation between the central banks (now much more numerous) of the Sterling Area have been continuous. Between European central banks (including the Bank of England) contacts have been developed especially in the monthly meetings of the Bank for International Settlements at Basel. European central bank cooperation received great impetus in the management of the European Payments Union; and the arrangements of the European Common Market, under the Treaty of Rome, involve consultations that may develop into concerted action.

Varied philosophies. While these international functions of central banks have been rapidly developing in the same direction in all countries, and the pattern of technical powers of domestic operation has been becoming almost common form throughout the world, the philosophy of central banks has shown little sign of falling into a common pattern. Only a systematic survey of a large number of countries would fully expose the range of ideas; the more important ideas can, however, be found in the development of central banking in the United States and in England.

The Federal Reserve. In the United States, since 1951, Federal Reserve control has been directed primarily at the availability of credit. The reserve requirements of the commercial banks, fixed by the Federal Reserve, are mostly held stable, and the excess reserves of commercial banks increased, and their indebtedness at the reserve banks decreased, by purchases of short-term paper in the market, whenever an expansion of credit has been thought appropriate, and vice versa. Movements of the discount rate have been comparatively rare: when expansionist forces in the economy pull market rates of interest up, so that banks are inclined to lend freely even when their reserve positions are tight, the Reserve System raises the discount rate; correspondingly, the Reserve System reduces its rates, in times of slack trade, in order to reinforce the stimulus of easy reserve conditions in the banking system.

The open-market operations through the earlier years of this period were ordinarily confined to short-term government paper. Federal Reserve authorities held that this sufficed for their purpose, since their concern was with member bank reserves and not with the structure of interest rates. This was the famous "bills only" doctrine; in support, it was further argued that any proper effects on longer-term interest rates would be transmitted from the short end of the interest rate spectrum by the normal arbitrage adjustments of a free market, and that official intervention at the long end of the market would almost certainly give rise to false expectations and so would undesirably distort the structure of interest rates.

At the end of the 1950s the development of a serious balance-of-payments problem in the United

States destroyed the simplicity of aims of monetary policy. Conflict appeared between the internal aim of promoting full employment in a growing economy and the external aim of maintaining the international demand for dollars; the Reserve System was then forced to attempt a reconciliation of easy credit conditions and steady low long-term interest rates with some rise in short-term rates. Under the pressure of this conflict, the bills-only doctrine gave way and the authorities began to operate on a large scale in medium-term and long-term securities. Whether they succeeded in making the *structure* of interest rates different from what it would have been is much disputed; the facts are inconclusive.

This modification of Federal Reserve doctrine, under the pressure of events, nevertheless leaves unchanged the position that the system's crucial powers are considered to be, in open-market operations, the fixing of reserve ratios for the member banks, and the fixing of the discount rates at which member banks can, by borrowing at the reserve banks, replenish their reserves. It is by the exercise of these powers that the Reserve System conditions the attitude of the commercial banks in lending to business firms throughout the country, and this is regarded as the main duty of the system.

In addition to these general methods of regulating the banking system, the Federal Reserve System has special powers to regulate the credit terms on which transactions in stock market securities are financed. The system was given these powers to enable it to attack directly any repetition of the 1928–1929 stock market boom. At times the system has been authorized to prescribe terms on which installment credit and certain real estate credit could be extended, and also to encourage lenders to restrict other types of credit voluntarily. Since 1951, although the stock market credit regulations have been used, all these possibilities of "selective" credit control have been rather out of fashion in the United States. This has been partly because the Federal Reserve authorities have felt themselves exposed to political pressures from sectional interests hurt by such controls. But the attitude has also been partly due to the confidence the Reserve System has felt in its broader powers to control the banking system and its belief that this is the proper business of the central bank. In many other countries, where the central bank has less confidence in its general powers, comparable measures of selective credit control have been greatly developed since 1945.

Another important activity of the Federal Reserve System is in the foreign exchange market. This activity, begun during World War I, was given new impetus by the events of the middle 1930s, and has been greatly developed since the International Monetary Fund was established and especially as part of the intensified international monetary cooperation that characterized the years 1958 to 1963.

Finally, the Federal Reserve System has extensive powers of inspection of its member banks. These powers have existed from the outset, and have been exercised not for direct support of the system's monetary policy but for the promotion of "sound" commercial banking.

For its own guidance in exercising all these functions, the Reserve System maintains a distinguished research division. The material produced by this division, besides being used internally, is in large part published. This is part of the effort of the system to foster an informed public opinion, an objective also sought by the efforts of the system's governors and officials to keep in touch with the banking and commercial communities all over the country.

The Bank of England. During the period 1951 to 1963, the functioning of the Bank of England has been quite different from that of the Federal Reserve System. The difference has been mainly due to the constant preoccupation of the Bank of England with the balance of international payments, a preoccupation that reinforced the traditional primacy of Bank Rate. At first the tradition itself was important, in that the use of Bank Rate affected international confidence in sterling and so had useful effects on international capital flows. Later, especially after 1958, Bank Rate operated in the traditional way of regulating international interest rate differentials. Although the Bank was moving Bank Rate primarily for the sake of influencing international capital movements, it has also entertained some hope that the changes in Bank Rate would affect the pressure of internal spending; in the 1950s these two objectives did not conflict.

Open-market operations have been further developed, particularly at the long-term end of the market. In the short-term market there has been no important departure from the pre-1939 and wartime technique. The Bank of England has operated to keep short-term rates in the desired relationship with Bank Rate; since 1951, this control has included action as lender of last resort ("front door" operations) as well as trading at rates below Bank Rate ("back door" operations). The implication of this technique is that the commercial banks' liquid assets ratio (conventionally "the 30 per cent ratio") rather than the cash ratio (8 per cent) has been the fulcrum for central bank influence on commercial bank liquidity. This has given new importance to operations in longer-term securities. These operations, carried out on the stock exchange by the Government Broker under daily instruction from the Bank, are at once the technical channel for management of the national debt and a device for operating on the reserve positions of the commercial banks. In effect, the Bank increases bank liquidity when the Government Broker buys bonds and decreases bank liquidity when he sells bonds. Throughout most of the postwar period, the desire of the authorities has been to reduce bank liquidity by selling more bonds and longer bonds, and to replace Treasury bills or very short bonds: this policy is usually referred to as "funding."

In pursuing its funding policy, the Bank has tried to avoid appearance of manipulation of market prices of securities. Unfortunately, since the Bank's policy on short-term rates tended over the 1950s to cause a gradual rise in long-term rates, the Bank was for long periods operating in a falling market and found itself unable to sell any large volume of longer-term bonds. It therefore continued to be embarrassed by the high level of liquid assets in the commercial banks. Concerned that this could add to inflationary pressures, the Bank, until 1960, resorted to increasingly stern instructions, of an informal kind, limiting lending by the commercial banks. Such instructions have been easy to use in England, where the banking system is characterized by geographical, political, and intellectual concentration. Complaints that these controls were ineffective and unfair, because as lenders the banks are competing with a variety of other financial intermediaries, have been met by extension of the range of financial intermediaries to which "requests" are addressed by the Bank of England.

Another innovation precipitated by the relative failure of the funding policy has been the imitation of a device common in other central banks, including the Federal Reserve: this is the variation of percentage reserve requirements imposed on the commercial banks. Throughout the 1950s, the Bank of England adhered to the percentages evolved by the commercial practices of the London Clearing banks: a fixed 8 per cent cash rate and a minimum of 30 per cent liquid assets. In 1960, however, a fresh bout of restriction was decided upon, at a time when the Bank's funding operations had still not entirely eliminated the excess liquidity of the commercial banks. The Bank raised the reserve requirements, eventually by 3 per cent, by requiring

the banks to make "special deposits" at the Bank of England. Two aspects of this special deposits system are noteworthy. First, the arrangements were made without any legal change, and the details were agreed upon between the Bank and the commercial banks. Second, although at the outset the banks were given no instructions as to how to adapt themselves to the raised requirements, when the weapon was pressed furthest (to 3 per cent) the banks were told precisely how they were to react. The new device had already become a piece of ritual, and the really effective step was the direct instruction to the banks on their lending policies. As much as ever before, the English authorities rely on moral suasion as a major technique.

When relaxation became appropriate in 1962–1963, the special deposits were reduced (by stages) to zero, and then the 30 per cent liquid assets ratio was reduced to 28 per cent. Announcement of this change implicitly left open the possibility of further flexibility in reserve requirements.

The Bank of England has also during the postwar period shown willingness to consider long-term interest rates as its proper concern. Until about 1955, the Bank's attitude was that its direct responsibility in interest rates was limited to the short end. This did not imply any denial of the Wicksell–Keynes view of long rates as instruments for controlling, via fixed investment, the pressure of total demand; rather it was that the Bank thought of itself as influencing long rates only through its action at the short end of the market (including both Bank Rate policy and its action on bank liquidity). From about 1957, however, the Bank began to pay some regard, in its operations in the gilt-edged market, to the possible effects of these operations on long rates. This shift of emphasis did not, however, go very far, and there appears to have been some retreat from it in 1962–1963.

Until the postwar period, the Bank of England was an extremely secretive body. At first this was because its business was essentially that of a private banker, but the tradition continued long after its public duties became paramount. In the postwar period, this attitude was strongly and persistently attacked, and a change has been evident. This change, associated with an effort to improve the economic information on which policies may be based, is to be seen in the Bank's quarterly bulletin. Thus, both the world's leading central banks now appear to accept the view that an informed public opinion is the surest foundation for monetary policy.

The developments in the functioning of the Bank

of England, described in these paragraphs, indicate that England has gone appreciably further than the United States in accepting the view that both the ends and the means of central banking are multiple and that there can therefore not be any golden rule for its conduct.

R. S. SAYERS

[*See also* MONEY; MONETARY POLICY; *and the articles under* INTERNATIONAL MONETARY ECONOMICS.]

BIBLIOGRAPHY

ASCHHEIM, JOSEPH 1961 *Techniques of Monetary Control.* Baltimore: Johns Hopkins Press. → The best detailed study of central banking techniques but almost exclusively related to American practice.

BANK FOR INTERNATIONAL SETTLEMENTS 1963 *Eight European Central Banks.* New York: Praeger. → Shows how central bank officials see the institutions in which they work.

BURGESS, WARREN R. 1927 *The Reserve Banks and the Money Market.* New York: Harper.

CHANDLER, LESTER V. 1958 *Benjamin Strong: Central Banker.* Washington: Brookings Institution.

CLAY, HENRY 1957 *Lord Norman.* New York: St. Martins.

COMMISSION ON MONEY AND CREDIT 1961 *Money and Credit: Their Influence on Jobs, Prices, and Growth.* Englewood Cliffs, N.J.: Prentice-Hall.

CRICK, WILFRED F. 1965 *Commonwealth Banking Systems.* Oxford: Clarendon.

Federal Reserve Bulletin. → Published since 1915 by the Board of Governors of the Federal Reserve System.

GOLDENWEISER, EMANUEL A. 1951 *American Monetary Policy.* New York: McGraw-Hill.

GREAT BRITAIN, COMMITTEE ON THE WORKING OF THE MONETARY SYSTEM 1959 *Report.* Papers by Command, Cmnd. 827. London: H.M. Stationery Office. → Known as the Radcliffe Report. Includes material from other countries.

HARDY, CHARLES O. 1932 *Credit Policy of the Federal Reserve System.* Washington: Brookings Institution.

HAWTREY, RALPH G. (1932) 1962 *The Art of Central Banking.* 2d ed. London: Cass. → Provides important material on British experience.

KEYNES, JOHN MAYNARD (1930) 1958–1960 *A Treatise on Money.* 2 vols. London: Macmillan. → Volume 1: *The Pure Theory of Money.* Volume 2: *The Applied Theory of Money.* Provides a pre-1935 view of central banking in the United States and Britain.

KISCH, CECIL H.; and ELKIN, WINIFRED A. (1928) 1932 *Central Banks: A Study of the Constitutions of Banks of Issue, With an Analysis of Representative Charters.* 4th ed., rev. & enl. London: Macmillan. → Documents central banking statutes in the interwar period.

PLUMPTRE, ARTHUR F. W. 1940 *Central Banking in the British Dominions.* Toronto Univ. Press; Oxford Univ. Press. → The best study of early central banking in the less developed systems.

REED, HAROLD L. 1922 *The Development of Federal Reserve Policy.* Boston and New York: Houghton Mifflin.

REED, HAROLD L. 1930 *Federal Reserve Policy: 1921–1930.* New York: McGraw-Hill.

RIEFLER, WINFIELD W. 1930 *Money Rates and Money Markets in the United States.* New York: Harper.

RITTER, LAWRENCE S. 1962 Official Central Banking Theory in the United States, 1939–1961; Four Editions of the Federal Reserve System: Purposes and Functions. *Journal of Political Economy* 70:14–29.

SAYERS, R. S. 1957 *Central Banking After Bagehot.* Oxford Univ. Press.

SAYERS, R. S. (editor) 1962 *Banking in Western Europe.* Oxford Univ. Press.

[U.S.] BOARD OF GOVERNORS OF THE FEDERAL RESERVE SYSTEM (1939) 1963 *The Federal Reserve System: Purposes and Functions.* 5th ed. Washington: The Board.

U.S. NATIONAL MONETARY COMMISSION 1909–1912 *Publications of National Monetary Commission.* 24 vols. Washington: Government Printing Office. → Includes material on early developments throughout the world.

WILLIS, HENRY P. 1923 *The Federal Reserve System: Legislation, Organization and Operation.* New York: Ronald.

BARANSKII, NIKOLAI N.

Nikolai N. Baranskii (1881–1963), the founder of Soviet economic geography, was born in Tomsk, Siberia, and died in Moscow. In his early years Baranskii was a professional revolutionary, participating in many underground activities of the Bolshevik movement. In 1918, after the establishment of the Soviet government, he began to occupy himself with economic geography and from 1926 devoted his time entirely to research, teaching, and publication in the field of geography. In 1929 Baranskii was appointed to the newly created chair of economic geography at Moscow State University, where he exerted great influence. He trained a body of specialists in economic geography and supervised more than a hundred candidate dissertations (roughly equivalent to American or German doctoral dissertations). He also founded or edited several important geographical periodicals and serials (*Geografiia v shkole, Voprosy geografii, Geografiia i khoziaistvo*), served as geographical editor for the first edition of the "Great Soviet Encyclopedia," helped secure important decrees by the government and the Communist party of the Soviet Union on the teaching of geography in schools (especially the decree of May 16, 1934), and led or aided in research expeditions from the university to various parts of the Soviet Union to investigate resources and potential projects.

His concepts in economic geography have had a wide influence in the Soviet Union and in other socialist countries. He developed a Marxist approach to economic geography. Geographers who use this approach are actively engaged in practical work in the development of the economy, in accordance with an over-all plan for the continuous expansion of production. Part of this plan is a "transformation of nature," or the offsetting of unfavorable natural conditions, such as drought, poor drainage, or permafrost, in order to create a more even areal distribution of population and production over the entire country. Baranskii stressed the need for concrete data based on direct field observation as a basis for comprehensive socialist planning. The regional orientation he established in Soviet economic geography emphasized the complex development of the economy by region rather than by type of economic activity.

In a closely related area, he analyzed the geographical division of labor in terms of two major variables, economic advantage and local variation in the productivity of labor. In agriculture, he noted variations in crop yields from place to place, according to differences in natural conditions (rainfall, temperature, or soil) or in social products and practices (reclamation, fertilization, or mechanization). He related variations in industry to proximity to raw materials (including fuel), to the extent of capital accumulation, and to the availability of a labor force. He emphasized also the effect of the historical evolution of human societies, with their differing cultures and attitudes, on the division of labor, as well as such factors as transportation and distance from major markets.

Another field that Baranskii developed was the study of the economic-geographic situation: the development of a particular economic activity in relation to routes, markets, scenes of war, and centers of industry, administration, or culture, as well as to the rate of social–political development.

Shifting the perspective, he studied the economic-geographic development of cities, viewing cities as commanders of a country who organize it in all respects, economic, political–administrative, and cultural. He worked out criteria for the classification of cities, such as characteristics of their economic-geographic situation, the functions they perform, and the size of territory over which a city exerts its influence.

Finally, Baranskii perfected methods of economic cartography and developed principles for depicting economic phenomena on maps. These principles were incorporated in a series of great Soviet atlases. To depict the distribution of manufacturing, he classified industries by branches and established indicators of the relative importance of manufacturing in particular areas. He also applied these principles to maps of ore deposits, energy, transportation and communications, and agriculture, and he examined the problems of pro-ducing a synthetic or comprehensive economic map, displaying all branches of the economy at once.

In 1935 Baranskii wrote the basic textbook on the economic geography of the U.S.S.R., which was used in the high schools of the Soviet Union for more than twenty years. He also played a role in the introduction of foreign concepts and methods into Soviet economic geography by his extensive published reviews, his consultation on books to be translated into Russian, and his own translation of some works. Altogether Baranskii published more than five hundred scientific books, monographs, articles, and reviews.

CHAUNCY D. HARRIS

WORKS BY BARANSKII

(1935) 1956 *Economic Geography of the U.S.S.R.* Moscow: Foreign Languages Publishing House. → First published as *Ekonomicheskaia geografiia SSSR.*

(1956) 1960 *Ekonomicheskaia geografiia; ekonomicheskaia kartografiia* (Economic Geography; Economic Cartography). 2d ed. Moscow: Gosudarstvennoe Izdatel'stvo Geograficheskoi Literatury.

1957 *Ekonomicheskaia geografiia v srednei shkole; ekonomicheskaia geografiia v vysshei shkole.* (Economic Geography in the Secondary School; Economic Geography in the University). Moscow: Gosudarstvennoe Izdatel'stvo Geograficheskoi Literatury. → A collection of Baranskii's key writings on the teaching of geography. Contains a comprehensive bibliography.

WORKS ABOUT BARANSKII

ARMAND, D. L. et al. 1961 Nikolai Nikolaevich Baranskii. Akademiia Nauk S.S.S.R., *Izvestiia* Seriia geograficheskaia [1961], no. 5:148–150.

GEORGE, PIERRE 1965 N. N. Baranski. *Annales de géographie* 74:195–197.

GOKHMAN, V. M.; and NAZAREVSKII, O. R. 1964 N. N. Baranskii i sovetskaia geografiia. Akademiia Nauk S.S.S.R., *Izvestiia* Seriia geograficheskaia [1964] no. 3:130–133.

HARRIS, CHAUNCY D. 1964 Nikolay Nikolayevich Baranskiy. *Geographical Review* 54:282–283.

KOROVITSYN, V. P.; NIKOL'SKII, I. V.; and RAKITNIKOV, A. N. 1961 Nikolai Nikolaevich Baranskii. Vsesoiuznoe Geograficheskoe Obshchestvo, *Izvestiia* 93:292–296.

MAERGOIZ, I. M.; and SAUSHKIN, IU. G. 1956 Nikolai Nikolaevich Baranskii. Akademiia Nauk S.S.S.R., *Izvestiia* Seriia geograficheskaia [1956], no. 5:56–60.

MAERGOIZ, I. M.; and TROFIMOVSKAIA, E. A. 1961 K vos'-midesiatiletiiu Nikolaia Nikolaevicha Baranskogo. Vsesoiuznoe Geograficheskoe Obshchestvo, *Izvestiia* 93:289–291.

Nikolai Nikolaevich Baranskii. 1950 Volume 4, pages 226–227 in *Bol'shaia sovetskaia entsiklopediia.* 2d ed. Moscow: Bol'shaia Sovetskaia Entsiklopediia.

N. N. Baranskii. 1963 *Izvestiia* December 1: p. 5, col. 1.

N. N. Baranskii. 1963 *Pravda* December 1: p. 6, cols. 6–7.

N. N. Baransky. 1963 *New York Times* December 1: p. 84, col. 5.

SAUSHKIN, IU. G. et al. 1964 Pamiati N. N. Baranskogo —osnovatelia *Voprosy geografii. Voprosy geografii* 65: 9–13.

Solov'ev, A. I. 1964 Nikolai Nikolaevich Baranskii. Moskva, Universitet, *Vestnik* Seriia 5: Geografiia [1964] no. 1:56–60.

Vitver, I. A. et al. 1964 Pamiati Nikolaia Nikolaevicha Baranskogo. Vsesoiuznoe Geograficheskoe Obshchestvo, *Izvestiia* 96:81–82.

Zimm, A. 1964 N. N. Baranskij. *Petermanns geografische Mitteilungen* 108:102.

BARGAINING

See Game theory, *especially the article on* economic applications; Labor relations, *article on* collective bargaining; Negotiation.

BARNARD, CHESTER I.

Chester Irving Barnard (1886–1961) was both a successful corporation executive and a powerful theorist about the nature of corporate organizations.

Born in Malden, Massachusetts, Barnard rose from humble origins, beginning a life of hard work at the age of 12. He supported himself while attending Mount Hermon School and during his three years at Harvard College. Upon leaving Harvard at the age of 23, he took a job as a statistical clerk with the American Telephone and Telegraph Company in Boston. He stayed with the Bell System for 39 years, from 1909 to 1948.

Barnard's first 13 years with the company were spent working as an expert on the economics of telephone rates. By 1922, when he was 36, he began performing what he was later to call "executive services," and by the age of 41 he had become the first president of New Jersey Bell Telephone. His 21 years as president were also the period of his most fruitful intellectual activity; both his books were written during those years. It may be remarkable that the Bell System tolerated such "deviant" behavior on the part of one of its chief executives, but Barnard surely separated his "personal decisions" from his "organizational decisions" (as he called them in *The Functions of the Executive*).

From 1931 to 1933, and again in 1935, Barnard served as state director of the New Jersey Relief Administration, an experience that allowed him to sample organization life outside of the Bell System. This experience inspired his only piece of formal research as a participant–observer: he recorded and analyzed his experiences in the form of a case for Lawrence J. Henderson's course at Harvard on "concrete sociology."

Barnard's association with Henderson brought him into contact with a wider group at Harvard that included Elton Mayo; Wallace B. Donham, then dean of the Harvard Business School; Alfred North Whitehead; A. Lawrence Lowell, the president of Harvard University; and Philip Cabot, a member of the business school faculty, whose social position gave him access to the elite in both the academic and the business community. All these men varied considerably in their principal academic interests, but they were all concerned with developing a new conceptual scheme to explain the behavior of men at work in modern organizations.

Until that time neither a commitment to interdisciplinary activity nor the recognition of intellectual ability without academic certification were at all common at Harvard. The leadership of Lowell and Henderson produced academic innovations. Henderson, whose researches in blood chemistry had brought him great distinction, gave seminars on Pareto to educate many of his colleagues and friends. Lowell organized the Society of Fellows, with Henderson, Whitehead, and himself as senior fellows and with junior fellows who were permitted to choose subjects for study on the basis of their interests rather than their disciplinary affiliations (Homans 1936–1961). The result of Barnard's encouragement by such men as Cabot, Donham, Lowell, Whitehead, and Mayo was his writing of *The Functions of the Executive* (1938), an examination of his own experiences as an executive in terms of the new conceptual scheme that they had been developing.

In this book, which was not a product of any formal research, Barnard analyzed organizations as "cooperative systems," that is, as open-ended natural dynamic systems of cooperative effort that had to meet two conditions in order to survive in the long run. The two conditions were that they must secure both their objectives and the cooperation of their individual contributors; that is, they must, in Barnard's terminology, be both effective and efficient. There were for Barnard three givens in any cooperative system: a common impersonal organizational purpose, individual motives that had to be satisfied in order to secure the individual's contribution, and the processes of communication by which these opposite poles of the system of cooperative effort would be brought into dynamic equilibrium.

Barnard re-examined the problems of organization and the dilemmas of leadership in terms of this model, studying such variables as the nature of authority, decision making, responsibility, and satisfactory exchange between the contributors to the system and the system of cooperative effort as a whole. He restated the functions of the executive as being the formulation of purpose, the securing of the essential services from the contributors by the maintenance of a satisfactory condition of exchange (organizational equilibrium), and the maintenance of organizational communication.

The contributors to the cooperative effort in a business organization were investors, suppliers, employees, distributors, customers, and managers. The principle of satisfactory exchange was to "give, so far as possible, what is less valuable to you but more valuable to the receiver; and [to] receive what is more valuable to you and less valuable to the giver" (1938, p. 254). This concept of satisfactory exchange was later developed by Herbert A. Simon in what he called the Barnard–Simon theory of organizational equilibrium, which for him was essentially a theory of motivation (Simon 1947), and by George C. Homans, who considered satisfactory exchange to be the condition for all human exchanges, even at an elementary social level (Homans 1961).

Barnard's book was received immediately with acclaim by academics. It became required reading in many sociology departments and business schools. But for many businessmen the new terminology and the level of discourse became serious barriers to understanding. Barnard was called upon to elucidate and amplify his ideas. He delivered papers to many professional groups—a good sample of which he published in *Organization and Management* (1935–1946).

One of Barnard's favorite themes was that the common understanding of organizational phenomena which skilled executives showed in their behavior at a practical level tended to disappear when these same phenomena were raised for consideration at a theoretical level. Much of his writing was addressed to this paradox.

Take, for example, management's seeming disregard of the fact and the necessity of informal organization. Barnard's theory stressed that informal organization emerges in any formal organization; that these two types of organization are interdependent aspects of the same cooperative phenomena; and that informal organization performs indispensable functions as a means of communication, of cohesion, and of protecting the integrity of the individual.

These phenomena of informal organization are recognized intuitively by executives in many of the actions they take. But when they were raised for serious consideration at a systematic level, Barnard found, executives would tend to deny their existence.

Equally paradoxical were the executives' ideas about the nature of authority, particularly what

Barnard called its subjective aspect. According to Barnard's formulation, authority resides in the person who receives the order and not in the person who gives it. In the final analysis it is the recipient of the order who decides to accept or reject the order as authoritative for him.

Again, this conception of authority in terms of cooperative phenomena is well understood intuitively by any skillful leader. He knows that not every order he gives is complied with but only those orders which the recipient can understand, which he feels are consistent with the purposes of the organization, and with which he is mentally and physically capable of complying. To give orders that cannot or will not be obeyed is the best way for him to lose the "authority" he is supposed to possess.

Yet Barnard found that because these phenomena could not be easily conceptualized by the executive and because they went against his legalistic notions of authority, he would misstate their nature and underestimate their importance. He would talk as though he got things done by "his" authority alone. He would fail to see how ineffective "his" authority was in particular situations and, thus, how many of his orders were not complied with.

Barnard was well on the road to becoming an academic. In addition to his other achievements, he received honorary degrees from many universities. World War II, however, caused him to change his direction, and from 1942 to 1945 he was president of the United Service Organization, Inc. (USO), for which he received the Presidential Medal of Merit in 1946. After the war the demands for his services did not cease. He became a member of the Board of Consultants to the State Department on Atomic Energy and coauthor of the department's report on international control of atomic energy in 1946.

In 1948 Barnard again faced the decision of whether or not to join a university. When he retired as president of New Jersey Bell, he chose to become president of the Rockefeller Foundation, a post he held from 1948 to 1952.

Those in the behavioral sciences in academe might be interested to note that at the death of Chester Barnard, the *New York Times,* a very faithful recorder of the facts of importance to our society, accurately cited Barnard's many accomplishments except two: there was no mention of his two books.

F. J. Roethlisberger

[*For the historical context of Barnard's work, see* Organizations, *article on* Theories of Organiza-

TIONS; *and the biographies of* HENDERSON; LOWELL; MAYO; *and* WHITEHEAD. *For discussion of the subsequent development of Barnard's ideas, see* ADMINISTRATION, *article on* ADMINISTRATIVE BEHAVIOR; LEADERSHIP, *article on* SOCIOLOGICAL ASPECTS; SOCIAL CONTROL, *article on* ORGANIZATIONAL ASPECTS.]

WORKS BY BARNARD

(1935–1946) 1956 *Organization and Management: Selected Papers.* Cambridge, Mass.: Harvard Univ. Press.
(1938) 1962 *The Functions of the Executive.* Cambridge, Mass.: Harvard Univ. Press.

SUPPLEMENTARY BIBLIOGRAPHY

Chester I. Barnard (obituary). 1961 *New York Times* June 8, p. 35, col. 4.
HOMANS, GEORGE C. (1936–1961) 1962 *Sentiments and Activities: Essays in Social Science.* New York: Free Press.
HOMANS, GEORGE C. 1961 *Social Behavior: Its Elementary Forms.* New York: Harcourt.
SIMON, HERBERT A. (1947) 1961 *Administrative Behavior: A Study of Decision-making Processes in Administrative Organization.* 2d ed. New York: Macmillan. → A paperback edition was published in 1965 by the Free Press.

BARNES, HARRY ELMER

Harry Elmer Barnes, publicist, cultural historian, and sociologist, was born in Auburn, New York, in 1889. He received his A.B. degree *summa cum laude* in 1913 and his A.M. degree in 1914, both from Syracuse University, and his PH.D. in 1918 from Columbia. In the academic year 1916/1917 he studied at Harvard on a fellowship. As a student, he centered his interest mainly on history, but at Syracuse, stimulated by Philip Parsons, he prepared a history of pre-Comtean sociological literature, and at Harvard, an extensive history of sociological contributions to political theory. Both studies furnished material for later works on historiography and the political, economic, and cultural aspects of Western thought and civilization, which are his chief claims to distinction.

Barnes taught in a number of colleges and universities across the country, usually in sociology departments; his longest tenure was at Smith College, 1922–1929. He was special commentator on social issues for the Scripps-Howard newspapers, 1929–1940, and during that time also lectured widely on penology, criminology, education, and other social issues and wrote numerous articles and book reviews and several of his most important works.

Most of his major contributions were made in the field of cultural history. He was well equipped for this work because of his tireless energy, prodi-

gious memory, and strong ego drive as well as his excellent training. He had studied under outstanding scholars in history, sociology, political science, and anthropology, including, at Columbia, the founders of the New History, James H. Robinson, James T. Shotwell, and William R. Shepherd, the political scientist William A. Dunning, and the anthropologist Alexander Goldenweiser, and at Harvard, the historian Edwin F. Gay, the physiologist Lawrence J. Henderson, and the anthropologist Earnest A. Hooton.

Barnes became, especially through his book *The New History and the Social Studies* (1925), an outstanding advocate of the New History, which was seeking a deeper understanding of the origin and development of Western culture. Contending that traditional history, with its emphasis on wars, dynasties, diplomacy, politics, and spectacular deeds, was "mostly bunk" because it threw little light on the basic causal factors and processes of historical trends, he argued that the "newer dynamic and synthetic history" should utilize the advances of all the sciences relating to man, from human geography through biology and psychology to the social studies, in search of a deeper and more socially meaningful understanding of the genesis and evolution of civilization. He saw in such history the cultivation of the informed intelligence in public affairs needed to undermine outworn myths, false assumptions, and illusory doctrines that retard cultural advancement. Noting also that social problems can be well understood only in the light of their historical background, he advocated the integration and cross-fertilization of history and the social sciences.

His other contribution to historiography, first published in the *Encyclopedia Americana*, was revised and expanded into his *History of Historical Writing* (1937b). Widely recognized as a monument of learning, it was universally praised both at home and abroad as meeting a long-felt need and as henceforth indispensable for all advanced students of history.

In the broad area of intellectual and institutional history, which was his forte, both the volume and the scope of Barnes's writings were immense. Designed as compendia of a vast literature, they were in no sense detailed historical researches; they necessarily relied largely on secondary sources. Clearly written and instructively organized, they showed keen discrimination in the selection of matter presented. Taken together, they condensed the intellectual output of Western civilization relating to its economic, political, religious, and other social institutions and problems from primitive to modern social organizations. They thus supplied for a large body of students and instructors essential orientation material, otherwise either inaccessible or unduly time-consuming.

In the area of intellectual and institutional history also belongs *The Twilight of Christianity* (1929), a controversial book that aroused wide interest, was highly esteemed by intellectuals and not a few liberal Protestant clergymen, but was roundly denounced by religious conservatives. It found Christian beliefs and theology to be based largely on myths and quite irreconcilable with higher criticism of the Biblical records, Near East history, and advancing knowledge of man and his universe, especially the universe of universes of modern astronomy.

His lifelong interest in penology and criminology began with a history of penal institutions in New Jersey (1918), which was followed by a similar history of Pennsylvania penology (1927). He was a sharp critic of the jury system as giving a basic judicial function to untrained and inexpert citizens. He strongly favored the indeterminate sentence, the wider extension of the probation system, reduction in the use of prisons except for incorrigibles, the extended use of specially trained psychiatrists for diagnosis and individualization of treatment, and the use of sterilization as a eugenic measure.

Writing in a period of rapid and revolutionary social changes, Barnes has often been engaged in public controversy over his statements of both fact and interpretation. This is due in part to his reformist urge, his polemical zeal, and his slight regard for the popular "eternal verities" of tradition or for their sponsors. It is due mainly, however, to the vigor of his language, his pointed comparisons, often having a personal reference, his use of adjectives that seem to label his opponents as prejudiced, incompetent, dishonest, or otherwise disqualified, and the dogmatic assurance, the doubtful validity, and sweeping nature of some of his generalizations on moot issues. His academic career was deeply affected by the fact that he alienated a considerable number of professional historians by his debunking efforts in behalf of the new historical approach and especially by his spirited espousal of revisionism after both world wars.

Some critics have charged that Barnes tried to cover too wide a range of literature, both in time and subject matter; that his works lacked any interpretative, theoretical framework; and that they were prolix in style and repetitious in substance. In general, however, his major works have been judged commendable both in reliability and scope, though some of them would have profited by judi-

cious pruning. He was admittedly neither philosopher nor statistician. In treating numerous social problems in his college texts, he tended to present an array of the current solutions, often merely logical utopias, with too little analysis of their cultural feasibility. No doubt much of his writing represents a combination of the publicist–reformer with the conscientious scholar, but of his unflinching courage and his devotion to historic truth there cannot be the slightest doubt.

FRANK H. HANKINS

WORKS BY BARNES

1918 *A History of the Penal, Reformatory and Correctional Institutions of the State of New Jersey.* Trenton, N.J.: MacCrellish & Quigley.

1924 *Sociology and Political Theory: A Consideration of the Sociological Basis of Politics.* New York: Knopf.

1925 *The New History and the Social Studies.* New York: Century.

1926 *History and Social Intelligence.* New York: Knopf.

1927 *The Evolution of Penology in Pennsylvania.* Indianapolis: Bobbs-Merrill.

1928 *In Quest of Truth and Justice: Debunking the War Guilt Myth.* Chicago: National Historical Society.

1928 KNIGHT, MELVIN M.; BARNES, HARRY E.; and FLÜGEL, FELIX. *Economic History of Europe in Modern Times.* Boston: Houghton Mifflin.

(1929) 1931 *The Twilight of Christianity.* New York: Vanguard.

1930 *World Politics in Modern Civilization: The Contributions of Nationalism, Capitalism, Imperialism and Militarism to Human Culture and International Anarchy.* New York: Knopf.

1935 BARNES, HARRY E.; and DAVID, HENRY. *A History of Western Civilization.* 2 vols. New York: Harcourt.

1937a *An Economic History of the Western World.* New York: Harcourt.

(1937b) 1962 *History of Historical Writing.* 2d rev. ed. New York: Dover. → A paperback edition was published in 1963 by Dover.

(1937c) 1961 *Intellectual and Cultural History of the Western World.* 3d rev. ed., 3 vols. New York: Reynal-Hitchcock. → A paperback edition was published in 1964 by Dover.

1938 BARNES, HARRY E.; and BECKER, HOWARD. *Social Thought From Lore to Science.* 2 vols. Boston: Heath. → A paperback edition was published in 1963 by Dover.

(1939) 1952 *Society in Transition: Problems of a Changing Age.* 2d ed. Englewood Cliffs, N.J.: Prentice-Hall. → A comprehensive social-problems text.

1940 BARNES, HARRY E.; BECKER, HOWARD; and BECKER, F. B. (editors). *Contemporary Social Theory.* New York: Appleton-Century.

1942 *Social Institutions in an Era of World Upheaval.* Englewood Cliffs, N.J.: Prentice-Hall. → Our cultural inheritance under the impact of the scientific and technological revolutions.

(1943) 1959 BARNES, HARRY E.; and TEETERS, NEGLEY K. *New Horizons in Criminology.* Englewood Cliffs, N.J.: Prentice-Hall.

1948 BARNES, HARRY E. (editor). *An Introduction to the History of Sociology.* Univ. of Chicago Press.

1953 BARNES, HARRY E. (editor). *Perpetual War for Per-*

petual Peace; A Critical Examination of the Foreign Policy of Franklin Delano Roosevelt and Its Aftermath. Caldwell, Idaho: Caldwell Printers. → Summary of World War II revisionism.

BARONE, ENRICO

Enrico Barone (1859–1924) was an Italian mathematical economist who made lasting contributions to modern international trade theory, the theory of the firm, welfare economics, and the theory of general economic equilibrium. Barone's mathematical background was superior to that of Walras and Pareto, who were laying the foundations of modern mathematical economics in the last quarter of the nineteenth century; Barone was therefore able to refine some of their important analyses. Moreover, his deliberate subordination of personal antagonisms to the desire to develop a scientific economics (see Walras [1857–1909] 1965, pp. 661–662) led him to draw upon British economics for inspiration to a greater extent than Walras or Pareto, although he did his most significant work within their context of general economic equilibrium. However, he cannot be viewed merely as an embellisher of the constructions of other economists or as a mediating agent between different architectural modes in economic theory.

Barone was a career army officer until the age of 48, attaining early eminence in this profession. When he was only 35, he was appointed a professor at the War College in Turin, which prepared officers destined for general staff duty. He wrote extensively in the field of military history and strategy. However, like Pareto, he had been introduced to economic theory by Maffeo Pantaleoni, and his involvement with it during his army career was far greater than that even of the passionately devoted amateur. He began as early as 1895 to seek a chair in economics in order to devote his full attention to the field, but not until 1907, when he received a professorship at the Istituto di Scienze Economiche in Rome, was he to achieve his desire. (At this time he resigned his commission as general staff colonel.) Paradoxically, all his lasting contributions to economics were made in the period of his army career.

The theory of international trade. Barone joined Marshall and Pareto in moving the analysis of international trade away from the classical labor quantity theory, or barter basis, toward the determination of trade flows by price differentials. Employing consumer surplus reasoning, Barone demonstrated rigorously that protective tariffs always reduce consumer welfare, yet he added that the im-position of such tariffs with their attendant reduction of welfare may prevent the imposition of policies even more damaging to welfare (Barone 1894–1924, vol. 2).

The theory of the firm. Barone played a significant role in developing marginal productivity analysis as the basis of the firm's supply functions for output and demand functions for inputs (see the discussion of the theory of general equilibrium, below). However, Barone never truly resolved the dilemma which plagued the analysis of the entire Lausanne school: in pure competition, how can the firm be maximizing profit when by the very nature of the market structure it must earn zero profits in equilibrium? As a consequence of the inability to solve this seeming paradox, Walras, Pareto, Barone, and their followers confused the maximum profit conditions on marginal value productivities with minimum cost conditions and the maximum profit requirement that price be equated to marginal cost with the condition that it be equal to average cost (Kuenne 1963, pp. 138–140, 180).

Barone's full role in the marginal productivity controversy during the last quarter of the nineteenth century is difficult to judge because much of his analysis seems not to have been published and his papers were not preserved. However, at least a translation of a most revealing document did escape destruction and has in recent years become available. It is a review of Philip Wicksteed's *Essay on the Coordination of the Laws of Distribution* which Barone wrote for the *Economic Journal*, but which was rejected in 1896 (for unclear reasons) by its editor, F. Y. Edgeworth. Fortunately, although the original manuscript was lost, a careful French translation by Walras survived (see Barone 1896; Walras [1857–1909] 1965, pp. 644–648).

In this review Barone attempted to generalize the exhaustion-of-product proposition for a linear homogeneous production function to the case of nonhomogeneous production functions in purely competitive environments. It is well known, following Euler's theorem, that for functions which are homogeneous of degree one, if every factor of production is paid its marginal product, the entire product will be exhausted in such payments. Homogeneity of this degree implies that for a fixed set of allowable input prices, average costs are independent of the scale of output if all factors are variable in quantity and, consequently, that average costs equal marginal costs.

Barone, in his attempt to show that this condition holds in the nonhomogeneous case, began with the assumption that pure competition implies the equation of price and average cost of a product, and therefore the absence of profits for the firm. Let $\bar{x}$ be the amount of output for the firm, P the price of the output per unit, X_i the firm's demand for input i, and P_i the price per unit of input i. Then, if price equals average cost,

$$(1) \qquad \bar{x}P = \sum_i X_i P_i \qquad i = 1, 2, \cdots, m.$$

Output is related to inputs by the following continuous smooth function:

$$(2) \qquad \bar{x} = F(X_1, X_2, \cdots, X_m).$$

To maximize profits for an interior maximum and under proper constraints concerning the shape of the production function in (2), it is necessary to equate the "marginal value product" of every input to its price. That is, it is necessary that

$$(3) \qquad \frac{\partial F}{\partial X_i} P = P_i$$

and Barone derived these conditions. By substituting them into (1) and eliminating P, he derived the relation of Euler's theorem:

$$(4) \qquad \bar{x} = \sum_i \frac{\partial F}{\partial X_i} X_i.$$

He believed he had thus freed Wicksteed's analysis from the restrictive assumption of linear homogeneity for (2).

Barone's analysis fails first of all because it implicitly assumes that linear homogeneity holds exactly or at least approximately at the equilibrium. Equation (1) is not the fundamental relation of price and cost in purely competitive equilibrium. His belief that pure competition implies the equality of price and average cost led him to substitute into (1) from (3) to eliminate the P_i and to obtain (4). But (1) need not hold in short-run pure competition, profits may be earned, and (1) is not a universal implication of that market structure.

There is, however, a second source of Barone's failure. Even if one consents to deal only with long-run pure competition, in which event (1) *is* a correct assumption, Barone did not establish the exhaustion-of-product proposition in the general case. The crucial price–cost relationship in pure competition is that of the equality of price and *marginal* cost. This relationship is necessary in order to derive (3)—a fact which escaped Barone. Therefore, given (1) and (3), Barone's proof of exhaustion-of-product requires that price equal both average and marginal cost. This set of conditions rules in Wicksteed's case of linear homogeneity (exactly) or in the case where all firms are oper-

ating at the minimum point of a U-shaped average cost curve (approximately). In the general case, however, it is impossible to have the firm equate price to both average and marginal costs.

It is symptomatic of the analytical uncertainty in this field at the time that Barone was writing that he affirmed the necessity of (3) in the firm's equilibrium, but that instead of explaining it as an *internal* adjustment of the firm necessary to maximize profits, he asserted that it must hold if factors are to be allocated properly among uses. This is true and its interpretation in this manner was quite insightful, but this external aspect of the firm's adjustment has little relevance to its own discretionary decision making.

The confusion was aggravated by Walras, who, in a letter to Barone, dated October 30, 1895 (Walras [1857–1909] 1965, pp. 650–651), insisted that the conditions of (3) were imposed to guarantee minimum average cost for the firm. Barone dropped his former interpretation of them and agreed, too readily, with Walras that this was indeed their genesis (Walras [1857–1909] 1965, pp. 652–653). From this time forward Barone seems invariably to have identified pure competition with the firm's equilibrium at zero profits and minimum average cost.

We now know that it is possible to state the firm's maximum profit conditions in this form only if the conditions of linear homogeneity hold exactly or approximately. If a firm is constrained to earn zero profits under these conditions and it is minimizing its costs, it is in fact maximizing its profits at zero. In this method of stating the conditions, therefore, Barone was once more implicitly assuming special cases, not developing the general theory, which permits profits to be earned.

The theory of general equilibrium. Yet, in a letter to Walras, written September 20, 1894, Barone had indeed already stated the problem correctly and solved it for the general case (Walras [1857–1909] 1965, pp. 619–621). He recognized the possibility of profit in pure competition, the role of the conditions of (3) in explaining it, and, most importantly, the method of deriving supply curves of output and demand curves for inputs from these conditions. In three short paragraphs, Barone there indicated the manner in which profit maximization under marginal productivity considerations determines the values of variable coefficients of production for the firm, supply-of-output and demand-for-input functions for the firm, and their integration into the functions and equations of general equilibrium.

These three rich paragraphs indicate that Barone

had by 1894 discovered the proper method of eliminating constant coefficients of production from the Walrasian structure and of making the desired integration described above. Indeed, the firm was given a real existence within the industry for the first time in general equilibrium theory, since it was allowed determinate outputs and input demands. It is an interesting question why he did not persist in this interpretation of the firm's decision making; perhaps it was because he was misled by his attempt to bring the entrepreneurial factor under the regime of marginal productivity.

Collectivist economic planning. There can be no doubt that Barone's most widely known contribution is his demonstration that a ministry of production in a collectivist economy would be able, through the use of instrumental "shadow prices" for the establishment of purely competitive equilibrium conditions, to plan production rationally. Although Barone was not himself sympathetic to socialism, his famous article, published in 1908 but translated into English only in 1935, furnished a theoretical basis to counter the arguments of those who urged that such planning is impossible in the absence of market prices.

Barone limited himself to consideration of production conditions by assuming that income distribution in the collectivist state is determined by ethical considerations. Income redistribution is effected by differential payments to classes of consumers from the earnings of state-owned means of production (and, he should have added, profits) to supplement private earnings. In Barone's treatment, profits occur only as differential rents to managerial ability, which he incorrectly argued should be eliminated by reductions in average cost of the product over the industry. As already pointed out, he should have included the usual concept of short-run profits in his collective income.

Barone's first step is to show that there exists a function, Φ, whose dimension is "units of money per period," such that when the conditions of pure competition rule throughout the economy it is true that $d\Phi = 0$ and $d^2\Phi < 0$, when prices are treated as fixed. Continuing to assume that there exist m factor service inputs i, that n consumer goods j are produced, that m capital goods Z_i exist to produce the respective factor services i, and that E is the value of new capital goods produced per period, Barone then defined

$$(5) \qquad \Phi = \sum_j D_j P_j + \sum_i D_i P_i + E$$

where the D-terms define total consumer demand. Further, on the assumption that new capital goods are eternal and will sell in equilibrium at the value

of their services rendered per period capitalized at the rate of interest, r, he obtained

$$(6) \qquad \Phi = \sum_j D_j P_j + \sum_i D_i P_i + \sum_i D_{z_i} \frac{P_i}{r}.$$

Under conditions of pure competition, (*a*) all consumers are adjusting marginal rates of substitution between goods to the same price ratios, (*b*) the prices of all goods equal minimum marginal costs, and (*c*) the prices to which firms adjust are the same as those to which consumers adjust, $d\Phi = 0$, and, with well-behaved functions, $d^2\Phi < 0$. This in turn implies that for the given distribution of income, small changes in the goods produced taken in conjunction with the implied changes in the factor services consumed or small changes in some factor services and compensating changes in the opposite direction for others with outputs constant will result in no change in consumer welfare, and larger changes will take the economy away from Pareto optimality.

Despite the fact that Barone, in his analysis of the collective economy, refused to employ marginal utility or even indifference curve concepts, preferring to remain with demand-and-supply functions, he implicitly relied upon the equality of marginal rates of substitution and prices for all consumers in his interpretation of this function (Barone [1908] 1935, pp. 254–255). Barone asserted, properly, that when the conditions of pure competition rule, and the differentials of Φ meet the above conditions, consumers cannot all benefit from such changes as were discussed above, nor can the gainers benefit to the extent of having net gains after compensating the losers.

He then showed how the ministry of production in a collectivist economy can set shadow prices on goods and services in such fashion as to employ all resources and, by iterative corrections of the prices within these resource constraints, lead the economy to the position where the equivalent of Φ has a first-order differential equal to zero. With the setting of the interest rate in the public interest by the ministry and the distribution of collective income, the equilibrium will resemble that of pure competition; that is, the ministry will have maximized social welfare when, subject to the availabilities of resources, all goods-prices equal minimum marginal costs and all capital goods earn the same net return as a percentage of costs. During the approach to an equilibrium, as well as at equilibrium, consumers are given the freedom within their earnings and social dividends to purchase what they wish.

Reflecting the unsatisfactory state of analysis of

the Paretian school in the area of savings and investment, Barone's analysis of the state's role in crucial savings–investment decisions is vague. Indeed, his analysis of these processes even in the purely competitive economy is almost impossible to decipher, particularly as it concerns the nature of "new working capital" and the determination of the interest rate. It does seem clear that he believed that in the collective economy individuals are required to deliver their savings to the state, that they are entitled to the earnings of their savings, and that the state sets an interest rate in the public interest.

Barone expressed some pessimism concerning the practical operational feasibility of a ministry of production performing the necessary iterative process, reserving his most severe misgivings for the case of variable coefficients of production. What he did succeed in doing, however, at a higher level of abstraction, was to point to the logical consistency of the ministry's tasks, the possibility and indeed rational necessity of using prices to guide allocation, the ability to use numerical analytical iterative techniques to approach an operationally definable equilibrium rather than having to solve many equations simultaneously, and the formal similarity of the solutions for the market and collective economies.

ROBERT E. KUENNE

[For the historical context of Barone's work, see the biographies of MARSHALL; PANTALEONI; PARETO; WALRAS; WICKSTEED; for discussion of the subsequent development of Barone's ideas, see FIRM, THEORY OF THE; PRODUCTION; WELFARE ECONOMICS.]

WORKS BY BARONE

(1894–1924) 1936–1937 Le opere economiche. 3 vols. Bologna (Italy): Zanichelli. → Volume 1: Scritti vari, 1894–1924. Volume 2: Principi di economia politica, 1908. Volume 3: Principi di economia finanziaria, 1911–1912.

(1896) 1964 Sur un livre récent de Wicksteed. Cahiers Vilfredo Pareto 3:68–73. → Léon Walras' French translation of Barone's unpublished review of 1896.

(1908) 1935 The Ministry of Production in the Collectivist State. Pages 245–290 in Frederick A. von Hayek (editor), Collectivist Economic Planning: Critical Studies on the Possibilities of Socialism by N. G. Pierson, Ludwig von Mises, Georg Hahn, and Enrico Barone. London: Routledge. → First published as "Il ministro della produzione nello stato collettivista."

SUPPLEMENTARY BIBLIOGRAPHY

BERGSON, ABRAM 1938 A Reformulation of Certain Aspects of Welfare Economics. Quarterly Journal of Economics 52:310–334.

JAFFÉ, WILLIAM 1964 New Light on an Old Quarrel. Cahiers Vilfredo Pareto 3:61–102.

KUENNE, ROBERT E. 1963 The Theory of General Economic Equilibrium. Princeton Univ. Press.

SAMUELSON, PAUL A. (1947) 1958 Foundations of Economic Analysis. Harvard Economic Studies, Vol. 80. Cambridge, Mass.: Harvard Univ. Press.

SCHUMPETER, JOSEPH A. (1954) 1960 History of Economic Analysis. Edited by E. B. Schumpeter. New York: Oxford Univ. Press.

WALRAS, LÉON (1857–1909) 1965 The Correspondence of Léon Walras and Related Papers. 3 vols. Selected and edited by William Jaffé. Amsterdam: North-Holland Pub. Co. → See especially Volume 2: 1884–1897.

WALRAS, LÉON (1874–1877) 1954 Elements of Pure Economics: Or, the Theory of Social Wealth. Translated by William Jaffé. Homewood, Ill.: Irwin; London: Allen & Unwin. → First published in French as Éléments d'économie politique pure.

BARTLETT, F. C.

F. C. Bartlett was born in 1886 at Stow-on-the-Wold, Gloucestershire. He was educated privately and at St. John's College, Cambridge, where he came under the influence of W. H. R. Rivers, the physician, anthropologist, and psychologist. Bartlett's early leanings were toward anthropology, in which he retained a lifelong interest, but circumstances led him to a career in psychology. In 1922 Bartlett succeeded C. S. Myers as director of the Cambridge Psychological Laboratory and nine years later became the first professor of experimental psychology in the university, a post that he held until his retirement, in 1952. Bartlett was elected a fellow of the Royal Society in 1932 and was knighted in 1948. He received honorary doctorates from the universities of Athens, Louvain, London, and Edinburgh and from Princeton and Oxford.

Bartlett's early work was concerned chiefly with perception and memory, and for this he owed a good deal to the influence of James Ward. In his work on memory, Bartlett was quick to see that the conditions of psychological study must be as lifelike as possible if light is to be thrown on the realities of human behavior. For this reason he rejected the use of artificially simplified material, of the kind introduced by Ebbinghaus, and arranged his experimental conditions to approximate as closely as possible those of everyday life. Although this involved some sacrifice in quantitative precision, it led to an important gain in psychological realism. Bartlett's methods and results were brought together in his noteworthy book Remembering—published in 1932—which had wide influence.

The main thesis of Bartlett's study is that remembering cannot properly be regarded as a reproductive process. He pointed out that much use is made of inference and judgment, with the result that what is remembered may come to differ remarkably from the events as originally experienced.

Typically, the original experiences undergo extensive changes governed by factors of interest, emotion, and cultural background. Indeed, Bartlett went so far as to speak of recall as a reconstructive rather than as a reproductive process, placing particular emphasis on the unwitting alterations in memory brought about by habit and social convention. This inevitably led him to explore the social background of memory and its dependence on cultural elements. Indeed, the view that no psychological response, at least above the level of sensation, can be profitably studied in isolation from its social context has always been central to Bartlett's thinking.

Bartlett's interest in anthropological issues is even more explicit in an earlier, if less important, book entitled *Psychology and Primitive Culture* (1923), the aim of which was to provide a groundwork of basic psychological principles applicable to the study of society, primitive or not so primitive. Throughout, Bartlett stressed that the underlying psychological mechanisms determining group activity remain the same at all levels of social development, advanced societies being characterized principally by the number and diversity of their component social groupings. He was therefore led to seek an analysis of group processes in terms of a relatively small number of basic human tendencies (in particular, comradeship, assertiveness, and submission) and to trace their expression and interaction in social groups at various levels of complexity. In opposition to the view of Lévy-Bruhl and others, Bartlett insisted that there is no true antithesis between primitive and civilized man, but that primitive culture, in virtue of its relative simplicity, forms the best introduction to the psychology of contemporary social life.

Although Bartlett produced no subsequent work of major proportions in social psychology, a number of the themes expressed or foreshadowed in his earlier writings are taken further in later papers. In a paper on "Psychological Methods and Anthropological Problems" (1937), he returned to the contribution that quite simple methods of psychological measurement—even the determination of sensory thresholds—might make to our understanding of cultural differences. At the same time, he came out strongly against the use of intelligence tests, which he felt lacked adequate theoretical foundation. Unaccompanied by any investigation of temperament, character, and personality, and devised without reference to the pattern of culture under inquiry, such tests might, he urged, give seriously misleading results. This warning was repeated, on the basis of wartime experience of personnel selection, in a Maudsley lecture on "Intelligence as a Social Problem" (1947b). Bartlett returned on several occasions (e.g., 1939; 1943a) to the general relations between psychology and anthropology, invariably stressing the extent of common ground, the promise of interdisciplinary inquiry, and the need for greater precision in research method.

Although the extent of Bartlett's interest in the social sciences was remarkable, it is his work as an experimental psychologist that has the highest claims to distinction. While his earlier work on memory remains his best-known single contribution, he was later responsible for initiating new and fruitful work on the analysis of human skill, much of it prompted by practical issues arising in the course of World War II. This work, it is true, owed much to the singular genius of his gifted pupil K. J. W. Craik, 1914–1945, but Bartlett was responsible for many of the guiding ideas and for the general development of the research program. He laid particular stress on the need to study not only the final *level* of performance, that is, the degree of skill achieved, but also the timing, grouping, and stability of the component responses involved in the performance itself (1947a). This emphasis on the detailed structure of human skill made possible a new and important analysis of the effects of fatigue and other adverse circumstances upon high-level motor activity (1943b). Bartlett's ideas were given experimental substance by his many pupils, who used methods a great deal more sophisticated than had been attempted before in the laboratory. Although much of the detailed work was undertaken by others, Bartlett's leadership may be said to have opened a new chapter in British experimental psychology.

Bartlett's book *Thinking* (1958), published after his retirement from the Cambridge chair, may be regarded as in some respects a natural sequel to *Remembering*. Again Bartlett stressed the constructive character of higher mental processes and their close relation to social activities. The book takes its departure, however, less from the earlier work on memory than from the more recent studies of human skilled performance. In Bartlett's view, thinking can properly be regarded as a high-level skill, sharing with bodily skill many of its most characteristic properties. With a wealth of pertinent illustration, some of it experimentally derived, Bartlett outlined the ways in which processes of interpolation and extrapolation play their part in thinking and how thinking comes to acquire its directional properties. Characteristically, he added chapters on adventurous thinking, as displayed more especially in the original thinking of artists and scientists. He also devoted attention to everyday thinking of the kind that governs decision in regard to current social issues. Although it presents no new theory, the book provides an original and stimulating approach to some of the most recalcitrant problems in experimental psychology.

Bartlett's work combines a belief in experimental method with a degree of imagination rare in contemporary psychology. Although he advanced no theory of sufficient precision to command general acceptance and founded no school built around a systematic approach to psychological issues, his originality, enterprise, and wise guidance have had a remarkable influence on the development of experimental psychology in Great Britain. In particular, his concern for the social application of psychology has ensured the development of the field into a responsible discipline in close contact with practical reality. As a teacher, his strong yet gentle personality and his exceptional tolerance and modesty endeared him to successive generations of students of psychology at Cambridge. His work touched contemporary science at many points and left its mark on the wider stage of public life in Britain.

O. L. ZANGWILL

[For the historical context of Bartlett's work, see the biographies of LÉVY-BRUHL; RIVERS; WARD, JAMES. For discussion of the subsequent development of his ideas, see CREATIVITY; FORGETTING; GESTALT THEORY; THINKING.]

WORKS BY BARTLETT

1916 An Experimental Study of Some Problems of Perceiving and Imaging. *British Journal of Psychology* 8:222–267.
1923 *Psychology and Primitive Culture.* Cambridge Univ. Press; New York: Macmillan.
1925 Feeling, Imaging and Thinking. *British Journal of Psychology* 16:16–28.
1932 *Remembering: A Study in Experimental and Social Psychology.* Cambridge Univ. Press; New York: Macmillan.
1936 F. C. Bartlett. Volume 3, pages 39–52 in Carl Murchison (editor), *A History of Psychology in Autobiography.* Worcester, Mass.: Clark Univ. Press; Oxford Univ. Press.
1937 Psychological Methods and Anthropological Problems. *Africa* 10:401–420.
1939 Suggestion for Research in Social Psychology. Pages 24–45 in F. C. Bartlett et al. (editors), *The Study of Society: Methods and Problems.* London: Routledge; New York: Macmillan.
1943a Anthropology in Reconstruction: The Huxley Memorial Lecture for 1943. *Journal of the Royal Anthropological Institute of Great Britain and Ireland* 73:9–16.
1943b Fatigue Following Highly Skilled Work. Royal Society of London, *Proceedings* Series B 131:247–257.
1947a The Measurement of Human Skill: Oliver-Sharpey Lecture. *British Medical Journal* 1:835–877.
1947b The Twentieth Maudsley Lecture: Intelligence as a Social Problem. *Journal of Mental Science* 93:1–8. → Now called the *British Journal of Psychiatry.*
1958 *Thinking: An Experimental and Social Study.* London: Allen & Unwin.

BARTOL'D, VASILII (BARTHOLD, WILHELM)

See RADLOV, VASILII, AND BARTOL'D, VASILII.

BARTON, JOHN

John Barton (1789–1852), British economist, was born in Southwark, London, into a Quaker family. His father died before he was born, and he was brought up in Tottenham and London, in the homes of Thomas Horne, his maternal grandfather, who seems later to have left him a handsome fortune. There is evidence that Barton received a good education; he knew French, German, and Latin, and his brother, Bernard, spoke of his "mathematically demonstrative turn of mind."

After his marriage, Barton and his family seem to have lived at Stoughton, a charming village some six miles northwest of Chichester, Sussex. About 1833 the household moved to Eastleigh, Hampshire. It remained there until 1851, when Barton became paralyzed; he died the following year, at Chichester. An unsigned obituary notice in the *Gentleman's Magazine* (1852, p. 431) describes him as "one of the original promoters of the Chichester Savings Bank, the Lancasterian School, and the Mechanics' Institution, of which he was treasurer until its union with the Philosophical Society. For many years he lectured within its walls in an able and popular manner."

Barton's first essay, *Observations on the Circumstances Which Influence the Condition of the Labouring Classes of Society,* appeared in June 1817. It is more than probable that both Ricardo and Malthus read this essay at once, without grasping, however, the full significance of Barton's criticism of their free-trade doctrine. Ricardo published his *Principles of Political Economy and Taxation* in the spring of 1817, and Malthus announced that he too intended to publish such a book. Ricardo read Malthus' book as soon as it became available, in 1820. Ricardo noticed, among other things, a footnote referring to Barton, which reminded him of some correspondence he had had with Barton three years earlier. Thus reminded of Barton's views, Ricardo revised his own views on the adverse effects of machinery on the income of the laboring classes and introduced a new chapter on this subject into the 1821 (third) edition of his *Principles*, virtually abandoning the free-trade doctrine.

The significance of Ricardo's shift cannot be overemphasized, nor the importance of Barton's role in producing that shift. It is important to remember that when Barton published his first essay, the free-trade doctrine was sweeping Britain and western Europe. Ricardo, in his *Principles*, seemed to have proved that free trade raised productivity to a maximum and created a necessary and sufficient prerequisite for permanent and lasting prosperity. Freedom of trade implies freedom to invest. Barton was the first writer to demonstrate that investment, or the "increase of fixed capital," as it was then called, results in the displacement of part of the labor force, which becomes unemployed. The economy can reabsorb the unemployed workers only if additional demand for labor appears from an external source. Barton pointed out that in the case of Great Britain it was the influx of precious metals from America via Spain that created new demand for manufactured articles, providing employment. This was also the cause of the population increase observed at this time.

In his *Inquiry* (1820) and in his essay on the excess of population (1830), Barton examined the consequences of rapid population growth—the expression "population explosion" had not yet become fashionable. He deplored the fact that "the great majority of political economists direct their attention almost exclusively to the circumstances which influence the accumulation of *wealth*, abstractedly speaking. Not only do they seem to forget that wealth is not happiness, they even leave out of their consideration the manner in which that wealth is distributed" (1830, p. 42). As an immediate solution to the unemployment problem Barton recommended government-sponsored emigration to Canada.

In his essay *In Defence of the Corn Laws*, Barton took issue with the promoters of the Anti-Corn Law League. He questioned the theory according to which workers who had lost their jobs could easily find employment in other industries. "Is it supposed, then," he asked, "that the ploughmen no longer wanted in Sussex might travel to Manchester, and there find employment as cotton-spinners? . . . The slightest attention to facts might shew that a district overburdened with population is scarcely ever relieved, unless by the cruel process of extermination" ([1833] 1962, p. 29).

On the Continent, Barton's first two essays were given a favorable review by Simonde de Sismondi. His essay on the corn laws was also mentioned favorably in a report by Dr. L. R. Villermé, commissioned by the French Academy of Moral and Political Science (1840). The *Observations* were referred to several times in the writings of Karl Marx, who gave Barton credit for his, Marx's, analysis of the conversion of circulating capital into fixed. More recently, Barton's original and perceptive studies have been noticed by Edwin Cannan (1893) and Stephan Bauer (1925). An article on Barton appeared in the *Encyclopaedia of the Social Sciences* (1930), over the signature of W. H. Dawson. In 1934, Barton's *Observations* was reprinted by the Johns Hopkins Press in Baltimore. A letter from Ricardo to Barton, dated May 20, 1817, is appended to this reprint. A two-volume edition of Barton's *Economic Writings* (1817–1850), with an introduction and notes by the undersigned, was published in 1962.

G. SOTIROFF

[*For discussion of the subsequent development of Barton's ideas, see biographies of* MALTHUS; RICARDO; SIMONDE DE SISMONDI.]

WORKS BY BARTON

(1817) 1962 Observations on the Circumstances Which Influence the Condition of the Labouring Classes of Society. Volume 1, pages 25–112 in John Barton, *Economic Writings*. Regina (Canada): Lynn. → Also published in 1934 as *Condition of the Labouring Classes of Society* by the Johns Hopkins Press.

(1817–1850) 1962 *Economic Writings.* 2 vols., with an introduction and notes by G. Sotiroff. Regina (Canada): Lynn. → Contains two posthumous essays that were first published in 1954 and 1955.

(1820) 1962 An Inquiry Into the Causes of the Progressive Depreciation of Agricultural Labour in Modern Times. Volume 1, pages 115–240 in John Barton, *Economic Writings*. Regina (Canada): Lynn.

(1830) 1962 A Statement of the Consequences Likely to Ensue From Our Growing Excess of Population If Not Remedied by Colonization. Volume 1, pages 241–294 in John Barton, *Economic Writings*. Regina (Canada): Lynn.

(1833) 1962 In Defence of the Corn Laws; Being an Inquiry Into the Expediency of the Existing Restrictions on the Importation of Foreign Corn: With Observations on the Present Social and Political Prospects of Great Britain. Volume 2, pages 5–136 in John Barton, *Economic Writings*. Regina (Canada): Lynn.

SUPPLEMENTARY BIBLIOGRAPHY

BAUER, STEPHAN (1925) 1963 John Barton. Volume 1, page 822 in Robert H. F. Palgrave, *Dictionary of Political Economy*. Rev. ed. New York: Kelley.

CANNAN, EDWIN (1893) 1953 *A History of the Theories of Production and Distribution in English Political Economy, From 1776 to 1848.* 3d ed. London and New York: Staples.

DAWSON, W. H. 1930 John Barton. Volume 2, page 472 in *Encyclopaedia of the Social Sciences*. New York: Macmillan.

Obituary. 1852. *Gentleman's Magazine* New Series 37: 431 only.

SOTIROFF, G. 1962 Introduction. Volume 1, pages 5–24 in John Barton, *Economic Writings*. Regina (Canada): Lynn.

VILLERMÉ, LOUIS RENÉ 1840 *Tableau de l'état physique et moral des ouvriers employés dans les manufactures de coton, de laine et de soie*. 2 vols. Paris: Renouard.

BASTIAN, ADOLF

Adolf Bastian (1826–1905), early ethnographer, was born in Bremen, the son of a wealthy merchant. He studied law at the University of Heidelberg and natural sciences and medicine in Berlin, Jena, and Würzburg. In 1850 he received a medical degree from the Charles University in Prague.

The following year Bastian began the first of the long series of voyages throughout the world that was not to end until his death. For several years he traveled as a ship's doctor and visited Australia, Peru, the West Indies, Mexico, China, the Malay archipelago, India, and Africa. In 1860 he published his major work, the three-volume *Der Mensch in der Geschichte*. He spent the next five years exploring various Asiatic countries and produced as a result of these explorations *Die Völker des östlichen Asien* (1866–1871).

Bastian then accepted a teaching position at the University of Berlin and founded the Königliche Museum für Völkerkunde in Berlin, for decades the most important ethnographical museum in the world. In collaboration with Rudolf Virchow he founded the Berlin Society for Anthropology, Ethnology, and Prehistory, which established the *Zeitschrift für Ethnologie* as its organ. Collecting exhibits for his museum, Bastian in 1875–1876 visited Ecuador, Colombia, Peru, Guatemala, and the Antilles. *Die Kulturländer des alten Amerika* (1878) is his account of this voyage. His travels continued during the next 25 years: he revisited some parts of the world, such as India, Australia, and the Malay archipelago, and saw some for the first time, such as the Fiji Islands, Hawaii, California, Yucatan, Ceylon, and the Near East. At the end of his life he returned to the West Indies, and in Port of Spain, Trinidad, on the voyage home, he died.

Bastian's concept of "elementary ideas." Bastian's life was dedicated to conquering the world ethnologically, to collecting materials from the greatest possible number of cultures. Despite the diversity of such cultures, he believed in uniform laws of growth and a general psychic unity of mankind. Essentially it is this psychic unity that is responsible for the elementary ideas (*Elementargedanken*) that are common to all individuals. Karl von den Steinen (1905, p. 245), Bastian's student, recalls Bastian's comparing an elementary idea to a chemist's element or a botanist's cell. It can be abstracted from the religious and aesthetic concepts of primitive peoples and from their social institutions and techniques. The number of such elementary ideas is relatively small. They are the primary units of which the *Völkergedanken* (folk ideas) are composed. The *Völkergedanken* develop differently from each other under the influence of varying physical surroundings (*geographische Provinzen*) and historical events. Bastian thought that the *Völkergedanken* were conceptually identical with *Weltanschauungen* (Steinen 1905, p. 244).

Jensen (1963, p. 71) observes that the concept of elementary ideas assumes a mechanistic functioning of the human mind, an assumption that was common in the nineteenth century but has become generally unacceptable. However, Bastian argued that the individual could think only if he functioned in a social group (1881b, p. 169).

Bastian and evolution. It is not surprising that a nineteenth-century anthropologist like Bastian had modes of thought that have led some historians of ethnology to call him an evolutionist. However, unlike orthodox evolutionists, he did not think that the pattern of development of the elementary ideas was unilinear; rather, this pattern of development was that of a multiplicity of *Völkergedanken* developing in different physical surroundings. According to Mühlmann (1948, pp. 98–99), Bastian's wide ethnographic experience was enough to prevent his ever becoming an evolutionist in the Spencerian sense. In fact, he differed sharply from the predominant view of his time in that he conceived of development as a spiral, an image that foreshadows modern concepts.

Predecessors, opponents, and successors. The influence of both Wilhelm and Alexander von Humboldt on Bastian is evident. Wilhelm von Humboldt's influence can be seen in the theoretical aspects of Bastian's work, whereas Alexander von Humboldt served him as a model of the explorer and scholar. Alexander von Humboldt also influenced Bastian through his *Kosmos*, the book in which he presented a synthesis of his observations and readings in various branches of science and which culminated in a universal law that harmonized the philosophy of idealism with the exact sciences.

Bastian's views were strongly opposed by the famous biologist Ernst Haeckel. In antithesis to

Bastian's monogenetic view of human origins, Haeckel believed the main human races to be descended from different anthropoid species. The diffusionists also attacked Bastian.

Among those who were influenced by Bastian are a number of distinguished anthropologists, Alfred Cort Haddon, Franz Boas, Richard Thurnwald, A. R. Radcliffe-Brown, and Bronislaw Malinowski. C. G. Jung's concept of a collective unconscious was directly derived from Bastian's elementary ideas (Mühlmann 1948, p. 181). Finally, Bastian's campaign to save data from cultures that are in the process of disappearing is being continued by the International Committee on Urgent Anthropological and Ethnological Research, organized by Robert Heine-Geldern.

HERBERT BALDUS

[For the historical context of Bastian's work, see ANTHROPOLOGY and the biography of HUMBOLDT. For discussion of the subsequent development of his ideas, see the biographies of BOAS; HADDON; MALINOWSKI; RADCLIFFE-BROWN; THURNWALD.]

WORKS BY BASTIAN

1860 Der Mensch in der Geschichte: Zur Begründung einer psychologischen Weltanschauung. 3 vols. in 1. Leipzig: Wigand. → Volume 1: Die Psychologie als Naturwissenschaft. Volume 2: Psychologie und Mythologie. Volume 3: Politische Psychologie.

1866–1871 Die Völker des östlichen Asien. 6 vols. Leipzig: Wigand.

1868 Das Beständige in den Menschenrassen und die Spielweite ihrer Veränderlichkeit: Prolegomena zu einer Ethnologie der Kulturvölker. Berlin: Reimer.

1870 Sprachvergleichende Studien mit besonderer Berücksichtigung der indochinesischen Sprachen. Leipzig: Brockhaus.

1874 Offner Brief an Herrn Prof. Dr. E. Häckel, Verfasser der "Natürlichen Schöpfungsgeschichte." Berlin: Wiegandt.

1875 Schöpfung oder Entstehung: Aphorismen zur Entwicklung des organischen Lebens. Jena (Germany): Costenoble.

1878 Die Kulturländer des alten Amerika. 3 vols. in 4. Berlin: Weidmann.

1881a Die heilige Sage der Polynesier: Kosmogonie und Theogonie. Leipzig: Brockhaus.

1881b Der Völkergedanke im Aufbau einer Wissenschaft vom Menschen und seine Begründung auf ethnologischen Sammlungen. Berlin: Dümmler.

1881c Die Vorgeschichte der Ethnologie: Deutschland's Denkfreunden gewidmet für eine Mussestunde. Berlin: Harrwitz & Gossmann.

1884 Allgemeine Grundzüge der Ethnologie: Prolegomena zur Begründung einer naturwissenschaftlichen Psychologie auf dem Material des Völkergedankens. Berlin: Reimer.

1886 Zur Lehre von den geographischen Provinzen. Berlin: Mittler.

1893–1894 Kontroversen in der Ethnologie. 4 vols. in 1. Berlin: Weidmann. → Volume 1: Die geographischen Provinzen in ihren kulturgeschichtlichen Berührungspunkten. Volume 2: Sociale Unterlagen für rechtliche Institutionen. Volume 3: Über Fetische und Zugehöriges. Volume 4: Fragestellungen der Finalursachen.

1895a Ethnische Elementargedanken in der Lehre vom Menschen. 2 parts in 1 vol. Berlin: Weidmann.

1895b Zur Lehre vom Menschen in ethnischer Anthropologie. 2 vols. Berlin: Reimer.

1898 Elementargedanken und Entlehnungen. Globus 74: 322–323.

1902–1905 Die Lehre vom Denken zur Ergänzung der Naturwissenschaftlichen Psychologie, für Überleitung auf die Geisteswissenschaften. 3 vols. Berlin: Dümmler.

SUPPLEMENTARY BIBLIOGRAPHY

JENSEN, AD. E. 1963 Mythos und Erkenntnis. Paideuma 9:63–75.

KLUCKHOHN, CLYDE; and PRUFER, OLAF 1959 Influences During the Formative Years. Pages 4–28 in Walter Goldschmidt (editor), The Anthropology of Franz Boas: Essays on the Centennial of His Birth. Memoir of the American Anthropological Association, No. 89. San Francisco: Chandler.

LOWIE, ROBERT H. 1937 The History of Ethnological Theory. New York: Farrar & Rinehart.

MÜHLMANN, WILHELM E. 1938 Methodik der Völkerkunde. Stuttgart: Enke.

MÜHLMANN, WILHELM E. 1948 Geschichte der Anthropologie. Bonn: Universitäts-Verlag.

STEINEN, KARL VON DEN 1905 Gedächtnisrede auf Adolf Bastian. Zeitschrift für Ethnologie 37:236–249.

BASTIAT, FRÉDÉRIC

Frédéric Bastiat (1801–1850), the spokesman for the liberal, optimistic school of French economics, was born in Bayonne. The son of a merchant, he was orphaned at the age of nine. Bastiat went to school at Sorèze, where he received an encyclopedic education, learned English, won a prize for poetry, and devoted himself to philosophical studies. At 17, the aspiring poet had to become an "aspiring businessman" in the firm of an uncle, which led to his reading J. B. Say and Adam Smith and gave him a taste for political economy. In 1825 an inheritance brought him back to his birthplace, and he began to manage his property at Mugron, discharging also, conscientiously and independently, his duties as justice of the peace and general councilor of the Landes.

With a friend, Bastiat set up a study circle in his village. It was an argument about England with a member of this circle that caused him to subscribe to an English newspaper and thus to learn of the Manchester League and of Richard Cobden's battle against protective tariffs. Bastiat became a "French Cobden," and the first article that he sent to the Journal des économistes in Paris (1844), an article on French and English customs duties, created a sensation. As a polemicist in Paris, he began to set forth his ideas in a number of magazines and newspapers, especially in *Libre-Échange*, the weekly organ of the Associations pour la Liberté des Échanges (Associations for Free Trade), which he founded in 1846. At the time of the revolution of 1848, he was elected representative of the Landes in the constituent assembly, and later, in the legislative assembly, and he gave lectures, made public addresses, and generally fought socialism with as much vigor as he had fought protectionism. But he fell ill and went to Italy, where he died, in Rome.

Bastiat as pamphleteer. Bastiat is noted primarily for his work as a pamphleteer. He had an exceptional talent for making his opponents' doctrines look ridiculous and, in general, for popularizing economic doctrines. Something of the quality of his mind is revealed by the fact that he was said to have both the wisdom of Franklin and the intelligence of Voltaire.

He was a thoroughgoing liberal and a believer in the virtues of competition, anxious to defend the individual against the state; his main targets were protectionism, socialism, and Ricardian economics. His parables showing the absurdity of protectionism, for example, his "Petition From the Manufacturers of Candles . . ." (1845) or his "The Right Hand and the Left" (1847), have remained famous. In such pamphlets as "L'état" (1849), *The Law* (1850*a*), and "What Is Seen and What Is Not Seen" (1850*b*), he attacked the Proudhonian forms of statism and socialism. He attempted to undermine confidence in government intervention and to show how onerous were the services ostensibly rendered gratuitously by the state. "That Bastiat from the Landes," as Proudhon called him contemptuously, wrote, in a famous lapidary phrase: "The state is the great fiction by means of which everyone tries to live at the expense of everyone else."

Bastiat and the French classical school were convinced that liberty and private property are the pillars on which the best of all possible worlds rests. They deplored the pessimism of those economists whose predictions destroyed faith in natural law. Their goal, therefore, was to rid the science of economics of the doctrines of Malthus and Ricardo by showing that their laws were without foundation. This anti-Ricardianism and optimism went so far as to constitute a belief in universal harmony.

Bastiat as theoretician. Bastiat held that the most liberal society is at the same time the most prosperous and the most progressive; that the perfectibility of man depends on his steadily increasing mastery of nature; and that social progress depends on economic progress. Harmony is a state in which the laws of nature and existing institutions such as liberty and property converge to increase what is good. Only man can disturb this harmony by undermining these two basic institutions through oppression and spoliation, for he alone is responsible for conflict in the economic world.

In order to reconcile the conflict between Ricardo's labor theory of value and the theory of value as utility, Bastiat erected a theory of value as service. The measure of the exchange value of a product is the service that it renders the buyer in terms of trouble saved: "Value is the ratio of two services exchanged."

In Bastiat's optimistic view, land produces not value but utility, which is, as is everything that nature provides, gratuitous. According to this theory, then, Ricardo's theory of ground rent is invalid. What is more, in the total amount of production, the part attributable to nature increases, while the part attributable to labor decreases, so that the extent of gratuitous utilities common to all expands at the expense of earned and appropriated utilities. This process continues until it culminates in the collective enjoyment of goods.

As wealth becomes increasingly gratuitous, property becomes better distributed, and the interests of capital and labor come to coincide. With progress, the rate of interest falls, and although the incomes of both the capitalist and the worker rise in absolute value, that of the capitalist increases less, proportionately, than does that of labor. Liberty has a natural tendency to create that equality which socialists want to institute by other means; Bastiat's quarrel with Proudhon on the interest rate is famous.

Finally, Bastiat denounced protective tariffs as robbery of the consumer, and insisted, even on his deathbed, that the subordination of the producer to the consumer is necessary if private interest is to be subordinate to the general interest and harmony is to prevail.

Influence. In his own time, Bastiat had considerable influence, but his fame is now in eclipse. He was surrounded by a group of economists who supported his ideas—in particular, Charles Dunoyer, Michel Chevalier, Adolphe Blanqui, and Joseph Garnier—and by other admirers. After 1860, Francis A. Walker introduced his doctrines into the United States. At the turn of the century, Charles Gide expressed his admiration for Bastiat, and such pre-World War I French liberals as Pierre Paul Leroy-Beaulieu, Gustave de Molinari, and Yves Guyot relied on Bastiat's authority.

It is all too easy a task for twentieth-century economists to demolish Bastiat's theories, and even the claim that he anticipated the theory of the multiplier cannot easily be defended. Bastiat won over his contemporaries but disappointed his successors.

HUGUETTE DURAND

[*For the historical context of Bastiat's work, see the biographies of* MALTHUS *and* RICARDO.]

WORKS BY BASTIAT

1844   De l'influence des tarifs français et anglais sur l'avenir des deux peuples. *Journal des économistes* 9:244–271.

(1845) 1877   Petition From the Manufacturers of Candles, Wax-lights, Lamps, Chandeliers, Reflectors, Snuffers, Extinguishers: And From the Producers . . . of Everything Used for Lights. Pages 73–80 in Frédéric Bastiat, *Sophisms of Protection.* New York: Putnam. → First published in French.

(1847) 1877   The Right Hand and the Left. Pages 309–318 in Frédéric Bastiat, *Sophisms of Protection.* New York: Putnam. → First published as "*La main droite et la main gauche*" in *Sophismes économiques.*

(1849) 1878   L'état. Volume 4, pages 328–342 in Frédéric Bastiat, *Oeuvres complètes.* 4th ed. Paris: Guillaumin.

(1850a) 1950   *The Law.* Irvington, N.Y.: Foundation for Economic Education. → First published as *La loi.*

(1850b) 1859   *What Is Seen and What Is Not Seen: Or Political Economy in One Lesson.* London: Smith. → First published as *Ce qu'on voit et ce qu'on ne voit pas.*

(1854–1855) 1862–1864   *Oeuvres complètes.* 7 vols., 2d ed. Paris: Guillaumin.

1889   *Oeuvres choisies.* Paris: Guillaumin.

SUPPLEMENTARY BIBLIOGRAPHY

BAUDIN, LOUIS 1962   *Frédéric Bastiat.* Paris: Dalloz.

GIDE, CHARLES; and RIST, CHARLES (1909) 1948   *A History of Economic Doctrines From the Time of the Physiocrats to the Present Day.* Boston: Heath. → First published in French.

GONNARD, RENÉ (1921–1922) 1941   *Histoire des doctrines économiques.* Paris: Librairie Générale de Droit et de Jurisprudence.

JAMES, ÉMILE 1955   *Histoire sommaire de la pensée économique.* Paris: Montchrestien.

NOUVION, GEORGES DE 1905   *Monopole et liberté: Frédéric Bastiat, sa vie, ses oeuvres, ses doctrines.* Paris: Guillaumin.

PIETTRE, ANDRÉ 1959   *Histoire de la pensée économique et analyse des théories contemporaines.* Paris: Dalloz.

RONCE, P. 1905   *Frédéric Bastiat: Sa vie, son oeuvre.* Paris: Guillaumin.

VILLEY, DANIEL 1944   *Petite histoire des grandes doctrines économiques.* Paris: Presses Universitaires de France.

BAYES, THOMAS

Thomas Bayes (1702–1761) was the eldest son of the Reverend Joshua Bayes, one of the first nonconformist ministers to be publicly ordained in England. The younger Bayes spent the last thirty years of his comfortable, celibate life as Presbyterian minister of the meeting house, Mount Sion, in the fashionable town of Tunbridge Wells, Kent. Little is known about his personal history, and there is no record that he communicated with the well-known scientists of his day. Circumstantial evidence suggests that he was educated in literature, languages, and science at Coward's dissenting academy in London (Holland 1962). He was elected a fellow of the Royal Society in 1742, presumably on the basis of two metaphysical tracts he published (one of them anonymously) in 1731 and 1736 (Barnard 1958). The only mathematical work from his pen consists of two articles published posthumously in 1764 by his friend Richard Price, one of the pioneers of social security (Ogborn 1962). The first is a short note, written in the form of an undated letter, on the divergence of the Stirling (de Moivre) series $\ln(z!)$. It has been suggested that Bayes' remark that the use of "a proper number of the first terms of the . . . series" will produce an accurate result constitutes the first recognition of the asymptotic behavior of a series expansion (see Deming's remarks in Bayes [1764] 1963). The second article is the famous "An Essay Towards Solving a Problem in the Doctrine of Chances," with Price's preface, footnotes, and appendix (followed, a year later, by a continuation and further development of some of Bayes' results).

The "Problem" posed in the Essay is: "*Given the number of times in which an unknown event has happened and failed: Required the chance that the probability of its happening in a single trial lies somewhere between any two degrees of probability that can be named.*" A few sentences later Bayes writes: "By *chance* I mean the same as probability" ([1764] 1963, p. 376).

If the number of successful happenings of the event is p and the failures q, and if the two named "degrees" of probability are b and f, respectively, Proposition 9 of the Essay provides the following answer expressed in terms of areas under the curve $x^p(1-x)^q$:

$$(1) \qquad \int_b^f x^p(1-x)^q \, dx \bigg/ \int_0^1 x^p(1-x)^q \, dx.$$

This is based on the assumption (Bayes' "Postulate 1") that all values of the unknown probability are equally likely before the observations are made. Bayes indicated the applicability of this postulate in his famous "Scholium": "that the . . . rule is the proper one to be used in the case of an event concerning the probability of which we absolutely know nothing antecedently to any trials made concerning it, seems to appear from the following consideration; viz. that concerning such an event I have no reason to think that, in a certain number of trials, it should rather happen any one possible number of times than another" (*ibid.*, pp. 392–393).

The remainder of Bayes' Essay and the supplement (half of which was written by Price) consists of attempts to evaluate (1) numerically, (*a*) by expansion of the integrand and (*b*) by integration by parts. The results are satisfactory for *p* and *q* small but the approximations for large *p, q* are only of historical interest (Wishart 1927).

Opinions about the intellectual and mathematical ability evidenced by the letter and the essay are extraordinarily diverse. Netto (1908), after outlining Bayes' geometrical proof, agreed with Laplace ([1812] 1820) that it is *ein wenig verwickelt* ("somewhat involved"). Todhunter (1865) thought that the résumé of probability theory that precedes Proposition 9 was "excessively obscure." Molina (in Bayes [1764] 1963, p. xi) said that "Bayes and Price . . . can hardly be classed with the great mathematicians that immediately preceded or followed them," and Hogben (1957, p. 133) stated that "the ideas commonly identified with the name of Bayes are largely [Laplace's]."

On the other hand von Wright (1951, p. 292) found Bayes' Essay "a masterpiece of mathematical elegance and free from . . . obscure philosophical pretentions." Barnard (1958, p. 295) wrote that Bayes' "mathematical work . . . is of the very highest quality." Fisher ([1956] 1959, p. 8) concurred with these views when he said Bayes' "mathematical contributions . . . show him to have been in the first rank of independent thinkers. . . ."

The subsequent history of mathematicians' and philosophers' extensions and criticisms of Proposition 9—the only statement that can properly be called Bayes' theorem (or rule)—is entertaining and instructive. In his first published article on probability theory, Laplace (1774), without mentioning Bayes, introduced the principle that if p_j is the probability of an observable event resulting from "cause" j ($j = 1, 2, 3, \cdots, n$) then the probability that "cause" j is operative to produce the observed event is

$$(2) \qquad p_j \left/ \sum_{j=1}^{n} p_j \right. .$$

This is Principle III of the first (1812) edition of Laplace's probability text, and it implies that the prior (antecedent, initial) probabilities of each of the "causes" is the same. However, in the second (1814) edition Laplace added a few lines saying

that if the "causes" are not equally probable a priori (2) would become

$$(3) \qquad \omega_j p_j \left/ \sum_{j=1}^{n} \omega_j p_j \right. ,$$

where ω_j is the prior probability of cause j and p_j is now the probability of the event, given that "cause" j is operative. He gave no illustrations of this more general formula.

Laplace (1774) applied his new principle (2) to find the probability of drawing *m* white and *n* black tickets in a specified order from an urn containing an infinite number of white and black tickets in an unknown ratio and from which *p* white and *q* black tickets have already been drawn. His solution, namely,

$$(4) \quad \int_0^1 x^{p+m} (1-x)^{q+n} \, dx \left/ \int_0^1 x^p (1-x)^q \, dx \right.$$
$$= \frac{(p+m)! \, (q+n)! \, (p+q+1)!}{p! \, q! \, (p+q+m+1)!},$$

was later (1778–1781; 1812, chapter 6) generalized by the bare statement that if all values of *x* are not equally probable a factor $z(x)$ representing the a priori probability density (*facilité*) of *x* must appear in both integrands. However, Laplace's own views on the applicability of expressions like (4) were stated in 1778 (1778–1781, p. 264) and agree with those of Bayes' Scholium: "Lorsqu'on n'a aucune donnée *a priori* sur la possibilité d'un événement, il faut supposer toutes les possibilités, depuis zéro jusqu'à l'unité, également probables. . . ." ("When nothing is given a priori as to the probability of an event, one must suppose all probabilities, from zero to one, to be equally likely. . . .") Much later Karl Pearson (1924, p. 191) pointed out that Bayes was "considering excess of one variate . . . over a second . . . as the determining factor of occurrence" and this led naturally to a generalization of the measure in the integrals of (1). Fisher (1956) has even suggested that Bayes himself had this possibility in mind.

Laplace's views about prior probability distributions found qualified acceptance on the Continent (von Kries 1886) but were subjected to strong criticism in England (Boole 1854; Venn 1866; Chrystal 1891; Fisher 1922), where a relative frequency definition of probability was proposed and found incompatible with the uniform prior distribution (for example, E. S. Pearson 1925). However, developments in the theory of inference (Keynes 1921; Ramsey 1923–1928; Jeffreys 1931; de Finetti 1937; Savage 1954; Good 1965) suggest that there are advantages to be gained from a "subjective" or a "logical" definition of probability and this approach gives Bayes' theorem, in its more general form, a central place in inductive procedures (Jeffreys 1939; Raiffa & Schlaifer 1961; Lindley 1965).

HILARY L. SEAL

[*For the historical context of Bayes' work, see* STATISTICS, *article on* THE HISTORY OF STATISTICAL METHOD; *and the biography of* LAPLACE. *For discussion of the subsequent development of his ideas, see* BAYESIAN INFERENCE; PROBABILITY; *and the biographies of* FISHER, R. A.; *and* PEARSON.]

BIBLIOGRAPHY

BARNARD, G. A. 1958 Thomas Bayes: A Biographical Note. *Biometrika* 45:293–295.

BAYES, THOMAS (1764) 1963 *Facsimiles of Two Papers by Bayes.* New York: Hafner. → Contains "An Essay Towards Solving a Problem in the Doctrine of Chances, With Richard Price's Foreword and Discussion," with a commentary by Edward C. Molina; and "A Letter on Asymptotic Series From Bayes to John Canton," with a commentary by W. Edwards Deming. Both essays first appeared in Volume 53 of the *Philosophical Transactions*, Royal Society of London, and retain the original pagination.

BOOLE, GEORGE (1854) 1951 *An Investigation of the Laws of Thought, on Which Are Founded the Mathematical Theories of Logic and Probabilities.* New York: Dover.

CHRYSTAL, GEORGE 1891 On Some Fundamental Principles in the Theory of Probability. Actuarial Society of Edinburgh, *Transactions* 2:419–439.

DE FINETTI, BRUNO 1937 La prévision: Ses lois logiques, ses sources subjectives. Paris, Université de, Institut Henri Poincaré, *Annales* 7:1–68.

FISHER, R. A. (1922) 1950 On the Mathematical Foundations of Theoretical Statistics. Pages 10.307a–10.368 in R. A. Fisher, *Contributions to Mathematical Statistics.* New York: Wiley. → First published in Volume 222 of the *Philosophical Transactions*, Series A, Royal Society of London.

FISHER, R. A. (1956) 1959 *Statistical Methods and Scientific Inference.* 2d ed., rev. New York: Hafner; London: Oliver & Boyd.

GOOD, IRVING J. 1965 *The Estimation of Probabilities: An Essay on Modern Bayesian Methods.* Cambridge, Mass.: M.I.T. Press.

HOGBEN, LANCELOT T. 1957 *Statistical Theory; the Relationship of Probability, Credibility and Error: An Examination of the Contemporary Crisis in Statistical Theory From a Behaviourist Viewpoint.* London: Allen & Unwin.

HOLLAND, J. D. 1962 The Reverend Thomas Bayes, F.R.S. (1702–1761). *Journal of the Royal Statistical Society* Series A 125:451–461.

JEFFREYS, HAROLD (1931) 1957 *Scientific Inference.* 2d ed. Cambridge Univ. Press.

JEFFREYS, HAROLD (1939) 1961 *Theory of Probability.* 3d ed. Oxford: Clarendon.

KEYNES, J. M. (1921) 1952 *A Treatise on Probability.* London: Macmillan. → A paperback edition was published in 1962 by Harper.

KRIES, JOHANNES VON (1886) 1927 *Die Principien der Wahrscheinlichkeitsrechnung: Eine logische Untersuchung.* 2d ed. Tübingen (Germany): Mohr.

LAPLACE, PIERRE S. (1774) 1891 Mémoire sur la probabilité des causes par les événements. Volume 8, pages 27–65 in Pierre S. Laplace, *Oeuvres complètes de Laplace.* Paris: Gauthier-Villars.

LAPLACE, PIERRE S. (1778–1781) 1893 Mémoire sur les probabilités. Volume 9, pages 383–485 in Pierre S. Laplace, *Oeuvres complètes de Laplace.* Paris: Gauthier-Villars.

LAPLACE, PIERRE S. (1812) 1820 *Théorie analytique des probabilités.* 3d ed., rev. Paris: Courcier.

LINDLEY, DENNIS V. 1965 *Introduction to Probability and Statistics From a Bayesian Viewpoint.* 2 vols. Cambridge Univ. Press.

NETTO, E. 1908 Kombinatorik, Wahrscheinlichkeitsrechnung, Reihen-Imaginäres. Volume 4, pages 199–318, in Moritz Cantor (editor), *Vorlesungen über Geschichte der Mathematik.* Leipzig: Teubner.

OGBORN, MAURICE E. 1962 *Equitable Assurances: The Story of Life Assurance in the Experience of The Equitable Life Assurance Society, 1762–1962.* London: Allen & Unwin.

PEARSON, EGON S. 1925 Bayes' Theorem, Examined in the Light of Experimental Sampling. *Biometrika* 17:388–442.

PEARSON, KARL 1924 Note on Bayes' Theorem. *Biometrika* 16:190–193.

PRICE, RICHARD 1765 A Demonstration of the Second Rule in the Essay Towards a Solution of a Problem in the Doctrine of Chances. Royal Society of London, *Philosophical Transactions* 54:296–325. → Reprinted by Johnson in 1965.

RAIFFA, HOWARD; and SCHLAIFER, ROBERT 1961 *Applied Statistical Decision Theory.* Harvard University Graduate School of Business Administration, Studies in Managerial Economics. Boston: The School.

RAMSEY, FRANK P. (1923–1928) 1950 *The Foundations of Mathematics and Other Logical Essays.* New York: Humanities.

SAVAGE, LEONARD J. 1954 *The Foundations of Statistics.* New York: Wiley.

TODHUNTER, ISAAC (1865) 1949 *A History of the Mathematical Theory of Probability From the Time of Pascal to That of Laplace.* New York: Chelsea.

VENN, JOHN (1866) 1888 *The Logic of Chance: An Essay on the Foundations and Province of the Theory of Probability, With Special Reference to Its Logical Bearings and Its Application to Moral and Social Science.* 3d ed. London: Macmillan.

WISHART, JOHN 1927 On the Approximate Quadrature of Certain Skew Curves, With an Account of the Researches of Thomas Bayes. *Biometrika* 19:1–38.

WRIGHT, GEORG H. VON 1951 *A Treatise on Induction and Probability.* London: Routledge.

BAYESIAN INFERENCE

Bayesian inference or Bayesian statistics is an approach to statistical inference based on the theory of subjective probability. A formal Bayesian analysis leads to probabilistic assessments of the object of uncertainty. For example, a Bayesian inference might be, "The probability is .95 that the mean of a normal distribution lies between 12.1 and 23.7." The number .95 represents a degree of belief, either in the sense of *subjective probability coherent* or *subjective probability rational* [*see* PROBABILITY, *article on* INTERPRETATIONS, *which should be read in conjunction with the present article*]; .95 need not correspond to any "objective" long-run relative frequency. Very roughly, a degree of belief of .95 can be interpreted as betting odds of 95 to 5 or 19 to 1. A degree of belief is always potentially a basis for action; for example, it may be combined with utilities by the principle of maximization of expected utility [*see* DECISION THEORY; UTILITY].

By contrast, the sampling theory or classical approach to inference leads to probabilistic statements about the method by which a particular inference is obtained. Thus a classical inference might be, "A .95 confidence interval for the mean of a normal distribution extends from 12.1 to 23.7" [*see* ESTIMATION, *article on* CONFIDENCE INTERVALS AND REGIONS]. The number .95 here represents a long-run relative frequency, namely the frequency with which intervals obtained by the method that resulted in the present interval would in fact include the unknown mean. (It is not to be inferred from the fact that we used the same numbers, .95, 12.1, and 23.7, in both illustrations that there will necessarily be a numerical coincidence between the two approaches.)

The term Bayesian arises from an elementary theorem of probability theory named after the Rev. Thomas Bayes, an English clergyman of the eighteenth century, who first enunciated a special case of it and proposed its use in inference. Bayes' theorem is used in the process of making Bayesian inferences, as will be explained below. For a number of historical reasons, however, current interest in Bayesian inference is quite recent, dating, say, from the 1950s. Hence the term "neo-Bayesian" is sometimes used instead of "Bayesian."

An illustration of Bayesian inference. For a simple illustration of the Bayesian approach, consider the problem of making inferences about a Bernoulli process with parameter p. A Bernoulli process can be visualized in terms of repeated independent tosses of a not necessarily fair coin. It generates heads and tails in such a way that the probability of heads on a single trial is always equal to a parameter p regardless of the previous history of heads and tails. The subjectivistic counterpart of this description of a Bernoulli process is given by de Finetti's concept of exchangeable events [*see* PROBABILITY, *article on* INTERPRETATIONS].

Suppose first that we have no direct sample evidence from the process. Based on experience with similar processes, introspection, general knowledge, etc., we may be willing to translate our judgments about the process into probabilistic terms. For ex-

ample, we might assess a (subjective) probability distribution for $\tilde{p}$. The tilde ($\sim$) indicates that we are now thinking of the parameter p as a random variable. Such a distribution is called a *prior* (or *a priori*) distribution because it is usually assessed prior to sample evidence. Purely for illustration, suppose that the prior distribution of $\tilde{p}$ is uniform on the interval from 0 to 1: the probability that $\tilde{p}$ lies in any subinterval is that subinterval's length, no matter where the subinterval is located between 0 and 1. Now suppose that on three tosses of a coin we observe heads, heads, and tails. The probability of observing this sample, conditional on $\tilde{p} = p$, is $p^2(1 - p)$. If we regard this expression as a function of p, it is called the *likelihood function* of the sample. Bayes' theorem shows how to use the likelihood function in conjunction with the prior distribution to obtain a revised or *posterior* distribution of $\tilde{p}$. Posterior means after the sample evidence, and the posterior distribution represents a reconciliation of sample evidence and prior judgment. In terms of inferences about $\tilde{p}$, we may write Bayes' theorem in words as follows: Posterior probability (density) at p, given the observed sample, equals

$$\frac{\text{Prior probability (density) at } p \times \text{likelihood function}}{\text{Prior probability of obtaining the observed sample}}.$$

Expressed mathematically,

$$(1) \quad f''(p|r, n) = \frac{f'(p)\, p^r (1 - p)^{n-r}}{\int_0^1 f'(p)\, p^r (1 - p)^{n-r}\, dp},$$

where $f'(p)$ denotes the prior density of $\tilde{p}$, $p^r(1 - p)^{n-r}$ denotes the likelihood if r heads are observed in n trials, and $f''(p|r,n)$ denotes the posterior density of $\tilde{p}$ given the sample evidence. In our example, $f'(p) = 1$ for $0 \leqslant p \leqslant 1$ and 0 otherwise; $r = 2$; $n = 3$; and

$$\int_0^1 f'(p)\, p^r (1 - p)^{n-r}\, dp = \int_0^1 p^2 (1 - p)\, dp$$
$$= 1/12,$$

so that

$$f''(p|r = 2, n = 3) = \begin{cases} 12\, p^2(1 - p), & 0 \leqslant p \leqslant 1, \\ 0, & \text{otherwise.} \end{cases}$$

Thus we emerge from the analysis with an explicit posterior probability distribution for $\tilde{p}$. This distribution characterizes fully our judgments about $\tilde{p}$. It could be applied in a formal decision-theoretic analysis in which utilities of alternative acts are functions of p. For example, we might make a Bayesian point estimate of p (each possible point estimate is regarded as an act), and the seriousness of an estimation error (loss) might be proportional to the square of the error. The best point estimate can then be shown to be the mean of the posterior distribution; in our example this would be .6. Or we might wish to describe certain aspects of the posterior distribution for summary purposes; it can be shown, for example, that, where P refers to the posterior distribution,

$$P(\tilde{p} < .194) = 0.25 \quad \text{and} \quad P(\tilde{p} > .932) = .025,$$

so that a .95 *credible interval* for $\tilde{p}$ extends from .194 to .932. Again, it can easily be shown that $P(\tilde{p} > .5) = .688$: the posterior probability that the coin is "biased" in favor of heads is a little over $\frac{2}{3}$.

The likelihood principle. In our example, the effect of the sample evidence was wholly transmitted by the likelihood function. All we needed to know from the sample was $p^r(1 - p)^{n-r}$; the actual sequence of individual observations was irrelevant *so long as we believed the assumption of a Bernoulli process*. In general, a full Bayesian analysis requires as inputs for Bayes' theorem only the likelihood function and the prior distribution. Thus the import of the sample evidence is fully reflected in the likelihood function, a principle known as the likelihood principle [*see* LIKELIHOOD]. Alternatively, given that the sample is drawn from a Bernoulli process, the import of the sample is fully reflected in the numbers r and n, which are called *sufficient statistics* [*see* SUFFICIENCY]. (If the sample size, n, is fixed in advance of sampling, it is said that r alone is sufficient.)

The likelihood principle implies certain consequences that do not accord with traditional ideas. Here are examples: (1) Once the data are in, there is no distinction between sequential analysis and analysis for fixed sample size. In the Bernoulli example, successive samples of n_1 and n_2 with r_1 and r_2 successes could be analyzed as one pooled sample of $n_1 + n_2$ trials with $r_1 + r_2$ successes. Alternatively, a posterior distribution could be computed after the first sample of n_1; this distribution could then serve as a prior distribution for the second sample; finally, a second posterior distribution could be computed after the second sample of n_2. By either route the posterior distribution after $n_1 + n_2$ observations would be the same. Under almost any situation that is likely to arise in practice, the "stopping rule" by which sampling is terminated is irrelevant to the analysis of the sample. For example, it would not matter whether r successes in n trials were obtained by fixing r in advance and observing the rth success on the nth trial, or by fixing n in advance and counting r successes in the n trials. (2) For the purpose of statistical reporting, the likelihood function is the

important information to be conveyed. If a reader wants to perform his own Bayesian analysis, he needs the likelihood function, not a posterior distribution based on someone else's prior nor traditional analyses such as significance tests, from which it may be difficult or impossible to recover the likelihood function.

Vagueness about prior probabilities. In our example we assessed the prior distribution of $\tilde{p}$ as a uniform distribution from 0 to 1. It is sometimes thought that such an assessment means that we "know" $\tilde{p}$ is so distributed and that our claim to knowledge might be verified or refuted in some way. It is indeed possible to imagine situations in which the distribution of $\tilde{p}$ might be known, as when one coin is to be drawn at random from a number of coins, each of which has a known p determined by a very large number of tosses. The frequency distribution of these p's would then serve as a prior distribution, and all statisticians would apply Bayes' theorem in analyzing sample evidence. But such an example would be unusual. Typically, in making an inference about $\tilde{p}$ for a *particular* coin, the prior distribution of $\tilde{p}$ is not a description of some distribution of p's but rather a tool for expressing judgments about $\tilde{p}$ based on evidence other than the evidence of the particular sample to be analyzed.

Not only do we rarely know the prior distribution of $\tilde{p}$, but we are typically more or less vague when we try to assess it. This vagueness is comparable to the vagueness that surrounds many decisions in everyday life. For example, a person may decide to offer $21,250 for a house he wishes to buy, even though he may be quite vague about what amount he "should" offer. Similarly, in statistical inference we may assess a prior distribution in the face of a certain amount of vagueness. If we are not willing to do so, we cannot pursue a *formal* Bayesian analysis and must evaluate sample evidence intuitively, perhaps aided by the tools of descriptive statistics and classical inference.

Vagueness about prior probabilities is not the only kind of vagueness to be faced in statistical analysis, and the other kinds of vagueness are equally troublesome for approaches to statistics that do not use prior probabilities. Vagueness about the likelihood function, that is, the process generating the data, is typically substantial and hard to deal with. Moreover, both classical and Bayesian decision theory bring in the idea of utility, and utilities often are vague.

In assessing prior probabilities, skillful self-interrogation is needed in order to mitigate vagueness. Self-interrogation may be made more systematic and illuminating in several ways. (1) *Direct judgmental assessment*. In assessing the prior distribution of $\tilde{p}$, for example, we might ask: For what p would we be indifferent to an even money bet that $\tilde{p}$ is above or below this value? (Answer: the .50-quantile or median.) If we were told that $\tilde{p}$ is above the .50-quantile just assessed, but nothing more, for what value of p would we now be indifferent in such a bet? (Answer: the .75-quantile.) Similarly we might locate other key quantiles or key relative heights on the density function. (2) *Translation to equivalent but hypothetical prior sample evidence*. For example, we might feel that our prior opinion about $\tilde{p}$ is roughly what it would have been if we had initially held a uniform prior, and then seen r heads in n hypothetical trials from the process. The implied posterior distribution would serve as the prior. (3) *Contemplation of possible sample outcomes*. Sometimes we may find it easy to decide directly what our posterior distribution *would be* if a certain hypothetical sample outcome were to materialize. We can then work backward to see the prior distribution thereby implied. Of course, this approach is likely to be helpful only if the hypothetical sample outcomes are easy to assimilate. For example, if we make a certain technical assumption about the general shape of the prior (beta) distribution [*see* DISTRIBUTIONS, STATISTICAL, *article on* SPECIAL CONTINUOUS DISTRIBUTIONS], the answers to the following two simply stated questions imply a prior distribution of $\tilde{p}$: (1) How do we assess the probability of heads *on a single trial*? (2) If we were to observe a head on a single trial (this is the hypothetical future outcome), how would we assess the probability of heads on a second trial?

These approaches are intended only to be suggestive. If several approaches to self-interrogation lead to substantially different prior distributions, we must either try to remove the internal inconsistency or be content with an intuitive analysis. Actually, from the point of view of subjective probability coherent, the discovery of internal inconsistency in one's judgments is the only route toward more rational decisions. The danger is not that internal inconsistencies will be revealed but that they will be suppressed by self-deception or glossed over by lethargy.

It may happen that vagueness affects only unimportant aspects of the prior distribution: theoretical or empirical analysis may show that the posterior distribution is insensitive to these aspects of the distribution. For example, we may be vague about many aspects of the prior distribution, yet feel that it is nearly uniform over all values of the parameter for which the likelihood function is not essentially zero. This has been called a diffuse, informationless, or locally uniform prior distribution. These terms are to be interpreted relative to the spread of the likelihood function, which depends on the sample size; a prior that is diffuse relative to a large sample may not be diffuse relative to a small one. If the prior distribution is diffuse, the posterior distribution can be easily approximated from the assumption of a strictly uniform prior distribution. The latter assumption, known historically as Bayes' postulate (not to be confused with Bayes' theorem), is regarded mainly as a device that leads to good approximations in certain circumstances, although supporters of subjective probability rational sometimes regard it as more than that in their approach to Bayesian inference. The uniform prior is also useful for statistical reporting, since it leads to posterior distributions from which the likelihood is easily recovered and presents the results in a readily usable form to any reader whose prior distribution is diffuse.

Probabilistic prediction. A distribution, prior or posterior, of the parameter $\tilde{p}$ of a Bernoulli process implies a probabilistic prediction for any future sample to be drawn from the process, assuming that the stopping rule is given. For example, the denominator in the right-hand side of Bayes' formula for Bernoulli sampling (equation 1) can be interpreted as the probability of obtaining the particular sample actually observed, given the prior distribution of $\tilde{p}$. If Mr. A and Mr. B each has a distribution for $\tilde{p}$, and a new sample is then observed, we can calculate the probability of the sample in the light of each prior distribution. The ratio of these probabilities, technically a marginal likelihood ratio, measures the extent to which the data favor Mr. A over Mr. B or vice versa. This idea has important consequences for evaluating judgments, selecting statistical models, and performing Bayesian tests of significance.

In connection with the previous paragraph a separate point is worth making. The posterior distributions of Mr. A and Mr. B are bound to grow closer together as sample evidence piles up, so long as neither of the priors was dogmatic. An example of a dogmatic prior would be the opinion that $\tilde{p}$ is exactly .5.

In an important sense the predictive distribution of future observations, which is derived from the posterior distribution, is more fundamental to Bayesian inference than the posterior distribution itself.

Multivariate inference and nuisance parameters. Thus far we have used one basic example, inferences about a Bernoulli process. To introduce some additional concepts, we now turn to inferences about the mean μ of a normal distribution with unknown variance σ^2. In this case we begin with a *joint* prior distribution for $\tilde{\mu}$ and $\tilde{\sigma}^2$. The likelihood function is now a function of two variables, μ and σ^2. An inspection of the likelihood function will show not only that the *sequence* of observations is irrelevant to inference but also that the magnitudes are irrelevant except insofar as they help determine the sample mean $\bar{x}$ and variance s^2, which, along with the sample size n, are the sufficient statistics of this example. The prior distribution combines with the likelihood essentially as before except that a double integration (or double summation) is needed instead of a single integration (or summation). The result is a joint posterior distribution of $\tilde{\mu}$ and $\tilde{\sigma}^2$.

If we are interested only in $\tilde{\mu}$, then $\tilde{\sigma}^2$ is said to be a *nuisance parameter*. In principle it is simple to deal with a nuisance parameter: we integrate it out of the posterior distribution. In our example this means that we must find the marginal distribution of $\tilde{\mu}$ from the joint posterior distribution of $\tilde{\mu}$ and $\tilde{\sigma}^2$.

Multivariate problems and nuisance parameters can always be dealt with by the approach just described. The integrations required may demand heavy computation, but the task is straightforward. A more difficult problem is that of assessing multivariate prior distributions, especially when the number of parameters is large, and research is needed to find better techniques for avoiding self-contradictions and meeting the problems posed by vagueness in such assessments.

Design of experiments and surveys.   So far we have talked only about problems of analysis of samples, without saying anything about what kind of sample evidence, and how much, should be sought. This kind of problem is known as a problem of *design*. A formal Bayesian solution of a design problem requires that we look beyond the posterior distribution to the ultimate decisions that will be made in the light of this distribution. What is the best design depends on the purposes to be served by collecting the data. Given the specific purpose and the principle of maximization of expected utility, it is possible to calculate the expected utility of the best act for any particular sample outcome. We can repeat this for each possible sample outcome for a given sample design. Next, we can weight each such utility by the probability of the corresponding outcome in the light of the prior distribution. This gives an over-all expected utility for any proposed design. Finally, we pick the sample design with the highest expected utility.

For two-action problems—for example, deciding whether a new medical treatment is better or worse than a standard treatment—this procedure is in no conflict with the traditional approach of selecting designs by comparing operating characteristics, although it formalizes certain things—prior probabilities and utilities—that often are treated intuitively in the traditional approach.

Comparison of Bayesian and classical inference. Certain common statistical practices are subject to criticism, either from the point of view of Bayesian or of classical theory: for example, estimation problems are frequently regarded as tests of null hypotheses [*see* HYPOTHESIS TESTING], and .05 or .01 significance levels are used inflexibly. Bayesian and classical theory are in many respects closer to each other than either is to everyday practice. In comparing the two approaches, therefore, we shall confine the discussion to the level of underlying theory. In one sense the basic difference is the acceptance of subjective probability judgment as a *formal* component of Bayesian inference. This does not mean that classical theorists would disavow judgment, only that they would apply it informally after the purely statistical analysis is finished: judgment is the "second span in the bridge of inference." Building on subjective probability, Bayesian theory is a unified theory, whereas classical theory is diverse and *ad hoc*. In this sense Bayesian theory is simpler. In another sense, however, Bayesian theory is more complex, for it incorporates more into the formal analysis. Consider a famous controversy of classical statistics, the problem of comparing the means of two normal distributions with possibly unequal and unknown variances, the so-called Behrens–Fisher problem [*see* LINEAR HYPOTHESES]. Conceptually this problem poses major difficulties for some classical theories (not Fisher's fiducial inference; see Fisher 1939) but none for Bayesian theory. In application, however, the Bayesian approach faces the problem of assessing a prior distribution involving four random variables. Moreover, there may be messy computational work after the prior distribution has been assessed.

In many applications, however, a credible interval emerging from the assumption of a diffuse prior distribution is identical, or nearly identical, to the corresponding confidence interval. There is a difference of interpretation, illustrated in the opening two paragraphs of this article, but in practice many people interpret the classical result in the Bayesian way. There often are numerical similarities between the results of Bayesian and classical analyses of the same data; but there can also be substantial differences, for example, when the prior distribution is nondiffuse and when a genuine null hypothesis is to be tested.

Often it may happen that the problem of vagueness, discussed at some length above, makes a formal Bayesian analysis seem unwise. In this event Bayesian theory may still be of some value in selecting a descriptive analysis or a classical technique that conforms well to the general Bayesian approach, and perhaps in modifying the classical technique. For example, many of the classical developments in sample surveys and analysis of experiments can be given rough Bayesian interpretations when vagueness about the likelihood (as opposed to prior probabilities) prevents a full Bayesian analysis. Moreover, even an abortive Bayesian analysis may contribute insight into a problem.

Bayesian inference has as yet received much less theoretical study than has classical inference. Such commonplace and fundamental ideas of classical statistics as randomization and nonparametric methods require re-examination from the Bayesian view, and this re-examination has scarcely begun. It is hard at this writing to predict how far Bayesian theory will lead in modification and reinterpretation of classical theory. Before a fully Bayesian replacement is available, there is certainly no need to discard those classical techniques that seem roughly compatible with the Bayesian approach; indeed, many classical techniques are, under certain conditions, good approximations to fully Bayesian ones, and useful Bayesian interpretations are now known for almost all classical techniques. From the classical viewpoint, the Bayesian approach often leads to procedures with desirable sampling properties and acts as a stimulus to further theoretical development. In the meanwhile, the interaction between the two approaches promises to lead to fruitful developments in statistical inference; and the Bayesian approach promises to illuminate a number of problems—such as allowance for selectivity—that are otherwise hard to handle.

HARRY V. ROBERTS

[See also the biography of BAYES.]

BIBLIOGRAPHY

The first book-length development of Bayesian inference, which emphasizes heavily the decision-theoretic foundations of the subject, is Schlaifer 1959. A more technical development of the subject is given by Raiffa & Schlaifer 1961. An excellent short introduction with an extensive bibliography is Savage 1962. A somewhat longer introduction is given by Savage and other contributors in Joint Statistics Seminar 1959. This volume also discusses advantages and disadvantages of the Bayesian approach. An interesting application of Bayesian inference, along with a penetrating discussion of underlying philosophy and a comparison with the corresponding classical analysis, is given in Mosteller & Wallace 1964. This study gives a specific example of how one might cope with vagueness about the likelihood function. Another example is to be found in Box & Tiao 1962. A thorough development of Bayesian inference from the viewpoint of "subjective probability rational" is to be found in Jeffreys 1939. A basic paper on fiducial inference is Fisher 1939.

BAYES, THOMAS (1764) 1963 *Facsimiles of Two Papers by Bayes.* New York: Hafner. → Contains "An Essay Toward Solving a Problem in the Doctrine of Chances, With Richard Price's Foreword and Discussion," with a commentary by Edward C. Molina, and "A Letter on Asymptotic Series From Bayes to John Canton," with a commentary by W. Edwards Deming. Both essays first appeared in Volume 53 of the Royal Society of London's *Philosophical Transactions* and retain the original pagination.

BOX, GEORGE E. P.; and TIAO, GEORGE C. 1962 A Further Look at Robustness Via Bayes's Theorem. *Biometrika* 49:419–432.

EDWARDS, WARD; LINDMAN, HAROLD; and SAVAGE, LEONARD J. 1963 Bayesian Statistical Inference for Psychological Research. *Psychological Review* 70:193–242.

FISHER, R. A. (1939) 1950 The Comparison of Samples With Possibly Unequal Variances. Pages 35.173a–35.180 in R. A. Fisher, *Contributions to Mathematical Statistics.* New York: Wiley. → First published in Volume 9 of the *Annals of Eugenics.*

JEFFREYS, HAROLD (1939) 1961 *Theory of Probability.* 3d ed. Oxford: Clarendon.

JOINT STATISTICS SEMINAR, UNIVERSITY OF LONDON 1959 *The Foundations of Statistical Inference.* A discussion opened by Leonard J. Savage at a meeting of the Seminar. London: Methuen; New York: Wiley.

LINDLEY, DENNIS V. 1965 *Introduction to Probability and Statistics From a Bayesian Viewpoint.* 2 vols. Cambridge Univ. Press.

MOSTELLER, FREDERICK; and WALLACE, DAVID L. 1963 Inference in an Authorship Problem: A Comparative Study of Discrimination Methods Applied to the Authorship of the Disputed Federalist Papers. *Journal of the American Statistical Association* 58:275–309.

MOSTELLER, FREDERICK; and WALLACE, DAVID L. 1964 *Inference and Disputed Authorship: The Federalist.* Reading, Mass.: Addison-Wesley.

PRATT, JOHN W.; RAIFFA, HOWARD; and SCHLAIFER, ROBERT 1964 The Foundations of Decision Under Uncertainty: An Elementary Exposition. *Journal of the American Statistical Association* 59:353–375.

RAIFFA, HOWARD; and SCHLAIFER, ROBERT 1961 *Applied Statistical Decision Theory.* Graduate School of Business Administration, Studies in Managerial Economics. Boston: Harvard Univ., Division of Research.

SAVAGE, LEONARD J. 1962 Bayesian Statistics. Pages 161–194 in Symposium on Information and Decision Processes, Third, Purdue University, 1961, *Recent Developments in Information and Decision Processes.* Edited by Robert E. Machol and Paul Gray. New York: Macmillan.

SCHLAIFER, ROBERT 1959 *Probability and Statistics for Business Decisions: An Introduction to Managerial Economics Under Uncertainty.* New York: McGraw-Hill.

BEARD, CHARLES A.

Charles A. Beard (1874–1948), historian, political scientist, and educator, was, from about 1912 to 1941, one of the most influential social thinkers in the United States. He helped to transform the discipline of political science in the early twentieth century, and came close to dominating the study of American history between the two world wars. He was ranked by a group of liberal intellectuals of that era as second only to Thorstein Veblen among the writers who had influenced their thought, and in a poll taken shortly after Beard's death by *Survey* magazine, a group of editors and educators voted his masterpiece, *The Rise of American Civilization* (1927), the book that best explained American democracy. Altogether, he published over three hundred articles and about sixty books, some in collaboration with his wife, Mary Ritter Beard, some with other associates. His textbooks on European and American history and on American government sold many millions of copies. The product of an age of reform, he was always the scholar *engagé*, assailing conventional myths and shibboleths, pronouncing continually on current events, and plunging repeatedly into policy making. The force of his personality penetrated not only his writings but every dimension of his life; for Beard enjoyed his power and bore himself with the authority of an ancient sage.

The son of a substantial landowner and building contractor, Beard was raised on a farm near Knightstown, Indiana. His parents were old-fashioned rationalists and descendants of Quakers; this heritage gave Beard a lifelong sense of close personal and intellectual kinship with eighteenth-century America. The down-to-earth, humane cast of mind that he derived from his upbringing was broadened at DePauw University through acquaintance with the writings of Karl Marx and especially John Ruskin, whose portrait always hung in Beard's study. A summer in Chicago, spent partly at Hull House, brought Beard into direct involvement with current social unrest. On graduating from DePauw in 1898, he went to England to study English and European history at Oxford. There he associated with cosmopolitan and radical spirits and had a large share in organizing a workingmen's college, Ruskin Hall. His first book, *The Industrial Revolution* (1901), explained current social problems to British working-class readers. His Oxford experience gave Beard a considerable familiarity with English literary culture, a distinctly uncommon attribute among American social scientists.

These moral and humane enthusiasms came increasingly under the discipline of an austere scientific methodology. From his Oxford professors, notably Frederick York Powell, Beard learned of the growing aspiration for a science of man that would furnish empirical understanding of human affairs without the intrusion of value judgments. Further graduate study at Columbia University, where Beard acquired the PH.D. degree in 1904, confirmed his adherence to a value-free social science.

From one point of view Beard's whole career can be seen as a struggle to maintain a fruitful union between his belief in science as a rigidly objective inquiry and his ardent commitment to moral action.

At Columbia in the early twentieth century, such a union was not hard to maintain. Empiricism was then the watchword throughout the social sciences in America, and at Columbia Beard joined a notable company of scholars who were convinced that the advance of democracy depended on a social science that would replace dogmatic or speculative statements with concrete, practical knowledge of particular situations and techniques. This view—at once scientific, utilitarian, and "present-minded"—was spelled out in philosophy by John Dewey and in history by James Harvey Robinson. The latter propounded a "New History," which would be a synthesis of the results of more specialized sciences and which would thereby reach out into the whole context of human activity instead of dwelling on the slow unfolding of formal institutions. New Historians would study the technique of progress and, in general, concentrate on the aspects of the past most relevant to the great public problems of the present. Thus Robinson's history emphasized change rather than continuity and invoked the authority of science for the reform of scholarship and society. All of this appealed strongly to Beard, who grew rapidly from a protégé to a partner of the older man.

Although Beard's training was primarily in history, his appointment at Columbia after 1907 was in the department of public law. Over the next decade his teaching and writing related primarily to American constitutional history and public administration. He constantly stressed the social and economic "realities" discoverable behind legal principles and governmental forms. To Beard the abandonment of an abstract, largely a priori analysis of law and sovereignty permitted political science to look more closely into motives, interests, and practical results. In the new field of public administration his work was very practical indeed. As a leader in the pioneering New York Bureau of Municipal Research, he directed a number of major state and municipal surveys designed to rationalize governmental machinery and establish clear criteria of public responsibility. Later, in 1922–1923, he acted as adviser to the Bureau of Municipal Research in Tokyo and also advised the Japanese government on the rebuilding of the city after a disastrous earthquake.

In constitutional history Beard's research flowed from an equally practical, contemporary interest. A series of conservative, laissez-faire decisions by the Supreme Court had aroused a heated debate over its legitimate powers. In *The Supreme Court and the Constitution* (1912) Beard made a more intensive investigation than anyone had previously done of the intentions of the Founding Fathers with respect to judicial review. He concluded that the framers had intended the Supreme Court to exercise control over legislation. Judicial control was just one facet of the larger purpose of the framers to protect property rights against turbulent popular majorities. Yet Beard ended by acclaiming the tough-minded intelligence with which the makers of the constitution grounded it on the rock of self-interest. Where others discerned idealism, Beard saw a more praiseworthy realism.

Beard's most famous monograph, *An Economic Interpretation of the Constitution* (1913), examined with care the Founding Fathers' motives. Inspired partly by the quantitative studies of sectional voting patterns that Frederick Jackson Turner and his students were making, Beard surveyed the distribution of economic power in the United States in 1787 and itemized the property holdings of every delegate to the Constitutional Convention of that year. He concluded that at least five-sixths of the delegates stood to gain personally from the adoption of the constitution, chiefly because it would protect the public credit and raise the value of the public securities they held. This thesis was a striking demonstration of a research technique—collective biography—that has only recently come into common use in historical studies; but Beard's analytical design seems crude compared to subsequent refinements. He proceeded as if conscious material self-interest were the only determinant of political behavior and thus assumed what he proposed to demonstrate. Moreover, he imposed a simplistic social dualism on his findings about individuals: he presented the constitution as the instrument of capitalistic creditors arrayed against landowning debtors. Beard further documented the same cleavage in a third significant monograph, *Economic Origins of Jeffersonian Democracy* (1915). Here he tried to demonstrate that the alignment of 1787 reappeared in the political parties of the 1790s: Jeffersonian democracy simply meant the transfer of federal power from the holders of fluid capital to the agriculturalists.

In the writing of American history Beard's capitalist–agrarian dichotomy quickly assumed im-

mense importance, for it asserted a pattern of conflict that was refreshingly "realistic" without being alien to traditional American political rhetoric. In effect, Beard's economic interpretation of American history provided a tangible class basis for the old idea that American politics was essentially a contest between Jeffersonian democracy and Hamiltonian privilege. By postulating a basic antagonism between two coalitions of interest groups, one dominated by urban capitalists, the other by farmers and planters, he used a flexible dualism in place of the more complex Marxist scheme that was influencing the writing of European history.

During the 1920s and 1930s the best of the books Beard wrote, together with those of such major scholars as Vernon L. Parrington, Arthur M. Schlesinger, and Howard K. Beale, amplified this conceptual scheme. Thus Beard's *The Idea of National Interest* (1934a) attributed differences between Hamiltonian and Jeffersonian traditions of foreign policy to economic interests, and the capitalist–agrarian struggle supplied the underlying dynamics for *The Rise of American Civilization* (1927). Among the special features of this panoramic volume were an interpretation of Jacksonian democracy as a farmer–labor uprising and of the Civil War as a "Second American Revolution," in which northern businessmen drove the planter aristocracy from power.

Yet there were significant differences between *The Rise of American Civilization* and Beard's prewar writings. He had resigned from Columbia in 1917 in protest against wartime infringements on academic freedom, and during the 1920s he became deeply disturbed both by the threat that modern war posed to democratic values and by the loss of confidence in progress and human nature then spreading in many intellectual circles. Instead of simply trusting in scientific inquiry to solve social problems, Beard began explicitly to defend his basic values. Living independently in the hills of Connecticut, he was increasingly removed from the behavioralist trend in political science; his writing assumed a more humanistic cast. *The Rise of American Civilization* combined the economic determinism he had developed before the war with an unashamed celebration of the cultural achievements of the American people. Specifically, it vindicated their collective energy and their undaunted faith in progress.

The depression and the spread of totalitarianism intensified Beard's concern with values. His herculean activities in the 1930s were an attempt to reanimate in America by creative thought that progress which science and world history no longer seemed to assure. In *The Open Door at Home* (1934*c*) and other writings he sketched an ambitious blueprint for a planned economy. He exercised a major and perhaps decisive influence on the 16-volume *Report* of the American Historical Association's Commission on the Social Studies in the Schools, 1932–1937, which declared that education in primary and secondary schools should be attuned to the advance of collectivistic democracy. He became the principal intellectual spokesman of isolationism. And he began to study the philosophy of history.

Until the 1930s very few American scholars in any discipline had paid serious attention to the basic problems of historical thought. Pragmatic Americans accepted science rather than philosophy as the key to historical knowledge. While Beard continued to insist that history must be useful, he now declared that it could not also be scientific and objective and that it must cease to be deterministic. His thunderous address as president of the American Historical Association, "Written History as an Act of Faith" (1934*d*), urged historians to recognize the subjectivity of history in order to restore the primacy of values in the study of man and thereby guide history in the making.

Beard's loss of confidence in the ability of scientific techniques to solve the great problems of the day inspired a general revolt against scientific history. His new conception of history, along with similar views expressed by Carl Becker, plunged U.S. historians into a great debate on relativism. The debate, which continued through the 1940s, created much confusion, partly because Beard drew his arguments from Italian and German philosophers, notably Benedetto Croce, whose idealist epistemology he never really understood or shared. Ultimately, most historians decided that Beard went too far in denying objectivity and thereby made history too "present-minded." Yet his agitation left a lasting impact. It upset the complacent assumption of professional historians that moral judgment has no legitimate place in their work. It awakened a philosophical consciousness and renewed American receptivity to European historical theory.

Beard's death in 1948 touched off a general reaction against his interpretation of American history. Much of the best scholarship since that time has gone to revise his stress on materialistic causation, on conflict rather than consensus, on the domestic rather than the international context of events. Attention has turned in good measure from interest groups to status groups and from rational to irrational motivation. Ironically, the history that Beard himself wrote in his old age prefigured this change

of outlook: in the 1940s he put a new emphasis on ideas in history and on the role of individuals. He largely abandoned interpretation in economic terms. One characteristic that remained unaltered, however, was a lifelong rationalism, a determination to control power by reason.

JOHN HIGHAM

[*For the historical context of Beard's work, see* CONSTITUTIONS AND CONSTITUTIONALISM; NATIONAL INTEREST; *and the biographies of* CROCE; DEWEY; MARX; ROBINSON; TURNER.]

WORKS BY BEARD

(1901) 1927 *The Industrial Revolution.* London: Allen & Unwin.

(1912) 1962 *The Supreme Court and the Constitution.* With an introduction and bibliographies by Alan F. Westin. Englewood Cliffs, N.J.: Prentice-Hall.

(1913) 1935 *An Economic Interpretation of the Constitution of the United States.* New York: Macmillan → A paperback edition was published in 1962 by Macmillan.

(1915) 1952 *Economic Origins of Jeffersonian Democracy.* New York: Macmillan.

(1922) 1945 *The Economic Basis of Politics.* 3d ed. rev. New York: Knopf. → A paperback edition was published in 1957 by Random House.

(1927) 1933 BEARD, CHARLES A.; and BEARD, MARY R. *The Rise of American Civilization.* New ed., rev. & enl. 2 vols. New York: Macmillan. → Volume 1: *The Agricultural Era.* Volume 2: *The Industrial Era.*

1934*a* *The Idea of National Interest: An Analytical Study in American Foreign Policy.* New York: Macmillan.

1934*b* *The Nature of the Social Sciences in Relation to Objectives of Instruction.* New York and Chicago: Scribner.

1934*c* *The Open Door at Home: A Trial Philosophy of National Interest.* New York: Macmillan.

(1934*d*) 1959 Written History as an Act of Faith. Pages 140–151 in Hans Meyerhoff (editor), *The Philosophy of History of Our Time: An Anthology.* Garden City, N.Y.: Doubleday.

1939 BEARD, CHARLES A.; and BEARD, MARY R. *America in Midpassage.* New York: Macmillan.

1942 BEARD, CHARLES A.; and BEARD, MARY R. *The American Spirit: A Study of the Idea of Civilization in the United States.* New York: Macmillan. → A paperback edition was published in 1962 by Collier.

1943 *The Republic: Conversations on Fundamentals.* New York: Viking.

1948 *President Roosevelt and the Coming of the War, 1941: A Study in Appearances and Realities.* New Haven: Yale Univ. Press.

SUPPLEMENTARY BIBLIOGRAPHY

BEALE, HOWARD K. (editor) 1954 *Charles A. Beard: An Appraisal.* Lexington: Univ. of Kentucky Press. → Contains a bibliography of Beard's writings.

BENSON, LEE 1960 *Turner and Beard: American Historical Writing Reconsidered.* Glencoe, Ill.: Free Press.

BORNING, BERNARD C. 1962 *The Political and Social Thought of Charles A. Beard.* Seattle: Univ. of Washington Press.

CRICK, BERNARD 1959 *The American Science of Politics: Its Origins and Conditions.* Berkeley: Univ. of California Press.

HIGHAM, JOHN; KRIEGER, LEONARD; and GILBERT, FELIX 1965 *History.* Englewood Cliffs, N.J.: Prentice-Hall.

JOSEPHSON, MATTHEW 1949 Charles A. Beard: A Memoir. *Virginia Quarterly Review* 25:585–602.

PRESSLY, THOMAS J. 1954 *Americans Interpret Their Civil War.* Princeton Univ. Press. → A paperback edition was published in 1962 by Collier.

STROUT, CUSHING 1958 *The Pragmatic Revolt in American History: Carl Becker and Charles Beard.* New Haven: Yale Univ. Press.

WHITE, MORTON 1949 *Social Thought in America: The Revolt Against Formalism.* New York: Viking. → A paperback edition was published in 1957 by Beacon.

BECCARIA

There have been few more reluctant heroes in the history of ideas than Cesare Bonesana, marquis of Beccaria (1738–1794). He was the creator of modern penal theory, but his classic *An Essay on Crimes and Punishments* (1764) was rather extracted from him than freely written by him. Bored and idle after leaving school, yet fired by Enlightenment ideals, the young Milanese joined a congenial radical discussion group, the Punch-hards. They saw themselves as north Italian Encyclopedists, so many Voltaires and Diderots joined to attack the abuses of the Austrian regime. Each member was expected to study, master, and report on a special subject. Beccaria chose criminal law but dawdled over it, until at last, goaded by his friends, he amazed them all and produced a masterpiece.

The book was immediately celebrated all over western Europe as the bible of legal reform. Within a few months d'Alembert and Voltaire had become enthusiastic converts. The Abbé Morellet's French translation went through seven printings in six months. Voltaire added a chapter-by-chapter commentary, and the book was soon hailed from Lisbon to St. Petersburg. The Berne Society awarded Beccaria its gold medal of honor; Catherine the Great invited him to Russia to codify criminal law; American and English editions followed; and Sir William Blackstone and Jeremy Bentham were eager celebrants.

Here, then, was irony: This small treatise on crime and punishment was written casually and reluctantly by an unknown, indolent aristocrat of 26, a stranger to legal studies who had no special knowledge of penal law and no experience whatever of criminal administration. Yet he succeeded where dozens of learned and experienced scholars and jurists had failed. Not only did all enlightened reformers and monarchs read and praise his book, they heeded it; and by the turn of the century every major nation of Europe had slowly or more quickly followed his road to criminal law reform. Why was he so successful?

His was first of all a master stroke of timing. The law is always conservative and even in quiet times lags behind other social changes, but in that critical progressive Age of Enlightenment the gulf between humanitarian ideals and barbarous practice became ever more notorious and at last intolerable. Throughout the Continent the heritage of the Inquisition lay heavily. Secret accusations, *lettres de cachet,* "confessions" extracted by brutal tortures, mere charges considered prima-facie evidence of guilt, convictions without appeal, arbitrary pardons, and tyrannical punishments were all commonplace. Capital offenses multiplied with frivolous abandon; there were over two hundred in England, including stealing turnips and damaging fishponds. The penalties were atrocious. Men were done to death by the gibbet, the axe, the lash, burning, breaking on the wheel. They were consigned to galleys, branded, or pilloried or had their limbs amputated. It was a nightmare of horrors that demanded reform, and by the 1760s many men had cried out against it.

It was Beccaria's genius, however, to gather up all those poignant cries and shape them into a simple, rational, elegant, and passionately humane theory, moving and persuasive to all men of good will. He thought his principles as clear and demonstrable as Euclidean geometry. His two basic axioms were those of all good utilitarians: pleasures and pains are the springs of human action; the end of good legislation must be the greatest happiness of the greatest number. By ascending to these general principles, a "political arithmetic" could now, for the first time, be created, "a calculation of probabilities to mathematical exactness" (Beccaria [1764] 1953, p. 29). It was clear, then, that both crimes and punishments are pains and therefore evil; that a scale of crimes can be formed according to the extent of the social evil they produce, from the highest crime of violent revolution down to the smallest private civil injustice; and that the test is always social injury and not private intention. From the new science of political arithmetic it also followed that there ought to be a fixed ratio between crimes and punishments, that its measure is prevention, not vengeance, and its axiom is minimum pain. It is enough that for any given crime the pain of punishment minimally exceed the pleasure gained from its commission. More is superfluous; all excess is tyrannical and barbarous. Cruel, secret, arbitrary punishments are not preventive; clearly written, known, certain, and immediate ones are.

Axioms in hand, Beccaria applied them one by one to the infamies of eighteenth-century criminal law—secret accusations, torture, banishments, confiscation, proceedings in bankruptcy, capital punishment. All miserably failed the test of his lucid humane aphorisms, which he summed up in a concluding general theorem: "That a punishment may not be an act of violence . . . against a private member of society, it should be public, immediate, and necessary, the least possible in the case given, proportioned to the crime, and determined by the laws" ([1764] 1953, p. 160). And the leading minds and monarchs of Europe agreed with him.

But Beccaria was more than the Italian Jeremy Bentham; he was also the Italian Adam Smith. Impressed with his fame, in 1768 the Austrian government created a chair of economics for him at Milan. Although he held it only two years, after which he became a high and valued official in the Milanese administration, he left behind a set of lectures remarkable for their analytic and mathematical power and their sophisticated foreshadowing of some modern economic theory. He began his analysis as Adam Smith did, with a normative definition of economics, and then moved on to the evolution of technology, division of labor, and population. His principle of economic action was of course utilitarian, the standard doctrine of egoistic hedonism. The second and third parts dealt with agriculture and manufactures, and the fourth with commerce and theory of value and price: barter, money, competition, interest, foreign exchange, banks, and credit. Here he gave prescient analyses of the indeterminateness of isolated barter and the transition to a determinate competitive market and thence to indirect exchange.

Rough, unfinished, not meant to be published, these lectures did not appear until 1804, ten years after Beccaria's death. Although he was a brilliant analyst, it was inevitable that he should forsake theory for practice and become a working administrator. The principle of utility demanded it, but we are the poorer for it.

MARY PETER MACK

[For discussion of the subsequent development of Beccaria's ideas, see CRIMINOLOGY.]

BIBLIOGRAPHY

BECCARIA, CESARE BONESANA, MARCHESE DI   (1764) 1953   An Essay on Crimes and Punishments. Stanford, Calif.: Academic Reprints. → First published in Italian under the title Dei delitti e delle pene. A new American edition was published in 1963 by Bobbs-Merrill (Indianapolis).

PHILLIPSON, COLEMAN   1923   Three Criminal Law Reformers: Beccaria, Bentham, Romilly. London: Dent.

SCHUMPETER, JOSEPH A.   1954   History of Economic Analysis. Edited by E. B. Schumpeter. New York: Oxford Univ. Press.

BECHER, JOHANN JOACHIM

Johann Joachim Becher (1635–1682) was the most important German mercantilist of the seventeenth century. He was born in Speyer, the son of a Lutheran minister, and was orphaned at an early age. Becher was largely self-taught, developing his versatile talents in Germany, Sweden, Italy, and Holland. Converting to Catholicism, he served the elector of Mainz as *mathematicus et medicus* from 1660 to 1664, and also served for a short time as professor of medicine at the University of Mainz. There, he laid the foundation for his natural philosophy, occupied himself with philological and pedagogical problems, and tried his hand at invention. Inspired by a trip to Holland, he also began to plan the establishment of factories. In 1664 Becher entered the service of the elector of Bavaria in the same capacity he had had in Mainz. In 1666 he was temporarily an imperial councilor and councilor for commerce at the court of Emperor Leopold I; he later held those positions uninterruptedly from 1670 to 1676. In Munich and in Vienna he became more and more of a political economist, influencing Bavarian and Austrian economic policy directly as well as through his writings.

Becher's works reveal his versatility. In 1668 he published his major work, *Politischer Discurs von den eigentlichen Ursachen des Auff- und Abnehmens der Städt, Länder und Republicken*, which was given the subtitle *Commercien-Tractat* in the second, greatly enlarged, edition (1673) and which went through many editions until 1759. In his *Moral Discurs* (1669a), he expounded his ethics, which was greatly influenced by the Stoics; and in his *Physica subterranea* (1669b), he presented a completely organic, natural philosophy, untouched by the mechanistic explanation of nature that was gaining ground at that time in western Europe.

Becher established silk factories in Munich and Vienna, and in the latter city he founded a company for trade with the Orient and a state-owned "House of Arts and Crafts," which was planned as a model workshop. He also made plans in Vienna for a company to engage in trade with Holland and planned the establishment of colonies in South

America. At his suggestion, Leopold I set up a council of commerce for the unified management of all national economic policy. As with his other institutional creations, it was of brief duration and did not survive him because of inadequate financial support from the state. Moreover, Becher's projects were often ahead of his time, and his erratic and intense personality gained him many enemies.

In 1677 Becher failed to implement an embargo ordered by the emperor on the importation of French goods, and he was compelled to spend the last years of his life wandering through Holland and England as an inventor and author. As a typical man of the baroque period, Becher included among his many and diverse talents an interest in technical and alchemical experiments. Shortly before his death in 1682, he published a summary of his inventions and a survey of the technical problems of the seventeenth century in his book *Närrische Weisheit und weise Narrheit* ("Mad Wisdom and Wise Madness").

As a political theorist, Becher was hardly original, since his doctrine stemmed from that of Justus Lipsius of the Netherlands, the leading representative of Neo-Stoicism. But in the *Politischer Discurs* he did make a significant start toward a theory of political economy. Also, inspired by the writings of the Dutch Pieter de la Court, he developed an abundance of ideas on economic policy to deal with the special problems facing mercantilism in Germany—a result of territorial fragmentation and the serious population losses during the Thirty Years' War. It was this depopulation that moved Becher to regard a populous state as a powerful one. But he did not blindly consider population as the decisive factor, for he was aware of the interrelation between population growth and economic opportunity.

Becher's conception of the state had both medieval and modern elements. He did not abandon the idea that the political estates were an essential correlate of princely authority, but he assigned functions to the state that were of so great a scope that the absolute ruler of the eighteenth century could hardly perform them, even with an enlarged bureaucracy. In his conception of the state, five agencies were to take care of the welfare of the subjects, covering all their material and spiritual needs. In this connection, Becher elaborated his pedagogical plans, which were deeply indebted to Luther's ideas on vocation and education. Becher felt that education ideally should be civic- and vocation-oriented, concentrating especially on the fields of economic and technical training.

If the material welfare of its subjects is only one of the functions of a state, it is nevertheless the principal topic of the *Politischer Discurs*. The work contains an early conception of the state as an economic community, with the peasants, artisans, and merchants as the economic estates. The principal estate is that of the merchant; for as the distributor, he personifies the market relationships between the estates. In Becher's study of the factors that disturb the equilibrium of the estates and the growth of population, he developed the remarkable rudiments of a theory of market forms. In this theory he added "polypoly," i.e., overproduction, to monopoly and "propoly," which he viewed as artificial restrictions of competition rather than as aspects of the urban economy of the Middle Ages. The major aims of his economic policy were the elimination of all those factors interfering with the market and the promotion of productive forces. This goal was to be achieved by means of state storage, workhouses, factories, trading companies, and commercial banks organized as joint-stock corporations, all under the supervision of a council of commerce. In general, Becher regarded problems of the function of money and of the balance of trade as subordinate to the promotion of the productive forces. He took protective tariffs for granted.

Thus, Becher's *Commercien-Tractat* deals with economic problems that traditionally had not been part of economic theory but had been treated within the traditional framework of political science—hence the title *Politischer Discurs*.

Becher's work influenced, to a greater or lesser degree, all subsequent German mercantilists, especially Philipp Wilhelm von Hörnigk, his younger brother-in-law, who was his secretary for some years and applied Becher's ideas, which were intended for all of Germany, to the Hapsburg monarchy in particular (*Oesterreich über alles wann es nur will* 1684).

HERBERT HASSINGER

[*For the historical context of Becher's work, see* ECONOMIC THOUGHT, *article on* MERCANTILIST THOUGHT.]

WORKS BY BECHER

(1668) 1759 *Politischer Discurs von den eigentlichen Ursachen des Auff- und Abnehmens der Städt, Länder und Republicken.* 6th ed., enl. Frankfurt am Main (Germany): Gselius.

1669a *Moral Discurs von den eigentlichen Ursachen des Glücks und Unglücks.* Frankfurt am Main (Germany): Zunner.

(1669b) 1738 *Physica subterranea.* Leipzig: Weidmann.

(1682) 1707 *Närrische Weisheit und weise Narrheit.* 2d ed. Frankfurt am Main (Germany): Zubrodt.

SUPPLEMENTARY BIBLIOGRAPHY

HASSINGER, HERBERT 1942 *Die erste wiener oriental-ische Handelskompagnie 1667–1683. Vierteljahr-schrift für Sozial- und Wirtschaftsgeschichte* 35:1–53.

HASSINGER, HERBERT 1951a *Johann Joachim Becher, 1635–1682: Ein Beitrag zur Geschichte des Merkan-tilismus.* Vienna (Austria): Holzhausen. → Lists all of Becher's writings.

HASSINGER, HERBERT 1951b *Johann Joachim Bechers Bedeutung für die Entwicklung der Seidenindustrie in Deutschland. Vierteljahrschrift für Sozial- und Wirt-schaftsgeschichte* 38:209–246.

HÖRNIGK, PHILIPP WILHELM VON 1684 *Oesterreich über alles wann es nur will.* Nürnberg (Germany).

SOMMER, LOUISE 1920–1925 *Die österreichischen Ka-meralisten in dogmengeschichtlicher Darstellung.* 2 vols. Vienna (Austria): Konegen.

BECKER, HOWARD

During most of his career, Howard Becker (1899–1960) taught at the University of Wisconsin. He is best known as a sociological theorist and methodologist. His work is most closely related to that of the German sociologists Max Weber and Leopold von Wiese and of certain Americans, particularly R. E. Park and G. H. Mead.

For Becker, the study of values constitutes the core of sociology; indeed, he regarded them as indispensable tools for sociological interpretation (1950). Judgments of right and wrong, good and bad, superiority and inferiority, and usefulness and uselessness determine the ends and means of human action and thus of institutions, customs, folkways, and so on. Valuation, for Becker, is not the reflection of social processes but arises primarily in the processes by which personality is acquired; the human propensity to form values is thus determined by the inner structure of the personality itself. Following Weber's leads closely, Becker divided situations of human action into four types: (1) expedient rationality, where any means can be used to achieve any end; (2) sanctioned rationality, where the means chosen are limited by the nature of the ends; (3) traditional nonrationality, in which means become the ends of action; and (4) affective nonrationality, where the distinction between means and ends is lost.

Human actions occur within social and cultural contexts, which are, at base, systems of values and which determine the preponderance of one type of action over the others. These contexts also determine the latitude the individual has in substituting ends and means within the rubric of one type of action and in shifting from one type of action to another.

There are two major contexts, the sacred and the secular. Sacred societies manifest an inability or unwillingness to respond to the new and are dominated by traditional nonrationality and sanctioned rationality. Two major subtypes of sacred society may be distinguished, folk and prescribed. Folk societies are marked by geographical, social, and mental isolation. Such societies are often, though not always, nonliterate. They are dominated by tradition and strong kinship ties. Prescribed sacred societies are governed by written and rigidly prescribed rules, laws, and sacred texts. Ties of kinship are replaced by ties of race, ethnicity, or language. Prescriptions may arise from the slow systematization of folk wisdom and deductions from it, or they may have their source in charismatic leadership. Thus, sacred societies are not necessarily small, isolated, nonliterate, and technologically backward. On the contrary, very large, literate, and technologically advanced societies may also be sacred societies. Modern large-scale totalitarian movements and societies provide examples (1946).

Secular societies, in Becker's view, demonstrate receptivity to change. Expedient rationality and affective nonrationality are the prevailing modes of action. Such societies are not completely lacking in traditions or prescriptions, but these are much looser than in sacred society. Here again Becker described numerous subtypes of secular societies; the main distinction is between the "principled" and the "normless" types (also called stable and unstable). In the principled type, some sacred prescriptions remain, but these are of a kind that permit a wide latitude for change. A stable democracy, for instance, is based on sacred principles. In the normless type, virtually all prescriptions have been lost; at the extreme such a society approaches a state of anomie. Normless societies are generally found in areas of intense culture contacts, such as large cities, where isolation is at a minimum.

Sacred and secular societies are not actually found in "pure form." For instance, all secular societies have sacred elements. Furthermore, many societies are in a process of change from a sacred to a secular type. Secularization may occur as the result of migrations or increased communications. Definite social and psychological manifestations accompany these changes.

The construction of such concepts as "sacred" and "secular" societies exemplifies what Becker called "constructive typology," a methodology he advocated for all sociological investigation. There is an indefinite number of ways in which the world may be regarded, of which the scientific way is one. Each manner of regarding the world is defined by the questions it poses and consequently reflects the values of the observer. The supreme values of science are the prediction (and, if possible, the control) of natural phenomena. Science asks the following kind of question of nature: "If and when certain conditions hold, what results will follow?" This approach is to be contrasted with that of the idiographic historian, who seeks to determine what actually happened in a particular instance, but no approach is intrinsically superior to any other. The merit of each depends on the purposes and values of the investigator.

Constructive typology is a scientific approach to human events; it seeks to pose "if and when" questions about these events. There are several stages in the process of constructing types. First, the sociologist frames a provisional hypothesis about causal, related, or prior conditions of some phenomenon he wishes to study. He then makes an investigation of the case itself or of a series of cases—"culture case studies" in Becker's terminology—and abstracts from these a "typical set of typical personalities, processes, and structures" (1950, p. 107) which seem adequate to explain the case or cases studied. It should be emphasized that although constructed types are composed of elements abstracted from a single concrete phenomenon or a set of closely related phenomena, they are neither ideal types nor fictions. The components of the constructed type must be found in reality, and the manner in which they are related to each other must not contravene empirical reality, logic, or established scientific theory.

The final stage in the process is to check the validity of the constructed type by applying it to other empirical instances. A failure to predict accurately or to explain these other instances indicates that they are basically different from the concrete phenomenon first studied and that the initial constructed type should be modified or abandoned. However, should prediction prove possible, and still further application reveal the continued utility of the constructed type, a genuine sociological generalization of the "if and when" type will have been achieved. It is in this way that sociology will gradually accumulate a set of valid laws, which may then be combined into a more general theoretical system.

EUGENE V. SCHNEIDER

[*For the historical context of Becker's work, see* TYPOLOGIES *and the biographies of* MEAD; PARK; SCHELER; TROELTSCH; WEBER, MAX; WIESE.]

WORKS BY BECKER

1932 Processes of Secularisation: An Ideal-typical Analysis With Special Reference to Personality Change as Affected by Population Movement. *Sociological Review* 34:138–154, 266–286.

(1938) 1961 BARNES, HARRY E.; and BECKER, HOWARD *Social Thought From Lore to Science.* 3d ed., rev. & enl. New York: Dover.

1940 BARNES, HARRY E.; BECKER, HOWARD; and BECKER, F. B. (editors) *Contemporary Social Theory.* New York: Appleton.

1941a Supreme Values and the Sociologist. *American Sociological Review* 6:155–172.

1941b The Limits of Sociological Positivism. *Journal of Social Philosophy* 6:362–369. → A critical review of George Lundberg's *Foundations of Sociology.*

1942 BECKER, HOWARD; and HILL, REUBEN (editors) *Marriage and the Family.* Boston: Heath.

1946 *German Youth: Bond or Free.* London: Routledge; New York: Oxford Univ. Press.

1950 *Through Values to Social Interpretation: Essays on Social Contexts, Actions, Types and Prospects.* Durham, N.C.: Duke Univ. Press.

1957 BECKER, HOWARD; and BOSKOFF, ALVIN (editors) *Modern Sociological Theory in Continuity and Change.* New York: Dryden.

SUPPLEMENTARY BIBLIOGRAPHY

WIESE, LEOPOLD VON (1924–1929) 1932 *Systematic Sociology: On the Basis of the* Beziehungslehre *and the* Gebildelehre *of L. von Wiese.* Adapted and amplified by Howard Becker. New York: Wiley. → First published as *System der allgemeinen Soziologie.*

BEHAVIOR GENETICS

See GENETICS, *article on* GENETICS AND BEHAVIOR.

BEHAVIOR THERAPY

See *under* MENTAL DISORDERS, TREATMENT OF.

BEHAVIORAL SCIENCES

The behavioral sciences study human behavior by scientific means; as a preliminary approximation, they can be distinguished from the social sciences as designating a good deal less but, at the same time, somewhat more. The term "social sciences" typically includes the disciplines of anthropology, economics, political science, sociology, and most of psychology. As a case in point, the scholarly associations in these five disciplines—along with history and statistics—provide the core membership of the (American) Social Science Research Council. The behavioral sciences, as that term was originally intended and as it is usually understood, include sociology; anthropology (minus archeology, technical linguistics, and most of physical anthropology); psychology (minus physiological psychology); and the behavioral aspects of biology, economics, geography, law, psychiatry, and political science. The edges of any such broad concept tend to be fuzzy—as are the edges of the social sciences themselves—but the center seems to be reasonably clear. Given time, the term will probably settle down to one or two generally accepted meanings, if it has not already done so.

The term "behavioral sciences" came into currency, one might even say into being, in the United States in the early 1950s. A decade and a half later, it appears to be well established in American universities and disciplines and is well on its way to acceptance abroad. Before 1950 the term was virtually nonexistent; since then it has come into such general use that it appears in the titles of books and journals, of conference sessions, programmatic reports, university departments, professorships, and courses, as well as in the names of a book club, a book prize, several publishers' series, and in the mass media of communication.

What happened to give rise to the term? The key event was the development of a Ford Foundation program in this field. The program was initially designated "individual behavior and human relations" but it soon became known as the behavioral sciences program and, indeed, was officially called that within the foundation. It was the foundation's administrative action, then, that led directly to the term and to the concept of this particular field of study.

The story begins with a committee that undertook a study for the Ford Foundation in the late 1940s, when the foundation was about to enter on the enlarged program that made it, overnight, the largest private foundation in the world. This study committee, given the task of suggesting how "the Ford Foundation can most effectively and intelligently put its resources to work for human welfare," concluded that "the most important problems of human welfare now lie in the realm of democratic society, in man's relation to man, in human relations and social organizations"; and it recommended that the over-all objective be pursued in five "program areas—the establishment of peace, the strengthening of democracy, the strengthening of the economy, education in a democratic society, and individual behavior and human relations." Among the social science disciplines, political science became involved in the first and second programs, economics in the third, and, in a more or less residual way, anthropology, psychology, and sociology in the fifth. In the study committee's report appeared the term that soon became current, "the behavioral sciences," and the beginnings of a definition to distinguish them from the social

sciences: "We have in the social sciences scientifically-minded research workers who are both interested in, and equipped for, the use of such techniques. Among these are the psychologists, sociologists, and anthropologists. In addition, there are psychiatrists and psychoanalysts, as well as natural scientists, including geneticists and other biologists" (Ford Foundation 1949, p. 92).

The conception was developed further in a staff paper, approved by the foundation's trustees in early 1952, that put forward the first plan for the foundation's program in this field. In that paper, hitherto unpublished, the notion of the behavioral sciences was characterized as follows:

1. It refers primarily to a program of *research*. A major part of Program Five is conceived as a program for research on human behavior, not as an "action program." Furthermore, it is not expected that the staff of Program Five will itself conduct behavioral research; rather, it will help to initiate and to support such activities.

2. It refers to the *scientific approach*. It encourages the acquisition of behavioral knowledge under conditions which, so far as possible, ensure objectivity, verifiability, and generality. It calls for conformity to high standards of scientific inquiry.

3. It refers to the acquisition of basic knowledge of human behavior and thus it is considered as a comparatively *long-range* venture. Basic study of the tremendously complicated problems of man cannot be expected to yield significant results in a short period of time.

4. It refers to the interest of the Foundation not in knowledge of human behavior as such but rather in knowledge which promises at some point to serve *human needs*. The program is thus oriented to social problems and needs.

5. It refers to an *interdisciplinary approach* and not to any single conventional field of knowledge or a single combination of them; traditional academic disciplines as such are not included or excluded. The program's goal is to acquire scientific knowledge of human behavior from whatever sources can make appropriate contributions. Social scientists, medical scientists, and humanists, singly and in combination, can be engaged on the program. The intention is to use all relevant knowledge, skills, concepts and insights.

6. It refers to a broad and complex *subject matter*, since the program aims at a scientific understanding of why people behave as they do. "Behavior" includes not only overt acts but also such subjective behavior as attitudes, beliefs, expectations, motivations and aspirations. The program seeks knowledge which is useful in attacking problems of an economic, political, religious, educational or personal nature by studying the behavior of human beings as individuals or as members of primary groups, formal organizations, social strata, or social institutions. The program is vitally concerned with the cultural heritage by which

men live, the social structures they have devised to organize their societies, the goals they pursue, and the means with which they pursue them.

7. Finally, it is definitely not considered as a cure-all for human problems but rather as a *contributor* to their solution, along with other sources of knowledge and judgment. The goal of the program is to provide scientific aids which can be used in the conduct of human affairs; it seeks only to increase useful knowledge and skills and to apply them wherever appropriate.

In short, then, Program Five is conceived as an effort to increase knowledge of human behavior through basic scientific research oriented to major problem areas covering a wide range of subjects, and to make such knowledge available for utilization in the conduct of human affairs. (Ford Foundation 1953, pp. 3–5)

The report went on to identify the topics that constituted the subject matter of the behavioral sciences, at least insofar as the foundation's interests were then concerned: political behavior, domestic and international; communication; values and beliefs; individual growth, development, and adjustment; behavior in primary groups and formal organizations; behavioral aspects of the economic system; social classes and minority groups; social restraints on behavior; and social and cultural change.

It was in this way that an administrative decision having to do with the programming and organization of a large foundation influenced at least the nomenclature, and probably even the conception, of an intellectual field of inquiry. The history of science contains several instances of intellectual concepts becoming administratively institutionalized, for example, psychoanalysis and gross national product (GNP). The concept "behavioral sciences" represents the reverse: an administrative arrangement that became intellectually institutionalized.

In the 1940s there were some similar stirrings within the universities themselves. In 1946 Harvard University organized a department of "social relations," which was in fact, though not in name, a behavioral sciences department, even to the exclusion of economics, political science, parts of anthropology and psychology, and, after a brief experimental period, history. And about 1950 a group of social and biological scientists at the University of Chicago began to seek a general theory of behavior under the term "behavioral sciences"— "first, because its neutral character made it acceptable to both social and biological scientists and, second, because we foresaw a possibility of someday seeking to obtain financial support from persons who might confound social science with socialism" (Miller 1955, p. 513). Earlier still, a somewhat similar effort was launched at the Institute of Human Relations at Yale University, although the line-up of specialties was different from what is now known as the behavioral sciences.

It is perhaps obvious that the Ford Foundation's commitment of several million dollars to this program had something to do with the term's acceptance and spread. In fact, one observer, upon learning that John Dewey and Arthur Bentley had in 1949 come close to using the term by distinguishing the *physical*, *physiological*, and *behavioral* regions of science (Dewey & Bentley 1949, p. 65), remarked that "the term may have been coined by John Dewey but it was minted by the Ford Foundation!" It would be a mistake, however, to conclude that the availability of funds was the only factor at work. Indeed, the term became so firmly established that it survived the termination of the foundation's program in the behavioral sciences in 1957. While money helped to establish it, the term did not die the day the money stopped; there seems to have been a genuine need for a collective term in addition to the traditional "social sciences."

The reason for this acceptance was and is a sense of both substantive and technical unity within this segment of the social sciences as compared with conventional work in economics, political science, and history. Psychology, anthropology, and sociology are more or less after the same end, namely, the establishment of scientifically validated generalizations about the subject matter of human behavior—how people behave and why. They are thus interested in motivation, perception, values and norms, learning, attitudes and opinion, personality, social organization, group practices, social institutions, culture, and similar matters. In consequence, they typically have more communication with one another than with representatives of the other disciplines; indeed, when political scientists act like behavioral scientists, they are called the "political behavior" wing of the discipline. Moreover, behavioral scientists collect original data on the direct behavior of individuals and groups through the use of surveys, questionnaires, interviews, tests, psychological inventories, personal observations, and the like, whereas economists, historians, and political scientists are more likely to use aggregative, indirect, and documentary sources of data. The rough unity in methods of inquiry goes along with similar subject matter as indicated in the several titles on research methods listed in the bibliography below.

It is only natural that the edges and connotations

of such a broad term, especially a new one, are frequently obscure, always in change, and sometimes tendentious. Not everyone using the term uses it in just the same way. Some economists and political scientists have felt that the emergence of the behavioral sciences means that they are being read out of the community of scientific students of human behavior, as have some historians and even some students of literature. However, all of these disciplines have been well represented at the Center for Advanced Study in the Behavioral Sciences in Palo Alto, California, established by the Ford Foundation in 1952; only half the Fellows at the Center during its first ten years came from the three disciplines of anthropology, psychology, and sociology. Similarly, some biologists are eager to keep a place within the behavioral sciences for studies of animal as well as human behavior and for inquiry into the genetic basis or biochemical determinants of human behavior. Just as there has been confusion between "social science" and "socialism," so there has been an unwarranted confusion between "behavioral science" and the once influential school of psychology called "behaviorism" (associated with John B. Watson).

It is more important than at first seems evident to distinguish between the plural and singular versions of the term—between, that is, "the behavioral sciences" and "behavioral science." The Ford Foundation deliberately used the term in the plural to signify that it had not embarked upon the creation of a unified discipline where three or more already existed. The singular usage has sometimes implied intent to create a unified discipline, whether in place of, or in addition to, the existing disciplines, as for example, in the journal *Behavioral Science*, which represents the search for a general theory of behavior.

Within the universities, the concept of the behavioral sciences has taken organizational form more frequently at the periphery than at the center. The traditional departments of anthropology, psychology, and sociology have not been supplanted by departments of "behavioral science" at the major universities that do the bulk of graduate training in this field. Organized expression of the behavioral sciences is more likely to be found in two other places: in undergraduate programs, particularly in lower-division work, that seek to put together the behavioral disciplines on both intellectual and economic grounds; and in professional schools, especially schools of business, medicine, and public health, that seek to apply the findings of the behavioral sciences to their own problems without

concern for disciplinary lines or labels. In late 1964, for example, the Rockefeller Institute announced the appointment of a senior staff in the behavioral sciences, again signaling the relationship between this field and the biomedical disciplines.

That there is sufficient affinity within the behavioral sciences to maintain the usage of the term seems already indicated by its acceptance in the literature as a convenient and reasonably well understood designation of only one part of what is usually termed the social sciences. There is of course no reason for the two terms to war with one another, since, quite simply, they refer to different things—the one broader, the other narrower.

The behavioral sciences also differ from the other social sciences in age: they are much younger. There is, of course, a long history of study and thought about man in philosophy, literature, history, political theory, religion, law, and medicine—in many cases study and thought about the same kinds of problems now being investigated by behavioral scientists. However, it was not until the late nineteenth century that the empirical, experimental, systematic, operational, scientific investigation of human behavior really began. Political science can of course be dated from Aristotle, history from Herodotus or Thucydides, economics at least from Adam Smith; but it is fair to say that the scientific study of human behavior is largely a development of the twentieth century.

The achievements and the potential of the behavioral sciences are reviewed in many hundreds of articles in this encyclopedia; see especially the articles on the individual disciplines. An inventory of findings is contained in Berelson and Steiner (1964). The boundaries of the behavioral sciences are by no means fixed, either among different observers or through time, but neither are the boundaries of such terms as the social sciences, the natural sciences, or the earth sciences, despite their greater age and familiarity. Nevertheless, it does appear that the concept, born to meet the administrative need of a foundation, has met a genuine intellectual need as well. The term has a place and seems to be here to stay. The new field of the behavioral sciences will in all probability be ranked among the important intellectual inventions of the twentieth century.

BERNARD BERELSON

[*See also* ANTHROPOLOGY; POLITICAL SCIENCE; PSYCHOLOGY; SOCIOLOGY.]

BIBLIOGRAPHY

WORKS CITED

BERELSON, BERNARD; and STEINER, GARY A. 1964 *Human Behavior: An Inventory of Scientific Findings.* New York: Harcourt.

DEWEY, JOHN; and BENTLEY, ARTHUR 1949 *Knowing and the Known.* Boston: Beacon.

FORD FOUNDATION 1949 *Report of the Study for the Ford Foundation on Policy and Program.* New York: The Foundation.

FORD FOUNDATION, BEHAVIORAL SCIENCES DIVISION 1953 *Report.* New York: The Foundation.

MILLER, JAMES G. 1955 Toward a General Theory for the Behavioral Sciences. *American Psychologist* 10: 513–531.

EXAMPLES OF THE USE OF THE TERM

ABRAMS, ARNOLD et al. (editors) 1964 *Unfinished Tasks in the Behavioral Sciences.* Baltimore: Williams & Wilkins.

American Behavioral Scientist. → Published since 1958.

American Men of Science. 10th ed. Volume 5: The Social & Behavioral Sciences. 1962 Tempe, Ariz.: Cattell.

Behavioral Science. → Published since 1956.

BENNIS, WARREN, et al. (editors) 1961 *The Planning of Change: Readings in the Applied Behavioral Sciences.* New York: Holt.

BERELSON, BERNARD (editor) 1963 *The Behavioral Sciences Today.* New York: Basic Books.

FESTINGER, LEON; and KATZ, DANIEL (editors) 1953 *Research Methods in the Behavioral Sciences.* New York: Dryden.

Journal of Applied Behavioral Science. → Published since 1965.

Journal of the History of the Behavioral Sciences. → Published since 1965.

PEARSALL, MARION 1963 *Medical Behavioral Science: A Selected Bibliography of Cultural Anthropology, Social Psychology, and Sociology in Medicine.* Lexington: Univ. of Kentucky Press.

SIEGEL, SIDNEY 1956 *Nonparametric Statistics for the Behavioral Sciences.* New York: McGraw-Hill.

U.S. PRESIDENT'S SCIENCE ADVISORY COMMITTEE, LIFE SCIENCES PANEL 1962 *Strengthening the Behavioral Sciences.* Washington: Government Printing Office.

BEHAVIORISM

For material on behaviorism in psychology, see LEARNING, *especially the articles on* INSTRUMENTAL LEARNING, REINFORCEMENT, *and* AVOIDANCE LEARNING; LEARNING THEORY; *and the biographies of* BEKHTEREV; GUTHRIE; HULL; PAVLOV; WATSON. *For the behavioral approach in political science, see* POLITICAL BEHAVIOR.

BEKHTEREV, VLADIMIR M.

Vladimir Mikhaylovich Bekhterev (Bekhtereff, Bechterew, von Bekhterew) (1857–1927), was a Russian neurologist, psychiatrist, physiologist, psychologist, and reflexologist. He made significant contributions to the first four of these disciplines and founded the fifth. *Bekhterev's band* or *layer, Bekhterev's nucleus, Bekhterev's tract*—all defined in any medical dictionary—attest to his neurological, more specifically, neuroanatomical, discoveries in the cerebral cortex, medulla oblongata, and neural pathways. Medical dictionaries also almost invariably include *Bekhterev's disease, Bekhterev's reflexes* (five in number), *Bekhterev's sign, Bekhterev's symptom,* and *Bekhterev's test*—his contributions to clinical medicine, psychiatry, and physiology. And dictionaries contain only eponymic contributions. Bekhterev founded a laboratory of experimental psychology at the University of Kazan in 1886; and in 1896 he founded the periodical *Obozreniye psikhiatrii, nevropatologii, i eksperimental'noi psikhologii* ("Review of Psychiatry, Neuropathology and Experimental Psychology"), the first periodical to contain the term "experimental psychology" in its title. In 1904, he advocated "objective psychology" as a separate discipline. In 1912 he called it "psychoreflexology" and in 1917 simply "reflexology."

Bekhterev was born in a small village near Viatka (now Kirov). He was graduated with high honors from the St. Petersburg Military Medical Academy at the youthful age of 21. By age 27, the number of his scientific publications amounted to 40 and he was appointed professor of psychiatry at the University of Kazan, both extraordinary achievements. He began his duties at Kazan in 1886, after spending a year and a half abroad studying with the neurologists P. Flechsig and Westphal, the psychologist Wundt, and the psychiatrist Charcot, and publishing all the while. (In 1893 he left Kazan for a professorship at his alma mater.) His bibliography, in Russian, contains 982 entries, 14 of which are books over 200 pages long. Most of his writings have been translated, either by himself or by others, into German or French, and often into both. His two classic compendious textbooks of neurology, the two-volume "Conduction Pathways of Brain and Spinal Cord" (1896–1898) and the seven-volume "Fundamentals of Brain Functions" (1903–1907), as well as his 660-page "Objective Psychology" (1907–1910) and 544-page *General Principles of Human Reflexology* (1917) are available in both languages. Only the last book is available in English.

Both Bekhterev and Pavlov preceded American behaviorists, notably J. B. Watson, in the formulation of principles of objective psychology. These principles centered, in each case, on the objectification of psychology's age-old main explanatory principle of association. Pavlov effected this objectification through pairing neutral sensory stimuli with feeding and thereby producing salivation in response to the stimuli. Bekhterev brought it about through the pairing of such stimuli with electric shock and a consequent withdrawal in response to them. Pavlov preceded Bekhterev by one year, 1903 versus 1904, in the enunciation of objective principles and by four years, 1904 versus 1908, in the laboratory demonstration of the operation of what Pavlov called "conditioned reflexes" and Bekhterev "association reflexes." Watson's behaviorism, as first promulgated in 1913 in the article "Psychology as a Behaviorist Views It," gave no evidence that he was cognizant of the Russians' prior work and views. However, after having read the German and French translations that appeared in 1913 of Bekhterev's "Objective Psychology" and also some of Pavlov's articles (Pavlov's first book in the field appeared only in 1923), Watson incorporated the Russians' empirical findings into his system; indeed, he based his system on what they had started. His 1915 address as president of the American Psychological Association was entitled "The Place of the Conditioned Reflex in Psychology" (1916). Although Watson used Pavlov's term "conditioned reflex," the experiments he reported had been performed according to Bekhterev's shock technique; and his general systematic theories were also much closer to those of Bekhterev.

Early American behaviorism may thus be said to have been influenced considerably more by Bekhterev than by Pavlov. Bekhterev's influence may also be seen in two articles appearing in the *Journal of Philosophy, Psychology and Scientific Method*: one by F. L. Wells (1916), "Von Bechterew and Übertragung" (Freud's "transference") and another by H. C. Brown (1916), "Language and the Association Reflex," which suggested, respectively, the interpretation of psychoanalysis and of verbal learning and behavior in Bekhterevian terms. Later, however, when Pavlov's research became more widely known in this country, and particularly when his two books were translated into English in 1927 and 1928, the Bekhterev influence was overshadowed. For not only were the quantity and variety of empirical findings on conditioned or association reflexes several times greater in the Pavlov than in the Bekhterev laboratories, but Pavlov's theoretical integration of the findings was much more consistent and systematic than that of Bekhterev. Indeed, Bekhterev himself came to use Pavlov's interpretation, even as Pavlov later introduced Bekhterev's methods into his laboratories.

In the Soviet Union, too, Bekhterev's influence was predominant in the first decade after the Revolution. His *General Principles of Human Reflexology* went through four editions in Russia, the first in 1917, the last in 1928. "Collective Reflexology," interpreting social behavior in terms of reflexes and association reflexes, appeared in 1921 and was followed by a number of articles on genetic, individual, pathological, industrial, comparative, "zoo-," and other reflexologies. Indeed, for a while it looked as if reflexology would wholly supplant psychology in the Soviet Union. Beginning with the 1930s, however, reflexology lost ground and finally disappeared in favor of Pavlov's "higher nervous activity," on the one hand, and an independent reformulation of traditional psychology, on the other. A significant reason for reflexology's decline was what Soviet ideologists call Bekhterev's vulgar-mechanistic interpretation of both society and philosophy.

GREGORY RAZRAN

[*For discussions of the subsequent development of Bekhterev's ideas, see* NERVOUS SYSTEM, *article on the* STRUCTURE AND FUNCTION OF THE BRAIN; LEARNING, *articles on* CLASSICAL CONDITIONING, REINFORCEMENT. *Other relevant material may be found in the biographies of* PAVLOV *and* WATSON.]

WORKS BY BEKHTEREV

1896–1898 *Provodiashchie puti spinnogo i golovnogo mozga* (Conduction Pathways of the Brain and Spinal Cord). 2 vols. St. Petersburg (Russia): Ricker. → Translated into French as *Les voies de conduction du cerveau et de la moelle*, 1900.

1903–1907 *Osnovy ucheniia o funktsiakh mozga* (Fundamentals of Brain Functions). 7 vols. St. Petersburg (Russia). → Translated into German as *Die Funktionen der Nervencentra*, 3 vols., 1908–1911; translated into French as *Les fonctions nerveuses*, 2 vols., 1909–1910.

1907–1910 *Obiektivnaia psikhologiia* (Objective Psychology). St. Petersburg (Russia). → Translated into German as *Objektive Psychologie; oder Psychoreflexologie*, 1913; translated into French as *La psychologie objective*, 1913.

(1917) 1933 *General Principles of Human Reflexology*. London: Jarrolds; New York: International Publishers.

1921 *Kollektivnaia refleksologiia* (Collective Reflexology). Petrograd (Russia): Kolos. → Translated into German as *Die kollektive Reflexologie*, 1928; translated into French as *La reflexologie collective*, 1957.

1954 *Izbrannye proizvedeniia* (Selected Works). Moscow: Medgiz.

SUPPLEMENTARY BIBLIOGRAPHY

BROWN, H. C. 1916 Language and the Association Reflex. *Journal of Philosophy, Psychology and Scientific Method* 13:645–648.

WATSON, JOHN B. 1913 Psychology as a Behaviorist Views It. *Psychological Review* 20:158–177.

WATSON, JOHN B. 1916 The Place of the Conditioned

Reflex in Psychology. *Psychological Review* 23:89–116.

WELLS, F. L. 1916 Von Bechterew and Übertragung. *Journal of Philosophy, Psychology and Scientific Method* 13:354–356.

BELIEF

See ATTITUDES; IDEOLOGY; MYTH AND SYMBOL; NORMS; RELIGION; VALUES.

BELL, CHARLES

Charles Bell, physiologist and anatomist, was one of the founders of the field now called physiological psychology. He was born in Edinburgh in 1774, the son of the Reverend William Bell, and died in Worcestershire on a journey to London in 1842.

Bell studied anatomy and surgery with his elder and already famous brother John. He also studied painting and drawing and became well-known for his anatomical illustrations—and, indeed, for his paintings. While still in his twenties he published studies on anatomy and was established as a brilliant lecturer and demonstrator in anatomy as well as a fellow of the Royal Society of Edinburgh.

At the age of 30, he moved to London, where he soon became director of the famous Hunterian School of Medicine. At the formation of London University this school was discontinued and Bell accepted the chair of physiology in the new institution. At length, in the hope of securing more time for research, he returned to Edinburgh to accept the chair of surgery there. During his London period Bell was knighted by George IV and given the honorary degree of M.D. by the University of Göttingen.

Bell's greatest contribution to knowledge was his discovery of the structural and functional discreteness of the motor and sensory nerves.

The modern physiological psychologist so clearly recognizes that the response mechanism involves receptors, sensory nerves, the central nervous system, motor nerves, and effectors that he finds it hard to remember how recent this knowledge is. Galen, Descartes, Swammerdam, Thomas Willis, Robert Whytt, Stephen Hales, and others made early contributions to the knowledge of the reflex arc, but when Bell began his work, peripheral nerves were generally believed to transmit promiscuously the powers of motion and sensation. Bell's experiments on this subject were made by laying bare the roots of the spinal nerves of living animals and demonstrating experimentally that the posterior (dorsal) nerve roots are exclusively sensory and the anterior (ventral) roots are exclusively motor in function [*see* NERVOUS SYSTEM]. This discovery was reported by Bell in a monograph that was printed in 1811 under the title *Idea of a New Anatomy of the Brain: Submitted for the Observation of His Friends.* He had been lecturing on the facts reported in the monograph to large classes in London for some years before it was published.

Through the years there has been some controversy concerning Bell's priority in this discovery. The eminent French physiologist François Magendie independently published on this subject in 1822, but he later admitted Bell's priority. The great principle of the structural and functional discreteness of the motor and sensory nerves is therefore properly called Bell's Law. However, the term Bell–Magendie Law, which is also frequently used, does name the two most important early investigators of this phenomenon.

Bell was the first scientist to enunciate in a complete way the so-called doctrine of the specific energy of sensory nerves. The name "specific nerve energies" was coined later, in 1826, by the eminent German physiologist Johannes Müller. The nub of this doctrine, as Müller put it, is that human beings are directly aware, not of external objects, but rather of the activity of their own nerves [*see* SENSES]. In 1811, more than a decade before Müller wrote on this subject, Bell clearly stated:

It is admitted that neither bodies nor the images of bodies enter the brain. . . . If light, pressure, galvanism, or electricity produce vision, we must conclude that the idea in the mind is the result of an action excited in the eye or in the brain, not of anything received, though caused by an impression from without. The operations of the mind are confined not by the limited nature of things created, but by the limited number of our organs of sense. ([1811] 1911, pp. 18, 22)

This view, in a modern, modified scientific form, is still one of the foundation stones of physiological psychology and sensory physiology.

Bell was the first physiologist to demonstrate in an adequate way the parity of the muscle sense with the five senses of antiquity. He was possibly the first physiologist to give a clear theoretical and experimental demonstration of the reciprocal innervation of antagonistic muscles. His concept of the "sensory circle" anticipated in some ways the modern concept of cybernetics as it is applied to the control of muscles in adaptive behavior.

Bell also made important contributions to the

understanding of the human expression of the emotions. He first published on this topic in 1806. Darwin, in his book *The Expression of the Emotions in Man and Animals* (1872), praised Bell's work in this field.

Bell was the author in 1833 of one of the famous Bridgewater Treatises, *The Hand: Its Mechanism and Vital Endowments as Evincing Design*. In this interesting book he makes many important observations, such as a discussion of the role of muscle sensibility in what is commonly called touch.

Bell also published medical works. A special distortion of one side of the face is called Bell's palsy.

However, his chief fame rests on his clear demonstration that sensory and motor functions are carried on in anatomically different sets of nerves. For this he has been classed with Harvey as one of the world's greatest contributors to physiological science.

Leonard Carmichael

[*See also the biography of* Müller, Johannes.]

WORKS BY BELL

(1811) 1911 *Idee einer neuen Hirnanatomie; Idea of a New Anatomy of the Brain*. Original text and German translation. Leipzig: Barth. → The English version was reprinted in 1936 by Williams & Wilkins, Baltimore.
(1833) 1865 *The Hand: Its Mechanism and Vital Endowments as Evincing Design*. 7th ed. London: Pickering; Philadelphia: Carey, Lea & Blanchard.

SUPPLEMENTARY BIBLIOGRAPHY

Boring, Edwin G. (1929) 1950 *A History of Experimental Psychology*. 2d ed. New York: Appleton.
Carmichael, Leonard 1926 Sir Charles Bell: A Contribution to the History of Physiological Psychology. *Psychological Review* 33:188–217.
Darwin, Charles (1872) 1901 *The Expression of the Emotions in Man and Animals*. Edited by Francis Darwin. London: Murray; New York: Appleton.

BENEDICT, RUTH

Ruth Fulton Benedict (1887–1948), originator of the configurational approach to culture, was a mature woman when she entered anthropology. At Vassar College, from 1905 to 1909, her main training was in English literature. Then, after three years of teaching, she turned to research and experimental writing about women who were literary figures. Thus, she came to anthropology without previous experience in science. This discipline attracted her as one that made it possible to place in manageable perspective the contrasts between the cultures of different peoples and between different historical periods. With her background in the humanities, she approached a body of cultural materials as a whole, in the sense in which the productive output of a writer or a painter forms a whole, and she conceived of a group of human beings and their culture as forming a total intellectual, religious, and aesthetic construct (Benedict 1922).

A student first of Alexander Goldenweiser and Elsie Clews Parsons at the New School for Social Research from 1919 to 1921, she was led through them to Franz Boas at Columbia University. There in 1923 she received her doctorate on the basis of her thesis, "The Concept of the Guardian Spirit in North America" (1923). The focus of her interest was the integration of this theme, a pervasive one in North American Indian religions, with various tribal values, such as wealth, success in warfare, success in hunting. However, she had not yet developed a theory of how this integration came about, and she presented it as arbitrary and essentially random in character, a view that she herself later abandoned but that is sometimes still attributed to her.

From this study of the guardian spirit and the vision quest among North American Indians, she turned to comparative work on folklore and, in the same period, undertook the editorship of the *Journal of American Folklore*. In her folklore research she still stressed the fortuitous distribution of widely diffused traits and themes that, in various ways, became integrated into different cultures. In this she continued the tradition of Boas' students, who used the wide distribution and local stylistic adaptation of folklore themes and plots to illustrate the importance of diffusion as a mechanism of cultural development.

During this early period she learned inexplicitly and by example to do highly responsible scientific work, without as yet having a basic involvement in the wider issues of scientific method. She had no specific concern for method divorced from matter, and she became restless when her colleagues or students strayed from a holistic consideration of the data to questions that were solely methodological in intent—as when a psychologist suggested making a field trip not to explore the culture of a particular people but simply to "test a test." Trained as a scholar, with a great respect for words, syntax, and metaphor as precise tools of intellectual endeavor, she learned to be a first-class comparative ethnographer and field worker without any conscious shift in role from scholar to scientist, even when she wrote "The Science of Custom" (1929). This article emphasized the uses to which our understanding of human culture can be put, rather than the study of culture as a science. In its implications, this approach, which stressed man's ability to make rational use of his knowledge of culture, is a precursor of conceptions (such as those of Conrad H. Waddington and Julian S. Huxley) of man's increasing participation in the evolutionary process. Temperamentally opposed to the study of uniformities, she insisted throughout her work on the importance of maintaining a sense of openness in history, including the future as well as the past in any perspective.

Although the type of unpatterned diffusion study in which single traits or trait complexes could be traced in great variety and without integrative consistency fitted her sense of the irony and capriciousness of human life and history, it failed to satisfy her disciplined appreciation of creative holistic constructs. While doing field work among the Pima in 1927, she was struck by the tremendous contrast between the culture of the Pueblo Indians, with its behavioral emphasis on harmony, order, and restraint, and Pima culture, with its emphasis on extreme types of behavior. Now, for the first time, she felt she had found an organizing principle that would give form to the scattered observations coming out of diffusionist research and comparative studies of folklore.

She saw individual cultures as drawing differentially on the inherent potentialities of human beings, emphasizing certain potentialities in successive generations and ignoring or even disallowing other potentialities. Using the cultural content available to them—techniques, forms of social organization, religious themes, and so on—the heritors of each culture elaborate a particular personality style at the expense of other possible styles. Ruth Benedict used the terms "personality writ large" and "time binding" to describe characteristics of this process of selection, which she saw as occurring over many generations and as involving many individuals, whose participation in the development of a cultural style can be regarded as analogous to an individual's development of his own personality style on the basis of his own available tradition.

This major insight, first developed in her paper "Psychological Types in the Cultures of the Southwest" (1930), which she presented at the 23d International Congress of Americanists in 1928, laid the groundwork for all her later significant contributions. In her expansion of the insight that culture can be seen as personality writ large, she initially drew on classical figures invoked by Nietzsche and labeled Pueblo culture as Apollonian and the contrasting cultures of other North American Indians as Dionysian. These designations she treated as "categories that bring clearly to the fore the major qualities that differentiate Pueblo culture from those of other American Indians" (*Patterns of Culture* 1934a, p. 79).

True to her sense of open-endedness, she included in her analysis two other cultures (on neither of which, however, she had done field work) with different emphases—Kwakiutl and Dobu. For these, unfortunately, she drew not on classical imagery but on abnormal psychology for her labeling; the Kwakiutl she characterized as megalomaniac and the Dobuans as paranoid. This borrowing from the poorly developed science of psychiatry, coming at the same time that she published her famous paper "Anthropology and the Abnormal" (1934b), resulted in intradisciplinary controversy and confusion. To a certain extent this was, and remains, an obstacle to the appreciation of her major contribution in *Patterns of Culture*—the delineation of the forms in which human beings, reared in an ongoing society, selectively elaborate some human potentialities, at the expense of other potentialities that would be inconsistent with the central emphases of the particular society.

In "Anthropology and the Abnormal" she was concerned primarily with the ways in which particular cultures are able to integrate various forms of extreme behavior, such as epileptic seizure, trance, hallucinatory experience, and so on, rather than with the question of whether or not certain forms of mental disorder characterize some members of all human societies. Psychologists and psychiatrists who wished to disregard culture as an intervening variable construed this paper as an attempt to prove that mental disorders or homosexuality are completely determined by cultural mechanisms. The central issue, however, is a different one, that is, the way in which psychological capacities, such as memory in its different forms, or psychological mechanisms, such as displacement, sublimation, and projection, are related to ways in which cultural forms are patterned, with stress on the place of each stylized component of behavior in the pattern. The differences between the several ways in which the vision quest (in which American Indians seek their guardian spirits) is related, say, to a search for ecstasy or a search for power could now be placed in the context of the historically shaped, psychologically comprehensible cultural style.

This configurational formulation provided a theoretical framework for anthropologists who were interested in such problems as the relationship of constitution and temperament to culture, or different types of enculturation. Ruth Benedict was not a psychologist, and she was intrinsically uninterested in the establishment of general laws. This confused some, but it challenged other research workers whose primary interest in comparative studies of culture was in the possibilities they offered for establishing biopsychological universals. At the same time her ability to discern and describe an integrated central cultural pattern exasperated those who had neither the desire nor the ability to do so, and she was sometimes accused of an absolutism she never intended (Barnouw 1949; 1957).

With her sense of the infinite range of human potentialities, Ruth Benedict emphasized the great variety of cultural configurations that have been and still may be found; moreover, she insisted that each item of culture must be judged relative to the culture in which it occurs. Ironically, this disciplined combination, in which the detail must be judged within a specific configuration but which leaves open the number and types of configurations human culture may present, sometimes has led to another basic misinterpretation. For she has been treated as the great apologist of a very different form of cultural relativism, a cultural relativism of values which (because the values of one culture are contradictory to those of another) denies that there are ethical imperatives of any kind. Actually she was deeply convinced that the causes to which she entirely devoted her anthropological skills between 1939 and 1945 were founded in anthropological knowledge: those causes were the abolition of racial and ethnic discrimination, based on theories of race difference contrary to anthropological findings on the psychic unity of mankind (Benedict 1940), and the demonstration that warfare, which is not a basic biological trait but a cultural invention and which was compatible with some earlier forms of society, has become lethal to civilization.

The work of the last years of her life was the outgrowth of her work during World War II, when she conducted a series of studies of "culture at a distance," using anthropological techniques of work with cultural wholes and living informants in combination with the analysis of cultural products— films, plays, novels, works of history, and so on— to produce cultural descriptions relevant to the prosecution of the war and, later, the formulation of conditions of peace. After making preliminary studies on Rumania, the Netherlands, and Germany (not published) and a study on Thailand (1952), she did her major work on Japan. In 1945, when the war was over, she wrote *The Chrysanthemum and the Sword* (1946) as a contribution to an understanding of the cultural potentialities of Japan as part of a peaceful and cooperative world. The spirit of cultural appreciation and the humane understanding that pervade this book made it the most acceptable of all the wartime contributions by anthropologists to the field that has more recently come to be known as "national character" research. Although the accuracy of many small details has been criticized, the book has had an enormous influence both within Japan and among those who worked with the Japanese after the war. It is perhaps the best example of the use of a comparative cultural approach to intercultural communication in the reduction of nationalistic acrimony and ethnocentrism.

Soon after the publication of *The Chrysanthemum and the Sword*, Ruth Benedict was invited to join a working group of social scientists gathered under the auspices of the Office of Naval Research to plan further research. Members of this unique group were encouraged to design their own investigations related to a study of human resources. Out of this, in 1947, came Columbia University Research in Contemporary Cultures (Mead 1951). The organization of this large project expressed Ruth Benedict's special approach to work—her concern with the well-being of each individual student and colleague, her attentiveness to individual styles of field work and different interests in theory, her willingness to spend precious hours carefully editing a student's fumbling English. This concern and attentiveness now governed the selection of personnel to work on the new project. Through work on seven cultures (i.e., the national cultures of France, Czechoslovakia, Poland, Syria, China, and pre-Soviet Great Russia and, later, the *shtetl* culture of eastern European Jews), the research sought to explore further the methods of studying cultures at a distance that had been hastily improvised during the war, and to test and expand their possibilities of continuing usefulness. Some of the cultures selected were accessible to field work; others were not. Ruth Benedict invited collaborators into the project (and welcomed those who invited themselves) not as they met the formal requirements of a rigid interdisciplinary design, but on the basis of their research interests. From the beginning the focus of the work was on the sharing and integration of materials rather than the delineation of different methodological viewpoints. In consequence, some 120 people, having very different capabilities and levels of experience and representing 14 disciplines and 16 nationalities, worked together, some of them for as long as four years, without falling into the divisive and sterile cross-disciplinary arguments that have defeated so many multidisciplinary ventures (Mead & Métraux 1953). The project and related successor projects resulted in a series of model studies of the cultures of France, Germany, Poland, Russia, precommunist China, and the eastern European *shtetl*, and in the development of a manual, *The Study of Culture at a Distance*, which discussed and illustrated the branch of applied anthropology that is relevant to the relations of national governments to their citizenry as well as to relations among national groups.

After years of teaching at Columbia University, Ruth Benedict was tardily made a full professor in 1948. That summer she was invited to attend a UNESCO conference in Czechoslovakia on the cross-cultural study of child-rearing practices (Benedict 1949). The trip to Europe, her first since 1926, gave her an opportunity to assess at first hand some of the cultures she had studied at a distance. Late in the summer she also attended the international anthropological meetings held in Brussels. A week after she returned home, she died, leaving as a legacy a vast, sprawling research group and an array of projects to which those doing the research were sufficiently committed to be able to complete them.

Ruth Benedict's work constituted a bridge between anthropology and the humanities; this was her most valuable contribution (Benedict 1948). Her early training in English literature, the years she devoted to writing poetry (published under the pseudonym of Anne Singleton; see Benedict 1959), and her passionate interest in the relationship between creator and creation, whether the creator was Earthmaker in an Indian myth, the nineteenth-century rebel Mary Wollstonecraft, or a contemporary poet like Robinson Jeffers, peculiarly fitted her to become a link between the young science of anthropology and the living humanities. *Patterns of Culture* is written so lucidly that it makes an ideal introduction to the ideas of anthropology, for unlike other anthropological works on which humanists depend, such as James G. Frazer's *Golden Bough*, it is informed not only by scholarship but also by disciplined, although implicit, scientific method.

Ruth Benedict's profound effect on cultural anthropology has been blurred by the small parochial quarrels that have centered on such minor points as whether every recognized cultural trait can be fitted into a configuration; whether her use of labels taken from psychiatry was or was not appropriate, whether she was or was not influenced by the thinking of certain philosophers, and so on; and

also by the perpetuation of ill-informed interpretations of her earlier work.

But her identification of the relationships between cultural systems and the varieties of human temperament continues to underlie, however inexplicitly, all later work in the field of culture and personality. Her emphasis on human culture as an open system served as a transition from earlier conceptions of history and from attempts to fit all cultures into the Procrustean beds of limited conceptual systems—e.g., the frustration–aggression hypothesis (Dollard et al. 1939; Bateson 1941) or basic personality theory (Kardiner 1939) or the conception of dynamic equilibrium (Chapple & Coon 1942)—to our present-day inclusion within one conceptual scheme: transcultural regularities in the relations between biology and environment, the indeterminate events of history, and cultural regularities.

MARGARET MEAD

[*For the historical context of Benedict's work see the biographies of* BOAS; GOLDENWEISER; PARSONS, E. C. *For discussion of related ideas, see* CULTURE; CULTURE AND PERSONALITY; NATIONAL CHARACTER.]

BIBLIOGRAPHY

Ruth Benedict's work falls into several categories, overlapping in time and emphasis. There are intensive, detailed, scholarly cooperative studies of written sources on North American Indian ethnology. There is field work, emphasizing folklore: among the Serrano 1922; the Zuñi 1924, 1925, 1935; the Cochiti 1925, 1931a; and the Pima 1926. Ruth Benedict led two anthropological training groups: one among the Mescalero Apache 1931b; and the other among the Blackfoot 1939. She edited the Journal of American Folklore *(1925–1939); she originated and elaborated upon the idea of configuration in culture, work that culminated in* Patterns of Culture *1934a; in the decade 1935–1945 she was actively committed to causes to which she felt anthropology was relevant; and, finally, she participated, from 1943 to 1948, in the development of techniques whereby the methods of anthropology could be applied to the study of modern cultures, combining an intensive use of sophisticated informants and the analysis of cultural products.*

WORKS BY BENEDICT

(1922) 1959 The Vision in Plains Culture. Pages 18–35 in Margaret Mead, *An Anthropologist at Work: Writings of Ruth Benedict.* Boston: Houghton Mifflin. → First published in Volume 24 of the *American Anthropologist.*

1923 The Concept of the Guardian Spirit in North America. American Anthropological Association, *Memoirs* 29:1–97.

1924 Zuñi. Unpublished manuscript.

1925 Zuñi and Cochiti. Unpublished manuscript.

1926 Pima. Unpublished manuscript.

1929 The Science of Custom. *Century* 117:641–649.

(1930) 1947 Psychological Types in the Cultures of the Southwest. Pages 14–23 in Society for the Psychological Study of Social Issues, *Readings in Social Psychology.* New York: Holt.

1931a *Tales of the Cochiti Indians.* Smithsonian Institution, Bureau of American Ethnology, Bulletin 98. Washington: The Institution.

1931b Mescalero Apache: Student Training Under Auspices of Southwest Laboratory of Anthropology, Santa Fe. Unpublished manuscript.

1934a *Patterns of Culture*. Boston: Houghton Mifflin. → A paperback edition was published in 1961 by Houghton Mifflin.

(1934b) 1959 Anthropology and the Abnormal. Pages 262–283 in Margaret Mead, *An Anthropologist at Work: Writings of Ruth Benedict*. Boston: Houghton Mifflin. → First published in Volume 10 of the *Journal of General Psychology*.

1935 *Zuñi Mythology*. 2 vols. Columbia University Contributions to Anthropology, Vol. 21. New York: Columbia Univ. Press.

1939 Blackfoot: Student Training Direction Under Joint Auspices of Columbia University and University of Montana. Unpublished manuscript.

(1940) 1959 *Race: Science and Politics*. New York: Viking.

1946 *The Chrysanthemum and the Sword: Patterns of Japanese Culture*. Boston: Houghton Mifflin.

1948 Anthropology and the Humanities. *American Anthropologist* New Series 50:585–593.

1949 Child Rearing in Certain European Countries. *American Journal of Orthopsychiatry* 19:342–350. → Contains one page of discussion.

1952 *Thai Culture and Behavior: An Unpublished Wartime Study Dated September, 1943*. Cornell University Southeast Asia Program, Data Papers No. 4. Ithaca, N.Y.: Department of Far Eastern Studies, Cornell Univ.

1959 Selected Poems: 1941, by Anne Singleton [pseud.]. Pages 473–490 in Margaret Mead, *An Anthropologist at Work: Writings of Ruth Benedict*. Boston: Houghton Mifflin. → Published posthumously.

SUPPLEMENTARY BIBLIOGRAPHY

BARNOUW, VICTOR 1949 Ruth Benedict: Apollonian and Dionysian. *University of Toronto Quarterly* 18:241–253.

BARNOUW, VICTOR 1957 The Amiable Side of *Patterns of Culture*. *American Anthropologist* New Series 59:532–535.

BATESON, GREGORY 1941 The Frustration–Aggression Hypothesis and Culture. *Psychological Review* 48:350–355.

CHAPPLE, ELIOT D.; and COON, CARLETON S. 1942 *Principles of Anthropology*. New York: Holt.

DOLLARD, JOHN et al. 1939 *Frustration and Aggression*. Yale University Institute of Human Relations. New Haven: Yale Univ. Press.

Journal of American Folklore. → Published quarterly since 1888 by the American Folklore Society, University of Pennsylvania.

KARDINER, ABRAM 1939 *The Individual and His Society: The Psychodynamics of Primitive Social Organization*. New York: Columbia Univ. Press; Oxford Univ. Press.

MEAD, MARGARET 1951 Research in Contemporary Cultures. Pages 106–118 in U.S. Office of Naval Research, *Groups, Leadership and Men: Research in Human Relations*. Pittsburgh: Carnegie Press.

MEAD, MARGARET; and MÉTRAUX, RHODA (editors) 1953 *The Study of Culture at a Distance*. Univ. of Chicago Press.

MEAD, MARGARET 1959 *An Anthropologist at Work: Writings of Ruth Benedict*. Boston: Houghton Mifflin. → A critical study of Ruth Benedict, illustrated from her own writing.

BENINI, RODOLFO

Rodolfo Benini (1862–1956) was born in Cremona. At the very young age of 27 he was appointed to the chair of history of economics at Bari. His academic life led him from Bari to Perugia in 1896 and then to Pavia, where from 1897 to 1907 he taught political economics and statistics. In 1908 Benini went to Rome and there held the chair of statistics until 1928; from then until 1956 he taught economics at the same university. It is difficult to name any single predecessor or teacher who had a particularly strong influence on Benini, since he worked in a great variety of social science fields and showed in each a great degree of independent thought and creativity. As immediate predecessors of Benini we may certainly list Angelo Messedaglia, Ridolfo Livi, Maffeo Pantaleoni, and especially Vilfredo Pareto. In a broader sense we might well cite the whole system of Italian economic and social thought, which up to this century had developed quite independently and which was ahead of the rest of European thought in many instances. It is the connection of statistical knowledge and economic and social theory in Benini which led him to very constructive results in all the fields he engaged in.

Together with Süssmilch, Quetelet, and Achille Guillard, Benini can be regarded as one of the founders of demography as a separate science (1896; 1901a). In his *Principii di demografia* he distinguished between a qualitative and a quantitative theory of population. Both his concepts differ from the standard use in the literature. In the "qualitative" theory Benini elaborated the concept of descriptive statistics to include rates of birth and mortality; life expectancies; the fertility of women as a decreasing function of their age; and normal distributions of physiological characteristics of men and women. In the analysis of the cohesion of social groups Benini developed an attraction–repulsion index to measure the association between dichotomous characteristics of husbands and wives (1898; 1901a; 1928a). Classifying a population by any given characteristic (e.g., literate vs. illiterate males—m_1, m_2—and females—f_1, f_2), Benini arranged the relative frequencies ρ_{ij} ($i, j = 1, 2$) of the possible combinations in 2×2 tables such as Table 1. From this classification Benini then derived a first measure of attraction (repulsion) with

$$\gamma_{ij} = \rho_{ij} - \rho_i \cdot \rho_{\cdot j}, \qquad i, j = 1, 2$$

where $\gamma_{11} = \gamma_{22} = -\gamma_{21} = -\gamma_{12}$. The index of attraction (when $\gamma_{ij} > 0$) or repulsion (when $\gamma_{ij} < 0$), a later measure he put forth, is given by Benini as

$$\frac{\gamma_{11}}{\min \rho_{\cdot 1}, \rho_{\cdot 1} - \rho_{1} \cdot \rho_{\cdot 1}} \equiv \frac{\rho_{11} - \rho_{\cdot 1} \rho_{1} \cdot}{\min \rho_{1} \cdot, \rho_{\cdot 1} - \rho_{1} \cdot \rho_{\cdot 1}},$$

the absolute value of the index ranging from 0 to 1. This statistic was further elaborated on by Benini (1928a) and later by many others in Italy and elsewhere (Goodman & Kruskal 1954–1963).

In the "quantitative" theory Benini tried to discover evolutionary laws of aggregate societies and their latent structures. He denied the general validity of Malthus' theorem. Uniform predictions cannot be made from empirical evidence, said Benini. He expected, however, that the continuing process of urbanization of societies would lead to an adjustment of the growth rates of social aggregates, not so much by delayed marriages as by advanced education and new methods of birth control. Moreover, because of an instinct of imitation, the lower classes of urban centers would aspire to the behavior and social status of the next higher classes. This would cause a continual process of assimilation—a narrowing and adjustment of the average age of marriages within and between social groups; an adjustment of the proportion of unmarried people; and an adjustment of birth and death rates. Thus eventually, the evolution of societies will lead to a stationary state of social aggregates and a gradual elimination of structural differences.

Benini engaged in statistical research in economics similar to his statistical work in demography. He hoped to reduce economic science by systematization and by empirically verified formulas or laws to the concise system of expressions characteristic of physics and chemistry (1907, p. 1053; 1908, p. 17). In 1894 he tried to estimate the distribution of property among social classes (1894). After Pareto's work on the distribution of incomes appeared (1896; 1897), Benini extended this work and modified the Pareto distribution in his analysis of the distribution of property. The function proposed by Benini for the distribution of property values was

$$\log F(x) = \log k - a(\log x)^2, \qquad \text{for } x \geq x_0,$$

where $F(x)$ is the proportion of property values greater than or equal to x, that is, the distribution function cumulated to the right. There is a truncation point, x_0, forming a lower limit. Another way of expressing Benini's distribution is to say that it is that of a random variable, X, such that $[\log (X - x)]^2$ has a negative exponential distribution. [See DISTRIBUTIONS, STATISTICAL, *article on* SPECIAL CONTINUOUS DISTRIBUTIONS.] In contrast, Pareto's distribution is such that $\log (X - x_0)$ has a negative exponential distribution. The attraction–repulsion index and the modification of the Pareto distribution are Benini's most original contributions to statistics.

As early as 1907 Benini established empirical estimates of price elasticities, demand curves, and Engel curves (see 1907; 1908). The demand curve underlying his estimates was of the general hyperbolic form $\log y = a + b \log x$. In the case of prices and demand for coffee in Italy, Benini came to estimates of $a = 3.63161$ and $b = -0.384$. In an extension of this work (1908) Benini estimated, in addition to other demand curves, income-induced increases in expenditures for housing. The underlying model is similar to that shown above, with b now positive and ranging from 0 to 1 (for Dresden and Breslau $b = 0.617$). In this Benini preceded A. C. Pigou, Lenoir, Lehfeld, R. Frisch, and H. Schultz. Benini, however, had no means of establishing confidence intervals for his estimates, although the signs of his estimates agreed with what one would expect. [See DEMAND AND SUPPLY, *article on* ECONOMETRIC STUDIES.]

Benini's other economic ideas are spread over a long series of articles, and it is hard to consider them all. They can be reduced, however, to some few central results which underlie his writings. Most important among them is Benini's notion that in any exchange transaction there exist a minimum price and a maximum price (p min and p max) at which the transaction still can take place (1928b). According to Benini, the most likely price between two equally endowed parties (equality of bargaining power, in whichever way this is defined) would be the point equidistant from the boundary points p min and p max. Given, however, unequal endowment of the contracting parties, there would result a shift in the price and an exploitation of the weaker partner. On this basis Benini explained how profits arise at the expense of labor income.

Table 1

		MEN		
		m_1	m_2	Σ
	f_1	ρ_{11}	ρ_{12}	$\rho_1 \cdot$
WOMEN	f_2	ρ_{21}	ρ_{22}	$\rho_2 \cdot$
	Σ	$\rho_{\cdot 1}$	$\rho_{\cdot 2}$	1

Benini believed that protectionism in international trade is justified on three grounds: first, by the existence of the same kind of exploitation of a weaker party described above for the general market place (in this case the parties are foreign enterprises or foreign states); second, by the cumulative effect of that exploitation associated with the power of states in international relations; and third, by the vulnerability of infant industries. For all these reasons the state has to fulfill special functions and is therefore introduced by Benini as an additional factor of production.

In connection with the distribution of property and income Benini observed that in some countries, among them Italy, a doubling of property was associated with a threefold increase in total income (per person or household), at least as long as the income derived from labor constituted a significant part of total income derived from labor and property. From this Benini then derived his fiscal axiom that a proportional taxation of incomes would lead in those countries to a less than proportional taxation of property and that a proportional taxation of property would lead to a progressive taxation of incomes.

His empirical results also led him to extend Galton's law concerning the progressive elimination of economic and social divergencies (structures). This process occurs as extreme points are continuously eliminated. Their elimination induces an asymptotic approach to stationary states. This process was previously noted in Benini's quantitative theory of the growth of social aggregates.

In addition to his work in demography, sociology, and economics, Benini developed a unique interest in the works of Dante. He undertook to reveal a "second beauty" in Dante by uncovering the quantitative consistency of the structure of *The Divine Comedy*, which up to then had generally been neglected (there had been some exceptions—Busnelli, Angelitti, and Moore). (It is apparent that Dante did incorporate quantitative relations and symbols in the structure of *The Divine Comedy*, as is immediately apparent from the fact that each of the three parts of *The Divine Comedy* contains 33 canti and *The Inferno* an additional introductory one, bringing the total to exactly 100. Moreover, each of the three parts ends with the word "stelle," and so on.) Many enigmas and allegorical elements in *The Divine Comedy* have yet to be interpreted. To do so it is important to appreciate Dante's knowledge of astronomy and the way he incorporated this knowledge into *The Divine Comedy*. Similarly, by quantitative analysis the structure and dimensions of the Inferno and Purgatory may be ascertained.

In addition, this kind of analysis may explain the relationship of the calendar used by Dante and the dates he attributed to events in *The Divine Comedy*. The exact dates of Dante's poetic voyage with Vergil and, later, with Beatrice through the regions of the Inferno, Purgatory, and Paradise can thus be established. The main assumption on which Benini based his investigation is that the rigorous structure of the poem will not allow for obvious contradictions or omissions. Explanations may be found by applying medieval concepts to these enigmas. In addition to explanations of the above kind, Benini showed that Dante believed Purgatory to be located on Mount Sinai and established the date of birth of Cacciaguida, an ancestor of Dante, and the date when Cacciaguida's son Alighiero died. Benini also thought he had discovered that Dante's poetic technique differed, depending on the seriousness of the moral crimes he was describing. The new perspectives contained in Benini's contribution to the knowledge of Dante's poem lead to the very margin where one might discover something in Dante that the poet himself was unaware of. Benini knew of this danger and tried to avoid such pitfalls. It took some time for Benini's work on Dante to find support, just as Benini's achievements in combining statistics and social science were not immediately appreciated.

KLAUS-PETER HEISS

[For the historical context of Benini's work, see POPULATION, *article on* POPULATION THEORIES; *and the biographies of* PANTALEONI *and* PARETO. *For discussion of the subsequent development of Benini's ideas, see* STATISTICS, DESCRIPTIVE, *article on* ASSOCIATION.]

WORKS BY BENINI

1892   Sulle dottrine economiche di Antonio Serra: Appunti critici. *Giornale degli economisti* Series 2 5:222–248.

1894   Distribuzione probabile della ricchezza privata in Italia per classi di popolazione. *Riforma sociale* 1: 862–869.

1896   Di alcuni punti oscuri della demografia. *Giornale degli economisti* Series 2 13:97–128, 297–327, 509–534.

1897   Di alcune curve descritte da fenomeni economici aventi relazione colla curva del reddito o con quella del patrimonio. *Giornale degli economisti* Series 2 14:177–214.

1898   Le combinazioni simpatiche in demografia. *Rivista italiana di sociologia* 2:152–171.

1899   Gerarchie sociali: Contributo alla teoria qualitativa della popolazione. *Rivista italiana di sociologia* 3: 17–49.

1901a   *Principii di demografia.* Florence: Barbèra.

1901b   Tecnica e logica dei rapporti statistici. *Giornale degli economisti* Series 2 23:503–516.

1905a   I diagrammi a scala logaritmica (a proposito della graduazione per valore delle successioni ereditarie in

Italia, Francia e Inghilterra). *Giornale degli economisti* Series 2 30:222–231.

(1905*b*) 1923 *Principii di statistica metodologica*. Turin: Unione Tipografico–Editrice Torinese.

1907 Sull' uso delle formole empiriche nell' economia applicata. *Giornale degli economisti* Series 2 35: 1053–1063.

1908 Una possibile creazione del metodo statistico: "L'economia politica induttiva." *Giornale degli economisti* Series 2 36:11–34.

1912 L'azione recente dell' oro sui prezzi generali delle merci. Società Italiana per il Progresso delle Scienze, Rome, *Atti* 6:97–123.

1928*a* Gruppi chiusi e gruppi aperti in alcuni fatti collettivi di combinazioni. International Statistical Institute, *Bulletin* 23, no. 2:362–383.

1928*b* Un ritorno ai preliminari dell' economia politica. *Economia* New Series 1:411–428.

1952 *Dante tra gli splendori de' suoi enigmi risolti, ed altri saggi*. Rome: Edizioni dell' Ateneo.

SUPPLEMENTARY BIBLIOGRAPHY

BACHI, ROBERTO 1929 I principali scritti di Rodolfo Benini. *Giornale degli economisti* Series 4 69:1068–1076.

BARI (CITY), UNIVERSITÀ, FACOLTÀ DI ECONOMIA E COMMERCIO 1956 *Studi in memoria di Rodolfo Benini*. Bari: The University.

GOODMAN, LEO A.; and KRUSKAL, WILLIAM H. 1954–1963 Measures of Association for Cross-classifications. Parts 1–3. *Journal of the American Statistical Association* 49:732–764; 54:123–163; 58:310–364.

PARETO, VILFREDO 1896 La curva delle entrate e le osservazioni del Prof. Edgeworth. *Giornale degli economisti* Series 2 13:439–448.

PARETO, VILFREDO 1897 Aggiunta allo studio sulla curva delle entrate. *Giornale degli economisti* Series 2 14: 15–26.

[Rodolfo Benini]. 1929 *Giornale degli economisti* Series 4 69:837–966. → Contains articles on Benini by Corrado Gini and others.

BENTHAM, JEREMY

As a social scientist, Jeremy Bentham (1748–1832) was a visionary born 150 years too soon. A passionate advocate of quantitative method in social observation, he lived in an England where even an elementary census was unknown until 1801. Convinced that a fixed neutral vocabulary is a necessary condition of scientific advance, he spent his life in a gallant but futile effort to redefine the highly emotional and ambiguous language of morals and politics. He hoped in vain to create a science of human behavior, the objective study and measurement of passions and feelings, pleasures and pains, will and action. The Principles of Utility were the sum of these new definitions and working hypotheses.

But if utilitarianism was intended as a coolly detached science, its source was angry passion. Bentham was first and last a reformer, not merely a scientist, and he never spoke of "science" but always of "art-and-science." "Knowing without doing," he often said, "is worthless." He studied what is—the social facts—in order to create what ought to be. And the facts as he observed them in late-eighteenth-century England horrified him.

Bentham was a precocious child, who read history at the age of three, and whose pushing middle-class father intended him to become first a barrister, then lord chancellor and a member of the peerage. He was therefore sent to Westminster School, London, and Queen's College, Oxford, the two most fashionable schools in England and centers of Establishment orthodoxy. Everything he found there repelled him: the gloomy religion, the forced subscription to the Thirty-nine Articles, the arid classical curriculum, the brutality and snobbery of students and masters alike. But it was not until he began to read law at Lincoln's Inn, in 1766, that his disgust became rebellion, and he dedicated his life "to cleansing the Augean stable." Born of his hatred of English law, this passion for radical reform ultimately spread to all of man's ideas and acts: psychology, ethics, semantics, education, economics, sociology, and political theory.

English common law and equity seemed to Bentham archaic, uncodified, incomprehensible, arbitrary, irrational, cruelly vindictive, tortuously dilatory, and so ruinously expensive that nine out of ten men were literally outlawed. It seemed to him a labyrinth without a clue until he discovered the Principle of Utility. This he saw as an ethical commandment for rulers: act always to ensure the greatest happiness of the greatest number.

He then needed an effective definition of happiness and, reading avidly among the *philosophes,* found it in Helvétius. Happiness is a compound sum of pleasures and pains, the greatest amount of pleasure and the least amount of pain. But what is pleasure, and what is pain? Bentham was completely latitudinarian: Whatever a man chooses to consider so; the variety of motives is infinite. These principles of psychology and ethics he developed in his two earliest books, the only ones by which he is remembered today, *A Fragment on Government* (1776) and *An Introduction to the Principles of Morals and Legislation* (1780).

An enthusiastic amateur chemist, Bentham hoped to apply the verbal precision and quantitative methods so successful in the physical sciences to the social sciences. His notorious psychological "calculus" was an attempt to measure the varieties and dimensions of pleasure and pain, and he offered it humbly, not as an exact scale, but as a useful, if crude, working hypothesis for the legislator. He appealed to judges and legislators who inevitably do weigh and strike a balance between crimes and punishments to open their imaginations to the endless range and consequences of human action. Therefore, according to the Greatest Happiness Principle, the evil of a crime is proportionate to the number of people hurt by it. The less the social pain, the less the punishment. It follows that motives are largely irrelevant in criminal law, and that sexual "offenses" like homosexuality are not crimes and should not be punished.

But what Bentham gained in psychological breadth and tolerance, by the application of his principle, he lost in verbal precision and philosophical rigor; and critics have often scorned his hedonism as superficial, a laughable attempt "to plus and minus people to heaven and hell."

Bentham himself hurled a charge of superficiality at English judges and legislators. The psychology implicit in English law was, he thought, crudely reductionist. The only motive of human behavior it recognized was love of money. It totally ignored sex, for example, which he considered among the most powerful of all motives. He offered his own psychology, based on years of observation in the courts and the infinite variety of human drama enacted there, as a far more subtle and empirical improvement. In his monumental *Rationale of Judicial Evidence,* edited in 1827 by the young John Stuart Mill, Bentham applied the results of his psychological studies to the judge's problem of gathering valid evidence. None of his works more fully reveals his genius for exhaustive analysis, and this may well be his masterpiece.

In any case, his psychology and ethics were offered merely as incomplete introductory chapters to an exhaustive code of law, and ultimately to a complete encyclopedia of all human thought and action, science and art. This grand vision he borrowed from Sir Francis Bacon, whom he considered the greatest of all geniuses. Like him, Bentham wanted to create a Novum Organum. This new science of human behavior, eudaemonics (or the art-and-science of well-being), was analogous to the science of medicine. His codes of civil and penal law, procedure and evidence, constitutional and international law, were anatomies. The Greatest Happiness Principle was an ethical commitment, like the doctors' Hippocratic oath. His social and political reforms were prescriptive remedies to cure the ills and cancers of the body politic, and he foresaw a future golden age when crime and punishment will have disappeared, conquered by a science of social therapeutics or preventive legislation, analogous to preventive medicine.

This was a superhuman ambition, and of course Bentham failed to achieve it completely. Nevertheless he pursued it wherever possible, with varying success, and even his fragments are imaginative and tantalizing. As an ardent reforming social scientist the two insuperable obstacles that he faced were a deaf public, content with the *status quo,* and a complete lack of the empirical data necessary for valid social generalizations. The success of his enterprises was directly proportionate to his success in overcoming these obstacles. As far afield as he often ranged from his legal studies, he inevitably returned to them, through all sixty years of his working life, for there as nowhere else he found the data, the case records, he needed.

All of Bentham's reforms were governed by the Greatest Happiness Principle and its four subordinate ends of good government: subsistence, abundance, security, and equality. Subsistence is a necessary condition of all government, even the most tyrannical. Its absence means starvation and anarchy. The test of good government is the measure of abundance, security, and equality it provides. By this standard, eighteenth-century English mixed monarchy was bad government, unable to provide abundance and violently insecure and unequal. Bentham therefore sought to provide these good ends in a series of radical reforms.

In his social and economic reforms he added these principles of abundance, security, and equality to the doctrines of Adam Smith, and the sum was a welfare state with free education, guaranteed employment, minimum wages, sickness benefits, and old-age insurance. Perhaps his most imaginative flight into social policy, certainly his most visionary as a social scientist, was his scheme for "Panopticon Hills." By the 1790s the problem of poor relief had become critical. In the turmoil of the early Industrial Revolution, the number of paupers had vastly increased, and with them so had the tax rates and administrative chaos. Bentham proposed a national network of self-supporting "houses of industry," small manufacturing centers surrounded by farms, where all of society's victims —orphans, cripples, the impoverished, the aged, unemployed workingmen, pensioned sailors and soldiers, unwed mothers—would be welcomed and could flourish. In these earthly paradises everyone would be educated and trained to the top of his talent.

Here Bentham hoped to see the first social laboratory where experiments under controlled conditions could be undertaken. He suggested work and leisure studies and wanted to ask such questions as: How much better does a man produce whose work is varied and interesting than one whose work is tedious and repetitive? What is the best ratio between hours of work and hours of leisure? What are the best incentives to efficient production? How can full employment be guaranteed? He also suggested education studies and wanted to test his assumption that children learn best by seeing and touching and therefore should first be taught botany and zoology. Of course, nothing came of this visionary scheme, although he wrote thousands of pages on it. Indeed, he abandoned economics and social planning altogether around 1804, humbly admitting that in the absence of reliable economic and social data his hypotheses were guesswork.

But in administrative, legal, and parliamentary reform he was far more successful; indeed, seldom if ever in the history of ideas has a man's thought been so directly and widely translated into action. An enthusiastic disciple once credited Bentham with nearly all the great reforms of the first half of the nineteenth century, and many more sober judges, such as Sir Henry Maine, A. V. Dicey, and Leslie Stephen, later agreed. The secret of his immense influence was this: he gave a small scattered army of reformers not only an ideal, the greatest happiness of the greatest number, but also an exact plan to gain it. He gave his disciples a set of working hypotheses and rules to apply to any given social problem. Among the most important was the principle of single-seated responsibility and the priority of procedure and evidence in law. The legislator or administrator must have full central authority to gather every shred of relevant evidence, to conduct completely free inquiries, and to enforce his decisions.

Armed with these principles of central control and inspection, such ardent Benthamite civil servants as Edwin Chadwick and James Kay-Shuttleworth introduced them into British administration. Among the laws they shaped in Bentham's image were the 1829 Metropolitan Police Act, the 1833 Education Act, the 1833 Factory Act, the Poor Law Act of 1834, the 1840 Railway Regulation Act, and the 1848 Public Health Act.

In the reform of civil and criminal law Bentham again found an army of disciples, for by the end of the Napoleonic Wars, in 1815, the archaisms and anomalies of the law had become intolerable to many others besides him. Among them were younger contemporaries like Sir Samuel Romilly and Lord Chancellor Brougham and late-nineteenth-century legal scholars and judges like Sir Henry Maine and Fitzjames Stephen. In so vast a field of tradition and precedent the work was slow and piecemeal, but at last, by the great consolidating Judicature Act of 1873, the separate courts of law and equity were brought together under Bentham's principle of single-seated responsibility. Meanwhile, in a long series of acts between 1833 and 1898, the law of procedure and evidence was completely transformed, so that his ideal of efficient informed justice was no longer a vision but a commonplace.

Bentham came slowly to parliamentary reform. Preoccupied with his civil and penal codes through the 1780s, he had been indifferent to politics. But gradually he began to see the bitter inequality between rich and poor in England. He saw a government of, for, and by rich aristocrats and concluded that the common man's only hope was to fight for a share in it. By 1790 he had become a democrat, but during the Napoleonic Wars these were treasonable thoughts and he was silent. With peace the movement for parliamentary reform grew strong, and he then joined the old-time democrat Major Cartwright, the moderate Whig Earl Grey, and the radical Francis Place in calling for it. The Reform Bill of 1832 was the first installment of democracy.

Bentham died that same year, still hard at work at the age of 84, "codifying like any dragon." For over 40 years he had lived secluded in a charming little flower-encircled house only a few hundred yards from the Houses of Parliament. There he kept close watch on every event, wrote 15 folio pages every day, poured out reform proposals in an inexhaustible stream, welcomed dozens of informants and disciples, dined them well, amused them with gay and whimsical sallies, and spread the gospel of utilitarianism. He once said his ambition was to be "the most effectively benevolent man who ever lived." He may well have been so.

MARY PETER MACK

[*For the historical context of Bentham's work, see* UTILITARIANISM *and the biographies of* BACON; BLACKSTONE; SMITH, ADAM. *For discussion of the subsequent development of his ideas, see* LEGAL SYSTEMS; PARLIAMENTARY GOVERNMENT; WELFARE STATE; *and the biography of* MILL.]

WORKS BY BENTHAM

(1776) 1891 *A Fragment on Government.* Edited by F. C. Montague. Oxford: Clarendon. → The 1891 edition was reprinted in 1951.

(1780) 1823 *An Introduction to the Principles of Morals and Legislation.* New ed., corrected by the author. London: Pickering. → The 1823 edition has been reprinted frequently by Oxford University Press; also reprinted in 1948 by Hafner, New York.

1827 *Rationale of Judicial Evidence.* 5 vols. Edited by J. S. Mill. London: Hunt & Clarke.

1838–1843 *The Works of Jeremy Bentham.* 11 vols. Edited by John Bowring. Edinburgh: William Tait. → Reprinted in 1962 by Russell & Russell in a limited edition.

SUPPLEMENTARY BIBLIOGRAPHY

DICEY, ALBERT V.   (1905) 1962   *Lectures on the Relation Between Law and Public Opinion in England During the Nineteenth Century.* 2d ed. London and New York: Macmillan. → A paperback edition was published in 1962 by Macmillan.

HALÉVY, ÉLIE   (1901–1904) 1952   *The Growth of Philosophic Radicalism.* New ed. London: Faber. → First published in French. Indispensable for the economic, political, educational, and other ramifications of philosophic radicalism.

MACK, MARY P.   1962   *Jeremy Bentham.* London: Heinemann.

STEPHEN, LESLIE   (1900) 1950   *The English Utilitarians.* London School of Economics and Political Science Series of Reprints of Scarce Works on Political Economy, Nos. 9–11, 3 vols. London School of Economics and Political Science; Gloucester, Mass.: Smith. → A sequel to the author's *History of English Thought in the Eighteenth Century.* A detailed study of Bentham and the two Mills.

BENTLEY, ARTHUR F.

Arthur F. Bentley (1870–1957) was certainly one of the most controversial political scientists the United States has produced. However, he never taught a class in politics, and although *The Process of Government* was first published in 1908, his essays have only recently come under wide consideration by the general practitioners of the study of politics. The influence he had on the extensive literature on pressure groups is being debated, but Bentley himself disclaimed any primary interest in pressure groups. He wrote in 1950 that *The Process of Government* was "an inquiry much wider in scope than any study of pressure groups" (1950, p. 780), suggesting that the debate about the extent of his influence in this particular area does not touch his own principal preoccupation.

Bentley was, in fact, committed to the search for a framework for the study of social change. His work suggests a recognition of the important effects of agricultural discontent and rapid urbanization. His search for a systematic method to describe these processes explains his interest in history, economics, sociology, and political science. His technique was that of the caustic critic who sought to provide a scheme for the study of social change by improving the use of language as a tool for description and thought.

The details of Bentley's life provide a few clues to the understanding of his work. Born in Freeport, Illinois, he moved with his parents and brother and sister to Grand Island, Nebraska, where his father achieved prominence as a banker. His father was an English immigrant and his mother was of devout Pennsylvania Dutch stock; Bentley's relations with parents and siblings were generally close.

After brief periods at York College and the University of Denver, he was drawn to Johns Hopkins, in 1890, by the writings of Richard Ely, whose studies of socialism had gained some notoriety. However, within a year after Bentley's arrival, Ely moved to Wisconsin; and out of his education at Johns Hopkins, Bentley later valued only the occasional lectures of such campus visitors as S. N. Patten and J. B. Clark and his own reading of Carl Menger. He received an A.B. after two years, in 1892. In the academic year of 1893–1894 he studied in Germany, at Freiburg and at Berlin, under such notables as Georg Simmel, Adolf Wagner, Gustav Schmoller, Wilhelm Dilthey, and Herman Grimm. He secured his PH.D. from Johns Hopkins in 1895.

Bentley's studies in Germany are reflected in his first theoretical essay, "The Units of Investigation in the Social Sciences" (1895), in which his actionist or behavioral orientation is already noticeable. After receiving his PH.D. he went for a year as docent in sociology to the University of Chicago, but he profited principally from attending a seminar by John Dewey, with whom he was to collaborate some fifty years later. This seminar freed him from his mentalistic bias. It also concluded his academic career, and he began a career in the newspaper world.

News reporting and editorial work for the *Times-Herald* and the *Record-Herald* in Chicago gave him an opportunity to investigate his surroundings and left him with considerable time for thought and intellectual exploration. The John Crerar Library near his office contained useful scientific publications, and his friend Michael A. Lane offered him much critical counsel as he worked on *The Process of Government.* Bentley's intellectual debts for this book are indicated by the inscription to his 1906 outline and by the dedication of the published book; the inscription reads, "John Dewey, Georg Simmel, Ludwig Gumplowicz, Walt Whitman, and the many other joint makers of this book." The dedication is simply "To my father."

Bentley left newspapers and Chicago in 1910 for Paoli, Indiana, where he operated an orchard; he also built the house in which he was to live during the rest of his long life. His social concerns were expressed in his organizational and financial efforts for the American Red Cross in Indiana during

World War I and his leadership of the 1924 Progressive campaign in the same state. His interest in the effective organization of agricultural discontent resulted in an unpublished manuscript, "Makers, Users, and Masters in America."

Bentley's main concern during these years was with linguistic clarity and consistency of thought and description, and this concern is clearly expressed in all his subsequent writings. His contributions to linguistics, epistemology, and logic resulted in an invitation in 1941 to Columbia University, where Bentley shared the responsibility, with Irwin Edman, Ernest Nagel, and J. H. Randall, for a seminar on language, which elicited praise from the participants. Testimony to his broad impact may be found in *Life, Language, Law: Essays in Honor of Arthur F. Bentley* (Taylor 1957) and John Dewey and Arthur F. Bentley's *Philosophical Correspondence* (1932–1951).

General methodology. In each of Bentley's major writings he declared that his intention was methodological; indeed, he said in *The Process of Government*, "This book is an attempt to fashion a tool" (1908, p. vii). The volume begins with a methodological criticism of other social scientists; many of his later works begin with similar critical sections, in each instance followed by proposed constructive solutions.

Bentley's approach was remarkably consistent throughout his life. As early as 1908 he took exception to the prevailing use of feelings, faculties, and ideas as *independent causes* for social action. And when, toward the end of his life, he and John Dewey developed a systematic classification of current methods of social explanation, they considered "self-actional" and "inter-actional" presentations as inadequate and suggested their replacement by "trans-actional" descriptions. These three types of analysis are categorized as follows:

Self-action: where things are viewed as acting under their own powers. Inter-action: where thing is balanced against thing in causal interconnection. Trans-action: where systems of description and naming are employed to deal with aspects and phases of action, without final attribution to "elements" or other presumptively detachable or independent "entities," "essences," or "realities," and without isolation of presumptively detachable "relations" from such detachable "elements." (1949, p. 108)

Self-action analyses are prescientific explanations in terms of independent souls, minds, powers, or forces that operate as activating events; they are similar to other ineffective animistic rationalizations.

Inter-actional accounts correspond to the scientific procedure that was dominant until the end of the nineteenth century. The mechanistic systems following Newton in physics fit into this frame, and conventional pressure group studies in politics, like those done in the 1930s by Pendleton Herring and Peter Odegard also have a mechanical model. The common separation of organism from environment can be considered inter-actional, and this separation was frequently attacked by Bentley.

Although Dewey and Bentley approved the provisional examination of phenomena in inter-actional forms, both of them asked that such an examination allow for an awareness that results of the inquiry need to be reinterpreted in wider systems of description. The transactional view is the wider system that they proposed, and it requires the observation of the functioning of organisms within the environment under free postulation. In social and psychological research the postulated descriptive system is the following:

(1) The Cosmos: as system or field of factual inquiry; (2) Organisms: as cosmic components; (3) Men: as organisms; (4) Behavings of men: as organic–environmental events; (5) Knowings (including the knowings of the cosmos and its postulation): as such organic–environmental behavings. (Ratner 1954, p. xiv)

The knowing process, then, is as much subject to inquiry as are conventional subject matters.

The transactional approach does not presume a reductionism. In his work Bentley made explicit the separation of biological from physical research and of behavioral from biological research with an illustration from the area of communication. A portion of a conversation may be described in purely physical terms and again in biological terms, but neither description goes very far in helping us to understand the "speaking–heard" event; this requires behavioral tools as well, social and psychological descriptions of what makes communication possible (1935, pp. 224–225). Basic to this conception of transactional analysis is the postulate that knowledge is a social phenomenon, and Bentley saw as one of his major tasks the investigation of the social characteristics of knowledge.

Bentley's general approach, explicit only at the end of his career, was implicit in most of what he wrote in *The Process of Government*. At that time he was principally concerned with the methodology of political research. He devoted himself subsequently to similar methodological problems in other disciplines: in sociology (1926), in mathematics (1932), in psychology (1935), and in logic and epistemology (Dewey & Bentley 1949). At no time did he attempt a social theory, and it is as a methodologist that he should be judged.

A strategy for political inquiry. *The Process of Government* urges political inquiry to focus on overt behavior. The raw material of the political process is the activity of human beings. What people do is what requires explanation: how they talk and organize in order to achieve their goals. This raw material includes crude as well as subtle intellectual arguments; it includes instances of cooperation as well as of conflict; it includes a continuum of behavior from the unorganized to the highly organized and mobilized.

The starting point for inquiry should be the observation of activity. When possible this activity should be subjected to quantitative measurement, for Bentley believed that there "is no political process that is not a balancing of quantity against quantity." He explained:

If we can get our social life stated in terms of activity, and of nothing else, we have not indeed succeeded in measuring it, but we have at least reached a foundation upon which a coherent system of measurements can be built up. Our technique may be very poor at the start, and the amount of labor we must employ to get scanty results will be huge. But we shall cease to be blocked by the intervention of unmeasurable elements, which claim to be themselves the real causes of all that is happening, and which by their spook-like arbitrariness make impossible any progress toward dependable knowledge.   (1908, p. 202)

Three queries are appropriate: (1) How are the rich data to be arranged? (2) Is it possible that the "unmeasurable elements" are the crucial factors in some political processes? (3) To what extent has Bentley's proposed strategy been utilized by political scientists?

(1) The arrangement of data. In his early writings Bentley asserted that the most heuristic and systematic way of arranging political data is in terms of *groups*, *interests*, and *pressures*. The same activity may be considered as the activity of a group, as the expression of an interest, and as the exertion of pressure. To the annoyance of many critics, Bentley never precisely defined the three crucial terms, because he did not wish a premature definition to inhibit investigation.

In any particular struggle, two groups can be provisionally established, consisting of those who favor and those who oppose a given course of action. These groups are "cross sections" of activity, men looked at in terms of their position for or against something. Interest is nothing other than the same conflict looked at from a different angle,

namely that of the respective goals of the groups. Pressure is the third aspect of group activity and refers to its strength and energy. According to Bentley, these three aspects of the group–interest–pressure postulation must be empirically verified and explained in terms of the ongoing behavior.

Bentley never intended to formulate a comprehensive group theory, and his work has never produced such a theory. Moreover, Bentley was not so firmly wedded to the group–interest–pressure approach that he did not in later works admit that for many purposes the study of political activity can just as successfully begin with the examination of the individual. He suggested that it might be useful to change the focus and look at individuals and the extent to which they are involved in political processes. The activity of these individuals may be explained either as the consequence of complex motivations or by introducing Simmel's carefully developed concept of complex and occasionally conflicting group associations. These group associations Bentley conceived of as a large number of planes passing through the individual's life space [see INTEREST GROUPS].

For Bentley, the purpose of group explanation is clearly to make possible the incorporation of group activities in coherent descriptions of behavior without assuming a causal relationship between group membership and behavior. Thus Marx's and Gumplowicz' studies of classes may be combined with Simmel's concept of groups; and although the group theories of Durkheim and Schmoller depend on a theory of division of labor, they may also be used. However, no single basic determinant of group activity need be postulated.

Throughout *The Process of Government* the author is at great pains to warn that he has not made the kind of study he recommends, that he is writing without detailed verification, and that the reader should not use his illustrations as a base on which to erect prematurely a theory to replace the systems of explanation that Bentley criticized. In spite of these warnings, some casual readers have accused Bentley of not providing a complete theory of groups. Others have charged him with developing a naive behavioristic theory of groups balanced more or less decorously in an equilibrium. The first set of critics complains that he did not do what the second set accuses him of doing. All Bentley was, in effect, trying to do was to offer a provisional method for empirical research.

(2) "Unmeasurable elements." Students of the political process are concerned with the manner of political decision making, the patterns of authoritative allocation of values. It has been suggested

that by concentrating, as Bentley recommended, on overt behavior, more particularly, on overt and measurable behavior, the political scientist can overlook the possibility that some group may be able to confine decision making to relatively noncontroversial issues by excluding the more controversial ones from the scope of legitimate political action. Is it possible that by emphasizing the measurement of voter attitudes and behavior, or of legislative attitudes and roll calls, research may neglect more significant conditions of which votes and roll calls are only superficial manifestations? Are such conditions the spook-like elements that Bentley wished to exorcise? These questions strike hard at Bentley's strategy and method, and there is merit in the implied criticisms.

Bentley argued that ideally social inquiry should begin with measurable behavior, although in his later writings he conceded that in *The Process of Government* he had overstressed the "thing-like" aspect of behavior. Insofar as he regarded the relations between observed activities as "spook-like" he may indeed have led the profession into a scientific blind alley, for no science is possible except as it verifies relations between recognizable entities. It must be remembered, however, that his main concern was not theoretical but methodological: his method of starting from manifest activity challenged the Marxist assumption that the superstructure is less stable than the foundation on which it depends. He sought to outlaw such assumed, unverified relations from systematic description. And far from precluding a deeper understanding of human affairs, the study of political behavior was particularly suited to that purpose by its visibility: Bentley believed that social conflict had reached a condition that could easily be observed in political activity and that the study of conflict was a profitable avenue to the understanding of underlying structure.

Bentley believed not that his emphasis on overt activity prevented an understanding of latent conflict but rather that the study of palpable conflict could lead to such an understanding. He exemplified this conviction in his incomplete study of the Chicago streetcar conflict between 1902 and 1907 (1908, pp. 487–492). His concern with conflict extended to the uncovering of patterns of conflict resolution. His classification of activities in terms of groups was designed, in part, to prevent the premature conclusion that the government or agencies of the government are the only means of conflict adjustment. Rather, he felt that the executive, the legislative, the judiciary, the election, the party, and the organized pressure association were

differentially involved. He went on to argue that it is an empirical question how much of the conflict is carried on through discussion, formal organization, or public institutions and how much through unorganized, informal activity. His extensive examination of informal activity suggests his sensitivity to the necessity of using data other than votes, roll calls, and the like.

(3) *Bentley's influence.* "Bentley's maxim seems to have been this: meaning cannot be posited; it must be earned" (Jacobson 1964, p. 22). However, Arnold Brecht's complaint that "concentration on the trans-actional as distinct from inter-actional (causal) aspects of events in social life is as yet a vague program rather than an achievement" has merit (1959, p. 513). Although he influenced such contemporaries as Charles A. Beard, Arthur Holcomb, and Karl Llewellyn, it is only since World War II that Bentley's work has received wider recognition and his influence has been more intensely felt. This can be seen especially in the work in political science of Truman (1951) and Gross (1953) and in many of the research projects carried out by scholars associated with Charles B. Hagan and the University of Illinois political science department. Bentley's vitality is certainly expressed in many of the studies of group pressure.

His incorporation of recent European scholarly inventions should also be emphasized. He undoubtedly was one of the earliest to apply Georg Simmel's work successfully. Three leading ideas from this work that find expression through Bentley deserve summary: (1) that society can be divided into groups that cut across each other in many directions and hence nullify any sweeping classification of society into rigidly fixed and sharply divided "basic" classes or groups; (2) that there is no conflict except when partisans also have common ground to stand on (both culturally and physically); and (3) that in the *Geisteswissenschaften*, what scholars call the foundation, is almost always weaker than the superstructure. Truman uses the first of these ideas to great advantage in the *The Governmental Process* (1951); the second is often ignored; and the third is obviously a criticism of Marxist thought.

Outside political science, Bentley's ideas found resonance in Beard's historical work, in Llewellyn's studies of law ways, in George Lundberg's sociological theories, in John Dewey's logic, and in Ames's and Cantril's work in perception psychology. In each of these, Bentley's ideas assisted a new and fruitful turn of the discipline involved. In each instance he contributed to greater linguistic precision and methodological sophistication. Bentley's influence may continue to prevent scholars from advancing premature theories that foreclose fruitful inquiry and may encourage them, instead, to examine closely a complex world.

RICHARD W. TAYLOR

[*Directly related are the entries* PLURALISM; POLITICAL BEHAVIOR; POLITICAL GROUP ANALYSIS. *Other relevant material may be found in the biographies of* BEARD; DEWEY; GUMPLOWICZ; LLEWELLYN; SIMMEL.]

WORKS BY BENTLEY

1893   *The Condition of the Western Farmer as Illustrated by the Economic History of a Nebraska Township.* Baltimore: Johns Hopkins Press.

1895   The Units of Investigation in the Social Sciences. *American Academy of Political and Social Science, Annals* 5:915–941.

(1908) 1949   *The Process of Government: A Study of Social Pressures.* Introduction by H. T. Davis. Bloomington, Ind.: Principia Press. → The introduction to the 1949 edition provides the best brief summary of Bentley's general position.

1926   *Relativity in Man and Society.* New York: Putnam.

1932   *Linguistic Analysis of Mathematics.* Bloomington, Ind.: Principia Press.

(1932–1951) 1964   DEWEY, JOHN; and BENTLEY, ARTHUR F. *A Philosophical Correspondence: 1932–1951.* Selected and edited by Sidney Ratner and Jules Altman. New Brunswick, N.J.: Rutgers Univ. Press.

1935   *Behavior, Knowledge, Fact.* Bloomington, Ind.: Principia Press.

1949   DEWEY, JOHN; and BENTLEY, ARTHUR F. *Knowing and the Known.* Boston: Beacon. → A paperback edition was published in 1960.

1950   Kennetic Inquiry. *Science* 112:775–783.

1954   *Inquiry Into Inquiries: Essays in Social Theory.* Edited with an introduction by Sidney Ratner. Boston: Beacon. → The introduction provides a useful view of the transactional approach.

1957   The Word "Transaction." *Humanist* 17:17–21.

SUPPLEMENTARY BIBLIOGRAPHY

BRECHT, ARNOLD 1959   *Political Theory: The Foundations of Twentieth-century Political Thought.* Princeton Univ. Press.

DOWLING, R. E. 1960   Pressure Group Theory: Its Methodological Range. *American Political Science Review* 54:944–954. → Group theory is viewed as a translation of Newtonian physics into politics.

GOLEMBIEWSKI, ROBERT T. 1960   The Group Basis of Politics: Notes on Analysis and Development. *American Political Science Review* 54:962–971. → This is the best short summary of Bentley and explains that he did not intend a group theory.

GROSS, BERTRAM M. 1953   *The Legislative Struggle: A Study in Social Combat.* New York: McGraw-Hill.

HALE, MYRON Q. 1960   The Cosmology of Arthur F. Bentley. *American Political Science Review* 54:955–961. → Bentley's cosmology and his functionalism are said to support conservative political practice.

JACOBSON, NORMAN 1964   Causality and Time in Political Process: A Speculation. *American Political Science Review* 58:15–22.

LOVEDAY, PETER; and CAMPBELL, IAN 1962   *Groups in Theory and Practice.* University of Sydney Studies in Politics, No. 1. Melbourne: Cheshire.

MACKENZIE, WILLIAM J. M. 1955   Pressure Groups: The Conceptual Framework. *Political Studies* 3:247–255. → Emphasizes the narrow scope of Bentley's method.

RATNER, SIDNEY 1954   Introduction. In Arthur F. Bentley, *Inquiry Into Inquiries: Essays in Social Theory.* Boston: Beacon.

TAYLOR, RICHARD W. 1952   Arthur F. Bentley's Political Science. *Western Political Quarterly* 5:214–230.

TAYLOR, RICHARD W. (editor) 1957   *Life, Language, Law: Essays in Honor of Arthur F. Bentley.* Yellow Springs, Ohio: Antioch. → Deals directly with Bentley's early critics.

TRUMAN, DAVID B. (1951) 1962   *The Governmental Process: Political Interests and Public Opinion.* New York: Knopf.

BERKELEY, GEORGE

Like many of his contemporaries, George Berkeley (1685–1753) was a man of wide intellectual and practical interests. Although his most significant contributions to human knowledge are to be found in his philosophical works, Berkeley displayed more than a passing interest in questions that were of an essentially economic nature.

Berkeley's writings in the area of political economy are of a rather fragmentary nature. Two of his pamphlets, "An Essay Towards Preventing the Ruine of Great Britain" (1721) and "A Word to the Wise" (1749), contain some discussion of economic issues, but their main theme is moral or theological. His major work in political economy, "The Querist" (1735–1737), consists of 895 rhetorical questions reflecting the author's thoughts on a wide variety of economic and social problems confronting Ireland during the early period of his tenure as bishop of Cloyne (a position he held from 1734 until just prior to his death, in 1753). Berkeley did not write a comprehensive theoretical work in political economy, and as a consequence it is hardly surprising that his writings in this area fall far short of such eighteenth-century treatises as Richard Cantillon's *Essai sur la nature du commerce en général*, Sir James Steuart's *Inquiry Into the Principles of Political Economy*, and Adam Smith's *Wealth of Nations*.

Berkeley displayed a sound grasp of a number of important tools of analysis, but the real significance of his work is to be found in his attempt to bring economic, moral, and theological concepts to bear on the broad problem of man's material progress, that is, the question of economic development. In fact, Berkeley's "Querist" represents one of the earliest attempts to focus attention on this important question, the study of which grew out of seventeenth-century philosophical discussions centering upon the idea of progress and the nature of the evolution of man.

To Berkeley, Ireland represented a picture of abysmal poverty and backwardness. Yet this, he felt, could be attributed not to a paucity of natural resources but rather to a failure to exploit these resources adequately. What was required, he argued, was the provision of a large and growing supply of labor; a satisfactory rate of saving; a higher degree of specialization and division of labor; the provision, especially by the government, of vital investment projects, particularly in the area of transportation; and the establishment of a sociological environment conducive to a greater degree of industry, ingenuity, and frugality on the part of the Irish people.

In his attempt to seek a solution to Ireland's economic problems Berkeley made use of a number of important analytical concepts. Among these concepts were (1) the "relative" doctrine of luxury, which sought to distinguish between, on the one hand, that element of luxury expenditure, in the form of a modest amount of "conveniences and superfluities," which acts as an inducement to both productive effort and ingenuity and, on the other hand, that consumption of luxury goods and services which takes the form of prodigality and dissipation by the wealthier classes and therefore simply serves to check the rate of saving in the community; (2) the dichotomy between productive and unproductive consumption, which Berkeley accepted tentatively; (3) the division of labor and its role in the establishment and growth of an exchange, or market, economy; (4) the metaphor that money is simply a ticket facilitating exchange; and (5) the possibility of deriving economic gains from international specialization, even when the major obstacles to initiating and maintaining economic growth lie in the domestic rather than the international sector of the economy.

In contrast to Hume, Smith, and Francis Hutcheson, Berkeley rejected the doctrine of natural harmony. He was also sharply critical of the Mandevillean theory that private vices are public benefits. Rather, he saw the need for the government to intervene if the bottlenecks inhibiting Irish economic progress were ever to be removed. In order to facilitate the implementation of government policy, particularly in the area of money and credit, Berkeley advocated the establishment of a national bank. It is important to note, however, that the interventionist program outlined in "The Querist" appears to rest essentially on his pragmatic assessment of the problems facing the Irish economy rather than being a derivative of a commitment to any particular philosophical doctrine.

One important theme running through all of Berkeley's economic writings is the significance of sound moral values as a precondition for social and economic progress. Many of the problems facing Ireland, such as idleness and prodigality, might be traced, he felt, to an absence of moral fiber and public spirit. Thus, in Berkeley's view, it was not simply the government but also the church that would have to take the lead in initiating and maintaining the forces of economic growth.

One must be careful not to overemphasize the significance of Berkeley's contributions within the context of eighteenth-century economic thought. Although his work contains a number of analytical insights and a sound understanding of certain aspects of the development problem, his writings, compared to the work of some of the eighteenth-century economic thinkers mentioned above, seem to have had little impact upon later scholars. Nonetheless, in Berkeley we have a great scholar who, had he chosen to devote himself more fully to questions of political economy, would almost certainly have become one of the great figures in eighteenth-century economic thought.

IAN D. S. WARD

[For the historical context of Berkeley's work, see the biographies of HUME; SMITH, ADAM; for discussion of related ideas, see ECONOMIC GROWTH.]

WORKS BY BERKELEY

(1721) 1953 An Essay Towards Preventing the Ruine of Great Britain. Volume 6, pages 61–85 in *The Works of George Berkeley, Bishop of Cloyne.* London: Nelson.

(1735–1737) 1953 The Querist. Volume 6, pages 105–154 in *The Works of George Berkeley, Bishop of Cloyne.* London: Nelson.

(1749) 1953 A Word to the Wise: Or, an Exhortation to the Roman Catholic Clergy of Ireland. Volume 6, pages 231–249 in *The Works of George Berkeley, Bishop of Cloyne.* London: Nelson.

The Works of George Berkeley, Bishop of Cloyne. 9 vols. Edited by A. A. Luce and T. E. Jessop. London: Nelson, 1948–1957.

WORKS ABOUT BERKELEY

HUTCHISON, T. W. 1953 Berkeley's *The Querist* and Its Place in the Economic Thought of the 18th Century. *British Journal for the Philosophy of Science* 4, no. 13:52–77.

WARD, IAN D. S. 1959 George Berkeley: Precursor of Keynes or Moral Economist on Underdevelopment? *Journal of Political Economy* 67:31–40.

BERNARD, L. L.

Luther Lee Bernard (1881–1951), one of the most versatile and erudite American sociologists of the first half of the twentieth century, was born in a rich agricultural area of eastern Kentucky. When Bernard was a small boy, however, he and his family joined a trek to an undeveloped and parched region on the Texas frontier, where they subsequently had to struggle for sheer existence. The rigor of Bernard's childhood was at least in part compensated for by the intellectual stimulation he received from two unusually able high school teachers.

When Bernard was about 17 years old his family moved to Missouri, where he entered Pierce City Baptist College, receiving his B.S. degree in 1900. Eager for better training, he matriculated at the University of Missouri and received an A.B. degree there in 1907. While at Missouri he attracted the attention of Charles A. Ellwood, who enabled him to get a fellowship at the University of Chicago. He received his PH.D. in sociology from that university in 1910, highly esteemed by the Chicago faculty for his scholarship and industry.

The harsh struggles of his childhood and his laborious efforts to get a good education had a marked effect on Bernard's personality. Described by a friend as "the embodiment of the Protestant ethic," he was addicted to hard, unremitting work and was highly individualistic and very direct in his contacts with others, especially in his professional life. It is possible that his frankness, which attested to his integrity and honesty, may have hindered him in conventional academic advancement. As it was, his career embraced an unusually large number of professorships. He taught at Western Reserve University, the University of Florida, the University of Missouri, the University of Minnesota, Cornell, Tulane, the University of North Carolina, Washington University (St. Louis), and Pennsylvania State College. He remained longest at Minnesota, from 1918 to 1926, and at Washington University, from 1929 to 1946. He was one of the best teachers among American sociologists, and the fact that he moved so much among universities increased the number of students he influenced, but it did prevent him from founding a school at a major university. Among his better known students, in addition to his wife, Jessie, were George A. Lundberg, Carl C. Taylor, Carle C. Zimmerman, and Harold A. Phelps. Lundberg and Taylor became presidents of the American Sociological Association.

The work that contributed most to Bernard's professional reputation was his book *Instinct* (1924),

the product of some fifteen years of research and writing. The research chiefly took the form of an extensive survey of the relevant literature of psychology, anthropology, economics, political science, and sociology to determine how the concept of instinct was being used. Bernard developed an elaborate tabulating procedure to organize and analyze the results. The book was important especially because it distinguished habitual from instinctive behavior and so laid at rest the exaggerated and quasi-biological emphasis on instinct as a social force, which had developed great popularity after the publication of William McDougall's *Social Psychology* in 1908. While Bernard's book had much influence on sociological theory at the time, it made somewhat less of an impression on psychology. His writing in psychological sociology carried on and amplified the tradition of E. A. Ross, Ellwood, W. I. Thomas, and Charles Cooley. He summarized his work in the *Introduction to Social Psychology* (1926) and in an unpublished companion volume on the socialization of infant and child.

While Bernard was best known for his writings on psychological sociology, he also worked out a system of sociology based on what he called "coadaptation," a concept that includes man's twofold or two-way adaptation to the natural and cultural environments in which he operates as a socialized being. Bernard's conception of natural environments as an influence on human behavior was a pioneer contribution to the ecological approach in sociology. He divided the environments to which man coadapts in the socializing process into the natural, which comprises both the inorganic (climate, geography, natural resources) and organic (flora, fauna), and the cultural, which includes the material cultural environment, the biocultural or learned behavior patterns and skills, the psychocultural or symbolic environment made up of languages and the cumulative products, and the derived control environment, mainly the institutional organization of society.

To understand and analyze the processes of coadaptation, the sociologist must go beyond the data of conventional sociology and investigate *all* the factors, natural and cultural, that are involved in the coadaptive process. The ultimate purpose of this study is to organize and present the results in such a manner as to make clear their significance for the improvement of social life. Bernard thus repudiated the tendency to bar all value systems and ameliorative aims from sociology. A severe positivist in the tradition of Comte, and dedicated to the scientific method in sociology, he nevertheless held that sociology is important only to the extent that it can contribute to social guidance and the betterment of mankind. His complete system, developed over many years, was embodied in his comprehensive textbook, *An Introduction to Sociology* (1942*a*), which had little influence despite the fact that it is exceptionally erudite and well balanced.

Bernard's distinction in the field of psychological sociology distracted attention not only from his more systematic work in general sociology but also from his contributions to other specialized fields, among them ecology and rural sociology, economics, the use of sociological studies in practical attempts to promote social welfare, and above all the history of sociology and the other social sciences. His most impressive contribution to the history of sociology was his monumental *Origins of American Sociology* (1943), which he wrote with his wife, Jessie Bernard. It covered the development of sociological concepts and writings from the colonial period to the Ward–Sumner–Giddings–Small era and thus was an eye-opener to most American sociologists, who had believed that the subject started in this country with Ward and his successors. Bernard was also the only American sociologist who possessed a precise and comprehensive knowledge of Latin American sociology and its Spanish background.

Bernard was active in professional societies and in organizations for social betterment, and he did much valuable work as an editor. While he was president of the American Sociological Society in 1932 he took the first steps in the launching of the *American Sociological Review*. His integrity and candor may have reduced his popularity, but detracted neither from the importance of his writings nor from the impact of his stimulating teaching.

HARRY ELMER BARNES

[*For the historical context of Bernard's work, see the biographies of* COMTE; COOLEY; ELLWOOD; McDOUGALL; ROSS; THOMAS; *for discussion of the subsequent development of his ideas, see* MOTIVATION, *article on* HUMAN MOTIVATION; SOCIAL PROBLEMS.]

WORKS BY BERNARD

1909 The Teaching of Sociology in the United States. *American Journal of Sociology* 15:164–213.
1911 *The Transition to an Objective Standard of Social Control.* Univ. of Chicago Press.
1914 The Application of Psychology to Social Problems. Pages 207–231 in Geoffrey Rhodes (editor), *The Mind at Work: A Handbook of Applied Psychology.* London: Murby.
1918 The Teaching of Sociology in Southern Colleges and Universities. *American Journal of Sociology* 23:491–515.
1922 The Conditions of Social Progress. *American Journal of Sociology* 28:21–48.
1923a Invention and Social Progress. *American Journal of Sociology* 29:1–33.
1923b Neuro-psychic Technique. *Psychological Review* 30:407–437.
1924 *Instinct: A Study in Social Psychology.* New York: Holt.
1925a A Classification of Environments. *American Journal of Sociology* 31:318–322.
1925b Scientific Method and Social Progress. *American Journal of Sociology* 31:1–18.
1926 *Introduction to Social Psychology.* New York: Holt.
1927a The Psychological Foundations of Society. Pages 395–491 in Jerome Davis and Harry E. Barnes (editors), *An Introduction to Sociology: A Behavioristic Study of American Society.* Boston: Heath.
1927b Sociology and Psychology. Pages 346–368 in William F. Ogburn and Alexander Goldenweiser (editors), *The Social Sciences and Their Interrelationships.* Boston: Houghton Mifflin.
1927c Foundations of Society. Pages 517–603 in Jerome Davis and Harry E. Barnes (editors), *Readings in Sociology to Accompany* An Introduction to Sociology. New York: Farrar & Rinehart.
1928 Some Historical and Recent Trends of Sociology in the United States. *Southwestern Political and Social Science Quarterly* 9:264–293.
1929 Mind: Its Emergence as a Mechanism of Adjustment. Pages 402–460 in Frederick A. Cleveland (editor), *Modern Scientific Knowledge of Nature, Man and Society.* New York: Ronald.
1931a An Interpretation of Sociological Research. *American Journal of Sociology* 37:203–212.
1931b Attitudes and the Redirection of Behavior. Pages 46–74 in Kimball Young (editor), *Social Attitudes.* New York: Holt.
1932 Social Psychology Studies Adjustment Behavior. *American Journal of Sociology* 38:1–9.
1934 BERNARD, LUTHER L. (editor). *The Fields and Methods of Sociology.* New York: Long & Smith.
1934 BERNARD, LUTHER L.; and BERNARD, JESSIE *Sociology and the Study of International Relations.* St. Louis: Washington Univ. Press.
1938 The Unilateral Elements in Magic Theory and Performance. *American Sociological Review* 3:771–785.
1939 *Social Control.* New York: Macmillan.
1940 The Method of Generalization for Social Control. *American Sociological Review* 5:340–350.
1942a *An Introduction to Sociology: A Naturalistic Account of Man's Adjustment to His World.* New York: Crowell.
1942b Recent Discussions Regarding Social Psychology. *American Journal of Sociology* 48:13–28.
1943 BERNARD, LUTHER L.; and BERNARD, JESSIE *Origins of American Sociology: The Social Science Movement in the United States.* New York: Crowell.
1944 *War and Its Causes.* New York: Holt.
1948 *Principales formas de integración social.* Mexico City: Universidad Nacional Autónoma de México.

BERNOULLI FAMILY

The Bernoullis, a Swiss family, acquired its fame in the history of science by producing eight or nine mathematicians of the first rank within three generations. They were all descendants of Niklaus Bernoulli, a prominent merchant in the city of Basel. Each of these mathematicians was compelled by his parents to study for one of the established professions before being permitted to embark upon his real interest, mathematics. Within the group there were four in particular who contributed to the theory of probability and mathematical statistics: Jakob (Jacques) ɪ, Johann (Jean) ɪ, Niklaus (Nicolas) ɪ, and Daniel ɪ.

Jakob ɪ and Johann ɪ

The first in the line of the Bernoulli mathematicians, Jakob ɪ (1654–1705), was the son of the merchant Niklaus. He completed theological studies and then spent six years traveling in England, France, and Holland. Returning to Basel, he lectured on physics at the university until he was appointed professor of mathematics in 1687. His younger brother, Johann ɪ (1667–1748), studied for a medical degree, at the same time receiving instruction in mathematics from Jakob. Later Johann, too, became a professor of mathematics, teaching at the University of Groningen in Holland until he returned to Basel as Jakob's successor.

The brothers were inspired by the works of Leibniz on the infinitesimal calculus, and they became his chief protagonists on the Continent. The new methods enabled them to solve an abundance of mathematical problems, many with applications to mechanics and physics. They applied differentiation and integration to find the properties of many important curves: they determined the form of the catenary curve (hanging chain) and the isochrone, or tautochrone (cycloid), and the form of a sail subject to wind pressure. Jakob was particularly fascinated by the logarithmic spiral, which he requested be engraved on his tombstone. Both used infinite series as a tool; the Bernoulli numbers were introduced by Jakob.

Johann was perhaps even more productive as a scientist than was Jakob. He studied the theory of differential equations, discovered fundamental principles of mechanics, and wrote on the laws of optics. Although the first textbook on the calculus, *Analyse des infiniment petits* (1696), was written by Antoine de L'Hospital, it was largely based upon the author's correspondence with Johann.

The personal relations between the brothers were marred by violent public strife, mainly disputes about priority in the discovery of scientific results. Particularly bitter was their controversy over the brachystochrone, the curve of most rapid descent of a particle sliding from one point to another under the influence of gravity. The problem was of great theoretical interest, since it raised for the first time a question whose solution required the use of the principles of the calculus of variation (the solution is a cycloid).

During his stay in Holland, Jakob became interested in the theory of probability. In his lifetime he published very little on the subject—only a few scattered notes in the *Acta eruditorum*. His main work on probability, the *Ars conjectandi* ("The Art of Conjecturing"), was printed posthumously in Basel in 1713. It is divided into four books. The first is an extensive commentary upon Huygens' pioneer treatise: "De ratiociniis in ludo aleae" (1657; "On Calculations in Games of Chance"). The second gives a systematic presentation of the theory of permutations and combinations, and in the third this is applied to a series of contemporary games, some quite involved. For each, Jakob computed the mathematical expectations of the participants.

The fourth book shows the greatest depth. Here Jakob tried to analyze the events to which probability theory is applicable; in other words, he dealt with the basic question of mathematical statistics: when is it possible to determine an unknown probability from experience? He emphasized that a great number of observations are necessary. Furthermore, he pointed out "something which perhaps no one has thought of before," namely, that (in modern terminology) it is necessary to prove mathematically that as the number of observations increases, the relative number of successes must be within an arbitrarily small (but fixed) interval around the theoretical probability with a probability that tends to 1. This he did, with complete rigor and without the use of calculus, by examining the binomial probabilities and estimating their sums. Illustrations with numerical computations for small intervals are given. The author concluded with some philosophical observations which show the importance he attached to his theorem.

To the *Ars conjectandi* Jakob added a supplement on the *jeu de paume* (similar to the game of tennis), in the form of a letter to a friend. Here he computed the chances of winning for a player at any stage of the game, given players with equal skill and players with differing skill, and in the latter cases he determined how great an advantage the more skilled one can allow the other.

Niklaus ɪ

Niklaus ɪ (1687–1759) was a nephew of Jakob ɪ and Johann ɪ; his father was a portrait painter. True to the family tradition, Niklaus studied for one of the older professions, jurisprudence, while on the side he attended the lectures in mathematics of his two uncles. His law thesis straddled both fields: ". . . de usu artis conjectandi in jure" (1709). He accepted a professorship in mathematics at Padua in 1716 but disliked the university there and returned to Basel in 1719. In 1722 he was appointed professor of logic; in 1731 he changed to a chair of jurisprudence.

When Jakob I died, his *Ars conjectandi* was not in finished form and the publisher asked Johann I to serve as editor. When Johann refused, Niklaus was suggested. He refused also, doubting his competence, but he was finally prevailed upon to accept the undertaking. Niklaus published little in the field of mathematics, probably because of his excessive modesty. But, as editor of the *Ars conjectandi*, he entered into extensive correspondence with the two other pioneers in probability, Rémond de Montmort and Abraham de Moivre. Both appealed for his support in the priority feud that arose between them.

Niklaus also corresponded with the Dutch physicist van s'Gravesande on a curious statistical phenomenon that had first been pointed out by Arbuthnot. It was generally accepted that births of boys as compared to girls correspond to a game of chance, with the same probability, $p = \frac{1}{2}$, for each. Nevertheless, the birth records in London showed that for 82 successive years there had been more males born than females, a most unlikely occurrence under the assumption of equal probabilities. Van s'Gravesande and Arbuthnot were inclined to see this as an example of divine intervention in the laws of nature, while Niklaus took the view that it was more rational to assume that the probability for the birth of a male child is slightly greater than one-half.

Daniel I

Johann I had three sons who were mathematicians: Niklaus II (1695–1726), Daniel I (1700–1782), and Johann II (1710–1790). He compelled each one to acquire a professional degree. Niklaus II studied law and began his career in Berne, as a professor in this subject, in 1723. In 1725 he was appointed to a professorship of mathematics at the Imperial Academy in St. Petersburg, but he died shortly after his arrival there. Johann II also studied jurisprudence; eventually he became his father's successor as professor of mathematics in Basel. He continued the Bernoulli dynasty, having three sons who were mathematicians: Johann III, Daniel II, and Jakob II.

Daniel I studied medicine, but his first mathematical book had already appeared when he was 24 years old and the next year he was called to a mathematical professorship at the Imperial Academy in St. Petersburg, remaining there from 1725 to 1733. Upon his return to Basel he became professor of medicine and botany; in 1750 he was appointed to a professorship in physics, which suited him better.

Daniel I was a prolific writer, even by the standards of the Bernoulli family; no less than ten times were his works awarded prizes by the French Academy of Sciences. His main interests centered in theoretical physics, the foundation of mechanics and, later, probability. Some of his best-known papers deal with celestial mechanics, the tides, and the laws governing a vibrating string.

Most important among the papers on probability by Daniel I is the study *Specimen theoriae novae de mensura sortis* (1738). The basis for this work is the well-known Petersburg paradox, which at that time was a much discussed topic in connection with the concept of expected value. The paradox was first mentioned by Niklaus I in his correspondence with Montmort and is reproduced in the 1713 edition of Montmort's book *Essay d'analyse sur les jeux de hazard*. The fact that the expectation is infinite led Daniel to introduce a moral expectation or marginal utility, now fundamental in economic investigations. He assumed that for a person with a fortune of size x, the utility of an increase Δx is proportional to Δx and inversely proportional to x, giving an expression

$$u = a \log x + b$$

for the utility. In the same paper Daniel also pointed out that a similar idea had already been proposed by the Swiss mathematician G. Cramer in a letter of 1728 to Niklaus I. Daniel also wrote a few other papers on probability, but they are of lesser importance; a number of them are concerned with questions arising from mortality statistics.

OYSTEIN ORE

[*For the historical context of the Bernoullis' work, see* STATISTICS, *article on* THE HISTORY OF STATISTICAL METHOD; *and the biography of* MOIVRE; *for discussion of the subsequent development of their ideas, see* PROBABILITY.]

WORKS BY DANIEL I

1724   *Exercitationes quaedam mathematicae.* Venice (Italy): Apud Dominicum Lovisam.

(1738) 1954   Exposition of a New Theory on the Measurement of Risk. *Econometrica* 22:23–36. → First published as "Specimen theoriae novae de mensura sortis."

WORKS BY JAKOB I

(1713) 1899   *Wahrscheinlichkeitsrechnung (Ars conjectandi).* 2 vols. Leipzig: Engelmann. → First published posthumously in Latin.

1744   *Jacobi Bernoulli . . . Opera.* 2 vols. Geneva: Cramer & Fratrum Philibert. → Published posthumously.

WORKS BY JOHANN I

1742 *Johannis Bernoulli . . . Opera omnia.* 4 vols. Geneva: Bousquet.
Der Briefwechsel von Johann Bernoulli. Volume 1. Basel: Birkhauser, 1955.

WORKS BY NIKLAUS I

1709 *Dissertatio inauguralis mathematico-juridica de usu artis conjectandi in jure.* Basel: Mechel.

SUPPLEMENTARY BIBLIOGRAPHY

HUYGENS, CHRISTIAAN 1657 De ratiociniis in ludo aleae. Pages 521–534 in Frans van Schooten, *Exercitationum mathematicarum libri quinque.* Leiden (Netherlands): Elsevier.
L'HOSPITAL, GUILLAUME FRANÇOIS ANTOINE DE 1696 *Analyse des infiniment petits, pour l'intelligence des lignes courbes.* Paris: Imprimerie Royale.
[MONTMORT, PIERRE RÉMOND DE] (1708) 1713 *Essay d'analyse sur les jeux de hazard.* 2d ed. Paris: Quillau. → Published anonymously.

BERNSTEIN, EDUARD

Eduard Bernstein (1850–1932), one of the leaders of German revisionist socialism, came of a lower middle-class family in Berlin. He attended the Gymnasium until the age of 16, when he became first an apprentice and then an employee in a bank. In 1872 he joined the German Social Democratic party (SPD) and was soon active in the Berlin organization of the party.

Like so many socialists of this period, Bernstein was forced to move from country to country. Just before the adoption of the antisocialist laws in Germany in 1878, he seized an opportunity to go to Switzerland, and when the Swiss government, under pressure from Bismarck, interfered with a socialist publication he was connected with, Bernstein left Switzerland for England. His enforced residence in London led him to study the political climate of Britain and the British labor movement, and he came into contact with the Fabian Society, which had been founded in 1883. Although the antisocialist laws in Germany were repealed in 1890, Bernstein was not granted permission to return until 1901.

The 1890's were a period of considerable prosperity in Germany, during which the economy grew steadily, undisturbed by any major crisis. The prediction contained in the Erfurt program of the SPD, adopted in 1890, that the army of superfluous workers would become ever larger and that the crises intrinsic to the very nature of the capitalist mode of production would become ever more extensive and more devastating, was sharply contradicted by the economic realities of those years,

when workingmen, too, shared in the general prosperity. Influenced as he was by British realism, Bernstein found this discrepancy between theory and actuality more disturbing than did other Marxists. In several articles that appeared in Kautsky's *Neue Zeit* in 1898 (see Bernstein [1896–1898] 1904, pp. 167–286) he made a break with orthodox Marxism, and in a book published three years later (1899) he focused his criticism on the prognosis of the increasing impoverishment of the proletariat and on the notion that, inevitably, capitalist crises would become increasingly acute and result in the early collapse of the capitalist system. With the aid of carefully collected statistics, Bernstein demonstrated that the capitalist system had, on the contrary, developed several stabilizing factors that made its early collapse extremely unlikely. He pointed out a trend that was the exact opposite of impoverishment, i.e., increased production, accompanied by an increase in mass consumption as well as by an increase in the workers' real income. The alleged exacerbation of crises could be similarly refuted.

While a necessary component of the Marxist theory of the evolution of capitalist society was its polarization into two sharply conflicting classes—with increasing numbers of increasingly poor proletarians on one side and increasingly few increasingly rich capitalists on the other—Bernstein insisted that in fact society was becoming more and more differentiated. He sought to show, with the aid of comprehensive statistical data, that the trend toward big business was being resisted by the middle class. Furthermore, the process of concentration was most obviously not taking place in the service occupations (Bernstein early recognized the importance of repair and auxiliary services), in trade, and in agriculture. He was aware of the rise of a new middle class of white collar workers and civil servants, and he pointed out the importance of gaining this new class as an ally of the workers. He believed he could demonstrate a process of differentiation, rather than of polarization or concentration, not only in the class system but also in the distribution of income.

Bernstein's attack on the theory of historical materialism went much farther than the questioning of specific Marxist predictions. He denied the validity of the concept of the unilateral economic determination of the historical process, and he acknowledged the importance of noneconomic factors, even placing them on a par with the productive forces and the relations of production. With this view Bernstein built a bridge to so-called bourgeois sociology. His view is essentially the same as that expressed in the well-known sentences at the end of Max Weber's first essay on Protestantism.

In view of the tremendous confusion of interdependent influences between the material basis, the forms of social and political organization, and the ideas current in the time of the Reformation, we can only proceed by investigating whether and at what points certain correlations between forms of religious belief and practical ethics can be worked out. At the same time we shall as far as possible clarify the manner and the general *direction* in which, by virtue of those relationships, the religious movements have influenced the development of material culture. Only when this has been determined with reasonable accuracy can the attempt be made to estimate to what extent the historical development of modern culture can be attributed to those religious forces and to what extent to others. (Weber [1904–1905] 1930, pp. 91–92)

The acceptance by sociology of some of the insights of historical materialism owes much to Bernstein.

His break with Marxism became final in a lecture "Wie ist wissenschaftlicher Socialismus möglich?" ("Is Scientific Socialism Possible?"), which he delivered in Berlin shortly after his return from England in 1901. Throwing economic determinism overboard, Bernstein deliberately chose Kant's basic ethical formulation and shifted the justification for socialist struggle from the sphere of what is to that of what ought to be. For him, socialism was henceforth a postulate and a program rather than a scientific analysis of the laws of change.

Bernstein's views, which were soon labeled "revisionism," did not convince the German Social Democratic party. While the SPD often pursued a revisionist policy in practice, its official condemnation of revisionist theory at its Dresden congress in 1903 prevented it from achieving a satisfactory reconciliation of practice with theory. The discrepancy persisted even in the Weimar period, to the detriment of the effectiveness of the party.

When Bernstein died in 1932, he had long ceased to act as theoretician for the SPD. Only after their defeat by Hitler did the Social Democrats finally abandon the Marxist dogmas hallowed by tradition. Many of Bernstein's insights were incorporated in the official theory of the West German Social Democratic party, as witness the action programs of Dortmund in 1952 and Berlin in 1954, and especially the 1959 Bad Godesberg program of principles.

CHRISTIAN GNEUSS

[For the historical context of Bernstein's work, see ECONOMIC THOUGHT, *article on* SOCIALIST THOUGHT; *and the biographies of* KAUTSKY; LENIN; LUXEMBURG; MARX.]

WORKS BY BERNSTEIN

(1896–1898) 1904 *Probleme des Socialismus.* 4th ed. Berlin: Dümmler. → Part 2 of Eduard Bernstein, *Zur Geschichte und Theorie des Socialismus.*
(1899) 1909 *Evolutionary Socialism: A Criticism and Affirmation.* London: Independent Labour Party. → First published as *Die Voraussetzungen des Socialismus und die Aufgaben der Socialdemokratie.* A paperback edition was published in 1963 by Schocken Books.
1901 *Wie ist wissenschaftlicher Socialismus möglich?* Berlin: Socialistische Monatshefte.

SUPPLEMENTARY BIBLIOGRAPHY

GAY, PETER 1952 *The Dilemma of Democratic Socialism: Eduard Bernstein's Challenge to Marx.* New York: Columbia Univ. Press. → A paperback edition was published in 1962 by Collier.
GNEUSS, CHRISTIAN 1957 Um den Einklang von Theorie und Praxis: Eduard Bernstein und der Revisionismus. Volume 2, pages 198–226 in *Marxismusstudien.* Tübingen (Germany): Mohr.
GNEUSS, CHRISTIAN 1962 The Precursor: Eduard Bernstein. Pages 31–41 in Leopold Labedz (editor), *Revisionism: Essays on the History of Marxist Ideas.* New York: Praeger.
WEBER, MAX (1904–1905) 1930 *The Protestant Ethic and the Spirit of Capitalism.* Translated by Talcott Parsons, with a foreword by R. H. Tawney. London: Allen & Unwin; New York: Scribner. → First published in German. The 1930 edition has been reprinted frequently. See especially pages 35–92.

BERTILLON, JACQUES

Jacques Bertillon (1851–1922) was one of the most prolific and influential quantitative social scientists in France near the turn of the century. His work grew out of a tradition pioneered by Adolphe Quetelet and developed by Bertillon's grandfather, Achille Guillard, and father, Louis-Adolphe Bertillon. Two biographies of his brother, Alphonse—popularly known for developing ingenious methods of identifying criminals—show that the entire Bertillon household was preoccupied with quantification (S. Bertillon 1941; Rhodes 1956). Like his father, Jacques Bertillon received his formal training in medicine, but he soon turned to the young science of statistics, at that time broadly defined by its proponents as the "numerical study of social facts" (1895, p. 1).

In the 1870s, Bertillon began to publish articles on such topics as international comparisons of suicide and divorce rates in the *Annales de démographie internationale*; he became the editor of this journal in 1882.

Bertillon's lifelong association with organizations connected with social research began in 1883, when he succeeded his father as director of the statistical bureau of the city of Paris. During his thirty years as director, Bertillon's influence was reflected in the increasingly lengthy annual reports —the increase being due both to a greater quantity of data collected and to the application of more elaborate types of analysis. Drawing principally on data collected by his bureau, Bertillon published numerous articles on those aspects of the Parisian population for which quantitative information was available: the incidence of births, deaths, diseases, marriages, divorces, and so on, generally analyzed by sex, age, geographical district, and occupation.

Bertillon served as representative of the Paris statistical bureau on the Conseil Supérieur de la Statistique, an organization advising the government on statistical matters. One of the most active members on the council, he suggested new types of data to collect, innovations in data analysis, and broader applications of statistical knowledge in general. Through the council he attempted to persuade the various ministries to require statistical training of some of their employees; to facilitate this task, he prepared a treatise, the *Cours élémentaire de statistique administrative* (1895), on the organization of statistical bureaus, questionnaire construction, interviewing procedures, data-processing techniques, and types of statistical analysis.

Further recognition in statistical circles came in 1897, when Bertillon was elected president of the Société de Statistique de Paris, having been a member since 1879. The society's journal contains articles by Bertillon on topics such as the social origins and mortality rates of different occupational groups.

In addition to his activity in France, Bertillon played a leading role in the congresses of the International Statistical Institute, which he helped organize in 1885. He thereby revived the international statistical congresses initiated by Quetelet, which had been discontinued after 1876. Bertillon published constantly in the institute's bulletin, particularly on the standardization of the types of data collected and the different classifications employed by the various national statistical bureaus. Perhaps his best-known contribution in this area is his standardized classification of the causes of death— consisting of an abridged, an intermediate length, and a more detailed account of the factors leading to death—which combined the most widely used factors employed by national statistical bureaus. The "Bertillon classification," adopted by a large number of countries in 1900, was revised in 1909 and again in 1920.

In addition to his purely statistical work, Bertillon had ties with a broad variety of social scientists: at the Collège Libre des Sciences Sociales, which he helped found in 1895 and where he taught demography; at the École d'Anthropologie, where he was also professor of demography; and as a collaborator on the *Revue internationale de sociologie*, edited by René Worms. He did not, however, collaborate with Durkheim and his associates on the *Année sociologique*.

Bertillon was a deeply patriotic Frenchman with strong social convictions. Through his statistical work, he became aware of the extent of two phenomena which he came to consider as the most serious social problems that France had to face: alcoholism and "depopulation." Attempting to develop a more thorough understanding of each of these phenomena, he undertook careful analyses of the statistics available on them. In addition to his more scholarly works (1904; 1911), he also published numbers of articles in the popular journals and newspapers, expounding the dangers of these problems for the entire French nation.

Concerning alcoholism, Bertillon demonstrated that the per capita consumption of alcohol had increased rapidly over the course of the nineteenth century in France, while Sweden and Norway, of all the European countries, showed the largest decreases during the same period. Attempting to explain these differences, he examined with a broad variety of quantitative materials the relative importance of 15 different measures suggested or employed to reduce alcoholic consumption. He found that the size of the tax on alcohol had no effect on consumption; the elimination of small distilleries did reduce consumption; and a monopoly on the distribution and sale of beverages was highly effective, with the Norwegian monopoly system the most successful of all.

"Depopulation"—the decrease in the size of the French population relative to that of other more rapidly expanding European powers, particularly Germany—was sapping French economic and military strength, Bertillon argued. He presented five principal interrelated causes of the declining birth rate: poorly conceived inheritance laws, exaggerated frugality, a weakened entrepreneurial spirit, the burdens imposed by large families, and the strong desire for upward social mobility (1911, pp. 62–209).

Bertillon's efforts at publicizing the dangers of depopulation were unceasing—he founded the Alliance Nationale pour l'Accroissement de la Population Française in 1896 and a popular magazine, *La femme et l'enfant*, in 1918; he was also an active member of the Conseil Supérieur de la Natalité following its establishment in 1920. Although his efforts, along with those of a small number of other persons, helped to attract public attention to the problem, it was not until many years later that the government undertook any systematic action to increase the birth rate.

Bertillon's general impact was probably most significant in areas where he reanalyzed and synthesized large-scale statistical data to bring them to bear on a broad variety of social questions. His ability to demonstrate the utility of quantitative materials for general social analysis helped lead to their increasing acceptance by social scientists. Bertillon's work was one of the most important foundations for Durkheim's analyses of suicide and divorce. J. Bourdon (1922) was more or less a disciple of Bertillon, and W. F. Willcox (1891) at Columbia was, thanks to Bertillon, an enthusiastic convert to quantification. Virtually every writer on depopulation in France since Bertillon has had somehow to come to grips with his work on this subject.

TERRY N. CLARK

[For the historical context of Bertillon's work, see Sociology; Vital statistics; and the biography of Quetelet; for discussion of the subsequent development of Bertillon's ideas, see the biographies of Durkheim; Willcox.]

WORKS BY BERTILLON

1880 La statistique humaine de la France: Naissance, mariage, mort. Paris: Baillière.

1883 Étude démographique du divorce et de la séparation de corps dans les différents pays de l'Europe. Paris: Masson.

1892 Compte rendu sommaire des travaux scientifiques du Dr. Jacques Bertillon. Paris: Imprimerie de Chaix. → An annotated bibliography, compiled by Bertillon, of his works prior to 1892.

1895 Cours élémentaire de statistique administrative. Paris: Société d'Éditions Scientifiques.

1897 Le problème de la dépopulation. Paris: Colin.

(1904) 1913 L'alcoolisme et les moyens de le combattre jugés par l'expérience. 3d ed. Paris: Gabalda.

1906 De la fréquence des principales causes de décès à Paris pendant la seconde moitié du XIXᵉ siècle et notamment pendant la période 1886–1905. Paris: Imprimerie Municipale.

1911 La dépopulation de la France. Paris: Alcan.

SUPPLEMENTARY BIBLIOGRAPHY

BARRIOL, A. 1922 Jacques Bertillon. Journal de la Société de Statistique de Paris 63:267–269.

BERTILLON, SUZANNE 1941 Vie d'Alphonse Bertillon. Paris: Gallimard.

BOURDON, JEAN 1922 L'oeuvre démographique de Jacques Bertillon. Revue d'économie politique 36:638–642.

CLARK, TERRY N. 1964 Empirical Social Research by Contributors to the Année sociologique and the Revue internationale de sociologie. Unpublished manuscript, Columbia Univ., Bureau of Applied Social Research. → Contains a discussion of Bertillon's contributions to the development of empirical social research.

DURKHEIM, ÉMILE 1906 Le divorce par consentement mutuel. Revue bleue 5th Series 5:549–554. → A criti-

cism and reinterpretation of the "Bertillon law" concerning suicide and divorce rates.

MARCH, LUCIEN 1923 Dr. Bertillon, Jacques. Institut International de Statistique, Bulletin 21:300–302.

MORICOURT, C. 1962 Bibliographie analytique des oeuvres de la famille Bertillon (y compris Guillard), médecins et démographes, de Jean-Claude-Achille Guillard (1799–1876), à Georges Bertillon (1859–1917). Unpublished manuscript, Institut National des Techniques de la Documentation, Conservatoire National des Arts et Métiers. → Includes publications by Bertillon up to the time of his death.

RHODES, HENRY T. F. 1956 Alphonse Bertillon: Father of Scientific Detection. New York: Abelard-Schuman.

WILLCOX, WALTER F. 1891 The Divorce Problem: A Study in Statistics. Columbia Studies in History, Economics and Public Law 1:1–74. → The preface contains a testimonial to the influence of Bertillon.

BETROTHAL
See Marriage; Nuptiality.

BETTING
See Gambling.

BEVERIDGE, WILLIAM HENRY

William Henry Beveridge, Baron Beveridge (1879–1963), creator of Britain's post–World War II social security system, was born in Bengal. He was the son of Henry Beveridge of the Indian Civil Service, from whom, presumably, he learned to be a good administrator; one of the most human of Beveridge's books is the biography of his parents, published in 1947 under the title India Called Them. He came to England at an early age and was educated at the Charterhouse School and at Balliol College, Oxford. At Oxford his early studies in mathematics and classics were equally distinguished, and in 1902 he secured a first-class degree in the latter. He was elected to the Stowell civil law fellowship at University College, Oxford, which he held from 1902 to 1909, taking a Bachelor of Civil Law degree in 1904. From 1903 to 1905 he was also subwarden of Toynbee Hall in Whitechapel, an industrial section of London, where he acquired his first insight into the problems of modern society.

At this time he also met Sidney and Beatrice Webb. Although at first they did not get on very well, later, when the Royal Commission on the Poor Laws was appointed in 1905, Mrs. Webb enrolled Beveridge in the ranks of the assistant inquirers who helped her to produce, in 1909, the famous Minority Report, with its detailed scheme for what subsequently came to be called social security. Just prior to the issue of the Report, Beveridge published his first major work, Unemployment: *A Problem of Industry* (1909), which established him as an economist of parts. The Webbs having introduced him to Winston Churchill, then president of the Board of Trade, Beveridge entered this department in 1908, and the following year he was made director of the newly formed system of labor exchanges.

For the next ten years Beveridge was a civil servant; he went to the new Ministry of Munitions in 1915 and to the Ministry of Food the following year, becoming permanent secretary in 1919. In both these posts he was assisted by his cousin Janet (Jessy) Mair as personal secretary; she continued to serve him in that capacity long after he left the civil service, and in 1942, after the death of her first husband, they were married.

When World War I ended and the wartime ministries were dissolved, the Webbs, seeking a vigorous director to succeed William Pember Reeves at the London School of Economics, invited Beveridge to take on the job. He accepted, and during the 18 years of his administration, from 1919 to 1937, he succeeded in greatly expanding the scope of work and increasing the physical facilities at the school. He was not, however, always so successful in his personal relations. The student body, which had a distinctly radical tendency, sometimes resented his disciplinary methods, and he had several brushes with one of the most distinguished members of his staff, Harold Laski. In 1937 he left the school in order to become master of University College, Oxford.

Until World War II Beveridge was known mainly as a competent economist and statistician; the first volume of a large study called *Prices and Wages in England*, edited by him, appeared in 1939. With World War II his opportunity came. In 1941 he was appointed chairman of the Inter-departmental Committee on Social Insurance and Allied Services. This was in fact a one-man operation; the civil servants on the committee were no more than investigators who took instructions from the chairman. The following year brought the result of the committee's work, the Beveridge Report, which was an instant popular success and carried the name of Beveridge to millions, in and out of the armed services. The refusal of the government to declare unequivocally in its favor produced the only sizable antigovernment vote between 1940 and 1945. The report contributed in no small degree to the Labour party's victory in 1945, after which it was implemented by the Labour government's social legislation.

The Beveridge Report sought, as had Beatrice Webb 33 years earlier, to protect the individual against the poverty and destitution caused by the principal hazards of modern life. Its main differences from the earlier scheme were that it accepted the contributory principle, which had become part of the state insurance system, and that it did not deal with the prevention of unemployment. (Beveridge tackled the problem of unemployment in a subsequent book, *Full Employment in a Free Society,* 1944.) The report was an extremely competent piece of work, but its success was due as much to its timeliness as to its competence. The two other reports in which Beveridge had a part, one on fuel rationing (1942*a*) and one on the future of broadcasting, were not so impressive, and they were not put into effect.

In 1944 a by-election at Berwick-on-Tweed returned Beveridge triumphantly to Parliament as a Liberal, but when he stood as an independent in the following year he was heavily defeated. The local electorate preferred to vote for the candidate of the Labour party, which was pledged to introduce social security. Greatly disappointed, he accepted a peerage; he had resigned the mastership of his college on his election to Parliament. Later he took on the chairmanship of Aycliffe and Peterlee, two of the "new towns" set up under Labour government legislation; these were in the northeast, where he actually lived for a while. Beveridge wrote many articles in various journals, took a vigorous part in debate in the House of Lords, and in 1953 published a volume of autobiography, *Power and Influence.*

MARGARET COLE

[*See also* WELFARE STATE.]

WORKS BY BEVERIDGE

(1909) 1930 *Unemployment: A Problem of Industry (1909 and 1930).* New ed. London and New York: Longmans.

1939 *Prices and Wages in England From the Twelfth to the Nineteenth Century.* New York and London: Longmans. → Beveridge was the senior author.

1942*a* *Fuel Rationing: Report by Sir William Beveridge, K.C.B., to the President of the Board of Trade.* Papers by Command, Cmd. 6352. London: H.M. Stationery Office.

1942*b* GREAT BRITAIN, INTER-DEPARTMENTAL COMMITTEE ON SOCIAL INSURANCE AND ALLIED SERVICES *Social Insurance and Allied Services.* Report by Sir William Beveridge. London: H.M. Stationery Office; New York: Macmillan. → Known as the Beveridge Report.

(1944) 1945 *Full Employment in a Free Society.* New York: Norton.

1947 *India Called Them.* London: Allen & Unwin.

1948 *Voluntary Action: A Report on Methods of Social Advance.* London: Allen; New York: Macmillan.

(1953) 1955 *Power and Influence.* New York: Beechhurst.

BIAS

See ANTI-SEMITISM; PREJUDICE; STEREOTYPES. *For discussion of bias as a problem in research, see* ERRORS, *article on* NONSAMPLING ERRORS; FALLACIES, STATISTICAL; INTERVIEWING; RESPONSE SETS.

BIBLIOGRAPHY

See INFORMATION STORAGE AND RETRIEVAL.

BIENAYMÉ, JULES

Jules Bienaymé, statistician and mathematician, was born in Paris in 1796 and died there in 1878. He received his secondary education in Bruges and later at the Lycée Louis le Grand in Paris. His studies at the École Polytechnique, where he enrolled in 1815, ended the following year, because that institution was dissolved when its students persisted in their loyalty to the Napoleonic regime. In 1818 Bienaymé became lecturer in mathematics at Saint-Cyr, the French equivalent of West Point. In the end, he joined the civil service as a general inspector of finance.

After Bienaymé became a civil servant, he began his studies of actuarial science, statistics, and probability. Baron Louis, France's able minister of finance during the Bourbon restoration, was inclined to make use of technical advice, and Bienaymé became closely associated with Louis's work. Bienaymé's career in the civil service was not interrupted by the revolution of 1830, but after the revolution of 1848 he retired and devoted all his time to scientific work.

Bienaymé's retirement made possible his active participation in the affairs of various scientific societies. He became a member of the Société Philomatique (an association for the advancement of science) and, on July 5, 1852, he was elected a member of the Institut de France (Académie des Sciences). At the time of his death, he was a corresponding member of the Science Academy of St. Petersburg and of the Central Commission of Statistics of Belgium, and an honorary member of the Chemical Conference Association of Naples. As a member of the Académie des Sciences he acted for 23 years as a referee for the Montyon Prize, the highest French award for achievement in statistics, and his interesting judgments of the candidates for this distinction can be found in the records of the academy.

Bienaymé published many papers in the proceedings of the academy. Among these is an important one on runs, giving a theorem for the probable number of maxima and minima of a sequence of observed numbers. In 1853 Bienaymé discovered a very important inequality: the probability that the inequality $|X| \geq t\sigma$ is true is less than or equal to $1/t^2$, X being a random variable with mean zero and standard deviation σ (1853a). The Russian mathematician Chebyshev independently published the same discovery some twelve years later.

Scientific controversies had considerable appeal for Bienaymé. He debated with Cauchy about the relative merits of the least squares method and of an interpolation procedure proposed by the latter (1853b). He also criticized the extension by Poisson of a theorem of Jacques Bernoulli, the so-called law of large numbers (1855). In addition to the criticism of Poisson, this paper contains a keen analysis of meteorological data, especially those having to do with rainfall.

In spite of his retirement, Bienaymé had considerable influence, as a statistical expert, in the government of Napoleon III. In 1864 Napoleon's minister, Dumas, praised Bienaymé in the French Senate for the help he had given to the administration in connection with the actuarial work required for the creation of a retirement fund.

DANIEL DUGUÉ

[*For the historical context of Bienaymé's work, see the biographies of the* BERNOULLI FAMILY; POISSON. *For discussion of the subsequent development of his ideas, see* NONPARAMETRIC STATISTICS, *article on* RUNS; PROBABILITY.]

WORKS BY BIENAYMÉ

1837   De la durée de la vie en France depuis le commencement du XIXe siècle. *Annales d'hygiène publique et de médicine légale* 18:177–218.

1838a   Mémoire sur la probabilité des resultats moyens des observations: Démonstration directe de la règle de Laplace. Académie des Sciences, Paris, *Mémoires présentés par divers savants; sciences mathématiques et physiques* 2d Series 5:513–558.

1838b   Probabilité des jugements et des témoinages. Société Philomatique de Paris, *Extraits des procès-verbaux des séances* 5th Series 3:93–96.

1853a   Considérations à l'appui de la découverte de Laplace sur la loi de probabilité dans la méthode des moindres carrés. Académie des Sciences, Paris, *Comptes-rendus hebdomadaires des séances* 37:309–324.

1853b   Remarques sur les différences qui distinguent l'interpolation de M. Cauchy de la méthode des moindres carrés, et qui assurent la supériorité de cette méthode. Académie des Sciences, Paris, *Comptes-rendus hebdomadaires des séances* 37:5–13.

1855   Communication sur un principe que M. Poisson avait cru découvrir et qu'il avait appelé loi des grands nombres. Académie des Sciences Morales et Politiques, *Séances et travaux* 31:379–389.

1875   Application d'un théorème nouveau du calcul des probabilités. Académie des Sciences, Paris, *Comptes-rendus hebdomadaires des séances* 81:417–423.

SUPPLEMENTARY BIBLIOGRAPHY

M. de la Gournerie donne lecture de la note suivante, sur les travaux de M. Bienaymé. 1878 Académie des Sciences, Paris, *Comptes-rendus hebdomadaires des séances* 87:617–619.

Notice sur les travaux scientifiques de M. I. J. Bienaymé . . . inspecteur général des finances. 1852 Paris: Bachelier.

BINET, ALFRED

Alfred Binet (1857–1911), French psychologist, was born in Nice. His father was a doctor, as were many of his ancestors on both sides of his family. If he owed to this medical tradition the concern for observing facts that was to mark all his work, it was no doubt from his mother, a painter, that he derived the artistic inclinations that later led to his interest in the psychological aspects of literature and art. He also wrote some quite successful plays. He studied at the lycée in Nice and then at the Lycée Louis le Grand in Paris. Initially he studied law, received a diploma as licentiate, and at the age of 20 took his first examination for a doctorate in law. Then his intellectual interests shifted entirely.

The 1880s saw the beginnings of scientific psychology in France. Taine had blazed the trail in 1870 with the publication of *Intelligence.* Influenced by John Stuart Mill and English positivism, Taine laid particular stress on pathology. Charcot, a physician at the Salpétrière hospital, had begun to study hysteria in 1871, and then hypnosis. His clinical lectures attracted large audiences. Taine attended them, as did a young philosopher, Théodule Ribot, who was to become the true founder of scientific psychology in France. Ribot's program was set forth in an article in *Mind* in 1877 in which he severely criticized official doctrine and proclaimed his adherence to Mill and Taine. He advocated that French psychologists should emulate the work done in England and Germany and that they should use the natural sciences, physiology, and psychiatry as models. Psychology should be purely experimental and should not deal with the soul; its scope should include the behavior of animals and genetic development. This program was placed under the aegis of Herbert Spencer and Ribot was rewarded by appointment first to the Sorbonne in 1885 and then to a chair of experimental psychology at the Collège de France in 1892.

Binet met Ribot in 1877 and on his advice went into psychology, initially the field of psychopathology, which was traditionally French. "With a few rare exceptions," Binet wrote in 1889, "the psychologists of my country have left psychophysical research to the Germans and the study of comparative psychology to the English. They have devoted themselves almost exclusively to the study of pathological psychology" (Delay 1958, p. 86). And so he went to the Salpétrière and worked there with Charles Féré, a pupil of Charcot's. At that time the Salpétrière was the center of psychological research in France. In 1885 Charcot founded the Société Française de Psychologie Physiologique, and in 1889 the First International Congress of Psychology was held under his chairmanship. He was surrounded by eminent colleagues who were interested in psychology: the physiologist Charles Richet, a future Nobel laureate; the neurologist Babinski; Féré; foreign physicians like Sigmund Freud who came to him to study; young philosophers like Pierre Janet who, under Ribot's influence, were turning toward psychology.

The school of Charcot was interested above all in the neuroses, especially hysteria, and in hypnosis. It was to these subjects that Binet devoted himself; his resulting work is contained in a series of publications: *The Psychology of Reasoning* (1886); *Animal Magnetism,* in collaboration with Féré (1887); *On Double Consciousness* (1889); and *Alterations of Personality* (1892). It is hard to judge these works fairly without taking into consideration the atmosphere in which they were conceived. (Axel Munthe's *The Story of San Michele* gives a picturesque, if not entirely faithful, idea of that atmosphere.) Charcot's authoritarian personality, his proclivity for systematization, and his great prestige in both Parisian and international medical circles created in his students an attitude of complete submissiveness to his views. A result of this was the *hystérie de culture,* or artificially induced hysteria. Its symptoms accorded with Charcot's definitive description but were produced in part by more or less conscious suggestions made to the patient by Charcot's students during preliminary examinations prior to his appearance before Charcot himself. Later Binet was very critical of Charcot, accusing him of allowing his students to deceive him: "The masters of science," he wrote in 1909, "are like kings, surrounded by skillful courtiers, who tint the truth" (Binet & Simon 1910, p. 70). Binet himself, as a member of Charcot's court, was led, no doubt unconsciously, to believe in facts that supported his mentor's theory, as when he asserted that "the magnet and other aesthesiogenic agents may affect the transfer of cataleptic attitudes" (Binet & Féré 1887, p. 125). All the work Binet did before he was 30 is good work of its kind, but too much marked with the *Zeitgeist* to have other than historical interest.

While working at the Salpétrière, Binet decided that he needed biological training. No doubt his marriage to the daughter of Balbiani, professor of histology at the Collège de France, had something to do with this decision. He obtained a *licence ès sciences* and then a *doctorat ès sciences naturelles,* with a thesis, "Système nerveux sous-intestinal des insectes," written with Henneguy, the successor to his father-in-law. In 1888, when a chair of experimental psychology was created for Ribot at the Collège de France, a laboratory was attached to it. Ribot asked that it be given to the physiologist Beaunis, a professor in the faculty of medicine at Nancy. Beaunis, who knew Binet through his family, asked him to collaborate, and so in 1891 Binet abandoned the Salpétrière. The quarters of the laboratory were in the Sorbonne buildings, but administratively the laboratory was connected with a national research institution, the École Pratique des Hautes Études. Binet, at first *préparateur*, became assistant director and, upon the retirement of Beaunis in 1895, director, a position he retained until his death in 1911. The title was actually honorific, for practically no salary was attached to it. Fortunately, Binet had independent means that enabled him to carry on his work. His efforts to win more official university recognition were in vain. Although he was a candidate for the chair at the Collège de France left vacant by the departure of Ribot, Pierre Janet was chosen for it. He then applied for a chair at the Sorbonne, but the objection was raised that he was a doctor of natural sciences and not a *docteur ès lettres,* and Georges Dumas was elected. In 1895 his former fellow student Take Jonescu, a Rumanian who had become an important political figure in his own country, secured an appointment for him at the University of Bucharest, and Binet taught psychology there for several months.

Between 1891 and 1900, Binet in effect established experimental psychology in France. Trained as he was in the school of the Salpétrière and by his reading of Mill, Taine, and Ribot, he was not interested in psychophysiology or, in particular, in the study of sensation that absorbed the first German psychologists. In contrast to Wundt, he affirmed that higher psychic processes can be studied experimentally. While Wundt developed a "general psychology," Binet, for the rest of his life, was to construct an "individual," or as we would now say, a differential psychology.

The direction of Binet's interest derived from a number of sources. First, the scientific atmosphere of the time was dominated by evolutionist ideas. Spencer had acted as an intermediary between Darwin and Ribot. Now, evolution gave prominence to individual differences, which Darwin's cousin, Francis Galton, had taken as the subject of his researches. Second, the industrial revolution had brought with it a social transformation, one of its most obvious aspects being the specialization of tasks within the framework of the division of labor. At the same time, the industrial revolution had made universal primary education indispensable. This development made it necessary to take into consideration individual differences, and it was in this context that Binet tried to develop an experimentally based differential psychology.

Under the influence of Ribot, Binet declared that "there is nothing much to be gained by turning the pages of authors who work apart from observation and experimentation" (1900, p. 330). It is only facts that count, and more than that, "We must always be hospitable to the facts that go counter to our theories" (1903, p. 130). At the outset of his career, Binet gave priority to facts gathered by introspection. He thought that the higher processes were accessible only by "the act by which we directly perceive what is going on in us, our thoughts, our memories, our emotions" (1894a, p. 95). But although it is necessary to take into account what the subject experiences, and in particular what he says, it is at the same time necessary to observe what he does. From a position initially dominated by Taine's associationism, Binet's thought gradually evolved. In 1903 he published the *Étude expérimentale de l'intelligence,* undoubtedly his best book, in which he studied his two daughters, Madeleine and Alice, from the perspective of differential psychology. By the painstaking observation of behavior, coupled with introspection, he came to contrast two types of intellectual functioning, "subjective" and "objective," which foreshadowed Jung's "introversion" and "extraversion." But at the same time he recognized that "imageless thought" exists. Most important, he noted that the observation of an individual's behavior with regard to a set task provides the best information about his intellectual performance. This was the first step along the road that was to lead Binet, at the end of his life, to recognize that "there are very large portions of our psychic life that are by their very nature inaccessible to consciousness" (1911c, p. 9), and to declare that psychology "has become a science of action" (Binet & Simon 1909, p. 146).

In 1905 Binet made the discovery that brought him fame. After 1900 he virtually abandoned his laboratory in favor of work in the schools and institutions for the feeble-minded, and at his suggestion, a commission was set up in the Ministry of Education to study the establishment of classes for the mentally abnormal. It was soon found that clinical methods could not detect accurately those children who could not profit by normal instruction. Within less than a year, Binet proposed a diagnostic method for determining the intelligence of children. In an article written with the psychiatrist Th. Simon, "Méthodes nouvelles pour le diagnostic du niveau intellectuel des anormaux" (1905), which appeared in the *Année psychologique,* Binet presented a series of 30 intelligence tests of increasing difficulty; revisions and minor improvements appeared later (Binet & Simon 1908; Binet 1911*b*).

The success of Binet's diagnostic method was immediate, and Cyril Burt has humorously described the astonishment and admiration of the English psychologists, who were surprised that Binet's tests, unlike certain French wines, lost none of their qualities in crossing the Channel. Several factors contributed to this success. In the first place, Binet implicitly assumed the existence of a "general intelligence," a hypothesis which ran counter to the psychology of "mental functions" that he had himself used in his other works. This eclectic approach was noted with some acerbity by Charles Spearman, whose first article on factorial analysis had appeared a year earlier than Binet's article.

A little more than a year afterwards appeared the great work of Binet and Simon. Here, this paradoxical recommendation to make a hotchpot was actually adopted in practice. Nevertheless the elaborate correlational theory which had in point of fact generated the idea, and had supplied the sole evidence for its validity, was now passed over. The said authors employed a popular substitute. "Intelligence," as measured by the pool, was depicted as a "general level" of ability. So far as doctrine is concerned, this is the only thing introduced by them that was novel. And most surprisingly Binet, although in actual testing he took account of this "general level" alone, still in all his theoretical psychology continued to rely altogether upon his old formal faculties, notwithstanding that these and the "general level" appear to involve doctrines quite incompatible with each other.   (Spearman 1927, p. 60)

The second factor that contributed to Binet's success was his opportunity to use the method of comparing groups, i.e., normal school children and the mentally retarded children of the hospital at Perray-Vaucluse. To be sure, there had been many psychologists before Binet who had used this method, starting with Galton. The work published by Bolton (1892), Gilbert (1894), and Bagley (1901) in the United States had compared the subjects' test results with their performance in school. But here the third, and no doubt most important, factor in Binet's success enters in. His predecessors, in the tradition of Wundt's psychology, had employed tests that were presumed to be "elemental," i.e., psychophysical, and the correlations they obtained were too low to have any practical value. This was true for Cattell's researches in the United States as well as for those of Spearman in England. Binet declared instead that it was possible to get at the higher mental functions directly and above all to create suitable tests that would produce significant results. Finally, on the practical level, the success of the Binet scale was furthered by the discovery of the notion of mental age (which, incidentally, was not introduced until the 1908 revision). Whatever the drawbacks of this unit of measurement may be (and they have by now led to its almost total abandonment, even for children), when it was first proposed it could so easily be understood even by nontechnicians—e.g., teachers and physicians—that it facilitated the acceptance of the method of tests.

Within the total compass of Binet's work on differential psychology, the scale of intelligence, which gave Binet his fame, occupies, quantitatively, only a small space. The diversity of his interests led him to take up the most varied subjects, and in every case he made an original contribution.

Binet played an important role in the development of biometrics and psychometrics. His concern with individual differences led him to propose a technique for assessing the variability of a particular trait, either over a population or for a single individual over time. He understood the inadequacy of describing an empirical distribution by its arithmetic mean and its extreme values, and he therefore abandoned Broca's procedure (dividing the difference between the extreme values by the mean) and instead divided the difference between the means of the last and first quarters by the general mean. This method is characteristic of the period before the introduction into psychology of the standard deviation and the coefficient of variation as commonly used indexes of dispersion. Binet's solution "may seem arbitrary, even oversimple, but on second thought it is no worse than various other measures of variability" (Schreider 1957, p. 309).

Binet tackled the problem of correlation as well as that of dispersion. One way in which he approached the problem was to use the "method of numerical scores"; a second way was to measure association as a function of ranks (Binet & Vaschide 1897; Binet & Henri 1898). The first method consists in selecting for reference one of two traits and subdividing the population into four subgroups that show this trait in order, from "weak" to "strong." Then, for each subgroup one calculates the mean for the second trait. Inspection shows whether the variations for the two traits run parallel. The second method, which is more elaborate, is essentially identical with what was later called Spearman's foot rule. However, it was abandoned by Binet, even though it was developed by a mathematician at his suggestion (Sée 1904).

Binet was one of the inventors of the questionnaire method. He also made the first scientific studies of graphology, of the psychology of arithmetic prodigies and chess players, and of the psychology of small groups (he even used the term "leader"), to cite only a few achievements of this "Paganini of psychology," as Claparède called him. Toward the end of his life he again became interested in pathological psychology, having abandoned it after his days at the Salpétrière, and spent time at psychiatric hospitals and at a laboratory that he had set up in an elementary school in the Rue de la Grange aux Belles. He also studied pedagogical methods, to which his last book was devoted.

Binet had an essentially independent nature, and although he occasionally had collaborators, he never really had any students. Indeed, he lived in a kind of intellectual isolation that became painful to him toward the end of his life. He exerted an influence not so much by personal contacts, which he shunned (he never went to a scientific congress), as by his publications. In 1893 he established the *Bulletin du laboratoire de psychologie physiologique de la Sorbonne* as a vehicle for his works, and it was replaced two years later by the *Année psychologique*. This appeared annually, and most of it was edited by Binet, either alone or with some assistance, until his death. The *Année psychologique* played an important part in the diffusion of psychology, both by bringing together original work and by reviewing the world literature in the field.

PIERRE PICHOT

[*For the historical context of Binet's work, see the biographies of* CATTELL; CHARCOT; GALTON; MILL; SPEARMAN. *For discussions of the subsequent development of Binet's ideas, see* EDUCATIONAL PSYCHOLOGY; HYSTERIA; INTELLIGENCE AND INTELLIGENCE TESTING; STATISTICS, DESCRIPTIVE; TERMAN.]

WORKS BY BINET

(1886) 1901 *The Psychology of Reasoning.* London: Routledge. → First published as *La psychologie du raisonnement.*

(1887) 1892 BINET, ALFRED; and FÉRÉ, CHARLES. *Animal Magnetism.* New York: Appleton. → First published in French.

1889 *On Double Consciousness.* Chicago: Open Court. → Published in English.

(1892) 1896 *Alterations of Personality.* New York: Appleton. → First published as *Les altérations de la personnalité.*

1894a *Introduction à la psychologie experimentale.* Paris: Alcan.

1894b *La psychologie des grands calculateurs et joueurs échecs.* Paris: Hachette.

1897 BINET, ALFRED; and VASCHIDE, N. Corrélation des épreuves physiques. *Année psychologique* 4:142–172.

1898 BINET, ALFRED; and HENRI, V. *La fatigue intellectuelle.* Paris: Schleicher.

1900 *La suggestibilité.* Paris: Schleicher.

1903 *L'étude expérimentale de l'intelligence.* Paris: Schleicher.

1905 BINET, ALFRED; and SIMON, TH. Méthodes nouvelles pour le diagnostic du niveau intellectuel des anormaux. *Année psychologique* 11:191–244.

(1906) 1907 *Mind and the Brain.* London: Routledge. → First published as *L'âme et le corps.*

1908 BINET, ALFRED; and SIMON TH. Le développement de l'intelligence chez les enfants. *Année psychologique* 14:1–94.

1909 BINET, ALFRED; and SIMON, TH. L'intelligence des imbéciles. *Année psychologique* 15:1–147.

1910 BINET, ALFRED; and SIMON, TH. Hystérie. *Année psychologique* 16:67–122.

1911a *Les idées modernes sur les enfants.* Paris: Flammarion.

1911b Nouvelles recherches sur la mesure du niveau intellectuel chez les enfants d'école. *Année psychologique* 17:145–201.

1911c Qu'est-ce qu'un acte intellectuel? *Année psychologique* 17:1–47.

WORKS ABOUT BINET

[Alfred Binet.] 1957 *Revue de psychologie appliquée* 7:229–316. → Contains five articles about Alfred Binet by Cyril Burt, Pierre Oléron, R. Perron and J. de Gobineau, E. A. Fleishman, and Eugène Schreider.

BERTRAND, FRANÇOIS-LOUIS 1930 *Alfred Binet et son oeuvre.* Paris: Alcan.

DELAY, JEAN 1958 La vie et l'oeuvre d'Alfred Binet. *Psychologie française* 3:85–88.

[La vie et l'oeuvre d'Alfred Binet.] 1958 *Psychologie française* 3:85–121. → Contains five articles about Alfred Binet by Jean Delay, Henri Piéron, Pierre Pichot, Paul Fraisse, and René Zazzo.

PICHOT, PIERRE 1963 Alfred Binet. Volume 3, pages 209–220 in Kurt Kolle (editor), *Grosse Nervenärzte.* Stuttgart (Germany): Thieme.

SCHREIDER, EUGÈNE 1957 La place d'Alfred Binet dans l'évolution de la biométrie. *Revue de psychologie appliquée* 7:305–316.

SUPPLEMENTARY BIBLIOGRAPHY

Année psychologique. → Founded by Binet in 1894. Most of his work was published in this journal.

BAGLEY, WILLIAM C. 1901 On the Correlation of Mental and Motor Activity in School Children. *American Journal of Psychology* 12:193–205.

BOLTON, THADDEUS L. 1892 The Growth of Memory in School Children. *American Journal of Psychology* 4:362–380.

Centenaire de Th. Ribot: Jubilé de la psychologie scientifique française. 1939 Agen (France): Imprimerie moderne.

GILBERT, J. ALLEN 1894 Researches on the Mental and Physical Development of School Children. Yale Psychological Laboratory, *Studies* 2:40–100.

SÉE, A. 1904 Une formule mathématique applicable aux recherches sur la psychologie. Société libre pour l'étude psychologique de l'enfant, *Bulletin* 4:492–498.

SPEARMAN, CHARLES E. 1927 *The Abilities of Man: Their Nature and Measurement.* London: Macmillan.

BINGHAM, WALTER

Walter Van Dyke Bingham (1880–1952) profoundly influenced the development of applied psychology in America. For over forty years he worked for the establishment of an industrial and applied psychology based on rigorous experimental psychology. While he contributed to the understanding of a wide range of problems in applied psychology, he is best known for his significant contributions to the solution of problems centering on personnel selection in industry, military selection and manpower utilization, interviewing techniques, and psychological testing.

Bingham was born in Swan Lake, Iowa. He earned his B.A. degree at Beloit College, Wisconsin, in 1901; studied at the University of Berlin in 1907; and earned his M.A. degree at Harvard University in 1907. He received his PH.D. from the University of Chicago in 1908.

Bingham's distinguished academic career began with his appointment to Teachers College, Columbia University, in 1908. He was assistant professor of psychology at Dartmouth from 1912 to 1915 and also served as director of the summer session. In 1915 he was asked by the Carnegie Institute of Technology to establish a department of applied psychology, the first in America. From 1915 to 1924 Bingham served at Carnegie as professor of psychology, head of the division of applied psychology, and director of the division of cooperative research.

While at Carnegie he embarked on his pioneering venture of using psychology as a tool to help clarify the problems of some of the large industries in the Pittsburgh area. At the same time, with the founding of a division of applied psychology, he endeavored to provide instruction for students planning careers in industrial management and other fields where success depended in some measure on the ability to understand and influence people. He hoped the instruction would enable such students to have a better understanding of human behavior. This work antedated such well-known historical developments in applied psychology as the Committee on Classification of Personnel in the army in 1917–1918 and the formation in 1919–1923 of the Scott Company, the first personnel consulting firm of applied psychologists.

Bingham became director of the Personnel Research Foundation, Inc., in 1924. He served as president of the Psychological Corporation from 1926 to 1928 and was appointed professorial lecturer in psychology at Stevens Institute of Technology in 1930.

Applied psychology grew in importance during and immediately following World War I, and Bingham came to hold many responsible positions. He served as executive secretary of the Committee on Classification of Personnel in the army in 1917–1918; he held the rank of lieutenant colonel in the personnel branch of the U.S. Army General Staff in 1918–1919; and he was the first chairman of the division of anthropology and psychology of the National Research Council in 1919–1920. In 1927 he served as the American member of the board of the International Congress of Technopsychology. His planning and consulting services to the army in World War II are acknowledged by the inscription "architect of the classification system of the army, 1940–1947," which appears on his headstone in Arlington National Cemetery.

Another of Bingham's major concerns was the measurement of the abilities of able and brilliant students and the early identification of the gifted. This aspect of his work was honored after his death by the American Psychological Association with the establishment of an annual lectureship in his name. The lectures have two purposes: to bring to the attention of psychologists and others the great value of accurate identification of exceptionally promising young people; and to do honor to psychologists and institutions working in this field.

Bingham was the author of over two hundred articles and books. He wrote on a wide variety of topics ranging from articles on tonal fusion, vocal functions, and studies in melody to such topics as the search for skill and talent in the army, the accident-prone driver, and reliability, validity, and dependability. Two of his books, *How to Interview* (Bingham & Moore 1931) and *Aptitudes and Aptitude Testing* (1937), are classics in the field of personnel psychology and guidance.

Bingham's works have been widely used. His example helped make training in applied psychology a respectable and common part of the curriculum in institutions of higher learning. The testing movement has flourished. Research in industrial psychology, guidance and counseling, and personnel psychology has proceeded to develop in many of the problem areas along the lines he suggested. And his hope that more attention would be paid to students of high ability has certainly been realized in the greatly increased research and educational activity in this area. Bingham must be recognized as an important founding father of applied psychology whose vision and work have determined in large measure the directions applied psychology has taken and the considerable progress it has made since he started the Carnegie program in 1915.

LLOYD H. LOFQUIST

[*For discussion of the subsequent development of Bingham's ideas, see* APTITUDE TESTING; INDUSTRIAL RELATIONS, *article on* INDUSTRIAL AND BUSINESS PSYCHOLOGY.]

WORKS BY BINGHAM

1907   The Role of the Tympanic Mechanism in Audition. *Psychological Review* 14:229–243.

1910a   Studies in Melody. *Psychological Monographs* 12, no. 3.

1910b   The Use of Experiment in Teaching Educational Psychology: Report of the Meeting of New York Teachers of Educational Psychology, Held at Ithaca, N.Y., April 8–9, 1910. *Journal of Educational Psychology* 1:287–292.

1911   A Useful Demonstration of Tonal Fusion. *Psychological Bulletin* 8:57 only.

1914   Five Years of Progress in Comparative Musical Science. *Psychological Bulletin* 11:421–433.

1916   BINGHAM, WALTER; SCOTT, W. D.; and WHIPPLE, G. M.   Scientific Selection of Salesmen: A Report on the Demonstration of Scientific Methods in the Testing of Applicants. *Salesmanship* 4:106–108.

1917   Mentality Testing of College Students. *Journal of Applied Psychology* 1:38–45.

1919   Army Personnel Work: With Some Implications for Education and Industry. *Journal of Applied Psychology* 3:1–12.

1923   On the Possibility of an Applied Psychology. *Psychological Review* 30:289–305.

1924   BINGHAM, WALTER; and DAVIS, W. T.   Intelligence Test Scores and Business Success. *Journal of Applied Psychology* 8:1–22.

1926a   Measures of Occupational Success. *Harvard Business Review* 5:1–10.

1926b   Personality and Dominant Interest: Vocational Tendencies of Introverts. *Psychological Bulletin* 23:153–154.

1926   BINGHAM, WALTER; and FREYD, MAX.   *Procedures in Employment Psychology: A Manual for Developing Scientific Methods of Vocational Selection.* Chicago and New York: Shaw.

1927   BINGHAM, WALTER; and SLOCOMBE, C. S.   Men Who Have Accidents: Individual Differences Among Motormen and Bus Operators. *Personnel Journal* 6:251–257.

1929   The Personal Interview Studied by Means of Analysis and Experiment. *Social Forces* 7:530–533.

1931   Management's Concern With Research in Industrial Psychology. *Harvard Business Review* 10:40–53.

(1931) 1941   BINGHAM, WALTER; and MOORE, BRUCE V.   *How to Interview.* 3d ed., rev. New York: Harper.

1934   Abilities and Opportunities: Some Meanings of Trends in Occupational Distribution. *Occupations* 12:6–17.

1935   MacQuarrie Test for Mechanical Ability. *Occupations* 14:202–205.

1937   *Aptitudes and Aptitude Testing.* New York: Harper.

1938a   Halo: Its Prevalence and Nature in Estimates of Objective Traits and in Inferential Trait-judgments. *Psychological Bulletin* 35:641–642.

1938b   Testing in Vocational Guidance. *Education* 58:539–544.

1939   A National Perspective on Testing and Guidance. *Educational Record* 20 (Supplement): 137–150.

1941   Psychological Services in the United States Army. *Journal of Consulting Psychology* 5:221–224.

1944   Personnel Classification Testing in the Army. *Science* New Series 100:275–280.

1946   Inequalities in Adult Capacity: From Military Data. *Science* New Series 104:147–152.

1947   Military Psychology in War and Peace. *Science* New Series 106:155–160.

1948   Psychologists in Industry. *American Psychologist* 3:321–323.

BINOMIAL DISTRIBUTION

See DISTRIBUTIONS, STATISTICAL, *article on* SPECIAL DISCRETE DISTRIBUTIONS.

BIOLOGY, HUMAN

See EUGENICS; EVOLUTION; GENETICS; MENTAL DISORDERS, *article on* BIOLOGICAL ASPECTS; PHYSICAL ANTHROPOLOGY; RACE.

BIOMECHANICS

See ENGINEERING PSYCHOLOGY.

BIPARTISANSHIP

The concept of bipartisanship is chiefly associated with postwar American foreign policy. Although the concept is complex and difficult to define precisely, bipartisanship generally implies the attempt of governmental officials to achieve maximum national unity toward foreign relations, by the use of techniques and procedures designed to attain that end.

Meaning and implications. Ambiguity has always surrounded the meaning and implications of bipartisanship, a fact that has itself engendered considerable disunity among policy makers. Former Republican Senator Arthur H. Vandenberg of Michigan, perhaps the leading exponent of bipartisanship, variously called for an "unpartisan" or "nonpartisan" foreign policy (Crabb 1957, p. 1; Vandenberg 1952, pp. 547–552). Former Secretary of State Cordell Hull advocated a "nonpartisan" foreign policy to prevent "divided councils, confusion, and lack of popular support" for diplomatic measures (Hull 1948, vol. 2, p. 1734). Negative terms like "unpartisan" and "nonpartisan" imply the necessity to eliminate partisan discords altogether from the handling of foreign affairs. Other commentators prefer the term "extrapartisan," to suggest that foreign policy programs be formulated outside party lines, although political organization may be utilized to rally support for them (Westerfield 1955, p. 16).

The most widely used term, however, is "bipartisanship"—a more positive word suggesting (1) the desirability of affirmative cooperation, among major political groups, on needed global programs and (2) the expectation that at least a minimum degree of consultation between spokesmen for each major party will precede important undertakings in the foreign policy field.

Sources of disunity in foreign policy. Alexis de Tocqueville, writing early in the nineteenth century, questioned whether in foreign affairs a democracy was able to "regulate the details of an important undertaking, to persevere in a design, and to work out its execution in the presence of serious obstacles." As in all democracies, public officials in the United States must constantly reckon with a number of forces capable of disrupting the continuity of the nation's foreign relations: (1) poorly informed, often indifferent, sometimes emotionally aroused public opinion; (2) continuing partisan discords that reach crescendos of vituperation during national elections; (3) the possibility that the succession of one administration by another may radically alter the nation's overseas commitments; and (4) the readiness of well-organized and vocal public groups to advance their own conceptions of the national interest.

The peculiar nature of the American political system also contributes to disunity. Local issues and organizations tend to dominate the political scene. Although the president is the "leader of his party," party lines are loose, and party discipline (as it exists in parliamentary systems) is practically nonexistent.

Since World War II an ever-growing number of executive agencies have been drawn into the foreign policy process, making it extraordinarily diffuse, cumbersome, and vulnerable to conflicts among strongly entrenched bureaucracies. A parallel tendency has been evident in Congress, where there has been a marked proliferation in the number of legislative committees involved in foreign affairs. This tendency has seriously undermined the once almost exclusive positions of the Senate Foreign Relations and House Foreign Affairs committees (which customarily work closely with the White House) in this field. Legislative activities in foreign relations have thus become progressively fragmented and resistant to coordination, either by the president or by groups within Congress.

The concept of bipartisanship was evolved to overcome, or at least to mitigate, the harmful effects of disunity in foreign policy.

Evolution of bipartisanship. From the earliest days of the American republic, governmental leaders have realized the need for domestic unity on foreign policy and have utilized rudimentary bipartisan techniques to achieve it. The "isolationist" character of the nation's foreign policy for a century and a half meant that such efforts evolved on an *ad hoc* basis and that their results were usually mixed. President Washington sought the active "advice" of the Senate at an early stage in treaty negotiations; the frustration and interminable delay he experienced soon led him to abandon the attempt. President Madison, however, successfully utilized two legislators to negotiate the treaty ending the War of 1812. President Wilson sought unsuccessfully to mollify his Republican critics by appointing a nominal Republican, Henry White, to accompany him to Europe to negotiate the Treaty of Versailles. On the eve of World War II President Roosevelt appointed two Republicans to his cabinet—Henry L. Stimson, secretary of war, and Frank Knox, secretary of the navy—in order to mitigate partisan animosities over critical foreign policy issues.

Today there is widespread agreement that unity is the ultimate goal of a bipartisan approach to foreign relations. Far less agreement prevails over the means to achieve it. Several techniques have been employed, with varying degrees of success. Presidents routinely ask legislators of both parties to take part in international negotiations and to attend sessions of the United Nations. Prior consultation is also essential to bipartisanship; the White House is expected to consult with leaders of the opposition party, ideally *before* it acts to meet challenges abroad. Whether the president solicits the advice of those consulted or merely informs them of anticipated actions will depend upon the personality of the chief executive, the exact situation confronting the nation abroad, and the time available for decision. Bipartisanship also implies that criticism of governmental activities in foreign affairs be constructive rather than destructive, a demand easier to accept in the abstract than to fulfill in specific circumstances. Moreover, adherence to bipartisanship is widely believed to require that political parties not seek partisan advantage from diplomatic victories or defeats.

Continuing problems. Since World War II, bipartisanship has built a solid base of national unity to support many American foreign policy commitments. Creation of the United Nations, provision of economic assistance to western Europe, NATO, and other military aid programs, opposition to the recognition of communist China, and firm resistance to communist expansionism are notable examples. Public opinion in the United States has, however, been sharply divided over other diplomatic issues, such as policy on nationalist China, the Middle East, Cuba, and eastern Europe, tariff and trade questions, and efforts to resolve cold war tensions.

In addition to yielding mixed results, the bipartisan approach has raised persistent problems for the United States, some of which are sufficiently serious to challenge the value of the bipartisan principle. Clearer understanding, derived from continued research, is needed before definitive judgments can be rendered on the bipartisan concept. A number of fundamental questions can be identified. (1) Does bipartisanship erode the president's control of foreign relations by transferring decision making to legislators and party leaders who bear no constitutional responsibility for most actions in the sphere of foreign relations? (2) Does this render it impossible for the electorate to hold the president and his agents accountable for public policies? (3) Is it possible to arrive at a consensus on a definition of "bipartisanship" that can be applied to the diverse range of external issues confronting the United States?

Bipartisanship also raises serious problems related to the nature and function of the American political system. (1) A basic premise of bipartisanship is that internal and external policy questions can be clearly delineated and partisan contests may legitimately be waged over the former but not over the latter. However, since the impact of nearly all domestic developments upon foreign affairs is increasing, and vice versa, is this distinction still relevant? (2) Furthermore, does bipartisanship allow political parties to discharge their traditional function of informing the public on vital issues? (3) For the opposition party, does bipartisanship impose a unique handicap by fostering a tendency to accept prevailing policy, even when it is deemed to be inimical to the nation's interests? (4) By contrast, does the majority party compromise its claim to successful leadership by permitting the minority to share in the "credit" for successful policies?

Equally pertinent is the question whether bipartisanship facilitates or actually impedes diplomatic success. Postwar experience suggests that it may reduce the process of policy formulation to a search for the lowest common denominator of policy, advocated not because the national interest demands it but because the widest measure of unity can be obtained to support it.

CECIL V. CRABB, JR.

[*See also* DIPLOMACY; FOREIGN POLICY; *and* PUBLIC OPINION.]

BIBLIOGRAPHY

COHEN, BERNARD C. 1957 *The Political Process and Foreign Policy: The Making of a Japanese Peace Settlement.* Princeton Univ. Press.

CRABB, CECIL V., JR. 1957 *Bipartisan Foreign Policy: Myth or Reality?* Evanston, Ill.: Row, Peterson.

HULL, CORDELL 1948 *Memoirs.* 2 vols. New York: Macmillan.

JEWELL, MALCOLM E. 1962 *Senatorial Politics and Foreign Policy.* Lexington: Univ. of Kentucky Press.

ROBINSON, JAMES A. 1962 *Congress and Foreign Policymaking: A Study in Legislative Influence and Initiative.* Homewood, Ill.: Dorsey.

SELLIN, THORSTEN (editor) 1953 Congress and Foreign Relations. American Academy of Political and Social Science, *Annals* 289:1–177.

VANDENBERG, ARTHUR H. 1952 *The Private Papers of Senator Vandenberg.* Edited by Arthur H. Vandenberg, Jr. Boston: Houghton Mifflin.

WESTERFIELD, H. BRADFORD 1955 *Foreign Policy and Party Politics: Pearl Harbor to Korea.* New Haven: Yale Univ. Press.

BIRTH CONTROL

See FERTILITY CONTROL.

BIRTH RATES

See FERTILITY.

BLACKSTONE, WILLIAM

William Blackstone's *Commentaries on the Laws of England* (1765–1769) was the first attempt since Bracton's, in the thirteenth century, to put the whole of the laws of England into one, albeit four-volume, book and in readable form.

Blackstone (1723–1780) was born after the death of his father, a London merchant. Family connections were able to gain him admission to the Charterhouse School, and after the death of his mother he was able to complete his education because of a special provision in the school's charter for the orphans of gentlemen. In 1738 he entered Oxford, concentrating on the classics, and in 1740, under an arrangement not uncommon in his day, he enrolled in the Middle Temple while continuing his Oxford studies. His interests were wide, ranging from architecture to the works of Shakespeare.

He was elected a fellow of All Souls in 1744 and took the bachelor of civil laws degree in 1745.

It is often said that Blackstone turned to academic work after failure to establish a successful law practice in London. It is more probable that the reverse is true. After his admission to the bar in 1746, he continued to maintain his close connections with the university, particularly through a series of administrative positions that included an intensive effort to reform the Clarendon Press. In 1752 he was the leading candidate for the professorship of civil laws and was passed over for purely political reasons. Part-time barristers were apparently unpopular in London, and his devotion to Oxford duties made it impossible for Blackstone to cultivate a practice successfully. Thus, when he began to offer a course of lectures on the laws of England at Oxford, he was following a natural academic bent that culminated in his appointment to the newly created Vinerian chair. The *Commentaries* was derived directly from his lectures.

In 1761, Blackstone returned to the practice of law and was elected to Parliament. In the 1760s his law practice flourished, and in 1766 he resigned his professorship to devote full time to it. Although he did serve as solicitor general to the queen for part of this period, he declined the chief justiceship of common pleas in Ireland and the solicitor generalship. In 1770 he was appointed a justice of the Court of Common Pleas, where, except for a brief period on King's Bench, he served until his death.

In A. V. Dicey's much-quoted phrase, the *Commentaries* "live by their style." Dicey meant by style not only Blackstone's flowing prose but his literary discretion, his ability to select and arrange material so as to seize the reader's attention and carry it from point to point. The *Commentaries* is not advanced critical scholarship but an attractive and methodologically daring elementary text. Blackstone, to be sure, borrowed the outlines of his system from an earlier work by Sir Matthew Hale (1713), but his attempt to present the law in terms of substantive areas and in the light of underlying principles was a radical departure from the professional thought of his day. English lawyers tended to deal with the law as an armory of writs, statutes, and procedures, and the fledgling lawyer learned to thrust and parry with each of these without any particular concern for the legal system they were designed to implement.

Blackstone's principal concern was to select the interesting and instructive. His eminently readable work therefore has the weaknesses of its strengths. It deliberately avoids difficult details and often emphasizes not what is most important but rather what is most colorful or most intriguing. Although in some areas it offers a perceptive picture of what is actually going on in the law, in others it follows the majority of texts and expounds what is formally or theoretically, rather than actually, true.

Blackstone belongs to the intellectual tradition of the common lawyers. Indeed, his aim in the *Commentaries* was to present the common law in the literary and philosophical garb acceptable to the educated man of the eighteenth century. The dominant tone of self-satisfaction in the *Commentaries* was undoubtedly due largely to a unique conjunction in that period of the vocabulary and modes of thought of the common law with a broader moral and intellectual outlook: Burkean conservatism and the common-sense school of philosophy shared an ideology with the professional successors of Sir Edward Coke. Little wonder that Blackstone, both a lawyer and a gentleman–scholar, should feel content when he found that the prejudices and rationales of each of his intellectual bailiwicks were confirmed by those of the other.

It is this basic contentment, primarily, that has made Blackstone the butt of much latter-day criticism. But he has been criticized, and even maligned, for other reasons as well. The *Commentaries* appeared near the end of a long period of judge-made law and just prior to a period of statutory reform. Blackstone therefore summed up a body of case law that was not otherwise readily available, and it became convenient to loose all the reformist barbs at the law as summed up in the *Commentaries*. Dicey, for instance, simply uses Blackstone as a symbol of the chaotic state of the common law immediately before the utilitarian crusade. It was rhetorically easier to condemn Blackstone for what, in fact, he was only describing than to cite a gaggle of incomplete law reports. It is probably because Blackstone was such a convenient target that Bentham's first work was directed specifically against the *Commentaries* and that his attacks on Blackstone became increasingly vitriolic through the years. Bentham's polemics have created the traditional image of Blackstone as a bumbling antiquarian, an image that tends to be uncritically absorbed along with Bentham's more substantial contributions to jurisprudence.

Blackstone is, of course, frequently illogical and nearly always inconsistent and thus falls an easy victim to Bentham's systematic attack. The illogic and the inconsistencies stem from Blackstone's efforts to describe the law as it was and to give reasons for it that might be understandable, interesting, and convincing to the average reader. These reasons were designed not as units in a critical and coherent legal philosophy but as instructional devices for leading the reader to a grasp of common-law methods of thought. Blackstone was, moreover, largely unaware of and unconcerned with the numerous philosophic inconsistencies that pervaded the body of contemporary thought and his own work (Boorstin 1941, *passim*).

The principal target of the attack on Blackstone has been not his inconsistency but his excessive satisfaction with the state of things and his alleged role as conservative apologist. However, Blackstone was not a thoroughgoing conservative. As a member of Parliament and a barrister, he moved in Tory circles and owed his judgeship in part to Tory connections, but he never seems to have been a trusted party man. His political philosophy was Old Whig, and since the Old Whigs were trying to conserve a revolutionary settlement and a Lockean philosophy, their outlook necessarily consisted of a mixture of conservative and liberal ideas. The major theme in Blackstone's work is the preservation of the rights and liberties of Englishmen. Giving broad limits to the royal prerogative while supporting parliamentary sovereignty (itself a neat trick), he also emphasized that a mixed constitution and separation of powers were in principle England's grandest defense against oppression. He admitted that the possibility of oppression was not entirely precluded and conceded, albeit vaguely, a right of revolution.

Blackstone was a leader of the prison-reform movement, further evidence that his conservatism was qualified. He borrowed many of his ideas of punishment from Beccaria; characteristically, he was not as consistent in his dependence on Beccaria as was Bentham. While Parliament in his day was busily adding to the list of capital offenses, there was a strong countermovement in the courts, which Blackstone supported, to mitigate the harshness of the criminal law by various devices of pleading and statutory interpretation. Clearly, Blackstone did not always defend the existing law: he was critical of the poor laws, for example, and in his treatment of statutory devices and his search for a general theory of contract he was ahead of his time (Plucknett 1929, pp. 555–556 and 583 in the 1936 edition).

It is true that Blackstone was basically satisfied with the polity of England, but in the middle of the eighteenth century Great Britain was generally acknowledged to be the freest and most advanced nation of Europe. Moreover, Blackstone lived and wrote before the French Revolution had hardened British conservatism into complete resistance to change. Blackstone's conservatism tends to be exaggerated by juxtaposition with the radicalism of his utilitarian attackers. The *Commentaries* is basically a defense of the existing legal order, and it often seems to avoid or ignore necessary criticisms, but the purpose of an elementary text has generally been to explain and rationalize rather than to attack the material it presents.

The extent to which Blackstone's use of natural law is conservative has long been a subject for discussion. The traditional view was that the passages espousing natural law in the Introduction to the *Commentaries* were simply borrowings from—or, indeed, direct copying from—Pufendorf, Grotius, and especially Burlemarque and had no real connection with the main body of the work, which constantly contradicts natural-law tenets. However, it has recently been asserted that Blackstone's natural-law references were more than decorative asides (Hart 1956, *passim*). Blackstone acknowledged a natural law to which no positive law can be contrary and remain law. However, he also stripped natural law of most of its content by holding that the commands of natural law are few and simple and that, consequently, most positive laws deal with questions on which the natural law is silent. Thus, Blackstone turned natural law from a revolutionary instrument into a conservative one by asserting that the bulk of positive law can never be invalidated by natural law because most human (or positive) law deals with matters to which the natural law is indifferent.

Although Blackstone did rely heavily on Continental natural-law writers, he did not copy directly from them, and indeed he modified their pronouncements rather markedly to make them more compatible with his own work (Lucas 1963; McKnight 1959). A strong Hobbesian, positivist strain runs throughout the *Commentaries*, but the work is no more consistently Hobbesian than it is consistently anything else. It is true Blackstone did not specifically follow Coke's teaching that any offense against the common law is an offense *malum in se* (evil in itself) and thus did not specifically equate common law with moral law. It is also true that when he borrowed the scholastic definition of positive law as a right or just ordinance commanding what is right and forbidding what is wrong, he consciously struck out the "right" and "just" before "law." In so doing he moved away from the natural-law notion that positive law is really law only insofar as it is "right," that is, in accord with natural law, and moved toward the positivist position that human law itself defines what is right and wrong. Then again, Blackstone did occasionally lapse into natural-law language when describing the common law (1765–1769, vol. 3, p. 162); his view of pre-Norman England as a golden age of pure law embodying the wisdom of the ancestors was closely akin to natural law in that it suggested a body of higher law against which existing law must be tested, and his search for foreign analogies to English law suggested universal-law notions. He even went so far as to say that the "legislature, and of course the laws of England" (1765–1769, vol. 1, p. 127), was designed to protect Englishmen in "those absolute rights, which were vested in them by the immutable laws of nature . . . summed up in one general appellation, and denominated the natural liberty of mankind" (vol. 1, pp. 124–125).

Obviously, his semischolastic definition of positive law is a neat piece of fence straddling: if law is an ordinance commanding what is right and forbidding what is wrong, does this mean that whatever the law commands is by definition right —that there is no standard of right and wrong except the law itself? Or does it mean that the positive law adds social sanction to the dictates of morality? Blackstone, who adopted every contradictory concept of his day, naturally accepted the traditional equation of common law with natural law. The crucial question dividing positivists from believers in natural law, whether the law *creates* rights or defends *pre-existing rights,* was for Blackstone only a chicken-and-egg problem. For him an Englishman had only those rights acknowledged by law, but Englishmen have formed the law to acknowledge their rights. Because Blackstone resolutely refused to recognize that the positivist and natural-law positions on rights are mutually exclusive, he cannot finally be neatly labeled as belonging to one philosophical school or the other.

Blackstone saw himself not as a legal philosopher but as an educational reformer. In the eighteenth century the Inns of Court had ceased to be a quasi university and had largely ceased to give real legal instruction; most lawyers felt that law was best learned by apprenticeship and practice, not through academic instruction. Blackstone gave the first regular lectures on English law at Oxford and later held the first chair of English law there, although he was thwarted in his attempt to establish what would have been the first university-connected college of law in England. The *Commentaries* was designed not only to teach aspiring lawyers but also to present the principles of English law as part of the liberal education of English gentlemen—and incidentally to show that only gentlemen should practice law. Thus, the *Commentaries* contains a good deal of what purports to be history, comparative law, and political philosophy, much of it in fact more nearly anecdote, curiosity, and political fiction. Although the *Commentaries* is a precursor of the historical school of law, it is only with Sir Henry Maine, a century later, that real historical scholarship came to English law.

Blackstone undoubtedly raised the tone of English legal education, but it was a revival of the Inns themselves and not university training that largely accounts for improved legal training at the beginning of the nineteenth century. In the United States, however, the examples of Blackstone's teaching at Oxford and of the didactic quality of the *Commentaries* contributed significantly to the early founding of academic law schools and to the weight of his disciples James Kent and Joseph Story in legal scholarship. And although in English courts Blackstone's *Commentaries* has never had the authority of Bracton, Coke, and Hale, it was for many years the principal authority for English law in American courts. In revolutionary and postrevolutionary America the *Commentaries* was often the sole source of a lawyer's scholarly training.

It is, in the end, impossible accurately to assess Blackstone's influence on the development of either the law or legal education. He introduced so few original ideas that when we find putative traces of Blackstone we are never sure whether we are faced with the impact of the author of the *Commentaries* or with the influence of the common law itself, which might have evolved in the same way whether Blackstone had written or not. There is almost nothing in Anglo-American law that we can point to as uniquely Blackstonian. Blackstone is considered today, as he was in his own time, a teacher and elementary-text writer of great clarity rather than an influential legal philosopher.

MARTIN SHAPIRO

[*For the historical context of Blackstone's work, see* LEGAL SYSTEMS, *article on* COMMON LAW SYSTEMS; NATURAL LAW; *the biographies of* BECCARIA; BURKE; COKE; GROTIUS. *For discussion of subsequent reactions to Blackstone's ideas, see the biographies of* BENTHAM *and* DICEY.]

WORKS BY BLACKSTONE

(1765–1769) 1922 *Commentaries on the Laws of England.* 4 books in 2 vols. Edited by William Draper Lewis. Philadelphia: Bisel. → Originally published in four volumes.

(1781) 1828 *Reports of Cases Determined in the Several Courts of Westminster-Hall From 1746 to 1779.* 2 vols. 2d ed., rev. & corrected. Edited by Charles H. Elsey. London: Sweet.

WORKS ABOUT BLACKSTONE

BARKER, ERNEST (1945) 1960 Blackstone on the British Constitution. Pages 120–153 in Ernest Barker, *Essays on Government*. 2d ed. Oxford: Clarendon. → Still the best introductory study.

BENTHAM, JEREMY (c. 1774–1775) 1928 *A Comment on the* Commentaries: *A Criticism of Blackstone's* Commentaries on the Laws of England. Oxford: Clarendon.

BOORSTIN, DANIEL J. 1941 *The Mysterious Science of the Law: An Essay on Blackstone's* Commentaries. Cambridge, Mass.: Harvard Univ. Press. → The book struggles under an excessive weight of hypothesis, and in placing Blackstone firmly in the eighteenth century it fails also to place him firmly in the tradition of the common law.

DICEY, ALBERT V. (1905) 1962 *Lectures on the Relation Between Law and Public Opinion in England During the Nineteenth Century*. 2d ed. London and New York: Macmillan. → A paperback edition was published in 1962 by Macmillan.

DICEY, ALBERT V. 1930 Blackstone's *Commentaries*. *Cambridge Law Journal* 4:286–307.

HALE, MATTHEW (1713) 1716 *The History of the Common Law, With an Analysis of the Civil Part of the Law*. 2d ed. London: Walthoe.

HANBURY, HAROLD G. 1958 *The Vinerian Chair and Legal Education*. Oxford: Blackwell. → Devotes three excessively apologetic chapters to Blackstone.

HANBURY, HAROLD G. 1959 Blackstone as a Judge. *American Journal of Legal History* 3:1–27. → An excessively apologetic article.

HART, H. L. A. 1956 Blackstone's Use of the Law of Nature. *Butterworth's South African Law Review* 3:169–174.

HOLDSWORTH, WILLIAM S. 1938–1952 *A History of English Law*. Vols. 11–13. London: Methuen. → Devotes long passages to Blackstone, but Holdsworth was an Old Whig himself and he brought almost no perspective to his material.

LOCKMILLER, DAVID A. 1938 *Sir William Blackstone*. Chapel Hill: Univ. of North Carolina Press.

LUCAS, PAUL 1962 Blackstone and the Reform of the Legal Profession. *English Historical Review* 77:456–489.

LUCAS, PAUL 1963 Ex Parte Sir William Blackstone, "Plagiarist": A Note on Blackstone and the Natural Law. *American Journal of Legal History* 7:142–158.

MCKNIGHT, JOSEPH 1959 Blackstone, Quasi-jurisprudent. *Southwestern Law Journal* 13:399–411.

PLUCKNETT, THEODORE F. T. (1929) 1956 *A Concise History of the Common Law*. 5th ed., enl. & entirely rewritten. London: Butterworth.

WARDEN, LEWIS C. 1938 *The Life of Blackstone*. Charlottesville, Va.: Michie.

BLEULER, EUGEN

Eugen Bleuler (1859–1939), Swiss psychiatrist, was born in Zollikon, which today is a suburb of Zurich. After a short period of study at the Waldau Clinic in Bern and a brief stay at Burghölzli, he was appointed director of the Rheinau Psychiatric Hospital at the early age of 29. Twelve years later he was appointed full professor of psychiatry at the University of Zurich—against the wishes of the Zurich faculty of medicine. He occupied that chair until 1927.

Outwardly Bleuler's career was uneventful; his brilliant achievements are all the more startling by contrast. In 1911 the publication of his monograph *Dementia Praecox: Or the Group of Schizophrenias* made Bleuler famous. He took over where Emil Kraepelin, with his clinical definition of dementia praecox, had left off. Bleuler added new symptoms to the description of this disease and, by his subtle analyses, so enriched our appreciation of these symptoms that in the world of psychiatry, schizophrenia became the standard name of the syndrome. Of late it has even become fashionable to call many social and political crises schizophrenic —which is a misuse of a medical concept.

Schizophrenia was a term first proposed by Bleuler in his paper "Die Prognose der Dementia Praecox (Schizophreniegruppe)" (1908), which was read at a conference of German psychiatrists in Berlin in 1908. Bleuler, who was then 50, emerged as a brilliant, accurate clinical researcher. He based his findings on 647 cases treated at Burghölzli over a period of eight years. This is a classic paper in the best sense of the term. It contains a number of important statements. Bleuler observed, for example: "Acuteness (of illness) is apparently of great significance in determining the outcome. Of the cases whose onset was acute, 73 per cent were discharged as capable of outside employment, 11 per cent deteriorated severely, and the remaining 16 per cent represented cases between these two extremes. Of the cases whose onset was chronic, 30 per cent remained severely deteriorated, and only 50 per cent were able to work independently outside the mental hospital" (1908, p. 437). He noted that abnormal personalities "tend more to severe illness and less to mild illness than do normal or nervous cases" (1908, p. 439) and that "it is rare to find patients with . . . remission (of symptoms) deteriorating so severely as to require permanent institutionalization" (1908, p. 441). His statement, "The schizophrenic is not simply demented, but merely demented with respect to certain questions, at certain times, and in response to certain complexes" (1908, pp. 452–453), has not been outdated. And he was the first to note a fundamental problem that still concerns us: "Above all, we must endeavor to distinguish between the primary symptoms, which are part of the disease process, and the secondary symptoms, which develop only as a reaction of the afflicted psyche to the influences of its surroundings and to its own efforts" (1908, p. 454).

Of the numerous other papers by Bleuler, particular mention should be made of those based on psychoanalytical thinking and of his polemics against alcohol. Even today psychiatrists are willing to learn from Bleuler about the general problems of psychopathology and psychology, of schizophrenia and paranoia, and of reason and unreason in science and practice. Today as then, however, his writings on natural philosophy have less appeal. Bleuler, as a child of his time—very much like his contemporary Kraepelin—was too much impressed by a materialism that now seems naive. He was, however, sufficiently flexible to have been receptive to the existential analysis of his pupil Ludwig Binswanger, 1922–1957, and he certainly would have liked *Die Person des Schizophrenen* ("The Schizophrenic Personality"), a study by his pupil Jacob Wyrsch (1949). Indeed, in his clinical writings Bleuler had elaborated a psychopathology of the schizophrenic personality in existentialist terms. Long before World War I, before Karl Jaspers and the later epigoni of Heidegger, Bleuler sought to make the world of the schizophrenic more familiar and real. For Bleuler, the scientifically trained nosologist, human beings suffering from psychoses were, of course, sick, but they also represented instances of humanity whose existence under extraordinary conditions he explored, most often through psychoanalysis. He was fascinated by psychoanalysis and was among the first to grant it respectability in psychiatry.

These brief statements may cover Bleuler's major achievements. We gratefully remember, however, that it was Bleuler who added such pregnant concepts as autism, ambivalence, and *Verhältnisblödsinn* (a deficient sense of proportion) to our store of psychopathological terminology. These concepts are explained in Bleuler's *Textbook of Psychiatry* (1916). On autism he wrote: "Schizophrenics lose contact with reality, the mild cases inconspicuously in one respect or another, the severe ones completely" ([1916] 1951, p. 384). As for ambivalence, he commented that "schizophrenic splitting of function makes it possible for contradictions that are otherwise mutually exclusive to exist side by side within the psyche" ([1916] 1951, p. 382). And concerning *Verhältnisblödsinn*, he noted:

Without any sharp line of demarcation, schizophrenia shades into *Verhältnisblödsinn*. Here too, there is sometimes confusion of thought. The essential factor, however, is a disproportion between aim and ability.

Persons with *Verhältnisblödsinn* have sufficient intelligence for an ordinary position in life, sometimes even for one of somewhat more than average difficulty, but they are excessively active, always trying to do more than they can really handle, so that they make many mistakes and fail in life. ([1916] 1951, p. 617)

All these noteworthy scientific achievements should not obscure Bleuler's accomplishments as a practicing psychiatrist. Like his predecessor Auguste Forel, Bleuler cultivated the spirit of freedom in the institutionalization and treatment of patients that had been introduced into Germany from England by Ludwig Meyer. In contrast to his predecessors, who resigned their posts prematurely exhausted, Bleuler's personality enabled him to overcome all obstacles, and his work, both as researcher and physician, raised Burghölzli to the summit of its influence in the world of medicine. To many outstanding psychiatrists throughout the world Kraepelin and Bleuler were centers of attraction from whom psychiatry constantly received new stimulation. Bleuler, with Freud and Kraepelin, had a lasting influence on Henry Maudsley and Adolf Meyer, the English-speaking reformers of psychiatry.

A lively picture of an unusual personality emerges in the obituaries of Bleuler written by his students the Minkowski brothers, Robert Gaupp, and Ludwig Binswanger, and in the biography by Jacob Kläsi. The short, delicately built man with his expressive features was intellectually active to the last. The singleness of purpose and constancy of his character, governed by "practical reason," as Binswanger put it, never hindered him from displaying broad tolerance, though he was not without traces of fanaticism. Eugen Bleuler knew of only two tasks, to which he devoted himself with the entire strength of his unique personality: to be a rational psychiatrist and a genuine human being.

KURT KOLLE

[*For the historical context of Bleuler's work, see the biography of* KRAEPELIN. *For discussion of the subsequent development of his ideas, see* PSYCHIATRY; SCHIZOPHRENIA; PSYCHOANALYSIS; *and the biography of* MEYER.]

WORKS BY BLEULER

1908 Die Prognose der Dementia Praecox (Schizophreniegruppe). *Allgemeine Zeitschrift für Psychiatrie und Physisch–gerichtliche Medizin* 65:436–464. → Translation of extracts in text provided by the editors.

(1911) 1950 *Dementia Praecox: Or the Group of Schizophrenias.* New York: International Universities Press. → First published in German.

(1916) 1951 *Textbook of Psychiatry.* Authorized English edition by A. A. Brill, with a biographical sketch by Jacob Shatsky. New York: Dover. → First published as *Lehrbuch der Psychiatrie.*

(1919) 1921 *Das autistisch–undisziplinierte Denken in der Medizin und seine Überwindung.* 2d ed. Berlin: Springer.

SUPPLEMENTARY BIBLIOGRAPHY

BINSWANGER, LUDWIG (1922–1957) 1963 *Being-in-the-world: Selected Papers.* New York: Basic Books. → Translated from the German by Jacob Needleman. Contains a critical introduction to Binswanger's existential psychoanalysis.

BINSWANGER, LUDWIG 1940 Bleulers geistige Gestalt. *Schweizer Archiv für Neurologie und Psychiatrie* 46:24–29.

GAUPP, ROBERT 1940 Eugen Bleuler: Die Persönlichkeit und ihr Werk. *Zeitschrift für die gesamte Neurologie und Psychiatrie* 168:1–35.

KLÄSI, JACOB 1923 Beitrag zur Frage der Behandlung von Magenneurosen. *Zeitschrift für die gesamte Neurologie und Psychiatrie* 82:122–130.

MAIER, HANS W. 1923 Eugen Bleuler zur Feier seiner 25 jährigen Tätigkeit als Ordinarius der Psychiatrie und Direktor der Psychiatrischen Klinik in Zürich, April 1923. *Zeitschrift für die gesamte Neurologie und Psychiatrie* 82:1–9. → Contains a bibliography of Bleuler's works.

MINKOWSKI, E. 1939 Hommage à la mémoire du Professeur Bleuler. *Annales médico-psychologiques* 97:420–423.

WYRSCH, JACOB 1949 *Die Person des Schizophrenen: Studien zur Klinik, Psychologie, Daseinsweise.* Bern (Switzerland): Haupt.

BLINDNESS

Blindness and severe visual impairment occur everywhere in the world and at all social levels. They are least prevalent in the economically advanced nations and most prevalent in the emerging nations. But whatever their prevalence, these ancient scourges of mankind are enveloped in a mystique that often defies rational analysis and that promotes many social misconceptions to the detriment of both blind people and society. How any social group—from nuclear family to complex modern nation—treats its blind and severely visually impaired provides meaningful cues as to how it perceives the individual, impaired or not, in that social group. For this reason changes in the treatment of these severely limiting chronic conditions can be considered a sensitive barometer of social change at any level of society.

Estimates of prevalence. World-wide estimates of any chronic condition, including blindness, are notoriously unreliable because of differences of definitions and reporting procedures. There is some agreement throughout the world on what basically constitutes blindness: in the United States it is generally defined as a central visual acuity of 20/200 or less in the better eye (with correcting lenses); 6/60 acuity is the comparable standard used in Britain and by other members of the Commonwealth; and 3/60 has been recommended by some international groups. But beyond this basic agreement, there are endless variations of interpretations, additional conditions, and varying reporting procedures that make comparable statistics from one administrative unit to another unobtainable. Still, some estimates must be made because of the severity of blindness as a limiting chronic condition and the consequent need for medical and social services. The World Health Organization (WHO) estimated that in 1962 there were ten million blind persons in the world, or a rate of 3.2 per thousand, and in 1965 the estimate was fourteen million (Wilson 1965).

As to reporting procedures, the United Kingdom has a central registry in the Ministry of Health that is maintained by local health districts and consolidated at the national level; thus its estimate of 2.07 per thousand is considered fairly reliable. Canada has a reporting procedure similar to the United Kingdom's. The U.S.S.R. and Sweden report through local chapters of a national society for the blind that is supported by the government but that remains private; these estimates are probably less reliable than those of the United Kingdom but are still very useful. In the United States the usual bureaucratic maze exists, with 8 states having mandatory reporting, about 40 having central registers of the blind, and only 13 reporting through uniform procedures to the National Institute of Neurological Diseases and Blindness (according to an unpublished survey conducted by the American Foundation for the Blind). In addition, the United States Public Health Service periodically conducts nationwide household interview surveys on health conditions and impairments, including severe visual impairment (generally defining blindness as the inability to read newsprint with glasses); this agency estimates the national prevalence of severe visual impairments to be 1.98 per thousand, based on data from the household interview sample for July 1959 through June 1961 (U.S. Public Health Service 1962). In the emerging countries regular reporting procedures are rare and tend to be unreliable. They resort to occasional sample surveys, such as those undertaken in the 1960s in India and some of the countries of the Arabian Peninsula (Wilson 1965). A notable example of a thorough clinical screening is one that was under way in Egypt in 1965 (Around the World 1965).

Two factors are major influences on trends of blindness in the world today: increasing survival rates of the aged and of children. In the industrialized countries like the United Kingdom and the United States, two-thirds of the blind and severely visually impaired are estimated to be over 65. In underdeveloped countries survival rates of the aged are far below those reported for industrialized countries, and hence the prevalence of types of blindness associated with aging is also lower. Survival rates among children have made spectacular advances in all countries, particularly the emerging nations like India. One estimate for Africa and the Middle East has been that one per cent of all children there will be blind during childhood (Wilson 1965); the comparable estimate for children under five in the United States is .01 per cent (U.S. National Institutes . . . 1965).

Blindness as a social problem. While the numbers of blind and severely visually impaired persons are relatively small, the social implications of their existence are enormous, because they have always imposed peculiar strains on the social structure of the society of which they are a part. The blind person in every culture is a man set apart, who by reason of his impairment cannot move about, work, or read as can the majority of his sighted peers. Thus the expectations of his sighted peers set limits on his activities. If, as in some primitive societies, his impairment is considered a special mark of attention from the deity, he is favored. However, in most societies he is seen primarily as a public health problem. In the more economically advanced nations where society is work-oriented and where the major emphasis is on the employability of all citizens, including the sensory impaired, the blind person is an economic and a psychosocial problem.

While the emphasis may differ from society to society, several social correlates of visual impairment exist universally in greater or lesser degree: the religious–mystic element that attributes guilt or favor to impairment, the medical or public health problem, and the psychosocial aspects. To ignore any of these correlates in analyzing the impact of blindness on a culture would result in oversimplification of the problems that blindness and severe visual impairment introduce in society and in an impaired person.

In the United States the complex social problem of caring for the visually handicapped is generally placed in the context of two cultural themes: the work orientation that requires each person to be a contributing, functioning member; and Judaeo-Christian concepts of individual worth and dignity. The ideal, then, in the United States is that the blind or severely visually impaired person be encouraged and helped to become a contributing member of society within the limitations imposed upon him by his sensory loss and that this be done in such a way as to insure his sense of personal worth and his individual dignity. However, the fulfillment of this ideal becomes complicated by the rigorous demands made by a highly mobile and competitive society on its visually impaired members. Thus, in such a society several important program aspects become necessary: personal reorientation and adjustment of the newly blind; vocational training and placement services for both the born blind and the newly blind; instrumentation to aid the blind of all ages to get around and to read with a minimum of help from another person; and, finally, provisions for meeting the financial needs of blind persons who are not able to support themselves. In the United States so-called "work for the blind" programs and research and development programs are concerned with providing comprehensive services to meet these needs.

Most European nations have instituted some prevocational or adjustment training centers as well as vocational training centers. In Finland a very thorough medical and psychosocial examination lasting one week is made before adjustment and/or vocational programs are prescribed (Graham & Clark 1964). Although few European nations have services as thorough as those of Finland, most do provide at least medical care and vocational training for newly blind persons. In Poland a special training course on mobility is given using the "long cane," which was first employed in training American war-blinded veterans. In the U.S.S.R. special training courses are given the foremen of state industrial concerns where large numbers of blind workers are employed. As compared with programs in the United States and Europe, those in the emerging countries are far more general and traditional; schools for blind children and homes for the aged are ordinarily the only existing services. Of course, there are a few exceptions: for example, Israel provides courses in modern technology, and in Japan the blind are traditionally taught to be masseurs and musicians.

In general, programs for the blind and severely visually impaired throughout the world are limited by two major factors: the ideological and economic emphasis of each country and the extent of its resources. For example, in work-oriented countries like the United States and the U.S.S.R., considerable effort is expended to make the blind person a contributing member of society through employment. In the U.S.S.R. experimental vocational programs are instituted in the R.S.F.S.R. Academy of Sciences, and those that are validated become required courses throughout the Soviet Union. In contrast, American vocational programs at the secondary school level, like American education in general, are not centrally controlled and differ a great deal with the locale (Graham & Clark 1964). In Europe several countries have laws requiring the employment of handicapped persons, a model of which is the British Disabled Persons (Employment) Act of 1944. However, in general, except for the British law, such statutes are not rigorously enforced; and employment is less emphasized than programs to meet the financial needs of the blind, especially in the more welfare-minded countries. In less affluent countries the daily needs of the adult blind are less often met; but in all countries, rich and poor, considerable effort is made to educate the young blind population.

Demographic data for the United States. In 1963 the number of legally blind persons in the United States (those having clinically verified central visual acuity of 20/200 in the better eye or a peripheral field of 20 degrees or less) was estimated at about 400,000, or a prevalence of about 2 per thousand. About 10 per cent of these were estimated to be totally blind; the rest have some useful vision. Well over half of the legally blind are 65 years of age or older, and, following national population trends, there are more aged women than men; 7 per cent of the legally blind are under 20 years of age. Compared to national norms, the legally blind have less education and are in the lower income brackets. The principal causes of blindness among the group are cataracts, glaucoma, and diabetes, which account for 40 per cent of all blindness and none of which are infectious (Schloss 1963, pp. 111–116; Hurlin 1962, pp. 2–10). Congenital blindness among children is often associated with prematurity.

A more liberal set of criteria for defining blindness is applied to those who function as blind people, particularly as far as being able to read is concerned. By these criteria almost one million Americans, or 5.6 per thousand of the U.S. population, are considered to be blind or severely visually impaired (U.S. Public Health Service 1962). Two-thirds of the "functionally blind" are over 65, with a somewhat greater number of females than males; about 15 per cent are under 24. They are probably nearer the national norms on education and income than the smaller legally blind group.

Cataracts are reported by almost half of the aged as the cause of their visual impairment.

The legally blind are likely to be known to agencies serving the blind and to research projects, since they have become known to some reporting agency as being within the eligibility requirements for services for the blind. However, among the larger group of the functionally blind there are a large number of "hidden" blind who have not sought services from agencies for the blind. This hidden group (according to preliminary research results) is composed of several categories of blind people: those who are affluent enough to care for themselves, those who are ignorant of available services, isolates ("rocking-chair cases") who desire no care, and a much larger group of persons who are able to function as sighted people in many tasks and activities (Josephson 1963).

Service and research programs. These demographic data, inexact as they are, influence services and research. It is clear that the low prevalence of blindness and its being a function of general population characteristics mean that blind people are widely scattered in relatively small numbers throughout the country, with urban centers having the largest and most readily accessible populations. Consequently, the urban blind are most likely to have services provided for them and to participate in research projects. However, research shows that the rural blind function relatively effectively in their home communities as long as they have resided there over a long period of time and do not have to leave familiar territory often (McPhee & Magleby 1963).

If current population trends persist, the numbers of severely impaired persons aged 20 or less and aged 65 and over will increase by about 40 per cent over the next 10 to 15 years. This suggests that the proper educational training of young blind people is a particularly acute problem and that prevention and early detection campaigns for both the young and the aged will have to be stepped up.

Research also shows that more effective techniques are needed for diagnosing the pseudo-retardation of the blind child who is understimulated both at home and at school; unless we develop more successful techniques for finding these cases, increasing numbers of such children (many of whom are premature at birth) will be mistakenly assigned to institutional care of a custodial nature only. The evidence strongly suggests that when blind children are properly stimulated through their remaining senses and put in an atmosphere favorable to learning they develop in much the same way as their sighted peers (Hallenbeck 1954, pp. 301–307; Imamura 1965; Norris et al. 1957; Parmelee et al. 1962). There is an obvious need for new instructional materials in keeping with advances for teaching sighted children. Furthermore, severely visually impaired children need to be given systematic travel or mobility training before they reach maturity, rather than receive it later in adult rehabilitation training centers, as so often happens now (American Foundation for the Blind 1960).

For the adult blind, research on new vocational opportunities is needed. In the United States economy, which sustains a steady unemployment level of about 5 per cent of the working force, the non-professional blind worker is very likely to be a marginal worker. Moreover, it would appear that in the future more opportunities in highly professional jobs and fewer in industrial and semiskilled jobs will be available in competitive employment. In the United States, where there are approximately seventy workshops employing the visually impaired, the trend is toward more "terminal" employment in workshops and less training for competitive employment; this change of emphasis is implicit in the 1965 amendments to the Vocational Rehabilitation Act (U.S. National Institutes . . . 1965). According to National Industries for the Blind, in the period 1964–1966 less than one thousand workers each year have passed from workshop employment to competitive employment in the United States. To increase the effectiveness of the adult blind person, technological research will have to be expanded so as to offer instrumentation that will permit the blind man to travel better, to undertake increasingly more complex jobs, and to have direct access to the printed word. Present research and development projects in the United States, the United Kingdom, and the Soviet Union offer some promise even at present levels of financial support (International Congress . . . 1963).

Older blind persons, ever increasing in numbers, need assistance with three major problems: maintaining a reasonable income, acquiring more meaningful patterns of daily existence, and maintaining reasonably good health. Welfare programs based on means tests too often compromise individual dignity; an insurance program against sensory deprivation, much like the American social security system, should be considered. To help the aged blind in adjusting to new patterns of living, individual counseling is needed. The problems of health are largely geriatric and well known, except for the problem of the blind person's emotional resistance to medical advances, such as cataract surgery, and to low-vision aids; this resistance needs to be broken down among older people who stand to benefit from such programs (Miller 1964).

Through all of these unsolved problems of the severely visually impaired runs the thread of public attitudes that commonly support the exclusion of blind people from jobs and schools and thereby adversely affect their acceptance as functioning members of society. Most societies still consider their blind populations as health and welfare problems only. Recent research by Lukoff and Whiteman (e.g., 1963) has found that attitudes toward blindness are multidimensional and generally susceptible to modification through exposure to blind persons and better knowledge of them. With a focus contrary to that of conventional theory of attitude formation and change, Cutsforth (1933) and others in the last thirty years have stressed the vital importance of a healthy self-image on the part of the blind person if stereotypes are to be overcome. Following this tradition, Lukoff and Whiteman found that in large part the formation of public attitudes depends on three factors that are involved in the blind person's adjustment to his blindness: his self-image; his status set, that is, "the way a person orients himself toward the several positions he occupies that also identify him to other persons"; and his role set, which is "arranged along a continuum of independence–dependence."

New opportunities for the blind. In general, the most advanced research on blindness has been done in the United States, with the exception of certain experimental programs for vocational training conducted by the U.S.S.R. However, even in the United States a great deal more needs to be done to eliminate the age-old subcultures of "the blind," who are in effect a minority of the severely visually impaired population. It is apparent from the discriminatory practices, such as labeling "the blind" with arm brassards in some Scandinavian and western European countries or tolerating them as fakirs and beggars in the Far East, that generally enlightened national health and welfare plans are not sufficient, at least by American standards, to insure the full participation of blind and severely impaired people in the society in which they live.

There is some hope that research and the further development of services will improve the lot of blind people throughout the world. Among the emerging nations the emphasis for some time will undoubtedly be medical: the prevention of blinding eye diseases, such as trachoma, by public health measures and the early detection and treatment of such conditions as glaucoma. Among the more developed nations, both psychosocial and technological research offer promise. It is generally conceded now by both ophthalmologists and educational specialists that residual vision should be used to its fullest capacity, not "saved." In the United States today there are about thirty "near-vision" clinics, partially supported by federal government grants; and double this number are planned if, on evaluation, the near-vision clinic proves an effective means of introducing visual aids and training severely visually impaired persons to use them. This encouragement to use residual vision opens up new experimental opportunities for many people: more can be taught to read, and more can be taught to get around unaided.

The experience with the war-blind in many countries, particularly the United States and the U.S.S.R., has led to many achievements hitherto not considered possible for the blind and severely visually impaired. In the U.S.S.R. the widespread employment of the war-blind as skilled workers, even though they receive pensions, has helped negate the argument that pensions destroy initiative (see Zimin 1962). Almost half of all American war-blind are employed (or twice the percentage of civilian blind), although they receive generous compensation for their losses and injuries; their average household income is well above the national average. In general, the American blinded veterans (average age 46) show very few differences from their sighted peers: largely they own their own homes, are heads of their households, are in middle-to-high socioeconomic brackets, are well educated, read heavily, are active in civic affairs, are generally healthy in spite of their impairments, and enjoy themselves in cultural and recreational activities like their neighbors. The extensive training, equipment, and economic flooring given them has paid off in terms of realizing their potentialities as human beings and as contributing members of society (Graham 1965).

The other group in the United States that has contributed to the successful challenging of the traditional stereotype of blindness (that is, characterized by hopelessness, indigence, and disease) has been the group of premature children blinded or visually impaired by oxygen poisoning in incubators, resulting in retrolental fibroplasia (RLF). The RLF children, numbering perhaps eight thousand to ten thousand since the mid-1940s, are proving conclusively that, given the proper equipment and training, as well as favorable attitudes toward their endeavors by educators, parents, and

peers, they can compete successfully in their academic work and personal lives (Norris et al. 1957). Indeed, each year sees more RLF and other blind children enrolled in the public day schools, and schools for the blind are paying far more attention to multiply handicapped blind children, who hitherto have been too often committed to institutions for custodial care. In the last few years the United States and the U.S.S.R. have begun a concerted effort to aid blind children to travel and to acquire access to the printed word. Indeed, increasingly the emphasis is on the realization of the potentialities and abilities of blind and severely visually impaired people, particularly children, rather than on their limitations and problems.

There is some hope that through research it will be possible to find ways to eliminate the main social causes of discrimination against blind people, whether or not medical advances to cut their numbers are realized. That effort must be multidisciplinary and long-range in nature if it is to succeed (Graham 1960; National Committee . . . 1964). From the present modest beginnings, more research on visual impairment can be expected if research funds continue at present levels. In time the emerging countries can expect to benefit from this research and experience, which has been so notable in the past few years.

MILTON D. GRAHAM

[*See also* HEALTH; ILLNESS; MEDICAL CARE; PLANNING, SOCIAL, *article on* WELFARE PLANNING; VISION, *article on* VISUAL DEFECTS; VOCATIONAL REHABILITATION.]

BIBLIOGRAPHY

Amendments to Vocational Rehabilitation Act. 1965 *Rehabilitation Record* 6, no. 6:5–15.

AMERICAN ASSOCIATION OF WORKERS FOR THE BLIND *Blindness.* → Published annually since 1964.

AMERICAN FOUNDATION FOR THE BLIND 1960 *Services for Blind Persons in the United States.* New York: The Foundation.

AMERICAN FOUNDATION FOR THE BLIND 1961 *Report of Proceedings of Conference on Research Needs in Braille, September 13–15, 1961.* New York: The Foundation.

AMERICAN FOUNDATION FOR THE BLIND 1962 *Proceedings of the Mobility Research Conference.* Edited by James W. Linsner. New York: The Foundation.

Around the World. 1965 *Sight-saving Review* 35, no. 2: 112–114.

ASHCROFT, SAMUEL C.; and HENDERSON, FREDA 1963 *Programmed Instruction in Braille.* Pittsburgh: Stanwix House.

BARNETT, M. ROBERT 1960 Science Still Seeking True Electronic Substitute for Sight. *UNESCO Courier* 13, no. 6:7–9.

CUTSFORTH, THOMAS D. 1933 *The Blind in School and Society.* New York: Appleton.

GRAHAM, MILTON D. 1960 *Social Research on Blindness.* New York: American Foundation for the Blind.

GRAHAM, MILTON D. 1965 Wanted: A Readiness Test for Mobility Training. Pages 133–161 in American Foundation for the Blind, *Proceedings of the Rotterdam Mobility Research Conference.* New York: The Foundation.

GRAHAM, MILTON D.; and CLARK, LESLIE L. (editors) 1964 *Recent European Research on Blindness and Severe Visual Impairment.* New York: American Foundation for the Blind. → See especially pages 3–29.

HALLENBECK, JANE 1954 Pseudo-retardation in Retrolental Fibroplasia. *New Outlook for the Blind* 48:301–307.

HURLIN, RALPH G. 1962 Estimated Prevalence of Blindness in the United States and in Individual States, 1960. *Sight-saving Review* 32:4–12.

IMAMURA, SADAKO 1965 *Mother and Blind Child.* Research Series No. 14. New York: American Foundation for the Blind.

INTERNATIONAL CONGRESS ON TECHNOLOGY AND BLINDNESS 1963 *Proceedings.* Edited by Leslie L. Clark. New York: American Foundation for the Blind.

JOSEPHSON, ERIC 1963 An Epidemiological Survey of Visual Impairment. Unpublished manuscript, American Foundation for the Blind.

LAIRY, GABRIELLE C.; and NETCHINE, S. 1962 The Electroencephalogram in Partially Sighted Children Related to Clinical and Psychological Data. American Foundation for the Blind, *Research Bulletin* 2:38–56.

LUKOFF, IRVING F.; and WHITEMAN, MARTIN 1963 Attitudes and Blindness: Components, Correlates and Effects. Unpublished manuscript, Univ. of Pittsburgh.

McPHEE, WILLIAM M.; and MAGLEBY, F. LeGRAND 1963 *Activities and Problems of the Rural Blind in Utah.* Salt Lake City: Univ. of Utah.

MILLER, IRVING 1964 *Resistance to Cataract Surgery.* New York: American Foundation for the Blind.

NATIONAL COMMITTEE FOR RESEARCH ON OPHTHALMOLOGY AND BLINDNESS 1964 *Symposium on Research in Blindness and Severe Visual Impairment: Proceedings.* New York: American Foundation for the Blind.

New Pathways for the Blind. 1960 *UNESCO Courier* 13, no. 6. → The whole issue is devoted to the topic.

NORRIS, MIRIAM; SPAULDING, PATRICIA J.; and BRODIE, FERN H. 1957 *Blindness in Children.* Univ. of Chicago Press.

PARMELEE, ARTHUR H. JR.; FISKE, CLAUDE E.; and WRIGHT, ROGERS H. 1962 The Development of Ten Children With Blindness as a Result of Retrolental Fibroplasia. American Foundation for the Blind, *Research Bulletin* 1:64–88.

SCHLOSS, IRVIN P. 1963 Implications of Altering the Definition of Blindness. American Foundation for the Blind, *Research Bulletin* 3:111–116.

U.S. NATIONAL INSTITUTES OF HEALTH 1965 *1963 Statistical Report: Annual Tabulations of Model Reporting Area for Blindness Statistics.* Public Health Service Publication No. 1312. Washington: Government Printing Office.

U.S. PUBLIC HEALTH SERVICE 1962 *Selected Impairments by Etiology and Activity Limitation: United States, July 1959–June 1961.* Health Statistics from U.S. National Health Survey, Series B-35. Washington: Government Printing Office.

WILSON, JOHN 1965 The Blind in a Changing World. American Association of Workers for the Blind, *Blindness* [1965]:87–92.

World Blindness Rate. 1965 National Society for the Prevention of Blindness, *Prevention of Blindness News* [1965] Winter: 6 only.

ZIMIN, BORIS 1962 Employment and Vocational Training of the Blind in the USSR. *New Outlook for the Blind* 56:363–366.

BLOCH, MARC

Marc Bloch, French medieval and economic historian, was born at Lyons, July 6, 1886, the son of Gustave and Sara Ebstein Bloch. It was near Lyons, at Trévoux, that he and some of his companions in the Resistance were killed by the Gestapo only a few days before the German defeat.

Bloch's father came from an Alsatian family that was deeply attached to France; he was a student at the École Normale Supérieure and the French schools of Athens and Rome and was a professor in the faculty of letters at Lyons at the time of his son's birth. In the following year he was appointed *maître de conférences* at the École Normale and then professor of Roman history at the Sorbonne in 1904. He was the author of many articles and books, the best known being *La république romaine*, 1913, and *L'empire romain*, 1922. One of the most brilliant historians of his time, he was the first and most effective of his son's teachers.

Marc Bloch grew up in Paris in a highly intellectual, highly cultivated milieu. His older brother, a prominent physician and a talented musician, who died prematurely after World War I, had an undoubted influence on him. I have it from Lucien Febvre that it was from this older brother that Marc Bloch got the idea that he later developed in his book *Les rois thaumaturges* (1924). Still more important was the influence of his wife, Simone Vidal, whom he married in 1919. She relieved him of all the material and domestic cares for which, according to friends, Bloch was not very well fitted, and, acting as his secretary and assistant, enabled him to devote himself entirely to his intellectual tasks.

Bloch received his secondary education at the Lycée Louis-le-Grand in Paris, where he was an outstanding student. He entered the École Normale in 1904, leaving it as agrégé in history and geography in 1908. He took courses not only at the École Normale itself but also at the Sorbonne, the École des Hautes Études and the Collège de France, namely the courses of Christian Pfister, Gabriel Monod, Lucien Gallois, Gustave Lanson, Antoine Meillet, Charles V. Langlois, Charles Seignobos, and Alfred Croiset. At the École Normale, he was the friend of the mathematician Paul Lévy, of the future diplomat Louis Massigli, of the philosopher and grammarian Paul Etard, and of the sociologist Georges Davy, who later became dean of the faculty of letters and human sciences at Paris. Davy was at that time the closest of his comrades [see DAVY]. Without doubt, Bloch's years of apprenticeship were unusually rewarding, both in the fields of classical culture and of history proper. From 1909 to 1912 he held a scholarship from the Fondation Thiers in Paris and was free to begin his first researches; the papers he wrote at that time, which have come down to us, are among his best.

It was during these student years that Bloch came into contact with Henri Berr and the *Revue de synthèse historique;* both appealed to him very strongly. Also, he spent quite a long time at the University of Berlin, where he attended the remarkable lectures of Wilamowitz-Moellendorff and enjoyed their theatrical qualities as well as their content.

Following the usual career pattern of the French university system, Marc Bloch's initial appointments were as professor at the *lycée* of Montpellier in 1912 and at the *lycée* of Amiens in 1913. But his career did not really begin until after World War I. In 1919 he was appointed *chargé de cours* of medieval history in the faculty of letters at Strasbourg and professor in 1921. He remained there until his appointment in 1936 as *maître de conférences* of economic history at the Sorbonne. He was made titular professor in 1937. In 1940, forced to give up his post in Paris because of the German anti-Semitic measures, he became professor at Clermont-Ferrand (where the University of Strasbourg had withdrawn) and at Montpellier in 1941–1942. Finally, suspended from his position by the Vichy government, he declined the chance to go abroad that was officially offered him and went underground into the Resistance.

Bloch was already a master of his specialty, medieval history (even technically he was the foremost medievalist of the time) when he was turned toward general history and the economic and social sciences as a result of meeting Lucien Febvre (1878–1956), his senior colleague at Strasbourg. The great turning point of his intellectual life came in 1929, when he and Febvre founded the *Annales d'histoire économique et sociale,* which in the next ten years completely transformed French historiography. In this common achievement it is hard to distinguish the particular share of each; individually, neither Bloch nor Febvre was the greatest French historian of the time, but together

both of them were. Their joint battle had a pattern: if history was to be revitalized, it would have to relate to itself and, as it were, conquer the other sciences of man: geography, political economy, demography, political science, sociology, ethnography, anthropology, social psychology, and so forth. Bloch and Febvre received decisive help from geographers like André Siegfried and Albert Demangeon, from economists like François Simiand, from sociologists like Maurice Halbwachs, and from historians like Georges Lefebvre, André Piganiol, and Ch. E. Perrin [see HALBWACHS; SIEGFRIED; SIMIAND.]

Bloch's kind of history, like Febvre's, had its roots in the *Revue de synthèse* of Henri Berr, who was the first to maintain that history is the sum total of all the specialized histories, those of the political sector, of the economic sector, and so on. The *Annales,* too, sought to regroup these traditional areas of historical work and to draw on the related human sciences, making them, in effect, auxiliary sciences to history. That, at least, is how the present author construes the conception of history of the *Annales* (and perhaps somewhat distorts it). Bloch was inclined to be less aggressive and more prudent (as well as more practical and less romantic) than Febvre; thus, Bloch spoke of collaborating with "the observers of the present" and patiently became an economist, a sociologist, and a psychologist, as Huizinga did also [see HUIZINGA]. But his goal for history was clear: "History is not the accumulation of the events of all kinds that have taken place in the past. It is the science of human societies." These two statements, with which Fustel de Coulanges once concluded a lecture, constitute not a method but a program—an open declaration.

From 1929 to 1938, the *Annales d'histoire économique et sociale* were the focus of all of Bloch's intellectual activity and passion. The best of his thought went into the many articles he contributed. It is impossible to decide what is most important in this "volume" of over a thousand pages; everything in it is worth reading and rereading. Bloch's best-known articles are undoubtedly "Le problème de l'or au moyen âge" (1933) and "Avènement et conquête du moulin à eau" (1935). Even though the conclusions of the latter article have been called into question by subsequent research, to this day any discussion of the subject must refer to Bloch's views and closely reasoned arguments.

Bloch's relatively limited articles are especially revealing of his approach to history, more so even than his books. They permit one to surmise, as it were, what he might have said and written had he not died prematurely. Two characteristic terms emerge in these articles: *synthesis* (the term he borrowed from Henri Berr) and *comparative history* (a phrase more peculiarly his own and better suited to his intellectual temper). Indeed, Bloch always tried to avoid language that was unnecessarily antagonizing. For example, instead of saying *agrarian system* he used the term *agrarian regime*. (Bloch's disciples and those of Lucien Febvre like to refer to *global history*, but that lofty term does not add anything to the more modest *comparative history*.)

To understand Bloch's approach it is particularly important to note what he said in his paper "Les transformations des techniques comme problème de psychologie collective": "An historian cannot afford to ignore the teachings of the psychologists. But the opposite is equally true. The early Middle Ages, for example, with their proliferation of forged documents, are an instance of collective mythomania that no psychologist dealing with truthfulness or lying has, I believe, the right to neglect" ([1948] 1963, p. 792). Comparative history is the bringing together of history and contiguous disciplines, the exchanging of services between them, and their convergence on selected problems, whether these be problems in toponymy or geography, in sociology or psychology, or in political economy. Bloch explained his approach at the Institut Français de Sociologie in 1932, in connection with the "problem of agrarian regimes," and even better in 1939, in connection with the problem of the settlement of the Beauce: "We are working here under the banner of synthesis . . . in the convergent interplay of disciplines . . ." (p. 638).

Bloch's innumerable articles and reviews are, therefore, an invaluable supplement to his few, classic books, but these of course are the essential part of his work. *Les rois thaumaturges*, a study that is at once history, sociology, and social psychology, since it deals with the supernatural powers attributed to the kings of France to heal scrofula by the king's touch, is a highly original work, admirably executed. The greatest of Bloch's books is no doubt his analysis of *Les caractères originaux de l'histoire rurale française* (1931), based on the examination of the patterns of fields and the interpretation of rural landscapes. A whole series of studies by geographers and historians of the European peasantry have followed in the wake of Bloch's *Caractères originaux*. The last volume that Marc Bloch himself published, *Feudal Society* (1939–1940), refocuses and integrates many hundreds of earlier studies in the perspective of a new conception of history; it is a book that seeks to distinguish common patterns, diversities, and the general direction of development in European society of the Middle Ages. Two books found among his papers were published posthumously by his friends: *Strange Defeat* (1946) and *The Historian's Craft* (1949). The former is a strong and bitter polemic on the French defeat, made all the more bitter by Bloch's feeling that he shared responsibility for the catastrophe of 1940; the second was written rapidly during his enforced leisure and should be regarded as the first draft of a larger work he hoped to write.

Marc Bloch is undoubtedly one of the most widely read French historians, both in France and abroad. His work has been widely translated and diffused and, except on details, has not been challenged. There are many reasons for this: the breadth of his knowledge, his prudence in statement, the aversion he always felt for grandiose explanations. (Although he was a friend and admirer of Henri Pirenne, he was not inclined to formulate such brilliant but debatable theories as that concerning the opening and closing of the Mediterranean to the Latin Occident.) His curiosity was matched by his love of careful scholarship. His students Robert Boutruche, Michel Mollat, Pierre Goubert, Paul Leuillot, and Henri Brunschwig show the same prudence, or the same wisdom.

His political position was in a sense similar to his intellectual one. He hesitated to make any extreme commitment. The war had already begun when he wrote to Lucien Febvre on September 17, 1939: "Like you, I should abhor a propaganda task. Historians must keep their hands clean" (*Hommages . . .* 1945, p. 16). And yet he felt deeply the defeat, "the strange defeat," of France. After miraculously escaping execution as a prisoner in 1940, he was at Dunkirk, got to England, returned to Brittany, and then resumed his life as a professor. After 1940 the Vichy government treated him with respect, as they had treated Bergson. They suspended him but offered to let him leave the country: Marc Bloch could have gone to an American university or to the Algiers faculty, which invited him. He preferred to stay where he was. "The French people is our people and we have no other," he wrote. In the Resistance he played an exemplary role. On March 8, 1944, he was arrested by the Gestapo. After being mistreated and tortured, he and his fellow prisoners were shot several months later.

FERNAND BRAUDEL

[See also HISTORIOGRAPHY; HISTORY. Other relevant material may be found in the biographies of FEBVRE; HUIZINGA; VIDAL DE LA BLACHE.]

WORKS BY BLOCH

(1911–1948) 1963 Mélanges historiques. 2 vols. Paris: Service d'Édition et de Vente des Publications de l'Éducation Nationale. → A bibliography appears in Volume 2, pages 1031–1104.
(1924) 1961 Les rois thaumaturges: Étude sur le caractère surnaturel attribué à la puissance royale particulièrement en France et en Angleterre. Paris: Colin.
(1931) 1952–1956 Les caractères originaux de l'histoire rurale française. New ed., 2 vols. Paris: Colin. → Volume 2, Supplément établi d'après les travaux de l'auteur: (1931–1944), was written by Robert Dauvergne.
(1932) 1963 Le problème des régimes agraires. Volume 2, pages 648–669 in Marc Bloch, Mélanges historiques. Paris: Service d'Édition et de Vente des Publications de l'Éducation Nationale.
(1933) 1963 Le problème de l'or au moyen âge. Volume 2, pages 839–867 in Marc Bloch, Mélanges historiques. Paris: Service d'Édition et de Vente des Publications de l'Éducation Nationale.
(1935) 1963 Avènement et conquête du moulin à eau. Volume 2, pages 800–821 in Marc Bloch, Mélanges historiques. Paris: Service d'Édition et de Vente des Publications de l'Éducation Nationale.
(1939) 1963 Les problèmes du peuplement beauceron. Volume 2, pages 638–647 in Marc Bloch, Mélanges historiques. Paris: Service d'Édition et de Vente des Publications de l'Éducation Nationale.
(1939–1940) 1961 Feudal Society. Univ. of Chicago Press. → First published as La société féodale: La formation des liens de dépendance and La société féodale: Les classes et le gouvernement des hommes.
(1946) 1949 Strange Defeat: A Statement of Evidence Written in 1940. London and New York: Oxford Univ. Press. → First published as L'étrange défaite.
(1948) 1963 Les transformations des techniques comme problème de psychologie collective. Volume 2, pages 791–799 in Marc Bloch, Mélanges historiques. Paris: Service d'Édition et de Vente des Publications de l'Éducation Nationale.
(1949) 1964 The Historian's Craft. New York: Knopf. → First published as L'apologie pour l'histoire, ou métier d'historien.
1954 Esquisse d'une histoire monétaire de l'Europe. Paris: Colin.
1958 La France sous les derniers Capétiens: 1223–1328. Paris: Colin.
1960 Seigneurie française et manoir anglais. Paris: Colin.

SUPPLEMENTARY BIBLIOGRAPHY

BOUTRUCHE, ROBERT 1947 Marc Bloch vu par ses élèves. Pages 195–207 in Strasbourg, Université de, Faculté des lettres, Mémorial des années 1939–1945. Publication No. 103. Paris: Belles Lettres.
FEBVRE, LUCIEN 1964 Marc Bloch et Strasbourg: Souvenirs d'une grande histoire. Pages 171–193 in Strasbourg, Université de, Faculté des lettres, Mémorial des années 1939–1945. Publication No. 103. Paris: Belles Lettres.
Hommages à Marc Bloch. Annales d'histoire sociale, Nos. 7–8. 1945 Paris: Colin.

PERRIN, CHARLES E. 1948 L'oeuvre historique de Marc Bloch. Revue historique 199:161–188.
RAFTIS, J. AMBROSE 1962 Marc Bloch's Comparative Method and the Rural History of Mediaeval England. Mediaeval Studies 24:349–365.

BLOOMFIELD, LEONARD

Leonard Bloomfield was born in Chicago in 1887 and died in New Haven, Connecticut, in 1949. He came to linguistics when it was the dilettante preoccupation of a few "crow-baited students of literature"; he left it a branch of science.

Bloomfield was the son of Sigmund and Carola Buber Bloomfield and the nephew of the Indologist Maurice Bloomfield. In 1896 his family moved to Elkhart Lake, Wisconsin; the winters of 1898–1899 and 1900–1901 were spent in Europe. He did not do well in the village school but was tutored by his mother and gained admittance to the North Division School in Chicago, graduating in 1903 and going on to Harvard College. By his own account, his most important Harvard experience was the discipline of writing daily themes for the merciless scrutiny of Charles Townsend Copeland. His writings support this judgment: his prose is simply constructed and, despite technical subject matter, largely consists of everyday vocabulary.

In 1906 Bloomfield received the A.B. and went to the University of Wisconsin as a graduate assistant in German. The teaching of German was to be a prominent part of his duties for more than two decades; in 1923 he published an excellent elementary text. He was unsure whether to concentrate on literature or linguistics, but the influence of the Germanic philologist Eduard Prokosch, at that time an instructor in the Wisconsin department of German, was quickly decisive.

In 1908 Bloomfield transferred to the University of Chicago, to complete his work for the PH.D. under Francis A. Wood. In March 1909 he married Alice Sayers of St. Louis. They adopted two children.

Bloomfield's first position after receiving his PH.D. in June 1909 was as instructor in German at the University of Cincinnati; after one year he moved to the University of Illinois at the same rank. In 1913, doubtless in part because of his completion of An Introduction to the Study of Language (1914), he was promoted to assistant professor of comparative philology and German and was granted a year's leave of absence, which he spent at Leipzig and Göttingen with such scholars as August Leskien and Karl Brugmann. His respect for these scholars, as for Prokosch, was abiding. Once, thirty years later, he said to me that we had learned nothing important about language not already known to Leskien.

Superbly equipped for Germanic and Indo-European philology, Bloomfield continued to teach those subjects but turned his research largely in other directions. We may suspect two reasons: first, his belief that the major problems of those fields had been solved; second, his recognition that generalizations based only on Indo-European fall short of the inductive inferences we must seek about all language. The temper of the times may have helped in a left-handed way: German was unpopular during World War I, and Bloomfield perhaps had fewer and smaller classes. At any rate, finding on the Illinois campus a Filipino student, Alfredo V. Santiago, he enlisted his help in work on Tagalog. Existing reference materials on the language were unreliable. Bloomfield took down, from dictation, an extensive series of texts, which he then subjected to detailed analysis. The results were published in 1917.

In order to write down the words Santiago spoke, Bloomfield had to devise a way to spell them. Earlier treatments of the language were of no help: they failed to indicate differences of pronunciation that were distinctive in Santiago's speech. The slow development of a valid notation was Bloomfield's painful introduction to the phonemic principle, of which he was one of a small number of partly independent discoverers.

In his treatment of grammar, also, the Tagalog report was a sharp departure from tradition. The prevailing habit of Western scholarship facing a "peculiar" language had been to assume that it must be like Latin and that the obvious differences were only superficial. Subtle but important differences were therefore typically overlooked: a grammar of a "peculiar" language was cast in the format of a Latin grammar, and the odd ways of the language were noted as discrepancies. Bloomfield would have none of this. His collating of Tagalog text materials sought to reveal and record the patterns of *that* language, whether they were like or unlike those of any other. This has become the standard approach; it is hard for us to understand the disapproval some linguists expressed at the time. The issue is not whether a valid "universal grammar" exists, relative to which we can characterize each individual language, but whether we can blithely assume such a frame of reference or must seek it inductively. Bloomfield believed it had to be sought inductively.

Tagalog led Bloomfield into Malayo–Polynesian,

in which, despite much work, he published very little. Because of the low quality of available reports on these languages, he felt he would need precise texts before attempting extensive comparison. But that would have required long field trips. Instead of such prolonged field trips, however, Bloomfield conducted a lively correspondence with Otto Dempwolff, and when the latter's treatise appeared in the 1930s, laying the foundations of Malayo–Polynesian comparative linguistics, Bloomfield's influence was evident and amply acknowledged.

Meanwhile, Bloomfield turned to a more readily accessible language family: Algonquian. Edward Sapir, then at the National Museum of Canada, may have suggested the choice. Between 1917 and 1920 he excerpted the Fox and Ojibwa materials published by his chief predecessors in this field, William Jones and Truman Michelson, the former a native speaker of Fox and both trained by Franz Boas. In the summers of 1920 and 1921 Bloomfield worked with the Menomini, in Wisconsin, not far from his boyhood home. After the second summer he did not return to the University of Illinois but went instead to Columbus, where he had accepted an appointment as professor of German and linguistics at the Ohio State University.

Bloomfield's Algonquian research, although often interrupted, continued until his death. In 1925 he spent five summer weeks as assistant ethnologist for the National Museum of Canada (undoubtedly arranged by Sapir, who left the museum that year for the University of Chicago), with the Cree of the Sweet Grass Reserve near Battleford, Saskatchewan. In the summer of 1938 he took down texts from an Ojibwa who was in Ann Arbor to assist in a field-methods course at the Linguistic Institute. A steady flow of publications began in 1922 and is not yet finished: two major works appeared after his death, and extensive lexical materials still remain in manuscript.

One of the reasons for the Algonquian research was Bloomfield's distrust of a notion then current: that regularity of sound change, so obvious a feature of the history of the Indo-European languages, might be due to something peculiar to those languages. Bloomfield believed, rather, that regularity of sound change is either a language universal or does not exist at all. The fruitfulness of the regularity assumption for Algonquian (and, in Dempwolff's hands, for Malayo–Polynesian) went a long way to support the former alternative; indeed, for many, including Bloomfield, all doubt was removed. More recently it has been recognized that Algonquian is less conclusive evidence for our understanding of language design than Bloomfield believed: in some ways the languages in this family resemble remarkably the older stages of Indo-European, with highly inflected verbs and verb-centered syntax. Languages of a sharply different type, like Chinese or Thai, might have afforded Bloomfield a broader basis for generalizations—although, to be sure, he would still have been very cautious about making them.

The Ohio State years brought Bloomfield into close contact with the Hellenist George M. Bolling and the psychologist Albert Paul Weiss. In collaboration with the former and with Edgard H. Sturtevant of Yale, he sought to launch a professional society devoted wholly to linguistics: he himself wrote the Call for an Organization Meeting; the three signed it; the Linguistic Society of America was founded in 1924 and began its journal *Language* in 1925. Bloomfield contributed the first article, setting forth the reasons for such a society; 21 years later the last article he wrote was a survey of the society's achievements.

The association with Weiss was important for both, although Bloomfield later spoke as though all the influence had passed from Weiss to himself. Weiss's behaviorism, under Bloomfield's influence, soon came to differ from the naive sort then common among psychologists: he saw that human behavior could not be viewed in exactly the same way as that of other animals, since the human species has language and others do not. For his part, Bloomfield was led to abandon the pseudo-psychological "explanations" of language phenomena that had been customary: if human psychology rests on language, then our understanding of language must not, circularly, rest on human psychology but on simpler things. Beyond their special fields, both Bloomfield and Weiss were led to the general scientific view later called "physicalism," which rejects the hoary common-sense notions of a special mind-stuff in humans or a special entelechy in living matter and insists that life and man are wholly phenomena of the physical world and must be so understood. Philosophers had flirted with this view (or similar ones) for a long time; but Bloomfield and Weiss meant it. It is only this view that renders linguistics a branch of science—to wit, that branch devoted to the determination of the position of language in the universe.

The two developed their views in various articles, Weiss also in a book first published in 1925. Bloomfield's work culminated in his "Language or Ideas?" drawn from his presidential address to the Linguistic Society in 1935 (1936). Of course, this orientation, coupled with his deceptively simple manner of speaking, got Bloomfield into trouble. Many thought he was denying the existence of obvious realities, such as love and honor and intelligence, when he was in fact only challenging our customary confused ways of philosophizing about such things. The misunderstanding continues to this day, although to reject the physicalist view is to deny the possibility not alone of linguistics but of any social science.

In 1927 Bloomfield left Ohio State and joined Sapir at the University of Chicago (Sapir was to leave for Yale four years later) as professor of Germanic philology. Still busy with all the interests he had developed, he nevertheless found the time to write what is generally regarded as his magnum opus and is certainly his most widely known work, the book *Language* (1933). Modestly described in the preface as a revision of the 1914 *Introduction*, it was nothing of the sort. Almost everything of enduring value that had been discovered in a century and a half of the study of language found its way into the new book. Since 1933 it has hardly been possible to become a linguist without first having mastered Bloomfield's integrated presentation. Today there is scarcely a feature of the book that can stand unmodified; yet subsequent criticisms of Bloomfield's work are cogent and possible only because by standing on his shoulders we can see farther than he did.

The very excellence of Bloomfield's integration of the field was unfortunate in a minor way that was not his fault. There had been very few American linguists in the preceding two decades; beginning in the 1930s many more were trained. Some of them were of limited ability, able to do useful research on specific languages only because Bloomfield's book showed them the way. But they took Bloomfield's treatment as definitive (he himself never did). Consequently, they missed the few points on which his discussion was clearly in error. Bloomfield had presented a "single-stratum" model of language design: phonemes, directly observable in the speech signal, are the minimum though meaningless units of a language; small groups of phonemes, called "morphemes," are the minimum meaningful units; morphemes form words, words form phrases and clauses, and these form sentences. Saussure had long since, in 1916, come closer to the truth with a "two-stratum" model, in which arrangements of phonemes merely *represented* morphemes, much as, in telegraphy, two dots represent the letter "i." But Saussure's presentation was cast in mentalistic terms; Bloomfield, in his vigorous rejection of antiphysicalist modes of discussion, threw the baby out with the bath. The exposure of this mistake did not begin for almost two decades.

Bloomfield was led by his physicalist position to an interest in mathematics and its role in science. In *Language* he characterized mathematics as "the best that language can do"; this notion was the basis of an article (1935) and a monograph (1939), as well as of the paper "Language or Ideas?" He found a curious disparity between the power of mathematics and the cloudiness of most discussions of its "foundations." His view that mathematics springs from language and writing and is thus, in origins, empirical rather than purely "abstract" has since been independently espoused by some mathematicians, although there is surely no general agreement.

In the late 1930s Bloomfield turned to the teaching of reading to children. He found existing materials very confused, reflecting the educationists' total lack of technical knowledge of the nature of writing and its relation to speech. Bloomfield held that writing is a representation of speech; that the child starting school already knows his language and has only to learn the rules of the writing system; and that those rules, in the case of the complex and irregular orthography of English, are most quickly mastered if the child is started with the regularities and then slowly introduced to the irregularities (1942). Bloomfield's materials were tried, with considerable success, in some Chicago parochial schools in the early 1940s; but they were not published until long after his death, in a modified form of which he might not have approved—and too late to be of research value, since it has recently been shown that his understanding of the problem, while far better than that of the "reading specialists" of then or now, is in certain ways oversimplified.

In 1940 Bloomfield accepted a call to Yale University as Sterling professor of linguistics, once again following Edward Sapir—but this time sadly, for Sapir had died in 1939 and Bloomfield went as his successor. World War II was beginning, and Bloomfield turned away from his real research concerns to devote himself to the practical language teaching that the country needed. The American Council of Learned Societies was engaged in an extensive preparation of learners' texts in a wide variety of languages, about some of which there was no reliable scientific information. Yale was a center of this activity. Bloomfield trained and guided younger linguists and himself wrote three practical manuals, two for Dutch (1944; 1944–1945) and one for Russian (1945), as well as a grammatical introduction for a spoken

Russian dictionary. This grueling work undermined his health. On May 27, 1946, a stroke ended his career, and after three years of forced inactivity he died.

The foregoing says too little of Bloomfield's personality. Unlike Sapir, who wrote poetry, Bloomfield had no discernible avocation and perhaps needed none. His humor was whimsical, sometimes biting. He liked simple, honest people: in the preface to *The Menomini Language* (1962) he thanks his informants for some of the finest companionship of his life; for many years after 1921 he maintained his friendships among the Menomini via correspondence. He was painfully aware of the tragedy of such peoples as the Menomini, divested of the guiding principles of their own culture and supplied with nothing in their place but the worst features of ours. His only intolerance was for the pompous misuse of language. He saw natural English spoiled by the artificial niceties of schoolteachers and regretted a similar distortion of Tagalog. His physicalism was consonant with this; it was a protest against the confusion in the discussion of human affairs wrought by operationally undefinable mentalistic and finalistic terms. He would have approved Whitehead's aphorism: "Seek simplicity, and distrust it"; perhaps his one fault was that he did not distrust it enough.

CHARLES F. HOCKETT

[*For the historical context of Bloomfield's work, see the biographies of* BOAS; SAPIR; SAUSSURE; *for discussion of the subsequent development of his ideas, see* LANGUAGE, *article on* LANGUAGE AND CULTURE; LINGUISTICS.]

WORKS BY BLOOMFIELD

1914 *An Introduction to the Study of Language.* New York: Holt.

1917 *Tagalog Texts With Grammatical Analysis.* University of Illinois Studies in Language and Literature, vol. 3, no. 2–4. Urbana: Univ. of Illinois Press.

(1923) 1928 *First German Book.* 2d ed. Columbus: Adams; New York: Century.

1925a Why a Linguistic Society? *Language* 1:1–5.

1925b On the Sound-system of Central Algonquian. *Language* 1:130–156.

1928a *Menomini Texts.* Publications of the American Ethnological Society, vol. 12. New York: Stechert.

1928b A Note on Sound Change. *Language* 4:99–100.

(1933) 1951 *Language.* New York: Holt.

1935 Linguistic Aspects of Science. *Philosophy of Science* 2:499–517.

1936 Language or Ideas? *Language* 12:89–95.

(1939) 1955 Linguistic Aspects of Science. Volume 1, part 1, pages 215–277 in *International Encyclopedia of Unified Science.* Univ. of Chicago Press.

1942 Linguistics and Reading. *Elementary English Review* 19:125–130, 183–186.

1945   About Foreign Language Teaching. *Yale Review* 34:625–641.

1946   Twenty-one Years of the Linguistic Society. *Language* 22:1–3.

1957   *Eastern Ojibwa: Grammatical Sketch, Texts, and Word List.* Ann Arbor: Univ. of Michigan Press.

1961   BLOOMFIELD, LEONARD; and BARNHART, CLARENCE *Let's Read: A Linguistic Approach.* Detroit: Wayne State Univ. Press. → Published posthumously.

1962   *The Menomini Language.* New Haven: Yale Univ. Press. → Published posthumously.

SUPPLEMENTARY BIBLIOGRAPHY

BLOCH, BERNARD   1949   [Obituary of] Leonard Bloomfield. *Language* 25:87–98. → Contains a bibliography of Leonard Bloomfield's works.

DEMPWOLFF, OTTO   1934–1938   Vergleichende Lautlehre des austronesischen Wortschatzes. 3 parts. *Zeitschrift für eingeborenen Sprachen* Supplements 15, 17, 19.

WEISS, ALBERT   (1925) 1929   *A Theoretical Basis of Human Behavior.* 2d ed., rev. Columbus, Ohio: Adams.

BOAS, FRANZ

Franz Boas (1858–1942), American anthropologist, was born and educated in Germany. He visited the United States in 1884 and 1886 in the course of expeditions to the Arctic and British Columbia and began his American career in New York in 1887. He became the most influential anthropologist of his time, a major force in the academic and professional development of the science, considered by many the architect of its modern structure. To Boas can be credited a critical reconstruction of anthropology and its principal branches as well as the emergence of the modern concept of culture—a concept central to the integration of anthropology as the study of man "as a member of social groups," and fundamentally influential with respect to all modern thinking in behavioral sciences. Boas led physical anthropology from taxonomic "race" classification into a field of viable research in human biology, and he exposed and eliminated traditional ambiguities in the area of race and culture study. His leadership in the study of American Indian languages became the established reference point for the development of structural linguistics and for questions of the relation of language to thought and culture. His critique of nineteenth-century unilineal (orthogenetic) cultural evolution established both the historicity of cultural developments and the primary role of culture in human history.

Boas was born in Minden, Westphalia. At school and the Gymnasium in Minden, and at the universities of Heidelberg, Bonn, and Kiel, he received the thorough German education of his time in sciences, mathematics, languages, and humanities.

He took his doctorate at Kiel in 1881; physics and mathematics attracted him, and his principal doctoral thesis, *Beiträge zur Erkenntniss der Farbe des Wassers* (1881), led him into problems of psychophysics, the forerunner of experimental psychology. But he also wrote three theses in geography, his favorite subject in the Gymnasium, and he began his career as a geographer. It was as a geographer that he planned his Arctic expedition of 1883–1884 to Baffin Land. He later was appointed docent in geography at the University of Berlin.

Ethnology, however, had a stronger appeal. Even as a schoolboy he wanted to study cultural history, to travel to "unknown lands," to learn about primitive peoples; and these interests were nourished by his studies in human geography. In 1882, before his Eskimo trip, he frequented meetings of the Berlin Anthropological Society, contacting Adolf Bastian and Rudolf Virchow and arranging with Virchow for instruction in anthropometry. Among the Eskimos he carried out extensive ethnological research in addition to his geographical work, which became his monograph "The Central Eskimo" (1888). Sometime in 1885, as he came to understand his Eskimo experience, he turned to anthropology as his primary field. That year he was writing his Eskimo monograph and, as assistant in Bastian's Museum für Völkerkunde in Berlin, he was associating with leading anthropologists and deepening his relationship with Virchow. Working with British Columbia collections at the museum, and with two Bella Coola Indians then in the city, Boas found the "attraction" of North Pacific culture, and especially its art, "irresistible"; he planned the ethnological expedition which took him to British Columbia in 1886 to begin the study of the region, and especially of the Kwakiutl Indians, that he continued throughout his life. For some years after 1888 he carried on these studies under the auspices of the British Association for the Advancement of Science.

In New York in January 1887, after returning from the field, Boas made a major decision: he gave up his German career to become an American scientist and citizen; accepting an assistant editorship of *Science*, he married and settled in New York. It was not a sudden decision: he was unhappy with his immediate German position—his docentship in physical geography—and for personal and political reasons he had sought for some years to transfer his career to the United States. Coming from a home "where the ideals of the revolution of 1848 were a living force" and where, with parents who had given up their formal Jewish faith, he "was spared the struggle against religious dogma that besets the lives of so many young people" (1938*b*), Boas was alienated by the antiliberal climate of Bismarck's Germany. He had experienced its anti-Semitism at first hand, and he could not accept the state requirement that to hold a scientific position he must make a declaration of religious affiliation. In New York he found a congenial atmosphere of intellectual, personal, and political freedom. Relatives and friends of the Boas family who had left Germany after the revolution of 1848 were already there—among others, Dr. Abraham Jacobi, an uncle; Carl Schurz, who introduced Boas into academic and cultural circles; and Marie Krackowizer, Boas' fiancée, whom he had met four years earlier on a vacation in the Harz mountains.

Boas' work on *Science* was primarily geographical. Anthropology in the United States, still in a preacademic and largely preprofessional era, offered limited opportunities. From 1888 to 1892 Boas held a post in anthropology at Clark University; and from 1892 to mid-1894 he was chief assistant in anthropology at the World's Columbian Exposition in Chicago and then curator of the museum there established to house its permanent collections. (The museum was first called the Columbian Museum, later the Field Museum.) After he left the museum, Boas was without a regular position for eighteen months. In December 1895 he joined Frederic Ward Putnam at the American Museum of Natural History in New York, becoming assistant curator in 1896 and curator from 1901 until 1905. Concurrently, he joined Columbia University in May 1896 as lecturer in physical anthropology and became professor of anthropology in 1899, his lifetime post, from which he retired in 1936.

Early in his American career Boas became active in promoting the academic and professional development of anthropology. He established anthropology at Clark University and at Columbia; and among the men he trained at Columbia were A. L. Kroeber, who established a department at the University of California in 1903, and F. G. Speck, who did likewise at the University of Pennsylvania in 1909. The work of Putnam and Boas made the Chicago World's Fair a landmark in the development of anthropology: its collections founded a permanent museum and its "Congress of Anthropology" set the stage for basic research and professional organization to follow. Boas played a leading role in modernizing the *American Anthropologist* in 1898 and in founding the American Anthropological Association in 1902. In 1899–1900 he reorganized the American Ethnological Society in New York as a viable scientific society; founded in 1842, it had long been inactive. He was tireless in promoting research and in establishing and editing scientific journals and publications. From 1897 to 1902 he organized and directed through the American Museum of Natural History the Jesup North Pacific Expedition, a major research investigation of man in the Americas. He founded and edited the major American publications in anthropological linguistics, and he was a founder of the American Folk-lore Society in 1888 and of its *Journal*, which he edited from 1908 to 1925. He took the lead in developing anthropology in Mexico, collaborating on the establishment of the International School of American Archaeology and Ethnology there and directing it from 1911 to 1912. He was active in the development of the American Association of Physical Anthropologists and of its *Journal*.

Boas was equally indefatigable in his own scientific work, contributing year after year to all branches of anthropology. To these efforts he brought a commitment to empiricism and rigorous scientific methods, an awareness of the complexity of natural phenomena, and a readiness to re-examine traditional ideas. By 1911, when he published *The Mind of Primitive Man*, collecting some of his important studies "in revised form and enlarged," he had restructured anthropology, defining in modern terms the scope and problems both of the general field and of its separable branches. Boas' work thereafter, as that of most modern anthropology, built upon the new base lines he had established.

The science of anthropology

Before Boas, anthropology as a subject matter was little more than a miscellany of anthropometric, linguistic, ethnographic, and archeological data about the evolution of man and his works. Race and language, or race and culture, understood as phases of the same evolution, were treated as inherently interrelated. Culture was defined essentially as the expression of the rational thinking of the human mind, and it was considered a single phenomenon, humanistic and evolutionary, manifested by all mankind but in different degrees. Culture differences or similarities were explained by differences or similarities in racial factors, in geographical factors, or in stages of a progressive (orthogenetic) evolution.

Boas' work transformed the field by basing it on

the conception of cultures as the environments of both human biological and behavioral life, and by establishing the relative autonomy of physical anthropology, linguistics, and ethnology as branches of the general science.

Elementary today, although not at all obvious before his time, was Boas' demonstration that physical type (race), language, and culture have had relatively independent histories. Traditional classifications of man had assumed that race and language, race and culture, or all three, are interdependent, that they "are in a way interchangeable terms." Boas showed that classifications based upon racial or biological criteria cannot be reconciled with those based upon linguistic or cultural criteria, nor can linguistic or cultural classifications be reconciled with racial classifications or with one another. The principle established—that human biological history and classification must be based on biological data, linguistic history on linguistic data, and cultural history on cultural data—is fundamental in modern anthropology. Neither variations nor similarities of culture can be explained by considerations of race.

Critique of geographical determinism.   During the time that Boas was a university student, the dominant approach to cultural history was geographical determinism. Under Theobald Fischer, Boas wrote a thesis on geography as the foundation of history, and he planned an empirical demonstration of the theory for his Baffin Land expedition—specifically, an investigation of the relations between Eskimo migrations and the physical geography of their region. After his return he published results which he considered satisfactory (1885), unaware for some time of the impact of his Eskimo experience upon his thinking (Stocking 1965). Yet within two years he turned from anthropogeography toward ethnology as his primary work, and in retrospect he saw his Eskimo research on geographical determinism as "a thorough disappointment" and his Eskimo year as a turning point in his interests (1938b). He had found that Eskimo behavior could not be explained by geographical environment except in trivial and shallow ways and that Eskimos often did things not because of geographical conditions but in spite of them.

In his critique of geographical determinism Boas showed that its logical conclusion—"that the same environment will produce the same cultural results everywhere"—is untenable in the light of the facts. Human culture is not simply an adaptation to nature; similarities and differences cannot be explained by geography alone. Environments, Boas showed, interact with pre-existing cultures—cultures "which themselves are due to historical causes" and cannot be explained by "action of the environment alone."

Evolution.   Even in his early thought, Boas interpreted the evolutionary view of nineteenth-century ethnology in historical terms. In 1889 he wrote:

The development of ethnology is largely due to the general recognition of the principle of biological evolution. It is a common feature of all forms of evolutionary theory that every living being is considered as the result of an historical development. The fate of an individual does not influence himself alone, but also all the succeeding generations. . . . This point of view introduced an historical perspective into the natural sciences and revolutionized their methods. The development of ethnology is largely due to the adoption of the evolutionary standpoint, because it impressed the conviction upon us that no event in the life of a people passes without leaving its effect upon later generations. The myths told by our ancestors and in which they believed have left their impress upon the ways of thinking of their descendants. . . .   ([1889] 1955, p. 633)

To Tylor, Morgan, Spencer and other nineteenth-century cultural evolutionists, evolution was more than a principle of historical continuity and change. It derived not from Darwin—whose conception of natural selection recognized the historical character of evolutionary events—but from eighteenth-century and nineteenth-century ideas of inevitable progress, of order and direction in the events of history. Cultural history was viewed as a universal, unilineal, unfolding process; variations were expressions of differences in stage of development. To Tylor, for example, "civilization" among more evolved peoples was a higher manifestation of culture as a universal attribute of man.

Boas' critique was directed not against the principle of evolution as historical development, which he accepted, but against the orthogenesis of dominant English and American theory of the time. He opposed history to orthogenesis, showing that sequential developments of technology, religion, art, social organization, moral ideas, and language did not follow the single course required by the orthogenetic theories, or move necessarily from simple to complex. A particular development involved many historical factors and was not simply a realization of inherent potentials. Similarities on which evolutionary conclusions were being based had been torn from their meaningful cultural-historical contexts; the similarity of the phenomena was "more apparent than real"; they were in reality noncomparable. Alleged parallel developments used as evidence were in fact not parallel but convergent outcomes of different histories. The course of historical evolution, Boas argued, must be derived from the comparison of actual histories (1911b).

Historical evolution made the "progress" inherent in orthogenetic views a separate, additional question—namely, an evaluation of the historic record in terms of human ideals and standards inevitably culture-based and culture-bound. In some aspects of culture, as in social organization, religion, or art, "our own ideals are not uniform" and progress is difficult to define. There is a general consensus, however, that since earliest times there has been progress "in knowledge and control of nature. . . . If we should value progress entirely by the development of invention and knowledge, it would be easy to arrange the divisions of mankind in order of progress, beginning with the simplest cultures of early Paleolithic man and leading up to modern civilizations . . ." (1938a, pp. 676–677).

Boas' critique was thought by some to be an attempt to disprove the historical reality of evolution, but this is a reflection of the thought and usage of the time rather than of Boas' meaning. Evolution and orthogenetic development had been identified in biology as well as anthropology. In biology the present understanding of evolution as the history of genetic change was achieved only after a long critical struggle against orthogenetic evolution that lasted into the twentieth century. The critique of cultural evolutionary theory, which Boas led, was a parallel effort in anthropology to displace orthogenetic preconceptions and promote the acceptance of history.

Culture and man. Boas' work established the relative autonomy of cultural phenomena. Cultural forms are not expressions of differences in outer environment, inner biology, or some directive force within culture itself; they are diverse historical developments, each the outcome of a prior history in which many factors and events, cultural and noncultural, have played a part. Cultures rather than culture became fundamental to the study of man.

In addition to this critical work Boas added new dimensions to the understanding of the relation of cultures and man: psychological considerations, which defined cultures as the environments of human thought and behavior; and biological considerations, which established the role of cultural environments (and hereditary factors) in human biological life, growth, and variation. This conception of cultures gave anthropology its modern integration: "All the various aspects of human life: bodily form, language, culture, as well as the environment in which man is placed, are interrelated, and the form of culture is a result of this integration" (1930c, p. 98).

Boas brought to anthropology a knowledge of the German psychology of his time: he was familiar with psychophysics, on which he published several papers; and he had studied the folk psychology movement, especially in the work of Wilhelm Wundt, whose conception of a comparative psychology based on studies of language, myth, and custom influenced Boas deeply. Early in his life, the declaration of a theologian friend that "one [has] not the right to doubt what the past [has] transmitted" had made him sharply aware of "the psychological origin of the implicit belief in the authority of tradition" as a fundamental problem (1938b). In psychophysics he found that the experience of the subject plays an important part in perception: quantitative methods alone do not explain the phenomena; and Neo-Kantian philosophy raised fundamental questions in his mind about the role of subjective mental activity in the perception of the external world. A "desire to understand the relations between the objective and subjective worlds" became a lifelong interest of his work in anthropology (Boas 1938b; Benedict 1943). This desire is evident in the problem he studied among the Eskimos, and it drew him to the study of the North Pacific Coast. He was "struck by the flight of imagination" in Northwest Coast art and surmised that "a wealth of thought lay hidden behind the grotesque masks and the elaborately decorated utensils of these tribes" (1909, p. 307). Thus, in his work on Northwest peoples, as in a great deal of his lifework in ethnology, he focused on language, mythology, religion, and art—the symbolic aspects of the cultures, the objective cultural manifestations of inner thought (Codere 1959).

The new psychological dimensions which Boas gave to the relation of man and culture made a radical break with the rationalism of Tylor and the English school. In Tylor, customs and beliefs and culture itself are the rational products of the human mind. In Boas the emphasis is essentially reversed: cultures—the diverse, cumulative results of diverse complex histories—are the behavioral environments in which human thought and feeling are structured and operate. The traditional is learned as habits from childhood on; these habits of thought, of feeling, of behavior become largely unconscious and automatic; and the individual thinks and acts largely in conformity with the traditional and customary (1911b).

What is handed on varies from culture to culture, and the differences are not superficial but involve the fundamentals of human behavior and thought—the modes of experiencing phenomena, of grouping and organizing sense impressions, of understanding what are objects and what are qualities or attributes and how these are associated. The difference in types of thought and feeling between different peoples, as between primitive and modern, are not expressions of organic or biological differences but are the products "of the diversity of the cultures" (1904). The idea of instincts as factors in the adult behavior and thought of man is eliminated, being replaced by the concept of habits learned in society. The understanding of human nature is radically altered: no longer fixed and unchangeable, it is a function of culture, not nature, modifiable by changes in cultural institutions and forms (Dewey 1932).

Boas saw in this view an important implication for education. The comparative study of cultures offered a way to discover and expose the traditional elements in thought and belief, which is essential for freedom of thought and objective scientific inquiry. The philosopher and reflective thinker in any culture, as well as the average individual, reflect the attitudes and ideas current in their social and cultural environment (1902). Only by recognizing the "shackles" that tradition has laid upon us are we "able to break them" (1889; 1938b).

Limits of generalization. Boas' historical approach—which involved "the consideration of every cultural phenomenon as the result of historical happenings" (1927, p. 1)—conveys the infinite complexity of ethnological data, a complexity not easily factorable into components and determinable relations. It does not deny the possibility of regularities or "laws" in cultural phenomena, as is often asserted by critics of Boas, but stresses the inherent difficulty of discovering them. Boas himself called attention to regularities—for example, the relation of population size and density to food supply and mode of economic life, to complexity of culture, and to forms of political organization; the relation of economic conditions to social, political, and legal organization; the relation of technological complexity to division of labor (1911b; 1930c). But the complexity of the phenomena and the difficulty of controlled analysis of an almost unlimited number of variables made him doubt that the *degree* of general validity of laws achieved in the natural sciences can be attained in ethnology. "In short, the danger is ever present that the widest generalizations that may be obtained . . . are commonplaces" ([1930a] 1955, p. 268). He was less skeptical of discoverable regularities in social con-

ditioning than in "sequences of cultural achievement" or "the study of cultural integration." He wrote, ". . . if we look for laws, the laws relate to the effects of physiological, psychological, and social conditions . . ." (Boas [1920c] 1955, p. 287; Benedict 1943).

Boas saw the historical (ideographic) goal of science, rather than the generalizing (nomothetic), as the goal of ethnology (1887). The establishment of general abstract laws, as in physics, in which particular phenomena are significant only as the data of research, cannot satisfy the human interest in human phenomena. Only the thorough understanding of individual cultural phenomena, as found in history, will suffice. Toward that understanding, generalizations, when discoverable, are not the end of research but are instrumental and heuristic.

Methods of study.   By precept and example Boas made field work among living cultures a hallmark of American ethnology. In the course of his own research effort to understand and record cultural data from the native viewpoint—in particular, in his Northwest Coast studies—he developed new trends in field work, training natives as informants and investigators, recording all basic ideas in native texts, and gathering all relevant native views, however divergent.

He continued for more than forty years to focus on the culture of one people, the Kwakiutl, seeking on the one hand to understand Kwakiutl culture in the historical cultural context of the Northwest Coast and on the other hand to provide as comprehensive and rounded an archive record of a culture as he was able to obtain.

Under Boas' leadership, field work among nonliterate peoples had a special urgency. He had seen among the Eskimos how rapidly natives were changing or disappearing, and he felt a pressing need to record their languages and cultures before they became extinct.

Although Boas referred to the history of culture as an aim of ethnology, in practice "history" to him was more a dimension of the data than an end of research. He was less concerned with historical reconstructions than with techniques for dealing with the historicity of the phenomena involved in a particular problem. He saw in archeology a way to reconstruct history with some accuracy and contributed directly to its development: under his direction, stratigraphy, used for the first time in American archeology in excavations in the Valley of Mexico, revealed the sequence of prehistoric cultures that became the foundation of Central American archeology (Boas 1913; Mason 1943).

Distribution studies of similar phenomena on a world, continental, or area scale, supplementing archeology and used cautiously, make some historical inferences possible. For Boas such studies were simply instrumental, and he was critical of tendencies to make them ends of research or to make "culture areas" used in museum presentation into natural classifications.

Boas used distributions instrumentally in studies of mythology and art (1896a; 1903b; 1908; 1916b) and in his general approach to the understanding of an individual culture. Knowing what features a culture has acquired by diffusion and what it has invented independently can reveal the creative individuality of a particular culture, mythology, or art. Boas' contributions to mythology and folklore and his work on primitive art advanced modern methods in both fields of study (Benedict 1931; Jacobs 1959; Boas 1927). His works on Tsimshian and Kwakiutl mythology were pioneer studies of the ways in which the culture of a people is expressed in its mythology, and they revealed mythology as a rich source of native values and thought (1916b; 1935). His historical treatment of mythologies demonstrated the complexity and diversity of their sources, references, and meanings, and it showed that attempts to explain mythology as "symbolizing or anthropomorphizing natural phenomena" were inadequate ([1891] 1955, p. 445; 1933).

An individual culture was never a unified, organic system to Boas. Its long history, the diverse origins of its content and form, its continuing change, and the continuing influence of other cultures upon it all make complete integration virtually impossible. "Holism" for Boas therefore was not the idea, entertained by some, that a culture can be treated as a unified system; it referred to the importance of understanding a particular phase or pattern in relation to its entire relevant cultural background. It also referred to the necessary investigation of the interrelations of different aspects of culture within the whole cultural framework. Boas was critical of attempts to describe a culture or a society in unified, general terms. Such configurations, however suggestive, are inevitably partial and selective, not exhaustive, and affected by subjective attitudes of the observer (1938a; 1933).

Linguistics

It is difficult to overestimate the central importance of Boas' work. His contributions broke sharply with philological tradition, opening new horizons and establishing modern linguistic anthropology. Boas saw languages, like cultures, as diverse products of diverse histories, each an essentially unique configuration at a given time. He found in language a model of the way in which the traditional and the habitual in human behavior become virtually automatic and unconscious in individual minds. As Boas saw it, the scientific problem of linguistics—the thorough understanding of languages and their historical development and the intricate role of language in human thought and culture—called for an immense research effort in the study of individual languages, and especially of unwritten languages ignored in traditional philology. He devoted himself untiringly to that effort throughout his life, recording and analyzing many languages himself, inspiring the participation of others by precept and example, and finding sources of financial support for linguistic research and publication.

American Indian languages took a large part of his attention; many were on the verge of extinction, and both in phonology and morphology their features challenged the preconceptions of traditional philology. Boas founded and edited the *Publications of the American Ethnological Society*, begun in 1906, the *Handbook of American Indian Languages*, begun in 1910, and the *International Journal of American Linguistics*, established in 1917. In 1925 Boas organized with Sapir and Bloomfield the Committee on American Indian Languages of the American Council of Learned Societies, which for many years centralized research in this field.

"Inner form." Boas' empiricism—description and analysis of a language in its own terms—was directed by the conception of the "inner form" of a language, which he accepted from Heymann Steinthal, a nineteenth-century folk psychologist and linguist; the concept itself goes back to Wilhelm von Humboldt. In Boas' inductive approach, linguistic data are accepted as found, regardless of philological preconceptions. The effect of his approach was a breakthrough of traditional limits and the discovery of a wider range and diversity of linguistic phenomena in both phonetics and morphology than had been thought to exist. For example, such phenomena as words without vowels and unfamiliar principles of classifying nominal or verbal ideas were found. For discovering the "inner form" of a language, the limited phonetic and lexical data used by philology in historical reconstruction of genetic relationships were not enough; the process required description in a grammar "treated as though an intelligent [speaker] was going to develop the forms of his own thoughts by an analysis of his own form of speech" (1911a, p. 81). This requirement led Boas to stress the importance of native texts and the use of speakers who could be taught to write texts in their own language. Grammars of non-Indo-European languages, only occasional earlier, became after Boas an integral part of linguistic work in anthropology.

Boas maintained high technical standards in his own work in descriptive linguistics and contributed significantly to the development of modern linguistic techniques. His phonetic work laid the foundations for the development of modern phonemics by Sapir, as did his comparative morphological studies for the development of structural linguistics.

Language and thought. It has been said that "with Boas almost the total scope of American linguistic anthropology until the present time became defined and adumbrated" (Hymes 1964, p. 9). Of signal importance is how his attempt to understand and compare the "inner form" of different languages led him into considerations of language and thought, of language and culture—a phase of his lifelong concern with the problem of the "relation between the objective world and man's subjective world as it has taken form in different cultures" (Benedict 1943, p. 27). This approach has inspired the more recent work of others on what has become known as the Sapir–Whorf hypothesis of the determining role of language in human thought. Boas, it should be noted, demonstrated fundamental ways in which the structure of language influences the direction of thought of its speakers, but he took the position that culture influences language more than language influences culture.

Boas' conception of linguistic phenomena as part of ethnological phenomena in general, subject to similar influences, led him, in historical linguistics, to challenge traditional naturalistic views of genealogical classification of languages. In American Indian languages he found distributional evidence that lexical, phonetic, *and* morphological borrowing had occurred, that languages can develop by convergence from diverse sources as well as, in the traditional view, by divergence from a common origin. Historical study therefore requires investigation not only "of the similarities of languages, but equally intensively" of "their dissimilarities": "the problem . . . is not one of classification but . . . [of tracing] the history of the development of human speech. . . . Classification is only a means to an end" ([1920*b*] 1955, pp. 212–213). His conclusion —that "the whole theory of an 'Ursprache' for every group of modern languages must be held in abeyance until we can prove that these languages go back to a single stock and that they have not

originated, to a large extent, by the process of acculturation" (*ibid.*, p. 217)—has not been adopted in linguistics, although there are indications in Indo-European philology that the fundamental question it raises has not been finally settled (Boas 1929; Jakobson 1944).

Physical anthropology

In physical anthropology, as in other areas, Boas' pioneer efforts opened up the modern field. His contributions to the study of human growth, hereditary and environmental influences in man, and race and the composition of human populations led physical anthropology from a static taxonomic field of anthropometric description and race classification into a dynamic science of human biology. Skilled in mathematics as no other anthropologist of his time, he devised techniques for handling problems that were innovations in statistics and biometrics (Howells 1959).

Race. Boas' work on race is transitional between the nineteenth-century tradition of viewing races as readily classifiable natural subdivisions of the human species and the contemporary trend toward a denial that race is a meaningful biological concept in the study of man. Although he saw taxonomy for its own sake as barren, he did not reject the concept of race, but rather refined and limited its meaning, avoiding naturalistic assumptions and making it instrumental in the analysis of human genetic history. He found in the biological phenomena of human populations a complexity that traditional views failed to recognize. Human groups —"local or social varieties," composed of "a series of individuals whose bodily form depends on their ancestry and environment"—cannot be scientifically described by subjective characterizations of type or by statistical averages alone; nor can groups be compared or classified by single features alone —like cephalic index—or by an arbitrary selection of a few features, even if the chosen features are stable and hereditary. Statistical description must include the variability of a group around the average, indicating its relative homogeneity or heterogeneity. And, since groups may be alike in one or a few features but different in others, Boas opposed a "cast-iron system" of selected measurements; more exhaustive description is an essential preliminary to the comparison and classification of groups (1899*a*).

Although Boas recognized that "the principles of biological science forbid us to assume a permanent stability of bodily forms," he accepted in his early work the dominant view that "anatomical characteristics of the present races" have been permanent at least since neolithic times (1911*b*, pp. 41, 44). Impermanence of features primarily involves variations within a race (1899*a*). Several considerations later led him to recognize a larger influence of environmental factors upon human types, a greater biological plasticity of the species: (1) the consideration of man as a self-domesticated animal form; (2) the discovery that head form (cephalic index) changes significantly with changes of environment; and (3) the phenomena of retardation and acceleration in human growth, involving environmental as well as hereditary factors.

Modification of bodily forms. Boas credited the idea that man is a self-domesticated animal form to two German scientists, Johannes Ranke and Eduard Hahn (Boas 1938*a*, p. 109). He noted that the domestication of animals and the development of human culture involve similar changes in nutrition and mode of life and that the great variability found in domesticated animal types when compared to related wild forms occurs especially in features used in racial description and classification, namely pigmentation, hair, eye color, head and body proportions (1911*b*; 1938*a*, pp. 108–110). Boas suggested that the environmental conditions of human cultural life and its diversification—the self-domestication of man—had been a factor in modifications of human anatomy and physiology.

The changes in head form which Boas reported in "Changes in Bodily Form of Descendants of Immigrants" (1912) surprised him as much as other anthropologists and influenced his thinking as profoundly as it affected the discipline. Boas had defended the cephalic index as a measure of a stable, hereditary trait (1899*a*; 1899*b*), but the assumption of its stability was based on data gathered in Europe, where no environmental change was involved. In the New York study Boas compared children with their European immigrant parents and compared parent–child measurements in cases of children born before immigration with cases of children born in America after immigration. Some 18,000 individuals were studied—Bohemians, Hebrews, Sicilians, and Neapolitans—and stature, weight, and head measurements were taken. The results showed significant changes in measurements of the head and in the cephalic index calculated from them.

The impact of this study on anthropology cannot be overstated. It ended the obsessive reliance of anthropologists upon cephalic index as a key to genetic history and, as no other work, it compelled

recognition of environmental influences upon human anatomy and physiology.

Initially Boas wrote that he had no adequate explanation of the changes but that they indicated "a great plasticity of human types" in response to changes of environment. Some of his remarks may have been overstatements, as Tanner has suggested, but the criticism aroused by publication of the study was directed indiscriminately both at his interpretations and at the validity of the study's methods and results. However, the findings have been confirmed by later work and are not challenged today. Similar changes have been found in studies of other migrant groups—in Hawaii, Mexico, Puerto Rico, Seattle, New York, and Philadelphia (Shapiro 1939; Goldstein 1943; Boas 1916*c*, 1920*a*, 1928*a*; Spier 1929; Tanner 1959; Herskovits 1943). Boas' own work on human growth clarified the meaning of the 1912 study, and he later wrote of a "limited plasticity," meaning that the results do not involve genetic changes but show "that the type as we see it contains elements that are not genetic but an expression of the influence of environment" (Boas 1936, p. 523; Tanner 1959).

Human growth. The study of human growth was new when Boas entered the field, its cross-sectional data compiled from height and weight measurements of different individuals, wherever and whenever gathered. Although the importance of longitudinal studies—successive measurements of the same individuals over a period of years—had been suggested in 1874, it was Boas' discoveries that made inevitable "the longitudinal studies which have been the chief characteristic of progress in the field in the first half of this century" (Tanner 1959, p. 107).

Boas began the first American longitudinal growth study in 1891, and in 1892 he questioned "in how far the results (of cross-sectional studies) have a physiological meaning and in how far they are purely statistical phenomena" (1892). He found that differences in the acceleration and retardation of individuals account for the increased variability at adolescence shown in cross-sectional data and for the distortion of the statistical curves from the "normal" or Gaussian form. Individuals differ in *tempo of growth*, and in later studies Boas showed that the variability at adolescence is greatly reduced when data on individuals are plotted by "time of peak velocity" of growth rather than by chronological age (1930*b*).

Boas' concept of physiological or developmental age in these studies gained currency through its use by Crampton (1908) as well as by others, and its impact on the social sciences (especially education) has continued, though it has not been fully accepted. Retardation and acceleration occur in mental as well as physical development, but, as Boas showed, physical and mental development do not determine one another; they are linked through common causes. The retarded child may develop, even accelerate, both physiologically and psychologically. Intelligence tests developed by Binet and others, based on chronological age and cross-sectional data, largely disregarded these findings, primarily because they assumed that they were testing innate, inherited intelligence. Recent intelligence studies, using longitudinal methods, indicate the presence of tempo of growth in mental ability (Tanner 1959).

Heredity and environment.   It has been erroneously asserted that Boas stressed the role of environmental factors in human biology at the expense of a recognition of heredity. The scientific problem, as he saw it, was to determine the *relation* between environmental and hereditary factors. He wrote: ". . . it seems justifiable to define racial characteristics as we do those of a variable plant, namely, by stating that under definite environmental conditions the bodily form of a race and its functioning are such as we observe, without prejudging . . . [the influence of environment]. The actual problem, then, would be to determine whether and how far the traits of the body may be so influenced" ([1922] 1955, p. 37). In pioneer studies in biometrical genetics Boas attempted to isolate the role of heredity in head form, face form, and other anthropometric traits (1899b; 1903a; 1907). Stimulated by Johannsen's work on beans, he analyzed populations into component family lines and showed that the variation of a population is composed of the variation of family lines (between-fraternity variance) and the variation of fraternities (within-fraternity variance) (Boas 1916a; Tanner 1959).

In this work Boas did not oppose Mendelian genetics, as is commonly thought. In his earliest effort, in 1894, he found in a bimodal distribution of face breadth in the offspring of French–Indian parents a "tendency to reproduce one of the ancestral types"—a phenomenon contrary to the traditional (Galton) conception of "blending" inheritance, which came to be known, after Pearson, as "alternating" inheritance (1894). This discovery predisposed Boas, after the rediscovery of Mendel's work in 1900, toward a limited acceptance of Mendelian principles. He found that while the simple ratios of "classical" Mendelian inheritance, with

their "unit" characters and evidence of dominant and recessive traits, do fit the genetic phenomena of some human traits, like eye color, they do not fit others, like stature. Actually, the apparent conflict between biometric studies of continuous variation, like stature, and Mendelian studies of discontinuous variation, like eye color, has been reconciled only more recently by developments in both biometrics and genetics (Tanner 1959).

Influence

Boas believed that truth, widely shared through publications and education, can serve to liberate the mind from traditional confusion, error, and prejudice. The findings of anthropology challenged traditional thinking at many points, and Boas spoke out boldly throughout his life against racism and race prejudice, against narrow nationalism and war, and for an internationalism based on "the common interests of humanity" (1928b; 1904–1943). Supplementing his own work on race and the situation of the American Negro, Boas stimulated or guided research by others, including the work of Klineberg on race differences, of Herskovits on the America Negro, and of Gilberto Freyre and Rudiger Bilden in their pioneer studies of race in Brazil. His influence was far-reaching; as Gossett has written: "It is possible that Boas did more to combat race prejudice than any other person in history" (Gossett 1963).

As a teacher, Boas' influence was profound. Between his years at Clark University and his retirement in 1936 he taught generations of anthropologists, including: A. F. Chamberlain, A. L. Kroeber, Edward Sapir, A. A. Goldenweiser, R. H. Lowie, Frank G. Speck, Fay-Cooper Cole, H. K. Haeberlin, Paul Radin, Leslie Spier, Erna Gunther, J. A. Mason, Elsie C. Parsons, Ruth F. Benedict, Margaret Mead, G. A. Reichard, M. J. Herskovits, Franz Olbrechts, A. I. Hallowell, R. L. Bunzel, M. J. Andrade, George Herzog, Frederica de Laguna, M. Jacobs, Ruth M. Underhill, Günter Wagner, Jules Henry, Rhoda Métraux, Marcus S. Goldstein, Alexander Lesser, G. Weltfish, M. F. Ashley Montagu, E. A. Hoebel, May M. Edel, Irving Goldman, as well as students in other fields who came to him for his teaching of anthropology. In his teaching Boas was consistently open-ended, moving from problem to problem in physical anthropology, linguistics, or ethnology, examining theoretical questions in the context of empirical data and handling data in the context of relevant theory (Mead 1959b).

Boas continued his scientific activity to the

moment of his death at an anthropology luncheon on December 29, 1942. His contributions, besides six books, include more than seven hundred monographs and articles (Andrews et al. 1943). He was honored during his lifetime throughout the scientific world by honorary degrees, by honorary memberships in scientific societies of many countries, by a *Festschrift* on the twenty-fifth anniversary of his doctorate (*Boas Anniversary Volume . . .* 1906), by membership in the National Academy of Sciences in 1900, and by election as president of the American Anthropological Association from 1907 to 1909, the New York Academy of Sciences in 1910, and the American Association for the Advancement of Science in 1931. His scientific legacy is the modern science of anthropology; his greater legacy the manner in which he changed our conception of man.

ALEXANDER LESSER

[*For the historical context of Boas' work, see the biographies of* BASTIAN; PUTNAM; SPENCER; TYLOR; WUNDT. *For discussion of the subsequent development of his ideas, see the biographies of* BENEDICT; COLE, FAY-COOPER; GOLDENWEISER; HERSKOVITS; KROEBER; LOWIE; PARSONS; ELSIE CLEWS; RADIN; SAPIR; SPECK; SPIER; *and the entries* ANTHROPOLOGY; ETHNOGRAPHY; EVOLUTION; LINGUISTICS; PHYSICAL ANTHROPOLOGY; RACE.]

WORKS BY BOAS

1881   *Beiträge zur Erkenntniss der Farbe des Wassers.* Kiel: Schmidt & Klaunig.

1885   *Baffin-Land: Geographische Ergebnisse einer in den Jahren 1883 und 1884 ausgeführten Forschungsreise.* Petermanns Mitteilungen, Vol. 17, Supplement 80. Gotha (Germany): Perthes.

(1887) 1955   The Study of Geography. Pages 639–647 in Franz Boas, *Race, Language and Culture.* New York: Macmillan. → First published in Volume 9 of *Science.*

(1887–1936) 1955   *Race, Language and Culture.* New York: Macmillan. → A collection of papers written between 1887–1936. First published in book form in 1940.

1883   The Central Eskimo. Pages 399–669 in U.S. Bureau of American Ethnology, *Sixth Annual Report, 1884–1885.* Washington: Government Printing Office. → A paperback edition was published in 1964 by the Univ. of Nebraska Press.

(1889) 1955   The Aims of Ethnology. Pages 626–638 in Franz Boas, *Race, Language and Culture.* New York: Macmillan. → First published in German.

(1891) 1955   Dissemination of Tales Among the Natives of North America. Pages 437–445 in Franz Boas, *Race, Language and Culture.* New York: Macmillan. → First published in Volume 4 of the *Journal of American Folk-lore.*

1892   The Growth of Children. *Science* 19:256–257, 281–282; 20:351–352.

(1894) 1955   The Half-blood Indian. Pages 138–148 in Franz Boas, *Race, Language and Culture.* New York: Macmillan. → First published in Volume 45 of *Popular Science Monthly.*

(1896a) 1955   The Growth of Indian Mythologies: A Study Based Upon the Growth of the Mythologies of the North Pacific Coast. Pages 425–436 in Franz Boas, *Race, Language and Culture.* New York: Macmillan. → First published in Volume 9 of the *Journal of American Folk-lore.*

(1896b) 1955   The Limitations of the Comparative Method of Anthropology. Pages 270–280 in Franz Boas, *Race, Language and Culture.* New York: Macmillan. → First published in *Science.*

(1899a) 1955   Some Recent Criticisms of Physical Anthropology. Pages 165–171 in Franz Boas, *Race, Language and Culture.* New York: Macmillan. → First published in the *American Anthropologist.*

1899b   The Cephalic Index. *American Anthropologist* New Series 1:448–461.

(1902) 1955   The Ethnological Significance of Esoteric Doctrines. Pages 312–315 in Franz Boas, *Race, Language and Culture.* New York: Macmillan. → First published in *Science.*

1903a   Heredity in Head Form. *American Anthropologist* New Series 5:530–538.

(1903b) 1955   The Decorative Art of the North American Indians. Pages 546–563 in Franz Boas, *Race, Language and Culture.* New York: Macmillan. → First published in *Popular Science Monthly.*

1904   Some Traits of Primitive Culture. *Journal of American Folk-lore* 17:243–254.

(1904–1943) 1945   *Race and Democratic Society.* New York: Augustin. → A collection of articles and lectures.

1907   Heredity in Anthropometric Traits. *American Anthropologist* New Series 9:453–469.

(1908) 1955   Decorative Designs of Alaskan Needlecases: A Study in the History of Conventional Designs, Based on Materials in the U.S. National Museum. Pages 564–592 in Franz Boas, *Race, Language and Culture.* New York: Macmillan. → First published in the *Proceedings* of the U.S. National Museum.

1909   *The Kwakiutl of Vancouver Island.* Jesup North Pacific Expedition, Publications, Vol. 5, No. 2. Leiden: Brill; New York: Stechert.

1911a   Introduction. Part I, pages 1–83 in Franz Boas (editor), *Handbook of American Indian Languages.* U.S. Bureau of American Ethnology, Bulletin No. 40. Washington: Government Printing Office.

(1911b) 1963   *The Mind of Primitive Man.* Rev. ed. New York: Collier. → A paperback edition was published in 1965 by the Free Press.

1912   Changes in Bodily Form of Descendants of Immigrants. *American Anthropologist* New Series 14:530–562. → A partial summary of this article was published in Boas' *Race, Language and Culture.*

(1913) 1955   Archaeological Investigations in the Valley of Mexico by the International School, 1911–1912. Pages 530–534 in Franz Boas, *Race, Language and Culture.* New York: Macmillan. → First published in the *Proceedings* of the 18th International Congress of Americanists.

1916a   On the Variety of Lines of Descent Represented in a Population. *American Anthropologist* New Series 18:1–9.

1916b   *Tsimshian Mythology.* Pages 29–1037 in U.S. Bureau of American Ethnology, *Thirty-first Annual Report, 1909–1910.* Washington: Government Printing Office.

(1916c) 1955   New Evidence in Regard to the Instability of Human Types. Pages 76–81 in Franz Boas, *Race,*

Language and Culture. New York: Macmillan. →
First published in the *Proceedings* of the National
Academy of Sciences.

1920a   Anthropometry of Porto Rico. *American Journal
of Physical Anthropology* 3:247–253.

(1920b) 1955   The Classification of American Languages.
Pages 211–218 in Franz Boas, *Race, Language and
Culture*. New York: Macmillan. → First published in
the *American Anthropologist*.

(1920c) 1955   The Methods of Ethnology. Pages 281–
289 in Franz Boas, *Race, Language and Culture*. New
York: Macmillan. → First published in the *American
Anthropologist*.

(1922) 1955   Report on an Anthropometric Investigation
of the Population of the United States. Pages 28–59
in Franz Boas, *Race, Language and Culture*. New
York: Macmillan. → First published in the *Journal
of the American Statistical Association*.

(1927) 1955   *Primitive Art*. New ed. New York: Dover.

1928a   Family Traits as Determined by Heredity and Environment. National Academy of Sciences, *Proceedings* 14:496–503.

(1928b) 1962   *Anthropology and Modern Life*. New York:
Norton.

(1929) 1955   Classification of American Indian Languages. Pages 219–225 in Franz Boas, *Race, Language
and Culture*. New York: Macmillan. → First published
in Volume 5 of *Language*.

(1930a) 1955   Some Problems of Methodology in the Social Sciences. Pages 260–269 in Franz Boas, *Race,
Language and Culture*. New York: Macmillan.

1930b   Observations on the Growth of Children. *Science*
New Series 72:44–48.

1930c   Anthropology. Volume 2, pages 73–110 in the
Encyclopaedia of the Social Sciences. New York:
Macmillan.

(1933) 1955   [Review of] G. W. Locher, *The Serpent in
Kwakiutl Religion: A Study in Primitive Culture*.
Pages 446–450 in Franz Boas, *Race, Language and
Culture*. New York: Macmillan.

1935   *Kwakiutl Culture as Reflected in Mythology*. American Folk-lore Society, Memoir No. 28. New York: The
Society.

1936   The Effects of American Environment on Immigrants and Their Descendants. *Science* New Series
84:522–525.

1938a   BOAS, FRANZ (editor)   *General Anthropology*.
New York and Boston: Heath.

1938b   An Anthropologist's Credo. *Nation* 147:201–204.

SUPPLEMENTARY BIBLIOGRAPHY

ANDREWS, H. J. et al.   1943   Bibliography of Franz Boas.
Pages 67–109 in *Franz Boas, 1858–1942*. American
Anthropological Association, Memoirs, No. 61. Me-
nasha, Wisc.: The Association.

BENEDICT, RUTH   1931   Folklore. Volume 6, pages 288–
293 in the *Encyclopaedia of the Social Sciences*. New
York: Macmillan.

BENEDICT, RUTH   1943   Franz Boas as an Ethnologist.
Pages 27–34 in *Franz Boas, 1858–1942*. American
Anthropological Association, Memoirs, No. 61. Me-
nasha, Wisc.: The Association.

*Boas Anniversay Volume: Anthropological Papers Written
in Honor of Franz Boas.*   1906   New York: Stechert.

CODERE, HELEN   1959   The Understanding of the Kwakiutl. Pages 61–75 in Walter R. Goldschmidt (editor),
*The Anthropology of Franz Boas: Essays on the Cen-
tennial of His Birth*. American Anthropological Asso-

ciation, Memoirs, No. 89. Menasha, Wisc.: The Association.

CRAMPTON, C. WARD   (1908) 1944   Physiological Age: A
Fundamental Principle. *Child Development* 15:3–52.

DEWEY, JOHN   1932   Human Nature. Volume 7, pages
531–536 in the *Encyclopaedia of the Social Sciences*.
New York: Macmillan.

FREEMAN, JOHN   1965   University Anthropology: Early
Departments in the United States. Kroeber Anthropological Society, *Papers* 32:78–90.

GOLDSCHMIDT, WALTER R. (editor)   1959   *The Anthro-
pology of Franz Boas: Essays on the Centennial of
His Birth*. American Anthropological Association,
Memoirs, No. 89. Menasha, Wisc.: The Association.

GOLDSTEIN, MARCUS S.   1940   Recent Trends in Physical
Anthropology. *American Journal of Physical Anthropology* 26:191–209.

GOLDSTEIN, MARCUS S.   1943   *Demographic and Bodily
Changes in Descendants of Mexican Immigrants,
With Comparable Data on Parents and Children in
Mexico*. Austin: Univ. of Texas, Institute of Latin-
American Studies.

GOLDSTEIN, MARCUS S.   1948   Franz Boas' Contributions
to Physical Anthropology. *American Journal of Physical Anthropology* New Series 6:145–161.

GOSSETT, THOMAS F.   1963   *Race: The History of an
Idea in America*. Dallas, Texas: Southern Methodist
Univ. Press.

HERSKOVITS, MELVILLE J.   1943   Franz Boas as Physical
Anthropologist. Pages 39–51 in *Franz Boas, 1858–
1942*. American Anthropological Association, Memoirs,
No. 61. Menasha, Wisc.: The Association.

HERSKOVITS, MELVILLE J.   1953   *Franz Boas: The Science of Man in the Making*. New York: Scribner.

HOWELLS, WILLIAM W.   1959   Boas as Statistician. Pages
112–116 in Walter R. Goldschmidt (editor), *The Anthropology of Franz Boas: Essays on the Centennial
of His Birth*. American Anthropological Association,
Memoirs, No. 89. Menasha, Wisc.: The Association.

HYMES, DELL H. (editor)   1964   *Language in Culture
and Society: A Reader in Linguistics and Anthropology*. New York: Harper.

JACOBS, MELVILLE   1959   Folklore. Pages 119–138 in
Walter R. Goldschmidt (editor), *The Anthropology of
Franz Boas: Essays on the Centennial of His Birth*.
American Anthropological Association, Memoirs,
No. 89. Menasha, Wisc.: The Association.

JAKOBSON, ROMAN   1944   Franz Boas' Approach to Language. *International Journal of American Linguistics*
10:188–195.

KLUCKHOHN, CLYDE; and PRUFER, OLAF   1959   Influ-
ences During the Formative Years. Pages 4–28 in
Walter R. Goldschmidt (editor), *The Anthropology of
Franz Boas: Essays on the Centennial of His Birth*.
American Anthropological Association, Memoirs,
No. 89. Menasha, Wisc.: The Association.

KROEBER, A. L.   1943   Franz Boas: The Man. Pages 5–26
in *Franz Boas, 1858–1942*. American Anthropological
Association, Memoirs, No. 61. Menasha, Wisc.: The
Association.

LOWIE, ROBERT H.   1947   Biographical Memoir of Franz
Boas: 1858–1942. National Academy of Sciences, *Biographical Memoirs* 24:303–322.

MASON, J. ALDEN   1943   Franz Boas as an Archeologist.
Pages 58–66 in *Franz Boas, 1858–1942*. American An-
thropological Association, Memoirs, No. 61. Menasha,
Wisc.: The Association.

MEAD, MARGARET   1959a   *An Anthropologist at Work:*

Writings of Ruth Benedict. Boston: Houghton Mifflin.
→ A critical study of Ruth Benedict, illustrated from
her own writing.

MEAD, MARGARET 1959*b* Apprenticeship Under Boas.
Pages 29–45 in Walter R. Goldschmidt (editor), *The
Anthropology of Franz Boas: Essays on the Centennial
of His Birth.* American Anthropological Association,
Memoirs, No. 89. Menasha, Wisc.: The Association.

SHAPIRO, HARRY L. 1939 *Migration and Environment:
A Study of the Physical Characteristics of the Japanese Immigrants to Hawaii and the Effects of Environment on Their Descendants.* New York: Oxford
Univ. Press.

SMITH, MARIAN W. 1959 Boas' "Natural History" Ap-
proach to Field Method. Pages 46–60 in Walter R.
Goldschmidt (editor), *The Anthropology of Franz
Boas: Essays on the Centennial of His Birth.* Amer-
ican Anthropological Association, Memoirs, No. 89.
Menasha, Wisc.: The Association.

SPIER, LESLIE 1929 *Growth of Japanese Children Born
in America and in Japan.* University of Washington
Publications in Anthropology, Vol. 3, No. 1. Seattle:
Univ. of Washington Press.

SPIER, LESLIE 1959 Some Central Elements in the Leg-
acy. Pages 146–155 in Walter R. Goldschmidt (edi-
tor), *The Anthropology of Franz Boas: Essays on the
Centennial of His Birth.* American Anthropological
Association, Memoirs, No. 89. Menasha, Wisc.: The
Association.

STOCKING, GEORGE W. JR. 1965 From Physics to Ethnology: Franz Boas' Arctic Expedition as a Problem in
the Historiography of the Behavioral Sciences. *Journal
of the History of the Behavioral Sciences* 1:53–66.

STOCKING, GEORGE W. JR. 1966 Franz Boas and the Culture Concept in Historical Perspective. *American Anthropologist* New Series 68:867–882.

TANNER, JAMES M. 1959 Boas' Contributions to Knowl-
edge of Human Growth and Form. Pages 76–111 in
Walter R. Goldschmidt (editor), *The Anthropology of
Franz Boas: Essays on the Centennial of His Birth.*
American Anthropological Association, Memoirs,
No. 89. Menasha, Wisc.: The Association.

BODIN, JEAN

Jean Bodin (1529 or 1530–1596), French jurist
and polyhistor, was born into a substantial and
well-connected middle-class family of Angers. He
managed to acquire an excellent humanist education at Paris in the course of preparing for the
priesthood—a career that ended in his teens, for
reasons still obscure, when the Carmelite order released him from his vows. In the 1550s he studied
civil law at the University of Toulouse and apparently hoped for a professorship. Ultimately de-
spairing of this goal and unsuccessful also in his
effort to promote a humanist college in the city of
Toulouse, he returned as an advocate to Paris,
where he had a moderately successful career in
politics. In the late 1560s he was entrusted by the
crown with several special missions of an administrative nature. In 1576 he appeared in the

Estates-General at Blois as a deputy of the Third
Estate from Vermandois and became, at some cost
to his ambitions, a highly influential critic of royal
fiscal policies. And from 1571 until the death of
his patron in 1584 he served in the household staff
of the duke of Alençon, an ambitious member of
the royal family, in which post he was privy to
much of the high intrigue and diplomacy of the
time. Bodin was not, however, a very skillful politician and failed to achieve what at one time he
most coveted, a high position in the royal household. He ended his career as *procurer du roi* for
Laon.

On the main political issue of his time, the demand for religious toleration by a large and powerful Protestant minority, Bodin stood with the party
of the Politiques, who sought to compromise the
issue of religious uniformity in the interest of political unity, and were therefore bitterly resented
by the party of militant Catholics united in the
Catholic League. In the recurring civil warfare,
which entered its final phase in 1588, it was often
extremely dangerous to hold such views as Bodin's
in public and, under heavy pressure at Laon, he
temporarily collaborated with the League. There
was, however, a considerable element of boldness
in Bodin's character that comes out most strongly
in his intellectual endeavors. After a series of spiritual crises, and amid recurrent charges of heresy,
he gradually worked out a highly unorthodox religious syncretism of his own, although he outwardly remained a Catholic. This religicus syncretism, furthermore, was but one aspect of an
encyclopedic synthesis of all existing knowledge,
which Bodin pursued with unflagging scholarly
devotion.

Jurisprudence and public law. Bodin's main
contributions to the development of social science
were in jurisprudence and public law. During the
sixteenth century the intellectual authority of Roman law, more or less unchallenged in the Middle
Ages, had been increasingly undermined by humanist criticisms of its relevance and logical arrangement. Among sixteenth-century jurists committed to the unification of French law there was
an influential party, which preferred an independently created code to direct reception of the
Roman law. Bodin was a member of this group,
and at one point in his career his highest ambition
was to construct a universal jurisprudence through
a comparison and synthesis of "the laws of all of
the most famous commonwealths" in order "to derive the best variety." In his *Six livres de la république* (*Six Bookes of a Commonweale*, 1576), this
program is actually carried out for what is roughly

the domain of public law. Bodin first attempted to find the universal and "necessary" principles of public order in those legal elements that "all or the better part" of peoples have in common. He then went on to classify and illustrate the different types of commonwealths and states encountered in history, producing what amounts to a comprehensive system of comparative public law. His final objective was to show which particular legislative and governmental policies are best adapted to the peculiar problems of each type of state and how all of these policies together should be adapted to a people's "natural temperament," which he attributed to the strong, but not determining, influence of climate and other geographic factors. This entire work is carried out with encyclopedic erudition and a profound, if not always fully realized, desire for system. It represents, therefore, a definite break with the exegetic jurisprudence of the Middle Ages and the adoption of a critical method. Bodin's historical universalism points toward the rationalist universalism of seventeenth-century natural law; and his comparative and sociological approach clearly, and often strikingly, anticipates various eighteenth-century developments.

The central theme in Bodin's doctrine of the state is the need, suggested by the disorders of his time, for complete concentration and centralization of political authority. Through a great number of historical examples he attempted to show that in every important and enduring commonwealth all legislative and executive functions are subordinate to some single center. This doctrine of the state questions the classical wisdom of the mixed constitution, at that time one of the most influential notions in political science. In order to demonstrate that famous "mixed" constitutions, such as those of ancient Rome and modern Venice, were in fact instances of concentration, Bodin introduced an ingenious and influential distinction between the form of state and the form of government, corresponding to a distinction between the ownership and the exercise of power. On this basis he was able to argue, with some degree of plausibility, that the Roman Empire was really a democracy governed aristocratically and that Venice was really an aristocracy with certain democratic features in its government.

Bodin did not deny that the old idea of "mixture" contained an important principle of policy when properly interpreted and instituted, not as a division in the ownership of power but as a balancing of aristocratic and popular interests in the arrangement of government and the distribution of rewards and punishments. And he argued that this balance in the exercise of power is most readily achieved in monarchies, where the ultimate owner of power can stand apart from the social interests to be harmonized. Bodin's critique and reinterpretation of the mixed state turns out, then, to be a highly sophisticated defense of absolute yet moderate monarchy, and it was to play an important role in the ideological conflicts of the old regime.

For Bodin, however, the fundamental condition of stability is that expressed in his celebrated principle of sovereignty, which holds that in every stable commonwealth there must exist a supreme or sovereign authority vested in some single individual or group. A sovereign authority is one whose power is "absolute and perpetual." And since power is, in Bodin's usage, absolute when it is unlimited in jurisdiction and perpetual when it is not held in trust for someone else, a sovereign authority is a group or person endowed with an intrinsic and inalienable right to exercise, or supervise the exercise of, all the powers that a government may legitimately claim. The absolutism of the sovereign, therefore, is but a guarantee of the concentration and unity of government and does not necessarily imply unlimited power over the person or property of subjects. Indeed, Bodin, in accord with medieval precedent, very strenuously insisted that the rights of sovereignty are restricted by natural law as well as other claims of the community. And he admitted that a subject may legitimately refuse to obey an unjust order of the sovereign, although he rejected any general right of active revolution. If Bodin's position on these issues is not always lucidly worked out, it is at least in part because he was less concerned with the moral grounds of obligation than with the legal conditions of effective governance.

Economic policy. On specific points of public policy most of Bodin's recommendations are mere bits of tactical wisdom in the style of Machiavelli, but there are many that have more far-reaching theoretical implications. In economic policy Bodin was an enlightened mercantilist who located the real wealth of a country not in bullion but in industry and natural resources. This distinction between real and money values is theoretically grounded in the quantity theory of money, which, despite anticipations by Copernicus, is fully developed only with Bodin. In his *Réponse aux paradoxes de M. de Malestroit* (1568), Bodin elaborately argued that the price inflation of his age was caused not by debasement of the coinage, a hypothesis advanced by Malestroit, but by the sudden increase in the supply of precious metals. This essay may also be regarded as a pioneering monograph in scientific social history, for Bodin, with great ingenuity, used economic records to reconstruct the movement of prices.

Religious policy. In religious policy Bodin recommended a strictly political approach to the religious conflicts of the time. Outward uniformity of worship should be enforced wherever possible, but toleration should be granted wherever a religious minority is too strong to be repressed conveniently. More interesting than these recommendations is Bodin's attempt to supply a theological foundation for this "politique" solution. In his *Colloquium heptaplomeres* (1588a), a series of conversations on the nature of the true religion between a proponent of natural religion, an apologist for paganism, a Jew, a Turk, a Catholic, a Lutheran, and a Zwinglian—the following conclusions, among others, are either stated or implied: that the various positive religions are degenerations of an original natural religion still known to speculative reason; that the positive religions were designed to counteract the ignorance and irrationality of the masses by supplying rituals and dogma adapted to circumstances and temperaments of different peoples; and that any one of the positive forms of worship is sufficient for salvation, because all that God demands is the attitude of piety as such. Theological truth and political expediency can therefore never be in conflict, since a double standard in religion is decreed by providence itself. It may also be noted that Bodin's position, although not unique, was especially radical for its time in that it contained an elaborate refutation of Christianity by the spokesman for Judaism, which, Bodin implies, is the purest of the positive religions. The *Colloquium heptaplomeres* may also be regarded as one of the earliest comparative treatments of religion. For obvious reasons the work was never published by Bodin, but it was known to scholars of the seventeenth and eighteenth centuries in manuscript copies. The first complete published version did not appear until 1857, and a truly definitive edition is wanting even now.

Universal history. Dedicated as he was to a comparative understanding of social institutions, Bodin was convinced that the study of universal history was a prime requirement of education and his *Methodus ad facilem historiarum cognitionem* (*Method for the Easy Comprehension of History*) was a sort of guidebook for prospective students. Among other things there is a chapter on evaluating historians that makes an important contribution to the emergence in this period of a methodology of historical criticism. In the seventh chapter there are two influential polemical essays defending what might be called a naturalistic view of historical change: one is a devastating refutation of a medieval periodization of history, based on a biblical prophecy, into four world empires, of which the Germano–Roman was supposed to be the last; and the other is a critique of the idea of a golden age and of the superiority of the ancients to the moderns, in which Bodin begins to enunciate a theory of cumulative progress in the arts and sciences.

Bodin's ultimate objective was a synthesis, broadly Neoplatonic in tone, of the entire realm of human knowledge; and the corpus of his writings covers not only what would now be called the social science disciplines, but natural philosophy, demonology, astrology, and numerology as well. The works on these latter topics are among his least enduring, and it may be said in general that Bodin, like the other encyclopedists of the period, was frequently loose and hasty in his "syntheses" and often lacked the critical resources to avoid superstition and credulity. But with all this, his social thought is so creative that he must be regarded as a central figure in the development of modern social science.

JULIAN H. FRANKLIN

[*For the historical context of Bodin's work, see* CONSTITUTIONS AND CONSTITUTIONALISM; SOVEREIGNTY; STATE; *and the biographies of* MACHIAVELLI; MARSILIUS. *For discussion of the subsequent development of his ideas, see the biography of* MONTESQUIEU.]

WORKS BY BODIN

(1559–1566) 1951 *Oeuvres philosophiques.* Edited and translated by Pierre Mesnard. Corpus général des philosophes français, auteurs modernes, Vol. 3. Paris: Presses Universitaires de France. → Text is in both Latin and French. This is the first volume—containing works up through 1566—of a projected series that may eventually include critical editions of the *Six livres de la république* and the *Colloquium heptaplomeres,* both of which are badly needed.

(1566) 1945 *Method for the Easy Comprehension of History.* Records of Civilization, Sources and Studies, No. 37. New York: Columbia Univ. Press. → First published in Latin as *Methodus ad facilem historiarum cognitionem.*

(1568) 1932 *La vie chère au XVIᵉ siècle: La response de Jean Bodin à M. de Malestroit.* Edited by Henri Hauser. Paris: Colin. → A new edition of *Réponse aux paradoxes de M. de Malestroit.*

(1568) 1946 *The Response of Jean Bodin to the* Paradoxes of Malestroit, *and the* Paradoxes. Chevy Chase, Md.: Century Dollar Press. → A limited edition, translated from the second French edition.

(1576) 1962 *The Six Bookes of a Commonweale.* Edited by Kenneth D. McRae. Cambridge, Mass.: Harvard Univ. Press. → A facsimile reprint of the English translation of 1606, corrected and supplemented in the light of a new comparison with the French and Latin texts.

(1588a) 1857 *Colloquium heptaplomeres de rerum sublimium arcanis abditis.* Edited by Ludov Noack. Schwerin (Germany).

(1588b) 1914 *Colloque de Jean Bodin: Des secrets cachez des choses sublimes entre sept sçauans qui sont de differens sentimens (traduction français du "Colloquium heptaplomeres").* Selected and edited by Roger Chauviré. Paris: Sirey. → Contains selections from a French translation of the *Colloquium heptaplomeres* made shortly after Bodin's death. It is probably a more accurate version of the lost original than the Latin text edited by Noack. However, Noack's is the only complete version.

WORKS ABOUT BODIN

Full-length works that attempt to give a reasonably comprehensive account of Bodin's political and social thought are Baudrillart 1853; Chauviré 1914; *and* Garosci 1934. *For an excellent account of his political doctrine, see* Mesnard 1951a; *and for a brief survey, see* Allen 1928. *Two biographical sketches that take full account of recent findings can be found in* McRae 1962 *and* Mesnard 1951b.

ALLEN, JOHN W. (1928) 1957 *A History of Political Thought in the Sixteenth Century.* London: Methuen.

BAUDRILLART, HENRI J. L. 1853 *J. Bodin et son temps: Tableau des théories politiques et des idées économiques au seizième siècle.* Paris: Guillaumin.

BROWN, JOHN L. 1939 *The* Methodus ad facilem historiarum cognitionem *of Jean Bodin: A Critical Study.* Washington: Catholic Univ. of America Press.

CHAUVIRÉ, ROGER 1914 *Jean Bodin: Auteur de* La république. La Flèche (France): Besnier.

DILTHEY, WILHELM (1914) 1957 Der religiös–universale Theismus: Bodins Vergleichung der Religionen. Pages 145–153 in Wilhelm Dilthey, *Gesammelte Schriften.* Volume 2: Weltanschauung und Analyse des Menschen seit Renaissance und Reformation; Abhandlungen zur Geschichte der Philosophie und Religion. Stuttgart and Göttingen (Germany): Teubner.

FRANKLIN, JULIAN H. 1963 *Jean Bodin and the Sixteenth Century Revolution in the Methodology of Law and History.* New York: Columbia Univ. Press.

GAROSCI, ALDO 1934 *Jean Bodin: Politica e diritto nel rinascimento francese.* Milan: Corticelli.

HAUSER, HENRI (editor) 1932 Introduction. In Jean Bodin, *La vie chère au XVIᵉ siècle: La response de Jean Bodin à M. de Malestroit.* Paris: Colin.

McRAE, KENNETH D. (editor) 1962 Introduction. In Jean Bodin, *The Six Bookes of a Commonweale.* Cambridge, Mass.: Harvard Univ. Press.

MESNARD, PIERRE 1929 La pensée religieuse de Bodin. *Revue du seizième siècle* 16:77–121.

MESNARD, PIERRE (1951a) 1952 *La république* de Jean Bodin. Book 5, pages 473–546 in Pierre Mesnard, *L'essor de la philosophie politique au XVIᵉ siècle.* 2d ed., rev. Paris: Vrin.

MESNARD, PIERRE (editor) 1951b Vers un portrait de Jean Bodin. Introduction in Jean Bodin, *Oeuvres philosophiques.* Paris: Presses Universitaires de France.

MOREAU-REIBEL, JEAN 1933 *Jean Bodin et le droit public comparé dans ses rapports avec la philosophie de l'histoire.* Paris: Vrin.

REYNOLDS, BEATRICE 1931 *Proponents of Limited Monarchy in Sixteenth Century France: Francis Hotman and Jean Bodin.* Columbia University Studies in History, Economics and Public Law, No. 334. New York: Columbia Univ. Press.

SABINE, GEORGE H. 1931 The *Colloquium heptaplomeres* of Jean Bodin. Pages 271–309 in *Persecution and Liberty: Essays in Honor of George Lincoln Burr.* New York: Century.

BODY IMAGE

"Body image" can be considered synonymous with such terms as "body concept" and "body scheme." Broadly speaking, the term pertains to how the individual perceives his own body. It does not imply that the individual's concept of his body is represented by a conscious image; rather, it embraces his collective attitudes, feelings, and fantasies about his body without regard to level of awareness.

Basic to most definitions of body image is the view that it represents the manner in which a person has learned to organize and integrate his body experiences. Body image concepts are important for an understanding of such diverse phenomena as adjustment to body disablement, maintenance of posture and spatial orientation, personality development, and cultural differences.

At a common-sense level, the pervasive significance of the body image is evident in widespread preoccupation with myths and stories that concern body transformation (such as the change from human to werewolf form). It is evident, too, in the vast expenditure of time and energy that goes into clothing and reshaping the body (for example, plastic surgery) for the purpose of conforming to idealized standards of appearance.

Historical background. Interest in the body image appeared first in the work of neurologists who observed that brain damage could produce bizarre alterations in a person's perception of his body. Patients suffering from brain damage manifested such extreme symptoms as the inability to recognize parts of their own bodies and the assignment of entirely different identities to the right and left sides of their bodies. Interest in body image phenomena was further reinforced by observations that neurotic and schizophrenic patients frequently had unusual body feelings. Paul Schilder (1935), neurologist, psychiatrist, and early influential theorist, reported the following kinds of distortions in the schizophrenic patient: a sense of alienation from his own body (depersonalization), inability to distinguish the boundaries of his body, and feelings of transformation in the sex of his body. Surgeons recorded unusual body experiences in patients with amputations and noted that amputees typically hallucinated the absent member as if it were still present. The hallucinated body member was designated a "phantom limb."

The neurologist Henry Head, another early influential theorist, took the view that a body schema was essential to the functioning of the individual (Head et al. 1920). He theorized that each person constructs a picture or model of his body that constitutes a standard against which all body movements and postures are judged. He applied the term "schema" to this standard. His description of the body schema underscored its influence upon body orientation, but he noted also that it served to integrate other kinds of experiences.

Equally prominent in early body image formulations was the psychoanalytic work of Sigmund Freud. Freud considered the body concept basic to the development of identity and ego structure. He conceived of the child's earliest sense of identity as first taking the form of learning to discriminate between his own body and the outer world. Thus, when the child is able to perceive his own body as something apart from its environs, he presumably acquires a basis for distinguishing self from non-self.

Freud's theory of libidinal development was saturated with key references to body attitudes. He conceptualized the individual's psychosexual development in terms of the successive localization of energy and sensitivity at oral, anal, and genital body sites. It was assumed that as each of these sites successively acquired increased prominence and sensitivity, corresponding needs were aroused to seek out agents capable of providing stimulation. Presumably, too, when a person failed to mature and was fixated at one of the earlier erogenous zones (oral or anal), he was left to deal with adult experiences in terms of a body context more appropriate to the way of life of a child.

Many of Freud's concepts of personality development assign importance to changes in the perceptual and erogenous dominance of body sectors. Psychoanalytic theorists continue to focus upon body attitudes as significant in understanding many forms of behavior deviance (for example, schizophrenia and fetishism). Indeed, psychoanalytical concepts have had a major influence upon body image theory and research.

Schilder drew attention to other body image phenomena in his book *The Image and Appearance of the Human Body* (1935), where he formulated a variety of theoretical concepts that were phrased largely in psychoanalytic terms. He suggested that the body image is molded by one's interactions with others, and to the extent that these interactions are faulty, the body image will be inadequately developed. Schilder's book contained rich descriptions of how the individual perceives his own body in diverse situations. He analyzed body experiences that characterize awakening, falling asleep, assuming unusual body positions, ingesting certain drugs, and undergoing schizophrenic disorganization. One idea he particularly emphasized was that sensations of body disintegration are likely to typify those who masochistically direct anger against themselves.

Schilder concerned himself with determining whether specific brain areas are linked with the body image. He was one of a group of neurologists who made persistent attempts to relate body image distortions observed in brain-damaged patients to the sites of the brain lesions. Considerable evidence has accumulated that damage to the parietal lobes selectively disrupts the individual's ability to perceive his body realistically.

Phantom limb. Historically, the phantom limb phenomenon has played a significant role in calling attention to the problems of organizing body perceptions. Such observers as Head and his colleagues (1920), Lhermitte (1939), and Schilder (1935) were puzzled by the fact that normal persons typically hallucinated the presence of body members lost through injury or amputation. Such hallucinations implied that the individual had a "picture" of his body which persisted even when it was no longer realistically accurate. Controversy still exists about whether the phantom experience is primarily a result of a compensatory process occurring in the central nervous system or of persisting peripheral sensations evoked by injured tissue in the stump. Evidence indicates that while stump sensations play a part in the phantom experience, central factors are of greater importance. Interesting questions have been stimulated by observations of the phantom limb: for example, why does the duration of phantom experiences vary markedly between individuals? And why does the phantom not appear when body parts are gradually absorbed (as in leprosy) rather than suddenly removed?

Research. Well-controlled experiments in the area of body image are relatively new, most scientific studies having been carried out since 1945.

Human figure drawing. One of the oldest and most frequently used techniques for the study of the body image makes use of human figure drawing. It has been suggested that when an individual is asked to draw a picture of a person, he projects into his drawing indications of how he experiences his body. Some investigators have proposed that such indicators as the size of the figure drawn and difficulty in depicting specific body areas provide information about the individual's body concept. There have been claims that the figure drawing can be used to measure such variables as feelings of body inferiority and anxiety about sexual adequacy. However, despite a profusion of studies, there is no evidence that figure drawing is an effective method of tapping body image attitudes. It is true that in some instances it has proved sensitive to the existence of actual body defects. For example, individuals with crippling defects have been shown to introduce analogous defects in their figure drawings. Moreover, there have been some demonstrations that figure-drawing indicators of body disturbance are higher in schizophrenic than in normal subjects. However, no consistently successful indices of body attitudes have been derived. Indeed, the problem of using the figure drawing to evaluate body image has been enormously complicated by evidence that artistic skill may so strongly influence the characteristics of drawings as to minimize the importance of most other factors.

Attitudes toward the body. Another approach to evaluating the body image has revolved about measuring the subject's dissatisfaction with regions of his body. Procedures have been devised that pose for him the task of indicating how positively or negatively he views his body. These procedures vary from direct ratings of dissatisfaction with parts of one's body to judgments regarding the comparability of one's body to pictured bodies. It has been found that men are most likely to be dissatisfied with areas of their bodies that seem "too small"; whereas women focus their self-criticism upon body sectors that appear to be "too large." Also, evidence has emerged that dissatisfaction with one's body is accompanied by generalized feelings of insecurity and diminished self-confidence.

Perceived body size. One of the most promising lines of body image research has dealt with perceived body size. This work concerns the significance to be attached to the size an individual ascribes to parts of his body. The individual's concept of his body size is often inaccurate and exaggerated in the direction of largeness or smallness as a function of either situational influences or specific body attitudes. It has been demonstrated that estimates of body size vary in relation to the total spatial context of the individual, the degree of sensory input to his skin, the nature of his ongoing activities, and many other variables (Wapner et al. 1958). For example, subjects judge their heads to be smaller when heat or touch emphasizes

the skin boundary than when such stimulation is absent. It has further been shown that subjects perceive their arms as longer when pointed at an open, unobstructed vista than when pointed at a limiting wall. The subject's mood, his attitudes toward himself, his degree of psychiatric disturbance, and a number of other psychological factors have been found to play a part in his evaluation of his own body size. For example, persons exposed to an experience of failure see themselves as shorter than they do under conditions of nonfailure. Schizophrenic, as compared to normal, subjects unrealistically exaggerate the size of their bodies. Normal subjects who ingest psychotomimetic drugs, which produce psychoticlike disturbance, likewise overestimate the sizes of their body parts. At another level, it has been noted that the relative sizes an individual ascribes to regions of his body (for example, right side versus left side, back versus front) may reflect aspects of his personality organization.

Aside from the formal research efforts that have highlighted the importance of perceived body size as a body image variable, there is a long history of anecdotal and clinical observation supporting a similar view. Vivid experiences of change in body size have been described in schizophrenic and brain-damaged patients, in patients with migraine attacks, and in various other persons exposed to severe stress demands. Clearly, there is a tendency for experiences to be translated into changes in perceived body size.

Projective techniques. Responses to ambiguous stimuli, such as ink blots, briefly exposed pictures, and incomplete representations of the human form, have been widely utilized to measure body attitudes. It is assumed that when a person is asked to interpret or give meaning to something as vague as an ink blot, he projects self feelings and self representations into his interpretations. In this vein, it has been found that persons with localized body defects focus their attention upon corresponding body areas when studying pictures containing vague representations of the human figure. The frequency of references to body sensations (such as pain, hunger, fatigue) in stories composed in response to pictures has been shown by D. J. van Lennep (1957) to vary developmentally and to differ between the sexes. Females were found to show a moderate increase in body references beyond the age of 15, whereas males were typified by a pattern of decline in such references. It has been suggested by van Lennep that in Western culture men are supposed to transcend their bodies and to turn their energies toward the world.

Women, on the other hand, are given approval for continuing and even increasing their investments in their bodies.

Fisher and Cleveland (1958) have developed a method for scoring responses to ink blots which measures how clearly the individual is able to experience his body as possessing boundaries that differentiate it from its environs. This boundary measure has been able to predict several noteworthy aspects of behavior, including the desire for high achievement, behavior in small groups, the locus of psychosomatic symptomatology, and adequacy of adjustment to body disablement.

Perspectives and problems. The investigation of body image phenomena has become a vigorous enterprise. One dominant fact that has emerged is that the individual's body is a unique perceptual object. The individual responds to his own body with an intensity of ego involvement that can rarely be evoked by other objects. The body is, after all, in a unique position as the only object that is simultaneously perceived and a part of the perceiver. In studying an individual's manner of experiencing and conceptualizing his body, one obtains rich data about him that is not readily available from other sources.

It is difficult to know what priorities to assign to the body image issues that still need to be clarified. Speaking broadly, one may say there is an emphatic need to ascertain the principal axes underlying the organization of the body image. It remains to be established whether the body image is built around the spatial dimensions of the body, the specialized functions of different body regions, or perhaps the private and symbolic meanings assigned to body areas by the culture. There is also a need to examine the relationships between body attitudes and socialization modes in different cultures. There is evidence in the anthropological literature that body attitudes may differ radically in relation to cultural context. Another important problem for research is the assessment of the role that body image plays in the development and definition of the individual's sense of identity.

SEYMOUR FISHER

[*Directly related are the entries* IDENTITY, PSYCHO-SOCIAL; SELF CONCEPT. *Other relevant material may be found in* FANTASY; SCHIZOPHRENIA.]

BIBLIOGRAPHY

CRITCHLEY, MACDONALD 1953 *The Parietal Lobes.* London: Arnold.

FISHER, SEYMOUR; and CLEVELAND, SIDNEY E. 1958 *Body Image and Personality.* Princeton, N.J.: Van Nostrand.

FREUD, SIGMUND (1888–1938) 1959 *Collected Papers.*
5 vols. Authorized translation under the supervision of Joan Riviere. Volume 5 edited by James Strachey. International Psycho-analytic Library, No. 7–10, 34. New York: Basic Books; London: Hogarth. → Translation of *Sammlung kleiner Schriften zur Neurosenlehre* and additional papers. A ten-volume paperback edition was published in 1963 by Collier Books.

HEAD, HENRY et al. 1920 *Studies in Neurology.* 2 vols. London: Hodder & Stoughton. → These papers consist mainly of a republication of papers published in *Brain* between 1905 and 1918.

LENNEP, D. J., VAN 1957 Projection and Personality. Pages 259–277 in Henry P. David and Helmut von Bracken (editors), *Perspectives in Personality Theory.* New York: Basic Books.

LHERMITTE, JACQUES J. 1939 *L'image de notre corps.* Paris: Éditions de la Nouvelle Revue Critique.

SCHILDER, PAUL (1935) 1950 *The Image and Appearance of the Human Body: Studies of the Constructive Energies in the Psyche.* New York: International Universities Press.

WAPNER, SEYMOUR; WERNER, H.; and COMALLI, P. E. 1958 Effect of Enhancement of Head Boundary on Head Size and Shape. *Perceptual and Motor Skills* 8:319–325.

WAPNER, SEYMOUR; and WERNER, HEINZ (editors) 1965 *The Body Percept.* New York: Random House.

BOGORAZ, VLADIMIR G.; STERNBERG, LEV Y.; and JOCHELSON, VLADIMIR

Vladimir Germanovich Bogoraz (1865–1936), Lev Yakovlevich Sternberg (1861–1927), and Vladimir Jochelson (1855–1937) were Russian revolutionaries and ethnographers who studied the peoples of Siberia. Together with such other Russian ethnographers as Moisei A. Krol' and Dmitrii A. Klements, they formed a group whose members were at once political comrades and scientific colleagues. When their political activities resulted in exile, they turned exile to advantage, focusing their creative energy on Siberian ethnography; "beyond the pale of culture," they set out scientifically to acquire knowledge of the indigenous peoples, and in what they considered to be an intellectual consequence of their studies, they sided with the people generally against tsarism. Ethnography was for them an intellectual path to populism: they belonged to Narodnaya Volya (Peoples' Will), a radical, populist, and terrorist political party that was connected in a general way to *narodnichestvo*, the identification of the intellectuals with the simple folk, from whom, according to their doctrine, national strength arose. Toward the end of the nineteenth century, when changing social conditions and increased international contact overcame populist nationalism, Bogoraz, Sternberg, and their colleagues shared the new internationalism of the revolutionary movement.

Bogoraz was born in Volhynia into a Jewish family, but for practical reasons he joined the Russian Orthodox church. While a student at St. Petersburg he participated in revolutionary activities; indeed, from the age of 17 on, he frequently suffered penalties for such activities. Exiled to Yakutia, he encountered Jochelson, and they began their long partnership in ethnographic and linguistic studies of Russian Sibiriaks and other indigenous peoples. Sternberg's ethnographic studies-in-exile were done on the island of Sakhalin. Bogoraz also wrote poems and stories while in exile. He was permitted to engage in ethnographic research through the intervention of such influential members of the Russian Academy of Sciences as Vasilii Radlov (or Radloff) and Pëtr Petrovich Semënov-Tianshanskii. Even while he was still in exile, Bogoraz was appointed to the 1895–1897 Sibiriakov expedition to northeast Siberia sponsored by the Russian Geographic Society; in 1900–1901 he participated in the Jesup North Pacific Expedition of the American Museum of Natural History, serving as head of the Anadyr (Siberia) section.

He returned to St. Petersburg in 1901 to pursue both scientific and revolutionary activities, and again Radlov and others came to his aid when he had to flee from police action. He settled in New York for three years, and with the support of Franz Boas obtained a position at the American Museum; his friendship with Boas continued for three decades. On returning to Russia he lived until 1917 by scientific and belletristic work. Although he kept aloof from all parties, he remained generally sympathetic to the Narodniki (Populists) and to the Social Democrats. In 1904 he helped organize the First Peasant Congress and the Labor group in the Duma.

In 1918 he was appointed professor at the University of Leningrad and curator of the Museum of Anthropology and Ethnography, where he had served prior to the revolution. With Sternberg he organized the ethnographic faculty of the university. He became director of the Institute of the Peoples of the North, Leningrad, an agency concerned with the development of Siberian peoples. Here Bogoraz and his colleagues produced grammars, readers, dictionaries, textbooks, as well as historical and ethnographic sketches, and established schools, folklore collections, and cultural centers in Siberia for the Soviet regime. He was active in these capacities until his death.

In the Jesup North Pacific Expedition, Bogoraz was responsible for the Chukchee and the Eskimo of Siberia, Sternberg for the Gilyak (Nivkh) of the lower Amur River and Sakhalin, and Jochelson for the Yukagir and Koryak. The expedition was directed by Boas and had as its geographic locus the Pacific rim, from Puget Sound to the Amur River. Established with funds from the American philanthropist Morris Jesup, it was designed to explore art and archeology, folklore, languages, material culture, and physical anthropology. It emphasized factual description and systematic coverage based on long-term residence, an approach that was congenial to Bogoraz, Sternberg, and Jochelson, at least insofar as this expedition was concerned; Boas was a strong advocate of precise data collection as an end in itself. Evaluation of the data was left to the future, when the crisis of recording rapidly disappearing cultures was past. Then the study of cultures of the North Pacific would surely shed light on the problems of the peopling of America and subsequent cultural processes, including the possible relation of high cultures of Asia and America. The expedition resulted in a great series of monographic studies by individual members, but no systematic comparison of intrinsic culture content was made.

The Russian ethnographers, together with Berthold Laufer, specialized on the Asian side of the Pacific; Boas and his collaborators—Livingston Farrand, Gerard Fowke, George Hunt, John R. Swanton, and James A. Teit—on the American side. The contributions of Bogoraz and Jochelson are masterly ethnographies of the Chukchee, Koryak, and Yukagir, and careful folkloric and linguistic collections of the Siberian Eskimo. Sternberg's Gilyak materials remain in the American Museum (it has not been practical to publish them). Theory and interpretation were not, to be sure, entirely lacking in these works: thus Bogoraz outlined a five-stage development of Chukchee religion. However, despite adversions to Tylor and others, this brief religiotheoretical excursus is not so much a stage-theory of religion per se as a view of how Chukchee religion specifically was structured and how it developed. (Nor is this a theory of religious survivals, although it has been criticized as such.) Doctrinal, ceremonial, sociofunctional, and psychological approaches to shamanism were systematically explored in various of these works, with a sophisticated interpretation by Bogoraz of the inner humanity of shamans and their devouts.

Independently of his ethnographic work, in the years 1926–1927 Bogoraz developed a theory of culture; it remained unpublished. He sought a new science of culture in which the motive forces of man were to be derived not from within culture but externally. He proposed a dual emphasis—on the natural environment and on human biology—

that would be applied to man's past (archeology and history) and present (ethnography).

After the revolution, Sternberg taught ethnography at the University of Leningrad. He adhered explicitly to Marxist theory, seeking through his ethnography to demonstrate the theories of Engels —e.g., group marriage in relation to primitive communism as a stage of cultural evolution—and of L. H. Morgan—e.g., the Turano–Ganowanian system of consanguinity in northeast Asia. An avid polemicist, he attacked the theories of Freud, Lévy-Bruhl, and Wilhelm Schmidt.

In an unpublished work, however, Sternberg propounded a psychological and social theory of cultural change that was not directly related to historical materialism. Unlike Bogoraz, he did not derive culture from biology and milieu but regarded it as a purely social heritage; culture is a creation of the human psyche, and its creator is one—mankind as a whole. Differences in culture are external to human nature; they are geographic and historical accidents.

Jochelson left Russia permanently during the Soviet period and spent his later years in the United States, attached to the American Museum of Natural History. Bogoraz and Sternberg remained in Russia, and they were sharply criticized by Soviet writers for views which stood outside Marxism in general (in Bogoraz' case) and outside Leninist Marxism (in Sternberg's). Bogoraz was attacked for a biomechanical approach to culture, Sternberg for eclecticism and idealism. Nevertheless, both were able to study and teach.

Bogoraz and Jochelson stood close to the positivist–naturalist movement in the cultural anthropology of their time; their aim was an objective science of mankind, free of values. They were convinced that this was attainable. Bogoraz, in the absence of direct historical evidence, sought to introduce time depth by understanding the inner systematics and dynamics of culture. His ethnography was in this limited sense evolutionary. But neither he nor Jochelson made projections into the past or the future, nor did they seek for inferential cultural constructions. Sternberg at first shared many of these views but later adopted the evolutionary system of Morgan and Engels.

Despite the divergent theoretical and political tendencies of their later lives, these three Russian ethnographers constitute a school of thought in anthropology. They shared a common background of revolutionary activity, exile, and ethnographic study. While they may have responded differently to this background, there nevertheless remained their common geographic area of specialization, common techniques and methods of ethnography, and common broad social aims. They achieved the highest level of exactness and reliability in field techniques: Bogoraz on Chukchee and Sternberg on Gilyak are ethnographic classics. And they were a vital force in the profound political changes in Russia, contributing knowledge and direction to the transition of the indigenous peoples and to the development of anthropology among their colleagues and students.

LAWRENCE KRADER

[*For the historical context of Bogoraz, Sternberg, and Jochelson's work, see the biographies of* BOAS; ENGELS; MORGAN, LEWIS HENRY. *For discussion of related work, see* ETHNOGRAPHY; HISTORY, *article on* ETHNOHISTORY.]

WORKS BY BOGORAZ

1900   *Materialy po izucheniiu chukotskogo iazyka fol'klora, sobrannye v kolymskom okruge* (Materials for the Study of the Chukchee Language and Folklore, Collected in the Kolyma Region). St. Petersburg (Russia): Akademiia Nauk.

1900   BOGORAZ, VLADIMIR G.; and JOCHELSON, VLADIMIR I. O sibirskom poliarnom otdele severo-tikhookeanskoi ekspeditsii (On the Siberian Arctic Section of the North Pacific Expedition). *Zhivaia starina* 10, no. 1/2:295–296. → Outline of an anthropological and linguistic investigation of the Chukchee, the Koryak, and the Yukaghir.

1902   The Folklore of Northeastern Asia, as Compared With That of Northwestern America. *American Anthropologist* New Series 4:577–683. → A comparison of 32 Chukchee and Eskimo tales and of 59 Chukchee, Koryak, and Kamchadal tales with American Indian plots.

1904–1909   *The Chukchee.* Jesup North Pacific Expedition Publications, Vol. 7, and American Museum of Natural History, New York, Memoir, Vol. 11, Parts 1–3. Leiden: Brill; New York: Stechert.

1910a   *Chukchee Mythology.* Jesup North Pacific Expedition Publications, Vol. 8, Part 1, and American Museum of Natural History, New York, Memoir, Vol. 12, Part 1. Leiden: Brill; New York: Stechert.

1910b   K psikhologii shamanstva u narodov severovostochnoi Azii (On the Psychology of Shamanism Among the Peoples of Northeastern Asia). *Etnograficheskoe obozrenie* [1910], no. 1/2:1–36.

1922   Chukchee. U.S. Bureau of American Ethnology, *Bulletin*, no. 40, part 2:631–903.

1925   Ideas of Space and Time in the Conception of Primitive Religion. *American Anthropologist* New Series 27:205–266. → An analysis of Chukchee, Koryak, and Yukaghir beliefs.

1927   Drevnie pereseleniia narodov v severnoi Evrazii i v Amerike (Ancient Ethnic Migrations in Northern Eurasia and America). Akademiia Nauk SSSR, Muzei Antropologii i Etnografii, *Sbornik* 6:38–62.

1928a   Chukchee Tales. *Journal of American Folk-lore* 41:297–452.

1928b   Ethnographic Problems of the Eurasian Arctic. Volume 6, pages 189–207 in *Problems of Polar Research.* New York: American Geographical Society.

(1928c) 1929   Neue Daten über die Ethnographie der

kleinen Völkerschaften des Nordens. *Anthropos* 24: 517–521. → First published in Russian.

1928*d* Paleoasiatic Tribes of South Siberia. Volume 1, pages 249–272 in International Congress of Americanists, Twenty-second, Rome, 1926, *Atti.* Rome: Garroni.

1929*a* Elements of the Culture of the Circumpolar Zone. *American Anthropologist* New Series 31, no. 4:579–601.

1929*b* Siberian Cousins of the Eskimo. *Asia* 29, no. 1: 316–322.

1936 Osnovnye tipy fol'klora severnoi Evrazii i severnoi Ameriki (The Basic Folklore Types of Northern Eurasia and Northern America). *Sovetskii fol'klor* [1936], no. 4/5:29–50. → The oral tradition of the Chukchee, the Koryak, the Kamchadal, the Yukaghir, and the Chuvantsy.

1937 *Luoravetlansko–russkii (chukotsko–russkii) slovar'* (Chukchee–Russian Dictionary). Institut Narodov Severa, Nauchno-Issledovatel'skaia Assotsiatsiia, Trudy po lingvistike, Vol. 6. Leningrad: The Institute.

Autobiography. Unpublished manuscript, Archives of the Leningrad Ethnographic Institute.

WORKS BY STERNBERG

1893 Sakhalinskie giliaki (The Sakhalin Gilyaks). *Etnograficheskoe obozrenie* 17:1–46.

1908 *Materialy po izucheniiu giliatskogo iazyka i fol'klora* (Materials for the Study of the Gilyak Language and Folklore). St. Petersburg (Russia): Akademiia Nauk. → Only Part 1 of Volume 1 was published.

1925*a* Divine Election in Primitive Religion (Including Material on Different Tribes on N.E. Asia and America). Part 2, pages 472–512 in International Congress of Americanists, Twenty-first, Göteborg, 1924, *Compterendu.* Göteborg (Sweden) Museum.

1925*b* Kul't orla u sibirskikh narodov (Eagle Worship Among the Siberian Peoples). Akademiia Nauk SSSR, Muzei Antropologii i Etnografii, *Sbornik* 5:717–740.

1927 Izbrannichestvo v religii (Divine Election in Religion). *Etnografiia* 3, no. 1:3–56.

1929 The Ainu Problem. *Anthropos* 24:755–799.

1933*a* *Giliaki, orochi, gol'dy, negidal'tsy, ainy* (The Gilyak, Oroch, Goldi, Negidal, and Ainu Peoples). Khabarovsk (Russia): Dal'giz.

1933*b* *Sem'ia i rod u narodov severo-vostochnoi Azii* (The Family and the Clan Among the Peoples of Northeastern Asia). Leningrad: Institut Narodov Severa, Nauchno-Issledovatel'skaia Assotsiatsiia.

1936 *Pervobytnaia religiia v svete etnografi: Issledovaniia, stat'i i lektsii* (Primitive Religion in the Light of Ethnography: Studies, Articles, and Lectures). Leningrad: Institut Narodov Severa, Nauchno-Issledovatel'skaia Assotsiatsiia.

WORKS BY JOCHELSON

1897 K voprosu ob izcheznuvshikh narodnostiakh kolymskogo okruga (On the Question of the Extinct Peoples of the Kolymskii Region). I. Russkoe Geograficheskoe Obshchestvo, Vostochno-Sibirskii Otdel, *Izvestiia* 28, no. 2:160–165.

1898 Predvaritel'nyi otchet ob issledovaniiakh inorodtsev kolymskogo i verkhoianskogo okrugov (A Preliminary Report on the Investigation of the Natives of the Kolymskii and Verkhoianskii Regions). I. Russkoe Geograficheskoe Obshchestvo, Vostochno-Sibirskii Otdel, *Izvestiia* 29:9–52.

1898/1899 Die Jukagiren im äussersten Nordosten Asiens

(The Yukaghir in Extreme Northeastern Asia). Geographische Gesellschaft in Bern, *Jahresbericht* 17: 1–48.

1900 *Materialy po izucheniiu iukagirskogo iazyka i fol'klora* (Materials for the Study of the Yukaghir Language and Folklore). Trudy Iakutskoi Ekspeditsii, snariazhennoi na sredstva I. M. Sibiriakova, Section 3, Vol. 9, Part 3. St. Petersburg (Russia): Akademiia Nauk.

1905–1908*a* Ethnological Problems of the Bering Sea. American Museum of Natural History, *Memoir* 10.

1905–1908*b* The Koryak. Jesup North Pacific Expedition Publications, Vol. 6, and American Museum of Natural History, New York, Memoir, Vol. 10, Parts 1–2. Leiden: Brill; New York: Stechert.

1907 Etnologicheskie problemy na severnykh beregakh Tikhogo Okeana (Ethnological Problems on the Northern Shores of the Pacific). I. Russkoe Geograficheskoe Obshchestvo, *Izvestiia* 43:63–92.

1926 *The Yukaghir and the Yukaghirized Tungus.* Jesup North Pacific Expedition Publications, Vol. 9, and American Museum of Natural History, New York, Memoir, Vol. 13. Leiden: Brill; New York: Stechert.

1928 *Peoples of Asiatic Russia.* New York: American Museum of Natural History.

1930 Leo Sternberg. *American Anthropologist* New Series 30:180–181.

SUPPLEMENTARY BIBLIOGRAPHY

JAKOBSON, ROMAN; HÜTTL-WORTH, GERTA; and BEEBE, JOHN F. 1957 *Paleosiberian Peoples and Languages: A Bibliographical Guide.* New Haven: Human Relations Area Files Press.

KAGAROFF, EUGEN 1929 Leo Sternberg. *American Anthropologist* New Series 31:568–571.

[KOSHKIN], IA. P. 1935 V. G. Bogoraz-Tan, by Ia. P. Al'kor [pseud.]. *Sovetskaia etnografiia* [1935], no. 4/5:5–29. → A French résumé appears on pages 29–31.

VINNIKOV, I. N. 1935 Bibliografiia etnograficheskikh i lingvisticheskikh rabot V. G. Bogoraza. *Sovetskaia etnografiia* [1935]: 225–241.

ZELENIN, D. K. 1937 V. G. Bogoraz: Etnograf i fol'klorist. Pages v–xviii in *Pamiati V. G. Bogoraza (1865–1936): Sbornik statei.* Moscow: Akademiia Nauk SSSR.

BÖHM-BAWERK, EUGEN VON

Eugen von Böhm-Bawerk (1851–1914) was an Austrian minister of public finance, a teacher at the University of Vienna, and an economic theorist. As a leading civil servant, he participated in the introduction of gold currency and in the elimination of the sugar subsidy (this latter in 1902). In 1904, when the increased financial demands of the Austrian army endangered the balancing of the budget, he resigned as minister of public finance and returned as a professor to the University of Vienna. In the field of economic theory, he was important as a critic and a systematic thinker. Of his critical papers, the best is his attack on Marxian value theory.

The publication of his three-volume *Capital and*

Interest (1884–1912) established Böhm-Bawerk's vast reputation among his contemporaries. Indeed, he was considerably overrated during his lifetime, but today he is insufficiently appreciated. Until about 1920, American economists compared his importance to that of Ricardo, but since then, his influence has been largely confined to Europe. To redress the balance is difficult. The main parts of his work are not completely integrated, and his way of thinking differs from that of recent, more rigorous, thinking.

Time and again, circumstances beyond his control interfered with the completion of his work. In 1888, his publisher began to print the second volume, the *Positive Theory of Capital*, even before the last chapters were completed. Böhm-Bawerk was under constant pressure to finish the remaining pages quickly. This unfortunate situation did nothing to improve either the clarity of his organization or the consistency of his thought. Later, his duties as public finance minister, his teaching obligations, and finally a serious illness prevented him from thoroughly revising two subsequent editions of the *Positive Theory*.

Theory of value. Böhm-Bawerk's thinking grew out of the Austrian intellectual tradition, which was far removed from the scientific methods and the political and intellectual assumptions that existed in the United States and England. In the Austria of his time, Aristotelianism and ontology took the place of Western empirical skepticism and pragmatism, and faith in an all-powerful monarch and an all-wise and benign bureaucracy took the place of belief in the rights of the free citizen. Böhm-Bawerk applied the Aristotelian concept of final cause to economics. Economic value is the *causa prima*; all other forces possess only a vicarious power derived from value; costs, for example, are intermediate causes (*Zwischenursachen*). This economic cosmos, with value as the central force, cannot be regulated exclusively by free competition; government intervention is necessary for large areas of the economy. (In his belief in government intervention, Böhm-Bawerk revealed himself as much the Austrian civil servant inspired by the enlightened reign of Joseph II as the economic theorist.)

Carl Menger, an older contemporary of Böhm-Bawerk, had postulated consumer value, or marginal utility, as the force that drives the social cycle (1871). He was the only Austrian economist who had an essential influence on Böhm-Bawerk; other inspirations came from William Stanley Jevons, Johann Heinrich von Thünen, and John Rae. Although Menger was a pioneer, he was unable to appreciate Böhm-Bawerk's originality in con-

structing a system that reinterpreted and combined Menger's marginal utility theory with Thünen's and Rae's concept of roundabout production.

Menger had discovered that the consumer value of any one unit in a group of consumer goods of equal form, quality, and quantity is equal to that utility that is lost in reducing this group by one unit—the marginal utility. This law is based on the principle that since equal units can be substituted for one another, the incidence of a real or imagined loss will fall where it hurts least, at the margin. The value of a good is therefore dependent on its marginal utility. Böhm-Bawerk gave Menger's law a more general interpretation: the dependent utility of a commodity is transferable between groups of entirely different goods. His example of the loss of an overcoat illustrates his enlargement of Menger's original law. An overcoat is stolen. In most cases, the person who suffers this loss will buy a new one; only a very poor man will be forced to go without a winter coat. Other consumers will make up the expense of replacing the coat from a relatively insignificant part of their budgets: they may give up visits to the theater or similar luxuries to pay for a new coat.

Another aspect of marginal utility theory that Böhm-Bawerk pursued in his own way is the analysis of total value. In this departure from accepted theory, he came into conflict with Friedrich von Wieser. This conflict aroused great interest in Oskar Kraus, an eminent member of the Austrian school of psychology, who was particularly interested in the relationship between the economic and the philosophical formulations of the problem of values (1901). Böhm-Bawerk and Wieser disagreed on the total value of a group of equal goods. Thus, if six pieces of bread, B_1, B_2, B_3, B_4, B_5, B_6 (the total bread supply of one person) have the utilities U_1, U_2, U_3, U_4, U_5, U_6, and the value of these utilities is ordered as $U_1 > U_2 > U_3 > U_4 > U_5 > U_6$, Wieser calculated the value of the whole group at $6U_6$, the marginal utility times the number of units. Böhm-Bawerk, on the other hand, considered the value of the whole group to be the *sum* of all the utilities: $U_1 \pm U_2 \pm U_3 \pm U_4 \pm U_5 \pm U_6$. If the consumer buys three units of a commodity, each at the price of 40¢, he buys the third unit because the utility of that unit is just a little higher than the utility of the 40¢. In case of need, he would have given $1.00 for the first and 80¢ for the second unit. The consumer's total utility is:

$$(\$1.00 - 40¢) + (80¢ - 40¢) + 0 = \$1.00.$$

Joseph Schumpeter later pointed out that Böhm-Bawerk's calculation had a strong similarity to Alfred Marshall's consumer surplus (Schumpeter

1954, pp. 1060–1062 and footnote 3) [*see* CON-
SUMER'S SURPLUS]. According to Schumpeter, Marshall and Böhm-Bawerk were correct in their analysis, under two restricting conditions: (1) the
consumer's marginal utility does not change, and
(2) the utility can be measured. Böhm-Bawerk
would probably have agreed with these conditions,
because he took the position that utility numbers
have a cardinal character, and utility therefore can
be measured. This method of calculating total
value together with his theory of substitution are
Böhm-Bawerk's essential additions to Menger's
value theory.

Böhm-Bawerk's explanations of costs, of imputation or national accounting (*Zurechnung*), and of
prices are all expanded versions of Menger's ideas.
Böhm-Bawerk surpassed Menger in his aggregate
approach, and in the construction of his economic
table. The picture of economic forces contained in
this table combines the technical description of
capitalistic production and the theory of revenue:
wages, interest, and rent.

Theory of capital. Capital, analyzed in real
terms, is the central phenomenon in the table.
Capital goods are not permanent, and capital is
therefore in need of continuous reproduction. Like
his forerunners Thünen and Rae, Böhm-Bawerk
defined capitalist production as roundabout or time-
consuming: the longer the process of production,
from the first injection of land and labor until the
completion of consumer goods, the larger and better is the final product. The time interval increases
faster than the quantity and improvement of the
product; that is, a law of diminishing return operates with respect to time. The following illustration,
first used by Wilhelm Roscher, demonstrates the
increase of productivity with the introduction of
capital: some poor fishermen increase their daily
catch per worker from three fish to thirty fish by
replacing hand fishing (without boat or net—production without capital) with boat fishing (with
boat and net—production with capital). The weaving of the net and the building of the boat cost
time and a supply of food, but the haul is ten times
higher than before. Table 1 (adapted from Böhm-
Bawerk) demonstrates the diminishing increase in
units of production when a month of labor is injected into production periods of different length.

So far, Böhm-Bawerk's theory is very similar to
that of Thünen and Rae, but he went beyond them
in two ways: he combined the idea of the wages
fund with that of roundabout production, and he
refined the marginal calculations. The goods that
the fishing economy accumulates to keep the fisherman alive until he has finished weaving his net are
the food reserve for the netmakers. Böhm-Bawerk

**Table 1 — Effect of a month of labor in 1964 upon sub-
sequent production**

Economic period ending in	Units of production
1964	100
1965	200
1966	280
1967	350
1968	410
1969	460
1970	500
1971	530
1972	550

identified this accumulation of consumer goods, the
food reserve, with the wages fund.

In a market economy, the same commodity structure exists but in a somewhat more complicated
form. Consumer and producer goods are available
in different stages of completion. In each stage,
intermediate goods are brought forward one step,
until they become finished consumer goods. At each
moment there are goods in different stages of production. Because production is staggered and there
are different starting points, it is not necessary to
supply the entire wages fund at the beginning of
roundabout production. Assume that the whole production process takes five years and that each
period in which goods are brought one step toward
maturity takes one year. In this case, Böhm-Bawerk
argued, the supply of food, shelter, and housing
must last more than half the length of the whole
process, or more than two and one-half years. For
workers who are busy with the five-year project,
consumer goods for five years are necessary; for
those workers engaged in a more advanced stage of
production that will take only four years, a supply
for four years is needed; and for the workers of the
third stage, an advance of three years' consumer
goods is needed. For the whole roundabout production process, not five years' provisions, but only
$(5 + 4 + 3 + 2 + 1)/5$, or three years' provisions,
are needed.

The length of the roundabout production and
the structure of the wages fund are not fixed: like
an accordion, each can be compressed or extended.
They become fixed only if a number of other factors
are also fixed: the available means of subsistence,
the number of producers, the productivity of the
different modes of roundabout production, the
number and demand for consumer loans, the rent
of land, the existence of capitalists, and, last but
not least, the economic attitude of the population.
All these factors together create a market where
entrepreneurs, workers, and farmers, who need
present goods to carry on production, meet bankers,
financiers, and the saving public, who accept payments in claims against future production. In this
market, the difference in value between present

and future goods is established. Of all the forces operating in the market, the economic attitude of the population is the most important.

Böhm-Bawerk believed that a single axiom governs the difference in value between present and future goods: present goods have a higher value than future goods of equal quality, quantity, and form. The value of future goods diminishes as the length of time necessary for their completion increases. Lottini and Galiani had earlier discovered this agio or discount theory (Galiani [1750] 1915; Lottini [1574] 1941, pp. 109–110, paragraph 196). Böhm-Bawerk's originality lies in identifying three reasons for this value discrepancy:

(1) *Market situation.* In a growing economy, the supply of goods is larger in the future than in the present; therefore, present goods have a higher value than do the same goods at any later time.

(2) *Psychological motivation.* Carelessness and shortsightedness induce people to underestimate their future needs.

(3) *Technical preference.* Roundabout production can be initiated immediately by the entrepreneur with present goods, while waiting for goods that become available only in the future will delay the beginning of production.

The third reason, which is very controversial, is a combination of the first and second reasons and Böhm-Bawerk's theory of capital. The first two reasons explain why future goods have a lower marginal utility than present goods. The later production begins, the stronger the effect will be. To achieve the highest return, the entrepreneur buys present goods at a price that is higher than the price of equivalent future goods.

The present goods are the wages fund. Entrepreneurs or capitalists—Böhm-Bawerk did not distinguish between them—transfer these commodities to workers in the form of wages. Table 2 shows his computation of the wage rate that is consistent with full employment, maximum profit, and the spending of the entire means of subsistence. Five factors determine the ideal length of roundabout production: (1) the production schedules of different length and different productivity, as indicated in column 2 of Table 2; (2) the length of each step in such staggered roundabout production—in this case, one year; (3) the number of workers—in this case, 10 million; (4) the number of entrepreneurs or capitalists—in this case, 1.5 million, owning equal shares; (5) the size of the wages fund—in this case, $15 billion. It is assumed that production in stages will cause twice the original wages fund to be used up in the course of the entire process of production. With full employment,

each capitalist employs $6\frac{2}{3}$ workers ($10 \div 1.5$). Each capitalist owns a share of the whole fund of $10,000, which for the whole production period has to be multiplied by 2 (see above). The product $10,000 \times 2$ has to be divided by $6\frac{2}{3}$ to find the total individual wages of $3,000 for the whole roundabout production period. In Table 2, $6\frac{2}{3}$ workers per capitalist are used for a period of 6 years; therefore, the annual wages are $500. For periods of production less than 6 years, there would not be enough members at a wage of $500; for periods of production longer than 6 years, not all workers would be employed at this wage. For this length of roundabout production, the maximum profit is 10 per cent. For Böhm-Bawerk, this state of multiple equilibrium and maximal satisfaction is that toward which the forces of the market tend to gravitate.

Table 2 — Roundabout production (annual wages, $500)

Roundabout production, in years	Product of one year per worker, in dollars	Annual gain per worker (product minus wages), in dollars	Number of workers per capitalist	Gain in percentage of the used capital
(1)	(2)	(3)[a]	(4)[b]	(5)[c]
1	350	−150	40.00	Loss
2	450	−50	20.00	Loss
3	530	30	13.33	4.00
4	580	80	10.00	8.00
5	620	120	8.00	9.60
6	650	150	6.67	10.00
7	670	170	5.71	9.77
8	685	185	5.00	9.25
9	695	195	4.44	8.67
10	700	200	4.00	8.00

a. $(3) = (2) - 500$.
b. $(4) = 20{,}000/[500 \times (1)]$.
c. $(5) = (3) \times (4)/100$.

Source: Adapted from Böhm-Bawerk 1889.

Table 2 is the appropriate climax of a bold and highly controversial composition. Böhm-Bawerk's opponents attacked each part of the *Positive Theory*: marginal utility, the agio theory, and roundabout production. Although he was a friendly and amiable man, Böhm-Bawerk enjoyed arguments; he answered his critics in a paternal and courteous way, but he did not always understand their views. He defended the Austrian concept of marginal utility in general, and his own interpretation of it in particular, against the remaining classicists, Wilhelm Lexis, Conrad, Dietzel, Achille Loria, Franz Oppenheimer, and others. The most important opponent of the agio theory was Ladislaus von Bortkiewicz, for a long time the only theorist of note at the University of Berlin. The target of Bortkiewicz's attack was technical preference, Böhm-

Bawerk's third reason for the value discrepancy between present and future goods: Bortkiewicz considered technical preference to be only an application of Böhm-Bawerk's first reason, the market situation (Bortkiewicz 1906).

The theory of roundabout production is still being debated. Even among Austrian theorists, there is disagreement about its validity. In the Anglo-American literature, capital analysis is carried on primarily, although not exclusively, in monetary rather than in real terms, and those economists who do deal with real capital follow the productivity theory of Leon Walras and John Bates Clark, according to which capital is a completely homogeneous factor yielding services without end in the process of production. As has been pointed out by Robert Kuenne (1963), Frank Knight, and Nicholas Kaldor, the productivity theory is at variance with Böhm-Bawerk's theory, since Böhm-Bawerk defined capital as nonpermanent produced goods that are periodically extinguished. Oskar Morgenstern, a member of the Austrian school, also rejects the roundabout production theory; he believes that production can be explained completely with the law of diminishing returns and that the idea of roundabout production is superfluous. F. A. Fetter, G. Åckerman, E. Lindahl, Walter Eucken, and Frederick von Hayek have all constructed capital theories based on Böhm-Bawerk's; they object to details in his theory, not to principles. For instance, Eucken and Hayek assert that averages for an individual share of investment and of the wages fund cannot be calculated. Ludwig M. Lachman (1956), one of the foremost interpreters of the *Positive Theory*, finds more validity in Böhm-Bawerk's tables than do the other writers. The table, Lachman claims, is a model of an economic world of restricted progress, where development is exclusively due to the accumulation of capital. The table has also been compared to the uniformly progressive economy delineated by Harrod and Hicks. Clearly, it is still possible to defend Böhm-Bawerk's approach.

EMIL KAUDER

[*For the historical context of Böhm-Bawerk's work, see* ECONOMIC THOUGHT, *article on* THE AUSTRIAN SCHOOL; VALUE, LABOR THEORY OF; *and the biographies of* BORTKIEWICZ; CLARK, J. B.; JEVONS; LEXIS; MENGER; RAE; RICARDO; THÜNEN; WALRAS. *For discussion of the subsequent development of his ideas, see* CAPITAL; UTILITY.]

WORKS BY BÖHM-BAWERK

(1881–1914) 1962 *Shorter Classics of Böhm-Bawerk.* South Holland, Ill.: Libertarian Press. → A collection of five essays translated from the German: "The Austrian Economists" ("Die österreichische Schule"); "Whether Legal Rights and Relationships Are Economic Goods" ("Rechte und Verhältnisse vom Standpunkte der volkswirtschaftlichen Güterlehre"); "Control or Economic Law?" ("Macht oder ökonomisches Gesetz?"); "Unresolved Contradiction in the Marxian Economic System" ("Zum Abschluss des marxschen Systems"); "The Ultimate Standard of Value" ("Der letzte Maasstab des Güterwertes").

(1884–1912) 1959 *Capital and Interest.* 3 vols. South Holland, Ill.: Libertarian Press. → First published as *Kapital und Kapitalzins.* Volume 1: *History and Critique of Interest Theories,* 1884. Volume 2: *Positive Theory of Capital,* 1889. Volume 3: *Further Essays on Capital and Interest* was first published as appendixes to Volume 2 of the 1909–1912 edition, and was printed in a separate volume in 1921.

(1886) 1932 *Grundzüge der Theorie des wirtschaftlichen Güterwerts.* London School of Economics and Political Science Series of Reprints of Scarce Tracts in Economic and Political Science, No. 11. London: The School. → First published in *Jahrbücher für Nationalökonomie und Statistik,* New Series, Volume 13, pages 1–82 and 477–541.

1890 The Historical vs. the Deductive Method in Political Economy. American Academy of Political and Social Science, *Annals* 1:244–271. → First published as "Historische und theoretische Nationalökonomie" in *Jahrbücher für Nationalökonomie und Statistik,* 1890; reprinted in Volume 1 of Böhm-Bawerk's *Gesammelte Schriften,* 1924.

(1892) 1924 Wert, Kosten und Grenznutzen. Volume 1, pages 309–374 in Eugen von Böhm-Bawerk, *Gesammelte Schriften.* Edited by Franz X. Weiss. Vienna: Holder. → First published in *Jahrbücher für Nationalökonomie und Statistik,* Series 3, Volume 58, pages 321–367.

1895–1896 The Positive Theory of Capital and Its Critics. *Quarterly Journal of Economics* 9:113–131, 235–256; 10:121–155. → A series of essays under the titles "Professor Clark's Views on the Genesis of Capital," 1895; "General Walker Against *Capital and Interest,*" 1895; and "The Views of Mr. White, Mr. Bilgram, Professor MacVane, and Mr. Hawley," 1896.

(1899) 1926 Einige strittige Fragen der Kapitalstheorie. Volume 2, pages 129–306 in Eugen von Böhm-Bawerk, *Gesammelte Schriften.* Edited by Franz X. Weiss. Vienna: Holder. → First published in *Zeitschrift für Volkswirtschaft, Sozialpolitik und Verwaltung,* Volume 8, pages 105–146.

(1914) 1924 Unsere passive Handelsbilanz. Volume 1, pages 497–515 in Eugen von Böhm-Bawerk, *Gesammelte Schriften.* Edited by Franz X. Weiss. Vienna: Holder. → First published in *Neue Freie Presse,* issues of January 6, 8, and 9, 1914.

1924–1926 *Gesammelte Schriften.* 2 vols. Edited by Franz X. Weiss. Vienna: Holder.

SUPPLEMENTARY BIBLIOGRAPHY

BETTELHEIM-GABILLON, LUDWIG 1936 Eugen von Böhm-Bawerk und die Brüsseler Zuckerkonvention (1903). *Zeitschrift für Nationalökonomie* 7:596–636.

BORTKIEWICZ, LADISLAUS VON 1906 Der Kardinalfehler der Böhm-Bawerkschen Zinstheorie. *Jahrbuch für Gesetzgebung, Verwaltung und Volkswirtschaft im deutschen Reich* 30:943–972.

EATON, HOWARD O. 1930 *The Austrian Philosophy of Values.* Norman: Univ. of Oklahoma Press.

EUCKEN, WALTER (1934) 1954 *Kapitaltheoretische Untersuchungen.* 2d enl. ed. Tübingen (Germany): Mohr.

GALIANI, FERDINANDO (1750) 1915 *Della moneta.* Edited by Fausto Nicolini. Bari (Italy): Laterza.

HAYEK, FREDERICK A. VON (1941) 1950 *The Pure Theory of Capital.* London: Routledge; Univ. of Chicago Press.

KAUDER, EMIL 1953 Genesis of the Marginal Utility Theory. *Economic Journal* 63:638–650.

KAUDER, EMIL 1957 Intellectual and Political Roots of the Older Austrian School. *Zeitschrift für Nationalökonomie* 17:411–425.

KAUDER, EMIL 1962 Aus Mengers nachgelassenen Papieren. *Weltwirtschaftliches Archiv: Zeitschrift des Instituts für Weltwirtschaft an der Universität Kiel* 89:1–28.

KAUDER, EMIL 1965 *The History of Marginal Utility Theory.* Princeton Univ. Press.

KRAUS, OSKAR 1901 *Zur Theorie des Wertes: Eine Bentham-Studie.* Halle (Germany): Niemeyer.

KUENNE, ROBERT E. 1963 *The Theory of General Economic Equilibrium.* Princeton Univ. Press.

LACHMANN, LUDWIG M. 1956 *Capital and Its Structure.* London: Bell.

LOTTINI, GIOVANNI FRANCISCO (1574) 1941 *Avvedimenti civili.* Edited by Guido Mancini. Bologna (Italy): Zanichelli.

MENGER, CARL (1871) 1950 *Principles of Economics.* Translated and edited by J. Dingwall and B. F. Hoselitz. Glencoe, Ill.: Free Press. → First published as *Grundsätze der Volkswirtschaftslehre.*

MENGER, CARL 1915 Eugen von Böhm-Bawerk. *Almanach der kaiserlichen Akademie der Wissenschaften* (Vienna) 65:481–499.

MONROE, ARTHUR ELI (editor) (1924) 1951 *Early Economic Thought: Selections From Economic Literature Prior to Adam Smith.* Cambridge, Mass.: Harvard Univ. Press.

MORGENSTERN, OSKAR 1935 Zur Theorie der Produktionsperiode. *Zeitschrift für Nationalökonomie* 6:196–208.

SCHUMPETER, JOSEPH A. 1927 Deutschland. Pages 1–30 in *Die Wirtschaftstheorie der Gegenwart.* Volume 1: Gesamtbild der Forschung in den einzelnen Ländern. Edited by Hans Mayer et al. Vienna: Springer.

SCHUMPETER, JOSEPH A. 1954 *History of Economic Analysis.* Edited by E. B. Schumpeter. New York: Oxford Univ. Press.

WEINBERGER, OTTO 1925 Eugen von Böhm-Bawerk. *Archiv für Sozialwissenschaft und Sozialpolitik* 53:491–508.

WICKSELL, KNUT 1928 Zur Zinstheorie. Pages 199–209 in *Die Wirtschaftstheorie der Gegenwart.* Volume 3: Einkommensbildung, allgemeine Prinzipien, Lohn, Zins, Grundrente, Unternehmergewinn, Spezialprobleme. Edited by Hans Mayer et al. Vienna: Springer.

BOOTH, CHARLES

Charles Booth (1840–1916) was an English reformer, social surveyor, and social scientist and, at the same time, a wealthy Victorian captain of industry. In many ways he combined within himself the themes and conflicts prevalent in late nineteenth-century England, where the problems implicit in the maturation of an urban industrial civilization were becoming increasingly evident.

Booth was the son of a prosperous Liverpool businessman of liberal politics and religion. He left school to work for a steamship company and later, with his brother, founded his own steamship business. As a young man he was a member of the younger set within a group of prosperous industrialist families who had lively intellectual interests and were endowed with great social consciousness: his wife was a cousin of Beatrice Webb and a niece of the historian Macaulay. Booth was familiar with Comte's positivistic theories but, typically, never became a disciple. Although a Conservative in later life, he remained sympathetic to the trade union movement.

In the 1880s the ubiquitous paradox of urban industrial society—poverty in the midst of plenty —became too patent to ignore; the conventional doctrine of economic liberalism was increasingly deserted in practice, and a variety of sheerly speculative socialist theories were loudly proclaimed. In this context Booth set out in businesslike and positivistic fashion simply to discover "the facts." He believed that the assumptions of orthodox political economy were "very imperfectly connected with the observed facts of life" and that intelligent social action must be based on "a true picture of the modern industrial organism" (1887, p. 376).

Booth began his research by investigating the occupational characteristics of the population of the United Kingdom and went on to study the inhabitants of a small depressed area of London. The results of these as well as other efforts were published in the *Journal of the Royal Statistical Society*, beginning in 1886 (see Booth 1886). Ultimately, he organized and directed at his own expense a plan of research that eventuated in his 17-volume classic, *Life and Labour of the People in London* (1889–1891). His aim was nothing less than to give a picture—extensive and statistical as well as intensive and qualitative—"of the whole of London society."

The work is divided into three major subject areas: *poverty, industry,* and *religious influences.* In the four-volume poverty series, Booth divided London's four million inhabitants into eight social classes on the basis of income. The family was the unit of inquiry, and the reports of School Board visitors, whose cooperation Booth secured, were the source of the data. His conclusion that over 30 per cent of the people of London were "below the line of poverty" was a shock to many; it was also in essential agreement with the estimates of such socialist critics of the time as H. M. Hyndman.

The five-volume industry series classified London's population by two new criteria: "crowding," as measured by the number of persons per room, in the case of the lower classes; and number of servants, in the case of the upper classes. The source of these data was the 1891 census, to which Booth had served as a consultant. In the interests of economy, the street, rather than the family, was taken as the unit of investigation. A complete picture of the economic organization of the city in terms of the demographic characteristics of each occupation was presented: significantly, the locus of each trade, as well as the residences of those engaged in each occupation, was analyzed in terms of "inner" and "outer" ring divisions of the city.

The religious influences series was really misnamed, for despite Booth's concern with discovering the influence of organized religious efforts on the poor, he gave more than half of the seven-volume series to an investigation of the way of life of the poor and the working classes. Indeed, Booth lived as a participant–observer in lower-class households on a number of occasions.

A major focus of the final volume, "Notes on Social Influences and Conclusions," was a statistical analysis of the relation of birth and death rates to poverty and crowding. Here Booth turned from the 30 census registration districts and constructed 50 areas, "fairly convenient for comparison," which he colored according to "mean social condition." The resulting "Index Map of London" was only one of a series of maps that portrayed the spatial pattern of various aspects of the social organization and functioning of the city: for example, the distribution of the inhabitants by social class; the location of "Places of Religious Worship, Public Elementary Schools, and Houses Licensed for the Sale of Liquor."

Although the original intention was simply to discover "things as they are," the time span that the work came to cover inevitably led to an interest in change. Therefore, in the final series and in the summary volume Booth often abandoned mere description and instead offered generalizations and causal interpretations of his findings. While he lacked academic training and theoretical interest, his empirical generalizations concerning the social and spatial structure of the modern urban community (as well as many of his methodological innovations) were hardly surpassed by American urban sociologists a generation later. For example, Booth

formulated a "general law of successive migration," which noted the "centrifugal movement" of the city's population; he also concluded that "residential London tends to be arranged by class in rings with the most uniform poverty at the center." His recognition of the trend toward the separation of workplace from residence and the development of a "metropolitan community" are just a few of the modern insights with which the work abounds.

Despite Booth's desire to remain objective, his findings disturbed his ethical sense. Especially concerned over the plight of the aged poor, he drew up and advocated a program of noncontributory state pensions. Some of his proposals were incorporated in an act of Parliament under the Liberal government in 1908. A privy councilor and member of several royal commissions, Booth was honored by Oxford, Cambridge, and Liverpool universities. He also served as a president of the Royal Statistical Society.

A careful study of *Life and Labour* reveals Booth as a major methodological (and, implicitly, sociological) precursor of the University of Chicago studies of the city carried on by Robert E. Park and his students in the 1920s. Indeed, Booth went far beyond his own predecessors in England—Sir Frederick M. Eden, *The State of the Poor* (1797), and Henry Mayhew, *London Labour and the London Poor* (1851)—precisely in his concern with developing and employing more meaningful areal units for comparative analysis. Undoubtedly Park's use of spatial patterns as an objective index of social structure was much influenced by Booth's work. Moreover, Booth's study was clearly a great force in inspiring the social-survey movement both in England and America, such as the community studies of B. S. Rowntree and Sir Hubert Llewellyn Smith and the Pittsburgh Survey. On the other hand, Booth's contribution to the study of social stratification has been almost completely overlooked by modern students.

In England, the practical and political influence of Booth's work outweighed his impact on academic social science. British sociology failed to follow the empirical lead of such surveyors as Booth and Geddes; rather, the tradition of social philosophy under Hobhouse dominated the scene for the subsequent generation.

HAROLD W. PFAUTZ

[*For the historical context of Booth's work, see* CITY, *article on* FORMS AND FUNCTIONS; PUBLIC HEALTH; STATISTICS, *article on* THE HISTORY OF STATISTICAL METHOD; *and the biography of* SIDNEY AND BEATRICE

WEBB. *For discussion of the subsequent development of his ideas, see the biographies of* GEDDES; PARK.]

WORKS BY BOOTH

1886 Occupations of the People of the United Kingdom, 1801–1881. *Journal of the Royal Statistical Society* Series A 49:314–435.

1887 The Inhabitants of Tower Hamlets (School Board Divisions), Their Condition and Occupations. *Journal of the Royal Statistical Society* Series A 50:326–391.

(1889–1891) 1902–1903 *Life and Labour of the People in London.* 17 vols. London: Macmillan.

1899 *Old Age Pensions and the Aged Poor: A Proposal.* London: Macmillan.

1910 *Poor Law Reform.* London: Macmillan.

1913 *Industrial Unrest and Trade Union Policy.* London: Macmillan.

SUPPLEMENTARY BIBLIOGRAPHY

Charles Booth: A Memoir. 1918 London: Macmillan. → Published anonymously.

EATON, ALLEN H.; and HARRISON, SHELBY M. 1930 *A Bibliography of Social Surveys.* New York: Russell Sage Foundation.

EDEN, FREDERICK M. (1797) 1928 *The State of the Poor.* London: Routledge.

LYND, HELEN M. 1945 *England in the 1880's.* New York: Harcourt.

MAYHEW, HENRY (1851) 1861 *London Labour and the London Poor.* London: Griffin.

SIMEY, THOMAS S.; and SIMEY, MARGARET B. 1960 *Charles Booth, Social Scientist.* Oxford Univ. Press.

SMITH, H. LLEWELLYN 1929 The New Survey of London Life and Labour. *Journal of the Royal Statistical Society* Series A 92:530–547.

WEBB, BEATRICE (1926) 1950 *My Apprenticeship.* London & New York: Longmans.

BORING, EDWIN G.

Edwin Garrigues Boring, psychologist, historian, teacher, author, and editor, was born in Philadelphia, Pennsylvania, on October 23, 1886, the youngest of four children and only son of Edwin McCurdy and Elizabeth Garrigues (Truman) Boring. Other than his father, he was the only male in a household consisting of three older sisters, his mother, a maiden aunt, and a grandmother. Religion was of importance in his family, but the affiliations were varied: his father was a member of the Moravian church; the women were either Orthodox or Hicksite Quakers.

Regarded by the members of this matriarchal family as a delicate child, Boring was not permitted to play with the children of the neighborhood. He was tutored at home and grew up without playmates of his own age, except for an imaginary one—a girl whom he called "Mamie." When he was nine years old, he entered the Friends Select School and remained there until he was ready for college.

He went to Cornell University in the fall of 1904 to study electrical engineering, magnetism and electricity having interested him since childhood. In his sophomore year he chose E. B. Titchener's course in elementary psychology as an elective. It made a lasting impression on him and eventually changed the entire course of his life. He received an M.E. degree in 1908 and spent the following year as a student apprentice at the Bethlehem Steel Company. He was offered a foremanship at the end of his training there, but he had discovered during his apprenticeship that he did not like the practice of engineering and accepted instead a position teaching science and physical geography at the Moravian Parochial School in Bethlehem, Pennsylvania.

To prepare himself for this new position, he returned to Cornell during the summer of 1909 to study physical geography. Recalling the excitement aroused in him by the course in elementary psychology he had taken four years before, he chose to take also the laboratory course in experimental psychology offered by Madison Bentley, which further increased his interest in psychology.

When he realized, during the following year, that his career as a teacher would be handicapped without an arts degree, he again resigned a secure position and returned to Cornell. His dilemma of whether to work in physics, for which his engineering training had prepared him, or in psychology, for which he had a firm inclination but poor preparation, was finally resolved in favor of psychology because the physicists, whom he did not know, gave him less encouragement than did Bentley, with whom he had worked the previous summer.

Among the courses in psychology that he elected during that fall was Bentley's laboratory course in comparative psychology; the subject so captivated him that he published a research work on planarians. His interest and proficiency in this course led to his appointment in February 1911 to an assistantship in the department. Since he could live comfortably on an assistant's salary, he decided to go forward to a PH.D.

He obtained his M.A. degree under Bentley in 1912, was appointed to an instructorship in 1913, and won his PH.D. under Titchener in 1914. He continued as an instructor at Cornell until February of 1918, when he was commissioned into the armed forces as a captain in the newly created Psychological Service in the Sanitary Corps of the Medical Department. He remained in the service until the fall of 1919, assisting its head, Major R. M. Yerkes, in the preparation of the service's final reports.

When he was returned to civilian life, Boring went to Clark University as professor of experimental psychology, filling the vacancy created by the death, in February 1919, of J. W. Baird. In 1923 he became involved in a controversy at Clark over freedom of speech. This controversy arose when the president of the university interrupted a lecture given under the auspices of the students' Liberal Club by a man reputed to be a communist. Though neither a member of the club nor of the audience, Boring, as a matter of principle, defended the student's right "to hear all sides." For his efforts he acquired a stomach ulcer, from which he suffered for many years. In the midst of the controversy, Boring was invited to Harvard; he went there that fall and has since remained there.

Boring's years at Cornell and Clark were highly productive experimentally. His researches on the sensation of the alimentary tract and the cutaneous sensations after nerve section are classics. After he transferred to Harvard, his administrative duties, his writing, his editorial responsibilities, and his wide participation in the psychological profession—he was president of the American Psychological Association in 1928 and secretary of the International Congress of Psychology held at Yale University in 1929—took him away more and more from the laboratory. He continued his research through his students, whose work he directed and prepared for publication. Eventually, however, even that contact with the laboratory was turned over to colleagues who had once been his students.

In 1925, when Titchener retired from the editorship of the *American Journal of Psychology*, Boring, with three others from the cooperating board, took over that responsibility. In addition he also accepted the sole responsibility of the necrological department. Boring has always had an abiding interest in people, in discovering what in their heredity, environment, training, and experience made them the kind and manner of men they were. This interest, together with the paucity of biographical material about psychologists, led him in 1928, when he was writing his *History of Experimental Psychology* (1929), to initiate the publication of a series of autobiographies, under the title *A History of Psychology in Autobiography*, which was patterned after the German series *Die Philosophie der Gegenwart in Selbstdarstellungen*. He served on the committee selecting the authors for the series, which was published by the Clark University Press. Four volumes of autobiographies have appeared: the first in 1930; the most recent, in which Boring's abridged autobiography is published, in 1952.

In addition to numerous articles on psychology, Boring is the author of four books. His first, *A History of Experimental Psychology*—the first of a contemplated historical triad—was published in 1929. It is his magnum opus, the book for which he will longest be remembered; a second revised and enlarged edition appeared in 1950. His second book, *The Physical Dimensions of Consciousness*, was published in 1933; his third, *Sensation and Perception in the History of Experimental Psychology*, in 1942; and his fourth, *Psychologist at Large*, published in the year 1961, brings his autobiography up to date and presents selections from his more important articles and his bibliography. He abandoned the final volume of the contemplated triad on feeling, emotion, learning, attention, action, and thought in 1955, when he accepted the editorship of the newly established review journal *Contemporary Psychology*.

A collection of his papers on history, psychology, and science, selected and edited by Robert I. Watson and Donald T. Campbell, was published in 1963.

Boring was a coeditor with H. S. Langfeld and H. P. Weld of three textbooks in elementary psychology (1935; 1939; 1948). He was chairman of the subcommittee on a textbook of military psychology, established in 1941 by the National Research Council's Emergency Committee in Psychology, which produced three books: *Psychology for the Fighting Man* (1943); *Psychology for the Returning Serviceman* (1945); and *Psychology for the Armed Services* (1945). Each succeeded in its purpose, but the first, coedited by Boring and Marjorie Van de Water, of Science News Service, enjoyed the greatest success: approximately half a million copies of it were sold in post exchanges in the United States and abroad.

Boring was also a member of the emergency committee's Subcommittee on Survey and Planning, which initiated, among many other proposals for the parent committee's consideration, the suggestion that an intersociety constitutional convention of psychologists be held to unite in a single association the various organizations represented on the emergency committee. At the subsequent convention, held under Boring's chairmanship in May 1943, the American Association for Applied Psychology was merged with the American Psychological Association. Other instances of his academic statesmanship were his effecting of the separation of psychology from philosophy at Harvard in 1934 and of the experimental and physiological branches of psychology from the social and clinical in 1945.

In 1934, when threatened with a nervous breakdown from overwork and anxiety over the resurgence of his stomach ulcer, Boring turned to psychoanalysis, both for aid and to gain firsthand knowledge of the therapy. In the course of 168 sessions extending over a period of two years, he obtained the latter but not the former.

Among his numerous honors are the presidency of the American Psychological Association in 1928; honorary presidency of the 17th International Congress of Psychology held in Washington, D.C., August 1963; D.SC. degrees awarded by the University of Pennsylvania in 1946 and by Clark University in 1956; the Gold Medal of the American Psychological Foundation in 1959; and memberships in the National Academy of Sciences and the American Philosophical Society.

He was coeditor of the *American Journal of Psychology*, 1926–1946 (cooperating editor, 1921–1925, 1947–   ), and editor of *Contemporary Psychology*, 1956–1961.

KARL M. DALLENBACH

[*For the historical context of Boring's work, see the biography of* TITCHENER. *For discussion of other relevant material, see* SENSES; SKIN SENSES AND KINESTHESIS.]

WORKS BY BORING
(1929) 1950 *A History of Experimental Psychology.* 2d ed. New York: Appleton.

1933 *The Physical Dimensions of Consciousness.* New York: Appleton.

1935 BORING, EDWIN G.; LANGFELD, HERBERT S.; and WELD, HARRY P. (editors). *Psychology: A Factual Textbook.* New York: Wiley.

1939 BORING, EDWIN G.; LANGFELD, HERBERT S.; and WELD, HARRY P. (editors). *Introduction to Psychology.* New York: Wiley.

1942 *Sensation and Perception in the History of Experimental Psychology.* New York: Appleton.

1948 BORING, EDWIN G.; LANGFELD, HERBERT S.; and WELD, HARRY P. (editors). *Foundations of Psychology.* New York: Wiley.

1961 *Psychologist at Large.* New York: Basic Books.

1963 *History, Psychology and Science: Selected Papers.* Edited by Robert I. Watson and Donald T. Campbell. New York: Wiley.

1965 HERNSTEIN, RICHARD; and BORING, EDWIN G. (editors). *A Sourcebook in the History of Psychology.* Cambridge, Mass.: Harvard Univ. Press.

SUPPLEMENTARY BIBLIOGRAPHY
NATIONAL RESEARCH COUNCIL 1943 *Psychology for the Fighting Man.* Washington: The Infantry Journal.

NATIONAL RESEARCH COUNCIL 1945 *Psychology for the Returning Service Man.* Washington: The Infantry Journal.

NATIONAL RESEARCH COUNCIL, COMMITTEE ON A TEXTBOOK OF MILITARY PSYCHOLOGY 1945 *Psychology for the Armed Services.* Washington: The Infantry Journal.

BORTKIEWICZ, LADISLAUS VON

Ladislaus von Bortkiewicz (first spelled Bortkewitsch as in the Russian transcription) was born of Polish descent in 1868 in St. Petersburg and studied at the university there. His first papers (1890 and 1891) were published in Russian. He continued his studies in Göttingen under Lexis, where he wrote his doctoral thesis (1893). In 1895 he became *Privatdozent* in Strassburg and subject to the influence of Knapp, but he returned in 1899 to Russia, where he taught at the Alexandrowsky Lyceum in St. Petersburg. He became associate professor at the University of Berlin in 1901, and finally in 1920 he became full professor *ad personam* of economics and statistics. He remained in Berlin for thirty years, until his death in 1931. With rare exceptions he wrote in German. He was one of the few representatives of mathematical statistics in Germany and as such a lonely figure, highly respected but rarely understood.

Besides classical economics, the work of Bortkiewicz covered population statistics and theory, actuarial science, mathematical statistics, probability theory, mathematical economics, and physical statistics—fields separate in content but analogous in methodology. He contributed to the process of consolidating each of these disciplines and did classic work in mathematical statistics.

Many of his investigations dealt with mortality tables. In a stationary population, the birth rate equals the death rate and the expectation of life of a newborn equals the reciprocal of the common value of the two rates. For increasing populations it was believed that the expectation of life could be obtained from the observed birth and death rates. Bortkiewicz showed (1893), however, that a correct answer can be obtained only by the construction of a mortality table. He returned to this problem when dealing with different methods of comparing mortality rates (1904b; 1911). In an increasing population there are more infants and fewer old people than in a stationary one. The first influence raises, the second lowers, the general mortality. Bortkiewicz showed that the second influence prevails in general so that the growth of the population tends to decrease the mortality rate. The study of life tables led him to actuarial science (see 1903; 1929).

The work that made his name widely known was a brochure (1898) of sixty pages, *Das Gesetz der kleinen Zahlen* ("The Law of Small Numbers"). Poisson had shown in 1837 that besides the usual normal limit for Bernoulli's distribution there is a second limit, requiring that the number (n) of observations increase and the probability (p) decrease so that the product (np) has a limiting value. In this distribution n and p enter only through their product $\lambda = np$, which is the expected number of happenings. (The Poisson limit is primarily useful as an approximation when λ is small.) Poisson's important derivation remained practically unknown for sixty years; at least, its importance was not recognized. Bortkiewicz was the first to note the fact that events in a large population, with low frequency, can be fitted by a Poisson distribution even when the probability of an event varies somewhat between the strata of the population. This is what he called the law of small numbers—the name refers to small numbers of events (see also 1915a).

A striking example was the number of soldiers killed by horse kicks per year per Prussian army corps. Fourteen corps were examined, each for twenty years. For over half the corps–year combinations there were no deaths from horse kicks; for other combinations the number of deaths ranged up to four. Presumably the risk of lethal horse kicks varied over years and corps, yet the over-all distribution was remarkably well fitted by a Poisson distribution.

In this distribution the variance, that is, the square of the standard deviation, is equal to the expectation. The corresponding observed quotient should therefore be near unity. This is called "normal dispersion" in the Lexis theory. The law of small numbers says that rare events usually show normal dispersion; for a mathematical explanation of this fact consistent with Lexis' theory, see Gosset (1919). Bortkiewicz computed tables of Poisson's distribution and discussed estimation of its expectation by the sample mean. In addition he discussed errors of estimation in quantitative terms and used them as criteria for the validity of the theory. Thus Bortkiewicz created an important instrument for mathematical statistics and probability theory. However, the name he gave it was unfortunate because it implied a nonexistent contrast to the law of large numbers and led to much confusion and unnecessary argument. [*For a discussion of the law of large numbers see* PROBABILITY, *article on* FORMAL PROBABILITY; *see also the biography of* POISSON.] It would have been better to speak of "rare events."

Many recent studies on the meaning of the different derivations and uses of Poisson's formula are linked to Bortkiewicz's discovery. The Poisson distribution has become the subject of important work that extends to statistically dependent events and varying probabilities. Large parts of operational research and queueing theory are based on the Poisson distribution.

Bortkiewicz also contributed to the theory of runs with the publication of his book *Die Iterationen* (1917). This work was motivated by an attack made by the psychologist Karl Marbe (1916–1919) on the easy assumption of independence in applications of probability theory, for example, to successive flips of a coin or to sequences of male and female births. Marbe believed that a run of male births leads to a heightened probability of a female birth, as nature tries to equalize or make uniform the sex ratio. Bortkiewicz showed, however, that Marbe's mathematics was wrong and that a mathematically correct approach gives agreement between theoretical independence and observed sequences in cases of the kind discussed.

Bortkiewicz devoted a book (1913) to the statistical interpretation of radioactivity. He showed that regularities considered as physical laws could be expressed by existing theorems on mean values of stochastic processes.

He also showed (1922a) that the extreme values, which had been considered unsuitable for the analysis and the characterization of a distribution, are statistical variables depending upon initial distribution and sample size. He gave the exact distribution of the normal range and computed its mean for sample sizes up to 20. With primitive equipment, he reached good numerical results (Tippett 1925) and checked them by many observations. The statistical importance of this work is obscured by mathematical complexities incident to the normal distribution.

The study of dispersion was central to the thought of Bortkiewicz. He confirmed and extended (1904b) the ideas of his teacher, Lexis, and strengthened them by his derivation of the standard error of the coefficient of dispersion (1918). He defended the importance and originality of Lexis (1930). The generalization of these methods led to the modern analysis of variance.

From the start Bortkiewicz worked on political economy and, like Lexis, he shared none of the usual vulgar prejudices to Marx. According to Schumpeter ([1932] 1960, p. 303) "By far his most important achievement is his analysis of the theoretical framework of the Marxian system [(1906–1907; 1907)], much the best thing ever written on it and, incidentally, on its other critics. A similar masterpiece is his paper on the theories of rent of Rodbertus and Marx [(1910–1911)]."

Bortkiewicz succeeded in embedding in a mathematical form both Marx's determination of the average profit rate for simple reproduction and

Marx's transformation, implicit therein, of value into price. According to Marx (*Das Kapital*, vol. 3), to yield the average profit rate the total surplus value is divided by the total capital, that is, the sum of constant and variable capital. In this solution, however, the input is measured in values and the output in prices. Bortkiewicz was the first of Marx's many critics to see this inconsistency. He made the necessary modifications that rendered the Marxian scheme of surplus values and prices consistent. However, his dry presentation prevented the Marxists (except for Klimpt) from accepting his method.

His investigations on price index numbers (1923–1924) are noteworthy contributions to mathematical economics. Irving Fisher (1922) had developed many such numbers. Bortkiewicz brought clarity and order into this system of index numbers by stating the requirements that such a number must satisfy in order to fulfill its purpose.

Bortkiewicz argued vigorously for his views. In 1910 he wrote an article attacking Alfred Weber's geometrical representation of the location of industries. His polemical article (1915*b*) against the Pearson school clarified his fundamental attitude —namely, that it is worthless to construct formulas to reproduce observations if these formulas have no theoretical meaning. In another polemic (1922*b*) against Pearson he insisted on Helmert's priority in discovering the distribution of the mean square residual when individual errors are normal. Yet Bortkiewicz's answer (1923) was quite mild when Keynes (1921, p. 403, note 2) wrote, ". . . Bortkiewicz does not get any less obscure as he goes on. The mathematical argument is right enough and often brilliant. But what it is all really about, and what it really amounts to, and what the premises are, it becomes increasingly perplexing to decide."

In his article (1931*a*) on the disparity of income distributions Bortkiewicz used Pareto's law. While Pareto had not been very clear about the role of his basic parameter α, Bortkiewicz established different measures of income concentration and showed that α is such a measure. Bortkiewicz's work on concentration was published in ignorance of the prior work of Gini.

Bortkiewicz had a characteristic way of working. He presented each problem from all sides with extreme thoroughness and patience after an extensive study of the literature. This multiple foundation makes the solution unassailable, but the reader can trace no single line from premises to conclusion: the central line of thought is entwined with numerous sidelines and extensive polemics, especially on matters of scientific priority. He criticized with equal zeal and profundity important

and insignificant mistakes, printing errors, and numerical miscalculations. A large part of his work appeared as reviews and critical analyses in remote journals. His writings stimulated numerous scientists in Germany, in the northern European countries and in Italy, but not in England. He did not create a school, perhaps because of his austere character and his poor teaching. He underestimated his own work and even doubted, wrongly, its practical significance. His cautious nature forbade him to strive for external honors. He was, from 1903, a member of both the International Statistical Institute, which then consisted mainly of administrative statisticians, and the Swedish Academy of Sciences. He maintained objectivity in the face of popular slogans as well as "untimely opinions." He was a true scholar of the old school and his life was passed in enviable quietness.

Four of his contributions are decisive: the proof that the Poisson distribution corresponds to a statistical reality; the introduction of mathematical statistics into the study of radioactivity; the inception of the statistical theory of extreme values; and the lonely effort to construct a Marxian econometry.

E. J. GUMBEL

[*Other relevant material may be found in* DISTRIBUTIONS, STATISTICAL, *article on* APPROXIMATIONS TO DISTRIBUTIONS; ECONOMIC THOUGHT, *article on* SOCIALIST THOUGHT; NONPARAMETRIC STATISTICS, *articles on* ORDER STATISTICS *and* RUNS; QUEUES; *and in the biographies of* LEXIS *and* PARETO.]

WORKS BY BORTKIEWICZ

1890   Smertnost' i dolgovechnost' muzhskago pravoslavnago naseleniia evropeiskoi Rossii (Mortality and Lifespan of the Male Russian Orthodox Population of European Russia). I. Akademiia Nauk, *Zapiski* 63: Supplement no. 8.

1891   Smertnost' i dolgovechnost' zhenskago pravoslavnogo naseleniia evropeiskoi Rossii (Mortality and Lifespan of the Female Russian Orthodox Population of European Russia). I. Akademiia Nauk, *Zapiski* 66: Supplement no. 3.

1893   *Die mittlere Lebensdauer: Die Methoden ihrer Bestimmung und ihr Verhältnis zur Sterblichkeitsmessung.* Jena (Germany): Fischer.

1898   *Das Gesetz der kleinen Zahlen.* Leipzig: Teubner.

1901   Anwendungen der Wahrscheinlichkeitsrechnung auf Statistik. Volume 1, pages 821–851 in *Encyklopädie der mathematischen Wissenschaften.* Leipzig: Teubner.

1903   Risicoprämie und Sparprämie bei Lebensversicherungen auf eine Person. *Assekuranz-Jahrbuch* 24, no. 2:3–16.

1904*a*   Über die Methode der "Standard Population." International Statistical Institute, *Bulletin* 14, no. 2: 417–437.

1904*b*   Die Theorie der Bevölkerungs- und Moralstatistik nach Lexis. *Jahrbücher für Nationalökonomie und Statistik* 82:230–254.

(1906–1907) 1952   Value and Price in the Marxian System. *International Economic Papers* 2:5–60. → First published in German.

(1907) 1949   On the Correction of Marx's Fundamental Theoretical Construction in the Third Volume of *Capital*. Pages 197–221 in Eugen von Böhm-Bawerk, *Karl Marx and the Close of His System*. New York: Kelley. → First published in German.

1909–1911   Statistique. Part 1, volume 4, pages 453–490 in *Encyclopédie des sciences mathématiques*. Paris: Gauthier-Villars. → Substantially the same as Bortkiewicz 1901, with changes by the translator, F. Oltramare.

1910   Eine geometrische Fundierung der Lehre vom Standort der Industrien. *Archiv für Sozialwissenschaft und Sozialpolitik* 30:759–785.

1910–1911   Die Rodbertus'sche Grundrententheorie und die Marx'sche Lehre von der absoluten Grundrente. *Archiv für die Geschichte des Sozialismus und der Arbeiterbewegung* 1:1–40, 391–434.

1911   Die Sterbeziffer und der Frauenüberschuss in der stationären und der progressiven Bevölkerung. International Statistical Institute, *Bulletin* 19:63–141.

1913   *Die radioaktive Strahlung als Gegenstand wahrscheinlichkeitstheoretischer Untersuchungen*. Berlin: Springer.

1915a   Über die Zeitfolge zufälliger Ereignisse. International Statistical Institute, *Bulletin* 20, no. 2:30–111.

1915b   Realismus und Formalismus in der mathematischen Statistik. *Allgemeines statistisches Archiv* 9: 225–256.

1917   *Die Iterationen: Ein Beitrag zur Wahrscheinlichkeitstheorie*. Berlin: Springer.

1918   Der mittlere Fehler des zum Quadrat erhobenen Divergenzkoeffizienten. Deutsche Mathematiker-Vereinigung, *Jahresbericht* 27:71–126.

1919   *Bevölkerungswesen*. Leipzig: Teubner.

1922a   Die Variationsbreite beim Gaussschen Fehlergesetz. *Nordisk statistisk tidskrift* 1:11–38, 193–220.

1922b   Das Helmertsche Verteilungsgesetz für die Quadratsumme zufälliger Beobachtungsfehler. *Zeitschrift für angewandte Mathematik und Mechanik* 2:358–375.

1923   Wahrscheinlichkeit und statistische Forschung nach Keynes. *Nordisk statistisk tidskrift* 2:1–23.

1923–1924   Zweck und Struktur einer Preisindexzahl. *Nordisk statistisk tidskrift* 2:369–408; 3:208–251, 494–516.

1929   Korrelationskoeffizient und Sterblichkeitsindex. *Blätter für Versicherungs-Mathematik und verwandte Gebiete* 1:87–117.

1930   Lexis und Dormoy. *Nordic Statistical Journal* 2: 37–54.

1931a   Die Disparitätsmasse der Einkommensstatistik. International Statistical Institute, *Bulletin* 25, no. 3: 189–291.

1931b   The Relations Between Stability and Homogeneity. *Annals of Mathematical Statistics* 2:1–22.

SUPPLEMENTARY BIBLIOGRAPHY

ANDERSON, OSKAR   1931   Ladislaus von Bortkiewicz. *Zeitschrift für Nationalökonomie* 3:242–250.

ANDERSSON, THOR   1931   Ladislaus von Bortkiewicz: 1868–1931   *Nordic Statistical Journal* 3:9–26. → Includes a bibliography.

CRATHORNE, A. R.   1928   The Law of Small Numbers. *American Mathematical Monthly* 35:169–175.

FISHER, IRVING   (1922) 1927   *The Making of Index Numbers: A Study of Their Varieties, Tests, and Reliability*. 3d ed., rev. Boston: Houghton Mifflin.

FREUDENBERG, KARL   1951   Die Grenzen für die Anwendbarkeit des Gesetzes der kleinen Zahlen. *Metron* 16: 285–310.

GINI, C.   1931   Observations . . . à la communication . . . du M. L. von Bortkiewicz. International Statistical Institute, *Bulletin* 25, no. 3:299–306.

GOSSET, WILLIAM S.   (1919) 1943   An Explanation of Deviations From Poisson's Law in Practice. Pages 65–69 in [William S. Gosset], *"Student's" Collected Papers*. Cambridge Univ. Press.

GUMBEL, E. J.   1931   L. von Bortkiewicz. *Deutsches statistisches Zentralblatt* 23, cols. 231–236.

GUMBEL, E. J.   1937   Les centenaires. *Aktuárske védy* (Prague) 7:10–17.

KEYNES, JOHN M.   (1921) 1952   *A Treatise on Probability*. London: Macmillan. → A paperback edition was published in 1962 by Harper.

KÜHNE, OTTO   1922   *Untersuchungen über die Wert und Preisrechnung des Marxschen Systems: Eine dogmenkritische Auseinandersetzung mit L. von Bortkiewicz*. Greifswald (Germany): Bamberg.

LORENZ, CHARLOTTE   1951   *Forschungslehre der Sozialstatistik*. Volume 1: Allgemeine Grundlegung und Anleitung. Berlin: Duncker & Humblot.

MARBE, KARL   1916–1919   *Die Gleichförmigkeit in der Welt: Untersuchungen zur Philosophie und positiven Wissenschaft*. 2 vols. Munich: Beck.

NEWBOLD, ETHEL M.   1927   Practical Applications of the Statistics of Repeated Events, Particularly to Industrial Accidents. *Journal of the Royal Statistical Society* 90:487–535.

SCHUMACHER, HERMANN   1931   Ladislaus von Bortkiewicz *Allgemeines statistisches Archiv* 21:573–576.

SCHUMPETER, JOSEPH A.   (1932) 1960   Ladislaus von Bortkiewicz: 1868–1931. Pages 302–305 in Joseph A. Schumpeter, *Ten Great Economists From Marx to Keynes*. New York: Oxford Univ. Press. → First published in Volume 42 of the *Economic Journal*.

TIPPETT, L. H. C.   1925   On the Extreme Individuals and the Range of Samples Taken From a Normal Population. *Biometrika* 17:364–387.

WEBER, ERNA   1935   *Einführung in die Variations- und Erblichkeits-statistik*. Munich: Lehmann.

WINDSOR, CHARLES P.   1947   Quotations: *Das Gesetz der kleinen Zahlen*. *Human Biology* 19:154–161.

WOYTINSKY, WLADIMIR S.   1961   *Stormy Passage; A Personal History Through Two Russian Revolutions to Democracy and Freedom: 1905–1960*. New York: Vanguard.

BOSANQUET, BERNARD

Bernard Bosanquet (1848–1923), English philosopher, was the youngest son of the Reverend R. W. Bosanquet, Rector of Alnwick, Northumberland, and his second wife Caroline. Bosanquet was educated at Sherburn, Yorkshire, and at Harrow. During the period 1866 to 1870 he was a classical scholar at Balliol College, Oxford, where he obtained a first in classical moderations, 1868, and a first in greats, 1870. For the next 10 years, he was both a fellow and a tutor at University College, Oxford.

The dominant influence on Bosanquet at Oxford were his tutors at Balliol, T. H. Green and R. L.

Nettleship. Green, who like Bosanquet came from an evangelical Protestant background, had introduced a liberalized form of Hegelian idealism into English thought. He had turned his back on traditional English empiricism and naturalism and expounded a view of ethics and politics based on Hegel's metaphysical conception of history as the process whereby the Absolute realizes itself, attaining this realization in the most self-conscious form in human consciousness. This spiritual principle led Green to propound a teleological view of history and of human conduct. Yet Green did not accept Hegel's exaltation of the role of the state in politics, which tended to diminish the status and value of the individual; indeed, he reversed the emphasis. For Green the state exists as a means whereby individuals achieve moral self-fulfillment, which they do by freely willing the common good. The contribution of the state is to "hinder hindrances," to maintain and expand individual rights, to reconcile individual and class conflicts, and to provide those conditions in which individuals can conceive and freely will the good of all. He believed that his philosophy logically implied certain practical conclusions. Green himself and his followers engaged in active social work, and he can be regarded as one of the major influences in the creation of the modern welfare state in Britain. Bosanquet, while agreeing with Green on the importance of individual responsibility in the achievement of the common good, nevertheless was more conservative in his interpretation of Hegel, both in the metaphysics and politics.

In 1881 Bosanquet resigned his post at Oxford; he lived in London for the next 22 years in order to have the leisure to write and to engage in social work. His half-brother Charles had helped to found the Charity Organisation Society (COS) in 1869 and had been its first secretary. Its aims were to coordinate and administer charitable funds to aid the poor, but to do so in such a way that the recipient maintained his self-respect and self-reliance and that unity of the family was secured. The society developed the system of casework and of district committees to investigate applicants for charitable relief in order to discriminate between deserving cases and those cases where poverty was due to fecklessness or drink. The COS constantly resisted the intrusion of the state as a welfare provider, and in 1905 C. S. Loch (who succeeded Charles Bosanquet as secretary) was one of the opponents of proposals to reorganize the Poor Law and to introduce state old-age pensions. In 1890 Bernard Bosanquet became a member of the administrative committee of the COS. In 1895 he married Helen Dendy, one of its district secretaries

in Shoreditch, who later edited the society's journal and wrote a number of works advocating its aims. In 1886 Bosanquet helped found the London Ethical Society and the London School of Ethics and Social Philosophy. He gave many public lectures on their behalf, as well as for the University Extension Board. He returned to academic life in 1903 and was appointed to the chair of philosophy at St. Andrews, but he retired in 1908 to prepare his Gifford lectures.

Bosanquet's logical theory. Bosanquet's work on logic is closely related to the work of his famous Oxford contemporary, F. H. Bradley, whose *Principles of Logic* was published in 1883. For each of them logic is based upon and is an explication of metaphysics. The function of logic is to expound the unity and coherence implied in human knowledge, for it is essential to their metaphysical beliefs that as knowledge becomes more coherent, so it becomes more "real"—hence, logic as the science of knowledge and metaphysics as the science of reality ultimately become indistinguishable. The basic logical unit is "judgment," and all judgments are to be regarded as partial definitions of reality as it reveals itself in the mind of man. While isolated judgment may be contradictory, the pursuit of logical consistency forces the further qualification of each judgment so that thought becomes more systematic and more rational in the sense that each judgment logically should entail all other judgments. Our actual thinking falls short of this: our attempts to be comprehensive succeed only in expressing "abstract" universals and fall short of the concrete universal. The abstract universal is a class concept like "red" and refers to partial aspects of many different particulars. The concrete universal is the unity-in-difference of the particular and is the clue to "reality" as a whole. It is a world "whose members are worlds." And the ideal of knowledge is, by becoming more systematically coherent and self-consistent, to see the whole as a "macrocosm constituted by microcosms."

Bosanquet's social philosophy. It is from the above metaphysical generalities that Bosanquet proceeded to set out his social philosophy, which he conceived as standing midway between metaphysics and practical social activity. This is expounded in his *Philosophical Theory of the State* (1899). His object was to show that society is itself a concrete universal, or "world," included in the all-comprehensive concrete universal of reality as a whole. Here he followed through the implications of Hegelianism more rigorously than Green had. He thought that Green had unduly limited the functions of the state (though Bosanquet attacked the socialists for their belief in the efficacy of state-run bureaucracies to own and manage industry). Also, Bosanquet was readier than Green to acknowledge the contribution of sociology and psychology to social understanding. As social sciences they adopt analytic and descriptive procedures and tend to explain more developed forms of behavior in terms of simpler and more primitive forms, whereas philosophy studies the lower forms as containing the potentialities of the higher and sees in the diverse and apparently conflicting facts a manifestation of a unified social purpose. This conception of philosophy, indeed, can be claimed as the main explanatory principle of Bosanquet's social theory. This theory can be broadly summarized as follows:

(1) Human action is the expression of will. But what we will at any one moment may be harmful to us or inconsistent with our other desires. These activities therefore are subject to criticism from the point of view of an end which will most fully and coherently fulfill our needs. Hence he distinguished between the "actual" will, the momentary desires we feel, and the "real" will, what will wholly satisfy us and what we truly desire.

In political terms the moral justification of the state is that it reinforces by its laws the claims of the real will of the individual. It is a false antithesis to set the interests of the individual against those of the state. The purpose of the state is the self-perfection or self-realization of the individual. The true interests of state and individual coincide. In this sense the individual is "forced to be free." His freedom lies not in the absence of restraint but in the correction of impulses and delusive wishes which may prompt him to action harmful to himself. As a rational being he wants to will what is conceived as a good for himself. The state fulfills a moral function in directing him to this end.

(2) The state is conceived as a "concrete universal" when it is apprehended as the manifestation of a general will (which is the expression of the real will of each individual in the state) and when each institution is apprehended as the manifestation of that general will. For the general will is the source of the sovereignty of the state and as such is the final arbiter of social decisions and the authority which can criticize the imperfections of all other social institutions. And though the state cannot directly affect human motives it can affect human intentions. By law the state can induce men to act in certain ways and to bring about such behavior as should preferably occur from any motive rather than not occur at all.

(3) Bosanquet therefore followed Hegel in adopting Rousseau's concept of the general but applied it to the nation-state and did not confine it (as Rousseau did) to a limited city-state. The result is that Rousseau's safeguard of the direct participation of each individual in arriving at collective decisions is no longer practicable. Also, the distinction between the state and the executive becomes less clear. In its place Bosanquet relied on the sentiment of nationalism as a collective sense of group unity. "The modern nation is a history and a religion rather than a clear-cut idea." And the state ideally should be the focal expression of this feeling of unity. In practice, however, he admitted that the actions of the agents and organs of the state may fall short of the ideal, particularly in respect to the moral function of the self-perfection of individuals which the state should promote, though the state cannot be held responsible for the blameworthy actions of its agents.

(4) The practical consequences of this theory led Bosanquet to deny that predictions of human behavior can be made on the assumption of an egoistic psychology. We are "members one of another." Social groups are communities, not associations. He insisted on the limits of international institutions in promoting human cooperation: the nation-state has a finality which no international body can possess. Although Bosanquet claimed that his views were a kind of Christian Hellenism, it is clear that he denied both a personal God and the immortality of the soul. "I cannot believe," he said, "that the supreme end of the Absolute is to give rise to beings such as I experience myself to be."

HUW MORRIS-JONES

[*See also* GENERAL WILL; STATE; SYSTEMS ANALYSIS, article on SOCIAL SYSTEMS; *and the biographies of* GREEN *and* HEGEL.]

WORKS BY BOSANQUET

1885 *Knowledge and Reality.* London: Routledge.

(1889a) 1951 *The Philosophical Theory of the State.* 4th ed. London: Macmillan. → The 1951 publication is a reprint of the 1923 fourth edition.

(1889b) 1899 *Essays and Addresses.* 3d ed. New York: Scribner.

(1892) 1934 *A History of Aesthetics.* 2d ed. New York: Macmillan. → The 1934 publication is a reprint of the 1904 second edition.

1893 *The Civilisation of Christendom and Other Studies.* New York: Macmillan.

1897 *Psychology of the Moral Self.* New York: Macmillan.

(1899) 1920 *The Philosophical Theory of the State.* 3d ed. London: Macmillan.

1913 *The Value and Destiny of the Individual.* London: Macmillan.

1917 *Social and International Ideals.* London: Macmillan.

1920a *Implication and Linear Inference.* London: Macmillan.

1920b *What Religion Is.* London: Macmillan.

1921 *The Meeting of Extremes in Contemporary Philoso-phy.* London: Macmillan.

1923 *Three Chapters on the Nature of Mind.* London: Macmillan. → Published posthumously.

1927 *Science and Philosophy.* Edited by R. C. Bosanquet and J. H. Muirhead. London: Allen & Unwin. → Published posthumously.

SUPPLEMENTARY BIBLIOGRAPHY

BOSANQUET, HELEN 1924 *Bernard Bosanquet: A Short Account of His Life.* London: Macmillan.

HALDANE, R. B. 1923 Bernard Bosanquet: 1848–1923. British Academy, *Proceedings* 10:563–575.

HEGEL, GEORG (1817–1829) 1905 *Introduction to Hegel's Philosophy of Fine Art.* Translated by Bernard Bosanquet. London: Routledge. → First published in German.

HOBHOUSE, LEONARD T. (1918) 1951 *The Metaphysical Theory of the State: A Criticism.* London: Allen & Unwin; New York: Macmillan.

LOTZE, HERMANN (1874) 1888 *Logic: In Three Books, of Thought, of Investigation and of Knowledge.* 2 vols. 2d ed. Translated and edited by Bernard Bosanquet. Oxford: Clarendon Press. → First published in German.

LOTZE, HERMANN (1879) 1887 *Metaphysics: In Three Books, Ontology, Cosmology and Psychology.* 2 vols. 2d ed. The English translation edited by Bernard Bosanquet. Oxford: Clarendon Press. → First published in German.

MILNE, ADAM 1962 *The Social Philosophy of English Idealism.* London: Allen & Unwin.

MOWATT, CHARLES L. 1961 *The Charity Organisation Society, 1869–1913: Its Ideas and Its Work.* London: Methuen.

MUIRHEAD, JOHN H. 1923 Bernard Bosanquet: Obituary Notice. *Mind* 32:393–407.

MUIRHEAD, JOHN H. 1931 *The Platonic Tradition in Anglo-Saxon Philosophy.* London: Allen & Unwin.

MUIRHEAD, JOHN H. (editor) 1935 *Bernard Bosanquet and His Friends: Letters Illustrating the Sources and Development of His Philosophical Opinions.* London: Allen & Unwin.

PFANNENSTILL, BERTIL 1936 *Bernard Bosanquet's Philosophy of the State.* Lund (Sweden): Gleerup.

RICHTER, MELVIN 1964 *The Politics of Conscience: T. H. Green and His Age.* Cambridge, Mass.: Harvard Univ. Press.

SPILLER, GUSTAV 1934 *The Ethical Movement in Great Britain.* London: Farleigh.

BOSSISM

See POLITICAL MACHINES; RULES OF THE GAME.

BOUNDARIES

See AREA; CULTURE AREA; ENCLAVES AND EXCLAVES; GEOGRAPHY.

BOWLEY, ARTHUR LYON

Arthur Lyon Bowley (1869–1957), British statistician, was born at Bristol and brought up in a conventional and religious family. Before he went to Trinity College, Cambridge, in 1888 with a major scholarship in mathematics, he spent nine years at Christ's Hospital, a boarding school of a strictly religious foundation where pupils wore a traditional costume and were subject to spartan conditions. The school left a lasting impression on his character; later in life he was governor of the school for some years.

Bowley followed a conventional course in mathematics at Cambridge, graduating as a wrangler in 1891, but an interest in economics and social problems, which was to be the mainspring of his life's work, was already evident in his undergraduate days. He was in contact with Alfred Marshall and others active in the developing social sciences, and he was deeply affected, not so much by refinements of economic analysis as by the problems of social reform in Britain at the end of the century.

In studying these problems Bowley used both contemporary and historical material. His first work was *A Short Account of England's Foreign Trade in the Nineteenth Century* (1893), for which he received the Cobden Prize at Cambridge in 1892. Foreign trade was a subject on which he continued to write throughout his life, but a more important early interest was the relation between movements of wages and prices, the subject of the first paper he read to the Royal Statistical Society in March 1895 (1895a). From 1895 to 1906 the *Journal* of the society and the more recently established *Economic Journal* published many papers by him on this topic, sometimes by Bowley alone and sometimes with G. H. Wood as coauthor. Bowley approached the subject with statistical and historical care verging on the pedantic, yet at the same time with a deep and sympathetic appreciation of the human problems involved.

It was on Marshall's recommendation that Bowley was invited to join the small and mainly part-time staff of the London School of Economics when the first session began in 1895. Thus was laid the main path of his professional career. Over a period of more than forty years, until his retirement in 1936, Bowley taught statistics to successive generations of students of the social sciences at the school. He developed an intimate friendship with Edwin Cannan and remained to take his place as an elder statesman in a large and distinguished faculty of economists, historians, and social and political theorists. He was never a socialist in the sense of Webb and other founding fathers of the school, but as a good liberal he found the senior common room a congenial and stimulating background to his activities in teaching and research.

The London School of Economics, although increasingly the locus of his work, did not for many years provide Bowley with his livelihood. In 1895, when living and teaching mathematics at a school in Leatherhead, he bicycled from there on the Wednesday half holidays to lecture at the London School in the early evening. Later, from 1900 to 1913, he was a member of the mathematics staff at University Extension College, Reading, and remained as a lecturer in economics there until 1919. Meanwhile he became a part-time reader in statistics at the London School in 1908, receiving the title of professor in 1915. It was only in 1919, with the establishment of a chair in statistics in the University of London, of which he was the first holder, that he became a full-time member of the school's faculty.

As a mathematician Bowley was competent without being very original, and he became increasingly old-fashioned in his mathematical formulations. He published relatively little, and nothing of real substance, either in mathematical statistics or in mathematical economics, although both fields developed rapidly in very exciting directions in his middle and later life. Much of his work was in mathematical form as a matter of convenience, but the mathematics itself was incidental to his main purposes. First and foremost Bowley was a practitioner in applied statistics, with the whole of the social sciences as his field, and for most of his career he had to make bricks with very little straw. Always a severe critic of British official statistics, and highly respected in official quarters, he was called upon far too seldom to advise on the development of government statistics. British economic and social statistics in the 1920s and 1930s would undoubtedly have been improved, particularly by the use of sampling techniques, if he had had more to do with them. His main influence was through his private researches and in discussions at the international level.

There can be little doubt that Bowley's major contribution was to the development of sampling techniques and their application to economic and social studies. While he was forming his ideas in the 1890s, the great debate on the "representative method" was taking place among official statisticians in Europe and the United States. It was from these discussions against the rather narrow background of official statistics that the modern corpus of sampling techniques developed, with applications in all fields of scientific inquiry. Anders N. Kiaer (1838–1919), the distinguished chief of the Norwegian Bureau of Statistics for 46 years, led the case for sampling at a series of sessions of the International Statistical Institute from 1895 (Bern) to 1901 (Budapest). He was at first opposed by a majority of leading official statisticians, but his ideas rapidly gained ground, being greatly supported by the report of Carroll D. Wright, at Budapest, on sampling experience in the U.S. Department of Labor. Bowley, elected to the institute in 1903, was immediately attracted by the possibilities of the "representative method." With characteristic care, he explored for himself both the appropriate mathematical formulation of sampling precision and the best ways of interpreting the results of sample surveys to laymen.

Between 1912 and 1914 Bowley directed sample surveys of working-class households in five English towns, and in presenting his results in *Livelihood and Poverty* (Bowley & Burnett-Hurst 1915), he was far ahead of his time in explaining both the method and the errors of sampling. He devoted a chapter to the four sources of error: incorrect information, loose definitions, bias in selection of sample, and the calculable errors of sampling. It is true that he did not distinguish the method of cluster or systematic sampling he adopted (selection of 1 in n down a listing of the frame) from simple random sampling. Even so, his exposition of 1915 would have been readily accepted two generations later.

It was only appropriate, therefore, that Bowley became a member of the committee set up by the International Statistical Institute in 1924, presenting their "Report on the Representative Method in Statistics" (Jensen 1926) at the Rome session in 1925. Bowley's hand is clearly visible in the major recommendation "that the investigation should be so arranged wherever possible, as to allow of a mathematical statement of the precision of the results, and that with these results should be given an indication of the extent of the error to which they are liable" (Jensen 1926, p. 378), as well as in Annex A to the report "Measurement of the Precision Attained in Sampling" (1926a). Bowley himself continued to practice what he preached, notably in his resurvey of the five English towns published in *Has Poverty Diminished?* (1925) and in *The New Survey of London Life and Labour*, Volume 3 (1932a; 1932b) and Volume 6 (1934).

Another pioneering work undertaken by Bowley was the estimation of the distribution of national income, a task in which he was in the end rather less successful than might have been expected. His first essays were "The Division of the Product of Industry" and "The Change in the Distribution of the National Income: 1880–1913." Later he worked with Josiah Stamp on the more elaborate "The National Income: 1924" (see Bowley 1919–1927) and with the National Institute of Economic and Social Research on *Studies in the National Income: 1924–1938* (1942), a series that was curtailed by the outbreak of World War II. This work was a natural development of his early interest in wages and of his continuing concern with the redistribution of income as a tool in social reform. In the years between the two world wars he found British data quite inadequate for his purpose; economists did not agree on even the concept of national income. His work was influential when the first official estimates of the British national income were made, under the inspiration of J. M. Keynes, during World War II. But it was not in his careful and precise nature to take undue risks in handling scattered data. This he left to others, notably to the more adventurous, almost buccaneering, spirit of Colin Clark.

A third area in which Bowley's pioneering was influential was his regular reporting on and analysis of the current economic position for the London and Cambridge Economic Service. This service began publication as a private venture, dependent on subscriptions for its bulletins, in January 1923. At first it was a cooperative project with the Harvard University Committee on Economic Research, which had issued its Harvard Economic Service bulletins for some time, and the aims were set out by William H. Beveridge in an introductory article on the study of business cycles. Bowley was the first editor of the service, serving in this capacity for more than twenty years, until 1945, and continuing as a regular contributor until 1953. Under his guidance the service was soon set on a very profitable course of its own, independent of its Harvard parent (which failed to survive the crisis of 1929) and of various schools of business cycle research.

Two characteristics of Bowley as an editor were outstanding. One was the skill with which he listened at editorial meetings to the diverse and outspoken views of economists before writing his own pithy assessment of the economic position in order to represent just as much as, and no more than, the majority of economists could agree upon at that moment. The other was his conviction that any analysis of the present or forecast of the future was dependent on long runs of carefully prepared statistical series covering the whole range of economic and social matters. He and his research associates were indefatigable in designing and improving index numbers and in devising ways of presenting them most effectively. From the beginning he showed his series in graphical form, often by the use of ratio scales and often after adjust-

ment for seasonal variations. He was one of the earliest champions of these now well-recognized devices. In these and other aspects he never shirked the task of explaining highly technical matters to a lay public.

Bowley was an effective if rather dour committeeman, and he held many offices, in the British Association, in the Royal Statistical Society, and in the International Statistical Institute, among others. He received many honors, which culminated in his appointment as knight bachelor soon after his eightieth birthday.

R. G. D. ALLEN

[*For discussion of the subsequent development of Bowley's work in sampling, see* ECONOMIC DATA; INDEX NUMBERS; SAMPLE SURVEYS.]

WORKS BY BOWLEY

(1893) 1922   *A Short Account of England's Foreign Trade in the Nineteenth Century: Its Economic and Social Results.* 3d ed. London: Allen & Unwin.

1895a   Changes in Average Wages (Nominal and Real) in the United Kingdom Between 1860 and 1891. *Journal of the Royal Statistical Society* 58:223–278.

1895b   Comparison of the Rates of Increase of Wages in the United States and in Great Britain: 1860–1891. *Economic Journal* 5:369–383.

1897   Relations Between the Accuracy of an Average and That of Its Constituent Parts. *Journal of the Royal Statistical Society* 60:855–866.

(1900) 1937   *Wages and Income in the United Kingdom Since 1860.* Cambridge Univ. Press.

(1901) 1937   *Elements of Statistics.* 6th ed. New York: Scribner; London: King.

(1910) 1951   *An Elementary Manual of Statistics.* 7th ed. London: Macdonald & Evans.

1911   The Measurement of the Accuracy of an Average. *Journal of the Royal Statistical Society* 75:77–88.

1915   BOWLEY, ARTHUR L.; and BURNETT-HURST, A. R. *Livelihood and Poverty: A Study in the Economic Conditions of Working-class Households in Northampton, Warrington, Stanley and Reading.* London: Bell.

(1919–1927) 1938   *Three Studies on the National Income.* London School of Economics and Political Science. → Contains "The Division of the Product of Industry"; "The Change in the Distribution of National Income: 1880–1913," by Arthur L. Bowley; and "The National Income: 1924," by Arthur L. Bowley and Josiah Stamp.

1924   *The Mathematical Groundwork of Economics: An Introductory Treatise.* Oxford: Clarendon.

1925   BOWLEY, ARTHUR L.; and HOGG, MARGARET H. *Has Poverty Diminished? A Sequel to* Livelihood and Poverty. London: King.

1926a   Measurement of the Precision Attained in Sampling. International Statistical Institute, *Bulletin* 22, part 1:6–62.

1926b   The Influence on the Precision of Index-numbers of Correlation Between the Prices of Commodities. *Journal of the Royal Statistical Society* 89:300–319.

1928   Notes on Index Numbers. *Economic Journal* 38: 216–237.

1930a   Area and Population. Pages 58–83 in London

School of Economics and Political Science, *The New Survey of London Life and Labour.* Volume 1: Forty Years of Change. London: King.

1930b London Occupations and Industries. Pages 315–340 in London School of Economics and Political Science, *The New Survey of London Life and Labour.* Volume 1: Forty Years of Change. London: King.

1932a The House Sample Analysis. Pages 29–96 in London School of Economics and Political Science, *The New Survey of London Life and Labour.* Volume 3: Survey of Social Conditions: 1. The Eastern Area. London: King.

1932b BOWLEY, ARTHUR L.; and SMITH, H. LLEWELLYN. Overcrowding. Pages 216–253 in London School of Economics and Political Science, *The New Survey of London Life and Labour.* Volume 3: Survey of Social Conditions: 1. The Eastern Area. London: King.

1934 The House Sample Analysis. Pages 29–117 in London School of Economics and Political Science, *The New Survey of London Life and Labour.* Volume 6: Survey of Social Conditions: 2. The Western Area. London: King.

1935 ALLEN, ROY G. D.; and BOWLEY, ARTHUR L. *Family Expenditure: A Study of Its Variation.* London School of Economics and Political Science, Studies in Statistics and Scientific Method, No. 2. London: King.

1942 BOWLEY, ARTHUR L. (editor). *Studies in the National Income: 1924–1938.* Cambridge Univ. Press.

SUPPLEMENTARY BIBLIOGRAPHY

JENSEN, ADOLPH 1926 Report on the Representative Method in Statistics. International Statistical Institute, *Bulletin* 22, part 1:359–380.

BOWMAN, ISAIAH

Isaiah Bowman (1878–1950), a leading American geographer of his time, was born in Waterloo, Ontario, the third of eight children in a large farm family. Shortly after his birth his parents moved to eastern Michigan, and there Bowman grew up. After a decision "to study geography professionally" he enrolled in Michigan State Normal College at Ypsilanti, studying under Mark Jefferson, who interested him in the human side of geography and encouraged him to go to Harvard to study under William Morris Davis, then a well-known physical geographer. After obtaining his B.A. from Harvard in 1905, Bowman went to Yale, where he taught for the next ten years, receiving his doctorate there in 1909. In 1915 he left Yale and went to New York to become director of the American Geographical Society, a research institution founded in 1851. He remained with the society until 1935, when he was appointed president of The Johns Hopkins University. He retired in 1948.

Bowman made original contributions not only to physical and human geography but also to the type of regional geography in which the two are blended, as in *The Andes of Southern Peru* (1916) and *Desert Trails of Atacama* (1924). These studies reflect his participation in three expeditions to South America, in 1907, 1911, and 1913, in the first and third of which he acted as leader.

His classic in physical regional geography of the United States, *Forest Physiography* (1911), came about as the result of a physiography course he taught in the Yale forestry school. The book was a synthesis of hundreds of papers and monographs; its generalizations followed the Davisian erosional-cycle theory of land formation.

Bowman became chief territorial specialist on President Wilson's staff at the Paris Peace Conference, after leading a research team called the Inquiry for a year. The Inquiry was organized by Colonel House to provide geographical background materials for the negotiators at Paris; the value of its work has been questioned (Gelfand 1963).

His experience with the Inquiry gave Bowman the inspiration and practical experience for his writings on political geography and for his advisory positions in the State Department during World War II. His book *The New World: Problems in Political Geography* (1921) treated international relations on a regional basis. It was very successful: a special reprinting was necessary to fulfill the demand for it for armed-services training units studying the background to World War II.

In the early 1930s Bowman presented his "pioneer fringe" thesis that new human settlements should be made only after a scientific evaluation of the proposed environment and of the social and political processes involved. Support and funds for this work came from the National Research Council and from the Social Science Research Council (SSRC).

Bowman's *Geography in Relation to the Social Sciences* (1934) was Volume 5 of the 16-volume *Report* of the Commission on the Social Studies in the Schools of the American Historical Association and grew out of an earlier conference of the SSRC. Bowman believed that the subject matter of geography had to be decided by individual geographers and asserted that his book contained no quotable definition of geography. He did, however, describe the role of the geographer: "Besides being an explorer, a measurer, a describer, and an interpreter of the features of the earth, the geographer is a synthesizer of the data of his subject according to those realities of experience called *regions*, and this brings him to fraternize with the historian, the economist, and the sociologist" (1934, pp. 2–3).

Bowman was one of the founders of the Council on Foreign Relations and served on the editorial advisory board of its organ, *Foreign Affairs*, for over two decades. He served as president of the Association of American Geographers, the International Geographical Union, and the American Association for the Advancement of Science. He was elected to the National Academy of Sciences in 1930.

GEORGE A. KNADLER

[*Directly related are the entries* GEOGRAPHY; REGION.]

WORKS BY BOWMAN

1911   *Forest Physiography: Physiography of the United States and Principles of Soils in Relation to Forestry.* New York: Wiley.

(1916) 1920   *The Andes of Southern Peru: Geographical Reconnaissance Along the Seventy-third Meridian.* London: Constable.

(1921) 1928   *The New World: Problems in Political Geography.* 4th ed. New York: World.

1924   *Desert Trails of Atacama.* New York: American Geographical Society.

1931   *The Pioneer Fringe.* New York: American Geographical Society.

1934   *Geography in Relation to the Social Sciences.* New York: Scribner.

1936   *A Design for Scholarship.* Baltimore: Johns Hopkins Press.

1937   *Limits of Land Settlement: A Report on Present Day Possibilities.* New York: Council on Foreign Relations.

1939   *The Graduate School in American Democracy.* U.S. Office of Education, Bulletin No. 10. Washington: Government Printing Office.

WORKS ABOUT BOWMAN

KNADLER, GEORGE A.   1959   Isaiah Bowman: Backgrounds of His Contribution to Thought. Ph.D. dissertation, Indiana Univ.

WRIGHT, JOHN K.; and CARTER, GEORGE F.   1959   Isaiah Bowman, December 26, 1878–January 6, 1950. Volume 33, pages 39–64 in National Academy of Sciences, *Biographical Memoirs.* Washington: Government Printing Office.

WRIGLEY, GLADYS M.   1951   Isaiah Bowman. *Geographical Review* 41:7–65.

SUPPLEMENTARY BIBLIOGRAPHY

GELFAND, LAWRENCE E.   1963   *The Inquiry: American Preparation for Peace, 1917–1919.* New Haven: Yale Univ. Press.

WRIGHT, JOHN K.   1952   *Geography in the Making: The American Geographical Society, 1851–1951.* New York: American Geographical Society.

BRAIN

See NERVOUS SYSTEM *and the biographies of* BELL; BROCA; FLOURENS; LASHLEY.

BRAINWASHING

The term "brainwashing" is used here to refer to the technique or process employed in communist-controlled states to attain either or both of two objectives: (1) to compel an innocent person to admit, in all subjective sincerity, that he has committed serious crimes against the "people" and the state; and (2) coercively to reshape an individual's political views so that he abandons his previous beliefs and becomes an advocate of communism. Both objectives, however dissimilar they may initially appear, are attempts to make an individual accept as true what he previously rejected as false and to view as false what he formerly saw as true. Both are achieved through the same techniques and procedures.

The European communists and the Chinese communists differ considerably in their respective emphases upon these two goals. The Europeans concentrate largely on the confessional aspect; the Chinese, especially in dealing with their own people, are more concerned with ideological conformance. In either variant, however, the subordinated aspect will usually be pursued as a means of achieving the primary end. Accordingly, the Europeans rely upon Marxist indoctrination to hasten the confession; the Chinese utilize confession as a means of facilitating ideological conversion.

Although a number of other terms—"thought control," "thought reform," "ideological reform," "menticide"—have also been employed to denote this process, "brainwashing" is probably the most common and will be used here. Unfortunately, considerable confusion has arisen from the tendency of many writers to employ these terms indiscriminately when dealing with analogous situations in which prisoners have been compelled to reveal military intelligence, to cooperate with their captors against their fellow prisoners, or to make knowingly false confessions of guilt. The above phenomena, although superficially similar in some respects, lack the unique characteristics of true brainwashing: the enforced but real conversion of political belief and/or the sincere confession of guilt for crimes of which one is actually innocent.

Viewed in a broader perspective, brainwashing is related to propaganda and political education, or socialization. All three seek to mold attitudes, to inculcate certain beliefs and minimize or destroy others. All three utilize, in varying combinations, the tools of reason and emotion, logic and faith, persuasion and coercion. In short, all three may be regarded as aspects of political indoctrination.

History

Two lines of development, essentially independent of each other, can be traced. The communist Chinese were employing a rudimentary type of brainwashing against captured enemy soldiers and, less frequently, against civilians in the late 1920s.

By the Yenan period (1935–1945) the practice had been sufficiently improved to be used to ensure the loyalties of intellectuals who, in increasing numbers, were making their way to communist-controlled areas of China. Early in the 1940s the party faced the dual task of stamping out unorthodoxy among its growing membership and "Sinofying" an essentially foreign ideology (Lifton 1961; Mu 1962). The technique was then brought to its present state of sophistication and has since been an established organizational device.

In the Soviet Union an early variant of brainwashing, based upon a rich legacy from the tsarist secret police, can be traced back almost to the civil war period. Major refinements seem not to have been worked out, however, until the great purges of the 1930s. At this time widespread attention was first drawn to brainwashing by the series of amazing confessions produced at the well-publicized Moscow "treason trials." Equally amazing and, to the outside world, incredible confessions came to be a predictable feature of the recurring purges that racked the communist states of Europe over the next two decades. The pattern was quite consistent: officials holding positions of high responsibility were arrested and charged with plotting against the regime. After an intervening period of interrogation, they would abjectly confess, either at public trials or at administrative hearings, to a long series of counterrevolutionary crimes. By the most conservative estimate, hundreds of similar admissions were extracted from persons of lesser stature and prominence. Although many of the confessions undoubtedly were knowingly false and contrived, there were a disturbing number of instances in which it seemed that the accused had actually been brought to believe his own declaration of guilt (Beck & Gosin 1951; Leites & Bernaut 1954).

This initial interest was subsequently greatly fanned by the events of the Korean War. Some American prisoners of war confessed that they had engaged in bacteriological warfare operations; some, together with prisoners of war from other nations, issued statements highly critical of United Nations policy; some became openly pro-communist. These and other forms of coerced behavior were popularly attributed to brainwashing, and although the actual number of such cases was relatively small, the ensuing public furor led eventually to official inquiries (e.g., Great Britain . . . 1955; U.S. . . . 1955). Although many prisoners had indeed been subjected to harrowing pressures, few had undergone true brainwashing; nevertheless, the term came into widespread, if highly imprecise, popular usage (see Biderman 1963).

The next series of related events occurred in the years immediately following the Korean conflict. Many Europeans and Americans who had been living in communist China were arrested and charged with espionage and related crimes. After lengthy periods of incarceration most of the accused publicly confessed that they had engaged in counterrevolutionary efforts, attributed their crimes to mistaken "reactionary" political views, and proclaimed their conversion to Marxism. At the same time, thousands of Chinese of uncertain party loyalty were sent to revolutionary "colleges" and "thought reform centers," from which many subsequently emerged as avowed communists. There is little question that a sizable percentage of these persons, Chinese and non-Chinese alike, had successfully been brainwashed (Hunter 1951; Lifton 1961; Sargant 1957).

Although brainwashing is a comparatively recent addition to the armory of political weapons, it has many points of similarity, both in behavioral manifestations and in psychological dynamics, to phenomena with which the Western world is quite familiar. Among these are spontaneous religious conversions, voodoo rites, hypnosis, conditioned reflex behavior, and, of course, the extraction of confessions from "witches" in earlier centuries. But although brainwashing shares some features with these phenomena, it differs considerably from each of them in techniques and objectives and can therefore correctly be regarded as *sui generis*.

The process

The techniques of brainwashing are fairly well standardized, although the nature and intensity of the pressures applied to any individual will vary with the personality of the subject, the circumstances and importance of the case, and the competence of the personnel assigned. But there are two notable differences between the Chinese and the European practices. First, the Chinese will try to brainwash small groups of persons, as well as a single individual; the Europeans normally limit a given effort to one person, although dozens of such operations may be going on simultaneously. Second, a sizable percentage of the subjects in the Chinese undertaking will be persons not actually under formal arrest; many will be so-called volunteers with the technical status of students. In Europe, on the other hand, the subject is invariably someone under arrest and charged with serious political crimes. These differences are reflected in the specific tactics employed, but, in general, brainwashing is accomplished by the utilization of the following measures:

(1) Total control. The prisoner's entire ex-

istence, down to the most intimate needs, is governed by strictly enforced rules that cover both waking and sleeping hours. The objectives are to keep the subject under constant psychological harassment and to drive home the lesson that his jailers are omnipotent and he is powerless.

(2) *Uncertainty.* In the weeks immediately following his arrest, the prisoner will not be informed of the specific charges against him, and his pleas for a bill of particulars are met by angry declarations that he is fully aware of the nature of his crimes and by a demand for immediate and full confession. The accused thus finds himself in an appalling dilemma: he can hardly conduct an effective defense, given his ignorance of the charges, and he cannot satisfy the demand for a confession, since he does not know what it is that he is alleged to have done.

(3) *Isolation.* Once arrested, the accused is completely cut off from the outside world and receives only such information about his family and friends as his custodians see fit to give him. Where the isolated unit is the group rather than the individual, the program design minimizes the possibility of relationships going beyond the group.

(4) *Torture.* The accused is also subjected to a variety of other mental and physical torments. He may be told that his wife has divorced him or that his closest friends have signed statements testifying to his guilt. Relays of questioners will work on him for 12 or 16 hours at a stretch, during much of which he will be kept in acute or chronic pain. The prisoner will be sent back to his cell, allowed to fall asleep, and promptly recalled for another session. This process will be continued until the prisoner finally reaches the desired degree of mental malleability.

(5) *Physical debilitation and exhaustion.* Prison diet is planned to ensure rapid loss of weight, strength, and stamina. Eventually the subject is so weakened that prolonged mental effort becomes increasingly difficult, if not impossible. The disruption of sleep, particularly under conditions of constant interrogation, tension, and terror, greatly accelerates this process of debilitation and exhaustion.

(6) *Personal humiliation.* From the moment of his arrest, the prisoner is made to realize that his "criminal" behavior has deprived him of any previous claim to personal dignity or status. His degradation will be almost in proportion to his previous eminence and importance.

(7) *Certainty of guilt.* Perhaps one of the most insidious devices employed is the complete and unyielding assumption of the prisoner's guilt manifested by his interrogators. This certitude par-

tially justifies, even in the prisoner's mind, the stringency of the measures applied to elicit a confession.

Sequence of events. The above are the conditions, then, under which brainwashing takes place. After an initial period of disbelief and shock, the prisoner begins painfully to reflect upon his past behavior, hoping to recall some chance act or remark that, grossly misconstrued, could account for the apparent certainty of his guilt. With the passage of time he becomes increasingly incapable of coping intellectually with his jailer's arguments. Eventually, he concedes that any past deed which might even remotely have had "objective" subversive consequences, intended or not, may reasonably be viewed as criminal by the regime.

One aim of brainwashing is to destroy the distinction between guilt and innocence, the other to obliterate the borderline between fact and fancy. This intellectual demolition does not proceed easily or swiftly, in either its confessional or its ideological aspect. The prisoner will fight desperately to maintain his faith in his innocence and in his previous values, but his strength is steadily sapped by physical debilitation, fatigue, pain, deprivation, humiliation, and degradation.

Concurrently he begins to sense, if only subconsciously, that life becomes slightly less unbearable during those periods when he shows progress in conceding the possibility of his guilt, or when he evidences a greater receptivity to Marxist doctrine. Living conditions improve and there is a lessening of physical pain; even his interrogators become more friendly and less impersonal. Contrariwise, intervals in which little progress is made or in which the prisoner "regresses" are promptly followed by a return to the old mode of existence, now all the more intolerable. In short, compliance is rewarded, resistance punished. Inevitably he reaches that stage of hope and despair where, in Orwell's classic example, he most desperately *wants* to believe that "two and two make five."

In all probability, acceptance of the concept of "objective" guilt marks the point of no return. What follows, however prolonged or harrowing, is really a slow piecing together of detail into a confession. Confessional verisimilitude may necessitate the incrimination or denunciation of others, but by this time the prisoner is as confused about the guilt or innocence of others as he is about his own.

Psychological mechanisms and dynamics

The earlier theory that brainwashing was systematically perfected in the laboratories of Soviet and Chinese psychologists, and that it represented a triumph of social science research, has now been largely abandoned. Rather, the technique seems to have been empirically developed, with little if any assistance from professional psychologists, to cope with immediate practical problems (Bauer 1952; Wortis 1950). Evidence also suggests that the Chinese and European variants developed essentially independently of one another, although there may have been some exchange of ideas and practices.

As yet there has been no generally accepted explanation of the psychodynamics underlying the brainwashing process. One school, contending that it is primarily an extension of the work done by Pavlov in the field of conditioned reflex behavior, sees the subject as the victim of a step-by-step conditioning process. Another argues that brainwashing can best be understood in terms of Freudian theory. A third suggests that group behavior formulations provide the most satisfactory interpretation. Recent writings tend toward an eclectic approach, with the author likely to present the alternative theoretical explanations that might account for the behavior observed. There is now also general agreement that the technique was not the outgrowth of a consistent or even conscious adherence to any single school of psychology (Hinkle & Wolff 1956; Lifton 1961). Psychologists and psychiatrists tend to agree more readily upon the nature of the specific psychological mechanisms utilized in the brainwashing process. Many of these are already well known in behavioral contexts other than brainwashing.

(1) Identification.   Isolated from human contact, the prisoner will often identify with his chief interrogator, who is usually more sympathetic and less brutal to the prisoner than are his subordinates. This identification, in which both subject and inquisitor may become emotionally involved, is often an important factor in effecting the subject's capitulation. The students in group political indoctrination will, of course, tend to identify with each other.

(2) Decrease of intellectual capacity.   As a result of fatigue and debilitation, the prisoner reaches a point of exhaustion, where he is literally too weak to think in any coherent manner.

(3) Disorientation arising from solitary confinement.   Few persons can endure prolonged isolation without suffering serious adverse emotional and intellectual consequences. The ensuing disorientation and confusion contribute measurably to the "softening-up" process. Severe sensory deprivation will also often produce a type of "stimulus hunger," leading in turn to greater suggestibility [*see* PERCEPTION, *article on* PERCEPTUAL DEPRIVATION].

(4) Suggestion.   The susceptibility of most persons to suggestion has long been recognized as an important factor in shaping both normal and abnormal behavior. It can be particularly effective where, as in brainwashing, the suggestions move in a single direction, where "countersuggestive" stimuli can be screened out, and where the subject is kept under great emotional and physical stress. Suggestion plays a key role in helping the prisoner construct his confession once he is no longer able to distinguish between his own actions and those suggested to him at an earlier point by his interrogators. The resulting admission, fully credible to the confessing person, will often be an admixture of the two.

(5) Repetition.   The importance of repetition is well known to students of the learning process and has been a mainstay, in particular, of Chinese pedagogy. The prisoner is told, over and over again, that he is guilty; the student is subjected to innumerable repetitions of the principles of Marxist ideology. Constant reiteration of an idea, especially if its acceptance has desirable social or personal consequences, eventually inclines all but the most obdurate persons toward greater receptivity.

(6) Guilt feelings.   Both prisoner and student are compelled minutely to review—and often to justify—their past lives, personal as well as political. Except for the infrequent saint, reflections of this nature are almost certain to arouse some feelings of guilt. In a communist society, where one often remains silent in the face of flagrant personal and social injustices, these feelings are not far below the surface. Once evoked, they often work to undermine the capacity or willingness to resist.

(7) Ego destruction.   Although he has no alternative but to submit, the humiliation and degradation endured by the subject result in a profound decrease of self-esteem, a loss all the more devastating if he was previously a person of some eminence. His weakness and helplessness contrast invidiously with the omnipotence and apparent omniscience of his interrogators. The resulting ego destruction seriously affects his ability to withstand the process.

(8) Conditioned behavior.   The extent to which brainwashing relies upon the mechanism of conditioned behavior is a matter of some controversy (Sargant 1957). There is no question, however, that the deliberate relating of punishment and reward to progress or the lack of progress is one way of "conditioning" the prisoner to make the type of response desired.

(9) Nonrational behavior in the face of sudden stimulus.   Faced with an unexpected massive stimulus—pain, fear, anger—many individuals are

emotionally overwhelmed. They can no longer control their behavior and will react in what seems to be a quite uncharacteristic manner, much as experimental animals do when they can no longer cope with the stimuli presented to them. Prisoners unexpectedly subjected to abuse, indignity, or pain may be so overcome that their most determined resistance will suddenly crumble and they capitulate in relatively short time.

(10) Alternation of fear and hope. The alternation of fear and hope is the classic carrot-and-stick device. No matter how cruelly the prisoner may be treated, his captors are careful to keep before him the hope of a better life, perhaps even freedom, if he yields to their demands. The technique is quite similar to that used by the revivalist who depicts, in vivid and harrowing detail, the eternal suffering to which his auditors are doomed—unless they repent and accept the true faith. The revivalist plays upon fears of a hell to come; the brainwasher exploits the horrors of a hell that is.

Political capabilities and limitations

We come, finally, to the two most important questions that arise in any discussion of brainwashing: What are its political capabilities? What are its political limitations?

Almost every serious student has agreed that very few persons are capable of indefinitely resisting brainwashing, given the present state of the art. Assuming the brainwasher has technical competence and the determination and willingness to invest the time and manpower necessary to carry brainwashing to completion, there is an overwhelming likelihood that any individual victim will succumb to the process (Meerloo 1956). The exceptions, other than persons of incredible fortitude and stamina, are the psychotic, the highly neurotic, and those who die or commit suicide in the course of events (Hinkle & Wolff 1956). Much the same conclusion can be drawn, given the same conditions, with regard to brainwashing efforts conducted on a group of persons, although the circumstances here permit a larger number of cases of successful resistance. For the great majority of men, especially when a single person is the target, brainwashing comes close to being an "absolute" weapon.

Fortunately, it is a weapon with serious practical limitations and shortcomings. The results achieved seem not to be permanent if the subject is allowed to return to a free society. Most returned prisoners have renounced both their confessions and their Marxist sympathies shortly after their repatriation (Lifton 1961). On the other hand, more lasting

effects may be achieved when the subject remains in a communist society, where the conversion is strengthened and reinforced by recurrent environmental stimuli. On this point adequate data are lacking. The second shortcoming is more serious. The conditions required for its success make brainwashing one of the most expensive and uneconomical techniques available to the modern state. To be successful, it demands a uniquely structured and controlled environmental setting and an inordinate investment of time and manpower. Despite the costs entailed, its effectiveness is limited to individual subjects or, even under optimum conditions, to a small group of persons. Certainly it is not yet a weapon that can be turned against large, let alone mass, audiences.

Moral issues aside, one might well ask if the confessions and conversions obtained are really worth the labor and expense that go into their achievement. Both the European and the Chinese communists obviously think they are. The position of the former is perhaps easier to understand, since brainwashing is used only to elicit confessions that can be politically exploited at home and abroad, although the manner in which the confessions are attained is now sufficiently well known to deprive them of much of their original propaganda value. The Chinese persistence in continuing to subject sizable numbers of persons to this form of political indoctrination can, in the final analysis, be explained only in terms of China's obsession with achieving total ideological conformity regardless of the costs entailed.

In conclusion, one must keep in mind that the foregoing assessment of the capabilities and limitations of brainwashing is, at most, valid only with regard to the present state of the technique. One must concede at least the possibility that technological advances may someday surmount these limitations and that mankind will then be able to remold the human mind on the same mass scale and with the same economy and efficiency which advances in nuclear technology have enabled us to use in dealing with the human body.

ALBERT SOMIT

[*See also* PROPAGANDA; SOCIALIZATION. *Other relevant material may be found under* ATTITUDES.]

BIBLIOGRAPHY

BAUER, RAYMOND A. 1952 *The New Man in Soviet Psychology.* Cambridge, Mass.: Harvard Univ. Press.

BECK, F.; and GODIN, W. [pseuds.] 1951 *Russian Purge and the Extraction of Confession.* London and New York: Hurst & Blackett; New York: Viking Press. → Translated from the original German.

BIDERMAN, ALBERT D. 1963 *March to Calumny: The*

Story of American Prisoners of War in the Korean War. New York: Macmillan.

BROWN, JAMES A. C. (1963) 1964 *Techniques of Persuasion: From Propaganda to Brainwashing.* Gloucester, Mass.: Smith.

ELLUL, JACQUES 1965 *Propaganda.* New York: Knopf.

GREAT BRITAIN, MINISTRY OF DEFENSE 1955 *Treatment of British Prisoners of War in Korea.* London: H.M. Stationery Office.

HINKLE, L. E., JR.; and WOLFF, H. G. 1956 Communist Interrogation and Indoctrination of "Enemies of the State": Analysis of Methods Used by the Communist State Police (a special report). *Archives of Neurology and Psychiatry* 76:115–174.

HUNTER, EDWARD 1951 *Brainwashing in Red China: The Calculated Destruction of Men's Minds.* New York: Vanguard.

LEITES, NATHAN; and BERNAUT, ELSA 1954 *Ritual of Liquidation: The Case of the Moscow Trials.* Glencoe, Ill.: Free Press.

LIFTON, ROBERT J. 1961 *Thought Reform and the Psychology of Totalism: A Study of "Brainwashing" in China.* New York: Norton.

MEERLOO, J. A. M. 1956 *The Rape of the Mind: The Psychology of Thought Control, Menticide, and Brainwashing.* New York: World.

MEYERHOFF, ARTHUR E. 1965 *Strategy of Persuasion: The Use of Advertising Skills in Fighting the Cold War.* New York: Coward.

MU, FU-SHENG 1962 *The Wilting of the Hundred Flowers: The Chinese Intelligentsia Under Mao.* New York: Praeger; London: Heinemann.

SARGANT, WILLIAM W. 1957 *Battle for the Mind.* London: Heinemann; Garden City, N.Y.: Doubleday.

U.S. SECRETARY OF DEFENSE'S ADVISORY COMMITTEE ON PRISONERS OF WAR 1955 *The Fight Continues After Battle.* Washington: Government Printing Office.

WEISSBERG, ALEXANDER (1951) 1952 *Conspiracy of Silence.* With a preface by Arthur Koestler. London: Hamilton. → First published as *Hexensabbat: Russland im Schmetztiegel der Säuberungen.*

WORTIS, JOSEPH 1950 *Soviet Psychiatry.* Baltimore: Williams & Wilkins.

YÜ, TÊ-CHI 1964 *Mass Persuasion in Communist China.* New York: Praeger.

BRANDEIS, LOUIS DEMBITZ

Louis Dembitz Brandeis (1856–1941) was born in Louisville, Kentucky. His parents had migrated in 1848 from Bohemia to the United States, where his father became a prosperous grain merchant. Neither of his parents had participated in the European revolutions of 1848, but they had suffered from the severity with which the revolutions were crushed. Finding in America the freedom Europe had denied them, Brandeis' parents passed on their liberal views to their son.

Brandeis' family had no formal religious affiliation and no racial–cultural interests, such as knowledge of Hebrew and the Talmud, and his friends were both Jew and gentile; nevertheless, in 1912 he became a Zionist. During his years on the United States Supreme Court (1916–1939), all his extrajudicial activities and interests were curtailed, but his belief in Zionism never faltered, and in the years immediately preceding his death, Zionism again became a matter of absorbing interest to him.

His mother and his uncle, Lewis Dembitz, a Kentucky lawyer and scholar of uncompromising integrity, were influential in shaping his moral and intellectual standards. In 1891 Brandeis married Alice Goldmark of New York, who encouraged his public welfare crusades. Brandeis credited his wife with reinforcing his determination to carry on when critics bitterly assailed him as a radical who waged war on cherished economic institutions.

Brandeis was educated at private and public schools in Louisville, at the Annen Realschule in Dresden, Germany, in 1874 and 1875, and at the Harvard Law School, from which he received his LL.B. degree in 1877. He was admitted to the St. Louis bar in 1878. After a few months there he returned to Boston, practicing first with his friend and Harvard Law School classmate, Samuel Dennis Warren, and later as partner in the firm Brandeis, Dunbar, and Nutter.

Brandeis began his professional and public career just as the free enterprise system was beginning to crystallize into a structure of corporate and supercorporate monopolies. As a corporation lawyer, Brandeis drew his clients primarily from the ranks of big business. He became a millionaire by 1907 and a multimillionaire by 1915. For a while he was welcome in high financial and professional circles, as well as among "Proper Bostonians." Early in his professional career, charitable and other good causes engaged his attention and imagination, as was conventional among Boston's financial and social elite. What distinguished Brandeis' reformism from that of other public-spirited citizens was his invariable habit of coupling disclosures of evil with specific proposals for their remedy.

His inventive genius is reflected in the so-called sliding-scale utility rate, the savings bank life insurance plan, and the preferential union shop. The sliding scale, adopted in Boston, permitted profit sharing between the utility company and the consumer and provided a bilateral bonus for efficiency. As the dividend to stockholders rose, the selling price of gas to the consumer fell. Savings bank life insurance, available in Massachusetts, New York, and Connecticut, provides an alternative to high-priced commercial insurance to those with low incomes. The preferential union shop was prescribed by Brandeis in 1910 for the New York garment industry as a more palatable substitute for the open shop, which had been making it difficult for the garment union to grow.

Public attention was first drawn to Brandeis in 1897, when he appeared before the Massachusetts legislature to urge that the Boston Elevated Railroad Company be curbed in its drive for monopoly and privilege. Other campaigns of the same kind brought him prominence both in the state and nationally. Undertaken without fee, these activities soon won for him the title, "people's attorney." Driving him on was the conviction that bigness and monopoly are inimical to efficiency, true laissez-faire, and democracy.

Brandeis saw the rise of the masses, organized in trade unions and other social groups, as the natural outcome of a changed and changing social order. Power was moving from the few to the many. It was not informed statesmanship to try to freeze privilege or to thwart change indiscriminately; neither was it desirable or safe to stand aloof from the struggle. The reformer's role was to guide the forces of social experimentation and thus to direct change along the lines of evolution rather than of revolution.

This approach is exhibited in Brandeis' argument in support of hours-of-labor and minimum-wage legislation. In 1908, after the Supreme Court had denied the possibility of establishing a factual relationship between poor health and long hours of employment in a bakery, he prepared, with the help of his sister-in-law, Josephine Goldmark, of the National Consumers' League, the famous "Brandeis brief" (Brandeis 1908). Only a few pages were devoted to the law; much factual data, foreign and domestic, was amassed to demonstrate that the Oregon legislature, when it enacted an hours-of-labor law for women, could reasonably have believed that a relationship existed between long hours and the health of the workers. In recent years this kind of brief has become the lawyer's stock in trade. Though factual exploration was characteristic of all Brandeis' public welfare activities, he recognized that facts alone furnish no panaceas. They are primarily helpful—indeed indispensable—in sharpening the questions to be asked and in choosing the methods to be followed in fashioning a cure.

In 1912 Brandeis became a sort of one-man brain trust for Woodrow Wilson in the New Jersey governor's successful bid for the presidency. Wilson seriously considered Brandeis for a cabinet post, but the public image of him as a radical made the choice seem politically ill-advised. In January 1916, President Wilson appointed Brandeis asso-

ciate justice of the Supreme Court, stimulating the fiercest protest ever lodged against a nominee for the high bench. After five months of debate the Senate confirmed the appointment by a vote of 47 to 22.

Brandeis brought to his judicial task a precise technical knowledge of constitutional issues, and an informed political outlook based on long study and experience in practical affairs. Except when basic freedoms were involved, he took a latitudinarian view of the power to govern. At a time when the constitution had become for reactionary judges an instrument for preserving the status quo, it was for him, as for Woodrow Wilson, a "vehicle of the nation's life" (Wilson [1908] 1917, p. 158).

There must be power in the States and the Nation to remold, through experimentation, our economic practices and institutions to meet changing social and economic needs. . . . To stay experimentation in things social and economic is a grave responsibility. . . . This Court has the power to prevent an experiment. We may strike down the statute which embodies it on the ground that, in our opinion, the measure is arbitrary, capricious or unreasonable. . . . But in the exercise of this high power, we must be ever on our guard, lest we erect our prejudices into legal principles. If we would guide by the light of reason, we must let our minds be bold. (*New State Ice Company* v. *Liebmann*, 285 U.S. 262, 1932, p. 311)

Few men live to see their ideas become realities, their views accepted, their philosophy enacted and upheld as the law of the land. That reward did come to Brandeis. By the time of his death, the scope of government action had been enlarged as judicially created barriers against the government's power to regulate the economy were erased. However, in another respect the government's power had been limited: Brandeis had joined Oliver Wendell Holmes, Benjamin Cardozo, Harlan F. Stone, and Charles Evans Hughes in laying the foundation for the assertion of judicial responsibility for a "fundamental principle of the American Government," the protection of freedom of speech, press, and assembly. "Those who won our independence by revolution," Brandeis had written in 1919, "were not cowards. They did not fear political change. They did not exalt order at the cost of liberty. . . . Only an emergency can justify repression. Such must be the rule if authority is to be reconciled with freedom" (*Whitney* v. *California*, 274 U.S. 357, 1927, p. 377).

Brandeis retired in 1939 and died in his Washington apartment in 1941, in surroundings more modest than he had known at the start of his life. Although he had never held political office or employed the techniques of politics or partisan organization, he had used his skills as a lawyer, publicist, and judge to promote change through the use of informed reason and the orderly processes of law. In cases involving government action to curb espionage and other alleged subversive activities, he upheld a man's freedom to think as he will and to speak as he thinks as "indispensable to the discovery and spread of political truth" (*Whitney* v. *California*, 274 U.S. 357, 1927, p. 375). This, he believed, was the only effective path to freedom and security.

ALPHEUS THOMAS MASON

[*For the historical context of Brandeis' work, see* JUDICIARY; WELFARE STATE; *and the biographies of* CARDOZO; HOLMES; POUND. *For discussion of the subsequent development of Brandeis' ideas, see* CONSTITUTIONAL LAW.]

WORKS BY BRANDEIS

(1908) 1912 *Women in Industry: Decision of the United States Supreme Court in Curt Miller* v. *State of Oregon.* Pages 558–563 in Josephine C. Goldmark, *Fatigue and Efficiency: A Study in Industry.* New York: Charities Publication Committee.

(1913–1914) 1933 *Other People's Money and How the Bankers Use It.* Washington: National House Library Foundation. → First published in *Harper's Weekly.*

(1914) 1933 *Business: A Profession.* Boston: Hale, Cushman & Flint.

1934 *The Curse of Bigness: Miscellaneous Papers of Louis D. Brandeis.* New York: Viking.

1942 *Brandeis on Zionism: A Collection of Addresses and Statements.* Washington: Zionist Organization of America.

SUPPLEMENTARY BIBLIOGRAPHY

GOLDMARK, JOSEPHINE C. 1912 *Fatigue and Efficiency: A Study in Industry.* New York: Charities Publication Committee.

MASON, ALPHEUS T. 1946 *Brandeis: A Free Man's Life.* New York: Viking. → Contains a list of Brandeis' major writings, as well as of books published about him.

MERSKY, ROY M. 1958 *Louis Dembitz Brandeis, 1856–1941: A Bibliography.* Yale Law Library Publications, No. 15. New Haven: Yale Law School.

WILSON, WOODROW (1908) 1917 *Constitutional Government in the United States.* New York: Columbia Univ. Press.

BRECHT, ARNOLD

Arnold Brecht has had two distinguished careers: as a professional civil servant in Germany he rose to the level of ministerial director; and after he left Germany in 1933, he became a creative and influential political scientist in the United States. Over a span of sixty years, Brecht, as a philosopher–administrator, has published some 150 books, monographs, and articles; in 1959, his magisterial *Political Theory* appeared, and a year later he was awarded the Woodrow Wilson Award of the American Political Science Association for his work.

Brecht was born into a professional family in Lübeck in 1884. His paternal grandfather, the son of a saddler, was a Protestant minister in a small town. His father, a lawyer, entered public service and became an administrator of railroads in the Ministry of Trade. His maternal grandfather was the first engineer to achieve directorial status in a Prussian ministry; he was ministerial director of railroads. Brecht grew up in an atmosphere that was liberal and where public service was considered a family tradition.

His formal education began in 1891 at the renowned Lübeck Gymnasium, the 400-year-old Catherineum, which Thomas Mann also attended and later described. As a student, Brecht enjoyed mathematics and writing, but the rest of the curriculum failed to inspire him. His later interest in political questions was singularly absent at this time. He read little in philosophy, politics, or history, and paid scant attention to current political problems. In his last year he developed a profound interest in the theater, frequently attending twice a day. Brecht has remarked that a major goal of his years at the Catherineum seems to have been avoiding and circumventing the authority of the faculty.

From 1902 to 1905, Brecht studied law at the universities of Bonn, Berlin, Göttingen, and Leipzig, where, in 1906, he received his law degree. He became fascinated by the consequences of the replacement of the multiplicity of local legal systems in Germany by a new civil code: the different sets of legal rules bred confusion and conflict, and the problem that Brecht posed to himself was the justification of legal rules in general. His approach to the problem began to take form in his doctoral dissertation, which dealt with "promises to deliver goods owned by other persons"; he subtitled it "a contribution to the theory of impossibility" (1906). He conceived of a legal system as a network of rules derived from a basic set of axioms and demonstrated that conflict and confusion resulted from contradictions in the axiomatic foundation of the law. A few years later, at 23, he wrote his "System of Contractual Liability" (1908) in which he reduced the rules of contractual obligation to a logic of great simplicity. This study was published in *Jherings Jahrbücher für die Dogmatik des bürgerlichen Rechts,* one of the most eminent journals of Continental jurisprudence. These early works by Brecht contain the first formulation of the theory of impossibility, which he employed so effectively in his later inquiry into the concept of justice.

Public service. In 1910, after four years of in-service training, Brecht became a judge in Lübeck, but he served only a short while before being called to the Ministry of Justice to begin an administrative career.

Until he entered government service, Brecht had read little outside of the areas of law, economics, and administration. But as his official duties took him closer to the center of policy decisions, his intellectual interests also turned to politics. When he was still a law student, Brecht had become interested in the meaning of "justice," filling a folder with notes and observations. Now, actively engaged in the preparation of war legislation, Brecht began to study such subjects as the relation between politics and justice, the respective demands of justice and of international obligation, the concept of a just peace, and the axiomatic base upon which the warring parties rested their aims.

During the Weimar Republic, Brecht's most important position was that of ministerial director of the Ministry of the Interior. His primary concerns were constitutional problems, administrative management, and the civil service. As an outspoken opponent of the Nazis, he was arrested in April 1933, but was freed because of the intervention of non-Nazi ministers. In November of that year he left Germany and, at the age of 50, started a new career in the United States. In 1946 he became an American citizen.

Brecht as a political scientist. At the invitation of Alvin Johnson, Brecht joined the graduate faculty of the New School for Social Research in New York City and remained a member of that faculty until his retirement in 1954. He has also served as visiting professor of political science at Harvard, Yale, Columbia, and other universities.

For Brecht, the study of politics, as distinct from the practical art, is a scientific discipline: in principle, there is nothing that precludes the application of scientific method to political phenomena. Accordingly, the task of the political scientist is to provide theoretical bases for further scientific development that will also yield solid blocks of knowledge that may be applied in the realm of the practical art of politics. The bulk of Brecht's academic life has been devoted to this quest.

In *Political Theory*, his most notable contribution, the full range and purpose of Brecht's scholarship is evident. He demonstrates the differences between scientific and nonscientific theory: they are validated by different rules of procedure. Scientific propositions can be warranted only in conformance with the rules of scientific procedure, and to practice science, therefore, requires understanding of, and rigorous adherence to, those rules. A good part of *Political Theory* is devoted to the clarification of the rules.

While Brecht insists that the rules of scientific procedure be rigorously followed, he allows for the use of intuition and speculation in the initial formulation of potentially relevant concepts. His distinction between the "context of discovery" and the "context of justification" is somewhat similar to that of Hans Reichenbach (*The Rise of Scientific Philosophy* 1951): it is only in the latter context that the rules of scientific warrant hold, and Brecht therefore deplores efforts to disparage "nonscientific impulses" in the initial stages of inquiry. In the preparatory stages of investigation, attempts to keep science on a physical or behaviorist basis unnecessarily close off hunches, which can be creative. After the starting point of an inquiry, hunches may enter the domain of science, however, only after they have been properly formulated and processed.

Scientific value relativism. Brecht uses the concept of scientific warrant to clarify the doctrine of scientific value relativism (SVR). The essence of SVR is that ultimate values cannot be validated scientifically. It is impossible to establish scientifically what goals or purposes are valuable without regard either to the value they have in the pursuit of other goals or purposes or to given ideas about ultimate goals or purposes. Conversely, the question whether something is valuable can be answered scientifically only in relation either to some goal or purpose for the pursuit of which it is, or is not, useful, or to given ideas about what is, or is not, valuable.

Brecht's elaborate treatment of SVR has several major purposes. His first purpose is to demonstrate that the derivation of "ought" statements from "is" statements, so characteristic of natural law theorists, is logically fallacious. His second purpose is to refute the notion that scientists are necessarily philosophical relativists, who hold that nothing is intrinsically valuable. Although value judgments cannot be scientifically validated according to SVR, it does not follow that SVR leads to the type of general relativism such as that implicit in social Darwinism, Marxism, and legal positivism. Brecht's third purpose is to show that the defeatism that took hold with the rise of Hitler was not justified. To deplore the failure of science to warrant ultimate values is to misunderstand the proper scope of science: it extends only to the relationship between a decision and a set of ends, since this constitutes a factual (or scientific) problem. Logico-empirical analysis, therefore, can do no more than clarify values and goals, indicate risks and consequences, and specify effective courses of action. It can also, from a set of alternatives, differentiate those probabilities and possibilities that are attainable from those that are improbable or impossible.

Justice. In his sixty years of intensive study of the problem of justice, only the most fugitive materials have escaped Brecht. His approach to justice is illustrative of his application of the concept of SVR, and of the theory of impossibility that underlies that concept. While it is impossible scientifically to validate any ultimate value as just, it may be possible to identify certain universally or transculturally held elements in the human sense of justice. Once such universal elements are identified, derivative values and goals may be dealt with scientifically, since they constitute decisions whose correctness is determinable as a matter of fact. (The same conception of the nature of decisions is crucial to modern decision-making theory.)

Brecht's effort to determine whether there are some common basic values in the variety of concepts of justice that have either been held operationally or formally idealized has led him to formulate a *prima vista* concept of justice that does appear to characterize human behavior. This concept has five essential postulates: (1) accordance with objective truth or veracity, that is, all relevant statements as to facts and relations must be true; (2) equal treatment of what is equal under the same system; (3) generality of the value system applied, that is, the same standards must be applied to all cases; (4) no restriction of freedom beyond the requirements of the accepted system; (5) respect for the necessities of nature, that is, no sanctions for nonfulfillment may be applied if fulfillment is impossible.

These five postulates are, in Brecht's phrase, "a minimum definition of justice," and he considers them to be hypothetically descriptive of human behavior. Accordingly, they must be investigated empirically, and subjected to extensive field research that must include phenomenological descriptions of subjective behavior. Brecht is confident that his hypothetical description not only permits and directs empirical research, but that it will stand empirical test. His willingness to subject such a proposition as this to the severe test of scientific warrant is most impressive.

Since justice is defined as an empirical problem, Brecht recognizes that science can get no closer to it than to determine whether certain values are, or are not, universally held. If science does estab-

lish their universality, this does not make them absolute; but they can be certified as "universally human." Thus, Brecht, the scientific value relativist, becomes the leader in the fight against relativist defeatism, since a common, cross-culturally held set of values can provide a universal standard.

The study of government. Brecht has invariably brought his vast European political experience to the study of problems of constitutionalism, federalism, and public administration. For the last 25 years, the political and constitutional problems posed by the rise of totalitarianism have been the major theme of his study of political institutions. This theme dominates his analysis of the fall of the Weimar Republic, which he attributes to certain structural weaknesses (1944). The intricate questions of federalism and administrative decentralization are examined with much rigor in his analysis (1945) of the complex organization of Germany from 1815 to 1945. It is interesting that in an essay on "Limited-purpose Federations" (1943) Brecht anticipated the principles on which the European Coal and Steel Community and the Common Market were to be founded. In the area of American public administration, he has made novel proposals for the organization and coordination of departments and bureaus. These have the purpose of strengthening policy direction without overcentralizing the bureaucracy.

For Arnold Brecht, the destruction of democracy in Germany provided a lesson that can be ignored only at great peril. To his profession, he has assigned the duty "to see, sooner than others, and to analyze, more profoundly than others, the immediate and the potential problems of the political life of society" (1946).

MARTIN LANDAU

[*For the historical context of Brecht's work, see* POLITICAL THEORY.]

WORKS BY BRECHT

1906   *Vom Verkauf einer fremden Sache: Ein Beitrag zur Unmöglichkeitslehre.* Borna-Leipzig (Germany): Noske.

1908   System der Vertragshaftung. *Jherings Jahrbücher für die Dogmatik des bürgerlichen Rechts* 53:213–302.

1918   *Geheim–diplomatie,* by Arnold B. Hanson [pseud]. Bern (Switzerland): Wyss. → Translated into French, Dutch, and Danish.

(1939–1954) 1954   *The Political Philosophy of Arnold Brecht: Essays.* Edited by Morris D. Forkosch. New York: Exposition Press. → This volume was presented to Brecht by former students. It contains six of his major articles on political and legal philosophy, and it carries an almost complete bibliography of Brecht's writings from 1906 to 1954.

1940 BRECHT, ARNOLD; and GLASER, COMSTOCK. *The Art and Technique of Administration in German Ministries.* Cambridge, Mass.: Harvard Univ. Press.

1942 European Federation: The Democratic Alternative. *Harvard Law Review* 55:561–594.

1943 Limited-purpose Federations. *Social Research* 10: 135–151.

1944 *Prelude to Silence: The End of the German Republic.* New York: Oxford Univ. Press.

1945 *Federalism and Regionalism in Germany: The Division of Prussia.* Institute of World Affairs, Monograph Series, No. 1. Oxford Univ. Press.

1946 Democracy: Challenge to Theory. *Social Research* 13:195–224.

1959 *Political Theory: The Foundations of Twentieth-century Political Thought.* Princeton Univ. Press.

SUPPLEMENTARY BIBLIOGRAPHY

REICHENBACH, HANS 1951 *The Rise of Scientific Philosophy.* Berkeley: Univ. of California Press.

BRENTANO, LUJO

The German economist Lujo Brentano (1844–1931) was born in Frankfurt am Main into a patrician family of Italian descent whose members left a strong mark on the cultural life of Germany. Clemens Brentano, the poet, was his uncle; Bettina von Arnim, the writer, his aunt; and Franz Brentano, the philosopher, his brother. The anti-Prussianism characteristic of south Germany during the second half of the nineteenth century and a home environment of strict Roman Catholicism were the dominant influences of his adolescence.

It was not until after 1866, when he had already received a doctor of law degree from the University of Heidelberg, that Brentano decided to become an economist. He spent a year at Göttingen and, after writing a thesis on Johann Heinrich von Thünen's theory of distribution, received a second doctorate in 1867.

His first appointment was with the Prussian Statistical Office, then under the direction of Ernst Engel (of Engel's law). Engel's concern for social questions influenced Brentano, who then became involved with two of the problems that were to concern him for the whole of his long professional career: improvement of the wage earner's lot and the preservation of harmony between capital and labor.

Engel was particularly interested in profit sharing as a method of at least attenuating, in an authoritarian and inflexible Prussian environment, some of the social tensions that were the by-product of rapid industrialization. To study this measure more thoroughly, he planned a visit to England and asked Brentano to accompany him. Brentano went, only to find the potentialities of profit sharing quite limited. Instead, he became interested in other reform movements, in particular the growing trade-union movement. Investigating the emergence of the trade unions and their role within the English framework, on his return to Germany Brentano published the celebrated *On the History and Development of Gilds, and the Origin of Trade Unions* (1870). In this essay, later attacked by Sidney and Beatrice Webb, Brentano argued that unions were the descendants of medieval guilds. He attempted to show that in every social setting the laboring man—whether corporate journeyman or free wage earner—must band together with his fellow workers to offset his basic weakness within the labor market and defend his interests against the employer, be he patrician burgher or capitalist entrepreneur.

The inherent disadvantages of the individual wage earner in the market for his services were a recurrent theme in Brentano's writings. Since the ordinary kind of buyer–seller relationship did not prevail in the labor market, he thought the classical economists were wrong in not exempting labor from their general laissez-faire prescriptions. Brentano believed that through trade-union activity workers were able to gain at the expense of the employers' monopsonistic position rather than at the expense of the earnings of the rest of the working class. Furthermore, insofar as very few markets are purely competitive, employees could, if sufficiently well organized to bargain effectively, share in the benefits of the employer's monopoly power to raise prices within an industry.

Brentano advocated higher wages and better working conditions as social expedients and as sound business, and he urged that they be established through collective agreements negotiated by vigorous and enlightened management. He was against preserving the employment contract as a private matter between capitalist and wage earner, as others, such as Bastiat, propounded. Moreover, Brentano regarded labor organizations and cooperatives as means for the raising of working-class morale and self-esteem. He further believed that higher earnings and shorter working hours would expedite mechanization and spur worker productivity and efficiency and thus reduce the unit costs of labor. In the same spirit of advancing both social peace and economic progress, Brentano pressed for the extension of social insurance as a way of alleviating the worst aspects of proletarian misery and insecurity that lead to demoralization.

Although in principle he was skeptical of state intervention, he considered factory legislation (above all, that covering the employment of minors) and the enactment of a minimum wage law prerequisites of a civilized industrial environment. He also supported all efforts to improve working-class housing and adult education. His population theory, which attempted to correlate rising standards of living with a declining birth rate, was meant both as an attack upon the Malthusian postulates and as an expression of faith in the possibilities of reform.

After leaving the Prussian Statistical Office, Brentano spent the rest of his life as a professor at the following German universities: Berlin, from 1871 to 1872; Breslau, from 1872 to 1882; Strassburg, from 1882 to 1888; Vienna, from 1888 to 1889; Leipzig, from 1889 to 1891; and finally Munich, where he remained until his death. A founding member of the Verein für Sozialpolitik, Brentano played a leading role in some of the important research projects undertaken by the Verein as background material for its policy recommendations on social and economic issues in general and industrial relations in particular. However, he never supported the pro-Prussian, imperialist attitudes of the majority of its members.

Brentano was neither an original theorist nor an economic historian whose basic research opened new vistas of the past. His forte was exposition (for example, his study of the development of value theory), and some of his writings are excellent popularizations of history. Judging by the memoirs of some of his students (notably those of Theodor Heuss and M. J. Bonn), Brentano must have been an effective teacher as well as a popular lecturer. Yet it is difficult not to conclude that, as a John Stuart Mill liberal in an environment that was a far cry from Gladstonian England, he could not exert much influence as a social scientist.

HERBERT KISCH

[*Other relevant material may be found in* LABOR UNIONS *and in the biographies of* ENGEL *and* MALTHUS.]

WORKS BY BRENTANO

1870 *On the History and Development of Gilds, and the Origin of Trade Unions.* London: Trübner.

(1876) 1894 *Hours and Wages in Relation to Production.* New York: Scribner; London: Sonnenschein.

(1877) 1898 *The Relation of Labor to the Law of To-day.* New York: Putnam.

1879 *Die Arbeiterversicherung gemäss der heutigen Wirtschaftsordnung.* Leipzig: Duncker & Humblot.

(1899) 1924 *Alte und neue Feudalität: Gesammelte Aufsätze zur Erbrechtspolitik.* Vol. 1. Leipzig: Meiner.

1904 *Wohnungs-zustände und Wohnungs-reform in München.* Munich: Reinhardt.

1908 *Die Entwickelung der Wertlehre.* Munich: Königlich Bayerische Akademie der Wissenschaften.

1909 *Die Malthussche Lehre und die Bevölkerungsbewegung der letzten Dezennien.* Munich: Franz. → Also published in volume 24 of the *Abhandlungen* of the Akademie der Wissenschaften, Munich, Historische Klasse.

(1910) 1911 *Die deutschen Getreidezölle.* 2d rev. ed. Stuttgart (Germany) and Berlin: Cotta.

1923 *Der wirtschaftende Mensch in der Geschichte.* Leipzig: Meiner.

1924 *Konkrete Grundbedingungen der Volkswirtschaft.* Leipzig: Meiner.

1927–1929 *Eine Geschichte der wirtschaftlichen Entwicklung Englands.* 3 vols. in 4. Jena (Germany): Fischer.

1931 *Mein Leben im Kampf um die soziale Entwicklung Deutschlands.* Jena (Germany): Diedrichs.

WORKS ABOUT BRENTANO

BARICH, WERNER 1936 *Lujo Brentano als Sozialpolitiker.* Berlin: Triltsch & Huther.

NEISSER, HANS; and PALYI, MELCHIOR 1924 *Lujo Brentano: Eine Bio-Bibliographie.* Berlin: Prager.

BRESCIANI-TURRONI, CONSTANTINO

Constantino Bresciani-Turroni (1882–1963) was the last internationally known representative of Italy's classical school of economics, which flourished in the early part of the century and continued to exert its influence between the world wars. Although he adhered to classical theories, his methodological innovations departed markedly from the traditions of the classical school.

Bresciani-Turroni was born in Verona. After completing humanistic studies in high school, he attended the law school at the University of Verona, specializing in statistics and economics. He soon became a professor, teaching first statistics and then economics in various Italian universities.

Between 1905 and 1907, Bresciani-Turroni published essays on Pareto and on income distribution in industrial and agricultural regions. In these he anticipated modern methods of analysis, attempting to confirm the hypotheses of classical theory by statistical studies instead of through the study of individual behavior.

The same methodological approach is evident in his later studies on the relation between the quantity of money, the rate of interest, and the price level. Through a rigorous and broad investigation of actual conditions, Bresciani-Turroni provided evidence that supported the classical theory, according to which the interest rate is related—in the long run—to the productivity of capital. This principle was to constitute a fixed point of reference in the studies of monetary theory and policy to which he dedicated the major part of his life.

During the years immediately following World

War I, Bresciani-Turroni was economic adviser to the Berlin office of the Reparations Commission. In his frequent and long visits to Germany, between 1920 and 1929, he could follow the vicissitudes of her inflationary economy and the destruction of her currency. From this experience emerged his most important study, *The Economics of Inflation*, published in 1931 in Italy and later translated into English and other languages. In this trail-blazing study, he conducted a rigorous and documented investigation into the circumstances which led to the drastic depreciation of the German currency; and he examined critically the policies of the Reichsbank, which did not restrain, but in fact encouraged the great inflation that led to the breakdown of the economic and social order of the country. The course of events in Germany presented an extraordinary opportunity for Bresciani-Turroni to attempt to confirm the classical theory of money. In the unrestricted expansion of the quantity of money, he saw the cause of the price increase; according to Bresciani-Turroni, this was a warning to the national authorities of every other country to adopt monetary measures necessary to suppress any inflationary tendencies. Subsequent events in Germany provided him with additional abundant material for another book, *Le previsioni economiche*, published in 1932.

In the 1930s Bresciani-Turroni, as professor of economics at the University of Cairo, conducted studies on the theory of international trade and finance, adding to his German work an examination of the balance of payments of Egypt. The course of the balance of trade seemed to him related to the monetary and credit policies followed in both of these countries by their respective authorities. His attachment to classical theory, supported by comparative studies and observations, led him to assume a critical position with respect to Keynesian theories. In his opinion, these induce inflationary pressures whenever and wherever they are adopted by the authorities as prescriptions for policy.

In 1942 Bresciani-Turroni published a book on *Economic Policy for the Thinking Man*, in which he expounded the rules that, according to his classical principles, should guide the actions of public officials. With the end of World War II, Bresciani-Turroni became one of the leaders of Italy's new economic policy. In 1945 he was appointed president of the Banco di Roma, one of the leading Italian banks, and from 1947 to 1953 he was also executive director of the International Bank for Reconstruction and Development. In 1953 he served the Italian government as minister for foreign trade.

In the postwar years Bresciani-Turroni continued his scholarly activities, contributing various articles to the *Review of Economic Conditions in Italy*, published by the Banco di Roma. In these writings he surveyed the principal economic developments, with special reference to Italy and to money and credit. He no longer concentrated on subjecting his theory to empirical tests; instead he used his theory to determine the most appropriate economic policy for existing conditions.

FRANK M. TAMAGNA

[*For discussion of the subsequent development of Bresciani-Turroni's ideas, see* MONEY, *articles on* QUANTITY THEORY *and* VELOCITY OF CIRCULATION.]

WORKS BY BRESCIANI-TURRONI

(1931) 1937 *The Economics of Inflation*. London: Allen & Unwin. → First published as *Le vicende del marco tedesco*.

1932a *Le previsioni economiche*. Turin: UTED.

1932b *Inductive Verification of the Theory of International Payments*. Cairo: Noury.

1934 Egypt's Balance of Trade. *Journal of Political Economy* 42:371–384.

1936 The Theory of Saving. *Economica* 3:1–23.

1938 The "Multiplier" in Practice: Some Results of Recent German Experience. *Review of Economics and Statistics* 20:76–88.

(1942) 1950 *Economic Policy for the Thinking Man*. London: Hodge. → First published as *Introduzione alla politica economica*.

1946 *Il programma economico–sociale del liberalismo*. Milan: Giuffrè.

(1947–1962) 1964 *Articles Contributed by Constantino Bresciani-Turroni to the* Review of Economic Conditions in Italy *in the Years From 1947 to 1962*. Rome: Banco di Roma.

(1949) 1960 *Corso di economia politica*. 2 vols. 5th ed., enl. Milan: Giuffrè.

1961 *Saggi di economia*. Milan: Giuffrè.

BREUIL, HENRI

Henri Édouard Prosper Breuil, French archeologist devoted to the study of prehistory, was born in 1877 in the very small town of Mortain (Manche) in Normandy. He began his scientific career by helping his father collect butterflies and other insects. In 1878 his father, who was a magistrate, was transferred to Clermont (Oise), north of Paris. There the young Breuil made the acquaintance of Geoffroy d'Ault du Mesnil, who was working on the "diluvial deposits" in the Somme valley; Breuil visited the valley with him and later published many papers on it.

In 1895 Breuil began his studies at the ecclesiastical seminary of Issy-les-Moulineaux, near Paris. One of his teachers was Abbé Guibert, who was interested in problems of human origins. At the seminary Breuil met Jean Bouyssonie, who in

1908 was one of the discoverers of the classic Neanderthal man of La Chapelle-aux-Saints. In 1897, having been ordained as an *abbé*, Breuil went with Bouyssonie to visit known sites of prehistoric habitation in southwest France. There he met one of the famous prehistorians of the time, Édouard Piette, whose magnificent collections, rich in paleolithic works of art, decided Breuil's vocation. Although his first publication, in 1898, was about anomalies among insects, in his subsequent work he touched upon almost every aspect of prehistory, in more than 800 publications. The main part of Breuil's activity, however, was devoted to Lower and Upper Paleolithic culture and cave art.

He first taught prehistory at the University of Fribourg in Switzerland, from 1905 until 1910, beginning as *Privatdozent* and later becoming extraordinary professor. He then became professor of prehistoric ethnography at the Institut de Paléontologie Humaine in Paris. In 1927–1928 he lectured at the Sorbonne and from 1929 to 1947 was professor at the Collège de France. In 1938 he was elected to the Académie des Inscription et Belles Lettres. During World War II he taught at the University of Lisbon and at the University of Johannesburg in South Africa. He died in 1961 at L'Isle-Adam (Seine-et-Oise) near Paris.

Only half in jest was Breuil called the "pope of prehistory." His influence on the development of prehistory was tremendous, not only in France but in the whole world. In his time he saw almost every important discovery or collection pertaining to his science; he had a phenomenal memory and wrote very detailed accounts of the things he saw and the men he met. He was always ready to put his inexhaustible supply of information at the disposal of colleagues and students. And he was always willing to discuss the validity of his theories, if new or anomalous facts were brought to his attention. His judgment in the choice of collaborators was not always good.

Lower Paleolithic. Like all long scientific careers, Breuil's had a good and a bad side. He was, for example, the first to point out the presence of worked-bone implements in the Lower Paleolithic at Choukoutien; he adopted and developed the theory of Hugo Obermaier that the Acheulean hand-ax cultures had not penetrated into central Europe, where greater emphasis was put on flake tools. This idea was certainly profitable, and today the view that the Clactonian flake technique evolved parallel to the Acheulean is generally accepted, although Breuil's definition of Clactonian, based only on the method of flaking flint, has been corrected by Hazzledine Warren.

On the other hand, Breuil certainly misled pre-history for a long time with the theory of the so-called Levalloisian culture. On the lowest terrace of the Somme River valley, rolled Levallois flakes were found associated with cold-climate fauna, without the presence of hand axes. Victor Commont, before World War I, had correctly dated this terrace as a Würm glacial deposit. Overlying these gravels, most of them deposited by solifluction, are fluvial sands, containing smaller, less rolled Levallois flakes. In these sands was found a unique molar of *Elephas antiquus*, on which Breuil based all his chronology. The layers that contained *Elephas antiquus* were dated as the last interglacial, and the solifluction deposits under them as the penultimate glacial. And as the layers contained only Levallois flakes, without hand axes, a sequence was posed in which Levalloisian culture was placed as early as Riss glacial times, existing independently of the Acheulean.

It is a tribute to the influence of Breuil that this theory, founded on so flimsy a base, was accepted for so long a time. This "chronology" of the Lower and Middle Paleolithic in the north of France was the basis for the dating given by English scientists to human remains at Swanscombe. Even after discoveries in Africa in which Levallois flakes were commonly found as an integral part of Acheulean culture, no prehistorians questioned Breuil's scheme. Of course, as Raymond Vaufrey had immediately pointed out, the single *Elephas antiquus* probably derived from an older deposit. It is now commonly accepted that this lowest terrace of the Somme is of Würm age, as Commont had said, and that no Levalloisian culture existed that was independent of hand-ax traditions.

Upper Paleolithic. In Upper Paleolithic studies, where knowledge of Pleistocene geology is somewhat less necessary, Breuil's work will remain fundamental for a long time; the mistakes he made in his work in Lower Paleolithic derived mainly from his lack of geological training.

As early as 1906, Breuil took a leading part in what is called "the Aurignacian battle." The Aurignacian culture, discovered in 1860 by E. Lartet at Aurignac in southwestern France, had been either forgotten or placed chronologically with the Magdalenian, after the Solutrean. This sequence was established on the basis of the absence of bone tools in the Mousterian, of few or no bone tools (known at that date) in the Solutrean, and of an abundance of bone tools in both the Aurignacian and the Magdalenian cultures. It was the merit of Breuil to show, by uncontrovertible stratigraphical evidence, that the Aurignacian culture invariably occurred earlier than the Solutrean. In 1912, at the International Congress of Anthropology and Prehistory in Geneva, Breuil presented an article entitled "Les subdivisions du paléolithique supérieure et leur signification," in which he established a classification of this period that was to remain unmodified until 1933, when Denis Peyrony demonstrated the independence of the Aurignacian and the Perigordian. Breuil's 1912 paper is one to which any archeologist dealing with this period must still refer very frequently. Very few scientific works have been as durable as this one.

Breuil wrote many articles dealing with the Upper Paleolithic, including site reports and more general studies. His knowledge of paleolithic flint typology was excellent, enabling him to discriminate at a glance among thousands of implements. Although the typological analysis of flint implements has changed greatly since Breuil, the typology of bone tools rests mainly on his work.

Cave art. To the general public, Breuil is best known for his work on cave art. As early as 1901 he published, in collaboration with Louis Capitan, a first note on the newly discovered cave of Combarelles, near Les Eyzies (1901a, 1901b). Even when he was no longer in good health, toward the end of his life, he remained willing to crawl into any cave where prehistoric drawings were said to exist. He was familiar with all known prehistoric art, in France and elsewhere. Altogether, the time he spent in caves copying engravings or paintings would surely amount to several years.

Breuil developed a theory of two "cycles" of prehistoric art, a theory that is no longer accepted. The style of the first cycle, corresponding to the Aurignacian–Perigordian period, was presumably characterized by the "twisted perspective": the body of the animal is drawn as seen from the side, while the hoofs and the horns or antlers are seen from the front. In the second style, belonging to the Magdalenian cycle, the animal is seen in absolute profile. This theory led Breuil to assign the Lascaux cave art to the Aurignacian–Perigordian cycle of the Upper Paleolithic. However, all the implements found in the cave seem to belong to the Magdalenian culture, and radiocarbon datings also seem to preclude anything earlier.

Breuil also studied cave paintings in northern Spain, which were allied to the culture of southern France, and the paintings on the walls of the rock shelters in southern Spain. These latter he believed to belong to yet another paleolithic culture, a view that is not shared by Spanish specialists, who see in them the work of much more recent men. Again, Breuil's theory that South African rock paintings were native representations of Mediterranean "foreigners" has aroused much recent controversy.

Although many of Breuil's theories are under severe attack, without these theories our knowledge of prehistoric art would be a mere collection of unrelated facts. The magnificent drawings he did in so many caves under difficult conditions will, of course, maintain their great value, and his publications will be, for a long time to come, the standard works for anyone interested in cave art.

Besides his work in his three main areas of interest, Breuil published some articles on neolithic and metal-age sites. He wrote numerous critical reviews. Although he was not a geologist, he immediately understood the importance of the phenomena of solifluction. Among his miscellaneous publications, there was one on the ways to poison foxes, two on the anomalies of tree leaves, and a famous book of drawings depicting the everyday life of prehistoric hunters, *Beyond the Bounds of History* (1949). He was one of the last men to try to encompass all the different aspects of prehistory.

FRANÇOIS BORDES

[*See also* ARCHEOLOGY; HUNTING AND GATHERING.]

WORKS BY BREUIL

1901a BREUIL, HENRI; and CAPITAN, LOUIS. Une nouvelle grotte avec parois gravées à l'époque paléolithique. Académie des Sciences, *Compte rendu* 133:478–480.

1901b BREUIL, HENRI; and CAPITAN, LOUIS. Reproduction de dessins paléolithiques gravés sur les parois de la grotte des Combarelles (Dordogne). Académie des Sciences, *Compte rendu* 133:1038–1043.

1906 CARTAILHAC, ÉMILE; and BREUIL, HENRI. La caverne d'Altamira à Santillane, près Santander (Espagne). Monaco: Imprimerie de Monaco.

1907 La question aurignacienne: Étude critique de stratigraphie comparée. *Revue préhistorique* 2:173–219.

1910 CAPITAN, LOUIS; BREUIL, HENRI; and PEYRONY, DENIS. *La caverne de Font de Gaume aux Eyzies (Dordogne).* Monaco: Imprimerie Chêne.

1913 Les subdivisions du paléolithique supérieur et leur signification. Volume 1, pages 165–238 in International Congress of Anthropology and Prehistoric Archaeology, Fourteenth, Geneva, 1912, *Proceedings.* Geneva: Kundig.

1924 BREUIL, HENRI; CAPITAN, LOUIS; and PEYRONY, DENIS. *Les Combarelles aux Eyzies (Dordogne).* Paris: Masson.

1931 Le feu et l'industrie lithique et osseuse à Choukoutien. Geological Society of China, *Bulletin* 2:147–154.

1931–1934 BREUIL, HENRY; and KOSLOWSKI, L. Études de stratigraphie paléolithique dans le nord de la France, la Belgique et l'Angleterre. *Anthropologie* 41:449–488; 42:27–46, 291–314; 44:249–290.

1932 Les industries à éclats du paléolithique ancien: I. Le Clactonien. *Préhistoire* 1:125–190.

1934a De l'importance de la solifluxion dans l'étude des terrains quaternaires de la France et des pays voisins. *Revue de géographie physique et de géologie dynamique* 7:269–331.

1934*b*   L'évolution de l'art pariétal dans les cavernes et abris ornés de France. Pages 102–118 in Congrès préhistorique de France, *Compte rendu de la 11*^{ème} *session.* Paris: Bureaux de la Société Préhistorique de France.

1939   Le vrai niveau de l'industrie abbevillienne de la Porte du Bois (Abbeville). *Anthropologie* 49:13–34.

1948   The White Lady of Brandberg, South West Africa: Her Companions and Her Guards. *South African Archaeological Bulletin* 3:2–11.

1949   *Beyond the Bounds of History: Scenes From the Old Stone Age.* London: Gawthorn.

1952*a*   *Four Hundred Centuries of Cave Art.* Paris: Sapho.

1952*b*   *Quatre cent siècles d'art pariétal: Les cavernes ornées de l'Age du Renne.* Paris: Sapho.

SUPPLEMENTARY BIBLIOGRAPHY

BRODERICK, ALAN H.   1963   *Father of Prehistory; the Abbé Henri Breuil: His Life and Times.* New York: Morrow; London: Hutchinson. → Published in London as *The Abbé Breuil: Prehistorian.*

BRINKMANN, CARL

Carl Brinkmann, whose work encompassed the fields of history (especially social and economic history), sociology, economic theory and policy (the latter with an emphasis on problems of agriculture), history of economic thought, and public finance, was born in 1885 in Tilsit into a distinguished family. His paternal grandfather had been a jurist and for a time a member of the Prussian diet and his father had been a mayor in Berlin. His maternal grandfather was a Protestant clergyman. Brinkmann studied at Breslau, Göttingen, Oxford, and Berlin, and in 1913 became *Privatdozent* at the University of Freiburg in Baden. In 1923 he went to Heidelberg as a full professor to succeed Eberhard Gothein, and in 1942 he moved to Berlin. In 1946, after the German collapse, he was teaching in Erlangen, but in 1947 he again became a full professor, at Tübingen, where he remained until his death in 1954.

The author of more than 170 books and papers, Brinkmann was widely recognized, successful, and influential. A glance at the bibliography below will reveal the breadth of his interests. Although he was one of those who found it distasteful to specialize, this did not mean that his work was superficial; whatever he undertook he treated with thoroughness and insight. His strong bent toward history, which he retained all his life, was typical of the German social scientists of his generation and reflected the influence of Gustav Schmoller and Adolf Wagner. His views on the relationship between history and economic theory were somewhat similar to those of his older contemporary, Arthur Spiethoff.

Brinkmann in his early years considered himself a historian, although even in those years he was attracted to sociology. He was deeply impressed by Max Weber, without becoming a blind follower, for he was equally influenced by Scheler, Litt, and Pareto. Furthermore, he recognized the importance of the American writers on social psychology for sociological studies.

His work in economics was, on the one hand, unlike that of the pure theorists, for Brinkmann had started as a historian and had come to economics by way of sociology and then of *Wirtschaftssoziologie.* Thus he was attracted to border areas between the social sciences and saw the importance of the state in setting the stage on which men live and do business. For heuristic and didactic reasons he thought historical studies should take precedence over model building, an outlook which again distinguished him from the pure theorists. On the other hand, his emphasis on the importance of the state in economic life led him to study public finance, a field in which his work gained great importance. Yet he did not neglect research on economic problems and on the thought of individual economists.

Brinkmann's apparent roaming over the whole field of the social sciences was in no way haphazard. Since he thought of theory as a category of history, it was natural that he would be simultaneously concerned with both fields. In the same way the fact that he was interested in all the social sciences reflected his belief in their common goal: the discovery of uniformities, regularities, and trends. Through continually changing his perspective and through systematically combining the observations he obtained, Brinkmann tried to approach the totality of the subjects he dealt with. It was his hope that it would be possible to achieve a synthesis of the social sciences, a synthesis in which sociology would be the key discipline around which the other social sciences pivoted.

FRITZ REDLICH

[*For the historical context of Brinkmann's work, see the biographies of* SCHMOLLER; WAGNER; WEBER, MAX.]

WORKS BY BRINKMANN

1912   *Freiheit und Staatlichkeit in der älteren deutschen Verfassung.* Berlin: Duncker & Humblot.

1919   *Versuch einer Gesellschaftswissenschaft.* Berlin: Duncker & Humblot.

1924   *Geschichte der Vereinigten Staaten von Amerika.* Leipzig: Teubner.

1925   *Gesellschaftslehre.* Enzyklopädie der Rechts- und Staatswissenschaft, Abteilung Staatswissenschaft, 48. Berlin: Springer.

(1927) 1953 *Wirtschafts- und Sozialgeschichte.* 2d ed. Göttingen (Germany): Vanderhoeck & Ruprecht.

1937 *Gustav Schmoller und die Volkswirtschaftslehre.* Stuttgart (Germany): Kohlhammer.

1939 Das Problem der sozialökonomischen Synthese. *Weltwirtschaftliches Archiv* 50:435–445. → Reprinted in Brinkmann 1944.

(1944) 1950 *Wirtschaftsformen und Lebensformen: Gesammelte Schriften zur Wirtschaftswissenschaft und Wirtschaftspolitik.* 2d ed. Tübingen (Germany): Mohr.

1948a *Soziologische Theorie der Revolution.* Göttingen (Germany): Vanderhoeck & Ruprecht.

(1948b) 1953 *Wirtschaftstheorie.* 2d ed. Göttingen (Germany): Vanderhoeck & Ruprecht.

1949 *Friedrich List.* Berlin: Duncker & Humblot.

1952 *Soziologie und Leben: Die soziologische Dimension der Fachwissenschaften.* Tübingen (Germany): Wunderlich.

SUPPLEMENTARY BIBLIOGRAPHY

BECKERATH, ERWIN VON (1955) 1962 Carl Brinkmann. Pages 52–64 in Erwin von Beckerath, *Lynkeus: Gestalten und Probleme aus Wirtschaft und Politik.* Tübingen (Germany): Mohr.

LÜTGE, F. 1956 Carl Brinkmann. *Historische Zeitschrift* 181:734–735.

MONTANER, ANTONIO 1954 Carl Brinkmann in Memoriam. *Finanzarchiv* New Series 15:205–211.

WEBER, ADOLF 1954 Carl Brinkmann. *Jahrbuch der Bayerischen Akademie der Wissenschaften* [1954]: 202–206.

WEIPPERT, GEORG 1959 Carl Brinkmann: Zur Frage der Verknüpfung ökonomischer und soziologischer Betrachtung. *Jahrbuch für Sozialwissenschaft* 4–10:8–37.

BROCA, PAUL

Paul Broca (1824–1880) was a French surgeon who made an important contribution to the understanding of the etiology of aphasia.

He was born to a Protestant family in the small township of Sainte-Foy-la-Grande in the Dordogne. His father was an army surgeon and had served at Waterloo. As a schoolboy and adolescent, Broca showed exceptional abilities as a linguist, a musician, an artist, and a poet. Nevertheless, he chose to go into medicine and at 17 began his studies at the Hôtel Dieu in Paris. His strained finances forced him for a time to take a part-time job as a tutor, work he disliked so much that he threatened to emigrate to America. However, by the time he was 24 he was a prosector, and at the age of 29 a *chirurgien des hôpitaux,* an *agrégé,* and a founder-member of the Société d'Anthropologie. This society had been established not without difficulty, since official sanction was held up by the apparently sinister connotations of the term "anthropology."

Broca's interest in craniology was initially aroused when he participated in an investigation of human remains in the ancient Cordeliers cemetery. Then, on April 4, 1861, at a meeting of the Société d'Anthropologie, he heard a carefully prepared paper by Ernest Auburtin to the effect that lesions of the frontal lobes of the brain were associated with "alalia," or impairment of speech. Auburtin was an enthusiastic follower of Franz Joseph Gall, and, even more, of Johann Spurzheim, in associating the faculty of language with the most forward segments of the brain. He cited a number of instances of alalia, including Adrien Cullerier's unusual case of an attempted suicide in which a shattered frontal bone exposed the subjacent brain: the patient could talk, but whenever the frontal lobe was lightly pressed with a spatula, speech was temporarily arrested.

Broca heard Auburtin's paper with particular interest: an old hemiplegic and speechless mental defective had just come under his surgical care. After the meeting, Broca took Auburtin to the hospital for a joint consultation. When the patient died, a day or so later, an autopsy revealed a superficial lesion in the left frontal lobe. A few weeks later, a similar case occurred in Broca's service, and once again post-mortem inspection of the brain revealed a lesion in the same place.

The demonstration of these two specimens created a sensation, and Broca's fame in this field soon overshadowed that of Auburtin. From many sides came both corroborative comments and objections. Pierre Gratiolet raised the question of negative cases, where unmistakable frontal lesions had not produced speechlessness. He challenged Broca also on the grounds that if a faculty of speech resides in the frontal lobes, monkeys—which are endowed with such lobes—should be able to speak. At first Broca protested mildly that he had no wish to participate in any debate about the location of centers for speech but had only called attention to two pathological specimens that chance had brought his way and that illustrated a rare and curious fact. He abandoned this cautious attitude, however, as his case material grew and as other observers, with their evidence and their prejudices, took sides on the issue.

Broca coined the term "aphemia" to denote the type of speech loss that he was observing. In the beginning of his studies, he thought that this speech loss was caused by a bifrontal lesion of a bifrontal speech center; subsequently, as his evidence accumulated, he came to realize that a unilateral lesion sufficed to cause speech loss and that it was the left cerebral hemisphere that was crucial. Sir David Ferrier suggested that the foot of the third left frontal convolution—the gyrus concerned—be named Broca's area. It was almost against his will that Broca found himself the protagonist of cerebral localization and a pioneer in the philosophy of language.

Broca was a busy and successful surgeon whose principal outside interests were ethnological. He did research in craniometry and steadily amassed a collection of skulls. After the Franco–Prussian war, he founded the department of anthropology at the University of Paris as well as an anthropological journal, the *Revue d'anthropologie*—all this despite the opposition of the clerical party, which disapproved of exhuming human remains and regarded Broca and his colleagues as Malthusians, atheists, and materialists. He wrote five volumes to prove that with increased breadth of the head the quality of the brain improved—and that the French had particularly broad heads!

When in 1880 the Republic decided to fortify the Senate by appointing a number of distinguished men of science and letters, Broca was included.

MACDONALD CRITCHLEY

[*For the historical context of Broca's work, see the biography of* FLOURENS; *for discussion of the subsequent development of his ideas, see* MENTAL DISORDERS, *article on* ORGANIC ASPECTS; NERVOUS SYSTEM; *and the biography of* LASHLEY.]

WORKS BY BROCA

1855   *Propriétés et fonctions de la moelle épinière: Rapport sur quelques expériences de M. Brown-Séquard.* Paris: Bonaventure.

1856   *Des anévrysmes et de leur traitement.* Paris: Labé.

1871–1888   *Mémoires d'anthropologie de Paul Broca.* 5 vols. Paris: Reinwald.

1886   *Paul Broca; Correspondance: 1841–1857.* 2 vols. Paris: Schmidt.

1888   *Mémoires sur le cerveau de l'homme et des primates.* Paris: Reinwald.

SUPPLEMENTARY BIBLIOGRAPHY

ACHARD, CHARLES   1924   Éloge de Paul Broca. Académie de Médecine *Bulletin* 3d Series 92:1347–1366.

CRITCHLEY, MACDONALD   1964   Dax's Law. *International Journal of Neurology* 4:199–206.

CRITCHLEY, MACDONALD   1964   La controverse de Dax et Broca. *Revue neurologique* 110:553–557.

GENTY, MAURICE   1935   Paul Broca: 1824–1880. Volume 9, pages 209–224 in *Les biographies médicales.* Paris: Baillière.

POZZI, SAMUEL   (1880) 1961   Bibliographie de Paul Broca. Volume 14, pages 60–86 in *Revue d'histoire des sciences et de leurs applications.* Paris: Presses Universitaires de France. → First published in *Revue d'anthropologie.*

BROWN, RALPH H.

Ralph Hall Brown (1898–1948), American geographer, was born in Ayer, Massachusetts. He graduated from the University of Pennsylvania in 1921 and received his PH.D. from the University of Wisconsin in 1925. For the next four years he served at the University of Colorado, first as an instructor and then as an assistant professor. In 1929 he moved to the University of Minnesota, where he served as an assistant, then as an associate, and finally as a full professor until his death. He produced a continuous series of articles and other publications, dealing with various parts of the United States and concerned mainly with historical geography, which he defined as the presentation of "the geography of the past"—the geographical reconstruction of the past, not the study of the influence of geography upon history or the examination of changing political boundaries. His work in reconstructing the past was characterized by the use of a wide variety of original sources, eyewitness accounts, and contemporary maps, published and unpublished. Among many contributions, the most outstanding were his two books, *Mirror for Americans* (1943) and *Historical Geography of the United States* (1948).

Mirror for Americans, subtitled *Likeness of the Eastern Seaboard, 1810,* with the word "likeness" being used in its old meaning of image or portrait, is an unusual reconstruction of the past geography of an area. Brown carried the idea of making an areal cross section of the past to its logical conclusion. He invented an imaginary author of the early nineteenth century, Thomas P. Keystone, and wrote the book that Keystone might have written in 1810, based upon the sources that were available at the time. These sources were treated with the understanding that could be expected of a man of 1810; and the thought, the style of presentation, the maps and illustrations, even the language, are those of the period.

In appraising the method of the book, two points must be borne in mind. In the first place, the idiosyncrasy of the treatment has a limiting effect in the sense that the reconstruction does not avail itself of our modern knowledge of the relief and soils and climate of the eastern seaboard. The imaginary Keystone was obviously a man who not only had something to say but who could say it well; yet a study by Brown himself would have given us, in some respects, an even clearer view of the geography of the area in 1810. Thomas P. Keystone's account partakes of the nature of genuine early sources, e.g., Thomas Jefferson's *Notes on the State of Virginia,* 1784–1785, or the geographical works of Jedidiah Morse, which appeared about 1800; these are sources that form some of the raw materials for a modern study of past geography. In the second place, the method of *Mirror for Americans* is not one that can be generally followed with the likelihood of any great success.

As one looks back in time, the language, the outlook, and the method of exposition in the receding ages become more and more different from our own, until one reaches a point when a "reconstruction" in Brown's manner could have but little value. It is difficult, for example, to envisage a very useful presentation, along these lines, of the geography of an area during the Middle Ages.

Yet, even when the full force of these points is allowed, who would wish *Mirror for Americans* to be any different? It is a magnificent tour de force and an intellectual exercise that throws light upon some of the problems involved in the creation of the "historic present." It is, moreover, a work of great charm that must delight all who read it.

Five years after *Mirror for Americans*, Brown published his *Historical Geography of the United States*. This pioneer study will always be of interest to students of American geography, however much later work amplifies and modifies its conclusions. The book contains six parts, each dealing with a particular area at a critical formative period in its development and in that of the United States: The Colonization Period; The Atlantic Seaboard at the Opening of the Nineteenth Century; The Ohio River and the Lower Great Lakes Regions, to 1830; The New Northwest, 1820–1870; The Great Plains and Bordering Regions, to 1870; From the Rocky Mountains to the Pacific Coast, to 1870. The terminal date of the volume is 1870, and there is a chapter devoted to a cross section of "The United States in 1870." This does not, however, appear at the end of the volume but as Chapter 13 at the end of Part Four—that is, at a point from which one can look backward to review changes in the East and forward to anticipate changes in the West.

It must have been an extremely difficult task to organize the material for the greater part of a continent into a coherent "historical geography"; and, inevitably, such a pioneer attempt is open to criticism. Four obvious points of criticism at once spring to mind, all arising from omission. In the first place, the Atlantic seaboard is not described after 1810 because, so we are told, of "limitations of space." In the second place, there is very little reference to Ohio, Michigan, Indiana, and Illinois after about 1830. Then again, not much is said about the Southwest before about 1850. Finally, there is scarcely any reference to the South (to states such as Louisiana and Mississippi) during any period. In view of these omissions, some such title as "Studies in the Historical Geography of the United States" might well have been more appropriate. But to be critical is not to be lacking

in appreciation, and one must salute this great study, based largely on original sources, as a landmark in the development of the study of American historical geography.

H. C. DARBY

WORKS BY BROWN

1927   A Method of Teaching Regional Geography. *Journal of Geography* 26:270–276.
1943   *Mirror for Americans: Likeness of the Eastern Seaboard, 1810.* New York: American Geographical Society.
1948   *Historical Geography of the United States.* New York: Harcourt.

SUPPLEMENTARY BIBLIOGRAPHY

DODGE, STANLEY D.   1948   Ralph Hall Brown, 1898–1948. Association of American Geographers, *Annals* 38: 305–309.

BRUNSWIK, EGON

Egon Brunswik (1903–1955) was one of several outstanding psychologists who came to the United States from Europe shortly before World War II. He was born in Budapest. In 1921 he graduated from the Theresianische Akademie after receiving training in mathematics, science, classics, and history. He then studied engineering and passed the state examinations but afterward enrolled as a student of psychology at the University of Vienna. Here he became an assistant in Karl Bühler's Psychological Institute (among his student colleagues were Paul F. Lazarsfeld and Konrad Lorenz) and received a PH.D. in 1927. While a graduate student in psychology, he also passed the state examination for Gymnasium teachers in mathematics and physics.

Brunswik established the first psychological laboratory in Turkey while he was visiting lecturer in Ankara during 1931–1932. He became *Privatdozent* at the University of Vienna in 1934. In 1933, however, Edward C. Tolman, chairman of the department of psychology at the University of California (Berkeley), spent a year in Vienna. He and Brunswik found that although they had been working in different areas of psychological research, their theories of behavior were complementary, and in 1935/1936 Brunswik received a Rockefeller fellowship that enabled him to visit the University of California. He remained at Berkeley: he became an assistant professor of psychology in 1937 and a full professor in 1947.

In 1937 Brunswik married Else Frenkel (also a former assistant in Bühler's institute), who became well known as a psychoanalytically oriented psychologist. Brunswik became an American citizen in 1943.

His work in Vienna had culminated in the publication of *Wahrnehmung und Gegenstandswelt* in 1934. All of his subsequent work was devoted to the extension and elaboration of the fundamental position set forth in this book, namely, that psychology should give as much attention to the properties of the organism's environment as it does to the organism itself. He asserted that the environment with which the organism comes into contact is an uncertain, probabilistic one, however lawful it may be in terms of physical principles. Adaptation to a probabilistic world requires that the organism learn to employ probabilistic means to achieve goals and learn to utilize probabilistic, uncertain evidence about the world. His "probabilistic functionalism" was the first behavioral system founded on probabilism, an approach that is attracting increasing attention in the fields of learning (Estes 1959), thinking (Bruner et al. 1956), decision processes (Edwards 1961), perception (Postman 1963), communication (Miller 1953), and the study of curiosity (Berlyne 1960). Brunswik's emphasis on the importance of the environment is reflected in the increasing development of "psychological ecology," best illustrated by the work of Roger Barker (1960).

Brunswik wrote a great deal about the history of psychology. His historical analysis is remarkable for its development in structural terms rather than in the customary longitudinal recapitulation of names, dates, and places. It consists of a general identification of the kinds of variables that have traditionally been employed in psychological theory and research and a description of the changes in the emphasis of these variables over time. Brunswik's theory stems as much from his analysis of the history of psychology as it does from his research. His historical as well as his theoretical analysis also led him to criticize orthodox methods of experimental design (particularly the "rule of one variable") and to suggest methods for avoiding what he believed to be an unfortunate artificiality inherent in classical experimental procedures.

His main field of empirical research was perception, but he also brought his probabilistic approach to bear on problems of interpersonal perception, thinking, learning, and clinical psychology. His research findings were published in *Perception and the Representative Design of Experiments* (1947), which also includes Brunswik's methodological innovations and related research by others.

Perhaps the most significant feature of Brunswik's work is its coherence. Each theoretical, his-

torical, and research paper is explicitly and tightly integrated with every other one. Brunswik's cast of mind compelled him to fit together with precision his conceptual framework, his methodology, and his views of the history of psychology. In 1952 he presented an overview of the field of psychology in *The Conceptual Framework of Psychology*—acknowledged to be remarkable both for its deep analysis and for its broad scope. Such an integration of ideas has seldom, if ever, been attempted by a modern psychologist, and in Brunswik's case it demonstrates a remarkable capacity for independent and creative thought.

Brunswik's ideas received wide attention during his lifetime and continue to do so. The extent of his direct influence on psychology, however, remains doubtful. Although his ideas are powerful and his research complicated and ingenious, the scope, depth, and integration of his work make it formidable. His unorthodoxy tends to discourage the timid and to offend those who think it mistaken. However, his history, theory, and methodology struck at key problems in psychology which remain unsolved, and it is too soon to appraise with finality Brunswik's contribution to their eventual solution.

KENNETH R. HAMMOND

[*For the historical context of Brunswik's work, see the biographies of* BÜHLER; FRENKEL-BRUNSWIK; TOLMAN. *For discussion of the subsequent development of Brunswik's ideas, see* ATTENTION; DECISION MAKING, *article on* PSYCHOLOGICAL ASPECTS; MODELS, MATHEMATICAL; MULTIVARIATE ANALYSIS.]

WORKS BY BRUNSWIK

1934 *Wahrnehmung und Gegenstandswelt: Grundlegung einer Psychologie vom Gegenstand her.* Leipzig: Deuticke.

1937 Psychology as a Science of Objective Relations. *Philosophy of Science* 4:227–260.

1943 Organismic Achievement and Environmental Probability. *Psychological Review* 50:255–272.

(1947) 1956 *Perception and the Representative Design of Psychological Experiments.* 2d ed., rev. & enl. Berkeley: Univ. of Calif. Press.

1952 *The Conceptual Framework of Psychology.* Univ. of Chicago Press.

1955 Representative Design and Probabilistic Theory in a Functional Psychology. *Psychological Review* 62:193–217.

SUPPLEMENTARY BIBLIOGRAPHY

BARKER, ROGER G. 1960 Ecology and Motivation. Volume 8, pages 1–49 in Marshall Jones (editor), *Nebraska Symposium on Motivation.* Lincoln: Univ. of Nebraska Press.

BERLYNE, D. E. 1960 *Conflict, Arousal, and Curiosity.* New York: McGraw-Hill.

BRUNER, JEROME S.; GOODNOW, J. J.; and AUSTIN, G. A. 1956 *A Study of Thinking.* New York: Wiley.

EDWARDS, WARD 1961 Behavioral Decision Theory. *Annual Review of Psychology* 12:473–498.

ESTES, WILLIAM K. 1959 The Statistical Approach to Learning Theory. Volume 2, pages 380–491 in Sigmund Koch (editor), *Psychology: A Study of a Science*. New York: McGraw-Hill.

HAMMOND, KENNETH R. (editor) 1966 *The Psychology of Egon Brunswik*. New York: Holt.

MILLER, GEORGE A. 1953 What Is Information Measurement? *American Psychologist* 8:3–11.

POSTMAN, LEO 1963 *Perception and Learning*. Volume 5, pages 30–113 in Sigmund Koch (editor), *Psychology: A Study of a Science*. New York: McGraw-Hill.

BRUSEWITZ, AXEL

Axel Karl Adolf Brusewitz (1881–1950), Swedish political scientist, was born in Vichtis, Finland, of Swedish parents who later resettled in Sweden. After his matriculation examination in 1900 he studied at the University of Uppsala and became docent in political science there in 1913. From 1906 to 1920 he was an assistant at the provincial archives at Uppsala; and from 1919 to 1923, he was lecturer at the elementary school teachers college at Uppsala. In 1923, with the support of many prominent men in the field, he became Skytteansk professor of rhetoric and political science at Uppsala. He held that position for 24 years, retiring in 1947 to become professor emeritus.

Brusewitz' scholarly work began, in effect, with several studies on the origin of the 1809 constitution and related problems. The most important of these were his doctoral dissertation, *Representationsfrågan vid 1809–10 års Riksdag* ("The Question of Representation in the 1809–1810 Riksdag Session" 1913), and *Studier öfver 1809 års författinngskris* ("Studies on the Constitutional Crisis of 1809" 1917). These works contained some new and revolutionary perspectives on the constitution. Thus Brusewitz emphasized that foreign doctrines, especially those of Montesquieu, had had an important influence on the founders of the Swedish constitution; he also maintained that the constitution was a compromise between opposing parties rather than the product of national unity, as had previously been thought.

As a member of a government-appointed committee on the popular vote Brusewitz was assigned to report on Switzerland, and the result was his book *Folkomröstningsinstitutet i den schweiziska demokratien* ("The Institution of the Popular Vote and Swiss Democracy" 1923). This study, which has unfortunately not been translated into any major language, is superior to anything else that has been written on the subject; especially remarkable is its analysis of the relationships between politics and the history of ideas.

As a professor, Brusewitz did a great deal of research on the relative position of the government and the Riksdag in matters of foreign policy. He wrote on the secret consultative committee in the 1809 constitution, the Scandinavian foreign committee, and the handling of foreign affairs in the Swedish Riksdag (1933–1941).

Brusewitz was a specialist in English parliamentary history, but his only published work on the subject was a brilliant little article on Palmerston (1944). For many years he accumulated data on Swedish political history—entries in diaries, letters, and other documents on recent political history—materials that are invaluable for further research, but which Brusewitz himself never used for the full-length biographies he had planned.

Brusewitz was a notable teacher. His authoritative, lucid summaries of seminar discussions were masterly. Perhaps even more important was his role as inspirer and adviser in private conferences with his students. Few teachers can have given so much time and interest to this work of guidance, and few can so fully have won their friends' and students' gratitude and warm personal devotion. Brusewitz edited the journal of the Political Science Society of Uppsala (the *Skrifter* of the Statsvetenskapliga Föreningen i Uppsala); it is excellent proof of the way in which he stimulated and led his students. It contains a large part of recent Swedish political science.

It can truly be said that, as a result of Brusewitz' work, Swedish political science is on a high level. The language barrier was the only thing that prevented his work as a scholar and teacher from achieving international importance.

Among the characteristics that gave Brusewitz stature as a man and as a scientist were his independence and self-reliance. When as a young man he did pioneering scientific work on the origin of the Swedish constitution and at the same time set parliamentary democracy in its historical context, he was also acting in terms of his intellectual and political radicalism and breaking with the conservative dogmas that had ruled the political science of the time. He was prominent as an enemy of traditional notions and was often regarded as something of a revolutionary and troublemaker, retaining this Jacobin trait all his life. Lacking respect for authority in all its forms, he invariably spoke his mind; no one found the doctrines of the modern dictators more reprehensible. But his seemingly strong and simple personality was not without complexities, and thoughts about transience, futility, and emptiness were always with him.

HERBERT TINGSTEN

WORKS BY BRUSEWITZ

1913   *Representationsfrågan vid 1809–10 års Riksdag.* Uppsala: Berling.

1917   *Studier öfver 1809 års författinngskris: Den idépolitiska motsättningen.* Uppsala: Akademiska Bokhandeln.

1923   Folkomröstningsinstitutet i den schweiziska demokratien. Sweden, *Statens offentliga utredningar* 10. → The entire volume is devoted to Brusewitz's work.

1933–1941   *Studier över riksdagen ock utrikespolitiken.* 3 vols. Uppsala and Stockholm: Almqvist & Wiksell. → Volume 1: *Hemliga utskottet i 1809 års författinng,* 1933. Volume 2: *Nordiska utrikesnämnder i komparativ belysning,* 1933. Volume 3: *Utrikesfrågors behandling i den svenska riksdagen,* 1941.

1944   Palmerston blir preiärminister (Palmerston Becomes Prime Minister). Pages 83–139 in Statsvetenskapliga Föreningen i Uppsala, *Statsvetenskapliga studien.* Skrifter No. 20. Uppsala and Stockholm: Almqvist & Wiksell.

SUPPLEMENTARY BIBLIOGRAPHY

Statsvetenskapliga Föreningen i Uppsala *Skrifter.* → Published since 1933.

BRYCE, JAMES

Viscount Bryce (1838–1922) is one of those figures whose importance in the history of thought is explained not by the originality or penetration of their ideas but by their pertinence to a certain time and place. He was surely one of the most successful cultivators of Anglo-American affinity to have yet appeared. In his major work, *The American Commonwealth* (1888), he left posterity an invaluable account of American politics and society in the late nineteenth century. To be sure, that account may be as much a description of America's self-image as of American reality, but a nation's vision of itself is vital historical data. Most important of all, Bryce helped set the terms of American political attitudes and American political science for several decades. He could have performed none of these functions if he had been a daring and unorthodox social critic and innovator rather than what he was—a diligent, highly intelligent and observant, but essentially conventional, British gentleman who loved America because he found there a great many people not very different from himself.

Bryce was born in Belfast but educated chiefly in Scotland and England. His father, a Scottish schoolmaster, was a mathematician and geologist of some distinction, and Bryce grew up in a bookish, pious atmosphere, which seems to have stimulated his natural precocity and nurtured a spirit of private and public virtue. He attended Glasgow University for three years, then went on a scholarship to Trinity College, Oxford. There his remarkable capacity for forming friendships and his evident intellectual gifts quickly won him an honored place. Albert Dicey, T. H. Green, Henry Nettleship, E. A. Freeman, and Matthew Arnold were among his friends. His academic career was punctuated by the bewildering succession of awards that so often identified men of future distinction in the Britain of his day. He took a first in both Greats and Modern History and received, among other accolades, the Arnold prize for his essay "The Holy Roman Empire," which was published "greatly changed and enlarged" in 1864. The book earned the young author an immediate and deserved scholarly reputation, but it is worth noting that the study was praised not for originality of insight but as the first erudite English synthesis of accepted historical knowledge on the subject.

He had been elected a fellow of Oriel College in 1862; in the same year he began to study law and was called to the bar in 1867. Although moderately successful as a lawyer, he had already developed a consuming passion for travel, inquiry, and public service, and he abandoned the bar in 1882 after his election to Parliament. Meanwhile he had found time not only for his legal practice but for journalism, scholarship, teaching, and an endless series of journeys on the Continent, in the Near East, and in America. Everywhere he went he gathered information, largely by word of mouth, about the government and mores of the countries he visited. The United States interested him most of all, and he began writing *The American Commonwealth* after his third visit to America in 1883. The first edition was published in 1888.

The book and the view of America that it presented faithfully reflected the quality of the man. Bryce had undertaken to produce the first over-all description of American democracy, treating not only the national constitutional structure but also state and local government, the party system, public opinion, and social institutions. From conversations during his American travels, he had accumulated a formidable body of detailed knowledge that he now poured into the work. He sought, as he said, "to present simply the facts of the case . . . letting them speak for themselves," and he hoped that philosophically inclined readers would find in the book not ready-made theories but material on which they could base their own bold generalizations. His great predecessor, Tocqueville, was of course always before his mind's eye, but Bryce consciously chose to eschew Tocqueville's deductive, speculative method, preferring to exploit his own talents and opportunities.

The choice was shrewd. He could never have matched Tocqueville's brilliant imagination, but he knew far more about the actual data of American political life, and much of the data had never been recorded before. There was little new in the section on the national government, but the synoptic descriptions of state governments and of the party system were unique, and the perspective Bryce provided was as useful to contemporaries as it has been to later historians. The account has all the qualities of its tireless and fair-minded author: it is balanced, never tendentious, thoughtful though seldom profound, and as accurate as objective descriptions of human institutions are likely to be.

But of course Bryce could not entirely suppress evaluations, however detached and objective he sought to be, and the value system of the book, stated or implied, is the one that might be expected, given his character and his sources. His outlook had been shaped by the England of Mill and Bagehot and by his own moderate and friendly temperament. His principal American friends and informants were kindred spirits like Charles Eliot of Harvard, and his view of American democracy was much like theirs—cautiously optimistic but troubled by its flaws, meliorative rather than revolutionary, institutional rather than comprehensive. Insofar as he could be said to have a fundamental point, it was that the party system, with its pattern of spoils and corruption, was the great blemish of the commonwealth, but that the excellence of the constitutional structure and the sovereignty of a basically right-minded populace prevented the blemish from ruining the polity and justified a favorable verdict for American democracy. It followed that the most urgent American problem was to reform politics and government and that this could be best accomplished by substituting good men for the rascally machine politicians who were the chief source of corruption and inefficiency. That the good men were at hand Bryce knew: they were his friends in Boston, New York, and elsewhere— the solid, Anglo-Saxon, natural leaders of the upper middle class, those among whom the mugwump movement was conceived. If more of them would turn their interest to civic affairs, the sensible electorate would support them, jobbery and dishonesty would be eliminated from government,

the merit system established, and the American republic purged of its faults.

Once put down on paper and stamped with the mark of Bryce's continually growing international fame, these judgments assumed independent authority and influenced the tone of political discourse for years to come. Bryce had become Regius professor of civil law at Oxford in 1870 and was under secretary for foreign affairs under Gladstone and British ambassador to the United States from 1907 to 1913. For the last-named role he was admirably equipped, and his affection and respect for America were reciprocated in full measure. In 1914 he was raised to the peerage. *The American Commonwealth* received attention not only because of Bryce's prestige but also because it was the first, and for a long time incomparably the best, textbook on American government. It is hardly surprising then that its influence, as it ran through successive editions from 1888 to 1909, can be traced in the political rallying cries of the progressive era and in the approach of American political scientists until very recent times.

Bryce was not as sanguine about the benevolence of direct popular democracy as some of the progressives were, for his instinct was to be moderate in both his enthusiasms and his fears. But his confidence in the fundamental goodness of the American populace (or at least what was then an Anglo-Saxon majority) implied a faith in direct popular rule that the progressives could draw on, and his reformist strictures against machine politics were echoed throughout the "age of reform." Those like Herbert Croly, who thought that "bosses" might be indispensable democratic leaders, or like the later Lincoln Steffens, who lacked faith in purely political reform, could not prevail against Bryce's great authority, particularly since Bryce had the common advantage of saying what America preferred to hear. His impact on academic political science was no less strong. When other texts on American government were written, they tended to take off from Bryce. Thus they reflected his concern with institutions rather than with underlying social forces, his view that the political could and should be sharply distinguished from the administrative and governmental, and his belief that political behavior was something to deplore and reform, rather than to study and live with.

However, by the time he published *Modern Democracies* in 1921, the wheel had turned. Characteristically, he had elected to produce a pioneer work in the field that is now called "comparative government"; again he could claim to have written the first synoptic treatment of a significant subject. But Bryce was still wedded to the assumptions of 1888, and modern social thought was not; and while the book was justly praised as a compendium of data, its outlook was respectfully criticized. Bryce was aware that representative democracy, which had seemed so promising in the Mill–Bagehot era, was now being challenged and that attempts were being made to appraise political systems in terms of root economic and social facts. Yet he steadfastly held to the view that democracy has nothing to do with economic equality, ignored the group basis of politics, continued to emphasize reforms like the abolition of the spoils system, and proposed as his chief remedy for democracy's ills an improved second chamber of the legislature. His values and attitudes continued to find some spokesmen for many years to come, but political science in general has gradually but surely drifted away from him, and he is now often dutifully cited but seldom read or heeded. Yet his books remain, as has been said, precious historical records of the facts and viewpoints of an earlier age, and few scholars can claim to have influenced their time more profoundly than Bryce did.

ROBERT G. MCCLOSKEY

[For the historical context of Bryce's work, see DEMOC-RACY; PRESIDENTIAL GOVERNMENT and the biogra-phies of BAGEHOT; DICEY; MILL; TOCQUEVILLE.]

WORKS BY BRYCE

(1864) 1956 *The Holy Roman Empire.* New ed., rev. & enl. London: Macmillan.
(1888) 1909 *The American Commonwealth.* 3d ed., 2 vols. New York and London: Macmillan. → An abridged edition was published in 1959 by Putnam.
1901 *Studies in History and Jurisprudence.* 2 vols. New York: Oxford Univ. Press.
1903 *Studies in Contemporary Biography.* New York: Macmillan.
1921 *Modern Democracies.* 2 vols. New York: Macmillan.

WORKS ABOUT BRYCE

Bryce's American Commonwealth: *Fiftieth Anniversary.* Edited by Robert C. Brooks. 1939 New York: Mac-millan.
FISHER, HERBERT A. L. 1927 *James Bryce (Viscount Bryce of Dechmont, O. M.).* 2 vols. New York: Mac-millan.

BUBER, MARTIN

Martin Buber (1878–1965) was primarily a re-ligious and social philosopher and a Zionist leader, whose work is of great relevance to the social sciences. He was professor of religion at Frank-furt until 1936. Moving to Israel (then Palestine),

he became professor of sociology of culture (social philosophy) and later the first chairman of the department of sociology at the Hebrew University in Jerusalem and taught such subjects as the so-ciology of religion and ethics, social philosophy, and the history of sociology. He was the first presi-dent of the academy of sciences and humanities in Israel.

Buber's studies ranged over a great variety of fields, beginning with his work on the Hassidic communities and traditions (*The Origin and Meaning of Hasidism* 1921–1954), which brought the stream of Jewish sectarianism and mysticism to the attention of a wide Western public. In his works on educational and religious philosophy (for instance, *Eclipse of God: Studies in the Relations Between Religion and Philosophy* 1952a; *Daniel: Dialogues on Realization* 1913; *For the Sake of Heaven* 1943–1944; "Rede über das Erzieherische" 1926; "Urdistanz und Beziehung" 1951; "Das Pro-blem des Menschen" 1948), and most explicitly in his book *I and Thou* (1936), he developed the principle of the "dialogue." He studied Biblical thought, especially the conception of kingship and polity in Biblical times (*The Prophetic Faith* 1942) and, mainly through his translation (with F. Rosenzweig) of the Bible into German, he be-came involved in Biblical exegesis. His publica-tions in social philosophy centered on Utopian so-cial thought and the experiments in collective life in Palestine and Israel (*Paths in Utopia* 1947) and on Judaism and Zionism (*At the Turning: Three Addresses on Judaism* 1952b; *Israel and the World: Essays in a Time of Crisis* 1921–1943). For a time he was editor of the series *Gesellschaft,* which published articles by leading German so-ciologists, for example, Tönnies (on custom), Simmel (on religion), and Oppenheimer (on the state).

Buber's methodological and analytical approach combined influences from many sources. In his philosophical emphasis he was close to the tradi-tions of social philosophy associated with Max Scheler and Martin Heidegger, and those of re-ligious existentialism identified with Paul Tillich, Reinhold Niebuhr, and Jacques Maritain. He was also close to those German sociologists, like Lorenz von Stein, who first asserted that the "social" is independent of the "political," and to such Utopian and religious thinkers as Saint-Simon, Proudhon, Landauer, and Eduard Heimann, who looked for regenerative forces in society.

However, Buber's approach to the problems of social and cultural transformation, creativity, and regeneration was different from the usual Utopian approach. Utopian views tend to be static, emphasizing a flight from various constraints of modern society or presenting an unattainable model of a desirable society. Buber's central sociological or social philosophical concern was to define the conditions of social and cultural transformation and the conditions of the stagnation or demise of cultures and societies rather than to prescribe simple structural or organizational change. He sought to identify the situations where creativity really can occur, and he believed that these situations exist to some extent in all cultures but that their fullest development occurs only rarely.

Cultural creativity, according to Buber, is the product of four basic forms of opposition: tradition versus innovation; the shaping of concrete, instrumental social relations versus the creation of an independent sphere of cultural products and values; the growth of forms of culture versus the development of self-awareness or self-consciousness on the part of the actors; and the plurality of institutional spheres versus the existence of some central common core of cultural tradition.

The possibilities of cultural creativity and social regeneration appeared to Buber to be greatest in those situations where the opposites exist in a state of tension that preserves the autonomy of each. The domination of any one element over the others may produce organizational or structural change unaccompanied by any cultural or value tranformation, or it may lead to the stagnation or demise of a society or culture. Buber was especially concerned with the possibility that the state might dominate the more generative forces of social and cultural spontaneity. He thought this an inherent possibility of all political systems, but one that had reached its culmination in modern totalitarianism. However, he refused to denigrate political activity as such; rather, he saw it as a basic, essential, autonomous component of social life, which if kept within proper limits—limits that change according to circumstances—constitutes a positive force in the process of social creativity.

The central characteristic of situations producing creativity is the existence of a dialogue, of communicative openness—a dialogue between man and man and between man and God. Such communicative openness is maximized in situations having certain structural characteristics: the participants have a strong commitment both to direct *personal* relations, transcending and cutting across more institutionalized and formalized

frameworks, and to direct relations to *the sphere of ultimate values*—that is, the realm of the sacred.

Buber never thought that the conditions of communicative openness and creativity were tied to any concrete social, organizational, or cultural contents. Historically, he saw the apex of cultural creativity in the great classic civilizations, China and Greece, during their periods of transition from tribalism to universalism. He also saw it in the instances of the historical Judaic political–religious community, of the Hassidic community, and of some modern Utopian communities, especially the communal settlements in Palestine. All these manifest a strong commitment to worldly activity, but an activity that transcends the goals of any given concrete community and that is based on general, universal, and transcendental orientations.

Unlike many of the Utopians, Buber also tried to identify situations that permit some creativity of this kind within the more routinized and formalized situations generally prevalent in societies, especially in modern ones. He found these favorable conditions in modern religious and international dialogue, in educational institutions, particularly those devoted to adult education, and, in fact, in any situation which promises to break up communicative closure among national, professional, and religious entities. Buber's search for the multiplicity of concrete situations in which communicative openness and dialogue can be maintained is evidence of his belief that these situations are not tied to any concrete contents: cultural and social regeneration does not come from a social system established according to some formula; rather, it results from a continuous, ongoing process.

Through his examination of the conditions of cultural creativity, Buber's analysis contributes to the understanding of the proper place of charisma in social processes and helps reveal both the creative and destructive possibilities inherent in charismatic orientations. Of crucial importance here is his analysis of the variety of social and cultural forms that permit the creative possibilities of charismatic orientations to find expression. By not limiting the charismatic to any given contents, such as the political or religious, Buber connected it directly with the total process of cultural creativity and social regeneration. This related the authenticity of charismatic attitudes to the existence of direct, unmediated relations of man to man and man to the sacred. Thus Buber defined the nature and structure of the open situations through which the charismatic quality can become effective in the processes of social and cultural transformation.

SHMUEL N. EISENSTADT

[Directly related are the entries PSYCHOLOGY, article on EXISTENTIAL PSYCHOLOGY; RELIGIOUS SPECIALISTS; UTOPIANISM. Other relevant material may be found in CREATIVITY, article on SOCIAL ASPECTS; JUDAISM; SOCIAL INSTITUTIONS; and in the biographies of SCHELER; STEIN.]

WORKS BY BUBER

(1913) 1964 *Daniel: Dialogues on Realization.* New York: Holt. → First published in German.

(1921–1943) 1963 *Israel and the World: Essays in a Time of Crisis.* 2d ed. New York: Schocken. → Contains essays originally published in German and Hebrew.

(1921–1954) 1960 *The Origin and Meaning of Hasidism.* New York: Horizon. → Contains essays originally published in German and Hebrew.

(1926) 1962 Rede über das Erzieherische. Volume 1, pages 787–809 in Martin Buber, *Werke.* Munich: Kösel.

(1936) 1958 *I and Thou.* 2d ed. New York: Scribner. → First published in German.

(1942) 1949 *The Prophetic Faith.* New York: Macmillan. → First published in Hebrew. A paperback edition was published in 1960 by Harper.

(1943–1944) 1953 *For the Sake of Heaven.* 2d ed. New York: Harper. → First published as *Gog und Magog.*

(1947) 1950 *Paths in Utopia.* New York: Macmillan. → First published in Hebrew.

(1948) 1962 Das Problem des Menschen. Volume 1, pages 307–407 in Martin Buber, *Werke.* Munich: Kösel.

(1951) 1962 Urdistanz und Beziehung. Volume 1, pages 411–423 in Martin Buber, *Werke.* Munich: Kösel.

1952a *Eclipse of God: Studies in the Relations Between Religion and Philosophy.* New York: Harper.

1952b *At the Turning: Three Addresses on Judaism.* New York: Farrar.

1957a Distance and Relation. *Psychiatry* 20:97–104.

1957b Guilt and Guilt Feelings. *Psychiatry* 20:114–129.

1962— *Werke.* Vols. 1–3. Munich: Kösel. → A projected multivolume work.

SUPPLEMENTARY BIBLIOGRAPHY

COHEN, ARTHUR A. 1957 *Martin Buber.* New York: Hillary House.

DIAMOND, MALCOLM 1960 *Martin Buber: Jewish Existentialist.* New York: Oxford Univ. Press.

FRIEDMAN, MAURICE 1955 *Martin Buber: The Life of Dialogue.* Univ. of Chicago Press.

BÜCHER, KARL

Karl Bücher (1847–1930), economist, statistician, historian, and sociologist, was born to lower-middle-class parents in Kirdorf, a village in the Prussian Rhineland. He studied political science, history, and classical philology at the universities of Bonn and Göttingen. In his early thirties, he spent several years in Frankfurt am Main on the staff of the *Frankfurter Zeitung.* Later he taught at the universities of Dorpat, Basel, and eventually, Leipzig, from which he retired in 1917.

While he was in Frankfurt, Bücher began research into archival materials relating to the demography of the city in the fourteenth and fifteenth centuries (1886). This and other research led to the publication of a series of monographs on a variety of subjects: medieval labor conditions ([1876–1894] 1922, pp. 245–258); the position of women in the Middle Ages ([1876–1894] 1922, pp. 259–299); medieval tax ordinances ([1876–1894] 1922, pp. 300–328); bookbinders' ordinances from the sixteenth to the nineteenth centuries ([1876–1894] 1922, pp. 400–457); and others. His work on population and his authoritative study of forms of organization of the handicrafts in the German town of the high Middle Ages ([1876–1894] 1922, pp. 373–399) established his eminence as an economic historian.

His famous theory of stages (1893) claimed to establish the "law" that governed the economic development of western and central Europe from antiquity to modern times: the town economy of the high Middle Ages, which was the principal object of his own studies, had been preceded in antiquity by a closed household economy, the *oikos,* and was followed in modern times by a national economy, the *Volkswirtschaft.* In the context of Bücher's writings, the term *Volkswirtschaft* may be considered synonymous with *Verkehrswirtschaft,* i.e., extensive exchange economy.

The role of exchange, then, serves as the criterion for determining what type of economy is under scrutiny. Primitive man, Bücher held, had an aversion to exchange rather than a propensity for it. In the *oikos*-dominated economy of antiquity, goods moved from producer to consumer without any intervening exchange. In the medieval town, there was some exchange, and craftsmen worked for the consumer either directly or indirectly by way of the local market. In the modern national market economy, everyone is engaged in multiple exchange.

Bücher found the factual basis for his *oikos* in Johann Karl Rodbertus' interpretation of the gigantic slaveholdings of later Roman antiquity. In the *familia rustica* and the *familia urbana* all phases of production, from raw materials to finished goods, were united, under the control of the master, in the *familia,* i.e., the *oikos.* Although technical specialization in crafts did exist, there was no exchange of goods in various stages of completion. After chattel slavery was modified, first to villenage and eventually to colonate, only the protective *Burg* was required to create the closed medieval town economy with its craftsmen-*Bürger*, who exchanged goods locally on a modest scale. The third stage, *Volkswirtschaft*, resulted when the modern centralized state rescinded the privileges of medieval towns, as well as those of local territorial rulers generally, and thus cleared the way for an unlimited exchange economy on a national scale.

Of Bücher's three stages, the last has proved to be conceptually of the greatest significance. Theories of the exchange economy were not new, but they lacked perspective and merely reflected the facts of contemporary life. Exchange was taken for granted as part of every economy. Bücher was the first to note the distortion that this assumption produced with regard to premodern economic history. In this sense, he rejected classical economics as a sound basis for the study of economic history.

His own more general and substantive concept of the economy evolved partly in reaction to classical economics and partly in response to some elements in Rodbertus' *oikos* economics, complemented by assiduous reading of travelers' accounts of early societies. (His *Arbeit und Rhythmus*, 1896, was a sociological by-product of his familiarity with this literature.) Classical economics, Bücher wrote, was concerned primarily with the circulation and distribution of goods, to the neglect of production and consumption. Money was conceived chiefly as a means of exchange, and its other uses were largely overlooked. In Rodbertus' *oikos*, the process of production was central, forming one uninterrupted exchangeless unit: not even labor had a market; money was mainly used for purposes other than exchange. Briefly, Bücher's approach makes exchange only a phenomenon of a particular stage of economic development, while the essence of the economy has to do with actual production, or, as one might say today, with the substantive element.

As to method, Bücher followed an entirely independent line. Although he was an institutionalist, he sided in the *Methodenstreit* with Carl Menger and the neoclassical theorists against Gustav Schmoller and the German historical school, with its preference for institutional description. He welcomed the return of the Vienna school to "isolating abstraction" and "logical deduction," for he was convinced that it was in these methods that the strength of classical economics lay. He objected to both classical and neoclassical economics on the grounds that these theories had a narrow, timebound concept of economy, a concept which they

assumed was applicable to all historical periods, including antiquity and the Middle Ages. Bücher's brand of institutionalism was fundamentally analytical; he called for further research into the working of the modern *Volkswirtschaft*, pressing all the while for theoretical treatment of the results of this research. He himself treated the forms of medieval craft organization as well as the *oikos* economy in this manner.

Bücher's genetic theory of the medieval urban economy was variously criticized by Schmoller, Georg von Below, Alfons Dopsch, and Werner Sombart. Eventually the impact of their criticism abated, and scholars of the rank of Henri Pirenne and Max Weber accepted Bücher's urban theory. As they interpreted it, the rationale of the town economy was the institutional securing of an appropriate standard of life for the citizen.

A second controversy, which is still not settled, has to do with whether the material civilization of ancient Greece was primitive or modern in character. This is the *oikos* controversy, in which Bücher and Max Weber clashed with the classical historians Eduard Meyer and Karl J. Beloch. Meyer adduced evidence that the economic life of classical Greece, even its commerce and banking, was "thoroughly modern." Max Weber held, on the contrary, that nothing would be more disastrous than to conceive of the conditions of antiquity in modern terms; such concepts as commercialism, factory, or industrial proletariat, he held, could not properly be used in a discussion that hardly transcended the level of cultural interpretation. Later, Johannes Hasebroek upheld and developed the primitivist case. He argued, for example, that the Solonic crisis was not caused by a revolt akin to the French Revolution, but rather by a disaffected peasantry revolting against the warrior rule of the landed aristocracy. On this decisive point, Michael Rostovtzeff, originally an antagonist of primitivism, came to agree with Hasebroek. But Rostovtzeff did not give way to Weber on another aspect of the controversy: he disagreed with Weber's view that capitalism, insofar as it existed at all in antiquity, was no more than a cultural phenomenon, and then only in the political, rather than the strictly economic, field. Quite recently, such scholars as A. L. Oppenheim (1957), W. F. Leemans (1960), Gelb, and Grandin have studied and modified the old *oikos* theory. Clearly, the problem originally formulated by Bücher still has intellectual vitality.

KARL POLANYI

[*For the historical context of Bücher's work, see* ECONOMIC THOUGHT; *and the biographies of* MENGER;

RODBERTUS; SCHMOLLER. *For discussion of the subsequent development of his ideas, see* GILDS; MANORIAL ECONOMY; SPECIALIZATION AND EXCHANGE; *and the biographies of* PIRENNE; WEBER, MAX.]

WORKS BY BÜCHER

(1876–1894) 1922 *Beiträge zur Wirtschaftsgeschichte.* Tübingen: Laupp. → Contains "Zur Arbeiterfrage im Mittelalter," 1876; "Die Frauenfrage im Mittelalter," 1882; "Zwei mittelalterliche Steuerordnungen," 1894; "Frankfurter Buchbinderordnungen vom 16. bis zum 19. Jahrhundert," 1888; and "Mittelalterliche Handwerksverbände," 1922.

1886 *Frankfurt am Main im XIV. und XV. Jahrhundert: Socialstatistische Studien.* Volume 1. Tübingen (Germany): Laupp. → Only Volume 1 was published.

(1893) 1901 *Industrial Evolution.* Univ. of Toronto Press. → First published as *Die Entstehung der Volkswirtschaft.*

(1896) 1924 *Arbeit und Rhythmus.* 6th ed., rev. & enl. Leipzig: Teubner.

SUPPLEMENTARY BIBLIOGRAPHY

BRODNITZ, GERHARD 1931 Karl Bücher (obituary). *Zeitschrift für die gesamte Staatswissenschaft.* 90:1–7.

HOSELITZ, BERT F. 1960 Theories of Stages of Economic Growth. Pages 193–238 in Bert F. Hoselitz et al. (editors), *Theories of Economic Growth.* New York: Free Press.

LEEMANS, W. F. 1960 *Foreign Trade in the Old Babylonian Period.* Leiden (Netherlands): Brill.

OPPENHEIM, A. L. 1957 A Bird's-eye View of Mesopotamian Economic History. Pages 27–37 in Karl Polanyi et al. (editors), *Trade and Market in the Early Empires.* Glencoe, Ill.: Free Press.

PEARSON, HARRY W. 1957 The Secular Debate on Economic Primitivism. Pages 3–11 in Karl Polanyi et al. (editors), *Trade and Market in the Early Empires.* Glencoe, Ill.: Free Press.

SWEET, RONALD F. G. 1958 On Prices, Moneys, and Money Uses in the Old Babylonian Period. Ph.D. dissertation, Oriental Institute, University of Chicago.

TROELTSCH, WALTER 1917 Zum siebzigsten Geburtstag von Karl Bücher. *Evangelisches Gemeindeblatt* [1917], no. 15.

WILL, ÉDOUARD 1954 Trois quarts de siècle de recherches sur l'économie grecque antique. *Annales* 9:7–19.

BUDDHISM

"Buddhism" is a Western term for the immensely diverse system of beliefs and practices centered on the teachings and person of the historical Buddha, who enunciated his message of salvation in India over two millennia ago. The general concept easily lends itself to a false sense of empirical unity remote from the complex history of the tradition and the varied faiths of the individual believers. In the centuries following the promulgation of the original teaching and the formation of the earliest community, Indian Buddhism underwent a massive process of missionary diffusion throughout the Asian world, assimilating new values and undergoing major changes in doctrinal and institutional principles. Today, under the impact of conflicting ideologies and of science and technology, Buddhism, like all the great religions, finds itself, amid the acids of modernity, undergoing vast internal changes which further prohibit simplistic stereotypes and definitions.

The traditional distinction between the major historical forms of Buddhism has centered on a threefold typology, based on doctrinal and institutional differences which seem to fall within relatively homogeneous geographical areas. They are (1) The Theravāda ("teaching of the elders"), located in the lands of southeast Asia—most importantly in Ceylon, Burma, Thailand, Laos, Vietnam, and Cambodia; (2) the Mahāyāna ("great vehicle"), in Nepal, Sikkim, China, Korea, and Japan; and (3) the Tantrayāna ("esoteric vehicle"), formerly prevalent in Tibet, Mongolia, and parts of Siberia. However, this classification is crosscut with atypical variations. The Theravāda, as it exists today, represents the sole survivor of the numerous ancient Indian schools. It has a fixed body of canonical literature, a relatively unified orthodox teaching, a clearly structured institutional distinction between the monastic order and laity, and a long history as the established "church" of the various southeast Asian states.

The Mahāyāna, on the other hand, is a diffuse and vastly complex combination of many schools and sects, based on a heterogeneous literature of massive proportions from which no uniform doctrinal or institutional orthodoxy can ever be derived. There are certain key scriptures which are sometimes regarded as typifying the more universal thrust of Mahāyāna principles over against Theravāda teaching, and Theravāda has traditionally been stigmatized as Hīnayāna ("small vehicle") by Mahāyānists; but Mahāyāna itself is also to be found on the southeast Asian mainland, in syncretistic fusion with Theravāda. In China and Japan its literature ranges from the most abstruse philosophy to popular devotional theism and magic, and it includes the Hīnayāna sources as well. Institutionally it has appeared both in monastic and in radically laicized forms, and it has occasionally served in well-defined church–state configurations.

Tantric Buddhism, dominantly identified with Tibetan Lamaism and its theocracy, is equally ambiguous. The esoteric Tantric teachings, which originated in India, persisted in several so-called Mahāyāna schools in China and Japan. In its Tibetan form Tantric Buddhism was richly fused with a native primitivism, and it underwent important and very divergent sectarian developments. The Tibetan monasteries contain (or did contain) superb collections of Mahāyāna and Hīnayāna sources in addition to the Tantric literature.

The statistics of Buddhist membership are even more deceptive. The total given has frequently ranged from 150,000,000 to 300,000,000—with the variation based principally on the fact that in Mahāyāna lands "orthodox" commitment to one religious faith was never a significant cultural characteristic. The populations of China and Japan could not be categorized as Buddhist, Taoist, Confucian, or Shintoist in the same way that Western religious history seems to lend itself to relatively clear confessional divisions between Protestants, Catholics, and Jews. In Japan, for example, Buddhism, Confucianism, and Shinto have frequently formed a single interlocking system for the specialized satisfaction of a wide range of personal and social needs. The same family that takes an infant to a Shinto shrine for a baptismal ceremony will, without any sense of conflict, have funeral rites conducted by Buddhist monks and maintain family ancestral worship and ethical standards largely dominated by Confucian values.

In southeast Asia approximately 90 per cent of the total population is Buddhist, monastic and lay. In China, just prior to 1949 less than one-fifth of the popular cults were recognizably oriented to Buddhism in some form, and only a small fraction of the total population (under 1 per cent) were specifically affiliated with the monastic orders. Since 1949 this percentage has been further reduced, as it also has, most recently and drastically, in Tibet, where over one-fifth of the total population once lived in the monasteries. In Japan more than three-quarters of the population have Buddhist affiliations, while in India and Pakistan—after an absence of many centuries—Buddhism has only recently, during the past few decades, begun to return in strength; however, it still numbers less than 1 per cent. Since the eighteenth century, with the first Asian emigrations to the West, Buddhism has found its way into Europe, Great Britain, South America, and the United States. The number of conversions among the populations of these countries is small in total number but is of considerable cultural significance, since conversions frequently reflect dissatisfaction with Western values and goals.

Amid this diversity there are a few central elements, which may be taken as generally characteristic of Buddhism throughout the larger part of its history. First, for all Buddhists the common point of unity has been in the symbol of the Buddha—whether revered chiefly as a human teacher, as in Theravāda, or worshiped as a supreme deity, as in certain forms of theistic Mahāyāna. In all cases the element of personal commitment in faith is present in some form. Second, Buddhism is one of the three major religions of the world which defines the human situation with sufficient universality for all mankind to fall within the scope of its message of salvation without prior criteria of social, ethnic, or geographic origin. The voluntary act of personal conversion in response to the teaching was from the very beginning and still remains one of the most decisive symbols of its missionary scope. Third, from the very beginning Buddhism was dominated by a religious elite for whom the monastic ideal and pursuit of a mystical, otherworldly goal were overriding concerns, frequently to the exclusion of consistent focus on mundane socioeconomic and political problems. However, even here there are many exceptions which must be noted and which require that Buddhism be "defined" with careful regard for its discrete historical forms.

The systematic study of Buddhism in full critical perspective began with the Enlightenment and the advent of Western colonialism in Asia during the seventeenth and eighteenth centuries. The arduous translation of Buddhist scriptures and basic historical and institutional reconstructions were sufficiently well advanced by the end of the nineteenth century to provide raw material for bolder attempts at comparative evaluation.

In general it may be said that today the major obligations of study include, first, the basic Buddhist literature, doctrines, and institutions considered internally—that is, within the community itself and among individual believers, as they understand it; second, the external relationship and exchange between Buddhism and the larger cultural environments of which it has been a part—including its relation to the goals of the state and its confrontation with other religions and ideologies; and third, what can be very broadly called the therapeutic contributions of Buddhist teaching to the human situation—both personal and social.

Early history

Historically, ancient Indian culture during the sixth century B.C. was to much of Asia what Hellenistic culture was to the West, and Buddhism was the missionary bearer of many of its values. The conditions underlying the emergence of Buddhism in ancient India were those generally characteristic of the wider process of sociocultural transition which took place during the first millenium B.C. across the face of the civilized world, from Greece to China. In the principal centers of the high cultures, archaic social and religious institutions were breaking down under the pressure of more complex forms of economic and political activity, associated with the urban revolution and the territorial expansion of new imperial states. In all cases, apparent economic and political advances were mixed with serious social disorders, hardship, and the loss of traditional religious moorings.

In this process of transformation, new philosophical and religious solutions were sought and attained by the formative thinkers whose teachings still lie behind the institutions and ways of life characteristic of the major civilizations of the world today. Socrates, the prophets of Israel, Confucius, and the Buddha were among the great innovators who, in distinctive ways, offered systematic critiques of the older values and redefined the meaning of existence and the nature of man and society within a more universal, transcendent framework, which became the basis for new cultural reconstruction.

In India during the seventh and sixth centuries B.C. there were significant developments in agricultural productivity, urban commerce based on a money economy, a new and increasingly affluent middle class, and the beginnings of rational bureaucracy. But these advances were offset by protracted power struggles between warring states for territory and economic resources. They resulted in the uprooting and extirpation of political minorities and the corrosion of the traditional forms of communal solidarity and religious legitimation—a situation that provoked a deep spiritual malaise and intensified earlier innovating speculations about the meaning of the self and the world. The value of all worldly activities and of life itself was questioned with unparalleled sharpness.

The new religious and philosophical teachers in India—most significantly those whose doctrines are embodied in the Upaniṣads, in Buddhism, and in Jainism—began their reconstructive enterprise quite paradoxically with a radical devaluation of the phenomenal world and the simultaneous affirmation of an otherworldly realm of absolute transcendence which alone is worthy to be the goal of all human striving. The normative religious problem emerged as one of personal salvation from bondage to phenomenal existence. The process of salvation was defined by a transmigrational metaphysic which forms an almost airtight theodicy: the soul (*ātman*) undergoes an endless cycle of rebirth (*saṃsāra*), in which the individual assumes a new physical form and status in the next life depending on the ethical quality of deeds (*karma*) in this life. The individual may attain salvation from this process by practicing the Yoga—an autonomous, ascetic discipline of the inner self, of body, mind, and motivations, designed to eliminate the karmic source of the transmigratory process.

Although this basic metaphysic was presupposed by many of the major schools, there were sharp sectarian disputes on the theoretical particulars. This conflict was heightened by disagreements over the prevalent theory of social stratification, the caste system. From the *brāhmaṇ* perspective all means of salvation were contained in the Vedas, and the law of *karma* was tied rigidly to the caste system: one is born in a particular caste as a result of deeds in the former life, and conformity to caste rules is the precondition of salvation or at least improvement in caste status in the next life. The non-*brāhmaṇic* schools, like Buddhism and Jainism, denied the ultimacy of the Vedas and the ritual significance of caste. Their messages of salvation were preached openly. Admission was based on personal conversion, usually without ascriptive limitations of caste, class, or sex. Their teachings found rich soil among upwardly mobile urban commercial groups, who held that both soteriological and social status should be based on achievement criteria rather than on hereditary right.

The Buddha and his teachings. Efforts to reconstruct the life and teachings of the Buddha and the institutions of the earliest Buddhist community run aground on many refractory critical problems. But the Buddha's life story, overlaid in its many versions with legend and myth, is nevertheless persuasive in basic outline. The historical Buddha ("enlightened one"), named Siddhārtha Gautama, was born a prince of an indigenous Indian clan in northern India about 550 B.C. In his early youth he displayed unusual sensitivity to the pressing enigmas of human existence. His family endeavored unsuccessfully to distract him from these concerns and to insulate him from the signs of human finitude—suffering, contingency, and death. But at the age of 29, still preoccupied with the ultimate questions, he left to search for a means of salvation. For some years he tested and rejected radical physical asceticism and abstract philosophy. Finally, in a single night of intensive meditation he achieved enlightenment and evolved his own unique diagnosis and teaching (Dharma). He then embarked on a missionary career, preaching his message of salvation openly to all "without a closed fist." He formed an ever-widening community (Saṅgha) of mendicant disciples from all castes, including women and lay devotees, and after a long ministry he died at the age of 80.

The major forms of the tradition represent the Buddha as teaching an exoteric, practical Yoga which followed the so-called "middle path"—a mean between the extremes of bodily indulgence, self-mortification, and speculative philosophy. This is a qualitative, not merely an expedient, mean. It is based on the conviction that neither ritual manipulation of external physical forms—including radical asceticism (e.g., Jainism)—nor abstract intellectualism can touch the real core of the human problem—the habitual errors of the mind and the inward perversion of the will and motivational processes. The Buddha's unique diagnosis and soteriology are embodied classically in the "four noble truths." (1) All creaturely existence is marked by *duḥkha* ("pain," "anguish"), an agonized bondage to the meaningless cycle of rebirths amid a transitory flux which is impermanent (*anitya*) and without essential being (*anātman*). (2) The cause of this agony is ignorance (*avidyā*) of the illusory nature of phenomenal existence and particularly the pernicious notion of the eternality of the soul, which ironically perpetuates the desire (*tṛṣṇā*) for life. As individual consciousness is dissolving in death, this residual ignorance and desire once again—in an inexorable causal sequence—form the empirical self from heterogenous phenomenal elements and chain it to the process of rebirth. (3) The removal of ignorance about and desire for phenomenal life will break the causal sequence and so precipitate final salvation. (4) For this purpose the proper Yoga is the "eightfold path," an integral combination of ethics (*śīla*) and meditation (*samādhi*), which jointly purify the motivations and mind. This leads to the attainment of wisdom (*prajñā*), to enlightenment (*bodhi*), and to the ineffable Nirvāṇa ("blowing out"), the final release from the incarnational cycle and a mystical transcendence beyond all conceptualization.

The Yoga is radically autosoteriological—an autonomous performance by the self-reliant individual. It demands total commitment, adequately expressed only in the role of the mendicant monk who has abandoned the aspirations of the everyday world and has undertaken a life devoted to full-time pursuit of the religious goal. Although the lay householder might practice the Yoga and originally was not excluded from the ultimate goal (the Buddha said only that it was "harder" for the householder to attain Nirvāṇa), it was inevitable that full spiritual perfection should be dominantly reserved for those whose deeper concern for salvation was institutionally defined by complete monastic commitment.

The rudiments of the teaching outlined here give only the barest suggestion of its innovatory and therapeutic potential. Always foremost is the paradigmatic grandeur of spiritual transcendence and renewal represented by the Buddha himself. His withdrawal from the givenness of the everyday world and his negation of it was the first step in gaining a new critical leverage over it. The principal symbols of world rejection and negation are not pessimism or nihilism. They negate and displace the archaic religious practices and forms of social organization in the name of a transcendent goal that places all men in a universal context of religious meaning through which the whole human situation can be comprehended and managed. Correlatively, it is possible to inculcate universal standards of conduct which establish expectations of interpersonal and intergroup relationships without particularistic, ascriptive limits of space or time.

The initial act of conversion, expressed in commitment to the Buddha, Dharma, and Saṅgha, not only allows for the dramatization of personal dissatisfaction with one's present life situation but projects a long-range program of spiritual recovery and maturation, including the cathectic transformation of the whole personality and the internalization of new values, which can be publicly acted out. Enlightenment is not only the result of incessant meditation on the truths and on the transitoriness of life, which will ultimately eradicate desire for it; it requires motivational purification through the practice of universal virtues, in addition to monastic poverty and continence, love (*maitrī*), and compassion (*karuṇā*) toward all living creatures, the elimination of a host of specific vices, and the obligation to promote friendship and concord. Within the community the ritual divisions of caste and all ascriptive divisions are obliterated before the universal force of love and the knowledge of the common condition of all men.

The Saṅgha. The solidarity of the earliest mendicant community was centered on the charisma and teaching of the Buddha himself, but the growing number of converts, the addition of lay devotees, and the settlement of a number of cenobitic communities around major cities in the Ganges valley forced the routinization of discipline and teaching. By the end of the Buddha's long ministry the Saṅgha was differentiated along several characteristic lines; most important was the class distinction between the monastic elite and the lay devotees. The tradition relates that after the Buddha's death a council was convened at Rājagṛha to regularize the teachings and monastic rule. The actual accomplishments of the council are uncertain, but it is apparent that a substantial body of the scriptures found in the present Theravādin canon and the residuals of other early schools already existed in oral form— including the nuclear disciplinary code (Prātimokṣa) of the later full monastic rule (Vinaya) and much of the soteriological teaching embodied in the Buddha's discourses (Sūtra). The major ceremonials of communal life were in practice, most importantly the bimonthly *uposatha*—a congregational assembly and confessional recital of the Prātimokṣa. As a result of the increasing generosity of the laity, the various monastic centers soon possessed extensive properties and dwelling places, with a highly differentiated system of specialized roles for administration and teaching.

By the third century B.C. the Saṅgha was in the process of sectarian proliferation, ultimately forming a number of schools, each of which emphasized different philosophical and doctrinal features of the received tradition. Their distinctive doctrinal positions were embodied in commentaries on the early teachings, finally forming—to take the Theravādin case—the Abhidhamma—the third part of the threefold Pāli canon (Tipiṭaka). According to uncertain tradition, a second council was convened at Vaiśālī one hundred years after the Buddha's death. There a series of sharp disagreements about the inner meaning of the teaching, the status of the laity, and the rigors of the monastic rule brought on the "great schism," a split chiefly between the conservative forerunners of the Theravāda and the more liberal Mahāsaṅghika, whose doctrines were significantly related to the rise of Mahāyāna Buddhism in the following centuries.

The apparent failure of the first councils to unite the Saṅgha has to be gauged against the basic values of the teaching itself, the nature of monastic constitution, and the conception of internal authority. The early Saṅgha was never a "church" under one centralized control or subscriptionist orthodoxy. At Rājagṛha, after the Buddha's death (and supposedly at his own request), the idea of routine patriarchal succession was deliberately rejected. In keeping with auto-soteriology, the primary function of the monastic rule was to protect the spiritual independence of each monk. It contains typically stringent rules and penalties dealing with sexual offenses, abuse of material possessions, and interpersonal disturbances and outlines legal–rational procedures for dealing with internal disagreements. But the overriding aim was to provide optimum conditions for pursuit of the ultimate religious goal, not to enforce ecclesiastical unity. Issues were discussed openly and decided by majority vote, with all ordained monks having equal franchise. The constitution of a monastery allowed free dissent in "good faith," and if controversies could not be resolved, the rules governing schism allowed the dissenters to depart and form their own monastic center. Formal routinization finally included a status system based upon degree of spiritual perfection, knowledge and capacity to instruct, and seniority reckoned in a sequence of three decades from the date of ordination. There was a preceptor system for the guidance of novice monks, but the authority of the senior monks was in principle strictly advisory. The novice joined the Saṅgha by confessing his inward spiritual intention, but not within the framework of a system of bureaucratic office-charisma, as in the Roman and Byzantine churches, or of monastic obedience, such as we find in the Benedictine rule.

Social and political ethic.   For the laity and for all secular spheres of social reality, the leadership of the Saṅgha developed a highly differentiated secondary soteriology, based on a merit-making ethic rationally oriented to the economic and political needs of the urban mercantile and artisan classes. In joining the Saṅgha, the lay devotees promised to conform to the "five precepts" (no killing, stealing, lying, adultery, or drinking of alcoholic beverages). By support of the monastic order and by their personal morality they could accumulate karmic merit and so be assured of better rebirth opportunities. By contrast with the archaic sacrificial rites which still persisted, Buddhism provided less-expensive religious media. The Buddhist laity were expected to make donations to the Saṅgha, but the soteriology stressed the autonomy of the self as the sacrificial agent.

In the Theravādin Sigālovāda Sutta, sometimes called the householder's Vinaya, the layman is exhorted to pursue a lifetime of ethical self-discipline, for the sake of a well-being in "this world and the next," including the maximization of economic efficiency. He must eliminate self-indulgent and wasteful vices which impair effective economic action: sensuality, hate, fear, and slothfulness. Undesirable business associates include those who lack self-discipline and waste human and physical resources. Slave trading and other dehumanizing practices are prohibited. The householder must train his children in socially useful occupations and carefully observe contractually defined ethical relationships with his family, servants, and business associates.

The lay theory of social stratification undercut caste criteria because it denied the religious ultimacy of the *brāhmaṇs*, the Vedas, and the ritual significance of caste divisions. The Buddha is represented as arguing that caste has no inherent sanctity because it arose historically as the result of occupational differentiation—"quite naturally, and not otherwise." The social status of women was much improved, and in theory women and men were equals within the Saṅgha. Political theory, though basically patrimonial, asserts that the power of the state is based on a historically evolved contractual relationship between the king and the people which requires that the king earn his keep by his executive skill and moral example.

By the end of the third century B.C., popular lay piety had begun to find its center of gravity in a semitheistic cult entailing the merit-making worship (*pūjā*) of saintly relics and of the Buddha himself—now exalted to a supramundane plane and surrounded with symbols of his previous incarnations. The places of cultic worship (*stūpas* and *caityas*) signify the pressure of the laity for religious means increasingly remote from the monastic autosoteriology. These cultic developments were accompanied by civilizing rationalizations of many indigenous archaic resources which facilitated missionary activity—myths, cosmologies, gods, demons, heavens, hells, and magic—all subjected to the overarching power of the Buddha and the monastic order and tied to higher educational and socializing aims.

From the viewpoint of the expanding state in ancient India, Buddhism was from the very beginning a potentially valuable asset. The organized clergy—sworn to poverty—was a powerful and relatively inexpensive medium for building social solidarity where traditional collectivities had been disrupted by force, and they could assist in more subtle forms of pacifist teaching where force was impractical. This was also particularly meaningful in an expanding economy dependent on a stable and pacified environment for efficient production and exchange. The Saṅgha could provide the legitimation for political leaders and bureaucrats who either did not have suitable ascriptive status or desired to increase their innovatory power against some traditional elite.

The supportive relationship between Buddhism and the developing state reached a climax in the third century B.C., with an event which determinatively affected the subsequent history of Buddhism. The expansion of the state of Magadha, which had begun in the sixth century B.C., culminated in the founding of the Mauryan empire, a patrimonially governed centralized bureaucracy which dominated the subcontinent. The third ruler of this empire, King Aśoka, who acceded to the throne about 270 B.C., converted to Buddhism after completing the military consolidation of his territorial holdings. He then issued a pacifistic ideology grounded on the universal achievement-based principles common to the Buddhist lay ethic and most of the other Indian religions. This ecumenical ideology, along with an autobiography of his own spiritual transformation from military coercer to pious layman, was inscribed on stones and pillars and promulgated by emissaries throughout the Indian subcontinent and beyond. Its goal was clearly not only to legitimize the innovatory authority of the royal house but also to provide a wider cultural base for a more viable social system. It exhorts all men in the empire to cooperative pursuit of socially and economically efficient virtues. It discourages the practice of archaic sacrificial and magical ceremonials, thus undercutting traditional religious customs that reinforced politically troublesome local solidarities and supported an entrenched class of archaic religious practitioners. The ideology makes no specific mention of *brāhmaṇ* caste criteria for social integration, urging only that *brāhmaṇs* be shown the same respect as other religious leaders.

Although Aśoka did not institute Buddhism as the state religion, he promoted Buddhist missionary movements, which spilled over the borders into other lands—most importantly into southeast Asia. Several of his edicts indicate that he tried to unify the Saṅgha and stem schismatic tendencies which threatened its effective support of the goals of the state. He may have instituted a doctrinal reform by convening a third council at the capital city of Pāṭaliputra, which then became the basis for the Theravādin orthodoxy that was carried to Ceylon and the southeast Asian mainland. But sectarian schisms in India persisted, for the doctrinal and institutional reasons noted above.

Within fifty years after Aśoka's death the Mauryan empire collapsed under a multitude of pressures—barbarian invasions, economic decline, internal political conflict, and a resurgence of *brāhmaṇ* power. Subsequently, the ascriptive principles of the caste system were further rationalized. The king's responsibility was increasingly tied to the maintenance of the social order in accordance with caste criteria, thus forming the permanent social base for the emergence of normative Hinduism. The specifics of Buddhist nonascriptive social theory remained only peripherally influential—allowing for occasional nontraditional legitimation of invading monarchs and their courts—most notably among the Greeks, the Śakas and Pahlavas, and the Kuṣāṇas.

The Mahāyāna. Mahāyāna Buddhism did not emerge identifiably as a self-conscious movement with its own distinctive literature and institutions until the first century A.D. Its earliest *sutras*—held to contain the true and restored teachings of the Buddha—cannot be dated with certainty before the beginning of the Christian era, and there is some indication of Western and Iranian influence on their doctrine and symbolism. However, many prominent Mahāyāna principles have their roots in the issues raised at the second council of Vaiśālī, which culminated in the schism of the Mahāsaṅghika school. Its doctrines and those developed by other forerunners of the Mahāyāna represented liberalizing solutions to cumulative tensions which had been present within the Saṅgha almost from the very beginning. Particularly controversial were the hardened dichotomy between the laity and the monastic elite and disagreements regarding the right of lay access to the full religious goal.

The issues at stake centered on the traditional conservative conception of monastic perfection, ideally embodied in the Arhant, the fully perfected monk who attains complete enlightenment only at the end of the long and arduous pursuit of self-perfection demanded by the Yoga. This ideal was held by liberals to be a "selfish" distortion of the original teaching, violating the Buddha's compassion for all men. In its place they introduced a new conception of spiritual perfection—the ideal of the Bodhisattva (being of enlightenment). The term, which was originally used chiefly to denote previous incarnations of the historical Buddha, was universalized. In its new configuration it means one who, although worthy of Nirvāṇa, sacrifices this ultimate satisfaction in order to help all sentient creatures with acts of love and compassion. All men are inherently capable of filling this role. It is not necessarily a monastic category, and the Arhant is lower on the scale of perfection.

This innovation significantly undercut the rigidities of the class distinction between monk and layman. Although monasticism continued as a central institution, the Bodhisattva ideal opened the soteriology to new symbolic forms, beliefs, and practices. It facilitated popular diffusion and provided the basis for new theistic and philosophical developments, reflected in the principal Mahāyāna *sutras* and schools. Equally important was the doctrinal affirmation of the divinity of the Buddha. He is not only the historical teacher; he is an omnipresent deity, an eternal spiritual being and force. This allowed for further rationalizations of the popular theistic movements.

The Perfection of Wisdom *sutras* are among the most important theoretical formulations of Mahāyāna soteriology. The Bodhisattva's distinctive marks are loving compassion and wisdom. This wisdom and its perfection are related not only to self-sacrificing love but also to a more accurate understanding of the real nature of Nirvāṇa. It is not an otherworldly goal, in polarity with the phenomenal world. This is a Hīnayāna distortion, which ironically reduces Nirvāṇa to an empirical spatiotemporal object and reinforces the desire inimical to salvation. Nirvāṇa is beyond all phenomenal and conceptual polarities—void and empty (*śūnya*). As one approaches inward realization of this truth and experiences enlightened insight, all distinctions between Nirvāṇa and the world are obliterated. One lives with pure, egoless compassion.

The "emptiness" motif in the Wisdom *sutras* was developed by the philosopher Nāgārjuna, founder of the Mādhyamika school. He evolved a negational logic designed to break the inveterate tendency of the finite human mind to impose spatiotemporal categories on the supreme spiritual ideal. The other major philosophical school—the Vijñānavāda (or Yogācāra)—based its teachings on *sutras* developed around idealistic conceptions: all objective perceptions are illusory projections of the mind. Salvation is achieved by exhausting the source of dualistic consciousness and sensory perception through a Yoga which leads to union with the purity of being.

The philosophical schools reached extraordinary heights of exaltation and subtlety. They liberated the mystical ideal and soteriology from their scholastic bondage, attracted many intellectuals, and provided new principles for theoretical development of Mahāyāna universalism. But the bulk of Mahāyāna practice found its popular social base through theistic means. The heavens were filled with saving Buddhas and Bodhisattvas, who transferred their own merit to the believer in response to prayer, provided richly differentiated objects for cultic worship, and satisfied a wide range of personal affective needs. Theistic piety inspired important artistic achievements, beginning perhaps as early as the second century B.C., in the friezes of the Bhārhut and Sānchī topes, and culminating in the Buddha statuary produced by the Mathurā and Gandhāra schools—the latter clearly influenced by Greco–Roman art forms.

Among many efforts to systematize this theistic profusion one of the most important was the formulation of the Trikāya ("three bodies") Buddhology. Here the Buddha exists in his eternal essence as a supreme heavenly deity and in worldly manifestations. He is both the absolute ground of being and the actional agent of salvation. He interpenetrates all discrete phenomena, assuring the universal presence of the Buddha-nature among all creatures, without distinction. This theory provided an integral basis for formal and functional differentiation of symbolic resources, and it was at the same time a dynamic metaphysic which could be adjusted to new social and cultural pressures.

Within the immensely rich theistic literature of Mahāyāna there are several important *sutras* which became the basis of the most popular cults and schools in China and Japan. The Lotus of the Good Law purports to reveal the ultimate teaching of the Buddha Śākyamuni, the transcendent father of all worlds, whose love bridges all finite limitations. The devotee is saved by faith in this *sutra* itself. There is a suggestion of sectarian exclusiveness in the dogma that this *sutra* alone embodies the *ekayāna* ("one vehicle")—the only efficacious means of salvation, which thus exhausts all other doctrines.

More radical are the Land of Bliss *sutras*. Here Amitābha Buddha presides over a heavenly paradise—the "pure land"—available to the faithful through the power of his grace. Eschatological and sectarian motifs appear, stressing the utter uselessness of all techniques of self-salvation in a world of utter degeneracy and emphasizing the need to rely absolutely on Amitābha.

Though Mahāyāna produced little in the way of systematic economic or political theory, there are some exceptions which deserve mention because of their demonstrable influence in China and Japan. The Exposition of Vimalakīrti glorifies the virtues of a paradigmatic layman who not only pursues a life of rational economic gain and sophisticated worldly well-being but simultaneously achieves a spiritual perfection excelling that of the most distinguished monks. In the area of political theory the Sūtra of the Excellent Golden Light, written some time prior to the expansion of the Gupta empire (319–540), outlines a modified doctrine of divine kingship. The king is called *devaputra* ("son of the gods"), a designation current in the Hindu theory of kingship, but he has no insulated cultic status. He stands under the Buddha's law and is obliged to promote universal peace and social order or by judgment of the gods forgo his right to rule—obviously a sanction for revolt. The patrimonial theory of kingship remained dominantly contractual. Only rarely did the incarnational Bodhisattva principle lend itself to caesaropapist or theocratic pretensions in India. Problems of social stratification receive only passing attention. Caste is presupposed as an institutional reality, and one looks in vain for a systematic critique comparable to that found in the scriptures of the early schools.

The missionary diffusion of Mahāyāna was greatly facilitated by a remarkable principle of rationalization which allowed for almost unlimited adaptability to given conditions. This was the idea of the Buddha's *upāyakauśalya* ("skill-in-means") —the ability to adjust teachings and institutions to the needs of all sorts and conditions of men through any means available. It was identified with the Buddha's universal love, and, combined with the conviction that all phenomenal forms are illusory and void, it allowed for expedient use of new techniques to further the message of salvation. It cut through traditional boundaries, textual literalism, orthodox formulations, and monastic regulations with remarkable innovatory power and carried the teaching forward, however adumbrated and transformed.

Tantric Buddhism. The assimilative diversity of popular Mahāyāna did not mark the end of the development of Buddhism in India but rather led almost imperceptibly to a metamorphosis. Beginning recognizably in the sixth and seventh centuries A.D. there took place an upsurge of a vast new repertoire of magical, ritualistic, and erotic symbolism, which formed the basis for what is commonly called Tantric Buddhism. Its distinguishing institutional characteristic was the communication through an intimate master–disciple relationship of doctrines and practices contained in the Buddhist Tantras (esoteric texts) and held to be the Buddha's most potent teachings, reserved for the initiate alone.

In content, Tantric Buddhism is fused in many areas almost indistinguishably with Mahāyāna doctrines and archaic and magical Hinduism. Cryptic obscurities were deliberately imposed on the texts to make them inscrutable except to the gnostic elite. But it took a number of identifiable forms, the most dramatic of which was Vajrayāna ("thunderbolt vehicle"). Vajrayāna had its metaphysical roots in the supposition that the dynamic spiritual and natural powers of the universe are driven by interaction between male and female elements, of which man himself is a microcosm. Its mythological and symbolic base was in a pantheon of paired deities, male and female, whose sacred potency, already latent in the human body, was magically evoked through an actional Yoga of ritualistic meditations, formulas (*mantra*), and gestures (*mudrā*) and frequently through sexual intercourse, which occasionally included radical antinomian behavior. The inward vitality of the sacred life force is realized most powerfully in sexual union, because there nonduality is experienced in full psychophysical perfection.

The philosophical justification for these developments was derived from adaptations of Yogācāra and Mādhyamika theory: since the objective phenomenal world is fundamentally identical with the spiritual universe of emptiness or is at most an illusory projection of the mind, the conclusion was drawn that all forms are not only devoid of real moral distinctions but, also, may serve as expedient means to an undifferentiated spiritual end: the overcoming of the illusory sense of duality between the phenomenal and spiritual world. For the adept it is not only necessary to say that there is no good or evil; it must be proved in an active way. The traditional morality is violated as behavior formerly regarded as reprehensible is found to speed the realization of nonduality.

Many Tantric sects practiced these rites only symbolically and in certain cases—most notably in the Sahajayāna ("innate vehicle") school—produced works of great ethical exaltation. The Mantrayāna ("true-word vehicle") school, which became influential in China and Japan, remained a rational paragon of restrained magico-religious esotericism. The social origins and class stratification of Tantric Buddhism are almost impossible to determine. Tantric Hinduism, also, was in vogue during this period, and its popularity suggests that a wide-ranging democracy of magical esotericism had broken through stereotyped pressures resulting from the development of state-controlled orthodox institutions during the Gupta era. In the sixth and seventh centuries there were sporadic persecutions of Buddhism, which may have promoted esoteric withdrawal.

After the tenth century A.D. Buddhism began a perceptible decline, for reasons which are still far from clear. The Mahāyāna philosophical schools became increasingly preoccupied with abstruse theoretical issues and hairsplitting polemics. In time theistic Mahāyāna and Tantric Buddhism became hardly distinguishable from the increasingly luxuriant garden of Hinduism. The great medieval Hindu philosopher Śaṅkara successfully incorporated the strong points of Buddhist philosophy in a decisive synthesis. Buddhist monasteries, schools, and cults began to lose their popular foundation, and we can see the slow but sure absorption of its symbolism, intellectual leadership, and laity into the richness of what Étienne Lamotte has called *l'hindouisme ambiant*. The Buddha was represented as one among many incarnations of the Hindu god Viṣṇu. The final blow came with the Turko–Muslim invasions in the twelfth century. Offended by monasticism in principle, shocked by polytheistic Mahāyāna and Tantrism, and coveting the wealth of the monasteries, the invaders systematically extirpated Buddhism by force. It was not to return as a significant institutional reality for eight hundred years.

Diffusion of Buddhism

Despite their stark contrast in doctrine and practice, the divergent missionary movements of Theravāda Buddhism into the lands of southeast Asia and of Tantric Buddhism into Tibet hide similarities which reveal the deeper potency of Buddhist universalism. In both cases Buddhism became the official state "church" and provided the religious base not only for evolutionary advances but also for long-lasting and relatively stable societies. In both cases Buddhism was introduced under favorable ecological, cultural, and political circumstances by rulers who controlled relatively small, homogeneous land areas and polities grounded on primitive and archaic religions. They saw in Buddhism an opportunity to innovate and to provide a broader religious base for legitimation and social integration.

With respect to the church–state relationship however, in Tibet this evolutionary movement finally took the form of a theocracy based on a unique rationalization of Mahāyāna and Tantric incarnational theology; while in southeast Asia the Theravāda—with its class division between celibate monk and layman and its highly routinized, orthodox version of the classical tradition—was able to maintain a structural distinction between church and state which had important consequences for later institutional developments.

Southeast Asia

In coordination with Aśoka's political and ideological universalism, Theravāda missions had penetrated southeast Asia by the end of the third century B.C., most importantly in Ceylon, where Theravāda was instituted as the official religion of the state. Ceylon became the chief citadel for Theravādin orthodoxy and its continued diffusion throughout the mainland. In all cases the introduction of Theravāda facilitated the development of more highly differentiated polities by freeing societal resources from their embeddedness in limited traditional and ascriptive ties. Moreover, the two-class system had certain advantages. The king was a lay "defender of the faith," working cooperatively with the superior charismatic and educative power of the monastic order, which provided state chaplains, missionaries, and teachers who crossed traditional boundary lines and created a new cultural milieu. The specialized performance of these tasks by the Saṅgha and the structural distinction between church and state also allowed for the formation of secular bureaucracies.

This rational *rapprochement* between the secular authorities of the state and the monastic leadership of Theravāda in southeast Asia did not take place without significant changes in the values and institutions of the ancient Indian Saṅgha, particularly in those factors which had precipitated its earlier sectarian instability. The radical soteriological independence of the individual monk was placed under routine controls by the introduction of a hierarchy of scholastic distinctions that marked out a chronological path through which the monk progressed toward the ultimate goal. This included grades of perfection based on seniority and routine acquisition of appropriate knowledge. Many of these modifications already appear in later portions of the Vinaya and in the Theravādin Abhidhamma and commentaries. This provided more real space and time for the individual monk to perform worldly tasks without being stigmatized as a spiritual weakling. In addition, in Ceylon the structure of monastic authority was redefined in a way which sets it off strikingly from the early mandate interdicting all forms of centralized ecclesiastical control. We find new rationalizations of the legitimacy of patriarchal authority. A uniform line of charismatic successors to the Buddha's authority was used to justify hierarchical control of the monastic orders, approaching that of a unified church backed up by the power of the state. Finally, a doctrinal orthodoxy was established. The key text is the Kathāvatthu, reputedly promulgated under King Aśoka's supervision and contained in the Abhidhamma. It simply declares 252 non-Theravādin teachings "heretical," with minimal discussion of the issues at stake. These relatively new dogmas and lines of authority now allowed for the definition of other essential forms. The councils at Rājagṛha, Vaiśālī, and Pāṭaliputra were approved as officially binding. At the fourth Theravādin council, in 25 B.C., the threefold canon of scriptures was established as the basis for a uniform ecclesiastical law.

In this newly stabilized form Theravāda was located on solid institutional and doctrinal ground, from which it could more effectively serve the goals of the state. The "four noble truths," the precepts, and the other rational socioeconomic and political teachings set generalized standards for interpersonal and intergroup relations at all levels of society.

In Ceylon the Saṅgha was partially fused with existing feudal institutions, forming a monastic landlordism pre-empting more than one-third of the land. But it also taught necessary technical skills and norms and provided a wider sphere for social consensus and the religious legitimation of the polity.

On the mainland—to take Thai as an example —the monarchs of some of the early Thai kingdoms which emerged in the mid-thirteenth century supported the Theravādin Saṅgha not only for internal integration but also for the acculturation of conquered non-Thai groups. The structurally differentiated status of the Saṅgha later facilitated the formation of a civil bureaucracy, which became the basis for Thai administration up to modern times. Specialized departments were set up under the titular rule of royal princes, with the actual administration performed by civilian officials. The Saṅgha was headed by a state-appointed patriarch, who coordinated the activities of the Saṅgha with the needs of the state, maintaining an important sphere for the management of tensions and the mediation of conflicting pressures from both sides. Although hereditary ascription, including discriminatory laws and penalties, remained an important integrative principle, the system was considerably opened to individual achievement because access to the civilian bureaucracy and the religious hierarchy was based on free education, provided by village monks. In addition, all young males were expected (as they still are) to spend at least several months living as novices in training with the monastic community. In general the Theravādin system represented a qualitative advance over the primitive and archaic systems which preceded it.

Tibet

In Tibet, Buddhism provided equally important evolutionary guidance and ecclesiastical support, chiefly through the medium of Mahāyana and Tantric values and under cultural conditions which resulted in a unique synthesis. The economy was agricultural and pastoral, with little in the way of commercial exchange and mobility. The native religion was a primitive magical animism (Bönism), marked by a labyrinthian demonolatry and controlled by Bönist shamans, who specialized in manipulatory magic, necromancy, divination, and exorcism. In the early seventh century A.D. Yogācāra teaching was introduced to the royal court by the monarch of a newly formed patrimonial state, but it was not until the eighth century, when Tantric missionaries arrived from Bengal, that the real cultural breakthrough occurred. Tantric success was due in part to the inherent grass-roots appeal of its theistic cosmologies and magical practices to those already steeped in the native religion. But compared with Bönism it provided a more highly differentiated and psychologically liberating system of beliefs and practices. The literate Buddhist clergy were armed with a charisma which overwhelmed local chiefs, sorcerers, and demons alike. The native deities were subordinated to the superior power of the Buddhist pantheon, and in time ethical standards were at least partially reformed and universalized through the karmic theodicy. Typically, many primitive indigenous practices were assimilated and placed under a suitable socializing hierarchy. Religious resources soon included a wide range of additional Indian Mahāyāna and Hīnayāna materials, and the monasteries became centers for the systematic translation and study of texts.

Authority was maintained by patriarchal succession, and the noncelibate Vajrayāna tradition, with its sexual–sacramental rationale, encouraged the monks to take spouses. This resulted in the institution of a hereditary "monastic" elite, which undermined and finally destroyed the secular monarchy itself. By the thirteenth century Tibet was controlled by *lamas* ("elders"), who ruled from their fortified lamaseries and dominated all political, economic, and religious activities. Theocratic power was hardened by an alliance with the emerging Mongol empire.

However, with the collapse of the Mongol empire in the fourteenth century, the inner resources of Buddhism found new creative outlets and produced a remarkable reforming movement. The monk Tson-Kha-pa, who initiated this reform, emerges as a genuine prophetic figure. He was a specialist in Mādhyamika negational philosophy and in the rules of the Vinaya, and he aimed at the elimination of Vajrayāna abuses and the restoration of monastic celibacy, discipline, and rational ethics. He organized the Ge-lug-pa ("virtuous sect"), the "yellow church." The color yellow signified his purifying reforms against the Vajrayāna practices of the traditional "red church," which soon lost its position of political power.

The reassertion of monastic celibacy in combination with the theocratic principle of political organization precipitated another series of innovations in the fifteenth century. Since patriarchal authority could no longer be defined by hereditary succession, charismatic legitimacy was maintained through a unique rationalization of incarnational theory: each of the chief lamas in the clerical hierarchy was held to be a worldly incarnation of a divine Bodhisattva, reborn as an infant in a lay household shortly after the preceding lama died. His spirit transmigrated into the newborn child, whose legitimacy was determined through elaborate rites of divination. The child was then trained in the monastery, under rigorous supervision. Theocratic authority was distributed between the Dalai Lama, who served as temporal ruler, and the Panchen Lama, who was authoritative in all doctrinal matters.

The metaphysical base of this system was further routinized by an emanational theology in which an original creator Buddha (Ādibuddha) produced and controlled all subdeities and discrete empirical forms. This was not only a soteriological hierarchy but a paradigm for the organization of the state, representing the order of the ecclesiastical bureaucracy and the organic participation of various subsects and all the people in the spiritual power of the chief lamas.

China

The decisive factor affecting the history of Buddhism in China was its confrontation with the religious values and institutions of a high civilization that differed markedly from the ascetic, otherworldly orientation of Indian Buddhism. The Buddhist world view made its own unique contributions to Chinese culture, while at the same time undergoing acculturation—a process that produced a new if not always stable synthesis of Indian and Chinese values.

In China during the first century A.D., Buddhism was confined mainly to foreign communities in the northern commercial cities. The Buddha was worshiped popularly as one among many deities considered worthy of petition and propitiation, and it was not until the end of the second century, with the arrival of Mahāyāna missionaries and texts, that systematic propagation was undertaken. Buddhism's deeper values and institutions began to assume relatively clear definition and to find a social base among members of the gentry.

The penetration of Buddhism was enhanced by the severe political and economic disorders which occurred at the end of the Later Han dynasty (A.D. 25–220). In this situation of general social breakdown, Buddhism provided therapeutic answers to pressing questions about the meaning of the times and of life itself, unanswerable within the indigenous religious framework. Han Confucianism formed the basis for a highly rational political system, and its ethic had immense integrative strength. However, its cosmological metaphysic was designed to reinforce worldly institutions, obligations, and goals. Awareness of the meaning of the self and the world and of the ambiguities of life was sometimes profound, as with Mencius and Chuang-tzu, but self-reflection and inward cultivation were aimed at better performance of the *li* (proper social action), rather than at personal salvation.

Taoism, with its naturalistic mysticism, provided an important outlet for the socially induced tensions and the pressures of conventional civilization. Equally significant was the *hsüen-hsüeh* ("mysterious learning"), an esoteric gnosis with a comparatively sophisticated metaphysic. But *hsüen-hsüeh* appears as a metaphysical capstone to Confucianism; and cultic Taoism was dominantly shamanistic—providing magical techniques and recipes for immortality in this world, not the next. Buddhism was something very different. With its devaluation of phenomenal life and rich repertoire of otherworldly symbolism and soteriologies, it placed infinite worth on the legitimacy of personal striving for salvation at the cost of all worldly concerns. By comparison the indigenous religions and philosophies were eminently life-affirming and naturalistic.

The Buddhist monastery, however worldly in fact, served as the institutional setting for full-time pursuit of an otherworldly goal. Despite important similarities between them, the Buddhist monk and the Taoist recluse, the "retired gentleman," could not be mistaken for each other. Even more striking was the stark contrast between the monk and the ideal Confucian gentleman, the *chün-tzu*. The decisive and ultimately victorious opponents of Buddhism in China were the Confucian literati. Their categorical affirmation of the inherent value of the phenomenal world and of the need for clearly structured human obligations and rational social order was deeply violated by the ideal of the celibate, ascetic monk who abandons the world, his family, and the principle of filial piety for the sake of an unknown, incompre-

hensible reward. The monastic ideal was regarded by many Confucians as an immense threat to the family, to the state, and to every sacred value.

The social disturbances at the end of the Han dynasty extended into the period of the Three Kingdoms and Six Dynasties (220–589). In the early part of the fourth century there were a series of barbarian invasions and settlements in the north which provoked a mass migration of Han gentry to the south. This long-lasting cultural split was important for the subsequent development of Buddhism in China. In the north, amid the chaos of the times, Buddhism was a relatively calm oasis of religious and social stability. The Hunnic warlords found in Buddhism the means of religious legitimation and of establishing their own political identity on a wide cultural base which broke through traditional social fissures. The merit-making ethic and magical therapy were valuable for expiating past sins, gaining practical ends, and sanctioning desired social standards, which still remained profoundly Confucian in depth despite the decimation of the literati.

Under state sponsorship a systematic and remarkably disciplined translation of Buddhist texts was undertaken, introducing many new *sūtras* and commentaries, around which schools and cults began to form. Among the first were the T'ien-t'ai, based on the Lotus Sūtra, and the San-lun, which centered on the Perfection of Wisdom *sūtras* and Mādhyamika materials. Popular theistic cults included the worship of many Bodhisattvas. However, by the fifth century the entrenched status of the monastic orders—free from taxation and *corvée*—had resulted in internal abuses which, from the viewpoint of the state, destroyed their rational cultural and integrative functions. Many of the monasteries had accumulated vast wealth and properties. They were regarded as sanctuaries for those who wanted to avoid secular obligations —including the transfer of land titles to avoid taxation—and as hotbeds of immorality and political subversion. As a result, efforts were made to break the power of the Saṅgha and to place it more directly under state control. A caesaropapist fusion of church and state was contemplated by the emperor of the Northern Wei. It was suggested that he declare himself an incarnate Buddha and thus pre-empt the charismatic authority and power of the order. The Saṅgha was able to resist this effort because the northern dynasties were inherently too unstable for a theocratic synthesis.

More successful was the effort to control the Saṅgha by systematic reorganization and occasional persecution. A clerical bureaucracy in the Confucian pattern was superimposed on the monastic orders to guarantee rational internal regulation; and persecutions initiated in A.D. 446 and 574 deprived the monasteries of much of their property, wealth, and personnel. However, these acts of coercion had important consequences for the development of the Pure Land cult—intensifying the emphasis on eschatological symbolism and the need for salvation through faith in Amitābha's grace alone and deepening its social grounding and universalism.

In the south the dynasties remained Chinese, and political and economic conditions were more stable. The primary cultural and ideological leadership remained dominantly in the hands of the Confucian literati, although Neo-Taoism was strongly represented at court. The leading Buddhist monks were for the most part learned, Confucian-trained intellectuals prepared to deal with Taoist and Confucian teachings in depth. They deliberately sought to maintain the political independence of the Saṅgha, while at the same time synthesizing and enrichening its soteriology in an endeavor to meet the spiritual and social needs of the laity. This independence of mind and synthetic flexibility are best typified by Hui-yüan (334–416). His monastery was a richly Sinified center of Buddhist–Confucian teaching. He was both an expert in the Confucian *li*—especially the mourning rites—and the traditional founder of the Pure Land school. In order to stabilize the lay ethic, he stressed the moral efficacy of the karmic metaphysic and insisted that the laity observe the five relationships and the law of land. Paradoxically, his rational accommodation of Buddhist teaching to Confucian norms was mixed with a strong sense of the independent dignity of the monk in contrast to the claims of the state cult. With remarkable courage he refused to conform to the traditional court ritual venerating the sacredness of the emperor. In a superb quasi-prophetic treatise entitled "A Monk Does Not Bow Down Before a King," he argued that the monk does not lack loyalty or filial piety but has a higher loyalty to the universal Buddhist law, to which all men are subject.

On the whole, however, the bifurcation between the soteriological status of monk and layman prevented the formation of a principle of secular or lay social criticism. Lay patrons were expected to conform humbly to the given political values of the state, and in the last analysis the Saṅgha's power in both the north and south was dependent on the attitude of the patrimonial monarch, which might range from pious support to savage persecution, depending on utilitarian need or personal whim.

The conquest of the south and the unification of China in A.D. 589 under the Sui dynasty was followed by a deliberate effort on the part of the Sui rulers to use the three major religions coordinately to attain a higher level of cultural unity. Buddhism not only supplied the religious imagery but also the ideology behind the conquests of the founder of the Sui. He deliberately drew on the Buddhist traditions about King Aśoka and justified the use of force by infusing it with cultic imagery: ". . . we regard the weapons of war as having become like the offerings of incense and flowers presented to the Buddha. . . ." Also of value was the psychological conditioning of the army through Buddhist-inspired emphasis on the otherworldly paradise and the trivial consequences of bodily wounds and death itself.

The Buddhist monasteries, patronized by wealthy aristocratic families, were important links between upper and lower status groups. They implemented a pietistic economic justice by distributing the wealth among the poor—a rational contribution in a time of low economic mobility. State supervision was tight. Monks were required to hold government-approved certificates of ordination and to submit to the supervision of a state-appointed Vinaya master.

In this situation of new political stability, which extended into the T'ang dynasty (A.D. 618–907), Buddhism underwent a remarkable institutional flowering. The T'ang capital was a great center of Sino-Buddhist art and ceremonial, gilding the power of the royal Son of Heaven with suitable charismatic and aesthetic beauty. The provinces and villages were dominated by Buddhist temples and staffed with clergy who tended to the personal affairs of the faithful, simultaneously reinforcing wider social solidarity.

By the eighth century the diffusion of Buddhism had in many ways broken through many of the old particularisms and created a relatively unified Buddhist culture, moderating the severity of the ferocious penal codes and promoting many charitable works. The major Buddhist philosophical schools—now emerging in full strength—provided varied outlets for personal choice and intellectual and soteriological satisfaction. These schools did not develop primarily out of institutional schism or sectarian dissent. Instead, they were formed around the teachings of one or more of the Indian *sūtras,* commentaries, and doctrinal systems expounded in China by a master and his designated successors. Confronted as the scholars were with the immense profusion of source materials, their practical goal was to reconcile and harmonize the texts. Some of the schools were based dominantly on the literature of the major Indian philosophical schools, Mādhyamika and Vijñānavāda. But others, like T'ien-t'ai and Hua-yen, had no specific Indian institutional counterpart except that implied by the existence of their key *sūtras,* around which they catalogued the other sources. Membership in the philosophical schools was necessarily limited to a relatively select literate group, although T'ien-t'ai had an extensive lay following, and Pure Land —for the reasons noted above—was inherently capable of wide popular diffusion.

The most remarkable synthesis of Chinese and Indian values was achieved in the Meditation school of Ch'an (Zen). While it was based on the autosoteriological principles of yogic action, its leadership developed a unique meditative technique, which stressed practical, nondiscursive, and naturalistic media for attaining enlightenment. Its teaching was conveyed through a master–disciple relationship founded rigidly on the principle of patriarchal succession, but the school split into two main sects in the seventh century. The Ts'ao-tung emphasized a gradual approach, including routine textual study in the traditional fashion, while the Lin-chi adopted an approach in which all residuals of abstract intellectualism, received texts, and dogmas were abandoned in favor of new techniques. Most notable was the "public case" (*kōan* in Japanese), a method of question and answer designed to shock the routine patterns of thought that inhibit intuitive insight and the realization of the Buddha nature latent in every man.

Although the Meditation school retained much of the traditional monastic discipline, the essential teaching was communicated largely without ecclesiastical or textual encumbrances. This proved helpful not only in facilitating missionary mobility but also in surviving persecutions which destroyed the edifices, property, and literature of the more traditional schools. The Meditation masters frequently required their disciples to do manual labor, and the antinomian potentials of the teaching were held in check by adherence to the Confucian ethic. In its practicality and its validation of the natural world by the very act of transcending it, there is much of native Chinese naturalism and mystical Taoism. The school exercised considerable influence on the arts and aesthetic values by stressing the inner spiritual depths of the natural form and act.

Buddhism reached its zenith in China during the eighth century. But in the latter part of the T'ang it began to weaken. The main factors in this decline were the rise of Taoist political power in the royal court and the renewed importance of Confucianism among the gentry, including the restoration of the bureaucratic examination system under new Confucian leadership. Internal rebellions and barbarian pressures on the frontiers contributed to the collapse of the great family systems on which Buddhism had relied. Equally important was the fact that once again the Buddhist temples and monasteries had become entrenched centers of irrational economic and political power, which from the viewpoint of the state outweighed their cultural contributions. In A.D. 845 a massive persecution was instituted during which—according to the Emperor Wu—over 44,000 temples and monasteries were demolished and their properties confiscated, releasing millions of acres of land and their laborers. Monks and nuns were compelled to return to productive lay occupations.

This disastrous deinstitutionalization of Buddhism in the late T'ang was capped in the Sung (960–1279) by the Neo-Confucian reform, which effectively broke the back of Buddhist intellectual pre-eminence in philosophy and placed Confucianism on a new and metaphysically satisfying base. It represents an attack on the Buddhist world view, while at the same time appropriating from Buddhism not only much of its deeper philosophical orientation but also a new concern for the individual and questions of personal meaning. In the philosophical perspective of the great Neo-Confucian thinker Chu Hsi (1130–1200), understanding leads to a salutary enlightenment. This new image of the Confucian sage encroached on the unique role of the Buddhist monk.

Specifically, the Neo-Confucian attack on Buddhism was in two directions. First, there was an assault on the idea that, since the world is in constant change and flux, it is nothing but meaningless suffering and illusion. On the contrary, all change shows order and permanence in the larger process if not in particular things. Second, there was an attack on the idea that the world is empty and that one should turn away from outer sensations and progressively realize the artificiality not only of the world but also of the mind's assertion of the independent reality of the world and the mind. On the contrary, instead of turning from the world, one must investigate its principles and discover its norms, as the basis for the active correction of worldly imperfection.

By the end of the Sung dynasty Buddhism lost much of its intellectual social grounding. The Mongols supported Tibetan Lamaism and Tantrism, as did the Manchus (1644–1911), for political reasons, but the long association of Buddhism with barbarian dynasties contributed to the general revulsion against it which characterized much of later Chinese intellectual thought. Monasticism continued, but under the closest government supervision. The Buddhist clergy were relegated to the service of popular religious needs and competed with the Taoist shamans for pre-eminence in magical therapy. Their main role was to pray for the souls of the dead, while the Taoists were specialists in the exorcism of demons and sickness. Individuals seeking their aid were not classified as Buddhists or Taoists but simply as Chinese consulting specialists who were essentially without congregations. A residue of Buddhist lay piety remained in several secret societies—most notably the White Lotus Society, which served largely as a low-level *Gemeinschaft* organization with little in the way of real devotional fervor or religious universalism.

Japan

Japan had not participated independently in the cultural revolutions of the first millennium B.C. For Japan, like Tibet and southeast Asia, this transition occurred much later, in the sixth and seventh centuries A.D., under the impact of Sino-Buddhist values and institutions imported from Korea.

At first Buddhism was valued primarily for its magical power and its prestige as the symbol of the great civilization of China. The real breakthrough to its deeper resources was initiated by one of the greatest figures in Japanese history, Prince Shōtoku (573–621). Shōtoku assumed the regency at a time when there was growing strife between the leading clans over imperial succession. He converted to Buddhism as a layman and, with the assistance of Korean monks, began to reconstruct his society on the broader ethical and cultural base provided by the new values. The innovatory significance of this conversion is suggested by a passage in one of the *sūtra* commentaries attributed to him: "The world is false— only the Buddha is true." In this ecstatic affirmation of the fundamental principle of world rejection, he appears to have taken the first step in the process of liberating his society from the burden of the archaic institutions which surrounded him.

His reconstructive enterprise was spelled out in a new ideology, embodied in a 17-article constitution —a fusion of Buddhist universalism and Confucian ethics.

Shōtoku actually ruled from the monastery, availing himself of its legitimation and the leverage provided by the monastic order. He sent embassies to China to bring back knowledge of Chinese civilization, which became the basis for the later Taika reform and codes based on T'ang law, land systems, and bureaucratic principles.

In the Nara period (709 to 784) Buddhist doctrine found institutional expression in newly imported schools, representing both Hīnayāna and Mahāyāna teachings, including the Mādhyamika (Sanron) and Vijñānavāda (Hossō). Buddhism dominated the religious life of the royal court and was patronized through the building of temples and monasteries and in other acts of merit-making piety. It provided important ceremonial media for reinforcing court solidarity. Significant contributions to state ideology were made by some of the more politically useful *sūtras:* The Lotus of the Good Law not only represented the unity of all forms of soteriological action in the "one vehicle" but also had a potential affinity for symbolizing national unity, which gave it a permanent place in Buddhist political theory. In 741 Emperor Shōmu ordered copies of the Sūtra of the Excellent Golden Light sent to all the provinces. He directed the building of provincial temples, staffed them with suitable personnel, and built a central shrine to house the immense statue of the Lochana Buddha. By the mid-eighth century Buddhism was the cultic center and metaphysical base of state authority.

However, the Saṅgha itself began to gain new political power—a process which culminated in an effort to institute a Buddhist theocracy under a master of the Hossō sect. This was finally blocked by opposing forces in the royal court, and at the close of the Nara and the beginning of the Heian period (794 to 1185) the Nara clergy was significantly discredited. Emperor Kammu deliberately undertook to dissociate the court from the Nara schools by moving the capital bodily to Kyoto and adopting the term *heian* ("peace," "tranquillity") to express his new political and cultural goals. He also encouraged the formation of a new Buddhist monastic order, under the leadership of Saichō (767–822), a reforming monk who had earlier withdrawn in disgust from the worldly meshes of Nara Buddhism. Saichō established his own charismatic and doctrinal independence by studying with T'ien-t'ai (Tendai) monks in China. He centered his teaching on the Lotus Sūtra and required his monks to undergo 12 years of study and discipline under the rules of the Vinaya. His specific social aim was to prepare them to assume positions of responsible leadership in joint support of the monastic order and the state.

With Kammu's death in A.D. 806, the new emperor asserted his own patrimonial independence by promoting a new teaching, expounded by Kūkai (Kōbō Daishi), a monk of aristocratic Japanese lineage who had studied in China and returned with Tantric doctrines culled from the Mantrayāna (Chen-yen) school. Kūkai, unquestionably a man of immense intellectual and artistic abilities, founded Shingon—the Japanese version of this school. Its esoteric teachings, rich ceremonial, and aesthetically satisfying symbolism appealed to the royal court. Shingon claimed to incorporate not only all the major Buddhist doctrines but also Confucianism, Taoism, and Brahmanism, forming a hierarchial system arranged in ten stages of perfection and capped by the esoteric mysteries. It thus provided an eclectic system of beliefs and practices capable of wide-ranging social penetration, which could be accommodated to the given social hierarchy through extension of the highest esoteric privileges to the elite. Shingon's synthetic potential also found one of its most important expressions in "dual" Shinto, in which Shinto gods were designated Bodhisattvas in an effort to form a unified cultic framework.

The syncretic power and popularity of Shingon moved Saichō and his successor, Ennin (794–964), to institute a Tendai esotericism, based chiefly on Ennin's studies in China. But Tendai itself was victimized by a sectarian disruption stemming principally from a dispute over the right of patriarchal succession which developed when the emperor selected a blood relative of the aristocratic Kūkai as abbot of the order. The conflict produced one of the most tragic periods in the history of Japanese Buddhism. The two camps not only split into hostile religious sects but also, in coordination with dominant clan-based feudal developments, formed fortresses of warrior-monks, who engaged in violent internecine warfare. During the medieval period this became a widespread characteristic. These hostilities were exacerbated by the fact that personal prestige and political status depended jointly on education in one of the monasteries and the monastery's respective position vis-à-vis royal or clan approval. Clan conflict was frequently defined along sectarian lines, with the great families supporting one feudal monastery

against another. Equally important was the free-wheeling legitimation allowed by the syncretic richness of the esoteric teachings—including suitable Shinto deities to signify the solidarity of each monastic fortress. The esoteric repertoire also gave rise to the Vajrayāna sexual sacramentalism of the Tachikawa school—a "heretical" movement bitterly opposed by Shingon leaders and ultimately suppressed by imperial order.

In all of this the resurgent Buddhism of the early Heian seemed to have undergone a compromising worldly domestication. However, toward the end of the Heian period, amid increasingly violent clan wars and social disruptions, there were countervailing forces at work. In the Heian court, clearly under the influence of Buddhism, we find the emergence of a self-reflective poetry, literature, and drama marked by an extraordinary sophistication of mood and expression. Awareness of the transience of life and the melancholy of impermanent beauty was coupled with symbolism of withdrawal and a nostalgia for the tranquillity of the past. This easily degenerated into sentimentality and became a sign of courtly refinement, but nevertheless it signified a growing uneasiness and a renewed sense of human finitude and guilt.

The feudal wars finally resulted in the overthrow of the old Kyoto aristocracy and the installation of military rule under the Kamakura shōgunate (1192–1333). However, effective stabilization of the society did not take place until the Tokugawa period, and during the intervening four centuries Japan continued to be devastated by protracted warfare. In this situation of deepening gloom and pessimism the energies of Buddhism were once again restored, in a new breakthrough which touched all social strata. Liberated from aristocratic ties to the defunct Kyoto court, it expressed its inherent universalism in ways which still dominate Japanese religious life today. The most important new movement was Pure Land Buddhism. The soteriology was basically the same as in the Chinese case. Self-salvation is impossible. The single efficacious act is the Nembutsu, the invocation and fervent repetition of Amida's (Amitābha's) name—a practice already introduced earlier by Ennin.

The institutionalization of Pure Land in Japan was promoted by three unorthodox Tendai priests, Kūya (903–972), Genshin (942–1017), and Ryōnin (1071–1132). Kūya left the monastery to preach to the masses and promote charitable public works. His missionary zeal even moved him to try to evangelize the primitive Ainus. Genshin popularized Pure Land in his book *The Essentials of Salvation.* Ryōnin expounded the teaching in songs and liturgy, intoning the Nembutsu and urging the unity of all men in the faith. His converts included monks, aristocrats, and common laity alike. Subsequent developments were even more radical. Ippen (1239–1289) followed the tradition of personal evangelism, preaching and singing in Shinto shrines and Buddhist temples about the omnipresence of Amida's compassion with a universalism which transcended all sectarian differences.

The sudden increase in the popularity of Pure Land during this period of hardship suggests that for the first time the meaning of the human situation—not merely the immediate conditions of personal well-being—was called into question on a large scale. There was an increasing obsession with the idea that the world is hell and the human situation totally corrupt. Although it is clear that for many the heavenly paradise of the "pure land" was an affirmation of worldly pleasures, there were practices symptomatic of deeper stresses. People of all classes practiced ascetic vigils and fasts while concentrating on Amida's compassionate image. There were radical acts of physical self-mortification—for example, gifts of a finger, hand, or arm to Amida or religious suicides by burning or drowning—all indicative of deep disturbance.

Hōnen (1133–1212) and Shinran (1173–1262) were responsible for the major forms of Pure Land, which still exist today. Prior to their efforts the images of Amida were to be found in the temples of almost every sect, and the Nembutsu had no orthodox exclusiveness. But Hōnen insisted on the inherent superiority of Pure Land. His radical sectarianism and his success in winning converts resulted in persecution and exile. His disciple Shinran went further: man's total sinfulness means that calling on Amida's name is a useless effort toward merit making unless it is done out of grace-given faith and gratitude. Suffering and sin are the preconditions for personal salvation: "If the good are saved, how much more the wicked." Monastic celibacy and the precepts are ineffectual and must be abandoned. The warrior, hunter, thief, murderer, prostitute—all are saved through faith alone. Shinran held that monastic celibacy was not required, and he formed the True Pure Land sect (Jōdo Shin) in reaction to some of the more conservative members of Hōnen's group, who still held to the celibate ideal and other traditional vows. The new sect was organized around Shinran's lineal descendants.

One of the consequences of Pure Land radicalism was that it provoked a counterreformation which brought new rigor to the Nara sects and reform movements within Shingon and Tendai. The most important reformer was Nichiren (1222–1282), a Tendai monk born the son of a fisherman, who took deep pride in his low birth and prophetic role. His reforming message was based on a call to return to the teaching of the Lotus Sūtra. The goal of his mission was a paradoxical combination of evangelical universalism, radical sectarianism, and fierce nationalism, demanding the cultural and political unification of Japan around Buddhism through faith in the Lotus alone. His position was sufficiently radical for him to form a new school, and his criticism of the incumbent regime resulted in the imposition on him of the death sentence, which was finally commuted to exile. His suffering he interpreted as inherently in keeping with the Buddha's message, and his disciples continued missionary activity despite continuous persecution, particularly during the Tokugawa shōgunate.

Zen Buddhism was the third major movement to emerge out of the Kamakura matrix, although it did not reach full strength until the Ashikaga shōgunate (1338–1573) and after. In its soteriology it was the reverse of the Pure Land and Nichiren sects, and it did not become equally popular, although it was immensely appealing to many individuals for whom neither otherworldly theism nor ascetic withdrawal were meaningful forms of religious action. It was successfully transplanted to Japan by Eisai (1141–1215) and Dōgen (1200–1253). Dissatisfied with the condition of Tendai Buddhism, Eisai left for Sung China, where he studied with a Lin-chi (Rinzai) master. After returning to Japan he settled in Kamakura, where his practical teaching found popular acceptance among the new warrior aristocracy. Later he went to Kyoto, with the intention of blending both Shingon and Tendai esotericism with his doctrine. His alliance with the new political order and his compromise with the other sects were major factors in the successful institutionalization of Zen in Japan.

Dōgen, a Tendai monk of aristocratic birth and Confucian training, studied with a master of the Ts'ao-tung (Sōtō) school. He tried to strike a balance between the patriarchal and scriptural traditions, approving both Hīnayāna and Mahāyāna sources and minimizing the importance of the *kōan*. His soteriology stressed rational modes of self-perfection through meditation and ethical and intellectual striving. He retained a strong sense of the dignity of physical labor and the discipline of work in the world, rejecting an easy accommodation of moral standards to given conditions.

Though Dōgen refused to lend open support to the incumbent political regime, Zen teaching in general provided a remarkably creative base for coordination with the secular needs and cultural goals of the state. Zen monks assisted the emperor in many tasks and helped to cement diplomatic and economic relations with China. They were instrumental in establishing a state-sponsored Buddhist church during the Ashikaga shōgunate, which imported and promulgated Sung Neo-Confucianism, provided educational services, and printed textbooks. Equally important was the liberalizing influence of Zen in the arts, including the military art of swordsmanship (stern discipline, selflessness, and spontaneity), the classical tea ceremony, and many aesthetic refinements which became part of the vital mainstream of Japanese cultural life.

The egalitarian thrust of these new religious movements initiated during the Kamakura period contributed richly to the moral and religious health of Japanese culture, but they were not basically reformist. They did not undercut the feudal or patrimonial basis of the society. Although at first they broke through the social boundaries of the old aristocracy, they later supported the ethic of the new warrior class, in many direct and indirect ways, by reinforcing the feudal leader–follower nexus. The demand for unswerving loyalty to the lord had structural and psychological parallels with the authority of the Zen master and the Pure Land hereditary patriarch. The early prophetic–critical tension was also siphoned off in other ways—through the aesthetic life, which Zen promoted by affirming the inner spiritual validity of the natural world as it is given, and in the otherworldly piety of the Pure Land devotee, which did not give rise to rational social criticism but rather to discrete philanthropies.

In the late medieval period, as the rationalization of state Shinto and the first glimmerings of a real national ideology began to emerge, Buddhism was increasingly regarded as a political menace because it reinforced clan particularism and, with the exception of Zen, seemed to add little to political or economic reason. In 1571 the military unification of Japan by General Oda Nobunaga was dramatized by the deliberate destruction of the Tendai establishments, including the razing of over 3,000 buildings and the massacre of all their inhabitants. His pretext was that Tendai had provided sanctuary for political rebels, but the more general reason given was that it obstructed "the maintenance of law and order in the country," a notion which presaged subsequent events affecting the fate of Buddhism in Japan during the next two centuries.

Influence of the West

The advent of European colonialism in the eighteenth century and the diffusion of Western values and institutions throughout Asia precipitated far-reaching strains and innovations, which have significantly modified the traditional social role and teachings of Buddhism. Under the impact of Western imperialism and acculturation, the major modernizing pressures took the form of resurgent nationalism, democratic aspirations, the development of rational science, and industrialization—all of which placed new pressures on the Saṅgha for critical self-reflection and reform.

In southeast Asia—to take the Thai case once again—an initial positive response by the royal house to French colonialism and Catholicism was followed by a conservative reaction, approved by the Saṅgha, resulting in usurpation of the throne. The fear of political and economic domination was directly tied to the fear of a loss of religious identity. The Theravādin base of national unity against Western encroachments has persisted and intensified, although it has been modified by modernizing rationalizations allowing for the introduction of Western political institutions and technical means which at the same time have been used to reinforce the central national role of the Saṅgha. These innovations were effected not only by external pressures from the royal house and a Westernized laity but also, occasionally, by movements within the Buddhist Saṅgha itself, which liberalized traditional values and educational techniques held to be incompatible with rational science and modernization.

Characteristically, throughout Theravādin lands the Buddha is now often represented as the first modern "psychologist" and "scientist," concerned with the analytical understanding of the human situation and the need for innovation and progress. The monastic leadership was placed under new pressures to jusify the immense drain on the economy which state support of the Saṅgha represented and to bridge the gap between its traditional values and the modernizing goals of the state. The principles of love and noninjury are now regarded as basic axioms for organized social action and reform, particularly in the new Buddhist youth movements and missionary activity. The value of the merit-making metaphysic has been refocused on the need for support of national ideology and new economic and technological goals.

The Saṅgha also sees itself as a harbinger of

international peace, apparently unattainable in Christendom, and as a bulwark against the erosions of Western secularism and materialism. For the fifth Theravādin council, in 1871, the canonical scriptures were inscribed in stone partly to symbolize the permanency of the teaching in the face of Western values. At the assembly of the sixth council, in Rangoon, Burma, in 1954–1956, there was a new stress on the international solidarity of all Buddhists with respect to the missionary goals of Buddhism in the modern world.

The Western-educated laity and certain members of the monastic elite have been the most influential factors in bringing about internal political reforms. Constitutional monarchies and the franchise were both introduced in the early 1930s, undermining the entrenched relationship between the traditional monastic order and the aristocracy. Many of the new reforming movements were initiated by native civil servants who had worked for the British and French bureaucracies. In this regard Ceylon represents a particularly interesting case because it is the only one of the principal Theravādin nations which did not institute Buddhism as the national religion following political independence. The refusal to support the Saṅgha at state expense is significantly related to a deep split between the bulk of the educated laity and the more conservative members of the monastic leadership. One finds evidence of protesting lay movements publicly excoriating the leadership of the Saṅgha for its backwardness.

With respect to the encroachments of communism in southeast Asia, Buddhism has played an ambiguous role. Buddhist hostility to the former Catholic regime in South Vietnam has added to political instability in that country, but on the whole Buddhist leadership has found communist materialism and aggression repugnant to its spiritual ideals.

Prior to the communist take-over in China, there were several indications of Buddhist resurgence, including lay social welfare services and various youth movements with social reform programs. Most striking was the work of the monk T'ai-hsü, who joined the revolutionary forces against the Manchus and founded voluntary lay groups for the promotion of democratic institutions, educational services, and Buddhist missions. He conceived of Buddhist universalism as the basis for internal social reform and ecumenical restoration of world peace and moral standards. The communist regime has not extirpated Buddhism but rather placed it under ideological controls. Many of the monastic orders ostensibly retain their traditional customs, edifices, and property, but most of the inmates are compelled both to work productively and to support a cultural image of pacifistic tolerance which serves the goals of the state. The Buddhist Association of China in Peking has encouraged the study of Buddhism as a culturally valuable asset, and it has maintained ideologically useful contacts with Buddhists in other lands. The present results of communist domination in Tibet are uncertain. The economically unproductive aspects of monasticism appear to have been eliminated, but residuals of the traditional theocracy have been retained to facilitate hierarchical distribution of ideological propaganda and lines of authority from Peking. Marx and Mao are now the supreme charismatic figures.

In India, Theravāda Buddhism has returned, partly under government sponsorship of a more general program of cultural restoration. King Aśoka is a key symbol of India's new national self-awareness. One of the most notable contributions which Buddhism has made in India is its emergence, under the leadership of the late B. R. Ambedkhar, as a social-protest movement against caste discrimination. As leader of the Untouchables in their bid for equal political and religious rights, Ambedkhar saw in Buddhism the innovating potential for formation of a new caste-free solidarity, and in 1956 he led a mass conversion of outcaste groups to the new faith. Buddhist anticaste polemic continues as an important element in the larger effort to break through the entrenched caste-oriented mentality, which persists despite official de-institutionalization in the new constitution.

In Japan, following Oda Nobunaga's short-lived dictatorship, the Tokugawa shōguns forced Buddhism into a utilitarian alignment with state policy. Through mandatory temple registration for all citizens, it was used to reinforce social controls against the encroachments of Christianity. After the Meiji restoration in 1868, it was further subordinated to the imperial Shinto–Confucian ideology. Shinto deities were divested of their "dual" association with Bodhisattvas, and Buddhism in general was briefly regarded as a foreign depredation on the purity of the indigenous religion.

There is some indication that Pure Land devotionalism, together with Confucian and Shinto values, may have contributed to the psychological ethos which facilitated later rapid industrialization. A functional analogue has been established between the work ethic of ascetic Calvinism and certain forms of self-sacrificing Amida devotionalism found among businessmen of the Tokugawa and Meiji periods. In the later Meiji and the early decades of the twentieth century the state promoted Buddhism extensively in Korea, for the purpose of pacifying the conquered territory, while at the same time it intensified state Shinto teaching at home, in support of nationalist aims. During the prewar military take-over and the subsequent events leading to World War II it is difficult to find significant examples of systematic political criticism from Buddhist leaders.

However, in philosophy the fusion of Western categories with the Buddhist world view produced some remarkably creative syntheses, as exemplified in the works of such men as Nishida Kitarō and Tanabe Hajime. Equally significant has been the influence in the West of D. T. Suzuki's interpretations of Zen teachings, particularly in correlation with certain dimensions of existentialist philosophy and psychology. Japan in the postwar situation is an extremely complex matrix of cultural ferment, within which Buddhism appears in many new forms. It ranges from the radical sectarianism of Soka Gakkai, which blends intense devotionalism with militant political goals, to the subtle historical reflection and self-criticism of intellectuals like Ienaga Saburō. Ienaga sees in the history of Japanese Buddhism—particularly in Shōtoku and Shinran—evidence of its transcendent universalism and capacity to cut through traditional forms with innovating power; but this is paradoxically mixed with an easy accommodation to the givenness of the world and a loss of critical tension, with worldly institutions regarded as inherently illusory and unreal. Ienaga's powerful critique of Buddhist tradition is itself a manifestation of the pristine ideals of prophetic negation, self-reflection, and reconstruction which the earliest teaching conveyed. For Buddhism throughout the world, it suggests the presence of the power of spiritual renewal and transcendence which continues to speak therapeutically to the human situation even as it seeks to re-create itself to meet the pressing challenges confronting all the major religions.

PETER A. PARDUE

BIBLIOGRAPHY

ANESAKI, MASAHARU 1930 *History of Japanese Religion.* London: Routledge.

BELLAH, ROBERT N. 1957 *Tokugawa Religion: The Values of Pre-industrial Japan.* Glencoe, Ill.: Free Press.

BORIBAL BURIBHAND, LUANG 1955 *A History of Buddhism in Thailand.* Bangkok: National Culture Institute.

CH'EN, KENNETH K. SH. 1964 *Buddhism in China: A Historical Survey.* Princeton Univ. Press.

CONZE, EDWARD 1951 *Buddhism: Its Essence and Development.* New York: Philosophical Library.

DASGUPTA, SHASHIBHUSAN (1950) 1958 *Introduction to Tāntric Buddhism.* 2d ed. Univ. of Calcutta.

DAYAL, HAR 1932 *The Bodhisattva Doctrine in Buddhist Sanskrit Literature.* London: Routledge.

DUTT, SUKUMAR 1924 *Early Buddhist Monachism: 600 B.C.–100 B.C.* London: Routledge.

ELIOT, CHARLES NORTON E. (1921) 1954 *Hinduism and Buddhism: An Historical Sketch.* 3 vols. London: Routledge; New York: Barnes & Noble.

FOCHER, ALFRED 1949 *La vie du Bouddha.* Paris: Payot.

HALL, DANIEL G. E. (1955) 1960 *A History of Southeast Asia.* New York: St. Martins.

HORNER, ISALINE B. 1930 *Women Under Primitive Buddhism.* New York: Dutton.

JASPERS, KARL (1957) 1962 *The Great Philosophers.* Volume 1: The Foundations. New York: Harcourt. → First published as *Die grossen Philosophen.* More volumes in progress.

LAMOTTE, ÉTIENNE 1958 *Histoire du bouddhisme indien: Des origines à l'ère Śaka.* Louvain (Belgium): Publications Universitaires.

LANDON, KENNETH 1949 *Southeast Asia: Crossroad of Religions.* Univ. of Chicago Press.

MURTI, T. R. V. 1955 *The Central Philosophy of Buddhism.* London: Allen & Unwin.

SUZUKI, D. T. 1959 *Zen and Japanese Culture.* New York: Pantheon.

WEBER, MAX (1921) 1958 *The Religion of India: The Sociology of Hinduism and Buddhism.* Translated and edited by Hans H. Gerth and Don Martindale. Glencoe, Ill.: Free Press. → First published as *Hinduismus und Buddhismus,* Volume 2 of *Gesammelte Aufsätze zur Religionssoziologie.*

WRIGHT, ARTHUR F. 1959 *Buddhism in Chinese History.* Stanford Univ. Press.

ZÜRCHER, ERIK 1959 *The Buddhist Conquest of China.* Leiden (Netherlands): Brill.

BUDGETING

I. GOVERNMENT BUDGETING	*Arthur Smithies*
II. BUDGETING AS A POLITICAL PROCESS	*Aaron B. Wildavsky*

I
GOVERNMENT BUDGETING

Budgeting may be described as the art of living within an economic constraint. Virtually every organization or individual has economic limits imposed on what it wants to do; exceptions are the professional ascetic or the sailor shipwrecked on an abundant island. Budgeting, however, may be passive or active. A traditional subsistence farmer will undertake the same production program year after year and always wants to consume more than he has of everything he produces. On the other hand, a modern commercial farmer has a number of alternative ways of employing his resources and actively chooses among them. In an organization, the process of budgeting is almost necessarily active and explicit, since the very nature of an organization is that its decisions result from the interaction of a number of individuals or groups. This article is concerned with government budgeting, but it is useful to recall that, in their budgetary processes, governments are reflecting the pervasive need to allocate scarce economic resources. [*For consumer budgeting, see* CONSUMERS, *article on* CONSUMPTION LEVELS AND STANDARDS.]

A government's budget is usually, and almost necessarily, its only comprehensive program of action for the period to which it relates. This is so because a program cannot be crystallized until the question of cost is taken into account, and virtually everything a government does costs money. The character of the administration of justice, for instance, depends critically on the amount of money spent on judges, prosecutions, and policemen. In the United States, varying political attitudes toward the antitrust laws find concrete expression in the appropriations made to the Department of Justice. The importance of the budget is clearly recognized in countries with the parliamentary system of government. The invariable British tradition is that the government (executive) resigns if its budget is defeated in Parliament.

The process of decision making that results in a budget, whatever its complexities, contains three necessary ingredients: (1) determination of the variety of policy objectives the government intends to pursue, such as defense, education, or law enforcement; (2) estimation of the cost of pursuing each of these objectives in varying degrees; and (3) an assessment of the willingness and ability of the public to pay for the government's program as a whole [*see* PUBLIC EXPENDITURES; TAXATION].

No government can exist without a policy, even though that policy may be largely passive. In the world contemplated by the English classical economists, government should restrict itself to "essential functions" in order to give maximum scope to private enterprise. Its budgetary problem would then be to determine the minimum cost of performing those necessary functions and to raise the taxes necessary to pay for them, while interfering to the minimum extent with private capital accumulation.

The task of modern governments is far less simple. Although classical considerations impose restraints on their action, governments are concerned with the active pursuit of goals that require expenditures for their attainment. Governments of today are preoccupied, in different degrees, with defense, development, and improving the economic welfare of their citizens. The way in which these objectives become formulated varies widely among countries, depending on their form of government. An authoritarian government can select its objectives and assess their relative importance with minimum reliance on the consent of the public. In

a democratic society, the process is far more complicated. Consent to government policies is given or withheld in free elections, and the goals established by government result largely from ideas and opinions that emerge from the whole society and are impressed on government by the groups actively interested. But, one way or another, a government does acquire a set of objectives and some idea of the relative weight to be given to each.

The extent to which an objective should be pursued, or whether one should be preferred to another, will depend on their costs. In a "classical" world, where governments were supposed to perform minimum functions, the question of costs could be approached by fairly crude methods. Finance ministers and officials won their reputations by frustrating the operation of Parkinson's Law. Treasuries acquired their reputation for saying "no." In a world of nuclear weapons, space flight, and economic development, the question of cost estimation becomes vastly more important and difficult.

Finally, governments must assess the willingness of the public to pay for government programs—to provide money, in the form of taxes or loans, that could have been used for something else. To win acceptance for its budget the government must persuade the legislature or the electorate that what it proposes is worth the cost.

The essential ingredients of the process of budgeting under "ideal" conditions can then be summarized:

(1) If the relative importance of spending money in pursuit, to varying degrees, of the different objectives can be ascertained, the government can prepare a series of "optimal budgets." For any level of total expenditures it can determine the best mix of its various programs. The mix, say between defense and social welfare, will normally vary with the size of the hypothetical budget. It will also vary materially among countries.

(2) The government can determine the method of paying for budgets of any given size that is least burdensome from economic and political points of view. It can thus estimate the cost of any of its hypothetical budgets in terms of private goods.

(3) The information provided under (1) and (2) provides the government with a basis for weighing the benefits to be derived from expenditures against the costs of expenditures, and hence for selecting a particular budget.

Traditional approach.   In practice, governments have attempted to organize themselves for budgetary purposes by attempting to make a basic distinction between "policy making" and "finance."

Policy makers decide what ought to be done. Financial agencies assert their views on how much the government can afford. There remains the task of achieving a compromise between the two views and producing a budget. In most governments, this third function is also considered to be within the province of finance. The budget is usually the immediate responsibility of the chancellor of the exchequer, the minister of finance, or the treasurer, as the case may be.

In countries with the parliamentary system of government, particularly in countries whose institutions are of British origin, policies are decided on by the cabinet in the general political context that obtains and are endorsed by parliament in legislation. Budget requests are submitted by the departments to the treasury, which produces a budget that allocates the total among the various activities. That total is arrived at in the light of the difficulties of financing it. The budget, prepared by the treasury, is then discussed to varying extents by the policy makers in the cabinet, which may accept or revise the treasury's budget as an adequate expression of the government's policy. The outcome depends on the relative strengths of the treasurer and other members of the cabinet in a collective bargaining process. It is fair to say, however, that the cards are stacked in favor of the treasury. Not only is the treasurer the authority on revenues, but he is more completely informed on the entire expenditure program of the government than is any other member of the cabinet. When the budget has been approved by the cabinet, it is submitted to the parliament, which must virtually accept the budget or dismiss the government.

In the United States Congress, the three steps in the process are explicitly recognized in the parallel committee structure of the House and Senate. Authorizing committees recommend legislation that both declares policy and authorizes expenditure. Moreover, committee hearings and reports constitute "legislative history" that establishes policy in more informal ways.

The Committee on Ways and Means of the House and the Senate Finance Committee are the bodies concerned with recommending tax measures. The traditional rule in the United States is that the entire budget be covered by taxation.

The task of budget making is assigned to the appropriations committees, which review estimates received from the executive branch in the light of the objectives declared by Congress and the availability of revenues. In practice, however, revenue considerations are implicit rather than explicit in the work of the committees.

Before 1921, the Congress was the main budget-making body in the United States. The executive departments submitted their estimates to Congress with very little coordination by the executive branch. In that year, however, legislation required a single executive budget to be submitted by the president and set up a Bureau of the Budget to prepare it. In line with tradition, the Bureau of the Budget was to be located in the Treasury. In 1939, however, this ambiguity was removed, and the Bureau of the Budget was transferred to the executive office of the president. His personal responsibility for the executive budget was thus unequivocally established.

The Bureau of the Budget has no independent authority; it is a staff agency of the president. Under this system, the Treasury is concerned with the revenue side of the budget. The president, in making his budget, weighs the claims of the departments against the reluctance of the Treasury. However, both the claimant departments and the Treasury are supposed to reflect the policy of the president. He is thus policy maker and budget maker. In principle at least, the distinction between policy making and finance has been blurred. Practice has been steadily catching up with principle. The Bureau of the Budget is slowly becoming increasingly concerned with policy as well as finance.

The distinction drawn between policy making and finance is unfortunate. It conveys the impression, reflected in practice, that a financial agency is concerned not with policy but merely with costs and revenues. In fact, the statement has frequently been made in the United States that the Congress determines what ought to be done, and the budgetary problem is to translate that policy into financial terms. In this view, the budget should be a document that merely expresses the minimum cost of doing the government's business and gives explicit directions to the executive agencies with respect to the personnel they can employ, the automobiles and typewriters they can purchase, and the buildings they can construct. Its preoccupation is with the means to be employed rather than the ends to be accomplished.

That view of the problem might be adequate in a simple society in which each agency of government performed well-defined functions to some specified extent. For instance, it might be firmly established policy that the post office make two mail deliveries per day or that there be a prescribed number of policemen on the beat. In the defense area, planning was long dominated by the concept of absolute requirements. Military men by military methods were supposed to be able, by applying planning factors, to determine the number of men, weapons, and ships and the amount of food and clothing needed for the "defense of the country." If all this were possible, policy throughout the government could be definitely determined. Budget makers would then review cost estimates submitted by the departments, cut out those costs that they deemed unnecessary, and then raise the revenues needed to finance the resulting budget. The process thus becomes a highly simplified special case of the more general theory of budgeting set out above.

Problems. This simplified view of the matter has never been more than a rough approximation, although it still underlies much budgetary practice. Treasuries have never accepted a military view of absolute requirements. Sometimes to the benefit and sometimes to the detriment of the country, they have cut military strength below the level deemed necessary. They have also cut the number of mail deliveries or the number of policemen in order to relieve the burdensomeness of taxation. In these activities they have, in the guise of a financial operation, assessed the relative merits of defense, postal service, and law enforcement, and at the same time compared the absolute merits of these programs with the burdensomeness of taxation.

Nevertheless, much of the distinction between policy making and finance could be preserved if the policy makers could give adequate instructions to treasuries with respect to the policy decisions the latter have to make. This could be done if it were possible to measure government programs like defense or welfare in precise quantitative terms. If, in addition, the policy makers could follow the economics textbook and draw up social utility curves of their programs, they could give precise instructions to the financial officials. If the latter could determine the costs of carrying out the different programs to varying extents, they could draw up the array of optimal budgets referred to above as a reflection of policy already determined. There would remain, however, the policy question of which optimal budget to select. That would require a policy decision.

The task of physical measurement of major programs, to say nothing of measuring social importance, is out of the question in any precise sense. Consider education as an example. At first sight it might appear that the numbers of students taught might serve as useful indicators of the quantities of school and college education provided. But although the numbers of students are an important dimension of the problem, it has other dimensions, such as the number and quality of teachers, buildings, and equipment. Even if all

measurable information were assembled, the educational value of it all would have to depend on an exercise of human judgment. Nevertheless, some unit of measurement is needed, and for major programs or program subdivisions, there seems to be no unit of measurement as satisfactory as money cost. In considering education, for instance, the question to be asked is not, How can a given amount of education be achieved at minimum cost? It is, rather, How can a given sum be spent on education in order to give the best educational results, under conditions in which education itself is not precisely defined? Although all available quantitative and qualitative information should be brought to bear on the decision, uncertainties concerning educational values render an element of human judgment necessary. The process of decision making should be organized so as to make this judgment as informed as possible.

What policy makers should do is conduct intellectual and practical experiments to determine the benefits of spending money in alternative ways. Can expenditures be shifted beneficially from social welfare to defense or vice versa, or can they be shifted usefully to alternative uses within the areas of defense and social welfare. Difficult though such comparisons may be, they would be intellectually impossible without using the common denominator, money. Thus, policy making penetrates far into the area traditionally assigned to finance.

Proposed solutions. The world survived for a long time with traditional views of the distinction between budgeting and policy making. But modern governments, preoccupied as they are with defense, development, and welfare, are coming to recognize that budgeting and policy making are part of the same process.

In the United States, in particular, efforts are being made to adapt budgetary methods to modern requirements. In consequence, conventional methods, particularly in the defense area, are being replaced or supplemented by "program budgeting."

In view of the world-wide interest and concern with economic development, investment budgeting, too, calls for special attention. In one respect investment is different from other government programs: the ends to be accomplished as well as the means employed can be expressed in economic terms. The problem of investment criteria has evoked extensive discussion. All that can be done here is to indicate the main principles involved and the relation of a government's investment program to other components of its budget.

A further important contemporary problem is the assessment of the economic impact of the budget. When budgets were small in relation to national revenue, the problem of financing them could be regarded as largely the political one of overcoming the reluctance of the public to pay taxes and ensuring reasonable standards of equity. In the United States in the latter part of the nineteenth century the problem was even easier than that. Customs revenues were so plentiful that the problem of the federal government was to avoid a surplus, which, if allowed to occur, might have led to a reduction of the tariff. At the present time budgets are so large that the methods of financing can have marked effects on levels of employment, income distribution, or economic growth. Consequently, simple rules of finance are gradually being replaced by analysis of the economic impact of the budget.

Program budgeting.   For the budget to serve its purpose as a policy-making instrument, it must be prepared and considered in terms that relate directly to the policy objectives to be furthered. This means a reversal of traditional practice whereby budgets are designed to allocate money to responsible administrative agencies. In some cases there need be no conflict between program and administrative objectives. For instance, the money appropriated to the post office is, or should be, the same thing as the cost to the government of the postal program. (Even this statement, to be true, requires that the post office pay what may be other government agencies, such as airlines or railways, for carrying mail. This is not universal practice.) In other cases there is a clear conflict. Tradition and administrative effectiveness require that the army, the navy, and the air force be maintained as separate services; yet important defense programs require the cooperation of the three services. Budgets for the separate services clearly fail to indicate the capacity of the services to perform a combined operation.

At first sight, it might appear that program budgets could be extracted from administrative budgets. But this practice would fail to do justice to the central problem of obtaining maximum program advantage from a given cost. Administrative budgets are necessary, but they should be derived from program budgets. Governments are only slowly coming to realize this point.

Progress toward a program budget has been most noticeable in connection with the defense budget of the United States in the early 1960s. The conventional defense budget has been submitted for each of the services and for the Defense Department as a whole, in the following categories: military personnel, operation and maintenance, procurement, research and development, military construction, and civil defense. These categories are designed essentially from the point of view of effective administration of the Department of Defense, and they tell very little about the relation of the defense program to the various missions it is supposed to accomplish. Military personnel of the air force, for instance, includes airmen on missile sites in Colorado and airmen in Laos, and the same holds for the other categories. The information contained in the conventional budget does not permit the reader, including members of Congress who have to review it, to form any adequate idea of the program for the defense of the United States itself. Reviewers therefore have to take the word of officials concerning the strategic adequacy of the budget and confine their specific review to small details that are likely to be irrelevant to the major issues. Yet their decisions have a vital bearing on strategy.

The Department of Defense has met these difficulties by preparing an alternative budget in terms of major "budget programs." These include strategic retaliatory forces, continental air and missile defense forces, general purpose forces (the army, the bulk of the navy, and the tactical air force), sealift and airlift forces, reserves and guard forces, research and development, general support, and civil defense. These programs, in turn, are built up from "program elements," which consist of complete weapons systems that contribute to the program objective.

The reforms, however, have not been able to accomplish a complete program budget at this time. The objectives of general purpose forces cannot be indicated with the same clarity as those of retaliatory forces. Transport and reserve and guard forces represent administrative rather than program categories. With respect to research and development, especially research, budgeting in terms of particular programs would presumably cause needless duplication.

The program budget permits the Congress and the president to address themselves to the important questions of strategy when they review the budget. Moreover, knowledge of the costs of these programs and program elements is an important aid in the original process of strategic planning. Defense in the modern world has multiple objectives: to prevent general war, to prevent or win limited war, and to prevent or eliminate internal subversions—so-called sublimited wars. Because resources are limited, substitutions among programs and program elements must be considered by the strategic planners. It is exceedingly difficult to think in terms of shifting a "unit" of general purpose forces to strategic retaliatory forces, or vice versa. It is easier, although still difficult, to consider the "cost effectiveness" of shifting a billion dollars of expenditure from one program to another. As Assistant Secretary of Defense C. J. Hitch observed (in a statement before the Military Operations Subcommittee of the House Committee on Government Operations, July 25, 1962): "The job of economizing . . . cannot be distinguished from the whole task of making military decisions."

The practical need to measure programs in terms of their cost has led to the new concept "cost effectiveness." Studies of cost effectiveness attempt to answer the question whether the purposes of a program will be better served if a given sum is spent in one way rather than another. To study cost effectiveness in simple situations may mean nothing more than to determine the cheapest way of performing some specific and well-defined operation. The more interesting cases, however, are those in which expenditures in different directions contribute in different ways to general and imprecisely defined program objectives. Here a study of cost effectiveness organizes the information on the basis of which the decision maker must make a judgment. Examples, arranged in order of the increasing importance of the judgment factor, are: Will expenditure of an additional sum on sea-based or land-based missiles more effectively contribute to the retaliatory forces? Will expenditure on the retaliatory forces or on air defense more effectively protect the United States from attack? Will expenditure on strategic forces or on general purpose forces more effectively contribute to the whole defense program? Will expenditure on defense or on social welfare more effectively serve the interests of the country? In the area of research, the problem becomes vastly more difficult, if not insoluble. Expenditures undertaken *now* yield unpredictable results in an unpredictable future. Estimates of their cost effectiveness may have to rely almost entirely on experienced judgment.

Defense budgeting in the United States has been selected for discussion because in that country and that area of government activity, the intellectual problems have been most extensively examined and faced. But the problems are pervasive, for budgeting is essentially concerned with the task of achieving a rational allocation of resources under conditions in which the objectives are imperfectly defined.

Program budgeting calls not only for new concepts and methods but for the application of human skills infrequently found in traditional ministries of finance or departmental budget offices. Budgetary staffs, wherever they are located, should include men of the highest professional competence, with respect both to the ends of policy and the economic analysis of costs.

Investment budgeting. Budgeting for economic development projects falls in a separate category because the objectives of the projects can be defined in economic terms. The problem also engages particular attention, not only because of the worldwide interest in development, but because it seems to be soluble by objective economic calculation.

From the point of view of the whole economy, the benefits of a development project consist of the contributions to the national income of the country that the project will make during the course of its life, which may be very long. In this respect, a public project is no different from a private project if the latter is considered from the social point of view: if the indirect benefits and costs to the economy are taken into account in addition to the direct returns from it. On the other hand, if as is sometimes appropriate, the public project is considered purely in terms of the direct monetary returns from it, the problem is similar in principle to that faced by the private investor. In either case, forecasting the distant economic future is notoriously difficult. Although there is no escape from making the attempt, the great uncertainty surrounding any estimates should be explicitly recognized. The evaluation of a project can be attempted by estimating what may be termed its economic "efficiency." Following Keynes, the efficiency of a project may be defined as the rate of discount which, when applied to future returns and future costs, will equate the present value of returns with that of costs [*see* INVESTMENT].

If the government assumes control over the entire investment program of the economy, both public and private projects can be ordered in terms of their efficiency and priority granted to projects in that order. (This statement assumes that the efficiencies of various projects are independent of one another. This assumption may be a fair approximation in a developed economy with free access to foreign supplies. It may be far from adequate in an underdeveloped economy in which the efficiency of an automobile factory depends on the existence of a steel mill.)

If the total supply of saving is known, the total investment program should be such as to absorb that supply; and the "rate of interest" will correspond to the efficiency of the lowest priority project undertaken.

This account of the matter, however, ignores the

critical factor of uncertainty of the estimates of future yields and costs. Allowance for uncertainty must be made either as a deduction from the measure of efficiency or as an increase in the rate of interest to be compared with the efficiency of particular projects. The latter is the more common approach, and it is sometimes argued that differences in the structure of rates that appear in the market are an adequate assessment of the risks and uncertainties that surround the investment projects of particular classes of borrowers. This point of view is not generally shared by private business. The rates of return that are used for internal planning purposes are normally much higher than the rates at which firms can borrow in the market. In government, however, there is a persistent tendency to regard the rate at which the government can borrow as that which should be applied in assessing particular investment projects. That rate is thoroughly inappropriate for the purpose; it is normally lower than other rates, mainly because the entire creditworthiness of the government is behind its loans, but also partly because governments are able to adjust the loan market in their favor. It is safe to say that the rate with which the efficiency of a public investment project should be compared is normally higher than the rate at which the government can borrow.

If it were true that the flow of saving available for investment in public and private projects were fixed, budgeting for public investment could be separated from the rest of the budget and dealt with as a matter of allocating investment among public and private projects in the manner suggested above. In fact, this assumption is the basis of the common practice of regarding public loans as the normal source of finance for public investment and taxation as the normal way to finance current expenditures.

That assumption, however, is unwarranted. The flow of saving is affected by the government's policies with respect to current expenditure and taxation. The flow of saving is increased or decreased if taxation exceeds or falls short of expenditures. Furthermore, a balanced increase of current expenditures and taxation will reduce saving, for taxation inevitably reduces private saving. An increase or decrease in total saving will lower or raise the structure of interest rates, including internal planning rates, which affects the rate of investment, public or private, or both. Hence, investment budgeting cannot be regarded as a separate operation. Current government expenditures compete with public investment expenditures, and both compete with private consumption and investment expenditures. The government must make a political choice between its desire for future development and its desire for benefits of defense, welfare, and law and order.

As a further complication, the government's contribution to economic development cannot be identified with public investment. As governments are coming to realize, expenditures on current items such as education or public health are equally relevant. Defense programs can yield important by-products in the form of technological knowledge that can be applied throughout the economy. They can also withdraw technical skills from employment elsewhere.

Economic impact of the budget. Governments, traditionally, have applied some simple rule of thumb to decide whether the budget as a whole is worth its cost. In the United States the rule has been that total expenditures should be covered by taxation. Other governments use the rule that current expenditure should be so covered, while capital expenditures should be financed by borrowing from the public. These rules are honored by their breach as well as their observance. They are inevitably broken in times of depression or war, when governments borrow for current purposes; but the rules persist as guides for normal prudent governmental conduct and, indeed, may serve some useful purpose in a complex political organism. Nevertheless, governments are gradually recognizing the need for a more comprehensive and rational approach to the question of economic impact. Reflections of modern economic theory are gradually appearing in budget documents, and many governments issue statements of the national accounts together with their budgets. These statements imply that the government sector of the economy should be considered in its relation to the entire national economy. This, indeed, is inevitable if large development expenditures are involved.

In financing a budget of given size, the government should decide on the method of withdrawing resources from the rest of the economy that will least impede the attainment of other economic objectives; or it may seek to further other objectives, such as distribution of income, through its method of financing. In deciding on the size of the budget, it must seek a satisfactory compromise between the ends to be attained by the budget itself and those other objectives.

The government can finance the budget by taxation or borrowing. Whether taxation or borrowing is used should depend not on the character of government expenditures—whether they can be classified as consumption or investment—but on the effects the government desires to produce, broadly speaking, on private consumption and investment.

In a fully employed economy, the government withdraws resources from private use when it applies them to public use. Whether it withdraws them from private investment or private consumption depends on how it compares the present with the future. Borrowing mainly affects private investment; and finance by borrowing means that the budget is being provided for at the expense of the growth of the private economy. Finance by taxation, on the other hand, normally means that both private consumption and investment are curtailed, although the relative degrees by which they are curtailed will depend on the nature of the taxation imposed. The appropriate combination of borrowing and various kinds of taxation can be determined only by explicit recognition of the objectives of government policy with respect to the private economy. The government may go further and, in the guise of financing the budget, may actively promote other objectives. For instance, it may levy taxes in excess of total expenditures and thus increase savings that may be made available for the private economy. Such action, in conjunction with an appropriate monetary policy, can increase the rate of growth of the private economy.

In a situation where resources are generally unemployed and likely to remain so, the immediate task of the government is not to withdraw resources from private use to make way for the budget, but to use the budget to increase both public and private expenditures. This it can do by borrowing and spending funds that would otherwise remain unused. So long as resources remain generally idle, budgeting ceases to be a matter of allocating scarce resources. Indeed, under such conditions budgeting and economic life as well lose their rationality. The objective of government through its budget or other measures should always be to ensure that a condition of scarcity prevails. Economic activity should always be increased to the point where it is limited by some scarce factors. Such factors may be labor, particular kinds of labor, capacity in critical industries, or foreign exchange. In a condition of scarcity, rational conduct is possible and the allocative principles of budgeting apply.

Technical summary. The foregoing argument represents an attempt to apply the principles of economic theory to the problem of budgeting, with minimum use of the language of economics. It may be useful to summarize the central argument in economic terms. If government activities can be expressed in quantitative terms, the government can draw up a preference map showing rates of substitution among its various activities. If it knows the relative costs of these activities, it can then draw up its series of hypothetical budgets. If it can produce from this information index numbers of public goods, and also of private goods, it can draw up another preference map, consisting of a family of indifference curves relating public to private goods. With its cost information it knows the rate at which private goods can be transformed into public goods. It can thus find its optimum budget. Under these circumstances there could be a clear division of labor between policy makers who determine the indifference curves and budget makers who determine the cost curves and make the computations.

In practice, the construction of index numbers for various programs would involve enormous difficulties. Initial weights of the various components would have to be determined, and the problem of the changing mix of optimal programs would have to be wrestled with. The relation of any index number to what it was supposed to indicate would be subject to change. The significance of the defense index would be affected by the capabilities of the enemy, and of the health index by the prevalence of disease. At all these points the construction of an index would depend heavily on judgment. But the construction of an index might give the impression that objective methods were possible and that the exercise of judgment was not necessary.

The same difficulties occur, in magnified form, if an index of all public goods is attempted. On the other side of the question, no index of private goods foregone would convey an adequate impression of the economic impact of budgets of varying size.

Because a large element of judgment must be exercised in any case and because the construction of aggregate indexes for programs would not facilitate that process, it seems clearly preferable to work with the more familiar notion of money optimally spent in various directions, with particular stress on the need for optimizing. (The standard index approach, however, may be feasible in many cases in solving problems at the "program elements" level, just as it is in many other economic problems.)

Consequently, the indifference curves should be established in terms of given amounts of money optimally spent on various programs, on the total government program, and on private goods. The transformation curves then simply become 45° lines. The processes of budgeting and policy making are thoroughly intermingled.

These conclusions concerning government budgeting suggest that the standard theory of consumer behavior might be usefully modified along similar lines. Although a consumer, planning his breakfast, may be able to establish preferences between bacon and eggs, the purchase of a house may be a different matter. A consumer with a limited budget may employ an architect to draw up a number of plans within his budget constraint. The purchaser then selects the plan he likes most; he may not know what kind of house he wants until he has inspected the alternatives available to him. Economics should be concerned not only with the allocation of scarce resources among alternative uses but also with the discovery of the alternative uses to which scarce resources can be put.

ARTHUR SMITHIES

[*See also* ECONOMICS OF DEFENSE.]

BIBLIOGRAPHY

BURKHEAD, JESSE 1956 *Government Budgeting.* New York: Wiley.

COLM, GERHARD 1955 *Essays in Public Finance and Fiscal Policy.* Oxford Univ. Press.

ECKSTEIN, OTTO 1958 *Water-resource Development: The Economics of Project Evaluation.* Harvard Economic Studies, Vol. 104. Cambridge, Mass.: Harvard Univ. Press.

HICKS, URSULA K. 1954 *British Public Finances: Their Structure and Development, 1880–1952.* Oxford Univ. Press.

HITCH, CHARLES J.; and MCKEAN, R. N. 1960 *The Economics of Defense in the Nuclear Age.* Cambridge, Mass.: Harvard Univ. Press.

MOOR, ROY E. 1962 *The Federal Budget as an Economic Document.* Prepared for the Subcommittee on Economic Statistics, 87th Congress, Joint Economic Committee Print. Washington: Government Printing Office.

NATIONAL BUREAU OF ECONOMIC RESEARCH 1961 *Public Finances: Needs, Sources, and Utilization.* Special Conference Series, No. 12; Universities–National Bureau Committee. Princeton Univ. Press.

NOVICK, DAVID 1961 *New Tools for Planners and Programmers.* Santa Monica, Calif.: RAND Corp.

SMITHIES, ARTHUR 1955 *The Budgetary Process in the United States.* New York: McGraw-Hill.

UN DEPARTMENT OF ECONOMIC AFFAIRS 1951 *Budgetary Structure and Classification of Government Accounts.* New York: United Nations.

II
BUDGETING AS A POLITICAL PROCESS

Budgets are predictions. They attempt to specify connections between words and numbers on the budget documents and future human behavior. Whether or not the behavior intended by the authors of the budget actually takes place is a question of empirical observation rather than one of definition. The budget of the Brazilian government, for example, has long been known as "a great lie" (Alionar Baleeiro, reported by Frank Sherwood), with little if any connection between what is spent for various purposes and what is contained in the formal document. Nor is there any necessary connection between the budgets of Soviet (Berliner 1957) and American (Argyris 1952; Sord & Welsch 1958) industrial firms and the expenditures they make or the actions they take.

Budgeting is concerned with the translation of financial resources into human purposes. Since funds are limited, a budget may become a mechanism for allocating resources. If emphasis is placed on receiving the largest returns for a given sum of money, or on obtaining the desired objectives at the lowest cost, a budget may become an instrument for pursuing efficiency (Smithies 1955). A proposed budget may represent an organization's expectations; it may contain the amounts which the organization expects to spend. A budget may also reflect organizational aspirations; it may contain figures the organization hopes to receive under favorable conditions. Since the amounts requested often have an effect on the amounts received, budget proposals are often strategies. The total sum of money and its distribution among various activities may be designed to have a favorable impact in support of an organization's goals. As each participant acts on the budget he receives information on the preferences of others and communicates his own desires through the choices he makes. Here a budget emerges as a network of communications in which information is being continuously generated and fed back to the participants. Once enacted a budget becomes a precedent; the fact that something has been done before vastly increases the chances that it will be done again (Wildavsky 1964).

For our purposes we shall conceive of budgets as attempts to allocate financial resources through political processes. If politics is regarded as conflict over whose preferences are to prevail in the determination of policy, then the budget records the outcomes of this struggle. If one asks who gets what the (public or private) organization has to give, then the answers for a moment in time are recorded in the budget. If organizations are viewed as political coalitions (Cyert & March 1963), budgets are mechanisms through which subunits bargain over conflicting goals, make side-payments, and try to motivate one another to accomplish their objectives.

Viewed in this light, the study of budgeting offers a useful perspective from which to analyze the making of policy. The opportunities for comparison are ample, the outcomes are specific and quantifiable, and the troublesome problem of a unit of analysis with which to test hypotheses— there is no real agreement on what a decision consists of—is solved by the very nature of the transactions in budgeting. Although a major effort has been made to collect budgetary material from many different countries, levels of government, and private firms, the results have only been fragmentary at best. Very little is available in any language on how budgeting is actually carried on. From Stourm's classic work on the budget (1889) to the present day, virtually the entire literature on budgeting has been normative in tone and content (Smithies 1955; Burkhead 1956; Buck 1929; 1934; Willoughby 1918; 1927). Yet the glimpses we do get of budgetary behavior in different systems suggest that there may be profound uniformities underlying the seeming diversities of form and structure.

Budgetary calculations

Decisions depend upon calculation of which alternatives to consider and to choose. Calculation involves determination of how problems are identified, get broken down into manageable dimensions, and are related to one another, and how choices are made as to what is relevant and who shall be taken into account. A major clue toward understanding budgeting is the extraordinary complexity of the calculations involved. In any large organization there are a huge number of items to be considered, many of which are of considerable technical difficulty. Yet there is little or no theory in most areas of policy which would enable practitioners to predict the consequences of alternative moves and the probability of their occurring (Braybrooke & Lindblom 1963). Man's ability to calculate is severely limited; time is always in short supply; and the number of matters which can be encompassed in one mind at the same time is quite small (Simon 1947–1956). Nor has anyone solved the imposing problem of the interpersonal comparison of utilities. Outside of the political process, there is no agreed upon way of comparing and evaluating the merits of different programs for different people whose preferences vary in kind and in intensity.

Simplification. Participants in budgeting deal with their overwhelming burdens by adopting aids to calculation. They simplify in order to get by. They make small moves, let experience accumulate, and use the feedback from their decisions to gauge the consequences. They use actions on simpler matters they understand as indices to complex concerns. They attempt to judge the capacity of

the men in charge of programs even if they cannot appraise the policies directly. They may institute across-the-board ("meat axe") cuts to reduce expenditures, relying on outcries from affected agencies and interest groups to let them know if they have gone too far (Wildavsky 1964, pp. 1–13). Hospital boards in Great Britain, unable to determine what costs should be in an absolute sense, rely on comparisons with comparable institutions. County councils keep close track of expenditures in only a few major areas to cut down on the bulk of overspending. The timing of new starts on projects is used as a simplifying device for regulating total expenditures. Another way local authorities keep spending within limits is through the practice of "rate rationing," or allowing committees so many pence or shillings of each pound of income (Royal Institute . . . 1959). Industrial firms use the percentage of total industry sales or some percentage of earnings on assets employed before taxes in setting budgetary goals. Many organizations use the number of personnel as strategic control points in limiting expenditures (Sord & Welsch 1958). Constraints are actively sought as in the common practice of isolating "prunable" items when looking for places to cut the budget (Royal Institute . . . 1959, pp. 115–116).

Incremental method.   By far the most important aid to calculation is the incremental method. Budgets are almost never actively reviewed as a whole in the sense of considering at once the value of all existing programs as compared with all possible alternatives. Instead, this year's budget is based on last year's budget, with special attention given to a narrow range of increases or decreases. The greatest part of any budget is a product of previous decisions. Long-range commitments have been made. There are mandatory programs whose expenses must be met. Powerful political support makes the inclusion of other activities inevitable. Consequently, officials concerned with budgeting restrict their attention to items and programs they can do something about—a few new programs and possible cuts in old ones.

When a British Treasury official warns in 1911 against "the habit of regarding each year's estimate as the starting-point for the next . . . ," (Higgs 1914, pp. 135–136) one can be sure that the practice has become well established. Both the practice and the complaints continue unabated in Great Britain (Mitchell 1935; Royal Institute . . . 1959). Incremental budgetary calculations can be found in such different places as Canadian provinces (McLeod 1953) and Michigan cities (where a sample budgetary guideline to department heads reads, "Budgets should be for the same level of service as the current year unless a variation is previously approved . . ." [Kressbach 1962, p. 41]).

Expectations of participants. Incremental calculations proceed from an existing base. By "base" we refer to commonly held expectations among participants in budgeting that programs will be carried out at close to the going level of expenditures. The base of a budget, therefore, refers to accepted parts of programs that will not normally be subjected to intensive scrutiny. Since many organizational units compete for funds, there is a tendency for the central authority to include all of them in the benefits or deprivations to be distributed. Participants in budgeting often refer to expectations regarding their fair share of increases and decreases (Wildavsky 1964, pp. 16–18). Argyris (1952, p. 16) quotes a supervisor as observing that employees had a well-developed notion of a fair output. In talking about the Philadelphia capital budget, Brown and Gilbert (1961) observe that every department got a share because projects were considered partly as contributions toward keeping the departments going. The widespread sharing of deeply held expectations concerning the organization's base and its fair share of funds provides a powerful (though informal) means of coordination and stability in budgetary systems which appear to lack comprehensive calculations proceeding from a hierarchical center.

Coordination and supervision

The most powerful coordinating mechanisms in budgeting undoubtedly stem from the role orientations adopted by the major participants. Roles (the expectations of behavior attached to institutional positions) are parts of the division of labor. They are calculating mechanisms. In American national government, the administrative agencies act as advocates of increased expenditure, the Bureau of the Budget acts as presidential servant with a cutting bias, the House Appropriations Committee functions as a guardian of the Treasury, and the Senate Appropriations Committee serves as an appeals court to which agencies carry their disagreement with House action. The roles fit in with one another and set up a stable pattern of mutual expectations, which markedly reduces the burden of calculation for the participants. The agencies need not consider in great detail how their requests will affect the president's over-all program; they know that such criteria will be introduced by the Budget Bureau. Since the agencies can be depended upon to advance all the programs for which there is prospect of support, the Budget Bureau

and the appropriations committees can concentrate respectively on fitting them into the president's program or paring them down. If the agencies suddenly reversed roles and sold themselves short, the entire pattern of mutual expectations would be upset, leaving the participants without a firm anchor in a sea of complexity. For if agencies refuse to be advocates, congressmen would not only have to choose among the margins of the best programs placed before them, they would also have to discover what these good programs might be. Indeed, the Senate Appropriations Committee depends upon agency advocacy to cut its burden of calculation; if the agencies refused to carry appeals from House cuts, the senators would have to do much more work than their busy schedules permit (Wildavsky 1964).

A writer on Canadian budgeting (Ward 1962, p. 165) refers to the tendency for an administrator to become "an enthusiastic advocate" of increased funds for his policies. When disagreements over departmental budgets arise, as they frequently do in private firms, the controller and the departmental representatives come to a meeting armed to the teeth to defend their respective positions (Argyris 1952, p. 9). The same interministerial battles go on in Great Britain (Brittain 1959, pp. 216–217), the Netherlands (Drees 1955, pp. 61–71), and the Soviet Union, where "serious clashes" arise when ministries and republics ask for greater funds to fulfill their plans (Davies 1958, p. 184).

In a discussion which deserves to be better known, W. Drees (1955, pp. 61–71) points out that agency heads can defend the interests of their sectors because it is so difficult for them to relate their modest part in total expenditures to the over-all budgetary situation. Anything they could save through a spirit of forbearance would be too small a portion of the total to make the sacrifice worthwhile. From their point of view, total expenditures are irrelevant.

The role of guardian or defender of the treasury apparently did not come naturally. In the early days of public finance in France, "Financiers appropriated to themselves without restraint the spoils of the nation, and used for their own profit the funds intended for the Treasury; the only restraint lay in the fact that when their plundering exceeded the measure of tolerance they were hanged. It was a summary procedure of control *a posteriori* . . ." (Stourm [1889] 1917, p. 536). It took centuries to develop a finance minister like Louis Thiers, whose definition of his role included that "ferocity . . . needed to defend the Treasury"

(Stourm [1889] 1917, p. 69). The members of the U.S. House Appropriations Committee consider themselves guardians of the Treasury who take pride in the high degree of frequency with which they reduce estimates (Fenno 1962). They reconcile this role with the defense of constituency interests by cutting estimates to satisfy one role and generally increasing amounts over the previous year to satisfy the other.

Among the legislatures of the world, however, guardianship appears to be quite rare. Drees (1955) reports that in the Netherlands the legislative specialists concerned with finance, by advocating higher appropriations, defend the interests of the policy areas over which they have jurisdiction to a degree overriding party lines. Much the same thing happened in France during the Fourth Republic (Williams 1954). It may be that guardianship depends, first, on appropriations committees that have continuing power to affect outcomes— a rare occurrence in the modern world—and, second, on the development of cultural values and legislative mores that support an insistent financial check on the bureaucracy. Legislative committees in nations like Mexico, where virtually complete budgetary power is in the hands of the president, who heads the single great party (Scott 1955), or Great Britain, where party responsibility overwhelms parliamentary initiative (Brittain 1959), are hardly in a position to develop a role of guardianship.

Budgetary goals

Possessing the greatest expertise and the largest numbers, working in the closest proximity to their policy problems and clientele groups, desirous of expanding their horizons, administrative agencies generate action through advocacy. But how much shall they ask for? Life would be simple if they could just estimate the costs of their ever-expanding needs and submit the total as their request. But if they ask for amounts much larger than the appropriating bodies believe are reasonable, the credibility of the agencies will suffer a drastic decline. In such circumstances, the reviewing organs are likely to apply a "measure of unrealism" (Royal Institute . . . 1959, p. 245), with the result that the agency gets much less than it might have with a more moderate request. So the first decision rule is: Do not come in too high. Yet the agencies must also not come in too low, for the assumption is that if agency advocates do not ask for funds they do not need them. Since the budgetary situation is always tight, terribly tight, or impossibly tight, reviewing bodies are likely to accept a low

request with thanks and not inquire too closely into the rationale. Given the distribution of roles, cuts must be expected and allowances made.

The agency decision rule might therefore read: Come in a little high (padding), but not too high (loss of confidence). But how high is too high? What agency heads do is to evaluate signals from the environment—last year's experience, legislative votes, executive policy statements, actions of clientele groups, reports from the field—and come up with an asking price somewhat higher than they expect to get (Wildavsky 1964, pp. 21–32). In Michigan cities, for example, city managers sound out councilmen to determine what will go or get by in their budgets (Kressbach 1962, p. 5). Departments and local authorities in Great Britain commonly make assessments "of how much spending is likely to be acceptable to the governing body" (Royal Institute . . . 1959, p. 57). After first determining what the mayor, finance director, councilmen, and other key participants will "die for," together with other projects which "cannot be moved," the men in charge of Philadelphia's capital budget let other projects by if they seem sound and if the request is not too far out of line (Brown & Gilbert 1961, pp. 71–88).

The Bureau of the Budget in the United States takes on the assigned role of helping the president realize his goals when it can discover what they are supposed to be. This role is performed with a cutting bias, however, simply because the agencies normally push so hard in asking for funds. The bureau helps the president by making his preferences more widely known throughout the executive branch so that those who would like to go along have a chance to find out what is required of them. Since Congress usually cuts the president's budget, Bureau figures tend to be the most the agencies can get, especially when the items are not of such paramount importance as to justify intensive scrutiny by Congress. Yet the power of the purse remains actively with Congress. If the Budget Bureau continually recommended figures which were blatantly disregarded by Congress, the agencies would soon learn to pay less and less attention to the president's budget. As a result, the Bureau follows consistent congressional action (Wildavsky 1964, pp. 4–42); it can be shown empirically that Bureau recommendations tend to follow congressional actions over a large number of cases.

In deciding how much money to recommend for specific purposes, the House Appropriations Committee breaks down into largely autonomous subcommittees in which the norm of reciprocity is carefully followed (Fenno 1962). Specialization is carried further as subcommittee members develop limited areas of competence and jurisdiction. Budgeting is both incremental and fragmented as the committees deal with adjustments to the historical base of each agency. Sequential decision making is the rule as problems are first attacked in the jurisdiction in which they appear and then followed step-by-step as they manifest themselves elsewhere (Wildavsky 1964, pp. 56–64). The subcommittee members treat budgeting as a process of making marginal monetary adjustments to existing programs, rather than as a mechanism for reconsidering basic policy choices every year (Fenno 1962). Fragmentation and specialization are further increased through the appeals functions of the Senate Appropriations Committee, which deals with what has become (through House action) a fragment of a fragment. When the actions of subcommittees conflict, coordination may be achieved by repeated attacks on the problem or through reference to the House and Senate as a whole when the appropriations committees go beyond the informal zone of indifference set up by the more intense preferences of the membership. When one thinks of all the participants who are continually engaged in taking others into account, it is clear that a great many adjustments are made in the light of what others are likely to do.

Budgetary strategies

Having decided how much to ask for, agencies engage in strategic planning to secure their budgetary goals. Strategies are the links between the goals of the agencies and their perceptions of the kinds of actions which their political environment will make efficacious. Budget officers in the U.S. national government uniformly believe that being a good politician—cultivating an active clientele, developing the confidence of other officials (particularly of the appropriations subcommittees), and using skill in following strategies that exploit opportunities—is more important in obtaining funds than demonstration of efficiency. Agencies seek to cultivate a clientele that will help them to expand and that will express satisfaction to other public officials. Top agency officials soon come to learn that the appropriations committees are very powerful; their recommendations are accepted approximately 90 per cent of the time (Fenno 1962). Since budgetary calculations are so complex, the legislators must take a good deal on faith. Hence their demand that agency budget officers demonstrate a high degree of integrity. If the appropriations committees believe that they have been misled, they can do grave damage to the

career of the offending budgeting officer and to the prospects of the agency he represents. While doing a decent job may be a necessary condition for success, the importance of clientele and confidence are so great that all agencies employ these strategies (Wildavsky 1964, pp. 65–98).

In addition to these ubiquitous strategies there are contingent strategies which depend upon time, circumstance, and place. In defending the base, for example, cuts may be made in the most popular programs so that a public outcry results in restoration of the funds. The base may be increased within existing programs by shifting funds between categories (Kressbach 1962, p. 51; Stourm [1889] 1917, p. 348). Substantial additions to the base may come about through proposing new programs to meet crises and through campaigns involving large doses of advertising and salesmanship (Wildavsky 1964, pp. 101–123). The dependence of these strategies on the incremental, increase–decrease type of budgetary calculation is evident. By helping determine the ways in which programs are perceived and evaluated, the forms of budgetary presentation may assume considerable importance.

One major strategy deserves separate attention—the division of expenditures into capital and expense budgets. In practice, as Mosher says, "The Capital budget is a catalogue of prospective budgets for which money may be borrowed . . ." (1956, p. 69). The attempted distinction between capital assets with future returns and ordinary expenditures soon breaks down under the pressure of avoiding tax increases or the appearance of deficits by borrowing for items designated in the capital budget (Burkhead 1956, pp. 182ff.; Mosher 1956, p. 70; Sundelson 1938, pp. 146–198). The ideological emphasis on the size and growth of the deficit in the United States makes it likely that the introduction of a capital budget would permit substantially greater expenditures as apparent deficits become converted into formal surpluses.

Organizations wish to maintain themselves in their environment. For governmental agencies this can be taken to mean maintenance of political support from clientele groups and other governmental participants. We expect that policies are chosen not only because of any intrinsic merit but also because they add to, or at least do not seriously detract from, the necessary political support. The heads of agencies can expect to lose internal control, to be fired, to see their policies overturned, or even to find their organization dismembered if their recommendations are continually disapproved. They therefore seek to maintain a reasonable record of success (to guard their professional reputation, as Richard Neustadt puts it) in order to maintain the confidence of the key people in and out of their agency. Thus, they are compelled to consider the probable actions of others differently situated who have a say in determining their income. These notions may be tested by observing how agency requests vary with the treatment they receive from the Budget Bureau and Congress.

Suppose that we wish to explain the level of appropriations which agencies request of Congress through the Bureau of the Budget and the amounts which Congress provides through appropriations laws. The goals of the participants may be conceived of as constraints which are represented by the role orientations adopted by members of the appropriations committees and by top agency officials. Moreover, we know that budgetary calculations are incremental. Thus, it becomes possible to create in symbolic form, as linear, stochastic differences equations, a series of simple decision rules embodying the relationships we expect to find. Given the availability of appropriations laws and of Budget Bureau requests for individual agencies, the decision rules can be tested for their fit in accommodating the times series comprising fifteen or twenty years' figures.

In the simplest form, for example, a decision rule might be that the funds requested by an agency in a particular year are a direct function of its appropriation in the previous year up to a normally distributed random error. A second decision rule might make allowance for the difference between what the agency asked for and actually received from Congress in the previous year. Should an agency decide to pad its request to make up for a cut, should it decide to insist on the worth of its programs despite congressional action—strategies such as these can be represented as separate decision rules. Davis, Dempster, and Wildavsky (1966) are now able to show that basic parts of the federal budgetary process can be precisely described by a small number of relatively simple decision rules.

Budgets of firms

Treatment of budgets as political instruments is justified not only in governmental activities but also in industrial enterprises. A more political phenomenon than budgeting in Soviet industrial firms has not been invented. Rewards to managers depend on meeting production quotas assigned in economic plans. But the supplies, skilled labor, and financial resources are often lacking. The first consequence is that the quota is not set from above

but becomes the subject of bargaining as the managers seek to convince the ministries that quotas should be as low as possible. The managers find it prudent not to exceed their quota hugely, for in that case next year's quota will be raised beyond attainment. The second consequence is that production is not rationalized to yield the greatest output at the lowest cost but is geared instead to meeting specific incentives. Heavy nails, for example, are overproduced because quotas are figured by weight. Maintenance may be slighted in favor of huge effort for a short period in order to meet the quota. Funds are hidden in order to provide slack that can be used to pay "pushers" to expedite the arrival of supplies. The list of essentially deceitful practices to give the appearance of fulfilling the quota is seemingly endless: producing the wrong assortment of products, transferring current costs to capital accounts, shuffling accounts to pay for one item with funds designated for another, declaring unfinished goods finished, lowering the quality of goods, and so on (Berliner 1957). The point is that the budgetary system arranges incentives so that managers cannot succeed with lawful practices. Communist China reveals the same pattern (Hsia 1953; Li 1959). When similar incentives are set up in American industrial firms similar practices result, from running machines into the ground, to "bleeding the line," to meeting a monthly quota by doctoring the accounts (Jasinsky 1956, p. 107).

As in the Soviet Union, American firms often use budgets not to reflect or project reality but to drive managers and workers toward increased production. Indeed, some firms base their budgets on historical experience plus an added factor for increased performance (Axelson 1963). Budgets are conceived of as forms of pressure on inherently lazy people so that (to paraphrase Mao Tse-tung) the more the pressure, the better the budget. Inevitably, managers and workers begin to perceive budgets as "perpetual needlers." In some cases this type of budget leads to discouragement because it is apparent that whatever the effort, the budget quota will be increased. Since accounting takes place by subunits in the firm, it is not surprising that fierce negotiations occur to assign costs among them. As a result, top officials find it necessary to engage in campaigns to sell budgets to the units. Otherwise, sabotage is likely (Sord & Welsch 1958, pp. 140–150). While some attention has been given to human relations in budgeting (Bebling 1961, p. 16), only Stedry (1960) has attempted to explore the essential motivational problems of budgeting within a political, institutional framework. Yet without an understanding of the impact of different goals and incentive systems on human activity, reliable statements about the likely consequences of budget documents can hardly be made.

Intensive study of budgetary behavior has just begun. Despite the relative paucity of comparative data, patterns of behavior appear to be remarkably consistent across private and public organizations (Wildavsky 1965) and national and state boundaries. After the appearance of monographs on different budgetary systems in various environments, it should be possible to create a small number of budgetary models specifying the elements of the organization coalition, the distribution of roles among the principal actors, the most prevalent aids to calculation, the strategies which appear as responses to types of incentives, and the outcomes to be expected in terms of amounts requested and received. Computer simulation may be used to test the effect of shocks to the budgetary systems. The study of budgeting as a political phenomenon in an organizational context may then become a major aid in the comparative analysis of governmental policy.

AARON B. WILDAVSKY

[*See also* DECISION MAKING; ORGANIZATIONS; POLITICAL PROCESS.]

BIBLIOGRAPHY

ARGYRIS, CHRIS 1952 *The Impact of Budgets on People.* New York: Controllership Foundation.
AXELSON, CHARLES F. 1963 What Makes Budgeting So Obnoxious? *Business Budgeting* 11, no. 5:22–27.
BEBLING, ARNOLD A. 1961 A Look at Budgets and People. *Business Budgeting* 10, no. 2:15–18.
BERLINER, JOSEPH S. 1957 *Factory and Manager in the U.S.S.R.* Cambridge, Mass.: Harvard Univ. Press.
BRAYBROOKE, DAVID; and LINDBLOM, CHARLES E. 1963 *A Strategy of Decision: Policy Evaluation as a Social Process.* New York: Free Press.
BRITTAIN, HERBERT 1959 *The British Budgetary System.* New York: Macmillan.
BROWN, WILLIAM H. JR.; and GILBERT, C. E. 1961 *Planning Municipal Investment: A Case Study of Philadelphia.* Philadelphia: Univ. of Pennsylvania Press.
BUCK, A. E. 1929 *Public Budgeting: A Discussion of Budgetary Practice in the National, State and Local Governments of the United States.* New York: Harper.
BUCK, A. E. 1934 *The Budget in Governments of Today.* New York: Macmillan.
BURKHEAD, JESSE 1956 *Government Budgeting.* New York: Wiley.
CYERT, RICHARD M.; and MARCH, JAMES G. 1963 *A Behavioral Theory of the Firm.* Englewood Cliffs, N.J.: Prentice-Hall.
DAVIES, ROBERT W. 1958 *The Development of the Soviet Budgetary System.* Cambridge Univ. Press.

DAVIS, OTTO; DEMPSTER, M. A. H.; and WILDAVSKY, AARON 1966 A Theory of the Budgetary Process. Unpublished manuscript.
DREES, WILLEM 1955 *On the Level of Government Expenditure in the Netherlands After the War.* Leiden (Netherlands): Stenfert Kroese.
FENNO, RICHARD F. 1962 The House Appropriations Committee as a Political System: The Problem of Integration. *American Political Science Review* 56:310–324.
HIGGS, HENRY 1914 *The Financial System of the United Kingdom.* London: Macmillan.
HSIA, RONALD (1953) 1955 *Economic Planning in Communist China.* New York: Institute of Pacific Relations, International Secretariat.
JASINSKY, FRANK 1956 Use and Misuse of Efficiency Controls. *Harvard Business Review* 34, no. 4:105–112.
KRESSBACH, THOMAS W. 1962 *The Michigan City Manager in Budgetary Proceedings.* Ann Arbor: Michigan Municipal League.
LEPPO, MATTI 1950 The Double-budget System in the Scandinavian Countries. *Public Finance* 5:137–147.
LI, CHO-MIN 1959 *Economic Development of Communist China: An Appraisal of the First Five Years of Industrialization.* Berkeley: Univ. of California Press.
MCLEOD, T. H. 1953 Budgeting Provincial Expenditure. Pages 11–19 in Institute of Public Administration of Canada, Annual Conference, Fifth, *Proceedings.* Toronto: The Institute.
MARRE, A. S. 1957 Departmental Financial Control. *Public Administration* 35:169–178.
MITCHELL, RONALD J. 1935 *State Finance: The Theory and Practice of Public Finance in the United Kingdom.* London: Pitman.
MOSHER, FREDERICK C. 1956 Fiscal Planning and Budgeting in New York City. Pages 65–84 in New York State–New York City Fiscal Relations Committee, *A Report to the Governor of the State of New York and the Mayor of the City of New York.* New York: The Committee.
ROYAL INSTITUTE OF PUBLIC ADMINISTRATION 1959 *Budgeting in Public Authorities.* New York: Macmillan.
SCHUBERT, GLENDON; and MCINTYRE, DONALD F. 1953 Preparing the Michigan State Budget. *Public Administration Review* 13:237–246.
SCOTT, ROBERT E. 1955 Budget Making in Mexico. *Inter-American Economic Affairs* 9:3–20.
SIMON, HERBERT A. (1947–1956) 1957 *Models of Man; Social and Rational: Mathematical Essays on Rational Human Behavior in a Social Setting.* New York: Wiley.
SMITHIES, ARTHUR 1955 *The Budgetary Process in the United States.* New York: McGraw-Hill.
SORD, BERNARD H.; and WELSCH, GLENN A. 1958 *Business Budgeting: A Survey of Management Planning and Control Practices.* New York: Controllership Foundation.
STEDRY, ANDREW C. 1960 *Budget Control and Cost Behavior.* Englewood Cliffs, N.J.: Prentice-Hall.
STOURM, RENÉ (1889) 1917 *The Budget.* New York: Appleton. → First published in French.
SUNDELSON, JACOB W. 1938 *Budgetary Methods in National and State Governments.* Albany, N.Y.: Lyon.
WARD, NORMAN 1962 *The Public Purse.* Univ. of Toronto Press.
WILDAVSKY, AARON B. 1964 *Politics of the Budgetary Process.* Boston: Little.

WILDAVSKY, AARON B. 1965 Private Markets and Public Arenas. *American Behavioral Scientist* 9, no. 1: 33–37.

WILLIAMS, PHILIP M. (1954) 1964 *Crisis and Compromise: Politics in the Fourth Republic.* 3d ed. Hamden, Conn.: Shoe String Press. → First published as *Politics in Post-war France: Parties and the Constitution in the Fourth Republic.*

WILLOUGHBY, WILLIAM F. 1918 *The Movement for Budgetary Reform in the States.* New York: Appleton.

WILLOUGHBY, WILLIAM F. 1927 *The National Budget System.* Baltimore: Johns Hopkins Press.

BÜHLER, KARL

Karl Ludwig Bühler (1879–1963), German psychologist, was born in Meckesheim, near Heidelberg; his father was a railway clerk and small peasant, and his mother came of Catholic peasant stock. Bühler grew up a Catholic and obtained a scholarship to the Tauberbischofsheim Catholic Gymnasium. In 1899 he matriculated at the University of Freiburg im Breisgau and in 1903 earned his M.D. with a dissertation on the physiological theories of color vision under Johannes von Kries. He also studied philosophy at Freiburg and continued his philosophical studies at the University of Strassburg. There he earned his PH.D. under Clemens Bäumker in 1904 with a dissertation on the psychology of Henry Home (Lord Kames), the eighteenth-century Scottish philosopher.

After returning to Heidelberg to serve as assistant to von Kries, Bühler went to Berlin to study under Erdmann and Carl Stumpf; in 1906 he went to Würzburg as an assistant to Oswald Külpe, obtaining his habilitation as docent in philosophy upon submitting experimental studies on the psychology of thought processes. Bühler followed Külpe when the latter moved to Bonn in 1909 and to Munich in 1913; there Bühler was appointed associate professor without tenure. During World War I he was for a time a captain in the medical corps, developing psychological aptitude tests for drivers and pilots and also treating brain injuries.

In 1916 Bühler married Charlotte Malachowski, who in the same year earned her PH.D. at the University of Munich. At the end of the war, in 1918, Bühler was appointed a full professor at the Dresden Institute of Technology, where his wife received the habilitation as a docent in 1920. Two years later, when Bühler was appointed professor in Vienna, Charlotte Bühler also transferred her docentship to Vienna and became his assistant. Between 1922 and 1938, Bühler, with his wife's support, established and ran a psychological institute in Vienna, as well as his own school of psychology, which soon achieved world-wide recognition. Concurrently he was visiting professor at the Pedagogical Institute of the City of Vienna.

In 1926–1927 and again in 1929 he taught in the United States as an exchange professor at Stanford, Johns Hopkins, Harvard, and Chicago universities. In 1938 he was briefly arrested by the Hitler regime in Vienna but released upon the intervention of Norwegian friends. Then he emigrated, first to Oslo and, in 1939, to the United States, where he became professor of psychology, first at the College of St. Scholastica in Duluth, Minnesota, and later, from 1940 to 1945 (with a brief interlude at Clark University in Worcester, Massachusetts), at the College of St. Thomas in St. Paul, Minnesota. At the end of World War II he moved to Los Angeles, serving as assistant clinical professor of psychiatry at the medical school of the University of Southern California until 1955 and as consulting psychologist at the Cedars of Lebanon Hospital. He died in Los Angeles in 1963.

In 1960 Bühler was elected honorary president of the Sixteenth International Psychological Congress in Bonn, where he was awarded the Wilhelm Wundt medal of the German Psychological Association. During his years in Vienna, Bühler had a number of European students who later made names for themselves, such as René Spitz, Alexander Willwoll, Hildegard Hetzer, Paul F. Lazarsfeld, Egon Brunswik, Else Frenkel-Brunswik, Konrad Lorenz, Albert Wellek, and Peter Hofstätter, and from the United States, Edward Tolman, David Klein, and Neal Miller.

When Bühler's Würzburg habilitation thesis on the psychology of thought was published in the *Archiv für die gesamte Psychologie* in 1907–1908, it gave rise to a celebrated controversy with Wilhelm Wundt, the old master of experimental psychology, concerning the methodological legitimacy of nonexact experiments and retrospective introspection. Next to Külpe, Bühler was the leading figure in the new psychology of thought that broadened and redefined experimental procedures. This psychology of thought was subsequently developed (beginning in 1919) into a psychology of speech.

During Bühler's years in Bonn, however, he was primarily interested in the work of the Graz school, particularly that of von Ehrenfels on visual gestalten. As early as 1912—simultaneously with the first similar statements of the Berlin psychologists who founded gestalt theory—Bühler read a paper at the Fifth German Psychological Congress on the comparison of spatial gestalten with respect to their proportions. His first major opus, *Die Gestalt-*

wahrnehmungen, which elaborated the initial "laws of gestalt," followed in 1913. Bühler claimed to have developed these laws before the Berlin school had; to be sure, the experimental holistic-psychological researches in the field of sound begun by Felix Krueger in 1900 anticipated all of them. Bühler even claimed priority for the concept of physical gestalten, although he regarded the concept merely as a hypothetical possibility and later rejected it quite decisively. Bühler's later work in the psychology of perception extended to optics and appeared in his *Erscheinungsweisen der Farben* (1922), which was announced as part 1 of a general theory of perception, though no further parts were published under this title. David Katz had earlier done such work on the appearance of colors. Bühler's polemics against the Berlin school became even more heated in 1926, when he wrote a critique of Koffka's new psychology (1926*a*).

By the early 1920s Bühler had progressed from the psychology of thought and of perception to his third major theme, developmental psychology. He wrote the first systematic exposition of this topic in 1919, following the work of William Preyer and William Stern, entitled *The Mental Development of the Child* (*Die geistige Entwicklung des Kindes*), which was followed in 1928 by a condensed version, or *Abriss*; both of these went through numerous editions. His investigations of the psychology of speech, which began at about that time, became part of the study of developmental psychology (1926*b*). In all of these areas, especially in developmental psychology, Bühler attacked the traditionally basic problem of the significance of feelings (or feeling tones) for motivation and action (1928). In sharp disagreement with Freud's broad concept of a general "pleasure principle," he made the concept only one of three such structures: he limited Freud's mechanism to "the pleasure of satisfaction," positing two others, "the pleasure of functioning" and "the pleasure of creating," alongside or above it.

Bühler combined these theories with others within the framework of a major evaluation of psychological methodology, which was published in 1926 as "Die Krise der Psychologie" (1926*c*) and appeared as a book in 1927 (second edition, 1929, with an important addition to the preface). The title was similar to the subtitle of a book by Hans Driesch that was published at the same time (*Grundprobleme der Psychologie: Ihre Krisis in der Gegenwart*, 1926) as well as to *Krisis der Geisteswissenschaften* by Josef Strzygowski (1923). Bühler's point of departure was the revolution caused by the victory of gestalt and holistic psychology over elementism and associationism, but he proceeded from this crisis in fundamental concepts to the crisis in methodology—in other words, to the plight of the psychology of consciousness, faced by behaviorism, on the one hand, and by humanistic psychology, on the other. Bühler found a solution in his doctrine of the three aspects of psychology: the three positions were not conceived as essentially antagonistic, nor was any one of them granted exclusive validity; rather, he demanded that all three be accorded equal validity and that they be treated as complementary. Bühler called his three aspects the experiential aspect, the behavioral aspect, and the cultural-achievement aspect. From the standpoint of methodology, the first proceeds from self-observation, or introspection, the second from the observation of others, and the third from humanistic analysis. These three aspects are the very substance of psychology—the stuff of cognition. They are "aspects" insofar as they define the possible bases of psychological cognition: points *toward* which one looks, rather than points *from* which one looks out.

In 1934 Bühler published *Sprachtheorie: Die Darstellungsfunktion der Sprache*. Starting out from Plato's *Cratylus*, he had, in 1918, already developed the concept of speech as an instrument (organon) of communication and had constructed a three-part "organon model" involving a transmitter, a receiver, and a designated object. These correspond to the threefold function of speech as utterance (symptom or sign), release (signal), and representation or information (symbol or sign of what is meant). In 1934 he chose new terminology: expression (by someone), appeal (to someone), and representation (of something). In this triad we again see the triad of the substance of psychology according to his doctrine of three aspects: expression has to do with experience, appeal with behavior, and representation with the object, the objective (*das Objektive*), the mental (*das Geistige*), and the cultural achievement. At the same time, the thetic nature of speech, as set agreement and construction, is emphasized, while its spontaneous and physiognomic nature, in the sense of coincidence of sign or symbol with what is designated or symbolized, is rejected. Accordingly, the physiognomics of speech, especially in the version of Heinz Werner (implicit also in that of Albert Wellek), is rejected or reduced to a "sound-painting," accessory in the body, or the whole, of speech. As early as 1931 Bühler advocated "phonology" as a humanistic science of speech sounds (as distinct from phonetics as a natural science of the same subject). In this he was joined by Prince N. S. Trubetskoi, his Viennese colleague in Slavistics and general linguistics, and by the Prague Linguistic Circle stimulated by Trubetskoi ("Phonetik und Phonologie," 1931).

After his enforced emigration in 1938, Bühler remained silent for a long time. His friends grieved as many of his profoundest interests appeared to have been extinguished, especially his interest in linguistics and phonology. At the age of 60 he was unable to establish himself firmly in the United States. His style of thought, his manner of lecturing, in fact his entire approach to psychology met with little understanding, and he was neither willing nor able to make an adjustment. His most famous pupil, Egon Brunswik, who had emigrated shortly before Bühler, had joined the Vienna Circle of Moritz Schlick and Rudolph Carnap while still in Vienna. In America Brunswik had come to advocate even more strongly a "unitary science" of operationism, of which he became the outstanding theoretician. Bühler regarded this as desertion, which in exile he found hard to bear.

Only in 1952 did he come forward again—hesitantly, only rarely, and without receiving much attention. He wrote several papers on spatial orientation in man and animals. His last book, *Das Gestaltprinzip im Leben des Menschen und der Tiere*, was published in 1960. Here he returned once again to large-scale (though no longer concise or even comprehensive) consideration of his old fundamental problem, the relationship between biology and psychology, between life and thought, "modernized" somewhat by investigations in the field of cybernetics. His final conclusion was that what is essentially human—thought and reason, gestaltic and holistic experience—is independent of the machine, or the mechanical principle, and also independent to some extent of what is merely biological in the animal kingdom.

This concept was consonant with the dual, in fact dialectical, underlying idea in all of Bühler's work: the notion of the creative nature of human thought, notwithstanding its biologically governed foundation. He found the concept of homeostasis was not sufficient to describe psychic life in full. Thus, the creative nature of life follows from the creative nature of mind and vice versa; both are differentiated, however, from the inanimate, which is mindless.

Bühler's *Krise* (1926c), his most important book, remains timely. The core of the book, the doctrine of three aspects, has proved to be a bold departure. It bridges and eliminates spurious and unnecessary contradictions and conflicts.

Leading psychologists have acknowledged the enduring fruitfulness of this doctrine. Increasingly, though implicitly, even psychologists in the United States have done so: only for a very short time did it seem possible that, as a final concession to behavioristic radicalism, the aspect of inner experience, the *horribile dictu* "subjective," might be banished entirely from psychological science. Similarly, the cultural-achievement aspect (the cultural and ethnopsychological), the humanistic, is beginning to acquire more methodological importance. In the Old World, almost every psychologist of importance has acknowledged the need to integrate and synthesize aspects and methods and has followed Bühler in viewing such a synthesis as a means of avoiding a disastrous one-sidedness, even a crippling, of psychology as a science.

ALBERT WELLEK

[*For the historical context of Bühler's work, see* GESTALT THEORY; *and the biographies of* KATZ; KOFFKA; KÖHLER; KÜLPE; STERN; WERTHEIMER. *For discussion of the subsequent development of Bühler's ideas, see* LANGUAGE; PERCEPTION, *article on* SPEECH PERCEPTION; VISION, *article on* COLOR VISION AND COLOR BLINDNESS; *and the biography of* BRUNSWIK.]

WORKS BY BÜHLER

1907–1908   Tatsachen und Probleme zu einer Psychologie der Denkvorgänge. *Archiv für die gesamte Psychologie* 9:297–365; 12:1–123. → Part 1: Über Gedanken. Part 2: Über Gedankenzusammenhänge.

1912   Vergleichung von Raumgestalten. Pages 183–185 in Deutsche Gesellschaft für Psychologie, *Bericht über den V. Kongress für experimentelle Psychologie*. Leipzig: Barth.

1913   *Die Gestaltwahrnehmungen*. Stuttgart (Germany): Spemann.

(1919) 1930   *The Mental Development of the Child*. New York: Harcourt. → First published as *Die geistige Entwicklung des Kindes*.

1922   *Erscheinungsweisen der Farben*. Jena (Germany): Fischer.

1926a   Die "Neue Psychologie Koffkas." *Zeitschrift für Psychologie* 99:145–159.

1926b   Les lois générales d'évolution dans le language de l'enfant. *Journal de psychologie* 23:597–607.

(1926c) 1929   *Die Krise der Psychologie*. Jena (Germany): Fischer. → First published in Volume 31 of *Kant-Studien*.

1928   Displeasure and Pleasure in Relation to Activity. Volume 8, pages 195–199 in International Symposium on Feelings and Emotions, First, Wittenberg College, 1927, *Proceedings*. Worcester, Mass.: Clark Univ. Press.

1931   Phonetik und Phonologie. Cercle Linguistique de Prague, *Travaux* 4:22–53.

1934   *Sprachtheorie: Die Darstellungsfunktion der Sprache*. Jena (Germany): Fischer.

1952   The Skywise and Neighborwise Navigation of Ants and Bees. *Acta Psychologica* 8:225–263.

1953   Der Atemfaktor in tierischen Geruchsspuren. *Jahrbuch für Psychologie und Psychotherapie* 1:479–483.

1954a   Essentials of Contact Navigation. *Acta Psychologica* 10:278–316.

1954b   Menschliche Fernorientierung. *Jahrbuch für Psychologie und Psychotherapie* 2:242–258.

1960   *Das Gestaltprinzip im Leben des Menschen und der Tiere.* Bern (Switzerland): Huber.

SUPPLEMENTARY BIBLIOGRAPHY

Beiträge zur Problemgeschichte der Psychologie. 1929 Jena (Germany): Fischer. → A publication honoring Bühler on his fiftieth birthday.

BÜHLER, CHARLOTTE 1965 Die Wiener psychologische Schule in der Emigration. *Psychologische Rundschau* 16:187–196.

DRIESCH, HANS 1926 *Grundprobleme der Psychologie: Ihre Krisis in der Gegenwart.* Leipzig: Reinicke.

Festschrift für Karl Bühler. With a dedication by Albert Wellek. 1959 *Zeitschrift für experimentelle und angewandte Psychologie* 6:1–165.

STRZYGOWSKI, JOSEF 1923 *Krisis der Geisteswissenschaften.* Vienna: Schroll.

WELLEK, ALBERT 1959 Ein Dritteljahrhundert nach Bühlers *Krise der Psychologie. Zeitschrift für experimentelle und angewandte Psychologie* 6:109–117.

WELLEK, ALBERT 1965 Der Einfluss der deutschen Emigration auf die Entwicklung der nordamerikanischen Psychologie. *Jahrbuch für Amerikastudien* 10:34–58.

BUONARROTI, FILIPPO

Filippo Michele Buonarroti (1761–1837) was an Italian Jacobin and Babouvist leader who survived to help perpetuate as well as reshape the revolutionary tradition in the Metternich era. The materials for his biography are still being quarried from archives pertaining to the conspiratorial underground of early nineteenth-century Europe. He was born in Pisa of patrician stock and, as heir to a long line of Tuscan magistrates and councillors of state, trained for a legal career. But his conversion to the doctrines of Rousseau, Mably, and Morelly as a law student at the University of Pisa and his subsequent role as an anticlerical radical journalist led to trouble with the Hapsburg authorities, which culminated in his abandonment of family and fortune to serve the Jacobin cause after the revolution broke out in France.

As an agent of the First Republic in Corsica, he was made a French citizen by the National Convention in May of 1793 and won a post as national commissioner in Oneglia (a region in the Maritime Alps occupied by French troops). He was arrested by the Thermidorian government in March of 1795 and was sentenced to a six-month term in the prison of Plessis, where he encountered and began to collaborate with "Gracchus" Babeuf.

Buonarroti's opposition to the *ancien régime* dif-

fered from that of the more plebeian self-educated Babeuf. His views were not grounded, as were Babeuf's, in personal and practical grievances against French provincial feudal customs but derived from academic studies of Enlightenment ideas and a philanthropic impulse akin to *noblesse oblige*. The two men also adopted different attitudes toward the revolutionary factions. Babeuf, who was an atheist, was alienated by the Cult of the Supreme Being and welcomed the fall of Robespierre. Only later did he exploit, for tactical reasons, the image of Robespierre as a popular republican, martyred by a small counterrevolutionary faction, whereas Buonarroti, a deist, adhered to this image. Both agreed, however, that the political institutions and economic legislation of 1793–1794 should be viewed not as transient emergency measures but as guidelines for the future permanent establishment in the most powerful nation on the Continent of an ideal egalitarian community.

Upon their release from prison, Babeuf and Buonarroti worked together closely in the so-called Conspiracy of Equals, a plot to overthrow the Directory. After the events of *Prairial*, they discarded as futile any effort to inspire another popular insurrection. Instead, they resorted to a *coup d'état* by a resolute minority which acted in the name of the helpless populace to install a provisional dictatorship. The Conspiracy of Equals failed no less than the *Prairial* uprising, but the Babouvist justification of avant-garde action in the popular interest became part of the revolutionary tradition, largely because Buonarroti, unlike Babeuf, escaped execution and survived his incarceration in a fortress.

During the Empire, Buonarroti participated in anti-Bonapartist plots, even while under police surveillance as a political prisoner. After Waterloo he moved from various residences in Switzerland to Brussels and then to Paris, recruiting agents for his own cosmopolitan secret society and infiltrating most of the others that honeycombed Europe at the time. Although he had long been deeply involved in Italian affairs (his clash with Mazzini led to a rift in the *risorgimento*) and had won disciples elsewhere in western Europe, his persistent efforts to revise the verdict of Thermidor bore fruit primarily in France. There, the July Revolution made it possible for him to return to Paris and created a political climate that favored the dissemination of his views. By collaborating closely with those who directed the activities of the radical wing of the republican opposition to the Orleanist monarchy and by exploiting the personal veneration he inspired among young Parisians like Louis

Blanc and Etiénne Cabet, Buonarroti contributed much to both the Robespierrist revival and the Neo-Babouvist agitation of the 1830s.

Upon his death, his personal reputation declined and his conspiratorial network collapsed. His written work *Conspiration pour l'égalité dite de Babeuf* (1828) nevertheless continued to serve many of the future men of 1848 (and later some of the Communards of 1870) as a "textbook and almost a breviary." This two-volume chronicle, interwoven with documents, traces the history of the Babeuf plot and expounds its ideology. It was inspired by debates with surviving officials of the First Republic whom the author encountered in Brussels, where it was written and first published in 1828. A Paris edition in 1830 was followed by Bronterre O'Brien's English translation in 1836, by several French abridgments, and in the twentieth century by German, Italian, and Russian versions issued under communist auspices. Suggesting that the same grand design to ensure the permanent redistribution of wealth guided both the Robespierrist policy and Babouvist conspiracy and that all social conflicts could be resolved by measures improvised during war and civil strife, this book explicitly associated avant-garde dictatorship and state communism with nineteenth-century aspirations toward social democracy. It also founded a long-lived school of revolutionary historiography which was perpetuated by Jean Jaurès and Albert Mathiez. Since the 1930s, Buonarroti has emerged from obscurity to become a focal figure for various scholarly controversies involving pre-Marxian socialism, the role of French Jacobinism in the *risorgimento*, the real or mythical nature of cosmopolitan conspiracy in Metternich's Europe, French revolutionary historiography, and the origins of a "totalitarian left."

ELIZABETH L. EISENSTEIN

[*See also* REVOLUTION; SOCIALISM; TOTALITARIANISM.]

BIBLIOGRAPHY

BUONARROTI, FILIPPO 1828 *Conspiration pour l'égalité dite de Babeuf.* 2 vols. Brussels: Librairie Romantique.

BUONARROTI, FILIPPO 1836 *Buonarroti's History of Babeuf's Conspiracy for Equality.* Translated by and illustrated with original notes by James Bronterre O'Brien. London: Hetherington. → First published as Buonarroti 1828. The English translation was reprinted in 1963 by Kelley.

EISENSTEIN, ELIZABETH L. 1959 *The First Professional Revolutionist: Filippo Michele Buonarroti (1761–1837).* Harvard Historical Monographs, No. 38. Cambridge, Mass.: Harvard Univ. Press. → Contains an extensive bibliography.

GALANTE GARRONE, ALESSANDRO 1948 *Buonarroti e Babeuf.* Turin (Italy): De Silva.

GALANTE GARRONE, ALESSANDRO 1951 *Filippo Buonarroti e i revoluzionari dell' ottocento, 1828–1837.* Turin (Italy): Einaudi.

LEHNING, ARTHUR 1956 Buonarroti and His International Secret Societies. *International Review of Social History* 1:112–140.

LEHNING, ARTHUR 1957 Buonarroti's Ideas on Communism and Dictatorship. *International Review of Social History* 2:266–287.

SAITTA, ARMANDO 1950–1951 *Filippo Buonarroti: Contributi alla storia della sua vita e del suo pensiera.* 2 vols. Rome: Edizioni di "Storia e Letteratura."

BURCKHARDT, JACOB

Jacob Burckhardt (1818–1897) was born and died in Basel, Switzerland. He was the son of a Protestant pastor and a member of a patrician family long socially and intellectually prominent in the city. After an extended period as a student, during which Burckhardt self-consciously turned himself into a "European" and a spokesman for European culture, he lived most of his life in Basel as professor of history and the history of art. Alienated by Prussian nationalism and preferring his small cosmopolitan city, he refused the invitation to follow his old teacher Leopold von Ranke in the chair of history at Berlin.

Life in Basel may have contributed to Burckhardt's Europeanism; a free commercial city since the Middle Ages, the town was a cosmopolitan center and a refuge for the dispossessed intellectuals of Europe. Burckhardt's parents were persons of deliberate culture: from his mother, he took his interest in the visual arts, manifest in his lifelong sketching; from his father his sense of history and his early piety—the latter, however, he later rejected. His Gymnasium education insured his classical competence; during those years, he became much interested in early modern history, especially the history of the Swiss Reformation, and began his many trips abroad. In 1836 he entered the university at Basel, continuing his Greek studies and translating Greek drama into German; during this period he also perfected his French. To please his father, in 1837 he began the study of theology, receiving an excellent grounding in church history and comparative religion, which later stood him in good stead in his studies of Greek culture and the age of Constantine. By 1839 Burckhardt had come to reject pietism and the study of theology and was regarded as a near-heretic by his professors and his father; his anti-religious bias remained with him for the rest of his life and is manifest in his preference for secularism in *The Civilization of the Renaissance in*

Italy (1860). He went then to Berlin, where from 1839 to 1843, with a short interval in Bonn to study ancient art, he studied history: under Franz Kugler (history of architecture), August Boeckh (comparative philology and Greek inscriptions), J. G. Droysen (modern history and historical method), and especially Ranke (medieval and modern history). Just at the end of this period he came in contact with Jacob Grimm, from whom he learned much about the "unthinking habits" of mankind and their place in "culture." In 1843 he took his doctorate with a study of Charles Martel and returned to Basel to teach history and art history, lecturing à la Ranke and Grimm on all sorts of topics—the idea of Europe, ancient art, the history of architecture, seventeenth-century painting and literature. From 1837 on, Burckhardt summered in Italy, where he made those precise academic architectural sketches and city scapes which occupied him wherever he went and may have sharpened his eye for detail; his observations in Italy were as important to his development as a historian as was the formal instruction he derived from his teachers.

At the time of the Revolution of 1848 Burckhardt was in Berlin, helping Kugler prepare a series of art history handbooks; the revolution horrified Burckhardt, who then abandoned the little liberalism he had picked up from his friends, retreated to Basel's security and remoteness, and concentrated on his own view of cultural history, stressing periods where tradition seemed especially ingrained and stable, like classical antiquity and the Renaissance. He continued to lecture, developing his courses in world history. He regarded these courses as propaedeutic for such studies as his own *Age of Constantine the Great* (1853), his first work in cultural history, a "pluralist" work, to use his own term, dealing with the political, social, religious, and artistic situation in Rome and the empire from Diocletian to the death of Constantine. His understanding of comparative religion enriched his work, but the book's greatest originality lay in his use of visual and literary art forms to illustrate generalizations drawn, more conventionally, from political and social sources. In 1855 he published *Der Cicerone*, a guidebook to Italian art objects, and, from then on, Burckhardt himself was a kind of cicerone both for Italian culture and for the culture of the West in general. He was called in 1855 to the chair of history at the Zurich Polytechnic, where he worked on his two books about the Renaissance, the famous *Civilization of the Renaissance in Italy* (1860) and its by-product, the

Geschichte der Renaissance in Italien (1867), a study of architecture omitted from the more general book. He then returned to Basel, lecturing on world history and on specific historical periods and problems and preparing the material for his posthumously published *Griechische Kulturgeschichte* (1898–1902) and *Recollections of Rubens* (1898).

Burckhardt wrestled with the relation of *Kulturgeschichte* to *Kunstgeschichte*. Although he pretended to regard them as separate disciplines, he welded them together in his own work. In *The Age of Constantine the Great,* art objects illuminate a style of life and a historical process; in *Der Cicerone,* history illuminates the disparate works of art scattered, regardless of time and relation to each other, over the Italian peninsula. Again, in *Constantine,* he demonstrated the decline of the empire —the bemused tolerance and eclecticism of the rulers, their self-aggrandizement, their whimsical warfare and arbitrary expenditure—from the art and architecture of the period even more precisely than from examples of political and social behavior.

Burckhardt's preference for "harmonious wholes," deepened by his revulsion from modern democracy whose mass media dull the senses and reduce men to automata, was qualified by his historical interest in multiplicity and variety. Although he never adopted Ranke's limited view of history as an archival enterprise, he rejected the prevailing Hegelianism because of its metaphysical predestinarianism, which, in his view, was too schematized to present the multiple activities of life and of history. Although Burckhardt was interested in "individualism," he differed from Hegel in his view of great men. His famous notion of "the emergence of the individual," developed in *The Civilization of the Renaissance in Italy,* has nothing to do with Hegel's notion of a great man "summing up" his period, a man "moved" by abstract historical forces to express the spirit of the age. Rather, Burckhardt's great individuals, for better (Raphael) or for worse (Michelangelo), shape the period into which they are born; he used great men as pivots for his interpretation of their periods. Nonetheless, there are some Hegelian traces in Burckhardt's work: the *Zeitgeist* certainly casts its shadow over his attempts to parallel manifestations in politics with those of art and of thought; and in his fragmentary historical lectures, he clearly preferred to present periods *sub specie analogiae* rather than *sub specie anomaliae.*

Burckhardt was more concerned for *Kultur* than for *Geist.* Thus, in *The Civilization of the Renaissance in Italy,* his most original if not his greatest work, he drew generalizations about life as it was actually led from all kinds of sources not usually awarded historical attention—the festivals, the music, the rules of etiquette of Renaissance Italy—although he did also draw heavily on literary sources —from Castiglione to Aretino, from Ficino to Cellini, from epics to epigrams. Even in his *Griechische Kulturgeschichte*, he did not see philosophy as a world of ideas autonomous and separate from the historical world, but he did use philosophy as historical evidence of cultural preferences, weights, and values. For him *Kultur* was no Hegelian abstraction, but a matter of living, breathing men.

Burckhardt's bill held more than anyone's belly can: intending to write a cultural history of all Western civilization, he left instead three large books: studies of antiquity, of Constantine, and of the Italian Renaissance. His *Griechische Kulturgeschichte* presents a narrative of political history, interlaced with moral comments by the author, and then devotes its great bulk to cultural matters: the *paideia*, religions and cults, philosophies, the natural sciences, rhetoric and oratory, literary and art forms. The mark of Vico is on this book, with its emphasis on language, poetry, and myth as the *Urgrund* of all culture (see also, "On the Historical Consideration of Poetry," in *Force and Freedom* 1905); so also is the mark of Ranke evident in the work's devotion to "facts," although the facts are art forms, cultural habits, and ideas which for Burckhardt were as irreducible as Ranke's archival "proofs."

In *Force and Freedom*, Burckhardt reduced the main elements of history to the state, religion, and culture, discussing the hypothetical and actual supremacy of each over the other two. "Culture" comes out best, religion worst in his value system, but the state has its dangers too. For Burckhardt, culture is consciousness and, therefore, *Bildung*—as he stated, "that millionfold process by which the spontaneous, unthinking activity of a race is transformed into considered action. . . ." In *The Civilization of the Renaissance in Italy*, Burckhardt's strongly secular preference is clear; to some extent, the same bias is visible in *Constantine*, where he plainly indicated his mistrust of the emperor's conversion and the motives of the hierarchy that converted him. Burckhardt commended the emperor's toleration, even though he also considered it evidence of weakening unity and conviction.

Burckhardt's theoretical interests were slight and his theoretical writings weak; his practice, however, altered historical disciplines thereafter. He is one

parent of the school of *Geistesgeschichte*—a name he would have deplored—which developed in the generation after his; yet his own view of cultural history was too hard, even positivist, to permit the concept of *Geist* (or abstract intellect), since, for him, ideas are significantly related to the culture which they serve. Further, cultural products have their own actuality and their own lives, develop their own traditions within their own disciplines (hence his interest in "styles"), and are only partially governed or influenced by abstract ideas. He preferred to make inferences from historical "facts" rather than to impose intellectual patterns upon such facts. In this he was a true historian; so also because he selected, for his three great works, periods in which change was crucial: the decline of Greek hegemony in the Mediterranean world, the grading of classical into religious culture in the age of Constantine, and the shift from that culture to a new secularism in Renaissance Italy. His proclivities are clear—he occasionally amplified his aestheticism by his choice of materials and by his organization of them, and he indulged his internationalism. In such societies as ancient Greece and Rome and Renaissance Italy, rather than in the narrow nationalisms of nineteenth-century Europe, he saw possibilities for humanism and culture: Greece, a loose collection of states and groups all calling themselves Hellenes; the Roman Empire, reaching from Africa to England and from Spain to the Byzantine hinterland; Italy, a warring agglomeration of political units of different structure, units sharing nonetheless a vision of a malleable and constructive antiquity and sharing a culture to which they made different contributions. His preference for these societies explains his prophetic pessimism about his own world. This pessimism has earned him, in our period, more admirers than it should have; his expansion of the legitimate activities of the historian is what makes him important.

ROSALIE L. COLIE

[*See also* HISTORY; *and the biographies of* HUIZINGA *and* RANKE.]

WORKS BY BURCKHARDT

(1838–1852) 1930 *Jacob Burckhardt—Gesamtausgabe.* Volume 1: *Frühe Schriften.* Stuttgart (Germany): Deutsche Verlags-Anstalt.

(1853) 1949 *The Age of Constantine the Great.* London: Routledge; New York: Pantheon. → First published as *Die Zeit Constantin's des Grossen.*

(1855) 1925 *Der Cicerone: Eine Einleitung zum Genuss der Kunstwerke Italiens.* Leipzig: Kröner. → Partially translated as *The Cicerone: An Art Guide to Painting in Italy for the Use of Travelers and Students* and published by Scribner in 1908.

(1860) 1955 *The Civilization of the Renaissance in Italy.* London: Phaidon. → First published as *Die Kultur der Renaissance in Italien.* A paperback edition in two volumes was published in 1958 by Harper.

(1867) 1891 *Geschichte der neueren Baukunst.* Volume 1: Geschichte der Renaissance in Italien. 3d ed. Stuttgart (Germany): Ebner.

(1898) 1950 *Recollections of Rubens.* Translation of Burckhardt's essay by Mary Hottinger. London: Phaidon Press. → Published posthumously as *Erinnerungen aus Rubens.*

(1898–1902) 1956–1957 *Griechische Kulturgeschichte.* 4 vols. Basel: Schwabe. → An abridged translation was published in 1963 by Ungar as *History of Greek Culture.*

(1905) 1943 *Force and Freedom: Reflections on History.* New York: Pantheon. → Contains lectures delivered between 1868 and 1871. First published posthumously as *Weltgeschichtliche Betrachtungen.* A paperback edition was published in 1964 by Beacon.

Briefe. Edited by Max Burckhardt. 5 vols. Basel: Schwabe, 1949–1963. → The volumes published thus far include letters dated 1820 to 1875.

Jacob Burckhardt—Gesamtausgabe. 14 vols. Stuttgart (Germany): Deutsche Verlags-Anstalt, 1929–1934.

Judgments on History and Historians. Translated by Harry Zohn. Boston: Beacon, 1958. → Contains lectures delivered between 1865 and 1882. First published posthumously as *Historische Fragmente* in 1957.

SUPPLEMENTARY BIBLIOGRAPHY

FERGUSON, WALLACE K. 1948 *The Renaissance in Historical Thought: Five Centuries of Interpretation.* Boston: Houghton Mifflin.

GILBERT, FELIX 1960 Cultural History and Its Problems. Pages 40–58 in International Congress of Historical Sciences, Eleventh, Stockholm, 1960, *Rapports.* Volume 1: Methodologie. Göteborg (Sweden): Almqvist & Wiksell.

KAEGI, WERNER 1947–1956 *Jacob Burckhardt: Eine Biographie.* 3 vols. Basel: Schwabe. → A multivolume publication in progress.

KAEGI, WERNER 1962 *Europäische Horizonte im Denken Jacob Burckhardts: Drei Studien.* Basel: Schwabe.

LÖWITH, KARL 1936 *Jacob Burckhardt: Der Mensch inmitten der Geschichte.* Lucerne: Vita Nova Verlag.

WEINTRAUB, KARL 1966 *Visions of Culture.* Univ. of Chicago Press.

BUREAUCRACY

This article deals with the historical development of bureaucracy as a mode of government. Some related aspects of governmental bureaucracies are discussed in CIVIL SERVICE. *Guides to more general and sociological topics in this area will be found under* ADMINISTRATION *and* ORGANIZATIONS.

The term "bureaucracy" is of recent origin. Initially referring to a cloth covering the desks of French government officials in the eighteenth century, the term "bureau" came to be linked with a suffix signifying rule of government (as in "aristocracy" or "democracy"), probably during the struggles against absolutism preceding the French Revolution. During the nineteenth century the pejorative use of the term spread to many European countries, where liberal critics of absolutist regimes typically employed it to decry the tortuous procedures, narrow outlook, and highhanded manner of autocratic government officials (Heinzen 1845). Since then this pejorative meaning has become general in the sense that any critic of complicated organizations that fail to allocate responsibility clearly, or any critic of rigid rules and routines that are applied with little consideration of the specific case, of blundering officials, of slow operation and buck-passing, of conflicting directives and duplication of effort, of empire building, and of concentration of control in the hands of a few will use this term regardless of party or political persuasion (Watson 1945). During the years following World War II this common stereotype was given a new twist by the witty, mock-scientific formulations of *Parkinson's Law,* which derided empire building, waste of resources, and inertia by implying that official staffs expand in inverse proportion to the work to be done (Parkinson 1957).

This popular, pejorative usage must be distinguished from "bureaucracy" used in a technical sense. Although the distinction is beset with difficulties, social scientists have employed the term because it points to the special, modern variant of age-old problems of administration, just as terms like "ideology" and "class" point to modern aspects of intellectual life and social stratification. The analytic task is to conceptualize this modern variant. At the macroscopic level, Max Weber's definition of bureaucracy under the rule of law provides the best available solution to this problem; none of the critics of Weber's analysis has as yet dispensed with his definition. According to Weber, a bureaucracy establishes a relation between legally instated authorities and their subordinate officials which is characterized by defined rights and duties, prescribed in written regulations; authority relations between positions, which are ordered systematically; appointment and promotion based on contractual agreements and regulated accordingly; technical training or experience as a formal condition of employment; fixed monetary salaries; a strict separation of office and incumbent in the sense that the official does not own the "means of administration" and cannot appropriate the position; and administrative work as a full-time occupation (Weber 1922a; Bendix 1960, pp. 423 ff.).

A government administration so defined must be understood, according to Weber, as part of a legal order that is sustained by a common belief in its legitimacy. That order is reflected in written regulations, such as enacted laws, administrative rules, court precedents, etc., which govern the employment of officials and guide their administrative behavior. Such authoritative ordering of the bureaucracy is never more than a proximate achievement; written regulations are often "out of step" with the conditions to which they refer, while codifications and legal and administrative reforms, although designed to cope with that problem, are subject to interpretation. The legal order remains intact as long as such difficulties are resolved through further elaboration of existing regulations and, in relation to the bureaucracy, as long as administrative behavior is oriented toward a system of regulations. In sum, these ideal types of administration and the rule of law are the more fully realized "the more completely [they] succeed in achieving the exclusion of love, hatred, and every purely personal, especially irrational and incalculable, feeling from the execution of official tasks" (Weber [1922b] 1954, p. 351).

A word is needed concerning the difficulties of these formulations. Weber himself always emphasized that an ideal type simplifies and exaggerates the empirical evidence in the interest of conceptual clarity. No actual government administration is bureaucratic in the strict sense of his definition; this follows from the simplifications needed to arrive at an ideal type. Concrete instances will, therefore, lack one or several of the constituent elements or possess them in varying degrees; thus Weber speaks of mixed types like "patrimonial bureaucracy" when referring to specific examples. This approach involves methodological problems still under discussion (cf. Lazarsfeld & Oberschall 1965; Schweitzer 1964; Machlup 1960–1961; Martindale 1959). However, for present purposes it is sufficient to distinguish among and to discuss three possible uses of Weber's definition: as a historical bench mark (modern bureaucracy); as a syndrome of social change (bureaucratization); and as a specification of the problems of bureaucracy in the modern nation-state.

The modern type of bureaucracy. Structures approximating Weber's definition of bureaucracy have existed from time to time in different parts of the world. The historical bureaucratic empires, such as ancient Egypt, the Roman empire, and ancient and medieval China, exemplify this point [see EMPIRES]. China, for example, witnessed a close approximation to bureaucracy in the sense

that appointment to office depended upon qualifications tested by examination, and authority relations were ordered systematically. On the other hand, Chinese officials qualified through humanistic learning rather than technical proficiency; in the absence of a legal order based on abstract, written norms, administrative performance was based ideally on considerations of equity; and administrative work was not a full-time occupation strictly separated from the official's personal and familial concerns—to mention at least three respects in which administration under the Chinese dynasties was nonbureaucratic or protobureaucratic (cf. Weber [1922c] 1951, chapters 2–4). In partial contrast with these approximations, Weber recognized a distinctive modern type of bureaucracy, and it is useful to follow him in this respect.

The several attributes specified in his ideal type have been approximated most closely under the conditions of the modern state. A product of absolutist regimes in Europe since the Renaissance and distinct from the bureaucratic empires mentioned above, the modern state is characterized by a government over a contiguous territory, which is stabilized on the basis of written regulations and the centralized appropriation of all means of administration. Such stability and centrally controlled administration are possible only on the basis of financial resources and revenue administration that are the exclusive prerogative of the central government. Similarly, an army and a police force are at the exclusive disposal of the government. This central appropriation of resources and means of coercion is paralleled by the establishment of a country-wide jurisdiction, both with regard to the creation and application of legal rules and with regard to the provision of public services considered to be in the general interest. It is in this sense that Weber defines the state as based on a monopoly of physical coercion, which is made legitimate by a system of legal norms binding on rulers and ruled alike and which entails the ultimate subordination of all less inclusive associations under this central jurisdiction (Winckelmann 1964). In the setting of the modern state, bureaucracy, as defined above, is the most characteristic form of governmental administration.

Both ideal types (of the state and of bureaucracy) may be considered historical bench marks designating over-all distinguishing attributes of an entire historical period. The meaning of these ideal types is most clear-cut when they are contrasted with their opposites. Political structures in pre-absolutist Europe, for example, lacked a central government with such attributes of states as exclusive financial resources, administrative apparatus, military force, and territorial jurisdiction. Similarly, administration lacked dependence on written regulations, separation of office and incumbent, and several other attributes of bureaucracy (Bendix 1964). Such distinctions are the results of comparative study and are useful at their general level, but they are also starting points of further analysis. For the attributes defining these ideal types are themselves the several by-products of changes which have culminated in the historical constellations that we call state or bureaucracy (Delany 1963).

Bureaucratization of government

One area of comparative sociological analysis consists in examining the substitution of bureaucratic conditions of governmental administration for nonbureaucratic ones. The term "bureaucratization" serves to designate this pattern of social change, which can be traced to the royal households of medieval Europe, to the eventual employment of university-trained jurists as administrators, to the civilian transformation of military controllers on the Continent, and to the civil-service reforms in England and the United States in the nineteenth century. These several changes were related to other social trends, especially the development of the universities, a money economy, the legal system, and representative institutions; but the present discussion is confined to governmental administration.

Development of European bureaucracies. Bureaucratization may be traced to the royal or princely households of the early Middle Ages, which were composed in part of retainers who made up the military following of the ruler and also performed administrative functions in his service (the German word *Amt*, meaning "office," goes back to a Celtic term meaning servant). Rulers would appoint these retainer–officials to the several offices of the royal household, including those charged with organizing and superintending supplies, finances, clothing, horses, weapons, written communications and records, etc. For a time the royal household traveled from place to place, administering the affairs of the realm, dispensing justice, and collecting (and in part consuming) the revenue owed to the ruler (Peyer 1964). However, eventually a separation occurred, in terms of personnel and location, between the offices of the royal household and the corresponding offices of government. In his classic work T. F. Tout (1920–1933) has shown for England, and in a briefer essay Otto Hintze (1908) has shown for several western Eu-

ropean countries, how the several functions of the royal household provided the starting points of a development eventuating in the establishment of the several ministries of a modern government. This change from personal to public service on the part of officials involved a century-long development.

From an organizational standpoint, this development was partly a by-product of the size and complexity of governmental affairs. As the territory to be governed grew in size and the complexity of affairs increased, the households of kings and princes grew larger, since they provided lodging, food, and clothing for the officials of the ruler as well as for members of his family and his personal retainers and servants. Sooner or later the corps of officials became too large to be maintained in this manner, and officials came to live in households of their own and to be paid for their services in money rather than in kind. Several factors, both tangible and intangible, facilitated this change. Among the more tangible factors were improved means of transportation, the increased use of money, and the growth of the economy and, hence, of revenue; for the control of officials at a distance depends on the incentives available to the ruler and on the ease with which the officials can be reached. A more intangible factor was the sense of obligation or awe with which subordinate officials regarded those above them. That this partly patriarchal feature remained a part of government employment long after government through the ruler's household had disappeared is suggested by the fact that until the nineteenth century public officials in Prussia were still obliged to obtain permission to marry from their official superior, who would pass judgment on the social standing of the prospective bride (Hintze 1911).

The development of modern public service has been less uniform in its political than in its organizational features. Service to a ruler in a capacity that combined household functions and official responsibilities soon resulted in honor and social standing for the incumbent, whether or not he originally possessed an aristocratic title. All royal officials came to constitute a lower nobility in contrast to a higher nobility, which was entitled to an autonomous exercise of authority on a hereditary basis. Yet the dividing line was neither clear nor stable, as high royal officials used their positions to gain more independence from the ruler in the conduct of government affairs as well as for their own advancement. This drive of high-ranking officials for greater independence was supported, moreover, by public demands for greater stability and for an administrative performance that was readily available. One can visualize the development as one alternating between a growing independence of one or another group of officials and a renewed endeavor by the ruler and his "party" to buttress his authority by increasing the dependence of his officials or obtaining the services of more dependent and dependable men. The vicissitudes of these struggles have much to do with the divergent development of representative institutions in the several European countries.

These vicissitudes could lead to nonbureaucratic as well as to bureaucratic conditions of government employment, which suggests that bureaucratization is neither an inevitable nor an irreversible development. The point may be illustrated by reference to developments in France. Under the Carolingian rulers, office holding and its attendant powers had been annexed to the fiefs granted by the king to his vassals, and these fiefs became hereditary. In this way dependent retainers and officials, exercising only a delegated authority, developed into a landholding aristocracy that exercised the powers of government autonomously, a process facilitated by the undeveloped condition of economy and transport (Peyer 1964). Later on, French rulers came to delegate authority by making grants of official functions directly rather than making grants of land, with its attendant powers. In so doing they followed the practice of the Catholic church, which had developed not only a well-organized, clerical officialdom but also a body of secular managers who exercised local authority over the extensive holdings of the church. From the twelfth to the fourteenth century, for example, French district officials (baillis) already possessed several characteristics of the modern bureaucrat: they were outside the fealty relationship, were frequently transferred or recalled, were subject to detailed controls by royal authority, were forbidden to acquire land where they performed their official duties or to have their children marry property owners in that locality, and were dependent upon a money income, albeit one partly derived from fees and tolls accruing to the office. These conditions of employment combined the personalized controls characteristic of the royal household with the personnel management (frequent transfers, detailed controls, monetary compensation) characteristic of bureaucracy.

In the sixteenth and seventeenth centuries France witnessed a further commercialization of government offices. In response to the need for revenue and the demands of a well-to-do middle class, most positions became a form of property that could be purchased and could also be made hereditary for an annual fee. Soon, offices were created as a means of raising revenue rather than in terms of the functions to be performed. Also, wealthy families came to consider the purchase of an office a form of investment. Salary and office fees yielded a rent income; officeholding itself was exempted from direct tax payments (taille); and hereditary occupancy of a higher office conferred an aristocratic title on the incumbent (Göhring 1938). Parts of this noblesse de robe became an estate of great dignity which was represented in the provincial parlements and which, by the mid-eighteenth century, constituted a resurgence of aristocratic privilege (Ford 1953). This commercialization of office went furthest in France, but in the early modern period, officeholding as a form of property and as an opportunity for family investment was prevalent in many countries (cf. Swart 1949).

So far we have considered the subdivision of administrative tasks and their separation from the royal household as aspects of bureaucratization. The feudalization and the commercialization of public office facilitated that subdivision and separation, because they represented steps away from personal service to a ruler. However, neither process contributed for long or unequivocally to bureaucratization, because each represented a type of private appropriation of public office. Accordingly, European rulers resorted early to the employment of clerics (hence the English word "clerk") in order to obtain the services of dependable men who possessed skills useful in administrative work. Owing to their celibate status, members of the clergy had no direct interest in using their position to enlarge a family inheritance, and from this viewpoint they were more reliable than landed aristocrats or men of wealth. On the other hand, in all conflicts between secular rulers and the church, the clergy's subordination to the authority of the church jeopardized their dependability as royal servants. Accordingly, toward the end of the fifteenth century, clerics were increasingly replaced by laymen trained in the universities as jurists and humanists, a development associated on the Continent with the reception of Roman law (Koschaker [1947] 1958, chapters 12 and 13).

The employment of trained laymen introduced or greatly furthered the practice of public employment as a contractual relation entered into on the basis of stipulated conditions of service in exchange for a salary and subject to cancellation by either party. This was clearly a major step in the process of bureaucratization. Until the fifteenth century public service had been a temporary matter, since the knight or cleric still remained a landlord or priest and expected a fief or benefice at the termination of his service. With the employment of university-trained councilors and secretaries, a new status group developed and was greatly strengthened during the sixteenth century when temporary public service was transformed into life-long employment on a contractual basis.

In the provinces of Prussia persons of bourgeois origin predominated among those acquiring a university education and hence among officials of the new type, a situation often exploited by secular rulers to combat the influence of the aristocracy. However, as sons of aristocratic families came to attend the universities and enter public employment, the prestige of these trained officials, their interest in regular conditions of employment, and their covert resistance to the arbitrary commands of the ruler also increased (Hartung 1942–1948). Hence the old tendency toward independence among officials recurred, albeit on the new contractual basis; this development paralleled the growth of independence of the *noblesse de robe* in France.

Following Otto Hintze (1910), one may consider the absolutist measures taken against these tendencies a third foundation of modern bureaucracy. The Prussian kings appointed special officials (*kommissarische Beamte*) who were recruited among natives of other provinces and among foreigners and had nothing in common with the indigenous aristocratic cliques. In France the new office of the provincial *intendants* was made completely dependent upon royal authority, subject to cancellation at will, and entirely free from the commercialization of office mentioned earlier. Both the Prussian commissars and the French *intendants* originated in the procurement officers who accompanied the armies in the field and were then charged with maintaining peace and order in the conquered provinces on the basis of dictatorial powers. The institutionalization of these quartermasters for purposes of civilian administration retained the patriarchal features of government employment but also introduced a new measure of centralized control, which has remained an important feature of Continental bureaucracy.

Three antecedents of modern bureaucracy have been mentioned so far: subdivision of tasks in the service to a ruler and the eventual separation of officials from the ruler's household; employment of university-trained jurists; and the transformation of military controllers into civilian officials. During the nineteenth century these antecedents even-

tuated in a regularization of public employment approximating the ideal type as defined by Max Weber. On the Continent, government officials themselves played a dominant role in this development in an endeavor to increase the security, remuneration, and social standing of their position. The independence and impartiality of administrators was also a political objective of groups seeking to curb royal prerogative and to combat privileged access to government employment. These developments on the Continent were paralleled by the civil-service reform movements in England and the United States, which exemplify recent antecedents of modern bureaucracy.

Administrative reform in England. Beginning as part of the royal household, English government administration was gradually separated out into the different branches of the executive, much as it had been in France and Germany. But in this process the cohesion of the country, the ease of communication, and the absence of a standing army and other factors combined to achieve a balance between royal authority and the local authority of the landed gentry. True, an administration approximating the Continental absolutist system was attempted, beginning with the Tudor monarchy in the late fifteenth century. Yet this absolutist interlude ended with the legislative supremacy of parliament rather than with the administrative absolutism of the king, while administration at local levels consisted of offices as a species of collective prerogative in the hands of the gentry and urban notables (Namier 1930, pp. 3–41 in 1961 edition). In France bureaucratization had already been advanced by royal absolutism, and when the revolution swept aside both the *pouvoirs intermédiaires* and the monarchy, the national system of administration that was instituted extended the bureaucratic measures of the *ancien régime* (Tocqueville 1856; Cobban [1957] 1965, vol. 2, pp. 18–38). In England, on the other hand, earlier bureaucratic developments had been arrested by the overthrow of royal absolutism, which was followed by a period in which the private appropriation of public office prevailed. Some reforms curbing a direct financial exploitation of public office and requiring the personal discharge of public duties by office-holders were instituted in the late eighteenth century, and some unsuccessful experimenting with examinations for the public service occurred during the 1830s (Cohen 1941). But administrative reform became effective only insofar as it was part of the movements for political reform and hence an attack upon the identification of office with family and property. Beginning in practice with the Poor Law Amendment Act of 1834 and the administrative centralization pioneered by Edwin Chadwick (Finer 1952), administrative reforms were extended to the personnel field on a programmatic basis by the Northcote–Trevelyan Report of 1853. Selection by competitive examinations and promotion by merit were instituted subsequently by Gladstone's Order in Council of 1870. English bureaucratization was, therefore, in part a manifestation of increasing equalitarianism and in part evidence of the desire to detach the public service from its previous ties with familial and political privilege at a time when governmental services and controls were being expanded rapidly to cope with the problems of a maturing industrial society [see CIVIL SERVICE].

The United States. Bureaucratization in the United States was also the result of a movement for administrative reform, but the setting and course of this movement differed from the experience of England. In the first decades after independence, political life was largely in the hands of notables, and presidential appointments to the public service reflected not only the privileged access of the dominant upper-class groups but also their competence. Partisan activity as a basis of appointment increased in importance under Adams and Jefferson; in this respect Jackson's administration merely continued previous practices, although because of the altered character of political life, family origin and connections as factors favoring appointment to office declined markedly in importance during this era (Aronson 1964). Jackson first articulated the ideology of the spoils system, but his reputation as its initiator is undeserved because the abuses incident to that system mounted rapidly only with the growth of machine politics (White 1954, pp. 347–362).

The movement for civil-service reform gained momentum in the years following the Civil War and had as its objective the elimination of machine politics from the public service. Accordingly, the reform measures, which were largely borrowed from abroad, were aimed at curbing the abuses of machine politicians rather than, as in England, at destroying privilege. Leadership of the movement for civil-service reform came from socially and politically prominent Eastern liberals. They saw in the destruction of the spoils system a needed emancipation from moral corruption that was second only to the earlier abolitionist movement, in which many had been active as well (Van Riper 1958, pp. 78–86).

The Western experience. The common denominator of bureaucratization is that the earlier involvement of public employment with family prerogative and the identification of office with property have been superseded, in the course of long and diverse developments, by the emergence of the nation-state in which public officials administer "a service-rendering organization for the protection of rights and the enforcement of duties" of a national citizenry (Barker 1944, p. 6). That is, government is in charge of the currency, the postal system, the construction of public facilities, the provision of social services, the adjudication of legal disputes, the national educational system, the defense establishment, and the collection of revenue to pay for these and other public services. Although the policies that should govern such public functions are often in dispute, the relative neutralization of the civil service and hence the conception of administrators as employees in charge of a public trust may be due ultimately to the growth of consensus concerning the idea of government as a service-rendering institution that should not be pre-empted by any one of the individuals and groups contending in the political arena. This consensus is both cause and consequence of the growth of government and public employment. Official statistics on these developments in several countries are conclusive in this respect, but they are not standardized enough to be suitable for comparative study (cf. Ule 1961 and the sources cited there).

Developing areas. The preceding discussion of bureaucratization, which has been confined to the "Western experience," has suggested the importance of at least two characteristics: the long-run continuity of this experience, and the central role played by the clergy and by law and legal experts in effecting the emancipation of government service from ties with personal service, kinship relations, and property interests. These and related preconditions have been absent from other types of bureaucratization, to which at least some reference ought to be made at this point. One type refers to problems of public employment in the so-called developing areas.

However diverse, these areas have at least three features in common. They are latecomers as far as industrial development is concerned. They show little of that diminution of "primordial" ties which preceded or accompanied the development of Western nation-states and their bureaucratization. At the same time, they greatly emphasize the importance of government and rapidly expand public employment (Shils 1959–1960; Fallers 1956, 1964; Chicago, University of . . . 1963, pp. 105 ff.). Under conditions of economic scarcity, government posts are much sought after, and the ideology of government initiative in economic development provides no basis for restricting public employment. As a result, such countries are characterized by top-heavy officialdom relative to economic growth; this severely strains the merit system of recruitment, which is a legacy of colonial regimes in many of these areas (Berger 1957, chapter 2; Braibanti 1963, pp. 360 ff.; Kingsley 1963, pp. 301 ff.).

Perhaps it is useful to consider public administration in these cases as an arena of fluctuating contests, in which the primordial ties between officials and the public, the exigencies of governmental planning under conditions of great poverty and in the context of the cold war, and the ideals of efficient public service by trained administrators all play a part. This novel setting calls for an analysis of bureaucratization in terms appropriate to it (Riggs 1964), but there is reason to think that these terms are as inappropriate to Western bureaucratization as concepts derived from the Western experience are inappropriate to the developing areas.

Communist countries. In the modern world the comparative study of bureaucratization must also deal with what may be called the "postbureaucratic" or "quasi-bureaucratic" type of governmental administration in communist societies. It is appropriate, but also easily misleading, to apply Weber's definition of bureaucracy to these societies. Such criteria as experience or training as a condition of public employment, the separation of office and incumbent, the strict exclusion of familial ties, and administrative work as a full-time occupation are clearly applicable in the communist countries. Indeed, these countries appear to be "superbureaucratic," in the sense that centralized planning swells the ranks of governmental employees. At any rate, in the Soviet Union organizations have been set up to deal in coordinated fashion with problems of personnel administration throughout the government hierarchy (Fainsod [1953] 1963, pp. 414–417).

Nevertheless, it would be misleading to treat communist countries as if their governments simply represented other instances of bureaucratization in the sense discussed above. This is evident in the policies governing the placement of executive personnel, which depends not only on the standards developed by the Soviet Ministry of Finance and on the separate procedures adopted by the various ministries and agencies concerned but also on decisions of the Central Committee of the Communist party. Agencies of the party work out lists of jobs that may not be filled without prior party clearance,

and they also prepare rosters of trusted personnel available for placement (DeWitt 1961, pp. 463–466). The principle that decisions of any importance require political clearance in addition to their appropriate administrative surveillance applies throughout Soviet society; indeed, it is the distinguishing characteristic of this "postbureaucratic" society.

In order to mount the desired degree of political mobilization and control over the decision-making centers of an entire society, the Communist party is itself obliged to undergo a process of bureaucratization. In 1962 between 150,000 and 200,000 persons, or some 4 per cent of the membership, were paid party workers; the actual number was probably higher, since many held temporary assignments in various institutions. Through higher party schools, first established in 1946, this cadre of activists has become increasingly professionalized; by 1956 there were 29 party schools officially rated as institutions of higher education, offering a four-year curriculum and affording selected students a stipend from five to eight times higher than stipends at ordinary schools (Brzezinski & Huntington 1964, pp. 140–173; DeWitt 1961, p. 300; Armstrong 1959). Thus, the most characteristic feature of the "postbureaucratic" structure of communist societies is the bureaucratization not only of the public service but also of political life, so that the ruling party has the trained activists it needs to politicize the executive and the judicial branches of government and much of civilian life as well.

This degree of centralized, political manipulation indicates that these societies lack a concept of law in the sense of a system of relatively stable, impersonal, and nonpolitical norms and procedures. They are also distinguished from the societies whose further bureaucratization is considered below by their determination to centralize decision making under the auspices of a single party, by their injection of political controls at all levels of the administrative hierarchies, and by their effort to prevent the uncontrolled emergence of organized interests.

Problems of modern bureaucracy

We have seen that Weber's concept of bureaucracy is serviceable as a macro-historical bench mark and that "bureaucratization" is a useful term to characterize an important pattern of social change. But it is also true that, in the course of that change, several elements of Weber's definition have been transformed from political issues into administrative techniques. As long as government administration was in the hands of a social elite or a group of political partisans which had privileged access to office and conducted the "public" business as a species of private prerogative, administrative reforms were aimed at equalizing access, diminishing arbitrariness, and reducing private profiteering. The separation of office and incumbent, appointment by merit, the contractual regulation of appointment and promotion, fixed monetary salaries, and other, related measures can be understood as *preventing* the intrusion of kinship relations, property interests, and political partisanship upon the conduct of the public business. This negative effect was bound to decline in importance to the extent that government administration by a social elite or by party politicians became a thing of the past. The exclusion of "every purely personal feeling" remains an important desideratum as well as a proximate characteristic of official conduct. So does the effective separation of office and incumbent. But in most modern governments in the countries of Western civilization these and related aspects of public employment are handled routinely, if only proximately, by departments specializing in the several branches of personnel administration, which are themselves an example of bureaucratization as well as a means of promoting it.

Social composition of the civil service.   In practice, appointment to public office on the basis of competitive examinations has succeeded in its primary objective of separating officeholding from partisan politics and the vested interests of a social elite. But recruitment to public office on this basis is not a "neutral" instrument, if we mean by this that it would result in a corps of public officials whose social composition corresponds to that of the general population. Rather, under the merit system, recruitment reflects the unequal distribution of opportunity characteristic of society at large. This implication has been the subject of several studies. Generally speaking, higher civil servants come from families in which the father is in an administrative, professional, managerial, or related middle-class occupation at a high or intermediate level, and they do so far in excess of the proportions of these occupational groups in the working population. By contrast, sons of families in which the father is a manual laborer are "underrepresented" among higher civil servants. Since the merit system makes educational qualifications a condition of entry into the public service, it tends to favor recruitment from social groups with a high level of education (Kelsall 1955; Bottomore 1952; Warner et al. 1963; Bendix 1949). Marked regional differences in economic development, as in Italy,

may superimpose their own effects on these patterns: Italian higher civil servants come in disproportionate numbers from the disadvantaged south, and their social origin appears to be considerably below that of officials recruited from the north (Cappelletti 1966).

There have been efforts to make public employment at all levels more "representative" of the general population by adopting quota systems of selection favorable to those who come from disadvantaged families. In the Soviet Union and in other communist countries this policy was adopted for a time in order to dispense as quickly as possible with the dependence of the revolutionary regime upon old-time public officials. Subsequently, such quotas have been adopted from time to time when political considerations have suggested the advisability of populist appeals and measures against new "pockets of privilege." However, experience has shown that an administrative apparatus dependent upon a skilled staff is limited in the degree to which it can manipulate quotas favoring the disadvantaged without jeopardizing its level of performance. As a result, educational policies favoring the disadvantaged tend to be preferred to quota systems in public employment (Fainsod 1953; Inkeles 1950; Feldmesser 1960). In India a public-employment policy *and* an educational policy are incorporated in the constitution. Quotas for positions in government employment and at the universities are reserved for members from "backward classes," leading to the paradoxical result that various castes, tribes, and other groups seek to be classified as "backward" in order to provide their members with additional opportunities for employment and education (India . . . 1955–1956).

These instances are cited to suggest that the merit system reflects existing social differences in various ways and that within narrow limits it can be used deliberately to alter such differences. In either case, studies of the social composition of higher civil servants have more to teach us about the social and political structure of a society than about the exercise of governmental authority. The organizational problems encountered in that exercise and some of the divergent solutions found for them are discussed elsewhere. Such technical problems are bypassed here in order to discuss the critical question of political control.

Political control of public officials

The basic issue of control was formulated by Hegel in his *Philosophy of Right* in 1821, in which he pointed out that the bureaucracy will be prevented "from acquiring the isolated position of an aristocracy and [from] using its education and skill as a means to an arbitrary tyranny" by the sovereign working on it from the top and corporation-rights working on it from the bottom (Hegel [1821] 1942, pp. 296–297). Despite its dated and parochial references, the statement identifies three dimensions that should be considered in an analysis of control over the exercise of governmental authority: the tendency of high public officials to develop and display a consciousness of special rank and the dangers of an abuse of authority implicit in the secrecy that is a by-product of expertise; the problems thereby posed for the "sovereign" who seeks to control officials from on high; and, conversely, the problem of the influence on administrative procedure and decision making exercised by the individuals and organized groups who are subject to governmental authority.

The bureaucratic culture pattern. Consciousness of rank among public officials is part of a historically derived "bureaucratic culture pattern." It may reflect the degree to which public office has been associated with the established privileges of a ruling class (Kingsley 1944, chapter 7), although an element of this consciousness may remain as an attribute of high public office even in the absence of such traditions (Shils 1965). Consciousness of rank is probably related to the prestige accorded to public employment and the confidence or trust with which the public at large regards the work of governmental officials (Almond & Verba 1963; Kilpatrick et al. 1964).

But there is no systematic evidence to indicate how public opinion concerning government is related to the discretionary exercise of authority. It is as plausible to assume that public officials will make responsible use of their public trust because they have high prestige and sense the confidence placed in them as it is to assume that they will do so in the absence of prestige and trust because they fear the consequences of abusing their power. One is probably on safe ground only with the empty assertion that both too much and too little prestige and privilege tend to be correlated with abuse, either because the incumbent official assumes that anything *he* does must be right or because he is so needy as to use his office "for all it is worth." Generally, civil-service systems have provided public officials with a high degree of economic security and special legal protection in order to enhance their sense of responsibility in the exercise of discretionary powers. Yet such measures bear an uncertain relation to the conduct of the public business and specifically the exercise of discretion; with bureaucratization the importance of professional skills and administrative expertise increases, as

does the difficulty of implementing the principles of accountability.

Bureaucracy and accountability. In his discussion of bureaucracy Max Weber noted one major obstacle standing in the way of accountability: the tendency of officials to increase their intrinsic superiority as experts by keeping their knowledge and intentions secret (Weber [1922a] 1946, p. 233). More recent analyses have examined the tensions typically arising in the relations between experts and top administrative officials in public bureaucracies (Merton [1949] 1957, pp. 219–224; Leighton 1949, pp. 129–173) and, more generally, the inherent difficulty of distinguishing between policy decisions and administrative implementation where executives must rely on professionals (Parsons 1960, pp. 66–69; Friedrich 1963, pp. 309–314). The intrinsic dilemma appears to be that ultimately all professional services involve an element of trust in the skill and wisdom with which the professional makes his judgments, whereas accountability of all administrative actions implies that on principle these actions are subject to scrutiny and criticism by higher authority. It is only somewhat exaggerated to say that the trust implicit in the employment of professionals is at odds with the distrust implicit in the accountability of administrators. This incompatibility is enhanced as governments make increasing use not only of technical and scientific expertise but also of professional administrative skills. To be "modern" a government must rely on such skills, but to be responsible it must nevertheless check on the discretionary judgments that are indispensable for both professional work and good government.

Genuine as this dilemma is, it should not be exaggerated. The unchecked exercise of discretion by administrators with professional training is *not* simply synonymous with an abuse of authority. A substantial part of such discretion is usually called for by the general legislative mandate under which officials do their work. Much of what is kept secret by government officials concerns types of information involving legitimate personal and social concerns of individuals, which under the rule of law should not be divulged despite periodic demands to this effect by partisans of all kinds. It may be the fundamental tendency of all bureaucratic thought, as Karl Mannheim has stated, to turn all problems of politics into problems of administration (Mannheim 1929–1931, p. 105 in 1949 edition). Similarly, professionals tend to turn every problem of decision making into a question of expertise. However, such tendencies occur not only (or even primarily) because officials with professional training wish to exceed their authority but also because the perennial difficulties of decision making at higher political levels leave a vacuum of action. Then, indeed, officials will proceed in keeping with *their* interpretation of the public interest. In so doing they may be influenced by their professional preoccupations, but they are still acting in the context of public authority. Under a system of laws, that context is circumscribed by the controls to which public officials are subject and by their own belief in legitimacy. Such controls and beliefs exert a constraining pressure upon them even in the absence of any direct checks on their performance.

The civic position of public officials. Among the controls to which public officials are subject are the rules pertaining to their civic position. Should these officials be permitted to retain all the rights enjoyed by private citizens, or should certain special restrictions be imposed on them in view of their powers and responsibilities as public employees? The question pertains to those political systems that give legal recognition to the rights of citizens against the government. Under these conditions one viewpoint would concede to public officials the full exercise of their rights as private citizens and hence reject any restriction on the political or trade-union activities of public employees. The other position demands of public officials that they accept special restrictions upon their expression of political views and their participation in partisan political activities in order to safeguard the impartiality of governmental administration as well as public confidence in that impartiality.

According to this second view, governmental employment involves a public trust that can be jeopardized if public officials make injudicious use of their rights as citizens; hence, efforts are made to draw a legally binding distinction between permissible and impermissible political activities (Kirchheimer 1941; Esman 1951). Related to this second position are the various efforts to regulate the relations between public officials and elected representatives, including the question whether and under what conditions officials should be permitted to stand for elective offices (Werner Weber 1930). Efforts to control the political activities of public officials have the same objective as the merit system, namely, to ensure the quality and impartiality of the public service. Hence, the importance of these efforts will diminish in proportion to the success of the merit system of personnel recruitment.

Legislative and executive supervision. Direct checks on the performance of administrators are, of course, a more important means of ensuring the responsible execution of policies than are general rules concerning the civic status of officials. In his incisive critique of Prussian bureaucracy, Max Weber emphasized parliamentary inquiries as a means by which politicians could check upon the administrative implementation of the legislative intent. He saw such inquiries as a proving ground for politicians in parliament. They would match wits with expert administrators in order to vindicate the supremacy of political decisions over the official's use of his education and skill to preserve the technical integrity of an administrative program (Weber [1921] 1958, pp. 308–357). The problems that Weber noted have become, if anything, more complex. Under the conditions of the modern welfare state, legislatures increasingly delegate authority to administrative agencies. With the consequent proliferation of governmental functions and reliance on expertise, the difficulties not only of parliamentary but also of executive control over the administrative process mount. Elected representatives are too few in number in comparison with the officials under their authority, less expert than the latter, and necessarily restricted to spot checks on performance. Moreover, in a context of expanding government functions, political decisions already involve the active participation of top administrators and are then embodied in service-rendering institutions. To an extent, parliamentary control of officials is circumscribed, because past political decisions tend to engender a popular demand for the continuation of government services once these are initiated, even aside from the self-perpetuating momentum of the administration.

It is true that legislative controls have proliferated, as in the annual authorization of agencies or in statutory provisions requiring agencies to obtain legislative clearance for particular programs. But the result has not only been further legislative control of the administrative process. Legislative committees are also transformed into champions of particular administrative agencies, in part because politicians and administrators compete for the allegiance of the same constituency, albeit for different ends. In this way legislative committees combine control and advocacy in their relations with administrative agencies. At the same time the executive branch (in particular, the office of the president) has had to develop its own methods of supervision through the Bureau of the Budget and other instrumentalities, in order to keep pace with the expansion and decentralization of the administrative process (Neustadt 1965).

The influence of interest groups. We have noted several concurrent and interrelated developments of bureaucracy in the industrialized societies of Western civilization: the relative success of the merit system and the consequent decline of direct political interference with administration; the professionalization of public administration and the consequent difficulties of parliamentary and executive supervision; and the expansion of governmental functions and the consequent delegation of authority.

The mounting difficulties of supervision are associated, in turn, with the process of democratization. As long as a politics of notables prevailed, it was more or less accurate to think of decision making as a legislative and ministerial prerogative and of administration as an implementation of policies. Even in this setting, voluntary associations like the Anti-Corn Law League in England and the *Bund der Landwirte* in Germany were used to influence public policy. However, representatives of such associations had close social ties with political decision makers and thus appeared as little more than a specially organized section of the ruling elite. With democratization the number of those engaged in political activities has increased; organized interests have proliferated in interaction with the proliferation of governmental functions (Kaiser 1956), and so have the opportunities of individuals and groups to contact and influence administrators as well as legislators. Delegation of authority to administrators has developed along with the mobilization of interest in the government process on the part of the public (Selznick 1949).

Close and frequent contacts between bureaucracy and organized interests are encouraged where policies are general, where effective administration requires information that is often at the disposal of these interests, and where governmental responsiveness to the public, together with freedom of association, are considered major desiderata of a pluralistic polity. The result is policy formation at many levels of government and outside the government proper, as in licensing boards, advisory committees, and other such institutions. Under these conditions contacts between administrators and the interested public on matters of policy as well as on matters of procedure become frequent, especially if the legislature and the political executive fail to make needed decisions. With only very general policies to guide them, officials may function as resolvers of conflicting claims not previously resolved at higher political levels. In these and other cases there is reason to question how deeply the available controls can still penetrate into the network of interaction between organized interests and the bureaucracy, and it cannot be taken for granted that by gaining ascendancy over the controls exercised by politicians the administrator is also increasing his own autonomy.

Where interest groups do not exist, officials may help to create them in order to have organs of consultation and cooperation, and under certain conditions frequent contacts may lead to a mutual support between interest group and clientele administration (Ehrmann 1961; Woll 1963a; 1963b). Even in this case, it may be said that groups which obtain a hearing in the executive agency directly concerned with their affairs probably also endorse the political system which grants them that hearing, so that here again it is appropriate to emphasize the important, if imponderable, belief in legitimacy. A spirit of moderation may be created by the consensus of the public as well as by the prudential neutrality of the administrators, but this certainly need not happen. And even where it does, there is still the question of how much decision making can be decentralized without jeopardizing the capacity for concerted action on the part of the national political community.

The developments sketched here have recurred in the several countries usually considered together under the term "welfare state," and they have evoked certain predictable responses. In the United States, as direct political interference with the administrative process has become less and the influence of interest groups has become more important, conflict-of-interest legislation has been elaborated. By distinguishing between acceptable and unacceptable types of contact between officials and the spokesmen for interest groups, such laws seek to safeguard the impersonal character of public employment and day-to-day administration (Perkins 1963; Manning 1964). Where such controls are successful, they probably do more than provide general discouragement and occasional penalties for the worst abuses engendered by close relations between administrators and the interested public. For they also provide the administrator with a ready buttress to his neutrality, which he can use in his handling of the conflicting claims pressed upon him. The same consideration applies to the established legislative and executive controls over the administrative process, which vary in the degree to which they penetrate the contacts between administrators and private interests [see OFFICE, MISUSE OF].

That this penetration is felt to be insufficient is perhaps best exemplified by the Scandinavian institution of the *ombudsman*, a parliamentary commissioner who is charged with the task of screening complaints against the administrative arm of the government and of vigorously prosecuting transgressors, whether they have violated the law or merely neglected the performance of their official duties. The need for an opportunity to redress individual grievances is widely recognized, but the institution of the *ombudsman* is not easily transferred from one constitutional framework to another, in part because similar functions may be performed in other ways (Rowat 1965). It remains to be seen whether such new devices, as well as old ones like administrative courts, will be sufficient to counteract the unwitting and undesired effects of interest-group activity upon the impartiality and effectiveness of a corps of professional administrators.

The study of bureaucracy

The preceding discussion of recruitment patterns and political controls has certain general implications for the comparative study of bureaucracy. The old argument over the amateur generalist versus the expert technician is a case in point. At one time, the former tended to be the man of privilege, while the latter was the man of technical reasoning. But with the disappearance of privilege, the generalist may be open to considerations of broad policy, while the technician, with his commitment to expertise and perhaps a disinclination to entertain political considerations, may be open to influence by special interests clothed in technical arguments. In an increasingly specialized administration, considerations of technical efficiency can hide a political judgment (Selznick 1957). Hence, the view that bureaucracy is the most efficient type of administrative organization remains valid only on the very narrow ground that it is more efficient than an administration governed by kinship ties and property interests. Such considerations suggest that today we are less concerned with bureaucratization as such than with the exercise of administrative authority.

With this shift in orientation the study of bureaucracy comes close to the analysis of organizations, although this is no warrant for neglecting the separate significance of governmental authority. The analysis of organizations has called into question the utility of assuming the unequivocal unity of organizational goals, the unilateral determination of administrative conduct by the commands of superiors, the hierarchical ordering of superior–subordinate relationships, and hence the significance of hierarchical organizations as a means to the attainment of well-defined ends (Long 1962; Crozier 1963). Oriented as it is to the macroscopic contrast with patrimonialism, Weber's model of bureaucracy does not provide guidelines in these respects, but three elements of his analysis may be noted (Bendix 1956; 1964; Luhmann 1964).

The emphasis on the belief in legitimacy as the foundation of administrative conduct already precludes an interpretation of organizational behavior in terms of specific ends. Thus, democratic beliefs in legitimacy implicitly endorse the many diverse ends that are pursued in the interaction between bureaucracy and interest groups. A second basic characteristic of bureaucracy is the emphasis on an orientation toward abstract norms as an integral part of the rule of law. Organizational analysis can be related to the study of bureaucracy if it takes cognizance not only of informal relations in hierarchical organizations but also of the continuing efforts to offset their effects on the organization or to subject these relations to norms developed for this purpose. Third, the defining characteristics of bureaucracy have one common denominator, namely, the effort to insulate officials from all effects of society that militate against the probability of a faithful and efficient implementation of policies. This is necessarily a proximate achievement that requires continuous reinforcement. We have seen that its original objective—the insulation of officials from the effects of kinship ties and property interests—has become less important with time, while the new problems posed by the contact between officials and interest representatives may not be amenable to over-all solutions. In this respect the managements of large industrial organizations have been more successful, to the extent that they have insulated their top officials by providing their families with a luxurious but manipulated style of life. These perspectives suggest the possibility of linking the study of bureaucracy, with its historical and comparative approach, and the study of organizational behavior, to the benefit of both.

REINHARD BENDIX

[*Directly related are the entries* ADMINISTRATION; CIVIL SERVICE; EMPIRES. *Other relevant material may be found in* INTEREST GROUPS; LAW, *article on* THE LEGAL SYSTEM; LEGITIMACY; MASS SOCIETY; ORGANIZATIONS, *article on* THEORIES OF ORGANIZATIONS; *and in the biographies of* HEGEL; HINTZE; WEBER, MAX.]

BIBLIOGRAPHY

ALMOND, GABRIEL A.; and VERBA, SIDNEY 1963 *The Civic Culture: Political Attitudes and Democracy in Five Nations.* Princeton Univ. Press.
ARMSTRONG, JOHN A. 1959 *The Soviet Bureaucratic Elite.* New York: Praeger.
ARONSON, SIDNEY H. 1964 *Status and Kinship in the Higher Civil Service.* Cambridge, Mass.: Harvard Univ. Press.
AYLMER, GERALD E. 1961 *The King's Servants: The Civil Service of Charles I, 1625–1642.* New York: Columbia Univ. Press.

BARKER, ERNEST 1944 *The Development of Public Services in Western Europe: 1660–1930.* Oxford Univ. Press.

BENDIX, REINHARD 1949 *Higher Civil Servants in American Society.* Boulder: Univ. of Colorado Press.

BENDIX, REINHARD 1956 *Work and Authority in Industry: Ideologies of Management in the Course of Industrialization.* New York: Wiley.

BENDIX, REINHARD 1960 *Max Weber: An Intellectual Portrait.* Garden City, N.Y.: Doubleday.

BENDIX, REINHARD 1964 *Nation-building and Citizenship.* New York: Wiley.

BERGER, MORROE 1957 *Bureaucracy and Society in Modern Egypt: A Study of the Higher Civil Service.* Princeton Oriental Studies: Social Science, No. 1. Princeton Univ. Press.

BOTTOMORE, THOMAS B. 1952 La mobilité sociale dans la haute administration française. *Cahiers internationaux de sociologie* 13:167–178.

BRAIBANTI, RALPH 1963 Bureaucracy and Judiciary in Pakistan. Pages 360–440 in Joseph G. LaPalombara (editor), *Bureaucracy and Political Development.* Studies in Political Development, No. 2. Princeton Univ. Press.

BRZEZINSKI, ZBIGNIEW; and HUNTINGTON, SAMUEL P. 1964 *Political Power: USA/USSR.* New York: Viking.

CAPPELLETTI, LUCIANO 1966 The Italian Bureaucracy: A Study of the Carriera Direttiva of the Italian Administration. Ph.D. dissertation, Univ. of California.

CHICAGO, UNIVERSITY OF, COMMITTEE FOR THE COMPARATIVE STUDY OF THE NEW NATIONS 1963 *Old Societies and New States: The Quest for Modernity in Asia and Africa.* Edited by Clifford Geertz. New York: Free Press.

COBBAN, ALFRED (1957) 1965 *A History of Modern France.* Rev. ed., 2 vols. New York: Braziller.

COHEN, EMMELINE W. 1941 *The Growth of the British Civil Service: 1780–1939.* London: Allen & Unwin.

CROZIER, MICHEL (1963) 1964 *The Bureaucratic Phenomenon.* Univ. of Chicago Press. → First published as *Le phénomène bureaucratique.*

DELANY, WILLIAM 1963 The Development and Decline of Patrimonial and Bureaucratic Administration. *Administrative Science Quarterly* 7:458–501.

DEWITT, NICHOLAS 1961 *Education and Professional Employment in the U.S.S.R.* Washington: National Science Foundation.

EHRMANN, HENRY 1961 Les groupes d'intérêt et la bureaucratie dans les démocraties occidentales. *Revue française de science politique* 11:541–568.

EISENSTADT, SHMUEL N. 1958 Bureaucracy and Bureaucratization: A Trend Report and Bibliography. *Current Sociology* 7:99–164.

ESMAN, MILTON J. 1951 The Hatch Act: A Reappraisal. *Yale Law Journal* 60:986–1005.

FAINSOD, MERLE (1953) 1963 *How Russia Is Ruled.* Rev. ed., Russian Research Center Studies, No. 11. Cambridge, Mass.: Harvard Univ. Press.

FALLERS, LLOYD A. 1956 *Bantu Bureaucracy: A Study of Integration and Conflict in the Political Institutions of an East African People.* Cambridge: Heffer.

FALLERS, LLOYD A. (editor) 1964 *The King's Men: Leadership and Status in Buganda on the Eve of Independence.* Oxford Univ. Press.

FELDMESSER, ROBERT (1960) 1962 Equality and Inequality Under Khrushchev. Pages 223–239 in Problems of Communism, *Russia Under Khrushchev: An Anthology.* London: Methuen. → First published in Volume 9 of *Problems of Communism.*

FINER, SAMUEL E. 1952 *The Life and Times of Edwin Chadwick.* London: Methuen.

FORD, FRANKLIN L. 1953 *Robe and Sword: The Regrouping of the French Aristocracy After Louis XIV.* Cambridge, Mass.: Harvard Univ. Press.

FRIEDRICH, CARL J. 1963 *Man and His Government: An Empirical Theory of Politics.* New York: McGraw-Hill.

GÖHRING, MARTIN 1938 *Die Ämterkäuflichkeit im Ancien Régime.* Historische Studien, Vol. 346. Berlin: Ebering.

HARTUNG, FRITZ (1942–1948) 1961 Studien zur Geschichte der preussischen Verwaltung. Pages 178–344 in Fritz Hartung, *Staatsbildende Kräfte der Neuzeit: Gesammelte Aufsätze.* Berlin: Duncker & Humblot.

HEGEL, GEORG WILHELM FRIEDRICH (1821) 1942 *Philosophy of Right.* Translated with notes by T. M. Knox. Oxford: Clarendon.

HEINZEN, KARL 1845 *Die preussische Büreaukratie.* Darmstadt (Germany): Leske.

HINTZE, OTTO (1908) 1962 Die Entstehung der modernen Staatsministerien. Pages 275–320 in Otto Hintze, *Staat und Verfassung.* 2d ed. Göttingen (Germany): Vandenhoeck & Ruprecht.

HINTZE, OTTO (1910) 1962 Der Commissarius und seine Bedeutung in der allgemeinen Verwaltungsgeschichte. Pages 242–274 in Otto Hintze, *Staat und Verfassung.* 2d ed. Göttingen (Germany): Vandenhoeck & Ruprecht.

HINTZE, OTTO (1911) 1964 Der Beamtenstand. Pages 66–125 in Otto Hintze, *Soziologie und Geschichte.* 2d ed. Göttingen (Germany): Vandenhoeck & Ruprecht.

INDIA, BACKWARD CLASSES COMMISSION 1955–1956 *Report.* 2 vols. New Delhi: Manager of Publications.

INKELES, ALEX 1950 Social Stratification and Mobility in the Soviet Union: 1940–1950. *American Sociological Review* 15:465–479.

KAISER, JOSEPH H. 1956 *Die Repräsentation organisierter Interessen.* Berlin: Duncker & Humblot.

KELSALL, ROGER K. 1955 *Higher Civil Servants in Britain, From 1870 to the Present Day.* London: Routledge.

KILPATRICK, FRANKLIN P.; CUMMINGS, MILTON C.; and JENNINGS, M. KENT 1964 *The Image of the Federal Service.* Washington: Brookings Institution.

KINGSLEY, JOHN D. 1944 *Representative Bureaucracy: An Interpretation of the British Civil Service.* Yellow Springs, Ohio: Antioch College Press.

KINGSLEY, JOHN D. 1963 Bureaucracy and Political Development, With Particular Reference to Nigeria. Pages 301–317 in Joseph G. LaPalombara (editor), *Bureaucracy and Political Development.* Studies in Political Development, No. 2. Princeton Univ. Press.

KIRCHHEIMER, OTTO 1941 The Historical and Comparative Background of the Hatch Law. *Public Policy* 2:341–373.

KOSCHAKER, PAUL (1947) 1958 *Europa und das römische Recht.* 3d ed. Munich: Beck.

LaPALOMBARA, JOSEPH G. (editor) 1963 *Bureaucracy and Political Development.* Studies in Political Development, No. 2. Princeton Univ. Press.

LAZARSFELD, PAUL F.; and OBERSCHALL, ANTHONY R. 1965 Max Weber and Empirical Social Research. *American Sociological Review* 30:185–199.

LEIGHTON, ALEXANDER 1949 *Human Relations in a Changing World.* New York: Dutton.

Long, Norton E. 1962 *The Polity.* Chicago: Rand McNally.

Luhmann, Niklas 1964 Zweck–Herrschaft–System, Grundbegriffe und Prämissen Max Webers. *Der Staat* 3:129–158.

Machlup, Fritz 1960–1961 Idealtypus, Wirklichkeit und Konstruktion. *Ordo* 12:21–57.

Mannheim, Karl (1929–1931) 1954 *Ideology and Utopia: An Introduction to the Sociology of Knowledge.* New York: Harcourt; London: Routledge. → First published in German. A paperback edition was published in 1955 by Harcourt.

Manning, Bayless 1964 *Federal Conflict of Interest Law.* Cambridge, Mass.: Harvard Univ. Press.

Martindale, Don 1959 Sociological Theory and the Ideal Type. Pages 57–91 in Llewellyn Gross (editor), *Symposium on Sociological Theory.* Evanston, Ill.: Row, Peterson.

Merton, Robert K. (1949) 1957 *Social Theory and Social Structure.* Rev. & enl. ed. Glencoe, Ill.: Free Press.

Namier, Lewis B. (1930) 1962 *England in the Age of the American Revolution.* 2d ed. New York: St. Martins. → A paperback edition was published in 1961.

Neustadt, Richard E. 1965 Politicians and Bureaucrats. Pages 102–120 in David Truman (editor), *The Congress and America's Future.* Englewood Cliffs, N.J.: Prentice-Hall.

Parkinson, C. Northcote 1957 *Parkinson's Law, and Other Studies in Administration.* Boston: Houghton Mifflin.

Parsons, Talcott 1960 *Structure and Process in Modern Societies.* Glencoe, Ill.: Free Press.

Peabody, Robert L.; and Rourke, Francis E. 1965 Public Bureaucracies. Pages 802–837 in James G. March (editor), *Handbook of Organizations.* Chicago: Rand McNally.

Perkins, Roswell B. 1963 The New Federal Conflict-of-Interest Law. *Harvard Law Review* 76:1113–1169.

Peyer, Hans K. 1964 Das Reisekönigtum des Mittelalters. *Vierteljahrshefte für Sozial- und Wirtschaftsgeschichte* 51:1–21.

Riggs, Fred W. 1964 *Administration in Developing Countries.* Boston: Houghton Mifflin.

Rowat, Donald C. (editor) 1965 *The Ombudsman.* London: Allen & Unwin.

Schweitzer, Arthur 1964 Vom Idealtypus zum Prototyp. *Zeitschrift für die gesamte Staatswissenschaft* 120:13–55.

Selznick, Philip 1949 *TVA and the Grass Roots: A Study in the Sociology of Formal Organization.* University of California Publications in Culture and Society, Vol. 3. Berkeley: Univ. of California Press.

Selznick, Philip 1957 *Leadership in Administration: A Sociological Interpretation.* Evanston, Ill.: Row, Peterson.

Shils, Edward (1959–1960) 1962 *Political Development in the New States.* The Hague: Mouton.

Shils, Edward 1965 Charisma, Order and Status. *American Sociological Review* 30:199–213.

Swart, Koenraad W. 1949 *Sale of Offices in the Seventeenth Century.* The Hague: Nijhoff.

Tocqueville, Alexis de (1856) 1955 *The Old Regime and the French Revolution.* Garden City, N.Y.: Doubleday. → First published as *L'ancien régime et la révolution.*

Tout, Thomas F. 1920–1933 *Chapters in the Administrative History of Medieval England.* 6 vols. London: Longmans.

Ule, Carl H. (editor) 1961 *Die Entwicklung des öffentlichen Dienstes.* Cologne (Germany): Heymanns.

Van Riper, Paul P. 1958 *History of the United States Civil Service.* Evanston, Ill.: Row, Peterson.

Warner, W. Lloyd et al. 1963 *The American Federal Executive.* New Haven: Yale Univ. Press.

Watson, Goodwin 1945 Bureaucracy as Citizens See It. *Journal of Social Issues* 1:4–13.

Weber, Max (1921) 1958 *Gesammelte politische Schriften.* 2d ed. Tübingen (Germany): Mohr.

Weber, Max (1922a) 1946 Bureaucracy. Pages 196–244 in *From Max Weber: Essays in Sociology.* Translated and edited by H. H. Gerth and C. Wright Mills. New York: Oxford Univ. Press.

Weber, Max (1922b) 1954 *Max Weber on Law in Economy and Society.* Edited, with an introduction and annotations, by Max Rheinstein. Cambridge, Mass.: Harvard Univ. Press. → First published as Chapter 7 of Max Weber's *Wirtschaft und Gesellschaft.*

Weber, Max (1922c) 1951 *The Religion of China: Confucianism and Taoism.* Glencoe, Ill.: Free Press. → First published as "Konfuzianismus und Taoismus" in Volume 1 of Weber's *Gesammelte Aufsätze zur Religionssoziologie.*

Weber, Werner 1930 Parlamentarische Unvereinbarkeiten. *Archiv des öffentlichen Rechts* New Series 19:161–254.

White, Leonard D. 1954 *The Jacksonians.* New York: Macmillan.

Winckelmann, Johannes 1964 Max Webers historische und soziologische Verwaltungsforschung. Fondazione Italiana per la Storia Amministrativa, *Annals* 1:27–67.

Woll, Peter 1963a *Administrative Law: The Informal Process.* Berkeley: Univ. of California Press.

Woll, Peter 1963b *American Bureaucracy.* New York: Norton.

BURGESS, ERNEST W.

Ernest W. Burgess, American sociologist, was born in 1886 in Ontario, Canada. That same year his parents moved to the United States. He received his A.B. from Kingfisher College in Kingfisher, Oklahoma, in 1908 and his Ph.D. from the University of Chicago in 1913.

Burgess is so completely associated with the University of Chicago that it is easy to forget that before he began teaching there in 1916 he had taught at the universities of Toledo (Ohio) and Kansas and at Ohio State University. He became a professor of sociology at Chicago in 1927 and professor emeritus in 1951. He died in 1966.

The strongest influences on Burgess' academic development were those of W. I. Thomas, Robert E. Park, and George Herbert Mead. Thomas urged his students to go out into the city, as he did, to study the behavior of people in actual social situations. Park also insisted that a sociologist study life as it really exists. Mead's primary concepts—the social self, conversation of gestures, and taking the role of the other—were incorporated into Burgess' thinking. Burgess' idea that family unity arises out of the interaction and communication of family members can be traced to Mead's influence.

Burgess' two dominant interests were the family and the aged. It was he who virtually opened up the subject of the family as a field of sociological inquiry. His interest in the family began when he was asked to teach a course in the subject at the University of Chicago in 1916. Determined to break with romanticized conceptions of the family and of marriage, he conceptualized the family as "a unity of interacting personalities" (1926a).

In 1928 Burgess participated in a study that attempted to predict the success or failure of parole (1928a). This study led him to focus on the problem of predicting the success or failure of marriages. When he first began his study on this subject, in 1931, he used data obtained from only one spouse. Before that project was completed, however, he had embarked on a more ambitious one, with more satisfactory data, which included gathering data during the engagement of couples, predicting their adjustment in marriage, and reinterviewing the couples three to five years after marriage (Burgess & Wallin 1953). He concluded that the quality of adjustment depended primarily on the homogeneity of attitudes and social characteristics of the husband and wife.

Studying the life cycle of the family led Burgess to his concern with the aged. He was primarily interested in the decline in the economic role of the aged, the roles of husband and wife in old age, problems associated with the husband's retirement, changing expectations of support of the aged on the part of the aged themselves and of their children, and government programs for the aged.

Burgess had a considerable impact both on the development of sociology in general and on the field of the family in particular. One source of his broad influence on the social sciences was the immensely successful textbook he coauthored with Park (1921). In addition, he was president of the American Sociological Association, the Sociological Research Association, the National Conference on Family Relations, and the Gerontology Society. It is hard to overestimate the importance of his research and his theories in establishing the sociological study of the family. While more recent work in this field has devoted somewhat more attention than Burgess did to the family as an element in the larger structure of a society, his objective, tough-minded approach raised the study of the family to a high level in the field of sociology.

HARVEY J. LOCKE

[*For the historical context of Burgess' work, see* SOCIAL DARWINISM *and the biographies of* MEAD; PARK; THOMAS. *For discussion of the subsequent development of Burgess' ideas, see* CITY, *article on* COMPARATIVE URBAN STRUCTURE; ECOLOGY, *article on* HUMAN ECOLOGY; MARRIAGE; *and the biography of* WALLER.]

WORKS BY BURGESS

(1921) 1929 PARK, ROBERT; and BURGESS, ERNEST W. *Introduction to the Science of Sociology.* 2d ed. Univ. of Chicago Press.

1926a The Family as a Unity of Interacting Personalities. *Family* 7:3–9.

1926b The Romantic Impulse and Family Disorganization. *Survey* 57:290–294.

1926c BURGESS, ERNEST W. (editor) *The Urban Community: Selected Papers From the Proceedings of the American Sociological Society, 1925.* Univ. of Chicago Press.

1928a Factors Determining Success or Failure on Parole. Pages 203–249 in Illinois, Committee on Indeterminate-sentence Law and Parole, *The Workings of the Indeterminate-sentence Law and the Parole System in Illinois.* Springfield, Ill.: Division of Pardons and Paroles.

1928b Family Tradition and Personality Development. *National Conference of Social Work* 55:322–330.

1928c The Family and the Person. Pages 133–143 in American Sociological Society, *The Relation of the Individual to the Group.* Publications, Vol. 22. Univ. of Chicago Press.

1939 BURGESS, ERNEST W.; and COTTRELL, LEONARD S. *Predicting Success or Failure in Marriage.* New York: Prentice-Hall.

(1945) 1963 BURGESS, ERNEST W.; LOCKE, HARVEY J.; and THOMAS, MARY M. *The Family: From Institution to Companionship.* 3d ed. New York: American Book Co. → See especially Chapter 22 on "Family Relations in the Middle and Later Years."

1953 BURGESS, ERNEST W.; and WALLIN, PAUL *Engagement and Marriage.* Philadelphia: Lippincott.

(1953) 1954 BURGESS, ERNEST W.; WALLIN, PAUL; and SCHULTZ, GLADYS D. *Courtship, Engagement and Marriage.* Philadelphia: Lippincott. → First published as *Engagement and Marriage,* by Ernest W. Burgess and Paul Wallin.

1955 COUNCIL OF STATE GOVERNMENTS *The States and Their Older Citizens.* Chicago: The Council. → A study directed by Ernest W. Burgess and Sidney Spector.

1960 BURGESS, ERNEST (editor) *Aging in Western Societies.* Univ. of Chicago Press.

1964 BURGESS, ERNEST W.; and BOGUE, DONALD J. (editors) *Contributions to Urban Sociology.* Univ. of Chicago Press.

SUPPLEMENTARY BIBLIOGRAPHY

CAVAN, RUTH [Shonle] 1949 *Personal Adjustment in Old Age.* Chicago: Science Research Associates.

DENTLER, ROBERT A.; and PINEO, PETER 1960 Sexual Adjustment, Marital Adjustment and Personal Growth of Husbands: A Panel Analysis. *Marriage and Family Living* 22:45–48.

PINEO, PETER C. 1961 Disenchantment in the Later Years of Marriage. *Marriage and Family Living* 23: 3–11.

BURKE, EDMUND

Edmund Burke (1729–1797), British statesman and political writer, was born in Dublin, Ireland. His father, an attorney of some former prominence, may possibly have descended from gentry but enjoyed only modest wealth by the time Burke was born. Perhaps it was a yearning for lost status that motivated one aspect of Burke's character, his lifelong desire for a high social station.

Another natural outgrowth of Burke's background was religious tolerance: he, like his father, was an Anglican, but his mother and sister were Roman Catholics, and his schoolmaster and closest childhood friend were Quakers. He possessed a generous nature, a lofty sense of moral obligation, and unusual devotion to family and friends.

Burke received a thorough secondary school education and was enrolled in Trinity College, Dublin. Then, in 1750, at the age of 21, he left for London to study law. But although he completed his legal studies, he was more interested in debating clubs and a literary career than he was in the law. It was his *Philosophical Enquiry Into the Origin of Our Ideas of the Sublime and Beautiful* (1757), a work on the relation between aesthetics and emotions, that established his reputation. In 1759 he agreed to edit the *Annual Register*, a new encyclopedic review of politics and literature. During these early years Burke became a charter member of Samuel Johnson's "Club," and he always retained the close association with the literary world that his own prose mastery so clearly merited.

Burke's political career began in 1759, when he became private secretary to William Gerard Hamilton, a member of Parliament. When the two men quarreled in 1765, Burke obtained a similar position with the marquis of Rockingham, leader of an important group of Whigs in Commons and, at the time, head of the government ministry. The following year friends provided Burke with a seat in Parliament, where he was immediately acclaimed for his informed, incisive, and polished analyses of political problems.

The Rockingham ministry fell in 1766, and it was Burke, the new Whig theoretician, who converted the Rockingham clique into an opposition party committed to distinctive political principles. In 1774 he was elected to sit for Bristol, a major commercial center, but he lost the seat in 1780. From then on he sat for one of Rockingham's pocket boroughs.

By 1782 Burke had made numerous enemies, and he held only minor office during Rockingham's short-lived second administration. When the marquis's death, later in the year, removed the protection of that powerful patron, Burke's influence in the House of Commons waned further. Then, as a new generation moved in, his decline accelerated.

Burke had always had a quick temper, and constant personal attacks led him to an increasingly uncritical defense of his emotional commitments. His intense personal and family affections developed into a blind refusal to believe that his kinsmen and friends could be guilty of the irregularities which others knew they had committed. His aspiration for high status had led him to buy a landed estate that he could not afford. Under continued criticism for financial embarrassment, and longing for the security of a peerage, he became a more intense apologist for aristocracy than the aristocrats themselves.

It was Burke's uncompromising condemnation of the French Revolution that precipitated his break with the Whig party. In 1791, climaxing a dramatic scene in Parliament, he severed his ties with Charles James Fox, Rockingham's young successor. Although after 1792 public opinion tended to support his position, Burke felt obliged to resign his parliamentary seat, delaying his resignation only until the end of the trial he had initiated against Warren Hastings, the former governor of India. The tragic death of his only surviving son in 1794 not only robbed him of the most cherished object of his love but also ended his hopes for a hereditary peerage, so that in one blow the two most important personal devotions of his life were destroyed. He lived only a short while longer.

Approach to politics. Burke's theories synthesize the Whig aspirations of the eighteenth century as Locke's do those of the seventeenth. During the seventeenth century English constitutional traditions turned brittle from the refusal of Cavaliers and Tories to temper the "divine right of kings." Blocked from access to the power centers that interpreted those traditions, Roundheads and Whigs who sought the extension of political consent and freedom had to abandon argument from national custom and rest their case instead on the abstract principles summed up in the Lockean theory of "natural rights," a "social contract," and the legislative sovereignty of a representative Parliament. By Burke's time, however, the successful Whig revolution had made the commitment to freedom an integral part of a reformulated national tradition. It was now the unreconciled Tory, like Bolingbroke, and the more radical, democratic Lockean, like Paine, who argued from abstraction. Whig theory therefore had to be restated in terms of the new tradition without being made vulnerable to attack from the right or the left, and Whig theorists had to use the new formulation to redefine the collective interests of a society that was rapidly raising its level of secular expectations. Burke provided the theoretical basis for this new orientation.

A distaste for speculative argument permeated all of Burke's writings and speeches. Politics and morality, he was always ready to point out, are matters of prudence and practicability. If we insist on imposing the simple perfection of a logical ideal on an imperfect, complex reality, we shall only succeed in destroying both the amount of good that already exists and the limited improvements that are feasible. Moral principles must be adjusted to the feelings and emotions of a people, to their conflicting interests, their interrelated institutions, and the complicated realities of circumstance. The integration of all these strands requires an element of political artistry, an act of creation that is something more than a moral arithmetic. It is destructive, therefore, to criticize on the basis of an abstract ideal, unless something better can actually be put into effect.

Social order.   With this prudential approach to politics Burke offered a new theoretical synthesis of the Whig principle of freedom and the Tory principle of order. There were important occasions when Burke spoke of order in instrumental terms as the condition of freedom and prosperity. On these occasions he was prepared to urge that the existing order be redefined to make it more compatible with freedom. But order, especially social order, was also an intrinsic good, to be defined and valued in its own terms, as it was in Tory theory. Four principles recur and are elaborated in Burke's theory of order:

(1) Social order is a part of the natural order that God has created in the universe, and it exists prior to the individuals who are born into it. Obedience and tranquillity in society rest ultimately on man's reverence for God, on the religious obligation to restrain his selfish desires and passions, on the faith that gives "dignity to life and consolation in death." Social order must hence be built on a religious establishment, because it is in itself divinely ordained, quite apart from the human advances and benefits it makes possible.

(2) Man is a social animal. Therefore, the family, not the individual, is the proper unit of social order. Families are organized into classes that reflect social functions and into regional communities that reflect geographic conditions. The pre-eminently effective community is the nation; the nation is the vehicle that expresses the unique character of a people in history, that integrates classes and localities in space and links them in time to generations both past and unborn.

(3) A nation must have rules of behavior to bring unity of purpose out of the mutual adaptation of conflicting interests and emotions. In time these unifying rules become prescriptive traditions that assign rights and privileges and transmit them to the next generation through the principle of family inheritance. The more ancient the tradition, the more profound the respect it evokes, because it embraces the accumulated collective wisdom of the ages. Such ancient traditions must therefore be examined only with great caution and veneration.

(4) Inequality is inescapable in society. But social leadership is most properly founded on the natural sense of dependence, subordination, and affection, which respond to ability, virtue, age, and graciousness. These qualities of leadership are best institutionalized in a hereditary aristocracy, because aristocracy combines training in expert knowledge and self-discipline with a gracious, humane code of social behavior and with the ancient, hallowed institution of nobility. Since aristocracy offers its members the highest social honors for public service, the aristocrat develops the strong sensitivity to reputation and personal honor that leads him to identify the public interest with his own.

Burke's emphasis on the emotional responses that social order evokes and his view of the nation as a unit of historical time were original ideas. But established religion, hereditary aristocracy, reverence for ancient traditions, and a familistic basis for social organization were conceptions of social order that derived from old Tory principles and, beyond them, from medieval social theory.

To build his Whig superstructure Burke modified the old Tory principles of order with liberal attitudes more appropriate to his own age: (1) religious establishment should respect the conscience of the dissenter; (2) aristocracy should leave some limited room for the upward mobility of new talent; (3) tradition must be adjusted, however cautiously, to the new circumstances and problems for which there is no solution in precedent; (4) an imperial nation can maintain order only by respecting the distinctive character and traditions of its colonies.

Economic theory. On questions other than that of social order Burke's viewpoint diverged more radically from Tory principles. This was especially true of his economic theory, which was almost identical with the advanced position held by Adam Smith. In economics Burke was prepared to define order entirely in terms of individual freedom: free trade, free competition, and reward for individual work and thrift. Given a system of competitive capitalism, God and nature lead men, "whether they will or not, in pursuing their own selfish interests, to connect the general good with their own individual success" (1800, p. 11). If nobility was the "soul" of the social order, freedom was the "vital spring" of economic energy and the key to national prosperity.

Political principles. The task of good government was to combine both principles, to provide "liberty, connected with order," as Burke described the English system. He spoke of political authority in general terms as an accountable trust, granted by the community to its leaders for the purpose of pursuing the common good. But more specifically, this meant (1) fulfilling and expanding the traditional interests of the nation; (2) adhering to the rule of law, with respect for the prescriptive rights of the citizens, and cautiously expanding political liberties; (3) balancing landed and commercial political interests under aristocratic leadership; and (4) developing a "mixed government" consisting of a representative legislature and a hereditary monarchy.

Monarchy was the central institution of political order because it was, to Burke, the "natural" object of political obedience and reverence, the symbol of national continuity. Although these characteristics made monarchy a primary condition of good government, the ultimate significance of monarchy lay in its potential for developing into mixed and balanced government. The principle of continuity by inheritance guaranteed peaceful succession to the throne. But the same principle became, for Burke, the guarantee of the inherited rights of the citizens. When these rights were violated, an oppressed community could, by political revolution, withdraw its grant of trust. The conditions for such withdrawal of trust were prolonged and great

abuse, with no prospect for improvement, under pressure so heavy that no delay was possible, and the absence of any clearly better alternative to revolution.

Needless to say, Burke found his political principles best expressed in the English constitutional tradition, last clarified by the Whig revolution of 1688–1689. Burke proceeded further to clarify this tradition for the late eighteenth century. The traditional rights of Englishmen, he insisted, applied to all citizens—rights such as habeas corpus, private property, and some elements of a free press and of religious conscience. But the right to vote or to hold office was based primarily on property qualifications, he argued, not only because property expresses the economic element in the national interest but also because it instills in its possessors both respect for order and an attitude of independence. These property interests were represented in the House of Commons. The nobility in the House of Lords represented the nation's interest in social order and rank. At both levels of government the aristocratic sense of honor stood as a kind of collateral to guarantee performance of the public trust with which government is endowed. Parliament thus represented social rank and economic interests, not individuals. It was the uniquely English class ties between landed aristocracy and urban commerce, as Burke realized, that generated the unifying force of English politics and made possible the integration as well as the balance of prescriptively protected interests.

Although the king retained control over executive appointments, Burke explained, Parliament held legislative sovereignty as the representative body through which the public spoke. Therefore, it could properly reject a ministry by refusing to allocate funds to it. Similarly, the public itself could reject parliamentary representatives by refusing to re-elect them. But just as the legislature should not try to administer, so the public should not try to legislate. It is important that popular grievances be voiced, but only the government can provide the necessary remedies, and it cannot dispense with independent judgment.

Critique of government policy. In this synthesis of Whig and Tory political principles, Burke was articulating views widely held at the time. It was in his application of these principles to the new problems of the day that he departed from the majority, for he charged the king's government with major failures of national policy and systematic perversion of the English constitution.

Since it was Burke's position that one social

group should never benefit at the expense of the traditional interests of another, a progressive national policy was one that meant a general increase of benefits for the whole society and the individuals in it. In his analysis, such progress could best be achieved by (1) commercial expansion through freer trade and economic competition, and (2) imperial unity maintained by careful attention to the character, traditions, and interests of the colonies.

It was essential, Burke reasoned, that the government hold the affections of the American colonies and preserve the commercial relations which made England the imperial manufacturing center. But the administration had stubbornly insisted on imposing unprecedented taxes upon Americans, ignoring those elements in the American character which would lead them to resist in the name of freedom. The resort to coercive acts would not only violate the colonists' rights as Englishmen but would also produce such intense resentment that imperial order and the whole commercial system would be endangered, no matter how successfully disturbances might be repressed (1775a; 1775b).

In Ireland also, the government had enforced harmful trade restrictions and violated civil rights far too long, Burke charged. The systematic oppression of the Catholic majority left it without either sympathetic representation or protection against the small minority that ruled in its own interests. Irish policy too would one day end in disaster, he warned.

Burke argued that these dangers to the common interest were the consequences of a constitutional imbalance which had illicitly given unchecked control of the government to King George III and his court faction. This faction had used political patronage as an instrument for the systematic control and corruption of the electorate, which in turn meant control of Parliament. Civil rights had been violated and "natural" leaders ignored. The entire English constitution had been turned upside down by making electoral consent and legislative criticism objects of irresponsible and secretive executive manipulation, instead of effective instruments of popular control.

Burke neglected to point out that it was originally the Whigs themselves who, under Walpole, had created this perversion of their doctrine. George III had merely taken over the system by reasserting his royal prerogatives. Only after they were out of power had the Whigs become sensitive to this problem. But Burke did provide the theoretical remedies for the constitutional imbalance that were to pass into English tradition.

First, he supported wider political rights, such as publication of parliamentary debates, less government discretion in political libel cases, more exact voter lists, and effective protest against the seating of a minority candidate by Commons (as in the Wilkes election of 1769). Second, he called for permanent disciplined parties, organized within the House of Commons, to provide a continuous channel of responsibility to the political public. Party government, he insisted, is not subversive of order, and it is essential to freedom. A party, however, needs more than personal loyalties and common economic or social interests. It needs common political principles consistently expressed in a clear doctrine on which national policy can be based. With this kind of doctrinal party unity, he concluded, it becomes possible for the party in power to have responsible administration and for the opposition to produce responsible criticism (1770). Reapportionment and more frequent elections appeared to Burke to be irrelevant to the task of enforcing political responsibility. He did admit that party government would not in itself eliminate executive control of elections, and in 1782 he provided a third remedy—a program of "economical reform" to reorganize government finance and reduce the whole system of electoral patronage, though it was Pitt who later made financial reform effective.

Burke, in effect, formulated the principles for reversing the whole flow of power to the executive: financial reorganization to give Parliament more effective control of the executive, broader political rights to enlarge public information, and a redefinition of the national interest around freer trade and less coercive imperial unity. Above all, organized, disciplined parties with clear programs were to provide the active public with an instrument of control over both the legislature and the executive, linking them together in an effective system of responsible government. He may have refused to take the final step of pushing toward the universal franchise, and most of his arguments against democracy may seem unconvincing to our age, but he supported his position forcefully when he pointed out that the English people were simply not interested in democracy at the time.

After 1782 Burke's criticisms grew steadily more bitter and emotional in tone, and his facts were more apt to be exaggerated or otherwise distorted. But he still had vital messages to deliver. During the rest of the decade he became increasingly absorbed in the problems of India, specifically in the prosecution of Warren Hastings. He accused the Hastings regime and the East India Company of plundering India for private profits without giving anything to India in return. Not satisfied with destroying the country's social order, they had depressed its economy, despoiled the private property of its citizens, and returned with their loot to corrupt English politics, further undermining the authority of the Parliament whose instructions they had repeatedly ignored. Although the personal charges against Hastings were finally dismissed in 1795, Burke had created for Britain's Indian policy a national conscience that it was never to shake off.

French Revolution.   It was the French Revolution that drew Burke's heaviest and most sustained fire. This was the catalyst that forced Burke to crystallize his whole theory of social order. With a passion matched only by his eloquence, he charged the revolutionaries with every social and political crime in his catalogue. In terrible contrast to the cautious political rebellion with which the English Whigs had regained their freedom, France had unleashed total chaos. From pure abstractions, he thundered, and with total indifference to their own national traditions, these inferior, factious Frenchmen of the middle class were launching a Continental social revolution. They were destroying the spirit of chivalry and nobility; they were undermining religion and the established church; they were subverting property and the family; they had already murdered a legitimate monarch and loosened the bonds of political allegiance. And having disintegrated the base on which responsible freedom is built, Burke warned, French individualism would be forced to turn to a new despot to save it from total anarchy; moreover, the new despotism would soon overflow with barbaric savagery into all of Europe (1790). Before long he had issued his call for a crusade against revolutionary France and for the repression of French ideas in Great Britain.

There is no doubt that Burke's theoretical framework enabled him to see more clearly than many others the explosive consequences of a total social revolution, as distinguished from a limited political rebellion. The events that culminated in the rise of Napoleon seemed the fulfillment of his prophecy. But in his frenzy to fasten all the blame on the revolutionaries he failed to understand the extent to which revolutionaries are molded by the system against which they revolt, and he made statements very difficult to reconcile with those he had made during the American and Irish controversies.

Burke had begun with an important generalization about his country—that the edifice of British freedom stood on a foundation of social order which preserved selected elements from its medieval past. But the traditional order *had* changed, as he well knew. In the United States it had changed still further; the American constitution abolished monarchy, nobility, and an established national church. Yet Burke raised no public objections to these experiments that redefined order for the sake of expanding freedom: Implicitly, and often explicitly, he held that continuity was preserved because of a traditional Anglo-Saxon readiness to alter the older order when it conflicted with the extension of freedom, and usually to do this before the conflict became explosive.

Burke seemed unable, however, to understand the corollary to this analysis: that the moderate principles of Anglo-Saxon development might be inapplicable in a tradition-oriented social order which repressed any strong internal or external movement toward individual freedom; he was quite incapable of shedding British standards when dealing with totally alien conditions. In spite of the many years he devoted to studying India, he always tended to equate Indian institutions with European counterparts that were, in fact, only remotely similar, and he was therefore able to indulge in the comforting illusion that the British could stay in India indefinitely without radically altering the country's traditions. For all his insistence that allowance be made for differences in national character, Burke's indictment of the French Revolution adds up to blaming France for not being Britain.

The many difficulties Burke had in defending his position led him to attribute the profound upheavals in India and France to personal conspiracies, but he simply refused to believe that his own friends and those he admired merited as large a share of "blame" as his enemies. Parliament knew this when it dismissed his charges against Hastings. Many contemporaries knew it when they contrasted his generous sympathy for the fate of French royalists with his seeming indifference to the plight of less privileged Frenchmen. Outmatched though Tom Paine was in his debate with Burke over the French Revolution, he hit the mark when he noted the ease with which Burke "pitied the plumage and forgot the dying bird."

Influence on later thought.   Burke was not one of the really great political theorists of Western civilization. His theories were fruitfully tailored to eighteenth-century Britain and British imperial problems, but his insights were not systematic and his formulations not universal. In the early nineteenth century his influence was largely confined on the Continent to the defenders of the medieval *ancien régime* against the liberalism of the French

Revolution and in Great Britain to some of the literary figures of the early romantic movement. The democratic movement of the later century made the antidemocratic Burke seem irrelevant to the new problems facing Great Britain, and his ambiguous party affiliations did not endear him to the political spokesmen of the period.

By the twentieth century, partisan reaction to Burke was being superseded by a willingness to draw piecemeal on his many insights without any necessary commitment to his particular conclusions. The list of social and political theorists in twentieth-century Britain and America who have referred approvingly to particular of Burke's formulations includes such diverse political thinkers as Harold Laski, Woodrow Wilson, Reinhold Niebuhr, Walter Lippmann, Hannah Arendt, and Ernest Barker. In the 1950s there appeared in America a number of books whose authors, such as Russell Kirk, Peter Viereck, and Clinton Rossiter, affirmed intellectual descent from Burke.

There are few contemporary works on political parties or on the nature of political representation that do not refer to Burke's analyses of these subjects, and his discussions of prudential considerations in political policy are probably of even more lasting significance. Certainly, there is much in Burke that is indispensable for an understanding of the long-term dynamics of British political development. Beyond the purely political, scholars will continue to find fruitful insights in his appreciation, however overdrawn and unqualified, of the more intangible elements of social order.

M. Morton Auerbach

[*For the historical context of Burke's work, see* Consensus; Conservatism; Parliamentary government; Representation, *article on* representational behavior; Revolution; *and the biographies of* Locke; Paine; Smith, Adam.]

WORKS BY BURKE

(1744–1782) 1958–1963 *The Correspondence of Edmund Burke.* 4 vols. Univ. of Chicago Press; Cambridge Univ. Press. → Four volumes of a projected ten-volume work.

(1757) 1958 *A Philosophical Enquiry Into the Origin of Our Ideas of the Sublime and Beautiful.* New York: Columbia Univ. Press.

(1769–1796) 1949 *Burke's Politics: Selected Writings and Speeches on Reform, Revolution, and War.* Edited by Ross J. S. Hoffman and Paul Levack. New York: Knopf.

1770 *Thoughts on the Cause of Present Discontents.* London: Dodsley.

1775a *Speech of Edmund Burke, Esq., on American Taxation, April 19, 1774.* London: Dodsley.

1775b *Speech of Edmund Burke, Esq., on Moving His Resolutions for Conciliation With the Colonies, March* 22, 1775. London: Dodsley; New York: Rivington.

(1790) 1960 *Reflections on the Revolution in France, and on the Proceedings in Certain Societies in London Relative to that Event.* New York: Dutton; London: Dent.

1800 *Thoughts and Details on Scarcity.* London: Rivington. → Originally presented to William Pitt in 1795 and first published in 1800.

1803–1827 *The Works of the Right Honourable Edmund Burke.* 16 vols. London: Rivington.

SUPPLEMENTARY BIBLIOGRAPHY

Barker, Ernest 1931 *Burke and Bristol: A Study of the Relations Between Burke and His Constituency During the Years 1774–1780.* Bristol (England): Arrowsmith.

Canavan, Francis P. 1960 *The Political Reason of Edmund Burke.* Durham, N.C.: Duke Univ. Press.

Cobban, Alfred (1929) 1960 *Edmund Burke and the Revolt Against the Eighteenth Century: A Study of the Political and Social Thinking of Burke, Wordsworth, Coleridge and Southey.* 2d ed. London: Allen & Unwin; New York: Barnes & Noble.

Cone, Carl B. 1957–1964 *Burke and the Nature of Politics.* 2 vols. Lexington: Univ. of Kentucky Press. → Vol. 1: *Age of the American Revolution.* Vol. 2: *Age of the French Revolution.*

Copeland, Thomas W. 1949 *Our Eminent Friend Edmund Burke.* New Haven: Yale Univ. Press.

Graubard, Stephen R. 1961 *Burke, Disraeli and Churchill: The Politics of Perseverance.* Cambridge, Mass.: Harvard Univ. Press.

Hoffman, Ross J. S. 1956 *Edmund Burke: New York Agent; With His Letters to the New York Assembly and Intimate Correspondence With Charles O'Hara, 1761–1776.* Philadelphia: American Philosophical Society.

MacCunn, John 1913 *The Political Philosophy of Burke.* London: Arnold.

Magnus, Philip M. 1939 *Edmund Burke: A Life.* London: Murray.

Mahoney, Thomas H. D. 1960 *Edmund Burke and Ireland.* Cambridge, Mass.: Harvard Univ. Press.

Morley, John M. 1867 *Edmund Burke: A Historical Study.* London: Macmillan.

Morley, John M. 1879 *Burke.* London: Macmillan; New York: Harper.

Osborn, Annie M. 1940 *Rousseau and Burke: A Study of the Idea of Liberty in Eighteenth-century Political Thought.* Oxford Univ. Press.

Parkin, Charles 1956 *The Moral Basis of Burke's Political Thought.* Cambridge Univ. Press.

Stanlis, Peter J. 1958 *Edmund Burke and the Natural Law.* Ann Arbor: Univ. of Michigan Press.

BUSINESS CYCLES

I. General — Arthur F. Burns
II. Mathematical Models — Trygve Haavelmo

I

GENERAL

Economic change is a law of life. Nowadays, we commonly associate economic instability with business booms and recessions, and we have become accustomed to speaking of these vicissitudes in economic fortune as the "business cycle." However, economic instability has been man's lot through the ages, whether he has made his living by hunting and fishing, by cultivating crops, or by practicing the arts of commerce, industry, and finance. Economic history discloses endless variations of economic conditions. Even the meaning of "good times" keeps changing as the aspirations of people and their performance undergo changes. But relative to the standards of each age and place, some years are prosperous, others dull, still others depressed.

Types of economic movement.   The outstanding feature of modern industrial nations is the growth of their economies. Thus, the population of the United States has risen steadily, year in and year out. So too, with very few exceptions, has the stock of housing, industrial plant, machinery, school buildings, highways, and other major forms of capital. The gross national product—that is, the total output of commodities and services—has fluctuated continually, but has done so along a rising secular trend. So also has output per capita, per worker, or per man-hour worked. In short, the American economy, viewed in the aggregate, has been basically characterized by growth of resources, growth of output, and growth of efficiency.

When we look beneath the surface of aggregate economic activity, we find some industries and communities growing rapidly, others growing only gradually, and still others declining. These divergent trends reflect a host of influences—among them, business innovations, population changes, shifts in consumer preferences, the discovery of new mines or oil fields, the exhaustion of old mines or timberlands, and changes in governmental policies. For example, the capital invested in American railroads and their volume of traffic increased rapidly during the nineteenth century, responding to the economic growth of the country and in turn stimulating it. But the railroads also grew at the expense of coaches, canals, and other waterways, which they gradually superseded by offering better service or charging a lower price. Years later the competitive trend was reversed, as new methods of transportation came into being—first, trolley lines, then buses, trucks, passenger automobiles, pipelines, airplanes, and improved waterways. These battled the railroads for traffic as vigorously as railroads in their youth had fought their commercial rivals. More recently, railroads have begun to retaliate through the use of radically new freight cars and other innovations. Such divergence of industrial trends is one of the expressions of economic progress.

Business cycles have been intimately connected with the lopsided surges of development that mark economic progress. However, business cycles are not the only type of fluctuation to which economic life is subject. During certain hours of the day, most of us are at school or at work; during other hours we relax in whatever way suits our tastes or needs. This daily cycle in activity is so regular and dependable that we take it for granted. The same is true of the weekly cycle which brings its day or days of rest. Whatever difficulties or opportunities the daily and weekly cycles may have posed for our remote ancestors, our own lives and social institutions have become adjusted to their repetitive course. We know that shops will be closed at certain hours and on certain days, and we plan our shopping accordingly. We know that the nation's production will decline abruptly when factory workers put down their tools in the late afternoon, but we also know that their jobs do not cease on that account and that they will take up their tools again the next morning or when the weekend is over. In view of the extreme brevity and regularity of these cyclical movements, we pay no attention to them in judging whether business is improving or worsening.

Much the same is true of the seasonal fluctuations that run their course within the period of a year. Partly because of vagaries of the weather or the calendar, partly because of changes in business practice, the annual cycle is less regular than the daily or weekly cycle. Nevertheless, we expect business in general to be more brisk in the spring than in the summer or winter, and we ordinarily find it so. We expect department store sales to reach a peak during the Easter shopping season and a still higher peak before Christmas, and so we find it. We expect unemployment to be at its highest in February and at its lowest in October, and so it usually is. Workers in seasonal trades may not cherish the fluctuation to which they are subject, but they can reasonably count on returning to their jobs when the dull season ends and can plan their lives accordingly. In view of the substantial regularity of seasonal fluctuations, businessmen as well as economists usually put them out of sight when they seek to determine whether a particular branch of trade—or the economy as a whole—is expanding or contracting.

Business cycles differ in vital respects from these daily, weekly, and annual cycles. First, the recurring sequence of changes that constitutes a business cycle—expansion, downturn, contraction, and upturn—is not periodic. In other words, the phases of business cycles repeat themselves, but their duration varies considerably and so too does their intensity and scope. Second, since business cycles last from about two to ten years, they are considerably longer than the other cycles. Third, business cycles have a more powerful tendency to synchronize industrial, commercial, and financial processes than do the shorter cycles. Thus, the daily and weekly cycles in total production have no counterpart in inventories, bank loans, or interest rates, while seasonal fluctuations vary widely from one business activity to another. Fourth, although custom has left its imprint on the daily and annual cycles, they are part of the natural environment of man. Business cycles, on the other hand, are a product of culture. They are found only in modern nations where economic activities are organized mainly through business enterprises and where individuals enjoy considerable freedom in producing, pricing, trading, and saving or investing.

When economic plans and decisions are made independently by millions of business firms and households, some imbalance is frequently bound to occur between output and sales, or between output and the stock of equipment, or between inventories and outstanding orders, or between costs of production and prices. This much can be reasonably anticipated by everyone. However, the locus of the imbalance, its timing and magnitude, and the adjustments to which it leads can rarely, if ever, be foreseen with precision. In short, the business cycle lacks the brevity, the simplicity, the regularity, the dependability, or the predictability of its cousins. For all these reasons, although the business cycle is often the vehicle of progress, it also spells instability for society. When the economy starts on a downward course, no one can be sure how many months the recession will last, whether it will degenerate into a depression, how many business firms will go bankrupt, how far prices will decline, and—most important of all from a human standpoint—how many men and women will become unemployed. Although the United States and other countries are learning rapidly how to adapt to business cycles and to bring them under control, they remain troublesome.

Business cycles are not merely fluctuations in aggregate economic activity. They are also fluctuations that are widely diffused throughout the economy, and this fact distinguishes them from the convulsions of economic fortune that characterized earlier times as well as from the other short-term variations of our own age. Continuous and fairly pervasive fluctuations do not arise in a nation's economy until its activities of production, distribution, and consumption have become closely interwoven through division of labor, the making and spending of money incomes, a system of banking and credit, a mode of production relying extensively on fixed capital, and some ease in communication and transportation. Since these institutions emerged gradually in the Western world, the phenomenon of business cycles itself developed gradually and no precise date can be assigned for its first mature expression. It appears, however, that business cycles have existed in the United States, Great Britain, and France for nearly two hundred years, and that they have marked the economies of other modern nations practicing free enterprise since the latter part of the nineteenth century—if not longer. Earlier centuries, while free from business cycles, did not escape the ordeal of economic instability. This is evident from the hardships that frequently accompanied or followed bad harvests, epidemics, wars, earthquakes, monetary upheavals, high-handed acts of rulers, civil disorders, and similar fortuitous events.

In recent decades, the Soviet Union and other nations that organize economic activity through state enterprises and governmental edicts have also escaped business cycles; but they have not escaped economic fluctuations. Variations in harvests, political purges, wars, monetary revolutions, and misadventures, as well as successes of planning, have left their mark on the aggregate economic activity of these nations. Of course, episodic or erratic disturbances also powerfully influence the course of economic activity in the United States and in other developed nations that practice free enterprise, but they appear to do so by hastening or retarding, by strengthening or opposing, the economic processes that of themselves tend to generate cyclical movements. The ragged contours of most business cycles testify to the role of random disturbances, and so too does the strong individuality of successive business cycles.

Business cycles also need to be distinguished from specific cycles—that is, cycles in specific activities, such as mining coal or trading in securities, which have about the same order of duration as the business cycle but may or may not match its timing. Occasionally, specific cycles appear to be superimposed, so to speak, on longer cycles marked by their own rises and declines. Huge swings, lasting about 10 to 25 years, have been common in building construction in various countries. Waves of this order of duration, but consisting of accelerations and retardations of growth rather than of actual rises and declines, also appear to have characterized aggregate economic activity in the United States. These Kuznets cycles, as they are often called, reflect variations in the intensity of successive business cycles. A distinction between major and minor cycles, such as Hansen makes, likewise involves a grouping of successive business cycles. On this view, the interval between the troughs of severe depressions is a major cycle, so that some major cycles may include only one business cycle while others include two or more. Long waves of about fifty years—usually called Kondratieff cycles—have also been alleged to characterize aggregate economic activity of Western nations. The existence of these waves, while suggested by price movements, has not yet been established.

The terms used by economists to describe the phases of business cycles are rich in diversity but are gradually becoming standardized. The "peak" of a business cycle marks the end of "expansion" and the beginning of "contraction." The "trough" marks the end of contraction and the beginning of expansion. Frequently, "prosperity" is used interchangeably with "expansion," although it is better practice to restrict terms such as "prosperity" or "boom" to the higher reaches of particular expansions when full employment is closely approximated. The term "recession" does double duty. It is widely used to refer to the transition from expansion to contraction, just as "recovery" or "revival" is used to refer to the transition from contraction to expansion. Contractions of varying intensity are also commonly distinguished by the terms "recession" and "depression"; the former refers to a moderate contraction of aggregate activity that lasts in the neighborhood of a year, while the latter refers to a severe contraction or to one which, while moderate, lasts distinctly longer than a year. The term "crisis" originally was used to denote the financial disturbances that frequently occurred during the transition from expansion to contraction, but later it came to be applied to any transition from expansion to contraction. Nowadays, the term "crisis" is usually reserved for a violent disruption of financial markets without regard to the stage of the business cycle in which such a disturbance occurs.

Growth of knowledge about business cycles. In view of the complexity of business cycles and the innumerable differences between them, their essential features and causes have long been a matter of debate. The lack of full or precise economic statistics, which was especially serious before World War I, inevitably contributed to uncertainty about the actual course of business cycles and their causes. But as public concern about crises, inflation, depressions, and unemployment grew, economists have also pressed their investigation of this range of problems.

During much of the nineteenth century, interest was focused on commercial crises—that is, the sharp rise of money rates, scramble for liquidity, drop of prices, and spread of bankruptcies that frequently marked the culmination of a boom. With the emergence of the concept of a business cycle, various economists became concerned with the entire round of events that preceded and followed a crisis. The business cycle itself, however, was still viewed as centering, in the main, in activities of commerce and finance. Some economists traced its causes to natural forces, others to psychological factors, and still others to the workings of the monetary and banking system. Toward the end of the century, interest began to shift to phenomena of industry and employment, and more particularly to the great fluctuations that characterized the capital goods industries. This change of outlook reflected the growth of manufacturing, transportation, and public utility enterprises in modern nations, the relative decline of agriculture, and a growing realization that the transition from prosperity to recession could occur without a crisis or panic but not without a substantial increase of unemployment. In later decades, numerous explanations of the business cycle were developed that gave a large role to investment—usually to investment in fixed capital but sometimes to investment in inventories. Economists stressed different factors that had a bearing on the investment process—such as population growth, territorial expansion, stock of capital, the state of optimism, new technology, bunching of innovations, the rate of change in consumption, variation of interest rates, and changes of costs, prices, and profits. Or else they attributed primary significance to particular features of economic organization—such as industrial competition, uncertainty of demand, or the inequality of incomes. More frequently than not, the various theories differed mainly in their points of emphasis and therefore served to supplement one another.

The truly outstanding contributions to knowledge of business cycles were made by a small number of economists. Clément Juglar, 1819–1905, pioneered by demonstrating, in the course of a massive factual study of prices and finance, that crises were merely a passing phase of a recurring, wavelike fluctuation in business activity. Mikhail Tugan-Baranovskii, 1865–1919, was the first influential economist to see in the fluctuating rate of growth of the fixed capital of a country the main cause of its business cycles. Knut Wicksell, 1851–

1926, clarified the cumulative processes of the business cycle by analyzing the consequences of a discrepancy between the rate of return on investment, which was liable to shift because of technological or other real changes in opportunity, and the market rate of interest. Albert Aftalion, 1874–1956, developed the implications for the business cycle of certain industrial facts—the long period required to bring new fixed capital into being, the long life of capital goods, and the capacity of minor changes in consumption to generate large changes in the net additions to the fixed capital required by business firms. Joseph A. Schumpeter, 1883–1950, viewed economic growth itself as a cyclical process and attributed the business cycle to the bunching of innovations, which forced difficult readjustments on old enterprises but in the end resulted in a more effective use of existing resources. Wesley Clair Mitchell, 1874–1948, carried factual investigation of business cycles far beyond earlier efforts, sharpened the concept of a self-generating cycle in a business system, and clarified the interrelations of costs, prices, and profits during a business cycle. John Maynard Keynes, 1883–1946, stressed the dynamic role of investment in altering the level of national income, formulated a consumption function which treats consumer spending as a passive response to national income, and with the aid of this function clarified the process whereby an increment of investment, besides adding directly to a nation's income, raises it indirectly by stimulating larger consumer spending. Through the contributions of these pioneers and of many other economists and economic statisticians, notably Warren M. Persons, Simon Kuznets, and Jan Tinbergen, significant advances have been made in recent decades in describing with some precision the major features of business cycles and also in understanding the processes whereby they are generated.

This paper presents in nontechnical language the main results of modern research on the nature and causes of business cycles. It should be borne in mind, however, that the concrete manifestations of the business cycle keep changing and that numerous aspects of business cycles are still obscure. These facts justify extensive new research. The investigations that economists have currently under way focus on speculative model building, econometric model building, historical studies of individual cycles, statistical studies of fluctuations in individual processes or in the economy at large, experiments with forecasting techniques, and studies of business-cycle policy. This variety of approaches sometimes leads to methodological controversies. But no serious student of business cycles any longer questions that empirical research must be guided by an analytic framework or that speculative theorizing must be tested by an appeal to experience.

Cyclical behavior of aggregate activity. The business cycle involves to some degree the entire system of business—the formation of firms and their disappearance, prices as well as output, the employment of labor and other resources, costs and profits, the flow of incomes to individuals and consumer spending, savings and investments, exports and imports, trading in securities as well as commodities, the extension and repayment of loans, the money supply and its turnover, and the fiscal operations of government. Since there is no unique way of combining all these activities, the business cycle cannot be fully depicted by any single measure. However, the behavior of the entire congeries of fluctuations is indicated reasonably well for recent decades by statistical series of fairly comprehensive economic coverage—such as industrial production, total or nonagricultural employment, the flow of personal income, bank clearings or debits, and the gross national product.

The picture of a typical business cycle which emerges from these statistical records and also from earlier historical descriptions is that of a sustained rise in aggregate economic activity followed by a sustained, but smaller and shorter, decline. Activity at the peak of a business cycle is not merely higher than at the immediately preceding and following troughs. With very rare exceptions, it is also higher than at the preceding peak and lower than at the following peak. Likewise, the trough of a business cycle is usually higher than its immediate predecessor. In view of these typical characteristics, a business cycle almost always includes a visible element of growth. It is not merely an oscillation. The expansion, which ultimately carries aggregate activity to new heights, is typically most rapid in its early stages—the more so when it follows a severe contraction than when it follows a mild one. Although the rate of advance usually tapers off as the expansion proceeds, at times it reaccelerates as an expansion draws to a close without, however, regaining its initial speed. During contractions the rate of decline is usually fastest in the middle stages.

Between 1854 and 1961 the average length of business cycles in the United States was 49 months, with the average expansion lasting 30 months and the average contraction 19. The duration of individual cycles varied considerably—from 10 to 80 months for expansions, from 7 to 65 months for contractions, and from 17 to 101 months for full cycles. In a sense, aggregate activity was "depressed" over longer intervals than the duration of contractions may suggest, since some time must elapse before recovery can restore activity to the level attained at the preceding cyclical peak. On the other hand, the level of activity in the months immediately following a peak is often only a little lower than at the peak. During the ten business cycles from 1919 to 1961, when expansions averaged 35 months and contractions 15, the increases of industrial production ranged from 18 to 93 per cent and averaged 38 per cent, while the declines ranged from 7 to 66 per cent and averaged 26 per cent. Total output and employment, however, have fluctuated within decidedly narrower ranges. The reason is that they encompass, besides volatile activities like manufacturing and mining, relatively stable activities such as re-

tailing, the service trades, and governmental work. Thus, during the business-cycle contraction of 1957–1958, when industrial production declined 14.2 per cent, total real output fell only 4.6 per cent and employment in nonagricultural establishments 4.3 per cent (see Table 1 and Figure 1).

In other industrial countries the average duration of business cycles has been somewhat longer than in the United States. For example, between 1879 and 1932, 15 business cycles ran their course in the United States, but only 10 in Germany, and 11 in Great Britain and France. Typically, the amplitude of business cycles has also been smaller in other countries than in the United States. Although the business cycles of individual countries often synchronize, some divergence of economic fortune has always been present. In general, the minor cycles of individual nations have followed a relatively independent course, while the larger cyclical movements have tended to be of international scope.

Table 1 — A partial chronology of business cycles*

UNITED STATES		GREAT BRITAIN		GERMANY		FRANCE	
Peak	Trough	Peak	Trough	Peak	Trough	Peak	Trough
	1834	1792	1793		1866		1840
1836	1838	1796	1797	1869	1870	1847	1849
1839	1843	1802	1803	1872	Feb. 1879	1853	1854
1845	1846	1806	1808	Jan. 1882	Aug. 1886	1857	1858
1847	1848	1810	1811	Jan. 1890	Feb. 1895	1864	Dec. 1865
1853	Dec. 1854	1815	1816	Mar. 1900	Mar. 1902	Nov. 1867	Oct. 1868
June 1857	Dec. 1858	1818	1819	Aug. 1903	Feb. 1905	Aug. 1870	Feb. 1872
Oct. 1860	June 1861	1825	1826	July 1907	Dec. 1908	Sept. 1873	Aug. 1876
Apr. 1865	Dec. 1867	1828	1829	Apr. 1913	Aug. 1914	Apr. 1878	Sept. 1879
June 1869	Dec. 1870	1831	1832	June 1918	June 1919	Dec. 1881	Aug. 1887
Oct. 1873	Mar. 1879	1836	1837	May 1922	Nov. 1923	Jan. 1891	Jan. 1895
Mar. 1882	May 1885	1839	1842	Mar. 1925	Mar. 1926	Mar. 1900	Sept. 1902
Mar. 1887	Apr. 1888	1845	1848	Apr. 1929	Aug. 1932	May 1903	Oct. 1904
July 1890	May 1891	1854	Dec. 1854			July 1907	Feb. 1909
Jan. 1893	June 1894	Sept. 1857	Mar. 1858			June 1913	Aug. 1914
Dec. 1895	June 1897	Sept. 1860	Dec. 1862			June 1918	Apr. 1919
June 1899	Dec. 1900	Mar. 1866	Mar. 1868			Sept. 1920	July 1921
Sept. 1902	Aug. 1904	Sept. 1872	June 1879			Oct. 1924	June 1925
May 1907	June 1908	Dec. 1882	June 1886			Oct. 1926	June 1927
Jan. 1910	Jan. 1912	Sept. 1890	Feb. 1895			Mar. 1930	July 1932
Jan. 1913	Dec. 1914	June 1900	Sept. 1901			July 1933	Apr. 1935
Aug. 1918	Mar. 1919	June 1903	Nov. 1904			June 1937	Aug. 1938
Jan. 1920	July 1921	June 1907	Nov. 1908				
May 1923	July 1924	Dec. 1912	Sept. 1914				
Oct. 1926	Nov. 1927	Oct. 1918	Apr. 1919				
Aug. 1929	Mar. 1933	Mar. 1920	June 1921				
May 1937	June 1938	Nov. 1924	July 1926				
Feb. 1945	Oct. 1945	Mar. 1927	Sept. 1928				
Nov. 1948	Oct. 1949	July 1929	Aug. 1932				
July 1953	Aug. 1954	Sept. 1937	Sept. 1938				
July 1957	Apr. 1958						
May 1960	Feb. 1961						

* The dates given are subject to revision. Work on the extension of the chronologies for Great Britain, Germany, and France is under way.

Source: Based on studies of the National Bureau of Economic Research.

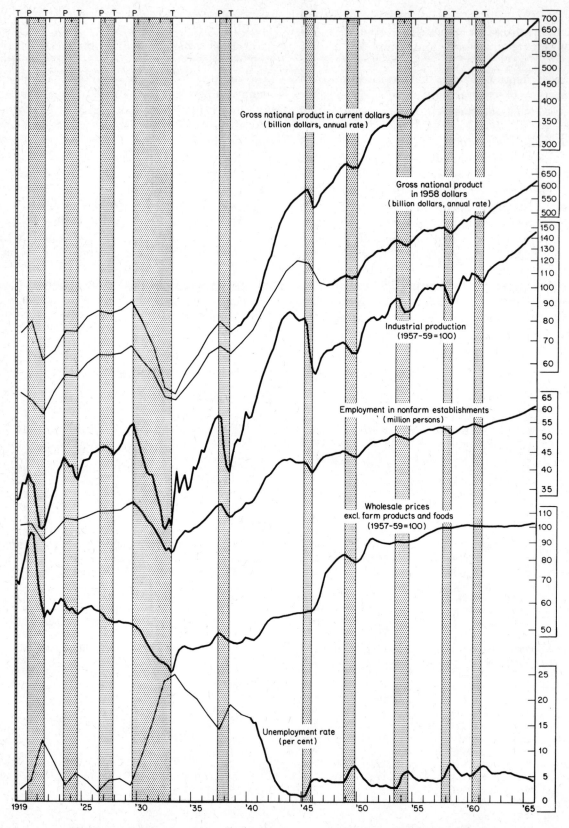

Figure 1 — Production, prices, and employment in the United States, 1919–1965*

* **T** indicates trough; P indicates peak; shaded areas represent business-cycle contractions; unshaded areas represent expansions. Data are
quarterly, except for the following, which are annual: GNP in current dollars, 1919–1938; GNP in 1958 dollars, 1919–1946; employment,
1919–1928; unemployment rate, 1919–1939.

Cyclical behavior of individual activities. Many, but by no means all, individual activities reflect the cyclical movements of comprehensive aggregates of economic activity. The fortunes of individual firms are often dominated by personal factors or conditions peculiar to their industry or locality. Activities like the production of wheat experience fluctuations that are heavily influenced by the weather and bear little relation in time to business cycles. Activities involving the production of new products, like radio tubes in the 1920s or transistors more recently, may defy business-cycle contractions during the early and rapidly growing stage of their history. Some financial magnitudes, like the money supply, decline during severe contractions but merely experience a reduced rate of growth during ordinary contractions. Others, like commercial bank investments or the cash balances of corporations, tend to move contracyclically. Even activities that generally move with the business cycle sometimes skip a cycle, or undergo an extra fluctuation of their own, or move especially early or late during recessions or recoveries. In short, some economic activities are free from cyclical fluctuations over extended periods or are subject to an independent rhythm, while even the numerous activities that tend to keep in step with the business cycle have specific cycles whose turning points are scattered.

This diversity of movement in various branches of the economy means that expansion in some activities is always accompanied by contraction in others. We find, for example, that expansions in individual branches of production run side by side with individual contractions, whether business as a whole is depressed or prosperous. The turns of the specific cycles are not, however, distributed at random through time. On the contrary, they come in clusters, so that at a time when the troughs in production are bunched the peaks are few, and vice versa. But when the number of troughs in a given month exceeds the peaks, the number of expanding activities must also be larger the following month. Hence, the bunching of cyclical turns results, so to speak, in protracted periods when a majority of individual branches of production experience expansion, followed by protracted periods when a majority experience contraction. Empirically, the periods when expansions preponderate are virtually coterminous with the upward phases of the cycle in aggregate production; that is to say, aggregate production expands when individual expansions dominate. Moreover, when the expanding activities constitute a large majority, the amplitude of the cyclical rise in total production is apt to be larger than when the majority is small. To put this relationship another way, when the cyclical rise of total production is especially large, the industrial scope of expansion also tends to be especially broad. The scope of individual contractions, while usually less extensive than that of expansions, is similarly correlated with cyclical declines in aggregate production. All these relations in the sphere of production hold, and in the same way, between individual branches of employment and total employment, between individual branches of expenditure and total expenditure, and, indeed, between individual business processes and business as a whole.

The shift from a widening to a narrowing scope of expansions usually takes place gradually and follows a cyclical course. Rising activities are only a bare majority at the beginning of a business-cycle expansion. Their number swells as aggregate activity increases, though expansion reaches its widest scope not when aggregate activity is at a peak but perhaps six months or a year earlier. In the neighborhood of the peak, crosscurrents are the outstanding feature of the economic situation. Once the economy turns down, the number of expanding activities becomes smaller and smaller, but the scope of contraction does not widen indefinitely. Perhaps six months or a year before aggregate activity reaches a trough, the proportion of contracting activities is already at a maximum. Thereafter, the majority of contracting activities dwindles, while the minority of expanding activities keeps growing and before long becomes the ruling majority. About the time when that happens, the tide of aggregate activity begins rising again. A continual transformation of the economic system thus occurs beneath the surface phenomena of aggregate expansion and contraction.

The degree of clustering and the precise sequence of the cyclical turns of individual branches of production or employment vary from one business-cycle turn to the next. New and rapidly growing industries tend to move down late at downturns and to move up early at upturns. Activity in the machinery trades tends to move somewhat late at both upturns and downturns. Apart from these tendencies, the sequence within any cluster of cyclical upturns in individual branches of industry usually bears little resemblance to the sequence within the next cluster of either downturns or upturns.

Rather strong repetitive tendencies emerge, however, when production and employment are viewed in relation to other economic processes. Activities preparatory to investment expenditure—such as the formation of new firms, appropriations for capital expenditure by corporations, issuance of building permits, contracts for residential building, orders for machinery and equipment, contracts for commercial and industrial construction, additions to private debt, and new equity issues—typically begin declining while total production, employment, the flow of incomes, and the average level of wholesale prices are still rising. Similarly, these visible preparations for investment typically recover several months before production, employment, incomes, and wholesale prices end their cyclical decline. Cyclical fluctuations in profit margins, in the proportion of corporations achieving rising profits, and in prices of common stocks also tend to lead the tides of aggregate activity, and so too—although less consistently—do the fluctuations of total corporate profits. Other activities that tend to move up early in recoveries and to move down early in recessions are investment in inventories of materials, spot prices of industrial raw materials, and certain marginal adjustments of the work force, such as the average length of the work week and the rate of new hirings.

On the other hand, many economic processes or activities tend to lag in the course of business cycles. Outstanding among these are labor costs per unit of output, interest rates charged by banks on business loans, mortgage yields, retail prices, business expenditures on new plant and equipment, the installation of new industrial facilities, and aggregate business inventories. Of course, the cyclical turns in these lagging processes tend to precede opposite turns in aggregate activity.

The internal composition of the economy keeps changing in the course of a business cycle but not only on account of differences in cyclical timing. Just as individual activities do not rise or fall in perfect unison, so also they do not rise or fall by any uniform percentage during a business cycle. Some economic magnitudes—for example, retail sales and bank interest rates on business loans—move within a range that is narrow relative to their level. Others—especially business profits, capital gains or losses, and orders for investment goods—have enormous fluctuations. These and many other differences of cyclical amplitude are a recurring feature of business cycles. The turmoil that goes on within aggregate economic activity during a business cycle is, therefore, in no small part systematic.

In a typical business cycle, aggregate production fluctuates over a wider range than do aggregate sales. Moreover, sales by manufacturers fluctuate more widely than sales by wholesalers, while the latter fluctuate more than sales by retailers. The production of durable goods—both those destined for producers and those destined for consumers—fluctuates more widely than that of nondurables. Industrial production usually fluctuates more than the level of industrial prices at wholesale, which in turn fluctuates more than the level of retail prices or of wage rates. The cyclical fluctuation in the number of man-hours worked is larger than the fluctuation in the number employed, and the latter is larger in commodity-producing industries than in the service trades. Wage disbursements fluctuate within a wider range than salary payments or the flow of property income to individuals but within a much narrower range than profits. Corporate profits also fluctuate much more widely than dividend payments or total personal income. Consumer expenditures fluctuate still less than personal income, while personal savings fluctuate more than personal income but less than corporate savings. Cyclical amplitudes are larger in private investment expenditure as a whole than in consumer expenditure and they are also larger in consumer spending on durable goods than on nondurables or services. Again, amplitudes are typically larger in construction contracts than in the volume of construction executed, larger in business orders for machinery and equipment than in their production or shipments, larger in additions to inventories by business firms than in gross or net additions to their fixed capital, and larger in additions to inventories of the firms manufacturing durable goods than of those manufacturing nondurables. Finally, new security issues fluctuate more widely than trading on the stock exchanges, stock prices more than commodity or bond prices, short-term interest rates more than bond yields, open market interest rates more than customer rates, extensions of consumer installment credit more than repayments, imports more than exports, governmental revenues more than expenditures, and so through the gamut of processes that make up the economy.

Since disparities of cyclical amplitude and timing, such as those just noted, tend to be repeated in successive business cycles, the proportions that critical economic factors bear to one another tend to change in a systematic manner during a business cycle. For example, investment expenditure fluctuates much more widely relative to its size than does consumer spending; hence the ratio of investment to the gross national product tends to move with the business cycle, while the ratio of consumer spending to gross national product traces out an inverse movement. The amplitude of cycles is larger in total production than in sales; hence, inventory investment passes through a cycle of accumulation and liquidation that closely matches or even leads the cycle in aggregate activity, while the movement of total inventories lags both in recoveries and recessions. Government expenditures usually fluctuate within a smaller range or bear a much looser relation to the business cycle than do revenues; hence, the budgetary surplus, taken in an algebraic sense, tends to move with the business cycle. One more illustration will have to suffice. The rate of increase of the labor force varies little between expansions and contractions of aggregate activity; employment, on the other hand, moves strongly and synchronously with the tides in activity but typically rises more slowly than the labor force both at the beginning and toward the very end of expansion. Unemployment, therefore, typically turns up before aggregate activity starts receding and turns down only after economic recovery is already under way.

The empirical features of business cycles will be further elucidated in later pages. The point to note now is that our generalizations are largely based on intensive studies of the business cycles that have occurred in the United States during recent decades, although considerable confirmation has also been provided by studies of other countries—notably, Great Britain, Canada, Italy, and Japan. It is also well to keep in mind, first, that the generalizations emphasize the repetitive features of the economic changes that take place during business cycles; second, that they merely express strong tendencies toward repetition—not invariant rules of behavior. Diversity and individuality are no less characteristic of business cycles than the family resemblance among them, and this fact inevitably complicates the task of understanding the nature and causes of business cycles. Fortunately, there is less uncertainty about the broad processes that typically generate business cycles than about the specific causes of this or that cyclical episode.

The cumulative process of expansion.   The continual transformation of the economy during a business cycle, which we have just reviewed, indicates that once the forces of recovery have taken hold, they will cumulate in strength. In other words, the expansion will spread out over the economic system, gather momentum, and for a time become a self-reinforcing process.

The proximate impulse to expansion may come from an increase of spending by business firms, consumers, or the government, or it may originate outside the domestic economy. The source or sources of the expansive impulse will be considered later. For the moment, let us assume merely that the economy is jarred out of its depressed level by an appreciable rise in the volume of newly initiated construction. A chain of familiar consequences will then be set in motion. Contractors will hire additional labor, disburse larger sums in wages, place larger orders for materials, supplies, and equipment with dealers or manufacturers, and finance at least a part of their rising outlays from new bank loans. The employment of labor on construction sites will at first increase only a little but after a few weeks or months—as the sequence of technical operations permits—more rapidly. Sales by retail shops and service establishments that cater to consumers will follow suit; for most construction workers will soon spend all or part of their larger income, and some will even feel encouraged to buy on the installment plan. The impact of the additional spending by contractors and their workmen will be spotty and uneven, but the effects will gradually spread out. Although some dealers or manufacturers will be content to meet the enlarged demand by drawing down their inventories, others will want to maintain inventories at their current level, and still others will seek to expand them in order better to accommodate a rising volume of sales. Here and there, therefore, there will be a stimulus to production not only of services and of goods made to specification but also of staples that are normally carried in stock.

In response to larger construction spending, the rough balance between expanding and contracting enterprises that had previously ruled in the economy will thus be tipped, albeit irregularly, toward expansion. As firms revise their production schedules upward, they also will often increase their purchases from other firms, give fuller work to their present employees, perhaps recall some former employees or hire new ones, but in any event disburse larger sums in wages. Thus, each expanding center of production will stimulate activity elsewhere, including lending by the banks, in ever-widening circles. The spread of expansion from these centers will serve to check or counteract spirals of contraction that meanwhile are being generated at other points. With the scope of the expansion gradually becoming wider, retailers will be more prone to place orders with their suppliers in quantities that exceed their current sales, wholesalers and manufacturers will behave similarly, working hours will lengthen here and there, the work force will grow in an increasing number of firms and in the aggregate, and so too will income disbursements and sales to consumers.

We have supposed thus far that the higher volume of newly initiated construction will merely be maintained. In fact, construction work will tend to grow and so too will the activity of those making all sorts of machinery and equipment. Business firms, viewed in the mass, will still be operating well below capacity; but some firms—and their number is now increasing—will be operating at or close to full capacity. Moreover, as production rises, the profits of these firms, and indeed of business generally, will tend to improve. For a time, service enterprises—shops, theaters, buses, airlines, etc.—can handle more customers without adding appreciably, if at all, to the aggregate hours worked by their employees. That is much less likely to happen in manufacturing and other commodity-producing establishments. However, since these enterprises also rely heavily on overhead types of labor, their labor requirements per unit of output will tend to fall as output expands, thus reinforcing increases of productivity stemming from improvements of organization or technology. Experience shows that the swiftest advances of output per man-hour typically occur in the early stages of a business-cycle expansion and that they then usually outweigh such increases as may occur in wage rates. The result is that unit labor costs of production tend to decline rather sharply, at least for a few months. Depreciation charges per unit of output will also be falling. Meanwhile, such increases as occur in other cost items are as yet apt to be quite moderate, and they can frequently be offset by advancing selling prices. Hence, an increasing number of firms will find that their profit margins are rising handsomely and, since their volume of business is also growing, that their total profits are rising still more. With business profits and consumer incomes improving on a wide front, with shortages of capacity looming more frequently, with delivery periods lengthening, and with interest rates, machinery and equipment prices and construction costs still relatively favorable, it is only natural that contracts and orders for investment goods should rise briskly. Investment expenditures will follow suit, though with an irregular lag and diminished amplitude.

Moreover, as the expansion spreads, it generates in more people a feeling of confidence about the economic future—a mood that may gradually change from optimism to exuberance. As people become more optimistic, they respond more strongly to such increases of sales, prices, or profits as keep occurring. In other words, a given increase of sales, prices, or profits evokes a larger business response. An advance of prices, whether in commodity markets, business salesrooms, or on the stock exchange, is now more apt to encourage expectations that prices will go still higher. Increases of sales, improvements of profits, and delays of deliveries are similarly projected. In this sort of environment, dishoarding and borrowing become easier to rationalize and buying rises briskly all around. Many firms, fearing that they may not get all of the supplies they will soon need, begin bunching their orders more heavily and some actually order more than they expect to get. Not a few investors who had previously postponed action on attractive projects because the time did not seem right, now decide to go ahead. The new spirit of enterprise fosters more new projects that are related loosely, if at all, to the specific shortages of facilities that keep arising. More business firms brush up their long-range plans for expansion or modernization. More promoters push projects to exploit new products or techniques. More new firms are organized to share in the growing markets. More legislatures authorize improvements worthy of an era of prosperity. More families decide to buy a new automobile, to refurnish their home, or to build or buy a new house. Thus, the widening scope of expansion and the improved outlook that goes with it foster both investment and consumption, with advances of the one reinforcing the other in a cumulative process.

Even an adverse development, such as a strike in a major industry or a deliberate effort to reduce inventories of some major product, may now be taken in stride. At an early stage of the expansion, any such reversal of fortune could have sufficed to terminate it. Now, in view of the high level of business and consumer optimism and the large backlog of outstanding commitments for capital goods, a brief inventory adjustment is merely apt to bring a pause to the growth of aggregate economic activity; once this adjustment is completed the economy can resume its advance in spirited fashion.

Gathering forces of recession.   And yet, as history so plainly teaches, a general expansion of economic activity sometimes lasts only a year and rarely lasts more than three or four years. Why does not the process of expansion continue indefinitely? And if the expansion must end, why is it not followed by a high plateau of economic activity instead of a decline? A partial answer to these questions can sometimes be found in disturbances that originate outside the mainstream of the domestic economy—such as political developments that threaten radical changes in property rights, or a drastic cut of military expenditures at the end of a war, or a major crisis abroad. Developments of this nature are entirely capable of cutting short an expansion that otherwise would have continued. However, experience strongly suggests that even in the absence of serious external disturbances the course of aggregate activity will in time be reversed by restrictive forces that gradually but insistently come into play as a result of the expansion process itself.

First, as the expansion continues, the slack in the economy is taken up and reduced. Although improvements of technology and new installations keep adding to the capacity of the nation's workshops, production generally rises still faster; hence, idle or excess capacity diminishes in a growing majority of the nation's businesses. Although the nation's labor force keeps growing, jobs increase faster; hence, unemployment declines. Although the reserves of the banking system may be expanding, bank loans and investments generate deposits at a faster rate; hence, the ratio of reserves to deposits keeps falling. Although producers of metals and other materials and supplies respond to the brisk demand by raising production schedules, they are frequently unable to move quickly enough; hence, deliveries stretch out or become less dependable. The pecuniary expression of the mounting shortages is a general rise of prices—of labor, credit, raw materials, intermediate products, and finished goods; but that is not all. The shortages are real and their physical expression is a narrower scope of the expansion itself. Rising sales by a particular firm or industry still release forces of physical expansion elsewhere, but their effects are blunted since more and more businessmen must now contend with bottlenecks. Once labor is in short supply in a community, an increase of employment by one firm must often result in some reduction of employment elsewhere in the same community. Once this or that material is in short supply, some firms must get along with less than they need or wait longer for deliveries. Once the banking system stops expanding credit or materially reduces its rate of expansion, any new loans to some firms will affect adversely the ability of other firms to get the credit they need. Instances of this sort multiply as the economy moves toward full employment. At some point, therefore, the scope of the expansion stops widening and begins to narrow. Although aggregate activity is still growing, it can no longer maintain its initial rapid pace.

Second, the advance of prosperity tends to raise unit costs of production and therefore threatens profit margins—unless selling prices rise sufficiently. Taking the business system as a whole, much the largest item in costs and one which businessmen watch with the greatest care is labor—more pre-

cisely, the cost of labor per unit of output. This cost depends, first, on the hourly wage of labor and, second, on output per man-hour. Both tend to rise as the expansion progresses, but at unequal rates. The price of labor moves sluggishly in the early part of the expansion, but advances of wages tend to become more frequent and larger as competition for labor increases and trade unions take advantage of improved market conditions. Increasing resort to overtime work at premium rates of pay accentuates the rise in the average price of labor, and so too does the faster upgrading of workers. On the other hand, output per man-hour, which improved sharply early in the expansion, tends to increase more gradually as the expansion lengthens, and it may also decline before the expansion is over. To be sure, improvements in organization and technology continue to be made at a thousand points at this as at every stage of the business cycle. However, their effectiveness in raising productivity is offset by developments that increasingly grow out of prosperity—such as a decline in the average quality of newly hired labor, fatigue of both workers and their managers, restlessness among workers and rapid turnover of labor, the need to put some obsolete plants or equipment back into use, the need to operate some highly efficient plants beyond their optimum capacity, and the need or wish to add liberally—once substantial increases of business have occurred—to indirect or overhead types of labor. Thus, as the expansion of aggregate activity continues, increases of productivity tend to diminish or even vanish, while the price of labor not only rises but tends to rise faster than productivity. The result is that unit labor costs of production tend to move up persistently.

Third, the increases of construction costs, equipment prices, and interest rates that are generated by the expansion process gradually become of more serious concern to the investing community. After all, a rise in long-term interest rates tends to reduce the value of existing capital goods at the very time that it raises the carrying charges on new investments. Higher costs of new capital goods likewise serve to raise fixed charges. For a time, optimistic expectations concerning the earnings stream from new investment projects overpower the restraining influence of higher costs of capital goods or of higher interest rates, but they will not do so indefinitely. A firm that expects to earn 20 per cent annually from a new project can overlook a modest rise of construction costs or interest rates, especially when it plans to finance the investment from retained earnings or depreciation reserves. Not all investors, however, are in such a fortunate position. Home builders, in particular, are sensitive to a rise of construction and financing costs, partly because their activities are largely financed by borrowing and partly because interest charges are a very considerable fraction of the total cost of operating a dwelling. Experience shows that contracts for residential construction typically turn down before commitments for any other major category of investment. Business orders for machinery and equipment, as well as contracts for new factories, commercial buildings, and public utility plants still keep rising for a time. These types of investment are more responsive to prospective demand than to conditions of supply; but as the expansion of economic activity becomes more intense, they too begin to feel the pressure of rising costs. In deciding to invest in a particular project, a business firm may have given little heed to recent increases in costs. That decision, however, must still be followed by another, namely, whether to get the project under way now or later. Investors know that they will have the new plant or equipment on their hands for a long time and that their annual carrying charges will depend on the cost of the new capital goods, if not also on the rate of interest. They have got along thus far without the desired investment, and they will have to manage in any event without it for some months or years. If, therefore, they expect costs to be appreciably lower a year or so from now, they may well bide their time. Such postponements in placing orders and contracts become more frequent even as business decisions to invest continue to accumulate.

The rise in construction, equipment, and financing costs during an expansion impinges so broadly on the investing class that it would eventually check the investment boom even if prosperity were diffused uniformly over the economic community. However, this is not the case, and the uneven spread of profits is still another major development that impedes the continuance of expansion. At every stage of the business cycle there are bound to be some firms whose profits are declining or whose losses are increasing. But these firms are not a steady fraction of the business population, and there are cogent reasons for expecting their numbers to increase as the expansion of aggregate activity stretches out. To protect profit margins, selling prices must rise sufficiently over the entire range of business enterprise to offset higher unit costs of production. Since business conditions are good, many firms can and do raise prices that much or more. But there are always some firms

that find it hard to advance selling prices, and their number tends to grow at an advanced stage of the expansion. In some industries, sales have recently been pushed with such vigor that the markets for their products are approaching saturation at existing prices. In other industries, exaggerated notions concerning the volume of sales that could be made at a good profit have led to overstocking or overbuilding, so that prices come under pressure. Errors of this type occur at all times, but they are likely to be bunched when enthusiasm has infected a large and widening circle of businessmen. In still other cases, business custom, long-term contracts, or governmental regulation make it difficult or inexpedient to raise selling prices. Of course, firms that cannot advance selling prices will try all the harder to resist increases in costs, but such efforts meet with limited success at a time of extensive shortages. With the rise in unit costs of production continuing across the business front, more and more firms therefore find that their profit margins are becoming narrower, thus offsetting the influence on profits of rising sales or reinforcing the influence of declining sales—instances of which now become more numerous. We thus find in experience, as we should expect, that after a business expansion has run for some time, the proportion of firms enjoying rising profits begins to shrink, although profits of business in the aggregate still continue to advance.

These developments—the narrowing scope of expansion as full employment is approached, the rise of unit labor costs, the rise of financing costs, the rising cost of new capital goods, the spread of these cost increases across the economy, and the shrinkage in the proportion of business firms experiencing rising profits—tend gradually to undermine the expansion of investment. Prominent among the first to reduce investment commitments are the firms whose fortunes are waning. Their curtailments spread doubt among businessmen whose profits are still rising, many of whom have also become concerned about prospective profits or have come to feel that construction and financing costs will recede before long from the abnormal level to which they have been pushed by prosperity. These attitudes and responses are likely to be reflected in some weakening of stock exchange prices, which in turn will stir fresh doubts. With investment commitments declining, but actual expenditures still rising, backlogs of unfilled orders for capital goods and of uncompleted contracts for business construction must sooner or later turn down. Meanwhile, uncompleted contracts for residential construction have, in all probability, already been declining for some time. The decline in these several backlogs induces reductions in orders for raw materials and parts, and the reduced pressure on suppliers in turn serves to stabilize, if not lower, prices. Since many of the consumer trades can now also count on faster deliveries, the orders placed with their suppliers are likely to turn down as well. These changes reinforce efforts to adjust inventories that have already been induced at numerous points by the narrower scope of expansion and the reduced rate of growth of aggregate activity. For all these reasons, while inventories on hand still keep rising, investment in inventories begins declining. In view of the smaller backlogs, business expenditures on fixed capital will themselves gradually move to a lower level a little later. Public expenditures may still rise, but they are unlikely to do so on a sufficient scale to offset the declines of private investment. The growth of consumer spending, therefore, is retarded, if it does not actually stop. As these adjustments proceed, the balance between expanding and contracting economic activities tips steadily toward contraction. The need for overtime is much reduced, unemployment begins to rise, aggregate production soon turns down—in short, a business recession gets under way.

The process of contraction. The course of a typical recession is well known. A decline of production is accompanied by a reduction in the number of jobs, besides a reduced work week for many. The flow of incomes to individuals, therefore, tends to decline, and consumer spending—at least for expensive durable goods—follows suit. Retailers and wholesalers are now more apt to place orders for merchandise that are below the level of their respective sales. Many manufacturers, in their turn, also attempt to reduce their inventories. Taking the economy as a whole, the broad result of these efforts is that production declines more than sales, and that inventory investment not only declines but is soon succeeded by liquidation. Meanwhile, quoted prices of many commodities, especially of raw materials, tend to soften, and discounts or concessions from list prices become more numerous and larger. Wage rates, however, are generally maintained and actually rise here and there. Even when they decline somewhat, unit costs of production still tend to rise, perhaps sharply, because it takes time before overhead costs, including the employment of indirect types of labor, can be adjusted to the lower volume of business. Many firms that are already experiencing lower profit margins therefore find that they must put up with still lower margins, while others first begin to feel the profit squeeze. With sales more often than not also declining, an increasing majority of businesses now experience falling profits, bankruptcies become more frequent, business profits in the aggregate—which probably began shrinking before sales did—decline further, and stock exchange prices extend their fall as well. In view of these developments, many businessmen and consumers, even if they are not actually poorer, become more concerned about the future. New business commitments for investment in fixed capital therefore tend to become less numerous, and—unless forces of recovery soon come into play—investment expenditures of this type as well as outlays on consumer durables will extend their decline, which is as yet modest, and reinforce the contraction process.

As a decline in one sector reacts on another, the economy may begin spiraling downward on a scale that outruns the magnitudes that we ordinarily associate with recession. The likelihood that a depression will develop depends on numerous factors —among them, the scale of speculation during the preceding phase of prosperity, the extent to which credit was permitted to grow, whether or not the quality of credit suffered significant deterioration, whether any major markets became temporarily saturated, how much excess capacity had been created before the recession started, whether and in what degree the balance of international payments has become adverse, the organization of the financial system and its ability to withstand shocks, the shape of political developments, and the aptness and scale of monetary actions and other governmental efforts, if any, to stem the economic decline. If the onset of the contraction is marked by a financial crisis or if one develops somewhat later, there is a substantial probability that the decline of aggregate activity will prove severe and perhaps abnormally long as well. For when businessmen and their bankers begin to scramble for liquidity, both trade credit and bank credit will decline and so too will the money supply; commodity prices at wholesale and retail will slump and wage rates decline, while interest rates for a time rise sharply; confidence will become impaired and many investment projects will be abandoned instead of merely being postponed; business losses and bankruptcies will multiply; more workers will earn less or become totally unemployed; and, since spells of unemployment also lengthen, more and more families will deplete their savings and be forced to reduce their spending drastically. Even if the shift from expansion to contraction is made gradually, untoward disturbances originating outside the economy may still strike with great force and transform a mild contraction into a depression.

Forces of progress and recovery.   Normally, however, a contraction in aggregate activity does not lead to depression. A contraction is not a mirror image of expansion, as it might well be if the business cycle were merely an oscillation. A contraction does not usually cumulate and feed on itself in the manner of an expansion. Normally, many progressive developments continue, and some even become stronger, during the contraction phase of the business cycle; in other words, the forces making for contraction are powerfully counteracted by forces of growth that limit the degree to which it can cumulate.

What are these forces of growth? First, businessmen and consumers in a modern nation are accustomed to seeking and to expecting economic improvement. This optimistic state of mind generally continues during a contraction, provided its dimensions remain moderate. Investment opportunities, connected with new technology or market strategy, always keep arising in the minds of imaginative and resourceful men. Not a few of these opportunities are acted on promptly in spite of the recession. Second, most people are extremely reluctant to give up the standard of living that they have managed to attain, and in any event they cannot quickly readjust family expenditures. Hence, consumer spending is well maintained in the face of declines of income that are judged to be temporary. Third, the pitch of both interfirm and interindustry competition becomes more intense during a recession. Unlike investment commitments, which are at their highest level before aggregate activity turns down, the bunching of installations of new plant and equipment is likely to be heaviest when the recession is well under way. The newer facilities typically serve new products or permit lower costs of production of old products. Many progressive enterprises are therefore able to extend their markets even when business as a whole is falling off. Firms that suffer from shifts of demand or from an outworn technology may have managed to limp along or even do reasonably well when activity was brisk. Now, finding that competitors are penetrating their markets on a scale that threatens survival, the hard-pressed firms are more likely to move with energy to modernize their plant, acquire new equipment, improve their products, try out new marketing strategies, and eliminate waste. Meanwhile, vigorous businesses whose plants are

operating at or close to optimum capacity do not stand still. Not a few of them anticipate a large expansion of sales when the dull season is over, and therefore undertake additions or improvements to their plant and equipment. Fourth, a nation's resources normally continue to grow even during a recession. Since the population is still growing, the stabilizing force of consumption is reinforced. Since the number of business firms is still increasing, the formation of new businesses contributes, although at a reduced rate, to the demand for capital goods. Since the stock of housing, consumer durables, and industrial facilities is still expanding, a large market is assured for repairs, improvements, and replacements, although there is undoubtedly some postponing of this type of expenditure. Fifth, public efforts to promote economic growth and the general welfare are customary in a well-governed nation. These efforts may not always be wise or geared closely to the business cycle, but neither are they confined to times of prosperity. On the contrary, they are more likely to come during recessions—especially in recent times when full employment has become an increasingly firm objective of the public policy of nations.

The progressive forces that operate during recessions serve as a brake on the cumulative process of contraction. True, aggregate activity falls below the level reached at the peak of prosperity. The decline, however, is usually of moderate proportions. Not only that, but sales decline much less in the aggregate than production and the level of sales soon becomes higher than that of production. For a while, the liquidation of inventories proceeds at an increasing rate, but this cannot continue. To handle the volume of business on hand, especially if sales stabilize or decline very gradually, manufacturers and distributors must soon slow down, if not halt, the decline of their inventories. Taking the economic system as a whole, once inventory disinvestment declines more rapidly than the decline of sales, production must begin rising. Of course, a recovery of production will be preceded by an increase of orders, and an early upturn of orders is precisely what occurs when dealers and manufacturers take steps to slow down appreciably the decline of their inventories.

While business firms keep bringing inventories into better alignment with their sales, other developments that grow out of the recession also favor an early recovery. Since the reserves of commercial banks tend to pile up again, reserve ratios improve. Hence, interest rates decline and credit becomes more readily available. The effects of easy credit are likely to be felt most promptly by smaller businesses and the homebuilding industry, but they tend to ramify as banks put their reserves to use. When the demand for loans is still deficient, banks seek out customers energetically. At the same time, they augment their investments in bonds, thereby strengthening the bond market and stimulating a renewed interest in preferred stocks and gilt-edged common stocks. Meanwhile, numerous readjustments in the nation's workshops serve to lower unit costs of production. In view of the decline of aggregate demand, wage rates often stop rising and sometimes decline a little, overtime operations become less frequent, not a few of the less efficient enterprises go out of business, production is increasingly concentrated in the most modern plants and on the best equipment, many of the less efficient workers are let go, the ranks of the overhead types of labor are thinned here and there, and workers generally become more attentive to their duties. These changes reinforce the improvements of organization and technology which always occur in a progressive economy and which are often speeded up during a recession, in response to the keener competition that develops at such a time. Of course, the beneficial changes in the costs of production of individual businesses are frequently offset or nullified by declining selling prices. However, once the adjustments of inventories have made good headway, commodity prices tend to stabilize. Hence, more and more firms are apt to find that their profit margins begin improving. With the prospect of profits brightening, interest rates declining, and costs of capital goods lower, some of the numerous investment projects that had previously been postponed are now revived and they supplement the new crop of active projects. As these developments become stronger, the decline of investment commitments ceases, new firms are established in larger numbers, orders and contracts for investment goods turn up, inventory disinvestment continues to ebb, and a recovery of aggregate production and employment soon gets under way.

Thus, corrective forces released by the recession combine with the more persistent forces of growth to bring the contraction of aggregate activity to a halt. Typically, the process works fairly speedily and the contraction is over in about a year or a year and a half. However, as previously noted, a contraction sometimes develops into a spiraling depression. When that happens, declining investment in fixed capital supplants inventory disinvestment as the principal drag on the economy.

Worse still, the stubborn human trait of optimism begins to give way, so that a mere readjustment of inventories may bring only an abortive recovery. Once many men begin to lose faith in themselves or in the institutions of their society, full recovery may need to wait on substantial innovations or an actual reduction in the stock of fixed capital, unless powerful external influences come into play— such as a reorganization of the monetary system, massive governmental expenditures, or a sudden increase of exports on account of foreign developments. Fortunately, no industrial country has suffered a spiraling depression since World War II, and the likelihood of such a development—as will be noted later—has been greatly reduced.

Differences among business cycles. The preceding sketch of the nature and causes of business cycles has stressed typical behavior. Yet no business cycle of actual experience corresponds precisely to our sketch, and some cycles bear only a faint resemblance to it. What history discloses is a succession of business cycles that differ considerably in length, in the intensity of their phases, in the industrial and financial developments that gain prominence during their course, and in their geographic scope. In American experience, for example, while expansions have normally run longer than contractions, there is no peacetime expansion on record before 1960 that lasted as long as the decline from 1873 to 1879. Industrial production has typically fluctuated over a wider range than industrial prices, but the opposite is true of several business cycles associated with wars. Interest rates have commonly risen during expansions of aggregate activity, but they continued to decline during almost the entire expansion from 1933 to 1937. Broad indexes of wholesale prices have generally declined during contractions of activity, but they failed to do so during the recession of 1890–1891 or 1957–1958. Contracts and orders for investment goods have typically moved up before total production or employment in the recovery process, but they did not do so at the upturns of 1914 or 1933. Declining stock prices have frequently signaled the approach of a recession, but the stock market crash of 1929 came after aggregate activity had already turned down. Some economic declines, such as those of 1887–1888 and 1926–1927, were merely pauses in the growth of the domestic economy. Others, such as the depression of 1920–1921, attained international scope, while the depression of the 1930s became a world-wide upheaval of catastrophic proportions.

In view of these and countless other variations

among business cycles, the causes of any particular cycle are always in some or large degree peculiar to it. One prolific source of cyclical variation in the United States, as elsewhere, is found in the behavior of money, foreign trade, and the balance of payments. For example, good harvests in 1879, when crops abroad were poor, stimulated large exports of grain at favorable prices, thereby improving farmers' incomes, enlarging the business of shippers, inducing an inflow of gold, and otherwise speeding economic recovery. In 1891 and 1892, fear that political agitation for free silver would result in abandonment of the gold standard led to domestic hoarding of gold, to massive gold shipments abroad, and finally to a financial crisis in the spring of 1893. The expansion of 1891–1893, therefore, developed nothing like the vigor suggested by our account of the cumulative process of expansion. The outbreak of war in Europe in 1914 soon caused a sharp upsurge in American exports, thereby checking a contraction in aggregate activity that otherwise might have dragged on. To cite one more illustration, the expansion of 1958–1960 proved incomplete, in large part because of the restrictive monetary and fiscal policies that were undertaken by the government to curb inflationary pressures and to prevent further deterioration in the balance of international payments.

Business-cycle movements often spread from one country to another and sometimes engulf almost the whole world economy. Foreign trade, commodity prices, stock prices, and interest rates play a vital role in this process of transmission, both directly and through their influence on business psychology. The economies of most commercial nations are far more closely tied to the course of foreign trade and investment than is the economy of the United States. In view of the large role of foreign trade in small countries like the Netherlands or Norway, conditions abroad can have a decisive influence on domestic prosperity. Even in a larger country like Great Britain, an improvement of exports has not infrequently been the immediate cause of economic recovery. However, as the economic activity of a nation expands, its imports also tend to rise, partly because of a larger need for foreign raw materials and partly because of larger purchases abroad of equipment and consumer products. Meanwhile, since domestic markets keep improving, some firms find it more profitable or more convenient to cultivate home trade than to push exports. If, in response to the upswing of activity, domestic costs and prices advance more rapidly than prices charged by foreign

enterprises, exports will probably suffer and monetary reserves—whether of gold or foreign currencies—will tend to diminish. A restriction of credit often follows, because under a regime of stable exchange rates the state of a country's balance of payments and the size of its monetary reserves and borrowing facilities may leave little room for an independent financial policy. This pattern of developments has become familiar to the nations of western Europe and to Japan.

Many nations of Latin America, Asia, and Africa derive their foreign exchange mainly from the export of one or at most a few raw materials, supplemented by investments made in these countries by foreigners or, perhaps, by gifts from abroad. But the prices of internationally traded raw materials tend to fluctuate widely, in part because of variations in the state of demand in the industrial countries. These price fluctuations often have a critical bearing on the ability of the raw-material producing nations to acquire from abroad the capital goods and supplies needed to develop their economies.

Not only are the economies of different nations tied together, but as various theories of long waves or major cycles have sought to suggest, no business-cycle movement can be understood solely in terms of what happened during that phase or the one just preceding it. Thus, the American contractions of 1923–1924 and 1926–1927 were merely minor interruptions of a great onrush of economic activity from 1921 to 1929. The period began with a rapid increase of production, was followed by a stretch of slower growth, and ended on a note of reacceleration. Financial activities followed a different and more hectic course. Emerging as an international creditor after the war, the United States played its new role with exuberance. Through 1924 the volume of foreign loans was substantial, yet the loans were on the whole of sound quality—as attested by later experience. The next few years witnessed a further expansion of foreign loans and a sharp deterioration of their quality. The speculative craze expressed itself also in other financial areas, notably in the real estate market and superlatively in the stock market. Consumer credit shared in the general upsurge and made possible a huge expansion in the output of durable consumer goods during the 1920s, not only absolutely but also relative to total output, thus adding a new hazard to economic stability. The financial situation was also made vulnerable by the great pyramiding of international credits that developed under the gold exchange standard. Governmental policies in the United States after 1929, which brought on tax increases and—worse still—tolerated the destruction of a third of the nation's money supply, cannot escape a very large part of the responsibility for the Great Depression; but neither financial developments abroad nor the course of policy, private and public, in the decade prior to the depression can go blameless.

Progress toward economic stability. Besides such differences among business cycles as we have noted, which largely reflect episodic influences, there are other differences of a more persistent kind. Just as the business cycle itself emerged gradually in the course of economic evolution, so many of its features have undergone changes as the economy has continued to evolve.

The structure of a nation's economy and its institutions inevitably leave their stamp on the character of its cyclical fluctuations. Thus, after the introduction of the Federal Reserve System, the fluctuations of short-term interest rates in the United States became narrower, while the lag of long-term interest rates during recoveries and recessions became shorter and of late has virtually vanished. With the growth of trade unions and increasing resort to long-term labor contracts, wage rates have become less responsive to cyclical contractions of activity. More important still, the precise relations among the movements of production, employment, and personal income have kept changing as the structure of the American economy and its institutions have evolved. During the early decades of the nineteenth century, when agriculture was the dominant occupation, occasional declines in the nation's total volume of production, whether large or small, had little effect on the number of jobs and sometimes had slight influence even on the flow of money incomes. Later, as wage-jobs gained rapidly in importance, the movements of employment and personal income fell into step with production. In recent times, however, numerous changes in the structure of the American economy have served powerfully to reduce the impact of a cyclical decline of production on the lives and fortunes of individuals.

Important among these changes is the vast expansion of government, the greatly increased role of the income tax in public revenues, the shift of income tax collection to a pay-as-you-go basis, the rapid growth of unemployment insurance and other programs of social security, the growing frequency and scale of private pensions, the spread of business corporations, and their increasing pursuit of stable dividend policies. As a result of these and related developments, the movement of personal income is no longer closely linked to the fluctuations of production. For example, in the course of the recession of 1957–1958, the physical volume of industrial production fell 14 per cent and of total production nearly 5 per cent. In the early decades of this century, aggregate personal income would have responded decisively to such a decline in production. This time government receipts and expenditures offset the drop in the flow of income from production, first, because much less was collected in taxes from corporations and individuals, second, because the amount of unemployment insurance and other social security payments rose. Corporations in turn reacted to the decline in profits by reducing their savings rather than the flow of dividends or pensions to individuals. In the end, the aggregate of personal incomes, whether before or after taxes, declined less than 1 per cent, and in the case of after-tax incomes even this decline was over before the recession ended.

Major structural changes have also occurred in the sphere of employment. Manufacturing, mining, construction, and freight transportation are the cyclically volatile industries; but their relative importance as providers of jobs has been gradually declining in recent decades, while that of the more stable service industries has been increasing. In addition, the proportion of people who work as managers, engineers, scientists, accountants, secretaries, salesmen, or in kindred "white-collar" occupations has been steadily rising. Much of this type of employment is of an overhead character and therefore less responsive to the business cycle than are the jobs of machine operators, craftsmen, truck drivers, laborers, and others in the "blue-collar" category. It appears, therefore, that changes in the structure of the labor force have of late been loosening the links which, over a considerable part of economic history, tied the short-run movements of total employment in the United States rather firmly to the movements of production. We can no longer suppose, moreover, when employment falls during a recession, that there will be a corresponding decline in the number of people receiving an income. On the contrary, as a result of the widening sweep of social security programs, the number of income recipients actually increased during each recession of the postwar period.

These developments have left an imprint on the behavior of consumer spending in recent business cycles. First, consumers have maintained their spending at a high level even after business activity had been declining for some months, so that the cumulative process of contraction has been curbed. Second, retail trade has tended to turn up before production or employment, instead of lagging during the recovery stage as it did in earlier times. Thus, consumer spending has emerged as one of the active factors in arresting recession and hastening recovery. Of course, if the fluctuations of production had been larger in the postwar period, the impact of recessions on the lives of working people would have been greater. On the other hand, the more stable behavior of personal income and consumption has itself been a major reason why recent contractions of activity have been brief and of only moderate intensity.

Many other factors have contributed to this result. The need to overhaul the financial system became clear during the 1930s and led to numerous reforms, among them the development of the long-term amortized mortgage, the regulation of stock exchanges, the insurance of mortgages, the creation of a secondary market for mortgages, the insurance of savings and loan accounts, and—most important of all—the insurance of bank deposits. These financial reforms have served to prevent crises or the propagation of fear. Even more basic has been the change in political attitudes that emerged during the 1930s and which the Congress later articulated in the Employment Act of 1946. It is now generally agreed that mass unemployment is intolerable under modern conditions and that the federal government has a continuing responsibility to promote a high and rising level of employment and production. In recent times, therefore, the business cycle has no longer run a free course, and this fact has figured prominently in the plans of businessmen as well as consumers. The general expectation of the postwar period has been that the government would move with some vigor to check any recession that developed, and that its monetary, fiscal, and regulatory actions would contribute to that objective. By and large, this confidence has been justified by events. Not only has monetary policy in the main been shaped with a view to promoting stable prosperity, but fiscal policy—which previously had been handicapped by the convention of annually balanced budgets—has lately also been guided by the state of the economy. Business firms too have been paying closer attention to the business cycle. There is evidence, in particular, that inventories are being better managed and that this is helping to moderate the cyclical swings in production. On the other hand, governmental policies have often served to intensify inflationary expectations or pressures, and this has become a recurring problem.

The nations of western Europe have also experienced structural changes in the postwar period that, on balance, have worked in a stabilizing direction. White-collar occupations have gained in importance, and so too have systems of social security and of tax collection on a pay-as-you-go basis. Some countries, especially Sweden, achieved notable success with contracyclical policies well before the United States. Of late, all of western Europe has been striving energetically and ingeniously to promote economic expansion and full employment, and these efforts have been attended by great success. Even before World War II, the business cycle was a milder type of fluctuation in western Europe than in the United States, and the difference has persisted in the postwar period. Indeed, the main problem facing European nations in recent years has not been unemployment but rather the difficulties caused by inflation and balance-of-payments disequilibria. Japan has also been struggling with this problem.

It would, nevertheless, be premature to conclude that the older hazards of the business cycle belong to the past. True, the business cycle has become milder as a result of a favorable conjuncture of structural changes and of both better and wider understanding of the requirements of business-cycle policy. Certainly, there is increasing recognition of the desirability of preventing recessions, rather than merely acting to moderate them once they occur. However, the forces that tend to generate cyclical movements have not vanished in western Europe or Japan any more than in the United States. It is possible that in the future a "recession" will mean merely a reduced rate of growth of aggregate activity instead of an actual and sustained decline, but there is as yet insufficient ground for believing that economic developments will generally conform to this model in the near future. Hence, the wise course for economists is to continue basic research on the nature and causes of business cycles, to remain watchful of developments that seem likely to bring on a slump in activity, and to extend the search for acceptable pathways to prosperity without inflation.

ARTHUR F. BURNS

[See also EMPLOYMENT AND UNEMPLOYMENT; FISCAL POLICY; INCOME AND EMPLOYMENT THEORY; MONETARY POLICY. Other relevant material may be found in the biographies of HANSEN; KEYNES, JOHN MAYNARD; MITCHELL.]

BIBLIOGRAPHY

ABRAMOVITZ, MOSES 1950 Inventories and Business Cycles, With Special Reference to Manufacturers' Inventories. New York: National Bureau of Economic Research.

AFTALION, ALBERT 1913 *Les crises périodiques de sur-production.* 2 vols. Paris: Rivière. → Volume 1: *Les variations périodiques des prix et des revenus: Les théories dominantes.* Volume 2: *Les mouvements périodiques de la production: Essai d'une théorie.*

AMERICAN ECONOMIC ASSOCIATION 1944 *Readings in Business Cycle Theory.* Edited by Gottfried Haberler et al. Philadelphia: Blakiston. → Includes an article by Kondratieff. A bibliography appears on pages 443–487.

AMERICAN ECONOMIC ASSOCIATION 1965 *Readings in Business Cycles.* Edited by Robert A. Gordon and Lawrence R. Klein. Homewood, Ill.: Irwin.

BURNS, ARTHUR F. 1954 *The Frontiers of Economic Knowledge: Essays.* Published for the National Bureau of Economic Research. Princeton Univ. Press.

BURNS, ARTHUR F.; and MITCHELL, WESLEY C. 1946 *Measuring Business Cycles.* New York: National Bureau of Economic Research.

CLARK, JOHN J.; and COHEN, MORRIS (editors) 1963 *Business Fluctuations, Growth and Economic Stabilization: A Reader.* New York: Random House. → A bibliography appears on pages 623–669.

FRIEDMAN, MILTON; and SCHWARTZ, ANNA J. 1963 *A Monetary History of the United States: 1867–1960.* National Bureau of Economic Research, Studies in Business Cycles, No. 12. Princeton Univ. Press.

HABERLER, GOTTFRIED (1937) 1958 *Prosperity and Depression: A Theoretical Analysis of Cyclical Movements.* 4th ed., rev. & enl. Harvard Economic Studies, Vol. 105. Cambridge, Mass.: Harvard Univ. Press; London: Allen & Unwin.

HANSEN, ALVIN H. (1951) 1964 *Business Cycles and National Income.* Enl. ed. New York: Norton. → A bibliography appears on pages 699–710.

HICKS, JOHN R. (1950) 1956 *A Contribution to the Theory of the Trade Cycle.* Oxford: Clarendon.

JOHNS HOPKINS UNIVERSITY, DEPARTMENT OF POLITICAL ECONOMY 1957 Business Fluctuations. *Economic Library Selections* Series 2, No. 4.

JUGLAR, CLÉMENT (1862) 1889 *Des crises commerciales et de leur retour périodique en France, en Angleterre et aux États-Unis.* 2d ed. Paris: Guillaumin. → Partially translated as *A Brief History of Panics and Their Periodical Occurrence in the United States*; published by Putnam in 1916.

KEYNES, JOHN MAYNARD 1936 *The General Theory of Employment, Interest and Money.* London: Macmillan. → A paperback edition was published in 1965 by Harcourt.

KUZNETS, SIMON 1961 *Capital in the American Economy: Its Formation and Financing.* National Bureau of Economic Research, Studies in Capital Formation and Financing, No. 9. Princeton Univ. Press. → See especially pages 316–388.

MITCHELL, WESLEY C. 1913 *Business Cycles.* Berkeley: Univ. of California Press. → Part 3 was reprinted by the University of California Press in 1959 as *Business Cycles and Their Causes.*

MITCHELL, WESLEY C. 1927 *Business Cycles: The Problem and Its Setting.* New York: National Bureau of Economic Research.

MOORE, GEOFFREY H. (editor) 1961 *Business Cycle Indicators.* 2 vols. National Bureau of Economic Research, Studies in Business Cycles, No. 10. Princeton Univ. Press. → See Volume 1, pages 736–744, for a list of business-cycle reports by the National Bureau of Economic Research, which has led for many years in this field of study.

PERSONS, WARREN M. 1919 Indices of Business Conditions. *Review of Economics and Statistics* 1:5–107.

PIGOU, ARTHUR C. (1927) 1929 *Industrial Fluctuations.* 2d ed. London: Macmillan.

ROBERTSON, DENNIS H. (1915) 1948 *A Study of Industrial Fluctuations.* London School of Economics and Political Science Series of Reprints of Scarce Works on Political Economy, No. 8. London: Aldwych.

SCHUMPETER, JOSEPH A. 1939 *Business Cycles: A Theoretical, Historical, and Statistical Analysis of the Capitalist Process.* 2 vols. New York and London: McGraw-Hill. → An abridged version was published in 1964.

THORP, WILLARD L. 1926 *Business Annals.* New York: National Bureau of Economic Research.

TINBERGEN, JAN 1938–1939 *Statistical Testing of Business-cycle Theories.* 2 vols. Geneva: League of Nations, Economic Intelligence Service. → Volume 1: *A Method and Its Application to Investment Activity.* Volume 2: *Business Cycles in the United States of America: 1919–1932.*

TUGAN-BARANOVSKII, MIKHAIL I. (1894) 1913 *Les crises industrielles en Angleterre.* 2d ed. Paris: Giard & Brière. → First published as *Promyshlennye krizisy v sovremennoi Anglii, ikh prichiny i vliianie na narodnuiu zhizn'.*

UNIVERSITIES–NATIONAL BUREAU COMMITTEE FOR ECONOMIC RESEARCH 1956 *Policies to Combat Depression.* Princeton Univ. Press. → A report of the National Bureau of Economic Research, Special Conference Series, No. 7.

WICKSELL, KNUT (1898) 1936 *Interest and Prices: A Study of the Causes Regulating the Value of Money.* London: Macmillan. → First published as *Geldzins und Güterpreise.*

II
MATHEMATICAL MODELS

A mathematical model of business cycles is not necessarily a special kind of business cycle theory as far as economic content is concerned. The mathematical formulation is an instrument for organizing our factual knowledge and our hypotheses. For this purpose, mathematical tools may be not only useful, but indispensable. Use of these tools may produce fruitful theories that could not have been discovered by verbal reasoning, and a precise mathematical formulation may serve to verify or reject previous theories set forth in a loose, verbal form and to clear the way for more systematic empirical studies.

It is not easy to date the origin of mathematical business cycle models. Fragments of such models may be found in even classical economic theory. However, it is probably fair to say that the development of explicit and complete mathematical business cycle models does not date further back than the early 1930s (see Frisch 1933; Kalecki 1935; Tinbergen 1935). These first models were of a highly macroeconomic type, involving only a few key variables to characterize the economic system. Subsequently, a very large number and variety of such models have been developed (see, for example, Samuelson 1939; Metzler 1941; Hicks 1950; Goodwin 1951). A good survey of some of these models is found in Allen's textbook on mathematical economics (1957, pp. 209–280).

More detailed models, involving a large number of economic variables, have also been developed by Tinbergen (1938–1939), Klein (1950), and others. The purpose of these detailed models has been not only to furnish a more detailed theoretical explanation of business cycles but also to pave the way for verification and measurement by means of principles of statistical inference. Electronic computers play an increasingly important role in this kind of business cycle research.

General features.   Facts and data concerning the ups and downs of business activity constitute a bewildering mass of information. Any attempt to write "the whole story of what happens" during booms and depressions is not only hopeless but also rather unrewarding as far as gaining real understanding is concerned. Somehow one has to look for principles of systematic classification and for simplifying ideas of *simulation* that can help to reduce the number of things to be taken into account. With this in mind, what are the general features of the dynamic process we call business cycles?

Apart from some relatively crude theories that explain business cycles as something "coming from the outside" (sunspot theories or the like), all theories of business cycles focus attention on the idea that what we observe is a result of human decision and action. The *driving force* is the prospect of profit or economic advantage, of one kind or another. The release, strength, and direction of such forces can be regarded as reactions to a system of *signals* that guide the economic activities of the various individuals or groups. These signals are prices of goods and services or other data that enter into the calculations of economic gains or losses for each decision unit.

The forces thus released are counteracted by various elements of inertia and friction due, in part, to human hesitation and slowness and to constraints set by nature or by rigid institutions.

There is also an intricate network of "feedbacks," with the characteristic property that the feedback line from the activity of *one* decision group usually connects with the signal system guiding some *other* decision unit. Clearly, if elements of inertia and delay are present in such a system, a continued process of adjustment of some kind is almost unavoidable.

If we view the process of booms and depressions through the framework just described, the analogy with models of force and motion in mechanical engineering and related fields becomes striking. To utilize the idea of such analogies while at the same time being on guard against stretching the analogy too far is one of the main principles of mathematical model building in the field of business cycle analysis.

The notion of dynamic equilibrium.   Economists have long had a deeply rooted feeling that a "normal" situation in business activity is a state of affairs where *motion is absent* (except, perhaps, for some kind of trend). Strangely enough, the use of mathematics to set up systems of general market equilibrium may have strengthened the hold that this notion of normality has on so many economists. Given the wide acceptance of this notion, it is understandable that ups and downs in business activity are often looked upon as "deviations from normal," as imperfections of the market, as unforeseeable and unwanted exceptions to the rule. But such ideas are not particularly fruitful as a basis for understanding business cycles.

The point is, of course, that in a stationary situation, such as the equilibrium of the Walrasian system, the forces in operation are not zero. They are in fact very strong, but they happen to *balance at zero motion*. This is, however, a very special case of a balance of forces. The more general case is a balance brought about by sustained *motion* of certain elements of the economy. This explains why it is indeed possible to represent the process of change in business activity by means of mathematical equations based on the principle of forces in balance. The economic forces may be in balance at various rates of motion of the economic magnitudes involved, and this general idea of dynamic equilibrium is fundamental in mathematical business cycle theories.

Explanation of turning points.   A central problem in business cycle theory has, of course, been to explain the turning points, i.e., to explain why expansion should turn into contraction, and vice versa. One of the major contributions of the mathematical approach to business cycle theory has been to demonstrate that the explanation of turning points is no more difficult than the explanation of any other phase of cyclical movements. Employing the notion of dynamic equilibrium, one can simply say that the relative strength of the economic forces in operation at any time will determine whether the motion necessary for balance will be up or down.

The reason why the mathematical approach is superior to a verbal analysis is obvious. By verbal reasoning it is simple enough to enumerate the various economic forces involved in a process of development, but it is often difficult, if not impossible, to determine the direction of the motion resulting from the relative strengths of the various forces.

Effects of learning—irreversibility. One objection to business cycle theories in the form of rigid mathematical models has been that they lead to a monotonous recurrence of booms and depressions of the same kind, while in fact "history never repeats itself." Certain mathematical models are indeed open to this criticism, but others are not.

One of the remedies for this deficiency is the explicit introduction of elements of learning into the model. For example, the pattern of consumers' demand may gradually change as a consequence of accumulating experience, or the way in which producers form their expectations (their basis for action) may gradually change as a result of their comparing past expectations with realizations. In recent years, more and more attention has been given to such elements as necessary parts of mathematical business cycle models (cf. Goodwin 1951).

While it is possible to introduce elements of irreversibility into a model in this way, it should be realized that a model must be based on the assumption that there are *some* aspects of economic development that repeat themselves. Otherwise, no theory, mathematical or verbal, is feasible.

Main types of models. By classifying the various business cycle models according to the principles involved rather than according to the particular economic variables dealt with, it is possible to group the models in a two-by-two table. First, we consider whether the principal active forces responsible for motion are assumed to come from the *outside* or are assumed to be *endogenous* parts of the economic system itself. The first type of model is sometimes called an *open* model, and the second type is called *closed*. Second, for each of these two types of models, we consider whether the cycles are produced because *the driving force is itself cyclical* ("forced oscillations") or because of the particular way in which the *economic system responds* to the stimulating forces ("free oscillations").

These principles of classification are helpful, even though a really comprehensive business cycle model may contain elements that would place it in all four categories simultaneously (cf. Samuelson 1947, pp. 335–349).

Some explicit examples will illustrate many of the points discussed above.

The cobweb model with external forces. Let $x^d(t)$ be the demand for product x at time t, and let $p(t)$ be the price of x at time t. Assume that

$$(1) \qquad x^d(t) = f[p(t)].$$

Let $x^s(t)$ be the supply of x at time t, and assume that

$$(2) \qquad x^s(t) = g[p(t - \theta)] + v(t),$$

where θ is positive and $v(t)$ is some external force that independently influences $x^s(t)$. For example, $v(t)$ may be some weather factor or perhaps some influence from another economic sector that is independent of the one considered here. For market clearance at time t, $x^d(t)$ must equal $x^s(t)$. Let $x(t)$ be the quantity of x at which the market clears at time t. From (1) and (2) and the market-clearance condition, it will generally be possible to derive

$$(3) \qquad x(t) = G[x(t - \theta)] + v(t).$$

The usual shape of supply and demand curves would imply that the first derivative of the function G is negative.

If $v(t)$ were a constant, independent of t, this model would be the usual textbook case of the "cobweb" (Allen 1957, pp. 2–6). In such a model, there could be business cycles of period 2θ, which would either eventually die out or go on vigorously forever.

Now let us consider the effect of changes in $v(t)$. If $x(t)$ oscillated but tended toward some constant when $v(t)$ was constant, a change in $v(t)$ to a new level would generally set the variable $x(t)$ in motion again; and $x(t)$ would go on oscillating for some time, even if $v(t)$ were to remain constant at the new level. In other words, the driving force $v(t)$ need not itself oscillate systematically in order to generate oscillations in $x(t)$. It is sufficient that $v(t)$ change occasionally, perhaps in a quite irregular manner.

If $v(t)$ should have a cycle of its own, this would, of course, have certain consequences for the resulting time shape of $x(t)$. But $x(t)$ would, in addition, have cyclical properties that are not present in $v(t)$, but are a consequence of the functional form G and of the lag θ. In this case, the model is one of "free" oscillations with an external driving force.

Consider now the special case where θ is equal to zero. From (3) it can be seen that in this case $x(t)$ can be expressed directly as a function of $v(t)$, assuming (3) permits such a solution. Thus, $x(t)$ could not move except when $v(t)$ is in motion. If $v(t)$ had a cyclical nature, these cycles would, in some manner or other, be reflected in $x(t)$ as "forced" oscillations.

Investment cycles—a closed model. Let $C(t)$ denote consumption, $I(t)$ net investment, and $Y(t)$ income at time t in a closed economy. Then we have

$$(4) \qquad Y(t) = C(t) + I(t).$$

Consider a simple "Keynesian" consumption function:

$$(5a) \qquad C(t) = f[Y(t)],$$

or, as an alternative, a dynamic version:

$$(5b) \qquad C(t) = F[Y(t), Y(t-1)].$$

Suppose that for some reason there are outside forces causing independent oscillations in the rate of investment $I(t)$. Then, in the case of the consumption function $(5a)$, we should have *forced oscillations* in $C(t)$ and $Y(t)$. If the consumption function were $(5b)$ instead of $(5a)$, consumption and income could be subject to both free oscillations and forced oscillations.

The model above would be called *open*, because it does not "explain" the behavior of investment. The idea of the acceleration principle can be used to close the model. Let us first consider a very simple version of this idea.

Let $K(t)$ be the (physical) amount of capital present in the economy at time t, and let $K^*(t)$ denote the amount of capital that producers *would like to have* at that time. If these two amounts of capital are equal, producers would be satisfied. If, on the other hand, $K^*(t)$ is larger than $K(t)$, the demand for new capital *per unit of time* would be unlimited, i.e., producers would be willing to buy any rate of investment that could be supplied. Assuming that there is a capacity limit on total production in the economy, there would be an upper limit, a "ceiling," on the amount of output of capital goods. In other words, the rate of investment would be restricted on the *supply* side. If, instead, $K^*(t)$ is below $K(t)$, there would be no demand for new capital goods, not even for replacement purposes. In this situation it is, therefore, *demand* that determines investment, and the rate of depreciation establishes a (negative) *floor* under which demand cannot fall (unless capital is purposely destroyed).

The model now "explains" investment, provided we know the determinants of the desired capital stock, $K^*(t)$, and how existing capital depreciates. But if this knowledge is lacking, the model is still an *open* model and the question is how to close it. The simple assumptions that have been introduced

for this purpose (cf. Allen 1957, pp. 242–247) are that the desired capital stock is a function of total net output; more specifically, that $K^*(t)$ and $Y(t)$ are proportional and that there is a constant rate of depreciation.

Under these assumptions, it is easy to indicate the characteristic properties that the model would have. Suppose that consumption is given by $(5a)$ and that the capacity to produce investment goods is sufficiently high for the amount of capital to *reach and to exceed* the amount of desired capital. After the desired amount of capital has been reached, output obviously must fall below capacity. But as output falls, so does the desired amount of capital, and this decline cannot stop until gross output of investment goods is zero. This would then lead to a minimum level of net output and thus to a minimum level of desired capital. Only after the existing amount of capital has been worn down below the minimum desired level could there be any demand for new capital goods. But *when* that situation eventually occurs, output must increase again. The amount of desired capital must then increase, and output will again reach full capacity. Thus, we have a *closed model, with free and maintained oscillations.*

This version of the model is, however, unsatisfactory in several respects. First, an explanation of why the desired amount of capital should be a function of output is needed. Second, there is some question as to whether it is safe to assume that the level of desired capital will ever actually be reached. And third, there is some question as to whether the closed model is not a somewhat artificial product, obtained by neglecting such things as wage policy and monetary policy.

It may be of interest to indicate briefly how some of these defects could be remedied. Let $X(t)$ denote total gross output, and let depreciation be equal to $\delta K(t)$, where δ is a constant. We then have

$$(6) \qquad X(t) = Y(t) + \delta K(t).$$

Assume that $X(t)$ is the output of a "classical" production function:

$$(7) \qquad X(t) = \phi[N(t), K(t)],$$

where $N(t)$ is employment and where complementarity is assumed to exist between inputs N and K. Let the (real) wage rate, $w(t)$, be an increasing function of employment:

$$(8) \qquad w(t) = W[N(t)].$$

Finally, let $r(t)$ be the rate of interest.

Consider two different situations:

Situation 1. Suppose, tentatively, that there is no limit on $X(t)$ from the demand side. Then we may assume that employment is determined by setting the marginal productivity of labor equal to the wage rate, provided total wages are below current revenues. If the marginal productivity of capital is greater than or equal to $r + \delta$, the demand for X will in fact be unlimited, because of the demand for an increased amount of capital.

Situation 2. Suppose, tentatively, that output, $X(t)$, is limited by effective demand, the role of producers being simply that of producing to order. Then employment follows from (7), with $K(t)$ given, provided total wages according to (8) are below current revenues. If the corresponding marginal productivity of capital is less than or equal to $r + \delta$, demand for $X(t)$ will in fact be limited and will be equal to consumers' demand, because producers will not want any new capital.

Whether in this model there will be a switching back and forth between the two situations, similar to that in the simpler model previously discussed, depends in an essential way on policy concerning the rate of interest. If situation 1 exists but is about to break down, lowering the rate of interest could prolong the situation. It should be noted that if situation 2 is allowed to occur, the reduction of the rate of interest that could then get us back to situation 1 would generally be much greater than the reduction that would be sufficient to maintain a situation 1 already in existence.

This model has a great deal of flexibility and can be extended to include technical progress, rachet effects in consumers' demand, and so on.

TRYGVE HAAVELMO

[*Directly related are the entries* ECONOMETRIC MODELS, AGGREGATE; STATICS AND DYNAMICS IN ECONOMICS.]

BIBLIOGRAPHY

ALLEN, R. G. D. (1957) 1963 *Mathematical Economics.* 2d ed. New York: St. Martins; London: Macmillan.

FRISCH, RAGNAR (1933) 1965 Propagation Problems and Impulse Problems in Dynamic Economics. Pages 155–185 in American Economic Association, *Readings in Business Cycles.* Edited by R. A. Gordon and L. R. Klein. Homewood, Ill.: Irwin.

GOODWIN, R. M. 1951 The Nonlinear Accelerator and the Persistence of Business Cycles. *Econometrica* 19:1–17.

HICKS, JOHN R. 1950 *A Contribution to the Theory of the Trade Cycle.* Oxford: Clarendon.

KALECKI, M. 1935 A Macrodynamic Theory of Business Cycles. *Econometrica* 3:327–344.

KLEIN, LAWRENCE R. 1950 *Economic Fluctuations in the United States: 1921–1941.* New York: Wiley.

METZLER, LLOYD A. (1941) 1965 The Nature and Stability of Inventory Cycles. Pages 100–129 in American Economic Association, *Readings in Business Cycles.* Edited by R. A. Gordon and L. R. Klein. Homewood, Ill.: Irwin.

SAMUELSON, PAUL A. (1939) 1944 Interactions Between the Multiplier Analysis and the Principle of Acceleration. Pages 261–269 in American Economic Association, *Readings in Business Cycle Theory.* Edited by Gottfried Haberler. Philadelphia: Blakiston. → First published in Volume 21 of the *Review of Economic Statistics.*

SAMUELSON, PAUL A. (1947) 1958 *Foundations of Economic Analysis.* Harvard Economic Studies, Vol. 80. Cambridge, Mass.: Harvard Univ. Press. → A paperback edition was published in 1965 by Atheneum.

TINBERGEN, JAN 1935 Annual Survey: Quantitative Business Cycle Theory. *Econometrica* 3:241–308.

TINBERGEN, JAN 1938–1939 *Statistical Testing of Business-cycle Theories.* 2 vols. Geneva: League of Nations, Economic Intelligence Service. → Volume 1: *A Method and Its Application to Investment Activity.* Volume 2: *Business Cycles in the United States of America: 1919–1932.*

BUSINESS HISTORY
See under HISTORY.

BUSINESS MANAGEMENT

Management is a term that is used to describe a particular kind of behavior *within* an organization. Specifically, the term describes the behavior of those responsible for the decisions that determine the allocation of the physical and human resources within an organization. It is increasingly recognized that the management function is built upon the social sciences and provides them with interesting problems. Management bears the same relationship to the social sciences that medicine does to such fields as chemistry, physiology, and anatomy.

The central core of the management function, which has made this area of great interest to social scientists, is decision-making behavior. Since this behavior governs the allocation of the resources of a firm, economists in particular have been attracted to the study of management. There is an obvious relationship between the theory of the firm and the field of management. In the theory of the firm under perfect competition, the economist has abstracted significantly from the problems of management and has substituted a simple decision rule for determining price and output. In markets that deviate from the perfectly competitive, the internal structure of the firm and the role of the manager as a decision maker become important. Market forces may no longer dominate the decision but may become only one set of variables in a process that must involve a number of other variables (Cyert & March 1963).

Recognition of the importance of management to the theory of the firm has led to an increase in field studies concentrating on decision making. Concurrently, there has been an increase in interest on the part of social scientists in particular decisions within certain areas of management (Simon 1960). Economists, for example, have become interested in the financial decisions of the firm, and psychologists have become interested in certain marketing decisions. This interaction has been extremely fruitful for the field of management. [*See* ADMINISTRATION, *article on* ADMINISTRATIVE BEHAVIOR; INVESTMENT, *article on* THE INVESTMENT DECISION.]

General management. Traditionally, social scientists have viewed the managerial function in simplified terms. Economics has generally posited a single owner whose function it is to make decisions on price and output by using highly rigid decision rules. If one examines the general management function, however, one discovers a much wider and richer range of behavior. To understand this behavior it is necessary to examine briefly the nature of the business firm.

The business firm in the American economy does not have the autocratic organizational structure attributed to it in popular writing. The management cannot exercise disciplinary power over the members of the organization in the manner of a military organization. Rather, the general management of the business firm should be viewed as a coalition of members, each of whom brings to the coalition a set of preferences that represent his model for the firm's behavior. In the process of making decisions for the firm as a whole, coalition members will have their preferences modified, ignored, or incorporated as goals (constraints) for the decisions the coalition makes.

Membership in the coalition is an operational definition of general management. In most large organizations this membership would include the president of the firm and the vice-presidents. However, in very large organizations this membership might include only a subset of vice-presidents, and in smaller organizations others, such as plant managers, might be included.

The general functions of the coalition, or general management, fall into the two broad categories of decision making and decision implementation.

Decision making. The decision making of the coalition will be concentrated in areas involving the allocation of the resources of the firm to broad categories of activities. These decisions may involve changing or modifying an old activity; for example, investing in new equipment for an established plant. The decision may involve the elimination of an old activity; for example, the elimination of a particular product line because it does not meet the profitability constraints determined by the coalition. Finally, the decision may involve allocating resources to a new activity; for example, acquiring another firm through purchase or merger.

In all these classes of decisions it is clear that the firm's goals must be defined by the coalition. A business firm does not have a stated list of goals that governs all decisions; rather, the process of decision making includes the process of determining goals. A continuous bargaining–learning process takes place among the members of the coalition. The goals of the organization are not a weighted function of the individual members' preferences. In general, the coalition continues to exist by utilizing some preferences of members as goals (constraints) and by making policy side-payments to others. The preferences that are used as goals define the criteria which a proposed solution or alternative must meet. The determination of the goals of the organization for a particular decision is also a function of the alternatives discovered by the search activity of the organization.

The preferences of coalition members may be in direct conflict and, therefore, some preferences of some members will have to be ignored. In such cases, the firm may make side-payments to keep those members within the coalition. Side-payments may take many forms. For example, at the next budget period the individual whose preferences have been ignored may get a relatively large increase in his department's budget. The side-payment might take the form of an expansion in the size of his department to give him more power, or he might be put on additional committees and given more voice in the management. In short, he will usually be given inducements to remain within the coalition in compensation for having his preferences excluded in the decision.

Decision implementation. Implementation is the procedure by which general management accomplishes its goals. The procedure can be viewed as a process of programming the firm (in the sense of computer programming). These programs are known as standard operating procedures and can be classified into four major types.

(a) Task performance rules. To keep a firm operating smoothly, over time and with changing personnel, it is necessary to specify the methods for accomplishing the tasks assigned to individuals and subgroups within the organization. When the task is a recurring one, the task performance rules represent the results of past learning. The rules

represent the firm's attempt to educate new employees in the firm's methods.

(*b*) *Records and reports.* A firm's records and reports are its written history. Current records and reports contain most of the quantitative data that are the basis for making decisions and for controlling the behavior of individuals and subgroups within the organization.

(*c*) *Information-handling rules.* These rules define the formal communication system within the firm. They cover three kinds of information: (1) Information about the environment relevant to the firm. (2) Information about the firm for internal use. (3) Information about the firm for external use. The information-handling rules specify the distribution pattern of the information as well as the security measures on information leaving the firm.

(*d*) *Plans and planning rules.* We do not include within this category strategic, long-run planning for the firm. We include activities, such as budgeting, which involve repetitive planning that lends stability to the organization's activities. Such planning results in schedules for behavior over a period of time and puts constraints on acceptable alternative behaviors. General management tends to continue existing decisions on resource allocation from year to year, except in cases where achievement is unsatisfactory.

We have defined management in broad terms, but it is necessary to look more closely at some of the substantive areas of management to gain a better understanding of the field. A convenient way of analyzing management is by functional fields. Although there is no hard and fast classification system, we shall examine finance, marketing, and production. These three describe important segments of the management function and will serve to illustrate the interrelations of the management field with the social sciences.

Finance. In general, the field of finance is concerned with the problems and decision-making processes involved in the allocation among competing uses of the scarce financial resources of the firm. This concept of the field is in contrast to the approach which dominated the finance field until the last ten to fifteen years (Solomon 1963) and which emphasized description of the institutional aspects of financial markets and the various financial instruments available to a corporation. The problem focus was almost entirely one of determining the kinds of securities that might be used in particular financing situations.

The modern approach, on the other hand, investigates such questions as the following: (1)

What are the financial constraints that determine the rate of growth and the ultimate size of the firm? (2) What is the optimum portfolio of assets and liabilities for the firm? (3) What considerations are involved in obtaining external funds and what is the optimum method of obtaining them? Such problems are characterized by a concern for choosing among alternative uses and sources of funds.

The distinguishing feature of the finance problem is the emphasis on maximizing the return to invested funds. From the finance point of view, the importance for production or marketing of an investment is not taken into account. It is up to other members of the firm to show that an investment should be made when the return does not meet the financial standards.

Cash management. While the problems described above are, in one sense, the crux of financial decision making, the short-run problems of cash management are also significant. Cash management involves forecasting the amount of cash that will be available for expenditures at particular points in time. This kind of forecasting is closely related to accounting and is one of the ties between finance and accounting. The first step in planning cash receipts is to forecast cash sales and the expected collections from credit sales. In addition, one has to look at other sources of cash, such as interest and dividends, sales of assets, and tax refunds. In a similar fashion it is necessary to set out anticipated expenditures for such things as raw materials, labor, travel, and miscellaneous supplies. Expected receipts and disbursements are then matched, usually on a monthly basis for six months or a year in advance, so that the firm knows its planned cash balance for each month.

Working-capital management. A similar planning problem exists in the management of working capital. The expected amount of working capital at various points in time must be projected. Working capital is defined as the difference between current assets, which include cash, marketable securities, accounts receivable, and inventories, and current liabilities, which include accounts payable, notes payable, and other debts that must be paid in a short period of time.

Managing short-term credit is another important aspect of working-capital management, as is the planning of inventories. In recent years, much work has been done on the problem of determining an optimal inventory level (Holt et al. 1960). This involves an analysis of the costs of holding inventory, which include insurance, taxes, interest, and warehousing costs. Against these must be weighed the cost of lost sales which come about when a customer wants an item that is not in stock. [*See* INVENTORIES.]

Cost of capital. Another major concern of finance is the evaluation of investment alternatives. The general approach used in choosing among alternatives is to determine the present worth of each alternative (Solomon 1963). To find the present value of the investment in question, its net earnings for each year are computed and discounted to the present according to the following formula:

$$PW = \frac{E_1}{(1+K)} + \frac{E_2}{(1+K)^2} + \frac{E_3}{(1+K)^3} + \cdots + \frac{E_n}{(1+K)^n}.$$

Here K is the discount rate, E_i the net earning in year i, and PW is the present worth. The discounted value for any year, $E_i/(1+K)^i$, is the amount that has to be invested now at rate K in order to equal E_i in year i. For example, where i is equal to 1, let K equal .25 and E_i equal one dollar. Then $PW = \$1.00/1.25 = \$.80$.

There are obvious problems in this analysis, when uncertainty is taken into account, because both E and K must be estimated. The more difficult concept is K; it is currently the source of controversy. The prevailing view is that the proper K to be used in a calculation such as the one above is the rate which measures the cost to the firm of obtaining new capital.

But the cost of capital is difficult to measure because capital is raised in a wide variety of ways, ranging from bank borrowing to issuing stock. It is, therefore, difficult to determine a precise cost. This difficulty is compounded because one is interested in the cost of raising additional capital; in an uncertain world it is difficult to forecast this cost for some unknown time in the future when a firm may want to raise capital. Much work in finance is concerned with determining the cost of particular kinds of capital, such as equity capital, debt, and retained earnings.

One of the cost-of-capital controversies concerns the use of borrowed capital, which is said to give "leverage" to the owners of the firm. Modigliani and Miller (1958) have contended that under the assumptions of certainty, perfect markets, and maximizing behavior on the part of investors, the amount of leverage bears no significant relationship to the market value of a company. This would mean that the financial structure does not need to be examined in order to determine the cost of capital. The argument about this position has not been settled, and it has reached something of an impasse because of the difficulties of doing empirical work to test the hypothesis precisely.

The total plan. Finally, there is the problem of integrating financial planning with the over-all objectives of the firm. This involves the integration of plans from all parts of the firm and bears specifically on decisions involving the outflow of cash, the desired level of liquidity, and additional financing. It requires a more elaborate analysis than is used to deal with the cash account alone. Sophisticated mathematical techniques are being applied to this problem, and new developments in capital budgeting give promise of producing a relevant analytical framework (Weingartner 1963; Beranek 1963).

Marketing. Marketing is concerned with all of the variables affecting the sale of the product to the customer, whether the customer is a household or a firm. This range of concerns is broken up into the following broad categories:

(1) Understanding consumer behavior.

(2) Responsibility for variations in product quality and design.

(3) Price determination.

(4) Selection of distribution channels.

(5) Choice of advertising media and the level of advertising.

Consumer behavior. In economics, one way of summarizing consumer behavior is through the use of a demand curve, which relates the amount of a product a consumer will buy to its price [*see* DEMAND AND SUPPLY]. The curve is based on the assumption that income, the prices of related products, and consumer tastes are all fixed. To make sound marketing decisions, however, it is necessary to investigate the process by which consumers decide what to buy.

Work on this problem has taken essentially two paths. The first attempts to observe and survey consumers and to discover their goals. It relies heavily on sociological and psychological theory. The type and source of the buyer's information have been investigated in the context of the whole communication problem. For example, Katona and Mueller found that 50 per cent of the consumers in their sample received information about durable products from friends (Mueller 1954, p. 45). This line of research is attractive and shows promise. The major difficulty to date lies in the integration of the results into broader decision models; that is, in transforming explanatory propositions into normative operational propositions on which a firm can act.

Another approach in the analysis of consumer

brand choice utilizes the concept of consumer learning (Kuehn 1962, pp. 390–392).

Product decision. Decisions must be made about the addition of a new product or the elimination of an old one. Also existing products may be modified. Increasing expenditures for research and development have made decisions about products more important. One line of attack attempts to determine the characteristics that buyers are seeking in new products and the way in which buyer decisions about new products are made. Unfortunately, there are few studies in this area, and they are not directly applicable to marketing problems. Most of them are diffusion studies on the use of innovations, done by sociologists and anthropologists. Marketing students are seeking help from these studies in the development of the proper strategy for introducing new products.

There are a number of other interesting problems in this area, of which we will mention two. The first involves testing the marketability of new products before they are added to the company's product line. Here two basic approaches have been used. One attempts through questionnaire and interview data to determine consumer reaction to the new product through comparisons with other products on the market. The difficulties with this approach stem from the problem of eliciting accurate answers from the consumer. The consumer is asked in an artificial setting to describe his potential behavior in a real situation. The measurement of the reliability of response in such situations is a fruitful area of research for psychologists. The other approach primarily utilizes statistical analysis. The product is test marketed and predictions of the success of the product are made from the analysis of such phenomena as repeat purchases. The market areas are usually picked with the aid of sampling theory.

The second problem is that of deciding the amount of funds that should be invested in research for new product development. This problem is clearly not the sole concern of the marketing group; however, marketing considerations must play an important role in the solution. Currently, this decision is made by some rule of thumb, such as allocating a fixed percentage of sales to research and development. To improve such decisions, more knowledge is needed about the desired frequency of new product introduction. Answers to this will probably be obtained through an application of behavioral science and mathematical techniques.

Pricing. One of the most important problems for the marketing manager is to determine the price to charge for a product or the items in a product line (a set of related products, each differing from the other primarily in quality—for example, men's suits in a department store). There are no firm rules that will guarantee proper pricing. The best that can be done, given the current state of knowledge, is to indicate some variables that should be examined and to review some current practices.

Some of these variables are considered in economic analysis. It is clear, for example, that the prices of competitive products must be taken into account and that potential competitors exert a downward pressure on price. The latter force is more important in markets where there are only a few sellers and where new competitors may enter freely. The characteristics of the demand must be investigated, particularly its price elasticity (the percentage change in quantity demanded divided by the percentage change in price). If price is lowered by a given percentage, will quantity demanded increase relatively more or less than price? [*See* ELASTICITY.] If quantity increases relatively more, it may be profitable to lower the price. In this case, of course, cost considerations become important.

Since the marketing manager must come to a decision, he uses some practical techniques that give him specific, but imperfect, information. Experimental methods have been used in which different prices are set in a number of similar markets to determine the influence of prices on sales. Interviewing has been used for the same purpose as has the analysis of sales data in situations where prices have been changed. All of these techniques give useful but not decisive information.

Distribution channels. Producers must determine the route by which their product reaches the consumer. A variety of ways are possible, of which the simplest is that in which the consumer buys directly from the manufacturer at his plant. The most complicated distribution channel might include four different middlemen—sales agent, wholesaler, jobber, and retailer. The marketing manager generally decides upon the best channel for the product on the basis of a qualitative analysis that examines the characteristics of the product and of the various possible channels. He considers such factors as the need for demonstration of the product, the amount of repair and maintenance, and the number and variety of the items that must be shown to the customer. In other words, he must decide how to make the product easily accessible to the customer under conditions in which the selling effort can be effective. [*See* INTERNAL TRADE.]

Promotion.   Promotion generally covers the entire selling effort, and promotion expenses include all expenditures specifically aimed at increasing sales. Promotion problems can be summarized by the following set of questions:

(1) What is the optimum level of funds to allocate to promotion?

(2) How much should be allocated to advertising and how much to other forms of promotion?

(3) How should advertising expenditures be allocated among various media?

In addition, there are problems in measuring the effectiveness of advertising and other promotional devices. As yet, no completely satisfactory techniques have been developed for solving these problems. [See ADVERTISING, *article on* ECONOMIC ASPECTS.]

In this whole area, however, the use of mathematical and statistical techniques is increasing rapidly. Until about 1950 there was no indication that advertising problems were amenable to quantitative analysis. Currently, many attempts at such analysis are being made, and the outlook for improving management decisions is hopeful.

Production.   Production is concerned with the operations by which inputs of men and materials are converted into goods and services through the use of machines and other fixed equipment. Recent definitions of production include all of the physical operations of the firm. In addition, a systems concept is developing which relates previously disparate parts of the firm. Thus, a production or operations system would include the following range of problems (Buffa 1963, pp. 26–28):

(1) Forecasting sales.

(2) Converting these forecasts into plans for a relatively stable production rate, inventory level, and work force.

(3) Specific plans for the mix of items in the inventory and development of a control system to insure against "running out" of items.

(4) Detailed scheduling of transportation facilities, machines, and men.

(5) Development of control systems to insure the quality of the product and the viability of the whole production process.

Within this framework a number of decisions have to be made:

(1) The product must be designed and production costs must be estimated as they may in turn affect the design.

(2) The processes to be used must be determined and equipment selected. Decisions to replace equipment must also be made.

(3) The layout of the production facility must be designed. Capacities must be determined and the flows of materials and men within the system organized.

(4) Provision must be made for maintenance of the system.

These problems and decisions constitute only a brief overview of the production problem. In economic theory it is assumed that surviving firms in the long run use the optimum production function and operate at the lowest average cost curve possible for the given plant. It is the broad goal of production management to achieve this state; it studies the techniques and develops the methods for attaining the position that is assumed in economic theory.

Production, like other functional areas of management, relies heavily on still other disciplines. Production management since about 1946 has in particular utilized psychology, mathematics, statistics, and computer technology.

Psychology is used in problems of machine design, job design, and general work environment. Much work has been done by psychologists in designing and positioning the dials and meters used by workers. The object is to design the information and control panels so as to minimize errors and the time required to do the job. Work schedules have been examined and redesigned to minimize fatigue. The effect on productivity of noise, temperature, and lighting in the work environment has also been investigated.

Use of linear programming.   Perhaps the most important impact on the production area has come as a result of the application of a particular mathematical technique, linear programming. By means of linear programming a linear function subject to certain inequality restrictions can be minimized or maximized. A number of problems can thus be solved mathematically that in the past were handled on a judgmental basis:

(1) *Mix problems.* Frequently, in making a product such as gasoline, alternative inputs can be used to meet specific product requirements. With linear programming the minimum cost combination can be found.

(2) *Production scheduling.* Production can be scheduled over time to minimize storage costs and to obtain a relatively stable work force.

(3) *Shipping problems.* Frequently products must be shipped from several locations (warehouses) to other points (customers). Linear programming can help to achieve minimum transportation costs [see PROGRAMMING].

In the inventory problem, classical mathematical and statistical methods have been used. The general approach is to start with a probability distribution for sales in a given period. Taking into account such variables as sales, losses incurred if the producer is out of inventory, losses on items left in inventory, interest, and warehousing costs, a solution for the desired inventory level can be determined. Significant work has been done in this area, especially the development of the linear decision rule [see INVENTORIES; see also Holt et al. 1960].

Use of computers. Computers are becoming increasingly important in production in two primary uses. The first is in simulating a process in order to determine a policy. For example, job-shop simulators are used to determine the results of various scheduling rules. In a job shop, where each job has different characteristics and goes through different operations, there is no "best" rule for scheduling the various jobs when there is competition for the facilities. One approach is to program the computer to simulate the shop and then, using different scheduling rules, schedule a series of jobs that is similar to an actual series. The simulation can help to evaluate the results of following any of the rules or some set of them. An analogous procedure has been followed for determining the optimal maintenance force. [See SIMULATION.]

Computers have also been used as decision-making devices. Programs have been written for assembly-line balancing (designing successive operations so as to minimize waiting time) as well as warehouse location problems (Tonge 1961; Kuehn & Hamburger 1963). These applications fall in the category of heuristic programming and have been used for problems in which a mathematical optimum cannot be found. The programs utilize decision rules suggested by an analysis of previous human attempts to solve the problem. By a systematic use of the rules and greater processing ability the computer is able to improve on the unaided human solution.

Education for management. We have described briefly three areas in which much of the work of management is done. Other areas such as personnel and accounting (particularly controllership) could have been mentioned. The trend in education for management, however, has been to reduce the emphasis on specialized training and to stress training for general management.

Courses valuable for business management fall into two categories: the disciplines on which management is based and management courses as such.

In the first category we include psychology, economics, mathematics, and statistics.

Psychology is important in human relations and in organization theory. The student of human relations is given an adequate background in psychology, especially individual psychology. He is then taught to use this background in understanding human behavior. The aim is to establish the attitude that problems of human relations should be approached scientifically.

Organization theory also builds on psychology. It seeks to give the student an understanding of human behavior in the context of organizations as well as a better understanding of the administrative process. In particular, the student learns the importance of organizational structure in the implementation of decisions and in the changing and designing of organizations.

Economics courses are oriented toward giving the future manager an understanding of the economic environment in which he will operate. He needs to become familiar with the operation of the economy as a whole—with the determinants of the level of gross national product, employment, and the price level and with the relation of these aggregates to actions of the government and the banking system. He must also study economics to understand the role of the firm in the functioning of the economy.

In mathematics the student should, at a minimum, know elementary calculus and matrix algebra. More importantly, he must be able to relate the mathematics to management problems. He need not be able to develop new theorems or invent new mathematics. An analogous statement can be made for statistics. It is important that future managers have a working knowledge of both disciplines, as well as the ability to know when to call in an expert and how to use him.

The student of management must understand the role of the computer in management decision making and in the development of information systems within the firm. This knowledge should be developed through course work in which some programming language is taught and where the computer is used by the student.

The three functional areas of business management described above must also be covered. In addition to required work in each, there should be an opportunity for the student to go somewhat deeper into at least one of the areas. It is important, however, that this depth be limited, since the student is training for general management and not a specialty. Accounting must be covered, with an emphasis on the managerial uses of accounting —the use of accounting data for decision making and control.

There is also need for a course in the techniques of management science, the most important of which is linear programming. This course should build directly on the mathematics course, and the techniques learned should be used in the functional courses.

We have tried to sketch briefly the basic ingredients of an education oriented toward general management. We have not tried to describe a curriculum in detail but rather to mention some of the principal courses that any curriculum should cover. In general, there are three guiding principles for the construction of a curriculum in management. The first is that the disciplines underlying the practice of management must be present. Courses in the social sciences and mathematics and statistics give the student the basic knowledge and techniques he will need. The second principle is that the emphasis should be on breadth rather than on specialization. The specialization can generally be learned as necessary on the job, but breadth is acquired more efficiently in the classroom. The third principle is that the management curriculum must anticipate changes in management practices and not reflect only past management practices (Cyert & Dill 1964, p. 223). The faculty should know current management practices as well as have the objectivity to stand off and speculate on new techniques. The student, after all, will not ordinarily reach a top management position until fifteen or twenty years after his graduation (Bach 1958, p. 351).

RICHARD M. CYERT

BIBLIOGRAPHY

BACH, G. L. 1958 Some Observations on the Business School of Tomorrow. *Management Science* 4:351–364.
BERANEK, WILLIAM 1963 *Analysis for Financial Decisions.* Homewood, Ill.: Irwin.
BOWMAN, EDWARD H.; and FETTER, ROBERT B. (1957) 1961 *Analysis for Production Management.* Rev. ed. Homewood, Ill.: Irwin.
BUFFA, ELWOOD 1963 *Models for Production and Operations Management.* New York: Wiley.
CYERT, RICHARD M.; and DILL, WILLIAM R. 1964 The Future of Business Education. *Journal of Business* 37:221–237.
CYERT, RICHARD M.; and MARCH, JAMES G. 1963 *A Behavioral Theory of the Firm.* Englewood Cliffs, N.J.: Prentice-Hall.
FRIEDMAN, LAWRENCE 1961 Game Theory in the Allocation of Advertising Expenditures. Pages 230–244 in *Mathematical Models and Methods in Marketing.* Edited by Frank M. Bass et al. Homewood, Ill.: Irwin.
HOLT, CHARLES C. et al. 1960 *Planning Production, Inventories, and Work Force.* Englewood Cliffs, N.J.: Prentice-Hall.
HOWARD, JOHN A. (1957) 1963 *Marketing Management.* Rev. ed. Homewood, Ill.: Irwin.
KUEHN, ALFRED A. 1962 Consumer Brand Choice: A Learning Process? Pages 390–403 in Ronald E. Frank (editor), *Quantitative Techniques in Marketing Analysis.* Homewood, Ill.: Irwin.
KUEHN, ALFRED A.; and HAMBURGER, MICHAEL J. 1963 A Heuristic Program for Locating Warehouses. *Management Science* 9:643–666.
MODIGLIANI, FRANCO; and MILLER, MERTON H. (1958) 1959 The Cost of Capital, Corporation Finance and the Theory of Investment. Pages 150–181 in Ezra Solomon (editor), *The Management of Corporate Capital.* Glencoe, Ill.: Free Press. → First published in the *American Economic Review.*
MUELLER, EVA 1954 A Study of Purchasing Decisions. Part 2: The Sample Survey. *Consumer Behavior* 1: 38–87.
SIMON, HERBERT A. 1960 *The New Science of Management Decision.* New York: Harper.
SOLOMON, EZRA 1963 *The Theory of Financial Management.* New York: Columbia Univ. Press.
TONGE, FRED M. 1961 *A Heuristic Program for Assembly Line Balancing.* Englewood Cliffs, N.J.: Prentice-Hall.
WEINGARTNER, H. MARTIN 1963 *Mathematical Programming and the Analysis of Capital Budgeting Problems.* Englewood Cliffs, N.J.: Prentice-Hall.

BUSINESS PSYCHOLOGY
See under INDUSTRIAL RELATIONS.

C

CAIRNES, JOHN ELLIOTT

John Elliott Cairnes (1823–1875), an Irish economist, was born at Castlebellingham, County Louth. After some years reluctantly spent in his father's brewing business, Cairnes entered Trinity College, Dublin, in 1842 and received his primary degree in Arts in 1848. He was at first uncertain where his career lay—his interest in economic studies seems only to have developed around 1854, the year in which he received his M.A. degree. Two years later he took the competitive examination by which the Whately professorship of political economy was then filled and as a result was appointed to the chair for the usual five-year tenure. He was admitted to the Irish bar in 1857 but did not practice law. From this time on, he devoted himself wholly to academic economics. In 1859 he was appointed professor of political economy and jurisprudence at Queen's College, Galway, and retained this post until 1870, discharging its duties through a deputy after he moved his residence to London in 1865. In 1866 he became professor of political economy at University College, London, but resigned in 1872, having been reduced to almost helpless invalidism by the rheumatic complaint that caused his death three years later.

Although Cairnes's active career as an economist extended over less than 20 years, he quickly established himself in the front rank of the profession; his contemporaries recognized him as second only to John Stuart Mill, whose close friend he was from 1859 onward.

Cairnes's first work, *The Character and Logical Method of Political Economy* (1857), stands as the definitive statement of the methodology of the Eng-lish classical school. In it Cairnes laid stress on the primacy of the deductive method, emphasized the hypothetical character of political economy, and stressed its independence of any particular political or social system. He was, in fact, defining the scope and method of economic analysis rather than of political economy in its fullest sense. Although this approach later brought criticism from advocates of the historical method, such as his fellow countryman Cliffe Leslie, Cairnes could not properly be charged with neglecting the study of economic facts. He was, above all, a theorist, but one who could employ his analytical powers to great advantage in dissecting the essential elements of a current problem.

A notable example of his use of this approach is found in his papers on the depreciation of gold, published between 1858 and 1860 and subsequently reprinted with other papers in his *Essays in Political Economy, Theoretical and Applied* (1873a). Another instance, and one that gained him much wider repute, was in *The Slave Power* (1862), in which he outlined both the requisite conditions for the operation of a slave economy and its inevitable social consequences. The book was a strong indictment of the social system of the American South and did much to influence public opinion in Britain in favor of the Northern cause in the Civil War.

Cairnes also took a strong interest in the problems of his native Ireland, notably land tenure and university education, and there is evidence that on these and other questions of his day he indirectly exerted considerable political influence through his friends Mill and Henry Fawcett. Yet ultimately Cairnes's main interest and strength lay in the field

257

of economic theory, to which he returned in his last and best-known work, *Some Leading Principles of Political Economy Newly Expounded* (1874). This was avowedly designed "to strengthen and add consistency" to the structure of the Ricardo–Mill system and included an attempt to rehabilitate the wages-fund doctrine, which Mill had "recanted" in 1869. Perhaps the most permanently significant feature of this book is the modification of the cost-of-production theory of value to take account of the existence of noncompeting industrial groups, primarily in the case of labor. Cairnes pointed out that the cost-of-production theory could be applied only in cases where complete mobility of factors existed. Where this condition was not fulfilled, in domestic as in international trade, the principle of reciprocal demand must be invoked, in addition to the cost-of-production theory, to explain the determination of normal values. This concept of noncompeting groups did not originate with Cairnes, but it was he who first recognized and gave it its full importance.

Although in this and other respects Cairnes endeavored with some success to improve on accepted classical theory, he had no sympathy for attempts at radical reconstruction of the science, as his uncomprehending review (1872) of Jevons' *The Theory of Political Economy* (1871) clearly showed. Since on the central issues of economic theory his approach was essentially backward-looking, there seems no reason for altering the conventional estimate of him as "the last of the classical economists."

R. D. COLLISON BLACK

[*For the historical context of Cairnes's work, see the biographies of* LESLIE; LONGFIELD; MILL; RICARDO. *For discussion of the subsequent development of his ideas, see* PRICES *and* WAGES.]

WORKS BY CAIRNES

(1857) 1875 *The Character and Logical Method of Political Economy.* 2d ed. London: Macmillan.
(1862) 1863 *The Slave Power: Its Character, Career, and Probable Designs.* 2d ed. London: Macmillan.
1872 New Theories in Political Economy. *Fortnightly Review* New Series 11:71–76.
1873a *Essays in Political Economy, Theoretical and Applied.* London: Macmillan.
1873b *Political Essays.* London: Macmillan.
1874 *Some Leading Principles of Political Economy Newly Expounded.* London: Macmillan.

SUPPLEMENTARY BIBLIOGRAPHY

BLACK, R. D. COLLISON 1960 Jevons and Cairnes. *Economica* New Series 27:214–232.
FAWCETT, HENRY 1875 Professor Cairnes. *Fortnightly Review* New Series 18:149–154.
JEVONS, WILLIAM S. (1871) 1965 *The Theory of Political Economy.* 5th ed. New York: Kelley.
LESLIE, T. CLIFFE (1879) 1888 Professor Cairnes. Pages 60–62 in T. Cliffe Leslie, *Essays in Political Economy.* 2d rev. ed. Edited by J. K. Ingram and C. F. Bastable. Dublin: Hodges & Figgis; London: Longmans.
O'BRIEN, GEORGE 1943 J. S. Mill and J. E. Cairnes. *Economica* New Series 10:273–285.

CALVIN, JOHN

John Calvin (1509–1564), one of the major leaders of the Protestant Reformation, was born in Noyon, France, and died in Geneva. His work will be considered in this article only insofar as it has implications for the development of political theory.

Calvin's undergraduate career at the University of Paris was followed by legal training at Orléans and Bourges and by a period of intensive study of classical authors under the royal lecturers at Paris. A religious struggle ended with his "sudden conversion," early in 1532, which led him to become a biblical theologian. He published his *Institutio religionis Christianae* at Basel in 1536 and was thereafter identified with the Reformation in Geneva.

His first published treatise, a commentary on Seneca's *De clementia*, revealed a mind familiar with ancient political thought, and his interest in politics was not diminished by his later devotion to theological studies. In all editions of the *Institutio* (1536) he included a more or less systematic treatment of civil government. His commentaries on the books of the Scriptures contained searching political passages, and his extensive correspondence is abundantly sprinkled with informed references to political events of his day and with characterizations of chiefs of state and their policies, especially as these related to the prospects of the Reformation.

Calvin raised political relationships and duties to a high level of importance by bringing them completely within the sphere of religious motivation. The dominion of kings and magistrates is "a holy thing," and they should be obeyed as "vicars of God" unless they command what God forbids. He sought a mutuality of service and obligation sanctioned by religion: civil obedience is an expression of the Christian law of love, since it makes for the safety and peace of all, while magistrates, for their part, are "responsible to God and to men." Government exists both to protect the church in its integrity and to promote the civil virtues and public peace. "In short, it provides that a public manifestation of religion may exist among Christians and that humanity be maintained among men" (*Institutio*, IV, xx, 3). The coercive power of rulers is to be exercised under God's authority and with clemency. If they observe these two conditions, they may resort to war to save their people, and they may levy taxes, remembering always that their revenues are received in trust and are, as it were, the blood of the people.

The duty of obedience applies even when the ruler is not Christian. It is not affected by variation in the form of government. Anyone entrusted with a ruling function is to be revered and must act responsibly.

Calvin in 1536 impartially compared the forms of government described by classical writers, but in the 1543 edition of the *Institutio* he stated a decided preference for "aristocracy, or a system compounded of aristocracy and democracy" (*vel aristocratiam vel temperatum ex ipsa et politia statum aliis omnibus longe excellere—Institutio*, IV, xx, 8). In 1559 he explained this preference by a further insertion: since kings lack the requisite justice and prudence, it is preferable that a number of people exercise power, so that they may help, teach, and admonish one another and together censure and restrain willful individuals (*Institutio*, IV, xx, 8). Thus the main motive for plural responsibility is not representation of all interests, but the opportunity for mutual criticism and the sharing of opinions.

Calvin inserted the "aristocracy–democracy" phrase at a time when he was also cooperating in the revision of the constitution of Geneva, whereby the four chief magistrates (syndics) were elected by vote of all citizens from a list of eight names presented by the Little Council. Membership in the Little Council was by co-optation with the approval of the Council of Two Hundred, a body that was also selected by the Little Council. Here we have aristocracy, although not of lineal descent, with an element of democracy. Calvin's mind seems to have continued to move in the direction of democratic government. In 1560, writing on Micah 5:5, he noted that hereditary kingship seems out of accord with liberty and added that a well-ordered government is derived from a general vote of the people. In one of his sermons he observed that the choosing of judges and magistrates is not a formality or a ceremony, but a "holy thing" that should be done with reverence.

Most of what Calvin wrote on politics is marked by a deep respect for stable government and a cautious avoidance of any suggestion of resistance or revolution. Even under oppression the Christian is to submit and pray for deliverance. Calvin observed, however, that in the course of history God has sometimes raised up his agents to "break the bloody sceptres." In this context he introduced a striking sentence on the high importance of constitutional guardians of the people's liberty. As ex-

amples of *populares magistratus* he cited the Spartan ephors, Roman tribunes, and Athenian demarchs and suggested, apparently for the benefit of France, that perhaps the three estates in modern realms could serve the same purpose. He declared it "nefarious perfidy" for those so commissioned to fail to withstand wicked kings and thereby betray the people's liberty, which they were bound by God's ordinance to maintain. The "ephors" passage found its echo in the bolder stands of many later advocates of resistance to tyranny.

It would be easy to show that most of Calvin's political ideas had found previous expression in classical and medieval writers. Yet a certain originality is discernible in him. This is partly due to the informed clarity of his judgments, partly to the fact that he wrote from a Protestant position. He had the advantage of being fully equipped with the language skills of the Renaissance, which permitted him to use with sharpened effectiveness both the classical treatises on the state and the appropriate passages of Scripture. As a Protestant who had repudiated the papacy and dismissed all the claims to divinely bestowed supernatural authority made on its behalf, he assumed the autonomous civil community or national state as the environing framework within which the citizen functions politically. There is thus a sense in which his teaching was prophetic of the Peace of Westphalia in 1648, by which the papacy was thrust out of any determining role in international affairs. At the same time his thought ran wholly counter to the influence of Machiavelli's *Prince,* a work in which the sanctity of the ruler's office, as seen in both the classical and the Christian traditions, was frankly cast aside. Calvin would have said, "This nation under God," but never, "My country right or wrong." His ideal was that of a church-associated political community in which interaction between church and state would be fruitful for the common good.

Many elusive factors would be involved in any attempt to estimate Calvin's influence on later political thought and action. Writers who made use of his ideas invariably drew also from other sources. Writers influenced by him would certainly include not only such contemporaries and successors as John Ponet, François Hotman, Philippe de Mornay, and Hugo Grotius but also, nearer to the American Revolution, John Locke, Jean Jacques Burlamaqui, and to a lesser degree, Jean Jacques Rousseau. It will be remembered that John Witherspoon, the one clergyman to sign the Declaration of Independence, was theologically a strong Calvinist and politically a disciple of Locke and that the secretary of the Continental Congress, Charles Thompson, praised by John Adams as "the life of the cause of liberty," was a Presbyterian minister of similar views. We may easily exaggerate Calvin's affinity with modern exponents of representative government, but that he gave some impetus to its development is undeniable.

JOHN T. MCNEILL

[For the historical context of Calvin's work, see CHRISTIANITY. *For discussion of the subsequent development of his ideas, see* PROTESTANT POLITICAL THOUGHT *and the biographies of* GROTIUS *and* LOCKE.]

WORKS BY CALVIN

(1536) 1960 *Institutes of the Christian Religion.* 2 vols. Edited by John T. McNeill. Philadelphia: Westminster Press. → First published as *Institutio religionis Christianae.*

(1863–1900) 1964 *Ioannis Calvini opera quae supersunt omnia.* 59 vols. Edited by Johann W. Baum, August Eduard Cunitz, Eduard W. E. Reuss. Corpus Reformatorum, Vols. 29–87. New York: Johnson Reprints.

1926–1959 *Joannis Calvini opera selecta.* 5 vols. Edited by Petrus Barth. Munich: Kayser. → Volume 1: *Scripta Calvini ab anno 1533 usque ad annum 1541 continens,* 1926. Volume 2: *Tractatus theologicos minores ab anno 1542 usque ad annum 1564 editos continens,* 1952. Volume 3: *Institutionis Christianae religionis 1559 libros I et II,* 1957. Volume 4: *Institutionis Christianae religionis 1559 librum III continens,* 1959. Volume 5: *Institutionis Christianae religionis 1559 librum IV continens,* 1936.

(1950) 1956 *John Calvin on God and Political Duty.* Edited with an introduction by John T. McNeill. 2d ed. New York: Liberal Arts Press. → Selections from Calvin's *Institutes of the Christian Religion; Commentaries on Romans;* and *Commentaries on Daniel.*

SUPPLEMENTARY BIBLIOGRAPHY

CARLYLE, ROBERT W.; and CARLYLE, ALEXANDER J. (1903–1936) 1950 *A History of Medieval Political Theory in the West.* 6 vols. Edinburgh and London: Blackwood; New York: Barnes & Noble.

CHENEVIÈRE, MARC É. 1937 *La pensée politique de Calvin.* Paris: Éditions "Je sers."

HARVEY, RAY F. 1937 *Jean Jacques Burlamaqui: A Liberal Tradition in American Constitutionalism.* Chapel Hill: Univ. of North Carolina Press.

HUNT, GEORGE L.; and MCNEILL, JOHN T. (editors) 1965 *Calvinism and Political Order: Essays Prepared for the Woodrow Wilson Lectureship of the National Presbyterian Center, Washington, D.C.* Philadelphia: Westminster Press.

MCNEILL, JOHN T. 1964 John Calvin on Civil Government. *Journal of Presbyterian History* 42:71–91.

CAMPAIGN FUNDS
See POLITICAL FINANCING.

CANNON, WALTER B.

Walter Bradford Cannon (1871–1945) was a most productive physiologist who exerted an important influence on the development of medical investigation in the United States. He was born in Prairie du Chien, Wisconsin, and was fond of tracing his own interest in scientific exploration to the fact that his forebears came from the French Canadian and Scotch–Irish pioneers who explored and settled this continent.

After graduating from the public schools of St. Paul, Minnesota, he put himself through Harvard College and Harvard Medical School, from which he graduated in 1900. The rest of his life was spent as a member of the faculty at Harvard, where he held the George Higginson professorship of physiology from 1906 until he became professor emeritus in 1942. During World War I, he did important work on surgical shock, first with Sir William Maddock Bayliss at University College, London, and later in the surgical research laboratory at Dijon. Briefer absences from Harvard enabled him to serve as visiting professor at the Sorbonne in 1929, in Peiping in 1935, and as visiting investigator at the Instituto de Cardiologia in Mexico City in 1944.

Cannon's investigations into the functioning of living organisms began while he was an undergraduate, rapidly rose to a level of international distinction during his first year in medical school, and continued virtually without interruption until his death. Although the total body of his contribution appears to range over a number of fields, it all grew by a series of closely connected steps from his studies as a medical student on the motions of the digestive tract. For these, he employed the newly discovered X rays to reveal the course of swallowed food rendered radiopaque by mixing with the salts of heavy metals. Unhappily, little was then known about the dangers of radiation, and later in life he suffered severely from a degeneration of the tissues of his hands and arms that required an almost endless series of plastic operations. It is not improbable that the early exposure to X rays also contributed to the malignant lymphoma that was originally diagnosed in 1929 and caused him uninterrupted discomfort until his death nearly two decades later.

The early work on gastrointestinal motility laid the practical and theoretical groundwork for modern understanding of the digestive process and for the use of the barium meal as a diagnostic tool. More importantly, perhaps, it gave to Cannon a lifelong interest in the way the autonomic nervous system helps to maintain the constancy of the internal environment.

Initially, during his work on digestion, he was sometimes frustrated by a sudden cessation of all gastrointestinal movement in the animal under observation. Soon, however, he noticed that these interruptions could be correlated with the onset of emotional tension. Even simple pain, as well as the more complex states of fear and anger, seemed to lead to a prompt cessation of the digestive process. By successive elimination of different parts of the autonomic nervous system, he was able to show quite clearly that the inhibition of digestive activity is carried largely by the splanchnic nerves, which constitute the sympathetic supply to a large portion of the abdominal organs including the adrenal glands. Conversely, the parasympathetic nerves, especially the vagus, were shown to bring about an increase in motility and, as Pavlov had demonstrated a little earlier, an increase in gastric secretion.

From here, Cannon went on to elaborate the hypothesis that the sympathetic nervous system and the adrenal glands together form a more or less unitary arrangement for adjusting the body to certain emergency situations. Conversely, the parasympathetic includes a number of more discrete elements, each of which is primarily concerned with one or another part of the body's normal household economy—the digestion of food, the elimination of wastes, and even the protection of the eye against excessive light. His experiments and thoughts on these matters were brought together in the book *Bodily Changes in Pain, Hunger, Fear and Rage* (1915).

The idea that an endocrine gland, such as the adrenal, could be turned on and off according to circumstances encountered bitter opposition. In the course of an elaborate set of experiments designed to settle this controversy, which at times became unpleasantly warm both for participants and onlookers, Cannon devised the denervated heart as a sensitive indicator of adrenal secretion in the otherwise intact, unanesthetized animal. Three important lines of investigation grew out of this experimental preparation. First, Cannon used it to demonstrate that the sympathetic nerves produce their effects through the mediation of an adrenalin-like substance, which he called sympathin, that circulates in the blood after release. Second, he, and later his students, went on to show that many organs and even individual nerve cells become more susceptible to chemical influences after degeneration of their normal nerve supply. Finally, the same series of experiments led to the preparation of animals without any sympathetic nervous system at all. A large number of observations on such animals showed that they were entirely capable of leading satisfactory lives in the sheltered circumstances of the laboratory. What was lacking was

the ability to adjust to abnormal or threatening circumstances. Extremes of temperature, vigorous exercise, hemorrhage, and a number of other stresses quickly resulted in serious dislocations of the general state of the animal and especially in the composition of its body fluids.

Building on these observations and on Claude Bernard's famous dictum—*La fixité du milieu intérieur est la condition de la vie libre*—Cannon went on to make his most important theoretical contribution. Coining the term "homeostasis" to identify the tendency of all complex organisms to maintain a steady internal state, he detailed in a series of reviews and monographs the various mechanisms by which such constancy is achieved. His own experiments were, of course, primarily concerned with the role of the autonomic nervous system in determining the course of the assimilative, circulatory, respiratory, and excretory reactions involved. Certain subsidiary features of the theory, such as the previously mentioned distinction between the roles of parasympathetic and sympathetic divisions of the autonomic nervous system, have been considerably modified by further study; but Cannon's over-all view has greatly influenced clinical practice as well as theory building in both physiology and psychology.

Cannon's influence on the behavioral and social sciences may be clearly seen in current discussions of the nature of emotion and its physiological expression. Most important, perhaps, is the firm experimental foundation he provided for what is now referred to as "psychosomatic medicine."

His early work on hunger called attention to the important role played by contractions of the stomach in the elaboration of the subjective sensation, a concept that was taken up and greatly elaborated by his contemporary, Anton J. Carlson (1916). Nevertheless, the bulk of his work, as he was at considerable pains to show, argued against the James–Lange conception that the subjective aspects of emotion result directly from sensations arising in organs and muscles involved in overt emotional responses. Later work has not yet completely clarified the nature of hunger, let alone that of more complex emotional awareness. However, it is certain that hunger involves factors other than mere awareness of gastric contraction, and theories of emotion cannot be categorized as either James–Lange or some obvious alternative. Nevertheless, Cannon's work is still important for having shown us how to frame parts of these questions in clear experimental terms.

Cannon's attempt to extend the theory of homeostasis into the social and economic sphere, undertaken most fully in the last few chapters of his book *The Wisdom of the Body* (1932), is not generally regarded as anything more than a stimulating but limited analogy.

Cannon's influence on students and colleagues was very great. Fortunately, much of what he meant to them has been made readily available in his short but profound autobiography, *The Way of an Investigator* (1945), written a few years before his death. Here he put together with his usual economy a distillation of what he had found important, interesting, and diverting—both about his work as an investigator and about life in general. He was never particularly concerned with metaphysics; and his philosophy of science was primarily a matter of day-to-day common sense. Rather than defining knowledge, Cannon's writings concentrate on its acquisition. His description of "serendipity" added a new word to the vocabulary of scientific discourse and has no doubt alerted the senses of innumerable investigators to the importance of the chance observation (Merton [1949] 1957, pp. 103–105).

Cannon's outlook was basically that of the enlightened nineteenth-century liberal, and his attitude toward life as a whole was similar to his approach to laboratory investigation—simple, direct, devoted, and optimistic.

His liberalism was clearly evident in the interest he took in the Soviet Union during his visit there in connection with the International Physiological Congress of 1935. Although fully and painfully aware of the many restrictions on political liberty and basic human rights, he concerned himself mainly with the efforts being made to improve the health, education, and general welfare of the Soviet people. A little later, his personal friendship with a fellow physiologist, Juan Negrín, who was head of the Spanish government at the outbreak of the Falangist revolution, caused him to take an active interest in providing medical aid to the Loyalist armies and to the numerous refugees.

His laboratory attracted students and postdoctoral fellows from all over the world and thus contributed markedly to the increased international stature of American medical science during the 1920s and 1930s. For many years, Cannon helped guide the development of the American Physiological Society, serving on the council from 1905 to 1912 and as president from 1914 through 1916. As a charter member of the National Research Council's Committee on Physiology, set up in 1916, he was an active participant in most of the council's activities from then until his death and was one of the first Harvard scientists to help shape national scientific policy.

Although Cannon never sought the kind of intimacy with students and junior colleagues that became common in a later period, he was held in affectionate regard by all of them. He would go to great lengths to guide graduate students and fellows through the early difficulties of a research career, and all of them will recall the pains he took to teach them how to write succinct and informative scientific papers. Almost daily he presided over a kind of scientific salon at the departmental tea table. It was here that most of his associates learned to share not only his scientific experiences and outlook but also his warm and quietly humorous approach to life in general.

ROBERT S. MORISON

[*For discussion of the subsequent development of Cannon's ideas, see* EMOTION; HOMEOSTASIS.]

WORKS BY CANNON

(1915) 1953 *Bodily Changes in Pain, Hunger, Fear and Rage: An Account of Recent Researches Into the Function of Emotional Excitement.* 2d ed. Boston: Branford.

(1932) 1963 *The Wisdom of the Body.* Rev. & enl. ed. New York: Norton.

1945 *The Way of an Investigator: A Scientist's Experiences in Medical Research.* New York: Norton.

SUPPLEMENTARY BIBLIOGRAPHY

BERNARD, CLAUDE (1878) 1930 Leçons sur les phénomènes de la vie communs aux animaux et aux végétaux. Pages 307–309 in John F. Fulton (editor), *Selected Readings in the History of Physiology.* Springfield, Ill.: Thomas.

CARLSON, ANTON J. 1916 *The Control of Hunger in Health and Disease.* Univ. of Chicago Press.

LINDSLEY, DONALD B. 1951 Emotion. Pages 473–516 in S. S. Stevens (editor), *Handbook of Experimental Psychology.* New York: Wiley.

MERTON, ROBERT K. (1949) 1957 *Social Theory and Social Structure.* Rev. & enl. ed. Glencoe, Ill.: Free Press.

STELLAR, ELIOT 1960 Drive and Motivation. Volume 3, pages 1501–1527 in American Physiological Society, *Handbook of Physiology.* Baltimore: Williams & Wilkins.

CANON LAW

The term "canon law" usually refers to the law of the Roman Catholic and Orthodox churches, although it is sometimes applied analogically to the law of other religious groups, particularly Islam. The word "canon" is derived from the Greek κανών, meaning a rule or measure (originally an architectural instrument), and it has been used in several senses. The canon of sacred Scripture is the body of those sacred writings that have received official approval as divinely inspired. The decrees of the church councils are also known as canons; a saint is canonized when he is placed on the official list or canon of the saints, and a member of a cathedral chapter in the Anglican and Roman Catholic churches is called a canon. (Originally the term applied to all priests on the official list of a bishop.)

Early collections

The body of law known as canon law developed out of the collections of canons of the early church councils. The first such collections were made in the Eastern church beginning with the Council of Nicea (A.D. 325). A collection of Apostolic canons supposedly dating from the time of the apostles but actually much later in origin (fourth century) had great authority in the East. The collection made by the Council of Constantinople, *In Trullo* (A.D. 691), and 22 canons from the Council of Nicea that were added to it in A.D. 787 form the basic texts for the canon law of the Greek and Russian Orthodox churches.

In the West, however, the collections made by Dionysius Exiguus around A.D. 500 were the first important texts of canon law. They included the canons of the ecumenical councils held in the East (omitting one adopted at Chalcedon that equated the patriarch of Constantinople and the pope), 50 of the Apostolic canons, the canons of the councils held by the north African church, and 39 papal letters or decretals containing interpretations of doctrine made by popes of the fourth and fifth centuries. Another collection, the *Hispana,* made in Spain in the seventh century, also included the decrees of councils held in Gaul and Spain as well as many more papal decretals. In the ninth century, the pseudo-Isidorean or false decretals, supposed to have been collected by St. Isidore of Seville (560–636), drew on this collection and added apocryphal letters said to have been written by the popes in the first three centuries. Subsequent collections in the West in the period between the ninth and twelfth centuries began to be organized on an analytical rather than chronological basis, and the collection of Yves de Chartres made in 1095 gave rules for the interpretation of conflicting canons.

Around 1240 a new collection was published that was a systematic attempt to use Yves's method to analyze and harmonize the conflicting elements in the conciliar decrees, papal decretals, and writings of the church fathers that had appeared in previous collections. Attributed to Gratian, a Bolognese monk, its original title was the *Concordantia discordantium canonum* ("Concordance of Discordant Canons"), but it is usually referred to as the *Decretum* ("Decree"). While it was never officially endorsed by the papacy, it formed the basis for the teaching and study of canon law in the West for many centuries and was included in the corpus of canon law along with the later official collections, the decretals of Gregory IX (1234), the *Liber sextus* ("Sext") of Boniface VIII (1298), and the *Clementinae* of Clement V (1317). Two further unofficial collections complete the medieval texts—the *Extravagantes* of John XXII and the *Extravagantes communes* of the later popes of the fourteenth and fifteenth centuries. Together these collections form the body of law that governed the Roman Catholic church down to the twentieth century, when Pope Benedict XV issued a formal code of canon law in 1917.

Medieval canon law and political thought

The writings of the canon lawyers in the three centuries that followed the publication of the *Decretum* are of special interest to the social scientist, particularly to the student of political theory. In the thirteenth century, canon law became the object of specialized study in the new universities of western Europe, and the questions that were discussed by the "decretists," as the commentators on the *Decretum* were known, and the "decretalists," or commentators on the later collections of papal decretal letters, included many of the fundamental problems of political thought and institutions. Since the ablest intellects were attracted to the church as a career, and the church's legal system developed rapidly in this period, it is not surprising that the solutions that they gave to these problems have had a lasting influence on Western political thought. The "civilians," or commentators on the civil, i.e., Roman, law were also active in this period, and the two groups influenced each other (it is still possible today in Europe to receive a doctorate in "both laws"—the degree of J.U.D., *juris utriusque doctor*), but the important writing on most questions was done by the church lawyers in the glosses they wrote on the texts of the *Decretum* and the decretals, and in their *summae,* or general treatises, on the canon law.

Papal sovereignty. In the hands of the canon lawyers, the claims of the papacy to supremacy over the Christian church were steadily expanded by judicious selection of materials and by interpretation of the texts in the glosses. For example, where an earlier text referred to the selection of a bishop by the prince or the cathedral chapter, a canonist commentator inserted after the reference to the prince the words "of the church, that is, the pope." In another instance, where Pope Innocent III (1198–1216) had claimed the right to intervene in temporal matters *casualiter*, "incidentally," the canonist who became Pope Innocent IV (1243–1254) added the word *saltem*, "at least," thereby claiming a much broader papal jurisdiction. Probably the best known of the canonist attempts to buttress the claims of the papacy was the appeal to the spurious Donation of Constantine —the alleged transfer of the western empire by Constantine to Pope Sylvester in gratitude for his cure from leprosy. The account of the donation was included among the forgeries in the pseudo-Isidorean decretals, and although it was not mentioned by Gratian, it was inserted as a postscript to a section of the *Decretum* by his pupil, Paucapalea. Attempts were also made to claim jurisdiction for the burgeoning system of ecclesiastical courts not only over doctrinal matters but also over wills, marriages, widows, orphans, usury, contracts, and treaties (on the grounds that an oath was involved). The furthest extensions of the claim for papal legal supremacy included in the canon law were Innocent IV's claim to be ordinary judge (*judex ordinarius*) over all mankind and the bull *Unam sanctam* of Boniface VIII, which claimed both the "material and spiritual swords" for the pope. Some decretalist commentators, however, went still further and claimed for the pope the right to grant dispensations from the requirements of the natural law (Ullmann 1949, chapter 3).

Recent research (see especially Tierney 1955) has compelled a revision of the earlier view of the canonists as mere apologists for the papacy. Gratian had included in the *Decretum* the statement by Pope Gelasius (492–496) that there are two powers by which the world is governed, and it strained the logical powers of the canonists to reduce this dualism to unity—although some were able to do so. In the *Decretum* too was the specific statement (distinction 40, chapter 6) that the pope was subject to judgment by the church "if he is found to have departed from the faith." The increasing legalization of relationships that had assisted papal centralization and expansion also resulted in a more precise analysis of the relations of the pope and other bodies within the church and led to an exploration of the cases in which the church could assert control over an errant pope. Thus, although some canonists identified the pope and the church so completely that it was impossible for the church to act against him, the analysis by the decretalists of the relations of the head (*rector*) and members of an ecclesiastical corporation (*universitas*) paved the way for the claim by later conciliarist writers with a canonist

background (e.g., John of Paris, Henry of Langenstein, Franciscus Zabarella, and Nicholas of Cusa) that the church as a whole had a corporate right to act against its head in certain cases.

The development of corporation theory was recognized in the nineteenth century by Otto von Gierke as a significant contribution of the medieval canonists to political and legal thought, although Gierke's theories about the real personality of corporate groups led him to criticize their views as inadequate. In a statement that was to have ramifications for American constitutional law (the Slaughterhouse Cases), Innocent IV described a corporation as a fictitious person (*persona ficta*) and recognized that it could be represented in legal action. The thirteenth-century and fourteenth-century canonists discussed how the corporation could act and thereby became involved in problems of consent, representation, and election.

Representation. A century earlier, Gratian had stated that the prelate was the representative of his church, but this representation was considered a personal one rather than the result of any corporate act. However, by the thirteenth century the popes were calling on corporate groups in the church to elect representatives to such meetings as the Fourth Lateran Council in 1215, with full powers to bind those who had elected them. The exercise of this right to elect representatives by ecclesiastical corporations in turn influenced theories of the representation of corporate communities in the emerging parliamentary institutions in England, France, and Spain. The interaction of canonist and secular law was facilitated by the fact that those engaged in administration (the clerks) were at least in minor orders (and therefore clerics). Ernest Barker (1913) has tried to develop a more direct relationship between the theory and practice of representation in the Dominican order and the development of the English parliament, noting especially the action of Simon de Montfort, a friend and possible pupil of the Dominicans, who called on the towns to send representatives to the parliament of 1265. This theory has been criticized by historians, but it is not necessary to be as specific as this in tracing the influence of canonical thought, since there was and had been a general borrowing of ecclesiastical concepts and practices both in England and on the Continent for at least a century. (For further details, see the essays collected in Post 1964.)

Consent. A similar development can be observed in canonical theories of consent to corporate action. Particularly on questions of the disposition of ecclesiastical property, the canonists spelled out the cases in which the consent of the cathedral or monastic chapter was necessary to actions by the bishop or abbot, the *rector* of the corporation. They distinguished between cases involving the corporate group as a whole, for which consent was required, and those involving the head of the corporation alone, for which he was required only to seek counsel. In this connection, the discussion of the precept "What touches all, should be approved by all" was of great importance for the history of democratic thought. Originally found as a Roman legal principle governing the rights of guardians and of those who shared a common source of water, it was given a broader extension by the canonists in their attempts to define the rights of the members of a corporate group, and in 1298 it was incorporated as one of the rules for the interpretation of the canon law in the *Liber sextus* of Boniface VIII. It was also cited by the Italian city-states in the thirteenth century to assert a right to participate in legislation, and its most famous use was by Edward I in the summons to the Model Parliament in England in 1295. (It should be noted that Edward would not have recognized a right to withhold consent, only to haggle about terms.) The conciliar theorists of the fourteenth and fifteenth centuries appealed to the maxim to assert a right of consent by the council to ecclesiastical legislation. The commentators on Gratian's *Decretum* also discussed popular consent to legislation when they glossed distinction 4, chapter 3 of the *Decretum*, which states that "laws are confirmed when they are approved by the custom of the people using them."

Elections.   The canonists were obliged to discuss electoral procedures, since many of the church officers, including the pope, were chosen by election. While it was recognized that elections could be unanimous, acclamation following divine inspiration, the normal method was to take a vote (*per scrutinium*). However, a simple majority did not suffice, for the *maior pars* also had to be *sanior* (sounder), a requirement originally contained in the Benedictine rule and extended to all episcopal elections by the Fourth Lateran Council in 1215. In the mid-thirteenth century, Pope Gregory X decided that a vote in which the prevailing side was twice as large as those opposed—a two-thirds majority—could be assumed to fulfill both the requirements of numbers and merit. This decision was incorporated in the *Liber sextus* (C. 9, I, 6) in 1298 and extended to episcopal elections a requirement that had already been applied to the election of the pope in the twelfth century (1179). Subsequently, the two-thirds requirement found its

way into the proceedings of many deliberative bodies, but its origin seems to be the canonistic requirement of approval by the *maior et sanior pars*.

Reason of state.   The canon lawyers also helped to develop the modern conception of reason of state. The term *ratio status* was, of course, Roman in origin, as were many of the legal and political concepts of the canonists. The *status* of the church and the "reason of the utility of the church" were often appealed to, both to limit the pope when he was conceived to be acting against the interest of the church and to extend his power in cases of "necessity," when the requirements of the church demanded it. Thus the pope could give dispensations from church law (although not from articles of faith) when "necessity" required it, but he could never act against the *status* of the church. Secular rulers also could take action on the basis of necessity, especially in waging just wars in which the reason of the matter (*ratio rei*) made it necessary to fight for the defense of the fatherland. In such cases, the canonists also recognized that the church had to contribute taxes to the common defense.

Natural law and equity.   The ideas of natural law and of *jus gentium*, or the law of the peoples, contained in the opening passages of Justinian's *Institutes* were reflected in the canonist discussions. The canonists tended to reject Ulpian's definition of natural law as what nature has taught all animals and to confine it specifically to man. However, the fact that at the beginning of the *Decretum* Gratian defined natural law as that which is contained in the Mosaic Law and the Gospels created some confusion, and the natural and divine law are not as carefully distinguished in canonist writings as they are by St. Thomas Aquinas in his discussion in the *Summa theologica* (2, 1, question 91). The canonists also borrowed the Roman conception of *aequitas* in the interpretation of the law, and this became an important influence on English law, when, beginning in the fourteenth century, it became the guiding principle of the court of the lord chancellor, usually a clergyman, whose decisions were based on equity rather than on the common law.

Authority and legitimacy.   Although all authority was considered to be derived ultimately from God, the canon lawyers adopted the Roman law theory that the authority of the emperor was derived from an original transfer by the people. Even before the introduction of Aristotle's *Politics* to western Europe, the canonists accepted government as a natural institution and recognized the legitimacy of infidel rulers. (See the documentation in Tierney 1964, chapters 3 and 6; and Post 1964, pp. 521–535.) However, they were still concerned with justifying papal intervention, and they therefore argued that papal excommunication made it necessary for the people to withdraw from their ruler and that the pope alone, as vicar of Christ, had full power over all men, including infidel rulers.

Legislation. When so much legislation was being made by the pope, it is easy to understand why the canon lawyers were also the first in the medieval period to recognize the role of lawmaking in government. As early as the *Decretum* the pope's right to make new laws was clearly stated, and in 1163 Pope Alexander III stated that "new ills demand the discovery of new medicines." The theory that law was "found, not made" in the Middle Ages reflects neither papal practice nor the canon lawyers' understanding of its meaning.

The same thing can be said about the medieval myth of a universal empire. In the same decretal in which he asserted the right to intervene "incidentally" in temporal affairs, Innocent III observed that "the king [of France] recognizes no superior in temporal affairs" (*Per venerabilem* 1202). This text was included in the decretals of Gregory IX and gave the decretalists an opportunity to comment on the claims of the European kingdoms to be independent of the jurisdiction of the Holy Roman Empire.

The theories of the clerical legal writers in the golden age of canon law, from the twelfth to the beginning of the fifteenth century, profoundly influenced the political thought of the West. Their discussions of papal sovereignty and the rights of the church, of election, representation, and consent, of the state, nature, and law, influenced the theory and practice of secular government and developed and refined many of the most important conceptions of Roman law.

Canon law in modern religions

Roman Catholicism. Canon law in the Catholic church in recent years has aroused less interest on the part of social scientists. In addition to the collections that formed the *Corpus juris canonici* until its codification in this century, church law also included papal laws or constitutions, the authoritative opinions of papal congregations, and the decrees of the Council of Trent and the First Vatican Council. Since 1918, this legislation has been superseded by the code of canon law, although the decrees of the Second Vatican Council should certainly be included in any listing of the basic law of the church, along with papal decrees and official definitions of dogma after 1918, such as that on the Assumption of the Blessed Virgin in 1950. The apostolic constitution of Vatican II, *De ecclesia*, marks a reversal of the general process over the last millennium of centralization of authority and explicitly associates the bishops with the pope in the government of the church (the principle of collegiality), affirming that this right belongs to the bishops by virtue of their succession to the "college of the apostles" (and not derivatively from the pope).

Although the code of canon law has reorganized and systematized the law of the Roman Catholic church, it maintains continuity with the earlier legal texts. (Gratian's *Decretum* alone is cited 8,400 times.) Like the earlier texts it is concerned with the internal government of the church, the qualifications for priests and members of the hierarchy, the administration of the sacraments, and the maintenance of a system of ecclesiastical justice. The sanctions at its disposal include excommunication—cutting off the violator of the law from the corporate life of the church, especially from participation in the sacraments; suspension—prohibition of a church officer from exercising his office; and interdict—the cessation of worship and the administration of the sacraments in a given geographical area. A system of church courts administers the code, culminating in the judicial bodies of the sacred congregations, especially the Sacred Roman Rota in Rome. The legalistic emphasis in much of Roman Catholic theology and moral teaching was much criticized at the Second Vatican Council; an attempt is being made to reduce the influence of the legal approach in these areas, but in a hierarchical church with a legal tradition of many centuries, it is evident that canon law will continue to play a major role.

Protestantism. Canon law does not have a significant position in the Protestant churches; in fact, the excessive legalization of the church was one of the abuses against which the reformers reacted. In a symbolic act to demonstrate this, Luther burned the *Corpus juris canonici* in front of the church at Wittenberg, denouncing the canon law as "heretical, anti-Christian, and unnatural." However, all Protestant denominations have basic creeds or statements of faith that might be compared to the dogmatic canons of the church councils, and most of them have constitutions or by-laws that set forth the organization of local, regional, or national groupings variously called synods, jurisdictions, conferences, assemblies, or conventions.

Unlike the Roman Catholic example, the Protestant governing bodies invariably include lay representatives. For those denominations, such as the Baptists or Congregationalists, in which the basic unit of church organization is the local congregation, a highly developed system of church law is seen as an infringement of the autonomy of the individual congregation. Some central group is necessary, however, for such activities as the organization of the foreign missions, but in theory the local congregation is the final authority. For the Presbyterians, the presbyteries, the synods, and the General Assembly are higher bodies with judicial power, and the way in which their judicial proceedings are to be conducted in the Presbyterian church in the United States is prescribed in *The Book of Discipline*, first adopted in 1788 but often revised and amended since. The Methodist church has its *Doctrines and Discipline,* which has a section on judicial administration that specifies procedures for the trial of bishops and preachers and establishes a judicial commission to be elected by the quadrennial General Conference. The Episcopal church in the United States is closer to the Roman Catholic system both in terminology and substance. Its *Constitution and Canons* can be amended by a triennial General Convention composed of a House of Bishops and a House of Deputies, the latter including both clergy and laymen.

In the case of the Church of England, there is, in theory, a continuity with medieval canon law. However, by the Act of Submission of 1532, the English clergy agreed not to make any new canons without royal permission and to authorize a commission to reorganize the existing church law. In 1604, 141 new canons were drawn up and approved by the church convocations and the king. Other efforts at reform, however, ended in failure. In the intervening centuries most of the medieval canon law has been ignored, and Parliament has steadily reduced the jurisdiction of the church courts, successively abolishing the benefit of clergy (the right of clergymen to be tried in church courts), the practice of tithing, and control by church courts over wills, marriages, and the affairs of the laity. Since 1919, the assembly of the Church of England, made up of bishops, clergy, and laity, has acquired some autonomy in legislating for the church, but all major decisions must nevertheless be approved by Parliament. [*See* CHRISTIANITY.]

Judaism. In Judaism, the ceremonial and legal precepts of the Bible, particularly those contained in the Pentateuch or Torah, were also developed and interpreted by the great rabbis shortly before, and for several centuries after, the beginning of the Christian era. At first these interpretations were transmitted orally; only later were they committed to writing in the Talmud (teaching). The Talmud is divided into two sections: the Mishnah, a collection of decisions on the interpretation of the laws contained in the Torah, and the Gemara, which is a later commentary on the contents of the Mishnah. Since there is no central legislative authority in Judaism, the Talmud should be compared with the canonist commentaries rather than with the canon law itself. For orthodox Jews, it has great authority, but the modern reform movement has tended to give the Talmud much less attention. [*See* JUDAISM.]

In the modern state of Israel, canon law plays an important and controversial role. The conservative religious parties are committed to the establishment of Jewish religious law as the sole law of the state. Their opposition has been one of the principal reasons that Israel has not adopted a written constitution, and they have been responsible for the application of several religious laws. For example, only kosher food may be imported into Israel; Jewish dietary laws are observed in the army; the Sabbath is officially recognized, and neither the railroads nor shipping operates on that day. Most important, rabbinical courts have sole jurisdiction over all Jews in matters of marriage, divorce, alimony, and wills, and the determination of a person's status as a Jew is made by these courts on the basis of religious law.

Some of these practices have been criticized by the secular parties, particularly the application of a marriage law that clearly discriminates against women. While there have been proposals to convene the Sanhedrin to modernize the law, there is some doubt as to how this can be done. In addition to the archaic character of some of its provisions, the fact that the religious parties are in a minority in Israel makes it unlikely that they will succeed in extending greatly the jurisdiction of religious law.

Islam. The Islamic legal system, as contained in the Koran and its subsequent interpretations, is not called canon law, but it fulfills many of the same functions and has undergone a similar evolution. The Koran contains some six hundred verses with ethical content and eighty on legal topics. These are considered to be the basis of Islamic law and to have eternal and immutable validity. Polygamy is permitted, and divorce is possible by simple dismissal by the husband and a prescribed waiting period. Drinking of wine is forbidden, and games of chance are discouraged.

Severe penalties, including death by stoning and cutting off a hand or foot, are laid down for sexual offenses, theft, and apostasy. A fast is commanded in the month of Ramadan that is so strict that nothing may pass the lips between sunrise and sunset. A religious tax, the *zakat*, is imposed on the faithful, and they are commanded to "obey God, his apostle, and the established authorities" (Sura 14, 59, 83).

During the three centuries after the death of Muhammad, the Islamic conquests spread the knowledge of the *Shariyah* (way) of Allah over the Middle East and north Africa and into Spain. Legal specialists commented upon the commands and prohibitions contained in the Koran, and the possible ethical and legal implications of cases from the life of the Prophet. By about A.D. 900 all essential questions of interpretation had been settled, and four schools of interpreters had emerged with varying emphases on each of the four sources of legal interpretation—the literal Koran, tradition, the agreement of the people, and analogical reasoning.

The *ulama*, or legal scholars, authorized Muslim rulers to make changes in the law in cases of necessity, but in reality two systems of law emerged: one, public and criminal law, under the control of the ruler and based on custom and his decrees; and the other, private and religious law, the object of study by *ulama*, who were roughly equivalent to the canon lawyers in the West but even more important, since there was no priesthood. The latter system was chiefly concerned with regulating family life, inheritance, and religious ritual in accordance with the Koran as interpreted by the great legal schools. The judges, or *kadis*, of the Islamic courts that applied this law were drawn from the *ulama*, although the ruler retained ultimate control and the right of review of their decisions.

From the tenth to the twentieth century, Islamic law underwent no significant development, and the *ulama* relied on the jurisprudence developed in the first three centuries of Islam. In the twentieth century, with the emergence of modern Islamic states in the Middle East and north Africa, an effort is being made to modernize its provisions, but this is often opposed by the traditionalist *ulama*. However, the Koranic rules on inheritance have been modified by the governments of Pakistan, Syria, and Iraq, and in Tunisia an attempt is being made to change many of the provisions of Islamic law by appealing to principles of interpretation that would lead to the abandonment of polygamy and of the fast of Ramadan and bring about a stricter legal regulation of divorce. Another alternative is to reject the whole system of Islamic law as Atatürk did in Turkey. More commonly, synthesis and adaptation of Islamic and Western law are being attempted, and such institutions as Al Azhar University in Cairo continue to train students in Islamic law with the support of the modernizing Islamic states in the Middle East and north Africa. [*See* ISLAM.]

A common element of all canon law systems is their literalism—the insistence on the observance of the letter of the law combined with an elaborate exegesis to determine its exact meaning. This can be understood if one recalls that the original texts that are being interpreted are usually considered to be divinely inspired. Yet at the same time, under the guise of interpreting the law, the commentators have often developed and changed its meaning. The canon lawyers have profoundly influenced the life, culture, and politics of their societies—at least in cases, as in medieval Europe and the Islamic world, where those societies are overwhelmingly of a single religious persuasion. In the pluralistic world of the West, canon law continues to exert an influence on the clergymen and adherents of the religious groups in which it plays an important role.

PAUL E. SIGMUND

[*Relevant material may be found in* NATURAL LAW; RELIGION; *and in the biographies of* AQUINAS; GIERKE.]

BIBLIOGRAPHY

BARKER, ERNEST 1913 *The Dominican Order and Convocation: A Study of the Growth of Representation in the Church During the Thirteenth Century.* Oxford: Clarendon.

BOUSCAREN, TIMOTHY L.; and ELLIS, ADAM C. (1946) 1951 *Canon Law: A Text and Commentary.* 2d rev. ed. Milwaukee: Bruce.

CARLYLE, ROBERT W.; and CARLYLE, A. J. 1903–1936 *A History of Medieval Political Theory in the West.* 6 vols. Edinburgh and London: Blackwood. → See especially Volume 2, *The Political Theory of the Roman Lawyers and the Canonists, From the Tenth Century to the Thirteenth Century* and Volume 5, *The Political Theory of the Thirteenth Century.*

CATHOLIC CHURCH, CORPUS JURIS CANONICI (1879–1881) 1959 *Corpus juris canonici.* 2d ed., 2 vols. Edited with critical annotations by Emil Friedberg. Graz (Austria): Akademische Druck & Verlags-anstalt.

CICOGNANI, AMLETO GIOVANNI (1925) 1934 *Canon Law.* Philadelphia: Dolphin. → First published as *Ius canonicum.*

COULSON, NOEL J. 1964 *A History of Islamic Law.* Edinburgh Univ. Press.

FEINE, HANS E. A. 1950 *Kirchliche Rechtsgeschichte auf der Grundlage des Kirchenrechts von Ulrich Stutz.* Volume 1: *Die katholische Kirche.* Weimar (Germany): Böhlaus.

LEWIS, EWART (editor) 1954 *Medieval Political Ideas.* 2 vols. New York: Knopf. → See especially Volume 1.

MAITLAND, FREDERIC W. 1898 *Roman Canon Law in the Church of England.* London: Methuen.

MORTIMER, ROBERT C. 1953 *Western Canon Law.* Berkeley: Univ. of California Press.

POST, GAINES 1964 *Studies in Medieval Legal Thought: Public Law and the State, 1100–1322.* Princeton Univ. Press.

RACKMAN, EMANUEL 1955 *Israel's Emerging Constitution: 1948–1951.* New York: Columbia Univ. Press.

SCHACHT, JOSEPH 1964 *An Introduction to Islamic Law.* Oxford: Clarendon.

TIERNEY, BRIAN 1955 *Foundations of the Conciliar Theory: The Contributions of the Medieval Canonists From Gratian to the Great Schism.* Cambridge Univ. Press.

TIERNEY, BRIAN 1964 *The Crisis of Church and State 1050–1300, With Selected Documents.* Englewood Cliffs, N.J.: Prentice-Hall. → See especially "The Age of the Lawyers," pages 97–157.

ULLMANN, WALTER 1949 *Medieval Papalism: The Political Theories of the Medieval Canonists.* London: Methuen.

CANTILLON, RICHARD

Richard Cantillon (1680?–1734), author of the *Essai sur la nature du commerce en général* (1755), is considered by many to be the earliest writer on economic matters who might appropriately be described as an "economist," because his analysis encompassed the price system and its workings. He was of Irish birth, directly descended from Roger Cantillon, who in 1556 married Elizabeth Stuart (the Cantillons were Stuart partisans). The family had been established in County Kerry, Ireland, since the twelfth century and could trace its ancestry to a companion of William the Conqueror. In 1716 Cantillon settled in Paris (where many Stuart supporters lived) and successfully engaged in banking and trade. A shrewd and perceptive financier, Cantillon foresaw the failure of John Law's scheme. (Law's animosity caused Cantillon to quit Paris temporarily in 1719.) Cantillon undertook to profit from the failure and, upon the collapse of Law's scheme in 1720, realized a great fortune. The remaining 14 years of his life were spent largely in the Low Countries, France, Italy, and London; he died in London in 1734, murdered by his recently discharged cook.

In his *Essai* Cantillon dealt with many of the topics subsequently of concern to classical and neoclassical economists. Among these topics are population growth and its distribution; the determination of prices, wages, and interest; the role of the entrepreneur (which he was the first to isolate); banking operations and the financing of trade; and the response of exchange rates and the price structure to changes in the supply of money. He seems to have conceived of a state's economy as an essentially autonomous subsystem in which the major functions are performed by landowners, entrepreneurs, and persons working for hire. Unlike the medieval writers on the subject, he was little concerned with ethical considerations; he found them "outside my subject." When possible, he reduced his analyses to terms of supply and demand.

Population movements in space and time reflect underlying costs and demands. Variation in mortality, internal migration, and (above all) nuptiality and (hence) natality adjust population to the means made available for its support within social classes and regions, given prevailing standards of living and the structure of demand. The structure of demand is dominated by the expenditure patterns of rich landowners. Cantillon thus made the size of a closed economy's population depend mainly upon the domestic food supply and prevailing (although variable) standards of life; but he showed that this supply is susceptible of augmentation through the importation of land-embodying produce or of diminution through its exportation in exchange for labor-embodying wrought goods. He examined the relation between the distribution of population in space and the conduct of marketing and transport, noting, among other things, that too much activity is concentrated in cities with the result that transportation costs are excessive.

Although Cantillon did not put forward a functional theory of distribution, he did attempt to explain commodity and factor prices. He defined the "intrinsic value" of goods in terms of the land and labor entering into their production; but he noted that actual or "market" price may exceed or fall short of this value. He treated land rent as a surplus. Interest varies not with the supply of money but with the comparative number of lenders and borrowers and their circumstances. The price of labor tends to approximate its cost; it varies with the workers' standards of living (which can be elastic upward) and in some instances with other supply-regulating conditions, such as costs of training craftsmen. He looked upon profit (or loss) as a concomitant of the risks and "uncertainty" that entrepreneurs bear when organizing production and distribution, for while they contract for land, labor, etc., at stipulated prices, they can dispose of their output only at such prices as rule at the time of sale.

The value of money is but a special case of value in general. The amount of real cash for which a state or economy has need approximates in value one-ninth "of all the produce of the soil," given ruling habits of payment and monetary velocity together with equilibrium in international payments. The purchasing power of gold and silver coins normally corresponds closely to their intrinsic value, although their purchasing power is sensitive to a country's debtor or creditor status, which conditions both its rate of exchange and the domestic market price for gold. A country's rate of exchange depends mainly upon the state of its trade balance.

Cantillon's analysis of the impact of increases in the money supply was particularly insightful. He distinguished the principal sources of such increase (that is, mines, a favorable trade balance, foreign travelers) and then traced, for each type of increase, its distribution and its various effects upon wages, salaries, rents, patterns of expenditure, and different prices. Although he believed it advantageous to a state to have an abundance of money, he indicated that increase in its supply would eventually elevate costs and prices expressed in money and result in a flow of precious metals abroad. Conversely, falling prices would attract money from abroad. He thus recognized the self-regulating specie-flow mechanism, although he did not define it as precisely as did Hume.

The *Essai* was not published until 1755, though a manuscript copy was known and used by Malachy Postlethwayt and Mirabeau, and may have been known to others (for instance, Joseph Harris, David Hume, Josiah Tucker). It became known after publication to a number of important eighteenth-century writers and influenced some of them, although only one translation, in Italian, was made (in 1767). Representative of the writers who knew or were influenced by the *Essai* were some of the physiocrats, a variety of other French authors (for example, J. C. M. V. Gournay, Accarias de Serionne, Turgot, Condillac, André Morellet, G. B. de Mably, Abbé F. A. A. Pluquet, G. Garnier), Arthur Young, Adam Smith, James Steuart, G. A. Will, J. A. Graumann, J. G. Busch, J. F. von Pfeiffer, C. M. de Jovellanos, Beccaria, F. Ferrara, and (apparently) C. Filangieri and A. Genovesi. During the first three-quarters of the nineteenth century Cantillon's work was referred to only occasionally, although some of his ideas continued to exercise influence anonymously. Interest revived, however, after W. S. Jevons called the *Essai*'s merits to the attention of economists in

1881. Since then at least five new editions have been published, a facsimile in 1892, and editions in German and French–English in 1931, Spanish in 1950, and French in 1952.

Joseph J. Spengler

[*For the historical context of Cantillon's work, see the biography of* Aquinas. *For discussion of the subsequent development of his ideas, see the biographies of* Condillac; Hume; Law, John; Smith, Adam; Steuart; Turgot.]

BIBLIOGRAPHY

Cantillon, Richard (1775) 1952 *Essai sur la nature du commerce en général.* Paris: Institut National d'Études Démographiques.

Estapé, Fabián 1951 Algunos comentarios a la publicación del *Ensayo sobre la naturaleza del comercio en general,* de Cantillon. *Moneda y credito* 39:38–77.

Jevons, W. S. 1881 Richard Cantillon and the Nationality of Political Economy. *Contemporary Review* 39: 61–80.

Spengler, Joseph J. 1954 Richard Cantillon: First of the Moderns. *Journal of Political Economy* 62:281–295, 406–424.

CAPITAL

Capital is necessary because production takes time (Smith 1776; Ricardo 1817; Fisher 1907). The inputs have to be put in and paid for over an interval before they result in outputs available for sale. This is true whether the input consists of equipment that is needed right at the beginning (*fixed capital*) or of materials that have to be put in continuously during the process of production (*working capital*). A producer therefore needs a stock of *money capital* out of which to pay for input over this interval. Only after the interval, during which he will have turned his money capital into *real capital* (the stock of goods in process from input to output), can he begin to use the inflow of proceeds from output to cover the outflow of payments for input, and he will therefore not need any more capital.

The existence of the interval is obscured by the continuous flows of input and output in "sausage machine" types of production. (We are leaving for later consideration the need for acquiring the machine itself and, for the moment, are concentrating on the working capital alone.) The interval between the input of a particular piece of "meat" into the machine and the output of the "sausage" containing that piece of meat may seem insignificant, and the quantity of real capital (the meat that is at any moment on the way from the input point to the output point of the production process) may seem negligible. The two flows may even be said to be "synchronized," or "simultaneous," which suggests that there is no interval between them at all (Stigler 1941, chapter 11).

"Width" and "depth" of capital.   The quantity of capital needed for a productive process depends, of course, on the volume of production. Two factories instead of one, working in exactly the same way, with twice the input and twice the output, will naturally require twice as much capital as well. This has been called the "width" of capital. But the quantity of capital needed is also directly related to the length of the interval between input and output. This has been called "depth" of capital (Hawtrey 1937). If it takes five minutes for the meat put into the machine to come out as sausage, the "meat capital" will correspond to the quantity of meat put in during five minutes. If the interval is ten minutes, twice as much meat capital is required for the same rate of input and output. This may seem negligible, but if the meat has to be brought to the factory each morning and the sausages produced are taken away the next morning, the interval for the factory is 24 hours and the meat capital corresponds to a day's input of meat.

The relationship between the length of the interval and the quantity of capital needed is seen most easily in imaginary cases of "point input–point output" production (of which our sausage machine is an example if we consider only the meat input). If we suppose that the making of wine requires nothing more than one day's work in making the barrel and squeezing the (freely available) grapes and one year of waiting for the juice to turn into wine, then an established winery will consist of a capital stock of 365 barrels of maturing wine for each barrel in the daily input of grape juice or output of one-year-old wine. The depth of capital corresponds to the length of the interval or, its equivalent, the ratio of the *stock* of capital to the *flow* of input or output.

The average period of production.   There may also be many different intervals between input and output. If the meat is brought to our sausage factory every morning but the sausages are collected and paid for only on Monday mornings (and the factory works a continuous seven-day week), then the capital needed corresponds to the *average interval*. For the meat brought in on Sunday morning the interval is one day; Saturday's meat has a two-day interval and Monday's meat a seven-day interval until it is taken away as sausage the following Monday. The average interval is four days, and the quantity of meat capital needed will be equal to four units (four days' input of meat), since

that will be the *average stock* of meat in the factory. On Mondays there will be just one unit, on Tuesdays two units, and on Sundays seven units.

It might seem that seven units of capital are needed, corresponding to the *total* period of seven days, since the producer has to buy meat for seven days before he gets any proceeds from the sale of sausages. But this is true only if he has to have on hand every Monday morning all the money to pay for the whole week's purchases of meat. In that case the appropriate input is not the daily input of meat but the input of the *money* for a whole week's meat every Monday morning. The interval from input to output is then from Monday morning to Monday morning, or seven days. But if the producer does not need to hold any money idle, he needs only the four units of capital corresponding to the average interval of four days. In the first three days of the week he needs as capital only one, two, and three units, respectively, and he can lend to others the difference between this and his four units of capital: namely three, two, and one units. During the last three days of the week, when he needs five, six, and seven units, he can borrow the difference of one, two, and three units from others—an exactly equivalent amount.

Another way of seeing this is to suppose that a producer sets up seven such factories, each selling its sausages on a different day of the week. For this he would need one unit of capital the first day for the first factory, two more units on the second day (one for the second day of the first factory and one for starting the second factory), three more units on the third day (one for starting the third factory and two for the first two factories), and so on: one unit more each day than the previous day until the seventh day when he would need seven more units. On the eighth day the first factory's weekly output of seven units becomes available, and its proceeds can pay for the daily input of all seven; every day after that another factory's output becomes available. The total amount of capital required is therefore $1 + 2 + 3 + 4 + 5 + 6 + 7$, or 28, which is just four units per factory and equal to four times the daily input of the seven factories.

All this of course refers only to the "meat capital," which stands for the raw materials and other inputs involved in current production and in the maintenance of the factory—the labor, the raw materials, the electricity, the window cleaning, and all such things. There remains the capital needed for equipment, which usually comes to a much greater amount. It corresponds to the average interval between the input (elsewhere) of resources into the production of the equipment and the output (in our factory) of the services of the equipment.

Capital and ownership.   It would be possible for an individual producer to manage without any capital if he could *buy the services* yielded by all the capital items involved in his line of production without owning any of them (or, what comes to the same thing, if he could *rent* the capital items from their owners). He would then be paying out a current flow of money for the current flow of input to his factory, and he would be receiving a current flow of money from the current flow of his output, earning the excess of the money inflow over the outflow (or losing the deficiency).

But to manage in this way without any capital he would have to find others who own all the capital items, including the working capital or goods in process—the "meat capital." Such arrangements are unusual. Normally the producer finds it more convenient and more economical to acquire ownership of most of the capital goods—at the very least, the working capital—even if he has to borrow money capital for this. He needs capital to the extent that he finds it more convenient, more efficient, or more economical to *own* the sources of services involved in his productive activity than to *buy* the services or to rent the sources.

Capital and accumulation.   This difference between owning the sources and renting them (or buying their services) from someone else is crucial to the individual producer. But it is of no use whatever from the social point of view, because from the social point of view *there is no someone else.* Society can acquire additional productive services only by bringing into existence additional sources of such services. This involves the slow process of *accumulation,* or *net investment,* which is the production of more than is being used up during a period—that is, a period in which input exceeds (final consumption) output.

The social average period of production.   It is obvious that society must have accumulated in previous periods all the capital in existence at any point in time. This includes both the "meat," or "working," capital and the fixed capital involved in the equipment, which may come to many times the working capital. Not quite as obvious is the fixed capital that normally has to be sunk in learning how to operate the factory smoothly and efficiently.

Nor is this all. From the social point of view it is also necessary to consider the capital that must have been accumulated for industries that produce the sausage-making equipment, including their working capital, their equipment, and their initial growing pains. These industries in turn depend on more generalized industries such as transportation, electricity, fuel, and so on. A similar proliferation appears when we consider what is necessary for the provision of the current input. The "meat" producers need both capital and current input, and their providers depend on yet other industries whose capital must have been accumulated, and so on.

Still another set of proliferations appears if we look in the other direction—that in which the output of our factory goes. In some cases our "sausages" are in turn the raw material of other industries, which cannot take our supply until they have built up their own stock of capital. Even then these industries cannot be our regular customers until their own customers have themselves built up capital and made connections with suppliers and customers and so on.

However, this seemingly endless proliferation does not make our problem unmanageable. We are saved by two considerations. First, the different proliferations overlap. Many of them involve links to the same industries, and their total number is no greater than the finite number of industries in the economy as a whole. Second, the social point of view cannot limit itself to the input and the output from our sausage factory. The *social output* is the net product of all the final goods and services that constitute consumption and accumulation in the economy as a whole—those products that are consumed by the citizens and those that are not consumed but are added to the capital stock of the economy. The *social input* is the total of productive services available to the economy from its labor force, its natural resources, and its accumulated stock of capital. The *social capital* corresponds to the average interval between the application of the productive services and their emergence (as either consumption or accumulation) after passing through the different industries that are the stages in the production of the final social output. (We stipulate *net* and *final* to avoid double, or rather multiple, counting. We do not want to count the meat, the sausage that contains it, and the restaurant meal that includes the sausage.) This average interval for the economy as a whole, to which the social capital stock corresponds, is called the *social average period of production* (Böhm-Bawerk 1884–1912; Dorfman 1959).

"Corresponds" is a deliberately ambiguous expression. Under certain assumed special conditions the ambiguity disappears. One then can say that the value of the net flow of input is equal to the value of the net flow of output and that the average period of production is equal to the ratio of the value of the capital stock to the value of each of these flows—namely, to both the *capital–input ratio* and the *capital–output ratio*. If the average period of production is three years then the capital–input ratio and the capital–output ratio will each be 3:1 (the input and the output flows being measured at annual rates).

The assumptions under which these relationships hold are indeed abstract and unreal, but they help us to see the nature of more complicated, but more realistic, conditions. The special assumptions are *a stationary economy* and *a zero rate of interest*.

The stationary economy

Implicit in a stationary economy are an unchanging technology, a constant supply of labor services, a given stock of land yielding a constant flow of land services, and an unchanging stock of capital goods.

The constant supply of labor services implies not only a constant population but in addition the absence of changes in skills, education, training levels, and the proportion of workers in the total population. The given supply of land constitutes the "original and indestructible properties of the soil" of the classical economists, where "original" means that land can never be produced (by men) and where "indestructible" means that in the normal course of events the supply and the fertility of land never diminishes.

The unchanging stock of capital goods existing at any moment has been produced by labor and land services in the past and is contributing to the production of consumption goods and services that will become available only in the future. It is unchanging in its composition because each item, as it gets a day older, takes the place of a similar item one day older and is replaced by a similar item one day younger. The very oldest item of each kind is completely used up and disappears, while the one-day-old item is replaced by a newly created one. The stock of capital goods may thus be viewed as consisting of congealed past labor and land services waiting to be turned into future consumption goods or services.

The existing stock of capital goods, of course, has been produced by land and labor services, working not by themselves but in cooperation with other capital goods that existed in the past; but this does not change the essence of the matter. We need only go back further into the past to the land and labor services that went into the making of the other capital goods, then to those that went into the still more remote capital goods that contributed

to the production of these later goods, and so on. Similarly the currently existing capital goods will be used not only to produce future consumption goods and services but also to make further capital goods in the future. This again means only that we must go still further into the future to the consumption goods and services that will be produced by these capital goods, then to those that will be produced by the capital goods that these future capital goods will help to produce, and so on. The longer the interval between the original application of land and labor services and their final emergence in consumption goods and services, the larger the capital stock constituting the volume of congealed past services that at any moment in time are still on their way to their final transformation into future consumption goods.

This stationary economy is essentially a very simple model, but many find it very difficult to use because they tend to forget that it is only a model of an imaginary economy that has been in exactly the same condition since time immemorial and that is expected to remain so for ever. They are therefore disturbed at its being nothing like a true account of the actual past and nothing like a plausible prognosis of the future.

This model contains the essence of the theory of capital as developed by Eugen von Böhm-Bawerk (1884–1912). Since the 1930s there has been a tendency to neglect Böhm-Bawerk because without the implausible assumption of a zero-interest rate (which would induce the owners of capital and of land to consume more than their possibly very small incomes and, thus, to disrupt the stationary economy) it seemed impossible to maintain his basic tenet—the equality of the capital–input ratio, the capital–output ratio, and the average period of production. [*See* BÖHM-BAWERK.]

A zero-interest model. The assumption of a zero rate of interest in the model is what gives us the equality between the value of the *present* capital stock and of the *past* flow of land and labor services congealed in it. Unless these values are just equal, it would be profitable to increase or decrease the stock of capital goods, rather than maintain the stationary economy by merely replacing them when they wear out. Similarly, the zero rate of interest is what makes the value of the *present* capital stock just equal to the value of the *future* flow of consumption into which the capital stock will be transformed. Thus, it is only at a zero rate of interest, when the *date* on which goods or services exist or are performed does not matter, that the capital–input ratio, the capital–output ratio, and the average period of production are equal to one another.

A positive-interest model.   It is possible to construct a slightly less implausible model of a stationary economy with a positive, instead of a zero, rate of interest. At a sufficiently high rate of interest, the owners of property would on the average want to keep it for the sake of its yield and not consume any of it. The stationary economy could then persist. The capital stock would still incorporate a quantity of past land and labor services equal to their rate of flow of input over the average period of production and would still be the source of an aggregate future consumption equal to the rate of flow of output over the same average period of production. But the *values* would no longer coincide.

In this model the value of the current stock of capital goods must *exceed* the value of the incorporated land and labor services by the interest that can be earned on them during the interval between their input and the current date. Otherwise it would pay to increase or to decrease the capital stock. The capital–input ratio is *greater* than the average period of production. At the same time the value of the future consumption output from the capital stock must exceed the value of the current capital stock by the interest that can be earned on this stock from the present until the appearance of the future consumption output. The capital–output ratio is therefore *less* than the average period of production.

These apparent departures from the average-period-of-production theory of capital are however only the result of an *incomplete* introduction of interest into the theory. If there is a positive rate of interest *the services of the capital stock* cannot be disregarded (as they quite properly were disregarded in the zero-interest model, in which such services are free goods and not economic goods). They must be treated as input on a par with land services and labor services. Bringing these into the model removes the excess of the value of the flow of output over the value of the flow of input, since that excess is precisely equal to the missing value of the flow of the uncounted input of capital services and thus restores the equalities of Böhm-Bawerkian capital theory.

In such a model, properly corrected for a positive rate of interest, we have stocks of land, labor, and capital yielding flows of land services, labor services, and capital services. Every capital good begins to yield capital services from the moment of its creation and continues to do so until the moment of its complete disappearance into consumption. The average interval between the application of land, labor, and *capital* services and the emergence of the final output of consumption goods is *shorter* than the average period of production, in terms of the "original" factors of production (land and labor) alone, because the capital services continue to be applied *later* in the productive process by the stock of congealed past labor, land, and capital services. The value of the capital stock is just equal to the value of the current flow of input (or the value of the current flow of output) multiplied by the corrected average period of production, which in turn is just equal to the corrected capital–input ratio as well as to the corrected capital–output ratio (Lerner 1965).

Private capital and social investment.   So far we have been following the traditional simplifying assumption that every nonhuman source of productive services is either both producible and consumable, in which case we called it capital, or is neither producible nor consumable ("original and indestructible"), in which case we called it land. But there are also sources of productive services that are producible but not consumable, such as tunnels through hard rock or land reclaimed from the sea, and there are sources that are consumable but not producible, such as fossil fuels or ore deposits, which are *used up* when they are used. Such phenomena do not fit into the classical average-period-of-production theory of capital. We also touched on a somewhat disturbing difference between the individual and the social aspects of capital when we noted that the individual producer is concerned with the extent to which he should *own* sources of productive services, while society is concerned with the extent to which it is possible and desirable to *produce* (or to refrain from consuming) such sources. Both of these difficulties can be settled at the same time by a clarification of the relationships between *capital* and *investment*.

For the individual it does not matter whether the sources of productive services are producible or consumable or both or neither. If he does not want to own the sources, preferring to buy the services (or rent the sources) from someone else, he needs no capital. But if he wants to own *any* source of productive services he needs *capital funds* to enable him to buy it.

For society as a whole, which cannot buy productive services (or rent their sources) from someone else, the only problem is how much to produce of producible sources and how much to consume (or refrain from consuming) of consumable sources. This is another way of saying that society is never faced with problems of acquisition or disposal of stocks of *capital goods* against money or credit. It can only decide on the rates at which it *invests* in the production of producible sources and *disinvests* by consuming consumable sources.

The productivity of capital and the return on investment. The theory of capital is necessary to explain why investment yields a positive return. The explanation is that a period in which input exceeds output, which is the essence of investment, increases the quantity of sources of capital services (and therefore the supply of these services also) in relation to other services. If the economy had all the capital goods that could be of any use, then investment could not increase productive capacity and would not yield any positive return. But as long as a longer average period of production (which means having a larger stock of producible and consumable sources of productive services) or a larger stock of other nonhuman sources of productive services permits a larger total output, capital is productive. The increase in total output due to the existence of a larger stock of capital (with its larger flow of productive services) constitutes the marginal productivity of capital.

The marginal productivity of capital is denied by the labor theory of value, which says that only labor produces value. But in recognizing that the total product is greater when there is more capital (or more land), the supporters of the labor theory of value in essence confess their failure to provide a tenable theory of exchange value (as distinct from postulating an ethical judgment as to how the product ought to be distributed). The marginal productivity of labor means only that a larger quantity of labor (used together with the same amount of other productive services) results in a larger product, which is true as long as labor is not a free good but is "scarce." But a larger quantity of capital also results in a larger product, as long as capital is not a free good but is "scarce." To say that only labor is productive and that an increase in capital merely increases the productivity of labor makes no more sense than to say that only capital (or only land) is productive and that an increase in the quantity of labor merely increases the productivity of capital (or of land). [*See* PRODUCTION *and* VALUE, LABOR THEORY OF.]

It is possible for the marginal productivity of labor to fall to zero (in countries that prevent extreme poverty), because of a natural tendency for population to increase indefinitely. But it is not possible for the marginal productivity of capital to fall to zero, because there seems to be no natural tendency for capital to increase indefinitely. The preference for current, over future, consumption and the expectation that technical progress will make future consumption levels higher than pres-

ent levels will stop any net investment, and therefore any increase, in the capital stock as soon as the rate of return on investment falls below that required to offset these considerations.

The rate of return on investment measures the extent to which a sacrifice of (potential) current consumption permits future consumption to be increased by more than the current sacrifice. If the sacrifice of 100 units of consumption goods this year permits an increase of 110 units in next year's consumption (all other future outputs remaining the same), then the rate of return is 10 per cent per annum. Consumption of the 110 units available next year can be postponed for another year. If there is no change in the general situation, this will again yield 10 per cent for a combined total of 121 units from a two-year postponement of 100 units. It is also possible to consume 10 of the 110 and to reinvest the remaining 100, which would yield 110 again the following year. Each successive year the same procedure can be repeated. In this way there can be a permanent return of 10 per cent per annum on the investment.

Investment and interest. The marginal rate of return on investment will vary inversely with the volume of investment, since at a higher rate of return (required, say, to pay interest at a higher rate on the money borrowed for the investment) fewer investments will qualify.

For the individual, perfectly competitive firm this tendency would not show itself as a downward sloping investment curve with respect to the rate of interest. A fall in the rate of interest would cause the firm to reconsider the technique it was using and to buy (or rent) more capital goods at once so as to have the greater ratio of capital (and of capital services) relative to other productive services that is appropriate at the lower interest rate. But for the economy as a whole (unless there are unemployed productive resources freely available, in which case all of the economics that deals with scarcity is irrelevant) additional capital goods can be provided only by the slow process of shifting resources from the production of consumption goods and services to the production (or preservation) of sources of productive services. This is *investing.*

Investing by the economy as a whole comes about through the attempts of firms to increase their capital. Suppose that increased thriftiness causes the monetary authorities to lower the rate of interest in order to prevent unemployment. The reduction of the rate of interest makes it worth while for the competitive firms to try to buy more capital. They cannot *succeed* in increasing the total of the capital stock owned by all of them together, since they can only buy capital goods from one another. But their *attempt* has the effect of raising the prices of the capital goods. This induces the manufacturers of capital goods to increase their output, drawing the needed extra resources from a reduction in the output of consumption goods. The increase in the rate of output of capital goods raises their costs of production. An equilibrium is reached at that increase in the rate of output of capital goods which makes marginal costs equal to the higher prices. This determines the increase in the rate of investment, for the economy as a whole, that goes with a reduction in the rate of interest (and conversely, of course, for a decrease in thriftiness).

If the process starts from a stationary equilibrium, with zero net investment, the rate of net investment becomes positive. As this proceeds the stock of capital goods increases, while their prices fall, and the rate of investment begins to move down again. Meanwhile, the firms can succeed in increasing the ratio of capital services to other productive services. When the stock of capital goods has increased enough to satisfy the greater thriftiness, consumption will have increased enough to absorb the whole net output of the economy once more and investment will have fallen to zero again in a new stationary equilibrium with a lower rate of interest.

Nonstationary models

To make the analysis "dynamic," let us substitute for the implausible assumption that the future is unchanging and known the much more implausible assumption that the future is continually changing but is still known. We may then imagine that each firm, given a known time shape (i.e., the value at every future date) of all prices (including interest rates), will fix on that dynamic time shape of all planned future inputs and outputs which maximizes the present value of the firm. The time shape of net investment, instead of being constant at zero (with gross investment just enough to offset the constant depreciation and depletion of capital), will be changing over time (and will be equal to the changing difference between input and output). But in both cases this time shape will be different for different expectations. In both cases a change in expectations would make the firms want to revise their (static or dynamic) plans, beginning with an immediate adjustment of their stock of capital. In both cases there will be a determinate limit to the change in the *social* rate of investment,

as a result of increasing costs in the capital goods industries as their rate of production increases. In both cases we see that from the social point of view changes in prices (including interest rates) are not exogenous data (as they appear to be to the perfectly competitive firm) but are part of the mechanism through which changes in the basic conditions (including expectations) work themselves out on the firms' demand for capital goods, on the prices of these goods, and thus on their *net supply,* which constitutes the social investment (Stigler 1941).

Marginal productivities and efficiencies.   A country, industry, or firm will be interested in *both* capital and investment if it is not so small as to have no significant effect on the prices at which it buys or sells or if it has internal resistances to changes in the proportion between the factors of production (so that any change is more difficult if it is done more rapidly). To deal with this difficulty we must define four concepts: the marginal productivity of investing (mpI), the marginal productivity of capital (mpK), the marginal efficiency of investing (meI), and the marginal efficiency of capital (meK).

We define mpI as the additional quantity of investment goods (i.e., capital goods or sources of productive services) that can be produced by the sacrifice of an additional unit of current consumption goods. (For consumable, but nonproducible, sources of productive services it is the additional quantity that remains as the result of sacrificing an additional unit of consumption.)

We define mpK as the additional flow of output due to the use of an additional unit of sources of productive services.

The product of these two is meI—the additional flow of future output from that addition to the stock of productive sources that results from the reduction of current consumption by one unit. The rate of investment will be in equilibrium when meI is equal to the rate of interest. This will be the case when expected additions to future output, discounted at the appropriate rates of interest, are equal in value to the unit of current consumption sacrificed. The meI is what Keynes called "the marginal efficiency of capital" (Keynes 1936).

Every firm will have a planned time shape of its future activities and, consequently, of its capital stock, in which the size of the latter will at each point in time be such as to make the marginal rate of return on owning it—the value of the marginal (flows of) output plus the expected increase in its price—equal to the expected rate of interest for the corresponding period; otherwise the firm would want to have a larger or a smaller stock of capital goods. The firm's marginal rate of return on the capital goods it owns might therefore be called the *meK*. However, we have seen that the attempts by firms to change the size of their capital stocks does not directly affect the total quantities—only the prices. It is therefore better to keep *meK* to describe a condition where not only *the rate of investment* but the *stock of capital* in the economy is in equilibrium.

Steady growth models. One situation of equilibrium is that in which there is a constant rate of growth for the economy as a whole with no changes in the ratio between any two of its elements. The ratio of net investment to capital stock constitutes the rate of growth of capital and must therefore be equal to the rate of growth of the entire economy. The quantity of capital can then be said to be in a moving equilibrium.

Therefore *meK* is best defined as the *meI* when the quantity of capital is in equilibrium. Only then will *meK* and *meI* both be equal to the rate of interest (Lerner 1965).

A special case of the steady-growth model, which was at the center of most capital theory until the "post-Keynesian" developments in economic theory (mainly in Cambridge, England), is the *stationary state*, in which the absolute quantity of capital has reached equilibrium and in which the ratio of investment to the capital stock is not merely constant but zero (i.e., equal to the zero rate of growth). The actual world is seen as one of disequilibrium, in which the quantity of capital has not reached the equilibrium level, so that *meK* is above *meI* and above the rate of interest. This is why investment takes place. The rate of investment is that which brings *meI* into equality with the rate of interest. The continuing positive investment is, however, continually increasing the stock of capital and using up the opportunities for investment. The rate of investment asymptotically falls to zero as *meK* asymptotically falls to equality with both *meI* and the rate of interest.

A satisfactory level of employment therefore depends on the maintenance of investment sufficient to absorb all the saving that would be undertaken at such an employment level. This could be attained by any of the following factors in sufficient strength: reduction of total saving through government dissaving; encouragement of private investment through reduction of the rate of interest; an excess of capital-using, over capital-saving, inventions; investments or grants from rich countries for the development of poor countries; the destruction of capital in wars or in natural catastrophes; or some combination of such factors. [*See* ECONOMIC GROWTH, *article on* MATHEMATICAL THEORY.]

Modern mathematical models. The foregoing is becoming an old-fashioned approach. Modern capital theory tends more to the development of mathematical models of growth that attempt to deal with many kinds of capital goods and consumption goods; with independent changes in population, given the stock of land (which in the constant-rate-of-growth models was supposed to have grown in step with capital in efficiency terms); with technical progress, both neutral (on various definitions) and biased, as between being capital saving or capital using; and with the introduction of uncertainty about the future. It is hoped by these means to arrive at growth models that will be more directly related to the actual world than are the traditional disequilibrium models that were assumed to be moving toward imaginary stationary states. If these efforts are successful, some light may be thrown on the still unsolved problems of how to bring more rapid economic growth to the poorer countries, whose apparent falling further and further behind the richer countries threatens the future of all.

ABBA P. LERNER

[*See also* INTEREST *and* LAND.]

BIBLIOGRAPHY

BLAUG, MARK 1962 *Economic Theory in Retrospect.* Homewood, Ill.: Irwin. → See especially Chapter 12. Also contains useful notes on the literature.

BÖHM-BAWERK, EUGEN VON (1884–1912) 1959 *Capital and Interest.* 3 vols. South Holland, Ill.: Libertarian Press. → First published in German.

DORFMAN, ROBERT 1959 Waiting and the Period of Production. *Quarterly Journal of Economics* 73:351–372.

EDELBERG, VICTOR 1933 The Ricardian Theory of Profit. *Economica* 13:51–74.

FISHER, IRVING 1907 *The Rate of Interest: Its Nature, Determination and Relation to Economic Phenomena.* New York: Macmillan.

HAAVELMO, TRYGVE 1960 *A Study in the Theory of Investment.* Univ. of Chicago Press.

HAHN, F. H.; and MATTHEWS, R. C. O. 1964 The Theory of Economic Growth: A Survey. *Economic Journal* 74:779–902. → Contains an extensive bibliography.

HAWTREY, RALPH G. (1937) 1952 *Capital and Employment.* 2d ed. London and New York: Longmans. → See especially Chapters 2 and 3.

INTERNATIONAL ECONOMIC ASSOCIATION 1961 *The Theory of Capital: Proceedings of a Conference Held by the International Economic Association.* Edited by F. A. Lutz and D. C. Hague. New York: St. Martins.

KALDOR, NICHOLAS (1937) 1960 The Controversy on the Theory of Capital. Pages 153–305 in Nicholas Kaldor,

Essays on Value and Distribution. Glencoe, Ill.: Free Press.

KEYNES, JOHN MAYNARD 1936 *The General Theory of Employment, Interest and Money.* London: Macmillan. → A paperback edition was published in 1965 by Harcourt.

LERNER, ABBA P. 1944 *The Economics of Control: Principles of Welfare Economics.* New York: Macmillan. → See especially Chapters 20 and 25.

LERNER, ABBA P. 1965 On Some Recent Developments in Capital Theory. *American Economic Review* 55, no. 2:284–295.

RICARDO, DAVID (1817) 1962 *Principles of Political Economy and Taxation.* London: Dent; New York: Dutton. → A paperback edition was published in 1963 by Irwin. See especially Chapter 1, sections 2, 4, and 5.

SMITH, ADAM (1776) 1952 *An Inquiry Into the Nature and Causes of the Wealth of Nations.* Great Books of the Western World, Vol. 39. Chicago: Encyclopaedia Britannica. → See especially Book 2, Chapters 1 and 3. A two-volume paperback edition was published in 1963 by Irwin.

STIGLER, GEORGE J. 1941 *Production and Distribution Theories: 1870–1895.* New York: Macmillan.

WICKSELL, KNUT (1901) 1951 *Lectures on Political Economy.* Volume 1: General Theory. London: Routledge. → First published in Swedish. See especially Part 2.

WICKSELL, KNUT (1911) 1958 Böhm-Bawerk's Theory of Capital. Pages 176–185 in Knut Wicksell, *Selected Papers on Economic Theory.* London: Allen & Unwin. → First published in *Ekonomisk tidskrift.*

CAPITAL, HUMAN

The idea of capital has long had a strong materialistic bent that is evident in the dominance of material capital in economic thinking. The logical basis of an all-inclusive concept of capital, which includes human capital, was established by Irving Fisher (1906). This concept treats all sources of income streams as forms of capital. These sources include not only such material forms as natural resources and reproducible producer and consumer goods and commodities but also such human forms as the inherited and acquired abilities of producers and consumers. Yet the core of economics with respect to this matter concentrates on producer goods, particularly on structures, equipment, and inventories, with little or no attention to the abilities of human beings, even though human resources are much the larger source of income streams.

An approach to capital that includes human capital has two major advantages. The first arises out of the fact that by taking both human capital and material capital into account, a number of biases in economics would be corrected. The overemphasis of material sources of income streams is one of them. Closely related are the imbalances in investment programs of countries where investment in human capital is not an integral part of such programs. Another is the mistaken inference that the real capital–income ratio is necessarily declining over time when the observed ratio of material capital to income falls. Still another is the belief that the productivity of the economy as a whole increases as rapidly as total output rises, relative to measured inputs, although the estimates of inputs fail to include many improvements in the quality of both material factors and human agents. These improvements in quality are the product of investment and thus are forms of capital. There are strong reasons, both theoretical and empirical, to support the inference that in value terms the productivity of the U.S. economy, for example, has remained approximately constant for many decades. [*See* PRODUCTIVITY.] An all-inclusive concept of capital also provides a framework for determining how closely the private and public sectors of an economy come to an optimum in investing in each of the sources of income streams.

The other major advantage of the concept of human capital is in analyzing the various organized activities that augment those human abilities which raise real income prospects. People acquire both producer and consumer abilities. Many of these abilities are clearly the product of investment. There are important unsettled questions about economic growth, changes in the pattern of wages and salaries and the personal distribution of income, that can be resolved once investment in human capital is taken into account. There are also biases in the way the labor force is measured, and in the treatment of public expenditure for education and medical care that can be corrected by using the concept of human capital.

Inherited and acquired abilities. The philosopher–economist Adam Smith boldly included all useful abilities of the inhabitants of a country, whether inherited or acquired, as part of capital. These two sorts of abilities, however, differ importantly in the formation of human capital.

Migration and population growth aside, inherited abilities of a population are akin to the original properties of land in the sense that they are "given by nature" in any time period that is meaningful for economic analysis. Any genetic drift that affects the distribution and level of these abilities occurs so slowly that it is of no relevance in economic analysis. It seems to be true also that the distribution of inherited abilities within any large population remains, for all practical purposes, constant over time and that the distribution of these abilities is approximately the same whether a country is poor or rich, backward or modern, provided the population is large.

But the picture is quite otherwise in the case of acquired abilities having economic value. The formation and maintenance of these abilities are analogous to the formation and maintenance of reproducible material capital. These abilities are obviously subject to depreciation and obsolescences. The distribution and level of acquired abilities can be altered importantly during a time span that matters in economic analysis. Historically they have been altered vastly in countries that have developed a modern economy. In this respect the difference between poor and rich, backward and modern, countries is indeed great. The level of acquired abilities that have economic value is very high in a few countries while it is still exceedingly low in most countries. The truth is that the amount of human capital per worker, or per million inhabitants, varies greatly among countries.

The acquired abilities that raise income prospects are of many types and differ from country to country, depending upon differences in the demand for these abilities and upon differences in the opportunities to supply them. They also are augmented in different ways, depending in part on the type of abilities and in part on the process of investing in them. Some abilities are acquired through informal and essentially unorganized activities, which is the case with most learning in the home and learning from informal community experiences. Others are acquired through organized activities that are, as a rule, also specialized; these include schooling, most on-the-job training, and many adult programs to improve the skills and knowledge of those participating [see ADULT EDUCATION; LABOR FORCE, article on PARTICIPATION]. People also improve their future earning abilities through medical care, by acquiring job and other types of information about the economic system, and by migrating to take better jobs.

The formation of human capital, especially through those activities which have become organized and specialized in a modern economy, is of a magnitude to alter radically the conventional estimates of savings and capital formation. These forms of human capital are the source of many additional income streams contributing to economic growth. They also alter wages and salaries, in both absolute and relative terms, and the share of the national income from earnings relative to that from property over time.

Biases related to the omission of human capital

Instead of developing and using a general concept that includes human capital, economists have predominantly used a concept restricted to classes of wealth that are bought and sold. Irving Fisher, in a series of papers published just before the turn of the century and then in his excellent but neglected book, *The Nature of Capital and Income* (1906), clearly and cogently established the economic basis for an all-inclusive concept of capital. But the prestige of Alfred Marshall was too great; his ideas on this matter prevailed. Marshall dismissed Fisher's approach in these words: "Regarded from the abstract and mathematical point of view, his position is incontestable. But he seems to take too little account of the necessity for keeping realistic discussions in touch with the language of the market-place" (Marshall [1890], 1916, pp. 787–788). Marshall concluded his appendix "Definitions of Capital" by stating, ". . . we are seeking a definition that will keep realistic economics in touch with the market-place . . ." (*ibid.*, p. 790). Marshall's market place restriction had the effect of excluding all capital that becomes an integral part of a people.

In this respect five of the more serious biases that thwart economic analysis and limit its usefulness require a brief comment.

Materialistic orientation.   It has been said that the economists have had a rather unfavorable image in the public mind. Whether true or not, there have been many protests contending that the policy implications of economics are primarily concerned with the value of material things. Unquestionably, economics has been strongly and persistently biased in favor of producer and consumer goods and commodities. For this reason it is justly charged as having a materialistic orientation. This orientation is all too evident in the treatment of capital, where producer goods are treated as if they were the sum and substance of capital and as if economic growth were dependent wholly on investment in such goods. Accordingly, there is much merit in the protest that the rise of human capital in capitalism is not seen or that increases in human capital, which have become a crucial feature of the economic system, are neglected.

Labor inputs inadequately specified.   Economists have found it all too convenient to think of labor as a homogeneous input free of any capital components. Much theory rests on a presumed dichotomy between labor and capital. But it is a treacherous dichotomy when analyzing economic growth, for the reason that the acquired abilities of labor that contribute to growth are as much a product of investment in man as growth is a product of investment in material forms of capital. The bias here is also clearly evident in the conventional approach to the measurement of labor as a factor of production.

In this approach it suffices to count the number of workers in the labor force or the number of man-hours worked. Differences in the acquired abilities of a labor force that occur over time are not reckoned. This particular bias has fostered the retention of the classical notion of labor as a capacity to do manual work requiring little skill and knowledge, a capacity with which, according to this notion, laborers are endowed about equally. But this notion of labor is patently wrong. The size of the labor force or the number of man-hours worked is not a satisfactory measure of increases in the productive services rendered by labor over time because of changes in the human capital component.

Misinterpretation of declines in capital–income ratios. The empirical foundation of economics has been much strengthened by studies of wealth and income [see NATIONAL INCOME AND PRODUCT ACCOUNTS; NATIONAL WEALTH]. One of the uses made of these studies has been to show that the capital–income ratio has been declining in countries with a modern economy. The decline in this ratio is then frequently viewed with apprehension because of the inferences that are drawn with respect to savings and investment and with respect to economic growth. Here, too, there is obviously a bias arising out of the restricted concept of capital on which these estimates are based.

There are no compelling reasons why the stock of any particular class of capital should not fall (or rise) relative to national income over time. Producer goods—structures, equipment, and inventories—are such a class. It is this particular class of capital that has been declining relative to income in the case of these estimates. Leaving aside the fact that the estimates of producer goods omit many improvements, they are at best only a part of all capital. The most serious omission in them is human capital, which has been increasing at a much higher rate than that of material reproducible capital. In the United States between 1929 and 1957, for example, while national income was increasing at about 3 per cent per annum, the stock of reproducible tangible capital rose only 2 per cent per annum. But the stock of educational and of training-on-the-job capital in the labor force rose between 4 and 5 per cent per annum. It turns out that the sum of this class of material capital and

of the human capital just mentioned rose about 3 per cent per annum, that is, at the same rate as national income. The ratio of this more nearly all-inclusive concept of capital to national income was about the same in 1929 and in 1957; in both of these years it was about six. Thus the apparent substantial declines in capital relative to income, which are based on estimates covering a number of modern countries, are an illusion in the sense that they are not valid indications of what has been happening to the ratio of all capital to income.

Savings and investment–income relation. Another closely related issue has been the concern about the amount of savings and investment relative to income, the concern being that as national income rises, savings and investment decline relatively [see CONSUMPTION FUNCTION]. Here, too, conventional estimates are very misleading because they omit investment in human capital. They understate the amount of savings and investment that occurs in any given year, and they show a decline in such savings and investment over time relative to income, when in fact there may have been no decline in all savings and investment in relation to income. Again, an appeal to more all-inclusive estimates for the economy of the United States is instructive. Based on the sum of the investment in reproducible material capital and in educational and on-the-job-training capital in the labor force, the amount of capital thus formed was equal to about 26 per cent of net national product in both 1929 and 1957.

Seeming rise in aggregate productivity. Another bias that has come to thwart economic analysis is the belief that the productivity of capital and labor has been rising very substantially over time, especially in countries that have developed a modern economy. There are estimates to support the belief that output has been rising not only relative to capital and to labor, respectively, but also relative to all inputs of capital and labor treated as an aggregate. The output of a particular industry or sector may, of course, rise in relation to material capital or to the size of the labor force. Nor is it implausible, under the circumstances that characterize economic growth, for an entire industry or sector to lag in its adjustments and thus to operate for a considerable period at a disequilibrium. This would cause the value of its output to decline relative to all inputs valued at equilibrium prices as the disequilibrium becomes established, and then to rise as such an industry or sector reattains an equilibrium.

But there is no strong theoretical or empirical basis for believing that the productivity of all factors of production treated as an aggregate, where the economy grows at an even pace, should either rise or fall. A much more plausible hypothesis is that it remains approximately constant over time. Why are there so many estimates that seemingly show total national output rising relative to total inputs? In a real sense it is because more of the additional capital that is formed over time *is concealed* than is income. This explanation is undoubtedly too cryptic, and therefore some elaboration is in order.

The analytical game that most economists have been playing in studying economic growth has been to take an index of reproducible material capital that omits changes in quality, in the sense that it abstracts from improvements in material capital. The next move is to take the size of the labor force, or man-hours worked, which also omits changes in quality, in the sense that improvements in the capabilities of labor are not fully reckoned. These two measures of inputs are then aggregated and related to total output. This game always shows the total input of such capital and labor as falling relative to total output over time. The inference is then drawn that the productivity of the economy as a whole rises over time, and this rise in productivity is generously attributed to "technological change," which according to this game would appear to account for most of the observed economic growth.

The finding that the over-all productivity of the economy increases in this manner is due to two types of illusions. The first is simply a consequence of the fact that many factors of production which are added to the resources of an economy over time are not included among the inputs; they are frequently and conveniently swept under the rug of "technological change." Here, basically, the analytical problem is one of specifying and identifying the improvements in human and material resources that occur over time. Undoubtedly most of the seeming rise in over-all productivity, which is based on estimates of the conventional measures of material capital and labor, is a result of omission of a large array of these quality components [*see* AGRICULTURE, *article on* PRODUCTIVITY AND TECHNOLOGY].

The second type of illusion is based on an apparent change in the capital–income ratio of a country. The observed ratio declines for reasons already noted, namely, because only a part of all capital is reckoned and because this part of the stock of capital is not increasing at as high a rate as either all capital or income. To avoid this type of illusion, an all-inclusive concept of capital is

necessary. The crucial question is as follows: When all the sources of income streams are treated as capital, is the rate of return on capital, so conceived, rising persistently over time? There is no theoretical basis for an affirmative answer, even though economic instability or forms of disequilibrium are postulated. Nor is there any empirical evidence that would support an affirmative answer to this question. The rate of return to investment that entails a "standard" component of risk and uncertainty is probably no higher presently in the United States than it was, say, during the 1920s. Nor should it come as a surprise that this rate of return has not been rising *secularly*.

With regard to motives and preferences of people for holding and acquiring sources of income streams, the most plausible assumption is that they have remained essentially constant. With respect to the behavior of suppliers of the sources of income streams, the equally plausible assumption is that these suppliers have been successful in providing enough new sources to increase national income, as it is now measured, at a rate of, say, between 3 and 4 per cent per year; however, they have not succeeded in increasing the supply at so fast a rate as to cause the price of these sources per dollar of income per year to decline, given the growth in demand consistent with the underlying preferences of the demanders. From these two very plausible assumptions it follows that the rate of return to investment would tend to remain approximately constant over time; and in this critical sense, the value of capital in relation to income has not been rising.

Both of these types of productivity illusions are in large part a consequence of the neglect of human capital and of its contribution to production, although improvements in the quality of other forms of capital are also a part.

But there is a sense in which real income can rise in a way that would alter the productivity of an economy that is beyond the two illusions already examined, although it is closely related analytically. There are consumer satisfactions that people derive from better health, from more education, and from more leisure time. These satisfactions also increase in most countries as economic growth occurs. Are they to be treated as a consumer surplus? [*See* CONSUMER'S SURPLUS.] Or are they concealed income from particular forms of capital that have been augmented over time? Surely a part of education has the attribute of an enduring consumer component that renders a stream of consumer satisfactions. These satisfactions from education, at least in principle, can be treated as a product of investment in schooling, akin to the satisfactions derived from investment in conventional consumer durables. But none of them appear in national income as it is presently measured. If they were included and if the sources were omitted from capital, it would tend once again to reduce the capital–income ratio. Contrariwise, if the stock of additional education capital represented by these enduring consumer abilities were to be identified and measured and thus made a part of the total stock of capital, and if the stream of income from this part of educational capital were omitted from national income, it would tend to increase the apparent capital–income ratio over time. Obviously the reason for the apparent rise of such a ratio would be the use of a partial concept of income. Unquestionably the same reasoning is applicable to consumer satisfactions from better health.

It is not obvious, however, that the additional satisfactions that come from more leisure time, from decreases in hours of work per week or in days worked per week and during a year, can be treated in the same way. But since more time for leisure has a value, the value of it can be included in income. The source of this leisure is an integral part of total production that provides enough income so that people can afford the leisure time. Thus, when all sources of income are treated as capital, the source of leisure is already reckoned. Accordingly, if the income component represented by leisure were to be omitted, and if all capital were reckoned, it would tend to increase the apparent capital–income ratio over time.

Public "welfare" expenditures. A long-standing bias permeates the treatment of public expenditures for health facilities and services and for education, treating them as if they were wholly for consumption, as welfare measures that in no way enhance the abilities of people as producers. Even vocational training and public funds to retrain workers in depressed areas for new jobs are often treated as welfare programs, although they are predominantly an investment in the productive abilities of the recipients. Conversely, most of the notions for attaining an optimum rate of economic growth in poor countries are seriously biased because of their strong emphasis on investment in new steel mills and in other modern industrial structures and equipment, with no comparable emphasis on providing for the complementary investment in human agents to administer and to do the skilled work which these installations require.

Economic attributes of human agents

Human beings are both consumers and producers. To production they contribute either entre-preneurship or work. In classical economics the producer attribute of human agents is that of a factor of production, referred to simply as labor. In modern analysis it is that of an input, or of a coefficient of production [see PRODUCTION]. In accounting for increases in national income over time, labor is treated as one of the sources of economic growth. As a source of income streams, the acquired abilities of human agents have, as we have argued, the attribute of an investment. All of these attributes of human agents are in one way or another a form of capital. Viewed as capital, they are a stock that renders services of economic value. The services are either consumer or producer services. Human capital is not, of course, bought or sold where men are free and none are slaves, as are the material forms of capital; but its producer services are generally for hire, the price being a wage or a salary. These producer services of human agents can be augmented by means of investment, which increases their income prospects. The additional income that is realized from an investment in human capital implies some rate of return.

The logical approach to determining the economic value of any of these attributes of human agents will differ depending upon the aim of the analysis, the theory and estimating technique that are used, and the limitations of the data. Much, of course, depends upon the aim. To see this, three different aims will be considered briefly.

Inputs. What are the inputs in an economy, sector, or industry? A basic difficulty arises at once out of the fact that an input has two economic faces; one is the income value of its productive services, and the other is its capital value. In the case of a parcel of land, for example, there is the rent paid for its use and the price at which the land sells.

The aim of many studies is to determine the economic value of the productive services of the inputs. Suppose we begin with a net national product for a given year and ignore all increases or decreases in inputs that occur during the year. Suppose also that the inputs are of two sorts, namely, labor and producer goods. Such a gross dichotomy may show that a fourth of the net national product is functionally contributed by producer goods and three-fourths by human agents. There is then the temptation to transform the productive services of the inputs into stocks of capital by using a naive approach that treats their services as permanent income streams and that capitalizes each of these income streams at the same rate of return. This approach would, of course, imply that the stock of human capital is three times as large as that of producer goods.

But this *is* obviously a naive way of transforming income streams into capital stocks, since estimates of net national product, as presently determined, are far from net—especially so for human capital —and thus in this important respect these estimates do not represent permanent income streams. It is also true that it would be a rare coincidence in a dynamic, growing economy to find an equality in the real rates of return to investment.

Nevertheless, in pursuing this aim there may be analytical reasons for concentrating on the magnitude and value of the productive services of these inputs while leaving aside the problem of determining their capital value. To do this, what is required is the price and the amount of the respective input services employed. With regard to these requirements, economists have treated human agents more adequately than producer goods. The difference is a consequence partly of inadequacies of the theory used and partly limitations of data. In aggregating producer goods, the differences in the quasi rents, or the relative prices of the services of these goods, are not as a rule reckoned; nor are the improvements in quality of new producer goods generally taken into account [see RENT].

In this sense it is true that most estimates of material capital conceal a part of the additional capital that is formed over time. The problem of aggregation in this connection is not only conceptual but is also confounded by the lack of price data of the productive services of different classes of producer goods [see AGGREGATION]. Fortunately these analytical inadequacies are not nearly so pronounced in the case of the productive services of human agents. Wages and salaries provide price data; and human agents can be classified into fairly homogeneous groups by occupations, or levels of skills, and by age, sex, and schooling. Nevertheless, this picture of the productive services of inputs will not reveal the differences in investment opportunities among the reproducible inputs.

Sources of economic growth.   National income increases at, say, a rate of 3 per cent per year between two dates. What are the sources of that growth? The matter of investment, rates of return to investment, and whether net savings are allocated optimally among investment opportunities can be put aside in determining the part of growth associated with each source. If the income value of the productive services of human agents and of producer goods were known, it would entail only a little simple arithmetic. But such is not the case, mainly for the reasons already considered. For human agents it is fairly straightforward to the extent that there is a linkage between what they contribute to production and what they earn in wages and salaries, although to determine what part of the increase in wages and salaries over time comes from more schooling, on-the-job training, better health, and from still other sources is far from easy. But not all of the additional income from these sources accrues to the individuals who have acquired these abilities. Some of it accrues to their co-workers, employers, and neighbors. In addition, there is an array of consumer satisfactions from these sources that accrues partly to the individuals who have acquired the relevant abilities and partly to others in the community. In general these consumer satisfactions are omitted from national income as presently measured.

For producer goods, it is as yet most difficult to ascertain this linkage because of the manner in which these forms of capital are identified and measured and because of the lack of price information on the services of producer goods. Improvements in the quality of such capital are largely omitted, and they become a major part of a "source" that appears as a residual, an increase in "output per unit of input." Thus, until this residual is properly allocated, it is obvious that producer goods (material capital) are underrated as a source of growth. Capital embodied in human agents is in this respect on a much stronger footing.

While this knowledge of the sources of economic growth is indeed useful in serving the aim of Edward F. Denison's comprehensive study (1962), it is not an approach to determining the underlying costs and returns to the investment that produced the additional sources that account for this part of economic growth. The important matter of an optimum allocation of total net savings among investment opportunities is not a part of the aim of this approach.

Investment in human beings

Acquired abilities that have economic value usually entail identifiable costs. Each process of acquiring abilities that enhance income prospects has the attributes of an investment. Viewed as an investment, what is the rate of return? The aim implied by this question cannot be realized by obtaining a picture of inputs or by ascertaining the sources of economic growth as they are treated above. An investment approach is required to attain this aim, which is important because knowledge about investment and the rate of return in this connection is essential in making the economic decisions necessary to achieve an optimum allocation of savings among investment opportunities. The relevance of this approach for a large array of economic problems is set forth by this writer in "Investment in Human Capital" (Schultz 1961*b*).

The theoretical "relations between earnings, rates of return, and the amount invested" and "how the latter two can be indirectly inferred from earnings" are investigated by Gary S. Becker (1962) in a paper that appears in the supplement referred to below.

The investment approach is central in a number of recent studies, the results of which are presented in a supplement, "Investment in Human Beings," to the *Journal of Political Economy*, October 1962. It includes the theoretical analysis by Becker just mentioned and the findings of several major empirical studies. These studies pertain to education, on-the-job training, health, information about the labor market, and migration when migration is treated as investment in human beings. Only two of these forms of investment, on-the-job training and education, will be considered here.

Investment in job training. By treating "training" as an "investment in acquisition of skill or in improvement of worker productivity" and by using a procedure akin to that used in determining investment in education, Jacob Mincer (1962) has identified and measured what appear to be costs of on-the-job training. His study, which also considers returns to this training, is restricted to males in the United States.

The investment in this training during 1939 was $3,000 million and during 1958, $13,500 million. In constant 1954 dollars, it was $5,700 million and $12,500 million, respectively. Mincer's study reveals two major shifts. One is toward higher skill levels; for example, males who already had a college level of education by 1939 accounted for one-third of all this training acquired that year; during 1958 they received nearly two-thirds of it. The other shift is toward formal schooling relative to on-the-job training; the investment in this training declined from about four-fifths to three-fifths of that in schooling between 1939 and 1958.

Estimates of the rate of return to investment in on-the-job training are very fragmentary. Those reported range from 9.0 to 12.7 per cent per year. The apparent reasons for the two shifts referred to above and the implications of on-the-job training as a factor in income and with respect to employment behavior are also examined by Mincer.

Investment in education. Education is unquestionably the largest source of human capital consisting of acquired abilities. But the road to an analysis of the economic value of education is not paved. The costs of education are surprisingly well concealed. Not all of the benefits accrue to students; they are frequently widely dispersed. The rates of return depend on earning profiles of many

different shapes, extending over many years. The responses to new, profitable investment in education are subject to some long lags; they are blunted in the case of public decisions by other matters and in the area of private decisions by incomplete information and by uncertainties that are inherent in a long future. There is also the uncertainty inherent in the fact that no student knows his abilities for schooling prior to putting himself to the test. In addition, the capital market is not well organized when it comes to lending funds for schooling.

Seemingly the task is simplified when it comes to formal education, since it is organized and presumably can be viewed as an industry that produces schooling. The difficulty with this simplification is that the functions of the educational establishment include activities other than schooling. One of the important functions of higher education is research. On-campus research has been increasing rapidly, and much of it is an integral part of graduate instruction. Another function consists of extension activities, notably, in the United States, the far-flung state agricultural extension services. There is also activity akin to an advisory service, especially to public agencies. Then, too, universities have been entering upon programs of instruction and research abroad with so-called sister universities in the cooperating country. And not least of these other functions is that of discovering and cultivating talent, which is quite distinct from formal schooling.

Costs. Much has been done recently to clarify the cost components of education. Opportunity costs are large, especially the earnings foregone by mature students, which were concealed in the way costs of schooling were formerly estimated. In the United States, for example, earnings foregone account for fully half to three-fifths of the total costs of high school and higher education. Because of the importance of earnings foregone, education beyond the elementary level is far from free to students. In poor countries and also in some low-income communities in the United States, for instance, in some agricultural areas and in city slums, earnings foregone have been and still are a factor even for children during the latter years in the elementary grades. When earnings foregone are brought into the picture, a part of the educational scene that always appeared blurred becomes clear. The distinction between private costs incurred by the student or his family and total costs to the economy is important analytically in explaining differences in incentives to invest in schooling, the shift in favor of formal schooling relative to on-the-job training over time, and in ascertaining the rates of return that matter in determining optimum investment decisions.

Total costs also provide clues to the amounts invested and changes in stocks. Leaving aside the education of persons who are not in the labor force, in the United States, as already noted, the amount spent on the schooling of persons who are 14 years and older rose at a rate of 4 per cent per annum between 1929 and 1957, measured in constant 1956 dollars. Investment in reproducible tangible wealth rose at 2 per cent per annum. When these rates of growth are applied to the respective stocks of 1957, the net annual investment implied is $21,900 million for this schooling and $25,500 million for this form of material capital.

Benefits. The future benefits from schooling accrue in part to the student and in part to others in society. Burton A. Weisbrod (1962) has substantially clarified the distinction between these two parts, although other investigators are fully aware that there are these two classes of benefits from schooling. As yet there has been little empirical success in determining the value of the benefits from schooling that accrue to co-workers and employers of the students and to the students' neighbors. There is a strong presumption that universal literacy of a population in a modern economy has large external economies [see CAPITAL, SOCIAL OVERHEAD; EXTERNAL ECONOMIES AND DISECONOMIES].

Furthermore, not all the benefits from schooling that accrue to the student are revealed in his future earnings, in wages, salaries, and entrepreneurial income from work. The benefits that accrue to the student are of three sorts. One consists of current consumption; the other two are an investment. That which is current consumption consists of satisfactions that the student obtains from schooling while in attendance. This benefit is undoubtedly small, for school days entail much hard work and long hours. There is next a class of enduring consumer abilities acquired through schooling; from these abilities the student derives satisfactions throughout his remaining life, for example, the ability to appreciate and enjoy the fine arts, the masterpieces of literature, science, and logical discourse. The source of these satisfactions is an investment in particular consumer abilities; but the value of the stream of satisfactions from this source, although substantial, is not a part of future wages and salaries. The third set of benefits consists of increases in the student's productivity, the source being the producer abilities acquired from schooling. While most of these appear in future

earnings, there are nevertheless some that are derived from production activities that the student does for himself over the years, like preparing his income tax returns, which do not enter into his earnings or into national income as it is presently measured.

Earnings. Investigations of investment in education have concentrated on earnings while leaving aside the other benefits from schooling. Even so, it is no simple matter to identify and measure these earnings. They are beset by the effects of differences in the inherited abilities of workers, of race, sex, and age; by unemployment; by the content and quality of schooling; and by the effects upon earnings of job training, health, and other forms of investment in human beings. Difficult as it is to isolate and adjust for these effects, some fairly satisfactory estimates have been obtained. These estimates make it possible to determine the rates of return to schooling, which are considered briefly below. They show also that at least one-fifth of the economic growth of the United States between 1929 and 1957 came from additional earnings connected with schooling.

Rates of return. Available estimates on rates of return are limited to money returns, that is, to money earnings from schooling that accrue to the student. Accordingly, all other benefits from schooling are omitted in these estimates; and to this extent the real rates of return to education are underestimated. For a more complete review and appraisal, see *The Economic Value of Education* (Schultz 1963).

Rates of return to total costs of schooling support several important generalizations. Costs here consist of all direct and indirect costs, including earnings foregone, whether borne privately or publicly; returns are restricted to monetary earnings from schooling. For males in the United States the following generalizations emerge: (1) the rate of return to elementary schooling is higher than to high school education, and in turn the rate of return to high school education is higher than to college education; (2) the rate of return to high school education (completing the twelfth year) rose persistently and very substantially between 1939 and 1958, while that to college education (completing at least the sixteenth year) declined somewhat between 1939 and 1956 and then began to rise; and (3) the lowest of these rates of return has been about 12 per cent per annum.

New knowledge pertaining to investment in human capital is already quite satisfactory with regard to the behavior of the supply and the rates of return to on-the-job training and to education.

Little is known, however, about the factors that have been increasing the demand for these acquired abilities—an integral part of economic growth.

THEODORE W. SCHULTZ

[*See also* CAPITAL; PRODUCTIVITY.]

BIBLIOGRAPHY

ANDERSON, C. ARNOLD; BROWN, JAMES C.; and BOWMAN, M. J. 1952 Intelligence and Occupational Mobility. *Journal of Political Economy* 60:218–239.

ASHBY, ERIC 1960 *Investment in Education: The Report of the Commissions on Post-school Certificate and Higher Education in Nigeria.* Lagos (Nigeria): Federal Ministry of Education.

BECKER, GARY S. 1960 Underinvestment in College Education? *American Economic Review* 50:346–354.

BECKER, GARY S. 1962 Investment in Human Capital: A Theoretical Analysis. *Journal of Political Economy* 70, no. 5 (Supplement):9–49.

BECKER, GARY S. 1964 *Human Capital: A Theoretical and Empirical Analysis, With Special Reference to Education.* New York: National Bureau of Economic Research.

BENSON, CHARLES S.; and LOHNES, PAUL R. 1959 Skill Requirements and Industrial Training in Durable Goods Manufacturing. *Industrial and Labor Relations Review* 12:540–553.

BLANK, DAVID; and STIGLER, GEORGE J. 1957 *The Demand and Supply of Scientific Personnel.* National Bureau of Economic Research General Series, No. 62. New York: The Bureau.

BONNER, J.; and LEES, D. S. 1963 Consumption and Investment. *Journal of Political Economy* 71:64–75.

BOWEN, WILLIAM G. 1964 *Economic Aspects of Education: Three Essays.* Princeton Univ., Department of Economics, Industrial Relations Section.

BOWMAN, MARY JEAN 1962 Human Capital: Concepts and Measures. U.S. Office of Education, *Bulletin* [1962] no. 5:69–92.

COLBERG, MARSHALL R. 1965 *Human Capital in Southern Development: 1939–1963.* Chapel Hill: Univ. of North Carolina Press.

COMMISSION ON HUMAN RESOURCES AND ADVANCED TRAINING 1954 *America's Resources of Specialized Talent: A Current Appraisal and a Look Ahead.* New York: Harper.

DENISON, EDWARD F. 1962 Education, Economic Growth, and Gaps in Information. *Journal of Political Economy* 70, no. 5 (Supplement):124–128.

DEWITT, NICHOLAS 1955 *Soviet Professional Manpower, Its Education, Training, and Supply.* Prepared in cooperation with the National Academy of Sciences–National Research Council for the National Science Foundation. Washington: Government Printing Office.

EDDING, FRIEDRICH 1958 *Internationale Tendenzen in der Entwicklung der Ausgaben für Schulen und Hochschulen; International Trends in Educational Expenditures.* Kiel (Germany): Institut für Weltwirtschaft. → Contains a summary in English.

Education and the Southern Economy. 1965 *Southern Economic Journal* 32, part 2:1–128.

THE FALK PROJECT FOR ECONOMIC RESEARCH IN ISRAEL 1961 *Report: 1959 and 1960.* Jerusalem (Israel): The Project. → See especially pages 138–146 on the profitability of investment in education and pages 146–150 on the measurement of educational capital in Israel.

FISHER, IRVING (1906) 1927 *The Nature of Capital and Income.* New York and London: Macmillan.

FRIEDMAN, MILTON; and KUZNETS, SIMON 1945 *Income From Independent Professional Practice.* National Bureau of Economic Research General Series, No. 45. New York: The Bureau.

HANSEN, W. LEE 1963 Total and Private Rates of Return to Investment in Schooling. *Journal of Political Economy* 71:128–140.

HARBISON, FREDERICK; and MYERS, CHARLES A. 1964 *Education, Manpower, and Economic Growth: Strategies of Human Resource Development.* New York: McGraw-Hill.

Investment in Human Beings: Papers Presented at a Conference Called by the Universities–National Bureau Committee for Economic Research. 1962 *Journal of Political Economy* 70, no. 5: Supplement. → The entire supplement is devoted to the problem of human capital.

KELLOGG, CHARLES E. 1960 Transfer of Basic Skills of Food Production. American Academy of Political and Social Science, *Annals* 331:32–38.

KENEN, PETER B. 1965 Nature, Capital and Trade. *Journal of Political Economy* 73:437–460.

MACHLUP, FRITZ 1962 *The Production and Distribution of Knowledge in the United States.* Princeton Univ. Press.

MARSHALL, ALFRED (1890) 1916 *Principles of Economics.* 7th ed. New York: Macmillan; London: St. Martins.

MILLER, HERMAN P. 1960 Annual and Lifetime Income in Relation to Education: 1939–1959. *American Economic Review* 50:962–986.

MINCER, JACOB 1958 Investment in Human Capital and Personal Income Distribution. *Journal of Political Economy* 66:281–302.

MINCER, JACOB 1962 On-the-job Training: Costs, Returns, and Some Implications. *Journal of Political Economy* 70, no. 5 (Supplement):50–79.

MUSHKIN, SELMA J. (editor) 1962 *The Economics of Higher Education.* U.S. Office of Education, *Bulletin* [1962], no. 5. → The entire issue is devoted to the topic. See especially pages 69–92 and pages 281–304.

NICHOLSON, JOSEPH S. 1891 The Living Capital of the United Kingdom. *Economic Journal* 1:95–107.

ORGANIZATION FOR ECONOMIC COOPERATION AND DEVELOPMENT 1962 *Policy Conference on Economic Growth and Investment in Education.* Paris: The Organization. → Also published in Volume 36 of the *Bulletin* of the International Bureau of Education.

ORGANIZATION FOR ECONOMIC COOPERATION AND DEVELOPMENT 1964 *The Residual Factor and Economic Growth.* London: H.M. Stationery Office.

PRINCETON UNIVERSITY, INDUSTRIAL RELATIONS SECTION 1957 *High-talent Manpower for Science and Industry: An Appraisal of Policy at Home and Abroad,* by J. Douglas Brown and Frederick Harbison. Research Report Series, No. 95. Princeton, N.J.: The Section.

SCHULTZ, THEODORE W. 1960 Capital Formation by Education. *Journal of Political Economy* 68:571–583.

SCHULTZ, THEODORE W. 1961a Education and Economic Growth. Volume 60, pages 46–88 in National Society for the Study of Education, *Yearbook.* Part 2: Social Forces Influencing American Education. Univ. of Chicago Press.

SCHULTZ, THEODORE W. 1961*b* Investment in Human Capital. *American Economic Review* 51:1–17.

SCHULTZ, THEODORE W. 1963 *The Economic Value of Education.* New York: Columbia Univ. Press.

STIGLER, GEORGE J. 1962 Information in the Labor Market. *Journal of Political Economy* 70, no. 5 (Supplement):94–105.

STIGLER, GEORGE J. 1963 *Capital and Rates of Return in Manufacturing Industries.* A Study of the National Bureau of Economic Research. Princeton Univ. Press.

TAWNEY, RICHARD H. 1938 *Some Thoughts on the Economics of Public Education.* Oxford Univ. Press.

VAIZEY, JOHN 1958 *The Costs of Education.* London: Allen & Unwin.

WEISBROD, BURTON A. 1961 The Valuation of Human Capital. *Journal of Political Economy* 69:425–436.

WEISBROD, BURTON A. 1962 Education and Investment in Human Capital. *Journal of Political Economy* 70, no. 5 (Supplement):106–123.

WILES, P. J. D. 1956 The Nations's Intellectual Investment. Oxford University, Institute of Statistics, *Bulletin* 18, no. 3:279–290.

CAPITAL, PRIVATE INTERNATIONAL MOVEMENTS OF

See under INTERNATIONAL MONETARY ECONOMICS.

CAPITAL, SOCIAL OVERHEAD

The concept of "social overhead capital" (SOC) is used to identify the source of certain "basic" services required in the production of virtually all commodities. In its most narrow sense the term refers to transportation, communication, and power facilities. Such forms of capital as railroads, ports and harbors, hydroelectric plants, and telephone lines are always included in the SOC category. In broader but less common usage, facilities for such things as education and health, for maintenance of law and order, and for research are included. The discussion here is concerned only with the narrower concept.

The terms "economic overhead facilities" and "economic infrastructure" are frequently used as synonyms for SOC. The services supplied by such facilities are called "basic" to industrial activity because their use is generally required for production independently of the nature of the output of the industry. SOC may be contrasted with "directly productive capital." The latter term refers to physical capital in the form of plant and equipment designed to produce a given product. The directly productive capital is used for the production of those products that add directly to final output, while SOC is assumed necessary to provide the service that makes possible the operation of all forms of directly productive capital. Another category of capital that is usually isolated for separate treatment is inventories and goods in process.

Characteristics. There are several characteristics of SOC that distinguish it from other capital (plant and equipment and inventories) and that warrant its isolation for special analysis:

(*a*) The services supplied by SOC are so widely used and their effectiveness is so dependent on what takes place in other sectors of the economy that the full contribution to the economy of such facilities is difficult to identify and even more difficult to measure. Thus, SOC is said to generate external economies [*see* EXTERNAL ECONOMIES AND DISECONOMIES] in that its existence results in reduced input costs to other sectors and the rewards arising from these reduced costs can rarely be captured by the enterprise originating them.

(*b*) The capital involved does not lend itself to very much divisibility, and the initial outlays to create SOC are often large relative to other forms of capital and relative to the total quantity of resources available to the economy for investment. Entry into the field is therefore difficult, and marginal costs are usually constant or declining over a wide range of output levels.

(*c*) An economy's SOC facilities (in the narrow sense) are usually either owned outright by the government or their construction and operation are closely regulated by the government. The reasons for this are implicit in the two characteristics just noted. External economies, large initial outlays and technical indivisibilities, the difficulty of entry, and the likelihood of declining costs over a wide range all mean that the conventional competitive market mechanism does not produce acceptable results. Hence, government ownership or regulation is accepted as necessary. In a more general sense, SOC is often said to be in the public interest. This vague term is used to mean that, independent of specific costs and input considerations, the existence of SOC is thought to contribute to the achievement of an economic climate and environment that encourages and facilitates the development of the economy as a whole. The argument then is simply that as SOC is in the public interest, it should be controlled by public authority.

(*d*) Very few of the services provided by SOC can be imported. This characteristic follows from the very nature of the service—transportation, power, etc. The consequence of this is the important one that an economy does not have the option of importing these services and must allocate domestic resources to their construction and operation no matter what the productivity of these resources is in this type of activity.

Quantitative significance.   Since about 1950 interest in SOC has centered almost exclusively on its role in economic development and in development planning in the low-income countries of the world. [See PLANNING, ECONOMIC.] That this role is widely considered to be extremely important is evidenced by the proportion of available investible resources allocated to the creation of SOC in most development plans. For example, during the 1950s India allocated about 40 per cent of her total public investment to the building of transportation, communication, and power facilities. For Ghana the allocation for the same time period was 41 per cent, for Mexico 38 per cent, for Thailand 51 per cent, Ecuador 49 per cent, the Philippines 40 per cent, and Colombia 74 per cent. Percentages for other developing countries are similar.

Although the collection of data on capital formation always involves many rather arbitrary decisions, and the classification into transportation, communication, and energy may not be exactly comparable among all the countries, the percentages do show quite unambiguously that most governments are heavily committed to this form of investment. Since public investment usually amounts to at least one-half of total investment in these countries, the data show that a significant part of available investible resources is allocated to the creation of SOC. To understand its role in the development process is therefore of great relevance in the making of development plans.

Role in economic development.   The importance of SOC in the development of an economy rests on several considerations. Its creation results in reduced costs for a wide range of producing units and may thereby encourage the expansion of existing units and the creation of new ones. The encouragement may be especially strong in those instances where the SOC creates external economies and the user of the service pays less than its value to him and possibly pays nothing at all directly for the service. For example, the construction of a new hard-surface highway in an area where previously only a dirt road existed is expected to reduce transportation costs directly. It may also reduce the appropriate size of inventories a firm must carry, as well as extend the geographic size of the firm's market. All of these freely available economies may be expected to add to the firm's profitability and thereby induce expansion. Thus a common strategy of planning is for the government to concentrate its own resources on the building of SOC and to rely on the private sector to respond to the incentives created by the new SOC. In this kind of strategy, the influence of investment in SOC on the development process depends largely on the extent to which the other sectors respond to the new profit opportunities.

The heavy dependence of the success of such a strategy on the ability of nongovernmental sectors to perceive and respond to the new opportunities has led a number of economists to question the effectiveness of a development program built around the argument of the preceding paragraph. In a contrary approach, the assumption is made that the chief obstacle to the development effort is not a lack of investible resources as such, but rather an inability to perceive and exploit newly arising profit opportunities.

The argument is further made that the opportunities produced by new SOC are neither clear enough nor demanding enough to induce the formation of the directly productive capital necessary to make the creation of the SOC profitable to the community. On the other hand, if the directly productive capital is constructed (possibly by the government) before the SOC, the need for the latter will be so evident to all observers that pressures—pecuniary and otherwise—will develop that force the building of the SOC. The conclusion then follows that if the time sequence of investment projects is directly productive capital first, then SOC, total investment will be larger and the development program more likely to be successful than if the sequence were the other way. The question is one of sequence of investments, not of whether SOC is required for development.

The empirical questions in this conflict of strategies have to do with the validity of the assumption about the ability of economic agents in the developing country to perceive and exploit economic opportunities and the extent to which resource limitations constitute a prior barrier to development. The situation will not be the same in all countries or even in the same country in all periods as development proceeds. Within the constraints of present knowledge the only safe generalization seems to be that the best strategy depends very much on the situation prevailing at the time the plan is made.

Few, if any, development programs accept either strategy completely. Much the most common practice in arriving at decisions on the size and timing of SOC in development plans is for the planners to estimate the directly productive capital formation to occur, and then to estimate the requirements for SOC services if the full advantages of the directly productive capital are to be realized. Thus a "balance" between SOC and directly productive capital is sought, of such a nature that there is no unused capacity in either type of capital good and the directly productive capital is not forced to operate at extremely high costs. In the forecasting of directly productive capital formation some emphasis is placed on inducements created by the assumption that whatever SOC is needed will be available. At the same time other inducements are introduced as well, and the possible inducement effect of SOC is not the key to the plan's effectiveness.

That this balance is frequently not achieved is evidenced by the existence of excess capacity in both kinds of capital in most developing countries. Thus in one developing country a manufacturing plant may operate below capacity because of an inadequate supply of power or because the transportation network cannot provide a steady inflow of raw materials. In another country or another part of the same country a large irrigation facility may be virtually unutilized because no further directly productive capital has been created by the individual farmer units for whose use the irrigation facility was built.

The empirical evidence suggests that neither role attached to SOC in the development strategies outlined above is alone sufficient to assure an appropriate rate and composition of capital formation. The formulation of development plans that accomplish the task of producing that quantity of SOC services that will enable the directly productive capital to operate at planned capacity and planned costs is difficult, not only because of technical indivisibilities in the production of SOC but also because of the difficulty of appraising the need for these services. To do the latter includes trying to appraise the inducement effects of the creation of SOC.

Along with its role in the problem of balance in the composition of output, investment in SOC also has important consequences for the regional pattern of development within a country. The creation of an SOC facility in one part of a country will necessarily give advantage to that area over other areas in attracting further capital formation. Since the high initial costs prevent supplying appropriate SOC simultaneously to all areas of the country, some regions of the country will lag behind others. The immediate effects of regional imbalances are social and political, but efforts to prevent or alleviate these imbalances also have effects on the rate at which the economy is able to develop. There are, of course, many factors that affect the pattern of regional development, but the building of SOC is perhaps one of the most strategic and the one most susceptible to control by central authorities.

A problem associated with SOC that has long occupied the attention of economists is that of the pricing of the services provided by such capital. The general dictum to equate price to marginal cost is not as widely accepted now as it was prior to World War II, largely as a result of developments in the theory of welfare economics [see WELFARE ECONOMICS]. The price equal to marginal cost case is especially vulnerable in a declining cost situation where a subsidy is necessary to make up the difference between price and average costs. In this case the economy must be taxed to subsidize the unit utilizing the SOC service, and the welfare implications of such a tax and subsidy are extremely difficult to establish. Although there is ample evidence that the average costs of SOC services are frequently not covered by the price paid by the user of the service, there is little evidence of conscious effort at marginal-cost pricing among the countries pursuing development plans. On the other hand there is evidence that some of the services of SOC are provided at a cost meant to encourage expansion of use by the private sector, but the argument supporting such a policy is rarely the marginal cost argument. This particular problem of pricing has not, however, occupied a great deal of the attention of individuals working on the problems of development, and to introduce explicit welfare considerations greatly complicates its solution. At the same time the practice actually followed in pricing SOC services has major repercussions on the role that this capital plays—for example, in inducing expansion in the private sector—in the development process.

Areas of research. Empirical research into the effects of the construction of SOC on economic development is difficult because of the indirect nature of the returns to be realized. For example, measurement of the inducement to further investment produced by the creation of SOC can be accomplished only in a rough and ready fashion. The major need, however, is for empirical data on just this kind of question. As an increasing number of large-scale projects are completed, data may become available that will permit testing the effects in a more satisfactory manner than has been possible in the past. Such data are necessary before firm views can be established on how much SOC to provide, on the timing of its construction relative to that of directly productive capital, and on the most effective pricing policy for a country to follow. Until these data are available, the large source of potential error in the allocation of scarce investment resources will continue to plague the development programer.

HENRY J. BRUTON

BIBLIOGRAPHY

In addition to the works cited below, consult the serial publications of the Economic Commission for Latin America, the Economic Commission for Asia and the Far East, and the Economic Commission for Africa—all of the United

Nations; also the published development plans of any of the developing countries.

GRAAFF, JOHANNES DE VILLIERS 1957 *Theoretical Welfare Economics.* Cambridge Univ. Press.

HIRSCHMAN, ALBERT O. 1958 *The Strategy of Economic Development.* New Haven: Yale Univ. Press.

NURKSE, RAGNAR 1953 *Problems of Capital Formation in Underdeveloped Countries.* New York: Oxford Univ. Press.

CAPITAL PUNISHMENT

Capital punishment means the officially authorized execution of the death penalty on persons determined by appropriate legal procedures to have committed a criminal offense. So defined, capital punishment is presently a prominent feature of the administration of criminal justice in many nations of the world and has typically, although not invariably, characterized the criminal law since the beginnings of recorded history.

This definition of capital punishment, while serving most utilitarian purposes, emphasizes the difficulties of tracing its origins in primitive society. Capital punishment, as it emerges in civilized communities, presupposes a system of criminal law predicated on the assumption that certain harms committed by one individual upon another represent injuries to the interests of the corporate society and, hence, are punishable by the society. Evidence suggests that among the primitive societies of western Europe such a conception of the criminal law was slow in developing. Even more slow to develop were the modern distinctions between the idea of crime and of private harms encompassed in the law of torts. In general, social control of private wrongdoing was principally concerned with the avoidance or regulation of private warfare rather than with the direct imposition of penalties by the organized community upon the offender. Accordingly, retribution for serious wrongs, such as homicide and major offenses against property, was left largely to the injured party or his family—subject, however, to elaborate social regulations of the manner and quantum of retribution that might be exacted. Typically, retribution was regulated by composition, wherein the injured party or his clan exacted compensation for the injury from the offender or his clansmen according to stipulated procedures. Thus, in England as late as the Norman Conquest, homicide could be composed by payment of the dead man's wergild. If the wergild was not paid, the obligation to avenge the death rested on the injured family, not the state.

This, of course, is not to say that primitive society reveals no instances of the infliction of death upon its members by the direct authority of the organized community. Many such instances, however, cannot confidently be represented as examples of capital punishment as that term is currently understood, but appear more closely related to primitive religious belief and ritual. It has been suggested that the authorization of the death penalty in some early legal codes reflects the substance and forms of earlier religious practices relating to human sacrifice and the infliction of death on persons deemed guilty of sacrilege (Bonner & Smith 1930–1938).

Ancient legal codes. The antiquity of capital punishment is clearly revealed, however, in provisions of the earliest written legal codes. Thus the Code of Hammurabi (c. 1750 B.C.) applied the death penalty to some 25 offenses, such as corruption in government service, theft, and various sexual offenses. The omission of murder is probably to be explained by the persistence of the blood feud in cases of homicide. Not only did the code authorize the penalty of death but in some cases it specified the mode of execution: drowning, burning, or impaling. In the Assyrian laws (c. 1500 B.C.) death was a specified penalty, but mutilation appears to have been the more common penalty. Both the Hittite Code, dating from the mid-fourteenth century before Christ, and the Covenant Code of the Hebrews specified the death penalty for a variety of offenses. The early Greek law reveals a strong tradition of self-help on the part of clan and tribal groups. The earliest written codes, however, authorize the death penalty for numerous offenses, many of them of a religious character; and capital punishment became an established feature of Greek law in the period of its maturity.

In Rome the first capital offenses to gain recognition appear to have been treason and murder, the latter representing an effort on the part of the community to suppress the blood feud. The Twelve Tables, enacted in the fifth century before Christ, contain provisions authorizing the death penalty for such offenses as libel, arson, bearing false witness, and certain forms of bribery. During the republic the penalty of death, although authorized in the written laws, seems rarely to have been imposed upon citizens. Execution of slaves, however, was a much more frequent occurrence. In the first two centuries after Christ, capital punishment appears to have been more frequently imposed for political crimes and for other offenses committed by members of the lower classes. During the last stages of the empire, when Christianity became the state religion, heretics were frequently condemned and executed, and the criminal law was generally expanded into the area of what had previously been regarded as private delicts. The Code of Theodosius (A.D. 438) specifies over eighty crimes punishable by death.

Penal practice in premodern Europe

From the fall of Rome until the beginnings of the modern era, capital punishment was widely practiced throughout western Europe. An astonishing variety of methods to produce death were employed. In English history the methods of greatest importance were burning, beheading, and hanging, sometimes accompanied by such refinements as drawing and quartering. One reason for the widespread use of capital punishment in preindustrial societies was the apparent lack of feasible alternative methods to deal with serious criminality. A system of long-term imprisonment, for example, requires outlays of resources that an impoverished society is unable or unwilling to make. Nevertheless, the history of capital punishment suggests that in any society certain countervailing tendencies based upon practical and humanitarian considerations are likely to develop and to limit the imposition of the death penalty. In the Middle Ages, for example, mutilation of the offender was frequently employed as an alternative to capital punishment. This phenomenon can be observed in the laws of William the Conqueror, in which mutilation rather than death was prescribed for most serious crimes. Although mutilation was conceived as a mitigation of punishment, its use was attended by serious social disadvantages. Thus, the loss of hands, eyes, or tongue often prevented the offender from resuming productive occupations; and the stigma and disabilities produced by mutilation tended to encourage the commission of new crimes by those upon whom it was practiced.

The seventeenth and eighteenth centuries. Although penal practice in the Middle Ages was often savage and unrestrained, it appears clear that the most extensive use of capital punishment occurred in western Europe during the period marked by the onset of the industrial revolution. Sir William Blackstone, writing in the middle of the eighteenth century, estimated that 160 crimes were punishable by death in England. A half-century later probably as many as one hundred additional offenses had been added to the list. Some historians have calculated the number at an even higher figure. This increase in the number of offenses punishable by death may not provide a wholly accurate index of the increases in the execution of the death penalty. It fails, for example, to take into account the num-

bers of convicted English felons transported during these years to America and later to Australia. Nevertheless, there have been few periods in the history of Western civilization when penal policy placed so great a reliance on capital punishment.

The reason for the increased resort to capital punishment in the seventeenth and eighteenth centuries are no doubt many and varied. Two, however, are of prime importance. First, the industrial and agricultural revolutions produced social dislocation and unrest and resulted in real and apparent increases in serious criminality. The Draconian penalties of this era represent the response of the propertied classes to these developments. Second, despite the rise in importance of overseas transportation of felons in some European countries, such as England, penal policy during the period was marked by a dearth of acceptable secondary punishments capable of being employed as alternatives to the death penalty. Long-term penal incarceration is for the most part a development of the nineteenth century.

The abolition movement

The eighteenth century, which accorded capital punishment the position of dominance in the penal policy of western Europe, also produced the beginnings of the movement to abolish it or greatly to restrict its use. The unsatisfactory state of the criminal law, the use of torture, the widespread use of capital punishment, and other brutal and degrading penalties received the critical attention of writers of the Enlightenment. These abuses were effectively satirized by Montesquieu in his *Lettres persanes*, 1721. Even more explicit denunciations were launched by Voltaire. But the most important work of the period was *An Essay on Crimes and Punishments* (1764), written by the youthful Cesare Bonesana, marquis of Beccaria (1738–1794). Beccaria was the first writer to urge the complete abolition of capital punishment, and his is perhaps the most influential volume on the reform of criminal justice ever published.

The impact of Beccaria's work was immediate and profound. Its influence was felt in England, where the work of law reform was undertaken by a remarkable group of men, the most prominent of whom was Jeremy Bentham (1748–1832). Many of Bentham's proposals were introduced in Parliament by Sir Samuel Romilly (1757–1818), who became the most distinguished legislative advocate of the restriction of capital punishment in English history. Although he did not live to see a substantial reduction in the number of crimes punished by death, which was his great objective, his work and that of Bentham prepared the way for the reforms achieved in Parliament in the next generation. The effectiveness of these efforts is demonstated by the fact that, whereas at the beginning of the nineteenth century well over two hundred offenses were punishable by death in England, by 1861 the number had been reduced to four.

The movement to restrict or abolish the death penalty, launched in the eighteenth-century Enlightenment, exerted important influence throughout the civilized world, and that influence persists to the present day. The reasons for these developments are many. First, the abolition movement was consistent with nineteenth-century humanitarian sentiment and, indeed, represented one of its most important expressions. Second, limiting or abolishing capital punishment became one of the important political objectives of the popular governments that came to power during the course of the century. Third, the rise of long-term penal incarceration throughout the civilized world, although it produced a plethora of new problems, provided a feasible alternative to the death penalty. Finally, a widespread conviction developed that a penal policy founded on extensive and indiscriminate use of capital punishment not only failed to achieve a reduction of serious criminality but in some respects rendered law enforcement less effective.

The United States. Capital punishment was brought to North America by the colonizing powers. In the American colonies legislation characteristically applied the death penalty to a long list of offenses, and in most colonies executions were frequently carried out. In the years following the American Revolution the number of offenses punishable by death declined. One manifestation of this tendency was the Pennsylvania statute of 1794, which for the first time divided murder into degrees and authorized capital punishment only for first-degree murder. Similar legislation has been enacted in most American states.

There has been agitation for the abolition of capital punishment in the United States for more than a century and a quarter. The first state to abolish the death penalty (except in cases of treason) was Michigan in 1847. Other states that have abolished the death penalty in all, or virtually all, cases include Rhode Island (1852), Wisconsin (1853), Maine (1876, 1887), Minnesota (1911), North Dakota (1915), Alaska (1957), Hawaii (1957), Oregon (1964), Iowa (1965), Vermont (1965), West Virginia (1965), and New York (1965). Both Puerto Rico and the Virgin Islands have also abandoned capital punishment. A number of states, including Kansas, South Dakota, and

Delaware, at one time abolished the penalty and later restored it. The federal government applies the death penalty to a variety of offenses.

In the considerable majority of American states that have retained the death penalty, there is some diversity in the offenses to which it is applied. Capital punishment is most commonly applied to murder and treason, but no executions under state authority have occurred for the latter offense in the modern period. Other offenses to which the death penalty has been attached by some American jurisdictions include forcible rape, kidnaping, armed robbery, certain narcotics crimes, and (in the case of the federal government) espionage and theft of military secrets.

In spite of the only moderate success of the American abolition movement, the actual execution of the death penalty has declined precipitously for more than a generation and a half. Thus, between 1930 and 1964, 3,849 persons were executed under civil authority in the United States (U.S. Bureau of Prisons 1964). The nature of the decline is revealed by the fact that in 1930, 155 persons were executed, whereas in 1964 the figure was only 15. Considerable regional variations may be observed in the number of executions. In the years 1950–1954, 27 persons were put to death in the populous state of New York, while 72 persons were executed during the same period in Georgia. No executions occurred in the 1950s and 1960s in the states of Massachusetts, South Dakota, Delaware, Montana, and Wyoming.

World-wide trends. In the mid-1960s a majority of the nations of the world retained the death penalty for certain categories of offenses. Capital punishment is recognized in Australia (except in Queensland), in Africa, and in most Asiatic nations. In Europe the death penalty is applied in the countries of eastern Europe and the Balkans, but it has been substantially abolished in all of the nations of western Europe except France, Greece, and Spain. In Britain the abolition movement came to fruition when, in 1965, the House of Commons approved a bill providing for the elimination of the death penalty in murder cases during a five-year trial period. The act would lapse after July 31, 1970, unless its life were extended by resolutions of both houses of the Parliament. In Latin America capital punishment has been abolished in Argentina, Brazil, Colombia, Costa Rica, the Dominican Republic, Mexico (under the federal law and in all but four of the states), Panama, Uruguay, and Venezuela. It is retained in Canada. A report submitted to the United Nations in 1962 clearly revealed a world-wide tendency toward a considerable reduction of the number and categories of offenses for which capital punishment may be imposed (United Nations 1962).

Effectiveness of capital punishment

In the controversy over capital punishment that has persisted throughout the civilized world since the eighteenth century, the arguments have generally been of two sorts. The first are assertions based upon conflicting versions of moral, religious, and humanitarian imperatives; and the second may be described as utilitarian arguments advanced to demonstrate social gains or losses deriving from a system of capital punishment.

Of all the utilitarian arguments, the ones advanced most frequently are those relating to the deterrent consequences of the death penalty. It should be observed that the crucial issue is not whether any deterrent potential can fairly be ascribed to the death penalty, but whether capital punishment possesses a deterrent efficacy lacking in other less drastic, nonlethal sanctions available to the state when performing its obligations of public order. Typically, those arguing for the retention of capital punishment have not attempted to establish its unique deterrent efficacy by empirical demonstration but have relied primarily on expressions of opinion by experienced police and prosecuting officials.

The abolitionists, on the other hand, have produced a large array of studies designed to test the deterrent consequences of the death penalty. These studies have taken a variety of forms: comparisons of homicide rates in countries or American states that have abolished the death penalty and those that have retained it; comparisons of homicide rates in jurisdictions before and after abolition; broader studies of general crime rates in abolition and death-penalty jurisdictions (Sellin 1959, pp. 19–52). These and similar studies have in general failed to identify any meaningful correlation between the presence of the death penalty and rates of serious criminality. Although abolitionists have sometimes claimed more of these studies than their significance warrants, the temperate observation of the Royal Commission on Capital Punishment seems clearly justified: "[T]here is no clear evidence of any lasting increase [in the murder rate following abolition] and there are many offenders on whom the deterrent effect is limited and may often be negligible" (Great Britain 1953, p. 274).

Another aspect of the deterrence argument has sometimes been slighted. Even if it be supposed that there are some conceivable circumstances in which the death penalty might enhance the deter-

rent consequences of the criminal law, the more important question is whether, under the circumstances actually surrounding the administration of justice, these effects can sensibly be anticipated. It may be assumed that realization of any unique deterrent gains from capital punishment would require that certain conditions be satisfied. These include reasonable certainty in the detection and apprehension of offenders, reasonable speed and certainty of conviction, and reasonable speed and certainty in the execution of the death penalty once it is imposed. In the United States, at least, none of these conditions is fulfilled at present or is likely to be in the years ahead.

Although arguments centering on deterrence have dominated discussion of capital punishment, many other issues have been canvassed. Abolitionists have frequently pointed to the irrevocable nature of the death penalty, which prevents the state from rectifying miscarriages of justice in cases of conviction of the innocent. Retentionists, on the other hand, have urged that the death penalty is essential to the safety of police officers; and murder of policemen was retained as a capital offense in the New York act of 1965, which generally abolished capital punishment in that state. A recent study conducted in the United States, however, indicates no correlation between the murder of policemen and the presence of the death penalty (Sellin 1959, pp. 52–57).

In most modern jurisdictions the imposition of the death penalty is discretionary rather than mandatory. There are no reliable data on the percentage of persons sentenced to death among those convicted of offenses for which capital punishment might be imposed. It is clear, however, that the percentage is very small. Furthermore, there is reason to believe that selection of persons for execution often proceeds on the basis of inadequate or improper criteria. The poverty of the offender and the consequent inadequacies of his legal defense appear to be important factors in an indeterminate number of cases. That the race of the offender has also played a role is at least suggested by the fact that 54.7 per cent of all offenders executed in the United States in the years 1930–1964 were nonwhite (U.S. Bureau of Prisons 1964). Other consequences of capital punishment on the administration of justice also merit concern; for example, the distorting effects of capital punishment on the development of the substantive criminal law have frequently been noted. In the Anglo–American world the result has been a legacy of legal rules intelligible only as devices to mitigate the severity of penalties. The rules so developed, however, cannot always be restricted in their application to capital cases, and the consequence is the introduction of anomalies and irrationalities in the development of legal principle.

It is clear that throughout the world the consensus of opinion among those professionally concerned with the treatment of offenders is strongly in favor of abolition of the death penalty. Study of the administration of capital punishment and its consequences has left more careful students skeptical of the claims of social advantage made in its behalf. Moreover, the death penalty is clearly at war with the principle of rehabilitation of offenders that has come to dominate modern correctional thought. Although capital punishment is an ancient and hardy institution, the trend toward reduction of its scope and application may be expected to continue.

FRANCIS A. ALLEN

[*Directly related are the entries* CRIMINAL LAW; PENOLOGY. *Other relevant material may be found in* CRIME, *article on* HOMICIDE; CRIMINOLOGY; PUNISHMENT; *and in the biography of* BECCARIA.]

BIBLIOGRAPHY

ALLEN, FRANCIS A. 1964 *The Borderland of Criminal Justice: Essays in Law and Criminology.* Univ. of Chicago Press.

BECCARIA, CESARE BONESANA (1764) 1953 *An Essay on Crimes and Punishments.* Stanford, Calif. Academic Reprints. → First published in Italian as *Dei delitti e delle pene.* A paperback edition was published in 1963 by Bobbs-Merrill.

BEDAU, HUGO A. (editor) 1964 *The Death Penalty in America: An Anthology.* Chicago: Aldine.

BONNER, ROBERT J.; and SMITH, GERTRUDE 1930–1938 *The Administration of Justice From Homer to Aristotle.* 2 vols. Univ. of Chicago Press.

CALVERT, ERIC R. (1927) 1936 *Capital Punishment in the Twentieth Century.* 5th ed., rev. London: Putnam.

CEYLON, COMMISSION OF INQUIRY ON CAPITAL PUNISHMENT 1959 *Report.* Colombo: Government Publications Bureau.

GREAT BRITAIN, ROYAL COMMISSION ON CAPITAL PUNISHMENT, *1949–1953* 1953 *Report.* Papers by Command, Cmd. 8932. London: H.M. Stationery Office.

HART, HERBERT L. A. 1957 Murder and the Principles of Punishment: England and the United States. *Northwestern University Law Review* 52:433–461.

JOLOWICZ, HERBERT F. (1932) 1961 *Historical Introduction to the Study of Roman Law.* 2d ed. Cambridge Univ. Press.

KOESTLER, ARTHUR 1957 *Reflections on Hanging.* New York: Macmillan.

MAITLAND, FREDERIC W.; and MONTAGUE, FRANCIS C. (1894–1898) 1915 *A Sketch of English Legal History.* New York: Putnam.

MUIRHEAD, JAMES (1886) 1916 *Historical Introduction to the Private Law of Rome.* 3d ed., rev. & enl. London: Black.

PHILLIPSON, COLEMAN 1923 *Three Criminal Law Reformers: Beccaria, Bentham, Romilly.* London: Dent.

RADZINOWICZ, LEON 1948 *A History of English Criminal Law and Its Administration From 1750.* Volume 1: The Movement for Reform. London: Stevens.

SELLIN, THORSTEN 1959 *The Death Penalty: A Report for the Model Penal Code Project of the American Law Institute.* Philadelphia: American Law Institute.

SMITH, JOHN M. P. (1931) 1960 *The Origin and History of Hebrew Law.* Univ. of Chicago Press.

STEPHEN, JAMES F. 1883 *A History of the Criminal Law of England.* 3 vols. London: Macmillan.

UNITED NATIONS, DEPARTMENT OF ECONOMIC AND SOCIAL AFFAIRS 1962 *Capital Punishment.* New York: United Nations.

U.S. BUREAU OF PRISONS 1964 *Executions: 1930–1963.* U.S. Bureau of Prisons, National Prisoner Statistics, No. 34. Washington: The Bureau.

CAPITALISM

Capitalism is the economic and political system that in its industrial or "full" form first developed in England in the late eighteenth century. Thereafter, it spread over Europe, North America, Australia, New Zealand, and South Africa. Together with its colonial manifestations, it came to dominate the world during the nineteenth century. A limited form of "early" or commercial capitalism, already known in the ancient world, had developed in Italy as early as the thirteenth century and in the Low Countries a century later. This commercial form developed in England in the sixteenth century and began to change into industrial capitalism while elements of feudalism and the guild system still existed.

The United Kingdom during the nineteenth century so facilated the development and dominated the functioning of capitalism that this country might well have been called the business manager for international capitalism. With the outbreak of World War I, the dominant role in capitalism passed to the United States, coincident with the emergence of changes in the structure and functioning of capitalism. These changes were to culminate, after the Great Depression of the 1930s in the United States, in more important alterations that placed a period to old-style capitalism. The Bolshevik Revolution of 1917 had already ushered in the present era of hostile competition between modified capitalism and collectivist economic and political systems.

The precepts of Adam Smith with respect to the politico–economic system most effective in increasing the wealth of nations furnish the best analysis of the nature of capitalism as it emerged from its commercial or mercantile form into the age of industrial capitalism. Self-interest as ultimately the servant of society, the minimization of the role of the state, and the institution of private property constituted the essence of capitalism in the nineteenth and early twentieth centuries. Yet neither Smith nor his successors among the classical and neoclassical economists used the term "capitalism." While Karl Marx rarely, if ever, used the noun "capitalism," his use of the adjectives "capitalist" and "capitalistic" fastened the term on the modern economic systems of Europe and the United States.

Although it is useful to follow the Marxist pattern to some extent in the analysis of capitalism and its development, it is even more useful to compare capitalism with existing collectivist economic systems. These two comparisons are not at all the same thing. While the Soviet, the Chinese, and the Yugoslav economic systems owe their origins to Marx, they all depart in the most drastic fashion from the kind of society which Marx had envisaged as the successor to capitalism. Not only do they depart from the model, however incompletely shadowed forth by Marx, but they depart by different roads.

Preconditions and development

The seeds of capitalism can be found in the propensity in human nature "to truck, barter and exchange one thing for another" (Smith [1776] 1952, p. 6). There was doubtless never a stage in human history in which this propensity did not exist. It is a long step, however, from this to the entrepreneur who becomes a specialist in trucking and bartering and makes his living by the turnover of his stock of capital. History is replete with examples of the energy and ingenuity with which the rising merchant classes adapted existing laws and customs to their needs. The sea loan in Genoa in the twelfth and thirteenth centuries, devised under the guise of marine insurance to circumvent the laws against usury, is a case in point.

A surplus above subsistence is the precondition for the existence of all even slightly advanced forms of social organization, but neither the resulting economic system nor the political system need be capitalistic. The political system largely determines what classes and what individuals will be the recipients of the surplus above subsistence. Thus, "surplus value" in this sense existed both in feudal society and in the Egypt of the Pharaohs, but in neither case was a bourgeois class its recipient. Capital accumulation took place under commercial capitalism out of the profits of merchants, quite independent of the employment of workers for wages.

History shows extremely diverse patterns of economic development. In Babylonia, in the city-states of classical Greece, in Phoenicia, in Carthage, in the Hellenistic states of the Mediterranean littoral, and in the Roman Empire, there developed, during different ages, what might be called commercial capitalism. There was, however, little uniformity of economic and political institutions in these variant national forms of commercial capitalism. In ancient Egypt, for example, there existed a monarchic state capitalism, with the surplus above subsistence put at the disposal of the priestly and military bureaucracy in the service of the Pharaoh.

Even where merchant capitalism existed in the ancient world, large-scale applications of improved technology to goods production did not occur. In Rome, where many of the elements of commercial capitalism existed and where Roman law had become in some respects more "capitalistic" than current English and American law, the "next stage of capitalism" did not develop. Without an industrial technology, there could be no industrial capitalism.

It is equally true that until the political and economic institutions of modern capitalism developed, there could be no application of improved technology to large-scale production. We know that, repeatedly, national forms of commercial capitalism were destroyed by foreign conquest, by social conflict, and by barbarian invasion, or they simply died out. Instead of organic growth from a simpler to a more complex form of politico–economic system, there was until the eighteenth century in western Europe, in every case, a relapse.

Nor is feudalism an inevitable stage in the development of capitalism. Commercial capitalism existed in various countries in the ancient world without a prior stage resembling the feudalism of the Middle Ages in Europe. Industrial capitalism came into existence in the United States, in Canada, and in Australia without a prior stage of feudalism. By a rather heroic oversimplification, the precapitalistic era in Japan might be termed feudalism. In these cases, capitalism was an importation from more advanced countries. In some of the presently underdeveloped countries of the world, which were previously colonial, the stage of capitalism is now being "skipped" in favor of some form of collectivism.

Capital accumulation and the entrepreneur. The entrepreneur, assuming the risk in return for the expectation of profits of mercantile ventures in the early stages of capitalism, and of introducing new technology in the stage of industrial capitalism, played the crucial role in the development of capitalism. Schumpeter (1942) has pointed out that the entrepreneur was always dependent upon not only the accumulation of his own capital but also the aggregation of the capital of others. The financial resources upon which industrial capitalism was based had to pass directly or indirectly into the hands of entrepreneurs, through withholding or transferring income from the nonbourgeois elements—feudal landlords, monasteries, peasants, and laborers. Capital thus came into the hands of the *bourgeoisie*, who would save it, and then passed into the hands of entrepreneurs, who invested it, rather than remaining in the hands of those who would have consumed it.

For capital to be saved and invested by entrepreneurs, a minimum level of peace, law, and order was, and is, necessary. Capitalism has survived numberless wars, domestic disturbances, and even revolutions. There have been international rivalries involving struggles for colonies and spheres of influence. Innumerable individual capitalist entrepreneurs have, indeed, made huge profits out of war. Yet capitalism cannot function if violence is too great or if it is continuous. There must be substantial pauses between wars and revolutions. Government must be able to prevent mob violence. The typical entrepreneur of early capitalism, unlike the feudal lord, was unwarlike by temperament and motivated by the search for profit. Bourgeois civilization, compared with the forms of social organization that preceded it or with the totalitarian forms that now compete with it, has remained inherently peaceable, rationalistic, and materialistic.

Liberty and democracy. The enforcement of commercial contracts by the state and the extension and protection of property rights—all essential to the development of capitalism—required a strong government. The process of saving, investment, risk-taking, and profit-making flourished best, however, when the powers of the state were restricted so that their exercise would not be arbitrary. The modern parliamentary, democratic state, with a "bill of rights" protecting the individual against the arbitrary power of the state, was the eventual product of capitalism. The democratic political aspects of the later capitalistic state did, indeed, often result from the demands of the noncapitalistic classes of the population and were reluctantly accepted by capitalists. The capitalist then came to realize that the more democratic the parliamentary state became, the more limitations on the power of the state were necessary to protect him against the masses. Political democracy and a government of limited powers thus came to be closely linked with modern capitalism. This kind of political system is

obviously not characteristic of the collectivist states which are in competition with capitalism as alternative politico–economic systems.

Competition and laissez-faire. A formalized model of old-style capitalism would be characterized by pure and perfect competition in factor and product markets, complete laissez-faire, absolute private-property rights, individual enterprise, and a zero level of all but frictional involuntary unemployment. This formal model, however, has inherent limitations and contradictions that prevented its existence as an actual economic system.

Complete laissez-faire and pure and perfect competition have never been attained, even during the early stages of industrial capitalism. Not all of the laws and customs of feudalism, the guild system, and mercantilism had been eliminated when there began to develop new processes and institutions that also were inconsistent with a formal model of laissez-faire and competition. Some forms and degrees of competition were essential if unregulated production, exchange, and distribution were to be relied upon to maximize the social product. Yet the new processes and institutions either reduced competition or profoundly changed its nature. Large corporations, while reducing the number of competitive enterprises, were essential to lowered costs of production and prices. The formation of trusts, cartels, and a multiplicity of other forms of restraint of trade manifestly reduced competition. Antitrust legislation might protect competition, but these laws obviously involved a breach of the principle of laissez-faire. [*See* COMPETITION; LAISSEZ-FAIRE.]

The organizational economy. In the United States, the political decision, accompanied by much argument among economists, was to attempt to maintain competition by legislation, even at the cost of the principle of laissez-faire, in those industries that were not natural monopolies. Where the maintenance of competition was obviously impossible, state and federal regulation was substituted. In Great Britain, where until very recent times there was no such antitrust legislation, only the unenforceability of contracts in restraint of trade was relied upon to supplement the self-eroding tendencies of such agreements. Thus, in Great Britain, laissez-faire was maintained at the expense of competition. In Germany, cartels were not only permitted, but their contracts were in some cases enforceable at law. Both laissez-faire and competition were largely emasculated. Yet in all three countries large-scale corporate industry grew and the role of individual enterprise diminished. Quasi-monopolistic and oligopolistic institutions and practices, "price leadership," "administrative pricing," and other forms of imperfect competition in the markets for factors, goods, and services, as well as the transfer of control of corporations from capitalist-owners to management, meant that the capitalism had undergone a profound change. [See ANTITRUST LEGISLATION; CARTELS AND TRADE ASSOCIATIONS; CORPORATION; OLIGOPOLY.]

There was still another contradiction with respect to the role of competition under capitalism. Technological progress under capitalism depends upon the possibility of a temporary monopoly profit for the innovator. Schumpeter's picture (1942) of the temporarily high rate of profit attained by the innovator serving to rescue the economy from the depressing effect of competition upon the rate of return from capital has substantial validity. J. M. Clark (1961) has also pointed out that for competition to be "workable" it need not be perfect, and this position is generally accepted by most economists.

Modified capitalism

The institution of private property, so basic to capitalism and so essential to its functioning, had always involved a serious contradiction in its claim to serve the best interests of society by the allocation of personal income through the market. "From each according to his ability, to each according to his productivity" was obviously defective so long as one's distributive share was also determined by the productivity of one's property. The institution of private property could be insulated for a long time against the ultimate logic of political democracy by a variety of legal devices. In the United States, for example, the fifth and fourteenth amendments to the constitution were used for this purpose. With the coming of the New Deal in the early 1930s, however, it became impossible to maintain the sacrosanct character of private property. A series of decisions by the Supreme Court validating New Deal legislation removed the constitutional barrier to governmental action in the economic field.

In Europe, by the late nineteenth and early twentieth centuries, the growing power of the lower-income classes was responsible for the amelioration, through political action and labor union activity, of conditions of work and of inequality in the distribution of wealth and income. This insistence by the working classes on departing from the European variant of old-style capitalism reflected a real hostility to the system. There was, indeed, not only hostility to capitalism, but hope of attaining some sort of socialism as an alternative.

The New Deal. In the United States the combination of massive unemployment and the collapse of farm prices in the 1930s brought about popular demand for governmental intervention in, and control of, many elements in the economy not previously controlled. The great series of legislative and administrative measures by which the government came to play a larger and larger role in the economic system was never admitted to be anticapitalistic by the Roosevelt administration. On the contrary, all of these measures were represented as essential to prevent the collapse of capitalism. The charge by conservatives that these measures represented "creeping socialism" never received popular support.

The series of economic measures of the New Deal, including control of agricultural prices, production, and marketing; the sanctioning and support of collective bargaining; social security legislation; the increase in the progressivity of income taxes; regulation of the security exchanges; increased governmental control over money and banking; the conscious use of deficit financing; the great increase in the proportion of national income flowing through the governmental budget; and the great increase in the proportion of the labor force in governmental employment, meant a significant change in the capitalistic system. The later legislative acceptance, which came about after World War II, of the responsibility of the federal government to attempt to maintain full employment represented another step in the same direction. All these changes served to differentiate modified capitalism from old-style capitalism. [See WELFARE STATE.]

While these changes in American capitalism brought about by the New Deal were generally resisted by upper-income classes in the United States, they were eventually accepted as inevitable. American industrialists even began sometimes to refer to the existing economic system as "people's capitalism." Another approach saw capitalism in the United States as the "affluent society," with both old-style competition and old-style monopolistic practices superseded by "countervailing power" that could be relied upon to maintain a balance between large buyers and large sellers and between labor unions and industrial giants—with governmental power exerted to aid economic groups whose organizational potentialities were small (Galbraith 1952). Communists deny vehemently the concepts of a "people's capitalism" or of a Galbraithian affluent society and insist that the United States is still in the last stage of capitalism—"monopoly capitalism."

Renewed support for free market capitalism. There has arisen, however, since the end of World War II, a group of economists in the United States, West Germany, and Switzerland, organized as the Mont Pelerin Society, who deny the existence of a third stage of capitalism by whatever name. In particular, they deny that the capitalistic system is less competitive than it ever was. They point out that there has been no sharp increase in industrial concentration in the United States during recent decades. They argue that the larger size of corporations means lower costs of production, particularly through massive research expenditures, and hence more effective competition than ever. [*See* ECONOMIES OF SCALE; INDUSTRIAL CONCENTRATION.] They do not concede that the pricing process of "competition among the few" differs from the atomistic competition of individual enterprises; or they do not admit the significance of such a difference if it does exist.

They consider almost all of the recent extension of the sphere of government to have been unnecessary and to have caused mal-allocation of resources. Although it would be politically difficult to accomplish, they believe most governmental controls could be stripped away, as was done with much of the system of controls in West Germany after the destruction of the Nazi system and the end of the Allied occupation. These economists have idealized and vigorously advocated the "social free market economy."

Capitalistic pluralism. In any case, the current forms of capitalism in all countries are characterized by a high degree and wide extent of pluralism. The role of the individual, within and among the corporate organizational forms that have come to characterize capitalism, remains important. Corporations still compete with each other even though the forms of competition have changed. The managements of corporations and the managements of labor unions carry out collective bargaining, not without governmental intervention, but at least without continuous government dominance. The process by which the managements of corporations and of labor unions come into power is highly complex and differentiated, but it is not dominated by government. Separation of economic and political powers is still characteristic.

The freedom of individuals under capitalism to undertake the production of any product or service where profit appears attainable is accompanied by the widest diversity in organizational forms. In collectivist economic systems only state authority can sanction production, and organizational forms are rigidly prescribed. Totalitarian regimes do not tolerate the existence of associations which are not closely controlled by the one-party state. Voluntary and spontaneous organization of individuals consequently cannot exist. Since capitalism can hardly be said to have an ideology, its economic pluralism is complementary to its pluralism in political, social, and cultural activities and organizational forms.

Capitalism and collectivism

Economists who conceived of a third stage of "late capitalism" as did Sombart (1902) and Schumpeter (1942), thought of capitalism as being on the eve of replacement by quite a different economic system. To this limited extent, they were in agreement with Lenin who had alluded in his *State and Revolution* (1917) to "monopolistic capitalism" as the latest phase of capitalism. There was both divergence of views and uncertainty about the nature of the successor economic system, but there was agreement that it would be a collectivist economic system. Whether such a collectivist economic system would take the form of democratic socialism or of a Soviet or a Nazi type of totalitarian state was a cardinal point of disagreement. Those who visualized the successor system to capitalism as democratic socialism assumed that the transformation would be gradual and peaceful. Those who foresaw the coming of a totalitarian economic and political system inevitably visualized the change as revolutionary and violent.

It is clear that there is no one historical process operative in all countries that eliminates capitalism and produces basically identical economic and political systems that could be called socialist. The communists looked upon the Nazi economic and political system in Germany as the very embodiment of monopoly capitalism, the last stage, to be followed by its revolutionary overthrow and the dictatorship of the proletariat. The Nazis visualized their form of the totalitarian state as the successor to bourgeois capitalism, but different from it in the most basic way. Yet, the economic system of the economically most important part of Germany today conforms neither to the Nazi nor to the Soviet forms of the totalitarian state, any more than the Soviet totalitarian state conforms to the Marxist model. Instead, the current economic system of West Germany approaches the economists' theoretical model of competition and laissez-faire more nearly than did the pre-Hitler German economic system.

It is equally clear that where collectivist economic systems have come into existence, they did not follow upon any stage of "late capitalism." Whether in the case of Soviet Russia, of communist China, of the communist states of eastern Europe, or of Cuba, the predecessor economic system in no instance had been characterized by highly developed industrialism and often could hardly have been designated as capitalistic. Furthermore, the economic systems of these noncapitalistic countries differ radically each from the other. The economic system of communist China is very different from that of Soviet Russia, and the economic system of Yugoslavia differs from both. Their political systems do have similarities. Since they are totalitarian, they are one-party states. They have neither free elections nor real parliamentary government. There is no protection of the individual against the power of the state. The personal dictator plays a major role. It is in the political systems of these collectivist economic systems that the greatest differences from capitalism exist.

The process of change from "old-style capitalism" to modified capitalism differed in detail between the United States and western Europe. At one time it appeared that the Social Democratic parties of western Europe and the Labour party of the United Kingdom might bring about the transformation of modified capitalism into democratic socialism through the gradual nationalization of industry. The movement toward further nationalization of industry in both the United Kingdom and in western Europe has now lost momentum. It is not even any longer seriously advocated by the socialist parties of western Europe. There is little evidence that nationalization in those industries where it occurred materially reduced inequality in income distribution or that it improved the productivity of labor through any change in motivation. Govermental planning of investment and wage and price levels, in cooperation with labor organizations and employer organizations, varying in kind and detail from country to country, has afforded a psychological substitute for nationalization. The high rate of increase in real wages, even if causing serious problems of "cost-push" inflation, has likewise greatly strengthened popular support for the current "mixed" form of economic system. Consequently, the prospect in western Europe for a change from the existing forms of capitalism to some form of collectivist economic system by democratic and parliamentary means has faded.

The majority of the underdeveloped countries, such as India, Burma, Indonesia, Egypt, Algeria, and the sub-Saharan countries of Africa, which have just emerged from colonial rule, have repudiated capitalism and have proclaimed a socialist economic system as a goal to be attained as soon as feasible. These countries, however, cannot nationalize nonexistent industries and hence cannot go over at once to a modern type of collectivized economy. Radical movements in Latin America, sometimes dominated by communists, are also anticapitalistic. They tend to favor "socialism" on the Cuban model. Whether the goal of socialism, of a democratic or totalitarian form, will remain the national objective depends in part upon the rate of economic growth of countries that adhere to the current form of capitalism, compared with that of nations such as the Soviet Union, China, and Yugoslavia with their variant forms of collectivist economic systems. [See NATIONALIZATION; PLANNING, ECONOMIC.]

Economic organization in capitalistic and collectivist systems. The organization of modern capitalistic business corporations has come to resemble that of governmental corporations and bureaus. There are also obvious similarities in organization and operation between a Soviet trust and a large capitalistic corporation, just as there are similarities between governmental bureaus or public corporations, such the Tennessee Valley Authority or the Port of London Authority, and private corporations, such as the United States Steel Corporation or the Imperial Chemical Company, Ltd.

The role of profits and interest in capitalistic countries remains, indeed, vastly more important than in Soviet-type economic systems. Nevertheless, crude substitutes for the interest rate as an allocator of investment funds in the Soviet economy have been developed, and there have recently been proposals for allowing profits to play a role in Soviet industry more nearly like that in capitalistic countries. There has likewise been some effort through the reorganization of Soviet industry to allow the market to have a greater role in price determination. [See COMMUNISM, ECONOMIC ORGANIZATION OF.]

The managerial class. The "New Class" that makes up the bureaucracy which manages the Soviet or the Chinese or the Yugoslav economy and the governments of these countries as well, decides on the division of the social product between consumption and investment and between labor in industry and labor in agriculture. It decides as well on the more detailed divisions between the different branches of industry, between skilled and unskilled labor, and so on. This "New Class" has obvious similarities to the managerial class of current capitalism. The compensation of the managers of a collectivist economy in salaries, bonuses, and other fringe benefits is of major importance in their decision making. They are not restricted by the market or by the managers of labor unions when they decide how much they should withhold for themselves from laborer-consumers. Government and party officials, army and police officers, labor union leaders, managers of collective farms, and industrial managers are all part of an undifferentiated ruling hierarchy. The constraints of free elections and of parliamentary government upon managerial decisions are absent.

The managerial class under corporate capitalism, like the "New Class" in Soviet-type economies, also determines in large measure its own compensation—but within the constraints of the market, of government, and of the counterclaims of the managers of labor unions. To the extent that top management of corporations is independent of stockholder control, however, salaries, "incentive" stock options, expense accounts, and other fringe benefits are not effectively limited by market constraints.

Comparative ethics. Critics in the past attacked capitalism especially on the ground that an economic system based upon self-interest and the pursuit of profit was essentially without social ethics. It was confidently asserted that a system of socialism would increase social motivation. In consequence, the coercive functions of the state could then be greatly curtailed or even eliminated. The record of the countries having collectivist types of economic systems affords no evidence to support this conclusion. There is no evidence that workers or managers in collectivist economic systems work more willingly and efficiently than do those under capitalism. The Soviet Union and every other collectivist type of economic system have had to resort to incentive payments to compensate for higher skills, greater productivity, or greater responsibility in management. There has been no evidence at all that economic crimes such as embezzlement, speculation, and theft have declined in Soviet Russia as the "heritage of capitalistic motivation" faded into history.

In every society, whether capitalistic or collectivist, the ethical problem of how the managerial class is to determine its own compensation arises. Since the managements of modern capitalistic corporations typically are autonomous with respect to their stockholders, new ethical problems inevitably have arisen. Is profit maximization for the benefit of the stockholders to continue to be the primary goal of management, as was true under old-style capitalism? Even if profits are maximized, what are the ethical limits on the management's power

to withhold these profits from the stockholders—in the form of stock options, large pension arrangements, and the like—for the benefit of management? There have been innumerable flagrant cases of such withholding in the United States in recent decades.

Economic stability. Capitalism is currently not plagued, as it seemed to be during the economic depression of the 1930s, by the threat of a Keynesian-type depression. There is currently no lack of investment outlets for savings. These investment outlets have earnings above that minimum rate of interest which Keynes envisaged as inhibiting further saving in an affluent society and which "can interfere, in conditions mainly of laissez-faire, with a reasonable level of employment and with the standard of life which the technical conditions of production are capable of furnishing" (1936, p. 219). Capitalistic countries have learned to cope with this kind of general deficiency in purchasing power, but they are still periodically faced with the choice between unemployment and rising prices.

Economic growth rates. In statistical comparisons of the annual rate of economic growth of capitalistic countries with that of the Soviet economy, the rates the Soviets claimed, in the early years, of 15 and even 20 per cent must be discarded as quite unreal. A rate of increase of some 6 per cent per annum during the period of the 1950s may be taken to represent reality. This was almost double the United States rate of increase of some 3½ per cent during the same period. While the higher rates continued, they reduced somewhat the relative disparity between the standard of living of the Soviet Union and capitalistic countries. The absolute disparity remains great and in the most recent years has even been growing. In recent years the rate of increase in Japan, for example, has been substantially higher than that of the Soviet Union. By the early 1960s, the rate of economic growth in the Soviet Union had begun to decline and has now fallen to a rate little, if any, above that of the United States or the countries of western Europe. Very slow capital construction has largely offset high rates of saving and investment.

The rate of economic growth in the Soviet Union, as in all other collectivist economies, has been held down by the extremely low efficiency of agricultural production. By contrast, the increase of efficiency in agricultural production in substantially all capitalistic countries has led to serious surplus problems. Access to the surplus agricultural production of capitalist countries has frequently saved communist countries from serious shortages. The failure of the "great leap forward" has, at least temporarily, discredited Chinese communism as a means of attaining economic growth.

Income distribution. Statistical evidence indicates the extent to which the masses of the population of capitalistic countries have benefited from economic growth. Improvements in productivity as a result of better technology and education have played a much larger role in increases in per capita production in the United States than have increases in the quantity of capital. A recent study for the National Bureau of Economic Research (Kendrick 1961) estimates that in the United States improvements in productivity accounted for about four-fifths of the per capita increase in production over the period 1919–1957. The same study estimates that labor obtained over 90 per cent of this productivity increment and that labor's share of the national income increased from a little more than 70 per cent in 1919 to slightly more than 80 per cent in 1957. This estimate is supported by another study of the bureau, which found that wages in manufacturing in the United States in 1954, the last year of the study, were about 86 per cent of total income, with capital receiving 14 per cent (after taxes). For the period 1939–1954, the average of the wage share was above 80 per cent (Stigler 1963). Efforts have been made to explain away the increase in labor's share which the raw data show. Some economists even claim that the shares have remained virtually unchanged over time.

It has become ever more difficult in current capitalism to separate capital as a factor of production from capital as merely the functional recipient of a distributive share. New capital construction reflects new technology rather than simply quantitative replacements of, or additions to, the stock of capital. Investment in research, which in accounting terms is a corporate expense rather than an addition to capital, has enormously increased. Similarly, labor is losing its identity as a factor purchased by the capitalist for its physical productivity. Clerical workers, salesmen, managerial personnel, engineers, and research scientists and their assistants constitute a larger and larger proportion of the labor force as automation progresses.

The findings of Simon Kuznets (1963) with respect to the decline in inequality of income in the United States are consistent with the trend of an increase in labor's share. Some recent indications of a partial reversal of this trend toward greater equality in income distribution do not offset the declining trend in inequality during the last 40 years. Kuznets has conjectured that the early effects of capitalistic industrialization may have been to increase inequality in income distribution while the later effects tend to narrow inequality. He has found that inequality is greater now in the underdeveloped countries than in the developed countries characterized by the current forms of capitalism.

In spite of obesity taking the place of hunger as a problem in modern capitalistic countries, poverty remains a problem for a substantial fraction of the population. In the United States, perhaps 20 per cent of the population still receive incomes below an adequate minimum. These people are largely the aged, those from broken families, minority groups, the undereducated, and the unemployed. These are, of course, overlapping categories. It is not capitalism's inability to produce national income that is responsible for these remnants of poverty. It is rather sectoral, organizational, and distributional difficulties, which have not yet been overcome. [*See* INCOME DISTRIBUTION; POVERTY.]

Prospects for the survival of modified capitalism. There is no longer any prospect for the outright, peaceful replacement of capitalism by socialism. Capitalism in all countries where it still exists has come to contain elements formerly associated with socialism. The further development of social security legislation; a continuation of redistribution of income through legislative measures and labor union activities; and the development of institutions for tripartite economic planning by government officials, the management of labor unions, and corporate managements have blurred the separation between socialism and capitalism.

Although the Soviet press still retains the habit of speaking of one "socialist camp" as opposed to the "capitalist camp," the recent histories of Soviet Russia, Yugoslavia, and communist China demonstrate that no such homogeneous "socialist camp" exists, either in terms of the organization and functioning of the economic systems, or in terms of the degree of hostility toward capitalistic countries.

The possibility of the overthrow of capitalistic governments by armed force cannot be excluded. Yet, it is no longer inevitable, or even likely, that in the event of armed conflict all communist countries would be united against capitalistic countries. The likelihood of global nuclear devastation if war does break out, however, removes this eventuality from the realm of economic or political analysis.

CALVIN B. HOOVER

BIBLIOGRAPHY

BERGSON, ABRAM; and KUZNETS, SIMON (editors) 1963 *Economic Trends in the Soviet Union.* Cambridge, Mass.: Harvard Univ. Press.

CLARK, JOHN MAURICE 1961 *Competition as a Dynamic Process.* Washington: Brookings Institution.

COMMONS, JOHN ROGERS (1924) 1959 *Legal Founda-*

tions of Capitalism. Madison: Univ. of Wisconsin Press.

DJILAS, MILOVAN 1957 The New Class: An Analysis of the Communist System. New York: Praeger.

Economic Systems of the Commonwealth. 1962 Edited by Calvin B. Hoover. Durham, N.C.: Duke Univ. Press.

FREI, RUDOLF (editor) 1957–1959 Wirtschaftssysteme des Westens. 2 vols. Tübingen (Germany): Mohr; Basel: Kyklos.

GALBRAITH, JOHN KENNETH (1952) 1956 American Capitalism: The Concept of Countervailing Power. Rev. ed. Boston: Houghton Mifflin.

HOOVER, CALVIN B. 1959 The Economy, Liberty and the State. New York: Twentieth Century Fund.

KENDRICK, JOHN W. 1961 Productivity Trends in the United States. National Bureau of Economic Research, General Series, No. 71. Princeton Univ. Press.

KEYNES, JOHN MAYNARD 1926 Laissez-faire and Communism. New York: New Republic.

KEYNES, JOHN MAYNARD 1936 The General Theory of Employment, Interest and Money. London: Macmillan. → A paperback edition was published in 1965 by Harcourt.

KUZNETS, SIMON 1963 Quantitative Aspects of the Economic Growth of Nations: 8. Distribution by Income Size. Economic Development and Cultural Change 11, no. 2 (part 2): 1–80.

LAMPMAN, ROBERT J. 1962 The Share of Top Wealth-holders in National Wealth 1922–56. National Bureau of Economic Research, General Series, No. 74. Princeton Univ. Press.

LENIN, VLADIMIR I. (1917) 1964 The State and Revolution: The Marxist Theory of the State and the Tasks of the Proletariat in the Revolution. Volume 25, pages 381–492 in Vladimir I. Lenin, Collected Works. 4th ed. Moscow: Foreign Languages Publishing House. → First published in Russian.

MARX, KARL (1867–1879) 1925–1926 Capital: A Critique of Political Economy. 3 vols. Chicago: Kerr. → Volume 1: The Process of Capitalist Production. Volume 2: The Process of Circulation of Capital. Volume 3: The Process of Capitalist Production as a Whole. Volume 1 was published in 1867. The manuscripts of Volumes 2 and 3 were written between 1867 and 1879. They were first published posthumously in German in 1885 and 1894.

MASON, EDWARD S. (editor) 1960 The Corporation in Modern Society. Cambridge, Mass.: Harvard Univ. Press.

RÖPKE, WILHELM 1958 Ein Jahrzehnt sozialer Marktwirtschaft in Deutschland und seine Lehren. Cologne (Germany): Verlag für Politik und Wirtschaft.

ROSTOVTSEV, MIKHAIL I. (1926) 1957 The Social and Economic History of the Roman Empire. 2 vols. 2d ed., rev. Oxford: Clarendon.

ROSTOVTSEV, MIKHAIL I. 1941 The Social & Economic History of the Hellenistic World. 3 vols. Oxford Univ. Press.

SCHUMPETER, JOSEPH A. (1942) 1950 Capitalism, Socialism, and Democracy. 3d ed. New York: Harper; London: Allen & Unwin.

SMITH, ADAM (1776) 1952 An Inquiry Into the Nature and Causes of the Wealth of Nations. Great Books of the Western World, Vol. 39. Chicago: Encyclopaedia Britannica. → A two-volume paperback edition was published in 1963 by Irwin.

SOMBART, WERNER (1902) 1924–1927 Der moderne Kapitalismus: Historisch-systematische Darstellung des gesamteuropäischen Wirtschaftslebens von seinen Anfängen bis zur Gegenwart. 3 vols. Munich and Leipzig: Duncker & Humblot. → Volumes 1 and 2 are the fourth edition; Volume 3 is the third edition.

STIGLER, GEORGE J. 1963 Capital and Rates of Return in Manufacturing Industries. A study of the National Bureau of Economic Research. Princeton Univ. Press.

CARDOZO, BENJAMIN

It is noteworthy that President Hoover's choice, in February 1932, of Benjamin Nathan Cardozo for a place on the Supreme Court as the successor to Justice Oliver Wendell Holmes was greeted with well-nigh universal acclaim. As Cardozo's colleagues on the New York Court of Appeals said in their affectionate farewell to their "beloved Chief Judge," "You were appointed neither for political nor geographical considerations, but in defiance of them and because the whole country demanded the one man who could best carry on the great Holmes tradition of philosophic approach to modern American jurisprudence." Cardozo's 18 creative years on New York's highest tribunal and the profound scholarship of his extrajudicial writings had won him an international reputation as a humane, imaginative, and learned judge.

Cardozo (1870–1938) was born in New York City of Portuguese-Jewish parentage. His father, a judge on the New York Supreme Court, resigned from the bench because of his connection with the notorious Tweed ring. This tragic episode, far from discouraging Cardozo from entering the legal profession, seems to have spurred him on to vindicate his family's good name.

Cardozo received his undergraduate education at Columbia College and studied for two years at Columbia Law School. Without waiting to receive a law degree, he was admitted to the bar in 1891.

By the time his first book appeared in 1903—The Jurisdiction of the Court of Appeals of the State of New York—he had already achieved a wide reputation for his brilliant work in arguing before the state's appellate courts. He had become "a lawyer's lawyer." In 1913 he was elected to the Supreme Court of New York but served for only a few weeks. On the request of the members of the Court of Appeals of New York, Governor Glynn designated him to serve as an associate judge on that court. With the endorsement of both major political parties, he was elected for a full 14-year term in 1917, and with similar backing he was elected chief judge in 1926.

Both his distinctive attitude toward modern problems and his felicitous (some have called it elegant or florid) style of expression were evident in Cardozo's utterances as a state judge. Whatever the subject matter—torts, contracts, crimes—these opinions were marked by a considered effort to bend the law to the needs of people living in a society that had been transformed by changing industrialism and technology.

Probably his most celebrated opinion on the Court of Appeals was that in *MacPherson* v. *Buick Motor Company* (217 N.Y. 382), and it well illustrates his approach. The MacPherson case was a suit for damages for personal injuries resulting from the collapse of the defective steering wheel of a 1914 Buick. It was argued by the company's lawyers that the manufacturer was not liable because the contract was with the dealer from whom the car had been purchased. They relied on an old English case in which the court had held that the contractor who had sold the post office department an imperfect stagecoach was not liable for the injuries sustained by the driver of the coach. Cardozo spoke for a majority of the Court of Appeals in refusing to be bound by this precedent and stated: "Precedents drawn from the days of travel by stagecoach do not fit the conditions of travel to-day. The principle that danger must be imminent does not change, but the things subject to the principle do change. They are whatever the needs of life in a developing civilization require them to be."

But the student of Cardozo's philosophy of law and of justice need not depend only on inferences to be gleaned from judicial opinions. While serving on the Court of Appeals, Cardozo found time to write four books in which he systematically set forth his fundamental ideas. Although most apparent in his now classic little volume, *The Nature of the Judicial Process*, published in 1921, Cardozo's deep concern with the subtleties of the function performed by judges permeates his other major extrajudicial writings—*The Growth of the Law* (1924); *The Paradoxes of Legal Science* (1928); and *Law and Literature* (1921–1930). As Justice Felix Frankfurter wrote soon after Cardozo's death: "Perhaps a few, but at best a very few, judges had as keen an insight into the peculiar rôle of the judge in the American scheme" (Frankfurter 1939, p. 440). And Edwin W. Patterson, the first Cardozo professor of jurisprudence at Columbia Law School, described *The Nature of the Judicial Process* as "the most original and significant of his works" (see Patterson in Cardozo [1921–1939] 1947, p. ix).

Cardozo confessed that he spent many "moments of introspection" searching for the answer to his own simply worded question: "What is it that I do when I decide a case?" In most instances, as he saw it, lawyers and judges are merely busy looking for applicable precedents; they are engaged in a more or less mechanical process of, figuratively speaking, "matching colors." There are occasions, however, when the constitutional provisions that have been invoked are not at all clear, or legislation on the subject is either lacking or ambiguous, or there are conflicting precedents. When such situations arise, the judge has an opportunity to fill in the "gaps" by inventing new principles or by resourcefully adapting old ones. Cardozo suggested that in these cases there were four possible roads to decision:

The directive force of a principle may be exerted along the line of logical progression; this I will call the rule of analogy or the method of philosophy; along the line of historical development; this I will call the method of evolution; along the line of the customs of the community; this I will call the method of tradition; along the lines of justice, morals and social welfare, the *mores* of the day; and this I will call the method of sociology. (1921, pp. 30–31)

In discussing the role of the judge as a legislator (1921, pp. 98–171), Cardozo made it clear that to the modern jurist considerations of social utility are particularly challenging. "The final cause of law," he observed categorically, "is the welfare of society" (1921, p. 66). In pursuing that goal, the judge must feel free to consult all available sources of knowledge and insight: "Courts know today that statutes are to be viewed not in isolation or *in vacuo*, as pronouncements of abstract principles for the guidance of an ideal community, but in the setting and framework of present-day conditions, as revealed by the labors of economists and students of the social sciences in our own country and abroad" (1921, p. 81).

Although his tenure on the Supreme Court was unfortunately of short duration (a mere six years), Cardozo succeeded in leaving a permanent imprint on the Court's constitutional jurisprudence. On the great issues that deeply divided the court during the years of the depression, he aligned himself with Justices Louis D. Brandeis and Harlan Fiske Stone, who were occasionally joined by Chief Justice Charles Evans Hughes and Justice Owen J. Roberts. More than once he spoke for the dissenters in vindicating the right of government, national and state, to foster programs of economic regulation and social welfare.

When, in the spring of 1937, the Court began to be more receptive to New Deal experiments, he helped to form the new majorities, as in the cases upholding the constitutionality of the National

Labor Relations Act and the Social Security Act. Indeed, Cardozo was the Court's spokesman in the two principal social security cases (*Steward Machine Company* v. *Davis,* 301 U.S. 548, 1937; *Helvering* v. *Davis,* 301 U.S. 619, 1937). His assertion in the first of these cases, "It is too late today for the argument to be heard with tolerance that in a crisis so extreme the use of the moneys of the nation to relieve the unemployed and their dependents is a use for any purpose narrower than the promotion of the general welfare," may justly be regarded as a reversal of the interpretation of the general welfare clause of the constitution that had served as the basis for the invalidation of the Agricultural Adjustment Act the year before (*Steward Machine Company* v. *Davis,* 301 U.S. 548, 586–587, 1937).

It was in the same year that Cardozo also wrote his best-known opinion in a civil liberties case. Although he led the Court in denying the particular constitutional right claimed by the criminal defendant, he used the occasion to analyze the philosophy (the "rationalizing principle," he called it) that has served as the justification for an important doctrinal innovation. This is the basis of the process by which the Supreme Court, beginning in the 1920s, has been reading into the "liberty" that the fourteenth amendment protects against violation by the states some of the rights guaranteed by the federal bill of rights against abridgment by Congress. His words explaining this significant development have come to be widely quoted:

We reach a different plane of social and moral values when we pass to the privileges and immunities that have been taken over from the earlier articles of the federal bill of rights and brought within the Fourteenth Amendment by a process of absorption. These in their origin were effective against the federal government alone. If the Fourteenth Amendment has absorbed them, the process of absorption has had its source in the belief that neither liberty nor justice would exist if they were sacrificed. . . . This is true, for illustration, of freedom of thought and speech. Of that freedom one may say that it is the matrix, the indispensable condition, of nearly every other form of freedom. . . . So it has come about that the domain of liberty, withdrawn by the Fourteenth Amendment from encroachment by the states, has been enlarged by latter-day judgments to include liberty of the mind as well as liberty of action. (*Palko* v. *Connecticut,* 302 U.S. 319, 326–327, 1937)

SAMUEL J. KONEFSKY

[For *the historical context of Cardozo's work, see* JUDICIARY; JURISPRUDENCE; LEGAL REASONING; *and the biographies of* HOLMES *and* POUND.]

WORKS BY CARDOZO

(1903) 1909   *The Jurisdiction of the Court of Appeals of the State of New York.* 2d ed. Albany: Banks.

(1921) 1960   *The Nature of the Judicial Process.* New Haven: Yale Univ. Press.

(1921–1930) 1931   *Law and Literature and Other Essays and Addresses.* New York: Harcourt.

(1921–1939) 1947   *Selected Writings.* Edited by Margaret E. Hall, with a foreword by Edwin W. Patterson. New York: Fallon.

1924   *The Growth of the Law.* New Haven: Yale Univ. Press.

1928   *The Paradoxes of Legal Science.* New York: Columbia Univ. Press.

SUPPLEMENTARY BIBLIOGRAPHY

Essays Dedicated to Mr. Justice Cardozo.   1939   *Columbia Law Review* 39, no. 1.

FRANKFURTER, FELIX   1939   Mr. Justice Cardozo and Public Law. *Harvard Law Review* 52:440–470. → Also published in Volume 39 of the *Columbia Law Review* and Volume 48 of the *Yale Law Journal.*

HELLMAN, GEORGE S.   1940   *Benjamin N. Cardozo: American Judge.* New York: McGraw-Hill.

LEVY, BERYL H.   (1938) 1965   *Cardozo and Frontiers of Legal Thinking: With Selected Opinions.* Port Washington, N.Y.: Kennikat.

POLLARD, JOSEPH P.   1935   *Mr. Justice Cardozo: A Liberal Mind in Action.* New York: Yorktown.

CAREERS

See OCCUPATIONS AND CAREERS; POLITICAL RECRUITMENT AND CAREERS; PROFESSIONS; VOCATIONAL INTEREST TESTING; VOCATIONAL REHABILITATION.

CAREY, HENRY C.

Henry Charles Carey (1793–1879), American social scientist, was born in Philadelphia. A pervasive influence in his life was his father, Mathew Carey (1760–1839), an immigrant from Ireland who made a name for himself as a Catholic spokesman, reformer, humanitarian, anti-British and protectionist publicist, supporter of Hamilton's and Clay's American system, and founder of a great publishing house, which was used to disseminate his and his son's copious writings. Even though the son broke with the ancestral faith and became a wavering Episcopalian, his life was in many respects the fulfillment of that of the father. He started work in the paternal firm at the age of eight, became its head in his early thirties, and retired after less than ten years to devote himself to the promotion of his widespread business interests in manufacturing, real estate, and utilities. Side by side with these activities he found time for a literary career that yielded more than 13 substantial books and about six thousand pages of pamphlet and newspaper material. He was one of the leading citizens of Philadelphia, and as an influential figure in state and national politics his advice was sought by more than one president. Had he been willing he could probably have held high public office himself. On his death he was referred to as America's most widely known private citizen.

Not since the time of Thomas Mun and Josiah Child had a businessman's economic writings exerted as strong an appeal as did Carey's. In substance, too, with their emphasis on economic nationalism and protectionism, there is a parallel with the thought of the mercantilists, as there is also in the insinuation that they helped to serve the author's own business interests.

Carey never failed to preach the harmony of economic interests. His optimistic outlook was typically American and marked a sharp break with the "dismal science" of Ricardo and Malthus, with whose views about free trade, population, rent, and wages he found as much fault as he did with the institutions and policies of Britain.

Initially, Carey embraced protectionism only haltingly. In his first book, *Essay on the Rate of Wages*, he depicted restrictions on foreign trade as a "disgrace" frustrating "the beneficent designs of the Deity" ([1835] 1960, p. 14). In other respects this work anticipated many ideas that were more fully worked out in Carey's later writings, such as the harmonious "law of distribution," which makes the accumulation of capital the all-important instrument of concordant economic progress: with capital increasing more rapidly than population and with increasing production, profits rise absolutely and wages absolutely and relatively. Soon thereafter, Carey published his *Principles of Political Economy* (1837–1840), in which he developed a reproduction cost theory of value. In this work he extended the harmony between capital and labor to the relationship between these and the landowner, interpreting the landowner's return as a reward for the application of capital to land rather than as the mere result of the operation of the forces of nature. In this harmonious ordering of the economic universe, in which the landowner appears in a better light than he does in the Ricardian tradition, population growth need not constitute a serious problem: it is not governed by a law of nature but is subject to social conditioning in the form of restraint. Carey's harmony doctrine and his value theory invited comparison with similar views of Bastiat, and there was a protracted controversy about the respective priorities.

The break with Ricardo and Malthus—but not with Adam Smith, whose views Carey ostensibly upheld and which he considered perverted by Ricardo and Malthus—becomes complete in *The Past, the Present, and the Future* (1848), in which Carey further developed his theory of rent and revealed himself to be a thoroughgoing protectionist. Basic to his theory of rent is the idea that cultivation moves from inferior to superior land, an order that reverses the one postulated by Ricardo, with resulting increasing rather than diminishing returns. Carey advocated protection because it conformed to his law of association: it encouraged "commerce," an associative link between producer and consumer, rather than "trade," which required middlemen, and facilitated centralization and combinations. Commerce, therefore, produced the kind of diversification of economic activities that was an important element in Carey's law; other elements were the diffusion of an increasing population and a decentralized organization of society. Carey made much of this law in his writings.

In *The Harmony of Interests* (1851) the protectionist argument is again developed and given popular appeal. In *The Slave Trade* (1853) Carey argued that protectionism was even more badly needed in the South than in the North in the United States: it would reduce the dependency of the South on foreign trade, stimulate its industrial development, put an end to slavery, and bring about its economic integration with the North.

Carey's later works go beyond the boundaries of economics, branching out into social and cosmic science. They are in line with the rise of sociological thought elsewhere and reflect the influence of Comte and possibly also of Spencer. The *Principles of Social Science* (1858–1860) restates many of Carey's earlier ideas and demonstrates the harmonious order of the cosmos. *The Unity of Law* (1872) claims a providential identity of cosmic and social laws. An unfriendly critic called it "a work which offers a rich harvest of blunders in physics" (Cossa [1876] 1893, p. 468).

In his method Carey aimed to support his theories with abundant references to historical and statistical material and to natural science. He was a pioneer in the use of quantitative data as well as in their graphic presentation. His works may be rhetorical and redundant, but the patient reader is rewarded with occasional insights. Carey's writings were widely translated, and his fame spread far beyond his homeland. For some time he had considerable following in Continental Europe, especially in Germany, where he found a faithful apostle in Eugen Dühring, whom he remembered in his will. Carey had some academic adherents, especially in Philadelphia, but his influence on the later development of a more disciplined and specialized economic science was slight.

HENRY W. SPIEGEL

[*For the historical context of Carey's work, see* ECONOMIC THOUGHT, *article on* MERCANTILIST THOUGHT; LAISSEZ-FAIRE; *and the biographies of* BASTIAT; COMTE; MALTHUS; RICARDO; SMITH, ADAM. *See also* ECONOMIC GROWTH; INTERNATIONAL TRADE.]

WORKS BY CAREY

(1835) 1960 *Essay on the Rate of Wages.* New York: Kelley.

(1837–1840) 1960 *Principles of Political Economy.* 3 vols. in 1. New York: Kelley.

(1848) 1859 *The Past, the Present, and the Future.* Philadelphia: Carey & Hart.

(1851) 1890 *The Harmony of Interests, Agricultural, Manufacturing and Commercial.* Philadelphia: Skinner.

(1853) 1862 *The Slave Trade, Domestic and Foreign: Why It Exists and How It May Be Extinguished.* Philadelphia: Carey & Hart.

(1858–1860) 1963 *Principles of Social Science.* 3 vols. New York: Kelley.

1872 *The Unity of Law: As Exhibited in the Relations of Physical, Social, Mental and Moral Science.* Philadelphia: Baird.

SUPPLEMENTARY BIBLIOGRAPHY

BERNARD, LUTHER L.; and BERNARD, JESSIE 1943 *Origins of American Sociology: The Social Science Movement in the United States.* New York: Crowell.

COSSA, LUIGI (1876) 1893 *An Introduction to the Study of Political Economy.* London and New York: Macmillan. → First published as *Economia politica.*

DORFMAN, JOSEPH (1946) 1965 *The Economic Mind in American Civilization.* Volumes 1–2: 1606–1865. New York: Kelley. → See especially Chapter 29.

GREEN, ARNOLD W. 1951 *Henry Charles Carey: Nineteenth-century Sociologist.* Philadelphia: Univ. of Pennsylvania Press.

JENKS, JEREMIAH W. 1885 *Henry C. Carey als National-ökonom.* Jena (Germany): Fischer.

KAPLAN, ABRAHAM D. H. 1931 *Henry Charles Carey: A Study in American Economic Thought.* Baltimore: Johns Hopkins Press.

SMITH, GEORGE W. 1951 *Henry C. Carey and American Sectional Conflict.* Albuquerque: Univ. of New Mexico Press.

SPIEGEL, HENRY W. (editor) 1960 *The Rise of American Economic Thought.* Philadelphia: Chilton.

TEILHAC, ERNEST (1928) 1936 *Pioneers of American Economic Thought in the Nineteenth Century.* New York: Macmillan. → First published as *Histoire de la pensée économique aux États-Unis au dix-neuvième siècle.*

TURNER, JOHN R. 1921 *The Ricardian Rent Theory in Early American Economics.* New York Univ. Press.

WALKER, FRANCIS A. (1883) 1888 *Political Economy.* 3d ed., rev. & enl. New York: Holt. → See especially pages 395–407.

CARGO CULTS

See articles on MASS PHENOMENA; NATIVISM AND REVIVALISM.

CARIBBEAN SOCIETY

The Caribbean area comprises the islands extending from Trinidad, Aruba, Margarita, and others off the coast of Venezuela in the south, to Jamaica, Cuba, Hispaniola (formerly, and in Spanish, Española, the western third now being the Republic of Haiti and the rest the Dominican Republic), and Puerto Rico (the Greater Antilles) in the north. The main groupings are the four Greater Antilles, the Lesser Antilles (about forty inhabited islands), and Trinidad and Tobago. A few units such as Colombia's San Andrés y Providencia and Honduras' Bay Islands, lying outside the 1,800-mile arc stretching from Cuba to Trinidad, are included, though the Bahamas are not.

Modern Caribbean societies are largely the products of nearly five centuries of European colonial policies. First as colonies, again as plantation settlements, they were forcibly modified to satisfy the strategic, political, and economic aims of the mother countries. To a significant extent their populations were imported to fulfill decisions made elsewhere, especially in order to maintain or change the relationship of labor supply to land (Lowenthal 1961).

The islands lie within the zone of coastal subtropical New World lowlands and share important general historical and sociological features: (*a*) aboriginal populations were either sparse or were destroyed or assimilated soon after 1492; (*b*) plantation agriculture developed early as an emergent phase of European overseas capitalism; (*c*) slavery and contract labor were the main means for productively relating the work force to the land; (*d*) under the plantation system and until about 1835, Africa was the principal source of labor; (*e*) local cultures often exhibit a substantial (but unevenly distributed and by no means exclusive) African component; and (*f*) political dependence and European control have persisted with fewer interruptions than elsewhere in the history of the New World.

The Conquest and its impact

The Spanish Conquest transformed Caribbean aboriginal life. In 1492 three major Indian groups were discernible: (*a*) pioneer fishermen–gatherers, who inhabited transient seaside camps in western Cuba (the Ciboney) and southwestern Hispaniola, where they had apparently been pushed by much larger numbers of (*b*) Arawakan-speaking horticulturists (the Island-Arawak), invaders who gradually occupied all of the Greater Antilles; and

(c) Arawakan-speaking cultivators and fishermen (the Island-Carib), who held the Lesser Antilles.

These three groupings probably entered the islands from mainland South America in the order given above. The first migration began perhaps 4,500 years ago; earliest dates for Greater Antilles occupation are about 4,000 years ago, while Island-Arawak penetration of the big islands began perhaps 2,300 years later. Island-Carib occupation of the Lesser Antilles dates from about a millennium ago, while Island-Carib movement into the Greater Antilles was stopped by the Spanish invasion (Rouse 1964).

Post-Columbian Spanish commentators (Las Casas 1552; 1561; Oviedo 1526; 1535–1557) reported cultural distinctions among the natives corresponding roughly with the archeological record, but almost all that is known of aboriginal social life is based on inference. Especially enigmatic are the nonhorticultural pioneer settlers of Hispaniola and Cuba; the subject of only scanty and uncertain Spanish commentary, they swiftly disappeared. Better known were the Island-Arawak of the Greater Antilles, especially the Taino of Hispaniola.

The Island-Arawak lived in villages and multivillage districts whose leaders directed group economic and religious activities. The people cultivated manioc (*Manihot utilissima* Pohl), from which they made cassava "bread," sweet potatoes (*Ipomoea batatas* [L.] Poir), maize (*Zea mays*), tobacco (*Nicotiana tabacum*) for smoking, cotton (*Gossypium* spp.), from which sleeping hammocks were woven, and other plants, probably by swidden agriculture (Sturtevant 1961). Native and probably uncultivated were fruit trees such as the mammee (*Mammea americana* L.), jagua (*Genipa americana* L.), and icaco (*Chrysobalanus icaco* L.). Fish were caught by hook and line, shellfish were collected, and the sea cow (*Tricechus manatus*) harpooned. Birds and animals, including the large hutia (*Capromys oedium*) and iguana (*Iguana tuberculata*), were hunted. The only domesticated animals were the guinea pig, which was eaten, and the dog, used for hunting.

Island-Arawak village headmen were under district leaders; each highest chief (Spanish *cacique*, from the Taino term), of whom there were five in Hispaniola, controlled up to 30 subchiefs and 70 to 80 village headmen. Social distinctions between chiefs and "commoners" were reflected in behavior and material culture (ritual deference, chiefly endogamy, and gold-inlaid chiefs' chairs), and a bottommost serflike group (*naborias*) also existed.

Spanish feudal preconceptions may have influenced these descriptions of a rigidly stratified social system.

Island-Arawak religion centered on supernatural spirits that could move about freely or settle in objects or places; a principal religious aim was their conciliatory lodging in artifacts or special sites. Chiefs' spirits, especially powerful, sometimes resided in anthropomorphic wooden figures.

By 1492 the Island-Carib, latecomers to the Lesser Antilles, had occupied all the small islands from Tobago to Vieques except Trinidad and Barbados. Though once Cariban-speaking, by 1492 the Island-Carib spoke an Arawakan language, presumably acquired during conquests from the captured Igneri (Lesser Antilles Arawakan-speaking) women. Island-Carib Arawakan was not mutually intelligible with Island-Arawak, and in fact, Island-Carib men and women were said to speak different languages. Available evidence suggests that the main difference between these "languages," however, was the presence of many Cariban words in men's speech, supporting the supposition as to how the Island-Carib language took shape (Taylor 1961).

Spanish (and later, other European) settlement of the Lesser Antilles was delayed, both because of the absence of precious ores and because of the Island-Caribs' fame as fierce fighters and cannibals. Their reputation for bloodthirstiness may have been exaggerated to serve European political ends, however, and to justify enslavement.

The Island-Carib cultivated most of the same crops as the Island-Arawak and fished and hunted. Their villages consisted of single extended families, headed by male leaders with limited authority. Both headmen and war leaders were chosen on grounds of achievement. The social order was democratic, absolute authority being exercised only on war parties.

Island-Carib cosmology included benign and evil spirits; offerings were made to good spirits, who had belonged to various human groupings before becoming supernaturals. Shamanistic specialists warded off malevolent spirits, worked countermagic against sorcerers, and prophesied. The couvade was practiced to protect the health of parents and the newborn (Taylor 1949; 1950).

Between 1492 and about 1622 when serious English and French colonization began in the Lesser Antilles, the Island-Carib were attacked by the Spaniards and seized as slaves, but the islands were uncolonized; the Island-Arawak of the Greater Antilles, however, received the full brunt of Spanish power. Subjugated Indians were used for mining, agriculture, and domestic labor, and Indian women were taken as concubines and occasionally as wives by the Spaniards. Spanish policy after 1512 granted the Indians nominal protection against enslavement (unless they made war, were cannibals, or resisted Spanish dominion), but in fact they were swiftly eliminated by maltreatment, disease, war, and suicide. By 1514 the number of able-bodied adult Island-Arawak in Hispaniola had decreased to 23,344 (Zavala 1935) from an estimated 100,000 or more; much the same occurred in Puerto Rico and Jamaica. In Cuba culturally identifiable Indian communities are believed to have endured until the end of the eighteenth century (Rouse 1948), though much later introductions of Yucatecan Maya laborers may have had an effect on this interpretation.

In the Greater Antilles the Spaniards first imposed the *repartimiento* (allocation of Indian labor) and *encomienda* (granting of Indian wards to the crown's vassals). Aimed at guaranteeing protection and religious guidance to the Indians, these administrative practices merely provided controllable servile labor and the land on which mines and plantations were located. Indian rebellions began in 1504 on Hispaniola and recurred there and elsewhere for half a century, but Spanish arms and superior organization invariably prevailed.

The confrontation of European with Indian was one of the more dramatic moments in modern world history: destruction and genetic assimilation of the Indians were rapid. A Spanish administrative policy advocating humane treatment proved more effective on the mainland; the brilliant appeals of the friars Montesinos and Las Casas (Hanke 1949) on behalf of the Indians created a theological and legal controversy in Spain that thereafter deeply affected European philosophy.

Many aboriginal cultural features (foods, crops, medicinal plants, agricultural techniques, plant and place names, and architectural and craft practices) were transferred to Europe or interwoven with European elements in the islands. Though later migrations swamped aboriginal stocks, the Indian ancestry of modern populations, especially in the Hispanic Caribbean, is still apparent, and the native cultures contributed richly to the Caribbean synthesis.

Post-Conquest history to 1800

From 1492 until about 1800, island history was written chiefly in terms of the struggles of European imperial powers. These three centuries may be summarized under five headings: (*a*) the Span-

ish shift to the mainland; (*b*) the era of piracy, buccaneering, and privateering; (*c*) north European penetration of the Lesser Antilles; (*d*) north European seizures in the Greater Antilles; and (*e*) the beginnings of island autonomy.

Spanish interest in the Caribbean waned after the discovery and conquest of the densely populated and metal-rich highlands of mainland America. Mainland entrepôts soon supplanted Havana, San Juan, and other insular centers, and from 1520 until 1790, Spain used her island possessions principally as military bastions and fueling stations. After 1520, the Hispano-Caribbean population fell because of migrations to the mainland. But Spain introduced livestock, European crops (including sugar cane), water power and cattle power, African slaves, and plantation production to the Greater Antilles. With the first generation born of Spanish fathers and aboriginal mothers, "creole culture" emerged, and the distinction between European and creole, thereafter politically and culturally important, was established.

Piracy against Spanish ports and ships began in the sixteenth century and persisted for nearly 200 years; it overtaxed Spanish naval strength and was welcomed by north European monarchs. More important than brigandage, however, was the smuggling trade. The first known exploit, in 1527, exposed colonial needs for goods and slaves, which were inadequately filled by Spain because of restrictive mercantile policies. Such smuggling, mixed with military action unofficially but strongly supported by north European heads of state, created the official piracy called privateering: privateers recruited crews and were outfitted in north European ports; rulers invested in ships and supplies and shared in the spoils. Thus privateering united commerce and plunder while serving the national aims of Spain's enemies until the mid-seventeenth century.

Buccaneering, a third type of marauding, began early in the seventeenth century and disappeared before 1800. Its original aim was settlement. Many buccaneers were Frenchmen (often religious and political dissenters) who occupied northwestern Hispaniola about 1620, and later, when harassed by the Spaniards, moved off the north coast to Île de la Tortue. As the first non-Spaniards to settle in the Greater Antilles, the buccaneers eventually threatened Spain more than did pirates and privateers. They lived by killing semiferal cattle and selling tallow, hides, and barbecued meat to passing ships. The buccaneers maintained a martial, predatory, and largely womanless form of society by constant recruitment of anti-Spanish volunteers; attacked by the Spaniards, they turned sailors, using small, fast barks to attack Spanish ports and shipping. After 1640 Britain and France dispatched colonial governors to Tortue, thus transforming buccaneering into an arm of official policy. As north European power expanded in the Caribbean, the buccaneers were stamped out or assimilated into colonial officialdom.

North European settlement in the Lesser Antilles began in the seventeenth century through chartered companies, which defied Spanish claims to all the islands. Unable to breach Spanish defenses in the Greater Antilles, the English settled St. Kitts in 1622–1623, Barbados and St. Croix in 1625, Nevis in 1628, San Andrés y Providencia in 1629, and Antigua and Montserrat by 1632. The Dutch had ensconced themselves in Curaçao by 1633, when they were driven out by the Spaniards; but they retook the island in 1634, meanwhile garrisoning nearby Bonaire and Aruba. Between 1630 and 1648 they also laid claim to Saba and St. Eustatius, the latter island becoming a major center of non-Spanish trade. The French, together with the English, settled St. Martin in 1635 and began colonizing Martinique and Guadeloupe. Spanish retaliatory expeditions against such settlements were usually successful, but new colonies would spring up again almost immediately. Hence the early decades of the seventeenth century marked the irreversible penetration of north European political and military power into the Caribbean (Newton 1933). By the mid-seventeenth century, these tiny islands became economically vital to the mother countries, and European naval wars for a century thereafter centered on their possession.

North European settlement in the smaller islands was accomplished mainly by indentured servants employed by chartered companies producing tobacco, indigo, ginger, and other commodities for growing European markets. Such laborers worked for a fixed period (usually three to seven years), after which they were granted land in freehold and became yeoman farmers. But the introduction of advanced sugar-making technology by the Dutch soon led to the decline of small-scale farming and its replacement by the plantation system. After 1650 plantations spread through the Lesser Antilles, and except in those islands unfit for the system, yeoman cultivation nearly vanished.

In 1655 Cromwell's navy attacked Jamaica, and England established *de facto* control, which was confirmed by treaty in 1670. This first successful territorial seizure in the Greater Antilles was followed in 1697 by the cession of western Hispaniola (Saint-Domingue) to France. Plantation development in these two colonies proceeded rapidly; by the early eighteenth century both were among the richest colonial possessions in the world. They were governed according to the mercantilist policies of their respective metropolises, changing little politically for almost a century.

In 1791, however, trouble began in Saint-Domingue; from a political conflict between two master classes this disturbance was transformed by the slaves into a national revolution. After a long and complex struggle, Haiti gained its independence in 1804, becoming the second free nation in the Western Hemisphere.

The presence of even a weak sovereign state in the islands signified that Caribbean peoples would now have a greater role in making their own history. Slave trade to the other islands was soon made illegal (Denmark, 1802; England, 1808; Sweden, 1813; Holland, 1814; France, 1814; Spain, 1820), though illicit trade remained very important until well into the nineteenth century. Slavery itself, which began to excite opposition near the end of the eighteenth century, ended in the British colonies in 1838, in the French islands in 1848, and in the Dutch islands in 1863; thereafter, only the Hispanic islands had slavery.

Thus the Haitian revolution marked a turning point in Caribbean affairs. Though it led to increasing repression in other colonies, it was exploited politically by European enemies of slavery, the plantation system, and the mercantilist philosophy. Except for the Hispanic islands, the mid-nineteenth century was a time of economic contraction, depression, and growing isolation. In Cuba and Puerto Rico (Spanish Santo Domingo had previously won nominal independence in 1844) the plantation system expanded as the British, Dutch, and French islands deteriorated economically.

Modern history

In the nineteenth century, United States interest in the Caribbean mounted as a geopolitical consequence of growing North American power; toward the close of the century, in 1898, the United States asserted this power militarily, seizing Puerto Rico and Cuba from Spain. Cuba soon received formal independence, while Puerto Rico has remained a United States dependency, long governed through the U.S. Department of the Interior. Both islands became prime centers of United States economic expansion, principally of large-scale sugar interests accompanied by investment in mining, railroads, wharf facilities, and shipping. The United States also occupied Haiti and the

Dominican Republic, both of which had been much isolated in the nineteenth century, maintained basic politico–military control in Cuba, and defined the noncolonial Caribbean as essential to its national interest (Munro 1964).

The British, Dutch, and French Antilles changed little until the world depression of the 1930s, when economic decline stimulated political activity; European-traincd political leaders hastened the growth of national political parties, often originating in trade union activity. World War II had important consequences for the Caribbean, partly embodied in the pledges of embattled European powers to their long-neglected colonies. Direct steps toward political independence culminated in independence for Jamaica and Trinidad-Tobago in 1962. A decade earlier Puerto Rico established a commonwealth relationship with the United States. The French Antilles became *départements* of the Republic in 1946, securing direct representation in the French assembly as integral portions of metropolitan France. The Dutch islands, by different legislative arrangements, became limited self-governing parts of the Kingdom of the Netherlands.

Since the war, political events occurring in the Caribbean include the emergence of a revolutionary socialist state in Cuba, the fall of the dictatorial Trujillo regime in the Dominican Republic, and the rise of the Duvalier political monolith in Haiti. Oil and oil refining have brought relative prosperity to Trinidad and the Dutch offshore islands; Puerto Rico's Operation Bootstrap, lubricated by private and official capital and aided by unimpeded immigration to the United States, has facilitated limited industrialization and brought about a sharp rise in living standards; bauxite mining in Jamaica has improved that country's economic position; and the growth of the tourist industry has benefited most of the Caribbean except (for political reasons) Cuba, Haiti, and the Dominican Republic.

European and North American political and economic interest in the Caribbean continues under significantly changed circumstances. The existence of socialist Cuba and its links to the communist powers of Europe and Asia; the debate over Puerto Rico's eventual status; the declining influence of the United States; the role of the new island nations, the greatly increased European interest in the economic possibilities of Caribbean trade; and the growing ideological ties among underdeveloped countries everywhere are all part of the new situation.

Any effective pan-Caribbean consciousness is still lacking, in large part because of the traditional cultural links between particular islands and their former or present mother countries. The possible entry of the new nations into the Organization of American States, the growth of important centers of higher education in the islands, and the emerging understanding of collective political influence lead toward pan-Caribbeanism. Though the federation of the West Indies endured for a brief time, from 1958 to 1962, lessening of international tension may produce regional federations of a more substantial character.

Typology of Caribbean plantations

For most of Caribbean history the major basis of colonial economic and social organization was the plantation system. Its nature can be delineated in terms of five major types: (1) the Mediterranean (e.g., Canary Islands) archetype, introduced experimentally by Spain in all the Greater Antilles (c. 1512–1560); (2) an intensified north European variant, developed by the English and French in Barbados, Guadeloupe, and elsewhere (c. 1640–1660); (3) the enlarged north European plantation, launched by these and other powers in both Greater and Lesser Antilles (c. 1655–1790); (4) the modified transfer of the enlarged form to the Hispanic Caribbean (c. 1790–1882); and (5) the corporate land-and-factory combine, pioneered by the United States in Cuba and Puerto Rico and by European powers elsewhere (post 1899).

Beginning about 1512 Spain undertook type 1 experiments in plantation production of sugar and other products in the Greater Antilles. Use of slave labor, also essential in types 3 and 4, was made practical by the plenitude of land relative to the number of freemen to work it. It early became clear that freemen in new colonies preferred agricultural self-employment to plantation labor; without legislative devices to bind them to the soil, plantation labor needs could not be filled. From the Conquest until the mid-nineteenth century, slavery provided the principal basis for such labor; it was not considered morally or politically inadvisable, and the slave trade itself was highly profitable.

Though important in Spanish type 1 plantations, slaves were little used in early British and French colonies in the Lesser Antilles, since indenture systems afforded agricultural capitalists adequate labor supplies for set periods. Indentured laborers could eventually become freeholders, however, and a growing yeoman class appeared early in the seventeenth century in British (e.g., Barbados) and French (e.g., Guadeloupe) colonies.

But expanding plantation production and a declining European labor supply after about 1670 stimulated slave importations; thereafter, throughout the Lesser Antilles, expanding slave-based type 2 plantations displaced yeoman settlements. By 1700 such settlements had vanished, except for a few island interiors and on islets too barren or mountainous to support plantation agriculture. Meanwhile African slave importations climbed sharply.

In the Hispanic Caribbean, type 1 plantations declined after about 1560. The creoles of Jamaica (until 1655), Hispaniola (until 1697), Puerto Rico, and Cuba sold or traded lard, tallow, leather, and cassava "bread" to passing ships, producing most of their own subsistence as well. The Hispanic insular highlands were internal frontiers, settled by squatter subsistence cultivators living in substantial isolation; merging African, Amerind, and European traditions gradually solidified into Hispano-Caribbean folk cultures. As refuge areas for military deserters, the shipwrecked, and escaped slaves, the Hispanic island interiors facilitated such syntheses. Slavery here had become economically minor; manumission was common; the free population of African origin was large; genetic intermixture of Indian, African, and European stocks occurred freely; and color lines did not sharply divide freemen from slaves or Europeans from non-Europeans.

Type 3 plantations were launched in Jamaica by Britain after 1655, in Martinique and Guadeloupe at about the same time by the French, and in French Saint-Domingue after 1697. By then the lucrativeness of plantations and the slave trade had stimulated other competitors: the Dutch and the Danes sought island colonies; the Swedes obtained a temporary foothold in tiny Saint-Barthélemy; the Knights of Malta briefly claimed parts of the Virgin Islands; even the Duchy of Courland made an abortive attempt to hold Tobago. Only after 1800—by which time the Caribbean economic contribution to the growth of European capitalism had been immense—did this intense European interest wane.

The Haitian revolution actually stimulated plantation production by France's rivals, but the decline of type 3 plantations soon followed. The perfection of beet-sugar production, growing movements to abolish the slave trade and then slavery itself, and the eventual political triumph of industry-oriented free-trade supporters over agriculture-oriented mercantilists all contributed to this decline (Williams 1944).

Spain, however, now struggling to satisfy the economic ambitions of her remaining New World colonies, strongly supported the growth of type 4 plantations in Cuba and Puerto Rico. This final resurgence of slave-based Caribbean plantations depended on slave smuggling as late as the 1860s; in Puerto Rico, in addition, "vagrancy laws" drove landless white freemen into forced plantation labor. Though seventeenth-century and eighteenth-century Spanish slavery was mild, it has been said that the system began and ended (Puerto Rico in 1873, Cuba in 1882) as the worst in the world.

Plantations operating with free and contract labor remained important in many islands, but the type 5 land-and-factory combine was not launched until nearly 1900. The United States pioneered this modern capitalist variant, especially in Cuba and Puerto Rico; comparable developments occurred in the British and French islands. Heavily capitalized modern plantations using free wage labor and intensive scientific agriculture differed qualitatively from their forerunners and signified the genuine proletarianization of many Caribbean populations (Mintz 1953a; 1953b).

Sociology of the plantation system

The classic plantation was a politico–economic invention, a colonial frontier institution, combining non-European slaves and European capital, technology, and managerial skill with territorial control of free or cheap subtropical lands in the mass, monocrop production of agricultural commodities for European markets. The plantation system shaped Caribbean societies in certain uniform ways: (a) the growth of two social segments, both migrant, one enslaved and numerous, the other free and few in number; (b) settlement on large holdings, the choicest lands (mainly coastal alluvial plains and intermontane valleys) being preempted for plantation production; (c) local political orders excluding the numerically preponderant group from civil participation by force, law, and custom; and (d) a capitalist rationale of production, with the planter a businessman rather than a farmer–colonist, even though the investment of capital in human stock and the code of social relations lent a somewhat noncapitalistic coloration to enterprise.

Almost everywhere slaves were systematically denied political rights, education, most religious instruction, opportunities to accumulate or to invest capital, and the rights to socialize or interbreed with their masters as equals. Hence plantation regions were markedly deficient in democratic political institutions, schools, churches, hospitals, stores, and the professionals, entrepreneurs, artisans, teachers, and service suppliers to staff them. A probable major contemporary consequence of the system is the persisting lack of strong community cohesion in plantation areas.

The plantation system effectively counterposed the two major sectors of each society; especially important in maintaining the division was the attribution of social and intellectual inferiority to certain physical traits. But the fact that masters and slaves were usually of differing physical types is overshadowed by more significant distinctions in behavior patterns, political power, and life chances. Each group, owners and owned, could bring only incomplete and imperfect renderings of its ancestral culture to the islands. The subordinate mass, unable either to maintain their cultural heritages and societal forms or to acquire the masters' models, eventually contrived very flexible solutions to their personal problems, perforce adapted to a repressive social environment. The masters could hardly maintain genuine continuity with European culture; they rarely came to the islands with the intention of remaining and often lacked European wives; most of them remained Europeans in exile. Hence the cultural and societal accompaniments of the plantation system were simplified, innovative, circumstantial, and dichotomous.

The rigidity and repressiveness of the system varied with time, colonial administration, and level of economic intensity. The formal Spanish slave code was, for most of the time and in most colonies, more liberal than the others. In practice, milder treatment probably originated in a less mature and more irregular capitalistic agriculture, strong metropolitan control of local affairs, the benefits of missionizing Catholicism (slaves in Spanish and French islands were usually baptized and permitted to marry as Catholics), and the relative lack of pure race prejudice.

French Saint-Domingue's liberal slave code led to the growth of an influential slaveholding free colored class. The Haitian revolution originated in a political struggle between these *affranchis* and the several classes of French settlers, among whom the least successful aimed to reduce growing *affranchi* power. In spite of the nominally humane French slave code, however, cruelty was common and notorious in Saint-Domingue.

British and Dutch slave systems provided rather less protection to slaves. In British colonies, where local legislatures were more autonomous than in Spanish and French islands, slaves effectively had no legal personality in spite of the relatively liberal consolidated slave codes enacted after 1800. Though the extreme harshness of British slavery has been attributed to the lack of a slavery tradition and of a missionizing religion, at least as important were the early and rapid development of plantations as the mainstay of British Caribbean life and the great local political power of the planters.

Other qualifications originate in the actual workings of the plantation system itself. The development of small groups of slave artisans and the use of slaves as domestics produced social and economic differentiations recognized in practice by slaves and masters alike. Subsistence agriculture, craft production, and marketing by slaves (where permitted by the masters to reduce operating costs, as in Jamaica) enabled slaves to accumulate some capital and buying power and, rarely, to buy their own freedom. Though female slaves were often sexually defenseless against their masters (probably a basic conditioning aspect of the forms of slave domestic organization and marital patterns), the masters' illegitimate offspring were sometimes provided educational and economic opportunities. These circumstances led to the growth in most colonies of intermediate "mulatto" groupings, sometimes having substantial economic and political power. In each instance, then, the plantation system differed somewhat from others, both in its operation and in the sort of society it helped to create.

The slaves themselves played important roles in changing their long-term situations by violent and nonviolent resistance. While rebellions were usually short-lived, the successful Haitian revolution strengthened the abolition movement elsewhere and probably encouraged slaves in other colonies to rebel. Slaves engaged in malingering, practiced self-induced abortion and self-mutilation, feigned stupidity, and misused equipment and stock, thus raising production costs and lowering profits. The long-term effects of such sabotage were to hasten the decline of the entire system, even though slave resistance intensified cruelty and led to the claim by proslavery elements that slaves were congenitally unfit for freedom. Successful escapes in Cuba, Jamaica, Hispaniola, and elsewhere led to the establishment of refuge communities and special opportunities for perpetuating parts of the African heritage. Though the most remarkable runaway communities developed in Dutch Guiana and Brazil, the Jamaican maroons successfully resisted the English; Cuban and Puerto Rican runaways established palisaded highland villages; and some Haitian *marron* bands lasted for fifty years or more. Thus the plantation system did not completely preclude either cultural continuity with the past or the growth of intermediate social segments within island societies, though the development of distinct subcultures had to take place in the interstices of tightly controlled social orders.

Only fragmentary portions of African cultural traditions could be perpetuated. These generally included religious, lexical, musical, folkloric, culinary, agricultural, and craft items and practices. The contention (Herskovits & Herskovits 1947, pp. 6, 303) that the slaves perpetuated what they valued most highly (e.g., religious beliefs and practices) may be correct; more likely, however, the slaves were able to preserve only those items that did not interfere with the plantation regimen. In many cases, moreover, it is not possible to attribute a present-day practice to the African tradition, since it may equally well be of European or American Indian origin. In any case, derivative elements were rewoven into a wholly new synthesis under the conditions of plantation life. Taken in their entirety, New World slavery and the plantation system constituted what may have been one of the most dramatic acculturational phenomena in world history until the twentieth century, a phenomenon that can hardly be matched even by contemporary events.

History and sociology of the yeomanry

From its very inception in Hispaniola less than two decades after the discovery, until the present, the plantation system has been counterposed against small-scale cultivation by freeholders. In almost every regard plantation and yeoman systems are contrastive. Hence the complementary profile of the plantation system's career (and of the "plantation islands" where it flourished) is that of the independent, small-scale freeholders and squatter farmers who escaped or resisted it.

Early Spanish plantation development limited the growth of a yeomanry in the Greater Antilles. As the plantations declined, squatter cultivators rapidly increased in the Puerto Rican, Cuban, Jamaican, and Hispaniolan interiors. Such growth was halted in Jamaica by English conquest in 1655 and in Saint-Domingue by French occupation in 1697; it continued in the remaining Hispanic possessions until the early nineteenth century. The elimination of the flourishing yeoman settlements that had preceded plantation growth in the Lesser Antilles signified the spread and expansion of populations of African provenience at the cost of those of European background.

In the great plantation colonies of Jamaica and Saint-Domingue, yeoman adaptations evolved under slavery, however, because the slaves usually grew their own foods and sold the surpluses. While still slaves, then, Haiti's and Jamaica's peoples acquired yeoman skills. Such developments were contradictory, even while representing savings to the plantations, since they ran counter to the social need under slavery for the total submission of the labor force and enabled the slaves to make individual decisions and to use their intellects productively.

Throughout the non-Hispanic Caribbean, emancipation signified an expansion of small-scale freehold cultivation except on those islands where no land at all could be acquired. Caribbean yeomen maintained the production of such cash export commodities as annatto (*Bixa orellana* L.), nutmeg (*Myristica fragrans* Houtt), arrowroot (*Maranta arundinacea* L.), bananas (*Musa paradisiaca* subsp. *sapientum* L.), and coffee (*Coffee arabica* L.), thus supporting a class of market intermediaries; created or expanded vigorous local exchange systems centering in large market places; and expanded their consumption of imports, only barely possible before emancipation. Mainly confined to upland interiors by continued plantation activity on fertile coastal plains, yeomen engaged in mixed farming to produce subsistence, local exchange items, and exports. Food crops included Amerind cultigens (e.g., sweet potatoes), African (e.g., sorghum, *Pennisetum glaucum* R. Br.) and Oceanian (e.g., breadfruit, *Artocarpus incisa* L. f.) transplants, and European vegetables and legumes. Cattle, horses, and donkeys became important, and goats, chickens, and swine served as foods and as means of saving. Cultivation involved no plows, little rotation, terracing, or manuring, and no clean tillage. Variants of swidden agriculture predominated; hilly slopes were planted, and substantial erosion and deforestation have typified Caribbean yeoman land use. But the destructiveness of such practices is attributable in part to the need to work hillsides because of plantation control of the lowlands, as well as to land pressure caused by increasing population and traditions of equal inheritance.

Post-emancipation migration

The growth of Caribbean yeomanries in the nineteenth century coincided with determined efforts by the planter classes to immobilize the labor force. In order to keep labor cheap and readily available, massive contract labor importations were begun. The major sources were India and China, though many workers came from Africa, Java, and southern Europe. Nearly 500,000

Indians (called "East Indians" in the Caribbean, to distinguish them from "West Indians" or "creoles" and from American Indians) entered the islands (and the Guianas) between 1835 and 1928; over 135,000 Chinese reached the British West Indies, Cuba, and Surinam; about 33,000 Javanese came to Surinam between 1891 and 1939. Free Africans were also imported—over 13,000 to British Guiana and many to Trinidad and elsewhere; even a few Annamese reached the French islands. In some islands, such as Jamaica, labor importations were financed by taxes levied on local imports and exports by island legislatures; thus local yeomen were compelled to finance the immigration of their competitors in the labor market.

Under the impact of North American power and with the advent of land-and-factory combines, more recent intraregional movements have occurred. Large numbers of Jamaicans, for instance, migrated to Central America after 1900 to work on banana plantations and on the Panama Canal. Between 1912 and 1924, Cuba received 110,000 Jamaican and 120,000 Haitian laborers. More recently, substantial numbers of Puerto Ricans have migrated to the U.S. Virgin Islands, as have small numbers of white fishermen from the French islands. With few exceptions (e.g., Japanese and refugee Jewish migration to the Dominican Republic), movement into the Caribbean has been wholly in accord with foreign economic decisions.

Mass emigration has become important only since World War II, as in the flow of Puerto Ricans to the United States mainland, and of British West Indians to the United Kingdom and Canada.

Modern Caribbean society and culture

All Caribbean societies are economically stratified (Simpson 1962a) and racially heterogeneous, and many contain diverse and identifiable ethnic groups. Ethnic and racial succession, fostered particularly by the plantation system, has produced some societies whose ethnic groupings are also largely distinct physically and whose behaviors may differ along ethnic, as well as class, lines. Where behavioral differences in forms of mating and domestic organization, religious persuasion and practice, language or dialect, and values express the presence of different institutional subsystems within a single Caribbean society, some analysts have labeled the society "plural" (M. G. Smith 1955), suggesting societal similarities with such Old World societies as Malaya, Fiji, or Mauritius.

Nearly all Caribbean societies show a dual or bipolar distribution of cultural forms, probably often stemming from (or paralleling) the traditional spheres of the masters and the slaves. Thus the uppermost segments, whose members are usually of European origin, are typified culturally by civil or sacramental marriage and European domestic organization, membership in an established religious body, and the use of a standard dialect of an Indo-European language. The bottommost segments, whose members are usually predominantly of non-European origin, are typified culturally by consensual unions and (often) matrifocal domestic organization, membership in folk religions or cult groups, and the use of creole languages or nonstandard dialects of Indo-European languages. The total societal structures may be analyzed in class, racial, or ethnic terms and are often best understood when these three (and other) variables are employed (Simpson 1962b).

It is not easy to order Caribbean societies along any continuum of lesser-to-greater pluralism or to generalize in more detail concerning their internal structures. Differing social and political histories, demographic patterns, and cultural origins have endowed each society with a somewhat distinctive character. Variations in economic opportunity and individual mobility and in the social utility of hypergamy have complicated traditional master–slave societies, as has the presence of large new ethnic enclaves in some instances. The following data on mating and kinship, religion, and language illustrate some of these complexities.

Kinship, domestic organization, mating forms

The best analyses of kinship, domestic organization, and mating forms treat rural lower-class populations of African origin, particularly in the British or formerly British islands. While data from Puerto Rico and the French Antilles hint at broad underlying structural similarities, data from the other islands are too sparse for controlled comparison.

Basic studies (e.g., for Jamaica, Davenport 1961) show that kinsmen are reckoned bilaterally; each individual (ego) is the center of a noncorporate assemblage of blood relatives shared only with full siblings; the group usually has little social coherence except with reference to ego. Such assemblages are rarely more than three generations deep, and collateral reckoning of kinsmen does not normally go beyond first cousins; normative taboos on sexual activity and unions usually hold within these groupings. Comparative data suggesting corporateness and patrilaterality cannot be reviewed here; where they occur, land or ritual or both are important (Clarke 1957; Davenport 1961; M. G. Smith 1962).

At the core of the kinship system is the mother–child tie; three linked generations of females are common, such linkages often showing themselves as units of domestic organization. Distinctions between domestic composition and the familial group are essential in analyzing West Indian social structure, since residence patterns vary widely and often do not coincide with lines of kinship (Solien 1960; Greenfield 1961). Developmental cycle studies (R. T. Smith 1956; Otterbein 1963; 1965) indicate that apparently alternate modes of domestic organization and mating may really be stages in a single sequence, but whether different sequences may coexist in the same subcultural setting is not wholly clear.

According to some observers, mating systems can be reduced to three predominant forms: sacramental or civil marriage, coresidential consensual unions, and stable but not coresidential consensual unions. In some cases marriage and consensual coresidence appear together as viable alternatives; consensual coresidence and nonresidential consensual unions may or may not. The cultural value put on neolocality, greater female longevity, the male's defined obligation (in at least some cases) to provide a socially acceptable house for coresidential mating, the chronic economic insecurity of males, and the existing disproportions of females to males because of male emigration influence domestic-unit composition and the establishment of new unions nearly everywhere among lower-class groups.

Explanations for these patterns range from references to the polygynous African past, through concerns with the impact of plantation slavery, to synchronic functional analyses of the demography, race relations, and economic conditions of contemporary Caribbean life. Careful interpretation of the importance of different slave codes and other historical influences has not yet been undertaken. Many more data are needed on cases of seeming patrilateral emphasis or suggesting the presence of patrilineages.

East Indian systems in British Guiana, Trinidad, and elsewhere differ from those of their creole (i.e., of African origin) class equals. Since the socioeconomic position of the East Indians does not diverge enough from that of the creoles to explain these differences—expressed particularly in the function of first marriage as a means for ritual incorporation in the East Indian subculture—historical factors are probably relevant (Jayawardena 1962). Some observers, however, believe East Indian patterns will be assimilated to those of the creoles and that wider contemporary influences

such as the social importance of physical differences, chronic economic insecurity, and the politics of ethnicity need to be taken into account (R. T. Smith 1956; 1963).

Most outstanding research on these subjects has been done by British-trained social anthropologists; some critics feel the importance of kinship, domestic organization, and mating forms may have been overstressed in Caribbean research. The forms themselves contrast sharply with those reported for many other world areas studied by anthropologists (e.g., Africa), while showing interesting similarities to those for peripherally Westernized areas (e.g., parts of mainland Latin America) and to some urban proletarian subcultures.

Religion and the supernatural

As with social structure most research on religion has been done with rural lower-class groups; and these religious forms differ from the patterns of the Caribbean upper classes as much as those of social structure do.

In the history of the Hispanic Caribbean, natives and African slaves were regularly proselytized; Hispano-Caribbean societies remain predominantly Roman Catholic. But while the elites maintained a formal Catholicism, the rural folk developed a simplified faith involving saints' cults, elimination of the sacraments except baptism, and intermixture of regional Spanish, African, and possibly Amerind elements.

In the twentieth century Protestant missionaries converted numerous middle-class Catholics in the Hispanic Caribbean. And since World War II, Pentecostal, Church of God, and other revivalist groups have gained many converts in Puerto Rico and Cuba. These faiths employ self-denial, public testimony, and ritual abstention, and their services are marked by trance, possession, and glossolalia.

Catholic influence was strong in the French islands, including Saint-Domingue; here, too, slaves were proselytized. During Haiti's isolation after 1804, however, vodun, which synthesized Catholic belief with African religious elements, became the popular faith. Vodun ceremonies include possession and the feeding of the gods, who are attached to individuals and to families, reside in the land, and require sustenance and commemoration. Many vodun believers attend Catholic services; Haiti's elite, while mainly Catholic in faith, is apparently more attracted by the "national" folk religion than is true elsewhere in the Caribbean.

In British or former British islands such as Jamaica, slaves were denied missionization almost until emancipation. Baptist and Methodist prose-lytization proved very successful, but after 1838 many persons lost their formal church affiliation; cults combining Christian elements with some features of African belief multiplied. Like vodun, these faiths lack any national institutional structure and vary locally; they compete for new adherents, partly by ceremonial innovation, but never entirely lose their Christian elements.

In Puerto Rico, the lower-class movement toward fundamentalist sects is a special aspect of the Americanization process. These sects, unlike the cult groups of the British islands, the "Afro" cults of Cuba, Trinidad, and elsewhere, and Haitian vodun, maintain national affiliations and are bottom rungs in the ladder of Protestantism.

East Indian migrants in Trinidad, British Guiana, and elsewhere often maintain simplified versions of their original Muslim or Hindu faith. However, as with all Caribbean folk religions, significant changes in form and meaning have occurred.

Religious activity has had important political overtones in the Caribbean area. Political organization sometimes has a quasi-religious cast, and, rarely, religious revivals have had racist or nationalistic, as well as millenarian, qualities. In this sphere of life, as in the sphere of social structure, some features are reminiscent of North American lower-class (especially Negro) subcultures.

Throughout the Caribbean area magic has some importance, perhaps particularly among lower-class persons and connected especially with agriculture, fishing, and life crises. Amerind, European, and African origins for particular magical elements have been identified in some cases.

Language

Languages of the Caribbean include dialectal variants of familiar Indo-European tongues, especially Spanish, French, English, and Dutch; intra-insular differences associated with class or regional divisions are common. Many people, however, have a creole language as their native tongue. Creole languages may have originated in a Portuguese-based pidgin (Taylor 1961); today most of them appear to consist of the combination of Indo-European lexicons and non-Indo-European (possibly African) syntactic forms. A lexically French creole is spoken in Haiti, the French Antilles, and several former French islands (e.g., Dominica, St. Lucia); the Dutch Leeward Islands use Papia-mento, a creole having Spanish, Portuguese, and English elements but syntactically similar to none of them. The folk of the English islands use non-standard dialects of English, which are not regarded by most scholars as creole languages because they apparently intergrade with standard dialects (Taylor 1961). In Dominica (Arawakan) Island-Carib is no longer spoken by the few surviving Island-Carib; only traces remain of the distinction between men's and women's speech. American Indian elements in Caribbean languages are confined to lexical items.

Studies of Caribbean sociolinguistics are but barely begun, though bilingual problems are serious. Thus, for example, while French is Haiti's official language, only a few Haitians can speak French, while everyone speaks creole. Language is a mark of class; the native use of a substandard dialect or a creole carries pejorative implications and also hampers education, because the student must learn in an essentially foreign tongue.

Communities and informal groupings

The preceding sections demonstrate the social polarity of many Caribbean peoples in terms of several spheres of belief and behavior. But the subordinate or "lower-class" groupings are not themselves culturally or socially homogeneous. Racial, ethnic, occupational, and other bases of difference greatly affect the organization of the masses of Caribbean societies into communities and other social groupings.

Some variants in community type originate from physical and/or ethnic difference, as in East Indian villages in Trinidad (Klass 1961) and British Guiana. Communities of phenotypically white fishermen or yeomen, such as the "Red Legs" of Barbados or the "Parratees" of Jamaica, represent peripheral survivors of early yeomen villages or later experimental settlements of European migrants. In Martinique some highland communities stem from early Negro freedman occupation; in Puerto Rico and Cuba a few isolated villages might have begun in the resettlement of Island-Arawak; in Jamaica several maroon villages still exist, while many highland settlements arose from the land-buying activities of Baptist and Methodist missionaries who resold small plots to their parishioners.

In economic terms the main contemporary community types are plantation settlements, freehold villages, haciendas (large estates, mainly in coffee, often with landless share-tenants and neighboring small-scale yeoman holdings, as in Puerto Rico), fishing villages, and more rarely, cattle-producing and dairy-producing settlements. The complexity and variety of shareholding, tenancy, squatting, and freehold arrangements are notable.

Small-scale agricultural settlement varies from widely dispersed to densely concentrated groupings, partly determined by land pressure and land distribution; in countries such as Haiti and Jamaica, the lack of concentrated communities probably results in the absence of numerous community-level services. Almost everywhere, however, yeoman villages are found in the uplands and plantation communities on the coasts, and the two forms of economy produce divergent patterns of settlement and of social life. Many communities, such as those Jamaican and Puerto Rican hill villages bordering coastal plantations, have populations that straddle both economic forms; men alternately work their own land and for wages. Many fishing villages near plantations show a similar adaptation.

Mineral industries in Jamaica (bauxite) and Cuba (tungsten, nickel) and oil refineries in Trinidad and Aruba have created new sorts of company towns; in Puerto Rico industrialization has produced urban proletarian communities, as well as affecting those outlying towns where factories have been opened. Urban slums are sociologically and politically important in Kingston, Jamaica; Port-au-Prince, Haiti; San Juan, Puerto Rico, and elsewhere; their populations are mainly unskilled, of recent rural origin, irregularly employed, and politically labile.

Most studies of Caribbean rural communities suggest only minor or fragmentary community-wide organization, with few institutional devices or traditions to express group sentiment or community will. Diffuseness of kin ties and looseness of community organization argue for a characterization of rural lower-class island folk as highly individualistic in their life styles. Few studies have taken full account of the importance of informal groupings lacking any institutional articulation. In the absence of either firm or well-developed kinship structures or of strong community cohesion, Caribbean societies have proved difficult to analyze sociologically; most social scientists have approached them with the study of one or the other of these bases of social assortment in mind. This may mean that an adequate interpretation of Caribbean rural lower-class subcultures must await greater theoretical exploration of the nature of informal and highly flexible social linkages, especially as expressed in polydyadic units with one individual or family at the core. Psychologically oriented studies in the islands often stress the weakness of familial bases of social affiliation as explanatory for the finding that personality disturbance is common and serious. Such interpretations may fail to cope adequately with the peculiar character of Caribbean social life, measuring behavior by norms largely derived from the study of more developed Western societies on the one hand and of kin-based primitive or non-Western societies on the other.

Politics and nationalism

The Caribbean islands include the hemisphere's second oldest nation (Haiti), two newly fledged sovereign states (Jamaica and Trinidad-Tobago), and some of the oldest colonies of the Western world. Though land hunger has played a certain part in political struggles (as in Jamaica's Morant Bay "rebellion" of 1865), and though slavery underlay much basically political disturbance (as in the Haitian revolution, the maroon "wars" of Jamaica, and many lesser conflicts), most political activity has originated in the colonial relationship itself. Colonial legislatures and creole leaders have struggled for total independence (e.g., Martí in Cuba) or for greater autonomy within the metropolitan framework (e.g., Betances and Ruíz Belvis in Puerto Rico) but not always in the context of needed reform within their island societies. In some instances (e.g., nineteenth-century Jamaica) local legislatures proved more conservative politically than the metropolis itself, for extensive reform might have threatened the existing insular structure of wealth and power.

In the twentieth century, rapid proletarianization of Caribbean populations accelerated political activities, often given a nationalistic complexion by the continued exercise of foreign economic and political power. The trade union movement, particularly among plantation workers, has provided a basis for national political organization, and many contemporary leaders began as union officials. Strong nationalist movements have frequently been associated with plantation activity, as in British Guiana and Cuba, though this obvious fact has escaped the attention of many experts. As elsewhere in the underdeveloped world, bourgeois professionals and union leaders have often joined forces in creating political change in the Caribbean.

Caribbean politics has also been marked by color consciousness, stimulated by persisting differences in wealth and power along radial lines and by sharp ethnic and racial differences—for example, as in British Guiana (Despres 1964). Political leadership often has a strong personal cast, the leader's own views sometimes taking the place of a formal platform. Widespread illiteracy, grinding poverty, rural isolation, and the wealth and power gap between small elites and vast subordinate majorities have delayed political democratization in most islands.

At the same time a brilliant stimulus has been provided to the political movements of other less developed areas by the writings of such Caribbean intellectuals as C. L. R. James, George Padmore, Aimé Césaire, Frantz Fanon, Fidel Castro and, of a less radical cast, Luis Muñoz Marín and Eric Williams. The association of Caribbean leaders with political struggle is ancient; more than 150 years ago independent Haiti twice gave aid and haven to Simón Bolívar; later, the impact of Cuba's Martí was felt throughout Latin America; and in recent years, Williams of Trinidad, Muñoz of Puerto Rico, and Castro of Cuba have stirred the colonial world. Political action in the Caribbean ranges, it is true, from sheer demagoguery to sophisticated democratic maneuvering within complex power spheres. But the lengthy colonial experience of the area early gave rise to new varieties of political thought and action. In spite of its present "backwardness," some of the Caribbean area's leaders today are probably those best prepared within the less developed and dependent world to deal with the political complexities of modern colonialism.

SIDNEY W. MINTZ

[See also LAND TENURE; PEASANTRY; PLANTATIONS; SLAVERY.]

BIBLIOGRAPHY

CLARKE, EDITH 1957 *My Mother Who Fathered Me: A Study of the Family in Three Selected Communities in Jamaica.* London: Allen & Unwin.

DAVENPORT, WILLIAM H. 1961 The Family System of Jamaica. *Social and Economic Studies* 10:420–454.

DESPRES, LEO A. 1964 The Implications of Nationalist Politics in British Guiana for the Development of Cultural Theory. *American Anthropologist* New Series 66: 1051–1077.

GREENFIELD, SIDNEY M. 1961 Socio-economic Factors and Family Form. *Social and Economic Studies* 10: 72–85.

GUERRA Y SÁNCHEZ, RAMIRO (1927) 1964 *Sugar and Society in the Antilles: An Economic History of Cuban Agriculture.* New Haven: Yale Univ. Press. → First published as *Azúcar y población en las Antillas.*

HANKE, LEWIS 1949 *The Spanish Struggle for Justice in the Conquest of America.* Philadelphia: Univ. of Pennsylvania Press.

HERSKOVITS, MELVILLE J.; and HERSKOVITS, FRANCES S. 1947 *Trinidad Village.* New York: Knopf.

JAYAWARDENA, CHANDRA 1962 Family Organisation in Plantations in British Guiana. *International Journal of Comparative Sociology* 3:43–64.

KLASS, MORTON 1961 *East Indians in Trinidad.* New York: Columbia Univ. Press.

LAS CASAS, BARTOLOMÉ DE (1552) 1909 *Apologética historia de las Indias.* Madrid: Bailly & Baillière.

LAS CASAS, BARTOLOMÉ DE (1561) 1951 *Historia de las Indias.* 3 vols. Mexico City: Fondo de Cultura Económica. → First published in Madrid in 1875–1876.

LOWENTHAL, DAVID 1961 Caribbean Views of Caribbean Land. *Canadian Geographer* 5, no. 2:1–9.

MCKENZIE, H. I. 1966 The Plural Society Debate: Some Comments on a Recent Contribution. *Social and Economic Studies* 15:53–60.

MINTZ, SIDNEY W. 1953a The Culture History of a Puerto-Rican Sugar Cane Plantation: 1876–1949. *Hispanic American Historical Review* 33:224–251.

MINTZ, SIDNEY W. 1953b The Folk–Urban Continuum and the Rural Proletarian Community. *American Journal of Sociology* 59:136–143.

MINTZ, SIDNEY W. (compiler) 1960 *Papers in Caribbean Anthropology.* Yale University Publications in Anthropology, Nos. 57–64. New Haven: Yale Univ., Department of Anthropology.

MUNRO, DANA G. 1964 *Intervention and Dollar Diplomacy in the Caribbean: 1900–1921.* Princeton Univ. Press.

NEWTON, ARTHUR P. 1933 *The European Nations in the West Indies: 1493–1688.* London: Black.

OTTERBEIN, KEITH F. 1963 The Household Composition of the Andros Islanders. *Social and Economic Studies* 12:78–83.

OTTERBEIN, KEITH F. 1965 Caribbean Family Organization: A Comparative Analysis. *American Anthropologist* New Series 67:66–79.

OVIEDO Y VALDÉS, GONZALO FERNÁNDEZ DE (1526) 1959 *Natural History of the West Indies.* Translated and edited by Sterling A. Stoudemire. Studies in the Romance Languages and Literature, No. 32. Chapel Hill: Univ. of North Carolina Press. → First published as *De la natural historia de las Indias (Sumario de historia natural de las Indias).*

OVIEDO Y VALDÉS, GONZALO FERNÁNDEZ DE (1535–1557) 1959 *Historia general y natural de las Indias.* 5 vols. Madrid: Atlas.

PARRY, JOHN H.; and SHERLOCK, PHILIP M. 1956 *A Short History of the West Indies.* London: Macmillan; New York: St. Martins.

ROUSE, IRVING 1948 The Arawak. Volume 4, pages 507–546 in Julian H. Steward (editor), *Handbook of South American Indians.* Bureau of American Ethnology, Bulletin No. 143. Washington: Government Printing Office.

ROUSE, IRVING 1964 Prehistory of the West Indies. *Science* 144:499–513.

SIMPSON, GEORGE E. 1962a Social Stratification in the Caribbean. *Phylon* 23:29–46.

SIMPSON, GEORGE E. 1962b The Peoples and Cultures of the Caribbean Area. *Phylon* 23:240–257.

SMITH, MICHAEL G. 1955 *A Framework for Caribbean Studies.* Mona (Jamaica): University College of the West Indies.

SMITH, MICHAEL G. 1962 *Kinship and Community in Carriacou.* New Haven: Yale Univ. Press.

SMITH, RAYMOND T. 1956 *The Negro Family in British Guiana: Family Structure and Social Status in the Villages.* London: Routledge.

SMITH, RAYMOND T. 1963 Culture and Social Structure in the Caribbean: Some Recent Work on Family and Kinship Studies. *Comparative Studies in Society and History* 6:24–46.

SOLIEN, NANCIE L. 1960 Household and Family in the

Caribbean: Some Definitions and Concepts. *Social and Economic Studies* 9:101–106.

STEWARD, JULIAN H. et al. 1956 *The People of Puerto Rico: A Study in Social Anthropology.* Urbana: Univ. of Illinois Press.

STURTEVANT, WILLIAM C. 1961 Taino Agriculture. Pages 69–82 in Johannes Wilbert (editor), *The Evolution of Horticultural Systems in Native South America; Causes and Consequences: A Symposium.* Caracas: Editorial Sucre.

TAYLOR, DOUGLAS 1949 The Interpretation of Some Documentary Evidence on Carib Culture. *Southwestern Journal of Anthropology* 5:379–392.

TAYLOR, DOUGLAS 1950 The Meaning of Dietary and Occupational Restrictions Among the Island Carib. *American Anthropologist* New Series 52:343–349.

TAYLOR, DOUGLAS 1961 New Languages for Old in the West Indies. *Comparative Studies in Society and History* 3:277–288.

WILLIAMS, ERIC (1944) 1961 *Capitalism and Slavery.* New York: Russell.

ZAVALA, SILVIO A. 1935 *La encomienda indiana.* Madrid, Centro de Estudios Históricos, Sección Hispanoamericana, Publication No. 2. Madrid: Helénica.

CARR-SAUNDERS, A. M.

Alexander Morris Carr-Saunders, British sociologist, was born in 1886, the son of J. Carr-Saunders of Dorking, Surrey. He was educated at Eton and at Magdalen College, Oxford, where he excelled in biology and was awarded a biological scholarship to study in Naples in 1908/1909. But even then his attention was shifting from biology to sociology, and he became deeply interested in social work among the underprivileged of the East End of London. He followed in the footsteps of William Beveridge, Clement Attlee, and many other social reformers by becoming subwarden of Toynbee Hall, an East End residential social club and cultural center for working people. He held this post in the year 1912/1913; during this time he also studied law and was called to the bar in 1913. He was a volunteer in the earliest days of World War I and served with the Royal Army Service Corps in France, Egypt, and Palestine, from 1914 to 1919. He married in 1929 and had three children.

In his first major work, *The Population Problem: A Study in Human Evolution* (1922), he used his biological training to assess relationships between resources and population in the past, thereby laying the foundation of modern demography. In the following year he was appointed Charles Booth professor of social sciences at the University of Liverpool, a post he held for 14 years. *Eugenics* (1926), *A Survey of the Social Structure of England and Wales* (written jointly with P. Caradog Jones, 1927), and *The Professions* (written jointly with P. A. Wilson, 1933) enhanced Carr-Saunders'

reputation and furthered the development of social science as a study at the university level. *The Professions* was the first comprehensive study of the development of the professions in Britain and is still invaluable. It was one of the first scholarly attempts to define the essential sociological characteristics of the professions and to point out their very special importance in the modern world—and to do both in a richly empirical work whose historical and demographic data are valuable in their own right. It was one of the very early contributions to what has since become the flourishing field of the sociology of the professions. At the request of Chatham House (Royal Institute of International Affairs), Carr-Saunders undertook an investigation into world population at a time when few facts about the population of many countries were known and there had been very few attempts to survey the development of population through the ages. The result was a relatively slim volume, *World Population* (1936), which laid a firm foundation for subsequent studies by many workers and remains a standard work.

Carr-Saunders' manifold but impartial interests in the field of the social sciences rendered his tenure of the directorship of the London School of Economics and Political Science (University of London), from 1937 to 1957, a very successful one, despite the interruption of World War II and the removal of the school to Cambridge from 1939 to 1945. Carr-Saunders served a term as vice-chancellor of the University of London, and he will always be remembered for the active part he played in the establishment of university colleges in the developing countries. As described in his *New Universities Overseas* (1961), semiautonomous colleges in special relationship with the University of London were designed eventually to become independent universities, which has in fact happened. Carr-Saunders may be regarded as the "father" of universities in Malaya, the Sudan, Uganda, Kenya, Rhodesia, Nigeria, Ghana, and Jamaica.

Carr-Saunders retired from the London School of Economics in 1957 at the age of 70, and although he has spent most of his time in his cottage in the Lake District near his beloved mountains (he was a keen mountaineer and listed mountain climbing as his chief hobby), he has remained active. He enjoys country life and has occupied a succession of large country houses. From his collection of old masters—chiefly landscapes—he has loaned many paintings to the London School of Economics, where they have graced the walls of the social rooms. He has worked hard to enable all students to enjoy a wider social life in which music, art, and literature play a part.

Like many others vitally interested in the progress of mankind, Carr-Saunders has always been remote and detached in manner. Unwilling to suffer fools gladly, his own high standards of scholarship are largely responsible for the present status of sociology and demography. For his academic work he was elected a fellow of the British Academy in 1946 and was awarded honorary doctorates by the universities of Glasgow, Dublin, Grenoble, Columbia, Natal, Liverpool, and London, as well as by the University of Malaya, his own creation. He was knighted in 1946 and raised to knight of the British Empire on his retirement.

L. DUDLEY STAMP

[*For the historical context of Carr-Saunders' work, see* POPULATION *and the biographies of* BEVERIDGE *and* WEBB, SIDNEY AND BEATRICE. *For discussion of the subsequent development of Carr-Saunders' ideas, see* POPULATION, *article on* POPULATION THEORIES; PROFESSIONS.]

WORKS BY CARR-SAUNDERS

1922   *The Population Problem: A Study in Human Evolution.* Oxford: Clarendon.
1926   *Eugenics.* New York: Holt.
(1927) 1937   CARR-SAUNDERS, A. M.; and JONES, P. CARADOG. *A Survey of the Social Structure of England and Wales as Illustrated by Statistics.* 2d ed. Oxford: Clarendon.
(1933) 1964   CARR-SAUNDERS, A. M.; and WILSON, P. A. *The Professions.* London: Cass.
1936   *World Population: Past Growth and Present Trends.* Oxford: Clarendon.
1938   CARR-SAUNDERS, A. M.; FLORENCE, P. S.; and PEERS, R. *Consumers Co-operation in Great Britain: An Examination of the British Co-operative Movement.* London: Allen & Unwin.
1961   *New Universities Overseas.* London: Allen & Unwin.

CARTELS AND TRADE ASSOCIATIONS

Business enterprises in the same trade collaborate with one another in numerous ways and for varied purposes. The term "cartel" characterizes those institutions or mechanisms of collaboration that serve to limit or suppress competition. Trade associations are organizations of enterprises in a particular line of business. They may function as cartels; indeed, their proliferation during the last century in advanced capitalist countries has been an important aspect of the cartel movement. But just as cartels take numerous forms, of which trade associations are but one, so trade associations engage in many activities, of which the suppression of competition is only one.

From the standpoint of both economic analysis and public policy, the important distinction is between those interfirm collaborations that significantly limit competition and those that do not. This distinction does not, however, necessarily provide sufficient basis for appraising their social impact: since free competition does not always produce optimum results, even collaborations that substantially impair competition—and, a fortiori, those that merely moderate or rechannel competitive endeavors—may in some circumstances improve the social performance of industry.

Types of cartels.   The principal activities in which cartels engage are price fixing, market sharing or output limitation, joint selling, patent and process cross-licensing, and profit pooling. They do these things sometimes by simple agreement, sometimes with such enforcement procedures as penalties for exceeding production or sales quotas and subsidies for falling short, sometimes by formal organizations like joint ventures in selected markets. All agreements of the above types are not necessarily cartels: marketing cooperatives may not seek or achieve monopoly power; patent cross-licenses may be nonexclusive and unrestrictive. It is a familiar task of antimonopoly policy to determine in such instances whether the collaboration effects a substantial or merely an incidental or minor limitation of competition.

Cartels vary widely in the extent of governmental involvement, which may take the form of reinforcement by tariffs, licensure of entrants, judicial enforcement of the compacts, compulsion of membership, or of direct participation in prescribing prices or quotas. They vary also in their formality, from verbal understandings and "gentlemen's agreements" to formal organizations—selling syndicates, *comptoirs*, patent holding companies—with written constitutions and prescribed powers and procedures. There is an inevitable arbitrariness in defining cartels in this respect, and usage varies. At the one limit, most authorities would require an explicit contractual organization or relationship, thus excluding the parallelism of action that may flow from mere recognition of interdependence among oligopolists. At the other extreme, the profit-pooling cartel, like the German *Interessengemeinschaften*, is only with some arbitrariness distinguished from the financial combination.

Origins and purposes.   It is generally assumed that cartels are typically children of necessity—defensive alliances in atomistically organized industries plagued or threatened by destructive competition. It is certainly true that the more numerous the producers in an industry, the more they will need formal price-fixing or output-regulating organizations with powers of enforcement if they are to escape the vicissitudes of competition. In contrast with the situation in relatively concentrated industries, it pays no one producer to exercise self-restraint in his price or output policies in order to avoid "spoiling the market"; and the conflicts of interest between high-cost and low-cost, large and small, financially strong and financially weak, and established and newly entering producers militate against any informal acquiescence in a uniform, noncompetitive course of conduct. And so it usually takes a period of severe, industry-wide distress to force upon these numerous firms a willingness to accept the restraints on individual action required by their collective interest in restraining competition and, perhaps, to induce governments to intervene. With relatively little adjustment in each instance, this skeletal description could be made to fit the intergovernmental commodity agreements in rubber, tea, coffee, sugar, tin; the British Coal Mines Act of 1930 and the Cotton Industry Reorganization Bill of 1939; the American Guffey Coal Act of 1935; and the institution of petroleum prorationing in the United States in the early 1930s.

But this explanation is far from universally valid. As for the type of industry structure conducive to cartelization, if atomistically organized industries typically have the greater *need*, concentrated industries have the greater *opportunity*. They will ordinarily find it much easier to collude effectively, and secretly if necessary, merely because their members are fewer, hence more conscious of their interdependence. Nor is their "need" typically negligible: few oligopolistic industries consistently achieve markedly supernormal profits without some direct collusion. Such moderately to highly concentrated industries as aluminum, cellophane, diamonds, dyestuffs, electrical equipment, explosives, incandescent lamps, oil (outside the United States), quebracho, synthetic rubber, and titanium dioxide all have long histories of effective cartelization. On the other hand, it is true that in some of the most highly concentrated industries —for example, nickel, molybdenum, automobiles, and (American) shoe machinery—cartels have been of minor importance because they were unnecessary.

As for the circumstances favorable to cartelization, excess capacity and subnormal profits do strengthen the incentive to bridle competition; witness, for example, the German Compulsory Cartel Law of 1934 and the American National Recovery Act of 1933. Most cartels have originated when an imbalance between capacity and demand at previously prevailing prices threatened intensified price rivalry. The modern cartel movement must be traced to the 1870s and 1880s, when improved transportation, industrialization, and freer trade threw theretofore geographically insulated companies into conflict with one another. But excess capacity also undermines cartels by tempting firms to cut prices in order to get more business. And the carrot of supernormal profits can be as effective a stimulus as the stick of subnormal ones.

It is not necessary to choose between these alternative hypotheses. Together they provide the necessary range of explanations of why practically every industry has at some time or other essayed some kind of cartelization. The purpose of all these efforts was to ward off competition, and in this sense all were defensive, by definition. But this purpose and method have recommended themselves to businesses in widely divergent situations, during prosperity and depression and in concentrated and unconcentrated, profitable as well as unprofitable, industries. At the same time, there are few industries that have not also seen cartel attempts founder because the forces impelling firms to behave competitively, each seeking to augment its own profits, proved more powerful than those impelling them to collaborate in order to augment the profits of the group. Cartelization is not a static phenomenon, and most attempts have been short-lived.

Economic consequences. The functioning and economic consequences of cartels will vary widely, depending on the character of the alliance and the structure and circumstances of the industry involved.

Price agreements in atomistic industries. The simple price agreement in an atomistic industry producing a standardized product is usually short-lived and has slight economic effect. As already indicated, it pays no individual participant to honor the agreement, and the number of participants is large. So in the absence of output controls or powerful policing devices (e.g., government stockpiling, trade union boycotts, or organized violence) prices cannot long remain above the competitive level.

Output or sales limitations in atomistic industries. Cartels in atomized industries have, therefore, either collapsed or adopted limitations on output or sales. Because of the large number and geographical dispersion of producers, this has usually necessitated government intervention. Such controls set in motion the following tendencies:

(1) Prices are raised above the marginal costs of those producers whose output is restricted.

(2) Higher profits are earned, at least transitionally.

(3) Consequently, entry of new firms, often in areas outside the cartel's jurisdiction, and expansion of capacity by established ones are encouraged.

(4) To the extent this new capacity remains outside its jurisdiction (and the more successful the cartel, the greater the advantage of remaining outside, benefiting from the raised price without having to pay the cost of restricted output), the cartel's members suffer a decline in market share. In any event, if the price is to be sustained, the quotas attached to existing capacity must be correspondingly reduced.

(5) Thus, excess capacity is generated, unit costs are adjusted upward to the artificially sustained price, and supernormal profits tend to be eliminated because of the encouragement to new entry and investment and the progressive curtailment of output from existing plant. Consequently these cartels rarely maximize aggregate industry profits. When the costs of existing firms differ, maximization requires, in the short run, greater cutbacks in output of the higher-cost than of the lower-cost firms and plants (until their respective marginal costs are equated); and in the long run, maximization requires restriction of investment and concentration of production in lowest-cost plants of optimum size. But achievement of this requires industry profit sharing to compensate those whose output and capacity are the most severely restricted. Such schemes have proved difficult to devise and implement in unconcentrated industries. Probably more often the very opposite happens: output of low-cost producers is restricted more severely than that of the high-cost producers in order to ensure the survival of the latter operators, which are usually smaller.

(6) In consequence, cartels of this kind tend to be self-destructive. Their major attraction to members is their promise of enhanced industry profits. When they fail to keep that promise and, instead, impose increasing burdens on established, and especially low-cost, members, the likelihood is increased that at some point a large enough group will become sufficiently dissatisfied with their allotted share to feel that they can do better by resorting to independent action. Their disaffection, reinforced by the growth of uncontrolled production, can break the cartel and usher in a regime of often violent competition. These tendencies, inherent in cartelization itself, have in practice been powerfully reinforced by fluctuations in demand, technological breakthroughs, and the opening up of new producing areas.

Do cartels, then, tend to stabilize market prices? Prices of primary products produced and marketed under competitive conditions have been exceptionally unstable historically. The reasons are complex, but the principal proximate cause is inelasticity of supply [see AGRICULTURE, article on PRICE AND INCOME POLICIES]. Ideally, cartels seek to remedy this defect with their output and marketing controls. But in practice these stabilizing tendencies have often been more than offset by fluctuations in the strength and effectiveness of the cartels themselves. Formed in periods of glut, they push prices up. This success in turn encourages new investment and entry, and exaggerates the disparity between capacity and demand at remunerative prices, and this in turn aggravates the price declines that follow the collapse of the control schemes.

Cartels in atomistic industries with entry restrictions. Some unconcentrated, cartelized industries have escaped some of the foregoing vicissitudes because of restrictions on entry, for example, by government licensure or trade union boycott. The main distinctive characteristics of this case are the following: (1) When the cartel is internally effective, the barriers to entry prevent the erosion of monopoly profits. (2) If the licenses are transferable, the monopoly profits come to be capitalized in their purchase price, so that new entrants may earn only normal returns on their investments. (3) The overinvestment, chronic excess capacity, and instabilities of the output or sales limitation case may be to some extent avoided. (4) But the barriers to entry of new firms and competing products and the elimination of price competition typically retard technological progress and the weeding out of the inefficient. These phenomena can be observed in the building trades, the service and trucking industries (medicine, barbering, taxicabs, funeral services), and some branches of retail distribution and agriculture.

Price agreements in concentrated industries. The more concentrated the industry and the higher the barriers to entry, the greater the likelihood that simple price fixing or similar agreements (e.g., exchanges of detailed price data) can be effective in sustaining price above cost for extended periods of time. To the extent that the individual sellers, recognizing their interdependence, offer for sale only what the market will take at the quoted price, explicit output controls cease to be necessary.

Even in quite highly concentrated industries, however, such agreements are rarely fully effective in maintaining monopoly prices and profits. Conflicts of interest and opinion remain, and to the extent that the respective products are mutually substitutable, the firm that prefers the lowest price is the one whose opinion tends to prevail. Secret, usually discriminatory, price concessions may abound in periods of weak demand; and the price collusively set will be limited by such "chiseling" and the possibility of entry. Investment and innovation policies remain uncoordinated; therefore capacity will tend to be expanded to a higher level, and innovation and product development will be pressed more rapidly and in a greater variety of directions than if the industry were dominated by a single firm.

Cartels in such situations are less likely to produce the instabilities and inefficiencies of the atomized cases above—the induced overinvestment, excess capacity, and preservation of firms of inefficiently small size. On the other hand, they may generate the wastes of monopoly and excessively concentrated oligopoly—insufficient attention to cost reduction, underinvestment, conservatism in radical innovation, excessive selling expenses, and frivolous and costly changes in product design. With prices fixed, market shares come to depend principally on sales promotion and product variations that catch the buyer's fancy.

Effective cartelization in concentrated industries. Thoroughgoing, effective cartelization is or sometimes has been found in concentrated markets where private parties control aggregations of patents (as in various chemical products or in the United States glass container industry) or strategic raw materials (as in nickel, diamonds, and world oil). In these instances, prices, profits, and efficiency sometimes come very close to those of single-firm monopoly, with all its attendant dangers and possible economies. At the same time, there remain (as in the preceding price-agreement case) important possibilities of rivalry. No such agreement remains eternally unchanged in the way it distributes its benefits, and dissatisfied members always have some possibility of going it alone. The distribution of benefits is therefore likely to bear some relation to what the participants could get outside the cartel, and any large and continued discrepancy will encourage the stronger parties to break the agreement. Therefore each member remains under pressure to innovate, accumulate patents, and secure control of raw materials and market outlets. On the other hand, the cartel will retard the competitive exploitation of these advantages and the quick passing on of their benefits to the consumer.

Do cartels contribute to stability in the economy at large? The relevant considerations are complex, and conclusive proof is unavailable. Other things being equal, price stability can be secured only at the cost of output and employment instability, i.e., by making supply more responsive to shifts in demand. But given relatively inelastic demand—and this is the situation in which collusive price fixing recommends itself—price stabilization means a tendency to stabilize the flow of money income to the cartelized industry; hence, in a one-crop, export-oriented country, to the entire national economy. This tendency is accentuated by the effect of price stabilization on buyer and producer expectations: tending to discourage speculative overbuying and underbuying on the one side, and cycles of overinvestment and underinvestment on the other.

But in diversified economies, where the effectiveness of competition differs greatly from one industry and one stage of the cycle to another, there are introduced numerous complicating factors. These factors relate to, for example, the effect of cartel-sustained prices during general recessions on the distribution of income, notably between profits and wages, hence on the propensity to consume; on the fortunes of buyers as well as sellers of the cartelized product; on incomes earned in the uncartelized sectors of the economy; on investment incentives; on the balance of payments; and on the willingness of governments to pursue expansionary macroeconomic policies.

The principal causes of economic instability in advanced market economies must be sought in the factors influencing the flow of aggregate demand; the competitiveness of markets does not rank importantly among these. Probably most economists feel that cartelization has comparatively little to contribute to macroeconomic stabilization.

Political–social consequences. Cartels almost inevitably produce a closer conjoining of political and economic centers of power. Many markets can be cartelized only with government help. Not only atomistic but also concentrated industries have sought such assistance and delegation of sovereign authority. The suppression of competition in turn makes the performance of industry a matter of direct public concern and invites regulation. Cartels are a step toward centralized planning; questions of planning by whom and for what and for whose benefit become vital political issues. There are corresponding social implications in a movement involving hierarchical and authoritarian organization of the economy.

Trade associations. Besides the direct control of competition, trade association activities include trade promotion, product standardization, exchange of price and other statistical information, industry cost analysis, technical collaboration and counseling, collective bargaining, employee training, prevention of fraud and unfair methods of competition, commercial arbitration, and providing a forum for the discussion of problems of mutual interest.

Some of these activities would seem unequivocally to bring market conditions more closely into line with the requirements of perfect competition. Yet in certain circumstances they could have just the opposite effect. For example, effective competition requires that full market information be available to buyers and sellers. But in an oligopolistic industry, the only achievable price competition may take the form of secret, discriminatory concessions. Agreements to provide detailed information of prices actually charged can, by removing the veil of secrecy and identifying price-cutters, produce more nearly the results of perfect collusion. The same possible consequences flow from compiling and sharing information about costs (average industry costs may serve as suggested uniform prices), inventories and shipments relative to production (which may serve as signals for coordinated, uniform changes in output), or uniform methods of cost accounting. Exchanges of credit information have produced suppression of competition in credit terms; and distribution of freight rate books has served as the basis of industry-wide uniform delivered pricing systems.

The efforts of trade associations to standardize products, impose quality standards, and prevent fraud all in a sense make markets more nearly perfect. Standardization enables buyers to make intelligent price comparisons; it may also reduce costs of production and distribution. Quality standards may protect buyers from their own ignorance, as well as scrupulous firms from losing business to the unscrupulous. But standardization is also essential if collusively fixed prices are to be truly uniform and may also suppress socially desirable quality competition. Particularly if they are enforced, as they sometimes are, by concerted refusals to handle the products of transgressors, quality standards may be employed to deny price cutters or product innovators access to the market. All too often trade association "codes of ethics" or of "fair competition" have really tried to suppress all effective rivalry.

Most trade association activities could be regarded also as making available to small but otherwise adequately efficient firms those economies of scale that they require for survival. Lobbying, trade promotion, the joint collection and dissemination of information, and joint research could all be so characterized. Yet, it is obvious, they may also suppress or serve as substitutes for independent, competitive efforts.

These ambiguous implications pose formidable problems for economic analysis and public policy. The basic difficulty is that the kind of imperfect competition achievable in the real world—given uncertainty, imperfect knowledge, immobilities of capital and labor, and fluctuating demand—often produces defective results, which can sometimes be improved by restraints on competition. The main defense of cartels is precisely that competition is often destructive, unstable, and wasteful. The question, then, is whether—either ever or under what circumstances—the possible contributions of cartels or trade associations in mitigating these ills outweigh their dangers, and if so, how to achieve the one while escaping the other.

One partial escape is to have the government undertake the socially beneficent functions. Government agencies collect and publish data on prices, costs, inventories, and sales; determine and prescribe quality specifications; prohibit fraud and unfair methods of competition; and provide technical and managerial assistance to small business. But government regulations too (e.g., product standards or rules of fair competition) may discourage competition and innovation. Moreover, it is inconceivable that in a pluralistic society government services could entirely supplant voluntary business collaboration. There is no escape, therefore, from the necessity of developing economic criteria and legal procedures for predicting, assessing, and sifting out the complex consequences of these various activities.

There are wide differences in the public policies adopted to this end; and there is in fact no wholly satisfactory solution, for several reasons.

(1) As we have already seen, the economic consequences of these activities will vary, depending in each instance not only on the nature of the collaboration but also on all relevant circumstances of the market in which it takes place; and these circumstances themselves constantly change over time. It is therefore extremely difficult to formulate general rules applicable to each individual instance.

(2) In economic terms, the ideal policy might be one that involves a comprehensive scrutiny of each individual situation, after the fact, to determine whether the collaboration was in practice doing more good than harm, on balance, and to institute whatever modifications seem to be required. But the law necessarily places heavy re-

liance on rules that are clear and readily enforceable: a case-by-case approach, ex post facto, would offer businessmen less guidance in advance about unacceptable courses of conduct; and regulatory processes would inevitably lag behind the dynamic forces they were seeking to control. The opposite extreme is the promulgation of per se prohibitions pertaining to specified interfirm collaborations; these fall afoul of the first objection but could be defended, on balance, as doing more good than harm. A familiar, intermediate course is to condemn only those arrangements whose impairment of competition as an effective force in the market place is direct and substantial. Such a rule requires an examination in some situations only of the nature of the collaboration and restraint; in others it requires a more comprehensive appraisal of its impact. Yet neither this nor any other solution can be economically perfect; in some situations direct and substantial concerted limitations on competition may prevent truly destructive rivalry.

(3) Finally, there is the difficulty that public economic policy is necessarily shaped by largely noneconomic considerations, and appropriately so. These include the attitude that society has toward the presence and exercise of private economic power and the respective weights it wishes to give to the goals of efficiency, equity, security, and progressiveness, all of which are affected by antimonopoly policy. There is no perfect resolution of these many, often conflicting, considerations.

ALFRED E. KAHN

[See also COMMODITY AGREEMENTS, INTERNATIONAL; OLIGOPOLY; PATENTS.]

BIBLIOGRAPHY

BRADY, ROBERT A. 1943 *Business as a System of Power.* New York: Columbia Univ. Press.

BURNS, ARTHUR R. 1936 *The Decline of Competition: A Study of the Evolution of American Industry.* New York and London: McGraw-Hill.

DEWEY, DONALD 1959 *Monopoly in Economics and Law.* Chicago: Rand McNally. → See especially Chapters 2 and 3.

EDWARDS, CORWIN D. (editor) 1945 *A Cartel Policy for the United Nations.* New York: Columbia Univ. Press.

EDWARDS, CORWIN D. 1949 *Maintaining Competition: Requisites of a Governmental Policy.* New York: McGraw-Hill.

FOG, BJARKE 1956 How Are Cartel Prices Determined? *Journal of Industrial Economics* 5:16–23.

HEXNER, ERVIN; and WALTER, ADELAIDE 1945 *International Cartels.* Chapel Hill: Univ. of North Carolina Press.

LEVY, HERMANN (1909) 1927 *Monopolies, Cartels and Trusts in British Industry.* London: Macmillan. → First published as *Monopole, Kartelle und Trusts.*

LIEFMANN, ROBERT (1927) 1932 *Cartels, Concerns and Trusts.* New York: Dutton. → First published as *Kartelle, Konzerne, Trusts.*

MASON, EDWARD S. 1946 *Controlling World Trade: Cartels and Commodity Agreements.* New York and London: McGraw-Hill.

MILLER, JOHN PERRY (editor) 1962 *Competition, Cartels and Their Regulation.* Amsterdam: North-Holland Publishing.

PATINKIN, DON 1947 Multiple-plant Firms: Cartels and Imperfect Competition. *Quarterly Journal of Economics* 61:173–205.

PEARCE, CHARLES A. 1941 *Trade Association Survey.* Washington: Government Printing Office. → U.S. Temporary National Economic Committee, Investigation of Concentration of Economic Power, Monograph No. 18.

PHILLIPS, ALMARIN 1962 *Market Structure, Organization and Performance: An Essay on Price Fixing and Combinations in Restraint of Trade.* Cambridge, Mass.: Harvard Univ. Press.

PLUMMER, ALFRED (1934) 1951 *International Combines in Modern Industry.* 3d ed. London: Pitman.

PRIBRAM, KARL 1935 *Cartel Problems: An Analysis of Collective Monopolies in Europe With American Application.* Washington: Brookings Institution.

STOCKING, GEORGE W. 1954 The Rule of Reason, Workable Competition, and the Legality of Trade Association Activities. *University of Chicago Law Review* 21:527–619.

STOCKING, GEORGE W.; and WATKINS, MYRON W. 1946 *Cartels in Action: Case Studies in International Business Diplomacy.* New York: Twentieth Century Fund.

STOCKING, GEORGE W.; and WATKINS, MYRON W. 1948 *Cartels or Competition? The Economics of International Controls by Business and Government.* New York: Twentieth Century Fund.

U.S. CONGRESS, SENATE, COMMITTEE ON MILITARY AFFAIRS, SUBCOMMITTEE ON WAR MOBILIZATION (1944) 1946 *Economic and Political Aspects of International Cartels,* by Corwin D. Edwards. 78th Congress, 2d Session, Monograph No. 1. Washington: Government Printing Office.

WHITTLESEY, CHARLES R. 1946 *National Interest and International Cartels.* New York: Macmillan.

CARTESIANISM

See INTERACTION, *article on* SOCIAL INTERACTION; *and the biography of* DESCARTES.

CARTOGRAPHY

Cartography is the science and art of map making as distinguished from assembling the data to be mapped, such as by surveying, by compilation from various sources, or by census-taking. It ordinarily encompasses a number of specialized technical phases: the scale of the mapping, the method of projection, the symbolization of the data being mapped, the map design, and the preparation of the map for duplication.

The primary function of a map is to serve as a reduction of all or part of the earth's surface for the purpose of recording, presenting, or analyzing the spatial positions and the interrelationships of phenomena occurring thereon. Cartography, therefore, is both a prime research technique and a medium of communication for all those social sciences in which the spatial distribution of phenomena play any part, such as geography, history, anthropology, and economics. Furthermore, much of the data used by social scientists is available only in map form.

Although the variety is almost infinite, maps are commonly grouped in two classes: (*a*) reference maps, such as topographic maps, charts, or the general maps in atlases, and (*b*) thematic maps, or those dealing with a selected class or classes of data arrayed on a special base of reference material.

History of cartography. The concepts of scale reduction, direction, and distance seem innate in man, and the earliest map that has survived is more than four thousand years old. By the second century A.D. cartography had reached a high state of development, being known especially through the treatise of Ptolemy. Thereafter, except for its navigational aspect, cartography languished until the sixteenth century, when it began to develop quite rapidly. By the end of the eighteenth century all modern classes of maps had been developed except for the thematic map, which originated with the growth of science and social consciousness in the first half of the nineteenth century. Cartography was profoundly changed by the rise of geography as a scholarly discipline, the extension of the basic survey, and the development of many new techniques, such as lithography, photoengraving, the use of color, and statistical methods. Today, in addition to its general use in the preparation of topographic maps and hydrographic charts, cartography is widely used in the social and physical sciences and is a discipline in its own right. It is regularly taught in institutions of higher learning throughout the world and is represented by national and international organizations, such as the Congress on Surveying and Mapping (U.S.) and the International Cartographic Association.

The principal kinds of maps. The variety of maps does not allow a strict classification; but in practice the uses made of maps and the methods involved in their preparation separate them into several general categories.

Reference maps contain, to the limit of their scale, the readily observable features of primary interest to man. These include the coasts, the drainage features, the terrain, administrative boundaries, settlements, transportation facilities, and occasionally such special information as land use or vegetation. When of large scale and prepared from survey or by photogrammetric methods, such maps are classed as topographic; when of small scale and prepared by compilation from larger scale maps, they are simply termed reference maps.

Topographic maps are generally prepared by large governmental agencies, either military or nonmilitary, and are usually made according to a precise plan with extreme regard for planimetric accuracy. In many countries, maps have the status of legal documents. The coverage available is usually indicated on an index map. In general, the more heavily populated areas of the world have been mapped topographically (Karo 1955).

Other reference maps are of several kinds. Of principal use to the scholar, and to the public at large, are the reference maps and the specialized atlases (Yonge 1962*a*; 1962*b*). They are compiled from various sources, including topographic maps, and in addition to those that are essentially topographic maps on a small scale, there are usually others showing individual distributions such as population, temperature, economic activities, and political status. In recent years, many atlases of national areas have appeared that contain a wealth of detail far surpassing the so-called world atlases (International Geographical Union 1960). Atlases usually contain gazetteers of named places and features, whereas topographic maps do not. There are literally hundreds of atlases (Yonge 1962*a*; 1962*b*).

Another type of reference map is the cadastral plan. It is usually of much larger scale than the topographic map and commonly shows property boundaries, owners' names, buildings, and roadways.

Thematic maps, which may also be used for reference, treat only a special class (or classes) of data, and the variety of other material included is carefully selected and is usually made subordinate to the primary data. Thematic maps commonly appear separately, but there are also thematic atlases of countries or of the world, such as historical, economic, and climatic atlases.

The sources of maps and map information are legion. Most libraries contain a file of atlases, and many institutions maintain a separate map library, the largest in the United States being the Division of Maps of the Library of Congress with its approximately 2.5 million maps.

The principal elements of cartography. All maps must be made to scale, and there are various aspects of scale that complicate their use. In its simplest form map scale refers to the ratio between some dimension on the map and the corresponding dimension on the earth stated as a proportion such as 1:250,000 or 1/250,000, the first element or numerator referring to the map and the second or denominator to the earth. This ratio, termed the representative fraction (RF), ordinarily refers to some linear relation; the squaring of the denominator in order that the RF may apply to areas is usually not stated. A large fraction, e.g., 1:50,000, is termed a large scale. The RF applied to a globe map is constant throughout the map; when scale is stated for a flat map, however, area scale can be held constant over the map area, but linear scale cannot. The amount of departure varies greatly with the system of map projection (Robinson [1953] 1960, pp. 26–28, 53–58).

All flat maps are based on a systematic framework that results from a transformation, to scale, of the earth's spherical surface to the plane of the map. On account of the nonapplicability of these two surfaces, variations of linear scale over the map are inevitable. This results in deformation of angles or sizes of areas, or both, and consequent distortion of the representation of various earth attributes, such as azimuths, dimensions, and shapes. An infinite number of systems of projection are possible, but relatively few are regularly employed. Among the more important classes of systems are equivalent (maintenance of correct sizes of all areas), conformal (maintenance of correct angles at each point), and azimuthal (maintenance of correct azimuths at one point). In general, the amount of the inevitable change of linear scale over a map varies inversely with the RF of the map. The methods of analysis of scale variation stem from the mathematical work of Tissot and have been applied to the description of specific map projections in various ways (ibid., pp. 59–94, 324–329). In addition to the geographical coordinate system of latitude and longitude, many large-scale maps carry also a superimposed rectangular coordinate grid (Mitchell & Simmons 1945) by which positions may be given by listing the x value first, followed by the y value.

Every map must contain a selection of basic reference data to show locational relations among the mapped information. These must be generalized to a degree consistent with the scale of the map. Only at the largest scales can true intricacies and planimetric relationships be represented. The generalization must involve a selection from among the elements of each category and a simplification of their representation; since this must be done at all scales in varying degree, a map reader must be alert when deriving information from maps.

The symbols used to convey the information to the reader consist of a variety of marks, commonly categorized as point, line, and area symbols. They may appear in one or more colors. Point symbols, such as dots, circles, and triangles, may portray qualitative aspects, such as the existence of a city, or, by variations of the size or number of the symbols, may also portray quantity. Line symbols range from the simple line representing a linear quality, such as a road, an air route, or a boundary, to a class having the generic name isarithm, which represents quantitative aspects that include a wide variety of variants with special names (Horn 1959). The isarithm is commonly used to portray distributions that vary in amount from place to place, such as elevation of the land surface above sea level (contour), but it may be employed for more abstract concepts (Robinson 1961). An isarithm is the line on a map that shows the orthogonal map position of the trace of an assumed horizontal plane with the surface of the actual or assumed three-dimensional distribution being mapped. The vertical spacing of the assumed planes (the interval), when combined with the map scale, provides information concerning the gradients of the distribution. This is shown directly by the spacing of the isarithms (Robinson [1953] 1960, pp. 178–194).

Gradients or actual flow may be represented by the "flow line," another class of line symbol, the width of which varies in direct proportion to the magnitude (slope, volume, speed, etc.) that occurs at each point or selected point along the line. Lines may be varied in appearance (dots, dashes, colors, etc.) to identify the classes of data to which they refer. Area symbols are various patterns of marks or colors applied to regions to show either the quality, e.g., vegetation or political affiliation, or the quantity included within a region. The boundaries of the region so designated may be defined by the qualitative limit, by isarithms, by the boundaries of enumeration districts (choroplethic), or by some internal characteristic of the distribution, such as zones of rapid gradient (dasymetric). The employment of map symbols is very complex and the map maker and user must be alert to their many implications (ibid., pp. 136–154).

The final element of the map is the lettering applied to identify specific locations or the characteristics of the mapped data. There are three major aspects of cartographic lettering. The first involves the style and size of the lettering. Lettering was formerly done freehand or sometimes by an engraver, but today it is usually done with the aid of mechanical devices, by the incorporation of photographically composed words, or by the application of preprinted lettering from type (ibid., pp.

243–263). All sizes and styles may be used on maps, but because the lettering is to be read it must be large enough, and because the various styles may provide subjective reactions and either harmonize or conflict with the other map data, the choice of lettering is an exacting process. The spelling of the words to be used is subject to numerous complications: local use may differ from official use; the alphabets employed may be different, as in the transliteration of Chinese characters; convention may depart from reality, e.g., Danube River; and official use may change from time to time, as countries are created or administrations change. Because of the confusion that results from these conditions, the United States has established a Board on Geographic Names in the Department of the Interior charged with deciding official use. The board publishes numerous lists, recommendations, and policy statements. Moreover, the positioning of the lettering on maps has many ramifications and must be done with care (Imhof 1962).

The design of a map involves many of the considerations already mentioned. For purposes of scientific communication the map, as a functional tool, must be appropriately designed. If the proper line weights, lettering styles, projection, scale distribution, colors, and patterns are not employed, the map reader may easily be misled; and it is not uncommon for maps to be designed for propaganda purposes, without due regard for intellectual honesty and without adequate understanding of the effects of design (Robinson 1952). The map reader and map maker, as Wright (1942) has pointed out, must be ever alert against the possibility of subjective impressions at variance with reality.

The reproduction of the map is usually necessary and may be accomplished by many methods (Robinson [1953] 1960, pp. 264–282). Except for very simple maps, the actual drafting and preparation of copy for the printer have reached such complex technical proportions that they are beyond the capabilities of the noncartographer. The person without cartographic training should never attempt this phase without seeking advice.

Cartography is an indispensable research tool in numerous ways. Its prime function is to make possible the analysis of the elements of spatial variation inherent in the distributional qualities of the data under consideration, such as the relation of distance to cost or time of transport, the relation of urban development to functional areas, or the relation of productive capacity of the environment to population distribution or character. Before analyses of this kind can be properly carried on, the spatial aspects of such data must be mapped so that they are capable of correlation with other distributional data. Techniques for correlating with some precision several quantitative distributions are now available (Robinson 1962), as are methods for mapping residuals from spatial regression (Thomas 1960). The development of location theory and spatial structure may be aided theoretically by methods of modifying the natural horizontal scale relationships of distributions in order to remove unwanted influences (Tobler 1963), but as yet this very complex process is in its infancy. Cartography is also a standard medium of communication, providing the social scientist with a means of displaying the areal relationship involved in his analyses as well as his conclusions. Such maps are usually quite different from those used for research purposes and must be carefully designed not to give wrong impressions (Robinson 1952).

Research in cartography is advancing along many lines. Of indirect concern to the social scientist are the many investigations into the methods of preparing the large-scale reference maps from which come all the basic data for the other forms of cartography. These are carried on primarily in government institutions. Of direct concern are the avenues of research relating to the map as a research tool and to its employment as a medium of communication. Currently under investigation are methods of deriving the error factor in quantitative mapping; the design of graduated quantitative point symbols, e.g., circles, so that the communication of data will fit psychophysical standards; the employment of statistical methods in the spatial (cartographic) context; the role and practice of cartographic generalization ranging from such linear elements as coastlines, drainage, and boundaries to the analysis of isarithmic and choroplethic intervals; and the design and employment of colors, patterns, and tones as area symbols. An increasing amount of research is being devoted to historical cartography, much of which is concerned with the developments in the post-Renaissance period, but an increasing awareness of the magnitude of the current revolution in cartography has stimulated investigations into the post-1800 developments.

ARTHUR H. ROBINSON

[See also AREA; CENTRAL PLACE; GEOGRAPHY; GRAPHIC PRESENTATION.]

BIBLIOGRAPHY

ECKERT, MAX 1921–1925 *Die Kartenwissenschaft: Forschungen und Grundlagen zu einer Kartographie als Wissenschaft.* 2 vols. Berlin and Leipzig: Gruyter.

EKMAN, GOSTA; LINDMAN, RALF; and WILLIAM-OLSSON, WILLIAM 1961 A Psychophysical Study of Cartographic Symbols. *Perceptual and Motor Skills* 13:355–368.

HORN, WERNER 1959 Die Geschichte der Isarithmenkarten. *Petermanns geographische Mitteilungen* 103:225–232.

IMHOF, EDUARD 1961 Isolinienkarten. *International Yearbook of Cartography* 1:64–98.

IMHOF, EDUARD 1962 Die Anordnung der Namen in der Karte. *International Yearbook of Cartography* 2:93–129.

INTERNATIONAL GEOGRAPHICAL UNION, COMMISSION DES ATLAS NATIONAUX 1960 *Atlas nationaux: Histoire, analyse, voies de perfectionnement et d'unification.* Moscow: Akademiia Nauk SSSR.

JENKS, GEORGE F.; and KNOS, DUANE S. 1961 The Use of Shaded Patterns in Graded Series. Association of American Geographers, *Annals* 51:316–334.

KARO, H. ARNOLD 1955 *World Mapping.* Washington: Industrial College of the Armed Forces.

MITCHELL, HUGH C.; and SIMMONS, LANSING G. 1945 *State Coordinate Systems (A Manual for Surveyors).* U.S. Coast and Geodetic Survey, Special Publication No. 235. Washington: Government Printing Office.

PANNEKOEK, A. J. 1962 Generalization of Coastlines and Contours. *International Yearbook of Cartography* 2:55–75.

RAISZ, ERWIN J. (1938) 1948 *General Cartography.* 2d ed. New York: McGraw-Hill.

Report of the Group of Experts on Geographical Names. 1962 *World Cartography* 7:7–18.

ROBINSON, ARTHUR H. 1952 *The Look of Maps: An Examination of Cartographic Design.* Madison: Univ. of Wisconsin Press.

ROBINSON, ARTHUR H. (1953) 1960 *Elements of Cartography.* 2d ed. New York: Wiley.

ROBINSON, ARTHUR H. 1961 The Cartographic Representation of the Statistical Surface. *International Yearbook of Cartography* 1:53–63.

ROBINSON, ARTHUR H. 1962 Mapping the Correspondence of Isarithmic Maps. Association of American Geographers, *Annals* 52:414–429.

THOMAS, EDWIN N. 1960 *Maps of Residuals From Regression: Their Characteristics and Uses in Geographic Research.* Iowa City: State Univ. of Iowa, Department of Geography.

TOBLER, WALDO R. 1963 Geographical Area and Map Projections. *Geographical Review* 53:59–78.

U.S. DEPARTMENT OF THE ARMY 1951 *The Universal Grid Systems: Universal Transverse Mercator and Universal Polar Stereographic.* TM 5–241/TO 16–1–233. Washington: Government Printing Office.

WRIGHT, JOHN K. 1942 Map Makers Are Human: Comments on the Subjective in Maps. *Geographical Review* 32:527–544.

YALE UNIVERSITY, MAP LABORATORY 1956 *Statistical Symbols for Maps: Their Design and Relative Values.* New Haven: The University.

YONGE, ENA L. 1962a Regional Atlases: A Summary Survey. *Geographical Review* 52:407–432.

YONGE, ENA L. 1962b World and Thematic Atlases: A Summary Survey. *Geographical Review* 52:583–596.

CARVER, THOMAS NIXON

From the late 1890s to the 1930s, Thomas Nixon Carver was one of America's leading economists. He was born in 1865 on his father's farm near Kirkville, Iowa, and after growing up there he became a farmer, first in Iowa and later in southern California. In 1889, in San Diego, he married an Iowa farm girl, Flora Kirkendall; the marriage lasted seventy years, until her death in 1959. Carver died in 1961.

Carver had some difficulty acquiring his education, but in 1891 he received his A.B. from the University of Southern California. In his senior year there he decided upon college teaching as his vocation, and the following fall he began graduate work at Johns Hopkins. Among his first economics teachers there were Richard T. Ely and John Bates Clark. Carver soon turned from the historical approach to economics advocated by Ely to the analytical approach represented by Clark. While still a graduate student he produced his first contribution to economic theory; his article "The Place of Abstinence in the Theory of Interest" (1893) established Carver's reputation as an economic theorist.

After completing his PH.D. at Cornell in 1894, Carver held the chair of economics and sociology at Oberlin until his appointment to Harvard in 1900. The period of his Harvard career, 1900–1932, was the period of his most important work.

Carver taught courses in many fields. In economic theory he specialized in problems in the distribution of income and wealth. He did important pioneering work in the economics of agriculture, and for many years his sociology course—in which he presented, with his own revisions and additions, the ideas of Herbert Spencer—was almost the only Harvard course available in the field. Finally, Carver taught a famous course on programs of social reform, including socialism, in which he "took on" the radicals among the undergraduates and tried to convert them to his own devotion to free-enterprise capitalism.

Carver was at once an economist and a rather homespun social, moral, and political philosopher. Inseparably blended with his presentation of economic theory of the neoclassical type (marginal analysis) was his preaching of a politico-economic "gospel" that to him was both scientific and religious truth: that national societies of free individuals under limited governments, with economic systems controlled mainly by the free competition of all in free markets, are at once the best means to achieve national prosperity and strength and, uniquely, morally right.

The range of Carver's writings was wide. *The Distribution of Wealth*, first published in 1904, was reissued many times. Carver wrote on agricultural economics, on sociology, and on more general problems of economic and political philosophy. He was the author of many elementary economics textbooks for high school and college and of numerous popular magazine articles.

Retiring from Harvard in 1932, he moved to Santa Monica, California, where he remained vigorously active until his death. He taught at the University of Southern California and continued to publish countless newspaper and magazine articles on economic problems. A lifelong, active member of the American Economic Association, whose president he had been in 1916, he regularly attended and took part in its annual meetings, generally contributing papers to their programs, to the last year of his life.

Although Carver's homely expression of his controversial views often invited ridicule, he must be recognized not only as a justly eminent economist in his time but also as a significant figure in American intellectual history. His simple (in the best sense), sterling character and mind dealt habitually with the fundamental, general problems of our society, and he made substantial contributions both to economics and other social sciences and to popular enlightenment.

OVERTON H. TAYLOR

[*For the historical context of Carver's work, see the biographies of* CLARK, JOHN B.; ELY; SPENCER.]

BIBLIOGRAPHY

1893 The Place of Abstinence in the Theory of Interest. *Quarterly Journal of Economics* 8:40–61.

1894 The Theory of Wages Adjusted to Recent Theories of Value. *Quarterly Journal of Economics* 8:377–402.

(1904) 1918 *The Distribution of Wealth.* New York: Macmillan.

(1911) 1932 *Principles of Rural Economics.* New ed. Boston and New York: Ginn.

1912 *The Religion Worth Having.* Boston and New York: Houghton Mifflin.

1915 *Essays in Social Justice.* Cambridge, Mass.: Harvard Univ. Press.

1923 CARVER, THOMAS NIXON; and HALL, H. B. *Human Relations: An Introduction to Sociology.* Boston: Heath.

1925 *The Present Economic Revolution in the United States.* Boston: Little.

1935 *The Essential Factors in Social Evolution.* Harvard Sociological Studies, Vol. 1. Cambridge, Mass.: Harvard Univ. Press.

CASE STUDIES

See ADMINISTRATION; FIELD WORK; OBSERVATION.

CASH BALANCES

See MONEY.

CASSEL, KARL GUSTAV

Karl Gustav Cassel (1866–1945), Swedish economist, was born in Stockholm. He received a doctor's degree in mathematics from the University of Uppsala in 1895, but after teaching mathematics and physics in schools in Stockholm for several years, he became interested in economics. Since at that time no economic training was available at the University of Stockholm, he went to Germany to study. He stayed there for many years, but basically his theoretical economics shows little German influence.

His first economic publications were essays on English classical economics, in particular Ricardian economics. He also wrote a programmatic theoretical article, "Grundriss einer elementaren Preislehre" (1899), which was to remain the basis of all his later work on price theory. Within a few years he had published a great many papers on social and economic questions, all of which were merged into a grand theoretical system, *The Theory of Social Economy* (1918).

This textbook gained a wide distribution and was translated into many languages (English, French, Japanese, Spanish, and Swedish). Its success seems to derive primarily from its pedagogical merits: without extensive theoretical detail, it develops a synthesis of the economic universe, illustrated by well-chosen, empirical examples. The relative lack of theoretical rigor is particularly apparent when Cassel's book is compared to the neoclassical textbooks of standing, for example, those of Alfred Marshall or Knut Wicksell. Cassel dismissed the marginalist approach: instead of using the principles of marginal utility and marginal productivity theory to explain the equilibrium of prices, he deduced (relative) prices with the help of the "principle of scarcity," which he used to bring consumption into agreement with scarce resources. In addition to the principle of scarcity, no less than four "supplementary principles" are required by Cassel's system, as well as the assumption that the conditions of production (given by the "technological coefficient") are fixed in the short run.

To explain money (or absolute) prices, Cassel generally used the quantity theory of money, a theory he considered confirmed by statistical evidence. Although he developed this theory primarily for stationary (and closed) economies, he believed that it could easily be turned into a dynamic theory for the so-called uniformly progressive society. Cassel stipulated that for equilibrium to be established the rates of exchange among countries must be in the same relation as their general price levels. In other words, he expounded the purchasing power parity theory, a theory that is still being given some consideration.

Writing on capital theory, Cassel dismissed the theories founded upon the work of Eugen von Böhm-Bawerk and instead based his writings on earlier economists, among them Nassau Senior. For Cassel, the purpose of capital theory is to explain the price of "capital disposition" or "waiting."

In general, Cassel's theoretical framework can be characterized as emanating from the neoclassical school, although certain "archaic" traits are still present. In the spirit of the neoclassical writers, he endeavored to put his work on a firm quantitative foundation, but he rejected their marginal apparatus. Fundamental to his system is the Walrasian method of considering all prices and incomes as constituting a closed model that can be described by a system of simultaneous equations. Cassel's work is weakened, however, by the fact that he did not analyze his particular functions with respect to derivatives of different orders and the solvability of the system.

Cassel's international reputation was enhanced after World War I by his participation in the discussions about German indemnity payments and the restoration of the gold standard. At this time, he wrote many books on foreign exchange and monetary policy. He was also actively engaged in writing on Swedish economic problems, concentrating at first on monetary and fiscal aspects. With the beginning of unemployment in the 1920s, he considered possible cures for it, harshly rejecting those based on directly increasing purchasing power, undertaking public works, or increasing relief payments. He rejected Keynesian economics and wrote a strongly negative review of Keynes' *General Theory* in the *International Labour Review* (1937).

KARL GUSTAV LANDGREN

[*For the historical context of Cassel's work, see* ECONOMIC EQUILIBRIUM; INTERNATIONAL MONETARY ECONOMICS; *and the biography of* SENIOR.]

WORKS BY CASSEL

1899   Grundriss einer elementaren Preislehre. *Zeitschrift für die gesamte Staatswissenschaft* 55:395–458.

1900   *Das Recht auf den vollen Arbeitsertrag: Eine Einführung in die theoretische Ökonomie.* Göttingen (Germany): Vanderhoeck & Ruprecht.

(1902) 1923   *Socialpolitik.* Stockholm: Geber.

1903   *The Nature and Necessity of Interest.* London and New York: Macmillan.

(1918) 1932   *The Theory of Social Economy.* New rev. ed. New York: Harcourt. → Translated from the fifth edition of *Theoretische Sozialökonomie.*

1921   *The World's Monetary Problems.* London: Constable. → Contains two memoranda originally written for the League of Nations.

1937   Keynes' *General Theory. International Labour Review* 36:437–445.

SUPPLEMENTARY BIBLIOGRAPHY

KROMPHARDT, WILHELM 1927   *Die Systemidee im Aufbau der Casselschen Theorie.* Leipzig: Quelle & Meyer.

MYRDAL, GUNNAR 1945   Gustav Cassel in memoriam. *Ekonomisk revy* 2:3–13.

SCHAMS, EWALD 1927   Die Casselschen Gleichungen und die mathematische Wirtschaftstheorie. *Jahrbücher für Nationalökonomie und Statistik* 127:385–400.

WICKSELL, KNUT (1919) 1951   Professor Cassel's System of Economics. Appendix no. 1, pages 219–257 in Knut Wicksell, *Lectures on Political Economy.* Volume 1: General Theory. London: Routledge. → Translated from the third Swedish edition.

CASSIRER, ERNST

Ernst Cassirer (1874–1945), German philosopher, was born in Breslau (now Wroclaw) in Silesia. He was educated at the universities of Berlin, Leipzig, Heidelberg, Munich, and Marburg. At Marburg he was the most gifted disciple of Hermann Cohen and later became an exponent of the Marburg school of Neo-Kantianism. He began his career as a *Privatdozent* at the University of Berlin and was a civil servant during World War I, but in 1919 he was made professor of philosophy at the newly established University of Hamburg, becoming *Rektor* (president) in 1930. A Jew, Cassirer resigned when Hitler came to power in Germany. After two years at Oxford, from 1933 to 1935, he went to the University of Göteborg, in Sweden. In 1941 he left for the United States, where he joined Yale's philosophy department and then, in 1944, that of Columbia University in New York. He died in New York on April 13, 1945.

In addition to Cohen's Neo-Kantianism, the important influences on Cassirer were Hegel's *Phenomenology of Mind*, Herder's philosophy of history, and Hertz's views of physics. Although he ranks foremost as a philosopher of culture, Cassirer also contributed more to philosophical anthropology than any of his contemporaries. His concept of man as the symbolizing animal led him not merely to work out a philosophy of language but also to write significantly on the methodology of the sciences, as well as on primitive culture, myth, politics, religion, and literature.

In his masterwork, the three-volume *Philosophy of Symbolic Forms* (1923–1929), he attempted a systematic analysis of the whole range of human creation. None of the areas of human culture— language, myth, knowledge, science, art, and religion—give us direct access to the world. Rather, they are different "forms of apprehension," which originate in primitive symbols, images, and acts. The very notion of human consciousness presupposes these "forms." Man does not find order and intelligibility in the world; his consciousness creates it. The categories of the understanding, therefore, need no longer be deduced theoretically (as in Kant) but can be empirically checked and verified. The methods and symbols of the (so-called) exact sciences derive no less from formal constructions than do those of mathematics. The creative activity of the human mind accounts for all human experience, and the significance of the role of symbols becomes nowhere more obvious than in the exact sciences. Physics developed from an initially crude realism to a highly symbolic construction, which does not so much "describe" the world as "order" it. This same movement away from concrete particularity to abstract structure characterizes all other endeavors and achievements of the human mind.

To understand man, therefore, we must understand his language, whose symbolic construction and function show the same development from the directly perceived to the abstract.

Cassirer's philosophy attempts to deal with every aspect of human experience. In his morphology of consciousness he shows that the human spirit moves in many directions, although the patterns in each differ. History, for Cassirer, is the story of man's growing awareness of himself as a being expressing its own autonomy. The tendency away from enslavement to matter and toward ever-increasing freedom is therefore always present. This freedom itself is never entirely absent; the extent of its existence depends upon the meaning-giving intelligible aspect of consciousness provided by the creative and liberating use of symbols.

Cassirer's work has influenced twentieth-century semantics, anthropology, and social psychology at least as much as it has philosophy. Although the idealistic strain of his Neo-Kantianism may be largely passé, his contributions to the philosophy of language and of culture promise to be of permanent value.

PAUL ARTHUR SCHILPP

WORKS BY CASSIRER

1902 *Leibniz' System in seinen wissenschaftlichen Grundlagen.* Marburg (Germany): Elwert.

(1906–1920) 1950 *The Problem of Knowledge: Philosophy, Science and History Since Hegel.* 3 vols. New Haven: Yale Univ. Press. → First published as *Das Erkenntnisproblem in der Philosophie und Wissenschaft der neueren Zeit.*

(1910–1921) 1953 *Substance and Function* and *Einstein's Theory of Relativity.* New York: Dover. → First published as *Substanzbegriff und Funktionsbegriff,* 1910, and *Zur Einstein-schen Relativitätstheorie,* 1921.

(1916) 1918 *Freiheit und Form: Studien zur deutschen Geistesgeschichte.* 2d ed. Berlin: Cassirer.

1918 *Kants Leben und Lehre.* Berlin: Cassirer.

1921 *Idee und Gestalt: Goethe, Schiller, Hölderlin, Kleist: Fünf Aufsätze.* Berlin: Cassirer.

(1923–1929) 1953–1957 *The Philosophy of Symbolic Forms.* 3 vols. New Haven: Yale Univ. Press. → A historical and critical analysis of the images, symbols, and function of the human mind to be found in every human culture. First published in German. Volume 1: *Language,* 1953. Volume 2: *Mythical Thought,* 1955. Volume 3: *Phenomenology of Knowledge,* 1957. The Index to the German edition, published in 1931, was not translated into English.

(1925) 1946 *Language and Myth.* New York: Dover. → First published as *Sprache und Mythos.*

(1927) 1964 *The Individual and the Cosmos in Renaissance Philosophy.* Translated with an introduction by Mario Domandi. New York: Barnes & Noble. → First published as *Individuum und Kosmos in der Philosophie der Renaissance.*

1932a *Goethe und die geschichtliche Welt: Drei Aufsätze.* Berlin: Cassirer.

(1932b) 1951 *The Philosophy of the Enlightenment.* Princeton (N.J.) Univ. Press. → First published as *Die Philosophie der Aufklärung.*

(1932c) 1953 *The Platonic Renaissance in England.* Austin: Univ. of Texas Press. → First published as *Die platonische Renaissance in England und die Schule von Cambridge.*

(1937) 1956 *Determinism and Indeterminism in Modern Physics: Historical and Systematic Studies of the Problem of Causality.* New Haven: Yale Univ. Press. → First published as *Determinismus und Indeterminismus in der modernen Physik.*

1939 *Descartes: Lehre-Persönlichkeit-Wirkung.* Stockholm: Bermann-Fischer.

(1942) 1961 *Logic of the Humanities.* New Haven: Yale Univ. Press. → First published as *Logik der Kulturwissenschaften.*

(1944) 1956 *An Essay on Man: An Introduction to a Philosophy of Human Culture.* New Haven: Yale Univ. Press. → A paperback edition in German was published by W. Kohlhammer Verlag (Stuttgart) in 1960.

(1945) 1961 *Rousseau, Kant, Goethe: Two Essays.* Princeton (N.J.) Univ. Press. → A paperback edition was published in 1963.

1946 *The Myth of the State.* New Haven: Yale Univ. Press; Oxford Univ. Press.

SUPPLEMENTARY BIBLIOGRAPHY

SCHILPP, PAUL A. (editor) (1949) 1958 *The Philosophy of Ernst Cassirer.* New York: Tudor. → A critical examination, by 23 American and European scholars, of every aspect of Cassirer's work. Also contains complete bibliography of Cassirer's writings and publications.

CASTE

I. THE CONCEPT OF CASTE   *Gerald D. Berreman*
II. THE INDIAN CASTE SYSTEM   *Adrian C. Mayer*

I
THE CONCEPT OF CASTE

The term "caste" has been widely used to describe ranked groups within rigid systems of social stratification and especially those which constitute the society of Hindu India. Debate over whether castes are found outside of India has intensified with increased knowledge and understanding of the Indian caste system. Among social scientists, and especially among those who have worked in India, there are basically two views: (1) that the caste system is to be defined in terms of its Hindu attributes and rationale and, therefore, is unique to India or at least to south Asia; (2) that the caste system is to be defined in terms of structural features which are found not only in Hindu India but in a number of other societies as well. Those who hold the latter view find caste groups in such widely scattered areas as the Arabian Peninsula, Polynesia, north Africa, east Africa, Guatemala, Japan, aboriginal North America, and the contemporary United States.

Either of these positions is tenable; which is preferable depends upon one's interests and purposes. The caste system of India is unique—in the religious ritual which explains it, in its complexity, and in the degree to which the constituent groups are cohesive and self-regulating. Indeed, there are significant differences in caste as it is exhibited within Hindu India from place to place and even from caste to caste within the same locale. However, caste can also be defined in terms which give the concept cross-cultural applicability, thus making possible certain generalizations. This is not to claim that all caste systems are identical but simply to assert that there are recurrent patterns of social organization, commonly termed caste, which exhibit significant similarities along with their differences. These similarities are the basis for analytic comparisons, leading to greater understanding of human social organization and human behavior. For

this purpose, similar social facts must be categorized together despite differences which, while not denied, are not critical to the generalization; thus, insights may be gained into the conditions which give rise to and perpetuate caste systems and into their social, cultural, and psychological concomitants.

A. L. Kroeber defined caste as "an endogamous and hereditary subdivision of an ethnic unit occupying a position of superior or inferior rank or social esteem in comparison with other such subdivisions" (1930, p. 254). Thirty-five years later, and with many times as much research literature available on India and on social stratification, this definition has not been significantly improved upon, although there has been greatly increased understanding both of the Indian caste system and of other systems of stratification.

Kroeber's definition, like other comparative definitions, describes caste systems as systems of social stratification, examples of ranked aggregates of people, that are unusually rigid, birth-ascribed, and permit of no individual mobility. Concepts and hypotheses derived from such comparative definitions stem primarily from the study of stratification, especially of stratification in the United States.

The application of concepts of stratification to the Indian caste system and to other caste systems as well is not wrong, but it fails to convey adequately the nature of these systems. This failing is not found in studies which define caste in a specific cultural framework; but these studies, in turn, do not say anything very relevant about man and society outside of the particular culture and the specific groups which have been described.

A more comprehensive approach, which makes for cross-cultural comparability without sacrificing cultural content, can be derived from three bodies of descriptive and analytical literature: studies of stratification, studies of cultural pluralism, and studies of social interaction. Caste systems are indeed rigid systems of social stratification, but they are also systems of sociocultural pluralism, and both of these facts can best be understood in terms of distinctive patterns of social interaction. In this way, it is possible to analyze a broader range of caste systems, castelike systems, and related phenomena than is possible with concepts derived only from stratification theory. In addition, processes of change in caste systems and changes to or from systems of caste organization can be analyzed, and the continuum from noncaste to caste organization can be described in terms of these defining dimensions.

A caste system, then, can be said to occur when a society is composed of birth-ascribed, hierarchically ordered, and culturally distinct groups (castes). The hierarchy entails differential evaluation, differential rewards, and differential association.

A society.   The groups constituting a caste system are differentiated, interacting, and interdependent parts of a larger society. Often, and perhaps universally, they are economically interdependent and/or occupationally specialized. Their members view themselves and are viewed by others as relatively homogeneous elements in a system of differentially ranked component parts rather than independent and mutually unranked self-contained systems. In a caste system, everyone belongs to a caste and no one belongs to more than one caste.

Composed of groups.   Each rank in the hierarchy of a caste system is occupied by socially distinct aggregates of people who recognize that they constitute discrete, bounded, and ranked entities. The size and degree of corporateness of such groups vary widely. The members usually share a group name; they interact with one another in characteristic ways; and there are identifiable symbols of group membership, ranging from skin color to cultural features such as language, occupation, dress, or place of residence. Only members of the group are one's peers. Where group affiliation is relevant, individual attributes are irrelevant.

Birth ascription.   Membership in castes is determined by birth. An individual is assigned his lifelong and unalterable status according to his parentage—status which he shares with others of similar birth who are, therefore, assigned to the same group (caste). A common means of guaranteeing this status is by prescribing endogamous marriage in the caste and ascribing to the child the caste affiliation of its parents. But this method, often cited as a defining characteristic of caste, is by no means universal. Even in India, caste, like kin-group affiliation, sometimes is assigned unilineally or according to other, more complex rules based on birth.

Hierarchy.   That a caste system is a hierarchy implies that it is a system of differential evaluation, differential power and rewards, and differential association; in short, a system of institutionalized inequality.

Castes are ranked ultimately in terms of the shared "intrinsic worth" that is ascribed by birth to the individuals who constitute them. This criterion of rank may be defined and expressed in many different idioms, such as purity (as in India), honor (as in Swat), or genetically determined capa-

bilities (as is putatively the case in the United States), but always those who are high regard themselves as more worthy than those who are low. Those who are low seem universally to question, if not the criteria of rank, then the judgment which relegates them to the low end of the hierarchy.

Caste systems rank people by birth-ascribed group membership rather than by individual attributes. Class systems, by contrast, define the rank of their members according to their individual attributes and behaviors. In a caste system, one displays the attributes of his caste because he is a member of it. In a class system, one is a member of his class because he displays its attributes. Individual mobility is by definition impossible in a caste system and possible (although in some systems statistically unlikely) in a class system.

Ranking is accompanied by differential power and other rewards contingent upon caste membership: access to goods, services, and other valued things. The ability to influence the behavior of others, the source of one's livelihood, the kind and amount of food, shelter, and medical care, of education, justice, esteem, and pleasure—all these things which an individual will receive during his life, and the very length of life itself, are determined in large measure by caste status.

A caste hierarchy is to a large extent an interactional hierarchy. Social interaction is inherently symbolic, that is, it has meaning. Rank is expressed and validated in interaction between persons. It is manifest in patterns of interpersonal behavior and in patterns of association. Who may be one's friend, wife, neighbor, master, servant, client, or competitor, is largely a matter of caste. Everyone is a superior, a peer, or an inferior, depending upon caste. Only within the caste is status equality found. Between castes any kind of interaction which defies or jeopardizes the rules of hierarchy is taboo, even when such behavior does not directly challenge the official bases of the rank system. Thus, there is always a more or less elaborate etiquette of intercaste relations which is stringently enforced from within and above.

It is becoming increasingly evident that castes cannot be defined adequately without reference to interaction patterns. An interactional definition of a caste system might be: a system of birth-ascribed groups each of which constitutes for its members the maximum limit of status-equal interaction and between all of which interaction is consistently hierarchical. A caste might then be defined as a network of status-equal interactions in a society characterized by a network of hierarchical interaction between birth-ascribed groups. The interactions range from informal social encounters to marriage and include a wide variety of networks, such as those based on occupation, economics, politics, ritual, and friendship.

Underlying hierarchical interaction between castes is the existence of what has been termed "status summation" (Barth 1960, pp. 144 ff.). The multiple roles played by individual members of a caste are equivalent in the status they confer. Thus, a person of high ritual status tends also to be of high economic, political, and social status. These statuses tend to coalesce, and people are thus enabled as well as enjoined to interact with members of other castes in an unambiguous, consistent, and hierarchical manner. Part of the dynamics of caste organization is the tendency for status incongruities, when they occur, to be rectified.

Because intensive and status-equal interaction is limited to the caste, a common and distinctive caste culture is assured. This is a consequence of the density and quality of communication within the group, for culture is learned, shared, and transmitted. More is inevitably held in common between those intimately communicating (that is, between caste members) than between such people and outsiders; and, because of shared culture, communication is easier and hence more intense within the caste than outside it.

Castes are discrete social and cultural entities. Caste hierarchies are discontinuous. This is a key factor in understanding the dynamics of caste systems as contrasted, for example, with class systems wherein the hierarchies are continuous. Caste systems are maintained by defining and maintaining boundaries between castes. They are threatened when boundaries are compromised. Even when interaction between castes is maximal and cultural differences are minimal, the ideal of mutual isolation and distinctiveness is maintained and is advertised among those who value the system. Similarly, even when mobility within, or subversion of, the system is rampant, a myth of stability is stolidly maintained among those who benefit from the system.

Caste and other social organizations

Caste systems resemble plural societies in the cultural distinctiveness and in the dissensus found among castes on many key values and attitudes, for cultural plurality obtains when "two or more different cultural traditions characterize the population of a given society" (Smith 1965, p. 14). This pinpoints an important difference between caste and noncaste systems of stratification. Smith (ibid., p. xi) has noted that "it is perfectly clear that in

any social system based on intense cleavages and discontinuity between differentiated segments, the community of values or social relations between these sections will be correspondingly low. This is precisely the structural condition of the plural society." It is also conspicuously the condition of caste systems.

Stratification theory presupposes, explicitly or implicitly, that among people who constitute a rank continuum there is a wide consensus on the criteria and expressions of rank in a society. It also implies a wide consensus on values, attitudes, motives, and goals. The concept of pluralism implies "a discontinuous status order lacking any foundation in a system of common interests and values while its component sections are genuine status continua, distinguished by their differing systems of value, action, and social relations" (ibid., p. 83). The plural society is held together by power rather than by consensus. Institutional distinctiveness and independence (except in certain spheres, notably, the economic and administrative ones) are also key features of pluralism.

Clearly, India falls short of being a plural society by these criteria of the ideal type, and probably all caste systems do. In fact, if the definition is taken literally, few societies fit it. But caste systems, and specifically that of India, have many plural features. Several contemporary social anthropologists have made the point, for example, that while castes in India share much by way of cultural traditions, values, attitudes, and goals, they are culturally distinct in each of these spheres as a result of their histories and associations. The nature of their shared culture is different, and its extent is considerably less than in societies which are culturally and socially continuous. Similarly, castes share some institutions with other castes, but each has important distinctive institutions as well.

We can suggest that all caste systems are characterized by plural features similar to those found in the Indian instance and that all caste systems are held together in large measure by considerations of relative power among castes—power expressed physically, economically, politically, and socially. India and the United States are typical in that the caste system of each functions as a result of sanctions in the hands of the dominant group(s) and is readily upset if the balance of power, as perceived by those in the system, changes (Berreman 1960). The dominant caste(s) exercises the power which maintains the status quo just as does the dominant group in a plural society. There is invariably an official rationale which indicates that the system functions by mutual consent—by consensus. Malfunctioning or change is likely to be attributed, therefore, to alien intervention. Actually, it is more often a result of changed power relations between groups, with consequent attempts by some of those groups to realize formerly suppressed aspirations.

Social cohesion need not rest entirely on common motives and values. It can, and more commonly does, rest on the articulation of divergent motives and values. Certainly this is true of caste systems. Consensus is not lacking between castes—they could not function within a society if it were—but it is a distinctly limited consensus. People largely agree on the facts of the behavioral and interactional hierarchy, on the membership of particular castes, and on their publicly accorded status. They agree on the hierarchical meaning ascribed in the society to particular attributes and behaviors. Where they disagree is on subjective and ideological matters: on the legitimacy of the hierarchy or, more commonly, on the place their group has been accorded in it; on the legitimacy of the criteria of ranking; and on the legitimacy of the requirements and rewards of rank. Such disagreements are often obscured by power relations and sanctions, threatened or applied.

In caste systems, as in all plural systems, highly differentiated groups get along despite widely differing subjective definitions of the situation because they agree on the objective facts of what is happening and what is likely to happen: on who has the power; and how, under what circumstances, and for what purposes it is likely to be exercised. They cease to get along when this crucial agreement changes or is challenged.

From a functional perspective, caste systems can be seen as facilitating cultural and socioeconomic differentiation. They provide mechanisms for incorporating distinct groups into a society and maintaining them as groups without incorporating their members into extant groups. Thus, they function to maintain cultural, occupational, and economic differences; to inhibit mobility; to maintain power relations; and to protect the *status quo*. Such systems provide blueprints for the articulation of sociocultural diversity and the protection of power and privilege.

Caste systems combine the principles of stratification and pluralism. A caste system resembles a plural society whose discrete sections are all ranked vertically. A plural society resembles a caste system wherein the groups (except the dominant one) are unranked relative to one another. In both instances there is a dominant group whose sanctions assure persistence of the system by articulating its component parts. In the village caste system of India this is the dominant caste or castes; in plural societies it is often the colonial power.

By utilizing the criteria of ranking and cultural distinctiveness (both expressed in patterns of interaction), caste systems as ideal types can be distinguished from three other important systems of organizing people in society: pluralism, class systems, and homogeneous systems wherein there are no culturally distinct or ranked aggregates (see Table 1).

Table 1

	Ranked	Unranked
Culturally distinct groups	Caste system	Plural society
Cultural continuum	Class or status system	Homogeneous society

Also, by utilizing the criteria of ranking and mode of recruitment, castes can be distinguished from other social aggregates, namely, consanguineal kin groups, classes, and community or residential groups. These are distinctive but not mutually exclusive social aggregates. All four, for example, occur in Indian society, even on the village level. Thus, a caste is generally also an extensive kin group; most castes are territorially delimited; and class distinctions commonly occur within castes as they do within kin groups and communities. Indian villagers can be defined, and can define themselves in many instances, by caste, kin, class, and community criteria (see Table 2).

Table 2

	Ranked	Unranked
Birth-ascribed membership	Caste	Consanguineal kin group
Acquired membership	Class	Community (locality)

Ranking and mode of recruitment appear to be especially important variables in the social psychology of groups and individuals, accounting in large measure for the widespread similarities in attitudes, values, beliefs, and behaviors discovered in societies sharing similar expression of these variables, for example, caste societies.

The definitions and discussion above should make it clear that "caste" and "caste system" are concepts describing one end of a continuum. Some instances fit the definition better than others. That is, some are more fully castelike than others, while some may be castelike in only certain respects. There is no mechanical rule by which all instances of social organization can be unequivocally and definitively judged as either caste or noncaste, no matter how perfectly documented or how well analyzed. In fact, by utilization of the concepts of stratification, pluralism, and interaction, this should be clearer, and the reasons should be more accurately specifiable, than if only the first of these were used.

Special types of caste organization

Each of two particular and peculiar types of caste organization have often been assumed by commentators to be either the only, or the characteristic, kind of caste organization. These are (1) caste in India and (2) pariah caste status. For the first, a culturally and regionally specific phenomenon, a term indigenous to that culture area of reference may profitably be used. *Jati* is a term widely applied in the Sanskritic languages of south Asia to those groups defined in English as caste or, sometimes, subcaste. South Asian caste is certainly unique and deserving of special study, but that fact should neither preclude nor inhibit its comparison with analogous systems in other societies.

Pariah status or "untouchability" is another special variety of caste organization; in this case structurally rather than regionally or culturally specific. It refers to the intrinsically polluted, stigmatized, denigrated, and excluded caste status found in many societies. It has been reported not only in south Asia but also in Japan, Korea, Tibet, pre-European Africa, contemporary South Africa, and the United States. Pariah castes and the relations between pariah and nonpariah castes are recurrent and interesting phenomena within the category of caste organization. But care must be exercised not to attribute the characteristics of these phenomena to all caste systems or to assume that they are diagnostic of caste organization. The general or universal characteristics of pariahs and their relations with nonpariahs may be quite different from—or at least may be only part of the picture when compared with—the characteristics and relations of castes not so widely separated in the hierarchy, such as the many intermediate castes and castes close to one another in the hierarchy in India. Pariah–elite relations highlight many of the general characteristics of caste systems, but they neither define such systems nor exhaust their range, and it is erroneous to assume even by implication that they do.

Perhaps dual systems, such as that of Negro–white relations in the southern United States and of *eta*–non*eta* relations in contemporary Japan, are sufficiently different from multiple caste systems, such as that in India, as to deserve to be treated as two major subtypes of caste organization. It may be, for example, that abolition of the system is the characteristic goal of ambitious low-status groups in dual caste systems (where they have nothing to lose but their inferiority), while upward mobility within the system is the aim of low-status groups in multiple caste societies (where, in the event of abolition, equality with superiors would be bought with the loss of superiority to inferiors).

An advantage of the comparative approach to the study of caste systems is that variety as well as consistency in their characteristics can be defined and studied and the consequences can be analyzed. The general concept of caste must not blind us to distinctive types of caste systems, just as it must not lead us to overlook or deny unique attributes of particular systems.

Concomitants of caste systems

The utility of a comparative concept of caste lies in the light it can throw on the sociocultural and psychological concomitants of a definable, recurrent type of social structure in the context of general social processes, universal human nature, and variant cultural and historical environments. That is, in addition to being a type of structure, a caste system is a peculiar pattern of human relationships and a peculiar state of mind. Some of the concomitants of caste organization can be suggested briefly (they have been reviewed in greater detail in Berreman 1966).

There appear to be common and distinctive patterns of life in caste systems which make it possible to speak of "cultures of caste organization." The imposition of birth-ascribed and unalterable membership in ranked, mutually isolated, but interacting groups with conspicuously different life experiences, life chances, and public esteem seems to have common psychological, attitudinal, and behavioral consequences wherever it occurs. Many of the common elements of caste cultures are doubtless characteristic of any sharply stratified society; others may be characteristic of any plural society; still others of any society with important inherited statuses. Caste cultures may be expected to exhibit a characteristic combination of elements from these three sources.

The consequences of caste systems surely include many of the responses, reactions, and mechanisms described in the literature on Negro–white relations in the United States, on touchable–untouchable relations in India, and on relations between rulers and ruled in colonial contexts. The similarities in these relationships is remarkable in view of the widely differing cultural environments in which they occur. Although members of any particular caste do not characteristically adopt a view of themselves entirely consistent with the view held by others in their society, they cannot avoid being influenced by those views and the associated behaviors. Common adjustments to low-caste status include avoidance, apathy, withdrawal, and over-compliance, as well as mobility, escape, and resistance, both passive and active. Self-justification, self-deception, rationalization, and fantasy serve both low and high castes. Those near the top of the hierarchy exhibit feelings of superiority relative to those beneath them. Prejudice, as it has been described and analyzed in American race relations, is a manifestation of this. Other attitudes and associated behaviors can be suggested by such terms as paternalism, *noblesse oblige*, condescension, segregation, discrimination, and exploitation.

The most striking examples of similarities between caste systems are found in social relations—in patterns of interaction. If an interactional definition of caste is used, these relations may be regarded as defining features; if a structural definition is used, they are concomitants. To maintain the sharp boundaries, the hierarchical ranking, and the power relations among castes, there are numerous rules restricting interaction between them. Most commonly these take the form of restrictions on marriage, on sex relations, on living together, on eating together, on sitting together, and on a variety of other forms of interaction symbolic of social equality. What constitutes status-equal interaction varies from society to society. What does not vary is the fact that some kinds of interaction and some kinds of behavior are defined as appropriate only between those who are equal in status (that is, within the caste), while others are defined as appropriate for superiors vis-à-vis inferiors and vice versa (that is, between castes). Each caste system, dominated as it is by high castes, has controls of variable effectiveness to assure that the rules are followed and the system is not jeopardized.

A closely related area is that of the processes of sociocultural change. Within caste systems there is constant mobility striving. It is generally sought through "status emulation" as groups attempt to imitate their social superiors (for example, "Sanskritization" in India). Another means to mobility is the adoption of reference groups wherein traditional considerations of status are irrelevant and new criteria are operative (for example, "Westernization" in India). Mobility striving, while intrinsic in caste systems, is a constant threat to the *status quo*. It is suppressed whenever possible, but the process of suppression is difficult and never completely effective. Caste systems are characterized not by consensus but by conformity. They are maintained not by agreement but by sanctions. It takes much physical and psychic energy to maintain an inherently unstable, conflictive situation in a semblance of working order. The dominant high-status groups must suppress mobility striving among others; rules restricting social interaction must be enforced; the purity and integrity of the group must be maintained; a myth of stability must be supported in the face of overt disconfirming evidence. On the part of low-status people, self-respect must be maintained despite constant denigration; resentment must be suppressed or carefully channeled. The social costs of such systems may be seen in in-group and intergroup conflict and violence. They might also be discovered in individual psychological disturbances. Certainly they are found in exploitative economic relations; in the waste of human resources resulting from discriminatory selection of occupational and other specialists; and in the distorted and inefficient distribution of goods, services, and opportunities. The social costs become manifest when the traditional hierarchy of power and privilege is confronted by democracy and equalitarianism and when pluralism is confronted by the homogenizing influence of mass media, public education, and the like. The resulting changes may take the form of group or individual mobility, of implementation of equalitarian practices, of elimination of traditional prerogatives, of wider dissemination of power and access to valued things in the society. Such changes are likely to be traumatic in their achievement. The fact that they are sought by some in the society and bitterly resisted by others belies the notion that caste systems are intrinsically consensus-based, equilibrium-maintained, personally satisfying, and conflictless.

Caste organization may seem to be an anachronism in the modern world. If so, it is at least an extremely important and quite widespread one whose human implications are becoming fully apparent as a result of the fact that such organization is being vigorously challenged and vigorously defended in many parts of the world. Unless it is understood, the problems it evokes are unlikely to be resolved. Recognition and understanding of it in its varied manifestations thus take on acutely practical significance in addition to theoretical importance.

GERALD D. BERREMAN

BIBLIOGRAPHY

BAILEY, F. G. 1959 For a Sociology of India? *Contributions to Indian Sociology* 3:88–101.

BAILEY, F. G. 1963 Closed Social Stratification in India. *Archives européennes de sociologie* 4:107–124.

BARTH, FREDRIK 1960 The System of Social Stratification in Swat, North Pakistan. Pages 113–146 in Edmund R. Leach (editor), *Aspects of Caste in South India, Ceylon and North-west Pakistan.* Cambridge Papers in Social Anthropology, No. 2. Cambridge Univ. Press.

BERREMAN, GERALD D. 1960 Caste in India and the United States. *American Journal of Sociology* 66:120–127. → See the subsequent exchange of letters with O. C. Cox in the *American Journal of Sociology* (1961) 66:510–512, and the exchange with L. Dumont in *Contributions to Indian Sociology* (1962) 6:122–125.

BERREMAN, GERALD D. 1965 The Study of Caste Ranking in India. *Southwestern Journal of Anthropology* 21:115–129. → Comprises a critical review of the literature.

BERREMAN, GERALD D. 1966 Caste in Cross-cultural Perspective. Pages 275–304 in George DeVos and H. Wagatsuma (editors), *Japan's Invisible Race.* Berkeley: Univ. of California Press. → See also the other chapters that describe and analyze pariah status in Japan.

COX, OLIVER C. 1945 Race and Caste: A Distinction. *American Journal of Sociology* 50:360–368.

COX, OLIVER C. (1948) 1959 *Caste, Class & Race: A Study in Social Dynamics.* New York: Monthly Review Press.

DOLLARD, JOHN (1937) 1957 *Caste and Class in a Southern Town.* 3d ed. Garden City, N.Y.: Doubleday.

DUMONT, LOUIS (1960) 1961 Caste, Racism and "Stratification": Reflections of a Social Anthropologist. *Contributions to Indian Sociology* 5:20–43. → An English version of a paper first published in French in *Cahiers internationaux de sociologie.*

GOULD, HAROLD A. 1960 Castes, Outcastes, and the Sociology of Stratification. *International Journal of Comparative Sociology* 1:220–238.

KROEBER, A. L. 1930 Caste. Volume 3, pages 254–257 in *Encyclopaedia of the Social Sciences.* New York: Macmillan.

LEACH, EDMUND R. (editor) 1960 *Aspects of Caste in South India, Ceylon and North-west Pakistan.* Cambridge Papers in Social Anthropology, No. 2. Cambridge Univ. Press.

MARRIOTT, McKIM 1959 Interactional and Attributional Theories of Caste Ranking. *Man in India* 39:92–107.

NADEL, SIEGFRIED F. 1954 Caste and Government in Primitive Society. *Journal of the Anthropological Society of Bombay* New Series 8:9–22.

PASSIN, HERBERT 1955 Untouchability in the Far East. *Monumenta nipponica* 11, no. 3:27–47.

POHLMAN, EDWARD W. 1952 Semantic Aspects of the Controversy Over Negro–White Caste in the United States. *Social Forces* 30:416–419.

SMITH, MICHAEL G. 1965 *The Plural Society in the British West Indies.* Berkeley: Univ. of California Press.

WEBER, MAX (1916–1917) 1946 India: The Brahman and the Castes. Pages 396–415 in *From Max Weber: Essays in Sociology.* Translated and edited by Hans H. Gerth and C. Wright Mills. New York: Oxford Univ. Press.

WEBER, MAX (1921) 1946 Class, Status, Party. Pages 180–195 in *From Max Weber: Essays in Sociology.* Translated and edited by Hans H. Gerth and C. Wright Mills. New York: Oxford Univ. Press. → First published as Part 3, Chapter 4 of *Wirtschaft und Gesellschaft.*

II
THE INDIAN CASTE SYSTEM

The term "caste" is used to designate each unit in the hierarchically arranged organic systems of closed groups to be found on the Indian subcontinent. Besides this, it has been applied to the classical division of Hindu society and to systems of ranked and closed populations found outside India.

The Indian caste system presents an extraordinarily complex social phenomenon. The great size and spatial extension of the population concerned and the close interlocking of religious and secular features have produced a luxuriance of local variation from which it is difficult to draw consistent features and give them their precise emphasis. Social scientists have been interested in the caste system as a type of social stratification. But for a long time their knowledge rested on the largely descriptive accounts of writers interested in providing general ethnographies, on official documents, such as censuses, and on the Hindu literary classics. It is only in recent years that detailed studies of local caste hierarchies have been made. Hence, the relation of the Indian caste system to other systems of stratification and social grouping has by no means been agreed upon, and it is debatable whether castes exist outside India and its immediate neighbors.

Units of very different scale have been denoted by the word "caste," as well as by vernacular terms, of which *jati* is the most common. Such units include reference categories extending throughout India, hereditary occupational units (such as potters, barbers, tanners), and the endogamous units within the occupational units. The terms *"varna,"* "caste," and "subcaste" will be used to distinguish these three broad levels, with a further distinction, where necessary, between the total population subsumed under the term and the operational local group.

Caste and "varna." The earliest written mention of division in Indian society refers to the distinction between the autochthonous Dasa and the immigrant Arya populations. Later texts specify a threefold and then a fourfold division of society into Brahmana (priestly), Rajanya or Kshatriya (warrior–ruler), Vaishya (merchant), and Shudra (servant) *varna*, with the population outside this scheme being subsequently categorized as Untouchable. The *varna* formed a hierarchy marked by differing material and spiritual privileges. Little is known about the internal structure of the *varna*, but individuals could change their *varna* membership.

The *varna* now form categories that have preserved their traditional hierarchical positions within Hindu society. They are not organized groups, although some attempts have recently been made to unite the people of a *varna* for political purposes. Because there is no formal mechanism for dealing with claims to *varna* membership, the *varna* provide at the local level a means for groups (although not for individuals) to gain a tradition-based validation of an achieved status. *Varna* membership enables people from distant parts of India to assess each other's approximate local status. *Varna* are socially significant, therefore, as a charter for hierarchical status and as a unifying feature of the system.

Caste and subcaste. Members of Indian caste society normally become members of one of its constituent units at birth. These units are local populations within which there is an effective implementation of the rules of caste behavior. Sometimes formal boundaries designate units that contain populations of between five and one hundred villages. But in other cases the size of the unit depends on the composition of informal gatherings that exert social control; since these are mainly of kin, such units are to some extent defined by the area and by the pattern of marriage ties of a family or local group. Units generally form part of a wider population bearing the same name and, at least in theory, following the same customs and allowing the intermarriage of members. Easier means of communication now make it possible for these larger units to regulate the behavior of members, at least in major matters. Nevertheless, variations often exist between the smaller local units, and minor differences can sometimes be observed even between nearby villages. The smaller, locally effective units can be called "subcaste groups," and the larger, named populations can be called "subcastes."

The subcaste group (which, of course, may compose the whole of a small or well-organized subcaste), besides controlling internal relations, regulates the behavior of members toward people of other subcaste groups in the area. Some of these may be subcaste groups of the same caste; others belong to different castes. Relations between two subcaste groups of the same caste may be close and may include intermarriage if the two subcastes are moving toward an amalgamation. In such transitional cases only the different name may distinguish the subcastes. More often, how-

ever, their relations are marked by endogamy or hypergamy and by many of the separations that characterize relations between the castes to which the subcastes belong.

Most castes contain a varying number of subcastes; in addition, a few are unitary and others have one or more intermediate sections composed of several subcastes. Caste membership seldom involves the regulation of internal relationships, for these are taken care of by the subcastes. Nevertheless, caste membership may influence behavior between people of different castes. The subcastes of a caste bear a common caste name, and they are not usually differentiated by outsiders, who therefore act in the same way toward them all, seeing them as parts of a single unit. This unit has been called a "caste-cluster" by scholars who wish to call the subcaste the "caste" and so stress the fact that subcastes are the basic units of action, which may have evolved independently and not from the fission of a larger unit (Karvé 1961). No single terminology is at present in use; other scholars designate the subcaste group by the vernacular word *jati*, a term the people themselves apply to all levels of the caste system.

Relations between members of different castes occur mainly at the local level, and whole caste populations seldom take concerted action. The same distinction can therefore be made between the caste group and the caste as has been drawn between the subcaste group and the subcaste. Until recently, analyses of the caste system have rested upon studies of relations between caste groups.

The caste hierarchy. The relations between caste groups (and, *mutatis mutandis*, between subcaste groups) can be characterized as hierarchical. They are based on evaluations of differences into which both religious and more mundane considerations enter. The belief in a differential innate purity of each caste is foremost in this evaluation. Purity is ascribed to caste members at birth and rewards them for the quality of their actions in their previous life. Thus, a belief in metempsychosis serves as an incentive for an individual to better his future rebirth. One way for him to achieve this is by adhering to the rules of society, in particular to those of his caste group as enforced by his subcaste group's council (*panchayat*).

Foremost among such rules are those that safeguard the level of caste group purity. Its pollution results from contact either with lower caste groups or with objects that are themselves impure. Contact with the former is avoided by restrictions on intermarriage and sexual relations with caste groups of less purity, sometimes on personal touch and approach, and on commensal relations, such as eating, smoking, and drinking. Impure materials include things having to do with the dead and with bodily emissions; hence, the practitioners of occupations connected with them (such as barbering and leatherworking) have a low status. This is especially important because castes are linked to hereditary occupations, whose degree of purity affects the members whether or not they are practicing these occupations. Members who become polluted involuntarily (through contact with the dead at funerals, through menstruation, etc.) undergo purificatory rites of varying complexity and, until these are completed, must stay apart from their caste group fellows. Those who pollute themselves by knowingly breaking caste group rules (by eating or having sexual relations with lower caste groups or by carrying on demeaning occupations) must also be purified and are barred from social intercourse until purification has taken place. The manner of their purification is decided by the subcaste group council, which also may determine the size of any fine that accompanies purification. There is a ceremonial meal at which a formal resumption of commensal relations readmits those who have been polluted to the subcaste group (and, in the eyes of outsiders, to the caste group). If they refuse to reform their behavior, they are excommunicated. An individual may then be recognized as a member of the lower caste group with which he has associated himself; a seceding local group will tend to form a separate subcaste group.

It is easy to see considerable variation of behavior at each end of the hierarchy and to recognize hierarchical differences. At the top the Brahman stands in an acknowledged position of purity and fulfills priestly duties, and at the bottom are caste groups that are traditionally associated with such occupations as scavenging and tanning and whose diet may contain beef (meat is more polluting than vegetables and beef is more polluting than other meats). But not all ranking is so easily distinguishable. Many caste groups have agriculture as their traditional occupation and follow similar dietary and other customs. Yet these groups may also claim to be higher than one another. In such cases, other factors may assist society to rank them. Land ownership and the wealth it brings, education, and hereditary positions of authority are attributes that may influence the assessment of rank and at the same time make it possible for others to distinguish ranks when dealing with two caste groups claiming equal status. Thus, the different economic and political positions of the same caste in different areas may account for variations in its hierarchical status.

These features are also often the mainsprings of mobility in the system. Although an individual cannot improve his caste affiliation, a caste group (or, more often, a subcaste group) can try to move upward by copying the behavior of either the ritually pre-eminent Brahman or of the castes that are economically and politically powerful. Thus, if the model group considers marriage to be a binding sacrament, an aspiring subcaste group will ban the remarriage of its widows. Again, many politically dominant castes do not object to alcohol, and their imitators also will not do so. To help it rise, a subcaste group may change its name and lay claim to a long-lost membership in a higher *varna*. This helps it sever relations with other subcaste groups in the caste in order to be recognized by outsiders as a separate, higher caste group. The impetus for such changes is frequently given by recently acquired wealth or political influence. However, success can only be gained slowly, for the traditional associations of the caste remain. Its members may no longer perform the traditional work, but their name will announce their former connection with it, and even after a change of name they must overcome tenaciously held memories. Modern conditions have made it possible for subcaste groups that have acquired economic and political power to disregard hierarchical status by leaning on the formally casteless institutions of the state. But a validation of power is still often sought within the caste system.

Theories of caste.   A number of theories about caste devote themselves to explaining its origin. These include the hypothesis that the system was created by the Brahmans for their own benefit (Sherring 1872–1881, vol. 3, p. 231) and the classical view (Manu, chapter 10) that castes developed from unions between members of different *varna*. It has also been suggested that castes were formed on "a community of function" through common occupation in a division of labor (Nesfield 1885, p. 88). An alternate theory claims that the underlying principle was a physical antipathy of Arya for Dasa, resulting in an endogamy that produced measurable physical distinctions, so that one could almost say for at least certain regions of India that "a man's social status varies in inverse ratio to the width of his nose" (Risley 1891, vol. 1, p. xxxiv). Hocart ([1938] 1950, p. 68) suggests that the functions and concomitant purity of participants in court rituals became hereditary, and when this organization later spread to meet the ritual requirements of the rest of the population a ritually ranked hierarchy was created. Such theories tend to center upon a single factor as basic to the origin of the caste system. Others are less sweeping, such as that which maintains that the system arose from Aryan institutions that were adapted to the conditions found in India (Senart [1896] 1930, p. 213). Hutton ([1946] 1964, p. 164) is even less ambitious, giving only a list of 15 factors whose concatenation (perhaps with others) contributed to the emergence of the system, and Weber ([1921] 1958, pp. 130–131) suggests that the institution could have been produced only by the convergence of several major factors.

Whatever the validity of such theories, it is clear that many of the features they stress are basic to caste. These include the emphasis on hereditary occupation, with its resulting functional interdependence and lack of competition, and the opposition of purity and impurity. Such features are also prominent in studies of present-day caste. These studies deal with caste groups as units linked to one another in a system, rather than with individual caste groups, and are based on analyses of the qualities of these connections. Many years ago Bouglé (1908) distinguished the basic principles of hierarchy, hereditary specialization, and repulsion (better expressed as separation); these are still considered to be primary, with intercaste links characterized as organic and as containing some degree of summation of roles. It is, however, possible to emphasize as a fundamental feature of caste either the opposition of purity and impurity or an economic and political aspect that may then be expressed in ritual terms. The latter approach stresses that caste groups that do not follow the precepts of pure behavior may nevertheless have high rank. Meat-eating and liquor-drinking groups may, in some local hierarchies, find themselves placed above vegetarian groups. In such cases rank may depend less on the pure or impure attributes of the caste group's behavior than on the dominance it has in its economic and political interaction with other caste groups. On the other hand, it can be maintained that to stress the political and economic aspects at the expense of other elements of caste behavior is to ignore the way in which caste is regarded by the people themselves. Rather, notions of purity and impurity lie behind a hierarchic principle that is distinct from, although not unconnected to, the economic and political power structure and that gives the caste system its nature.

The different weight scholars give to these approaches has a bearing on the extent to which caste is viewed as a general social phenomenon existing outside of India. For a definition in political and economic terms is more easily applied to hierarchical situations in other societies, whereas that resting on a particular form of purity–impurity opposition is more likely to be restricted to the Hindu situation.

Present and future research. One focus of present research has been on the problem of caste rank. This arises where the criteria of rank conflict with one another. Such a conflict may lead the caste groups involved into a relation of equal separation rather than one of differential rank, but others in the community may weight the various factors so as to produce a generally acknowledged rank order. The problem consists in finding out what these weightings are. Attempts have been made to do this through the analysis of different interactional contexts of ranking, especially the commensal (Mayer 1956), and, recently, efforts have been made to assess a collective hierarchy through the statistical analysis of village opinion about ranking rather than through observed behavior (Freed 1963). At the same time, there is study of the factors underlying the number of ranks (the elaboration of the hierarchy) in different places (Marriott 1960). It is hoped that this work will lead to a greater knowledge about the determinants of rank and provide data against which hierarchical change can be measured.

Related research is concerned with the scales of power and prestige underlying caste hierarchies. Studies have been made of the system of socioeconomic services (*jajmani*) to evaluate its place in intercaste group relations. Here, artisans and other specialists render economic and social services to clients, for which those having land pay in kind at each harvest. Such ties between the families of client and specialist may continue for generations and may be treated as heritable property by the specialist. The system has been viewed by some as providing for the interdependence and social cohesion of the local group (Wiser 1936); others have stressed that greater power lies with the landholder, who is assured constantly available services (Beidelman 1959). The *jajmani* system is related to the caste hierarchy because many of its occupations are the monopolies of specific castes and because the major landholders usually belong to higher caste groups. Such caste groups are dominant politically as well as economically, and this has led to the exploration of the connections between economic and political power, through analysis of local political systems and discussion of the extent to which class and party interests link people of different castes and internally differentiate caste and subcaste groups. Such studies enlarge our knowledge of the patterns of summation of roles in intercaste group relations. The relation of caste to class and party is especially important for the study of caste in towns, where there may be a low summation of roles and a weak caste organization, part of whose place may have been taken by other associations (for example, trade unions).

Yet another series of problems arises from the study of the internal constitution of caste units. The extent of the effective subcaste group has by no means been fully ascertained. Where there are formal councils with authority over the subcaste populations of definite numbers of settlements, the boundaries of social control are easy to define. But it is difficult to delimit subcaste groups where control is exercised at *ad hoc* meetings of kin. Caste and kinship have, until recently, been largely considered as separate social fields. It is now clear that the two are closely linked; some work has explored this connection (for example, Dumont 1957; Mayer 1960; Orenstein 1965), but it has yet to be fully analyzed.

A last set of problems stems from the role of caste in independent India (see, for example, Srinivas 1962). New fields for caste distinctions and rivalries have been provided by the introduction of universal franchise, semiautonomous community development committees, and legislation against untouchability and by the augmentation of benefits for castes classed as backward. The lower castes and others not traditionally dominant may now have the chance to gain local and regional political power. At the same time, occupational specialization is tending to diminish, with castes being economically linked more through competition than through functional interdependence. There are many newly emerging social questions to be studied, such as the degree to which these changes have affected patterns of rank, the extent to which the caste system is still a factor of social organization, and the extent to which the new situation, added to a greatly increased ease of communication, has stimulated larger caste groupings in the form of regional and national caste associations. Some study has been made of caste associations (Rudolph & Rudolph 1960) and of the role of caste in local, regional, and national politics (Brass 1965; Harrison 1960, chapter 4), but much more needs to be done before a detailed assessment of caste's new role can be made and, indeed, before it can be decided whether these associations should be classified as caste bodies.

It has been suggested that they are interest groups based on caste membership rather than manifestations of caste, since they form competing units in a segmentary system rather than organically interdependent parts (Bailey 1963, p. 123). Social scientists may therefore be faced with the problem either of redefining caste to include situations where caste-named groups act in qualitatively new ways or of adopting a new term for these groups.

Each of these sets of problems is devoted to providing a deeper understanding of caste in specific situations. Questions of technique arise where these situations are spatially extended (as in the study of the boundaries of the subcaste group) or where they involve single-interest roles rather than those with a high degree of summation. Therefore, like their colleagues working in other "complex" societies, students of caste in India are concerned with the problem of adapting their methods and concepts to new situations. Further problems exist for those who wish to make general statements about the place of caste in Indian civilization, notably the problem that concerns the usefulness of traditional literary and historical sources not only for the question of the origin of caste but also for the ways in which they can enlarge the temporal and spatial framework of sociological inquiry.

Caste outside India.   The term "caste" has been applied to social strata in a number of societies outside India. There is disagreement, however, over whether it should be used in this way or retained to define the pan-Indian phenomenon. Supporting the latter view are those who see caste as a form of structural organization specific to India and, at most, castelike situations in Pakistan, Nepal, and Ceylon (and possibly overseas Indian communities). Others stress the difference between what can be called *de facto* and *de jure* stratification (Nadel 1954) and maintain that a definition of caste must take into account the values of the society and the meaning given to the term by the people themselves. According to this view, caste systems are based on *de jure* stratification, which is qualitatively different from stratification in societies in which equality is the ideal relationship (Dumont 1960). Caste systems are therefore to be found in relatively few societies outside India, and even then with little elaboration. On the other side, the view is put forward that institutions should be defined so as to facilitate comparison. For instance, Berreman (1960) shows that a limited definition of caste as a hierarchy of closed divisions can lead to a comparison between India and the southern United States. However, the need to limit the definition of caste for comparative purposes suggests that Indian caste has features only partially duplicated in other societies. A comparative approach to stratification, although sociologically valuable, should thus be distinguished from studies of the operation of Indian caste and of its relation to its pan-Indian context.

ADRIAN C. MAYER

[*See also* ASIAN SOCIETY, *article on* SOUTH ASIA; HINDUISM; POLLUTION.]

BIBLIOGRAPHY

BAILEY, FREDERICK G. (1957) 1958 *Caste and the Economic Frontier: A Village in Highland Orissa.* Manchester Univ. Press.; New York: Humanities.

BAILEY, FREDERICK G. 1963 Closed Social Stratification in India. *European Journal of Sociology* 4:107–124.

BEIDELMAN, THOMAS O. 1959 *A Comparative Analysis of the Jajmani System.* Monographs of the Association for Asian Studies, No. 8. Locust Valley, N.Y.: Augustin.

BERREMAN, GERALD D. 1960 Caste in India and the United States. *American Journal of Sociology* 66:120–127.

BLUNT, EDWARD A. H. 1931 *The Caste System of Northern India: With Special Reference to the United Provinces of Agra and Oudh.* Oxford Univ. Press.

BOUGLÉ, CELESTIN (1908) 1935 *Essais sur le régime des castes.* 3d ed. Paris: Alcan.

BRASS, PAUL R. 1965 *Factional Politics in an Indian State: The Congress Party in Uttar Pradesh.* Berkeley: Univ. of California Press.

Caste: A Trend Report and Bibliography. 1959 *Current Sociology* 8, No. 3:135–183.

DUMONT, LOUIS 1957 *Une sous-caste de l'Inde du Sud: Organisation sociale et religion des Pramalai Kallar.* Paris: Mouton.

DUMONT, LOUIS (1960) 1961 Caste, Racism and "Stratification": Reflections of a Social Anthropologist. *Contributions to Indian Sociology* 5:20–43. → First published in French in Volume 29 of *Cahiers internationaux de sociologie.*

FREED, STANLEY A. 1963 An Objective Method for Determining the Collective Caste Hierarchy of an Indian Village. *American Anthropologist* New Series 65:879–891.

GHURYE, GOVIND S. (1932) 1961 *Caste, Class and Occupation.* 4th rev. ed. Bombay: Popular Book Depot; New York: Heinman. → First published as *Caste and Race in India.*

HARRISON, SELIG S. 1960 *India: The Most Dangerous Decades.* Princeton Univ. Press.

HOCART, ARTHUR M. (1938) 1950 *Caste: A Comparative Study.* London: Methuen. → First published in French as *Les castes.*

HUTTON, JOHN H. (1946) 1964 *Caste in India: Its Nature, Function and Origins.* 4th ed. Oxford Univ. Press.

KARVÉ, IRAWATI 1961 *Hindu Society: An Interpretation.* Poona (India): Deccan College.

LEACH, EDMUND R. (editor) 1960 *Aspects of Caste in South India, Ceylon and North-west Pakistan.* Cambridge Papers in Social Anthropology, No. 2. Cambridge Univ. Press.

MARRIOTT, McKIM 1959 Interactional and Attributional Theories of Caste Ranking. *Man in India* 39:92–107.

MARRIOTT, McKIM 1960 *Caste Ranking and Community Structure in Five Regions of India and Pakistan.* Deccan College Monograph Series, No. 23. Poona (India): Deccan College.

MAYER, ADRIAN C. 1956 Some Hierarchical Aspects of Caste. *Southwestern Journal of Anthropology* 12:117–144.

MAYER, ADRIAN C. 1960 *Caste and Kinship in Central India: A Village and Its Region.* London: Routledge; Berkeley and Los Angeles: Univ. of California Press.

NADEL, SIEGFRIED F. 1954 Caste and Government in Primitive Society. *Journal of the Anthropological Society of Bombay* New Series 8:9–22.

NESFIELD, JOHN C. 1885 *A Brief View of the Caste System of the North-western Provinces & Oudh.* Allahabad (India): Government Press.

ORENSTEIN, HENRY 1965 *Gaon: Conflict and Cohesion in an Indian Village.* Princeton Univ. Press.

RISLEY, HERBERT H. 1891 *The Tribes and Castes of Bengal: Ethnographic Glossary.* 2 vols. Calcutta: Bengal Secretariat Press.

RUDOLPH, LLOYD I., and RUDOLPH, SUSANNE H. 1960 The Political Role of India's Caste Associations. *Pacific Affairs* 33:5–22.

SENART, ÉMILE (1896) 1930 *Caste in India: The Facts and the System.* Translated by E. Denison Ross. London: Methuen. → First published in French.

SHERRING, MATTHEW A. 1872–1881 *Hindu Tribes and Castes.* 3 vols. Calcutta: Thacker; London: Trubner.

SRINIVAS, MYSORE N. 1962 *Caste in Modern India, and Other Essays.* New York: Asia Pub. House.

STEVENSON, H. N. C. 1954 Status Evaluation in the Hindu Caste System. *Journal of the Royal Anthropological Institute of Great Britain and Ireland* 84:45–65.

WEBER, MAX (1921) 1958 *The Religion of India: The Sociology of Hinduism and Buddhism.* Translated and edited by Hans H. Gerth and Don Martindale. Glencoe, Ill.: Free Press. → First published in German as *Hinduismus und Buddhismus* in Volume 2 of *Gesammelte Aufsätze zur Religionssoziologie.*

WISER, WILLIAM H. 1936 *The Hindu Jajmani System: A Socio-economic System Interrelating Members of a Hindu Village in Services.* Lucknow (India) Pub. House.

CATHOLICISM

See CHRISTIANITY *and the articles listed under* RELIGION.

CATTELL, JAMES McKEEN

James McKeen Cattell (1860–1944), although primarily a psychologist, probably did more than anyone else of his generation to foster the development in the United States of the sciences, especially the behavioral and biological sciences. He was one of the founders of the American Psychological Association and of several other scientific societies. He established the Science Press for the purpose of fostering the publication of both technical and popular scientific materials. He launched and published such scientific journals as the *Psychological Review*, *Science*, *Scientific Monthly*, *School and*

Society, and *The American Naturalist*. He prepared and published the first and subsequent editions of *American Men of Science* and *Leaders in Education*, and during his entire professional life he was the most vigorous promoter of the American Association for the Advancement of Science. He became a member of many scientific societies and was honored by most of them. He was one of the first psychologists to be elected a member of the National Academy of Sciences.

Cattell graduated in 1880 from Lafayette College, of which his father was president. As an undergraduate he majored in English, but in graduate study he shifted to philosophy and psychology, mainly under Lotze in Göttingen and Wundt in Leipzig. During three years of study with Wundt, Cattell invented some extraordinary and ingenious laboratory apparatus and improved many older devices. He undertook investigations that led to a quite new "objective approach" in psychological study. His purpose was to develop "psychology into a science rivaling in activity and fruitfulness the other great sciences" ([1888–1943] 1947, vol. 1, p. 9). He saw the values of the "introspective" methods of studying consciousness which then prevailed but declared that "psychology cannot attain the certainty and exactness of the physical sciences unless it rests on a foundation of experiment and measurement" (*ibid.*, vol. 1, p. 3). He became the champion of the idea that rigid, objective scientific work could be carried on in all the behavioral, biological, and social sciences. Thus he hastened the breakaway of psychology and other behavioral sciences from philosophy and promoted their comradeship with the physical and older biological sciences.

After his studies with Wundt and others on the Continent, Cattell moved to England for several years of work with Sir Francis Galton, whom he later rated as "the greatest man I have known" and who profoundly influenced his social and political as well as his psychological outlook. Galton's ideas about individual differences in human and animal equipment, about the possibilities of measuring all abilities and capacities, and about the use of the new statistical as well as experimental devices for determining the possible roles of heredity and environment fired Cattell with a new zeal for cultivating the behavioral sciences.

Cattell's vigor and enthusiasm were apparent in his early work at the University of Pennsylvania in 1888, when he developed a series of "mental tests" for college students. In 1891 he was called to Columbia and there first administered his "mental tests." Thus he introduced basic ideas that later, in the hands of his students, especially E. L. Thorndike, grew into the "testing movement" with its array of new statistical and psychophysical methods. Cattell foresaw the important contribution the sciences could make not only to education but to philosophy and public affairs in general, as exemplified by the work of William James, whom he admired enormously, and of John Dewey, whom he called "John the Baptist of Democracy." Cattell demonstrated the possibilities of fruitful cooperation among these disciplines during his years at Columbia, where he served at various times as head of the departments of anthropology, philosophy, and psychology.

After his retirement from Columbia in 1917, Cattell's Science Press published works in many fields of applied science. Among these publications was the journal *School and Society*, in which, as editor, he encouraged experimentation and innovations in education and social life. He tried out with his own children an intriguing form of tutorial and independent study that replaced attendance at school until the children were ready for college.

Cattell's purpose was to cultivate scientific methods for a wide range of subject matter. Although he favored "objective" methods, he recognized the value of other approaches, such as the introspective work of Edward B. Titchener and the observational methods of psychologist G. Stanley Hall and anthropologist Franz Boas. Cattell wrote no general text of psychology and developed no "system," but he held theoretical psychology in high regard and at Teachers College, Columbia, supported such theorists as Thorndike, Robert S. Woodworth, and Harry L. Hollingworth. He regarded theoretical work as indispensable and thought that the use of psychological methods in many practical fields was equally vital. He became a vigorous promoter of "applied psychology" as well as laboratory study. Thus, in his own institution he encouraged Thorndike and Hollingworth not only in their theoretical work but also in the former's application of psychology to education and the latter's to business and industry. Also at Teachers College Albert T. Poffenberger was applying psychology to advertising and selling; Leta S. Hollingworth was working in clinical and abnormal psychology; and others were involved in animal, social, and other areas of psychology. In 1921 Cattell established the Psychological Corporation to make the findings of applied psychology available to business and industry. It became a flourishing institution in the applied field.

Cattell's own shrewd contributions to psychophysical methods, such as the "order of merit" or "ranking" methods, led to the development of devices for measuring aesthetic and other intangible qualities. He demonstrated the fact that many words can be learned and later recognized more easily and accurately than most letters and that both are typically perceived on the basis of reduced or fragmentary cues. He showed that during reading, the eyes move along the line in a series of grasshopperlike jumps and that the words are perceived only when the eyes are at a standstill. He demonstrated that words and phrases can be read in a small fraction of a second. These and other of his earliest studies at Leipzig on reaction time, and his experimental analyses of his subjects' symbolic material, led to the revolution of many educational practices, such as methods of teaching reading and spelling [*see* READING DISABILITIES; VISION, *article on* EYE MOVEMENTS].

Cattell's constant encouragement of his students to devise objective procedures, rather than to use conventional anecdotal and observational methods, for studying the behavior of animals and infants led to conspicuously new movements in animal and child psychology. These ventures laid a foundation for several forms, or schools, of behaviorism, which appeared later. Thus, although Cattell did not try to develop a system of his own, his works produced important data for theoretical and systematic formulations of psychology. "Psychology is," he frequently reminded his students, "what good psychologists do." This conviction revealed his belief that psychologists should venture in many directions and pursue various types of study that could not be anticipated even by him.

Cattell invaded several practical areas with ideas and procedures developed in psychology. He was sarcastically critical of typical university teaching methods. Spoon-feeding by lectures and elaborate demonstrations he deplored. He did not "teach" in the ordinary sense. He left his students to their own resources and conducted most of his classes in the manner of the severe PH.D. oral. The student was expected to come up with new ideas and defend them against all present, including Cattell, who often appeared to be merciless but was in fact trying to challenge his students to think courageously and independently. He scorched many of his students but inspired all of them.

Cattell found college administration a field that gave full play to his penetrating insight and to what some persons, especially college presidents, might call his diabolic wit. In his address "Academic Slavery," he remarked: "The disease which is endemic in the university is subordination of the teacher to the academic machine, a kind of hook-worm disease which leaves the entire institution anaemic" (*ibid.*, vol. 2, p. 350). Irascible college presidents were advised not to listen to or read any of Cattell's comments on this topic. The head of his own university disregarded this advice and, after several years of poorly concealed combustion, took action to remove Cattell from his university post. But, as Cattell later noted, this appeared to have been an illegal action, for the university, on the advice of frightened trustees, paid heavy damages.

Cattell launched a typical attack on the U.S. political leaders who led the nation into World War I. Although he was himself "ever a fighter," he was a pacifist as far as international conflict was concerned. His stinging barbs were brilliant and devastating but not the kind to win popular political approval. They got him into much trouble, but in the course of time the university public, at least, arose to defend and applaud him.

Cattell died in 1944, in his 84th year. Shortly thereafter his colleagues and students published two commemorative volumes, which provide a most convenient and complete report of his life and work. Both carried the general title *James McKeen Cattell, Man of Science*, and were published in 1947 by his own Science Press, which one of his sons had taken over. Volume 1 contains his own reports of his researches, and Volume 2 his addresses and formal papers. Both contain expert appraisals of his characteristics and accomplishments. I have found no better brief characterization than the last paragraph of "An Appreciation" of Cattell by one of his students, Frederick Lyman Wells: "Agreeable associations await him on the *Houseboat*. Francis Galton and William Morton Wheeler will have arranged his introduction. With Plato, Freud and St. Paul he will have less in common; but Aristotle, Galileo, Francis Bacon and Voltaire—especially Voltaire—should find him highly congenial" (*ibid.*, vol. 2, p. 6).

ARTHUR I. GATES

[*For the historical context of Cattell's work, see the biographies of* GALTON; LOTZE; WUNDT. *For discussion of the subsequent development of his ideas, see* ACHIEVEMENT TESTING; APTITUDE TESTING; INTELLIGENCE AND INTELLIGENCE TESTING; PERSONALITY MEASUREMENT; *and the biographies of* THORNDIKE; WOODWORTH.]

BIBLIOGRAPHY

CATTELL, JAMES M. (1888–1943) 1947 *James McKeen Cattell; 1860–1944: Man of Science.* 2 vols. Edited by A. T. Poffenberger. Lancaster, Pa.: Science Press. → Volume 1: *Psychological Research.* Volume 2: *Addresses and Formal Papers.*

CAUDILLISMO

The word *caudillo* signifies "leader," or, in a more corrupted political sense, "boss." In Spain it has retained a less pejorative connotation than in Latin America, where it is invariably employed for purposes of denigration. In its broadest political sense, caudillismo in Latin America has popularly come to mean any highly personalistic and quasi-military regime whose party mechanisms, administrative procedures, and legislative functions are subject to the intimate and immediate control of a charismatic leader and his cadre of mediating officials. Outside Latin America, this broad usage of the term has slowly made caudillismo increasingly synonymous with any political system controlled by military personnel. The confusion between Spanish and Latin American usage has also taken the concept away from its historical roots in the early days of Latin American independence from Spain. Thus the designation of Generalissimo Francisco Franco of Spain as *el Caudillo* has been taken to be correlative with *der Führer* and *il Duce,* and in consequence not necessarily descriptive of the substantive differences between the political systems of Falangist Spain, Nazi Germany, and Fascist Italy.

This broadening of the sense of the term inhibits its more specific use in describing a particular type of authoritarianism—the kind found in varying degree and at different times throughout nineteenth-century Latin America. Although the Latin American experience is quite relevant to that of certain "new" nations of this century, care must be taken not to confuse the military component in caudillismo with that of all contemporary praetorian or other kinds of military governments in underdeveloped areas. Historically, the caudillo was a self-proclaimed leader, usually a military officer (although some were civilians) who was supported by an irregular or otherwise nonprofessional army. Although he generally found the source of his power in rural areas—recruiting his troops from among the peasantry and abetted in his undertakings by large landowners—the consolidation of his power demanded that he extend his sway over the national capital. In this curiously backward fashion, then, provincial caudillos served an integrating political function of a quasi-national nature.

The generalization, which may be historically drawn in the definition of caudillismo as a system of government, is that it is a personalistic, quasi-military government of provincial origin and economic interest serving a function of loose national integration in periods of decay or withdrawal of effective central authority. Caudillismo is not socially revolutionary, even though the caudillos themselves have not always been devoid of ideological commitment.

Origins and growth

The roots of caudillismo are found in the last years of the Spanish colonial period in Latin America. The personal and sometimes separatist ambitions of the more unruly conquistadors were handled most effectively by a crown legitimated by the strongly hierarchical values of the Iberian normative system and strengthened by the experience gathered from seven centuries of warfare with the Moors. Until the late eighteenth century, military units in Latin America were under the almost exclusive command of Spaniards, and a sharp status line was drawn between *criollos*, or "creoles," the children of Spaniards born in the New World, and *peninsulares*, or native-born Spaniards. In the 1760s, Charles III of Spain instituted a series of imperial reforms that included the establishment of a colonial militia and the regularized commissioning of creoles as military officers of the Spanish crown. The Spanish government was motivated not only by reasons of economy but also by its growing relative weakness among European powers and its increasing inability to prevent the inroads of pirates and other commercial adventurers on the Spanish economic monopolies in their colonies.

These creole officers were recruited from the colonial upper class and were granted the full privileges of Spanish officers, including the advantages of the *fuero militar*, or "military law." This legal privilege exempted them from trial by civil courts and entitled them to other special privileges giving them status midway between that of their colonial origins and that of the metropolitan upper groups. Such men as Simón Bolívar and José de San Martín, trained in the Spanish army, became the leaders of the independence movements of 1810–1823. But the number of such officers was insufficient for the long-drawn-out military contest of the wars of independence, necessitating the opening of officer ranks to many persons of lower social station. This popularization of the officer corps created the channel through which aspirants to higher social position gained access to power, although their position was in turn contested by waves of others equally ambitious and power-hungry.

By 1823, the disappearance of Spanish rule was complete everywhere in Latin America except Cuba. The first attempts to establish successor governments had begun as early as 1810 in many urban centers, where intellectual leaders and other members of the local aristocracies divided on ideological grounds, the clericalist Conservatives opposing the Liberals, who were the "radicals" of the period. The threat that the urban commercial and intellectual groups would consolidate national control evoked the coalition of interest between the caudillos and the landowning, provincial Conservatives, which gave form to the politics of most Latin American countries until the 1860s. Chile was an exception in that Diego Portales, a civilian Conservative caudillo, ruthlessly suppressed opposition elements in the military, thus giving his country a completely civilian integrative rule which has come to be known as the "Autocratic Republic." Brazil, too, followed a different path, in effect ingesting a Portuguese monarchy until 1889. Although the establishment of a republic in that year was followed by a very short period of caudillismo, civilian constitutionalism was reestablished by 1895. Every other nineteenth-century Latin American country followed a path from independence to short-lived Liberal victory to caudillismo.

Because some of the caudillos reigned for long periods and in some cases developed or represented specific schools of thought, they have left a deep imprint on their national histories and ideologies. Juan Manuel de Rosas ruled in Argentina from 1829 to 1852, for example, and remains a hero figure to authoritarian Conservatives. Rafael Carrera, an illiterate person of mixed Indian and white origin, held office in Guatemala from 1839 to 1865, and died in office. He must be counted among the more influential of the caudillos if for no reason other than his long tenure, but he has no appeal to any present Guatemalian intellectual groups, nor is he viewed as a national hero. Some of the other well-known caudillos are Jean Pierre Boyer (1818–1843) of Haiti, Ramón Castilla (1845–1851 and 1855–1862) of Peru, Juan José Flores (1831–1835 and 1839–1845) of Ecuador, Antonio López de Santa Anna (on and off the political scene from 1821 to 1855) of Mexico, and Francisco Solano López (1862–1870, inheriting power from his father) of Paraguay.

There were literally scores of other caudillos, however. Lieuwen (1960, p. 21), for example, points out that there were 115 successful revolutions in the Latin American republics between their independence and World War I; obviously there were many more unsuccessful rebellions. In the decade from 1849 to 1859 Ecuador had six presidents, four of whom were military men on active duty when they took office. Johnson says of the caudillos:

Their social and economic conformity and political orthodoxy in effect made them the tools of those landed elements dedicated to the survival of old ideas and old formulas. Because power was in this period based largely on personal magnetism, few were able to consolidate their control sufficiently to hand it on to a chosen successor. Their dictatorships tended to revert to civilian regimes controlled by the landed oligarchs. (Johnson 1964, p. 56)

By the 1860s, the instability inherent in caudillismo became untenable. Latin America's cities were growing, the educational systems were slowly expanding, new technology and ideas were coming in from Europe, and foreign capital was beginning to develop a new and sustained interest in Latin America. The Liberals then reasserted themselves and, following varying patterns, succeeded in gaining unequivocal control in all the Spanish American countries except Colombia by the end of the nineteenth century. The professionalization of the military, initiated in Chile in 1885 and extended virtually everywhere by 1910, changed Latin American armies into at least a semblance of modern, impersonal fighting forces. Traditional caudillismo was dead.

Contemporary meanings and research

In common usage, caudillismo as a concept has changed in Latin America. As was stated above, the name caudillo now is applied to any charismatic leader. Juan Perón, president of Argentina from 1946 to 1955, earned this sobriquet, as did General Alfredo Stroessner of Paraguay. Even though the term is also given to local political bosses, the Indian-derived *cacique* ("chief") is more commonly used to refer to ward leaders or relatively unimportant rural county or *municipio* politicians.

In the academic literature, however, caudillismo has retained its historical meaning. This consistency is due primarily to the fact that the Latin American experience is rarely used as prototypical for other underdeveloped regions. As a result, the concept has suffered no blurring from being generalized to other cultural settings. One recent study, in attempting to explain the inappropriateness of the Latin American case for comparative military studies, states:

Latin American countries . . . have many characteristics comparable to the new nations. Even more pointedly, it appears at first glance that Latin American nations are also confronted with similar crises of civil–military relations. But there are fundamental differences in the natural history of militarism in South

America. The forms of military intervention represent more than a century of struggle and accommodation which has produced political institutions different from those found in the new nations.   (Janowitz 1964, pp. v–vi)

It is doubtful that the turmoil in the Belgian Congo attendant on the withdrawal of the colonial government is in an entirely different family of events from the classical caudillismo of Latin America. Even from the histories of such complex and relatively developed countries as Argentina, significant parallels with certain new nations appear. It may be argued, for instance, that the first "Nasserist" government was in truth the Perón administration. Certainly both movements were led by nationalistic army officers using the military as a means of social ascent, both pursued populist and nationalistic ideological ends, and the political constituencies of both regimes were similar. The recent outpouring of research on Latin America may serve to remedy this disuse of the Latin American experience as supportive of the derivation of general comparative social theory.

Latin American historians, notoriously polemical in their approach to political affairs, have for long divided over the issue of whether the great caudillos were beneficial or harmful. Those writers who support caudillismo emphasize the nation-building functions some may have performed and tend to draw the conclusion that contemporary strongmen are desirable. Marcos Pérez Jiménez, military dictator of Venezuela, overthrown in 1958 after a six-year incumbency, expressed the standard justification for military tutelary rule that is also the contemporary justification for caudillismo: "I made every effort to give the Venezuelans the kind of government adapted to them. . . . We are still in our infant years and we still need halters. . . . There must be a leader who shows the way without being perturbed by the necessity of winning demagogic popularity" (cited in Johnson 1962, pp. 91–92). The counterarguments are advanced by *civilistas* opposed on all counts to military rule and concerned with the encouragement of democratic procedure.

An analogous schism separates non-Latin American writers. The post-World War II interest in military–civil relations has enriched the literature concerning caudillismo and subsequent military events in Latin America as elsewhere in the world. Although none of these authors looks with favor upon the caudillos as such, they are in implicit disagreement concerning the precise definition of the term and the meaning of caudillismo for contemporary events. One group (exemplified by Lieuwen 1960) equates the evils of classical caudillismo with the continued political interventionism of Latin American military leaders, a factor causing increasing perturbation in the Latin polities. The opposing view (most clearly expressed by Johnson 1962; 1964) argues that the caudillos were essentially irregulars spawned in the early national period of the Latin American republics, and that in this restricted sense caudillismo no longer exists. This kind of military phenomenon, they claim, is not to be confused with the later activities of professionalized military forces, whose political roles earn mixed critical judgments. The practical effect of these two views, of course, is that the "Lieuwen school" looks with much less favor on the military as a modernizing force than does the "Johnson school."

The political success or failure of given caudillos, with reference to the historical development of their countries, can be measured only in terms of whether they succeeded in imposing some degree of national integration, as in the case of Rosas in Argentina, or merely in compounding the confusion of the post-Independence times of trouble, as in the case of Santa Anna, the Mexican adventurer. Other criteria, of secondary importance in assessing the roles of individual caudillos, may be based on their civilian or quasi-military status, their attachment to Liberal or Conservative party doctrine, and their ability to survive through appreciable periods of time. Any extension of the caudillo type to the political experiences of other countries should be done with due care not to permit the concept to grow too broad.

Caudillismo, in its historical form, is made possible only by a disappearance or a breakdown of central authority, which permits private armies and other semiregular rural forces to attempt seizure of the nationwide political organization in order to maintain the economic and social power of provincial groups. The price paid by the latter for this protection is a sharing of political power and a recognition of the social ambitions of the caudillo. This type of political regime will become increasingly rare as more and more new nations enter periods of coherent national growth involving the presence of strong central governments, whether they be of a military stripe or not. Caudillismo, as a political product of social dissolution, can then reappear only in the event of severe institutional dysfunction and political retrogression.

K. H. SILVERT

[*See also* DICTATORSHIP; FASCISM; LATIN AMERICAN POLITICAL THOUGHT; MILITARISM.]

BIBLIOGRAPHY

BLANKSTEN, GEORGE I. (1951) 1964 *Ecuador: Constitutions and Caudillos.* University of California Publications in Political Science, Vol. 3, No. 1. Berkeley: Univ. of California Press.

BUSHNELL, DAVID 1954 *The Santander Regime in Gran Colombia.* University of Delaware Monograph Series, No. 5. Newark: Univ. of Delaware Press.

CHAPMAN, CHARLES E. 1932 The Age of the Caudillos: A Chapter in Hispanic American History. *Hispanic American Historical Review* 12:281–300.

GERMANI, GINO; and SILVERT, K. H. 1961 Politics, Social Structure and Military Intervention in Latin America. *Archives européennes de sociologie* 2:62–81.

HUMPHREYS, ROBIN A. 1957 Latin America, the Caudillo Tradition. Pages 149–166 in Michael Howard (editor), *Soldiers and Governments: Nine Studies in Civil–Military Relations.* London: Eyre & Spottiswoode.

JANOWITZ, MORRIS 1964 *The Military in the Political Development of New Nations: An Essay in Comparative Analysis.* Univ. of Chicago Press.

JOHNSON, JOHN J. (editor) 1962 *The Role of the Military in Underdeveloped Countries.* Princeton Univ. Press. → Papers of a conference sponsored by the RAND Corporation at Santa Monica, California, in August 1959.

JOHNSON, JOHN J. 1964 *The Military and Society in Latin America.* Stanford (Calif.) Univ. Press.

LIEUWEN, EDWIN (1960) 1961 *Arms and Politics in Latin America.* Rev. ed. Published for the Council on Foreign Relations. New York: Praeger.

McALISTER, LYLE N. 1957 *The "fuero militar" in New Spain, 1764–1800.* Gainesville: Univ. of Florida Press.

MASUR, GERHARD 1948 *Simón Bolívar.* School of Inter-American Affairs, Inter-Americana Studies, No. 4. Albuquerque: Univ. of New Mexico Press.

CAUSATION

A cause is something that occasions or effects a result (the usual lexical definition) or a uniform antecedent of a phenomenon (J. S. Mill's definition). When a question is asked in the form "Why . . .?" it can usually be answered appropriately by a statement in the form "Because . . . ." Thus, to state the causes of a phenomenon is at least one way to explain the phenomenon; and a careful explication of the concept of causation in science must rest on a prior analysis of the notions of scientific explanation and scientific law.

Explanations in terms of causation are sought both for particular events and for classes of events or phenomena. Thus, a statement of the causes of World War II might include references to German economic difficulties during the 1930s or to the failure of the League of Nations to halt the Ethiopian conquest. On the other hand, a statement of the causes of war might include references to the outward displacement of aggression arising from internal frustrations, the absence of legitimized institutions for legal settlements of disputes between nations, and so on.

Causal explanations generally involve a combination of particular and general statements. In classical price theory, for example, a drop in the price of a commodity can be caused by an increase in its supply and/or a decrease in demand. If an explanation is desired for a drop in the price of wheat in a particular economy in a given year, it may be sought in the unusually large wheat crop of that year. (The large wheat crop may be explained, in turn, by a combination of general laws asserting that the size of the wheat crop is a function of acreage, rainfall, fertilization, and specific facts relevant to these laws—the actual acreage planted, rainfall, and amount of fertilizer applied that year.)

A general paradigm can be given for this kind of causal explanation. Let a be a particular situation (for example, the wheat market in 1965); let $A(x)$ be a statement about situation x (for example, the supply in market x increases); and let $B(x)$ be another such statement about x (for example, the price in market x declines). Suppose there is an accepted scientific law of the form

$$(x)(A(x) \rightarrow B(x))$$

(for example, in any market, if the supply of the commodity increases, the price will decline). Upon substitution of a for x, this becomes $(A(a) \rightarrow B(a))$; if the supply of the commodity in market a increases, its price will decline (for example, if the supply of wheat increased in 1965, its price declined). Then $A(a)$ and $(x)(A(x) \rightarrow B(x))$ provide, conjointly, a causal explanation for $B(a)$. That is to say, $A(a)$ occasions or effects $B(a)$, while $A(x)$ is the uniform antecedent of $B(x)$. Thus, the paradigm incorporates both the lexical and Mill's definitions of cause.

Explication of causation along these lines gives rise to three sets of problems that have been discussed extensively by philosophers of science. The first of these may be called the "problem of Hume" because all treatments of it in modern times—both those that agree with Hume and those that oppose him—take Hume's analysis as their starting point (see Hume 1777). It is the logical and epistemological problem of the nature of the connection between the "if" and the "then" in a scientific law. Is it a "necessary" connection, or a connection in fact, and how is the existence of the connection verified?

The second problem may be called the problem of causal ordering or causal asymmetry. If $A(a)$

is the cause of $B(a)$, we do not ordinarily think that $B(a)$, or its absence, can cause $A(a)$ or its absence. But in the standard predicate calculus of formal logic, $(x)(A(x) \rightarrow B(x))$ implies $(x)(\sim B(x) \rightarrow \sim A(x))$, where "$\sim$" stands for "not." ("If much rainfall, other things equal, then a large wheat crop" implies "If a small wheat crop, other things equal, then not much rainfall.") While we accept the inverse inference, we do not regard it as causal. (The size of the wheat crop does not retrospectively affect the amount of rain; *knowledge* of the size of the wheat crop may, however, affect our *inference* of how much rain there had been.) Thus two statements corresponding to the same truth-function (that is, either both are true or both are false) need not express the same causal ordering. The asymmetry between $A(x)$ and $B(x)$ cannot, therefore, rest solely on observation of the situations in which either or both of these predicates hold. How can the causal relation be defined to preserve the asymmetry between cause and effect?

The third set of problems surrounding causation are the psychological problems. Michotte has explored the circumstances under which one event will in fact be perceived as causing another. Piaget and his associates have investigated the meanings that "cause," "why," "because," and other terms of explanation have for children at various ages. In succeeding sections we shall examine these three sets of problems: the problem of Hume, the problem of causal ordering, and the psychological problems of causal perception and inference.

The problem of Hume

David Hume pointed out that even though empirical observation could establish that events of type B had in each case followed events of type A, observation could never establish that the connection between A and B was necessary or that it would continue to hold for new observations. Thus, general statements like "If A, then B" can serve as convenient summaries of numbers of particular facts but cannot guarantee their own validity beyond the limits of the particular facts they summarize.

Hume did not deny, of course, that people commonly make general inductions of the form "If A, then B" from particular facts; nor that they use these generalizations to predict new events; nor that such predictions are often confirmed. He did deny that the inductive step from particulars to generalization could be provided with a deductive justification, or that it could establish a "necessary" connection between antecedent and consequent, that is, a connection that could not fail in subsequent observations. Modern philosophers of science in the empiricist tradition hold positions very close to Hume's. Extensive discussions and references to the literature can be found in Braithwaite (1953, chapter 10), Popper ([1934] 1959, chapter 3), and Nagel (1961, pp. 52–56).

In everyday usage, however, a distinction is often made between generalizations that denote "lawful" regularities and those that denote "accidental" regularities. "If there is a large wheat crop, the price of wheat will fall" states a lawful regularity. "If X is a man, then X's skin color is not bright greenish blue" states an accidental regularity. But since our basis for accepting both generalizations is the same—we have observed confirming instances and no exceptions—the distinction between laws, on the one hand, and generalizations that are only factually or accidentally true, on the other, must be sought not in the empirical facts these generalizations denote but in their relations to other generalizations, that is, in the structure of scientific theories.

Within some given body of scientific theory, a general statement may be called a *law* if it can be deduced from other statements in that theory. The connection between the quantity of a commodity offered on a market and the price is lawful, relative to general economic theory, because it can be deduced from other general statements in economic theory: that price reaches equilibrium at the level where quantity offered equals quantity demanded; that the quantity demanded is smaller (usually) at the higher price. These latter statements may be derived, in turn, from still others: statements about the characteristics of buyers' utility functions, postulates that buyers act so as to maximize utility, and so on.

Although lawfulness does not exempt a generalization from the need for empirical verification, a scientific law's logical connections with others may subject it to indirect disconfirmation; and its direct disconfirmation may affect the validity of other generalizations in the system. A scientific theory may be viewed as a system of simultaneous relations from which the values of particular observations can be deduced. When a reliable observation conflicts with the prediction, some change must be made in the theory; but there is no simple or general way to determine where in the system the change must be made.

Nothing has been said here about the issue of determinism versus indeterminism, which is often discussed in relation to the problem of Hume (see Braithwaite 1953, chapter 10; Popper [1934] 1959, chapter 3; Nagel 1961, chapter 10). The concept of causal ordering is entirely compatible with either deterministic or probabilistic scientific theories. In a probabilistic theory, events are only incompletely determined by their causes, and formalization of such theories shows that the causal relations implicit in them hold between probability distributions of events rather than between the individual events. Thus, in a system described by a so-called Markov process, the probability distribution of the system among its possible states at time t is causally (and not probabilistically) determined by the probability distribution at time $t - 1$. [See MARKOV CHAINS.] In this situation, disconfirming a theory requires not just a simple disconfirming observation but rather a sufficiently large set of observations to show that a predicted distribution does not hold.

Causal ordering

It was pointed out above that we cannot replace "A causes B" with the simple truth-functional $(x)(A(x) \rightarrow B(x))$ without creating difficulties of interpretation. For $(x)(A(x) \rightarrow B(x))$ implies $(x)(\sim B(x) \rightarrow \sim A(x))$, while we do not ordinarily infer "*not-B* causes *not-A*" from "A causes B." On the contrary, if A causes B, it will usually also be the case that *not-A* causes *not-B*. Thus, if a large wheat crop causes a low price, we will expect a small wheat crop to cause a high price. The appropriate asymmetrical statement is that "the size of the wheat crop is a cause of the price of wheat," and the example shows that the asymmetry here is different from that of "if–then" statements. Attempts (Burks 1951) to base a definition of the causal relation on the logical relation of implication have been unsuccessful for this reason.

The concept of scientific law, introduced in the last section, provides an alternative approach to explicating causal ordering. This approach makes the causal connection between two variables depend on the context provided by a scientific theory —a whole set of laws containing these variables (Simon [1947–1956] 1957, chapters 1, 3). This approach views the causal ordering as holding between *variables* rather than between particular *values* of those variables. As noted in the last paragraph, the variable "size of the wheat crop" (x) is to be taken as the cause for "price of wheat" (p), a large crop causing a low price and a small crop causing a high price ($p = f(x)$, with $dp/dx < 0$).

Linear structures. For concreteness, consider the important special situation where a scientific theory takes the form of a set of n simultaneous linear algebraic equations in n variables. Then, apart from certain exceptional cases, these equations can be solved for the unique values of the variables. (In the general case the system is called a *linear structure*.) In solving the equations, algebraic manipulations are performed that do not change the solutions. Equations are combined until one equation is derived that contains only a single variable. This equation is then solved for that variable, the value is inserted in the remaining equations, and the process is repeated until the values of all variables have been found. In general, there is no single, set order in which the variables must be evaluated. Hence, from an algebraic viewpoint, there is no distinction between "independent" and "dependent" variables in the system. The variables are all interdependent, and the linear structure expresses that interdependence.

However, it may be found in particular systems of this kind that certain subsets of equations containing corresponding subsets of variables can be solved independently of the remaining equations. Such subsets are called *self-contained subsets*. In the extreme case, a particular equation may contain only one variable, which can then be evaluated as the dependent variable of that equation. Substituting its value as an independent variable in another equation, we may find that only one dependent variable remains, which can now be evaluated.

A causal ordering among variables of a linear structure that has one or more self-contained subsets can now be defined as follows: Consider the minimal self-contained subsets (those that do not themselves contain smaller self-contained subsets) of the system. With each such subset, associate the variables that can be evaluated from that subset alone. These are the *endogenous* or dependent variables of that subset and are exogenous to the rest of the system. Call them *variables of order zero*. Next, substitute the values of these variables in the remaining equations of the system, and repeat the whole process for these remaining equations, obtaining the variables of order one, two, and so on, and the corresponding subsets of equations in which they are the dependent variables. Now if a variable of some order occurs with nonzero coefficient in an equation of the linear structure belonging to a subset of higher order, the former variable has a *direct causal connection* to the endogenous variables of the latter subset.

An example. The wheat price example will help make the above notions more concrete. Suppose a theory in the following form: (1) The amount of rain in a given year is taken as exogenous to the remainder of the system; that is, it is set equal to a constant. (2) The wheat crop is assumed to increase linearly with the amount of rain (within some range of values). (3) The price of wheat is assumed to move inversely, but linearly, with the size of the crop. The system thus contains three equations in three variables. The first equation, determining the amount of rain, is the only self-contained subset. Hence, amount of rain is a variable of order zero. Given its value, the second equation can be solved for the size of the wheat crop, a variable of order one. Finally, the third equation can be solved for the price of wheat, a variable of order two. Thus, there is a direct causal connection from the amount of rain to the size of the crop and from the size of the crop to the price.

Operational meaning—mechanisms. The causal ordering would be altered, of course, if before solving the equations the system is modified by taking linear combinations of them. This process is algebraically admissible, for it does not change the solutions, and, indeed, is employed as an essential means for solving simultaneous equations. If the causal ordering is not invariant under such transformations, can it be said to have operational meaning?

Operational meaning is assigned to the equations of the initial, untransformed system by associating with each equation a *mechanism* (meaning an identifiable locus of intervention or alteration in the system). "Intervention" may be human (for example, experimentation) or natural (for example, change in initial conditions). Just as the operational identity of individual variables in a system depends on means for measuring each independently of the others, so the operational identity of mechanisms depends on means for intervention in each independently of the others. Thus, in the wheat price model, the nature of the mechanism determining rainfall is unspecified, but the mechanism can be "modified" by taking a sample of years with different amounts of rain. Coefficients in the mechanism relating rainfall to the size of the wheat crop can be modified by irrigation or by growing drought-resistant strains of wheat. The mechanism relating the size of the crop to price can be modified by changing buyers' incomes.

When particular mechanisms can be identified and causal ordering inferred, this knowledge permits predictions to be made of the effects on the variables of a system of specific modifications of the mechanisms—whether these be produced by policy intervention, experimental manipulation, or the impact of exogenous variables. Thus, although there is algebraic equivalence between a system in which each equation corresponds to a separate mechanism and systems obtained by taking linear combinations of the original equations, the derived systems are not operationally equivalent to the original one from the standpoint of control, experiment, or prediction. In the statistical literature, the equations that represent mechanisms and causal ordering are called *structural equations;* certain equivalent equations derived for purposes of statistical estimation are called *reduced-form equations.*

Temporal sequence. The method described here for defining causal ordering accounts for the asymmetry of cause and effect but does not base the asymmetry on temporal precedence. It imposes no requirement that the cause precede the effect. We are free to limit our scientific theories to those in which all causes *do* precede their effects, but the definition of causal ordering does not require us to do so. Thus, in experimental situations, average values of the independent variables over the period of the experiment may be interpreted as the causal determinants of the values of the dependent variables over the same period.

Many scientific theories do, however, involve temporal sequence. In dynamic theories, the state of the system at one point in time is (causally) determined by the state of the system at an earlier point in time. Generally, a set of initial conditions is given, specifying the state of the system at a point in time taken as origin. The initial conditions, together wth the differential or difference equations of the system (the general laws), induce a causal ordering like that defined above.

Interdependence. If almost all the variables in a dynamic system are directly interdependent, so that the value of each variable at a given time depends significantly on the values of almost all other variables at a slightly earlier time, the causal ordering provides little information and has little usefulness. When the interrelations are sparse, however, so that relatively few variables are directly dependent on each other, a description of the causal ordering provides important information about the structure of the system and about the qualitative characteristics of its dynamic behavior (for example, the presence or absence of closed feedback loops). For this reason, the language of causation is used more commonly in relation to highly organized and sparsely connected structures —man-made mechanisms and organisms with their systems of organs—than in relation to some of the common systems described by the partial differential equations of chemistry and physics, where the interactions are multitudinous and relatively uniform.

Psychology of causal inference

The considerations of the preceding sections are purely logical and say nothing of the circumstances under which persons will infer causal connections between phenomena. Extensive studies of the psychology of causal inference have been made by Michotte and Piaget.

Michotte (1946) has shown that a perception of causal connection can be induced, for example, by two spots of light, the first of which moves toward the second and stops on reaching it, while the second then continues the motion in the same direction. Using numerous variants of this scheme, he has explored the circumstances under which subjects will or will not interpret the events causally. His evidence tends to show that the process by which the subject arrives at a causal interpretation is "direct," subconscious, and perceptual—that causal attribution is not a conscious act of inference or induction from a sequence of events perceived independently. While the general distinction intended by Michotte is clear, its detailed interpretation must depend on a more precise understanding of the neural mechanisms of visual perception. In particular, little is known as yet about the respective roles of peripheral and central mechanisms or of innate and learned processes in the perception of causality.

Piaget (1923; 1927) has brought together a sizable body of data on children's uses of causal language. A principal generalization from these data is that the earliest uses of "Why?" are directed toward motivation of actions and justification of rules; demands for naturalistic causal explanations appear only as the child's egocentrism begins to wane.

Spurious correlation

Previous sections have dealt with the principal problems surrounding the concept of causation. The remaining sections treat some significant applications of causal language to the social sciences.

It has often been pointed out that a statistical correlation between two variables is not sufficient grounds for asserting a causal relation between them. A correlation is called *spurious* if it holds between two variables that are not causally related. The definition of causal ordering provides a means of distinguishing genuine from spurious correlation [*see* FALLACIES, STATISTICAL; MULTIVARIATE ANALYSIS, *articles on* CORRELATION].

Since the causal orderings among variables can be determined only within the context of a scientific theory—a complete structure—it is only within such a context that spurious correlation can be distinguished from genuine correlation. Thus, to interpret the correlation between variables x and y in causal terms, either there must be added to the system the other variables that are most closely connected with x and y, or sufficient assumptions of independence of x and/or y from other variables must be introduced to produce a self-contained system. When this has been done, the simple correlation between x and y can be replaced with their partial correlation (other variables being held constant) in the larger self-contained system. The partial correlation provides a basis for estimating the coefficients of the self-contained system and hence can be given a causal interpretation in the manner outlined earlier. It can be shown (Simon [1947–1956] 1957, chapter 2) that all causal inference from correlation coefficients involves, explicitly or implicitly, this procedure.

Suppose, for example, that per capita candy consumption is found to be (negatively) correlated with marital status. Can it be concluded that marriage causes people to stop eating candy or that candy eating inhibits marriage? The question can be answered only in the context of a more complete theory of behavior (Zeisel [1947] 1957, p. 198). If age is introduced as a third variable, it is found to have a high negative correlation with candy consumption but a high positive correlation with marital status. When age is held constant, the partial correlation of candy consumption with marital status is almost zero. If age is taken as the exogenous variable, these facts permit the inference that age causally influences both candy consumption and marital status but that there is no causal connection between the latter two variables—their correlation was spurious.

Practical techniques for interpreting correlations and distinguishing spurious from genuine relations have been discussed by Blalock (1964), Hyman (1955, chapters 6, 7), Kendall and Lazarsfeld (1950, pp. 135–167), Simon ([1947–1956] 1957, chapter 2), and Zeisel ([1947] 1957, chapter 9).

Purpose and motivation

Since the social sciences are much concerned with purposeful and goal-oriented behavior, it is important to ascertain how causal concepts are to be applied to systems exhibiting such behavior. Purposeful behavior is oriented toward achieving some desired future state of affairs. It is not the future state of affairs, of course, that produced the behavior but the intention or motive to realize this state of affairs. An intention, if it is to be causally efficacious for behavior, must reside in the central nervous system of the actor prior to or at the time of action. Hence, present intention, and not the future goal, provides the causal explanation for the behavior. The influence of expectations and predictions on behavior can be handled in the same way: the expectations are *about* the future but exist at present in the mind (and brain) of the actor (Rosenblueth et al. 1943).

The simplest teleological system that illustrates these points is a house thermostat. The desired state of affairs is a specified air temperature. The thermostat setting is the thermostat's (present) representation of that goal—its intention. Measurements of the difference between actual temperature and setting are the causal agents that produce corrective action. Thus, the causal chain runs from the setting and the temperature-measuring device, to the action of a heat source, to the temperature of the room.

The term *function* (in its sociological, not mathematical, sense) can be analyzed similarly. To say that the family has the function of nurturing children is to say (*a*) that it is causally efficacious to that end; (*b*) that it operates in a goal-oriented fashion toward that end; and, possibly, (*c*) that it contributes causally to the survival of the society.

As Piaget's studies show, teleological explanation —explanation in terms of the motives for and justifications of action—is probably the earliest kind of causal analysis observable in children. Similarly, children tend to interpret causation anthropomorphically—to treat the cause as an active, living agent rather than simply a set of antecedent circumstances. Thus teleological explanation, far from being distinct from causal explanation in science, is probably the prototype for all causal analysis.

Influence and power relations. An influence or power mechanism, in the terms of the present discussion, is simply a particular kind of causal mechanism—the cause and effect both being forms of human behavior. The asymmetry of the causal relation is reflected in the asymmetry of these mechanisms, considered singly. This does not mean that there cannot be reciprocal relations and feedback loops but simply that the influence of A on B can be analyzed (conceptually and sometimes empirically) independently of the influence of B on A (Simon [1947–1956] 1957, chapter 4).

In sum, causal language is useful language for talking about a scientific theory, especially when the variables the theory handles are interconnected, but sparsely so, and especially when there is interest in intervention (for reasons of policy or experi-

ment) in particular mechanisms of the system. In a formalized theory, a formal analysis can be made of the causal relations asserted by the theory. When causal language is used in this way—and most everyday use fits this description—it carries no particular philosophical implications for the problem of Hume or the issue of determinism. Causal concepts are as readily applied to living teleological systems as to inanimate systems, and influence and power relations are special cases of causal relations.

HERBERT A. SIMON

[*See also* POWER; PREDICTION; SCIENTIFIC EXPLANATION.]

BIBLIOGRAPHY

BLALOCK, HUBERT M. JR. 1964 *Causal Inferences in Nonexperimental Research.* Chapel Hill: Univ. of North Carolina Press.

BRAITHWAITE, RICHARD B. 1953 *Scientific Explanation.* Cambridge Univ. Press.

BREDEMEIER, HARRY C. 1966 [Review of] *Cause and Effect,* edited by Daniel Lerner. *American Sociological Review* 31:280–281.

BROWN, ROBERT R. 1963 *Explanation in Social Science.* London: Routledge; Chicago: Aldine.

BURKS, ARTHUR W. 1951 The Logic of Causal Propositions. *Mind* 60:363–382.

Cause and Effect. Edited by Daniel Lerner. 1965 New York: Free Press.

HUME, DAVID (1777) 1900 *An Enquiry Concerning Human Understanding.* Chicago: Open Court. → A paperback edition was published in 1955 by Bobbs-Merrill.

HYMAN, HERBERT H. 1955 *Survey Design and Analysis: Principles, Cases, and Procedures.* Glencoe, Ill.: Free Press.

KENDALL, PATRICIA L.; and LAZARSFELD, PAUL F. 1950 Problems of Survey Analysis. Pages 133–196 in Robert K. Merton and Paul F. Lazarsfeld (editors), *Continuities in Social Research: Studies in the Scope and Method of* The American Soldier. Glencoe, Ill.: Free Press.

MICHOTTE, ALBERT (1946) 1963 *The Perception of Causality.* Paterson, N.J.: Littlefield. → First published in French.

NAGEL, ERNEST 1961 *The Structure of Science: Problems in the Logic of Scientific Explanation.* New York: Harcourt.

PIAGET, JEAN (1923) 1959 *The Language and Thought of the Child.* 3d ed., rev. New York: Humanities Press. → First published as *Le langage et la pensée chez l'enfant.*

PIAGET, JEAN (1927) 1930 *The Child's Conception of Physical Causality.* New York: Harcourt; London: Routledge. → First published as *La causalité physique chez l'enfant.* A paperback edition was published in 1960 by Littlefield.

POPPER, KARL R. (1934) 1959 *The Logic of Scientific Discovery.* New York: Basic Books. → First published as *Logik der Forschung.*

ROSENBLUETH, A.; WIENER, NORBERT; and BIGELOW, J. 1943 Behavior, Purpose and Teleology. *Philosophy of Science* 10, no. 1:18–24.

Simon, Herbert A. (1947–1956) 1957 *Models of Man, Social and Rational: Mathematical Essays on Rational Human Behavior in a Social Setting.* New York: Wiley.

Wold, Herman (editor) 1964 *Econometric Model Building: Essays on the Causal Chain Approach.* Amsterdam: North-Holland Publishing.

Zeisel, Hans (1947) 1957 *Say It With Figures.* 4th ed., rev. New York: Harper.

CENSORED DATA

See Statistical analysis, special problems of, *article on* Truncation and censorship.

CENSORSHIP

Censorship is essentially a "policy of restricting the public expression of ideas, opinions, conceptions and impulses which have or are believed to have the capacity to undermine the governing authority or the social and moral order which that authority considers itself bound to protect" (Lasswell 1930, p. 290). Censorship usually takes two forms: prior, which refers to advance suppression; and *post facto*, which involves suppression after publication or pronouncement has taken place. Although it is more frequently practiced under autocratic regimes, it is also present, in varied forms, in those states normally viewed as Western liberal democracies; and its execution is as variegated as are the states and governments involved. Broadly speaking, however, those who favor and those who oppose censorship normally bracket themselves with one of two approaches to society as represented by great names of the past. The former agree with Plato, St. Augustine, and Machiavelli that those who are qualified to identify evil should be empowered to prevent its dissemination. The latter, siding with Aristotle, Oliver Wendell Holmes, Jr., and John Dewey, maintain that a man is free only so long as he is empowered to make his own choices.

In its contemporary form, censorship is exercised both by public and by private authorities. Although it is still predominantly associated with governmental (public) action, its exercise by private groups—with religious as well as secular interests—is becoming more common. In the United States, since the end of World War II, the rise of private vigilante groups in a number of areas of everyday life clearly indicates this trend. The erstwhile dichotomy (Lasswell 1930, p. 291) of either political or religious censorship no longer suffices. Today, censorship, both public and private, may be generally grouped into four categories: political censorship; religious censorship; censorship against obscenity, i.e., censorship of morals; and censorship affecting academic freedom. It is important to remember, however, that these are merely categories of convenience and that a given act of censorship may, of course, embrace more than one category. Thus, the Tridentine Rules (formulated at the Council of Trent in 1564 under the guidance of Pope Pius iv) were religious in origin, but to some extent they were involved with obscenity; their enforcement was political; and there was then no academic freedom as we know it today. The investigations of alleged subversive influences in American schools, colleges, and universities in the years following World War ii had political, as well as educational, overtones.

History

The history of censorship, so closely linked with a basic sense of insecurity, represents a continuum of the battle between the individual and society and can be sketched only briefly here. Turning first to the Bible (Jer. 36.1–26), we find that the prophet Jeremiah encountered censorship when the book he had dictated to Baruch was mutilated by King Jehoiakim. During classical antiquity, censorship was sporadically applied. In the fifth century B.C., Sparta placed a ban on certain forms of poetry, music, and dance, because its rulers believed, or wished to believe, that these cultural activities tended to induce effeminacy and licentiousness. For their liberal thoughts on religious matters, Aeschylus, Euripides, and Aristophanes felt the censor's sting. Republican Rome considered itself devoted to virtue and assumed the right to censor any citizen who did not embrace that concept in the cultural realm. The theater was banned by the censor, except on the occasion of certain games (where tradition bestowed upon dramatic art a degree of license in both gesture and speech). Although there is no conclusive evidence of literary censorship either in Rome or Greece, the famed poet Ovid was banished to the Black Sea area by Emperor Augustus, allegedly because of his "licentiousness" but more likely because of his political views.

In the era of the Christian church, the earliest and most extreme manifestation of censorship is found in the Apostolic Constitutions, said to have been written in A.D. 95 by St. Clement of Rome at the dictates of the apostles. The constitutions forbade Christians to read any books of the gentiles, since it was thought that the Scriptures were all a *true* believer need read. There then followed a long series of prohibitions issued by the early church fathers, among them the death penalty edicts of the Council of Nicaea and the Emperor Constantine against the pens of Arius and Porphyry in 325; the decree of 399 by the Council of Alexandria under Bishop Theophilus, forbidding the Origens to read and own books; the stern punitive measures, akin to the book-burning days of the Hitler era, by Pope Leo I in 446; and the first papal Index, which made its appearance in 499 under Pope Gelasius. The concept of the Index, which was formalized by the amended Tridentine Rules, embracing a list of proscribed books for Roman Catholics, is still in existence today (see Gardiner 1958, pp. 51–54).

During the Middles Ages a new version of prior censorship commenced: the submission of manuscripts by writers to their superiors, both as a matter of courtesy and as a prophylactic against subsequent censure. But with the advent of printing and with steady cultural growth, the ecclesiastic authorities insisted upon formal, organized censorship. In 1501 Pope Alexander VI issued his famous bull against printing of books, which was designed to protect the vast domain of the Church of Rome against heresy. Even more drastic measures were taken by the Scottish Estates in 1551. By 1586, all books printed in England had to be read and approved by the Archbishop of Canterbury or the Bishop of London prior to publication. But the written word was not all that felt the censor's power in England; it was extended to drama by the public authorities, once religious drama, always under the control of the church, had become obsolete. In 1693, England substituted *punitive* for *prior* censorship of printing. This form essentially exists in many lands now and is generally much preferred to prior censorship, if there must be censorship. Probably the best-known illustration of this type of censorship is the John Peter Zenger case in 1735, often referred to as the birth of freedom of the press; for New York Governor William Cosby was unsuccessful in his gross attempt to silence and punish the courageous printer (see Zenger 1957, pp. 3–131).

It should be noted here that the triumph of Protestantism, and the subsequent rise of the nation-state, had brought about a significant switch in emphasis in the employment of censorship. Practically speaking, the monarchs became separated from the church, and to a considerable extent their interests in censorship no longer coincided. Thus, the compelling force necessary to sustain censorship was no longer concerned with religious beliefs. In those instances in which a state still guarded against blasphemy or heresy, it was from the conviction that these were often antecedent steps to sedition and treason, especially where the authority for the monarch's position came from the doctrine of the divine right of kings. Censorship was still aimed at beliefs and facts, but the orientation had switched from the religious to the political arena.

The seventeenth and eighteenth centuries were the transition years in the development of the freedoms and rights of men, which we value so much. Here the first voices began to ring out for the rights of the individual against the state, so that by 1695 the last formal governmental restraint upon literature in England had been withdrawn. Among the voices who made themselves heard in those centuries were Milton, Spinoza, Voltaire, and Locke.

Prior to this transition period, sundry intriguing devices had been employed to look after the interests of the monarch. King Henry VIII had entrusted the control of books to the infamous Court of Star Chamber. Queen Elizabeth maintained control by giving the Stationers' Company a monopoly on printing, for which they reciprocated by hunting out all undesirable books. Coincident with this she granted powers of suppression to the archbishops of Canterbury and York.

The Stuarts brought with their rule even more severe censorship, allowing their bishops control over the importation of books. The first breakthrough for free thought came in 1640 when the Long Parliament abolished the Court of Star Chamber. This brief respite lasted until 1643, when Parliament reintroduced licensing. This was the specific act that resulted in Milton's eloquent plea for free speech, his *Areopagitica*. In this work, he exposes the many absurdities, anomalies, and tyrannies inherent in literary censorship. During the Restoration, the devices of censorship employed by the former monarchs were maintained with the passage of the Licensing Act of 1662, which was aimed at "heretical, seditious, schismatical or offensive books or pamphlets."

The move toward individual rights being generated in England at this time reached its culmination in 1695, when the Licensing Act was not renewed, and governmental censorship temporarily disappeared from the English scene. Although the English had gained their freedom, in those nations where Catholicism still held sway, there was very little freedom to express ideas that would offend the church. This tradition has lasted even into the modern era in such nations as Spain.

The eighteenth century is conspicuous in historical perspective because of the freedom of expression that it attained. Even in the colonies, with the spread of the Great Awakening (dating from about 1740), the growth of freedom from the chains of Puritan control was evident. By 1789, the freedoms of the bill of rights were accepted as the natural heritage of all men. The remarkable feature of this phenomenon, both in England and America, was that it was a reality, not just an idea on a piece of paper.

It is in the field of morals—the area of censorship commonly classified as that of obscenity—that not only the most widespread but the most extreme forms of censorship and attempted censorship have transpired during the past two or three centuries. This censorship has been both on a public and private level, the former chiefly by virtue of a host of defense-against-obscenity statutes and ordinances, the latter by pressure groups, chief among them the Catholic church, whose emphasis in the realm of censorship has perceptibly changed from the old preoccupation with heresy to one that emphasizes morals, although the religious overtones are understandably present. But public and private aims and designs again merge here.

Although in certain types of censorship the political authority is concerned with defending the *status quo* and its position in it, this is not true of censorship of morals. More often than not, state action is not in defense of itself but in the form of a service to some influential members of the polity, in ridding the society of certain ideas that are considered offensive by these influential members. The common method of achieving these ends is the formation of watchdog groups that comb the arts and letters and upon finding works— books, plays, movies, etc.—that they consider obscene strive either for their official suppression or for private boycotts. The first of these societies, the English Society for the Suppression of Vice, appeared in London in 1802. It was to be the forebear of such American vigilante groups as Anthony Comstock's New York Society for the Suppression of Vice and the New England Watch and Ward Society (Craig 1962, pp. 138–139).

The effectiveness of these groups in the United States is evidenced by the vast amount of obscenity legislation that has been passed in the last century. Beginning with the clause in the Tariff Act of 1842 that barred the importation of obscene matter, American legislatures have produced a multitude of statutes designed to protect the minds and morals of both children and adults in our society. The 1920s through the 1940s marked the height of this moralistic legislation.

In England, the single most important piece of censorship legislation was the famous Campbell Act of 1857 (the Obscene Publications Act of 1857), named for its proponent, who was the lord chief justice. There was a great cry against it in Parliament, because in Campbell's attempt to strike down the sale of obvious hard-core pornography from the shelves of the bookstores of Holywell Street in London, he had left few safeguards to defend against similar attacks upon all literature that dealt with sex. The act was finally passed when Campbell defined an obscene work as written for the single purpose of corrupting the morals of youth, and of a nature calculated to shock the common feelings of decency in any well-regulated mind.

However, his successor, Lord Cockburn, in the grasp of the Victorians, did not so limit the obscene. In the famous Hicklin case he said, "the test of obscenity is this, whether the tendency of the matter charged as obscenity is to deprave and corrupt those whose minds are open to such immoral influences, and into whose hands a publication of this sort may fall" (L.R3/QB/371, 1868). Using standards such as this, the Comstocks on both sides of the Atlantic—indeed throughout the world—infiltrated various boards of censorship, and by the turn of the century succeeded in reducing "acceptable" literature to that fit for reading by children. At that time, more than one author was endangering his chances of publication if he referred to a leg as a "leg," rather than calling it a "limb." Starting in the late 1920s, however, American federal courts have been instrumental in salvaging some semblance of reasonableness in these matters.

In a series of opinions, the most important of which were the combined 1957 cases *Roth* v. *U.S.* and *Alberts* v. *California* (354 U.S. 476), the Supreme Court both defined the obscene and detailed the protections to which literature accused of being obscene was entitled. Associate Justice William Brennan, in his opinion, made clear that "obscenity is not within the area of constitutionally protected speech or press," because it is "utterly without redeeming social importance" (354 U.S. 484, 485). However, he cautioned that "sex and obscenity are not synonymous," and the portrayal of sex, for example, in art, literature, and scientific works, "is entitled to constitutional protection as long as it is not obscene." But his judicial test is not entirely helpful: Material is obscene when "to the average person, applying contemporary community standards, the dominant theme of the material taken as a whole appeals to prurient interest" (354 U.S. 487). This standard, and its later application by the courts to specific works, seems to indicate that the Supreme Court's view of what literature is obscene in modern America is limited to that genre of literature generally known as hard-core pornography. But the need to define hard-core pornography reintroduces the basic dilemma of drawing lines.

A categorized, comprehensive list of works censored in the United States was compiled in 1940 by Morris Ernst, one of the foremost crusaders against censorship. It includes some of the world's greatest classics, for example, works by Homer, Shakespeare, Whitman, and Darwin (Ernst & Lindey 1940, pp. 228–230).

The history of censorship in France and the other European nations has an amazing historical similarity to that of America. The giants of French literature, such as Baudelaire, Hugo, Verlaine, and Zola, have felt the same stings of censors as their counterparts in English. The modern laws regarding obscenity in France, Italy, Belgium, Germany, and the Netherlands, roughly parallel those of America; whereas those of the Scandinavian nations are a little more lenient. This is probably a reflection of the different attitudes toward sex prevailing in those nations.

Censorship in the world of dictatorships must be viewed from a different perspective, of course. Essentially, the rights of individuals in these nations are at a pre-Renaissance level in terms of the Western world. Consequently, censorship there is designed to propagandize as well as to forbid. This has been especially true in the totalitarian dictatorships, where complete control of the mind is a prerequisite for complete control of the society.

Critique

In its most general form, censorship is involved with the realm of ideas, ideas that naturally must take the form of something written or spoken in order to be censorable. Censorship implies that certain ideas are not only invalid, but that they should not be presented; that they constitute a genuine danger. In Lasswell's terms of "who gets what, why and how," censorship is thus concerned with controlling "dangerous" expression of ideas. It follows, then, that those who have been most successful in controlling ideas that endanger their interests are those who already possess authority. Hence, the most successful practitioners of censorship through the ages have been the authority figures themselves—church, monarchs, dictators. Those in nonpublic positions, who desire the suppression of certain ideas but do not of themselves have the necessary official authority to do so, will thus endeavor to enlist the aid of whatever authority may be promising. Because this is often difficult,

if not impossible, private groups in today's Western democracies then resort to personal pressure tactics, designed to intimidate those who have influence over, or who are in command of, channels of communication. A pertinent illustration of this technique, very successfully employed in the United States since the 1940s and 1950s (particularly during the McCarthy era), has been the so-called blacklisting of controversial literary figures as well as performing artists, thus blocking their employment in certain media of communication, notably the movies, radio, and television—the live stage having more successfully resisted that type of pressure (see Cogley 1956, *passim*).

Far less successful, especially in the United States, however, have been attempts to censor the press, which has enjoyed a unique position of communication freedom, even more so than in traditionally censorship-leery Britain. Although press censorship has continued in many lands even in the 1960s, not excluding certain Western democracies (France, for example), the Supreme Court of the United States again made quite clear in 1964 that the press is not only not censorable by way of prior restraint but that it cannot even be sued for allegedly libelous statements unless deliberate malice is proved conclusively in a court of law (*The New York Times Co.* v. *Sullivan*, decided March 9, 1964, 84 U.S. Sup. Ct. 710).

The bases of censorship are themselves largely repugnant to the ideas of Western liberal tradition, yet even the West must comprehend the three possible rationalizations that seem to exist for censorship.

The first rationalization is that ideas presented, or about to be presented, are "false" and/or "dangerous" by the standards of the authorities in power and that they must hence be suppressed or punished.

Related to this is the second rationale for censorship, equally obnoxious to Western traditions, that of elitism, the justification of which goes back to Plato and the *Republic*. Here, the belief is that the minds of those who would be subjected to the ideas to be censored are not capable of seeing the "falsity" and would hence be led astray. Western political tradition rejects this notion, but many a private pressure group in the West does not, as the persistent attempts by them, and at times by public authorities, to censor school textbooks demonstrate to this day. Yet any historical investigation will quickly prove that those who have set themselves up as being uniquely qualified to ferret out the truth have been no more capable of doing so than their adversaries.

The third rationale for censorship seems to be the one that stands on strongest grounds. Ideas that lead to "antisocial action"—for example, hard-core pornography—may be censored. Here, however, a crucial distinction enters: We are no longer so much in the realm of ideas as in the realm of overt action, and it is here that even the West may wish to, indeed may have to, draw a line between the cherished freedom of expression and the right of society to establish a modicum of standards of overt behavior. How, where, and by whom such a line is to be drawn is the peculiar dilemma of those who love and cherish the precious tradition of ordered liberty.

HENRY J. ABRAHAM

[*See also* ACADEMIC FREEDOM; CONSTITUTIONAL LAW, *article on* CIVIL LIBERTIES; FREEDOM; TOTALITARIANISM.]

BIBLIOGRAPHY

CHAFEE, ZECHARIAH, JR. 1941 *Free Speech in the United States.* Cambridge, Mass.: Harvard Univ. Press. → Supersedes Chafee's *Freedom of Speech,* 1920.

CLYDE, WILLIAM M. 1934 *The Struggle for the Freedom of the Press From Caxton to Cromwell.* St. Andrews University Publications, No. 37. Oxford Univ. Press.

COGLEY, JOHN 1956 *Report on Blacklisting.* 2 vols. New York: Fund for the Republic.

CRAIG, ALEC (1962) 1963 *Suppressed Books: A History of the Conception of Literary Obscenity.* New York: World. → First published as *The Banned Books of England and Other Countries: A Study of the Conception of Literary Obscenity.*

ERNST, MORRIS L.; and LINDEY, ALEXANDER 1940 *The Censor Marches On: Recent Milestones in the Administration of the Obscenity Law in the United States.* New York: Doubleday. → Still a classic.

ERNST, MORRIS L.; and SCHWARTZ, ALAN U. 1964 *Censorship: The Search for the Obscene.* New York: Macmillan.

FAULK, J. HENRY 1964 *Fear on Trial.* New York: Simon & Schuster.

GARDINER, HAROLD, S.J. (1958) 1961 *Catholic Viewpoint on Censorship.* Rev. ed. Garden City, N.Y.: Doubleday.

GELLHORN, WALTER 1956 *Individual Freedom and Governmental Restraints.* Baton Rouge: Louisiana State Univ. Press.

HANEY, ROBERT W. 1960 *Comstockery in America: Patterns of Censorship and Control.* Boston: Beacon. → Superb analysis of America's privately engendered drive for "morality" and "purity" in social action.

HART, H. L. A. 1963 *Law, Liberty and Morality.* Stanford Univ. Press.

KILPATRICK, JAMES J. 1960 *The Smut Peddlers.* Garden City, N.Y.: Doubleday.

LASSWELL, HAROLD 1930 Censorship. Volume 3, pages 290–294 in *Encyclopaedia of the Social Sciences.* New York: Macmillan.

LEVY, LEONARD W. 1960 *Legacy of Suppression: Freedom of Speech and Press in Early American History.* Cambridge, Mass.: Belknap Press.

McCORMICK, JOHN; and MacINNES, MAIRI (editors) 1962 *Versions of Censorship: An Anthology.* Chicago, Ill.: Aldine.

MacIVER, ROBERT M. 1955 *Academic Freedom in Our Time.* New York: Columbia Univ. Press.

PAUL, JAMES C. N.; and SCHWARTZ, MURRAY L. 1961 *Federal Censorship: Obscenity in the Mail.* New York: Free Press.

SWAYZE, HAROLD 1962 *Political Control of Literature in the USSR, 1946–1959.* Russian Research Center Studies, No. 44. Cambridge, Mass.: Harvard Univ. Press.

WIGGINS, JAMES R. (1956) 1964 *Freedom or Secrecy.* Rev. ed. New York: Oxford Univ. Press.

ZENGER, JOHN PETER 1957 *The Trial of Peter Zenger.* Edited and with introduction and notes by Vincent Buranelli. New York Univ. Press. → Trial in the Supreme Court of Judicature of the province of New York in 1735 for the offense of printing and publishing a libel against the government.

ZENGER, JOHN PETER 1963 *A Brief Narrative of the Case and Trial of John Peter Zenger, Printer of the New York Weekly Journal,* by James Alexander. Edited by Stanley N. Katz. Cambridge, Mass.: Belknap Press.

CENSUS

A census of the population—that is, a counting of the people within the boundaries of a country—has become indispensable to any modern government. How many people are there? What are their basic socioeconomic characteristics? Where do they live, and how are they affected by the processes of social and biological change? These questions arise daily in the governments of all industrially developed countries, not to mention the governments of those that are still developing.

Censuses have come to include many topics other than population. Censuses of manufactures, agriculture, mineral industries, housing, and business establishments are taken by many countries, often independently of the census of population.

The following discussion is concerned primarily with censuses of population, but many of the comments—especially the comments on methods, tabulation, and quality of results—apply with equal force to other kinds of censuses.

Some early censuses. Counting the people, or some portion of them, is a practice that is probably as old as government itself. No one knows which ruler first enumerated the men for military purposes, or drew up a list of households with a view to taxing them. Figures obtained from censuses have long served as items of political propaganda, particularly in order to justify territorial expansion.

Population counts were reported in ancient Japan and were taken by the ancient Egyptians, Greeks, Hebrews, Persians, and Romans. Many of these early censuses appear to have covered only part of the population, often the men of military age, and the results were generally treated as state secrets. In Europe censuses on a city-wide basis or, as in Switzerland, on a canton-wide basis, were reported in the fifteenth and sixteenth centuries. A 1449 census of Nuremberg presumably was taken to determine the needed food supplies when a siege was threatened. The city of Madras in India reportedly took a census in 1687.

Various censuses have been claimed as the first held in modern times with purposes and methods resembling those of today. Among these are a census in New France (the early possessions of France in North America) taken at intervals between 1665 and 1754 and a census in Sweden in 1749. Census taking began early in the North American and South American colonies. The British Board of Trade ordered 27 censuses in the North American colonies between 1635 and 1776, and censuses were taken by these former colonies between independence in 1776 and the establishment of the United States.

The oldest continuous periodic census is that of the United States, which has been conducted every ten years since 1790. The census of the United Kingdom dates back to 1801, and a census has been taken there every ten years except in 1941, during World War II.

If one were to define a modern census as one in which information is collected separately about each individual instead of each household, then the beginning of modern censuses would have to be dated about the middle of the nineteenth century. Censuses along these lines were taken in Brussels in 1842, in all Belgium in 1846, in Boston in 1845, and in the entire United States in 1850. This is the procedure that is now generally in use.

International activities. Toward the end of the nineteenth century, the International Statistical Institute recommended international publication of the results of all censuses. Around the turn of the century the institute repeated its recommendation, pointing out that the results of some 68 different censuses were available, covering about 43 per cent of the world's population. The institute had already adopted, in 1897, a set of rules for conducting censuses and presenting their results, while the whole topic had been discussed by the International Demographic Congress as early as 1878.

One of the early proposals considered by the United Nations was that it develop plans for a 1950 world census of population. Although it found that conditions were not ripe for such an effort, the United Nations took steps to foster census taking and made recommendations to improve the comparability of results. The Inter American Statistical Institute meantime had undertaken a program for the 1950 Census of the Americas, and 18 of the 21 countries in the Americas took censuses between 1945 and 1954. Throughout the world at least 150 areas took censuses in this period, collecting individual data on more than 2 billion people. For the decade centered on 1960, the number of censuses was about 180, including 2.2 billion people.

The use of censuses. The reasons for taking a census vary with the needs of the countries involved. The current concern with social and economic development is one of the prime reasons. Much information is needed in order to institute programs that will improve health, literacy, education, income, levels of living, supplies of food and other consumer goods, agricultural production, and industrial output. Census data are also collected in order to determine the representativeness of legislative bodies, the number of persons eligible to vote, and the areas or groups that have a claim to benefits deriving from the state.

The census provides a basis for much demographic, economic, and social research. It makes possible the identification and description of such groups as the labor force, economically dependent persons, recent migrants to cities, rural and urban populations, racial or religious minorities, refugees, scientific and technical workers, and others. Comparisons of successive censuses show changes in the numbers, characteristics, and location of the population. The census returns are also used as a frame from which samples are selected for subsequent inquiries.

The modern census

The United Nations (1958, p. 4) gives the following definition of a modern population census: "A census of population may be defined as the total process of collecting, compiling and publishing demographic, economic and social data pertaining, at a specified time or times, to all persons in a country or delimited territory."

It also listed six essential features of a census, as follows. (1) A census must have *national sponsorship*. Only a national government can provide the necessary resources and enact suitable legislation, although provincial and local governments may share a part of the responsibility and sometimes a part of the cost. (2) A census must cover a *precisely defined territory;* boundary changes that affect comparisons between successive censuses should be clearly and explicitly stated.

(3) *All persons* in the scope of the census must be included without duplication or omission. (4) The people must be counted as of a *fixed time*. Persons born after the census date are to be excluded, and persons who die after the census date are to be included. Some information, such as that relating to labor force participation or migration, may relate not to the census date but to another period, which must be clearly defined. (5) Census data must be obtained separately for *each individual*. This does not preclude making some entries for the entire household—and in exceptional circumstances summarized information for a group of persons may be acceptable—but the objective of a modern census, insofar as possible, is to collect data separately for each individual. (6) The data from a census must be *published*. Although at one time census reports were treated as state secrets, it is now recognized that a census is not complete until the data are compiled and published.

What is included.   The content of a census, no less than its purpose, is determined by the country's needs at the time. Questions of high importance in one country may be of relatively little importance in another, and questions of great significance at one time may be of little significance later. Every national census has changed over the years. Conditions in the country, alternative sources of information, and the ability of the census organization to provide the proposed information chiefly determine the census content.

The United Nations has approved a set of recommendations for national population censuses that includes the following list of question topics: location at time of census and/or place of usual residence, relation to head of household or family, sex, age, marital status, place of birth, citizenship, whether economically active or not, occupation, industry, status (as employer, employee, etc.), language, ethnic or nationality characteristics, literacy, level of education, school attendance, and the number of children born to each woman (Principles and Recommendations . . . 1958). For countries that could not include all items in the list, the following were suggested as a minimum: sex, age, marital status, and some indication of economic activity. Each item listed, of course, requires specific definition. Some items, such as marital status, type of economic activity, or level of education, apply to only part of the population.

Collection of data.   Discussions of census methods generally distinguish between a count based on the actual location of the population on the census date and one which relates each person to the place of which he is a resident. Frequently residence is interpreted as the place where the person usually lives, although "usual residence" has no statutory meaning. On either basis national totals are usually about equal; community totals, however, may differ substantially.

To facilitate international comparison, the United Nations (Principles and Recommendations . . . 1958) has suggested the adoption of an "international conventional total." This would include all persons present in the country on the census date except foreign military, naval, and diplomatic personnel: it would also include the country's own military, naval and diplomatic personnel and their families located abroad, and merchant seamen normally resident in the country but at sea on the census date. The same document recommends that counts or estimates of the following groups should be given where feasible: indigenous inhabitants and nomadic tribes, civilian national residents temporarily abroad on the census date, and civilian aliens temporarily in the country on the census date. This is because whether or not these groups are included in a national census is usually determined by the laws and needs of each country; thus detailed comparisons between national totals can be made only if separate enumerations of these groups are made available.

Customarily two basic methods of collecting census data are recognized—direct enumeration and self-enumeration. Under the direct enumeration system, an enumerator collects information directly from the individual concerned, the head of the household, or some other member of the household who may be authorized to report for him. Under the self-enumeration system, the questionnaire is given to the individual, or the head of the household, who is expected to enter the required information and return the questionnaire to the census office. In self-enumeration the enumerator often delivers and collects the questionnaire. He may assist persons in making the entries, and he is responsible for assuring the accuracy and completeness of the completed questionnaires.

In a few countries the people are required to present themselves at a designated place to be enumerated. In a few others the population is immobilized on the census date, and no one is permitted on the streets unless he has been enumerated. In the great majority of cases the census enumerator seeks out the potential respondents and delivers questionnaires to them or asks them directly for the required information.

Census legislation normally provides that respondents must give full and correct information. This information must be given confidential treatment by all census employees. For persons who do not wish to have other members of their households or local officials see the information about themselves, census offices have provided special forms on which the person can insert the information and send it directly to the local, regional, or national office.

Population registers and lists of households, where available, are often used to help make the census complete. In some censuses the first step in the field work is to establish a list of housing units. The numbers assigned to these units are then used to control the completeness of the enumeration.

The questionnaire must be designed to permit ready entry of the required information and also be adapted to the tabulation procedure. In self-enumeration there is customarily a separate form for each household, with space for entering information for each household member. When information is collected directly by enumerators they may carry a separate form for each household or a form on which information is recorded for a number of households. Sometimes a separate document is used for each person.

Some countries have a long-established tradition of taking a census once every ten years, a few countries require one every five years, but most countries take a census when it is needed and do not have a fixed date. In a few unusual situations censuses have been taken more often than once in five years. Whether by law or by custom, the ten-year term appears to be most common.

In an increasing number of countries a pilot census is taken before the full census to test the inquiries, the procedures, the development of the field organization, and sometimes the tabulation program.

Use of sampling. Sampling has been extensively used in connection with censuses, although a census in principle requires that information be collected for each person. The term "sample census," which is sometimes used, is a misnomer; a collection of information relating to only a specified part of a population should be termed a sample survey. In some censuses a part of the questions are asked of only a sample of all individuals; in this way more information can be collected without a comparable increase in respondent burden or tabulation work load. Many countries base some tabulations on a sample of the population instead of the total to provide preliminary totals for early release or to reduce the cost of some final tabulations. Sampling has been used to control the quality of the work at several stages of the processing of the data. In some countries a sample has been selected for a pretest and the resulting data have been used to validate the processing operations.

Tabulation of results. To be useful, individual census returns must be converted to statistical summaries. Tabulation methods vary from simple hand counts to processing on high-speed electronic computers. Processing may be done in the field, in provincial offices, or at the central office.

Questionnaires as received from the enumerators must be reviewed to locate incomplete or inconsistent entries. Procedures have been developed for correcting such errors by utilizing other information on the questionnaires or by using probability distributions based on data from other sources. In many instances the entries on the schedule must be converted to a numerical or other suitable code to facilitate counting and grouping into appropriate categories.

The most common procedure for grouping the entries is to punch cards and tabulate them by mechanical means. More recently, electronic computers have been adapted to this work, and devices have been developed to transfer the original questionnaire entries directly to the magnetic tape used in these computers. The capacity and speed of the computers have led to important advances in the amount of material tabulated and in the timeliness of the publications.

Completeness and accuracy. In view of the many public and private uses for census data, there is increasing concern with the quality of the results in terms both of completeness of coverage and accuracy of returns.

Completeness of coverage has received major attention. Unless special precautions are taken, some individuals may not be counted and some areas may not be enumerated. Undercounts of the population are more frequent than overcounts, although a few zealous census officials have been known to overcount the population of an area. Omission of individuals may arise from incomplete enumeration of a household or an area. Underenumeration has been particularly marked in the case of infants and young adults who are highly mobile or who lack firm occupational attachments. In cultures where men are considered more valuable than women, the number of women may be understated. In a few instances a fear that the census may be used for military conscription has led to some omission of men or to misreporting them as women.

Reporting residence may present problems. Some persons, such as migratory workers, have no usual place of residence. Others, such as college students, members of the armed forces, and persons engaged in long-distance transportation, may live away from their families for short or extended periods. Unless precise instructions are given for reporting these persons, they may be counted twice or not at all.

Age is often misreported either because people see some advantage in giving the wrong age or because they do not know their correct age. In many countries births are not recorded, and age is not precisely known. Some reasons for misreporting are that a person believes that despite pledges of confidentialness, the data will be used to his disadvantage; a parent believes that overstating a young child's age may gain him entrance to school or that overstating an older child's age may free him from compulsory school attendance; an older person may overstate his age to get social security benefits or to acquire the higher status sometimes accorded to the very old. Often people report a number ending in zero or five—even when asked for year of birth.

Nationality, citizenship, and mother tongue are particularly subject to misstatement when the correct answer may be considered detrimental in the context of the political situation of the group controlling the area.

Improvement of quality. Public confidence in the census greatly affects accuracy of returns. Public confidence can often be increased through an informational campaign, which explains that the data about any individual cannot be used to his detriment. Police officers, who are used as enumerators in some countries because of their availability and authority, are specifically excluded in others because they may give the impression that the information is not collected solely for statistical purposes.

To improve the quality of results, research has been devoted to reliability of response, role of enumerators, question wording, and attitudes of respondents in different situations. Increased attention is also being given to training the temporary field forces in census methods and concepts and in training the office staff in principles of editing and coding.

The quality of census statistics can often be determined by analyzing them after the complete census tabulations have been published. Formerly this work was performed mainly by scholars or by census officials willing to do scholarly work on their own time; but modern census offices increasingly are undertaking such analysis as part of their regular work. Checks are made for internal consistency of the census, for consistency with previous censuses, and also with other statistics, including estimates, that are entirely independent of the census. Both underenumeration and overenumeration of an age group can be determined by comparing the census results with the comparable age cohort for the previous census, adjusted for deaths and migration [see COHORT ANALYSIS]. Inaccuracies in age reporting that result from the preference of respondents for certain ages can be identified by internal analysis of the data. Sometimes the accuracy of census information for individuals is tested by comparison with information given for these same individuals in administrative records. Sample surveys may be taken to check on completeness of coverage and accuracy of census returns.

These evaluations aid in increasing the accuracy of future censuses, but they also provide users of the statistics with information about the reliability of the data. Although there has been some hesitation about revealing errors in the census, there is a growing recognition that full and frank disclosure leads not only to improvement in future censuses but also to increased public confidence.

CONRAD TAEUBER

[*See also* FERTILITY; GOVERNMENT STATISTICS; MORTALITY; POPULATION; VITAL STATISTICS.]

BIBLIOGRAPHY

BRUNSMAN, HOWARD G. 1963 Significance of Electronic Computers for Users of Census Data. Pages 269–277 in Milbank Memorial Fund, *Emerging Techniques in Population Research.* New York: The Fund.

CANADA, BUREAU OF STATISTICS 1955 *Ninth Census of Canada, 1951: Administrative Report.* Volume 11. Ottawa: Cloutier.

COALE, ANSLEY J. 1955 The Population of the United States in 1950 Classified by Age, Sex, and Color: A Revision of Census Figures. *Journal of the American Statistical Association* 50:16–54.

ECKLER, A. ROSS; and HURWITZ, WILLIAM N. 1958 Response Variances and Biases in Censuses and Surveys. International Statistical Institute, *Bulletin* 36, part 2: 12–35.

JAFFE, A. J. 1947 A Review of the Censuses and Demographic Statistics of China. *Population Studies* 1:308–337.

MAYR, GEORG VON (1895–1917) 1926 *Statistik und Gesellschaftslehre.* 3 vols. 2d ed., enl. Tübingen (Germany): Mohr.

Principles and Recommendations for National Population Censuses. 1958 United Nations Statistical Office, *Statistical Papers* Series M, No. 27.

STEINBERG, JOSEPH; and WAKSBERG, JOSEPH 1956 *Sampling in the 1950 Census of Population and Housing.* Bureau of the Census Working Paper, No. 4. Washington: U.S. Department of Commerce.

TAEUBER, CONRAD; and HANSEN, MORRIS H. 1964 A Preliminary Evaluation of the 1960 Census of Population. *Demography* 1, no. 1:1–14.

TAEUBER, CONRAD; and TAEUBER, IRENE B. 1958 *The Changing Population of the United States.* U.S. Bureau of the Census, Census Monograph Series, 1950. New York: Wiley.

UNITED NATIONS, STATISTICAL OFFICE 1958 *Handbook*

of Population Census Methods. Volume 1: General Aspects of a Population Census. New York: United Nations.

U.S. Bureau of Labor 1900 *The History and Growth of the United States Census.* Prepared for the Senate Committee on the Census. Washington: Government Printing Office.

U.S. Bureau of the Census *Bureau of the Census Catalog.* → Published since 1947.

U.S. Bureau of the Census 1909 *A Century of Population Growth From the First Census of the United States to the Twelfth: 1790–1900.* Washington: Government Printing Office.

U.S. Bureau of the Census 1955 *The 1950 Censuses: How They Were Taken.* Procedural Studies of the 1950 Census, No. 2. Washington: Government Printing Office.

U.S. Bureau of the Census 1960a *Inquiries Included in Each Population Census, 1790 to 1960.* Washington: Government Printing Office.

U.S. Bureau of the Census 1960b *The Post-enumeration Survey, 1950: An Evaluation Study of the 1950 Censuses of Population and Housing.* Bureau of the Census Technical Paper, No. 4. Washington: Government Printing Office.

U.S. Bureau of the Census 1964 *Evaluation and Research Program of the U.S. Censuses of Population and Housing, 1960: Accuracy of Data on Population Characteristics as Measured by CPS–Census Match.* Series ER 60, No. 5. Washington: Government Printing Office.

U.S. Bureau of the Census 1966 *1960 Censuses of Population and Housing: Procedural History.* Washington: Government Printing Office.

U.S. Library of Congress, Census Library Project 1950 *Catalog of United States Census Publications, 1790–1945.* Washington: Government Printing Office.

Willcox, Walter F. 1930 Census. Volume 2, pages 295–300 in *Encyclopaedia of the Social Sciences.* New York: Macmillan.

Zelnik, Melvin 1961 Age Heaping in the United States Census: 1880–1950. *Milbank Memorial Fund Quarterly* 39, no. 3:540–573.

Zelnik, Melvin 1964 Errors in the 1960 Census Enumeration of Native Whites. *Journal of the American Statistical Association* 59:437–459.

CENTRAL AMERICA

See Middle American society.

CENTRAL BANKING

See Banking, central.

CENTRAL NERVOUS SYSTEM

See Nervous system.

CENTRAL PLACE

Central place theory outlines the logic of systems of central places, focusing particularly upon the numbers, sizes, activities, and spatial distribution of such places and their associated regions.

The notion of "central place" may be explained as follows. A chief function of country villages and towns is to be centers for their rural surroundings as well as mediators between local commerce and the outside world. Larger cities play a similar role with respect to systems of smaller villages and towns, which find in the larger places goods and services that the local country villages and towns are too small to supply. Thus, villages, towns, and cities serve in a structural relationship as *central places* for tributary regions.

Central place theory is fundamentally concerned with the patterns through which wholesale, retail, service, and administrative functions, plus market-oriented manufacturing, are provided to consuming populations. Thus, it can also be designated as the theory of urban trade and institutions or the theory of location of tertiary production. As such, it complements the theory of agricultural production originally formulated by J. H. von Thünen, and the theory of location of industry, which has its roots in the work of Alfred Weber.

Origins of central place theory. The first formal statement of central place theory was made by the German economic geographer Christaller in his book on central places in southern Germany (1933).

There were, however, several antecedents and cases of independent invention. Some of the ideas were expressed by Léon Lalanne in his analyses of the structure of the French transportation and communication networks (1863). Christaller acknowledged his debt to the German geographer Robert Gradmann (1916). Models of the same kind were proposed by American rural sociologists in their studies of town–country relations and the rural community; notable among these were the contributions of Galpin (1915) and Kolb (1923 *et seq.*). Platt (1928, p. 83) looked at the "organized life" of an "areal unit of human activity" in his detailed study of a Wisconsin village. After examining the economic connections of the village's institutions with the surrounding area, he concluded: "It is these local connections which give the village enterprises their status as institutions of the community. Without these connections there would be no unified community" (*ibid.*, p. 92). Lösch, a German location economist working at the same time as Christaller, applied similar concepts to define economic regions; he subsequently attempted to generalize Christaller's model to entire "economic landscapes" (1938). Ullman (1941) introduced Christaller's work to American readers, and since then the largest part of both theoretical and empirical central place study has been American. A detailed review, bibliography, and synthesis of central place literature is provided by Berry and Pred (1961).

Some related theories.   The central place concept is related to other concepts used in studying the location and organization of cities, industries, and regions.

Location of cities.   On the basis of both distribution and function, human settlements on the face of the globe may be classified into two general types: *central places* and *specialized places* (Harris & Ullman 1945). Central places tend to have a more or less uniform, dispersed distribution over any area with homogeneous physical and economic characteristics, and are basically centers performing commercial functions. Specialized places tend to have highly localized distributions as individual cities or clusters of cities associated with specific resources or favorable sites: mining towns on the exploited part of a coal field; resort towns on the seacoast or in the mountains; industrial towns in manufacturing belts which have evolved as a result of a complex of natural, historical, and economic factors, including the cumulative advantages of specialization and agglomeration (Harris 1954). Linear arrangements of transport towns along a railroad, highway, river, or seacoast may be considered as special cases of the central place pattern.

Although the typology of central places and specialized places is clear in theory, most large cities actually combine activities of both types (Harris 1943). Thus, even specialized industrial towns in the manufacturing belt of the northeastern United States have some commercial functions; so, too, central place towns serving agricultural areas on the Great Plains may have some specialized activities.

Because of local variability in natural conditions, rural settlement, layout (and other characteristics of transportation networks), and, finally, evolution of urban settlements and of their functions (including political and industrial activities), centers of any given step in the central place hierarchy vary somewhat in size from place to place under actual conditions. As a result, the populations of urban centers, although conforming locally to central place hierarchies, tend in the aggregate to be arrayed in rank–size distributions, as described by Zipf [see RANK–SIZE RELATIONS]. The highest-order central place in the hierarchy of a country, or the largest city in the rank–size formulation, tends to develop a whole series of special economic, social, and political characteristics, activities, and qualities of leadership, as recognized by Mark Jefferson in his use of the term "primate city" (1939). The interlocking characteristics of rank–size distribu-

tions, central place hierarchies, and primate cities have been reviewed by Berry (1964).

Industrial location.   Any industrial process may be regarded as a continuum which begins with localized raw materials and moves through various stages of modification to finished products which are utilized directly by consumers. Corresponding to this continuum are locations of factories near raw materials, in intermediate positions, and near markets. It is the final, consumer- and market-oriented stages of production that tend to be located in central place cities and to have central place characteristics. In a special sense, the points of gathering or assembling any initial raw material also have these characteristics, although the concept of central place is usually applied to the whole bundle of associated activities at the consumer-service end rather than to specialized and localized activities of the early stages of processing or transportation.

Regions and areas.   Central places are associated with "regions of organization," or "nodal" regions, which derive their unity from contact with or movement through the central place. It may be noted that regions can be grouped into two great groups—regions of organization on the one hand, and uniform or homogeneous regions on the other. The latter are characterized by essential similarity of some physical, social, or economic feature.

The hierarchy of central places has its exact counterpart in a hierarchy of corresponding regions of organization. Thus, central places, considered as a system of points, fit into a global system of areal organization: tributary areas are seen as organized around these points, which are connected both with one another and with the tributary areas by lines of human movement.

The relations of central places to their zones of influence have been studied by geographers, sociologists, economists, planners, businessmen, and others, by many methods, in a large number of countries (Harris 1964). Among the overlapping concepts of these several disciplines are those of metropolitan dominance, retail gravitation, neighborhood and community organization, and areal functional organization.

The classic theory—postulates and theorems. Central place theory begins by considering two conditions that affect the variety of goods and services (*central functions*) which are to be provided to consumers. These are (*a*) conditions of entry (*thresholds*), the minimum market sizes (in quantity of sales) necessary to support establishments of each kind, and (*b*) maximum distances consumers are willing to travel to each kind of establishment (*outer ranges of goods*). In any area the maximum number of establishments of any kind is equal to demands for the commodity divided by threshold, while the minimum number of establishments (if all consumers are to be served) is equal to demands for the commodity divided by maximum possible size of the market. The last-named quantity is derived from the outer range of goods, as defined above.

Central functions may be arranged along a continuum at one end of which is the activity with the greatest threshold (the *highest-order* function) and at the other end, that with the lowest threshold (the *lowest-order* function). The problem is, therefore, to locate the varying numbers of establishments of each variety of central functions as *efficiently* as possible.

Efficiency, in terms of this model, requires (*a*) that consumers minimize costs of transportation by visiting the nearest location offering the good demanded; and (*b*) that there is active competition among businessmen to serve the consuming population. Under these conditions, supplying firms will spread out in a spatial pattern mirroring that of the spatial distribution of population. Each firm supplies the small region surrounding it (its *market area*) that is closer to it than to any of its competitors. *Market size* lies somewhere between the minimum size prescribed by thresholds (in volume of sales) and the maximum size prescribed by outer ranges (of areas that can be served). If perfect competition prevails and population is uniformly distributed on an unbounded isotropic plane, firms of each kind will be located in a perfectly uniform tessellation at the apexes of equilateral triangles (i.e., in a trigonal grid) serving hexagonal market areas of just-threshold size.

Generation of central place hierarchies. Assume that an area to be served is divided into the threshold market areas of the highest-order central function. Because consumers travel to the nearest place offering the good, the locations providing the highest-order good will be exactly "central" to their market areas; these locations are therefore central places in terms of the model. The problem then arises as to how lower-order functions will be provided.

Efficiency, of course, will be furthered if firms of different kinds group together in central places, for then aggregate consumer travel to obtain the variety of goods and services demanded will be minimized; each place offering the highest-order good therefore also offers all lower-order goods. But as the continuum of central functions is descended, threshold market sizes diminish. For which central function will a new competitor be able to squeeze in between the highest-order centers and carve out a profitable market area?

The answer is that it will be when the continuum of central functions has been descended to the point where a good is reached having an additional threshold located, as it were, in the interstices *between* the threshold market areas of the established central places. It is at this point on the continuum that a central place of second order comes into existence that will provide not only the good justifying its emergence but all goods of a lower order as well.

A similar argument can be used to generate third-order places between those of first and second order, fourth between those of the first three orders, and so forth. Highest-order places are the only ones providing those goods for which threshold market areas are too large for businessmen in second-level centers to squeeze a threshold amount of trade between the threshold market areas of the centers of highest order. Second-order places share with those of first order the provision of goods with thresholds large enough to be squeezed between the threshold market areas of the centers of highest order. Third-order centers share with those of the two higher levels provision of goods for which threshold market areas exist between the market areas of the two higher levels of centers, and so on. The highest threshold good at each level (i.e., that which justifies the emergence of that level of center) will be provided for market areas of just-threshold size.

It should be emphasized, however, that each of the lower-order goods supplied that do *not* justify emergence of lower-order centers in the process of spatial competition will have market areas exceeding threshold. This is because of imperfections in competition between businesses—imperfections introduced by the need to group stores in clusters in central places so as to minimize aggregate consumer travel. But there will not be enough excess demand in the interstices among existing centers to provide a compact, unserved area of threshold size that would make possible the rise of another center.

The net result of locating centers in this way is called a *central place hierarchy* or an *urban hierarchy*—a locational system comprising a steplike arrangement of centers and market areas patterned in a distinctive geometric manner. Higher-order centers do compete with lower-order centers in the provision of lower-order goods, but they are distinguished from the lower-order centers by the performance of a group of central functions for market areas that embrace the areas served by the lower-order centers. This takes place in a "nesting" pattern of dominance, subdominance, and competition; a hierarchy will exist even if population densities are uniformly spread over an isotropic plane. Under such "ideal" conditions, centers will be distributed spatially at the apexes of a regular tessellation of equilateral triangles, each with a surrounding hexagonal trade area. Each higher order of centers will then be spaced at $\sqrt{3}$ times the spacing of the next lower order; each higher order has three times the market area of each lower order, and so on.

Modifications of classic theory. Many studies testing various aspects of the central place theory have been carried out, particularly in the United States, Germany, Great Britain, and Sweden; but also in France, the Netherlands, Belgium, Switzerland, Austria, Finland, Poland, the Soviet Union, South Africa, Japan, India, New Zealand, Australia, Canada, and Brazil (Berry & Pred 1961; Harris 1964).

Shortcomings of geometric models. Christaller formulated central place theory largely in geometric terms, working out in detail the implications of uniform tessellations of triangles and hexagons for regular hierarchies of centers (i.e., hierarchies in which there is a uniform multiplicative relationship of phenomena at each successively lower order to the phenomena at the next highest level).

Unfortunately, however, the uniform conditions postulated as leading to regular hierarchies are never found in reality. Population densities, incomes, tastes, and lines of accessibility all vary considerably from place to place. If these variations were continuous over space, it would not be difficult to transform them back to uniformity to see if regular hierarchies actually exist. The problem is that geographic space contains many nongeographic discontinuities; authors talk, for example, about "income fronts" and a variety of "boundary" and "barrier" effects.

Mathematical models. In view of the above, much of the recent effort in central place studies has been directed toward constructing mathematical models rather than geometric ones. The logic of this is that properly formulated mathematical models can be used to facilitate both empirical and applied work in a variety of situations, whereas geometric models cannot. A mathematical statement of the geometric model was provided by Beckmann (1958), and an approach to a more general mathematical formulation is that of Berry and Barnum (1962) [*see* GEOGRAPHY, *article on* STATISTICAL GEOGRAPHY].

Empirical confirmation. Empirical workers have shown that most of the implications of central place theory are valid. Higher-order places offer more goods, have more establishments and larger populations and tributary areas, do greater volumes of business, and are fewer in number and more widely spaced than are lower-order places. Low-order places provide only low-order goods to small, low-order tributary areas; such goods are generally necessities requiring frequent purchase with little consumer travel. The converse is true for higher-order places, which, in addition to offering the low-order convenience goods, also offer shopping and specialty goods to larger market areas.

Moreover, higher- and lower-order places have been found to fall into a hierarchy comprising discrete groups of centers with the regular spatial patterns suggested by the theory. Most students suggest that the urban hierarchy has eight levels in advanced Western economies, roughly: the national capital; national metropolitan centers; regional metropolitan centers; regional capitals; small cities (e.g., county seats); towns; villages; and hamlets. A possible ninth level is that of the "world city," such as New York or London.

Systematic variations. Various kinds of systematic variation of the central place pattern have been recognized, although many of these have yet to be included in a more general theory. For example, as population densities fall, say as one proceeds westward in the United States, there is a thinning of centers, an enlargement of trade areas, and progressive upward shift of functions from lower- to higher-order centers. At the highest densities, within cities, the idea of central places as independent urban areas breaks down; but neighborhood, community, and regional shopping centers form a central place hierarchy. This extension of central place ideas to the case of business centers within cities is relatively recent but has proved useful (Berry 1963).

As income levels change from area to area or through time, there is a systematic change in the importance of higher- and lower-order centers. At higher income levels, more shopping and specialty goods are demanded, and people are willing to travel farther to obtain the goods they desire. Income, scale, and accessibility changes are all responsible for the progressive centralization of functions in the higher-level centers in the United States and the progressive decline of the smaller hamlets and villages.

Similarly, in Western societies in the past, and in the less developed non-Western parts of the world today, the central place hierarchy and attendant marketing system were and are much simpler than they are today in the West. The hierarchy has fewer levels. In the least developed peasant societies there is not enough trade to justify permanent market centers, which are replaced by a cyclical system of periodic markets. The periodicity of cycles varies markedly from one place to another, depending upon local custom. Merchants travel from market to market as they open on the appointed day of the cycle, and catch the limited trade of several small regions. Such periodic markets, the first step in the development of central place hierarchies, trade time for space, since within the maximum local area that potential consumers are willing to travel to any given location there is not enough trade to satisfy the thresholds of permanent markets open at all times (Skinner 1964/ 1965).

The mathematical formulations developed to date incorporate relatively few of these systematic variations. Thus, central place theory is at an intermediate level of development. At a given point in time in relatively advanced Western societies, it provides a useful analytic tool. In this context it has proved invaluable in marketing analysis, has aided in the location of new retail facilities, has been used in the planning of commercial redevelopment as part of urban renewal programs in older cities (Berry 1963), and is being used in rural redevelopment activities (Saskatchewan 1957). However, the theory is not general enough at present to account for variations among cultures or levels of economic development, nor does it permit very precise prediction of growth and change in central place systems, although first steps in the construction of more dynamic models have been taken (Morrill 1963).

BRIAN J. L. BERRY AND CHAUNCY D. HARRIS

[*Directly related are the entries* ECOLOGY, *article on* HUMAN ECOLOGY; REGION; REGIONAL SCIENCE; SPATIAL ECONOMICS. *Other relevant material may be found in* CITY; RURAL SOCIETY; *and in the biographies of* THÜNEN *and* WEBER, ALFRED.]

BIBLIOGRAPHY

BECKMANN, MARTIN J. 1958 City Hierarchies and the Distribution of City Size. *Economic Development and Cultural Change* 6:243–248.

BERRY, BRIAN J. L. 1963 *Commercial Structure and Commercial Blight: Retail Patterns and Processes in the City of Chicago.* Department of Geography, Research Paper No. 85. Univ. of Chicago.

BERRY, BRIAN J. L. 1964 Cities as Systems Within Systems of Cities. Pages 116–137 in John Friedmann and William Alonso (editors), *Regional Development and Planning: A Reader.* Cambridge, Mass.: M.I.T. Press.

BERRY, BRIAN J. L.; and BARNUM, H. GARDINER 1962 Aggregate Relations and Elemental Components of Central Place Systems. *Journal of Regional Science* 4, no. 1:35–68.

BERRY, BRIAN J. L.; and PRED, ALLAN 1961 *Central Place Studies: A Bibliography of Theory and Applications.* Bibliography Series, No. 1. Philadelphia: Regional Science Research Institute. → A reprint was published in 1965, with additions through 1964.

CHRISTALLER, WALTER 1933 *Die zentralen Orte in Süddeutschland: Eine ökonomisch-geographische Untersuchung über die Gesetzmässigkeit der Verbreitung und Entwicklung der Siedlungen mit städtischen Funktionen.* Jena (Germany): Fischer.

CHRISTALLER, WALTER 1962 Die Hierarchie der Städte. Pages 3–11 in IGU Symposium in Urban Geography, Lund, 1960, *Proceedings.* Lund Studies in Geography, Series B: Human Geography, No. 24. Lund (Sweden): Gleerup.

GALPIN, CHARLES J. 1915 *The Social Anatomy of an Agricultural Community.* Research Bulletin No. 34. Madison: Univ. of Wisconsin, Agricultural Experiment Station.

GRADMANN, ROBERT 1916 Schwäbische Städte. Gesellschaft für Erdkunde zu Berlin, *Zeitschrift* [1916]: 425–457.

HARRIS, CHAUNCY D. 1943 A Functional Classification of Cities in the United States. *Geographical Review* 33:86–99.

HARRIS, CHAUNCY D. 1954 The Market as a Factor in the Localization of Industry in the United States. Association of American Geographers, *Annals* 44:315–348.

HARRIS, CHAUNCY D. 1964 Methods of Research in Economic Regionalization. *Geographia polonica* 4:59–86.

HARRIS, CHAUNCY D.; and ULLMAN, EDWARD L. 1945 The Nature of Cities. American Academy of Political and Social Science, *Annals* 242:7–17.

JEFFERSON, MARK 1939 The Law of the Primate City. *Geographical Review* 29:226–232.

KOLB, JOHN H. 1923 *Service Relations of Town and Country.* Research Bulletin No. 58. Madison: Univ. of Wisconsin, Agricultural Experiment Station.

LALANNE, LÉON 1863 Essai d'une théorie des réseaux de chemins de fer, fondée sur l'observation des faits et sur les lois primordiales qui président au groupement des populations. Académie des Sciences, Paris, *Comptes rendus hebdomadaires des séances* 57:206–210.

LÖSCH, AUGUST 1938 The Nature of Economic Regions. *Southern Economic Journal* 5:71–78.

MORRILL, RICHARD L. 1963 The Development of Spatial Distributions of Towns in Sweden: An Historical–Predictive Approach. Association of American Geographers, *Annals* 53:1–14.

PHILBRICK, ALLEN K. 1957 Areal Functional Organization in Regional Geography. Regional Science Association, *Papers and Proceedings* 3:87–98.

PLATT, ROBERT S. 1928 A Detail of Regional Geography: Ellison Bay Community as an Industrial Organism. Association of American Geographers, *Annals* 18:81–126.

PROST, M. A. 1965 *La hiérarchie des villes en fonction de leurs activités de commerce et de service.* Paris: Gauthier-Villars.

SASKATCHEWAN, ROYAL COMMISSION ON AGRICULTURE AND

RURAL LIFE 1957 *Service Centers*. Report No. 12. Regina (Canada): Queen's Printer.

SKINNER, GEORGE 1964/1965 Marketing and Social Structure in Rural China. *Journal of Asian Studies* 24:3–43, 195–228, 363–399.

THOMAS, EDWIN N. 1961 Toward an Expanded Central-place Model. *Geographical Review* 51:400–411.

ULLMAN, EDWARD 1941 A Theory of Location for Cities. *American Journal of Sociology* 46:853–864.

CENTRAL TENDENCY

See STATISTICS, DESCRIPTIVE, *article on* LOCATION AND DISPERSION.

CENTRALIZATION AND DECENTRALIZATION

The following article deals with the administrative phenomena and problems of centralization and decentralization. Broader political and social aspects are treated in FEDERALISM; GOVERNMENT; POLITICAL PROCESS; STATE; STATELESS SOCIETY. *For related economic topics see* COMMUNISM, ECONOMIC ORGANIZATION OF; PLANNING, ECONOMIC; TRADE AND MARKETS. *For related urban and ecological processes see* CENTRAL PLACE; CITY; REGION; URBAN REVOLUTION.

Administrative centralization and decentralization principally describe a condition or a trend in an areal hierarchy of power. This condition or trend can be visualized in two ways. One view contrasts the powers of administrators whose formal authority extends over a large geographic area (for example, a nation) with the powers of administrators whose formal authority is confined to particular segments or subsegments of that area (for example, regions, states or provinces, districts, local communities). Here, the important dimensional setting is geographic, and the classic problem is that of the whole and the individual parts. The second view contrasts the powers of area administrators, arranged on a vertical series of "levels," with those at higher levels having correspondingly larger geographic areas (for example, relations between United States public health administrators at the national, state, and local levels). Here, the important dimensional setting is hierarchic, and the basic problem is perceived as distribution of authority among the levels.

Both visual images—one is of the segmented plane surface of a map and the other is of a pyramidal series of administrative levels—involve the factors of power distribution, areal jurisdictions, and a relating of the parts to the whole; but they emphasize them differently. Neither image is designed to prejudge how power should be distributed between large areas and their component areas.

Other usages. In broader practice, "centralization," "administrative centralization," and their opposites are used in a wholly nongeographic sense to characterize the distribution of power at the capital itself. Thus, "centralization," sometimes modified by "administrative," is found as meaning to some authors (*a*) existence or growth of the power of the chief executive or the bureaucracy at the expense of legislative and judicial institutions; (*b*) possession, gaining, or nonsharing of substantial power by the upper levels of an administrative hierarchy within the capital; or (*c*) an expanded or expanding role for the "central" specialized agencies for personnel, purchasing, and budgeting, at the expense of the program-administering executive departments.

Specialized terms. Even within the administrative sphere a single term is needed that will encompass and distinguish between situations where a program's administration is subdivided either functionally at the capital or areally in the field. Both approaches relate to a single concept: the delegation of power to a lower hierarchical level. Solutions for this terminological problem vary, from use of abbreviated symbols (Maass 1959, pp. 9–26, where *adp* and *cdp* refer to areal and capital division of powers) to choice of "decentralization" as the most inclusive term, with territorial and nonterritorial specified as types (Macmahon 1961, chapter 2; Waline [1944] 1963, part II, chapter 3).

In French usage *décentralisation* is a term reserved for the transfer of powers from a central government to an areally or functionally specialized authority of distinct legal personality (for example, the increase of the degree of autonomy of a local government or of a public-enterprise corporation). *Déconcentration*, on the other hand, is the French equivalent for "administrative decentralization" within a single government's hierarchy (Waline 1944). Efforts to obtain general acceptance of this neat distinction have been unsuccessful (Meyer 1957, pp. 56–61; United Nations 1962, p. 3; Maddick 1963, p. 23).

In both England and the United States "decentralization" is the generic term and as such even has some currency in France. Adjectives such as "administrative," "political," and "governmental" serve to specify narrower usage, whereas "federalism," "local self-government," and "intergovernmental relations" are alternative terms for special purposes. "Devolution," used by English, but rarely by American, scholars, generally is equal to the French *décentralisation* but occasionally embraces *déconcentration* as well.

Field administration. A government's or agency's administrative operations outside its national headquarters usually have a neutral designation. In the United States, "field administration" is the term, and the staff involved in such operations is the "field service." This appears a convenient usage but is not standard internationally. In England, "local and regional organization" is the term, sometimes preceded by "central" to distinguish it from local government proper. In France, the prefectoral system refers to the national government's field administration system, and the individual ministries' field services are identified as *services extérieurs*.

The centralization–decentralization continuum. Centralization and decentralization are best regarded as opposite tendencies on a single continuum whose poles are beyond the range of any real political system. Total decentralization would require the withering away of the state, whereas total centralization would imperil the state's capacity to perform its functions. It should be possible to compare individual political or administrative systems by noting their relative positions on the continuum. It should also be possible to characterize any single political or administrative system, over a given time period, as moving toward one or the other pole. Either of these possibilities would entail the use of relative terms like "more" and "less" in lieu of adherence to the popular dichotomous characterization of systems as "centralized" or "decentralized." Even the use of the last two terms would acquire scientific utility if one could specify a base point or segment in the middle range of the continuum, with centralist tendencies prevailing on one side and decentralist tendencies prevailing on the other.

Scientific discussion is handicapped by the lack of a single term for the phenomenon being examined: centralization–decentralization. To have a single objective term for the whole continuum or a third term designating its balanced middle range would have obvious advantages. Less obvious are the full consequences of this lack. Neither centralization nor decentralization is a neutral term; instead, each is freighted with value connotations. In England and the United States, centralization is seldom treated as good in itself or as the bearer of other goods; it is condemned *ab initio*, or is accepted reluctantly as a practical necessity, or is explained as the chance aggregate of a number of individually justifiable programmatic decisions. Decentral-

ization, on the other hand, is commonly advocated as a precondition for the achievement and preservation of the basic values of a free society. These prima-facie valuations of the alternatives are encountered more frequently in popular than in scholarly usage, and the decentralist bias is greater with respect to intergovernmental distribution of power than with respect to administrative arrangements within a single government. In France, jurisprudence and history both support a doctrine of the unity of the state and so contribute a centralist bias, although there has also been an eloquent literature of protest that pleads for regionalism, restoration of the ancient provinces, and greater local self-government.

History

For several millenniums administration was not consciously differentiated from other aspects of governance, either at the capital or in the provinces. Nonetheless, essentially administrative tasks required performance: maintenance of law and order, assessment and collection of revenues, raising of armies, construction of public works. In most states other than city-states, this required the stationing of central officials in the provinces. Their administrative functions were intermixed with military command (although more in the border provinces than in the interior), adjudication of disputes, an almost viceregal representation of the majesty and power of the distant ruler, and reporting of political intelligence to the capital.

Substantial powers had to be delegated to provincial governors, given the primitive state of communications, if the people and resources of a large nation or empire were to be effectively controlled and exploited. Yet such decentralization in itself involved risks for the stability of the state and the retention of power by its current rulers.

A variety of measures were adopted by prudent rulers to ensure the loyalty of their field officials. Among the more common were: initial choice of trusted central officials for field posts, frequent recall to the capital for renewal of loyalty, periodic rotation of field officials among provinces, dispatch of investigators from the central court to tour the provinces and report back or take remedial action on the spot, fragmentation of the provincial administration among parallel officials with independent avenues of communication to the capital, provision for appeals by aggrieved citizens, and, of course, rigorous penalties for disobedience.

Effectiveness and even merely formal maintenance of such controls, however, depended on the vigor of the ruler and his central officials and upon the varying pattern of power distribution in the society. Often the distributive pattern, being based on landholding or traditional local hierarchies, had a strongly geographic character, and neither the ruler nor his agent in the province could impose national will on the local magnate. The nation's principal magnates collectively might dominate the king's counsels and individually might claim the right to be the ruler's agents in their provinces.

Alternatively, the king's own field agents might use their decentralized authority to increase their private resources, including land, until they themselves became local magnates resistant to royal direction. This development was more likely when field posts were "farmed" (that is, granted to the highest bidder), and therefore exploited by the holder for private profit, or when compensation for service in such posts was by royal grants of land or its usufruct. These adverse features were reinforced whenever heritability of such profitable posts was successfully asserted.

The breakdown of royal authority, as in the Frankish kingdom before and after Charlemagne, and the growth of feudalism were in significant degree consequent on the privatization of the system of royal field administration. Conversely, the development of royal power and of the modern nation-state depended heavily on institution of a loyal and effective system of royal field administration (Fesler 1962a). This, in turn, rested on a growth of royal revenues and institution of the principle of a salaried civil service.

Historically, administrative centralization has often been associated with the growth of royal absolutism, with expansion of bureaucracy, and with impairment of local self-government. This association, however, is not invariable nor does it exhaust the relational patterns. It can be argued, for example, that a condition precedent for national democracies and constitutional governments was the existence of a national bureaucracy capable of carrying into effect whatever decisions might be made at the capital (Friedrich [1937] 1950, chapter 2). An even earlier necessary condition was the differentiation of public administration from private household or estate administration, a distinction that was advanced by a centrally controlled but far-flung bureaucracy administering public affairs over both the king's and the great lords' proprietary domains. Finally, local self-government often had been a parochial autocracy or oligarchy, rather than a democracy; displacement of self-serving local magnates and their agents by royal officials might have had a liberalizing effect for the people of the area.

Administrative centralization facilitates the operation of a central will and interest, as against the variety of wills and interests that are dominant in a variety of local areas. The substance of each set of interests and wills is the determinant of virtue or vice in administrative centralization. This substance, of course, may itself be consequent on procedures at the capital and these, history demonstrates, may facilitate one-man rule, oligarchy, or democracy. They may also vary in their accommodating of regional and local interests and wills, whether by territorial representation in the central legislature or conciliar body, by adaptation of laws to different local conditions, or by imposition of democratizing procedures on local governments.

Centralization and decentralization are apparently associated with historical stages of national integration, but the nature of the association has some ambiguities. A politically developing nation typically needs to emphasize integration in order to overcome parochial loyalties that threaten the breakup of the nation. National rulers' thrusts therefore tend to be centralist. But the geographically fragmented power situation often requires deference to holders of local power, which introduces a decentralist thrust. The successful balancing of these contrary impulses, with partial indulgence of the latter being used to build consent for the former, is often the essence of nation building. On the other hand, a politically developed nation, in which national loyalties are secure and a substantial social consensus prevails, is able to afford a governmental and administrative system that includes a number of formally decentralist arrangements. In one sense, however, this means that formal decentralization is possible only because there already exists a fundamental social centralization—in the fact of the people's national identification, widely shared values, and internalized restraints on highly parochial and norm-challenging actions.

Analysis

Delegation of power. Administrative decentralization of power is delegation of power in a geographic setting (except where power is already so diffused that mere continuance of the status quo is in itself decentralization). Accordingly, most of the doctrinal and pragmatic aspects of delegation are relevant. In doctrinal terms, since one may delegate or not delegate a particular portion of one's power, one can attach such conditions to the use of delegated power by the agent as one chooses; and one can even repossess delegated power. In pragmatic terms, however, power can escape one's grasp once it is delegated and the agent develops alliances with administrative, political, and economic groups that prefer the agent's decisional orientation to that of his principal. Both doctrinal and pragmatic considerations incline the careful delegator to specify the conditions governing the use of the delegated power, to establish informational procedures that permit his auditing of the performance of his agents, and to retain and apply sanctions for disapproved behavior [see DELEGATION OF POWERS].

The known hazards accompanying delegation of power are commonly deterrents to decentralization. A central official who bears legal and political responsibility for errors in administration of a program will hesitate to delegate portions of his power to local government officials or field agents whose integrity and competence are uncertain. In an elaborate bureaucracy the hesitancy is reinforced by members of the central staff organized in functionally specialized bureaus. Usually the degree of specialization at headquarters cannot be matched by local governments or field offices, and delegation to local and field generalists therefore sacrifices an important component of competence. It also attenuates the bureaus' direct responsibility for their portions of the national program. This is true because local agents will predictably adjust priorities of effort among program elements in response to heavy work loads, in pursuance of the obligation to adapt the program to the local area's particular needs, and perhaps in expression of their personal preferences.

Pseudo decentralization.   Decentralization of work load, however, is not identical with decentralization of administrative power. To move work load out of the capital may be efficient and convenient for the public and may even promote a feeling that government is close to the people. But it may not involve any decentralization of power, that is, it may not provide the opportunity to exercise substantial local discretion in decision making. The illusion of decentralization is partly the consequence of ease of quantitative measurement of work load (for example, volume of paperwork handled or number of employees needed for the work load), in contrast to the identification and application of indexes of discretionary power. The illusion is also made plausible by the difference between trying to administer everything by correspondence from the capital and administering by face-to-face contact between field official and citizen.

A large work load in the field, relative to that in the capital, may misrepresent the locus of decision making. This is true if most decisions on individual cases are made at the capital, even though field offices receive citizens' requests for decisions and gather, arrange, and perhaps analyze the data needed for decision making and, after the papers have moved to the capital and back, communicate the central decisions to the citizens concerned. The locus is also misrepresented, even though a large number of decisions are made by field officials, if the criteria to guide local decision making are prescribed so precisely and comprehensively that field officials can only perform the clerical operation of matching the characteristics of each decisional case against detailed rule-book prescriptions.

Gross indicators of decentralization of work load may provide broad hints as to whether some power has actually been decentralized. Thus, if there are no national field agents, the inference is reasonable that there is no administrative decentralization (although there may be because of delegation to provincial and local governments or to geographically specific tribes and fiefdoms), and if nine out of ten national civil servants are stationed in the field (as in the U.S. government), a plausible assumption is that some decentralization of power exists. However, even a very large ratio of field personnel to central personnel is not necessarily a useful index of *true* decentralization. Such ratios are often largest for the activities with the most centralized decision making, for example, the postal service.

Role of local and intermediate governments.   A national government must have contact with the people throughout the political community, even if only for tax collection, raising of armies, and maintenance of law and order [see LOCAL GOVERNMENT]. This can be either (*a*) indirect contact through feudal lords, tribal chiefs, or intermediate and local governments or (*b*) direct contact through direct agents of the national government itself.

Significantly, nation building has typically required the paralleling or supersedure of feudal lords and tribal chiefs by a corps of agents of the national government. The case is less clear with intermediate governments. In the second German *Reich* and in the Weimar and Bonn republics, the administration of national laws was largely entrusted to the governments of the constituent *Länder* (Jacob 1963). A somewhat similar arrangement under the American Articles of Confederation proved dysfunctional and was abandoned in the constitution. Political harmony between national and state governments facilitates the articulation of administration by the states with the goals of the national government (for example, development planning in India, where the Congress party has controlled both national and state governments).

Maintenance or extension of decentralization to intermediate and local governments is often the purpose of national grants-in-aid. Similar decentralist intentions are attributed to state grants-in-aid to local governments. But their effect may also be centralist. Conditional grants-in-aid, for example, often provide leverage for national influence on policies and administration of state governments in fields constitutionally or traditionally their own. State governments' grants-in-aid to local governments tend to freeze the existential and areal pattern of such governments, with the weaker and smaller ones surviving with state funds instead of consolidating to form viable units and areas for vigorous local self-government.

The tendency of national–state and state–local decentralization programs to be functionally specialized establishes or reinforces a vertical alliance among the departments at several levels when these departments are concerned with the same subject matter. This vertical alliance may come to be stronger than an agency's horizontal identification with the "family" of agencies, concerned with a variety of subject matters, that constitute the whole executive branch of a government at a particular level and for a particular area. Responsiveness to centralized functional forces may thus subvert responsiveness to the chief executive, the legislature, and the political community of the area, although preservation of their roles may be essential to political as well as administrative decentralization (U.S. Congress 1963, *The Federal System* . . .).

The degree to which a country's administrative system is centralized or decentralized is more readily gauged when the system has two, rather than three, tiers of government. The paired relations in a three-tier system are national–state, state–local, and national–local (and even state–state and local–local relations, when they involve voluntary surrender of some powers to a joint authority). In any of these paired relations, the centralist or decentralist forces may predominate, and consistency in this respect among the pairs is not assured. Consequently, the same state government that complains of inadequate decentralization by the national government may be attacked by local governments for centralization at the state

capital. And failure of state governments to use their powers to meet the needs of cities may create a vacuum that the national government is urged by city governments to occupy, resulting in direct national–local relations.

Intragovernmental decentralization. A government that wishes to administer directly through its agents, rather than through intermediate or local governments, operates through a field service. Two basic patterns of field services exist: the prefectoral and the functional. Each has a number of variations, and a combination of the two is common.

In a prefectoral system, such as that established by Napoleon, the national government divides the country into areas and places a prefect in charge of each. The prefect represents the whole government, and all specialized field agents in the area are under his supervision. The several ministries either directly or through a central agency issue instructions to the prefect, who then instructs his specialized subordinates, after adapting his instructions to the conditions of his area. Similarly, communications upward to the ministries flow through the prefect. Although it is convenient to refer to this as a prefectoral system, it had many precedents before Napoleon, both in Europe and in ancient empires. It has been widely adopted in recent times and has been the dominant pattern in colonial administration.

In a functional field service, such as that of the United States or the United Kingdom, each ministry (and sometimes many a bureau within ministries) establishes its own field arrangements, dividing the country into areas deemed suitable for the particular function and assigning its own staff members as field agents and directly supervising their work. No provision is made for a general representative of the government, such as a prefect, to supervise the totality of national activities in an area. In periods of national emergency an area coordinator, vested with coordinating powers, may be temporarily provided for; and both in such periods and in less critical times, committees and other devices may be instituted to promote cooperation in an area among ministries' agents on matters of common interest.

The two systems respectively emphasize area and function as the basis of field organization. Yet, because strong claims can be made for each of these bases, neither system is free of challenges to its purity of form. The prefectoral system seems to maintain its purity most successfully when serving an authoritarian order, as when a colonial power is imposing its rule on an alien population, a national elite is assuring its control of the mass of the people, or a national government confronts overt or latent dissidence in the local elites and general citizenry. Historically, it is associated with performance of a few functions that are critically important to stability of the regime: maintenance of law and order, collection of revenue, supervision of local governments, and appraisal of local opinion.

The functional system of field administration maintains its purity most successfully when governmental functions are numerous and burdensome, when they require specialized training for their performance, and, of course, when consensus is sufficiently high to make law and order and the collection of revenue ordinary, rather than critical, functions. The multiplication of governmental functions not only creates a case for specialized competence but also adds to the work load in the field so that channeling the work load through a single official in an area becomes impractical.

The purity of each system, however, is constantly threatened. The present-day prefectoral system in France conforms poorly to orthodox doctrine. Functional ministries insist on bypassing the prefect and even establish geographical areas not conforming to the prefects' areal *départements* (Diamant 1954). In 1964 the de Gaulle government designated 20 regional prefects and gave them authority over most, but not all, central ministries' field representatives having areal jurisdictions larger than *départements*. In developing countries the prefectoral systems inherited from French and British colonial regimes have been modified, partly because their orientation to law-and-order functions was poorly adapted to the functions of social and economic development.

In the American and British systems the claim of each function to a distinctive field service is generally allowed only for organization units at the ministry and bureau levels of the central hierarchy. Even so, area–function conflicts arise within individual ministries; the minister is likely to press for ministry-wide coordination in each field area, and the bureaus resist the subordination of "their" field agents to the coordinative role of a regional director for the whole ministry. The conflict is repeated in many settings, for example, in city health departments, whose specialized bureaus often oppose and sabotage district health centers that combine all specialized services under a prefectoral-type director (Kaufman 1963).

Mixed systems are common. The dual-supervision formula prescribes that a specialized field agent is administratively responsible to the generalized field director (for example, prefect or regional director) but technically responsible to his specialized counterpart bureau at headquarters (Macmahon et al. 1941, pp. 265 ff.; Millett 1945; Macmahon 1961, pp. 28–31, 39–42). The dividing line between administrative and technical, however, is difficult to draw and, once drawn, hard to maintain (Axinn 1957). Another formula is to maintain the functional system formally but to invest a coordinative area official with powers of persuasion only, in the hope that his personal qualities, the logic of the situation, and frequent committee meetings will build cooperation among field agents, whose functions should be mutually adjusted.

Intragovernmental decentralization, because it operates primarily through the bureaucracy, is often assumed to preclude participation by citizens and interest groups in decision making. In fact, such participation is often formally prescribed. In the United States some ninety thousand farmers serve on county and community committees of the Department of Agriculture, the selection of individuals for compulsory military service is made by local draft boards composed of citizens of the community, and important wartime economic controls have been administered by local price control and rationing boards and regional war labor boards. In France, prefects of both *départements* and regions have associated with them economic planning committees representing agricultural, commercial, industrial, and handicraft organizations, labor unions, and professional groups. In England, county and district agricultural executive committees (composed of farmers, landowners, farm workers, and others) serve the Ministry of Agriculture, Fisheries, and Food; and regional boards for industry, representative of employers' organizations and trade unions, serve under the national Board of Trade. Apart from formal provisions for representative bodies, national field agents are exposed to general and specific influences operative in their assigned areas and may consult extensively with spokesmen for local interests.

Extranational experience. Problems of administrative centralization and decentralization are not confined within national boundaries. Diplomatic and colonial services, programs of technical assistance, and international organizations encounter many of the same problems that are found in a nation's internal administration. The role of the ambassador involves questions of his scope of discretionary authority, the extent of his authority over other agents of his government who are stationed in the foreign country to which he is assigned, and the danger of his becoming too sympathetic to the interests of the foreign country to serve effectively his own nation's interests.

Imperial powers encounter critical problems in colonial administration. Although the prefectoral pattern prevailed generally, the British adopted a policy of "indirect rule," permitting large tribes and tribal federations to be self-governing under stated or implied conditions, and moved toward a "team" concept of district administration in lieu of the prefectoral concept.

The United Nations system confronts the problems of centralization and decentralization under peculiarly difficult circumstances. The fact that the several specialized agencies operate quasi-autonomously has naturally led to establishment of distinct field services throughout the world, with regional offices and, in some cases, country offices. Degrees of decentralization among these agencies vary: the World Health Organization appears to go furthest, vesting substantial program-deciding powers in regional committees aided by its regional offices; the United Nations Educational, Scientific, and Cultural Organization appears to be at the other extreme (Sharp 1961, p. 235).

Research trends and needs

Much of the best work on centralization and decentralization is of the monographic, case-study type, focused on a single country, agency, or substantive program. Almost none of the empirical experience recorded in these monographs and case studies has been synthesized. One result is that theoretical and prescriptive writing is rarely disciplined by clarification of the conditions under which various degrees and patterns of centralization and decentralization tend to occur, to have particular consequences, and to evolve toward other degrees and patterns. A further characteristic of the work on centralization and decentralization is the distinctness of several literatures, the result of which is that the relevancy of each to the others is largely neglected. The literature on any one country rarely draws on the descriptive and theoretical contributions made by other countries' political scientists and official commissions of inquiry. In addition, there is little mutual enrichment effected among the studies on the ambassador's role, the technical assistance mission's role, and the role of regional directors within a national field-administration system. For instance, the colonial-administration and French literatures are not brought together to explain the prevalence of the prefectoral pattern in both France and colonial areas; and the work on the currently developing countries and on the emergence of modern states in Europe is not correlated to clarify processes of national integration.

The literature on administrative centralization and decentralization has, in general, isolated a group of well-defined problems, and its cumulative impact establishes the similarity of these problems among countries and in different historical periods. Emphasis, however, has been placed preponderantly on problems within the governmental bureaucratic system and rarely with attention to how these problems are met within other large organizations, such as business corporations and church hierarchies. Except in France, few studies have been made of the origins and personal characteristics of field administrators or of their actual behavior when subjected to conflicting national and local influences. Political scientists have only recently given substantial attention to noncontemporary field-administration systems and to the dynamics of development through time (Fesler 1962*b*; Fried 1963; Jacob 1963), although professional historians of institutions have furnished a rich body of descriptive information from the Chinese, Roman, and Byzantine empires to the modern period. Many monographic studies, and some general treatments, have been narrowly administrative, neglecting the interplay between administration and other elements of the political system and of society itself—despite the fact that in many political systems the centralist or decentralist character of administration is explicable primarily as a reflection of, or counterweight to, the centralist or decentralist tendencies of the non-administrative portions of the political and social system.

The state of the literature may be summarized as follows: The large aggregate of descriptive and analytical studies has succeeded in identifying most of the problems relevant to administrative centralization and decentralization, but recorded empirical experience has not yet been ordered in such a way as to specify conditions under which particular responses to those problems are most appropriate. As such an ordering is attempted, gaps will be discovered in knowledge of important variables, and these may then be subjected to specifically focused research. Among the probable focuses are the origins, training, and behavior of field administrators; the dynamics of a field system's evolution over time; and the interplay between administration and other portions of the political and social systems. The development of empirically based theory will also require the drawing together of separate literatures on different settings of twentieth-century governmental experience, on the experience of earlier centuries, and on business and ecclesiastical administration.

A guide to research materials

A large number of contributions to the study of administrative centralization and decentralization are intermixed with treatments of federalism, local government, the region, and diplomacy.

Few cross-national studies have been made. The most useful are focused on developing countries (Maddick 1963; United Nations 1962). Cowan (1958) compares French and British local colonial administration in west Africa and the changes in the period since independence. Macmahon (1961), Meyer (1957), and Fesler (1949; 1962b) undertake general analyses of recurrent problems in administrative centralization and decentralization.

Individual countries' systems of administrative centralization and decentralization are extensively described and analyzed, both by scholars and by official bodies. The *International Review of Administrative Sciences* occasionally carries articles on particular systems. Annex III of the United Nations report (1962, pp. 133–243) gives separate descriptions of patterns of decentralization in 12 countries, including those of several "developed" countries. Descriptive information on provincial administration in 43 countries is included in Humes and Martin (1961). Particularly valuable are the numerous papers presented at the Sixth World Congress of the International Political Science Association (International Political Science Association 1964).

The French prefectoral system has probably a larger literature than any other system. The most helpful volume in English, with an extensive bibliography, is by Chapman (1955), and a useful historical and biographical account is given in French by Pierre Henry (1950). The journal *La revue administrative* contains relevant documentation and articles. The contrasting Italian prefectoral system's development and characteristic features are well set forth by Fried (1963).

For England, particularly, scholarly descriptions and analyses of decentralization are principally to be found in the abundant publications about local government. However, the English system of field administration is well, although briefly, described and a bibliography is provided in Mackenzie and Grove (1957, pp. 260–280) and more extensively in the earlier work by Dhonau (1938). A number of official reports have been illuminating; they are usually noted in the journal *Public Administration*.

A substantial literature in field administration in the United States has accumulated (see bibliographical references in Fesler [1946] 1959). Fresh approaches have been initiated by Axinn (1957), Freeman (1962), Gore (1956), and Kaufman (1960), who use empirical methodology to explore the interplay between organizational and local influences. Among the subject matter settings of decentralization, the ones attracting the greatest scholarly attention have been natural resources development and agricultural services and regulation. Intergovernmental administrative relations have been fully documented and analyzed by official bodies, with greatest attention being given to the grants-in-aid system. A good account of Germany's administrative adjustments to federalism, strongly contrasting with those of the United States, can be found in Jacob (1963).

Decentralization has been recently emphasized in the U.S.S.R., Yugoslavia, and eastern Europe generally, but scholarly analysis of its current impact and ultimate consequences has been highly tentative. This stems largely from insufficiency of data for judging the decentralization program's degree of harmonization with such centralist orientations as are implied by ideological conformity, one-party rule, and national economic planning.

Asian and African experience, both under colonial regimes and after independence, has been much studied, with the focus on the district officer (or comparable field agent) and on local government. The *Indian Journal of Public Administration* and the *Journal of African Administration* are especially valuable, giving much attention to methods and problems of administrative decentralization. Maddick (1963) provides a substantial bibliography for Asian and African nations.

The United Nations' arrangements and difficulties in field administration are comprehensively described in Sharp (1961), and the relevant problems encountered by both the United Nations and the United States in their technical assistance programs in Latin America are discerningly portrayed by Glick (1957). The role of the United States ambassador as a field agent has been touched on by a succession of official and quasi-official inquiries. One admirably conceived and documented study is that conducted by a subcommittee under the chairmanship of Senator Henry Jackson (U.S. Congress 1963–1964, *Administration of National Security . . .*).

JAMES W. FESLER

[*See also* ADMINISTRATION; FEDERALISM; GOVERNMENT; MODERNIZATION; NATION; POLITICAL PROCESS.]

BIBLIOGRAPHY

AXINN, GEORGE H. 1957 The Milieu Theory of Control. *Public Administration Review* 17:97–105.

BENSON, GEORGE C. S. 1941 *The New Centralization: A Study of Intergovernmental Relationships in the United States.* New York: Farrar & Rinehart.

CHAPMAN, BRIAN 1955 *The Prefects and Provincial France.* London: Allen & Unwin.

COWAN, L. GRAY 1958 *Local Government in West Africa.* New York: Columbia Univ. Press.

DHONAU, MAY L. 1938 *Decentralisation in Government Departments.* London: Institute of Public Administration.

DIAMANT, ALFRED C. 1954 The Department, the Prefect, and Dual Supervision in French Administration: A Comparative Study. *Journal of Politics* 16:472–490.

FESLER, JAMES W. (1946) 1959 Field Organization. Pages 246–273 in Fritz Morstein Marx (editor), *Elements of Public Administration.* 2d ed. Englewood Cliffs, N.J.: Prentice-Hall.

FESLER, JAMES W. (1949) 1964 *Area and Administration.* University: Univ. of Alabama Press.

FESLER, JAMES W. 1962a French Field Administration: The Beginnings. *Comparative Studies in Society and History* 5:76–111.

FESLER, JAMES W. 1962b The Political Role of Field Administration. Pages 117–143 in Ferrel Heady and Sybil L. Stokes (editors), *Papers in Comparative Public Administration.* Ann Arbor: Univ. of Michigan, Institute of Public Administration.

FREEMAN, J. LEIPER 1962 Some Characteristics of Field Officials in the Federal Civil Service. Pages 31–54 in Lynton K. Caldwell (editor), *Politics and Public Affairs.* Bloomington: Indiana Univ., Institute of Training for Public Service.

FRIED, ROBERT C. 1963 *The Italian Prefects: A Study in Administrative Politics.* Yale Studies in Political Science, Vol. 6. New Haven: Yale Univ. Press.

FRIEDRICH, CARL J. (1937) 1950 *Constitutional Government and Democracy.* Rev. ed. Boston: Ginn. → First published as *Constitutional Government and Politics.*

GLICK, PHILIP M. 1957 *The Administration of Technical Assistance: Growth in the Americas.* Univ. of Chicago Press.

GORE, WILLIAM J. 1956 Administrative Decision-making in Federal Field Offices. *Public Administration Review* 16:281–291.

HENRY, PIERRE 1950 *Histoire des préfets: Cent cinquante ans d'administration provinciale, 1800–1950.* Paris: Nouvelles Éditions Latines.

HUMES, SAMUEL; and MARTIN, EILEEN M. 1961 *The Structure of Local Government Throughout the World.* The Hague: Nijhoff.

INTERNATIONAL POLITICAL SCIENCE ASSOCIATION 1964 Papers on Decentralization Presented at the Sixth World Congress of the Association. Unpublished manuscript, International Political Science Association, Paris.

JACOB, HERBERT 1963 *German Administration Since Bismarck: Central Authority Versus Local Autonomy.* Yale Studies in Political Science, Vol. 5. New Haven: Yale Univ. Press.

KAUFMAN, HERBERT 1960 *The Forest Ranger: A Study in Administrative Behavior.* Baltimore: Johns Hopkins Press.

KAUFMAN, HERBERT 1963 The New York City Health Centers. Pages 609–628 in Inter-University Case Program, *State and Local Government: A Case Book.* University: Univ. of Alabama Press.

KHERA, SUCHA S. 1964 *District Administration in India.* New York: Asia Publishing House.

MAASS, ARTHUR (editor) 1959 *Area and Power: A Theory of Local Government.* Glencoe, Ill.: Free Press.

MACKENZIE, WILLIAM J. M.; and GROVE, J. W. 1957 *Central Administration in Britain.* London and New York: Longmans.

McKINLEY, CHARLES 1952 *Uncle Sam in the Pacific Northwest.* Berkeley and Los Angeles: Univ. of California Press.

MACMAHON, ARTHUR W. 1961 *Delegation and Autonomy.* New York: Asia Publishing House.

MACMAHON, ARTHUR W.; MILLETT, J. D.; and OGDEN, GLADYS 1941 *The Administration of Federal Work Relief.* Chicago: Public Administration.

MADDICK, HENRY 1963 *Democracy, Decentralisation and Development.* London and New York: Asia Publishing House.

MEYER, PAUL 1957 *Administrative Organization: A Comparative Study of the Organization of Public Administration.* London: Stevens.

MILLETT, JOHN D. 1945 Field Organization and Staff Supervision. Pages 96–118 in *New Horizons in Public Administration: A Symposium.* University: Univ. of Alabama Press.

REDFORD, EMMETTE S. 1947 *Field Administration of Wartime Rationing.* Washington: Government Printing Office.

RICHARDS, ALLAN R. 1953 *War Labor Boards in the Field.* The James Sprunt Studies in History and Political Science, Vol. 35. Chapel Hill: Univ. of North Carolina Press.

ROBERTS, J. L. (editor) (1961) 1963 *Decentralization in New Zealand Government Administration.* Studies in Public Administration, No. 7. Oxford Univ. Press.

SHARP, WALTER R. 1961 *Field Administration in the United Nations System: The Conduct of International Economic and Social Programs.* New York: Praeger.

TRUMAN, DAVID B. 1940 *Administrative Decentralization: A Study of the Chicago Field Offices of the United States Department of Agriculture.* Univ. of Chicago Press.

UNITED NATIONS, DIVISION FOR PUBLIC ADMINISTRATION 1962 *Decentralization for National and Local Development.* New York: United Nations.

U.S. ADVISORY COMMISSION ON INTERGOVERNMENTAL RELATIONS 1961— *Reports.* Washington: Government Printing Office.

U.S. COMMISSION ON INTERGOVERNMENTAL RELATIONS 1955 *Final Report.* Washington: Government Printing Office. → See also the study committee, subcommittee, and staff reports.

U.S. CONGRESS, SENATE COMMITTEE ON GOVERNMENT OPERATIONS 1963 *The Federal System as Seen by State and Local Officials: Results of a Questionnaire Dealing With Intergovernmental Relations.* A study prepared by the staff of the Subcommittee on Intergovernmental Relations of the Committee on Government Operations, U.S. Senate. Washington: Government Printing Office.

U.S. CONGRESS, SENATE COMMITTEE ON GOVERNMENT OPERATIONS 1963–1964 *Administration of National Security: Hearings Before the Subcommittee on National Security Staffing and Operations.* 88th Congress, 1st and 2d sessions. Washington: Government Printing Office. → See also other hearings, investigations and studies, and reports of the committee.

U.S. CONGRESS, SENATE COMMITTEE ON GOVERNMENT OPERATIONS 1964a *Administration of National Security; American Ambassador: Study Submitted by the*

Subcommittee on National Security Staffing and Operations. 88th Congress, 2d session. Washington: Government Printing Office.

U.S. CONGRESS, SENATE COMMITTEE ON GOVERNMENT OPERATIONS 1964*b* *Administration of National Security; Secretary of State: Study Submitted by the Subcommittee on National Security Staffing and Operations.* 88th Congress, 2d session. Washington: Government Printing Office.

WALINE, M. (1944) 1963 *Droit administratif.* 9th ed. Paris: Sirey.

CHANGE

See ATTITUDES, *article on* ATTITUDE CHANGE; CULTURE, *article on* CULTURE CHANGE; EVOLUTION; SOCIAL CHANGE.

CHARACTER

See CHARACTER DISORDERS; ETHICS; MORAL DEVELOPMENT; NATIONAL CHARACTER; PERSONALITY; PSYCHOPATHIC PERSONALITY; TRAITS.

CHARACTER DISORDERS

The diagnosis of character disorder is accepted generally as describing an individual whose behavior disturbances bring him into conflict with his immediate environment or society at large. Although a character disorder has certain similarities to a neurosis, it differs in the particular extent to which the disorder affects a person's entire behavior. The neurotic individual has a specific symptom, arising from internalized conflict and felt as alien and uncomfortable. The individual with a character disorder has a much more pervasive disturbance; most or all of his behavior and his responses are directed by the disorder, but he does not feel this as either pathological or uncomfortable. He is unaware that his way of coping with life is actually symptomatic of his conflicts, which are consistently externalized.

The range of aggressive and antisocial behavior patterns that sociologists designate as social problems—for example, juvenile delinquency, drug addiction, criminal recidivism—involve the actions of individuals who would be diagnosed by psychiatrists as having character disorders. The cost to society of these forms of illness is obvious, but there are other types of character disorder that tax society in much more subtle ways. The costs may lie in disturbed marital relationships; in difficult, if not disruptive, behavior in work situations; in the general inhibition of an individual's real capacities; and even in influence on the political attitudes and action of the individual.

The steady increase of character disorders in the general population has been recognized as a matter of concern to sociology as well as to the behavioral sciences, and the contributions of both may be needed to provide us with an accurate view of the etiology of these emotional disturbances.

Psychoanalytic theory of character structure

Any understanding of character disorders requires some background in the evolution of contemporary theories of character structure. In the United States, these theories are grounded primarily in Freudian concepts. The concepts of psychoanalytic theory originally were used to explain neurotic behavior and were not applied explicitly to the total picture of character structure; but as the theory later developed the term "character" began to be employed more frequently, and the literature began to refer to character traits, type, and structure; character neuroses; neurotic character; and character disorders.

Freud's earliest conceptions about character formation (see *The Interpretation of Dreams* and *Three Essays on the Theory of Sexuality*) were based on libido theory, with its emphasis on psychobiological factors, and proposed a classification of character in terms of the erogenous zones: oral, anal, phallic, and genital. In its later evolution, psychoanalytic theory employed the structural, libidinal concept of personality, in which the determining agencies were the id, the ego, and the superego. Freud viewed character as being an attribute of the ego, with the superego the most decisive element in its development.

But not until Wilhelm Reich's work (1925) did psychoanalytic theory and practice focus specifically on the problem of character. Reich, departing from Freud's psychobiological determinism, emphasized the influence of the social order on character formation, defining character structure as "the crystallization of the sociological processes of a given epoch."

Contemporary theories of character development tend to stress one of two directions. The first, begun by Freud and elaborated by the psychoanalysts who emphasized ego aspects, stems from Freud's instinctual drive theory. Karl Abraham, Isador Coriat, Sándor Ferenczi, Anna Freud (whose brilliant work on the defense mechanisms introduced a new dimension for the theoretical understanding and treatment of character disorders), Erik Erikson, Heinz Hartmann, Ernest Jones, Annie Reich, and Richard Sterba expanded this theory. The second was developed by the neo-Freudians—Erich Fromm, Karen Horney, Abram Kardiner, and Harry Stack Sullivan—and stresses the role of cultural factors rather than of instinctual roots in character formation.

Despite disagreements among schools, Gitelson's definition of character (1963, p. 4) as "an adaptive synthesis of forces stemming from the biological givens, the quality of the infantile environment, the psychic structure, the character of the identifications, and the mores of the social group in which later maturation and development occurs" would probably be acceptable to most behavioral scientists, who would agree with Gitelson that character "is an action and reaction pattern which has crystallized out of this flux of factors." Lustman, who views character as a dynamic process, a constantly evolving phenomenon throughout life, described the relationship between defense, symptom, and character and concluded that all symptomatic acts have intimately related characterological structures (1962). These are the relationships that must be understood in the character disorders.

Character types—whether those designated by Freud as the erotic, the obsessional, and the narcissistic, or, for example, those designated by Horney as the aggressive neurotic character, the detached character, the character with idealized self-image, and the character who externalizes—do not occur in pure form. The relatively arbitrary labels various disciplines and schools use to classify types refer to the traits that seem most prominent and powerful in influencing behavior, although each type would include mixtures from the others.

Types of character disorders

In the extensive psychoanalytic literature on the character disorders, the types are described in terms of the neuroses with which each is most closely allied, whether they be the hysterical (erotic), the compulsive (anal), or the narcissistic (oral). But, as in character typology, each type actually contains an admixture of responses that would have to be classified in the other categories.

The hysterical character. For reasons that are probably largely cultural, the hysterical character is found more frequently among women than men. In terms of behavior patterns, one finds in this type a tendency to coquetry in walk, expression, and speech; a general sexualizing of relationships in inappropriate situations; and often a pattern of frequent and unsuccessful sexual relationships. Other traits—lability of emotion, unexpected dramatic behavior, strong suggestibility, a tendency to represent fantasy as fact—are more concealed. In pure form, the hysterical character is nervous, agile, and lively. When the type appears with depressive, autistic, and retiring features, it is no longer specifically hysterical.

Psychoanalytic theory postulates that the hysterical character develops out of an unresolved Oedipus complex. The "normal" person, having successfully resolved the Oedipus complex and given up the wish for incest and the wish to eliminate the father (mother), is free to transfer his genital interests to a heterosexual object that has taken the place of the incest object. For the hysterical character, the heterosexual object merely represents the incest object. Frequent affairs, then, symbolize both the incest wish and the attempt to escape the anxiety it creates. In the depressive type of hysterical character, the genital–incestuous fixation is replaced to some extent by a regression to oral mechanisms [*see* HYSTERIA].

The compulsive character. Frugality, orderliness, and obstinacy, all of which were considered by Freud to be anal traits, are strongly intensified in the compulsive character. When the infant's toilet training is severe and rigid, the child may overcomply with this demand from his parents to master his instinctual drives. Orderliness, punctuality, and propriety, for example, are reaction formations of obedience; when these reaction formations break down, as they frequently do, an orderly person may become surprisingly disorderly. Frugality may represent a continuation of anal retention, motivated either by erogenous pleasure or by fear of loss. Stubbornness or obstinacy is often a rebellion against those early environmental demands, carried over into adult life, or else a method of resorting to passive aggression to attain one's way against superior forces.

Whereas the hysterical character constantly seeks to repeat the Oedipal incest wish, the compulsive individual copes with the unresolved Oedipus complex by maintaining rigidly the incest prohibition, producing a marked conflict between id and superego. This conflict results in the repression of aggressive and sexual impulses. The repressions may lead to the substitution of sadistic impulses, which are often converted into a harsh morality.

Underlying such obvious behavioral symptoms as compulsive orderliness or rigid obstinacy are marked feelings of impotence, against which the compulsive individual may try to defend himself by unusual striving for social achievements. Because they do not in reality provide enough compensation, he is caught in a circular process of striving and feelings of inadequacy, inferiority, and emptiness.

Perhaps the most striking symptom in the compulsive character is the characteristic dissociation of ideas from affects. His defense mechanisms are extremely effective, but they produce a restrained, self-controlled, cautious individual, incapable of spontaneity. Internalizing the early outer demands for self-control so that they no longer concern merely the demand for cleanliness but invade every aspect of his functioning, the compulsive character develops a rigid, chronic, intractable mode of reaction [see OBSESSIVE–COMPULSIVE DISORDERS].

The narcissistic character. Narcissism is an oral trait, in which there is an emphasis on taking and giving, which is associated with the "nursing mother." The normal traits of generosity and altruism, for example, represent identification with the person by whom one wants to be fed. Curiosity, too, may actually be an oral trait representing hunger transposed to mental activity. Oral neurotic characters, then, have an insatiable desire for supplies from the external world for the satisfaction of immediate needs. This demand can be expressed in two patterns of behavior, which are at first glance antithetical—the neurotically "independent" character and the neurotically "dependent" one. Both suffer from oral deprivation as the original trauma. The independent character, however, having regained the security of primary narcissism, feels that "nothing can happen to him"; the second is forever attempting to obtain restitution for the original deprivation and searches outside for all gratifications. A not uncommon type in this group is the chameleon character, who seems to need to fulfill all the assumed expectations of others and probably has multiple and evanescent identifications.

Both the pessimistic (depressive) and the sadistic (redress-demanding) character types fall into the group of narcissistic disorders. Both attitudes actually express a demand that the world should take care of one, although the depressive expresses the demand passively while the sadistic personality resorts to active aggression.

The psychopathic character. In psychobiologic psychiatry, the term character disorder refers specifically to the psychopathic personality. In psychoanalysis, psychopathic personality refers to one of the entire group of character disorders. Juvenile delinquency and criminal recidivism, for example, are usually considered forms of psychopathic behavior. Yet psychopathic personality is one of the least exact diagnoses in psychiatry and psychoanalysis, with little consensus as to the dynamic processes involved in producing it or its behavior.

If Freud's classification were broadened to include a urethral type as an opposite of the anal type, the range of pathological character types would expand to include the impulsive as an opposite of the compulsive. The impulsive type is characterized by a deficiency or weakness in the superego, expressed somatically in persistent enuresis, and might well be correlated with psychopathy.

It was suggested by Michaels (1955) that such impulsive disorders be divided into two types: the first, the impulsive psychopathic character, would embrace the psychopathic personality, Edward Glover's impulsive type, and the impulse disorders described by John Frosch and Joseph Wortis; the second, the impulsive neurotic character, would include Wilhelm Reich's impulsive character, Franz Alexander's neurotic character, and Glover's reactive neurotic group. The impulsive psychopathic type would be the individual who tends to externalize his conflicts, with superego disturbances less serious than those in the psychotic but more impairing than those in the neurotic; the impulsive neurotic form tends to have internalized conflicts and neurotic mechanisms closer to the compulsive (obsessional) kind.

The severe juvenile delinquent (aggressive, hostile, and antisocial—the boy who lies, steals, and is persistently truant) shows perhaps the clearest form of impulsive psychopathic behavior. This kind of child drives for immediate satisfaction without regard for the rights or feelings of others; he is incapable of sustained interest or effort or of profiting from experience. Unable to bind tension, such individuals are impelled to impatient action.

Michaels (1959a) suggested that a specific type of impulsive psychopathic character presents a clinical syndrome in which the cluster of identifying traits are maleness, aggressiveness, persistent enuresis, concrete language, reading disabilities, and acting upon impulse (primary acting out). With the hypothesis that this kind of character has a unique configuration of personality with a special psychosomatic disposition, from the viewpoint of libido theory one can regard the emotional disability as impulsiveness, and from the viewpoint of ego–superego organization as lack of control. He is the actor, rather than the thinker, whose style of behavior is characteristically motoric and action oriented.

Michaels (1959a; 1959b) provides an elaboration of Freud's original description of acting out (1914).

If, as suggested in a previous study (Michaels 1955), persistent enuresis and juvenile delinquency be considered character disorders of a functional nature, then the most primitive form of the impulsive psychopathic character would be an immature, undifferentiated pre-Oedipal personality, with poor object relationships, faulty identifications, a high degree of narcissism, a strong tendency to repetition compulsion, little ability to bind tension or tolerate anxiety, little sublimation of impulses, and a lack of differentiation in the ego and superego. He would have few feelings of shame and guilt, a minimum of conflict, and primitive defense mechanisms.

In contrast, the impulsive neurotic character has dormant psychopathic tendencies, which are held in check by the compulsive neurotic components in his character. Unlike the psychopathic character who comes into conflict with legal authority because of aggressive and antisocial acts, which express his unambivalent hatred, the neurotic individual would be apt to create friction at home and in marriage, as well as on the job, and show a history of provoking hostile responses from the environment. This character type suffers from his problems, his doubts, his ambivalence, and his guilt. He is, in effect, the impulsive psychopath with more maturity, greater differentiation in the ego and superego, and a greater internalization of conflict, so that his aggressive hatred is bound and neutralized by defensive reaction formations.

Kaufman and his collaborators (Kaufman 1963), in their studies of character disorders in juvenile delinquents, found that impulsivity is associated with ego mechanisms designed to protect the personality from being overwhelmed by a mass of uncontrolled anxiety. Where one person might deal with anxiety by running away from the situation that causes it, the juvenile delinquent acts impulsively, in denial of the anxiety. Much of the research indicates that these children are coping with separation anxiety or annihilation anxiety rather than castration anxiety.

Other character disorders.   More severe character disorders, which are related to borderline psychoses, have been described in children—particularly in autistic children, atypical children, symbiotic children, and children with ego variations.

Frosch (see Ross 1960) describes the psychotic character disorder—which is markedly different from the neurotic character disorder—in which there are disturbances in the relationship to reality, in the sense of reality, and in the capacity to test reality. The symptoms may resemble the process of an actual psychosis, but they are usually transient and reversible. Within the category of psy-chotic character disorders are such conditions as borderline states, ambulatory schizophrenia, and "pseudoneurotic" schizophrenia. Whatever the etiology of these conditions, they require specialized treatment because their severity may make even minimal functioning difficult. The symptomatology of these disorders is sufficiently bizarre to be recognizable to laymen, unlike neurotic character problems, which are usually perceived as "normal" variations and condemned or approved within a framework of moral and ethical value judgments.

Biological and social aspects

Since character structure seems to involve a combination of biological, social, and psychological phenomena, the problem of developing an integrating theory is a difficult one. Many biological factors—such as sex; age; race; organic disease; and the influence of drugs, hormones, and body build—need to be better researched and understood. The pioneers in psychosomatic research have made a start in this direction by trying to delineate the personalities characteristic of specific disease syndromes. In social psychology, Schachter and Latané's provocative research (1964) on the relationship between psychopathy and adrenal functioning in the criminal recidivist indicates the myriad possibilities for research along physiological and biological lines.

Benjamin's observations of infancy and childhood have contributed significantly to unraveling the problem of constitution, predisposition, and innate endowment (1961). Similar observations have been made in five main areas: sensation, motility, variations in instinctual drives, autonomic nervous system patterns, and ego variations. Although a psychoanalytic theory of character formation should include analyses of defensive styles, ego functions, and the operation of the energy principles, as well as a clear understanding of developmental considerations, this kind of integrating theory has yet to be formulated.

The complex problem of juvenile delinquency and its causes and treatment is approached differently by psychiatrists, criminologists, sociologists, and the police. Impulsive psychopathic behavior in any form demands more immediate and dramatic attention from society than do the results of the other forms of character disorder and consequently most vividly demonstrates the multiple theoretical viewpoints pertaining to human behavior. A sufficiently broadened psychoanalytic theory, offering a general systematic psychology of personality, would be pragmatically useful to the other specialists who must cope with the direct social consequences of these illnesses. What we need is a general synthesizer who has a dynamic psychology of human nature and who is at home with the disciplines of biology, psychology, and sociology.

Sociological interest in the juvenile delinquent has centered on that aspect of his behavior that is expressed in antisocial actions. In fact, Talcott Parsons and Edward Shils utilize action as a main bulwark of their sociological theory. Psychiatry has put forth three philosophical approaches to the understanding of this kind of problem: the psychobiologic, the psychoanalytic, and the combined psychobiologic and psychoanalytic.

Shaw (1929) and his collaborators among the sociologists center their theories about juvenile delinquency on the effects of general social disorganization; Robert K. Merton stresses socially induced deviations; Harrison G. Gough offers a sociological theory of psychopathy; and Albert J. Reiss, Jr., applying a sociological approach that incorporates psychoanalytic psychology (in a rapprochement with the clinician), views delinquency as a consequence of the type of relationship established among personal and social controls.

If we consider the character disorders as reflecting a continuum of control, we can move from deficient capacity to control (impulsive psychopathy, delinquency) to a high capacity to control (compulsiveness, obsessive–compulsive neurosis). The concept of control offers a common meeting ground for the biologist, the psychologist, and the sociologist. What remain to be determined are the relative strengths of the biological, psychological, and social factors in determining the development of control.

Anna Freud (1963) reformulated a position on the complementariness of heredity and environment in normal children, postulating that there are constitutionally inherent lines of development, including the maturational sequences in the development of libido and aggression (id) and, although less well-known, certain innate tendencies toward organization, defense, and structurization (ego). Accidental environmental influences single out individual lines for special promotion in development. The clinical problems of the choice of an organ for a psychosomatic disturbance, somatic compliance, and the choice of the symptom and form of the neurosis are one set of unsolved problems. Character choice is a much more difficult problem because it involves the question of social compliance. Hartmann (1950), for example, stated that "a given social structure selects and makes

effective specific psychological tendencies and certain developmental trends." David Riesman states the same hypothesis sociologically.

Until an interdisciplinary collaboration produces a theory that permits a reasonably scientific understanding of the causation and dynamics of character problems, treatment will remain extremely difficult because it is expensive and prolonged in the cases of the character neuroses. Nonetheless, once an individual develops sufficient insight to recognize that he has a problem, psychoanalytic therapy can sometimes produce constructive change, almost an impossibility in the case of psychopathy, where psychoanalysis is ineffective because the potential patient is too free of conflict or guilt to be amenable to therapy. Sociology may design social reforms that lead to a decrease in the incidence of psychopathic development, but it cannot alone find the answers to help the individual psychopath once his character choice has been made. Only an integrated theory will make it possible to predict, prevent, and ameliorate the wide-ranging character disorders that afflict society.

JOSEPH J. MICHAELS

[*See also* PSYCHOPATHIC PERSONALITY. *Other relevant material may be found in* CRIME; DELINQUENCY; PSYCHOANALYSIS.]

BIBLIOGRAPHY

BENJAMIN, JOHN D. 1961 The Innate and the Experiential in Child Development. Pages 19–42 in Conference on Experimental Psychiatry, Western Psychiatric Institute and Clinic, 1959, *Lectures on Experimental Psychiatry*. Univ. of Pittsburgh Press.

ERIKSON, ERIK H. (1950) 1964 *Childhood and Society*. 2d ed., rev. & enl. New York: Norton.

FREUD, ANNA (1936) 1957 *The Ego and the Mechanisms of Defense*. New York: International Universities Press. → First published as *Das Ich und die Abwehrmechanismen*.

FREUD, ANNA 1963 The Concept of Developmental Lines. *Psychoanalytic Study of the Child* 18:245–265.

FREUD, SIGMUND (1908) 1959 Character and Anal Erotism. Volume 2, pages 45–50 in Sigmund Freud, *Collected Papers*. International Psycho-analytic Library, No. 10. New York: Basic Books; London: Hogarth.

FREUD, SIGMUND (1914) 1959 Further Recommendations in the Technique of Psycho-analysis: Recollection, Repetition and Working Through. Volume 2, pages 366–376 in Sigmund Freud, *Collected Papers*. International Psycho-analytic Library, No. 10. London: Hogarth; New York: Basic Books.

FREUD, SIGMUND (1931) 1932 Libidinal Types. *Psychoanalytic Quarterly* 1:3–6.

FROMM, ERICH 1949 Psychoanalytic Characterology and Its Application to the Understanding of Culture. Pages 1–12 in Interdisciplinary Conference, New York, 1947, *Culture and Personality*. New York: Viking Fund. → Contains two pages of discussion.

GITELSON, MAXWELL 1963 On the Problem of Character Neurosis. *Journal of the Hillside Hospital* 12:3–17.

HARTMANN, HEINZ 1950 The Application of Psychoanalytic Concepts to Social Science. *Psychoanalytic Quarterly* 19:385–392.

HORNEY, KAREN 1945 *Our Inner Conflicts: A Constructive Theory of Neurosis.* New York: Norton.

KAUFMAN, IRVING 1963 The Defensive Aspects of Impulsivity. Menninger Clinic, *Bulletin* 27:24–32.

LUSTMAN, SEYMOUR L. 1962 Defense, Symptom and Character. *Psychoanalytic Study of the Child* 17:216–244.

MICHAELS, JOSEPH J. 1955 *Disorders of Character: Persistent Enuresis, Juvenile Delinquency, and Psychopathic Personality.* Springfield, Ill.: Thomas.

MICHAELS, JOSEPH J. 1959a Character Disorder and Acting Upon Impulse. Pages 181–196 in Morton Levitt (editor), *Readings in Psychoanalytic Psychology.* New York: Appleton.

MICHAELS, JOSEPH J. 1959b Character Structure and Character Disorders. Volume 1, pages 353–377 in Silvano Arieti (editor), *American Handbook of Psychiatry.* New York: Basic Books.

REICH, WILHELM 1925 *Der triebhafte Charakter.* Leipzig: Internationaler Psychoanalytischer Verlag.

ROSS, NATHANIEL 1960 An Examination of Nosology According to Psychoanalytic Concepts. *Journal of the American Psychoanalytic Association* 8:535–551. → Includes a discussion of John Frosch's paper, "A Specific Problem in Nosology: The Psychotic Character Disorder."

SCHACHTER, STANLEY; and LATANÉ, BIBB 1964 Crime, Cognition, and the Autonomic Nervous System. Volume 12, pages 221–275 in David Levine (editor), *Nebraska Symposium on Motivation.* Lincoln: Univ. of Nebraska Press. → Contains two pages of discussion.

SHAW, CLIFFORD R. 1929 *Delinquency Areas: A Study of the Geographic Distribution of School Truants, Juvenile Delinquents, and Adult Offenders in Chicago.* Univ. of Chicago Press.

CHARCOT, JEAN MARTIN

Jean Martin Charcot (1825–1893), specialist in neurology and hypnosis, was born in Paris in modest circumstances, the son of a carriage builder. Finishing secondary school at 19, he entered the medical school of the University of Paris. He served his internship at the Salpêtrière, a very large Parisian hospital for patients of all ages with chronic, incurable diseases, particularly those of the nervous system. The Salpêtrière had been one of the first hospitals to accept Philippe Pinel's beginning steps toward the reform of mental hospitals. In 1793, at the Bicêtre, another part of the Parisian medical service, Pinel had stopped the practice of keeping psychotic patients in chains, and the Salpêtrière had followed this example a few years later.

Charcot's connection with the Salpêtrière lasted throughout his life. In 1862, at the age of 37, he became a senior physician there. Up to that time, although he had been a competent physician and had published several papers, his work had been in no way remarkable nor had he shown any particular interest in the nervous system. Yet in the following eight years he produced what were to become the classic descriptions of multiple sclerosis, amyotrophic lateral sclerosis, and the localization of lesions of the spinal cord. It is said that in those eight years he founded the field of modern neurology (Guillain [1955] 1959, pp. 10–11). His method of diagnosis is, in its broad outlines, the one still being used. His appointment as professor of diseases of the nervous system at the University of Paris in 1882 represents the first recognition of neurology as a specialty in its own right.

Charcot was known for his ability as a clinician. Before him, no clinician could unequivocally recognize a given neurological disease in a living person, although the presence of such disease entities had been established by post-mortem study. Charcot was especially adroit at relating observable clinical signs and symptoms to the underlying neurological damage visible in a post-mortem examination. He was able to delineate the symptomatology of each disease in the living patient and to differentiate each syndrome from closely related disorders. Moreover, he succeeded in correlating each clinical picture with the post-mortem establishment of a set of lesions, thus founding what he called the clinical–anatomical method.

Although austere and reserved, Charcot was able to teach his diagnostic skill to his pupils by examining patients in their presence. These demonstrations were spectacular displays for which he soon became celebrated. Students came to him from all over the world, among them Pierre Janet and Sigmund Freud.

Charcot also made contributions to cerebral physiology. The doctrine that the cerebrum of the brain functions homogeneously, advocated by Pierre Flourens, a French physiologist, dominated medical science through the 1860s. Charcot, among others, did much to demonstrate that some functions of the cerebrum are localized in specific regions (1875).

Although Charcot maintained his interest in neurology, in the 1880s he began to devote considerable time to the study of hysteria and hypnosis. Hysterical patients show a host of bewildering symptoms: amnesia, paralysis, anesthesia, contractures, and spasms. Charcot studied these patients intensively, using hypnosis as one technique of investigation. Although his work with hysterics and his exploration of hypnosis were interrelated, it is necessary to consider them separately.

Charcot considered neuroses, including hysteria, to be diseases of the nervous system, but ones with no known organic lesions ([1872–1887] 1877–1889, vol. 3, pp. 13–14). Significantly, he believed, not that they are a separate class of nervous diseases but, rather, that they are governed by the same physiological laws as the "common" organically based neural diseases. He laid considerable stress on the importance of organic factors in causing neuroses, although he admitted the presence of functional components, notably in his conception of traumatic ideas.

Traumatic ideas, although dissociated from the consciousness of the patient and forgotten, continue to exert an influence on the patient and to determine the nature of his hysterical symptoms. A weakness, probably of a hereditary constitutional origin, would make some individuals subject to this hysterical dissociation. Charcot considered trauma, either physical or psychological, to be the precipitating etiological factor bringing on the dissociative process.

Conventional medical opinion held that hypnotism was at best a theatrical stunt and at worst sheer charlatanism. Consequently, Charcot was moving against medical opinion when he decided to employ hypnosis. He had read widely in psychology (Guillain 1955) and had familiarized himself with earlier work on hypnosis. A physiologist, Charles Richet, and a psychologist, Théodule Ribot, whose opinions Charcot respected, had upheld the scientific validity of hypnotic phenomena.

Hypnotism came to be his preferred method of investigating hysteria. Integral to his conception of hysteria was his belief that only hysterical persons can be hypnotized and that hypnosis itself is a manifestation of hysteria. To Charcot, the hypnotic trance and the hysterical crisis constituted essentially the same kind of alteration of personality. The trance, however, could be induced by the operator and could therefore be used for the study of hysteria.

Charcot distinguished three progressive stages in the depth of hypnosis, namely: lethargy (drowsiness), catalepsy (in which isolated suggestions are accepted without question since they can be acted upon without interference from other ideas), and somnambulism (the ability to carry out complicated activities with no recollection afterward, so that there is a splitting of personality by dissociation).

Charcot has been accused of being uncritical about the influence of suggestion, and it has been charged that he was duped by overzealous assistants (Guillain 1955). However, his writings show that he did appreciate the significance of both suggestion and malingering in hypnosis as well as in hysterical manifestations, although it is probable he underestimated the importance of their effects.

Charcot's contention that hypnosis is a psychopathological phenomenon was even then being disputed by the Nancy school of hypnosis, in the persons of Ambroise-Auguste Liébeault and Hippolyte Bernheim. The Nancy school argued that hypnosis is a normal behavioral experience arising from suggestion which can be induced in practically anyone and is continuous with waking behavior. Later findings support the position of the Nancy school, not that of the Salpêtrière school.

Although wrong in particulars, Charcot did much to make the study of hypnosis respectable (Wechsler 1953). He found that hypnosis can restore forgotten memories. He demonstrated so thoroughly that hysteria can occur in the male that after a few years such a statement was no longer seriously questioned. Freud, for example, who had worked under Charcot in 1885–1886 and referred to him later as "my master" ([1914] 1938, p. 943), was so impressed with Charcot's demonstrations of cases of male hysteria that he insisted on lecturing on this subject when he returned to Vienna. He was received with ridicule. In Vienna, medical authorities still held the view that hysteria was somehow due to a "wandering womb," and, consequently, male hysteria was a contradiction in terms. These lectures added to Freud's disrepute among Viennese medical men. It was a casual remark of Charcot's that reinforced Freud's later firmly established belief in the primacy of sexual difficulties as an etiological factor. According to Freud, on one social occasion Charcot insisted that a certain female patient's difficulties arose from the impotence of her husband.

Charcot prepared the way for much other fruitful psychological–medical collaboration. Above all, he contributed to the establishment of neurology as a scientifically based medical specialty.

ROBERT I. WATSON

[For the historical context of Charcot's work, see the biographies of BROCA; MESMER. For the subsequent development of his ideas, see HYPNOSIS; HYSTERIA; MENTAL DISORDERS, articles on ORGANIC ASPECTS and BIOLOGICAL ASPECTS; MENTAL DISORDERS, TREATMENT OF, article on SOMATIC TREATMENT; NERVOUS SYSTEM, article on STRUCTURE AND

FUNCTION OF THE BRAIN; *and the biographies of* FLOURENS; FREUD; JANET.]

WORKS BY CHARCOT

(1872–1887) 1877–1889 *Lectures on the Diseases of the Nervous System.* 3 vols. London: New Sydenham Society. → First published in French.

(1875) 1878 *Lectures on Localization in Diseases of the Brain.* New York: Wood. → First published in French.

SUPPLEMENTARY BIBLIOGRAPHY

FREUD, SIGMUND (1914) 1938 On the History of the Psycho-analytic Movement. Pages 933–977 in A. A. Brill (editor), *The Basic Writings of Sigmund Freud.* New York: Random House.

GUILLAIN, GEORGES (1955) 1959 *J-M Charcot, 1825–1893: His Life, His Work.* New York: Hoeber. → First published in French.

WECHSLER, I. S. 1953 Jean-Martin Charcot. Pages 266–269 in Webb Haymaker (editor), *Founders of Neurology.* Springfield, Ill.: Thomas.

CHARISMA

In all societies deference is accorded to authoritative roles, their incumbents, and the norms they promulgate in consideration of their capacity to create, maintain, and change the order of society. In all societies there is a propensity in most human beings, on occasion, to perceive, beyond immediate and particular events, the forces, principles, and powers which govern the immediate and the particular and which impose and necessitate an order which embraces them. Particularly serious attention and respect are given to what are thought to be those transcendent powers which are manifested in the orders of nature and society and in patterns of norms which intend the ordering of human action. Where institutions, roles, persons, norms, or symbols are perceived or believed to be connected or infused with these transcendent powers, we say that they are perceived as charismatic.

Charisma, then, is the quality which is imputed to persons, actions, roles, institutions, symbols, and material objects because of their presumed connection with "ultimate," "fundamental," "vital," order-determining powers. This presumed connection with the ultimately "serious" elements in the universe and in human life is seen as a quality or a state of being, manifested in the bearing or demeanor and in the actions of individual persons; it is also seen as inhering in certain roles and collectivities. It can be perceived as existing in intense and concentrated form in particular institutions, roles, and individuals (or strata of individuals). It can also be perceived as existing in attenuated and dispersed form.

The propensity to seek contact with transcendent powers and to impute charismatic qualities varies in any society; it is extremely strong in some persons, feeble in others. It also varies during the life span of individuals and in the history of particular societies. Some societies are characterized by a greater frequency of intense and concentrated charisma; others, by a greater frequency of attenuated and dispersed charisma. Both types exist in varying admixtures in all societies.

Intense and concentrated charisma

The propensity to impute charisma is a potentiality of the moral, cognitive, and expressive orientations of human beings. The propensity to seek contact with transcendent powers and to impute charisma is rooted in the neural constitution of the human organism. The intensity with which it is experienced and the strength of its motivation are also influenced by situational exigencies and by the prevailing culture. It can be deliberately cultivated by isolation from the routine environment, by instruction and self-discipline. It can be so prized that individuals are encouraged to allow it to come forward in their sensitivity. A culture can foster the discernment of charismatic signs and properties by focusing attention, providing canons of interpretation, and recommending the appreciation of the possession of these signs and properties.

Whatever the sources of the propensity to impute charisma—neural, situational, cultural, or any combination of these—when this propensity is intense enough to seek to penetrate beyond the immediate present, beyond the particular and the concrete to the more general categories and patterns which underlie and generate the vicissitudes of human existence, it results in a subjective experience of possession of charismatic quality or in a sensitivity and responsiveness to the subjectively experienced charisma manifested in the bearing, words, and actions of other individuals and institutions. Those persons who possess an intense subjective feeling of their own charismatic quality, and who have it imputed to them by others, we will call charismatic persons. In the charismatic persons it is "directly" experienced; in the others it is experienced only in "mediated" form through intensely and concentratedly charismatic persons or institutions. The authority exercised by these individuals who "experience" charisma directly, over all others in the society who experience it only in mediated form, we will call charismatic authority.

The concept of charisma derives from the reference in II Corinthians which describes the forms in which the gifts of divine grace appear. It was taken up by Rudolf Sohm in his analysis of the transformation of the primitive Christian community into the Roman Catholic church (Sohm 1892–1923); the emphasis there was on a "charismatic institution." The conception of charisma underwent its most important extension and formulation in the writings of Max Weber (1922*a*; 1922*b*). He treated charisma as a property attributed to great innovating personalities who disrupt traditionally and rational–legally legitimated systems of authority and who establish or aspire to establish a system of authority claiming to be legitimated by the direct experience of divine grace. Weber also applied the concept to creative, expansive, innovating personalities who are regarded as "extraordinary" even though they neither claim to possess divine grace nor have it imputed to them.

According to Weber's usage, charismatic quality may be attributed to religious prophets and reformers, to dominating political leaders, to daring military heroes, and to sages who by example and command indicate a way of life to their disciples. In such personalities, the charismatic quality is believed to be manifested in extremes of passionate and intense action or of willed passivity, in extremes of exultant or serene possession. Charismatic quality is attributed to expansive personalities who establish ascendancy over other human beings by their commanding forcefulness or by an exemplary inner state which is expressed in a bearing of serenity.

The "extraordinariness" (*Ausseralltäglichkeit*) of these charismatic persons is not simply statistical infrequency; rather, it is the intense and concentrated form in which they possess or are thought to possess qualities which are only slightly present in routine actions. Routine actions are those which are governed mainly by motives of moderate, personal attachment, by considerations of convenience and advantage, and by anxiety to avoid failure in conforming to the immediate expectations and demands of peers and superiors. Routine actions are not simply repetitive actions; they are uninspired actions in which immediately prospective gratifications and the demands of immediate situations and of obligations to those who are close at hand play a greater part than does the link with transcendent things. If any charismatic attribution is present in the pattern of routine action, it is not dominant and certainly is not vividly perceived.

Such uninspired actions maintain social structures, and they also change them through numerous minor adjustments. They do not impel drastic changes. Charismatic persons, and those who are responsive to charismatic persons, aspire to larger transformations. They seek to break the structures of routine actions and to replace them with structures of inspired actions which are "infused" with those qualities or states of mind generated by immediate and intensive contact with the "ultimate" —with the powers which guide and determine human life.

The charismatic person is a creator of a new order as well as the breaker of routine order. Since charisma is constituted by the belief that its bearer is effectively in contact with what is most vital, most powerful, and most authoritative in the universe or in society, those to whom charisma is attributed are, by virtue of that fact, authoritative. Charismatic authority is antipathetic to those forms of authority which invoke recently and currently acknowledged criteria of legitimacy and which call forth the performance of the previously performed. Even where such authorities command or recommend new actions, they legitimate the commands or recommendations by subsuming them under existing norms recently and currently accepted as valid. The bearer and the adherents of charismatic authority, in contrast, tend to think of their norms as legitimated by a source remote in time or timeless, remote in space or spaceless. The legitimacy of the norms enunciated by charismatic authority lies outside the norms practiced in the existing society. Although it is contained in the culture of the existing society, the source or the criterion of the legitimacy of charismatic authority occupies a position within that culture which, under the dominance of routine, is incompatible with the expansive aspirations of any charismatically asserted authority. Since it asserts the value of action which derives its impetus immediately, intensively, and unalloyedly from direct contact with "ultimate" sources of legitimacy, charismatic authority is of necessity revolutionary.

Charismatic authority denies the value of action which is motivated by the desire for proximate ends sufficient unto themselves, by the wish to gratify personal affections, or by the hope of pecuniary advantage. Charismatically generated order is order which acknowledges and is generated by the creativity which seeks something new, by discovery which discerns something new, by inspiration from transcendent powers.

The actions of men in all ongoing societies are impelled by a variety of considerations. Personal affections, primordial attachments, anticipations of advantage and fears of loss, destructiveness, responsiveness to obligations or expectations of role performance in corporate bodies, unimaginative acceptance of given norms where no alternative seems visible or practicable, respect for concrete, already-functioning authority—these, together with an intermittent flickering of charismatic responsiveness, form the complex of impulses from which any society reproduces itself and moves onward. Such charismatic elements as ordinary societies contain exist either in a highly segregated form or in a diffuse half life. Concentrated and intense charismatic authority transfigures the half life into incandescence. It involves a tremendous heightening of charismatic sensitivity. That is why charismatic authority, really intensely imputed and experienced charisma, is disruptive of any routine social order.

Segregation and discipline of intense charisma

All societies seek to make some provision for those persons whose actions are impelled by the possession of charismatic legitimacy. Within religious systems, the cenobitic or anchoritic monastic orders are institutional frameworks for the segregation and control of the charismatically endowed, i.e., those who are prone to experience a sense of direct contact with transcendent powers. This removes them from the scene of the routine and at the same time preserves and disciplines their charismatic quality within the legitimate order of the religious collectivity, in which a certain measure of attenuation and dispersal of charisma has been stabilized.

Universities, which must reproduce many established patterns of thought and evaluation and carry on traditions, face similar problems in dealing with young persons of highly charismatic intellectual and moral propensities. Through training and research, they attempt to discipline these charismatic propensities and to bring them to bear, at least at first, on the accepted problems and the accepted vision of the order of nature. The discovery of utterly new truths through intuition, unbridled by the accepted techniques of observation and interpretation, is rejected. Those who persist in practicing their intuition are either excluded or are constrained to submit to the prevailing discipline. This discipline involves learning and affirming what is already known and accepting the prevailing canons of assessment. Once this process of discipline has been accomplished, the acolyte is then freed to discern and create a new order through research.

In party politics, there is often apprehension among the party bosses about persons who are thought to be charismatic and who arouse the charismatic sensitivity of the mass of the party, because of the dangers which they represent to established interests within the party. But because of their wider appeal outside the party machine itself, which is concerned with routine practices, they will be tolerated and even sought in order to win the support of the charismatically sensitive for the party.

In armies, the charismatically heroic officers find a tolerated place among shock troopers and special units using unconventional methods of warfare in situations in which the routine procedures of military organization are thought to be inadequate. The military bureaucracy at higher staff levels does not find it easy to accommodate within its own circles the charismatically inclined soldier who tries to attain to new principles of warfare or who, as a hero, arouses the devotion of ordinary soldiers whose charismatic sensitivity is aroused by the danger of battle.

In bohemias, and in the circles of artists and literary men, aesthetically charismatic persons find a segregated environment congenial to the disregard for the rules of routine social life and for the creative transcendence of the traditional modes of artistic and literary expression. The authorities of the routine sectors of society are more inclined to tolerate these manifestations of aesthetic charisma as long as they do not intrude into the routine sectors. Nonetheless, because of the vagueness of the boundaries, friction is frequent.

By segregation, the custodians of the routine spheres of social life show both their apprehension of the disruptive nature of intense and concentrated charisma and their appreciation of a virtue requiring acknowledgment. Nonetheless, despite these efforts to contain those with intense charismatic propensities within situations where they can operate charismatically and to subject them to the discipline of institutionalization, the boundaries are sometimes infringed. A continuous reinforcement of the barriers against a free movement of charismatic persons is carried on by the custodians of routine order. They do not always succeed. Churches have been broken from within by charismatic prophets and have often suffered defeat, at least for a time, by a sectarian rival under charismatic leadership. States have been destroyed by charismatic revolutionaries, parties swept away from their traditional pattern by charismatic demagogues, constitutional orders supplanted by charismatic statesmen. Sciences have been revolutionized by unsuppressible charismatic intelligences; artistic genres have been transformed, against the resistance of orthodoxy, by the bearers of an original (charismatic) sensitivity.

Conditions of intense and concentrated charisma

Crises which discredit routine institutions and the authorities who govern them arouse in the more charismatically disposed persons a more acute awareness of the insufficiency of an organization of life in which contact with the ultimate powers and standards of right and wrong has become attenuated by mediation and segregation and by absorption into routine. Their demand for the right order of things is intensified; their sensibility to the divergence between this right order and the actually existing state of affairs is heightened.

These crises, which reveal to the afflicted members of the society in which they occur the inadequacy of the inherited and prevailing institutional systems and discredit the elites which have hitherto dominated them, operate on charismatic propensities in a twofold manner. Those in whom the charismatic propensity is strongest—out of intelligence, moral sensibility, metaphysical inclination, etc.—will be the promulgators of the new vision of a better order; those in whom the charismatic propensities, although not strong enough to permit charismatic originality, are strong enough to respond to such a vision when concretely embodied (and mediated) in a charismatic person, are the most likely followers.

Crises which are failures of the inherited order enhance the need of the potential followers for protective contact with the ultimately right and powerful. The incapacity of the hitherto prevailing institutions to afford moral and metaphysical nurture and succor to those who feel the need for it, and to afford it under morally and cosmically right auspices, generates in these defenseless persons a state of mind which is fertile for the seed of the more intensely creative charismatic persons. The result is a collective effort to establish a charismatically legitimate society—or church, or party, etc.—which will possess a greater authenticity.

Often these efforts are unsuccessful. Most of the movements are broken, after a brief period of excitation, into dispirited fragments which sometimes survive in segregation. Less often, the movement is successful, and the result is a charismatic order or at least an order in which a charismatic overlay covers the more tenacious routines of the older institutional system. The routine relations between superiors and subordinates in families, armies, workshops, and farms tend to reassert themselves after an initial adaptation to the pressures of charismatic visions and convictions. Once the crisis which generated the more intense charismatic sensibility is somehow resolved—often as a result of the intervention of the charismatic inspiration—routine actions return to the forefront of social life.

With the increased effectiveness and consequent stability of institutions, the need for protective charisma which puts their members into direct, or in any case less mediated, contact with the sources of inspiration and purification is reduced. The selection of prospective leaders is again institutionalized, reducing the likelihood that intensely charismatic persons will be chosen. Thus, the process of the imputation of charisma is restored to its normal state.

Attenuated and dispersed charisma

The intensely charismatic element of the new order never evaporates entirely. It can exist in a state of attenuation and dispersion. The very effort of a charismatic elite to stabilize its position and to impose a charismatic order on the society or institution it controls entails deliberate dispersion. It entails spreading the particular charismatic sensitivity to persons who did not share it previously. This means a considerable extension of the circle of charisma: more persons have to become charismatic; existing institutions have to have charisma infused into them; new institutions have to be created. All this brings with it not only a deliberate dispersion from a smaller to a larger number of persons but also produces an attenuation which is less intentional but more unavoidable.

The inevitability of death and the need to provide for succession call for dispersion of charisma from a few persons and institutions to institutional offices, lineages, governing bodies, electoral procedures, and groups of people. The last of these, although not absolutely or proportionately numerous in their societies, are considerably larger than the original bearers of the imputed charisma, and their charismatic sensibility is, of course, much less intense.

Then there is the tenacity of routine to be considered. Life cannot go on without routine, which is constantly reasserting itself. Thus, the charismatic founders of a new society might have elevated a particular norm of conduct—e.g., equality or saintliness—to a dominant position, to the practical exclusion of all others. As time passes, personal and primordial attachments, considerations of expediency, and loyalties within particularistic corporate bodies become more prominent again. The norms of equality or of saintliness might still be respected, but not exclusively respected. This is what is meant by attenuation.

Not all dispersions are the result of the changes in the situation of a new elite in which charisma was both concentrated and intense. One of the greatest dispersions in history is that which has taken place in modern states, in which an attenuated charisma, more dispersed than in traditional aristocracies (where it was already more dispersed than in primitive tribes or absolute monarchies), is shared by the total adult citizenry.

The extraordinary charisma of which Max Weber spoke was the intense and concentrated form. Its normal form, however—attenuated and dispersed charisma—exists in all societies. In this form it is attributed in a context of routine actions to the rules, norms, offices, institutions, and strata of any society. Though normal charisma plays a reduced part in the ordinary life of society, it is nonetheless a real and effective force. Quite apart from its manifestations in the routines of life which are loosely governed by religious attachments, it enters into obedience to law and respect for corporate authority. Furthermore, it provides the chief criterion for granting deference in the system of stratification and pervades the main themes of the cultural inheritance and practice of every society. Thus, normal charisma is an active and effective phenomenon, essential to the maintenance of the routine order of society.

EDWARD SHILS

[*See also* AUTHORITY; IDEOLOGY; LEADERSHIP; LEGITIMACY; SOCIAL CONTROL, *article on* ORGANIZATIONAL ASPECTS. *Further relevant material will be found under* RELIGION; *and in the biographies of* BUBER *and* WEBER, MAX.]

BIBLIOGRAPHY

DOGAN, MATTÉI 1965 Le personnel politique et la personalité charismatique. *Revue française de sociologie* 6:305–324.

MARCUS, JOHN T. 1961 Transcendence and Charisma. *Western Political Quarterly* 14, part 1:236–241.

OTTO, RUDOLPH (1917) 1950 *The Idea of the Holy: An Inquiry Into the Non-rational Factor in the Idea of the Divine and Its Relation to the Rational.* 2d ed. Oxford Univ. Press. → First published as *Das Heilige.*

RATMAN, K. J. 1964 Charisma and Political Leadership. *Political Studies* 12:341–354.

RUNCIMAN, W. G. 1963 Charismatic Legitimacy and One-party Rule in Ghana. *Archives européennes de sociologie* 4, no. 1:148–165.

SHILS, EDWARD 1958 The Concentration and Dispersion of Charisma: Their Bearing on Economic Policy in Underdeveloped Countries. *World Politics* 11:1–19.

SHILS, EDWARD 1965 Charisma, Order and Status. *American Sociological Review* 30:199–213.

SOHM, RUDOLF 1892–1923 *Kirchenrecht.* 2 vols. Leipzig: Duncker & Humblot.

WEBER, MAX (1922a) 1956 *Wirtschaft und Gesellschaft: Grundriss der verstehenden Soziologie.* 2 vols., 4th ed. Tübingen (Germany): Mohr. → See especially Volume 2, pages 832–873, "Die charismatische Herrschaft und ihre Umbildung."

WEBER, MAX (1922b) 1957 *The Theory of Social and Economic Organization.* Edited by Talcott Parsons. Glencoe, Ill.: Free Press. → First published as Part 1 of *Wirtschaft und Gesellschaft.* See especially pages 358–363, "Charismatic Authority"; pages 363–373, "The Routinization of Charisma"; and pages 386–392, "The Transformation of Charisma in an Anti Authoritarian Direction."

CHARITY
See PHILANTHROPY.

CHARTS
See GRAPHIC PRESENTATION.

CHECKS AND BALANCES
See CONSTITUTIONAL LAW, *article on* DISTRIBUTION OF POWERS.

CHEMICAL SENSES
See TASTE AND SMELL.

CHILD DEVELOPMENT
See DEVELOPMENTAL PSYCHOLOGY; EDUCATIONAL PSYCHOLOGY; INFANCY; INTELLECTUAL DEVELOPMENT; MORAL DEVELOPMENT; SENSORY AND MOTOR DEVELOPMENT; *and the biographies of* GESELL; HALL; MONTESSORI.

CHILD PSYCHIATRY
See under PSYCHIATRY.

CHILDE, V. GORDON

Vere Gordon Childe (1892–1957) was a scholar whose work commanded appreciation from many publics. Through his book *What Happened in History* (1942) he personified prehistoric archeology for several generations of college students. For professional archeologists, his masterly synthesis of European prehistory, *The Dawn of European Civilization* (1925), stated themes that were to pervade anthropological archeology for years to follow; and in *The Most Ancient East* (1928) he elaborated a view of cultural evolution that has stimulated interpretative archeology and refocused the attention of cultural anthropologists on problems that had characterized the earliest growth of the discipline but were then allocated to the discipline of history.

In the *Dawn,* Childe dealt the final scientific blow to the already faltering concept of a master Aryan civilization and in its place developed a view of man's early history that recognizes the infinitely complex nature of the cultural past. He brought to archeology a humanistic appreciation of the achievements of man throughout the reaches of time and clearly tried to deal with culture-historical processes. To this end, Childe explicitly identified himself as an anthropologist and insisted that artifactual remains be treated as the products of human sociocultural behavior. He was not afraid to propose hypotheses based on diffusionist principles, but his was not the ignorant "grand scale" diffusion of Elliot Smith and W. J. Perry. He was well aware of the interconnectedness of social institutions and was especially concerned with the relationship of the technological process and social structure. Childe's evolutionism was not universalistic; it sought to explain changes and emphasized the uneven tempo of cultural "progress," a concept he associated with the emergence of civilization.

Childe was probably the last archeologist able to range freely over so much of the world's early history, although his work was weakened by his lack of familiarity with New World prehistory. He was able to store and classify great quantities of detailed information, and this knowledge may have facilitated his extraordinarily nimble efforts at synthesis. However, his basic orientation to the museum laboratory rather than to field excavation prevented him from appreciating the theoretical significance of the ecological approach to archeological data.

Childe was born in New South Wales, Australia. The son of a pastor, he attended a Church of England grammar school and then the University of Sydney. He accepted a scholarship in classics at Oxford in 1914, completing his B.Litt. thesis, "Indo-European Elements in Prehistoric Greece," in 1916. His brief first stay in England proved intellectually explosive; he was caught up in a university atmosphere of fervent debate on the political and philosophical issues of the time. At Oxford he roomed with R. Palme Dutt, and the two "pursued [their] arguments on Hegel and Marx far into the night." His socialist sympathies made him a "friend" of the Soviet Union in the years following the revolution. He returned to Australia and immediately entered politics, joining civil liberties defense groups; in 1919 he became private secretary to the anticonscriptionist Labour leader John Storey, who was to become premier of New South Wales. In 1921 Childe accepted a post at the University of Queensland, but upon his arrival the university terminated the appointment on the grounds that his Marxist beliefs would endanger the school. Six months later, after writing How Labour Governs, a pioneer treatise on the history of trade unionism in Australia, Childe left again for Europe. He traveled widely in central and eastern Europe, finally settling in Britain.

In 1927, following publication of The Dawn of European Civilization, Childe was appointed the first Abercromby professor of prehistoric archeology at the University of Edinburgh. He directed numerous excavations in Scotland and Ireland, including the famous neolithic village at Skara Brae on Orkney, in 1935, 1940, and 1946. He was awarded an honorary doctor of letters by Harvard at the tercentenary celebration of 1936 and the doctor of letters by the University of Pennsylvania in 1937. Childe was elected a fellow of the British Academy in 1940 and was appointed director of the London Institute of Archaeology in 1945. He stayed in Britain until 1957, when he returned to Australia and lost his life in the Blue Mountains of New South Wales.

Throughout his career, Childe searched with intellectual passion for meaningful lessons in history, for vindication of his belief that the progress of man is rational and intelligible (1951, p. 179)—that it is progress in which "no trough ever declines to the low level of the preceding one; each crest out-tops its last precursor" ([1942] 1960, p. 282). He believed that the Marxist model of history best serves to explain the archeological evidence of man's past. Childe was strongly individualistic and maintained high standards of objectivity in his work and criticism; with many other intellectuals of the time, he expressed dismay at the rigid and dogmatic institutionalization of Marxism as an obstacle to the development of science.

Dawn of European prehistory. Childe wrote prolifically, albeit repetitively. The Dawn went through six editions, each considerably revised as Childe incorporated new data and asked new questions of his material. The book has been described as "not merely a book of incomparable archaeological erudition but . . . a new starting-point for prehistoric archaeology" (Daniel 1950, p. 247).

The avowed purpose of the argument presented in the Dawn is to demolish the idea of ex oriente lux, of the supremacy of Oriental civilizations, and to demonstrate the relevance of Europe's "barbarian" past to the understanding of the unique development of what has come to be called Western civilization. To accomplish this, Childe patiently compiled and compared the "insignificant bits of flint and stone, bronze and baked clay [in which] are revealed the preconditions of our gigantic engines and of the whole mechanical apparatus that constitutes the material basis of modern life" (1925, p. xv). In so doing, Childe evolved methods of classification and archeological exposition that prevailed until the 1960s. He combed masses of published data, including the little-known work of archeologists in eastern Europe, and identified assemblages of associated artifacts as "cultures." He then attempted to establish, partly on the basis of sequence dating techniques, partly by the intuitive recognition of stylistic similarities—but always with a control for functional equivalence—a relative chronology for the appearance, migrations, and disappearance of these cultures. Much of the work of cultural reconstruction presented in the *Dawn* has been superseded by the results of the scientifically controlled excavation which has flourished in Europe since the end of World War II and the use of radiocarbon techniques of dating (for bibliography see Gimbutas 1963, pp. 69–106; Piggott 1965). Especially important has been the way in which the map of prehistoric Europe has been filled in, particularly with regard to the early period of food production and the origins and diffusion of metallurgy. Yet much of this information has been gathered by archeologists seeking to answer the questions Childe posed.

In the *Dawn*, Childe organized his voluminous materials for two purposes. First, he conceived the "stages" of human cultures as "kinds of economies" ranged chronologically in terms of progress—a progress he defined by criteria of technological efficiency in extracting and distributing the means of subsistence. Second, he broke through the pervasive unitary, or holistic, view of prehistory and discerned the "cycles" of local development and adaptation that made up the European mosaic.

Childe assembled the evidence to answer Gustaf Kossinna and other German archeologists who believed that Europe had been colonized by Indo-Germanic peoples advancing from Scandinavia and Germany into south Russia. He examined the distributional patterns of very specific traits, especially the socketed battle-ax, and dissociated them from the megalithic complex, which he rightly saw to be of multiple origins. Using a careful method of archeological criticism, he formulated a hypothesis that sought the origins of the "peculiar vigour and genius" of the European metal ages in south Russia (1925, p. 151). Recent archeology has elucidated a picture of the Kurgan culture that seems to validate this view of Indo-European expansion (see Gimbutas 1963; Mongait 1955) and, while radiocarbon dates have considerably altered the supposed sequence of earlier cultures, Childe's culture areas—the Balkan, Mediterranean, Danubian, northern and western European—have largely withstood the test of time.

The food-producing revolution. Childe proposed a developmental prehistory derived in part from the Marxist economic model. He distinguished (1925, p. 1) the Paleolithic from the Neolithic period of prehistory, characterizing the latter as the time when man became the "master of his own food supply through the possession of domestic animals and cultivated plants, and shaking off the shackles of environment by his skill in fashioning tools for tree-felling and carpentry, by organization for co-operative labour, and by the beginnings of commerce." And he argued against the significance of a "mesolithic" period, claiming that such usage masks the true secondary, or imported, nature of the transition to food production. He repeated and expanded the theme of a food-producing revolution in *Man Makes Himself* (1936), *What Happened in History* (1942), and *Social Evolution* (1951). Thus he categorized the Paleolithic as a time of savagery, wherein man was not fundamentally differentiated in subsistence techniques from other herd animals, displaying superiority in degree rather than kind of dependency on the environment. He acknowledged the brilliance of the very specialized upper paleolithic adaptation to the conditions of the late Pleistocene, but, invoking the index of progress—biological survival in terms of increasing population size and density—he defined (1925, p. 38) the paleolithic failure not simply as resulting from inadequate technology but from an economic contradiction inherent in the balance between the institutions of savagery, including limited, or specialized, technological means, and the environment [*see* DOMESTICATION, *article on* THE FOOD-PRODUCING REVOLUTION].

The urban revolution. In *What Happened in History* (1942), and in *New Light on the Most Ancient East* (1928), Childe turned from Europe toward an appreciation of Oriental civilization. The accumulated evidence of much previous excavation provided the basic data from which Childe continued to construct his grand history; he formulated the concept of the second great revolution—the urban revolution—and explored the data in order to reveal the civilizing process. Childe described the urban revolution as a necessary consequence of food production: neolithic barbarism represented a major step in the human struggle for survival, but inherent in the neolithic economy were the pressures of an expanding population, its increasing need for cultivable land and fresh pasturage, and the inevitable resulting competition with hunting and gathering peoples. Neolithic barbarism was rooted in self-contained, largely self-sufficient villages capable of producing limited surpluses but not yet successfully in control of environmental circumstances. For Childe, the resolution of the neolithic contradiction came "when farmers were persuaded or compelled to wring from the soil a surplus above their own domestic requirements, and when this surplus was made available to support new economic classes not directly engaged in producing their own food" ([1942] 1960, p. 69).

The critical advance in the centuries preceding 3000 B.C. was the invention and development of a metallurgical technology; in turn, this produced a fundamental economic reorganization that destroyed the neolithic base and created the conditions of civilization. Childe's concern with metallurgy is illustrative of his approach to technology as part of a sociocultural system, in this instance an integrative system. Apart from the complex scientific knowledge required for the metallurgical process and the obvious superiority of metal tools—especially when the metal-edged plow was combined with harnessed animal labor—the skills involved required industrial craft specialization and gave rise to a class of metalworkers, freed from food production, who traveled widely, dispersing cultural information. Once introduced into the productive economy, metal tools destroyed neolithic self-sufficiency—trade became a regular feature of the social economy and specialization became a wedge in the familial structure of village society. Metallurgy was "socially expensive" and required greater surpluses of food to supply the needs of those engaged in it.

Childe was not unaware of the new patterns of appropriation and redistribution accompanying the economic changes wrought by this "revolution" and derived the stratification of class society from the concentration of surpluses in the hands of a minority: the kings, nobles, and priests. This stratification and craft specialization, the increasing size of permanent settlements, the construction of monumental public works, writing, and the predictive sciences compose Childe's "checklist" for civilization, a list much disputed since more recent archeological information has come to light, especially in the New World [see URBAN REVOLUTION; see also Adams 1966].

When Childe returned once again to the theme of European civilization (1958), he emphasized the role of an expanding metallurgical industry: the routes of diffusion traveled by artisans and merchants in the search for raw materials (tin and copper) required by the Aegean (Minoan–Mycenaean) markets. He contrasted the despotic, rigidly stratified and frequently theocratic Oriental civilizations with the market-oriented societies of Europe: "An international commercial system linked up a turbulent multitude of tiny political units. All these, whether city-states or tribes, while jealously guarding their autonomy, and at the same time seeking to subjugate one another, had none the less surrendered their economic independence by adopting for essential equipment materials that had to be imported" (1958, p. 172). Childe saw in this contrast the path to the florescence of European science, where creativity fed upon the inducements offered by a supranational economy and profited from the free exchange of knowledge. (See, for other views, Frankfort 1951; Wittfogel 1957.)

Social evolution.   His treatment of technological innovation is critical also to Childe's concept of archeological stages. Childe clearly distinguished a general evolutionary progression in human economic and social life from the homotaxial stages represented by archeologically known cultural sequences. In *Social Evolution* (1951) Childe explicitly set out to discover, through the comparison of cultures occupying roughly equivalent levels, the regularities of cultural evolution. In order to make this comparison objective, he made it clear that the technological criteria he derived from L. H. Morgan were taxonomic in nature and not processual: " 'evolution' does not purport to describe the mechanism of cultural change. It is not an account of why cultures change . . . but of how they change" (1951, p. 14). Thus he recognized "correlations" (*ibid.*, p. 118) between sociopolitical institutions and technicoeconomic stages, but he did not attempt to elicit from these correlations the functionally interrelated institutional structures common to each stage.

Eschewing simple parallelism in evolutionary development, Childe emphasized the phenomena of cultural divergence and convergence, and in so doing he came very close to the recent approach taken by the cultural ecologists. He repeatedly argued in favor of diffusion and assimilation in explaining convergences and partly recognized the differentiation that takes place as societies adapt cultural complexes (such as cultivation and stock breeding) to the requirements of differing environments (*ibid.*, pp. 173–175). However, it was in this regard especially that Childe was hampered in his interpretation by lack of familiarity with the comparative archeological data concerning the origins and unique development of New World cultures and civilizations. [See CULTURE, *article on* CULTURAL ADAPTATION; ECOLOGY, *article on* CULTURAL ECOLOGY; EVOLUTION, *article on* CULTURAL EVOLUTION.]

Culture history.   In his last works, as in his first, Childe insisted on the cultural interpretation of archeological data, demonstrating with example upon example the crucial methodology of inference.

He invoked ethnographical interpretations to clarify obscurities in material remains (his 1934 report on the site of Skara Brae is an excellent illustration), although he was aware of the dangers involved in equating archeological "cultures" with the ethnographer's "tribes": he admitted the limited nature of archeological assemblages, but because he conceived of artifacts not only as type fossils but as reflections of social habits conditioned by social traditions, his viewpoint was always anthropological rather than antiquarian. Indeed, recent developments in interpretive archeology and the use of statistical methods of analysis flow directly from this tradition.

JUDITH M. TREISTMAN

[*See also* ARCHEOLOGY; HISTORY, *article on* CULTURE HISTORY; *and the biography of* MORGAN, LEWIS HENRY.]

WORKS BY CHILDE

(1923) 1964 *How Labour Governs: A Study of Workers' Representation in Australia.* 2d ed. Melbourne Univ. Press.

(1925) 1958 *The Dawn of European Civilization.* 6th ed., rev. New York: Knopf.

(1928) 1953 *New Light on the Most Ancient East.* 4th ed. New York: Praeger. → First published as *The Most Ancient East.*

1935 *The Prehistory of Scotland.* London: Routledge.

(1936) 1965 *Man Makes Himself.* 4th ed. London: Watts.

(1942) 1960 *What Happened in History.* Rev. ed. Baltimore: Penguin. → A paperback edition was published in 1964.

1951 *Social Evolution.* New York: Schumann; London: Watts. → Based on a series of lectures delivered at the University of Birmingham in 1947–1948.

(1958) 1962 *The Prehistory of European Society.* London: Cassell.

SUPPLEMENTARY BIBLIOGRAPHY

ADAMS, ROBERT McC. 1966 *The Evolution of Urban Society: Early Mesopotamia and Prehispanic Mexico.* Chicago: Aldine.

BRAIDWOOD, R. J. 1958 [Obituary]. *American Anthropologist* New Series 60:733–736.

DANIEL, GLYN E. 1950 *A Hundred Years of Archaeology.* London: Duckworth.

DANIEL, GLYN E. 1962 *The Idea of Prehistory.* London: Watts.

FRANKFORT, HENRI 1951 *The Birth of Civilization in the Near East.* London: Williams & Norgate; Bloomington: Indiana Univ. Press. → A paperback edition was published in 1956 by Doubleday.

GIMBUTAS, MARIJA 1963 European Prehistory: Neolithic to the Iron Age. *Biennial Review of Anthropology* [1963]:69–106.

MONGAIT, ALEXANDER (1955) 1959 *Archaeology in the U.S.S.R.* Rev. ed. Moscow: Foreign Languages Publishing House. → First published in Russian.

PIGGOTT, STUART 1958 *Vere Gordon Childe: 1892–1957.* Oxford Univ. Press. → Reprinted from Volume 44 of the *Proceedings* of the British Academy.

PIGGOTT, STUART (1965) 1966 *Ancient Europe; From the Beginnings of Agriculture to Classical Antiquity: A Survey.* Chicago: Aldine.

SMITH, I. F. 1956 Bibliography of the Publications of Professor V. Gordon Childe. Prehistoric Society, *Proceedings* New Series 21:295–304.

WITTFOGEL, KARL A. 1957 *Oriental Despotism: A Comparative Study of Total Power.* New Haven: Yale Univ. Press. → A paperback edition was published in 1963.

CHINESE POLITICAL THOUGHT

The following article covers the period of pre-imperial history (Hsia, Shang, Chou) and the early (221 B.C.–A.D. 589), middle (589–960), and late imperial periods up to the time of the Ch'ing dynasty (1644–1911). For modern political thought, see CHINESE SOCIETY *and* COMMUNISM, *article on* NATIONAL COMMUNISM. *Also relevant is* HISTORIOGRAPHY, *article on* CHINESE HISTORIOGRAPHY.

From its historical beginnings, Chinese civilization has had a more wholly secular orientation than has any other traditional civilization. The religious element in Chinese life has remained largely unsupported by organization and religious institutions. Although religion's private and peripheral character was altered by China's mass acceptance of Buddhism, even Buddhism adapted itself quite thoroughly to China's secular values, and Neo-Confucianism strongly reasserted the primacy of traditional social values. Political thought thus has had a larger importance in the total intellectual life of the Chinese civilization than it has had in civilizations in which the state has had to compete with a church in institutional and ideological spheres. The ordering and bettering of human society by human means, or the cumulative human wisdom expressed in individual behavior and in social forms—in short, government—has been the great achievement of the Chinese civilization, both in its subjective view of itself and in the opinion of most modern historians of China.

In many ages of Chinese intellectual history, political thought has been virtually coterminous with philosophy. Chinese philosophy has not been compartmentalized into the classic divisions of logic, ethics, politics, ontology, and the like. Instead, ethics has been regarded as the individual's application of principles which on extension to society at large become politics; these principles have justified further speculation and learning within a framework of the "good society."

Politics and political thought were both the most useful and the most intellectually compelling of all activities. If the emphasis on history and on classical studies tended to impart a scholastic quality, the unity of the intellectual and the political worlds helped to preserve a pragmatic character as well. The same men who were the authorities on the Confucian canon also had to be experts on taxation, relief, and border defense; their political thought seldom became abstract, no matter how much they cited ancient classics for authority. A distinctive feature of China's political thought, and a perhaps serious limitation on it, however, is its intramural and self-contained character. It was all derived from the experience of one cultural tradition. Although it contains a wide range of political thought, including radical anarchism and extreme statism, it did not receive significant stimulus from outside cultures until the nineteenth century. China's thinkers knew only one civilization united under a single evolving tradition of government; unlike scholars in the classical Mediterranean or modern European world, they could not compare different cultures and institutions, and thus be stimulated to devise and create in their political theory. Perhaps for this reason, continuous vitality and originality could not be guaranteed throughout the 2,500 years of formal political philosophizing. But during the high points and the low, the role accorded government and speculation about government has given the study of political thought special importance. It is a kind of mirror, reflecting many intimately related aspects of social, economic, artistic, and intellectual development. And throughout, the continuing national absorption in the problems of society and government has at least brought about recurrent critical re-examination of basic issues, so that from time to time political theory has been enabled to close the gap between earlier formulations and later institutional developments. Change generally came about without revolution, until extramural elements were injected in the nineteenth century and produced the revolutions of the twentieth.

If the pace of change in traditional China seems slow to modern man, and if both political forms and their ideological underpinnings seemed to be badly in need of modernization by the end of the imperial era, that should not mislead us to believe that the old China was unchanging. It was not. We have referred above to growth and to periodic institutional accommodations to growth; each period of history acquired its distinctive character, whether observed with the focus on political thought, institutions, economic life, or the fine arts. But impatient modernizers at the end of the imperial era, observing the deepening gulf between the modern industrial West and apparently somnolent agrarian China, tended toward radical rejection of the past as static and moribund. Throughout the revolutionary contemporary period, one can observe that the intensity of the traditional emphasis on the problems of man in society undoubtedly has carried over, lending the same intensity to present-day China's search for a viable new political character.

In summary, the history of China's traditional political thought displays a basically humanistic orientation, reflecting the central role accorded politics in that secular-minded civilization; it gives evidence of the cumulative growth and periodic intellectual vitality of the whole civilization, and in particular it is marked by China's obsessive consciousness of continuity, making its past remarkably pertinent to its present in all periods of history, up to and including the present. This can be traced from its earliest beginnings in Chou times to the emergence of modern traditions during the Ch'ing dynasty.

The "Hundred Schools" of philosophy

The centuries preceding Ch'in unification in 221 B.C. were years of social and political upheaval. Early Chou rulers extended their hegemony over large areas of north and central China through a system of enfeoffing (*feng-chien*). This system lacked the kinds of legal contractual relationships which characterized European feudalism and is thus not strictly comparable. The Chou realm comprised some seventy principal vassals, of whom some fifty were members of the Chou kings' own clan. The number of smaller and less important states may have numbered two hundred or more. Over this loose federation of semiautonomous units, some from the beginning larger and more powerful than the royal Chou domain itself, the Chou kings maintained their hegemony less through exercise of the military power of the king and his "family states" than through the workings of a consciously cultivated mystique of legitimacy. This principle of legitimacy, probably originally required to validate the liquidation of Shang power, was deeply rooted in the social system and also was reinforced by the royal cult of ancestor worship. Chou sovereignty was acknowledged for centuries after Chou power had vanished, no holder of great power being willing to risk defying the legitimacy principle by displacing the Chou kings.

The Chou family system was the basis for many political institutions as the definitions of inter-family relations were extended to relations within the state. Clan law (*tsung-fa*) originally meant the systematization of the regulations and principles governing the members of the extended patriarchal clans of the ruling class, primarily the royal clan and allied clans, and the chief clans of retainers enfeoffed in each of the vassal states. The word *fa* translated as "law" should be taken in the sense of "pattern" or "way," since the system was in fact quite anti-Legalistic in spirit. In early Chou times the possession of a clan surname and the responsibilities toward a clan progenitor and successive ancestors distinguished the elite from the masses. Clan-law society was an upper-class society of inherited privilege, its family-centered mores expressed in elaborate ritual and its members exempt from the penal regulations, taxation, and labor service to which the masses were subject. Politically its greatest significance lay in the stress on mutual obligation and the sharing of authority in ritualized forms, hence definite limitations on the power of the kings and heads of states. Also important for government was the implicit repudiation of impersonal law in favor of ceremonial regulation of society according to the rites (*li*—originally the family ritual of ancestor worship, extended to include all behavior of the larger family of civilized man).

The Doctrine of the Heavenly Mandate.   The Chou had been a militarily powerful border dependency of the Shang state. To justify their conquest, they invoked an elaborately worked out Doctrine of the Heavenly Mandate (*t'ien-ming*), which may have been their invention but which was more likely based on Shang precedents. According to the doctrine, the ruler is the mediator between Heaven (or Nature) and man, a role he (or his clan) has earned by displaying virtue and the capacity to execute a benign Heaven's will. This role was to be retained within a dynastic line until Heaven found that store of virtue exhausted, as evidenced by disharmony in men's affairs and the natural world. The mandate then would theoretically be transferred to a new clan, Heaven would become its imperial ancestors, and the reigning bearer of the mandate would be known as a new "Son of Heaven." Heaven's will was made known somewhat vaguely and suggestively through portents and could be verified through divination, through which daily guidance also could be sought. Incumbent upon the ruler were the duties of performing in ritual propriety the ancestral sacrifices to Heaven on behalf of all men and of heeding Heaven's benevolent will in guiding the affairs of men. With the growth of philosophy in later Chou times, this doctrine was wholly secularized and philosophically developed; it remained the primary rationale of rulership and the only justification invoked for

any dynastic change until 1911. The word *ko-ming*, which means "changing the mandate" and derived from this concept, has become the modern word for "revolution."

The Chinese world view.   The Chinese probably are unique among all peoples, regardless of cultural level, in having had (within the 3,500 years of their cultural history that can be verified) no cosmogonical myth of a creator external to creation. Theirs was a naturalistic conception of the universe as an organismic, self-contained, and spontaneously self-generating entity. Such a cosmogony had important meaning for politics. There was no supreme being whose command or will or divine intelligence could be identified with natural law, or revealed as divine law which could, by extension, give authority and importance to human law; law never assumed the importance in Chinese civilization that it has had in most others. The dynamism of the cosmos was manifested in the harmony and complementariness of all its parts. In this cosmogony there was no contest between light and dark, good and evil, but, rather, a balance. Likewise, there could be no concept of sin as an offense against the divine will. In its place, there existed the much less serious error of human wrong-doing, a deflection of harmony, a source of shame but not of danger to the soul. While spiritual and religious values were provided for within this cosmos, there was no division of the "sacred" and the "profane" to be served in tandem by parallel organs of spiritual and temporal authority. Society needed only secular institutions, and the state did not have to share authority with a church.

Though this cosmogony provided for no beginning point in time, since the generative process was internal to the cosmos and cyclically continuous, with all its stages simultaneously present, there was a distinct concept of the emergence and gradual growth of human culture. Although the history of this human culture was somewhat mythologized, it remained a rational myth. The great achievement of the sages was entirely knowable and comprehensible through the study of historical records. It formed the chief guide to wise human action. Thus it was incumbent upon wise men to know the past and to apply its lessons to the present. Gradually the view appeared that the present must remain at best an imperfect emulation of a golden age in antiquity. Antiquity was regarded as historical; though we regard much of it as capsuled historical myth or as later idealization of the past, the great influence that it exerted on all subsequent Chinese history remained throughout a rational and humanistic one.

Out of such protophilosophical beginnings there developed in the late Chou era one of the great golden ages of philosophy of all human history. Confucius, its first great figure, anticipated that golden age in his overriding concern with political and ethical problems.

Confucius and early Confucianism.   The serious troubles which beset government at the time of Confucius (551–479 B.C.) reflected the deep changes in economy and society that were underway. A dozen great vassal states were warring with each other and absorbing their smaller neighbors. The old aristocracy faced the challenge of rising commoners, who pitted ambition and native ability against weakening aristocratic prerogative. It was a period of rapid cultural growth, of a great flowering of learning, accompanied by the dismaying dissolution of the old way of life. Confucius' profound study of tradition was motivated by the belief that tradition alone could provide rational man with the intellectual tools with which to reconstruct a sound social and political order. He said of himself that he was a transmitter, not a creator, perhaps purposely denying the imputation of creativity to himself because it would have decreased acceptance of his views, or perhaps because he really thought of himself in that way. If his attitude toward the past was genuinely nostalgic, however, it also was creatively selective and innovative, with implications for the future that Confucius himself may not have understood or fully intended. Living in the state of Sung, where the remnants of Shang aristocracy were given asylum, Confucius was heir to both Shang and Chou traditions. He was conscious of the contrasts between them and devoted his life to this study.

Confucianism, as perpetuated by its disciples, particularly by Mencius and Hsün Tzu, became a comprehensive humanistic philosophy. It was rational and skeptical, primarily concerned with ethics and with the realization of individual ethics in the spheres of society and government, Confucianism apparently was unsystematic, particularly in comparison with classic Greek or early Indian thought, but we can reconstruct the chief elements of Confucius' political thought.

The ideal of the superior man.   The Chinese term *chün-tzu* means literally "a son of a prince," hence, by extension, a gentleman. Confucius succeeded in imparting new meaning to this conception of the aristocrat by declaring that the term should be defined by individual worth, not by birth alone. Attempting to preserve something of the ancient ideal of the superior man (both nobly born and noble in characteristics) in the rough-and-

tumble open society that was emerging. Confucius acknowledged social mobility. Although himself of the aristocracy, Confucius accepted students from all social backgrounds, and of his known disciples all but two were commoners. The success of his teachings made education in subsequent ages virtually synonymous with Confucian education; this monopoly helped establish his ideals in practice. Confucianism became the uniform intellectual outlook of the educated; it molded the new elite in society and government. *Chün-tzu*, "superior man," was the self-identification of that elite of merit in traditional Chinese society. Though it suffered the fate of all institutionalized ideals in being often honored in the breach, the Confucian ideal was never lost. It provided a source of stability in the rather violent transformation of the *feng-chien* social order in the centuries immediately following Confucius' lifetime, and it helped to assure the enduring existence of the open society that came into being in that process.

The proper model of government.   Confucius said: "The Chou had the advantage of viewing the past two dynasties. How complete and elegant are its regulations! I follow Chou." That is, he accepted the normal viewpoint of his history-minded civilization in looking to the past, but he made that more specific, examining comparatively the political modes of the Shang and the Chou. In announcing his allegiance to the Chou, Confucius expressed his loyalty to the legitimate rulers, and perhaps a wish to harmonize Shang and Chou differences, to strengthen the symbols of cultural unity. But almost certainly the quotation expresses his genuine admiration for the duke of Chou and for his part in creating the *Institutes of Chou (Chou li)*, the great compendium of documents on the structure and the ritualization of society dating from the first reigns of the dynasty.

The rectification of terms (cheng-ming).   Despite the actual revolutionary import of much of his teaching, Confucius was conservative in outlook and cautious in method. His disciples were taught to serve worthy rulers when they could, and to withdraw and cultivate their own qualities when there were no worthy rulers to serve. Serving meant acting vigorously in the ruler's proper interests, making government benevolent, and influencing it by exercising moral suasion on the holders of power. The faults of human government were best analyzed by noting discrepancies between names and realities. For example, a "superior man," a member of the ruling class, was such when he acted according to the import of the name; when the reality of his conduct differed from the import of that name, he was no longer a "superior man" and should be regarded as an ordinary fellow—deprived of office, etc. Thus the famous saying: "Let the prince be a prince, the minister a minister, the father a father, and the son a son . . ." and then government would be accomplished. There are many anecdotes about Confucius and his later followers using this method to lecture rulers and kings on their faults, applying moral suasion and effective, if somewhat idealistic, argument.

Benevolence (jen).   The Confucian ethic is related to government primarily and most fundamentally in terms of *jen*, translated as "benevolence," "human-heartedness," "goodness," etc. It is a term that Confucius tried variously to define, and nowhere in the extant sayings is there a comprehensive statement of its meaning, yet there are repeated indications that he held it to be the most important concept of his thought system. *Jen* assumes the harmonious relations among all the members of the family of man, expressed in gradations of mutual affection and respect from those nearer and dearer to those farther away and less directly recipient of benevolent action. In early Chou times the identity of the state with the extended family of the Chou kings made proper family relations a necessity to government; as in other cases, a concept originally to be applied literally and narrowly was enlarged by Confucius to a metaphorical and idealized meaning. In his conceptualization of *jen*, perhaps consciously drawing on the lenient spirit of Shang tradition to correct a Chou tendency toward rigidity of form, Confucius made one of his most significant additions to the store of Chinese ethical and political concepts.

Moral suasion and ritual propriety versus regulating and punishing.   Confucius believed in a government of superior men whose cultivated minds would lead their behavior to be both benevolently concerned for other men and ritually correct. The rites harmonized men's spirits and led to harmonious relations among all men, thus contributing to the stabilizing harmony of the cosmos. A government of superior men would accomplish these things almost instinctively; superior laws and institutions had only a secondary place in Confucius' ideal. He ranked the techniques of government, giving foremost place to the suasive virtue of the ruler and lowest place to intimidation through punishments. Ideally, the good ruler should be able to govern without exerting himself and without the governed's being aware of government. Therefore, teaching the people to understand virtue was the essential act of government, providing for their material well-being was next in impor-

tance, and organizing them for defense against internal and external enemies was undertaken only as an acknowledgment of failure. Confucius was not so vague about human realities that he would eliminate laws, punishments, and weapons before human well-being could be assured by other means, but he retained a negative attitude toward these aspects of the state's activities. Moreover, he denied to the state an absolute command of the loyalties of its citizens; the "superior man" retained his own responsibility to judge the state and to judge for himself when it merited his services. One of the earliest Confucian texts says: "The administration of government lies in getting the right men, and such men are to be attracted through the power of the ruler's own character." A government of benevolence, functioning through the suasive power of virtue, embodying the cosmic harmony in the ritualization of relations, and relying on the judgment of cultivated men, ideally needed no law codes to be vindicated and no other defenses than the attachment to it that its people naturally would feel toward it, as members of a family toward the family head. Confucius never gained the opportunity to practice these lofty ideals as a chief minister of state or trusted adviser to a ruler, but he fixed this ideal so firmly in the minds of all men who received education through the canonical works and their Confucian school commentaries that all subsequent political theorizing had to take cognizance of it, and most, indeed, proceeded from it; at the very least, it became the established view against which other views must argue.

Mencius.   In many ways Mencius (c. 372–c. 289 B.C.) resembled Confucius. A native of the small state of Tsou, which was adjacent to Confucius' native Lu, pre-eminent in his command of the traditional learning, teacher of a large following of students, Mencius too traveled throughout China but had more success than Confucius in gaining recognition. He expounded his arguments, counseled kings and ministers, and debated with other philosophers. In the century following Confucius, philosophy had burgeoned, schools had appeared, and debate had become an important activity. But political and social dissolution also had progressed. Mencius lived in a world of still greater instability, more widespread warfare, and more intense social suffering. He appears to us as a great-spirited man of compassion in observing the people, a self-confident intellectual in dealing with the powerful, and a philosophical idealist in his political and social views.

In his political thought, Mencius especially developed the Confucian doctrine of benevolence (*jen*) and applied it to politics in ways that went significantly beyond Confucius' thought. This led him to state explicitly that human nature is fundamentally good (Confucius had not made the point explicit), that environment leads men to become bad but that benevolent government can encourage the innate goodness of man to assert itself. Therefore, government must first provide for man's material well-being and, second, teach man to observe family and social ethics. In this, Mencius reversed the order in which Confucius listed the chief responsibilities of government. Mencius also developed at great length the view that the state exists only for the well-being of the people, that they are, in fact, the "root of the state," in comparison with which the ruler is only the relatively unimportant "branch." No interest of the ruler or of the state could take precedence over the need to provide for the people's basic welfare. When the ruler of one state asked the learned Mencius what he could tell him that would profit his state, it brought forth an indignant lecture on the evils of the profit notion. So utilitarian a concept as "profit" was condemned because it destroys the benevolent sense of compassion for all men; ignoble goals could only produce political disorder. "Profit" to Mencius meant expediency in place of altruism and signified the end of benevolence. Mencius' view of the basic importance of the people also led him to the extreme view that "tyrannicide is not regicide."

Mencius' political thought was "liberal" and individualistic in some ways, but not in all. There was nothing in it of the democratic notion of "by the people." It was, rather, a radically idealistic and benevolent kind of paternalism.

The main faults in Mencius' political thought stemmed from carrying the idealistic view of human nature to logical extremes and from lack of realism about human institutions. He often gave vague or impractical political advice to the rulers of his time on specific details of administration. In isolation from his very realistic statements about the impossibility of the people's practicing virtue when they are hungry, such political advice would seem to mark Mencius as a man who knew nothing of social reality. Such was not the case. We must assume that some of his arguments were overdrawn for reasons deriving from particular circumstances. But in general his thought shows an impracticality about political institutions. The most important example of this is his espousal of the antique institution of the "well-field system" apportioning land to groups of eight families who would, in addition to their individual plots, work

a common field. The produce of the shared plot would become full payment of all obligations owed to the state. The model for this ideal system may never have existed, and Mencius may have known that. In any event, it was wholly unrealistic by Mencius' time, when private ownership had become general and when other forms of production than agriculture, demanding other kinds of organization, had grown to significant stature. Yet the idea, as outlined by Mencius, assumed considerable importance. It formed the basis for much later utopian thinking and in imperial times frequently became the springboard for liberal political theorists indirectly protesting the power of the state. In this, and in his denunciation of government by force, Mencius left a heritage of ideas built on Confucian foundations. They remained important elements of political theorizing, though they were not immediately as influential as the rather opposite views of Hsün Tzu.

Hsün Tzu.   The third and last of the great figures in the preimperial development of Confucian thought, Hsün Tzu (c. 300–c. 237 B.C.) lived on the eve of the political unification culminating in the imperial era after two centuries of the Warring States period. Like Confucius and Mencius, he was a man of immense learning, but unlike them, he also had long experience as an administrator, having served for many years as governor of a province.

Within the heritage of ideas developed by Confucius, several traditions emerged. Whereas Mencius stressed *jen*, Hsün Tzu emphasized the rites (*li*), the other principal area of Confucian political conceptualization. Confucius used the term *li* to include all the institutions and regulations by which the state is maintained and society is governed. Hsün Tzu's extensive and tightly reasoned philosophical writings are devoted largely to the exposition and defense of this vast conception of human culture. He is both the most systematic and the most profound thinker of the early Confucian school and is sometimes called its Aristotle. He was a man of great intellectual breadth—poet, musician, thinker, and scholar–bureaucrat, anticipating in these many roles the Confucian ideal elite type of imperial China.

Hsün Tzu disapproved of Mencius and disagreed with him on many basic issues. A tough-minded realist, he declared human nature to be basically animal, predisposed to antisocial, selfish pursuits of gratification and advantage. Like Mencius, however, he was optimistic about the capacity of all men to be perfected and molded by human culture, the highest expression of which was the rites. But whereas Mencius would leave human nature to realize its noble potential in self-expression and to recognize the value of ritual propriety through a cultivated but innate wisdom, Hsün Tzu believed in imposing normative controls and standards to curb innate tendencies and in enforcing their imposition through the power of the state. Though he started from the position that human nature is evil, Hsün Tzu was no less Confucian than Mencius in his stress on education and on the necessity of the state to nurture the people. His goal also was the greater happiness and prosperity of mankind in society. He did not propose the enhancement of the powers of the state for the sake of the state per se. However, his observation of and deep involvement in the disorders of the final stages of the Warring States period probably heightened his appreciation of the need for stability; he was willing to grant a more exalted position and authority to the ruler than had been typical of earlier Confucian thought, and he advocated a strong, centralizing governmental power exercised by or in the name of the legitimate ruler. Although two of his prominent disciples (Li Ssu and Han Fei) did abandon Confucian humanism to become leading figures in Legalism, the charge that Hsün Tzu was a Legalist is unfounded. Hsün Tzu established a view polarized from that of Mencius but one that fully shares in the basic Confucian values and attitudes.

Mo Tzu. Mo Tzu (c. 479–c. 381 B.C.) is interesting as a proponent of radical religious utilitarianism and as the organizer of a distinct social movement in late Chou society. His school is also of interest in the history of Chinese thought for its development of logical method in reasoning and for its epistemology. But in all of these things the Mohists are eccentric and atypical of Chinese civilization. Moreover, the school disappeared as an active element in Chinese political and intellectual life in the third century B.C. and had very little influence on subsequent political thinking. Interest in Mohism has re-emerged in the last two centuries, partly because of points of comparison with non-Chinese philosophies, particularly the interest Christian missionaries have shown in Mohist "universal love."

Mo Tzu probably was educated in the Confucian school tradition, but he revolted against that "elite" point of view and established his own. He attempted to create a rigidly organized company of followers among whom to perpetuate his views and to form the nucleus of the ideal society. He believed quite literally in gods and spirits, increasingly personalizing Heaven as a Supreme Being. He claimed that Confucian rational skepticism angered the gods, with disastrous results for mankind. He repudiated the rites, music, and learning of Confucianism on utilitarian grounds, claiming that they both interfered with productive activity and wasted the fruits of production, to the general impoverishment of mankind. His ideal society was to be one of austerity, permitting no wasted effort. He denied family ethics and family values, arguing that universal love (*chien-ai*) of all men for all men without the inequities of kinship ties would be of material benefit. His views were subject to three kinds of verification: they were the will of the gods and spirits; there were logical proofs of their correctness; they could be demonstrated to have utility in material terms. Mo Tzu cited naive evidence for the first and developed the logical arguments with considerable intellectual clarity, but he relied most heavily in all cases on the utilitarian argument.

Having religious and moral sanctions for his views, Mo Tzu further established a reasoned political form for his ideal society. It was to be organized into an all-embracing hierarchy under a leader exercising absolute authority. The leader would accede to that position naturally, because everyone in the society acknowledged authority for the sake of gaining order and peace; they would "conform to the Superior" both in principle and in the person of the one exemplifying superior qualities. This provided the political sanction for organizing a militaristic society of discipline, mutual surveillance, and total conformity. But it was to be organized for peace, since war is wasteful. Aggressive war was totally outlawed, but Mohists became experts in defensive warfare.

It is probable that some communities of Mohist organization came into being, and they may have persisted for decades. The ideas of Mohism became very important in the fourth and third centuries, during which period the later Mohists added to the book known as the *Mo Tzu*, in particular extending the logical tools needed for debating with Sophists and with the other philosophical schools. Mencius denounced Mohism for its utilitarian, hence amoral, character and also, no doubt, for its materialistic views, which were distasteful to his idealistic turn of mind. The Taoists found Mohism arid and lacking in aesthetic sense, but most of all they found its total organization and conformity to be the worst possible enemy of their ideal of natural freedom. In fact, Mohism could scarcely have been expected to have strong appeal for any significant segment of Chinese life; its appearance, not its disappearance, is the curiosity. However, it shared with other early Chinese schools of thought the overriding

Chinese concern for the problem of how to achieve social order and safety in an age of turmoil and, like Confucianism, its orientation was toward the welfare of the people, not the interests of state or ruler.

Taoism. *Tao* means "roadway," hence, "the Way," and it came to mean to Taoists the great Way of Nature, as opposed to the artifices and devices of human civilization. As a protophilosophical movement it apparently had its origins in early Chou eremitism. Traditionally, the man known as Lao Tzu was regarded as its earliest articulate philosopher. Efforts to discount his historicity and to date his book, the *Tao te ching* (*The Book of Tao*), as a late (i.e., fourth–third century B.C.) work have been strongly countered in recent scholarship. There now seem to be good reasons for considering him an older contemporary of Confucius and for dating the book roughly from that time. The second great figure in Taoism, Chuang Tzu, who lived from about 369 to about 286 B.C., is fully historical, though the known details of his life are rather scanty. Throughout all of Chinese imperial history and into our own time, the *Tao te ching* and the *Chuang Tzu* have been powerfully influential works, intimately known to all educated Chinese and the source of as many common speech images as the Confucian *Analects*. Taoism has functioned as a fascinating and particularly satisfying counterbalance to Confucianism, forming the traditional minor mode of Chinese thought, complementing if seldom seriously challenging the Confucian mainstream. Taoism is a naturalism, taking nature as its standard, whereas humanistic Confucianism takes man, especially the wise sages of antiquity. It is as antisocial, individualistic, and opposed to culture as Confucianism is the opposite. It advances a thoroughly amoral relativism in contrast with Confucianism's moral absolutism. And it includes views ranging from laissez-faire government of inaction to radical anarchism.

The political message of the *Tao te ching* is one of simple naturalism. A small work composed of 81 brief poems, mostly ambiguous lyrics, it has sometimes been described as a handbook for rulers, telling them that the way to govern is the great Way of not governing at all. The Way of Nature can be observed in the action of water, the book's favorite metaphor; water seeks low places, resists nothing, but fills and overcomes everything. "Reversal is the movement of Tao," the book says repeatedly, meaning that all movement is circular, from zenith to nadir and back, each point succeeded by the other. And from this it follows that all striving is vain, since it brings in time the opposite consequences of those directly sought. Hence, leave man alone rather than strive to regulate and guide him. The ruler who does nothing can accomplish everything; he who tries too much can only end up empty-handed. How literally should a metaphor be understood? Most Chinese have tended to regard this as a profoundly wise observation, cautioning simplicity and limitation of government.

Taoism, in keeping with the Chinese world view, is neither ascetic nor unworldly. It accepts life in this world, here and now, as man's real life. But the Taoist sage was one who reasonably limited his pursuit of material gain and pleasure and concentrated on the freedom of the mind. For all men, sage and clod, Taoism sought the greatest possible human happiness, which it equated with freedom. Chuang Tzu's anarchism would never lead to political movements, assassination of tyrants, or any other organized political or social action; it was the anarchism of extreme individualism, seeking the total liberation of the spirit from the fetters of civilization, not by destroying civilization but by ignoring it. It is clearly the antecedent of the typically Chinese movement within later Buddhism called *Ch'an*, best known in the West by the Japanese name of *zen*.

Taoist ideas, because of their great aesthetic and intellectual appeal, had influence on politics even while denying its validity. One curious example is seen in the fact that these ideas provided the image of the ruler who "does nothing and accomplishes everything," an image of the supreme ruler which was used by Legalism in a wholly perverted sense and which in slightly truer sense also helped to form the imperial concept of the emperor who is "above government." Taoist ideas emphasized the futility of government, thereby giving a kind of perspective with which to judge Confucianist activism. At its truest, Taoism could provide a nondisruptive pattern for political protest, for intellectual Taoists would withdraw rather than contest. But on the popular level Taoism—and unlike Confucianism, Taoism was susceptible to gross vulgarization—could spawn magical and superstitious religious and political movements that were frequently very destructive.

Legalism. Legalism is not a comprehensive philosophy; rather, it is primarily a set of methods and principles for the operation of the state which has the barest of ideological foundations. Legalists were content to justify their system by a single comment: "It works." And, unlike all the other thinkers of early China, the Legalists were concerned only with the ruler and his state apparatus; the happiness of the individual and the good of society were considered indirectly if at all. What philosophical foundations Legalism had were drawn largely from sociopsychological observations about human behavior, i.e., how to make people serve the state. It had no speculative interests like cosmology or metaphysics, could abandon logic since it need not worry about convincing people through argument, and abolished ethics as irrelevant. Yet Legalism drew to it some of the most brilliant minds of ancient China and produced a corpus of political writing without parallel for breadth and analytic perceptiveness. It failed ultimately when practiced on a large scale, perhaps because of its philosophical aridity; its understanding of human nature was overly cynical, unnecessarily limited. Even the most perceptive observations on how to manipulate humans through enticement and intimidation failed as a total system of controlled human behavior.

Legalists, too, faced the common problem of early Chinese philosophy: how to achieve stability in an age of turmoil. "Method men," experts on administrative law, economic organization, diplomacy, and other aspects of statecraft began to emerge as advisers to vassal rulers early in Eastern Chou. Shang Yang, who died in 338 B.C., wrote the earliest extant example of the important theoretical discussions of this statecraft.

The great synthesizer of Legalism was Han Fei (who died in 233 B.C.), a scion of the ducal house of Han, an ex-student of Hsün Tzu who repudiated even his authoritarian Confucianism, and an adviser at the court of the king of Ch'in. The state of Ch'in had officially adopted Legalist practice a century earlier, when Lord Shang had been chief minister. Finally, in 230–220 B.C., the decade of unification, the king of Ch'in took the title designed for him by his Legalist advisers, *huang-ti,* or "August Emperor," and inaugurated the imperial era as the first emperor of the Ch'in dynasty. Throughout, Legalist advisers played their important role, and Ch'in success was regarded as the success of a rigidly and ruthlessly applied Legalism. Han Fei became the synthesizer and theoretician of that culminating stage of development, and Li Ssu, his fellow rebel from the school of Hsün Tzu, as prime minister to the first emperor was its ultimate practitioner. Both were put to death under harsh Ch'in laws (misused, it must be admitted, in a non-Legalist manner), along with vast numbers of the suffering population, in one of the world's first experiments with totalitarianism. When popular revolts brought a quick end to the Ch'in dynasty, its Legalist doctrine was openly repudiated and "Legalist" became for all time a term of condemnation to be applied to a political enemy.

But Legalism had provided the actual means of organizing the vast machinery of Chinese government and of uniting the nation into a coherent, governable whole. Though officially and popularly repudiated, many of its features could not be abandoned. Officially, the successor dynasty (the Han, which held power from 206 B.C. to A.D. 220) launched an ideology called by modern scholars "imperial Confucianism," but government throughout the imperial millennia was in fact an enduring and very effective amalgam of Legalist methods and Confucian principles.

Legalist political thought is best seen in the extensive writings preserved in the book of Han Fei, *Han Fei Tzu.* Its inexorably logical analysis and exposition make it one of the universal classics of political theory. The essential elements are the definition of power; the analysis of the sources and the functions of power; the definition of the proper uses of power, namely, to enhance the ruler's position by making his state larger and stronger in economic and military spheres so as to permit him unrestricted attainment of his will; the analysis of the role of the people, who were to be made totally compliant and as productive and efficient as possible in agriculture and in warfare; the role of *fa* (laws, penal regulations, and administrative procedures), designed so perfectly that the state's machinery would run like clockwork, achieving the distorted version of the Taoist ideal of the ruler personally "doing nothing and accomplishing everything." In this state, the *fa* were to be above everything else, even above the ruler, who would not interfere arbitrarily with their design and operation. Moreover, the whole power of the state was to be used to enforce them. For example, it was decreed that refuse was not to be dumped on the streets, on pain of amputation of hands or feet, and the streets of Ch'in became spotless thoroughfares for cripples. Legalist planners well knew how to make such a system function at low administrative cost by involving the whole population in mutual responsibility, much like modern totalitarianism's mutual surveillance techniques.

Legalism is thus both a repellent view of human values and an effective political science. Fortunately, the Chinese empire was able to temper the former with Confucianism without losing too much of the latter.

Early imperial Confucianism

It has been suggested in the preceding section that the actual organization of the Chinese empire drew as much on Legalist practice as it did on Confucian principle. Most of the emperors of the imperial era whose achievements mark them as outstanding were themselves well aware of this and untroubled by it, realizing that the Legalist component strengthened their own position. Usually they recognized that the institutions of the imperial state were scarcely Confucian. Nonetheless, the conscious political theorizing and the formal imperial expressions alike were done in Confucian terms. And the political thought was produced in the overwhelming majority of cases by self-identified Confucians. The Confucian monopoly on education was virtually complete for the whole 2,000-year period. Everyone learned to read from the *Analects*, and then from the other Confucian classics. Service in government was somewhat irregularly controlled by civil service procedures and examinations in Confucian learning even before the seventh century A.D., and with increasing effectiveness after that time. Even during the centuries of Buddhist domination of Chinese intellectual life (especially the fourth to tenth centuries A.D.), Confucian formalism prevailed in the court and throughout the administration. The entire vocabulary of government and of political theory was drawn from Confucian contexts, and even those rare thinkers who consciously espoused non-Confucian ideas did so in Confucian terms. Even though it produced much sterile convention, this continuing presence of Confucianism also formed attitudes and influenced behavior. And occasionally it could come to life and arouse renewed Confucian intellectual vigor.

The political philosophers of the early Han dynasty had to make the initial Confucian adaptation to the needs of imperial China. They were confronted with the difficulty of rationalizing in Confucian terms a state that was a monstrosity in Confucian eyes. Moreover, their own "Confucianism" was strongly colored by contemporary intellectual currents of non-Confucian origin. Scholars throughout the centuries have repeatedly made the discovery that the elements of culture grow and change; only naive fundamentalists are troubled by the discovery. Tung Chung-shu's correlative thinking, with its tortuously devised relationships between man and the cosmos, could not have been anticipated by any Confucian thinker of the pre-imperial era, but it nonetheless constitutes the "Confucianism" of its time.

Tung Chung-shu (c. 179–c. 104 B.C.) stands out among many writers and statesmen of the Han dynasty as the great theorizer of the imperial world. Chief minister of state in the early Han, he established institutional adaptations which aided the Confucian ascendancy over the other schools of thought and helped to fix the acceptance of Confucian norms within the state's apparatus. His political theories were expressed in the form of commentaries on the Confucian canonical work, the *Ch'un ch'iu* ("Spring and Autumn Annals"). He is to be credited with the adoption in Han times of the principle of recruitment for public office that led ultimately, in later dynasties, to the highly rationalized and objective system of written examinations, of merit grading in office, and the other features of the famous Chinese civil service. Tung also helped to Confucianize the Legalist-derived institution of the emperor. On the one hand he drew on the *yin–yang* and Five Elements schools (minor philosophies of the fourth and third centuries B.C.), and on the other, on Confucian ethical concepts, to formulate a cosmology in which the emperor's supreme position, unjustifiable by any earlier political theory except for the repudiated Legalism, could be shown to be a necessary part of the moral Confucian cosmos. In Tung's system, the emperor played an indispensable role as the supreme mediator between mankind and *t'ien*, perhaps best translated in this context as "Nature." The Confucian social ethics, expressed in the three basic relationships (ruler–servitor, father–son, and husband–wife) and five constant ethical responsibilities (benevolence, righteousness, propriety, wisdom, and good faith), were both rigidified in conception and linked mechanistically to the cosmic function while being institutionalized in customary law. Perhaps the reversion to supermoral sanctions marks a degeneration of philosophical Confucianism, but in an age that seemed to call for religious attitudes, Tung Chung-shu's solutions to such problems were at least faithful to the Confucian concept of an ethical cosmos, and this makes it possible for us to speak of "imperial Confucianism" rather than of "imperial Legalism" as the ideological foundation of the Chinese empire. Tung's metaphysical justifications for the political and social order turned out to be of brief historical importance; far more important for imperial history was the firm establishment of at least partially effective Confucian norms for that political and social order.

The extremes of anti-intellectualism and credulity to which Tung's metaphysics could degenerate were attacked by many later Han thinkers, mostly in the name of a purer Confucianism. Most important are the skeptical critiques of Wang Ch'ung (A.D. 27–c. 100), who said of his great book of essays, the *Lun heng* ("Critical Essays") that its message could be summed up in the single phrase, "Hatred of fiction and falsehoods." Wang Ch'ung's

Confucianism reflected a new tendency to draw heavily on Taoist naturalism as an antidote against the mechanistically teleological cosmology of Tung's school of Han Confucianism. Confucian thought was capable of extravagant departures from basic Confucian attitudes, but it was always capable of producing its own self-criticism and corrective.

In the long period from the end of the Han dynasty to the beginning of the Sung, Chinese intellectual life was marked by the presence of a largely devitalized Confucian formalism, linked with the routine operation of the state and nominally conveying the norms of society. At the same time, intellectual vitality was manifested almost exclusively, first in Neo-Taoism (especially in the third century) and later in Buddhism. This long and philosophically rich period did not, however, contribute much to political thought, except indirectly, by enlarging the realm of the mind. Metaphysical speculation became an important part of the Chinese intellectual preoccupation, requiring even political thought thereafter to relate to metaphysical concepts.

Neo-Confucian political thought

Neo-Confucianism is the term by which one designates the ground of intellectual activity in the last thousand years of traditional Chinese history. It was a philosophical movement of the greatest possible breadth; at the same time it provided an entirely new direction and tone to many aspects of daily life beyond the reach of formal philosophy. The movement began in the ninth century as a segment of the scholar-officialdom's protest against Buddhist excesses in areas of social and political relevance. Chinese statesmen were concerned about conflicts of interest between the Buddhist church institution and the institutions of traditional Chinese state and society. Out of the opposition to the Indian (but by now long Sinicized) religion there appeared a general revival of Confucian values and of interest in classical Confucian ideas, hence the name Neo-Confucianism for the movement. We can regard Neo-Confucianism as a new synthesis of Chinese values and Chinese thought, consciously aiming at the recovery of pristine Confucian elements but in fact having become a much broader and somewhat differently oriented philosophy than early Confucianism had been.

Philosophically, Neo-Confucianism began by elevating the *Mencius* to a position second only to the *Analects*, while the *Hsün Tzu* was regarded simply as another Confucian school work, admirable though faulty. No doubt the Mencian idealism, with its overtones of mysticism, was more congenial, in pure philosophical terms, to the post-Buddhist mind of China. Yet the political theories of Neo-Confucian thinkers often seem much closer to the authoritarian spirit of Hsün Tzu, whose concept of the state more closely fit the realities of the long-established authoritarian empire.

Han Yü (768–824) is usually looked upon as the first great figure in the Neo-Confucian movement. He and his contemporaries began to reawaken interest in political theorizing, although their most important influence on subsequent history probably was simply to arouse the sense of rediscovery of pre-Buddhist ideas and values in philosophy and in literature (seeing the latter as the vehicle for the former), with which to launch a Chinese reaction against Buddhism. The formal Neo-Confucian philosophy saw its great flowering more than a century later, in the eleventh century, during which cosmological and metaphysical speculation was the major activity, and in the twelfth century, with the synthesizing work of Chu Hsi (1130–1200).

Neo-Confucianist rationalism. Ultimately most of the Neo-Confucianists resolved their understanding of the cosmos in terms of the dualism of reason and matter. Matter was thought of as being in a constant cycle of dispersion and concentration, dispersed in the formless ether and concentrated in the myriad forms of concrete reality. Matter assumed specific forms by the interaction of the polar modes (*yin* and *yang*) under the dynamism of cosmic harmony—a force that at the same time sustains human ethical conceptions. The Supreme Ultimate was a kind of comprehensive principle subsuming all of the specific principles of the myriad forms. Man did not invent objects or institutions but discovered their principles, which eternally exist whether or not material reality participates in their existence. Thus, there was a principle for government, for the ruler, for the state, and for all of the institutions of society and government. These made government possible but did not guarantee its quality. Man could improve the actual institutions of his time by perfecting his understanding of the ideal forms and causing their material counterparts to adhere more closely to the forms. Thus Chu Hsi discussed Mencius' distinction between the kingly government (*wang-tao*) and government by force (*pa-tao*), showing that the former embodied harmony and accorded with universal principle, whereas the latter deflected harmony and was divergent.

All of the Neo-Confucianist philosophers, widely split on many philosophic issues, more or less agreed in their basic political concepts. Given the foregoing rationalization of the state, they could readily subscribe to the Mencian doctrine of benevolent government, and indeed all of them positively advocated government by men deeply concerned about the moral rightness of their actions and about the welfare of the people. Yet in their moral zeal, and with their new metaphysical concepts of eternal principles serving as standards of human behavior, their thought could easily become more rigidly normative than was the case in early Confucianism, especially than was the case with Mencius. For example, the metaphor of the Supreme Ultimate in its hierarchy of cosmic forces, sustaining and ordering the myriad forms of life, was readily extended in literal fashion to the Supreme Emperor, Son of Heaven, exalted capstone of a hierarchy of political forces and social realities. Nothing so direct was consciously set forth by any of the Neo-Confucian cosmologists, but the detached character of their political discourses perhaps prevented this popular and even official misuse of the analogy from being repudiated by them. For another example, the old Confucian virtue of reciprocal loyalty between servitor and ruler, revived with moral zeal, came to be a one-way loyalty binding only the servitor and diminishing the play of his own judgment in deciding when the worthy ruler merited loyal service. For many reasons, of which conscious philosophizing may indeed be only one, the Neo-Confucian era was one of continuous enhancement of authoritarianism.

Reform and counterreform. During the Sung period, a distinctive feature of traditional Chinese society was the lack of specialization and differentiation of function of its elite; a vital Neo-Confucianism tended to impart an even greater uniformity of outlook. But commencing with the Sung dynasty (sometimes argued by cultural historians to be the beginning of modern China), one finds that the greatest figures in philosophy are not entirely identical with the great figures in active politics or with those in the more pragmatic political analysis and theory. And, if the political thought of the great metaphysicians and system builders is generally lacking in originality, that of their contemporaries who led the political factions of the day is of much greater interest. And there is the third group who were neither leading philosophers of the Neo-Confucian movement nor eminent statesmen but who produced a realistic

and analytically perceptive brand of utilitarian political theory. These latter two groups stimulated repeated political reform movements throughout the Sung period.

The most famous reform movement is that led by Wang An-shih (1021–1086). Wang used his position as chief minister in the years 1069–1076, when he enjoyed a rare degree of support from the throne, to promote sweeping reforms of government administration, of the fiscal and economic systems, and of military organization. He stirred up a mass of protest from within the scholar-officialdom, which led to a strong counterreform under the opposition leaders, with alternation in power of bickering factions for some decades thereafter. The political history of the period is itself quite revealing of the growth and change in Sung society. Wang An-shih's reform program was the second such major movement in Sung history, and still others followed. It is difficult to know the actual motivation of the reformers, and still more difficult to ascertain those of the counter-reformers. Their own statements on the subject are always admirably Confucian. Traditionally, and still in our own time, attempts to explain them have focused on regional factors, social backgrounds, economic interests, religion, and differing philosophic points of view. Whatever the factors causing political factionalism, reform thought tended to take a strongly utilitarian line. These reformers, masters of traditional scholarship themselves who insisted that their Confucian learning was both consistent and pure, felt that the Confucian society could survive only if the state were stronger, richer, militarily more efficient and powerful, and administratively more effective. Wang An-shih claimed to be reviving principles inherent in the *Institutes of Chou (Chou li)*, revered by Confucius. His enemies, however, called his ideas "Legalist."

The counterreform was at first led by the statesman-historian Ssu-ma Kuang (1019–1086), whose Confucian thought is very much of Hsün Tzu's authoritarian stamp; in fact, he took a position (remarkable among Neo-Confucians) seriously doubting the validity of the text of the *Mencius* where it is most outspoken in denying supreme power and dignity to the ruler and his state apparatus. He is the most extreme of Neo-Confucian spokesmen in upholding the exalted position of the supreme monarch and demanding of the loyal servitor an unquestioning subservience to him. Yet his concept of government is Confucian in its emphasis on benevolence and righteousness and, like much Neo-Confucian thought, is tinged with Taoism, especially noticeable in its laissez-faire economic views. He appears to have opposed Wang An-shih primarily on the grounds that radical innovation in institutions was reckless and ill-founded, though there undoubtedly were other, perhaps more personal, reasons as well.

Southern Sung utilitarian thinkers continued in the tradition established in the northern Sung and manifested most strikingly in Wang An-shih but did not succeed in gaining similar opportunities for experimentation at the highest level of government. Ch'en Liang (1143–1194) and Yeh Shih (1150–1223) are the most important.

Ch'en Liang found the political thought of contemporary Neo-Confucian philosophers like Chu Hsi too theoretical and too vague; he advocated more direct and realistic means of benefiting the people, thereby enriching and strengthening the state. He was particularly critical of administrative overcentralization, with resultant lack of initiative and efficiency in local government, and he was a harsh opponent of the compromise peace which left the Sung dynasty in insecure control of only its southern provinces, with the Jürched Chin conquerors in possession of the north. His political thought and criticisms of government were uncongenial to the Neo-Confucian philosophical trends, as well as to the intrenched interested of the scholar-gentry.

Yeh Shih had a distinguished early career as an administrator, but he ran afoul of factional politics and devoted much of his life thereafter to debating the meaning of classical political concepts with the Neo-Confucian philosophers. Although basically committed to the people's welfare, in the Mencian spirit, he dared to reject the Mencian distaste for the word "profit" or "benefit," attempting to demonstrate that good government in fact ensues from the realistic pursuit of material benefit. He was also critical of vague parallels with antiquity as drawn by more theoretical-minded Neo-Confucians. He was more clear-minded than most of his contemporaries about growth and change, and about the differences between the environment in which ancient models for institutions may have existed and the present. His focus on institutional development and analysis of institutional weaknesses marks him as a new kind of political scientist in the long history of Chinese political thought.

Neo-Confucian idealism.   In the Ming period, which lasted from 1368 to 1644, authoritarian government achieved a degree of despotic realization previously unknown. The Chu Hsi orthodoxy became one of the instruments of state control. Although nothing so comprehensive as modern totalitarian thought control could be realized in that society, the official orthodoxy became rigid and narrowly restrictive. Wang Shou-jen (1472–1528, also known as Wang Yang-ming), after a long period of intellectual search and in a moment of personal crisis, experienced a sudden enlightenment with the discovery of the truth that Mind is the single reality. This unorthodox idealist position was interpreted by Wang's followers as the discovery of individual freedom. Wang himself was an eminent literatus, governor, general, and pillar of the official world; his career and his personal behavior are unmarked by any departure from proper norms. But his thought implies radical rejection of all externally imposed norms and a reaffirmation of the Mencian freedom of the spirit to discover truth within the self. This had explosive results, especially among Wang's followers in the generation or two after his death. His idealism became a broad movement with a popular following and with a profound effect on society at large. It enhanced the conception of the dignity of the individual, and it led to greater opportunity for education of the common people. Eventually it produced extremes of libertarianism and eccentricity that demanded forceful suppression. The movement was somewhat discredited among thinkers and was recognized as a danger to the state. With the change of dynasty in 1644 it was effectively discouraged.

Wang's political thought as such is neither extensive nor explicit. It stressed the Mencian ideal of moral suasion and advocated broader education of the masses in order to help them realize their human potential for perfection. In maintaining that the awareness of truth and the sense of ethical correctness were minimally latent within all individuals, it was antiauthoritarian without intending to be revolutionary. He implied a degree of equality and of freedom in society quite in agreement with the Confucian concept of the "superior man," but it was socially dangerous when taken crudely and out of the context of Wang's ideas. It is significant that modern Chinese communist historians regard Wang as the voice of a newly emergent urban bourgeoisie, a kind of Chinese Rousseau. Among later followers of his school in the century after his death were many free-thinking radicals and some of the most interesting minds in Chinese intellectual history.

Continuity of traditional thought.   In the succeeding Manchu Ch'ing dynasty (1644–1912) the Neo-Confucian orthodoxy, defined in the synthesis wrought by Chu Hsi and functioning most directly in the bureaucratic civil service system, was rigidly and narrowly maintained. But particularly in the early years of the dynasty, some scholars remained independent of the elite career and, as private members of society more or less defying the government, reflected on Ming errors and wrote critically of the faults of authoritarianism.

The best-known figure in this connection is Huang Tsung-hsi (1610–1695) whose book *Ming-i tai-fang lu* (sometimes translated "A Plan for the Prince") is a thoroughgoing analysis of the faults of the imperial system as known in the Ming period. Although this book had no influence on politics at the time, its influence on thought was very great; moreover, it became a basic source book for the late nineteenth-century revolutionaries plotting the overthrow of the Ch'ing and the creation of a new moden society. Huang's basic political tenets are two: first, the Mencian doctrine of the primary importance of the people in any conceptualization of government, and second, the idea drawn from the *Book of Rites* (one of the ancient Confucian classics) that the empire is a great commonality, i.e., it is not the private property of the emperor, to do with as he wishes. Both of these clearly are aimed at the excesses of despotic emperors.

Huang Tsung-hsi saw the great fault in the gradual concentration of all powers in the hands of the emperor himself and the disappearance of supporting agencies and offices, through which administrative initiative and decision had been spread through a high level of responsible civil officials. This process culminated in the Ming period, with the abolition of the prime ministership in 1380. The Confucian ideal of wise ministers counseling and admonishing the ruler could never be realized in a court dominated by an arbitrary despot who shared none of his authority with his Confucian advisers, who intimidated them with force, and who regarded the operation of government as his private business. It is interesting that Huang's thought stemmed essentially from Wang Yang-ming's Neo-Confucian idealism; that of his great contemporary Ku Yen-wu (1613–1682) agreed with him in all essentials as far as the condemnation of authoritarianism is concerned but was in the tradition of Chu Hsi's rationalism. A third great figure of the time, Wang Fu-chih (who lived from 1619 to 1692) was perhaps the most original and independent-minded of all, with a more objective appreciation of the facts of historical development; he repudiated the excesses of despotism without being driven to seek ideal forms in an antique past. The three great figures show the scope of Confucian thought at the time and the resources it possessed for self-generated criticism and renovation. But none of these men launched a political reform movement that could seize power and bring his critical thought to bear on government. Throughout the century after their deaths, other thinkers continued to give evidence of the potential vitality of the Confucian heritage, but none could break through the crystallized forms of the Legalist–Confucian imperial institution. It might have happened, but in fact it did not, until the impact of the West and events external to the Chinese cultural world undermined its eternal verities and pointed the way to a radical transformation of Chinese civilization.

FREDERICK W. MOTE

BIBLIOGRAPHY

CLASSICAL WORKS

CHUANG TZU *Chuang Tzu: Mystic, Moralist, and Social Reformer.* Translated by Herbert A. Giles. 2d ed., rev. London: Quaritch, 1926.

CHUANG TZU *Chuang Tzu: A New Selected Translation With an Exposition of the Philosophy of Kuo Hsiang.* 2d ed. New York: Paragon, 1964. → A paperback edition, *Basic Writings*, was published in 1964 by Columbia Univ. Press.

CHU HSI *Dschu Hsi: Djin-si Lu: Die sungkonfuzianische Summa.* 3 vols. Tokyo: Sophia Univ. Press, 1953. → A German translation of *Chin-ssu lu.*

CONFUCIUS *The Ethics of Confucius: The Sayings of the Master and His Disciples Upon the Conduct of "the Superior Man."* New York and London: Putnam, 1915.

CONFUCIUS *The Conduct of Life: Or, The Universal Order of Confucius.* London: Murray, 1928.

CONFUCIUS *The Analects: Or, The Conversations of Confucius With His Disciples and Certain Others.* Oxford Univ. Press, 1937.

CONFUCIUS *The Wisdom of Confucius.* Edited and translated by Lin Yutang. New York: Modern Library, 1938.

HAN FEI *The Complete Works of Han Fei Tzu.* Translated with introduction, notes, glossary, and index by W. K. Liao. London: Probsthain, 1939. → The author is often referred to as Han Fei Tzu.

HAN YÜ *The Veritable Record of the T'ang Emperor Shun-tsung.* Cambridge, Mass.: Harvard Univ. Press, 1955. → A technical annotated translation of the *Shun-tsung shih-lu*, the only extant T'ang reign history.

HSÜN TZU *Basic Writings.* New York: Columbia Univ. Press, 1963.

HUANG TSUNG-HSI *A Plan for the Prince.* Translated by W. T. de Bary. Ph.D. dissertation, Columbia University, 1953. → Translation of the *Ming-i tai-fang lu.*

LAO TZU *The Book of Tao.* Mount Vernon, N.Y.: Peter Pauper Press, 1962. → Translation of the *Tao te ching.*

MENG TSU *Mencius.* Translated and annotated by W. A. C. H. Dobson. Univ. of Toronto Press, 1963.

MO TZU *Mo Tzu: Basic Writings.* New York: Columbia Univ. Press, 1963. → The author is often referred to as Mo Ti.

Ssu-ma Kuang *The Chronicle of the Three Kingdoms: 220–265.* Translated by Achilles Fang. Cambridge, Mass.: Harvard Univ. Press, 1952. → Translation of Chapters 69–78 of Ssu-ma Kuang's comprehensive narrative history of pre-Sung China, *Tzu-chih t'ung-chien.*

Wang Shou-jen *The Philosophy of Wang Yang-ming.* Translated by Frederick G. Henke. London and Chicago: Open Court, 1916. → Wang Shou-jen is also known as Wang Yang-ming.

Yang Kung-sun *The Book of Lord Shang: A Classic of the Chinese School of Law.* London: Probsthain, 1928. → A translation of the Chinese *Shang-chün-shu.* The author is often referred to as Kung-sun Yang or as Shang Yang.

MODERN WRITINGS

Bruce, Joseph P. 1923 *Chu Hsi and His Masters: An Introduction to Chu Hsi and the Sung School of Chinese Philosophy.* London: Probsthain.

Chan, Wing T. 1961 *An Outline and an Annotated Bibliography of Chinese Philosophy.* New Haven: Yale Univ., Far Eastern Pub.

Chan, Wing T. 1963 *A Source Book in Chinese Philosophy.* Princeton Univ. Press. → See especially pages 271–288, "Yin Yang Confucianism: Tung Chung-shu," and pages 692–702, "The Materialism of Wang Fu-chih."

Chang Chia-sen 1957–1962 *The Development of Neo-Confucian Thought.* 2 vols. New York: Bookman.

Fairbank, John K. (editor) 1957 *Chinese Thought and Institutions.* University of Chicago, Comparative Studies of Cultures and Civilizations. Univ. of Chicago Press.

Hucker, Charles O. 1962 *China: A Critical Bibliography.* Tucson: Univ. of Arizona Press.

Liang Ch'i-ch'ao 1930 *History of Chinese Political Thought During the Early Tsin Period.* New York: Harcourt; London: Routledge.

Lin Mou-sheng 1942 *Men and Ideas: An Informal History of Chinese Political Thought.* New York: Day.

Liu, James Tzu-chien 1959 *Reform in Sung China: Wang An-shih (1021–1086) and His New Policies.* Harvard University, Center for East Asian Studies, Harvard East Studies, No. 3. Cambridge, Mass.: Harvard Univ. Press.

Nivison, D. S.; and Wright, Arthur F. (editors) 1959 *Confucianism in Action.* Stanford Univ. Press.

Pott, William 1925 *Chinese Political Philosophy.* New York: Knopf.

Pulleyblank, Edwin G. 1960 Neo-Confucianism and Neo-Legalism in T'ang Intellectual Life: 755–805. Pages 77–114 in A. F. Wright (editor), *The Confucian Persuasion.* Stanford Univ. Press.

Thomas, Elbert D. 1927 *Chinese Political Thought: A Study Based Upon the Theories of the Principal Thinkers of the Chou Period.* New York: Prentice-Hall.

Williamson, Henry R. 1935–1937 *Wang An Shih: A Chinese Statesman and Educationalist of Sung Dynasty.* 2 vols. London: Probsthain.

Wright, Arthur F. (editor) 1953 *Studies in Chinese Thought.* University of Chicago, Comparative Studies of Cultures and Civilizations. Univ. of Chicago Press.

Wright, Arthur F. (editor) 1960 *The Confucian Persuasion.* Stanford Univ. Press.

Wright, Arthur F.; and Twitchett, D. C. (editors) 1962 *Confucian Personalities.* Stanford Univ. Press.

Wu Kuo-cheng 1928 *Ancient Chinese Political Theories.* Shanghai: Commercial Press.

CHINESE SOCIETY

Hegel spoke of China as the country *"des ewig wiederkehrenden Prinzips,"* meaning, in general, "eternal" China. Eternity, however, is not a concept much in vogue in a time when revolutionary changes are transforming almost every human society in the world. China appeared eternal to the French *philosophes* of the eighteenth century, many Sinologues of the nineteenth century, and some social scientists of the early twentieth century. Even at present some historians claim they see the re-emergence of old imperial patterns. There is continuity, but the changes have been more profound.

This article examines Chinese society in three stages. The first is traditional Chinese society, characterized by the social patterns that prevailed from the Sung dynasty (960–1279) until the beginning of the nineteenth century. However, it is necessary to begin with an account of the development of these patterns in the earliest centuries of Chinese civilization. The second stage is transitional Chinese society, characterized essentially by the patterns of Chinese society growing out of the dual impact of inland revolution and Western imperialism, which struck China almost simultaneously during the middle of the nineteenth century. The third is contemporary Chinese society—the patterns of Chinese society which arose after 1949, when the communists assumed control over the Chinese mainland.

Our main theoretical approach distinguishes between state and social system. By state we mean the macrosocietal structure of legitimate and organized political power. By a social system we mean a microsocietal structure of authority and human relationships deriving therefrom, whose boundaries can often be historically and culturally determined. The state, as a formalistic entity, ruled an aggregate of particular or local social systems. Chinese society represents a unity of state and social systems held together by institutionalized links. In traditional times, linkage between state and social systems was provided by a status group, known in the West as the gentry, which had substantive attachment both to the state and to a social system. In contemporary times, similar linkage is provided by the Communist party. The theoretical distinction between gentry and party is close to that made by Max Weber between status groups and parties ([1906–1924] 1946, pp. 194–195).

We regard this theoretical approach as an explanatory device to account for both the flexibility and changes in traditional Chinese society and the nature of the Chinese revolution. The three interlocking sectors of Chinese society (state, gentry, and local social system) historically gave it different options for maintaining the traditional patterns of power and authority. The state recruited from the gentry to fill its positions of power (notably bureaucratic). In turn, local elites reinforced their authority within the social systems through the exercise of state power roles. The cumulative effect of the interaction between state and social systems was the appearance and persistence of a distinct status group.

The main criterion for recruitment into the organizations of the state was education based on the ethos of Confucianism. Internalization of that ethos through the institutionalized educational system assured an individual society-wide status, on the basis of which he could obtain power roles within the state and also authority roles within the local social system.

In traditional times, the legitimacy of the state was sustained by the ethos of Confucianism, and its organization was concretely manifested in government (monarchy and bureaucracy). However, it is theoretically important to note that one segment of the state, the military, was independent of the complex of state, gentry, and social system. The military was attached to the monarchy, and for many centuries was non-Chinese. The dual nature of the traditional Chinese state has its counterpart in other traditional and modern societies.

The social systems were sustained by particular and local cultures, which included the ethos (Confucianism) but also other distinct cultural beliefs and values, and by patterns of human relationships based on status and authority.

The gentry, as the institutionalized link between state and social system, had a character of its own, but the composition of this status group varied from time to time. Since there were several options for achieving gentry status and recruitment was generally open, the gentry never developed the characteristics of a caste or an estate; it resembled more some of the "middle classes" of modern societies.

These structural elements are the core elements of traditional Chinese society. Since the core elements were either destroyed or profoundly transformed during the last one hundred years, we regard the Chinese revolution as a major transformation of Chinese society. The dominant ethos, Confucianism, was destroyed by the intellectual revolution of the early twentieth century. The dominant governmental organization of the traditional Chinese state disappeared with the 1911 revolution. The gentry was destroyed, as an elite and as a source of authority, by the revolutionary land re-

form of the late 1940s, thus doing away with traditional local stratification and status. Local cultures have changed more slowly, but the far-reaching liberation of women in modern times can be construed as having struck a deep blow to the traditional kinship system, so vital to all Chinese local cultures.

Since we regard change and not continuity as the main phenomenon to be explained in Chinese society, we have chosen to analyze it in the framework of the three mentioned stages.

Traditional Chinese society

The Chinese historically regard China both as a country and a culture, as evident in two words for China, *Chung-kuo* and *Chung-hua*. As a country, it occupies a large land mass in eastern Asia; except for Sinkiang and Tibet, both areas of non-Chinese peoples, its borders have not basically changed in two thousand years. As a culture, China extends to wherever there are ethnic Chinese. Since China's dual character as country and as culture is significant for understanding traditional Chinese society, let us first examine China's historical background.

During the second millennium B.C., the present area of China was inhabited by peoples belonging to at least eight different culture groups. Archeological comparisons suggest relationships between these cultures and those of proto-Tungusic peoples of the northeast, proto-Turkic peoples of the northwest, Tibetan peoples of the west, and the peoples of southeast Asia. During the middle of the second millennium B.C., tribal groups from the central and southern parts of Hopei invaded the rich agricultural regions of Honan. They founded several large cities, the most notable of which was Anyang. With Anyang as a political and military base, these tribal peoples created China's first empire—the Shang (Eberhard 1948; Needham 1954; Cheng 1959).

The development of empire and high culture occurred simultaneously. Although the cultural diversity of neolithic times continued well into the first millennium B.C., the Shang created China's first high culture, characterized primarily by the development of a system of writing that is the direct ancestor of the modern Chinese written language. The importance of writing in the subsequent high culture of China is reflected by the fact that the word *wen* in Chinese signifies both writing and culture.

During the latter part of the second millennium B.C., invaders from the northwest destroyed the Shang dynasty and established the Chou dynasty. The Chou dynasty created the first permanent system of political dominion; the rulers divided the country into appanages governed by relatives and allies of the dynasty. Each appanage was based on a town from which rule was exercised over surrounding villages and tribes. The links between dynasty and appanage were maintained through bonds of kinship, ritual, and loyalty. This system of personal indirect rule, in contrast to the impersonal bureaucratic rule which developed later, bears similarities to medieval European feudalism.

Although over-all Chinese cultural unity developed further during the Chou, largely through the linguistic unification of north China, the high-cultural achievements of the early Chou were not outstanding. A major reason was the downfall of the Shang priestly caste, which earlier had been the main creative element in Shang high culture. In contrast to the Shang religion of heaven worship and totemism, the Chou religion was essentially a politically oriented ancestor worship which tended to develop locally rather than nationally, thus impeding the formation of a unified high culture (Eberhard 1948, pp. 26–32 in 1950 edition; Reischauer & Fairbank 1960, vol. 1, pp. 49–52).

Great changes occurred during the middle of the Chou dynasty. The appanages became increasingly independent of central political authority. Economically, Chinese rural and urban life was transformed. Intensive agriculture replaced the extensive agriculture of the Shang. The use of irrigation led to stable villages. The introduction of wheat permitted a two-crop economy, which further consolidated village life. Iron not only revolutionized agricultural technology but made new types of warfare possible. The growth of trade led to an expansion of the towns. Socially, the increase in population led to migrations, which brought Chinese into the aborigine-settled areas of the Yangtze River basin and even farther south. All these changes laid the groundwork for the rise of China's classical age, a period of creative thought comparable to the Attic period in Greece. As in Greece, growing political disunity was accompanied by growing cultural unity. The language and concepts of the philosophers, although differing widely in content, came from the same cultural matrix. With few exceptions, almost all the philosophic currents explored paths that could lead to a new political unification (Reischauer & Fairbank 1960, vol. 1, pp. 53–84).

Unification came in the third century B.C. through the Ch'in dynasty. Though short-lived, it brought into being the organized state based on bureaucratic rule. The succeeding Han dynasty further expanded the Ch'in system of rule, which became the basis of the political structure in China for the next two thousand years. The political continuity and stability of the Chinese empire are unmatched anywhere else in the world; without the state bureaucracy, the history of China would indeed have been different.

If bureaucracy was the instrument of rule, the source of power was monarchy. From the Ch'in dynasty to the twentieth century, China was ruled by emperors who were regarded as the sole agents of heaven on earth. Despite the strong ties between monarchy and bureaucracy, the two remained distinct; many emperors, for example, held religious beliefs different from the predominant Confucianism of the bureaucracy. In later centuries, the monarchy became the preserve of alien conquerors; from the twelfth to the twentieth century the emperors were Chinese only during three centuries (Levenson 1958–1965, vol. 2, pp. 25–73).

During the Han dynasty China's traditional ethos of Confucianism was institutionalized. From the welter of philosophic currents of the preceding period, the teachings of Confucius emerged as doctrinal. Confucianism, in effect, became the ethos of bureaucracy. It was an ethos of legitimate authority, as expressed in the five basic human relationships: emperor–subject, father–son, elder brother–younger brother, husband–wife, and friend–friend (only the last relationship expresses egalitarian values). Its religious core combined belief in the natural law of heaven and the sanctity of descent and kinship (Yang 1961, pp. 244–257).

From the Han to the Ch'ing dynasty, China was essentially held together as an organized state based on bureaucracy and governed by the ethos of Confucianism. During the early decades of the Han, the Chinese empire began to assume the geographical form characteristic of modern China. In the process of expansion, the Han political and cultural system spread over large areas of central and south China, which were then inhabited by non-Chinese peoples culturally related to the peoples of southeast Asia. Over the centuries, a gradual process of cultural assimilation took place; aboriginal languages were replaced by the Chinese language, and Chinese high culture prevailed. Today there are still minorities who speak non-Chinese languages and have distinct particular cultures but who participate in the Chinese high culture.

Traditional China was a unified political and cultural entity. Was it a society? Despite political and cultural unity, considerable local diversity persisted and even increased over the centuries. The Chinese language split into many dialects, many of which became mutually unintelligible. Diversity was social as well as cultural, for customs differed widely across the country. This was traditionally reflected in law, which recognized local practices in the adjudication of offenses and disputes (Niida 1952, pp. 49–51; Wang 1937, p. 15).

In their joint memorandum on the concepts of culture and social system, Talcott Parsons and Alfred Kroeber defined a social system as "the specifically relational system of interaction among individuals and collectivities" (Kroeber & Parsons 1958, p. 583). In traditional China, such "specifically relational systems of interaction" were local rather than national. If marriage and kinship are taken as significant indicators of concrete relationships, then the boundaries of the social system rarely went beyond the *hsien* (district). In fact, in most instances the boundaries were marked by areas centering on market towns (Skinner 1964–1965).

One of the most important functions of social systems is the generation of authority, specifically in the form of status groups and notables. Western observers in the nineteenth century called the ruling status group they found throughout China the "gentry." However, modern scholars have objected to the word on grounds of false analogy with the gentry of eighteenth-century England. Ping-ti Ho contrasts the Chinese "class of officials and potential officials," often including men of modest means, to the English gentry, whose power and authority were based on the ownership of land (1962, p. 40). Wolfram Eberhard, on the other hand, regards local landowning as the chief mark of the Chinese gentry (1952, pp. 13 ff.). The long-continuing "gentry controversy" among Sinologists basically revolves around the question whether the ruling status group derived their power and authority from the state or from the local social systems. Since the Chinese themselves have no traditional term to designate the ruling status group, the controversy cannot be settled by reference to the Chinese sources. However, if one looks at the documents of China's numerous revolts during the nineteenth and twentieth centuries, one finds a recurrence of the words "officials, landlords, and notables" (*shen*) to designate the class enemies of the revolutionaries. The common phrases are "corrupt officials and venal clerks, local landlords and debased notables." Officials and their clerks made up the traditional magistracies. The word *shen*, which we render as "notable," has been responsible for much of the confusion surrounding the gentry. Strictly speaking, the *shen* were members of the scholar–official class who did not hold office in the state bureaucracy; the lowest members of this group were often little more than poor schoolteachers in the village (Fei [1947–1948] 1953, pp. 177 ff.). This indicates that gentry status had its roots both in the state and in the local social systems. G. William Skinner has suggested a solution to the controversy through "a recognition in future research that social structure in the middle range of traditional Chinese society is at once derivative of and enmeshed in two quite distinctive hierarchical systems—that of administration to be sure, but that of marketing as well" (1964–1965, p. 43). What Skinner calls "marketing" is what we call local social systems.

While all observers agree that China had a ruling status group linking state and society, the traditional Chinese designation of that group as "officials, landlords, and notables" suggests that there were three different sources of status—in effect, power, wealth, and prestige. At different periods of Chinese history, each of these factors had a different weight in the determination of status. Thus, during the first half of the first millennium A.D., landed wealth and genealogical prestige appear to have been the dominant factors, as evident in the existence of great aristocratic families. Subsequently, as the result of rapid socioeconomic development, a new landed meritocracy emerged, which acquired prestige through education, thus substituting official prestige for genealogical prestige. With the growth of political centralization during the Ming and Ch'ing, actual and potential bureaucratic position combined with education became the leading determinants of status (Ho 1962, pp. 259–262). However, regardless of the changing weights of the power, wealth, and prestige factors, acquisition of bureaucratic rank ultimately meant a rise in all three of these status determinants.

The ruling status group, which we shall henceforth call the gentry, enjoyed power, wealth, and prestige both within the state and within the local social systems. Because of the openness of membership, the gentry was neither an estate nor a caste, unlike the Japanese *bushi* and European nobles or the Indian Brahmins and Rajputs. Its members ranged from officials associated mainly with the state to landlords who belonged to prestigious and wealthy local families; the notables enjoyed mainly prestige as the result of education in the Confucian high culture. The gentry, with its large families, provided the model for those familistic values which have been considered so characteristic of traditional Chinese society. The clan, whose leading members were gentry but whose ordinary members were often poor peasants, symbolized the ideal solidarity of the traditional local social system (Hsu 1963, pp. 60 ff.).

We can thus say that traditional China consisted of a universal state characterized by a common high culture and a multiplicity of particular social systems of diverse local culture. The gentry formed the link between the two. Landed wealth gave the gentry access to higher education; internalization of the high culture allowed the gentry to assume positions in the state bureaucracy. Participation in the bureaucracy, in turn, contributed to the consolidation of local power, prestige, and wealth. The state recruited primarily from local status groups to fill the roles of organization. With the strict separation of monarchy and bureaucracy and of military and civil, local status groups were not endangered by alien competition for state bureaucratic positions. So entrenched had the system become that even foreign dynasties, such as the Mongol Yüan and the Manchu Ch'ing, had to accept it to consolidate their rule over China.

If we define a society as the broadest aggregate of people governed by common cultural, political, and social norms, traditional Chinese society coincided more or less with the territory of the Chinese empire. Prior to the development of the modern nation-state, there have been few instances in world history of the outer limits of society coinciding with those of political dominion. The ephemeral empires of the Islamic and Indian worlds, for example, were never able to bring state and society into line. Since the historical boundaries of the Chinese empire expanded more rapidly than those of the society, we can conclude that it was the political and cultural power of the state that unified the diverse local social systems and extended them to the outermost limits of the empire. Once the state established its dominion over territory, the assimilation and acculturation of local status groups brought them in line with those that were generally characteristic of China, thus creating Chinese society.

Theoretically, it appears more productive to regard Chinese society as the product of the interaction of the state with a multiplicity of local social systems than to see all of Chinese society as a single social system with differentiated parts. C. K. Yang agrees when he states: ". . . Traditional China may be thought of as having two major structural components: a national bureaucratic superstructure emphasizing centralization, standardization, formalism, a monocratically organized hierarchy of authority, and the norm of impersonality; and a vast substratum of heterogeneous local communities based on a morally common acceptance of the Confucian ideology, a national bureaucracy, and a weakly organized national economy" (1959, p. 135).

Thus, the modern Chinese nation-state may be seen as the unification of a particular state system with most, but not all, of the local social systems that can be considered Chinese. In traditional China, such a distinction was not too important, for the Chinese empire included virtually *all* areas of Chinese settlement. However, in modern times, the areas of Chinese settlement have expanded far beyond the borders of the Chinese nation. If society is regarded as the product of the interaction of state and social system, then, in the modern world, we have a number of distinct Chinese societies in formation. Presumably this process would be reversed if Taiwan and Hong Kong were eventually to be reunited with the mainland, which appears likely. However, in the case of the overseas Chinese areas, different processes are at work.

Traditional Chinese society achieved its classical form during the Sung dynasty (960–1279) and remained basically unchanged until the advent of the modern era. The Sung reunified China after a protracted period of political fragmentation, marked by an early form of warlordism. From then until 1911, despite dynastic changes and internal rebellions, China never again fell into political fragmentation.

Despite its benign character, the Sung contributed to the growth of absolute monarchy, which, in the Yüan, Ming, and Ch'ing became increasingly powerful. Since the main weapons of the monarchical institution were the large professional armies and various local paramilitary forces, political centralization brought with it growing military and police control. Thus, the *pao-chia* village control organization, which failed during the Sung, was institutionalized under the Ch'ing. The success of foreign dynasties (Liao, Chin, Yüan, and Ch'ing) in ruling over China was partly due to their abilities to command military power (Reischauer & Fairbank 1960, vol. 1, pp. 197–198; Liu 1959, pp. 90–91).

China's high culture achieved a stabilization under the Sung which subsequently led to a decline in creativity. Whereas there was a flowering of scientific and philosophical thought until the end of the Sung, later dynasties turned conservative; China's scholar–officials became mainly compilers and encyclopedists. Chu Hsi, who lived from 1130 to 1200, was China's last great philosopher (with the exception of the Ming scholar Wang Yangming); his writings on the classics were elevated to the status of orthodox doctrine (Levenson 1958–1965, vol. 1, pp. 3 ff.; Needham 1954, pp. 144–149).

General institutional stabilization was also reflected in the economy. During the T'ang and the Sung, the economy grew, not only quantitatively but qualitatively. New cities arose along with new forms of productive enterprise. However, from the Ming on, economic growth largely took the form of a continuing expansion of internal trade (Ho 1959, pp. 196 ff.). As Ping-ti Ho has stated, ". . . even during the period of steady economic growth [the economy] . . . was capable of small gains but incapable of innovations in either the institutional or the technological sense" (*ibid.*, p. 204). Thus, state and economy became routinized, but at the cost of their ability to deal creatively with the challenges that were to arise in later centuries.

Rapid social mobility in the T'ang and Sung periods led to counterforces that attempted to root the new landlord meritocracy in the local social systems. Many of the great clans of the early modern period had their beginnings in the Sung. In fact, most prestigious families of the modern period trace their genealogical roots to the Sung dynasty (Liu 1959, pp. 64–65).

While we have sketched a picture of traditional Chinese society as consisting of a state resting on a sea of local communities, one must remember that the core of the local social system was the village. During periods of tranquillity, the state made use of the local gentry to achieve its two main goals in the rural areas—the collection of taxes and the maintenance of order. However, the gentry, for the most part, did not live in the villages but in the towns and smaller cities, where it was in direct contact with the magistrates of the central government. The state needed the gentry, since it itself could not control the villages directly. However, at times, and particularly during the last centuries of the millennium of stability, the gentry, too, was unable to control the villages, or, if it did, it infringed on the interests of the state by failing to extract and deliver needed revenues. Thus, the state periodically stepped in and undertook direct organization of the villages (as in the case of the *she, li-chia,* and *pao-chia* systems). Ideally, the gentry functioned as a link between state and village, but when it failed, state and village directly confronted each other: the state tried to organize the village, and the village resisted with means ranging from noncompliance to open revolt (Hsiao 1960, pp. 43–83).

Transitional Chinese society

The word "transitional" implies a move from one base point to another. The two base points are the society of China as it was until the nineteenth century and as it is now in the People's Republic. What came in between was a period of change (Levy 1949, pp. 41–42). Although the roots of change can be traced to the eighteenth century, two great events of the nineteenth century symbolized the transition—the Opium war, from 1840 to 1842, and the Taiping rebellion, from 1851 to 1864.

The Treaty of Nanking in 1842 opened China's coastal ports to foreign penetration. As a result, a modern sector developed, essentially along Western lines. Great new cities, such as Shanghai, Tientsin, etc., grew up along the China coast, attracting immigration from the interior. With the opening of Manchuria in the middle of the nineteenth century, that rich underpopulated land was rapidly filled with immigrants, chiefly from Shantung. Russian and, later, Japanese economic penetration began a process of development that ultimately made Manchuria the center of China's heavy industry.

The rapid growth of a modern sector, on the coast and in Manchuria, based on an economy linked to the world market system or to particular foreign powers, notably Japan, created an ever-widening gap with the traditional sector of inland China. A new kind of Chinese society, based on Western principles, emerged in the modern sector. Education, from primary school on, was organized along Western lines. The mass media copied Western models. An urban business class appeared, often identified with particular cities, such as Canton, Hong Kong, Ningpo, and Shanghai. Industrialization brought a modern working class into existence. The modern cities, with their central business districts, surrounding slums, and suburban industries, resembled those of the West rather than the traditional cities of the interior. Intellectuals went to the West or to Japan to study; those that remained at home studied in Western-type universities. As in many modernizing countries, the cities became the social matrix for Westernization (Murphey 1953).

As the state became increasingly incapable of fulfilling its traditional role as a unifying force, China began to split into two different societies. The Chinese communists have recognized this split as one between the "semicolonialism" of the modern sector and the "semifeudalism" of the traditional sector. Both sectors evolved different social forces, thus giving a dual character to the great changes that marked the hundred years of transition.

If the Opium war launched the development of China's modern sector, the Taiping rebellion began the transformation of the traditional sector. Toward the end of the eighteenth century significant socioeconomic changes appeared in many parts of inland China. Population growth began to rise sharply, putting a great strain on resources. China's technology was stagnant; the ruling gentry was unable to introduce new forms of production. Moreover, outlets for internal migration declined in many inland regions. For example, during the seventeenth century, Szechwan became very crowded, and migration from Hunan to Szechwan dwindled. Undoubtedly, the rebellions that began to break out in the eighteenth century were linked to the changing economic conditions (Ho 1959, chapters 7, 9, 10).

Significantly, an ideology of foreign origin, Christianity, aroused the greatest rebellion in Chinese history. In 1850 a religious–military band, known as the "God-worshippers," began a rebellion which by 1853 had conquered much of China, including the early Ming capital, Nanking. The rebellion was led by a charismatic leader, Hung Hsiu-ch'üan, the son of a poor Hakka peasant family. Hung had come under the influence of Christian missionaries and, after a series of visions, came to believe that he was the younger brother of Jesus Christ. Although the original adherents were mainly Hakka, in a few short years large numbers of people in southern and central China rallied to the Taiping banners, as they were known after Hung was proclaimed the "heavenly king." The movement was egalitarian, puritanical, and socialistic (e.g., advocating the redistribution of land to the peasants). Like the communists who followed them a century later, the Taipings had a superb gift for organization. Although the movement almost succeeded in conquering all of China, internal decay and pressure from the combined forces of the Manchu dynasty, an aroused local gentry, and foreign mercenaries finally crushed them. The Taipings combined nationalistic hatred of the Manchus with an even fiercer hatred of the local gentry. The cry of the Taipings, carried throughout China, was: *Ta kuan* ("Smash the officials"). It is therefore not surprising that the gentry responded with counter-revolutionary ferocity (Michael 1966).

The gentry understood the threat and responded, in some cases with repression and in others with constructive measures. In the face of Manchu weakness, the provincial gentry and the Chinese bureaucracy recruited from it became increasingly powerful. Both nationally and locally, the gentry and the bureaucracy tried to improve conditions. Gentry-led economic development was by no means a rarity. However, sporadic reform could not resolve the fundamental problems. The inevitable result was the growing militarization of the provinces and the appearance of warlordism in the post-1911 period (Wright [1957] 1962, chapters 8–9; Feuerwerker 1958).

The Taiping rebellion revealed that the traditional state was in crisis. It was unable to bring about the pacification of the rebellion by its own resources. It was the combined forces of foreign powers and the local elites that finally led to imperial victory.

Although the decades that followed allowed hope for a reconsolidation of China's traditional system, the erosion of the state and of its ethos continued. The monarchy became increasingly obscurantist and impotent, and the bureaucracy could not give the country the leadership that it needed. In 1895 the monarchical armies of China were beaten by a resurgent Japan. In 1898 a reform movement emerged, which, despite its failure, revealed the growing lack of popular faith in the old system. Around the same time, intellectuals began to gnaw at the legitimacy of the ethos, first suggesting new ways of interpreting Confucianism and finally asserting its irrelevance for the modern world. The 1911 revolution was fairly bloodless, but it marked the death of a political system and an ethos that had held the country together for two millennia. The rise of the Chinese republic marked not the triumph of a new system, but the funeral of the old. China immediately fell into disunity (Teng & Fairbank 1954; Levenson 1958–1965, vol. 1, chapters 3–9).

However, the 1911 revolution did not disturb the power of the gentry. As bureaucratic positions in the new governments became unattractive, the gentry returned to their native provinces, where most were ready to collaborate with the rising warlords. The seeds of warlordism were planted in the post-Taiping period when the national armies were largely decentralized and placed under provincial control. When Yüan Shih-k'ai seized power in 1912, he found it only possible to rule through military commanders set up in different parts of the country. When his rule collapsed, these commanders became virtually independent and proceeded to construct their own military–political rule. Since the social revolution of the mid-1800s had subsided, the gentry had no reason to fear a challenge from the bottom again. Warlord rule combined with gentry administration appeared to be able to guarantee local stabilization until a new national unity could be achieved.

China's modern sector began to slip under the control of foreigners. Japanese influence in Manchuria grew until, in 1931, that land was detached from China. Despite Chinese participation in World War i, the Japanese emerged as the real winners at the Versailles Peace Conference. The big Western powers retained a firm grip on the concessions they owned in the Chinese treaty ports.

The existence of a unitary state and ethos for

so long a period of time could not but give rise to political movements that would seek to re-establish a new state and ethos. The Kuomintang, under the leadership of Sun Yat-sen, played a major role in the 1911 revolution, but its ideology was little more than a traditional antidynasticism: the Manchus must go. After 1911, the Kuomintang was reduced to a minor political movement. However, by the end of World War I, it was apparent that revolutionary ferment was arising in the cities, in particular a form of nationalism that, like all nationalisms, had a defined target of opposition—in this case, the Japanese. The Peking May Fourth Movement in 1919 and its successor in Shanghai revealed a deep hatred for the Japanese among the entire people; as during the French Revolution, the spearhead of popular opposition came from the intellectuals and the rising urban bourgeoisie. The Kuomintang took on a revolutionary character, made even more explicit by alliance with the newly formed Soviet Union. Protected by the liberal warlord of Kwangtung, Ch'en Chiung-ming, and aided militarily by the Soviet Union, the Kuomintang developed into a political and military force which, in 1925, was able to launch its "northern march" and capture Peking. Despite some efforts made in the area to organize peasant leagues, the Kuomintang was largely an urban revolutionary movement. By 1926 it was clear that the movement consisted of two wings—a disciplined military wing with power–political rather than revolutionary aims and an intellectual-dominated left wing, which saw revolution as the means to transform Chinese society (Chou 1960; Brandt 1958; Fitzgerald 1952).

The inevitable split came in 1927 when Chiang Kai-shek smashed the left-wing Kuomintang and the communists, who were allied with them. The new bourgeoisie rallied to Chiang and supported the Nanking government founded in 1928. Chiang's failure to unify the country, however, was due to the fact that the Kuomintang had few roots in inland China, which remained largely under the control of the warlords. Chiang Kai-shek attempted to bring inland China under his domination, much in the manner of the first Sung emperor, who, facing a similar heritage of disunity, pitted warlord against warlord, infiltrated their power bases with officials, and used the presence of an external threat to dissipate their power.

But there was one major factor that made the China of 1900 fundamentally different from the China of 900—the fermenting social revolution in the interior. The smoldering embers of peasant rebellion burst forth again in the mid-1920s. The Chinese Communist party, founded in 1920, func-tioned mostly as an organizational arm of the left-wing Kuomintang until 1927; its weakness was underscored by the ease with which Chiang destroyed its urban power base. However, in 1927, Mao Tse-tung united with dissatisfied units of the Kuomintang army and raised the banner of village revolution in Kiangsi and Hunan, classic areas of rebellion. The response was more than Mao could have hoped for. Rebellion burst forth in village upon village. Peasant *jacqueries* killed thousands of gentry and officials; the old Taiping cry of "Smash the officials" was revived. In 1931 the Chinese communists were strong enough to proclaim a Soviet republic on Chinese soil. Although short-lived, it revealed the immense revolutionary potential of the peasantry. The road to power for the Chinese communists lay in once again arousing and directing the peasant energies that had brought the Taipings close to victory (Ch'en 1965).

The gap between the two parts of China—coastal and inland—grew wider. The development of modern business and industry, the rise of Western education, and the ever-tightening linkage of coastal China to the world market system gave the cities a character sharply different from the backward villages of the interior. From 1928 to 1936 the nationalists succeeded in stabilizing conditions in the cities and even launching some social and economic reforms. However, coastal China gradually became prey for imperial Japan; the Sino–Japanese war, which began in 1937, led to the amputation of all of modern China and to Japanese occupation of all the major cities. Inevitably, the old nationalism reasserted itself, particularly among the intellectuals and the young army officers. Chiang's strategy of seeking accommodation with the Japanese until the country was unified met with opposition from intellectuals and young army officers. They triumphed after the Sian incident of 1936, when, in collaboration with the communists, they forced Chiang to accept a united front against the Japanese (Ch'en 1965, pp. 229–230; Ch'ien 1950, pp. 106–107).

In 1946 the civil war resumed, as did the great internal social revolution. In May 1946 the communists once again proclaimed a policy of radical land reform. Throughout rural China communist cadres revived the old hatreds within the village, and from the ensuing "struggle meetings," drew recruits for their armies. Within a few short years the nationalists lost their military superiority. The communist organizational build-up paid off handsomely, for when the challenge came, the communists knew how to turn guerrillas into regulars, make peasants into soldiers, and use the village base areas as powerful logistical support for the communist armies. The nationalist cause was also doomed by the attitude predominant among warlords, officials, and urban businessmen, one that led them to believe that they could return to their old ways. So vast was the social revolution that by 1949 China's gentry was destroyed. So violent was the land reform that the Chinese communist leaders tried to stem it in 1948, even before achievement of final victory. In 1949 the Chinese communists unified the entire mainland of China (Belden 1949).

In 1949 the last act of the Chinese revolution had been consummated. With the destruction of the gentry, the traditional local social systems ceased to exist: state, ethos, and gentry all disappeared. China stood at the threshold of a radically new era.

The main characteristic of transitional Chinese society was revolution—revolution against the state, the old ethos, and the gentry. Revolution first erupted in inland China, but by the beginning of the twentieth century it had spread to the cities. However, the urban revolution was mainly nationalistic in character; the uprisings that occurred in China's cities after 1919 were anti-imperialist, specifically anti-Japanese. The Kuomintang represented this tradition of revolution. In the mid-1920s, the revolution shifted back to the interior, where it became the instrument of communist victory. The communists, despite their nationalistic phases, represented the other tradition of revolution. Characteristically, the Kuomintang was mainly concerned with the acquisition of state power, after which it hoped to reform Chinese society. The communists, by contrast, first transformed the local social systems and then reached out for state power. Communist victory suggests that, in the end, the inland revolutionary tradition was a more powerful force than the nationalism of the cities. Nationalism needed an external enemy to remain alive, and the end of World War II did away with China's main enemy, Japan.

Transitional Chinese society saw great changes in the traditional patterns of social stratification. In the modern sector, new classes without precedent in Chinese history were created—a business class, a growing industrial proletariat, and the new intellectuals. As in most modernizing countries, the intellectuals played leading roles in the revolutionary movements. Discovering the power of direct political action during the May Fourth Movement, they became the ideologists of Chinese nationalism. Subsequently, large numbers went over to the communists, and became cadres in the rural war and revolution. In the rural areas young peasants coming from the poorest strata of the village population formed the bulk of the combat cadres of the Chinese Communist party. They not only spearheaded the revolution against the gentry but assumed positions of rural power after 1949.

Although the inland revolution had deep roots in the past, the ideology of revolution, brought to the peasants by urban intellectuals, was modern. While the Chinese communists often used traditional means to achieve their goals, the values underlying their ideology were radically different from those of the past. Communist victory in 1949, rather than signifying a dynastic restoration in modern garb, was a revolutionary transformation of the foundations of society.

Contemporary Chinese society

In October 1949 the Chinese communists established the People's Republic of China, thus creating a new political entity which launched a large-scale transformation of Chinese society. In this section we shall examine the transformation in relation to the key elements of Chinese society discussed in the section on traditional society—the state and its ethos, the local social systems, and the gentry (Schurmann 1966).

Whereas state and society in traditional Chinese society were governed by the ethos of Confucianism, China today is governed by the ideology of Marxism–Leninism. For Confucianism's world view of harmony the communists have substituted one of struggle. The functional importance of ideology cannot be separated from the main instrument of communist Chinese power—organization. After years of trial and failure, the Chinese communists realized that ideology serves to create and use organization and that organization is the only way to mobilize men to achieve goals. Chinese communist ideology consists of two parts—"theory" and "practice," or, in official terminology, Marxism–Leninism and the thought of Mao Tse-tung. The Chinese communists stress their membership in a global movement held together by common adherence to a fixed Marxist–Leninist theory. The core of that theory, as they see it, is the universality of class struggle: from the smallest village, where the poor fight the rich, to the whole world, where socialism and capitalism are in conflict, the human condition is one of class struggle. In this struggle, the poor will finally win. After the May Fourth Movement in 1919, Marxism spread rapidly among China's intellectuals; they were revolution-minded men, who lived in the modernizing cities of China, who realized that Sino-centric isolation was no longer possible, and who saw the emerging industrial proletariat as the prototype of the future population of China. The Chinese communists, in particular Mao Tse-tung, turned Marxism into "theory" by linking it with "practice," that is, organization and revolutionary action.

The traditional ethos, Confucianism, functioned mainly as a body of values, held by the state, by the gentry, and by the population as a whole, despite the diversity of local cultures. A brief comparison between Confucian and communist values will illustrate the changes. Instead of struggle, Confucianism preached harmony. Instead of organized power, Confucianism taught that networks of interpersonal relationships were the core of any political structure. Instead of modernization, that is, directed change toward set goals, Confucianism believed in *ad hoc* adaptation to situations. Instead of making the worker the human ideal, Confucianism sought the cultivation of man as a "gentleman" (*chün-tzu*). Instead of equality, Confucianism regarded legitimate authority based on unequal personal relationships as the foundation of the human order (as can be seen in the first four of the five basic human relationships: lord–subject, father–son, elder brother–younger brother, and husband–wife). Confucianism embodied these values in a unified ethos. Communism embodies its values in a unified theory.

It is through theory, with its ideological values of struggle, its political values of organized power, its economic values of modernization, and its social values of proletarianization and equality that the Chinese communists have transformed the value basis of Chinese society. But theory is also the spiritual cement that holds together the key organization of the country—the Chinese Communist party.

In contrast to theory, practice is flexible, changing, and nondogmatic. The thought of Mao Tse-tung, rather than fixed doctrine, is a manner of thinking that applies the theory of contradictions to the analysis and resolution of any human problem. Through actual experience, practice has evolved a series of principles and methods of organization and action. Although at times the Chinese have tended to dogmatize these methods, as in their teachings on world revolution, as a whole they have remained committed to the conviction that practice must be flexible and changing. The theory of contradictions has two variants—antagonistic and nonantagonistic contradictions. The first suggests that the juxtaposition of forces must lead to violent confrontation. The second suggests that the juxtaposition of forces can lead to peaceful resolution and even balance. Since practice is flexible and not doctrinaire, the quality of a particular contradiction can change from one day to the next (Mao 1917–1957; Cohen 1964; Holubnychy 1964).

One of the most important functions of ideology is the psychological transformation of individuals through group action. The primacy of organization means that every man must become a functioning member of a group linked to a larger organization. In the context of that group, ideology exerts spiritual pressure on the individual. The strong concern with the individual, which marks Chinese communism, can be seen in movements such as "thought reform" and "socialist education" (Lifton 1961).

The most startling change in China in the years following 1949 was the creation of a state power that emulated the Soviet Union down to the smallest details. There have been few instances in world history where political institutions that grew up in one society were so rapidly and effectively implanted in another with different traditions and practices. Revolutionary movements, once in power, often accept the given institutional framework, fill the top positions with their own men and the middle positions with elites ready to serve the new masters. Many in the West, in 1949, believed that a split between China and Russia would occur and that the Chinese communists, once in power, would revert to more traditional means of rule. Exactly the opposite happened. Despite reluctant Russian support during the civil war, and in the face of obvious Soviet intrigues to acquire power over Manchuria and Sinkiang, the Chinese communists chose to ally themselves unreservedly with the Soviet Union. They abolished almost every institutional structure remaining from Kuomintang times and substituted new Soviet-type ones.

The most important factor in the radical transformation of the state was the nationalization of private enterprise. As in the Soviet Union, the state became the administrator and manager of the economy. Indeed, to this day, the main function of the state bureaucracy is the administration of the economy. Nationalization meant the division of the economy into branches over each of which a national ministry was established. Almost immediately a large number of specialized ministries and agencies were set up, which had no counterpart in republican China. In the provinces and the cities miniature versions of the central government arose. Each of the regional departments was directly linked to a national ministry or agency, thus creating a straight-line span of control from center to region. By 1954, China had achieved a degree of administrative centralization that it had never known before in its history.

Clearly guided by Soviet influence and advice, the Chinese communists adopted the view that the state must manage and direct everything. Private businesses, for example, were nationalized and attached to a particular administrative hierarchy. It was no longer possible for managers to enter into free contractual relationships with other managers. The most striking evidence of the new managerial totalism was the extension of the bureaucratic apparatus into the smallest social units. City districts which hitherto had been loosely organized were now governed by street offices and residents' committees. In the rural areas the state extended its bureaucratic arms down to the level of the *hsiang* and the large administrative village. Administrative centralization served two basic purposes—political unification and economic development.

It is not unlikely that the speed with which administrative centralization was achieved was partly due to the fact that Manchuria, China's most advanced area, had already developed a functioning Soviet-style government by 1949. Whatever the reasons, it remains a remarkable achievement that the Chinese communists were able to create an entirely new type of state structure and make it work; Japan in early Meiji times is a comparable instance of such a transformation. Before 1868, Japan was ruled by a primitive bureaucratic organization thinly spread over the country and held together by a crude check-and-balance system (the *sankin kōtai*, or hostage-keeping practice) between the various feudal domains. Within a few years after the 1868 Meiji restoration, Japan had succeeded in building up a modern Western government with an efficient national bureaucracy. In 1949, China made a similar jump from an inefficient part-Western, part-traditional government to a Soviet-type government, comparable, even in details, to the foreign model. Sociologists tend to argue that no change in formal organization will work unless the informal organization, that is, the web of human relationships, also changes. We must remember that the Chinese communists came to power on the wave of a revolution which, as previously indicated, led to the destruction of the inland gentry and the far-reaching weakening of the urban bourgeoisie (through emigration and loss of position). Not only were the structures new, but new men were appointed to fill roles. For example, urban workers, rural cadres, and new intellectuals were given posts of responsibility. Although they were often unclear about how they were to operate, they at least were not burdened with older bureaucratic habits. Moreover, in many ministries and agencies Soviet advisers were on hand to extend help.

In the early years after 1949, the communists recruited mainly from two segments of the population—workers and intellectuals. Workers were put in positions of command, not only in factories but in the state administration. To improve the low level of their education, intensive training programs were inaugurated in schools, factories, and offices. Intellectuals, by which term the communists include all individuals with degrees from upper middle school and any more advanced institution, were taken into administrative, managerial, and technical positions at all levels. Since many of them were of bourgeois origin, special indoctrination programs were introduced ("thought reform") to elicit their full commitment to the new system. The Chinese communists, like the Russians, tried to create a workers' intelligentsia. However, whereas the Russians, from the early 1930s on, did this by bringing millions of workers' children into higher schools and excluding the bourgeois, the Chinese, true to their conviction that an individual's class identity could be changed by thought reform, tried to make workers into intellectuals and intellectuals into workers and so create a composite new elite.

From about 1955, however, the communists once again turned to the peasantry for cadre recruitment. Large numbers of peasants entered the party. Special educational programs for peasants were introduced—a policy which reached a high point with the rural "red and expert" universities of the "great leap forward." Peasant cadres now make up the bulk of party members.

In 1954 the Chinese communists completed the political unification of the country, save for Taiwan and Hong Kong, by eliminating the "independent kingdom of Manchuria." In 1955 they once again turned their focus from coastal to inland China. Having integrated the cities into the new system, they now undertook the difficult task of integrating the villages. By the summer of 1955 the rural party network had been extended over the whole country, and by late autumn collectivization began. Almost at the same time, the leaders began to demand a loosening of centralized administrative control, particularly a cutting down on the immense powers of the central ministries. During the eighth party congress in September several speakers intoned the theme of decentralization. Decentralization finally came late in 1957, but not in the form demanded by the moderates. The power of the big central ministries was drastically cut; new power was given to party-dominated provincial government. In 1958 the "great leap forward" was launched. Almost every province developed its own economic development program, which soon led to autarkic tendencies. In fact, so extreme was the assault on the state apparatus that, in the summer of 1958, many in China felt that the state was truly beginning to wither away.

Decentralization had gone to such extremes that Peking was forced to reverse the process. However, recentralization after 1960 has not led to a return to the conditions of 1949–1955. Although some ministries, notably in the fields of finance, transportation, and heavy industrial production, have reacquired power, provincial governments have retained their own share of power. Central planning continues in China, but in a context of much greater autonomy for regional governments and production units (Perkins 1966; Wu 1965; Tang 1957–1958, see esp. the 2d edition of volume 1).

The continuing decentralization is much more evident in the economic than in the political field, although there too we have some evidence to indicate that regional political leaders, while completely loyal to general policy made in Peking, can undertake autonomous initiative in some areas of "specific policy." If one looks at the published lists of provincial political leaders, one can discern a continuity of power, suggesting that provincial party machines have arisen. In the economy, Peking appears to have recognized that it must allow impulses to come from below. Enterprises, particularly in light industry and commerce, are allowed to develop their own economic programs, as long as they fulfill the demands of the state. Villages have much more autonomy in setting their own production plans than in the 1950s. Whereas the "great leap forward" policy tried to level differences between advanced and backward areas, Peking today quietly tolerates these differences. Thus today we see a generally centralized political system going hand in hand with a partially decentralized economic system. It is in this context that we must envisage the present decentralization.

In traditional China the concerns of the state were essentially exploitation and control: the state collected as much in taxes as it could and provided armies to maintain law and order. For the most part the state had few other administrative or managerial interests in society. The present state system has developed mechanisms for the extraction of surplus and certainly has created a powerful control apparatus, but it has also become an active manager. Fundamentally committed to change and growth, the state has taken the leadership in developing new economic, social, and cultural programs designed to make China into a modernized and industrialized nation. In the economic field, the state is striving to create a modern heavy industrial base, comparable in all respects to that of the Soviet Union and the United States. Efforts are being made to transform agriculture. Despite the inability of its social mobilization policy to realize more rapid agricultural progress, the state continues its commitment to agricultural development through programs of capital investment and rural education. In the social field the state has made strenuous efforts to improve living conditions. Here it is only since the recovery from the 1959–1962 crisis that progress has been made. Above all, state welfare efforts in the villages have been most notable. Culturally, the state has been consistently committed to the idea of universal education, a goal it has not fully attained but for which it expends major efforts.

Although some historians have regarded the new state as a modern version of a traditional dynasty, the similarities are superficial. A government agency in Communist China is a professional task-oriented bureaucracy, comparable to bureaucracies in other modern countries. As in the Soviet Union, agencies are responsible for management and production, in addition to administration, unlike the traditional Chinese bureaucracy which operated in a patrimonial fashion. Values of expertise and achievement, not Confucian harmony and stability, underlie the modern state system of Communist China.

Let us now turn to rural China. The Chinese communist leaders have consistently held the conviction that unless rural China could be transformed, the revolution could not ultimately succeed. Where traditional Chinese dynasties sought only to control and exploit the villages, the Chinese communists launched a great process of integrating the village into the nation, of unifying the traditional and modern sectors. The destruction of the local gentry through the revolutionary land reform did away with the traditional local social systems but provided no certain course for the future.

Land reform gave land to the peasant but did not fundamentally alter the conditions on the land. The poor peasant remained poor, but many peasants began to enrich themselves, much like the Russian kulaks during the New Economic Policy period—from 1921 to 1928. As early as 1948 the party modified its extreme revolutionary policies and adopted a more tolerant attitude toward the rich peasants.

The destruction of the local social systems also had the effect of forcing the natural village to rely on its own resources. The term "natural village" was used widely by the communists and even the nationalists in the sense of an ecologically unified farm settlement (e.g., unified through a common water system) in contrast to an "administrative village," which was a group of settlements so designated for purposes of political domination. The natural villages had a traditional socioeconomic unity; the administrative villages generally did not. Ever since the ties to the local landlord and official gentry had been snapped, the rich peasants became the chief traditional elements in the natural villages. Since the state administration did not effectively penetrate the natural village, the new rulers of the country had mainly administrative and military means at their disposal to enforce their commands. The Chinese communist leaders regarded this as an unsatisfactory situation, and in the early 1950s determined to lay the groundwork for breaking down the walls surrounding the natural village.

Until the great collectivization drive of late 1955, the Chinese communists followed two basic organizational policies toward the village. First, they encouraged the peasants voluntarily to form mutual-aid teams and cooperatives. Second, they expanded administrative control at the *hsiang* level. The word *hsiang* designates an administrative district covering a number of natural villages, generally centered on a market town. Although the government periodically changed the size of the *hsiang* from a very small unit, more or less the equivalent of what earlier were called administrative villages, to larger units coinciding with Skinner's standard marketing areas, in time the larger unit became institutionalized. Today there are approximately 80,000 *hsiang* in China. By 1954 it was clear that neither policy was very successful. Although teams and cooperatives were set up in large numbers, many dissolved again or came under the control of rich peasants. Similarly, the *hsiang* bureaucracy became increasingly repressive, concerned mainly with enforcing the "unified procurement" policies of the state.

Early in 1955 the Chinese communists took a major step toward the reorganization of agriculture: they launched a great campaign to build up the rural party organization. In 1955 they repeated what they had done during the Yenan period— penetrating the natural village through a party organization that recruited its cadres from among the poor peasants within the village itself. In July, Mao Tse-tung, in a secret speech not revealed until October, announced that collectivization would begin in the fall. Once the harvest was in, the party, in a spirit of mobilization called the "high tide,"

began a campaign to set up cooperatives in all villages. Though some were exceedingly large, going beyond the bounds of the natural villages, most were small, including only a portion of the population of the natural village. Since collectivization aroused the "class struggle" between rich and poor peasants, that is, essentially between traditional village leaders and the new party cadres, the former were excluded from the new cooperatives. However, after mobilization was succeeded by consolidation in the spring of 1956, official policy welcomed the inclusion of all elements in the village. What was called the transition from early to higher stage cooperatives was, in effect, the transformation of the natural village into an "agricultural people's cooperative" (APC): the APC became the equivalent of the natural village.

What the communists achieved in the 1955–1956 collectivization was the elimination of private property, a matter of most concern to the rich peasants. Every Chinese village had, in essence, two types of economy—a basic and a supplemental economy. The basic crops included grain, but also, on occasion, industrial and market crops. Even in the past the basic economy had required some degree of cooperation. Peasants grouped together for irrigation tasks and marketing, and they often shared tools and labor. Under the APC system, basic crop fields were amalgamated; the peasant no longer worked as an individual on his basic crop lands but as a member of a production team. The supplemental economy of the village (e.g., orchards, house animals, garden crops) remained a family or individual affair. The products of the supplemental economy traditionally provided the peasants with an income over and above the subsistence guaranteed by the basic economy. Collectivization reduced the scope of the supplemental economy but did not do away with it. The peasant retained his private plots.

Despite the success in collectivization, the APC based on the natural village did not yet constitute a functional equivalent of the old local social system. Although it had great promise for stability and productivity, it did not guarantee an automatic road for moving the village toward greater integration with the larger society. By collectivizing all land in the village and making everyone join the APC, the communists made the village a unified socioeconomic unit. However, the very unity of the village threatened to lead to self-isolation and a growing gap between it and the larger society. In traditional Chinese society, the village was part of a larger socioeconomic unit, as Skinner has indicated in his study of standard marketing areas. The destruction of the gentry by land reform and changes in traditional trading patterns had weakened the bonds holding these larger units together. Thus, the radical wing of the Chinese Communist party, hoping to find a new functional equivalent of the old local social system, sought ways of pulling the village out of its isolation and making it part of such a larger unit.

The greatest attempt to achieve this was made in the summer of 1958, when the communes were formed. The communes were amalgamations of APC's, generally equivalent to the administrative *hsiang*. Policy and operational controls were taken from the APC leaders and put into the hands of new commune committees, completely dominated by local poor peasant party cadres. The name "commune," taken from Marxist history, meant an armed egalitarian workers' community. So it was that the communes arose at the same time as the militarization of the peasantry, specifically in the form of a revived popular militia. The communes aimed at three things: (1) the creation of rural units encompassing several natural villages; (2) the creation of a new rural organization wherein production brigades and teams worked in different villages according to rational criteria of the division of labor; and (3) the transformation of the traditional work habits of the peasant—in effect, making him into a farm worker. Since communization took place in an atmosphere of utopian excitement, many of the results were unworkable. Indeed, as early as December 1958 the Chinese leaders ordered a retreat. The growing food crisis of 1959 and 1960 finally led to a widespread modification of the commune system. By late 1960, Peking ordered (or permitted) a decentralization of the commune system down to the team level. The team, a group of peasants living adjacent to each other, was little more than the early mutual-aid team. Moreover, Peking once again admitted that the natural village was the basis of the rural economy, and therefore the agricultural areas returned to the conditions of 1956.

Today it is the village that initiates its own production plans; the state exercises direction and control to insure fulfillment of its own procurement needs. The peasant retains his private lands, from which he makes an important "supplemental" living. However, the degree to which the communes were modified misled some observers to assume that the experiment had failed entirely. The fact is that the communes remain. For the most part, the commune is today the equivalent of the *hsiang*. The commune, for example, remains the headquarters of the important marketing and sales cooperatives which act as middlemen between the peasants and production and supply centers in the cities. Branches of the new agricultural bank are centered in the commune headquarters. The commune remains the center of disaster and relief work. Above all, the commune is the base area of the rural party organization.

In the past the traditional local social system was dominated by the gentry; today it is dominated by the party. However, what is significant is that Peking has succeeded in re-establishing a new version of what it earlier had destroyed, something it could not have done by allowing collectivization to remain at the 1956 level. Although it could be argued that the appearance of village-based production and commune-based marketing repeats the situation of traditional times, there have been basic changes. At least in some parts of China the government is making strenuous efforts to electrify and mechanize the villages. In 1958 the Chinese leaders felt that the organizational unification of the commune would eventually lead to its technological integration. During the first half of the 1960s, chastened by failures, they proceeded slowly on paths both of organizational and technological integration (Cheng 1963, pp. 22–59; Skinner 1964–1965). Given the continuing ideological and political campaigns of the mid-1960s, it remains to be seen whether another "leap forward" in the rural areas will occur.

Let us now turn to the third of the key elements in traditional Chinese society—the gentry. The party has replaced the gentry as the new ruling element in Chinese society. No two formations of human beings could be as different as gentry and party. The gentry constituted a status group, bound together by a common ethos, with roots in the local social systems and ties to the state through bureaucratic position. The party is an organization, bound together by ideology, from which the state recruits its leaders. Although one can see superficial similarities between gentry and party, the differences are more significant. (Max Weber's discussion of classes, status groups, and parties [(1906–1924) 1946, pp. 194–195] throws light on the differences between gentry and party.) The role of the party can only be understood in terms of the changes that have taken place in the society. The party stands as an *alter ego* alongside every unit of organization, e.g., factory, farm, school, office, etc. The unit of organization (of production, territory, or administration, as it is put in the official literature) is the basic social unit in China today. Everyone must be a member of one of these units, preferably of production or administration. A peasant in the village is first and foremost a member of a production team, as is a worker in a factory. We do not have enough information to state unequivocally whether these production units are new formations or formations superimposed on more traditional ones (the patterns undoubtedly are varied). Nevertheless, they are units of formal organization and have replaced all earlier units of formal organization. For example, if we remember that the traditional clan was part formal and part informal organization, as is evident in numerous studies of clan organization, then clearly the production teams and brigades have replaced, at least, the formal side of clan organization. If we also recall that the communists have made strenuous efforts to mix team membership in order to prevent "familism" and "cliquism" from reappearing, we can surmise that a good part of traditional informal organization has also been transformed. Since the social system depended heavily on traditional authority and kinship structures, the destruction of the former and the severe weakening of the latter has made possible the implantation of organization. Since organization has thus replaced the social system in China, the party, as the collective body of organizational leadership, has a built-in role in contemporary Chinese society.

The Chinese Communist party began in 1920 as a loose organization of several intellectual "study groups" in various Chinese cities. From 1925 to 1927 it developed a mass base of urban proletarians. In 1927, Chiang Kai-shek virtually destroyed its urban organization; it continued as a military–political movement in south-central China, where it acquired local power on the waves of peasant revolts. Late in 1934, Chiang once again virtually annihilated it, and the communists took their long march to northwest China. During the Yenan period, from 1935 to 1946, the communists turned the party into a disciplined organization based on villages in which party cadres had created deep organizational roots. In 1946, as the communist armies were caught in a life-and-death struggle with the Kuomintang, revolution burst forth in the villages. When the civil war ended, the communists had China, and the gentry had been destroyed.

In 1950 the communists decided on a far-reaching change in their organizational policy. Reducing the number of peasant members, they began to build up an urban-based party organization. The party underwent a certain "apparat-ization" and began to resemble the Soviet Communist party, with the top positions increasingly taken by men of education and skill. The party probably would have continued on this course but for the deep split between Manchuria and Peking. A quasi-independent party organization developed in Manchuria and was finally destroyed in the campaigns of 1954 and 1955 against Kao Kang, party chief of Manchuria. At the same time, the Chinese communist leaders resumed their earlier stress on a village-based party organization. Peasants again entered the party in large numbers. As the influence of Manchuria declined, that of the inland provinces, such as Honan and Szechwan, and later, Kwangtung, rose. By 1958, provincial party power had reached such a peak that many of the provinces began to "leap forward" as if they were small nations. A piecemeal rectification movement in 1960–1961 reduced the excessive power of regional party organizations, but by 1962 the party recovered some of its lost power. An organization with about 5 million members in 1950, it had, as of 1961, 17 million members.

The party is governed by the Central Committee, composed of about 100 regular members and an equal number of candidate members, who are representatives of party organizations throughout the country. The Central Committee meets periodically in formal or nonformal plenary sessions. In this sense, it has some resemblance to a parliament. Its purpose is to transform general policy decisions of the top leadership into concrete policy decisions which are later ratified by the National People's Congress.

Policy-making power is in the hands of the "politburo" or the standing committee of the politburo. The politburo functions somewhat like a cabinet or the circle of advisers of a prime minister.

There are small-scale versions of the central party structure at the levels of province, city, county, and *hsiang*. The secretariats function as the chain of command between different echelons.

At the lowest, or basic, level the party organization is attached to a unit of production, of territory, or of administration. Generally speaking, it includes the leaders of all areas within the organization to which it is attached. Thus it forms the leadership core of the organization (Lewis 1963).

It is hardly surprising that China has resumed some of the forms of the past. Decentralization, for example, has brought about a reappearance of certain traditional forms of business and industrial practices, as it has led to a recognition of the village as a basic unit of society. However, the core and substance of China has changed profoundly. China has experienced great progress in the development of its cities and villages. However, without the type of political organization it now has, it is exceedingly unlikely that inland China would have been brought closer to the modern world. Shanghai may have continued to modernize, as Hong Kong has done, but, as is the case in so many other developing countries, the gap between developing coast and retarded interior would most likely have grown wider. The gentry ultimately failed because of its impotence in the face of a changing world. The party that succeeded it has given inland China the needed leadership.

Despite the fact that a united party dominates both modern and traditional sectors, there are indications that a bifurcation of elites is developing, along the lines of "red" and "expert." As in the Soviet Union, a growing professional intelligentsia, almost entirely the product of the modern sector, is seeking positions of power and influence in opposition to the corps of party cadres, whose roots lie in inland China. The gap between a modern bourgeoisie and a traditional gentry, such as that which marked republican China, has its contemporary counterpart in this bifurcation of elites. However, the party acts as a unifying force, for both "reds" and "experts" are recruited, with the weighting of recruitment depending on particular policies of the leadership.

In the first section, we suggested that traditional Chinese society could be regarded as the product of the interaction of the state and a multiplicity of local social systems. If, traditionally, Chinese society coincided more or less with the bounds of the Chinese empire, this is not so today. There are areas of Chinese settlement outside the boundaries of the People's Republic of China—Taiwan, Hong Kong, Macao, and the areas of overseas Chinese settlement. Although most Chinese regard it as inevitable that the first three regions will ultimately be reunited with the mainland, they also agree that the areas of overseas settlement are not Chinese *irredenta*. In terms of our analysis, however, we can state that these areas, not having been subject to the same state power as the mainland, have developed in different directions. Thus we face not a single Chinese society but several.

Let us look first at Taiwan. Four hundred years ago, Chinese settlers, largely from Fukien, moved onto the island. By the late nineteenth century, the overwhelming majority of the islanders were Chinese, speaking a dialect akin to that of Amoy. Although a landlord class had developed, it was not comparable to the powerful gentry of the mainland. The Japanese occupation led to the growth of cities almost entirely Japanese in character and to the development of a plantation economy foreign to China itself. A new group of literate Taiwanese, strongly influenced by Japanese culture, arose in the cities and in some rural areas. The first Kuo-

mintang occupation in 1945 was little different from that of a hostile army; in 1947 a large-scale revolt broke out, which the Kuomintang brutally suppressed. In 1949 the Kuomintang army and a wave of mainland refugees, largely from the mainland cities, arrived on the island. Despite more than fifteen years of rule by the Republic of China, a sharp cultural gap persists between mainlanders and Taiwanese.

The land reform carried out with American aid did away with the remnant landlord class and paved the way for rapid agricultural development based on private farming. In time, a small entrepreneurial class arose which has launched industrialization. Thus today, despite a massive military superstructure, Taiwan has become a relatively prosperous area. The gap between mainlanders and Taiwanese and the role of the Kuomintang suggest some similarities to conditions in the People's Republic. The Taiwanese, as the new professional and entrepreneurial forces of Taiwan, have somewhat the same relationship to the politically dominant mainlanders as the mainland "experts" do to the "reds." The Kuomintang, through its political organization, tries to bridge the gap. However, as in comparisons with traditional China, the resemblances are more of form than of content (Formosa 1963).

The case of Hong Kong is different again. Originally a quiet trading port on the south China coast, it became, in the wake of the communist victory, a large urban area of three million people. It generally resembles the large cities of southeast Asia, which have heavy Chinese populations, notably Singapore. Hong Kong experienced an industrial revolution in the early 1950s under almost classical conditions of nineteenth century laissez-faire capitalism. Originally launched by a small group of Shanghai entrepreneurs, industrialization is now supported by a sizable middle class and a growing class of skilled and semiskilled workers. Like Shanghai, Hong Kong benefited from its membership in a world market system and an enlightened population strongly committed to education (Szczepanik 1958).

There are approximately 13 million Chinese living in countries outside China, mainly in southeast Asia. Most live in cities. With some exceptions, the Chinese have become an urban middle and working class and as such have greatly contributed to the economic development of southeast Asia, notably Malaysia. The predominant pattern of social development resembles that of Hong Kong (Purcell 1951).

From a comparative sociological point of view,

it may be concluded that the capacity of Chinese urban populations to modernize and industrialize appears to be independent of the particular type of political structure under which they live. Indeed, this capacity was already manifest in Shanghai during World War I, when industrialization developed in a city subject to several distinct political systems. However, the areas of Chinese settlement outside of China where economic development has been most rapid have also been the areas where traditional social ties have been most weakened, as in Hong Kong and Malaya. In southeast Asia, Chinese political organizations have arisen seeking to create new bonds of unity within the Chinese community. Thus, one finds political organization functioning there in a way analogous to the way it functions on the Chinese mainland. Just as the state traditionally has been the major unifying factor in Chinese society, today political organization aims at the same goal within the various contexts in which it operates.

Judging from the course modernization has taken in other societies, it appears to be only a matter of time before the traditional dichotomy of state and local social systems will be replaced by a new unity that will link village and city. The crucial factor underlying such a development is the completion of the economic and technological revolution on the land. However, without the political unity that the Chinese Communist party created at a time when the society was not yet economically integrated, village and city would have receded farther and farther from each other, as has happened in so many developing countries.

FRANZ SCHURMANN

[*See also* CHINESE POLITICAL THOUGHT; ECONOMIC DATA, *article on* MAINLAND CHINA. *Other relevant material may be found in* BUDDHISM; HISTORIOGRAPHY, *article on* CHINESE HISTORIOGRAPHY; JAPANESE SOCIETY.]

BIBLIOGRAPHY

BELDEN, JACK 1949 *China Shakes the World.* New York: Harper.

BENDIX, REINHARD (1960) 1962 *Max Weber: An Intellectual Portrait.* Garden City, N.Y.: Doubleday. → See page 476 for the distinction between society and polity.

BRANDT, CONRAD 1958 *Stalin's Failure in China, 1924–1927.* Cambridge, Mass.: Harvard Univ. Press.

CH'EN, JEROME 1965 *Mao and the Chinese Revolution.* New York: Oxford Univ. Press.

CHENG, CHU-YÜAN 1963 *Communist China's Economy, 1949–1962: Structural Changes and Crisis.* South Orange, N.J.: Seton Hall Univ. Press. → See especially pages 22–59 on "Agricultural Collectivization."

CHENG, TE-K'UN 1959 *Archaeology in China.* Volume 1: Prehistoric China. Cambridge: Heffer.

CH'IEN, TUAN-SHENG 1950 *The Government and the Politics of China.* Cambridge, Mass.: Harvard Univ. Press.

CHOU, TS'E-TSUNG 1960 *The May Fourth Movement: Intellectual Revolution in Modern China.* Harvard East Asian Studies, No. 6. Cambridge, Mass.: Harvard Univ. Press.

COHEN, ARTHUR A. 1964 *The Communism of Mao Tse-tung.* Univ. of Chicago Press.

EBERHARD, WOLFRAM (1948) 1960 *A History of China.* 2d ed. Berkeley: Univ. of California Press. → First published as *Chinas Geschichte.* See especially Chapter 1 on "Prehistory."

EBERHARD, WOLFRAM 1952 *Conquerors and Rulers: Social Forces in Medieval China.* Leiden: Brill.

FEI, HSIAO-T'UNG (1947–1948) 1953 *China's Gentry: Essays in Rural–Urban Relations.* Univ. of Chicago Press. → A collection of articles contributed by Fei to Chinese newspapers.

FEUERWERKER, ALBERT 1958 *China's Early Industrialization: Sheng Hsuan-huai (1844–1916) and Mandarin Enterprise.* Harvard East Asian Studies, No. 1. Cambridge, Mass.: Harvard Univ. Press.

FITZGERALD, CHARLES P. (1952) 1953 *Revolution in China.* London: Cresset Press; New York: Praeger. → See especially Chapters 1–4.

Formosa. 1963 *China Quarterly* (London) No. 15:3–114. → A collection of articles.

Ho, PING-TI 1959 *Studies on the Population of China: 1368–1953.* Harvard East Asian Studies, No. 4. Cambridge, Mass.: Harvard Univ. Press.

Ho, PING-TI 1962 *The Ladder of Success in Imperial China: Aspects of Social Mobility, 1368–1911.* New York: Columbia Univ. Press.

HOLUBNYCHY, VSEVOLOD 1964 Mao Tse-tung's Materialistic Dialectics. *China Quarterly* (London) No. 19: 3–37.

HSIAO, KUNG-CH'ÜAN 1960 *Rural China: Imperial Control in the Nineteenth Century.* Seattle: Univ. of Washington Press. → See especially pages 43–83 on "Police Control: The Pao-chia System."

HSU, FRANCIS L. K. 1963 *Clan, Caste, and Club.* Princeton, N.J.: Van Nostrand.

JAEGER, GERTRUDE; and SELZNICK, PHILIP 1964 A Normative Theory of Culture. *American Sociological Review* 29:653–669. → A theoretical discussion of the differences between high culture and culture.

KROEBER, A. L.; and PARSONS, TALCOTT 1958 The Concepts of Culture and of Social System. *American Sociological Review* 23:582–583.

LEVENSON, JOSEPH R. 1958–1965 *Confucian China and Its Modern Fate.* 3 vols. Berkeley: Univ. of California Press. → See especially Volume 2, *The Problem of Monarchical Decay.*

LEVY, MARION J. JR. 1949 *The Family Revolution in Modern China.* Cambridge, Mass.: Harvard Univ. Press.

LEWIS, JOHN W. 1963 *Leadership in Communist China.* Ithaca, N.Y.: Cornell Univ. Press.

LIFTON, ROBERT J. 1961 *Thought Reform and the Psychology of Totalism: A Study of "Brainwashing" in China.* New York: Norton.

LIN, PIAO 1965 On People's War. *People's Daily* (Peking) 3 September 1965.

LIU, HUI-CHEN WANG 1959 An Analysis of Chinese Clan Rules: Confucian Theories in Action. Pages 63–

96 in David S. Nivison and Arthur F. Wright (editors), *Confucianism in Action*. Stanford Univ. Press.

LIU, TZU-CHIEN 1959 *Reform in Sung China: Wang An-shih (1021–1086) and His New Policies.* Harvard East Asian Studies, No. 3. Cambridge, Mass.: Harvard Univ. Press.

MAO, TSE-TUNG (1917–1957) 1963 *The Political Thought of Mao Tse-tung.* New York: Praeger → An anthology of excerpts dated 1917–1957, edited by Stuart R. Schram.

MARSHALL, T. H. (1934–1962) 1965 *Class, Citizenship, and Social Development: Essays.* Garden City, N.Y.: Doubleday. → A collection of articles and lectures first published in England in 1963 under the title *Sociology at the Crossroads and Other Essays.*

MICHAEL, FRANZ H. 1966 *The Taiping Rebellion: History and Documents.* Volume 1: History. Seattle: Univ. of Washington Press. → The first of a projected three-volume series.

MURPHEY, RHOADS 1953 *Shanghai: Key to Modern China.* Cambridge, Mass.: Harvard Univ. Press.

NEEDHAM, JOSEPH 1954 *Science and Civilisation in China.* Volume 1. Cambridge Univ. Press. → See especially pages 79–90, "Chinese Prehistory and the Shang Dynasty."

NIIDA, NOBORU 1952 *Chûgoku hôsei-shi* (History of Chinese Law). Tokyo: Iwanami Shoten.

PERKINS, DWIGHT H. 1966 *Market Control and Planning in Communist China.* Harvard Economic Studies, Vol. 128. Cambridge, Mass.: Harvard Univ. Press.

PURCELL, VICTOR W. (1951) 1965 *The Chinese in Southeast Asia.* 2d ed. Oxford Univ. Press.

REDFIELD, ROBERT 1956 *Peasant Society and Culture: An Anthropological Approach to Civilization.* Univ. of Chicago Press. → The distinction between high culture and culture is analogous to that made by Robert Redfield between great and little traditions. A paperback edition, bound together with *The Little Community,* was published in 1961 by Cambridge Univ. Press.

REISCHAUER, EDWIN O.; and FAIRBANK, JOHN K. 1960 *A History of East Asian Civilization.* Volume 1: East Asia: The Great Tradition. Boston: Houghton Mifflin.

The Rise of the Modern Chinese Business Class: Two Introductory Essays. 1949 New York: Institute of Pacific Relations, International Secretariat. → Contains "The Social Background of Modern Business Development in China," by M. J. Levy, and "The Early Development of the Modern Chinese Business Class," by Kuo-heng Shih.

SCHURMANN, FRANZ 1966 *Ideology and Organization in Communist China.* Berkeley: Univ. of California Press.

SKINNER, G. WILLIAM 1964–1965 Marketing and Social Structure in Rural China. *Journal of Asian Studies* 24:3–43, 195–228, 363–399.

SZCZEPANIK, EDWARD F. 1958 *The Economic Growth of Hong Kong.* Oxford Univ. Press.

TANG, SHENG-HAO 1957–1958 *Communist China Today.* 2 vols. Washington: Research Institute on the Sino-Soviet Bloc. → A second edition of the first volume, revised and enlarged, was published in 1961.

TENG, SSU-YÜ; and FAIRBANK, JOHN K. 1954 *China's Response to the West: A Documentary Survey, 1839–1923.* Cambridge, Mass.: Harvard Univ. Press.

WANG, HUI-TSU 1937 *Tsochih yaoyen.* Shanghai: Commercial Press.

WANG, HUI-TSU 1939 *Hsüehchih ishuo.* Shanghai: Com-
mercial Press. → A traditional Chinese comment on the importance of local culture. See especially pages 22–23.

WEBER, MAX (1906–1924) 1946 *From Max Weber: Essays in Sociology.* Translated and edited by Hans H. Gerth and C. Wright Mills. New York: Oxford Univ. Press. → See especially pages 180–195 on "Class, Status, Party."

WRIGHT, MARY C. (1957) 1962 *The Last Stand of Chinese Conservatism: The T'ung-chih Restoration, 1862–1874.* Stanford Univ. Press.

WU, YUAN-LI 1965 *The Economy of Communist China: An Introduction.* New York: Praeger.

YANG, C. K. 1959 Some Characteristics of Chinese Bureaucratic Behavior. Pages 134–164 in David S. Nivison and Arthur F. Wright (editors), *Confucianism in Action.* Stanford Univ. Press.

YANG, CH'ING-K'UN 1961 *Religion in Chinese Society: A Study of Contemporary Social Functions of Religion and Some of Their Historical Factors.* Berkeley: Univ. of California Press.

CHI-SQUARE DISTRIBUTIONS

See DISTRIBUTIONS, STATISTICAL, *article on* SPECIAL CONTINUOUS DISTRIBUTIONS.

CHI-SQUARE STATISTICS

See COUNTED DATA; GOODNESS OF FIT; SIGNIFICANCE, TESTS OF.

CHRISTIANITY

This article will deliberately focus on the particular problem of the importance of Christianity for the modern phase of the development of societies. This is, of course, only one combination of aspects of the almost infinitely complex phenomenon that is Christianity.

What social scientists call the modern type of society does not have multiple independent origins but has originated in one specific complex, within the area broadly called western Europe, and has been diffused from there, now even to areas with altogether non-Western culture, the first notable case being Japan. On the religious side the area of origin of modern societies has been Christian, with direct involvement, in decisive periods, of numerically small Jewish subcommunities and with largely hostile, although still culturally significant, interaction with the Islamic world.

The main carrier of the Christian traditions significant to modern society was its Western branch, which developed around the Roman papacy in the area inherited from the western Roman Empire. Apart from the sense in which Eastern Orthodoxy underlies the recent importance of Russia in the modern world, the Eastern branch cannot be said to have been a main center of modernizing innovation, in a sense comparable to the Western.

A somewhat parallel, although different and in many ways more complex, differentiation took place in the Reformation period, with the Protestant sector taking the lead in the relation of religion to modernization. This situation came to a head in the movement of "ascetic" Protestantism (as Max Weber called it) and particularly in its more individualistic and "liberal" branches, especially as they matured in Holland and England and were extended to the United States and the English-speaking British dominions. These processes, however, have been intimately involved in complex interactions both with Catholic Europe and with the nonascetic, especially Lutheran, branches of Protestant Europe.

This article will stress two primary themes. The first is the basic *continuity* of the evolutionary trend. This begins with the Israelitic and Greek cultural backgrounds of Christianity, each of which laid certain decisive foundations of the movement. It then continues through the establishment and survival of the early church, the establishment of the Western church and its differentiation from the Eastern, the very gradual institutionalization of the Christian society of the High Middle Ages, the transition into the Renaissance, and then the Reformation and the developments that led to modern society. I will place special emphasis on the Protestant branch in what follows, because I believe the major turning point in the development of modern society was not, as has so often been held, the industrial revolution of the late eighteenth century but rather the developments of the seventeenth century, which centered in Holland and England and, in a special way, in France, which, although profoundly involved in the Reformation, ended up as a Catholic power.

The second primary theme is the analytical *complexity* of the explanation of what has occurred and what may be projected. This article does not assert that Christianity as a religious movement "produced" modern society; rather it holds that Christianity contributed a crucial complex of factors, which, because of its own internal trends of "transformative" development and because of the great diversity of nonreligious conditions at various stages of the process and in various areas, operated very differently at different points in the developmental process.

Incorporating and synthesizing elements from both of its two main cultural forebears, the Israelitic and the Greek, and developing a new religious pattern of its own, the Christian movement crystal-lized a new pattern of values not only for the salvation of human souls but also for the nature of the societies in which men should live on earth. This pattern, the conception of a "kingdom" or, in Augustine's term, a "city" of men living according to the divine mandate on earth, became increasingly institutionalized through a long series of stages, which this article will attempt to sketch. Later it became the appropriate framework of societal values for the modern type of society.

Christianity, through the societal values it has legitimized, has been *one* principal factor in the evolutionary process that has led up to modern society. At every stage, however, the religious system and its values have stood in complex relations of interdependence with other factors, notably economic and political organization and interests, the underlying institutions of kinship and social stratification, and certain aspects of secular culture. Several times, as in the rise of monasticism and the Puritan "errand into the wilderness," the main innovative trend has been associated with the withdrawal of its carriers from the main societal arena, rather than with short-run acquisition of control over them. Indeed, in the larger perspective the power of religiously grounded values to shape secular life has depended on the increasing structural differentiation of religion from the organization of the secular society, as is indicated in the great weakening and eventual abolition of the long-standing institution of established churches.

Although the present article is confined to Christianity, it is written in the perspective of the comparative status of Christianity among the historic "world" religions, in their relations to the development of the societies in which they have originated and to which they have become diffused. (This perspective derives, more than from any other source, from the work of Max Weber.) Some centuries before the origin of Christianity, not only in the world of the eastern Mediterranean but eastward through India to east Asia, there had developed the varied system of "historic" religions, including Judaism, Hinduism–Buddhism, and Confucianism–Taoism. All of them in varying ways and degrees sharply accentuated the differentiation between the profane and the sacred, temporal existence and eternity, worldly and otherworldly, natural and supernatural. These great cultural movements redefined the problems of the meaning of human life both for the individual as a personality and for human societies. One main axis of the problems concerned the relative devaluation of the profane, the temporal or the natural. Should the interests of temporal life be renounced in favor of some conception of radical salvation? Was there to be religious legitimation of those temporal interests or even of human societies with their necessary natural and secular anchorage? How were the two basic references to be balanced in relation to each other?

The general orientation and setting

Christianity developed a very special pattern of solutions to these questions. It was second to no other religion in emphasizing the transcendental character of its conception of divinity. The God which the Christians inherited from the Hebrews was the creator–ruler God, the *sole* creator and governor of the world, which included the human condition generally—the condition of *all* peoples. Not only was Christianity a transcendental monotheism, but its theology focused specifically on the conception of a divinely ordained, active mission for man. God created man "in His own image" in order for man to "do His will" on earth. That will, in turn, ordained the performance of a great collective task that eventually was believed to consist essentially of the building of a society in the temporal world in accord with the divine plan. This conception of the God–man relationship greatly influenced the social world through the commitments of its adherents to remake that world in accord with the divine plan. It contrasted very sharply with some of the Oriental religions that motivated "adjustment to" the immanent order of the nonempirical universe.

This transcendental–activistic attitude alone, however, does not account for the broad societal impact of Christianity. It has also characterized Judaism and Islam, but neither of these great movements originated the makings of a modern society on its own. Judaism, after a brief period in a politically independent, "divinely ordained," small kingdom, was dispersed into small enclaves widely scattered over the civilized world and too small, politically powerless, and insulated to exert a major influence on very large-scale societal developments. Islam so directly fused religious leadership and the government of large-scale, rapidly expanding empires that it could not (at least within a short enough period of time) adequately control the institutional conditions of social change to channel them in the religiously indicated directions. Furthermore, the development of the religious orientation system itself was not "rationalized" and systematized in a manner comparable with the Christian.

The theme of human imperfection, in acute contrast with the transcendence and thus in some sense the glory of God, is sharply accented in Judaism and became the basis of the Christian doctrine of sin. Such imperfection, however, was inherently relative to the deep theme of the goodness of the divine creation, of which man, "created in God's image," was clearly the highest part. Then even such expressions as the "total depravity" of sinful man are not to be taken so literally as to imply no basic potential for religiously legitimized good. It is not the "things of this world" or of the "flesh" which are inherently evil but primarily man's willfulness, his presumptuousness in disobeying the divine commandments and in thinking he can do without divine guidance.

The other essential ingredient of Christianity came from Greek culture, which had distant relations to Hebraic culture but was predominantly independent of it in development and pattern. The institutional structure of Roman society had sufficiently fused with Hellenistic culture in the area in which Christianity originated, so that we can consider the parts played in the shaping of Christian theology by Greek philosophy and by the institutionalized individualism and law of the Roman polity to be of a piece. Greek culture provided a major *constitutive* component of Christian religious orientations, and early Roman imperial society provided both an environment in which the movement could spread and institutional components, notably a legal system, which were eventually absorbed by the Christian religious system and the church itself.

Particularly important to the Christian orientation to human society was the Greco–Roman conception of a universalistically defined system of order in the "nature" of the world. In its more cosmic references it underlay the Greek contributions to the beginnings of natural science. But it also had relevance to human relationships, and in this connection, especially among the Stoics, the ideal of human society came to involve the ordering of these relations in accord with the "order of nature." The fullest institutionalization of this universalistic conception came with the systematization of Roman law, which, by including both the *jus civilis* (which defined the rights and obligations of Roman citizens) and the *jus gentium* (which defined the relations among persons of a different civic or ethnic allegiance) in a single, coherent legal system, transcended the parochial particularism that characterized previous conceptions of social order. Furthermore, this transcendence implies that the basic bindingness of such an order must be defined in general terms and not in highly specific prescriptions and prohibitions as has been characteristic of many systems of religious law, such as those of Talmudic Judaism and Islam. This universalism of the secular normative order could then be matched with the universalism of religious evaluation, which was one of the crucial religious features of the Christian movement.

The marriage of Hebraic and Greco–Roman elements that produced Christianity involved a crucial differentiation of the new sociocultural entity from both parent sources. Judaism and Greek and Roman religion had been the religions of already established sociopolitical communities, the People of Israel and the city-states of the Greek and Roman worlds. To use the terms loosely, they had been "ethnic," "civic," or "national" religions. On the level of social structure it was decisive that Christianity arose as a sect within Judaism, at a time when Palestine was Hellenized and Romanized—certainly the members of the elite were culturally quite Hellenized. Since all sectarian movements have a separatist tendency, it was natural that early Christianity raised questions about how its differences from the rest of the Jewish community were relevant to the general Greco–Roman matrix. These questions reached a crux when St. Paul initiated the church's historic break with the traditional Jewish community by declaring that the observance of Jewish law had no bearing on a convert's status as a Christian. This status was to be based only on the individual's act of commitment to the church and the saving message of Jesus (Nock 1938). It seems that this development was occasioned by problems stemming from the very success of Paul's mission to the Gentiles— that is, by the fact that many Christians were essentially alien to the particularities of Jewish tradition.

Its break with the Jewish community gave the church freedom to develop and expand. This freedom was realistically important, particularly because of two main features of the society of the Roman Empire at that time, perhaps especially of its eastern half. First, under the pattern of order just noted, this society was predominantly individualistic in a sense matched by no other society of comparable scale until modern times. In spite of its many regional and ethnic particularities, Rome effected its governmental authority over an exceedingly wide area and maintained substantial peace and internal order for a considerable period. A primary factor in this stability was the highly universalistic system of law, with its quite generalized principles allowing very substantial freedom within its framework. It was a society in which considerable mobility for migration and settlement

was feasible and in which the main urban centers, at least, were highly developed and cosmopolitan communities.

Second, the society was psychologically ready for the type of soteriological movement which Christianity represented. Within the Jewish community there had developed much interest in the salvation of the individual, in addition to the traditional primary focus on the destiny of the People of Israel, as recent research has particularly emphasized. Deutero–Isaiah emphasized the individual aspect, and the Christians were not the only sect within Judaism, as, for example, the Essenes show. Beyond the Jewish community there was also considerable ferment of this general character (Nock 1964). The Greek mysteries and various kinds of Oriental cults spread widely through the empire, for example, Mithraism and the Egyptian cult of Isis and Osiris, and schools of philosophy took on a quasi-religious, if not fully religious, character (Cumont 1910). All of these movements attracted individuals on terms ranging from the clientele of a simple cult to membership in relatively firmly structured associational groups.

The early movement—doctrine and organization

The church was the corporate vehicle of the implementation of a distinctive religious orientation. The God of the Christians was of course the God of Israel, in His transcendence as creator and ruler of the universe and as the One who defined man's mission on earth. Compared to the main lines of Judaism, however, there was a new centrality of the conditions of the salvation of the individual soul rather than of the fate of a community. The Saviour was not the Messiah—although partially identified with him—not a new Moses who would lead his people into a new Promised Land, but the bringer of eternal life to the souls of believers.

The critical thing was the Christ figure as the mediator between the divine and the human levels. As the conception of Christ became stabilized through its elucidation in terms of Neoplatonic philosophy, he was at the same time both divine and human; he was, as formalized in the Nicene Creed, of the *same*—not similar—substance as the Father. (For the importance of the *homousias* formula, see Lietzmann 1938.) But as mortal, as dying in the crucifixion, he was a man, sharing all the attributes of humanity. He was the "Word made Flesh."

The strict monotheism of Prophetic Judaism was thereby modified. God the Father had "begotten" his divine Son. The Son had the power to "save" the souls of men and they in turn could have access to this incomparable gift through faith, through commitment to him and his mission, not through belonging to the Chosen People. This conception in turn called for a third "aspect" of divinity, the Spirit which Christ emanated to the believers and by virtue of which they were reborn into eternal life. Hence the doctrine of the Trinity, which was at the same time one and three divine persons.

Against the background of Judaism the Christian doctrine can be seen to have preserved the transcendence of God, but at the same time broken the bond to the Chosen People as the sole basic vehicle of implementing the divine plan for man. The place of the People of Israel could be taken by the church, which by virtue of the role of the Holy Spirit could be conceived also as at once divine and human, the company of souls "in Christ," which after death were somehow in "eternity" but in this life on earth constituted a special sort of sacred association. Basically it could only be a collectivity grounded on belief, not an ethnic one (the "People"). This was the theological basis of a critical step of differentiation between the religious system and the main structure of secular society, without which the historic mission of Christianity could not have occurred.

It was crucial that the constitutive symbolism of Christianity was built about the problem of death. The central validating event of Jesus' mission was the crucifixion. That he died was the symbol of his humanity; that he was resurrected was the symbol of his divinity. The relation of the church to the risen Christ constituted a crucial break with Judaic tradition in that its promise to men was not the reward of a worldly collectivity (the Chosen People) in a future "land of milk and honey," but the spiritual participation of the individual believer in "eternal life" and "in Christ." Through the sacrificial death of Jesus, death in general was for the believer not denied but transcended (Nock 1964). The granting of divine status to the mortal human being, to the flesh, and to worldly concerns was perhaps more firmly repudiated than in any other religious tradition. However, in being given the opportunity for salvation, man was called to participate in the world of the divine, in his purely spiritual capacity. Thus, the great Christian step was to spiritualize man while still retaining the legitimation of a mission for him in *this* world. By contrast, what may be called archaic religions went much further in the direction of divinizing

the human—for example, by regarding the Egyptian pharaoh as a god. Indeed, the formula for the spiritualizing of man constituted the essential religious basis of the conception of the church.

Against the background of Hellenism the universalism of the conception of order in human relations in this world could be preserved. Even though the pagan society of imperial Rome could not be positively sanctioned, it could be negatively tolerated, as in the formula "render unto Caesar [a pagan emperor] the things that are Caesar's," and Paul could be proud of his Roman citizenship. The articulation with the Christian theology, however, could go beyond the conception of an immanent order of nature to that of a potential new order which developed through the penetration of human society by the Divine Spirit through the agency of Christ and his church and the souls which had been elevated by their Christianization. There was here a new source of leverage over the world of secular human life, a basis, over the long run, of profound influence over it, the efficacy of which depended on many conditions, one of the most important of these being preservation of the basic Israelitic conceptual pattern that the mission of mankind was divinely ordained. The dimensions of this basic cultural orientation can be illuminated by its relation to four of the heresies that had to be combated well down into the Middle Ages.

The Gnostic heresy was perhaps most formidable in the eastern area in the early centuries. Derived from Neoplatonism and certain elements stemming from Persian and Egyptian cults, without the correctives of Hebrew and Roman empiricism and realism, it would have deprived Christianity of its leverage over the secular world by denying the reality of nature in favor of a realm of idealistic symbolization.

The major initial crisis, however, was over the Arian heresy, which in a certain sense was the obverse of the Gnostic heresy. It would essentially have denied the divinity of Christ by making him in substance only "similar" to the Father and thereby have deprived the church of the primary source of its leverage over the world. The church would have been at best divinely legitimized rather than "inspired." Without the Athanasian victory over Arianism it is hard to see how the church could have maintained its independence under the pressures of institutionalization as the state religion of the Roman Empire.

The Manichaean and the Donatist heresies were particularly important in the developments from Augustine to the High Middle Ages. The Manichaeans, to whom Augustine at one time belonged, would have destroyed the integration of the divine and human spheres, which was so crucial to the mission of Christ and the church, in favor of a basic metaphysical dualism that saw human life as an unending struggle between the forces of light and darkness. The Augustinian doctrine, on the contrary, saw the Christian task as not merely to defeat the forces of evil, but to organize and eventually include the lower and worldly elements in the higher. Although the secular world of his time was only negatively tolerated, Augustine affirmed the potential of Christianization for the "City of Man."

Finally, the Donatist heresy, although it had presented a major challenge even at the time of Augustine, came to a head at the time of Pope Gregory VII in the issue of the status of the clergy. It located the religious efficacy of priesthood not in the Holy Spirit as infused in the church but in the state of grace of the priest as an individual. Had it prevailed, it would have destroyed the fundamental *collective* character of the church, its capacity to serve as the agent of reorganization of secular life in the service of the religious ideal.

Thus, the early Christian church became clearly *differentiated* from *any* collective structure of the secular societies in which it originated and into which it spread. It thereby achieved a position of independence from all the structures of secular society, which was to prove of the utmost importance (Troeltsch 1912). As a collectivity itself, it embodied a type of structure that both favored its spread in the societies of the time and provided societies which had a considerable Christian population with a model for their change. Thus, in the Middle Ages the church was far more nearly modern in structure than was feudal society. Change came to be the modification of secular society to resemble the church, far more than the accommodation of the church to the secular patterns.

Forms of Christian institutionalization

The Christian theological orientation provided the cultural grounding for establishment of the church as an association of believers committed through the faith and in a way that differentiated their status as church members from other elements of the status of the same people in the society in which they lived. The main patterns of institutionalization that the Christian church has assumed follow.

The first broad type is represented by the early church and in a considerably modified form by the many sectarian movements that have appeared throughout the history of Christianity. The common characteristic is the existence of the religious association of the Christian type as essentially a separate entity within a host society, without clearly stabilized relations to the rest of the society. It could, as the early church gradually did, move in the direction of establishment. It could also, like many pietistic sects, come to be stabilized in some kind of enclave within the society, under some kind of toleration—the Diaspora Jewish community is a model. Otherwise, it could fail to preserve its identity and could be dissolved or absorbed.

In the case of the early church the surrounding society was pagan. The church enjoyed a relatively high order of toleration, partly because in the earlier phases its members were relatively obscure people and were centered in the more impersonal urban communities. They supported themselves by work in the relatively ordinary ways; as Paul said, a man "must work that he may eat." This social situation was associated with the eschatological orientation of the early phase. Concern was overwhelmingly with eternal life and preparation for it. The Second Coming was, at least in a mythological sense (how literally is difficult to tell), paramount in Christian expectations and was to be associated with the Last Judgment and the end of the temporal world.

This orientation was repeatedly renewed, but most sects took positions short of this extreme dissociation from the environing society. In the first place, the society itself had become in some sense Christian; hence the differentiation was interpreted to mean that it was imperfectly so. Very broadly, we can say that the worldly "activism" that we have considered to be a major feature of the Christian movement generally has precluded full long-run stabilization in a sectarian status. An innovative movement within the Christian system would in the nature of the case be oriented to influencing the definition and structure of the system as such, including of course its relation to secular society. Many movements with a more or less sectarian origin have of course found a "niche" —for example, as religious orders within the Catholic system or as denominations within the Protestant.

The second primary type of Christian organization is the Catholic. This is interpreted in the sense of an established church, which is the "state" religion of a politically organized society. The critical difference here from other cases in which membership in the religious community coincides ideally with that in the secular is the *differentiation* of the church as a social collectivity from the secular political collectivity, the state in more or less the medieval sense. Church and state in this sense are distinct organizations. Their relations to each other, however, have necessarily been complex. Again very broadly, the Eastern Orthodox church, which took primary shape within the Byzantine political structure from Constantine on, was, as Harnack in particular has emphasized, oriented by the transcendental concerns of Christians. It therefore tended to be concerned eventually with its particular version of monasticism and to give the orders a kind of primacy over the secular priesthood, which did not exist for the Roman Catholic church. This in a sense gave by default a special position to the secular political authority, since there was no papal monarchy to match the secular. By contrast, the Roman papacy and secular priesthood gave the church a stronger organizational position, especially in the earlier phases, by contrast with the weak secular structures of the declining western Roman Empire.

Both were Catholic, especially in the sense of establishing a *sacramental* order, which gave the visible church a specifically transcendental character. The sacraments as the "power of the keys" were in fact the direct means of dispensing divine grace (Troeltsch 1912).

The third basic type is the Protestant. Here the break is fundamentally with the sacramental system, making the "true" church "invisible" and salvation dependent, from the human side, on faith alone. Again, there have been, in the broadest terms, two main forms of Protestantism. The first of these carried over the pattern of the established church from the Catholic versions, with its presumption of the coincidence of the religious and the secular political communities. This position carried with it the obligation of the enforcement, by ecclesiastical and political authorities in varying relations to each other, of doctrinal orthodoxy as a condition both of religiously acceptable standing and of secular citizenship.

The second type of Protestant orientation has basically differentiated the religious from the political systems, in a sense far more radical than that of the Constantinian church and its successors. It "privatized" religious adherence, introduced religious toleration, and eventually promoted denominational pluralism and the separation of church and state.

The special "sectarian" character of the early church was an essential condition of the church's institutionalization in the Roman Empire as differentiated from the secular "politically organized society." Moreover, of the two main versions of Catholicism, the Roman had the greater evolutionary potential because it could give a special, new meaning to the conception of the "City of Man," under the tutelary aegis of the church.

The shift to Protestantism essentially meant the abandonment of this tutelage with its special kind of religious paternalism. The Lutheran branch, however, had a sufficiently "inward" character, so that it entrusted the responsibilities for secular affairs to political authority in a manner somewhat similar to that of the Byzantine church and its Orthodox successor. The other main branch of Protestantism, the Calvinistic, was parallel to the Roman branch of Catholicism in developing in the activistic direction, placing the greatest emphasis up to that time on the conception of the kingdom of God *on earth*.

The trend to religious establishment

The spread of Christianity did not fail to occasion considerable disturbances, including the well-known persecutions of the Christians. However, the reign of the emperor Constantine the Great saw a consolidation of the social position of the movement. In 313 Constantine proclaimed full religious freedom for the Christians, in the Edict of Milan. He later took such an interest as to preside personally over the Council of Nicea (although perhaps partly for its political implications) and eventually was converted. By the end of the fourth century Emperor Constantine had established Christianity as the state religion of the Roman Empire.

When the church came to comprise a large sector of the upper class of the empire as well as the emperor and his court it was necessary to restructure the terms that had defined the distinction between Christians, who as such were free of the entanglements of the sinful world, and pagans, who constituted the secular society. By the third century, the spreading movement comprised a considerable proportion of the population of the Roman Empire and had begun to penetrate the higher social levels of the empire. The Roman upper groups may have been corrupt and pleasure-seeking, as legend of the Christian world has it to this day, but they were the carriers of the social responsibilities of their society, however badly they may have failed in their obligations. Clearly, not all of the upper-class converts to Christianity could withdraw from the secular world. Many of them, to be sure, did become anchorites. But some continued to be local magnates and even to hold imperial office.

The expansion of the church up to the critical

period of the early fourth century was a slow and complex process. The basic role was evidently performed by the apostles, who as missionaries went from community to community to make converts. Among them, the original apostles, who had been the personal followers of Christ, were only the first of a continuing series. Where the apostles succeeded local associations were formed, which at first were highly informal. However, "teachers" and "deacons" soon appeared to assume certain differentiated functions in maintaining the doctrine and in carrying on the simple administrative tasks of the group. The oldest and largest churches, usually those located in communities that were particularly important in the secular society, became pre-eminent, and their officials assumed a special importance, especially in relation to the secular political order. Such pre-eminence soon became involved in the relations between the separate churches, and hence the offices of the leading churches became the points of crystallization for the episcopal organization of the church (Harnack 1902). It was natural that the emerging sacramental system and the administrative functions should become consolidated in the same office at both parish and episcopal levels.

This was a classic case of success threatening the deeper foundations of the values for which the original great commitments were made—not the last such case in Christian history. There is little doubt that this development presented the Christian church with an exceedingly severe temptation and that it partly succumbed. It succumbed much more fully in the eastern half of Christendom than in the western, a differentiation which became crucial in the development of the Western world and had much to do with the great schism of the eleventh century.

A most important feature of the Christian movement, as so far analyzed, was its establishment of *independence* from the ascriptive ethnic and lineage ties—whether Jewish or Greco–Roman—in which its predecessors had been involved. This was accomplished by combining a specifically religious orientation *and* a type of collective social organization of the religious community, which was in some respects as great an innovation as the constitutive religious symbolism itself. This independence was, however, notably threatened by the very success of the movement in reorganizing the religious constitution of the Roman Empire. The development of organized collective monasticism, as distinguished from individualistic anchoritism, was in important degree a response to this critical situation. This process—the major innovations

being the work of St. Basil—resulted in a differentiation within the church that may be regarded as even more fundamental than that between clergy (administrators of the sacraments) and laity. This was the differentiation between the religious and the laity.

The religious, as members of the orders, became the elite of the church. Their withdrawal from the world, symbolized above all by the vows of poverty and chastity, insured the independence from secular ties which had been so basic to the early church but which had become so much more difficult for most Christians to attain under the new conditions. The vow of obedience can be seen as assuring selective obedience to religious authority, specifically of the abbot, and hence protection against non-religious influences and pressures.

In a sense this was a snobbish discrimination by "superior" Christians against "inferior" Christians. However, it differed crucially from the dualism of the early church in that the lay Christians were still Christians, not pagans, and were expected in principle to comprise practically the *whole* population of the relevant secular society, even though it took a long time to accomplish this. The pagan element had been religiously upgraded through its conversion by the Christian movement and had become eligible for *inclusion*, as a total society, in the category of Christian, at least potentially. Moreover, the society was not a small, precarious Chosen People in a vast sea of more powerful alien societies, but was the great Roman Empire, the secular organization of what then seemed to be practically the whole civilized world.

The conversion of Constantine was the event which symbolized concomitantly the enormous opportunity of the Christian church to shape the secular world and the equally enormous threat to its independence represented by its generalization to a great total population and by its conversion of the socially influential and responsible classes. The reality and importance of the threat is evidenced by the long series of conflicts between church and state and, more subtly and insidiously, the involvements of the clergy (and on occasion the orders) in the nexus of secular interests.

Formation of the Western church

The next great stage of Christian history was associated with the differential fate of the two halves of the Roman Empire. In its original cultural constitution Christianity was much more Greek than Roman (Nock 1964; Jaeger 1961). It seems that it *could not* have arisen and grown to the level it attained had it been confined to the western half of the empire, since not only the Judaic but the Hellenistic component of its heritage was essential. Nevertheless, its greatest mission materialized not in its eastern "homeland," but in the west. One condition of this lay in the fact that, for a longer period, the west proved to be politically less stable than the east. At the same time, the west was the focus of both the ancient origin and the medieval resurgence of the distinctively Roman institutions of autonomous legal order; in both respects it developed much further than the Greek and the Byzantine elements indigenous to the east.

The decline of the Roman Empire was in the first instance that of the western empire. The eastern portion became highly stabilized, surviving the western by a full millennium. Even though its structure was gradually undermined, the sheer length of this survival is an extraordinary fact. In the west, however, the new crisis of the disorganization of the secular society (beginning with the removal of the capital from Rome to Constantinople) was associated with a great and many-sided surge of organization and innovation in the church.

The tendency for the two halves of the empire to split politically was related to a parallel tendency within the church. At the time of the Council of Nicea, the Arian faction derived its main support from the eastern segments of the church and the Athanasian faction from the western (Lietzmann 1936). In accord with this division, the east moved broadly toward political stabilization without major cultural innovation, whereas the west tended more to foster cultural innovations within the church and organization changes partly determined by them. Four principal trends crystallized within a relatively short period.

(1) The highest levels of theological formulation were greatly transformed by the figure whose doctrines, more than those of anyone else, shaped the distinctive nature of western Christianity, namely, St. Augustine. He lived and worked in western north Africa and wrote in Latin, not Greek. As Harnack so clearly put it (Harnack 1916; Vasil'ev 1917–1925), Augustine's conception of the "City of God" was, in one of its two main references, a potentiality for human life on earth. It was not confined to the realm of eternal life after death. Although the emphasis on the basic metaphysical dualism between divine and human, spirit and flesh, remained as sharp as in the Alexandrian theology and was even sharpened in certain respects, salvation was conceived to be not only *from* the sinfulness of the flesh but also *for* participation in the divine mission that God had ordained for Christian man in and through the church. The use of the concept of city is particularly significant in that it emphasized the continuity of the conception of the church with that of the polis. This was indeed part of the larger framework within which Augustine produced a new level of cultural generalization in the synthesis of the Christian soteriological message and the main patterns of classical culture. The main orientations of the Eastern church remained at the level of theological concern established by the Alexandrine Fathers, whereas, with Augustine, the west began to build a new foundation, upon which grew the whole Western development, including both Scholasticism and the Reformation.

(2) We have noted that the monastic movement was first established in the east, emerging in close relation to the spread of Christianity, which culminated in its becoming the state religion of the empire. Basilian monasticism, which predominated in the Eastern church for many centuries, was overwhelmingly contemplative and devotional in its emphasis. But in the west there followed closely upon the theology of Augustine and certainly in connection with it a new turn in the monastic movement, starting with the establishment of the Benedictine order (Tufari 1965). The Benedictine Rule instituted a regime of secular useful work for its members, labor in agriculture and in crafts, as a religiously valued ascetic exercise—as Weber particularly noted. One might say that labor was no longer conceived as simply the "curse of Adam," but as an essential component of the most fully Christian way of life. It was patently connected with a synthesis of the transcendental focus of Christianity and the exigencies of Christian life in this world. Fostering this orientation, the Benedictine order was the first in a series of involvements by the monastic elements of the Western church with the problems, first, of firmly establishing the church in its relations with secular society and, second, of improving secular society itself from a Christian point of view.

(3) The west strongly consolidated the organizational structure of the church itself, with special reference to the position of the secular clergy and their control. In contrast to the Byzantine pattern, which placed the emperor religiously as well as politically above *any* bishop, the crucial factor in this development was the consolidation of the Roman papacy and the establishment of the primacy of the See of Rome and of the position of its bishop as the true head of the church in the west. Presumably the pope could not have assumed primacy had be been confronted with an emperor who claimed to be head of the church and was resident

in the same city. But with the emperor a thousand miles away and Italy in a condition of relative political chaos, the elevation was possible. Of course, the traditions of Peter's mission to and martyrdom in Rome provided cultural legitimation for this crucial organizational change.

(4) Underlying this organizational consolidation were developments in the sacramental system, especially its extension to all the laity. The core sacrament, the Eucharist, formally ritualized the central constitutive symbolism of Christianity, the sacrificial death of Jesus and its transcendence. The Mass was the primary occasion upon which the communal solidarity of all members of the church was demonstrated at the parish level. (Weber [1921a] especially emphasized that the *common* participation in the Mass included all social classes.)

The sacramental system required a formally ordained, professional priesthood. The episcopal system organized the priesthood in a firm way, and papal monarchy had an opportunity to hold the territorially scattered bishops to a common organizational focus. These features of the organization of the church, which gradually became increasingly formalized and systematized through the development of canon law and administrative agencies, was particularly important because of the decentralized, segmented nature of the emerging feudal society. In the face of these tendencies the church in the west maintained a fundamental unity and a relatively bureaucratic structure.

What was new in the Western church was the idea that the church was not only ordained for the salvation of souls for eternity, but that it also had a mission for this world, to establish the kingdom of God on earth. In the first instance, this was to be realized in the monastic life, then in the church as a whole, and eventually in the whole of secular society. In contrast, the Eastern church had only one focus: eternity and the afterlife of the individual (Harnack 1916). Even when secular society had been Christianized (in the fourth-century sense), the true Christian was to live by the tenet "in but not of" it, almost in the Pauline sense. At the same time the church as organization had to come to terms with secular society, a fact particularly conspicuous at the parish level in the status of the priesthood as both married and virtually hereditary. At the highest social level the direct involvement of the church with government was indicative of a similar mode of accommodation. There was never an independent status of the church, with respect to secular society as a whole, comparable to that attained in the west. The Eastern church remained, in Harnack's striking phrase,

"frozen" at the level of religious concern attained by Christianity generally in the third and fourth centuries under the influence of the theologians who had been Neoplatonists in philosophy. In these terms, a great turning point in the history of Christianity came in the west with the theology of Augustine.

The medieval system and the Renaissance

The first culmination of the Western development was what Troeltsch called the "Christian society" of the High Middle Ages. This was partly preceded but also accompanied by a major development in monasticism, centering first in the Cluniac order, and by a new surge of energy and organizational reform in the church itself, especially during the papacy of Gregory VII, who had probably been a Cluniac monk himself. Certainly one of the most significant reforms was the formal institutionalization of clerical celibacy for the secular priesthood, which contributed greatly to the organizational independence of the church. However imperfect the enforcement of celibacy may have been, the policy meant that no priest—including bishops, who were often men of great power—could have *legitimate* heirs, so that clerical office could not become hereditary. This was particularly important, as Lea (1867) made clear, because the institution of aristocracy was becoming so central to secular society at that time.

Monasticism was also very much involved in the new theological developments, under the stimulus of Scholastic philosophy, especially within the Dominican order. Culminating in the *Summa theologica* of St. Thomas Aquinas, Scholasticism carried the integration of theology and philosophy a long step forward and, through the influence of the rediscovered text of Aristotle, accomplished a new and more thorough incorporation of classical culture.

Greater involvement in the secular world was symbolized by the active building of churches, especially of cathedrals, all over Europe. This not only implied an increased concern for the lay Christian, providing better for his worship, but also gave him more opportunity to express his religious concern, since church building required immense efforts from whole communities. Great ecclesiastics competed for the services of architects; village stonemasons embellished the great piers of cathedrals with intricate carvings, and elaborate façades were peopled with sculptured figures, while painting and stained glass decorated interiors.

There was certainly a connection between these religious developments and the growth of urban communities. For example, the guilds, which were becoming ever more prominent in the secular organization of the cities, profited immensely in wealth and power from their part in building the cathedrals and great abbeys. Significantly, no less an authority than St. Thomas held the urban way of life more favorable to Christian virtue than the rural (Troeltsch 1912, p. 295 in vol. 1 of the 1960 edition)—an interesting contrast to some nineteenth-century religious views. A new level of concern for the laity was also shown in the increasing ecclesiastical emphasis on Christian charity, in which again monasticism, particularly the Franciscan movement, played the leading role. The material, as well as the spiritual, welfare of the economically disadvantaged Christian became more and more the concern of the church.

In growing measure the ecclesiastical development of the Middle Ages became Pan-European, at least from south to north. Italy, as the seat of the papacy, in many respects took the leading role, despite the fact that Scholasticism centered in Paris rather than in Rome; but in general the characteristic changes were as conspicuous north of the Alps as south. The Middle Ages developed a European society and culture far more than ever before, even at the height of Roman influence.

The medieval Christian system was hierarchical. At the top stood the members of the religious orders, who lived the fully religious life—with whatever lapses—and stored up "treasure in heaven" for the benefit of their less committed lay brethren. Not only did the orders exhibit an increasing concern for the world, both in church and in secular life, but also, in sharp contrast to Buddhist monasticism, this religious "upper class" was linked to the laity by an independent secular clergy that controlled the power of the keys.

The Christian laity were in religious terms all presumptive equals. Of course, one must recognize that at this stage there was no implication of secular, social or economic, equality. Not even slavery was morally condemned, although humane treatment of slaves was enjoined. Secular society was highly stratified, with rapidly crystallizing institutions of hereditary aristocracy. These changed gradually from predominantly feudal forms into territorial monarchies, with the monarchs heading the aristocratic classes. The mass of the common people were the tillers of the soil. However, European society differed from many others with a predominantly peasant base and an aristocratic elite in that, largely as a heritage of classical antiquity, corporately organized towns played a very important part. Their organization provided essential models and centers for the development of more egalitarian forms of political institutions and

of law, as well as of guild industry and commerce. Crucially, their bourgeois citizens were neither aristocrats nor peasants, but an essentially independent middle class.

Medieval European societies were the first in history to have basic religious uniformity for a very large population as a whole. At the same time they fundamentally differentiated the religious organization, the church, from the secular structure, what in this special sense has been called the state. Thus, within the context of the total society, the church was able to maintain its structural independence. This fact, combined with its organizational features and relatively this-worldly orientation, enabled the church to exert an unprecedented influence on the process of social development.

Both culturally and socially there were certain inherent elements of instability in the medieval system which a certain contemporary romanticism is prone to obscure. On the whole, however, these seem to have involved openness to progressive change rather than a tendency to breakdown or societal regression. On the cultural side, the Scholastic system was shot through with tensions and controversies. Certainly, the emergence of nominalism as a major movement on the borderline between theology and philosophy was highly significant (McIlwain 1932; Southern 1953; Kristeller 1955; Huizinga 1919). In accord with Thomas' example in seeking confirmation from Aristotle there was a general turning to classical sources and models—for example, the humanistic concern with classical literature and the revival of interest in Roman law which, especially in relation to the place of canon law within the church, began early in the Middle Ages (Gierke 1881). In fact, the high medieval culture merged almost imperceptibly into that of the Renaissance, however important certain dramatic advances may have been, such as those of Giotto and Masaccio in painting.

These processes of cultural elaboration and differentiation were grounded in the commitment of the Christian movement, especially accentuated in the west, to a genuine synthesis with classical culture. The critical development was the emergence of a differentiated system of secular culture more or less directly articulated with Christian orientations and, despite many tensions, legitimated in general by Christian values. Perhaps the most obvious field is that of art, where architecture was heavily oriented to the church and where painting, besides embellishing churches, dealt almost exclusively with religious subjects.

There was also instability in the relations between the church as organization and secular society. The imposition of clerical celibacy had been in one respect a measure to protect the autonomy of the church from over-involvement in the responsibilities, as well as the perquisites and privileges, of secular affairs. The "investiture controversy" was typical of the structural difficulties at the feudal core of the system, because the bishops, as the principal officers of the church, were responsible for both its political and its property interests. But in feudal terms, the church as corporation could not simply "own" property or enjoy political "rights" in the modern sense. The church was so interwoven with the feudal system that, as property holder, it also became the lord with temporal political jurisdiction, a circumstance that gave rise to a basic question of allegiance: Where did it lie, with the church or the secular authority? In medieval terms, no clear answer was possible (Troeltsch 1912, chapter 2, parts 3 and 4).

Thus, there was an unstable oscillation between ecclesiastical subordination to secular authorities and the direct assumption of secular power by the church, as in the papal states and in a few ecclesiastical principalities north of the Alps. It was inevitable that religious and ecclesiastical problems became intertwined with secular politics, so that the tensions in one sphere fed into the other. This situation goes far to explain the fact that the Reformation stimulated a full break in the unity of western Christendom rather than a "reform" of the church in the more usual sense.

The whole spectrum of cultural development, however, from the spheres of philosophy closest to the theology of the church to the most secular aspects of arts, letters, and eventually science, steadily eroded the cultural foundations of the medieval system. Socially, the feudal core of the society receded in relative importance before the rise of the Italian city-states with their commerce and manufacturing, the growth of the free cities of the Holy Roman Empire north of the Alps from Switzerland to the Netherlands, and the establishment of truly national states, particularly France and England.

The Reformation and its aftermath

The Reformation was the culmination in the strictly religious sphere of the general trend of social and cultural change away from the medieval system and toward modernity. Although it was hostile to certain of the Renaissance achievements (e.g., in art), its basic continuity with the Renaissance is the more impressive fact, as evidenced in the close following of the Italian initiatives in science by Protestant scientists in Holland and England and the hostility of the Protestant north to many of the artistic innovations coming from Italy. It is not unimportant that the founder of the more "progressive" wing of the Protestant movement, Calvin, was trained in law as well as in theology. The Reformation became intimately related to the development of nationalism—vernacular translations of the Bible multiplied—and some Protestant areas advanced very rapidly in economic development.

Although its consequences and implications took long to unfold, the Reformation constituted both a truly fundamental innovation and an authentic evolutionary development from the medieval Catholic base. The aspect of greatest interest here concerns primarily the relation of the religious system to the secular society.

At the strictly religious level the crucial development was the upgrading of the Christian laity. This was effected by ending the individual's dependence on sacerdotal mediation. The individual soul stood in *immediate* relation to God through Christ (Bellah 1964). With respect to the ancient triad of functions the effect was to throw emphasis strongly away from the institutional forms of the "cure of souls" and of "casuistry." It opened the door to an altogether new emphasis on "conscience," which emerged particularly in the Calvinistic branch, once the more subjective concerns of Lutheranism had given way to concern with objective activism in secular callings. Although it is true that the basic status *differential* was eliminated, this did not imply any lowering in the evaluation of the clergy or of the system, within which statuses had been "equalized."

The upgrading is expressed in the basic Protestant doctrine of the *invisibility* of the true church. The visible social organization, the concrete church with its priests and sacraments, is *not* the mystical body of Christ; the latter exists only in the souls of those who by faith are its true members in the eyes of God. The visible church has become "secularized." But in the true visible church the layman has been placed on equal footing with the religious. If the layman truly gives his commitment of faith and accepts the divine grace, his status of sanctification is fully equal to that which had previously been reserved to the monk.

The radical implication was that it is not necessary, in order to be sanctified, to lead a way of life apart from the secular world and under a special discipline (Weber 1904–1905). Religious merit was in principle compatible with any ethically acceptable worldly "calling." Moreover, as Luther himself deliberately dramatized, it was compatible with marriage. Thus, the two crucial vows of poverty and chastity were no longer preconditions of the "truly" Christian life. The same fate for the vow of obedience was inevitable because, in the monastic state, obedience was owed to a human ecclesiastical authority, in the first instance to the abbot. The differentiation of church and state clearly meant that ecclesiastical authority could not govern conduct in secular callings and presumably not in any complete sense in marriage and family life. The legitimation of monastic separatism as the *one* pattern of the fully Christian life was thereby destroyed.

The change in the status of the sacraments as administered by the secular clergy was parallel. The direct relation of the individual's soul to God in seeking grace through faith precluded *any* humanly administered mechanism from intervention in God's dispensation of grace. The minister became basically a teacher, counselor, and leader of his congregation (Troeltsch 1912, chapter 3 in vol. 1 of the 1960 edition).

The human individual was no longer conceived as a unitary entity, whose secular or worldly life was inseparable from its spiritual state, but as encompassing a much sharper differentiation between the two components. The aspiration to gain sanctification would yet have consequences for conduct in the secular world, but the commitment of the religious would no longer be embodied in a way of life concretely different from that of the nonreligious. The same principle obtained in regard to the sacraments. No concrete acts of human beings could automatically dispense or withhold grace. The only source of grace was directly divine, and grace could come to the individual only through his private, subjective acceptance of it.

To understand the potential significance of this shift it is essential to reconsider the whole development since early Christianity. The early church and its membership constituted a precarious island of sanctification in a sea of paganism, the latter comprising the whole structure of the secular society. With the successful proselytization of the whole of Western society and Christianity's emergence as the official religion of the Roman Empire, the newly differentiated religious orders became the elite vanguard of the church. They preserved the central Christian orientation from secularization by absorption in an environment that was not fully Christian in the religious sense and led the movement to the upgrading of the whole lay population on Christian terms.

The Christian society of the High Middle Ages was a class-stratified religious society in that the visible church was endowed with a kind of fundamental guardianship, first and foremost over secular society—the position of the state in this connection being highly equivocal. Within the church there was a parallel guardianship of the laity by the clergy, both regular and secular. Since the Reformation was in the first instance a "revolution" within the church, its primary consequence was, as noted, the emancipation of the laity from this guardianship by the clergy. The implications for secular society, however, were implicit and could not fail to become salient unless the whole development were suppressed.

Although events moved much more rapidly during the Reformation than during the spread of Christianity in the ancient world, there is a significant similarity of pattern. Once a movement apparently so alien to the Roman ethos as Christianity was able to reach a position to bid for religious ascendancy in the empire, an alliance with secular authority was inevitable. In this case, it took the form of conversion of the legitimate Roman emperor and the eventual proclamation of the official status of Christianity. It would have made some, but perhaps not a fundamental, difference if a Christian military leader had gained political supremacy by conquest, as was typical in the spread of Islam. In either case the secularizing influence of political involvement would have operated. As noted, the primary response of the Christian church was to protect its independence, first, by the development of religious orders that had considerably more independence from secular society than the secular clergy, and, second, by retreating into the politically disorganized west, where the secular authority was relatively weak.

The parallel events in the Reformation involve Luther's alliance with the German princes. (In certain contexts Luther may be considered the Constantine of his day—in the sense of being a politicized churchman, not a converted emperor.) Had not this religious innovation, too, enlisted political power during its crucial period, it could never have succeeded. It could not have become consolidated in strategic metropolitan centers and thus enjoyed the opportunity to spread into new areas. The price of this alliance, however, was a conservative turn—in the social sense—of the religious movement itself, exemplified by Luther's repressive attitude toward the peasant revolts and his general support of secular authoritarianism.

The developments of this period were the result of a complex combination of innovating and conservative elements at work. The princes were in fact pioneers in the construction of the national state, one of the institutional foundations of modern society. They were, however, at the same time markedly authoritarian in regard to independent movements within their jurisdictions. Luther's conservative position in economic affairs and especially affairs of political sovereignty vis-à-vis the subjects of the princes, accorded with this context. In an important sense, conservatism culminated in the Lutheran movement's acceptance of the Erastian principle that the political sovereign should also be the formal head of the church. Here, the development tended, as in Eastern Christianity, toward a symbiosis of church and state, severely compromising the religious potential for reconstructing the secular world. The parallel to the mystical, otherworldly orientation of Eastern monasticism was the Lutheran stress on "inwardness" of the Protestant Christian orientation, which also precluded undertaking major responsibilities in secular affairs. The truly Christian individual was to be primarily concerned with settling his accounts with God and hence relatively indifferent to the fate of secular affairs. The main responsibility for these affairs was to be left to a divinely ordained secular authority. Furthermore, the whole orientation was shot through with pessimistic convictions about the essential sinfulness of secular man, which would inevitably manifest itself in widespread unethical conduct, which could be checked only by a liberal resort to coercive measures on the part of the civil authorities (Troeltsch 1906; 1912, chapter 3, part 2 in vol. 1 of the 1960 edition). Although this conception was another version of the Christian society, it was not a very inspiring one from the viewpoint of secular idealism.

As must be expected of social movements directed toward such broad and generalized social change (Smelser 1962), Reformation Christianity has been characterized by a multiplicity of sectarian movements having a wide variety of orientational content and possibilities for influencing later social developments—as indeed has virtually every subsequent phase of Christianity. Some have been strongly chiliastic and sometimes antinomian and as such have generally failed to become permanently institutionalized—historically one of the most important was the Anabaptist movement (Cohn 1957; Knox 1950). Others have secured more or less stable interstitial positions (e.g., some of the Pietistic movements). Still others, like the two most important American movements, Mormonism and Christian Science, have been relatively close to the main line of ascetic Protestant development.

Ascetic Protestantism

The major Protestant alternative to the Lutheran development may be considered *the* main developmental line of Protestantism, if not of Christianity as a whole. Broadly, this started with the Calvinist wing of the Reformation. There is a striking parallel between this major differentiation within Protestantism and that between the eastern and western branches of the earlier church, even the geographical reference remaining stable in that the western was the more activistic branch. Indeed one might even suggest some significance in the fact of continuity with Rome; whereas Luther was a German monk steeped in Scholastic philosophy, Calvin was a Frenchman who had a predominantly lay education with special reference to law in the Roman tradition.

Asceticism within the Protestant framework had to be "this-worldly" in Weber's sense. Precisely by maintenance of the basic radical dualism between the transcendental and the "world" within that framework, the activistic potentials inherent in the whole Christian movement (and indeed back of it, in Judaism) were accentuated to a far higher degree than had been possible in the Catholic tradition. On the one hand, Calvinism, in common with the Lutheran branch, had emancipated secular society from ecclesiastical tutelage and put it "on its own"; on the other hand, the Calvinist version of the tensions between the divine mission and the human condition gave a far stronger anchorage to activistic orientations than did the Lutheran tendency toward resignation in the face of sin and divine Providence.

The Calvinist pattern centered on the conception, foreshadowed by Augustine but newly accentuated, of the holy community destined by divine mandate, but implemented by *human agency*, to bring into being a kingdom of God on earth (Miller 1956). This was from one aspect a collective orientation, but from another was perhaps the most radical expression of Christian individualism; at least it was an orientation to realistic possibilities of institutionalization in secular society rather than otherworldliness or antinomian expectations. Calvinism was, however, a developing religious system in a complex cultural and social environment, so that considerable time elapsed and many changes occurred before certain of the most important potentialities could emerge.

In the more immediate situation, the Reformation precipitated a critical period of conflict and reorganization in European society as a whole (Elton 1963)—to be sure, other factors were also involved, for example, the political impetus which led to and derived from the discoveries and extra-European expansion. The broad outcome of the tensions, which in secular terms operated mainly at the political level, was the creation of a northern European tier of predominantly Protestant communities. However, there were many crosscurrents in the political struggles, including those within the Protestant movement. The Catholic political bastions were Spain and the eastern Hapsburg domain, with disunited Italy being a continual battleground of interests. Northeastern Germany became solidly Protestant and with Scandinavia was the main focus of the institutionalization of Lutheranism. However, the most potent political unit of this system, the monarchy of Prussia, came to be dominated by a special version of Calvinism (Kayser 1961).

On the western wing, England, while also becoming, with her colonies in North America, the most important "mother" of institutionalized ascetic Protestantism, adopted in the Church of England the most nearly Catholic type of ecclesiastical organization of any Protestant church. France, after a bitter internal struggle in which the Protestant forces almost gained control, was carried by the most important Catholic victory during the wars of religion, but in a form which destroyed her religio–political "orthodoxy" and in some important respects paved the way for the French Revolution. Holland, in the heat of her struggle for independence from Spanish rule, was for a time the most Protestant of countries, only gradually to attenuate this characteristic in the subsequent period —a fact associated with the preservation, largely under French auspices, of the Catholicism of Flanders and of the German Rhineland, especially of its northern reaches.

The outcome of these complex restructurings, which was clear by the early eighteenth century, was politically inconclusive, but in one sense it was crucially decisive. The Reformation permanently broke the medieval form of the religious unity of western Christendom, and a Europe was created in which religious and political elements were interwoven in a very intricate, pluralistic fashion. Thus, in the mid-eighteenth century His Most Catholic Majesty, the king of France, could find himself first in an alliance negotiated by a cardinal with the Calvinist king of Prussia against the Hapsburgs and then in support of the very Protestant American colonies in their war of independence against the also Protestant British. After 1688 the danger of old-style political–Catholic domination of Britain was past. The position of Prussia made clear that there could be no Catholic reconquest of the eastern boundaries of the main European system—the Hapsburg monopoly was broken. Moreover, major societies of European origin and of predominantly ascetic Protestant orientation had been implanted overseas, beyond *any* basic control of the parent European system.

The main foundations of the ascetic Protestant religio–political system were laid in Holland and particularly in Great Britain (including Scotland) during the seventeenth century. The earlier version of the conception of the holy community was most dramatically embodied in the Commonwealth under the Protectorate of Oliver Cromwell. Although this drastic political innovation lasted only a few years, like the Calvinist movement in France, it left indelible marks on the whole future of the country. The Restoration brought back the monarchy and aristocracy and consolidated the position of the Church of England, but by the time of the Settlement of 1688, religious toleration was assured and opportunity was opened for nonconformism to develop further—a Catholic restoration of the French type would surely have precluded a Methodist movement so soon after the Stuarts.

Besides the religious movement itself, this enormous "effervescence" crucially advanced the development of the British parliamentary system, which eventually extended into a political democracy. It greatly aided the consolidation of the characteristic features of the common law and hence the establishment of the foundations of the legal component of modern citizenship, the famous "rights of Englishmen" (Little 1963; Marshall 1934–1962). It also created a social environment more congenial to the development of science than any hitherto found in the west—the century and country of Cromwell were also those of Newton (Merton 1938). Finally, the very fact that the political emphases of the Cromwellian venture failed to gain ascendancy probably shifted the balance in favor of the economic emphases, which Weber elucidated in his famous analysis. All of these factors—admittedly combined with various others—had much to do with the fact that in the later eighteenth century it was Great Britain that fostered the momentous beginnings of the industrial revolution.

The foregoing summary is not meant to imply that the development in seventeenth-century England was either unitary or independent of non-Protestant antecedents. The depth of the internal division which was manifested politically in the English Civil War is clear. However, the Stuart Restoration did not become consolidated and a new unity was achieved after 1688 which broke the chronic tendency of the crown under the Stuarts to ally itself with Catholic powers and to threaten the Protestant succession. The main framework of the legal system was established, as was religious toleration. In the case of science, of course, the main foundations of the modern development had been laid in Renaissance Italy with Galileo as the most notable figure, but England provided a newly favorable cultural and social environment for the next main phase, with Newton as the great symbolic figure, and the establishment of the Royal Society as the organizational focus.

England was thus unique in the combination of cultural and social factors which led toward modernization. Its only close rival was Holland. Here, however, the efflorescence was briefer and somewhat less widespread—for example, there was less development in the fields of law and parliamentary institutions. Moreover, the insular position of England encouraged the development of a solidary national community and protected her more fully against the inhibiting and disruptive influences of the complex Continental situation, such as the military threats that would encourage a large standing army and restrictions of economic access to trade with immediately neighboring countries. In particular, England was in a strikingly advantageous position to extend her politico–economic influence beyond Europe, and this included religious as well as other types of development overseas.

On the cultural side, another extremely important difference seems to have been established, broadly, between predominantly Catholic and predominantly Protestant Europe. It has been emphasized above that the relation between Christianity and the more secular elements of culture, with their special roots in the classical heritage, presented problems of great significance. The Christian capacity to synthesize with these cultural movements, which in its terms have been primarily secular, has been one of its most important features.

The rise of early modern science, in its connections with philosophy, presented a new set of problems for the nature of this synthesis. Here the more ascetic branches of Protestantism seem to have been able to develop a relation with substantially less immediate and overt conflict than the more predominantly Catholic cultures—with the exception of what later came to be defined as the "fundamentalist" trends in Protestantism. The somewhat special relation between science and Puritanism in seventeenth-century England is a prominent case (Merton 1938), although the situation in Holland was similar in the same period.

By contrast, there seemed to be a greater conflict between science, and more generally the "intellectuals," and religion in the Catholic sphere. This came to a head in eighteenth-century France in the Enlightenment. By and large, the orientation of the Enlightenment was antireligious, which of course meant anti-Christian. Since the religious structure was Catholic, it was also anticlerical because of the central place of the clergy in the Catholic system. On the whole, the antireligious

themes among persons committed to the secular intellectual disciplines have been much less prominent in Protestant areas, again especially those of ascetic Protestantism, although of course it has not been absent. This division still persists, especially between Continental European intellectuals and those of Anglo–American provenience. Thus, the resonance of Marxism has been notably weak in the latter area, which can almost certainly be associated with the militant anti-Christianism of the Marxists.

American Protestantism

There is an important sense in which the modernizing outcome of the European development of ascetic Protestantism occurred mainly in North America, although also in other places. In any case, the development there may serve to illustrate the second main subtype of Protestant institutionalization defined in the classification that was outlined above, namely, that characterized for a whole society by the "privatization" of organized religion and hence by the separation of church and state and the "spelling out" of religious toleration in a system of denominational pluralism, in which there is no distinction, as has persisted in England, between an established church and a set of "nonconformist" groups.

This development marks an important step in the general evolutionary trend of the Christian system from the "aspiration to Universal Brotherhood, to the institutionalization of Universal Otherhood" (Nelson 1949). The United States represents by far the largest scale of institutionalization of this type, and in addition, the fact of the American position of power and influence on the world scene, which has developed in the present century, gives this case a special empirical importance.

The case is, however, meant to deal with the realization of the "liberalizing" potentiality of Protestant development from a Calvinistic base, because of the special evolutionary significance of that trend in the total Christian picture. The role of this Protestant liberalism has been one of leading a trend, which could in turn be adopted by other groups, partly because of the generally modernizing developments in the respective societies, as in Scandinavia and much of Lutheran northern Germany and partly because of the impact of the "liberal" Protestant model which, for example, has certainly affected the development of the Catholic church.

Early Calvinism was predominantly collectivist in orientation. At the purely religious level it embodied the old Christian duality of spirit and flesh in the radical form of the doctrine of predestination. As interpreted in certain phases of Calvinism, this purported to categorize concrete human persons as either saved or damned, by divine decree, from eternity. Although the strict theological terms admitted of no visible signs of election, the social tendency was toward a certain kind of elitism, the rule of the presumptively elect over the presumptively damned, the reprobates. Nevertheless, this doctrine basically undermined the institution of aristocracy in the older European sense. There was never the slightest suggestion that God "predestined" persons to election by virtue of their ancestry; had there been, it would have been indefensible in theological terms. Moreover, the invisibility of the status of election raised the question of whether those who claimed it were not merely self-appointed.

Predestination tended continually to be confused with predeterminism and in this interpretation never could have been a genuinely Christian doctrine. It is one thing to assert that salvation comes to all men as a gift of God and that men are thus predestined to salvation. It is quite another to assert that some men are predestined to election and others to rejection. This latter interpretation was too radically in contradiction to the central conception of the mission of Christ to mediate the salvation of all humanity.

There is now clear evidence that the radical social elitism of original Calvinism should be regarded as characteristic only of an early phase of its development (Loubser 1965). In only two major cases has it actually lasted into the modern situation, namely, that of Prussia and that of the conservative wing of Dutch Calvinism in South Africa. In both the Prussian and the South African cases there was a crosscutting with religiously adventitious factors, which made anything like the relatively "pure" development of North American Christianity impossible. Both cases have in common an element of Christian militancy in facing a threatening environment on a frontier in such a way as to make their pattern of action religiously acceptable. Furthermore, in both cases the populations embodying the perceived threats were regarded as inferior by the bearers of the main tradition, namely, the Slavs on the eastern border of Germany and the "blacks" in South Africa.

American Protestant "fundamentalism" might be regarded as a third survival of "old Calvinism." In the South it has been intimately associated with racial segregation and the doctrine of the inferiority of the Negro. Like the South African and Prussian cases, it has been related to the frontier experience and indeed has recently been associated with the parts of the country where frontier traditions persist the most.

There can be little doubt, however, that the main line of development from the Calvinistic base has been a liberalizing one and, moreover, has not been predominantly secularizing in the sense of loss of religious commitment. Development along this main line has occurred in a number of nations, certainly in Holland and England, but most purely in the United States, with its earlier phases centering in Massachusetts.

As the general Protestant differentiation between the spiritual and secular components of an individual person matured, the predestination theology, with its categorization of total persons in temporal life as either sanctified or damned, became untenable. The basic Protestant tenet of salvation by faith then gained application to any individual who would make the commitment of faith. With this development, the conception of the church as in partnership with the political authority to enforce church discipline on the unregenerate also became untenable. The invisible church was a communion of souls in the faith, and the visible church of necessity became a voluntary association (Loubser 1964).

This development had gone so far by Independence that the provisions of the first amendment, separation of church and state and freedom of religion, were not seriously contested in the Constitutional Convention (Miller 1965). This fact was an index not of religious indifference, but of consensus on the religious principles involved. Another indication is that many local churches disapproved of taxation for support of the church well before it was held to be unconstitutional.

This article does *not* assert that on religious grounds alone the development that took place in America was inevitable. That, as contrasted with Dutch Calvinism in South Africa and, indeed, with much of American fundamentalism, it did take this direction was a function of a variety of social, economic, and political circumstances, some of which will be outlined. The crucial point here is that the religious system had the *potential* for this development, which was a religiously authentic and legitimate alternative. Its emergence, in stronger form than elsewhere, cannot be interpreted simply as the "rationalization" of a developing set of economic interests, as has so often been asserted.

This development was certainly favored by political decentralization, which predominated during the earlier phases of American society and gave wide scope for voluntary associations. The political structure also favored independent activity of the committed Christian in his calling—and not necessarily in any context of association—hence in that aspect of individualistic economic action associated with Max Weber's analysis of the relation between Protestantism and the development of capitalism. For a variety of reasons and under a variety of influences, America during the nineteenth century became in certain senses increasingly individualistic. However, this fact should not be placed outside the larger context of the conception of a holy community. The conception of the holy community was paramount among the early Protestant colonists, in Virginia as well as in New England (Miller 1956; 1959). As the scope of communication, trade, and common destiny grew the independent units tended to consolidate into a single community, a new "nation under God."

By the time of its establishment the new nation was religiously and politically pluralistic and was progressively developing increasing degrees of social and economic pluralism. Religiously, it went very far toward basing itself on the principle of voluntary association, a tendency that was virtually complete early in the nineteenth century. Although the exigencies that constrain political voluntarism are harsher, the trend was also toward a "free" polity more exposed to the hazards of populism than to those of traditional European authoritarianism.

The "individualism" of ascetic Protestantism should be understood in this context. It should be remembered that the Reformation eliminated the "two-world" system by virtue of which secular life in general and the secular callings of individuals in particular could not be valued equally with the "religious" callings. However, just as the religious calling and achievement of the individual in the monastic system occurred within the framework of the church, so the religiously critical performances of the Protestant layman in his calling occurred within the context of the holy community, which included *both* visible church and secular society, even though they were differentiated. Ascetic Protestant activism meant that "innerworldly" callings constituted the primary field for the individual to implement his religious commitments. The intensive activism of the general Christian commitment to regenerate (and hence upgrade) life was thereby channeled into achievement in worldly callings, among them, although by no means predominantly, business achievement.

This individualistic pattern bestowed the strong sanction of religious commitment on what is now often called achievement motivation and fostered the internalization of such motivation by typical individuals (Weber 1904–1905). It imbued the typical ascetic Protestant with a strong sense of responsibility for achievements in this-worldly callings, the obverse of which was the ambition to "succeed." This has not been primarily an anarchic individualism of impatience at all social restraint but an institutionalized individualism, the achievement of the individual ideally being a contribution to the building of the holy community. Thus, American individualism has been congruent with a prominent development of nationalism and the pervasive presence of many varieties of association, including much large-scale organization. What there is of the attempt to break down restraints in general—and there is a good deal—is more ideology than direct expression of the central cultural pattern.

American society has recently developed a trend that seems most important against the background of the historical trends sketched above. In its formative period the United States was an overwhelmingly Protestant society and one that developed its religious constitution in a liberal direction and toward a relatively advanced level of religious toleration. By immigration it acquired a large number of non-Protestants, so that by now about a quarter of the population is Roman Catholic and a very substantial number are Jewish. The change in the religious character of the immigrants culminated in the generation extending from about 1890 to World War I.

The crucial phenomenon is the *inclusion* of the non-Protestant groups in a national community which, though of course secular in government, still retains its religious character as a holy community in the transformed sense of a "nation under God." It has become a Judaeo–Christian ecumenical community having the positive form of religious toleration entailed in a denominational pluralism, which has been extended to all major groups in the population, including "secular humanists," who prefer to avoid involvement in organized denominational bodies (Herberg 1955; Parsons 1960). The important core of such groups is not the religiously "indifferent" who simply "backslide" in their religious principles, but the intellectuals who have severe reservations about commitment to any of the more traditional denominational positions. By contrast with much of Continental Europe, the American groups have generally not been characterized by militant atheism or anticlericalism.

We can thus speak of a near-consensus on a

"civic" religion—perhaps somewhere near the boundary between theism and deism—expressed in such conceptions as "One Nation Under God" and "In God We Trust" (Bellah 1965). This in turn articulates with and legitimates the broad moral consensus on what I have called the pattern of institutionalized individualism, most massively expressed recently in the civil rights movement, which had the conspicuous backing of *all* the important religious groups as well as of the "humanists" and agnostics.

The religion of the churches, on the other hand, has been both voluntarized and privatized. More detailed belief systems, more specific observances, variations in ecclesiastical polity, and the extent of the individual's commitment to them are largely confined to the denominational level and its embodiment in the particular parish. Broadly, all of the groups that historically have belonged in the established church tradition—for which a Jewish equivalent may be discerned in Orthodox Judaism —have "accepted" this situation, some of course more enthusiastically than others.

This process has been interdependent, as suggested above, with a structural pluralizing in the society as a whole: residence, socioeconomic status, occupation, and political attachment have become increasingly dissociated from religious affiliation and from the ethnic components which have historically been so closely associated with religion. This process is by no means complete, and it is unlikely that a society will ever completely "privatize" ethnicity and religion. However, there can be little doubt that recent American developments have reached an altogether new level, certainly if scale is taken into account. The new American "secular city," as Harvey Cox (1965) has called it, despite all its complex strains, conflicts, and imperfections (which from *any* religio–ethical point of view are many and serious), has been legitimized as a genuine holy community in the ascetic Protestant sense. Yet, it has undergone a development that few of its Protestant forebears could have expected in its ecumenical aspect, having come to include all those who live under the God of Israel and of Jesus Christ. The newly pluralistic framework has come to be *institutionally* established, however incomplete the implementation of its grand pattern.

It seems justified to consider this another version of the institutionalization of what Troeltsch called a Christian society. To be sure, Troeltsch did not deal with it, or any European variant, as such, but seemed to contend that such a conception implied the institutionalization of an established church. With his dichotomy of church and sect, he seems not to have understood the most important unit of such a pluralistic system, the denomination, which is a voluntary religious association that is nevertheless accepted, both by its members and by others, as an institutionalized unit in the social order. Furthermore, it is not only a Christian society, but a Christian–Jewish–humanistic society, with its very important inclusion of elements from beyond strictly Christian boundaries.

The modern ecumenical trend

If American society has produced the most highly developed version of the pluralistic ecumenical religious constitution that has so far appeared within a national framework, important developments have also continued in Europe. With the exception of the special fusion of Lutheran and Calvinistic elements in Prussia, perhaps the most obviously important movements have developed on a Lutheran base and have been more spiritual–cultural than organizational, from the point of view of the relation of religion to the secular society. However, they have already had a major impact on the contemporary situation.

Perhaps the most important reference point here is again the impact of the development of secular culture and, in particular, science. In the more western areas, in European terms, the two most important modes of coming to terms with science were the relatively full "synthesis" achieved, especially on an ascetic Protestant base—reaching a high point in the eighteenth century with Jonathan Edwards (Miller 1949)—and the antireligious orientation and acceptance of the challenge associated with the Enlightenment.

In the more eastern sector, centering in Protestant Germany, one main base was the movement of idealistic philosophy. This was intimately associated with Protestant theological concerns and also brought such traditions into close contact with the Enlightenment and its romantic counterpart. Against the background of Kant and Hegel, the more rationalizing theology was best exemplified by Schleiermacher. This trend also involved the philosophical grounding of Marxism, which is more central European than western European in its main cultural foundation, although it linked with the Enlightenment in being strongly anti-Christian. The other major trend took its departure from the "subjectivism" of the Lutheran tradition. Its great landmark was the Christian existentialism of Kierkegaard, which in its cognitive structure stressed the limitations on rational philosophy that had been highlighted in the Kantian tradition. This general orientation has also been involved in the "neo-orthodox" movements in Protestant theology, starting with Karl Barth. In broadest terms, the existentialist movement seems to serve as a major counterfoil to the relatively empirical rationalism and the conception of a legally ordered pluralistic society, which have characterized the influence of ascetic Protestantism. It has figured in the revolt of both religious and secular intellectuals whose points of reference have ranged from the ascetic Protestant to the secular, at certain points even being based on Marxist philosophy.

This complex welter of cultural movements could not but become closely involved with the status of the Catholic position. Catholicism has, in its orientation to the secular society, comprised an immense range of different subtypes, from positions, in such areas as northern France and part of Germany and Belgium, that were very close to the Protestant to those, in southern Europe, that often preserved an antimodern traditionalism that was close to medieval.

Doctrinally, the Counter Reformation had hardened the Catholic position, not only against Protestantism but also against the movements of secular philosophy that began prominently in the seventeenth century. Until relatively recently we could therefore speak of the dominance of Neo-Thomism in the church. Although it certainly enhanced the activistic elements in Catholicism, the main concern of the Counter Reformation was to bolster the sacramental position of the church as the core of a Christian society. Hence, it operated to preserve a structural element that tended to be fundamentally premodern.

It can, however, be said that although all of these movements have been at work within the Catholic world, it has felt the impact of two of them especially strongly. On the one hand, the ascetic Protestant pattern of institutionalization of religion, in relation to secular society, has gone far to provide a model sharply different from the traditional Catholic pattern of the relation of church and state. This situation is, perhaps, best exemplified by the fact that the very large Catholic minority in the United States has come to accept the separation of church and state and its own position in the system of denominational pluralism; but this is by no means an isolated phenomenon. On the other hand, the impact of the more subjective-existentialist orientations has worked to attenuate the rigidity of the older Catholic conceptions of sacramental order in favor of what may be called a "spiritual individualism."

These cultural movements have been associated with institutional changes that have broadly followed the American pattern. Thus, although in only a few European countries have historic Christian churches been totally disestablished, only in the most conservative Catholic areas of southern Europe has the religious freedom of other groups, including the secular humanists, been severely restricted. For the most part, European society has become religiously pluralistic. Even Spain has recently shown signs of an incipient pluralization. The aristocracy, which has been a most important factor in bolstering religious conservatism everywhere, has been considerably more prominent in Europe than in America; but major changes have taken place in the present century, so that aristocracy no longer counts heavily in the more "modernized" countries.

Although the structural changes in European society have been retarded relative to the relevant aspects of American society they have been considerable. How far they have gone has to a certain extent been masked by such factors as the segmentation of Europe into a sizable number of national states, the political disturbances of the present century (especially the two world wars, which had their primary centers in Europe), and the political movements of fascism and communism.

Fascism has been predominantly a regressive phenomenon in the context of the evolutionary scheme developed in this article and is not likely to have left any major mark on the sociocultural constitutions of the societies in which it has figured prominently; it is not the basis of a new fundamental variant of Western society, although it has been a major source of disturbance, and has inflicted severe social injury.

The communist movement is quite another matter. It certainly should be classified as at least a quasi-religious movement that has certain striking resemblances to Calvinism, both with respect to its mission as the agent of building an ideal secular society and with respect to the elitism of the two-class system, the party as the "vanguard" of the "proletariat" and the still socially unregenerate masses. Marxism is largely an offshoot of German idealistic philosophy and as such intimately associated with Protestantism. Indeed, the militant secularism of Marxism may be regarded as, in certain respects, the ideological accentuation of the importance of the kingdom of God on earth, or the "secular city"—God as the author of this great plan being replaced by the "dialectic of history." For these reasons it seems legitimate to treat the communist movement as part of the more general development of the relations between religiously grounded culture and the organization of secular society.

It is a striking fact that the communist movement has not—contrary to Marx's predictions—gained political ascendancy in any of the more advanced industrial countries, either in Europe or outside it. Its first great success was in Russia, which was a semi-European power, substantially backward industrially as compared with western Europe, and the largest single area whose Christian history had been dominated by the Eastern Orthodox church. Communism in the Soviet Union—and in China—has certainly been intimately connected with the problem of modernization. Its spread to the "satellite" countries is of course a direct function of Soviet political control in eastern Europe. The communist movement therefore cannot be regarded as a long-run basic alternative to the historic developments of Christianity, although this judgment may not be possible to confirm—or disprove—for a considerable time. At any rate, the acute mutual antagonism between virtually all Christian denominations, perhaps particularly Roman Catholicism, and "atheistic communism" seems to have begun to subside somewhat.

Against this background the catalytic influence of the brief papal reign of John XXIII and the council, Vatican II, which he called may well constitute a major breakthrough in the development of the Christian system, concerning the relation of the different branches to each other, of all of them to secular society and culture, and of Christianity to non-Christian religious movements and institutions. The fact that the initiative came from Rome seems to be particularly significant.

In the first place, this seems to indicate a further extension of the pattern of secular responsibility that the church had affirmed in the late nineteenth-century encyclicals on labor and related questions. Second, it seems to represent a major step in Catholic movement toward an ecumenical position. It seems to represent very considerable mitigation of the relatively rigid position that has officially obtained ever since the Counter Reformation. In addition to this, the action taken by the council on the problem of relation to the Jews has gone far toward including them in a wider religious community going beyond Christian boundaries. In this respect the Catholic church as a whole has moved appreciably closer to the position that had been crystallizing in the United States, brought to a head especially in connection with the

candidacy, election, assassination, and public mourning of John F. Kennedy, the first Roman Catholic to be president of the United States—indeed the first non-Protestant.

Third, the Vatican Council, along with parallel movements in Protestantism centering in the World Council of Churches, seems to represent a very important step in the direction of mitigating the exclusiveness of religious legitimation, even of the Judaeo–Christian complex, in favor of a still wider ecumenicism, which in particular has made overtures to the historic religious traditions of Asia. Pope Paul VI's visit to the Holy Land could be interpreted in a purely Christian context, although its break with the tradition of remaining in Italy was striking, and it brought him necessarily into official contact with Jewish and Muslim groups. His visits to India and to the United Nations, however, must be interpreted as symbolic gestures in the broadest ecumenical context.

It thus seems justified to consider that Christianity is entering on a new phase, part of the trend to institutionalization of Christian values in secular society. The proper type of this society, broadly called modern society, is widely valued. This is not to say that modern society is acceptable to Christian ethics in all detail and without any critical reservation. Quite the contrary, like any other actually existing human society, it is shot through with elements of "evil," which range from the deplorable to the intolerable. Moreover, differences of evaluation within the Christian community have by no means disappeared, although they have been substantially mitigated.

There seems, however, to be emerging a consensus on a broad framework of the institutions of the morally acceptable society and on social problems to be solved. Thus, high standards in the economic, health, and education fields, certain fundamental patterns of equality, notably of citizenship and opportunity, and certain aspects of freedom and autonomy for individuals and associational groups are almost universally valued. Conversely, the widespread problems of illness and poverty, of exclusion from educational, occupational, and many other opportunities, and of destruction due to the use of physical violence are more widely recognized and protested against than ever.

Many of the intrasocietal and intersocietal problems that distress the modern world owe much of their salience and form of statement to the processes of institutionalization of Christian values sketched above. The distress over them is not so much a measure of the irrelevance of the historic impact of Christianity as a measure of the incompleteness of institutionalization; a conception which implies that there has been in the past significant *relative* success. The magnitude of the tasks ahead often seems appalling, but they would not even have been defined as tasks if the attitudes of the earlier phases of Christian development still prevailed.

TALCOTT PARSONS

[*See also* PROTESTANT POLITICAL THOUGHT *and the related articles listed under* RELIGION. *Other relevant material may be found in the biographies of* AQUINAS; AUGUSTINE; CALVIN; ERASMUS; LUTHER; TROELTSCH; WEBER, MAX.]

BIBLIOGRAPHY

BELLAH, ROBERT N.   1964   Religious Evolution. *American Sociological Review* 29:358–374.

BELLAH, ROBERT N.   1965   Heritage and Choice in American Religion. Unpublished manuscript.

BLOCH, MARC   (1939–1940) 1961   *Feudal Society.* Univ. of Chicago Press. → First published as *La société féodale: La formation des liens de dépendance,* and *La société féodale: Les classes et le gouvernement des hommes.*

COHN, NORMAN   (1957) 1961   *The Pursuit of the Millennium: Revolutionary Messianism in Medieval and Reformation Europe and Its Bearing on Modern Totalitarian Movements.* 2d ed. New York: Harper.

COX, HARVEY   (1965) 1966   *The Secular City: Secularization and Urbanization in Theological Perspective.* New York: Macmillan.

CUMONT, FRANZ   (1910) 1956   *The Oriental Religions in Roman Paganism.* New York: Dover. → First published in German.

DUCKETT, E. S.   1938   *Monasticism.* Ann Arbor: Univ. of Michigan Press.

ELTON, GEOFFREY R.   (1963) 1964   *Reformation Europe.* Cleveland: World.

GIERKE, OTTO VON   (1881) 1958   *Political Theories of the Middle Age.* Cambridge Univ. Press. → First published as "Die publicistischen Lehren des Mittelalters," a section of Volume 3 of Gierke's *Das deutsche Genossenschaftsrecht.* Translated with a famous introduction by Frederic William Maitland.

HARNACK, ADOLF VON   (1902) 1908   *The Mission and Expansion of Christianity in the First Three Centuries.* 2 vols. 2d ed., rev. & enl. London: Williams & Norgate; New York: Putnam. → First published in German. The first British edition was published as *The Expansion of Christianity in the First Three Centuries.* A paperback edition was published in 1962 by Harper.

HARNACK, ADOLF VON   1916   *Aus der Friedens- und Kriegsarbeit.* Giessen (Germany): Töpelmann. → See especially the essay on "Der Geist der morgenländischen Kirche im Unterschied von der abendländischen."

HERBERG, WILL   1955   *Protestant, Catholic, Jew: An Essay in American Religious Sociology.* Garden City, N.Y.: Doubleday.

HUIZINGA, JOHAN   (1919) 1924   *The Waning of the Middle Ages: A Study in the Forms of Life, Thought and Art in France and the Netherlands in the 14th and 15th Centuries.* London: Arnold. → First published in Dutch. A paperback edition was published in 1954 by Doubleday.

JAEGER, WERNER W.   1961   *Early Christianity and Greek Paideia.* Cambridge, Mass.: Belknap.

KAYSER, CHRISTINE   1961   Calvinism and German Political Life. Ph.D. dissertation, Harvard Univ.

KNOX, RONALD A.   1950   *Enthusiasm: A Chapter in the History of Religion; With Special Reference to the XVII and XVIII Centuries.* New York: Oxford Univ. Press.

KRISTELLER, PAUL O.   (1955) 1961   *Renaissance Thought: The Classic, Scholastic and Humanistic Strains.* Gloucester, Mass.: Smith. → First published as *The Classics and Renaissance Thought.* A paperback edition was published in 1963 by Harper.

LEA, HENRY C.   (1867) 1957   *History of Sacerdotal Celibacy in the Christian Church.* New York: Russell. → First published as *An Historical Sketch of Sacerdotal Celibacy in the Christian Church.*

LIETZMANN, HANS   (1932) 1952   *The Beginnings of the Christian Church.* History of the Early Church, Vol. 1. New York: Scribner. → First published in German as a separate work. A four-volume paperback edition was published by World in 1961 as *A History of the Early Church.*

LIETZMANN, HANS   (1936) 1958   *The Founding of the Church Universal.* History of the Early Church, Vol. 2. 3d ed., rev. London: Butterworth. → First published in German as a separate work. A four-volume paperback edition was published by World in 1961 as *A History of the Early Church.*

LIETZMANN, HANS   (1938) 1958   *From Constantine to Julian.* History of the Early Church, Vol. 3. 2d ed., rev. London: Butterworth. → First published in German as a separate work. A four-volume paperback edition was published by World in 1961 as *A History of the Early Church.*

LITTLE, DAVID   1963   The Logic of Order: An Examination of the Sources of Puritan–Anglican Controversy and of Their Relations to Prevailing Legal Conceptions of Corporation in the Late 16th and Early 17th Century in England. Ph.D. dissertation, Harvard Univ.

LOUBSER, JOHANNES J.   1964   Puritanism and Religious Liberty: Change in the Normative Order in Massachusetts, 1630–1850. Ph.D. dissertation, Harvard Univ.

LOUBSER, JOHANNES J.   1965   Calvinism, Equality, and Inclusion: The Case of Afrikaner Calvinism. Unpublished manuscript.

McILWAIN, CHARLES H.   (1932) 1959   *The Growth of Political Thought in the West, From the Greeks to the End of the Middle Ages.* New York: Macmillan.

MARSHALL, THOMAS H.   (1934–1962) 1964   *Class, Citizenship, and Social Development: Essays.* Garden City, N.Y.: Doubleday. → A collection of articles and lectures first published in book form in England in 1963 under the title *Sociology at the Crossroads and Other Essays.* A paperback edition was published in 1965.

MERTON, ROBERT K.   1938   Science, Technology and Society in Seventeenth Century England. *Osiris* 4:360–632.

MILLER, PERRY   1949   *Jonathan Edwards.* New York: Sloane. → A paperback edition was published in 1959 by World.

MILLER, PERRY   1956   *Errand Into the Wilderness.* Cambridge, Mass.: Belknap. → A paperback edition was published in 1964 by Harper.

MILLER, PERRY (1959) 1965 *Orthodoxy in Massachusetts.* Gloucester, Mass.: Smith.

MILLER, PERRY 1965 *The Life of the Mind in America, From the Revolution to the Civil War.* New York: Harcourt.

NELSON, BENJAMIN N. 1949 *The Idea of Usury: From Tribal Brotherhood to Universal Otherhood.* Princeton Univ. Press.

NOCK, ARTHUR D. 1933 *Conversion: The Old and the New in Religion From Alexander the Great to Augustine of Hippo.* Oxford Univ. Press. → A paperback edition was published in 1963.

NOCK, ARTHUR D. 1938 *St. Paul.* London: Butterworth. → A paperback edition was published in 1963 by Harper.

NOCK, ARTHUR D. 1964 *Early Gentile Christianity and Its Hellenistic Background.* New York: Harper.

PARSONS, TALCOTT 1960 *Structure and Process in Modern Societies.* Glencoe, Ill.: Free Press. → See especially pages 295–321 on "Some Comments on the Pattern of Religious Organization in the United States."

SMELSER, NEIL J. (1962) 1963 *Theory of Collective Behavior.* London: Routledge; New York: Free Press.

SOUTHERN, RICHARD W. (1953) 1959 *The Making of the Middle Ages.* New Haven: Yale Univ. Press.

TROELTSCH, ERNST (1906) 1912 *Protestantism and Progress: A Historical Study of the Relation of Protestantism to the Modern World.* London: Williams & Norgate; New York: Putnam. → First published as *Die Bedeutung des Protestantismus für die Entstehung der modernen Welt.* A paperback edition was published in 1958 by Beacon.

TROELTSCH, ERNST (1912) 1931 *The Social Teaching of the Christian Churches.* New York: Macmillan. → First published as *Die Soziallehren der christlichen Kirchen und Gruppen.* A two-volume paperback edition was published in 1960 by Harper.

TUFARI, PAUL 1965 Authority and Affection in the Ascetic's Status Group: St. Basil's Definition of Monasticism. Ph.D. dissertation, Harvard Univ.

VASIL'EV, ALEKSANDR A. (1917–1925) 1928–1929 *History of the Byzantine Empire.* 2 vols. University of Wisconsin Studies in the Social Sciences and History, Nos. 13–14. Madison: Univ. of Wisconsin Press. → First published in Russian. Volume 1: *From Constantine the Great to the Epoch of the Crusades (A.D. 1081).* Volume 2: *From the Crusades to the Fall of the Empire (A.D. 1453).*

WEBER, MAX (1904–1905) 1930 *The Protestant Ethic and the Spirit of Capitalism.* Translated by Talcott Parsons, with a foreword by R. H. Tawney. London: Allen & Unwin; New York: Scribner. → First published in German. The 1930 edition has been reprinted frequently. A paperback edition was published in 1958 by Scribner.

WEBER, MAX (1921a) 1958 *The City.* Glencoe, Ill.: Free Press. → First published as *Die Stadt.*

WEBER, MAX (1921b) 1958 *The Religion of India: The Sociology of Hinduism and Buddhism.* Translated and edited by Hans H. Gerth and Don Martindale. Glencoe, Ill.: Free Press. → First published as *Hinduismus und Buddhismus,* Volume 2 of Weber's *Gesammelte Aufsätze zur Religionssoziologie.*

WEBER, MAX (1921c) 1952 *Ancient Judaism.* Glencoe, Ill.: Free Press. → First published as *Das antike Judentum,* Volume 3 of Weber's *Gesammelte Aufsätze zur Religionssoziologie.*

WEBER, MAX (1922a) 1951 *The Religion of China: Confucianism and Taoism.* Glencoe, Ill.: Free Press. → First published as "Konfuzianismus und Taoismus" in Volume 1 of Weber's *Gesammelte Aufsätze zur Religionssoziologie.*

WEBER, MAX (1922b) 1963 *The Sociology of Religion.* Boston: Beacon. → First published in German. A paperback edition was published in 1964.

CHURCH

See RELIGION; RELIGIOUS ORGANIZATION; SECTS AND CULTS.

CHURCH ATTENDANCE

See RELIGIOUS OBSERVANCE.

CITY

I
FORMS AND FUNCTIONS

Although the city as a form of human settlement dates back to the beginnings of civilization, it long escaped scholarly scrutiny; and its very definition is still under debate. Lévi-Strauss's attack on the ambiguities of "totemism" would apply equally to the term "city," but with less justification, since the city has undergone many changes without losing its architectural and institutional continuity. Meanwhile, new urban functions have modified and sometimes supplanted those that were originally formative. Morphologically, some of the changes in the structure of the city correspond to the different phases in any organic development. Since English lacks a neat vocabulary to distinguish the succession of urban forms from embryo to adult, their purely quantitative aspect is best rendered in German: *Dorf, Kleinstadt, Mittelstadt, Grossstadt, Millionenstadt.* In English, *eopolis, polis, metropolis, megalopolis,* and *conurbation* have been proposed as an equivalent series, with *regional city* and *regional urban grid* as possible emergent forms.

An adequate description of the city must not deal merely with structure, process, stage, and purpose but also with certain identifying characteristics reflected in layout and architectural symbolism. The city is both a collection of architectural forms in space and a tissue of associations, corporate enterprises, and institutions that occupy this collective structure and have interacted with it in the course of time. The size and complexity of the city bear a direct relation to that of the culture it assembles and passes on. Hence the inadequacy of attempts to define the city by a purely quantitative measure—area, density of occupation, range of communication—while passing over at least equally significant qualitative indications.

Admittedly, there is a point at which a village or a country town, by sheer accretion of numbers, may take on some of the characteristics of a city; but there is another point at which a metropolis, by unregulated congestion and expansion, loses its characteristic capacity to attract and integrate its varied components and turns into an amorphous mass, dynamic but increasingly dispersed and disorganized. In fifth-century Greece or thirteenth-century Europe, cities of two thousand were common and those of a hundred thousand rare; but in both, an institutional nucleus regulated and limited growth, as in a cell. Today a closely settled area containing tens of millions of people and covering thousands of square miles has been misidentified as a city and given the name "megalopolis" (Gottmann 1961). Such terminological inexactitude reveals a failure to understand the unique function of the city as a container and transmitter of culture. Only a more careful reading of the city's historic development will provide a sounder concept.

Research and study. Except for Aristotle's *Politics* and a few scattered essays, such as that of Giovanni Botero (1588), almost the sole appreciations of the city's essential role have been confined to utopian literature, from Plato and More to Buckingham and Bellamy, although local chronicles and histories of uneven value have abounded. Among the few studies of the city that appeared during the nineteenth century, Fustel de Coulanges' *The Ancient City* (1864), Adna Ferrin Weber's *The Growth of Cities in the Nineteenth Century* (1899), and the monumental *Life and Labour of the People in London* (1889–1891), by Charles Booth and his associates, remain notable. Possibly the earliest sociological analyses of the city, Patrick Geddes' papers for the Sociological Society, did not appear until 1905.

Early in this century, Werner Sombart and Max Weber, following studies of the medieval city by Hegel, Preuss, and others, attempted a general theory of urban development. Somewhat later, in the United States, Park and his associates (1925) and Wirth (1938) adopted an ecological approach to the city, but they tended to regard the contemporary American metropolis as a universal climax formation (Burgess 1927). Meanwhile, the French human geographers, led by Paul Vidal de la Blache and Jean Brunhes and supplemented by Kurt

Hassert, Maximilien Sorre (1952), and Robert E. Dickinson (1951), opened an investigation of the underlying geographic–economic factors in urban development. In urban history Emil Kuhn's early study of the Greek city (1878) paved the way for such comprehensive monographs as Ferdinand Gregorovius' work on Rome in the Middle Ages (1859–1872), Pompeo G. Molmenti's work on Venice (1880), and Marcel Poëte's work on Paris (1924–1931). Yet so completely had the city dropped out of political and historic discourse that in Arnold J. Toynbee's *A Study of History* (1934–1961) only a few passing references to the city appear. Since 1930, however, this neglect has been overcompensated for by a spate of sociological and economic treatises on urbanization, without sufficient further clarification of the problems surrounding the city's origin, nature, and historic transformations.

Archeological background. During the last century, excavations in the Near East have furnished the first clues to the origin of cities. These show that in the earliest stages of urban growth forces were at work similar to those more amply documented in the rise or resurgence of medieval Western cities. While the city's formation is contemporary with the introduction of cereal crops and therewith a storable food supply and a surplus population, Robert J. Braidwood and Bruce Howe (1962, p. 142) point out that "the way to urban life did not lie within exactly the same environmental zone as that in which the village–farming community made its first appearance." Such cities as have been uncovered owe their discovery to the fact that their public buildings were constructed of brick or stone; and it is chiefly by the monumental scale of these buildings that the city can be identified as a new collective artifact, multiplying by the fourth millennium, if not before, in Mesopotamia, Egypt, and the Indus Valley.

The studies of V. Gordon Childe (1936), Charles Woolley (1954), H. W. Fairman (1949), Kathleen Kenyon, Henri Frankfort (1948), Robert M. Adams, Richard E. Wycherly, and Roland Martin carry the emergence of the city into Egypt, the Near East, and the Aegean, with Mortimer Wheeler making a beginning in the Indus Valley and various other scholars, including Wheeler, working on Roman cities. But Childe's still widely accepted interpretation of a fourth-millennium urban revolution in the Near East (1936) does not account for early Jericho and its still undiscovered neighbors; nor does it account, as he realized, for the formation of Peruvian, Aztec, and Mayan cities, which presented significantly similar religious and political features but lacked many of the geographic advantages and technical inventions that Childe and others posited as necessary. Unfortunately, too little archeological work has been done in Iran, India, and the Far East, to say nothing of Africa and South America, to give a full account of the rise, growth, and spread of cities. What is more serious, the critical moment in the emergence of the city antedates the written record. Possibly more will be learned about the origins of the city by extrapolating backward from the fullest known urban remains to their original components, however remote in time and space from any fully formed city.

Historic beginnings

At the outset, two common impressions must be discarded; namely, that the city came into existence by a natural extension or concretion of village settlements or, alternatively, that the crossing of trade routes and the rise of specialized industries brought the city into existence as an economic convenience and detached it completely from its rural matrix. Mark Jefferson's observation as geographer that city and country are one thing, not two things, is supported by evidence from early Mesopotamian cities that their original population was composed largely of peasants who worked in the nearby fields or were drafted for forced labor on walls, dams, canals, and other public works. The village does indeed reappear within the city as the neighborhood group, sometimes composed of emigrants from the same rural background; but no enlargement of this village pattern or growth of the market could produce the complex of institutions that form the city proper.

The rise of the city was accompanied by other innovations, which the city helped to foster: systematic astronomical observation, the development of writing and arithmetic, the creation of monumental buildings and sculptures, the lifetime division and specialization of labor, and the compulsory organization of work in great "labor-machines" under central direction. But the over-all formative influence seems to have been the fusion of the surviving power-directed paleolithic hunting culture with the stable, life-oriented—but somewhat routinized—neolithic culture, whose culminating feats in domestication provided a surplus of manpower available for military exploits and public works on a scale never before even imaginable. These factors were recognized by Childe, but he left out the agent that brought them together within the city: the institution of kingship, which turned the earlier hunting chieftain into the all-powerful, semidivine representative of a cosmic deity, whose word was law (Frankfort 1948).

Documentary evidence from the founding of Memphis in ancient Egypt (Pritchard [1950] 1955, pp. 4–5) to the planning of St. Petersburg in the eighteenth century establishes the fact that cities were instituted as centers of royal and priestly power; and the first act of a king was the construction or the rededication of a temple to serve as the home of the god that ratified and sanctified his claims to absolute authority. In other words, the city first took form as a *Zwingburg*, or control center, rather than a market or a manufacturing center; and it is hardly an accident that the predynastic Narmer palette in Egypt contains not only one of the first representations of a city, sometimes dubiously identified as a fortress, but likewise a symbolic representation of the king as a destroyer of cities. This ambivalent magnification of the creative and destructive potentialities established through urban concentration has remained constant throughout the city's history.

The actual core of the ancient city, corresponding to the organizing nucleus in a cell, was the *citadel* or little city: its formidable walls enclosed the temple, the palace, and the granary or storehouse and incidentally protected the ruling group from assault by the surrounding inhabitants. This implosion of religious, scientific, political, military, and economic power within a symbolic collective container gave the city immense advantages over smaller and more loosely organized communities. The latter were accordingly subject to unscrupulous attack and exploitation, through raiding expeditions, taxation, and irregular tribute, well before more equitable market relations and codes of law became common. As against these negative features, the city was likewise a sacred precinct, the home of a god, itself a small-scale model of the universe, where law and order prevailed over chaos and where a common bond of association united a large population with varied cultural, occupational, and linguistic backgrounds (Éliade [1949] 1958, pp. 367–385; Müller 1961).

I first put forth this interpretation of the origins and nature of the city in an Oriental Institute symposium (Symposium 1960, pp. 224–242) and developed it further in *The City in History* (Mumford 1961, pp. 3–54). Although it has not yet been critically examined, still less generally accepted, it helps account for both the enlargement of human potentialities in the city, from the earliest period onward, and also for the perversions and destructions that have persistently plagued urban development. In addition, this theory gives a clue to the emergent functions and purposes of the city—both those that have been taken over by its political successor, the territorial state, and those that can still function only within the concrete urban container and await further development.

Urban components

Many of the institutions that were assembled and enlarged in the city were already widely distributed in more modest forms in simpler settlements. The earliest evidence of the attractive nucleus of the city as a ceremonial center lies in paleolithic burial places and sacred caves or grottoes: both often constituted the sacred core, as at Athens, of far later urban foundations. But many urban structures derive directly from the neolithic village, such as collective storage facilities for food; permanent hearths and houses in close proximity; open spaces for seasonal rituals, dances, and political assembly; and workshops for fashioning pots, tools, and images. Even long-distance trade, essential to a city's economic growth and social intermixture, is in evidence in the obsidian industry of Jarmo (fifth millennium B.C.). In the city the functions of the household (eating, drinking, sleeping) are translated into a specialized form: even sexual intercourse becomes professionalized in the house of prostitution (Braidwood & Willey 1962).

While the above traits have a village origin, a large group of other structures and institutions derive directly from the citadel. From the castle or palace come the military fortification, the barracks, the parade—also the park, the zoo, the museum, the law courts, the prison, the offices of the bureaucracy, and the hotel. From the temple comes the wall, possibly serving as a religious symbol before it became a military necessity, and the theater, the astronomical observatory, the library, the school, the university, and the hospital. The market, the workshop, the storehouse, and the bank come from both village and citadel; but when they achieve independence they first settle outside the wall, near river or harbor. From associations within these groups, craft guilds, merchant guilds, and burial societies emerge.

To describe the city in quantitative terms without reference to its institutions and their continued interaction is to ignore the most important role of the historic city: its assemblage and integration of these varied components, both public and private, both controlled and voluntary. Not the least significant part of the city's development since the Middle Ages in western Europe has been the multiplication of voluntary municipal organizations, churches, hospitals, guilds, almshouses, grammar schools, colleges, and, since the nineteenth century, a multitude of special-purpose clubs and societies. The classified telephone directory of any big city reveals, under the head of clubs and associations, how extensive this function has now become. By the scope of such enterprises, rather than merely by the volume of its commerce and industry or by the mechanization of its municipal services, the modern city distinguishes itself from its ancient urban prototypes. The fact that the scattering of population today over unlimited sub-urban areas reduces the possibility of forming such specialized associations is not the least disturbing factor in the breakdown of the modern metropolis.

Urban forms

Once the nuclear institutions of the city had crystallized, they constituted an urban model that, with various additions and subtractions, all subsequent forms of the city have followed. Two characteristic forms of city development were present almost from the beginning; and, properly interpreted, they help solve the problem of distinguishing the city from other types of human settlement. The first form, dominant until the seventeenth century A.D., is that of the classic *container*: an imposing mass of monumental buildings, usually protected by a wall and surrounded by closely built residential quarters, workshops, minor shrines or temples, and markets, threaded by alleys, streets, or processional ways, the whole area enclosed by one or more heavy walls, moats, and canals and entered only through massive gates (Woolley [1954] 1964, pp. 107 ff.). Such a city might cover a dozen or many hundred acres (Frankfort 1950).

But another, looser form, in which the *magnet* prevails over the container, is also visible. This open form, which possibly characterized the pyramid age in Egypt, appeared later in the Acropolis cities of the Aegean and the ceremonial centers of Meso-America. Here, priestly authority, rather than royal coercion, provided protection and controlled economic activities, giving dominance to the *temenos*, or sacred precinct. The population that served this area and periodically gathered there was distributed in neighboring villages, suburbs, and country estates. This open urban pattern preserved the institutional order of the citadel but by its salubrious spaciousness escaped the serious sanitary disadvantages of the closely built type. When war was in abeyance, as during the Augustan era of Rome, this more open urban plan often flourished.

In both urban forms, the original village component has persisted in the residential quarter or neighborhood unit—sometimes fully differentiated, as in ancient Mesopotamian cities, in late medieval Venice, or in contemporary British New Towns. Where the means of transport and communication are adequate, the separate parts of the city may even form distinct units or zones, spatially isolated as in the islands of Venice: Torcello (burial), Murano (glass industry), and Lido (aquatic sport). Thus, when the archeologist says that to be dispersed is not to be urban in the true sense of the city, he is arbitrarily ruling out a type of city that has had a long history and is again taking a new form today.

While these polar forms present contrasting spatial patterns, their institutional contents and their functional role are the same. Both urban types serve for the assemblage, storage, interchange, transmission, and further development of material products and symbolic cultural goods while widening the scope of human association through the continued interaction of functions and activities in time as well as in space. The superposition of many different functions and purposes within a limited common area not only provides a favorable basis for cooperation, communication, communion—and control—but also multiplies the number of chance meetings and encounters that challenge and enrich more orderly institutional routines. Although the concentration of cosmic and temporal power, rather than the diffusion of culture, was the original motive force for the city, it is now becoming clear that the cultural by-product has increasingly become the best reason for the city's long, if checkered, existence. This emergent function of the city still remains to be consciously explored and more systematically provided for.

Nucleation, specialization, and integration. The original constellation of urban institutions remains visible in the layout of historic cities: acropolis and agora; Forum Romanum and Palatine Hill; the cathedral, the castle, and the market place; the mosque, the palace, and the bazaar; and the New England meeting house, the town hall, and the common are just so many historic permutations of the organizing nuclei that brought the city into existence. It is by these attractive institutions at the center, rather than by its outer walls or other boundaries, that the city can continue to be identified. The many possible combinations of these institutions and buildings and their different expressions in plan and architecture give each city a marked individuality, indeed a collective personality. But the archetypal city, as distinguished from specialized enclaves like monasteries, garrison and factory towns, or residential suburbs, tends to completeness and balance, with a mixture of sexes, age groups,

and occupations large enough to carry on the principal political, religious, educational, and economic activities that characterize its culture. The assemblage and architectural embodiment of all these functions and institutions within a limited area constitute a complete city.

Although the city is distinguished by its orchestration of a diversity of social and cultural activities, sometimes one of its nuclear functions may be dominant: witness religious centers like Nippur, Mecca, and Benares; recreation or health resorts like Epidaurus or Bath; and industrial towns like Sheffield or Essen. But under the continued growth of such specialized urban centers, the undeveloped or suppressed functions tend to reappear, if only because the increase in numbers calls for many subsidiary occupations and services. If the great capitals, like Babylon, Rome, Athens, Baghdad, Peking, Paris, and London, have dominated the history of their respective countries, it is because they were capable of representing and passing on a larger portion of their total culture.

The role of the city as a container and transmitter of culture could hardly have been envisaged by its early founders. There is indeed no single urban activity that has not been performed successfully in isolated units located in the open country. But there is one function that the city alone can perform, namely the synthesis and synergy of the many separate parts by continually bringing them together in a common meeting place where direct face-to-face intercourse is possible. The unique office of the city, then, is to increase the variety, the velocity, the extent, and the continuity of human intercourse.

The greater the quantity of cultural artifacts and symbols accumulated, the more important becomes the city's function of organizing them and making them available for further use. Since writing and reading long remained the monopoly of a privileged minority, the city so far from being dependent upon the written record, as archeologists have sometimes assumed from their coincidental origin, has actually served until now as a concrete substitute for it. By attracting a varied population, the city transmuted and preserved ritual, dance, music, oral tradition, and, above all, occupational skills that would otherwise have remained isolated and undeveloped—possibly lost. This office remains important, despite the invention of the printing press, the camera, the tape recorder, and the computer. The cultural storage capacity of a city of only 100,000 population far exceeds that of any computer, if only because every human organism records and stores large areas of experience that cannot be reduced to quantitative symbols and programmed or transmitted to others except by direct human contact. Whether any complex culture can endure for long without maintaining a large number of integrated urban structures and substructures of sufficient capacity remains to be seen.

The city as a material artifact

In origin, the city is a Stone Age container, the largest of neolithic containers; and many of its original physical features, including the size of its house lots and the width of its streets, remained relatively constant, with only small variations, for thousands of years. The chief physical disabilities of the historic city were repeated destruction in war and failure to cope with the hygienic and sanitary problems of living in close quarters. Continued occupation of the city depends upon the systematic disposal of garbage, excrement, rubbish, and the dead. Success in providing a sufficient amount of space both within the house and within the city so as to limit the spread of diseases and in obtaining a sufficient amount of uncontaminated water for human consumption, personal hygiene, and industrial use is still far from realization even in technologically advanced countries. The bigger the urban unit, the more difficult the problems of environmental pollution have usually been. Today the lethal exhausts from factory and motorcar (to say nothing of nuclear fall-out and atomic wastes) have partly counteracted improvements in sanitation.

Some necessary inventions were, at an early date, brought into service for the occupants of the citadel: piped water, pavements, baths, and water closets or private toilets were available there thousands of years before they were passed on to the majority of urban inhabitants. But industrial towns grew up in nineteenth-century England without provision for drinking water or sanitary privies; and although later municipal ordinances have resulted in local gains, with a marked improvement in the survival rates of children, the cleansing of the city has only shifted the problem to the rural and the aquatic environment, whose pollution and spoilage constitute another problem, greatly aggravated by middens of industrial waste, bottles, cans, and motorcars.

During the nineteenth century, radical changes in industrial production, transportation, and communication altered the dimensions of the city and the tolerable density of population. With the introduction of sewers, water and gas mains, electric conduits, and underground public transportation, underground utilities competed for capital investment with the hitherto self-sufficient architectural shells. Meanwhile, the universal introduction of the paved street and permanent ways needed for rapid vehicular transportation facilitated the further extension of big cities, and by turn the railway, the electric streetcar, and the private motorcar widened the area within daily commutation distance of the center. This change was accompanied in the nineteenth century by the progressive abandonment of the wall and the seventeenth-century fortification as a means of military defense. Only by functioning as *social magnets* have the larger metropolitan centers survived.

Although the last century was marked by large-scale urbanization, the only significant change, apart from that of increasing scale, population, and intensity of congestion, lay in a widespread countermovement in which the upper economic groups took the lead, creating new suburban communities on an open pattern and restoring many aesthetic and hygienic features, including recreation space, that the city lacked. Such open building outside the city, which sacrifices the social benefits of the city for a healthier environment, goes back to the very beginnings of the city; it seems a spontaneous attempt at homeostasis, restoring necessary biological conditions that excessive urban congestion has destroyed. The notion that this is a purely modern phenomenon, a more or less automatic by-product of rail or motorcar transportation, runs contrary to ancient historic evidence. But a new factor has indeed appeared during the last two decades—a breakup of the central nucleus itself, with shopping centers, research centers, industrial parks, and even business offices establishing themselves as independent semifeudal enclaves in the megalopolitan intervals. This tendency, abetted by new methods of instantaneous communication, rapid transportation, and message storage, has led to sundry radically different pictures of the future form and function of the city.

Urban prospects

Until recent times one of the most conspicuous restrictions on the city's development was its confinement to a small fraction of the world's population. Yet this was a factor of safety, since it left a biological and cultural reservoir capable of restoring destroyed cities and replenishing populations decimated by sterility, disease, and war. Maximilien Sorre (1952) has estimated that even in the twentieth century four-fifths of the inhabitants of the planet still live in villages. Since the nineteenth century, however, this ratio has been reversed in such highly industrialized areas as Britain and the Low Countries; and a more general reversal of the historic ratio, with 90 per cent of the population dwelling in urbanoid areas if not in recognizable cities or metropolises, is theoretically in prospect.

Various recent urban studies confidently extrapolate this trend, as if the factors now in operation will continue indefinitely, unchecked by any appraisal and correction. This assumption ignores a growing body of contemporary evidence, supporting earlier historic observations, that uncontrolled urban expansion and congestion upset the ecological balance and produce most of the typical disorders noted in any overcrowded animal colonies, with an arrest or perversion of sexual activities, lapse of necessary social functions, together with suicidal desperation and aggression—although the animal failure to reproduce is not so far in evidence, except in the increase of homosexuality. In turn, the cultural changes thus brought about affect suburban and rural areas, with similar manifestations of crime and mental disease. Even without the possible cataclysmic arrest of growth through nuclear extermination, this process of continued urbanization may prove self-limiting.

Dispersal and concentration. On the prospective development of the urban community, two schools are beginning to emerge, although they are linked in different ways with a third, which believes that by continued patchwork—so-called urban renewal—the existing cities can and should be kept in being, even though many of their chief economic supports are being withdrawn and the population needed to maintain them is being dispersed or being replaced by automatic machines. The first school, the dispersionists, holds that the focal, synergizing functions of the city are either unnecessary or can now be performed without regard to topographic situation or any coherent assemblage of urban institutions and structures. Insofar as they would retain the existing urban structures, this school would treat the city as a disposable container, with its structures as transitory as their contents; no longer is it to be a means of maintaining continuity beyond the passing generation. Holding that only contemporary knowledge or culture is significant, this school believes that with the mechanical–electronic storage of messages, along with instantaneous communication and supersonic transport, the city as a unifying cultural center has lost its reason for existence. At most, the surviving components of the city will be scattered over the landscape, in specialized, spatially isolated, and unrelated enclaves.

Those who extrapolate existing tendencies may as an alternative concentrate upon the intensified congestion of existing metropolitan centers, despite the exorbitant cost of the mechanical equipment necessary to maintain even minimal transporta-

tion and communication activities. The grounds for concentration have been stated by Le Corbusier (see Jeanneret-Gris 1924) and Jane Jacobs (1961); those for dispersal have been presented by Jean Gottmann (1961), E. A. Gutkind (1962), and, more circumspectly and constructively, by Christopher Tunnard and Boris Pushkarev (1963). The highway building, housing, and urban renewal programs sponsored by the United States government since 1948 have dedicated enormous sums to both tendencies; and hence, so far, the predictions on which these plans have been based have been largely self-fulfilling.

Regional integration. The inertia of political and economic forces now favors both of the schools described above. In opposition to these almost automatic processes stand the urban integrationists: a school originated by the founder of the garden city movement, Ebenezer Howard (1898); carried further by George Unwin, Henry Wright, Sr., Clarence S. Stein (1951), and Frederic J. Osborn (1946; 1963); and abetted by the regionalism of Geddes (1915), MacKaye (1928), and Mumford (1938; 1961). This school was a generation in advance of rival doctrines in recognizing the factors that were promoting both metropolitan congestion and exurban dispersion—particularly, fast motor and air transport and instantaneous communication. But instead of regarding their forecasts as instructions to promote the existing tendencies and increase their tempo, they took them as warnings and, while showing how the new resources of science and technics could be utilized to improve the whole ecological pattern, sought to invent alternatives that would do justice to the unique role of the city.

The case for regional integration rests on two bases. That which has to do with the historic foundations of the city has already been outlined; but this in turn leads to the perception that the original pattern that favored the one-sided domination and magnification of a limited number of self-contained cities must be replaced by a more complex system fashioned on more organic lines and capable of wider diffusion. At our present state of cultural complexity, the integrationists hold that there is need for a hierarchical urban order that is composed of cellular units and organs, restricted in size and arranged in an ascending series, and that has stable intermediate units not only receiving directions and obeying orders but initiating actions and answering back in a give-and-take relation (Simon 1962).

While keeping the individual urban units limited in size and area—providing for growth by continued colonization instead of dispersion or congestion—the total effective coverage of a regional system composed of such units will be greater than that of the largest metropolis. Such a hierarchical pattern of small and large units, with the part reproducing the pattern of the whole and closely linked with it, has operated with unparalleled political success in the Roman Catholic church for almost two thousand years; and currently, it has been duplicated in the national lending library system in Britain, in the national film library system in Canada, in the organization of the state university of California, and, on a mechanical level, in the organization of the national telephone systems and electric power grids. For the integrationist school, the restriction of the constituent urban units and the organization of the whole into larger units are complementary processes. In such an organization, the advantages of both urban concentration and regional dispersal would be retained, and further growth and differentiation could take place without maximizing waste and disorder.

In this concept for controlling future urbanization by reconstituting the city, the many functions that were once clumsily handled by the physical massing of structures and populations will be "etherealized" over a much wider area. The preservation of a permanent rural matrix (both cultivated and wild) is an integral part of this new urban order. In this new model, individual cities, ranging ideally in size from 30,000 to perhaps 300,000, would be part of a regional grid embracing urban populations of an order of ten million and still containing smaller units serving purely rural or wilderness needs. This general pattern was first sketched out in the *Report* of the New York State Commission of Housing and Regional Planning (1926) and has been carried further in a report by the New York State Office for Regional Development (1964). By proposing to use the very mechanical and electronic agents that the dispersionists regard as a substitute for the city, the integrationists would reorganize our present technical resources so as to enable the city to perform its main historic task—the transmission of culture and the education of men.

LEWIS MUMFORD

[*See also* CENTRAL PLACE; COMMUNITY; PLANNING, SOCIAL, *article on* REGIONAL AND URBAN PLANNING; REGION; URBAN REVOLUTION; *and the biographies of* BOOTH; CHILDE; FUSTEL DE COULANGES; GEDDES; PARK; SOMBART; VIDAL DE LA BLACHE; WEBER, MAX; WIRTH.]

BIBLIOGRAPHY

BOOTH, CHARLES et al. (1889–1891) 1902–1903 *Life and Labour of the People in London.* 17 vols. London: Macmillan.

BOTERO, GIOVANNI (1588) 1956 A Treatise Concerning the Causes of the Magnificence and Greatness of Cities. Pages 225–280 in Giovanni Botero, *The Reason of State* and *The Greatness of Cities.* London: Routledge. → First published as *Delle cause della grandezza della città.*

BRAIDWOOD, ROBERT J.; and HOWE, BRUCE 1960 *Prehistoric Investigations in Iraqi Kurdistan.* Oriental Institute Studies in Ancient Oriental Civilizations, No. 31. Univ. of Chicago Press.

BRAIDWOOD, ROBERT J.; and HOWE, BRUCE 1962 Southwestern Asia Beyond the Lands of the Mediterranean Littoral. Pages 132–146 in Robert J. Braidwood and Gordon R. Willey (editors), *Courses Toward Urban Life: Archeological Considerations of Some Cultural Alternates.* Chicago: Aldine.

BRAIDWOOD, ROBERT J.; and WILLEY, GORDON R. (editors) 1962 *Courses Toward Urban Life: Archeological Considerations of Some Cultural Alternates.* Viking Fund Publication in Anthropology, Vol. 32. Chicago: Aldine. → The contents of this volume result from a symposium held at the European headquarters of the Wenner-Gren Foundation for Anthropological Research, Austria, July 3–11, 1960.

BURGESS, ERNEST W. 1927 The Determination of Gradients in the Growth of the City. Pages 178–184 in American Sociological Society, *The Progress of Sociology.* Publications, Vol. 21. Univ. of Chicago Press.

CHILDE, V. GORDON (1936) 1951 *Man Makes Himself.* Rev. ed. New York: New American Library.

Cities. 1965 *Scientific American* 213, no. 3. → The entire issue is devoted to cities.

DICKINSON, ROBERT E. (1951) 1962 *The West European City: A Geographical Interpretation.* 2d ed., rev. London: Routledge.

DICKINSON, ROBERT E. 1964 *City and Region: A Geographical Interpretation.* London: Routledge.

EGLI, ERNST 1959 *Geschichte des Städtebaues.* Volume 1: Die alte Welt. Zurich: Rentsch.

ÉLIADE, MIRCEA (1949) 1958 *Patterns in Comparative Religion.* New York: Sheed & Ward. → First published as *Traité d'histoire des religions.*

FAIRMAN, H. W. 1949 Town Planning in Pharaonic Egypt. *Town Planning Review* 20, no. 1:32–51.

FRANKFORT, HENRI 1948 *Kingship and the Gods: A Study of Ancient Near Eastern Religion as the Integration of Society and Nature.* Univ. of Chicago Press.

FRANKFORT, HENRI 1950 Town Planning in Ancient Mesopotamia. *Town Planning Review* 21, no. 2:99–115.

FUSTEL DE COULANGES, NUMA D. (1864) 1956 *The Ancient City: A Study on the Religion, Laws, and Institutions of Greece and Rome.* Garden City, N.Y.: Doubleday. → First published as *La cité antique.* . . .

GEDDES, PATRICK (1915) 1950 *Cities in Evolution.* New ed., rev. Oxford Univ. Press.

GOTTMANN, JEAN (1961) 1964 *Megalopolis: The Urbanized Northeastern Seaboard of the United States.* Cambridge, Mass.: M.I.T. Press.

GREGOROVIUS, FERDINAND A. (1859–1872) 1894–1902 *History of the City of Rome in the Middle Ages.* 8 vols. London: Bell. → First published as *Geschichte der Stadt Rom im Mittelalter.*

GUTKIND, ERWIN A. 1962 *The Twilight of Cities.* New York: Free Press.

GUTKIND, ERWIN A. 1964 *International History of City Development.* Volume 1: Urban Development in Central Europe. New York: Free Press.

HOWARD, EBENEZER (1898) 1951 *Garden Cities of To-*

morrow. Edited, with a preface, by F. J. Osborn. With an introductory essay by Lewis Mumford. London: Faber. → First published as *To-morrow: A Peaceful Path to Real Reform*.

JACOBS, JANE   1961   *The Death and Life of Great American Cities*. New York: Random House.

[JEANNERET-GRIS, CHARLES É.]   (1924) 1947   *The City of To-morrow and Its Planning*, by Le Corbusier [pseud.]. London: Architectural Press. → First published as *Urbanisme*.

KUHN, EMIL   1878   *Über die Entstehung der Städte der Alten: Komenverfassung und Synoikismos*. Leipzig: Teubner.

LAVEDAN, PIERRE   1926–1952   *Histoire de l'urbanisme*. 3 vols. Paris: Laurens. → Volume 1: *Antiquité: Moyen âge*. Volume 2: *Renaissance et temps modernes*. Volume 3: *Époque contemporaine*.

MACKAYE, BENTON   1928   *The New Exploration: A Philosophy of Regional Planning*. New York: Harcourt.

MOLMENTI, POMPEO G.   (1880) 1906–1908   *Venice: Its Individual Growth From the Earliest Beginnings to the Fall of the Republic*. 6 vols. Chicago: McClurg. → First published as *La storia di Venezia nella vita privata dalle origini alla caduta della repubblica*.

MÜLLER, WERNER   1961   *Die heilige Stadt: Roma quadrata, himmlisches Jerusalem und die Mythe vom Weltnabel*. Stuttgart (Germany): Kohlhammer.

MUMFORD, LEWIS   1938   *The Culture of Cities*. New York: Harcourt.

MUMFORD, LEWIS   1961   *The City in History: Its Origins, Its Transformations, and Its Prospects*. New York: Harcourt.

NEW YORK (STATE) COMMISSION OF HOUSING AND REGIONAL PLANNING   1926   *Report of the Commission of Housing and Regional Planning to Governor Alfred E. Smith. May 7, 1926*. Albany, N.Y.: Lyon.

NEW YORK (STATE) OFFICE FOR REGIONAL DEVELOPMENT   1964   *Change, Challenge, Response: A Development Policy for New York State*. Albany, N.Y.: The Office.

OSBORN, FREDERIC J.   1946   *Green-belt Cities: The British Contribution*. London: Faber.

OSBORN, FREDERIC J.; and WHITTICK, ARNOLD   1963   *The New Towns: The Answer to Megalopolis*. London: Hill.

PARK, ROBERT E.; BURGESS, ERNEST W.; and MCKENZIE, RODERICK D.   1925   *The City*. Univ. of Chicago Press.

POËTE, MARCEL   1924–1931   *Une vie de cité: Paris de sa naissance à nos jours. . . .* 3-vol. text and 1-vol. album. Paris: Picard.

PRITCHARD, JAMES B. (editor)   (1950) 1955   *Ancient Near Eastern Texts Relating to the Old Testament*. 2d ed., corr. and enl. Princeton Univ. Press.

SIMON, HERBERT A.   1962   The Architecture of Complexity. *American Philosophical Society, Proceedings* 106: 467–482.

SJOBERG, GIDEON   1960   *The Preindustrial City: Past and Present*. Glencoe, Ill.: Free Press.

SORRE, MAXIMILIEN   1952   *Les fondements de la géographie humaine*. Volume 3: L'habitat. Paris: Colin.

STEIN, CLARENCE S.   (1951) 1957   *Toward New Towns for America*. Rev. ed. New York: Reinhold.

SYMPOSIUM ON URBANIZATION AND CULTURAL DEVELOPMENT IN THE ANCIENT NEAR EAST, UNIVERSITY OF CHICAGO, 1958   1960   *City Invincible*. Edited by Carl H. Kraeling and Robert M. Adams. Univ. of Chicago Press.

TOYNBEE, ARNOLD J.   1934–1961   *A Study of History*. 12 vols. Oxford Univ. Press.

TUNNARD, CHRISTOPHER; and PUSHKAREV, BORIS   1963   *Man-made America: Chaos or Control? An Inquiry Into Selected Problems of Design in the Urbanized Landscape*. New Haven: Yale Univ. Press.

WEBER, ADNA F.   (1899) 1963   *The Growth of Cities in the Nineteenth Century: A Study in Statistics*. Ithaca, N.Y.: Cornell Univ. Press.

WEBER, MAX   (1921) 1958   *The City*. Glencoe, Ill.: Free Press. → First published as *Die Stadt*.

WIRTH, LOUIS   1938   Urbanism as a Way of Life. *American Journal of Sociology* 44:1–24.

WOOLLEY, CHARLES L.   (1954) 1964   *Excavations at Ur: A Record of Twelve Years' Work*. London: Benn.

II
THE MODERN CITY

The literature on the nature of the modern city is marked by disagreements. Social scientists not only employ a variety of theoretical orientations when interpreting the city's ecological and social structure but utilize diverse research procedures as well (Sjoberg 1965). Just as significant are the conflicting descriptions of the contemporary city or the divergent images of the ongoing changes therein—a problem on which most of our attention centers.

Theoretical orientations.   The study of the city, notably urban ecology, has been the focus of considerable debate between those scholars who believe that impersonal or "materialistic" forces shape its destiny and those who contend that sociocultural factors are the prime sources of change.

The first group traces its heritage back to the Chicago school—to Park (1916–1939) and Burgess (1923) in particular. Although Park recognized the existence of a moral order, he argued for the primacy of subsocial (or impersonal) forces in shaping man's spatial and temporal order. He drew heavily upon social Darwinism and the idea of the struggle for existence (the basis of Park's emphasis upon competition), whereas Burgess relied more upon classical economics in explaining the city's spatial structure.

Out of this group have emerged the neoclassical ecologists, represented by such prolific writers as Duncan and Schnore (1959) and Gibbs and Martin (1959). The former utilize the concept of "the ecological complex," which involves the study of the interrelationships among environment, population, social organization, and technology. For Gibbs and Martin the notion of "sustenance activities" becomes the key explanatory variable. Another view of the city that developed out of the writings of the early Chicago school culminated in the work of Wirth (1938) and Redfield (1941). Here the city—generally contrasted with the folk society (particularly by Redfield)—is seen as generating secularization, secondary group relations, tenuous social norms, and the like.

Standing somewhat between the proponents of impersonal forces and those who emphasize the more strictly sociocultural ones are sociologists such as Shevky and Bell (1955), who explain the changing urban scene in terms of stages of economic growth. Still another set of writers employs technology as the key explanatory variable. Some of them stress tools and energy per se, while others (like the author) believe that ideas, including those of science, must be viewed as an integral part of technology.

In sharp opposition to those who hold the impersonal or subsocial interpretation of the city are those who, sharing the view of Weber (1921), utilize cultural values as the primary variable. Firey's study of Boston (1947) has been the most influential sociological work in this tradition, although his argument has been elaborated upon and modified by Willhelm (1962). Still other scholars working within the sociocultural perspective have stressed social structure, with social power becoming the primary variable for explaining the patterns within urban communities [see COMMUNITY, article on THE STUDY OF COMMUNITY POWER].

Adherents of each of these theoretical traditions have carried out research that has been utilized by scholars of other persuasions. Even so, technology, cultural values, and social power appear to be the most useful variables for interpreting or predicting the changing patterns within the modern city—that is, one built upon the industrial and scientific revolution. But disagreements arise not merely over what variables should be given priority for purposes of analysis; sociologists also differ in their description and interpretation of the city's ecological and social patterns. To highlight the divergent images of the modern city we shall examine the tendencies toward centralization and decentralization and toward differentiation and "dedifferentiation" within the past few decades.

Centralization and decentralization

The tendencies toward centralization and decentralization are observable on both local and national levels. These social processes have several dimensions—the political–economic sphere being one of the most significant.

Changes in urban centers. The process of decentralization on the local level has been called "suburbanization" or "urban sprawl." Since World War II, notably in North America but in western Europe as well, there has been a marked growth of population outside of, rather than within, the central city. The pressures toward and reasons for this decentralization have been analyzed at con-siderable length. Modern technological advances (especially the automobile and the highway), along with the political and economic decisions of national and local governmental units (for example, regarding the tax structure), have supported and in turn been supported by a value system that idealizes the suburban way of life.

This outward flow of population has been associated with a decentralization of numerous economic activities, including some in manufacturing and the retail trade. Moreover, this movement has led to various political struggles—for example, over the kinds of governmental systems that can best manage the metropolitan area. The decentralization process has proved so disruptive that some planners, social scientists (e.g., Greer 1962), and government officials have in a sense "given up" on the city as a viable unit of social organization and on occasion speak of its "withering away." Although the decentralization of population and of certain functions is likely to continue (in some industrial orders it has still to reach full bloom), it is unlikely to lead to the demise of the central city—barring a nuclear holocaust.

Students of the city have generally downgraded the counterforces that are serving to sustain the central city. A number are worthy of special attention. First, a traditional value system or ideology continues to attach meaning to the central city as the locus of major social activities. This value system is perhaps most clearly defined in societies such as that of Japan and those of western Europe, where the tradition of the preindustrial city has stressed a socially dominant central core; yet this ideology also exists in nations that do not have a feudal heritage. In the face of pressures to decentralize, some groups cling to the traditional image of the central city and exert pressures to sustain its historical role.

Moreover, the very structural changes that have encouraged decentralization have also given rise to an organizational revolution that fosters certain kinds of centralization. Hoover and Vernon's study (1959) of the New York metropolitan area supports the proposition that managerial or administrative functions must to a degree concentrate in a limited area. Managers, whether in the public or the private sector, must sustain personal face-to-face relations in order to cope effectively with sensitive social issues, even in industrial cities dominated by the mass media. Although some sociologists believe New York is a unique case, it is clear that similar patterns have emerged in London and in other European cities. For as the economy is increasingly automated, the administrative functions assume ever greater significance within the city's political economy. Thus, Los Angeles—the symbol of the decentralized, automobile-dominated city—has begun building skyscrapers in the central city to house the expanding administrative apparatus. And a recent study of Chicago predicts a considerable increase in managerial functions within the downtown area during the next few decades (Nelson 1964).

Related to the expansion of managerial activities has been a vast proliferation of educational and scientific organizations. Although a number of these are locating outside the central city, many institutions of higher education and a variety of scientific laboratories are being built within the city center. In a number of nations the so-called revitalization of central cities has been directly related to the expansion of the educational–scientific complex. Modern Boston—symbolized by a skyline that attaches prominence to educational and scientific enterprises—is a case in point. And even where educational–scientific complexes are not concentrated in the central city, they become the nucleus for a host of other functions. As in the case of managerial activities, positive gains accrue from centralization and the resultant ability of key personnel to sustain face-to-face communication.

Although it is assumed that modern leisure-time pursuits encourage decentralization, clear counter-trends exist. Not only are urban universities rallying points for the cultural arts, but in many large metropolitan complexes, especially those in North America, we can observe the construction of large-scale cultural or civic centers within the city center. Moreover, such facilities as hotels have recently been constructed on a grand scale in Europe, Japan, and North America. These cater not only to the leisured and affluent classes but also to professional and administrative personnel who hold large-scale gatherings such as conventions.

High-rise apartment houses of the luxury sort are also increasing in the downtown areas of North American cities. There is some evidence that many members of the upper class have clung to the downtown areas of the major metropolises. Although they may have country homes, they continue to keep up residences in the city center.

Fundamental to the centralization–decentralization flux within industrial cities is the struggle to sustain or rebuild public transit systems in the face of the proliferation of the automobile and the highway. Even in the United States, where most fiscal policies (including the tax structure) have fostered an automobile culture, counterdecisions are emerging. And if a substantial degree of centralization is necessary to sustain the industrial complex as suggested above, we can anticipate continuing pressures in favor of mass transportation in the United States (see Dyckman 1965), western Europe, and elsewhere.

In general, then, contradictory structural requirements within the broader society account for various countervailing tendencies—some toward centralization and some toward decentralization. Yet we can advance a more specific hypothesis: the changes within industrial–urban centers are leading not to the central city's demise but rather to its continued dominance. The functions that have emerged—managerial, administrative, and cultural—are those that have been gaining ascendancy and will continue to do so in tomorrow's industrial–urban community. Thus the central city continues to reflect the functions and activities that command priority within the industrial order. The dominant economic, political, and educational bureaucracies have a vested interest in maintaining some control over, and integration of, the rather diffuse and complex metropolitan area, particularly the central city therein. Even symbolically —in terms of high-rise office buildings, hotels, etc.—the central city has sustained its traditionally dominant position.

Local and national decision making.   The strains between the decentralization and centralization processes appear not only on the local level but on the national one as well. Research in this area has been carried out by ecologist–demographers such as Duncan (Duncan et al. 1960); their attention, however, has been focused on industrial activities, largely within the framework of classical economics. In contrast, the emphasis here is upon the loci of decision making on the part of local and national bureaucracies, with the assumption that the classical economic model is of only limited value.

In the area of local and national decision making, considerable variation across nation-state systems can be discerned. Yet if we compare the United States and the Soviet Union, it is apparent that they are becoming more alike (rather than more different) in terms of their local and national decision-making patterns. A degree of autonomy and a modicum of national control are both essential to the maintenance of an industrial–urban order.

In the United States, what is essentially a decentralized system has become more centralized: since the 1930s local communities have lost some of their traditional autonomy. Centralization has not only been made possible as a result of the great advances in mass communication but, with the greater division of labor, it is actually required if the tasks of specialized functionaries who live and work in different cities are to be coordinated— especially during economic and political crises. Also, the local community has found it more and more difficult to finance needed functions without federal subvention. On the other hand, the Soviet leaders began with a strong commitment to centralized planning. However, especially in recent years, they have had to permit local authorities a degree of freedom in dealing with the special problems of their communities; thus the demands of efficiency and rationality have led to increased decentralization.

In all industrial systems the local urban center performs certain essential functions: as an educational or training center, a base for sustaining political authority, and as a locus for the production and exchange of goods and services. Thus national political decisions are, for example, reshaped to fit local conditions. Knowledge of the relationships between the local and national systems, especially in the legal sphere, is unfortunately limited. Yet it seems clear that if the national government's power is to be accepted as legitimate by the local urban center, and if its laws are to be enforced, it must gain the support of the local leadership.

A major dilemma arises from the difficulty of specifying just what is the optimum balance between local community autonomy and extracommunity controls. This balance varies not only along the political and economic dimensions but also among industrial–urban orders, depending upon the latter's value orientations. Moreover, all industrial–urban systems appear to enjoy considerable leeway in achieving a balance between the demands for autonomy and those for extracommunity controls.

Differentiation and "dedifferentiation"

One group of sociologists emphasizes the "cultural homogenization" of (or "dedifferentiation" in) city life and the rise of a "mass society" (Stein 1960), while another group focuses on the increased differentiation in the industrial city— particularly along occupational lines (e.g., Gibbs & Martin 1958). Indeed, industrial cities are becoming less diverse in some spheres and more differentiated in others.

Moreover, contradictory trends persist within the occupational structure itself. As scientific technology advances, new occupations demanding highly specialized knowledge emerge; yet we are also witnessing the "dedifferentiation" of large seg-

ments of the labor force. The evidence indicates that automation is destroying the need not only for unskilled and semiskilled laborers but also for skilled blue-collar and even some white-collar workers. These trends are of course complicated by the shifting tendencies in the direction of peace or of war.

Automation is perhaps falsifying traditional sociological generalizations about the industrial city as rapidly as it is displacing large segments of the labor force. We have only the most tenuous knowledge of this process that seems destined to revolutionize the urban community. But some scholars are even beginning to speak of the "postindustrial city." Cities of the future may contain large groups of people engaged in educational activities or occupations requiring a high degree of technical competence, along with a sizable percentage of unemployed workers or persons carrying out services that require less technical skill than is demanded by those occupations being displaced. At least in the short run, automation may widen the gulf between the upper and the lower occupational strata.

The assimilation of ethnic groups also gives rise to contradictory patterns. The sociologist's traditional theoretical model of this process was constructed upon the premise of continued assimilation of ethnic groups and the homogenization of urban life. Although this may occur over decades or centuries, it is not likely to happen in the immediate future. Surely, ethnic and religious groups persist within American cities (see, for instance, Glazer & Moynihan 1963); and in such European nations as the Netherlands and Belgium, Catholics and Protestants have for decades been living side by side within urban centers without loss of identity.

Indeed, the very process of assimilation (one form of dedifferentiation) leads to a heightened form of social identity. As the American Negro and the French-speaking Canadian, for example, have sought to enhance their over-all status and thus to hasten their assimilation, they have also attained greater group consciousness. For one thing, a group must have a well-defined concept of its past if it is to formulate a clear conception of its future. And in nations with value systems that stress equality, members of ethnic groups are able to climb the economic and political ladders more rapidly by sustaining their special affiliations than by functioning as isolated individuals.

Somewhat similar patterns can be identified in the Soviet Union, where studied efforts have been made to integrate Turkic groups, for instance, into the new industrial–urban order. While these minorities have relinquished many of their former economic, religious, and educational characteristics, their traditional folk arts have been revived—thus reinforcing their cultural identity along certain lines.

The differentiation–dedifferentiation processes (along with the trends toward decentralization and centralization of both functions and population) have been associated with constant struggles by such organizations as churches and schools to adapt themselves to the changing ecological and social conditions. One has only to examine, for example, the journal *Social Compass* to recognize that elements within the Catholic church in various European countries are endeavoring to reshape the parish structure, traditionally oriented around relatively self-contained subcommunities. But with the increased differentiation and decentralization (both of which foster spatial mobility), these communities have lost their former homogeneity. Thus the Catholic church is seeking to create a new conception of the parish in order to sustain itself in the modern city (see Reforming the Parish 1966).

The scope of this article has been limited to decades rather than centuries. If we had contrasted the industrial city with the nineteenth-century city or with the city of the preindustrial era, we could have observed marked changes in the social structure (Sjoberg 1960). Still, if we are to understand the modern city in relation to past forms, or if we are to predict the changes within present-day industrial centers, we must recognize the presence of contradictory trends within the social and ecological structure. Only then can we resolve some of the seemingly contradictory conclusions that sociologists have drawn about industrial city life.

GIDEON SJOBERG

[*Directly related are the entries* PLANNING, SOCIAL, *article on* REGIONAL AND URBAN PLANNING. *Other relevant material may be found in* CENTRAL PLACE; ECOLOGY, *article on* HUMAN ECOLOGY; NEIGHBORHOOD; SEGREGATION; TRANSPORTATION, *article on* SOCIAL ASPECTS.]

BIBLIOGRAPHY

BURGESS, ERNEST W. (1923) 1961 The Growth of the City: An Introduction to a Research Project. Pages 37–44 in George A. Theodorson (editor), *Studies in Human Ecology.* Evanston, Ill.: Row, Peterson.

Cities. 1965 *Scientific American* 213, no. 3.

DUNCAN, OTIS DUDLEY; and SCHNORE, LEO F. 1959 Cultural, Behavioral, and Ecological Perspectives in the Study of Social Organization. *American Journal of Sociology* 65:132–146. → A comment by Peter H. Rossi and a rejoinder by Duncan and Schnore appear on pages 146–153.

DUNCAN, OTIS DUDLEY et al. 1960 *Metropolis and Region.* Baltimore: Johns Hopkins Press.

DYCKMAN, JOHN W. 1965 Transportation in Cities. *Scientific American* 213, no. 3:162–174.

FIREY, WALTER I. 1947 *Land Use in Central Boston.* Cambridge, Mass.: Harvard Univ. Press.

GIBBS, JACK P.; and MARTIN, WALTER T. 1958 Urbanization and Natural Resources: A Study in Organizational Ecology. *American Sociological Review* 23: 266–277.

GIBBS, JACK P.; and MARTIN, WALTER T. 1959 Toward a Theoretical System of Human Ecology. *Pacific Sociological Review* 2:29–36.

GLAZER, NATHAN; and MOYNIHAN, DANIEL P. 1963 *Beyond the Melting Pot: The Negroes, Puerto Ricans, Jews, Italians, and the Irish of New York City.* Cambridge, Mass.: M.I.T. Press.

GREER, SCOTT A. 1962 *The Emerging City: Myth and Reality.* New York: Free Press.

HOOVER, EDGAR M.; and VERNON, RAYMOND 1959 *Anatomy of a Metropolis: The Changing Distribution of People and Jobs Within the New York Metropolitan Region.* Cambridge, Mass.: Harvard Univ. Press. → A paperback edition was published in 1962 by Doubleday.

NELSON, ROBERT C. 1964 Computer Changing Chicago. *Christian Science Monitor* July 30: p. 11, cols. 3–5.

PARK, ROBERT E. (1916–1939) 1952 *Human Communities: The City and Human Ecology.* Collected Papers, Vol. 2. Glencoe, Ill.: Free Press.

REDFIELD, ROBERT 1941 *The Folk Culture of Yucatan.* Univ. of Chicago Press.

Reforming the Parish. 1966 *Commonweal* 84, no. 1.

SHEVKY, ESHREF; and BELL, WENDELL 1955 *Social Area Analysis: Theory, Illustrative Application, and Computational Procedures.* Stanford (Calif.) Univ. Press.

SJOBERG, GIDEON 1960 *The Preindustrial City: Past and Present.* Glencoe, Ill.: Free Press.

SJOBERG, GIDEON 1965 Theory and Research in Urban Sociology. Pages 157–189 in Philip M. Hauser and Leo F. Schnore (editors), *The Study of Urbanization.* New York: Wiley. → This book includes citations to a wide range of relevant literature, including bibliographical surveys.

STEIN, MAURICE R. 1960 *The Eclipse of Community.* Princeton Univ. Press.

WEBER, MAX (1921) 1958 *The City.* Glencoe, Ill.: Free Press. → First published as *Die Stadt.*

WILLHELM, SIDNEY 1962 *Urban Zoning and Land-use Theory.* New York: Free Press.

WIRTH, LOUIS 1938 Urbanism as a Way of Life. *American Journal of Sociology* 44:1–24.

III
METROPOLITAN GOVERNMENT

Metropolitan government refers to the political mechanisms and processes through which local public decisions are made, covering areas approximately coterminous with the territories in which modern urban economic and social systems function. Historically, the term refers to efforts in many nations to redesign established local-government institutions by reducing the number of relatively autonomous units typically existing in heavily urbanized regions (metropolitan areas) or by introducing new levels or forms of government to make certain area-wide decisions. The concept has been broadened to include analysis of the ways in which the urban political process responds to pressures generated by the expanding scale of urbanization, regardless of the formal institutional arrangements involved. In this context, the emphasis is upon the properties and behavior of metropolitan political systems, and involves the characterization of the political actors and the types of conflicts, elite structures, political communication networks, and processes of conflict resolution in these areas.

Until about 1960, most professional studies of metropolitan political organization and behavior focused on the difficulties arising in governing the new urban regions through traditional local political institutions. They regarded those institutions as in many ways obsolete and incapable of providing effective public programs; and, implicitly or explicitly, the studies advocated major governmental reform. In the 1960s, however, a considerable number of social scientists suggested that these difficulties were exaggerated and that existing arrangements were useful in minimizing social and political conflict and in providing opportunity for individual participation in community affairs. They favored less extensive and more informal adjustments.

Metropolitan areas. The principal stimulus for proposals of establishing formal metropolitan governments and the evolution of informal metropolitan political systems is the rapid and continued expansion of urbanized territory beyond the boundaries of cities originally established as defense, trade, or manufacturing cities. In Great Britain, Europe, and the American Atlantic seaboard, urban populations spilled over boundary lines of such cities and into the countryside as early as the eighteenth century. However, the most dramatic increase in scale through widespread diffusion of households, industries, and commercial centers over a large number of local governmental jurisdictions is a phenomenon of the last one hundred years.

Previously, the technological advances in the early stages of industrialization that tapped new energy sources, created new manufacturing processes, and resulted in new building techniques had encouraged compact urban development. The first modern cities accommodated urban immigrants in limited areas that displayed a great variety of land uses and high population densities. Subsequent innovations, particularly in transportation and communication facilities, made possible a countertrend to population concentration within the original metropolis. Especially in the United States, the introduction of rapid transit, commuter railroad service, and the automobile allowed residents to settle in independent political jurisdictions outside the "mother" municipality. New communication devices and new public-utility, water, and sewage facilities reduced the dependence of residences and certain industries on downtown locations. Concomitantly, the process of population and economic diffusion was accelerated by rising incomes, changes in home-construction and home-financing patterns, new social aspirations, preferences for single-family residences with more open space for children, and the promotional techniques of land speculators.

Under the impact of these forces, the large urban areas became characterized by daily movements of the working population from home to place of employment, by steadily declining urban population densities, and by a rapid growth in the urban population living outside the central city. By 1960, there were over 1,000 metropolitan areas in the world, each consisting of a principal city of at least 50,000, with adjacent administrative territorial units within commuting distance of the city and with a labor force of which over two-thirds were engaged in nonagricultural industries. The populations in these areas are judged to be interdependent in economic and social activity, with such consistent patterns of interaction as to constitute organized systems of behavior.

In the United States, where the process is farthest advanced, the large metropolitan area typically consists of the old core city, now made up of a selected number of industries and businesses for which a downtown location is still economically desirable, the dwelling places of low-income and minority-group families, and a relatively small number of middle-income and wealthy household units. An inner ring of suburbs caters to warehousing, lower-priced commercial establishments, marginal industries, and lower-middle-income or low-income families, often in multiunit housing accommodations. In the outer ring of suburbs, middle-income and higher-income single-family residences predominate, together with large, standardized manufacturing plants, often grouped in industrial parks adjacent to major highways.

Since World War II, some of the largest American metropolitan areas have expanded to reach one another's boundaries. On the Atlantic seaboard, a continuous belt of densely populated urban counties six hundred miles long and between thirty and one hundred miles wide has arisen, containing five of the fifteen largest metropolitan areas in the country. Named "megalopolis" by the French geographer Jean Gottmann, this new type of urban region, interstate as well as intermunicipal in character, appears the prototype of the new physical form that urbanization is likely to take in the last half of this century.

The "metropolitan problem." The transformation of discrete cities into metropolitan areas and megalopolises ended the coincidence between social, economic, and political boundaries of urban territory. By 1962, the 212 standard metropolitan statistical areas (SMSA) in the United States defined by the U.S. Bureau of the Census encompassed over 18,000 local governments—counties, municipalities, townships, and special districts. Nine of the 24 largest SMSA's contained more than 250 governments apiece; the other 15 largest, between 200 and 249. The public affairs of metropolitan London were managed by the City Corporation, London County, 28 metropolitan boroughs, 5 administrative counties, 3 county boroughs, 39 municipal boroughs, 15 urban districts, and 5 special authorities. At mid-twentieth century, the metropolitan area of Rome included 100 communes, each a separate organ of local government; Montreal was surrounded by nearly 60 municipal governments; the Sydney area featured 33 municipalities and 5 shires. Throughout the world, wherever a historical tradition for autonomous local governments or highly decentralized administrative units existed, a number of separate jurisdictions carried on concurrently the public affairs of the new urban complexes.

The continuation of many separate units of local government within metropolitan areas that possess the social and economic properties of a single community constitutes "the metropolitan problem." Especially since 1900, many observers have concluded that effective and responsible local urban government is not possible where several units possess considerable discretion in controlling land use and in financing and directing public-service programs in the absence of a single frame of political authority.

Several effects of the multigovernment pattern in metropolitan areas are considered to be detrimental to effective governmental operations.

The first is administrative and financial in character. By conventional economic calculations, local units, operating independently, cannot realize presumed efficiencies of size and scale in the provision of important public services. Major public investment programs, such as those in water supply and distribution systems, transportation, and public utilities, by the inherent nature of the function involved, appear better planned and executed when managed by a metropolitan government than when each general-purpose government maintains its own facilities. Substantial improvements in administrative direction and financial savings also seem possible in the consolidation of many operating programs, such as fire, police, and health, to prevent duplication of services and competition for personnel. Evaluated according to administrative criteria of the optimum population or area, most local service activities appear expensive and ineffective.

A second consequence of continuing the established governmental arrangements is the unequal distribution of tax revenues that occurs where property taxation is the major source of local funds. Since individual jurisdictions possess different land uses, and hence different endowments of residential population and industrial and commercial property, sizable discrepancies in taxable resources exist among them, especially in relation to demands for public services.

The central cities of metropolitan areas often appear in a particularly disadvantageous position. They are required to maintain an elaborate array of services for the daytime working population but are unable to tax these users. Moreover, their tax bases are declining relative to suburban jurisdictions and are further reduced by the large number of tax-exempt civic and educational establishments that prefer to locate downtown. Extreme differences also appear among suburbs, depending on their predominant land use. Some, with large industrial properties within their borders that require few public services, have ample revenues. Others, with large, moderate-cost residential development, must devote a much greater proportion of their valuation to supporting government programs. Hence, the quality of services and the tax effort required of residences vary widely within metropolitan areas presumed to have the attributes of a single community.

Third, effective popular participation in major policy decisions with direct impact on the metropolitan population is often impossible. Suburban residents cannot vote in central-city elections, and central-city citizens cannot officially take part in suburban civic affairs. Further, where several units exercise concurrent jurisdiction, the citizen may often find it difficult to identify and evaluate the performance of elected officials. Although within suburban communities residents frequently find opportunity for direct political participation and easy access to public officials, their opportunity to influence public decisions of metropolitan consequence made outside their immediate jurisdictions is limited or nonexistent.

Finally, the absence of metropolis-wide political authority precludes or obstructs comprehensive planning and development activities on a metropolitan basis. General-purpose local governments within the area lack the geographical jurisdiction to adjust land uses to expected changes in population and in economic activities. Special-purpose authorities undertake area-wide activities only in terms of their dominant purposes, so that their planning is restricted to certain prime functions, for example, a particular mode of transportation or the provision of a major utility. As a consequence, anticipatory action by local government in guiding the character of physical development is most frequently defensive in nature (i.e., aimed at preserving or securing patterns of development desired by the local constituency for financial, aesthetic, or social consequences) and proceeds principally through voluntary cooperative efforts. In the United States, comprehensive public policy is rarely a significant factor in determining the shape of metropolitan areas.

Metropolitan governmental reform.   The identification of the political and administrative deficiencies of divided governmental authority in metropolitan areas has prompted an increasing number of efforts for institutional reform. Compared to the number proposed, few comprehensive changes in governmental structure have been achieved, but many structural and procedural adaptations have been implemented. These adjustments are customarily placed in five categories.

(1) *Special districts.*   The most popular device used to resolve administrative and financial difficulties has been the creation of special districts with jurisdictions and responsibilities different from those of the local general-purpose units. One type of special district provides service or developmental programs for entire metropolitan areas or large parts of them. The London Metropolitan Police District, established in 1839, and the Metropolitan Sewer Commission of Boston, established in 1889, represent prototypes of these arrangements. Typically, these units are designed to carry out a limited number of programs, such as transportation or water supply, with areal requirements different from those of the general-purpose governments. They have special financial and organizational arrangements designed to allow them to operate with considerable autonomy. For example, such prominent, large American special districts as the Port of New York Authority and the Bi-state

Development Agency for the St. Louis area are established by compacts between the affected states, are empowered to levy charges for use of their facilities, and are managed by boards directly appointed by state governors.

A second version of the special district is those districts which encompass much smaller areas, frequently only a segment of a general-purpose government's jurisdiction. They have been established to meet the service requirements in rapidly urbanizing areas where the special needs of a particular portion of the population can be separately identified. Usually, they provide utility distribution systems or refuse collection for new residential developments financed through special taxes, assessments, or levies applied only to the recipients of the services and calculated separately from general taxation. Thus, the special pressures of rapid growth upon the local public sector can be singled out and accommodated.

The special-district device, whether metropolitan or local in jurisdiction, has been criticized on the grounds that it fails to provide general-purpose government on a comprehensive basis, further complicates the pattern of divided authority, and is not democratic in character, since district officials often are not directly responsible to the constituencies served. But the effectiveness of the device in providing administrative and financial solutions to pressing service problems has usually outweighed these considerations in the minds of state and local policy-makers. Since World War II, the number of urban special districts in the United States has increased more rapidly than any other form of local government. Between 1952 and 1962, the number of special districts increased from 12,340 to 18,323.

(2) *Annexation.*   A more straightforward proposal for metropolitan reform than the special-district approach is the annexation of newly urbanized territory by the mother city. In the nineteenth and early twentieth centuries, this practice of extending municipal boundary lines to keep pace with urban population growth was extensively used by almost every large American city. It remains a popular instrument in southwestern and middle western regions of the United States.

Although effective in maintaining the coincidence of political, economic, and social boundary lines, annexation often creates substantial financial, organizational, and land-use problems. If a city annexes relatively undeveloped territory in anticipation of new development, it may have to undertake expensive investments in capital facilities long before any sizable revenues are forthcoming from the new area, and its administrative resources may be similarly strained. On the other hand, if a city waits until urbanization has occurred in outlying places, its opportunity to guide land-use policy is reduced or eliminated. Furthermore, it risks almost certain opposition to the annexation by fringe-area residents who value their status as citizens of smaller communities and oppose the higher taxes that annexation often brings. Frequently these citizens establish separate municipalities in preference to being absorbed by the metropolis. Even when the annexation device is extensively used, the metropolis typically assumes responsibility over areas with few tax resources but heavy service requirements, while the financially self-sufficient outlying parts of the metropolitan area retain their separate identities. In older metropolitan areas, when surburban municipalities have long been in existence, the annexation approach has proved almost completely impracticable.

(3) *Reallocations of functions.* In Great Britain and the United States, where the pattern of local governments is one of two levels, county and municipality, and in federal systems, where local governments are legally creatures of the states, an alternative approach is to reassign local programs from one governmental level to another, or to consolidate major units. In the smaller U.S. metropolitan areas, this type of reform has sometimes taken the form of separating central-city and county functions, and sometimes of their consolidation. More usually, the readjustments have been made for specific programs.

City–county separation, adopted in Baltimore more than one hundred years ago, has the disadvantage of seriously complicating the future expansion of central-city boundaries, for it often freezes the jurisdictions of the local governments involved. Only the state of Virginia in the United States has devised a practical means for municipal expansion under the separation philosophy by empowering the state judiciary to make such decisions. Consolidation plans, most recently represented by Baton Rouge, Louisiana, frequently achieve major structural simplifications, but neither separation nor consolidation has achieved integration of governmental functions in large, multicounty metropolitan areas. A new version of consolidation, adopted in 1960 by Nashville and Davidson County, Tennessee, establishes one expandable urban service district designed to overcome the jurisdictional inflexibilities of the older plans. This device may be applicable in other areas.

At present, however, the most popular type of functional adjustment is one of piecemeal mergers of specific functions. In many metropolitan areas, public health, welfare, highway, and recreational programs have been established on a joint basis, most usually involving the central city and the county and resulting in the emergence of the county as the principal metropolitan unit. This approach generally depends on voluntary agreements arrived at through a bargaining process between municipal and county officials and is widely heralded as a means by which politically autonomous units can overcome some of the administrative consequences of metropolitan fragmentation.

(4) *Metropolitan federation.* Given the difficulties inherent in the special-district, annexation, and functional-reallocation approaches, many experts have come to advocate metropolitan federation as the most satisfactory way to solve the metropolitan problem on a comprehensive basis. Metropolitan federalism calls for the establishment of a government with jurisdiction over the entire metropolitan area, but with limited responsibilities; most existing local units continue to perform "purely local" functions. Usually a federated plan provides for the participation of the smaller units in the policy-making process of the metropolitan government through some formula of representation on the latter's governing body.

The two-tier structure of government in London County, where 28 metropolitan boroughs plus the ancient City of London function alongside the London County Council, is an example of a partially federated structure. In 1963, this arrangement was extended to the other counties within the London metropolitan area, with a substantial strengthening of the powers of the boroughs; however, several important programs are excluded from the plan. New York City's five-borough plan, adopted in 1897, had the formal appearance of a federal system for the then urbanized area, but in practice the boroughs served principally as administrative units; no further extension of the city occurred by the 1960s. Miami and Dade County, Florida, adopted a two-tier form of government in 1957, but the experiment is limited to one county within a rapidly expanding area, and only cities with populations of more than 60,000 elect representatives to the county board of commissioners.

The most complete application of the federal principle in a metropolitan area was achieved in Toronto, Canada, in 1953, by prescription of the Ontario legislature. The Municipality of Metropolitan Toronto has jurisdiction over such area-wide functions as water supply and distribution, sewerage, principal highways, public transportation, and planning in an area encompassing the central city and twelve suburbs. A metropolitan council composed of the chief executives of the suburban governments and twelve elected public officials of Toronto directs the metropolitan municipality. The old units continue to provide health, library, and welfare services, although the assumption of police responsibilities in 1957 by the metropolitan government has given rise to charges that the plan is "creeping annexation" and that ultimately full consolidation is intended.

The Toronto plan has also been criticized because of its indirect and—on a population basis— unequal plan of representation and because it was established without a popular referendum. Nonetheless, the metropolitan government's activity in the first ten years of operation establishes it as a vigorous instrument.

(5) *Nonlocal governmental arrangements.* Besides the various changes and adjustments proposed or effected in the structure of loyal governments, two other lines of action have been employed to deal with metropolitan public-service and development problems. First, higher levels of government have directly undertaken some metropolitan programs and policy-making. The national governments of France and Britain, for example, operating through national ministries and departments, provide important health, welfare, housing, and public-works services without respect to local government jurisdictions. In France, the pattern of administrative organization within the departments is so constructed as to constitute a metropolitan government. The local communes are coordinated with national departments by the prefecture system: policy-making is centered at the national level; intercommunal syndicates are responsible for public works; limited participation by local communities is provided through the mechanism of departmental councils. In Britain, programs in health, education, and housing are nationalized to the degree that the policies of the respective ministries often assure uniform activities throughout metropolitan areas.

In federal systems the character of participation by nonlocal governments is more complex, for the states form an intervening level of government between national and local units. In the United States, for example, some state governments have established offices and agencies of their own to carry out metropolitan programs. New York and California have staff units of the governor's office that deal with local and metropolitan-area problems, and the planning departments of several states give special emphasis to urban development. Moreover, many of the large metropolitan-area districts are legally state agencies, and their chief executives and directors are appointed by the governor or the legislators. Major state line agencies, such as those dealing with highways and recreation, are similarly concerned with metropolitan planning and public works.

The national government in the United States, through its housing, urban renewal, highway, health, and public-works programs, has become increasingly concerned with the need to deal with metropolitan areas on a systematic basis. Interagency collaboration at the national level is increasing, as are efforts to develop a common approach to providing assistance to the many local governments involved.

There are also parapolitical enterprises at work on the American metropolitan scene that, while not formally governments, are becoming increasingly influential in public policy-making. Such an enterprise is the metropolitan planning agency, sometimes established by formal state action, but frequently a private organization supported by civic and business organizations and "floating" in the metropolitan area without official sanction. A companion activity has been the large-scale, professional research project, financed by private foundations and staffed by academic personnel, charged with the responsibility to study the pattern of metropolitan development and often to recommend new public policies and institutions. Local government officials have also come together to form a new instrument for metropolitan action on a voluntary basis, most commonly constituting themselves as an "area council."

The degree of formality of these organizations varies considerably, as does the scope of their interests and the character of their programs. Some are primarily discussion groups seeking solutions to common problems; some undertake fairly extensive research activities; a few have actually concluded agreements for the joint conduct of particular programs. While not committing their governments to any new formal structure, the emergence of these groups signals a growing awareness of the pressures of metropolitan growth and of the need for collaborative public action.

Metropolitan politics. While few major structural reforms of local government have taken place over the last century, the adjustments made in various areas suggest that a substantial evolutionary process has been under way.

Essentially, the rejection of comprehensive reorganization programs is due to the reluctance of the public at large and the political power structures within existing local government to relinquish political autonomy. Administrative efficiency and adequate financial resources have rarely been the main values of either the political leaders or the voters in metropolitan areas. Instead, the objectives of access to decision-making centers and of representation in policy deliberations have appeared as more important objectives. Hence, some students have emphasized that the present pattern of divided government has the important property of segregating the expanding urban population into political jurisdictions of small size and comparative homogeneity when measured by indices of income, ethnic groupings, religion, and occupation. These characteristics allow a stronger sense of community identity within the territory of each government and probably serve to minimize social conflict through the process of political isolation. Accordingly, the defeat of many plans drafted by administrative experts is explicable because they did not speak to the prime values of the major participants. Instead, they threatened the abolition of the positions of local public officials, the feeling of participation and informality of residents in the suburban jurisdictions, and the new political strength of minority groups within the central cities.

These separatist tendencies inhibit the development of formal institutions of metropolitan government, but there are also manifestations of at least embryonic metropolitan political systems. In recent years, it has been possible to identify major public figures and interest groups regularly participating in metropolitan decisions, communication networks existing among them, strategies and techniques by which they develop reasonable consensus on certain issues, and the general objectives they seek. Given the great number of governmental units involved, especially in federal nations where state and national levels participate, present metropolitan political systems are characterized by a large number of separate power centers and a substantial diffusion of influence. But with respect to decisions on transportation, public utilities, and general planning, more or less permanent coalitions of interests have appeared; it is these that account for the rapid rise in the number of special districts and parapolitical organizations. Moreover, the emergence of metropolitan planning organizations and councils of local officials suggests that developmental decisions concerning the growth and future character of the areas, in contrast with program or service decisions, are assuming new importance.

In several large American metropolitan areas, it is also possible to identify an interest-group complex committed to an area-wide perspective and approach, in contrast with those which defend traditional concepts of the appropriate role of urban government and the existing structure. These complexes are rarely powerful enough to provide widespread public support for reform, but they often succeed in introducing the metropolitan perspective into the preparation of transportation, public-utility, and land-use plans. Typically, they are most effective in modifying the behavior of professional bureaucracies within the present structure of government and in achieving some degree of cooperation and coordination among their activities.

Future developments. The present characteristics of metropolitan political systems suggest a continued expansion in cooperative arrangements among governments with large responsibilities in metropolitan areas and a further increase in governmental influence on major developmental decisions without radical readjustment in governmental form. In nations where popular approval of structural reform is not required, formal reorganization of the existing units may be achieved with some frequency. Where public referenda are required, however, a direct confrontation between pro-reform and anti-reform forces is likely to result in the former's defeat. Powerful leaders in the metropolitan system remain motivated by goals of continued separatism and autonomy. The ideological appeal of these goals remains popular with the public at large and is reinforced by desires to maintain communities that are occupationally, religiously, and ethnically homogeneous. In these instances, the coalition of interests seeking to broaden the scope of area-wide decisions is more effective in establishing quasi-public mechanisms or in increasing the involvement of state and national agencies than in attempting to modify the existing pattern of local government.

The outlook for the metropolitan political systems is that their behavior will grow more systematic and predictable and that area-wide decisions will be more influenced by parapolitical organizations. It does not seem likely, however, that the systems will decisively alter the pattern of urban growth as established by economic and technological forces or produce new physical forms for the metropolitan area. The establishment of area-wide governments will occur only occasionally, and the values and interests that emphasize the social and political benefits of present arrangements are more likely to prevail than are those committed to the more rationalistic objectives of administrative efficiency, policy control, and resource planning.

ROBERT C. WOOD

[*See also* LOCAL GOVERNMENT; LOCAL POLITICS.]

BIBLIOGRAPHY

BANFIELD, EDWARD C.; and GRODZINS, MORTON M. 1958 *Government and Housing in Metropolitan Areas.* New York: McGraw-Hill.

BOLLENS, JOHN C. 1956 *The States and the Metropolitan Problem: A Report to the Governors' Conference.* Chicago: Council of State Governments.

BOLLENS, JOHN C. (editor) 1961 *Exploring the Metropolitan Community.* Berkeley: Univ. of California Press.

CALIFORNIA, UNIVERSITY OF, INSTITUTE OF INTERNATIONAL STUDIES, INTERNATIONAL URBAN RESEARCH 1959 *The World's Metropolitan Areas.* Berkeley: Univ. of California Press.

CONNERY, ROBERT H.; and LEACH, RICHARD H. 1960 *The Federal Government and Metropolitan Areas.* Cambridge, Mass.: Harvard Univ. Press.

FORTUNE, THE EDITORS 1958 *The Exploding Metropolis.* Garden City, N.Y.: Doubleday.

GREER, SCOTT A. 1962a *The Emerging City: Myth and Reality.* New York: Free Press.

GREER, SCOTT A. 1962b *Governing the Metropolis.* New York: Wiley.

HIRSCH, WERNER Z. (editor) 1963 *Urban Life and Form.* New York: Holt. → Published for the Washington University Institute for Urban and Regional Studies.

JANOWITZ, MORRIS (editor) 1961 *Community Political Systems.* New York: Free Press.

JONES, VICTOR 1942 *Metropolitan Government.* Univ. of Chicago Press.

MCKENZIE, RODERICK D. 1933 *The Metropolitan Community.* New York: McGraw-Hill.

MARTIN, ROSCOE C. et al. 1961 *Decisions in Syracuse.* Metropolitan Action Studies, No. 1. Bloomington: Indiana Univ. Press.

STUDENSKI, PAUL 1930 *The Government of Metropolitan Areas in the United States.* New York: National Municipal League.

TAMIMENT INSTITUTE, NEW YORK 1961 *The Future Metropolis.* Edited by Lloyd Rodwin. New York: Braziller. → Essays originally published in the Winter 1961 issue of *Dædalus.*

U.S. ADVISORY COMMISSION ON INTERGOVERNMENTAL RELATIONS 1961 *Governmental Structure, Organization, and Planning in Metropolitan Areas.* Washington: Government Printing Office.

VERNON, RAYMOND 1960 *Metropolis 1985: An Interpretation of the Findings of the New York Metropolitan Region Study.* New York Metropolitan Region Study, No. 9. Cambridge, Mass.: Harvard Univ. Press.

WOOD, ROBERT C. 1959 *Suburbia: Its People and Their Politics.* Boston: Houghton Mifflin.

WOOD, ROBERT C.; and ALMENDINGER, VLADIMIR V. 1961 *1400 Governments: The Political Economy of the New York Metropolitan Region.* New York Metropolitan Region Study, No. 8. Cambridge, Mass.: Harvard Univ. Press.

WOODBURY, COLEMAN (editor) 1953 *The Future of Cities and Urban Redevelopment.* Univ. of Chicago Press.

IV

COMPARATIVE URBAN STRUCTURE

An urban settlement fundamentally consists of a collection of dwellings and other buildings plus a sizable resident population. The buildings are permanently situated, separated from other such settlements, and are compactly arranged with respect to each other—typically in blocks separated by streets or alleys. While there is no universal agreement as to how large the population must be before the settlement is classified as urban, the minimum is usually placed somewhere between 2,500 and 10,000 people.

Large, permanent assemblies of people have arisen historically in two sharply contrasting ways. Some settlements emerge because a group of people choose to live near each other in order to realize a way of life made possible by production activities carried on elsewhere. Other settlements arise because people who work within certain production facilities wish to live in the immediate vicinity of these facilities. In general, then, the population may be permanently assembled in order to *consume* the products and services of labor, regardless of where they are produced, or in order to *produce* goods and services, regardless of where they are consumed. The words "produce" and "consume" are used in their broadest senses, including not only traditionally economic activities, such as commerce and manufacture, but also religious, military, professional, educational, and other similarly organized activities.

Examples of consumption-oriented settlements include the modern residential suburb, the traditional rural village, the ceremonial capital or "court" city, and the urban community of the elite during the social season. Examples of production-oriented settlements include the manufacturing city, the market town, and the governmental administrative center (ranging from county seat to national capital). Of course, since the production-oriented settlement has a permanently settled population, it automatically becomes the site of many consumption activities. Prior to the industrial revolution most settlements were consumption-oriented, but today the production-oriented center is the more common. The consumption-oriented settlement usually has a more coherent social organization than the site of productive activity. The population assembled for production purposes is not necessarily well integrated; indeed, it may consist of many highly diverse and even antagonistic groups who live near each other only for the purpose of production. Creating a coherent and reasonably satisfactory mode of common social living (consumption) among disparate groups assembled for production purposes is one of the major problems facing the leaders of most modern urban settlements.

Two topics are of special interest in comparing

urban structures. One concerns the internal arrangement of the people and their dwellings within the settlement, and the other concerns the interrelationships between settlements in the area, region, nation, or world. These topics will be considered primarily in regard to the production-oriented settlement.

Internal spatial arrangements

Essentially, all human settlement patterns, whether single settlements or collections of settlements, display the phenomenon of centralization (Hawley 1950). In a single urban settlement the center is typically at or very near the site of the original community and is also typically at the local point of maximum access to other populations and settlements (Hurd 1903). The population of the settlement grows out in all available directions from this center, creating what is by far the most regular residential pattern found in urban places throughout the world, namely, the tendency for density (residents per unit of land) eventually to decrease as distance from the center increases. This density gradient is especially pronounced in very large cities, where densities of over 100,000 per square mile are common in centrally located neighborhoods; in Asian cities comparable densities sometimes reach 500,000. In many cities these maximum densities do not occur in the actual center of the city but rather in the area immediately adjacent to it. By contrast, densities in the peripheral areas of an urban settlement are often no more than 1,000 to 5,000 per square mile.

The concentration of residences near the center of an urban settlement is due primarily to the fact that until the twentieth century most local movement within a city was on foot. Since urban functions are relatively specialized, yet bound to one another by numerous interactions and interchanges, the entire settlement tends to be located in a relatively small area. If walking is the typical local means of transportation, the settlement's area will be particularly small; moreover, if such a settlement grows, it tends to grow almost entirely by making more intensive use of already settled land. Hence, central densities become very high, while outlying districts remain almost uninhabited. In many current non-Western urban settlements walking remains the major means of local transportation. Historically, the tendency toward a sharp density gradient was enhanced by the need for protection within a wall.

At the very center of most European or American urban settlements is an area called the central business district that contains many of the major production facilities of the settlement, whether in the form of factories, office buildings, or stores. The central business district is, therefore, the place where the bulk of the urban labor force works during the day. Preindustrial Western cities and most modern non-Western cities do not possess a central business district in quite the Western sense, although most of these cities have a major central market place (or bazaar) and possibly a collection of central office buildings for administration (Seminar on Urbanization in India . . . 1962). In general, however, the separation of places of work from places of residence has not proceeded as far in Asian as in European and American cities, except where Western influence has been dominant. When a central business district does exist, it provides a further stimulus to the build-up of central residential densities immediately around it, since the trip to and from work must be made each day.

In the Western world the appearance of a central business district coincided with the coming of the industrial revolution, especially the appearance of the large-scale factory and of the railroad with its highly centralized terminal facilities. (Some earlier port cities exhibited essentially a central business district pattern in the neighborhood of the harbor.) Thus, the very process that gave rise to new means of local transportation which could disperse the urban residents at first had precisely the opposite effect; namely, further concentrating population through the emergence of the central business district. Recent evidence suggests that in American cities the forces tending to centralize the urban population exceeded those tending to decentralize it until the early years of the twentieth century (Hawley 1956). Since then, however, the availability of more rapid and flexible means of transportation (especially the automobile and truck) has tended to decentralize both residences and places of work. Although the density gradient by distance from the center of the city is still very pronounced in American cities, it is not as steep as it was a few decades ago (O. D. Duncan 1957) and certainly not as steep as in most non-Western cities. Indeed, between 1950 and 1960 many large American settlements actually lost population in their central cities while gaining population in the suburban and fringe areas.

In many cities in South America and Asia settlement densities remain quite high to the outskirts of the settlement and then fall very rapidly almost to zero or to the rural base. The principal reason that densities remain high toward the outskirts is that migrants have been coming to these settlements in great numbers. These migrants are unable to find housing within the city proper and so cluster around it in large numbers, often in poor and relatively temporary housing accommodations. In general, new migrants to a city tend to flow into the immediate vicinity of the center when the demand for housing has resulted in the creation of tenements, flats, and apartments in that area; on the other hand, when the central areas have not been filled with suitable types of housing units, migrants tend to remain on the periphery. In older American cities movement to the center has tended to be typical, while in other areas of the world movement to the outskirts has frequently prevailed. In recent years the tendency for recent migrants to live near the center has declined.

Distribution of population subgroups. When attention is shifted from the distribution of the population as a whole to the distribution of various categories within the population (such as the well-to-do or the racially distinct), the existence of many different patterns is evident. Urban populations are usually very heterogeneous, consisting of many different religious and ethnic groups, as well as representatives of many different socioeconomic status levels. Moreover, in many cities, especially in the United States, the population contains at least two racial groupings. In every city that has been studied, there is a tendency for people who are similar socially or racially to live together and for people who are different socially or racially to live apart.

While comparative quantitative evidence is largely lacking, it is quite likely that the tendency to segregate different population subgroups was carried very far in preindustrial cities. Although persons of high socioeconomic status were very few in number, they were very sharply socially differentiated from the rest of the population and, with their indwelling servants, occupied one section of the settlement almost exclusively. Persons of deviant religious persuasion, such as Jews in European cities, were likewise highly segregated, typically in ghettos which were walled off to further the separation. Whether the bulk of the remaining population of preindustrial cities—artisans, shopkeepers, and laborers—was also sharply subdivided and segregated is not entirely clear (see Sjoberg 1960). However, in modern non-Western cities there is substantial residential differentiation and segregation even among these groups.

Studies of selected American cities have used an "index of dissimilarity" to measure the differences between the residential distributions of various groups; their results indicate that while the dissimilarity in the distribution of various ethnic

groups is almost 50 per cent, the comparable figure for the dissimilarity between Negroes and whites is about 90 per cent (O. D. Duncan & Lieberson 1959). Other segregation indices show similar results for the residential separation of racial groups in American cities. Relatively little is known about trends in this type of segregation, although there is evidence that it has been increasing during the last century (Taeuber & Taeuber 1965). It is difficult to measure the actual extent of segregation because it can take so many different forms. In American cities residential separation is likely to involve entire neighborhoods, whereas in European cities, as well as in the central areas of some large American cities, it is more likely to occur within neighborhoods—even within a block or a single building; for example, sometimes alley-fronting, cellar rooms are occupied by one group and street-fronting upper rooms by another, and there is little or no contact between them.

Patterns of segregation. Regardless of the extent to which patterns of segregation are carried, it is of interest to inquire where the various subgroups tend to live within the settlement. Four different patterns are frequently discussed. In the first pattern, persons of higher socioeconomic status tend to live near the city's center, while persons of low status live on the outskirts of the city. This pattern is found throughout the world, except in North America and in some parts of Europe. In a sense it can be considered the classic or traditional arrangement. It may result from the fact that the elite carry on a much more elaborate social life than do the poor; in most parts of the world this social life crucially involves the use of central facilities. On the other hand, this pattern may result historically from the fact that central areas of a city are more defensible militarily than are peripheral areas (although the protection factor is no longer significant, residues of its impact may still be strong). It may also result from the migration patterns discussed earlier.

The second pattern is just the opposite of the first. The poor are concentrated in the central residential areas, while those of high status occupy peripheral areas. This pattern is found to some extent in North American cities, where it has become known as the "concentric zone" pattern (Burgess 1923). It was especially prominent in the nineteenth century, when the central business district (or some other central location) was more likely to contain several large factories employing masses of laborers, when immigrants were constantly entering these cities, and when access to transportation facilities (notably the railroads at that time) was largely restricted to the more well-to-do. While this pattern can still be found, particularly in larger American cities, it is no longer as pronounced as it was in earlier manufacturing settlements, since factories have been dispersed to some extent, and modern transportation facilities are available to most residents. Municipal laws requiring that certain health and safety standards be met in new constructions have also had the effect of reducing the supply of cheap housing for the poor in central areas by raising the cost of construction (Anderson 1962).

The third pattern is called a "sectorial" arrangement: each population subgroup occupies a sector extending from the center to the edge of the settlement in a given direction (U.S. Federal Housing . . . 1939). This pattern is found in some American cities and is also typical of many cities in other countries, where the sectors are often called "quarters." It arises when a population subgroup that is already settled in a distinct location grows by adding new housing to the outer edge of its existing territory. In this way the subgroup's population extends farther and farther outward as it grows.

The final pattern is an "island," or localized pattern in which a subgroup occupies a territory within the settlement that is entirely surrounded by territory occupied by other subgroups. (The term "island" has not yet come into conventional usage to denote this pattern.) It is possible, of course, to visualize an island as an intersection of a sector and a concentric zone. On the other hand, it can also be visualized either as a sector that did not grow or as a sector whose spatial growth was inhibited despite growth in population. Most Negro housing areas in American cities today are of the latter type, as were many ethnic neighborhoods in earlier years. Such ethnic and racial islands are found within most of the world's cities.

Combinations of settlements

Cities tend to arise at points where major breaks in transportation facilities occur, such as at the point of transfer from land to water transportation (Cooley 1894), and at places which are central with respect to an interacting population (Loesch 1940). They also arise at points that possess decisive local advantages for carrying out some activity which requires the assembly of large numbers of people on a permanent basis. In the early nineteenth century, for example, textile manufacturing plants were located along rivers in New England near waterfalls, because these falls provided power that was impossible to transport.

Many manufacturing cities have arisen at points that provide easy access to the combination of materials required in manufacturing. Cities also tend to form and grow at locations which already contain urban populations. In particular, at any given time, the distribution of urban population is affected not only by conditions obtaining at that time but also by the location of population at some earlier time. A city that was originally (i.e., in terms of some past technology) a manufacturing center may grow and prosper, although the original advantage in the manufacturing process has disappeared with changing technology: the very existence of the population there often creates an advantage relative to other areas. The influence of population itself upon growth is represented in a simple form, for example, in the logistic curve of growth.

Within a country, individual cities grow primarily as a result of migration. Cities increase rapidly in size when many people are attracted to them, and they decline in size when many people already in them decide to live elsewhere. Cities also increase in size, though more slowly, as a result of the imbalance between local birth and death rates (see Bogue 1957).

Centralization. The growth and location of individual urban settlements is also a function of the growth and location of other such settlements in the vicinity or even at relatively remote locations. Urban life is highly interdependent, both within and between settlements. This interdependence makes the phenomenon of centralization just as important in understanding how cities are arranged with respect to each other as it is in understanding the spatial arrangements that exist within individual cities. Just as local centralization creates individual settlements, so does large-scale centralization create networks of settlements, or urban regions. Furthermore, the nature of these regions is also influenced by the efficiency of transportation services. There is a crucial difference between the local and the regional scene in this respect, however. Improvements in local transportation have tended to disperse the local population, whereas improvements in regional or long-distance transportation, on the other hand, have tended to concentrate more and more people in a small number of very large urban settlements. Roughly 25 per cent of the population of the United States lived in its ten largest urbanized areas in 1960, for example, in contrast with less than 10 per cent in the ten largest cities in 1860 (in 1860 the "urbanized area" concept did not exist, but most urban settlements were then contained within cities).

The tendency toward large-scale centralization has been augmented by another technological development. A productive activity is a city-building activity only as long as many people are required in the production process and as long as these people must be assembled in the same place to carry out the production. The industrial revolution ushered in a period when very large masses of people were assembled in factories and other industrial plants to carry out the manufacture of material goods, and for many decades the growth and development of these plants provided one of the major stimuli to the development of urban settlements. However, productivity (or goods produced per man hour expended) has increased steadily, especially in the area of manufacture, as man has increasingly learned how to substitute machine power for manpower. The result has been the shift of the main city-building impetus from the manufacture of material goods to the provision of services of one kind or another for human beings. This change is reflected, for example, in the relatively rapid growth of the white-collar segment of the population as compared with the much slower growth of the blue-collar segment throughout the industrial world. The principal spatial impact of this great technological movement has been further to concentrate the bulk of the population in a relatively few metropolitan areas. Manufacturing establishments must be distributed, in part at least, in relation to the location of raw materials, which tend to be scattered over the countryside. Service industries, on the other hand, are usually located where the people already are; hence the growth of these industries contributes strongly to the growth of pre-existing, large metropolitan areas. Thus, both increasing effectiveness of transportation and increasing human productivity, particularly with respect to the manufacture of material goods, contribute to the emergence of a relatively small number of very large urban settlements, each of which is increasingly spread over a larger and larger local territory.

The tendency for combinations of settlements to be centralized has been studied from two other major points of view. On the one hand, researchers have attempted to describe the spatial arrangement of networks of settlements. On the other hand, others have investigated the composition of cities of different sizes, with the joint objectives of classifying cities according to their functions, determining just how they are functionally interrelated, and ascertaining whether or not a "hierarchy" of cities can be established [see CENTRAL PLACE].

Regional networks. With respect to the spatial arrangement of settlements, three main regional networks have been identified: the metropolitan area, the metropolitan region, and what has been called the megalopolitan region (Gottmann 1961). Each form consists of a network of interrelated urban settlements, such that each performs relatively specialized functions with respect to the whole.

The smallest of these regions is the *metropolitan area*. It consists of a large central settlement and a variety of nearby smaller settlements (suburbs and satellites) which, taken together, form a relatively continuous pattern of urban settlements over the land occupied. Typically, several of the settlements in a metropolitan area have rather independent histories, merging into the same complex only as the population of the entire area grows and expands. The metropolitan area may be visualized as a single settlement, or it may be thought of as a compact arrangement of several settlements. It differs from the simple single settlement, however, in having many employment and shopping centers scattered through its territory—a phenomenon known as "multiple nucleation" (Harris & Ullman 1945).

The *metropolitan region* is a larger collection of urban (and rural) settlements, all of which are interrelated through relations with the metropolis that is dominant within the region. Generally speaking, the region is characterized by a series of gradients in various phenomena that are most pronounced in the central metropolis: for example, population density decreases throughout the region as distance from the metropolis increases (Bogue 1949). The tendency for individual settlements to be highly specialized also decreases as this distance increases. Furthermore, certain types of activity, such as wholesaling and banking, tend to be heavily concentrated in the metropolis, which serves as a distribution and accumulation center for the entire region. Increasingly, the metropolis also serves (at least in the United States) as an administrative center containing the headquarters of the major regional corporations and associations.

The *megalopolitan region* is a newer phenomenon that has not been as closely or elaborately studied to date. Indeed, there is even little agreement as to what it should be called, although there is no question that this form has really emerged in highly industrialized sections of the world. In these sections population growth has proceeded so far that many originally separate metropolitan areas have themselves tended to merge, as the outer fringes of one metropolis have interpenetrated the outer fringes of the next. In this way very extensive, relatively continuously urbanized land areas are created which contain not one massive center of population but rather many such centers. One such settlement pattern is found along the eastern coast of the United States, extending roughly from Boston, Massachusetts, to Washington, D.C., and many other similar conurbations are developing throughout the world. Much research remains to be done before the implications of this newest urban regional pattern will be properly understood.

Functional specialization of settlements. Cities in different size categories display substantial differences in their population composition, particularly with respect to their occupational–industrial composition (Duncan & Reiss 1950). There are many activities which are common to all cities, such as mechanisms for distributing food to the residents and for constructing various facilities within the settlement. Activities such as these are primarily local in character, in the sense that the persons who benefit directly from their performance are the residents of the city within which they are performed. Furthermore, since they are performed in essentially all cities, they do not tend to differentiate one city from another. Economists have called such activities *service* activities. On the other hand, there are also many activities which are very common in certain cities and very rare in others. The manufacture of automobiles is concentrated in only four or five American cities, for example. Insurance activities are likewise concentrated in a few cities, as are major book publishers. These activities, which tend to differentiate one city from another, also tend to be primarily regional or national in character, in the sense that the persons who benefit directly from their performance are found throughout a region or nation: that is, the products or services created by these activities are typically "exported" to other settlements (Andrews 1953–1956). While it is very difficult in practice to draw a sharp line between service and export activities, the distinction has proven of considerable value in the comparative study of cities. It underlies essentially all so-called functional classifications of cities. Export or base activities also tend to be crucial in the economic analysis of urban growth. Generally, a city's growth depends on the extent to which it can furnish products and services to outside populations in an efficient manner.

The relationship between the city size and composition is reflected primarily in the nature of the export or base activities characteristic of different sized cities. There are two major factors which appear largely to determine the extent to which an activity is concentrated in a few cities or widely dispersed through many cities. The first is the rate at which the user needs to be supplied with the good or service. Goods and services that are ordinarily supplied on a daily basis, such as newspapers, are produced in many more cities than are those goods and services which are ordinarily supplied on a weekly, monthly, or annual basis. Thus wholesaling, involving less frequent but larger shipments, is more concentrated than is retailing, which involves more frequent and smaller shipments. Insurance can be centralized partly because the insured make only occasional demands upon the companies involved. The second major factor concerns the size of the population required to generate a demand for the good or service that is sufficient to permit its efficient provision. So-called "economies of scale" vary widely from industry to industry, as does the volume of the demand for a product within a population of a given size. Products and services which can be efficiently provided by small organizations are performed in more cities than are those which require very large organizations. Likewise, products for which a great demand exists even in a small population (sidewalks) are produced in more cities than are products for which a relatively small demand exists even in relatively large populations (rockets or helicopters). Very large cities tend to be quite diversified with respect to their base activities. Most large cities serve as regional or national centers for networks of smaller cities, but for some large cities the "regional center" role is less important than are specialized production activities (Otis D. Duncan et al. 1960).

Many social scientists have considered the possibility that a hierarchy of cities (within a region or country) can be established on the basis of considerations such as functional specialization. The concept of hierarchy implies not only differentiation and specialization but also differential *control*. The hypothesis of metropolitan dominance, for example, is that a large city tends to control the distribution of people and facilities in a large region around it, primarily by centralizing these people and facilities so that gradients exist by distance from the center (Bogue 1949). Economists and geographers have long discussed a hierarchy of cities in respect to the accumulation and distribution of goods—a hierarchy that ranges from the farm market town to the metropolitan center. The large-scale centralization of such diverse activities as government, the new communication media, commercial corporations, and labor unions has given rise to the concept of a "mass society" in which control is exercised from a few very large centers (Vidich & Bensman 1958). In general, the hierarchical hypothesis is that it is possible to rank-order cities in such a way that cities of higher rank tend to determine the composition, growth, and character of available products and services in cities of lower rank. This hypothesis is an interesting and important one with major implications extending far beyond the scope of this article. In a general way, current evidence suggests that it is a reasonable hypothesis. However, there have been few analyses of historical trends in urban structure which are germane to the hypothesis, and thus it is very difficult to determine at the present time whether or not the extent to which a larger city exercises control over smaller cities in its region is increasing or decreasing.

THEODORE R. ANDERSON

[Directly related are the entries CENTRAL PLACE; NEIGHBORHOOD; SEGREGATION. Other relevant material may be found in COMMUNITY; ECOLOGY, article on HUMAN ECOLOGY; TRANSPORTATION.]

BIBLIOGRAPHY

For an excellent and detailed bibliography of contributions in the area of comparative urban structure, see Otis D. Duncan et al. 1960.

ANDERSON, THEODORE R. 1962 Social and Economic Factors Affecting the Location of Residential Neighborhoods. Regional Science Association, *Papers and Proceedings* 9:161–170.

ANDREWS, RICHARD B. 1953–1956 Mechanics of the Urban Economic Base. *Land Economics* 29:161–167, 263–268, 343–350; 30:52–60, 164–172, 260–269, 309–319; 31:47–53, 144–155, 245–256, 361–372; 32:69–84.

BOGUE, DONALD J. 1949 The Structure of the Metropolitan Community: A Study of Dominance and Subdominance. Ph.D. dissertation, University of Michigan.

BOGUE, DONALD J. 1957 *Components of Population Change, 1940–1950: Estimates of Net Migration and Natural Increase for Each Standard Metropolitan Area and State Economic Area.* Univ. of Chicago, Population Research and Training Center, and Scripps Foundation for Research in Population Problems.

BURGESS, ERNEST W. (1923) 1925 The Growth of the City: An Introduction to a Research Project. Pages 47–62 in Robert E. Park, Ernest W. Burgess, and Roderick D. McKenzie, *The City.* Univ. of Chicago Press. → First published in American Sociological Society, *Papers,* proceedings of the 1923 annual meeting.

CLARK, COLIN 1951 Urban Population Densities. *Journal of the Royal Statistical Society* Series A 114:490–496.

COOLEY, CHARLES H. (1894) 1930 The Theory of Transportation. Pages 15–118 in Charles H. Cooley, *Sociological Theory and Social Research, Being the Selected Papers of Charles Horton Cooley.* With an introduction and notes by Robert Cooley Angell. New York: Holt.

DICKINSON, ROBERT E. (1951) 1962 *The West European City: A Geographical Interpretation.* 2d ed., rev. London: Routledge.

DUNCAN, BEVERLY et al. 1962 Patterns of City Growth. *American Journal of Sociology* 67:418–429.

DUNCAN, OTIS D. 1957 Population Distribution and Community Structure. Volume 22, pages 357–371 in *Cold Spring Harbor Symposia on Quantitative Biology.* Cold Spring Harbor, N.Y.: Biological Laboratory.

DUNCAN, OTIS D.; and LIEBERSON, STANLEY 1959 Ethnic Segregation and Assimilation. *American Journal of Sociology* 64:364–374.

DUNCAN, OTIS D.; and REISS, ALBERT J. JR. 1956 *Social Characteristics of Urban and Rural Communities, 1950.* New York: Wiley.

DUNCAN, OTIS D. et al. 1960 *Metropolis and Region.* Baltimore: Johns Hopkins Press.

FIREY, WALTER I. 1947 *Land Use in Central Boston.* Cambridge, Mass.: Harvard Univ. Press.

GOTTMANN, JEAN (1961) 1964 *Megalopolis: The Urbanized Northeastern Seaboard of the United States.* Cambridge, Mass.: M.I.T. Press.

HARRIS, CHAUNCY D.; and ULLMAN, EDWARD L. 1945 The Nature of Cities. American Academy of Political and Social Science, *Annals* 242:7–17.

HAWLEY, AMOS H. 1950 *Human Ecology: A Theory of Community Structure.* New York: Ronald.

HAWLEY, AMOS H. 1956 *The Changing Shape of Metropolitan America: Deconcentration Since 1920.* Glencoe, Ill.: Free Press.

HURD, RICHARD M. (1903) 1924 *Principles of City Land Values.* 4th ed. New York: Real Estate Record & Guide.

ISARD, WALTER 1956 *Location and Space-economy: A General Theory Relating to Industrial Location, Market Areas, Trade and Urban Structure.* New York: Wiley; Cambridge, Mass.: M.I.T. Press.

LOESCH, AUGUST (1940) 1954 *The Economics of Location.* New Haven: Yale Univ. Press. → First published as *Die räumliche Ordnung der Wirtschaft.*

MUMFORD, LEWIS 1938 *The Culture of Cities.* New York: Harcourt.

MUMFORD, LEWIS 1961 *The City in History: Its Origins, Its Transformations, and Its Prospects.* New York: Harcourt.

SCHMID, CALVIN et al. 1958 The Ecology of the American City: Further Comparison and Validation of Generalizations. *American Sociological Review* 23:392–401.

SCHNORE, LEO F. 1957 The Growth of Metropolitan Suburbs. *American Sociological Review* 22:165–173.

SEMINAR ON URBANIZATION IN INDIA, BERKELEY, CALIFORNIA, 1960 1962 *India's Urban Future.* Berkeley: Univ. of California Press.

SHEVKY, ESHREF; and BELL, WENDELL 1955 *Social Area Analysis: Theory, Illustrative Application, and Computational Procedures.* Stanford (Calif.) Univ. Press.

SJOBERG, GIDEON 1960 *The Preindustrial City: Past and Present.* Glencoe, Ill.: Free Press.

TAEUBER, KARL E.; and TAEUBER, ALMA F. 1965 *Negroes in Cities: Residential Segregation and Neighborhood Change.* Chicago: Aldine.

THEODORSON, GEORGE A. (editor) 1961 *Studies in Human Ecology.* Evanston, Ill.: Row, Peterson.

U.S. FEDERAL HOUSING ADMINISTRATION 1939 *The Structure and Growth of Residential Neighborhoods in American Cities.* Washington: Government Printing Office.

VIDICH, ARTHUR J.; and BENSMAN, JOSEPH (1958) 1960 *Small Town in Mass Society: Class, Power and Religion in a Rural Community.* Garden City, N.Y.: Doubleday.

WEBER, MAX (1921) 1958 *The City.* Glencoe, Ill.: Free Press. → First published as *Die Stadt.*

CITY PLANNING

See under PLANNING, SOCIAL.

CIVIL DISOBEDIENCE

"Civil disobedience" will here refer to any act or process of public defiance of a law or policy enforced by established governmental authorities, insofar as the action is premeditated, understood by the actor(s) to be illegal or of contested legality, carried out and persisted in for limited public ends and by way of carefully chosen and limited means.

This is a descriptive rather than a formal definition; and it is a recommended definition rather than one that claims to represent current usage with maximal accuracy. One difficulty with this term is that it is rarely defined and never with great precision. Equally regrettable is the absence of systematic literature on the concept and the phenomenon, assuming that the term has a consensual core of meaning.

In this article neither a stringent definition nor a comprehensive survey of doctrines and practices can be attempted. What follows is, first, an attempt to clarify the concept; second, a brief and inevitably sketchy survey of political doctrines of civil disobedience from Socrates to the present time; third, a sketch of some campaigns of civil disobedience, mainly in modern times; and finally, a brief discussion of the prospects for civil disobedience and its justification in the modern world.

The concept

The notion of "disobedience" presupposes the concept of a norm to be disobeyed—typically a legal norm, but in any event a norm which is assumed by *some* people in power to be authoritative in the sense that transgressions would be expected to lead to punishment in one form or another. Disobedience can be active or passive; it can be a matter of doing what is prohibited or of failing to do what is required. But mere noncompliance is not enough; the action or nonaction must be openly insisted on if it is to qualify as civil disobedience, as the concept is interpreted here. For example, failure to vote in a country in which there is a legal obligation to vote does not in itself constitute civil disobedience; one would have to state in public that one did not intend to comply with the particular law; typically but not necessarily, one would publicly encourage others to disobey also.

The act of disobedience must be illegal, or at least be deemed illegal by powerful adversaries, and the actor must know this if it is to be considered an act of civil disobedience (for a contrary view, see Freeman 1966). Note the distinction between "conscientious objection" to military service and "civil disobedience" in countries that permit exemptions from otherwise obligatory service for reasons of conscience. The conscientious objector engages in civil disobedience only if he knowingly and explicitly objects to military service on grounds not recognized by the law or in a country that makes no exceptions for reasons of conscience.

"Civil" is the more ambiguous of the two terms. At least five different meanings would appear plausible, and in this area it would seem reasonable to cast the net wide and consider each of the following meanings equally legitimate:

(1) The term "civil" can imply a recognition of general obligations of citizenship and thus the legitimacy of the existing legal order as a whole; pains taken to limit defiance to a particular legal clause or policy, and/or to avoid violence, may (but need not) be construed as an affirmation of general citizenship duties.

(2) "Civil" can be taken to refer to the opposite of "military" in a broad sense. The customary stress on nonviolence (see below) may be construed to signify either (*a*) a recognition of the state's claim to monopoly with respect to legitimate use of physical violence, or (*b*) a rejection of all physical violence as illegitimate or morally wrong under all circumstances regardless of purpose.

(3) "Civil" can refer to the opposite of "uncivil" or "uncivilized"; acts of civil disobedience may seek to embody ideals of citizenship or morality that will inspire adversaries and/or onlookers, hopefully, toward more civilized behavior, or behavior more in harmony with the ideals that inspire a given campaign of civil disobedience. Most conceptions of civility and "more civilized behavior" stress a consistent respect for other people's—including one's adversaries—physical inviolability as a crucial attribute. Also, there may be an implied recognition of the probability that acts of violence, unless the civil disobedience activists are the sole victims, might divert attention from the intended message.

(4) "Civil" can also be taken to refer to public as distinct from private: as citizens we act in public. Acts of civil disobedience seek not only to affirm a principle in private but also to call public attention to the view that a principle of moral importance is being violated by a law or a policy sanctioned by public authorities. Acts of civil disobedience may be considered acts of public witness to the prior rights of conscience or of God. Defiance in private is not enough; at the very least, an act of civil disobedience must be communicated to representatives of the public order in an attempt to influence their thoughts and feelings on the general issues raised. An act of disobedience carried out with the intention of subsequently begging for mercy or for special consideration is outside the realm of civil disobedience; so is, of course, every act that attempts a surreptitious violation or evasion of the law.

(5) "Civil" can suggest that the objective of obedience is to institute changes in the political system, affecting not only one individual's or group's liberties but the liberties of all citizens. A religious sect persisting in outlawed practices of worship may insist only on being left alone or may at the same time consciously assert a principle to the effect that other sects, too, should enjoy equivalent rights. Degrees of consciousness about the wider implications of disobedient behavior are not well suited as conceptual demarcation lines, however, and it would seem most practical to include even very parochially motivated acts of disobedience within the scope of the concept of civil disobedience.

The ambiguities of the term "civil" are far from exhausted by this brief list, but the five meanings presented are probably among the more common. The chances are that most of those who practice civil disobedience think of their behavior as "civil" in a sense, whether articulated or not, which embraces more than one of these associations and perhaps others as well.

Returning now to the definition, let us note, first, that when there is a conflict of laws, acts of civil disobedience may be legal and illegal at the same time. Thus, campaigns were conducted against state segregation laws in the American South, in the belief that under the federal constitution such acts of disobedience will *eventually* be deemed legal in the federal courts.

The ends of civil disobedience must be public and limited. The ostensible aim cannot be a private or business advantage; it must have *some* reference to a conception of justice or the common good. (Individual motives for engaging in civil disobedi-

ence may, of course, be neurotic or narrowly self-seeking.) The proclaimed ends must also be limited, falling short of seeking the complete abolition of the existing legal system. Those who want a "nonviolent revolution" may engage in civil disobedience, but they too proclaim specific, limited ends each time. Also, according to the usage recommended here, the proclaimed aims must fall short of intending the physical or moral destruction of adversaries, even if at times a calculable risk of casualties may be tolerated. The ends of civil disobedience must be potentially acceptable to those in the *role* of adversaries even if the current adversaries are anathema to each other.

Above all, the proclaimed ends of civil disobedience, as the concept is understood here, must be formulated with a view to making them appear morally legitimate to onlookers and to the public. Educational objectives prompt most civil disobedience campaigns and are never wholly absent. If a trade union violates the law to gain equality or justice for its members, we may speak of civil disobedience, but not if a key position in the economic system tempts a union to violate the law for the purpose of extorting unreasonable privileges in return for obeying the law.

"Civil disobedience" should be kept apart from "nonviolent action." The latter concept by definition rules out violent acts while the former, as defined here, does not. (An opposite view is adopted by Bedau 1961; Cohen 1964; Freeman 1966.) For a variety of historical and psychological reasons, it appears that many believers in civil disobedience see themselves as wholly committed to nonviolent means, even in self-defense or in the defense of others against murderous assault.

Among some pacifist believers in civil disobedience it seems to be assumed that a complete commitment to nonviolence, even in the sense of avoiding the provocation of violence on the part of adversaries, is ethically superior to a more pragmatic attitude toward the possible use of violence. No such assumption is made here. "Carefully chosen and limited means" in the definition at the outset refers to choice of means rationally calculated to promote the limited ends. For many reasons it seems plausible that such rational calculation normally will suggest strenuous efforts toward either avoidance or reduction of violence. Civil disobedience activists and social scientists should be equally interested in research on the causation and consequences of violence and nonviolence under conditions of social conflict. The expansion of this type of knowledge is of crucial importance for calculating the most effective and economical means to achieve the chosen ends of civil disobedience campaigns and for evaluating the likelihood of the success or failure of such campaigns.

Political doctrines of civil disobedience

The term "civil disobedience" was given currency by Thoreau's famous essay (1849); the concept, however, is a composite of many developments in the history of human thought and action. The justification of civil disobedience has been attempted from a variety of philosophical premises.

Individual freedom.   To the modern political theorist it may seem that a prior problem is to justify obedience—a problem which in turn raises tangled issues on the nature of political authority, the state, sovereignty, the law, human rights, and so on. Yet in the history of political thought the notion of individuals having the freedom to *choose* whether to obey the state or not is a fairly recent phenomenon. Even today this idea is accessible to relatively few and acceptable to fewer still.

Socrates.   It is arguable whether Socrates was ever willing to concede that his teaching might have violated the laws of Athens; but it is certain that he would have felt compelled to continue his teaching had the court set him free, even in the event that it would have found him guilty.

Socrates may well be credited with having formulated the core of the modern argument for civil disobedience. In brief, he held that the only life worth living is the upright life, or the life committed to the search for truth and to obedience to the dictates of truth discovered. Justice was to him a matter of knowledge and therefore an aspect of truth. At the same time he acknowledged and honored his duty to obey the state, because he believed that a civilized order and therefore civilized persons can develop only in a well-ordered society, and he considered the Greek type of city-state the best kind of social order achieved so far. Yet the state, even the state of Athens, was capable of committing grievous injustice to the individual. Must the citizen obey unjust as well as just laws? Where should the line be drawn between the claims of the state and the claims of philosophy, of justice, of God, or of conscience?

In effect, Socrates drew the following limit on the state's claim to obedience: the citizen, bound by his implicit agreement to honor and respect the political order under which he was nurtured, and his parents before him, must be prepared to lay down his life if called on to serve his state, and he must submit to any punishment meted out to him, whether justly or unjustly. There is one realm, however, in which the claims of the state are void: the realm of conscience. The state cannot force Socrates to act unjustly; he is prepared to suffer evil but not to do evil. He respects the authority of the state to the extent of willingly giving up his life but not to the extent of being willing to act unjustly or to desist from acting justly—for example, by way of speaking out on public issues as his conscience dictates.

Early Christianity.   The early Christians represented the first spectacular—and highly successful—civil disobedience *movement* in the West. Their fundamental justification was that God must be obeyed before man. Religious and moral obedience required civil disobedience. On the whole, the movement was nonviolent at first, not only because any other course would have been foolish but also because Christ himself had urged his followers to turn the other cheek and to shun violence (see the following: Matthew 5.9, 20–22, 38–48, and 26. 50–52).

Countless individuals in the course of history have chosen to shed their blood rather than compromise in matters of faith or conviction. It is arguable, however, how many among them should be considered spokesmen for civil disobedience. Their acts of defiance may in many cases have been instinctual, even visceral, rather than premeditated; their goals may at times have been unlimited—say, the salvation of mankind, and their means may have not always been *chosen*, but at times they may have been the only ones subjectively and objectively available. Members of religious sects ready to die for their beliefs and to shun armed resistance under one set of circumstances may under new circumstances be ready to subjugate others with violence, as was seen in the early history of the New England colonies. Not every brave and for the time being nonviolent true believer is practicing civil disobedience when defying the law or the government; one would at the least require of him a reasoned determination not to repay injustice suffered with new injustice inflicted once victory has been won.

Thus understood, it is clear that the doctrine of civil disobedience as an instrument of sociopolitical change is a highly sophisticated one, for it requires a perspective that subordinates the dictates of one's specific cause to the prior requirements of certain general rules for civilized political conduct. Most true-believer movements are suspect on this score, unless their objectives are limited and conciliatory or unless they are resigned to remain a minority indefinitely.

The empiricists.   In one important sense it may be said that the modern concept of civil disobedience germinated with Thomas Hobbes, the first philosopher to espouse a doctrine of fundamental natural right as a basis for obedience to government. He distinguished right from law and asserted that laws should safeguard rights. He lived in a stormy age and was pessimistic about the prospects for civil peace, which he saw as the first prerequisite for the enjoyment of rights: without civil peace, lives will be "nasty, brutish and short." And Hobbes believed that only an all-powerful state could ensure civil peace. While Hobbes justified government as a means of preserving human lives "and a more contented life thereby" (1651, chapter 17), he emphatically rejected the right to dissent and, more so, the right to disobey (chapter 29). His explicit rejection of this right actually helped prepare the ground for its vindication [see HOBBES].

John Locke also saw government as a means for preserving human lives as well as liberties and properties. But Locke's idea of the social contract differed radically from the *carte blanche* Hobbes grants the sovereign: "Whenever the legislators endeavor to take away and destroy the property of the people, or to reduce them to slavery under arbitrary power, they put themselves into a state of war with the people who are thereupon absolved of any further obedience"; the people "have a right to resume their original liberty and to establish a new government" (1690, section 222). If revolution was justified against grave abuse of governmental power, then nonviolent as well as violent civil disobedience must be justified, although Locke never was clear on what criteria to use for judging the propriety of resistance. However, he did seek to rebut the expected argument that his doctrine would lay "a ferment for frequent rebellion": an open acknowledgment of the power of the (propertied) people to rebel against tyranny, since it will discourage the abuse of governmental power, is, he insisted, "the best fence against rebellion, and the probablest means to hinder it" [*ibid.*, section 226; *see also* LOCKE].

David Hume effectively demolished Locke's social contract theory, and his thought paved the way for an empirical utilitarian approach to determining the limits on political obligation and the right to resist. Hume himself adopted a libertarian position in the *Treatise*, and with considerable vehemence. But later, in his *Essays*, he came to fear anarchy much more than tyranny and advocated respect for and "exact obedience" to the authority of magistrates [1739–1742; *see also* HUME].

Jeremy Bentham, with his characteristic logic and style, argued that the conscientious citizen ought to enter into measures of resistance as a matter of duty as well as interest when, according to the best calculation he is able to make, the probable mischiefs of resistance—speaking with respect to the community in general—appear less to him than the probable mischiefs of submission [1776, chapter IV, sections 21–22; *see also* BENTHAM].

A paradoxical and rather unusual position on civil disobedience was taken by James Mill in his essay *Liberty of the Press*, in which he accepted Locke's argument that the right to argue for the overthrow of the government is a needed safeguard against abuse of governmental power. He held, as a believer in law and order, that it should be an offense to advocate the obstruction of any particular law or governmental operation but not to advocate resistance to all the powers of government at once. In effect he supported the right to advocate violent revolution while opposing the right to advocate limited civil disobedience.

Empiricists like Hobbes, Locke, Hume, Bentham, and Mill had in common a "negative" conception of individual freedom: they took "freedom" to refer to the relative absence of restraints, including (especially in Locke's case, when he defined "freedom" as "a standing rule to live by") the restraints imposed by unpredictability in social circumstances. While their views on the propriety of disobedience differed widely, their shared stress on freedom *from* unjustifiable coercion helped prepare the ground for modern theories of resistance to improper use of governmental authority.

The idealists.   On the whole, the mainstream of the idealist tradition in philosophy, from Aristotle to Rousseau and the Hegelians, as well as the Marxist offshoot, has been considerably less hospitable to the idea of civil disobedience. True, Aristotle was the father of the natural-law tradition, but in other respects all these philosophers have emphasized the importance of the state or the social class (or political party) over that of the individual; they have all stressed a "positive" concept of freedom, which allowed for meaningful individual lives only in terms of unconditional loyalty to a collectivity. "Freedom" to idealists and Marxists has meant "self-realization," and it has been assumed that only a recognition of common bonds could constitute the basis for a viable self. Rousseau talked of the need to "force men to be free," for freedom to him meant harmony between individual and public ("general") will. The Marxists speak of freedom as the recognition of (and acceptance of) necessity, meaning whatever the Marxist philosopher-kings hold to be necessities by virtue of a correct ("scientific") political diagnosis and prognosis.

Most idealists have insisted on obedience to the state, while most Marxists have urged a rival obedience; both persuasions have tended to discount the role of the individual conscience as a primary source of standards of political judgment. Marxists stress the need for discipline and believe in the necessity of a temporary dictatorship of the proletariat or of the party (Leninists). Among socialists, only anarchists have urged disobedience to the state and to every other authority, while syndicalists have urged obedience to democratic trade union leaderships only. Anarchists in the idealist (Tolstoi) or socialist (Bakunin, Kropotkin) traditions have been unique in their combination of a total rejection of every state with a positive concept of freedom as the realization of man's social self.

Natural law. The idea of natural law is the second principal basis, historically speaking, for the modern idea of civil disobedience. It would seem a short step from Aristotle's premise that "an unjust law is not a law" to the conclusion that an unjust law may be or even must be disobeyed. But it is remarkable how seldom this conclusion has been drawn by leading spokesmen for the natural-law tradition and how cautiously the issue has been approached even by those who chose not to ignore it.

Take Cicero, perhaps antiquity's most illustrious spokesman for natural law as "a true law—namely right reason—which is in accordance with nature, applies to all men, and is unchangeable and eternal" (*Republic*, III). "Neither the senate nor the people can absolve us from our obligation to obey this law" he says in the same context. Does this not mean that positive law in conflict with natural law ought to be disobeyed? It would seem to follow, but Cicero fails to develop a theory of civil disobedience.

Thomas Aquinas. St. Thomas Aquinas argues that unjust laws "are acts of violence rather than laws" and that "such laws do not bind in conscience." Yet he continues this last sentence as follows: ". . . except perhaps in order to avoid scandal or disturbance, for which a man should even yield his right." Only law contrary to *divine* law, like laws that would induce idolatry, must not be observed, according to Aquinas (*Summa theologica*), who clearly was far more fearful of anarchy than of tyranny. Disobedience to the church was rendered virtually unthinkable, while disobedience to the state was deemed proper only in extreme situations. The most memorable example of such a situation occurred almost three centuries later, when St. Thomas More died as a martyr to his Roman faith in 1535, having refused to countenance either the divorce and remarriage of King Henry VIII or his claim to supreme authority over England's clergy in defiance of the pope; More reportedly died with these words on his lips: "The King's good servant, but God's first." [*See* AQUINAS.]

The Roman Catholic church. Until recently, modern Neo-Thomists have tended to display the same caution as Aquinas on the issue of disobedience. Even in the event of a state power supposed to be "tyrannical and deprived of genuine authority" it is "a moral duty to give external submission . . . as long as one has not practically ascertained whether insurrection would not result in a greater evil for the community" (Maritain [1938] 1940, p. 105). This is a difficult task for most individuals, it would seem, unless advised and supported by the church.

After World War II the church was subjected to criticism for not having done enough to encourage its faithful to disobey or resist some aspects of Hitler's tyranny; Rolf Hochhuth, in his play *The Deputy* (1963), criticized Pope Pius XII himself for not having adopted and advocated a bolder stand against the genocide of Europe's Jews.

In recent years much soul-searching has gone on within the church, and it is likely that Pope John XXIII's bold stand on civil disobedience will become increasingly influential inside as well as outside the Roman Catholic church. "For to safeguard the inviolable rights of the human person and to facilitate the fulfillment of his duties, should be the essential office of every public authority. This means that, *if any government does not acknowledge the rights of man or violates them*, it not only fails in its duty, but *its orders completely lack juridical force*" (italics deleted, new italics supplied; see Catholic Church . . . 1963, pp. 60–61). This encyclical letter clearly states that laws which grievously violate the rights of man are not only immoral but are without the force of law: while one may risk actual punishment for acts of civil disobedience on behalf of human rights which have been violated, this punishment will be just as illegal, in terms of natural law, as the positive law or government orders which have been disobeyed. No longer is the right to disobey limited in scope to violations of divine laws. With Pope John the natural-law tradition has been moved toward actual union with the empiricist tradition of individual rights in defense of civil disobedience as a proper remedy against tyranny—i.e., against severe violations of human rights.

At least two additional sources of the modern doctrines of civil disobedience must be briefly noted. One is associated with rejection of the state—either the unjust state or every state; the other is associated with a commitment to nonviolence—either an aspiration to a completely nonviolent life or a more pragmatic dedication to nonviolence as a technique in the struggle for a just cause.

Rejection of the state. Henry David Thoreau, in his influential essay *Civil Disobedience* (1849), rejected the unjust state and by implication perhaps every state, calling for "not at once no government, but *at once* a better government." His own act of civil disobedience was inconsequential, but his ringing words have helped inspire thousands of others to go to jail cheerfully for many a just cause: "I cannot for an instant recognize that political organization as *my* government which is the slave's government also. . . . The only obligation which I have a right to assume, is to do at any time what I think right. . . . Under a government which imprisons any unjustly, the true place for a just man is also a prison" (1849).

Thoreau's rejection of the state's claim to moral authority belonged to the tradition of Tom Paine. William Godwin, whose *Political Justice*, first published in 1793, enjoyed a meteoric fame in England for several years and then was forgotten by the general public, was far more radical in rejecting every state and in expecting the millennium to result from an end to states. Subsequent generations of anarchists have preached disobedience to the state as a duty, but their objective was a total overthrow of the system rather than the limited aims that we associate with civil disobedience. And the means used were frequently uncivil; in fact, a number of terrorist acts in the name of anarchism, almost all of them prior to World War I, have made most people associate "anarchism" with bomb throwing [*see* ANARCHISM].

Commitment to nonviolence. There was at least one gentle anarchist who believed in Christ and in nonviolence, however, and that was Leo Tolstoi. A progressively deeper and more radical religious conversion, evident from around the age of fifty, made him sympathetic to anarchism; he admired Kropotkin but took exception to his belief in violence as a necessity in the struggle to eliminate the state. Because he was passionately opposed to every deliberate use of violence Tolstoi did not call himself an anarchist; however, he hated institutionalized violence just as much. If it is too much to ask of a rich man that he give his goods to the poor, or of the soldier to disobey orders and withdraw from the armed forces, Tolstoi does urge each person at least to recognize his guilt in his own conscience and to stop lying about it to himself and others (Tolstoi 1888).

Unlike Thoreau and Tolstoi, Mohandas K. Gandhi was a born organizer of men, and his India was ready for a mass movement that would defy the English masters. Gandhi was as profoundly religious and insistent on spiritual purity as was Tolstoi, by whom he was deeply influenced, and he considered himself a spiritual teacher first and a political leader second. What was unique in Gandhi was the combination of his uncompromising commitment to *ahimsa*, or nonviolence ("The principle of *ahimsa* is hurt by every evil thought, by undue haste, by lying, by hatred, by wishing ill to anybody"; cf. Gandhi [1951] 1961, pp. 41–42), and his firm commitment to political action and his shrewd tactical ability. Arne Naess aptly stresses Gandhi's "constructive imagination and uncommon ingenuity in finding and applying morally acceptable forms of political action" (Naess 1965, p. 6). [*See* INDIAN POLITICAL THOUGHT.]

Gandhi's techniques have been called "moral jiujitsu" (Gregg 1934). Gandhi himself speaks of *passive resistance* as "an all-sided sword . . . it blesses him who uses it and him against whom it is used. Without draining a drop of blood it produces far-reaching results. . . . Given a just cause, capacity for endless suffering and avoidance of violence, victory is a certainty" ([1951] 1961, pp. 52, 56).

Later on Gandhi abandoned the term "passive resistance" and chose the term *Satyagraha*, or "truth-force," with which to characterize his campaigns, because he had come to feel that the former term did not exclude feelings of hatred or violent means, which would render resistance less effective.

Satyagraha largely appears to the public as Civil Disobedience or Civil Resistance. It is civil in the sense that it is not criminal. The lawbreaker . . . openly and civilly breaks [unjust laws] and quietly suffers the penalty for their breach. And in order to register his protest against the action of the law givers, it is open to him to withdraw his co-operation from the State by disobeying such other laws whose breach does not constitute moral turpitude. In my opinion, the beauty and efficacy of Satyagraha are so great and the doctrine so simple that it can be preached even to children. ([1951] 1961, pp. 6–7)

Alienation—Albert Camus. The theme of alienation, drawn from modern existentialist philosophy, is also important to current theories of civil disobedience. Yet the major direct contributor to this area, Albert Camus, agrees with Jean-Paul Sartre and the secular existentialists only up to a point: there is no valid basis for any moral or political authority's claim to validity (or legitimacy) or to obedience. However, Camus believes in an essential human nature—he has been called an "essentialist"—and in a life committed to the goal of becoming more humane and thereby more fully human, more fully alive as a whole person. Camus sees every power elite and every government as a probable enemy of justice; as he asserted in his Nobel Prize address, the highest callings for a writer, and by implication for every man, are "refusal to lie about what we know and resistance to oppression."

Camus's ideal is the rebel—the man who feels revolted by oppression anywhere and who throughout his life makes common cause not with the makers of history but with their victims (see Camus 1951). For Camus, physical violence is the supreme evil, but he does not rule out its use entirely; violence must be used only to reduce or forestall far more or far worse violence in the immediate future, as a last, desperate resort, if no nonviolent means are available. To be a strict pacifist is in his view to condone the violence in the existing system; this amounts to a position of "bourgeois nihilism." Camus's may be called a position of permanent rebellion, or permanent civil disobedience: there will always be violence and oppression in this world, and the full-grown man must always be in revolt against men and laws and conditions that perpetuate oppression; but he must also be against men who, after a successful revolution, institute new patterns of oppression and violence. Camus does not say that this revolt must always take unlawful forms; that is a question to be settled empirically in terms of anticipated results of alternate tactics. What is crucial in Camus's thought is that respect for the dictates of justice must precede respect for the law.

Civil disobedience campaigns

One-man campaigns of disobedience like Thoreau's, Socrates', or the disobedience of early Christian and other religious martyrs, whether saints or heretics, will not be discussed here. Similarly, the illegal strikes conducted by labor unions will be ignored. Most illegal (as well as legal) strikes have aimed at improving labor contracts, not at changing laws or public policies. Some, including attempted general strikes, have had the aim of revolutionary changes, sufficiently sweeping to take us beyond the scope of civil disobedience as the term has been defined here. Others, however, have had more limited aims and should properly be considered campaigns of civil disobedience, especially since they have sometimes been organized in conjunction with other types of civil disobedience campaigns. Yet for reasons of space the subject of labor strikes must be left out in the present account. This leaves us with the main subject, Gandhi's *Satyagraha* campaigns, and with later campaigns which have been more or less influenced by Gandhi's teachings.

Gandhi. Among all the theorists of civil disobedience discussed above, only one name stands out in the history of mass civil disobedience *campaigns*—Mohandas K. Gandhi. He may be charged with being chiefly responsible for the confusion of civil disobedience with nonviolence in many people's minds; yet it may well be that it was Gandhi's insistence on nonviolence that has made mass organizing for disobedience possible, since most governments deal severely with violence-prone disobedience. Not the least of Gandhi's feats was the superior morale he established among his followers, who felt equally righteous about their means and ends.

The first real mass movement of civil disobedience, led by Gandhi, who had by then become known as the leading spokesman for Indian grievances in South Africa, was the November 1913 march to Transvaal to protest discriminatory laws, including a yearly tax on all Indians who chose to stay in South Africa after the end of the labor contracts that brought them there and an outrageous law that invalidated all non-Christian marriages. Mass arrests and police violence against nonresisting marchers created much opposition and protest in Britain as well as in India. Eventually, Prime Minister Jan Smuts consented to negotiations, which led to an almost complete victory for Gandhi, in the sense that nearly all the specific demands of the Indians were met. Gandhi had gone out of his way not to embarrass the government needlessly and had actually called off one projected mass march when Smuts was in deep difficulties with a railroad strike. In the end, "Gandhi had not won a victory over Smuts, he had won Smuts over" (Fischer 1954, p. 48).

Gandhi returned to India and after a year's study and meditation became involved in a number of successive campaigns of civil disobedience, including his 1918 campaign for Ahmadabad's textile workers, during which he for the first time put his life at stake by way of fasting. After four days of fasting his demands were met.

Gandhi was by no means anti-British, and he used his influence to hold back Indian demands for independence during World War I. But tensions rose after the war. At the same time, Gandhi's influence rose in the Indian National Congress, which in 1920 voted overwhelmingly to endorse Gandhi's program of nonviolent civil disobedience against obnoxious laws. He was given wide powers to pick the times and places for such campaigns. However, Gandhi felt strongly that education to nonviolence was an absolute necessity, and he decided in 1922, grieving over incidents of bloody mob violence in Uttar Pradesh, to call off the intended campaign of disobedience that millions had eagerly anticipated. He felt the Indian masses were not yet disciplined enough to shun violence when provoked. Nevertheless, Gandhi was sent to jail with a six-year sentence, found guilty of subversive writings; he served just under two years. The years following his release in 1924 were relatively quiet, while he prepared himself and his followers for large-scale nonviolent action against British rule.

The largest civil disobedience campaign was inaugurated on January 26, 1930, when the Indian National Congress unilaterally proclaimed India's independence from Britain and announced a program of peaceful struggles to induce the British to yield and eventually recognize Indian independence. The first law to be broken was the law that made it illegal to take salt from the ocean or from any source other than the British salt monopoly. On March 2, 1930, Gandhi sent a remarkable letter to inform the viceroy of the impending acts of civil disobedience, together with a last plea for negotiations. Ten days later the 26-day march of Gandhi and his followers began from his residence near Ahmadabad; the solemn and yet festive procession kept growing, and not only India's press, but the world's major newspapers followed the unfolding drama closely. At 6:30 on Sunday morning, April 6, about 4,000 followers watched breathlessly as Gandhi, after a brief swim, according to the London *Times*, "stooped down, scooped up a handful of sand and salt water, and returned to his bungalow with a broad smile on his face." This was the prepublicized launching signal for the all-Indian *Satyagraha* campaign for repeal of the salt laws and also, in Gandhi's words, "the repeal of the British bondage of which the salt tax is but an off-shoot" (Sharp 1960, pp. 89, 72).

Heartened by the nonviolent discipline achieved, Gandhi announced more radical acts of civil disobedience: salt would be taken from the government's salt depots. He was promptly jailed, on May 5. But on May 21, led by the poet Mes Sarojini Naidu and Gandhi's son Manilal, a dramatic "attack" on the Dharasana saltworks in Gujerat was launched. Wave after wave of peaceful "attackers" were clubbed down as they approached the depot by four hundred Indian policemen commanded by six British officers. These acts of government violence against nonviolent individuals were resented all over India and in Britain as well, and they soon led to somewhat more cautious and conciliatory British policies. In January 1931, Gandhi and most

other Congress leaders were set free, and in August Gandhi left for London for further negotiations, as sole representative of the Congress party.

The negotiations were fruitless, and soon Britain again had a Conservative government, which decided to get tough and declare the Indian National Congress illegal as well as institute numerous draconic penalties for even relatively trivial acts of disobedience. Gandhi, from his jail cell, chose to avoid another direct confrontation, and his next fast, in September 1934, pleaded the cause of India's Untouchables; he succeeded in securing for them access to the temples, first in Delhi and Calcutta, as well as fair political representation in the Indian parliament. This fast was primarily aimed at changing the attitudes and behavior of the Indian people, not the policies of the British government.

Gandhi's spiritual influence throughout India has remained undiminished; his sainthood was well established in his lifetime and accentuated by his tragic assassination by a young Hindu fanatic in 1948. But his political influence as a leader of Congress politics never again quite equalled his position just before 1931, when he went to London for his party and nation and returned almost empty-handed. His influence in the 1930s and 1940s no doubt saved tens of thousands of lives, for he kept preaching conciliation with the British and peaceful coexistence among the Hindu castes and between Hindus and Muslims. His influence did not suffice, however, to prevent the partition of India or the communal slaughter on both sides of the border after partition.

Gandhi's ideas as well as his example have kept spurring and also restraining civil disobedience movements outside India, although none of them has been on quite the same scale as the Indian campaigns of 1930–1931. A variety of causes have stimulated civil disobedience movements in many different countries, and no chronicle of even the major post-Gandhi events can be attempted. Some of the wide range of issues, conflicts, and geographic locations for civil disobedience campaigns of recent years will be indicated, followed by a brief account of civil disobedience campaigns in the United States, especially those for racial equality.

The range of modern campaigns. Outside India and the United States, South Africa has experienced the most widely organized and reported civil disobedience campaigns. Gandhi's influence has remained strong among the disenfranchised South African Indians and has become felt also in the African and Coloured population. The first major campaign which involved all three groups was, in

1952, aimed at the Apartheid policies of Malan; it must be rated unsuccessful, since it failed to reverse the trend toward increasingly oppressive discriminatory legislation. On the other hand, a beginning toward interracial solidarity among nonwhites was made, and there were gains in experience and in self-esteem within the oppressed majority.

In 1957 there was the spectacular and largely successful Johannesburg bus boycott, a spontaneous protest against higher fares. It was followed in the ensuing years by less successful campaigns against the passbook laws, which restrict the movement of Africans in particular. The last legally elected leader of the now outlawed African National Congress, Chief Albert J. Luthuli, has remained in confinement ever since his arrest in March 1960, after the Sharpville massacre, when the police had fired at a crowd of African antipassbook law demonstrators. Chief Luthuli was granted permission, however, to travel to Norway in November of the same year to receive the Nobel Peace Prize (Luthuli 1962; Kuper 1956).

Prospects for continued civil disobedience and especially for Gandhian nonviolence in South Africa in years to come are uncertain. Newly independent African states have openly campaigned for armed liberation of their South African cousins, and the conflict over white-ruled Rhodesia's declaration of independence may escalate demands for violence among Africans inside and outside South Africa and Rhodesia.

Another nonwhite population that has experimented with civil disobedience, and with some success, is the Buddhist population in South Vietnam's major cities. Led by Buddhist priests and inspired by ancient doctrines of nonviolence which had influenced Gandhi as well, their campaigns are waged in order to bring down or modify the policies of a succession of regimes imposed on the South Vietnamese by the United States. However, the Buddhists' actions have been only one element in a complex succession of events in which military and political violence has predominated and in which the dubious legitimacy of succeeding Saigon regimes makes it questionable whether the term "civil disobedience" is appropriate; what has been demonstrated in South Vietnam is that nonviolent resistance, with careful planning, can be a powerful force even when surrounded on all sides by military and police violence.

There are many reports of heroic nonviolent resistance against the German occupation in Denmark and Norway during World War II (Gregg 1934, pp. 28–35; Sibley 1963, pp. 156–186). It should be remembered, however, that the Nazis tended to treat their Nordic cousins with restraint, comparatively speaking, for the same racist reasons that made them decimate Slavs and exterminate millions of Jews; it should also be remembered that Danes and Norwegians accomplished a fair amount of violent resistance, too, and that the part played by nonviolent civil disobedience in defeating the Hitler regime must be rated as very minor. The Danish king's symbolic resistance to all measures against Danish Jews did not succeed in preventing their arrest but may well have been a crucial factor in saving their lives.

Resistance against poverty and other kinds of traditional oppression has been the domain of the labor movements, whose main weapon has been the strike, whenever satisfaction could not be won by way of collective bargaining or voting. Yet civil disobedience campaigns in our sense have occurred in this area, too. Best known, perhaps, are Danilo Dolci's "strikes in reverse" in Sicily. In the mid-1950s Dolci organized unemployed Sicilians to go to work, illegally, on improving public roads. The short-run objective was to shame the authorities into paying for the work done; instead, Dolci and some of his co-workers were arrested for trespassing. But the long-run objective of dramatizing the need for employment and the government's responsibility in this area was successfully achieved, in the sense that later Italian governments have been working more actively to combat unemployment.

The major type of civil disobedience campaign in western Europe in the last few decades has been that which urges resistance to armaments, above all to the nuclear arms race, and resistance to specific Western foreign policies deemed aggressive or threatening to world peace. While there have been sizable demonstrations in protest against the nuclear arms race and associated foreign policies, involving pacifists and nonpacifists alike, acts of civil disobedience have usually been resorted to by relatively few individuals each time. For example, some have walked into restricted military areas, having first notified the authorities about their plans. Increasingly, however, there has been a tendency in recent years for many demonstrators, especially if they feel provoked by the police, to sit down and block civilian as well as military traffic and then "go limp" when arrested.

In eastern Europe the 1956 nonviolent disorders in Poznan, Poland and the subsequent demonstrations against Polish laws and government policies may be credited with having effected without bloodshed the change of regime that led to much higher levels of political freedom in Poland; this result was not an example of Gandhi's principles at work, of course, but of a politically shrewd disobedience movement that challenged a weak government while scrupulously trying to avoid a confrontation with its ally, the Soviet Union.

Finally, in the Soviet Union, an example of successful use of civil disobedience, albeit under very special circumstances, was the largely nonviolent uprising in the Vorkuta prison camp in the summer of 1953, shortly after the death of Stalin (see Scholmer 1954).

American campaigns.   In the United States the chief instrument of Gandhi's influence in social action concerning race relations has been the Reverend Dr. Martin Luther King, Jr., who writes: "I had come to see early that the Christian doctrine of love operating through the Gandhian method of nonviolence was one of the most potent weapons available to the Negro in his struggle for freedom" (1958, p. 66). King was only 26 when he was thrust into a position of national prominence in 1955, in the midst of a civil disobedience campaign in Montgomery, Alabama. The campaign had been triggered by a seamstress, Mrs. Rosa Parks, who apparently on the spur of the moment had refused to move to the back of a bus and was arrested. To consolidate the spontaneous Negro boycott of Montgomery buses that followed, the Montgomery Improvement Association was formed, with King as president. The following year a hundred clergymen from the South formed the Southern Christian Leadership Conference (SCLC), of which King became the undisputed leader, following the clear victory that had been achieved under his leadership in the Montgomery bus boycott. And the SCLC has remained in the spotlight, under King's leadership, with numerous newsmaking marches and other acts, often involving disobedience, against Southern racist laws and enforcement policies. King's most momentous confrontation with Southern police power was in Birmingham, Alabama in 1963, where the principal Negro demands were desegregation in public accommodations, equal opportunity in jobs, and an interracial grievance machinery. Police brutality sparked unprecedentedly large and angry demonstrations, countered by segregationist bombs as well as electric cattle prods and police dogs; but in the end white business leaders took over effective power in the white community, forced the extremist mayor and police chief to yield, and accommodated most of the Negro demands.

The sit-in movement.   The most effective civil disobedience technique in the South has been the sit-in; we may well speak of the sit-in movement. This technique was developed under the auspices of the Congress of Racial Equality (CORE), founded with the help of the pacifist Fellowship of Reconciliation in 1942 and headed for 24 years by another disciple of Gandhi, James Farmer. Negro and white members of CORE during the 1940s successfully desegregated without much fanfare many restaurants in the Baltimore–Washington, D.C. area by the simple expedient of occupying tables and waiting for service until they either got it, were arrested, or could enter into negotiations with the managers.

However, it was in 1960 that a new generation suddenly took over the sit-in technique, greatly expanded it, and spread it all over the South. The trigger event was the decision of four Greensboro, North Carolina, Negro students to bring their books to a segregated Woolworth lunch counter and simply stay there and study when they were refused service. Within a year and a half, 70,000 persons had taken similar action, and over 100 Southern communities had desegregated one or more of their eating places (Quarles 1964, p. 253). A new organization of students was formed, the Student Nonviolent Coordinating Committee (SNCC), which was led by no single individual and in fact developed a kind of antiauthoritarian style and insisted on local leadership of local campaigns (Zinn 1964).

The Free Speech Movement.   Some of the SNCC momentum and style has carried over to other student protest movements and has led to new experiments in civil disobedience applied to issues of student rights and of peace. Mario Savio of SNCC became the undisputed leader of the explosive Free Speech Movement (FSM) on the Berkeley campus of the University of California during the academic year 1964/1965, which directly challenged the legitimacy of nonacademic, nondemocratic university governments and incidentally won the support of the academic senate and eventually saw its major grievances vindicated and remedied and the Berkeley chancellor replaced. At the same time, over eight hundred students were convicted for having participated in the crucial act of civil disobedience responsible for the FSM victory—an illegal sit-in in the campus administration building. The Berkeley experience with the FSM has visibly moderated the tone of many other university administrations in their dealings with liberal and radical student groups, and the self-assurance of student activists seems to have increased all over the country (Draper 1965; Lipset & Wolin 1965).

Protests against the Vietnam war.   Belief in the absurdity of the Vietnam war absorbed a large portion of student activist energies. Many activists subsequently engaged in civil disobedience on behalf of the Vietnam Day Committee (VDC), whose most spectacular acts of defiance were attempts to stop troop trains going through Berkeley. In the fall of 1965 the VDC leadership dramatically abandoned plans to march toward an army base in Oakland without a permit and instead filed a successful suit to force the city to grant the marching permit.

The teach-in movement which was launched at the University of Michigan in 1965 was originally planned as a civil disobedience movement, in violation of university regulations and perhaps of state laws as well. However, plans were changed, and the law-abiding could also participate in these protests.

The Vietnam Day Committee and some other war protest organizations elsewhere in the country have come close to outright violations of the draft laws in their occasional advocacy of draft refusal, but either they, the U.S. government, or both have so far avoided a head-on confrontation on this issue. Some nonpacifists have refused to fight in Vietnam, thus adopting a position of civil disobedience. In March 1966, the American Civil Liberties Union adopted the position that the courts ought to recognize moral opposition to a particular war as an additional ground for granting a conscientious objector status. Some pacifists, not satisfied with this status, have engaged in civil disobedience, refusing to register at all (a traditional stance for the most militant pacifists) or burning their draft cards (since 1965 a felony in the United States).

Politically speaking, a widespread challenge to a government's policy in a particular war would have a greater chance of success than a pacifist position which rejects participation in all wars. Perhaps for that very reason the courts, probably in every country, will be reluctant to grant to an individual the right to choose what national cause to kill for or die for—a right which in philosophical perspective may seem elementary but which could be a dangerous one to tolerate for almost any kind of government.

Another type of civil disobedience relating to peace and war issues is the refusal to pay all or a part of the income tax, unless or until the government abandons a particular policy. Following Thoreau's example, a good number of Americans have attempted this kind of protest, but if they have significant income or property the U.S. government usually is able to extract the tax money one way or another eventually, with fines and possible litigation costs added (Mayer 1964).

Prospects for civil disobedience

Three principal factors suggest the likelihood of a progressively expanding role for civil disobedience in the political life of modern democracies and somewhat later in communist countries, too, if their regimes become stabilized, their legal processes more dependably equitable, and their citizens more secure. One factor is our increasing knowledge of political behavior and political institutions in democracies; another is the impact of the Nuremberg verdicts and the Eichmann case on modern thought about the individual's political responsibilities; and a third factor, perhaps, is the influence of writers like Camus and some of the modern psychologists, who associate man's growth with a maturing independent social conscience and an increasing insistence on living according to its dictates.

Behavioral research has established the wide distance between the classical ideals of democracy and the modern realities of rule by contending minorities, some more privileged than others with respect to economic and political power. Most writers on democracy and virtually all American civics texts keep arguing, however, that in a democracy citizens have the right to vote and, therefore, are obligated, morally as well as legally, to obey the law. Bad laws must be obeyed while one goes to work to have them changed. Many defenders of liberal democracy write as if there were a social contract or some similar basis for a political obligation to obey the majority's will, as expressed in constitutional processes, even to the extent of subordinating one's personal sense of morality or one's firm conviction about vital issues concerning the public good.

A more liberal position is adopted by David Spitz, who recognizes three (but only three) exceptions to the general rule that citizens in a democracy are obliged to obey all laws, on the assumption that they have been enacted with their consent. First, from those who oppose democracy no consent can be assumed. Second, one cannot in fairness claim an obligation to obey on the part of those who believe in democracy as an ideal but who claim that the democracy under which they live is a fraud. For example, there can be no moral obligation for a disenfranchised American Negro to obey the law, whether or not he believes in the ideas of democracy. The state's claim to obedience with respect to such dissidents rests on power, not on a universal morality. A third category, Spitz continues, are those democrats who feel bound by most laws but consider a particular law or legally authorized policy patently unjust. What should a witness do when a congressional committee demands that he give names of individuals whom he once knew as communists? Spitz's position is that the mark of the good citizen—at least in a democracy—is not loyalty to the system, but to the principle of democracy itself (1954).

John H. Schaar takes issue with Spitz on the third category, arguing that a democrat must believe in the legitimacy of majority rule and that disobedience to a particular law in effect would substitute minority rule in this context. "The principle of majority rule knows only the limits that the majority sets upon itself. Any other form of limitation is undemocratic" (1957, p. 51). An implication of this not uncommon view would seem to be that a disenfranchised Negro or an American communist would violate no political obligation by exercising civil disobedience but that almost any other citizen would. Schaar's argument seems to assume not only that "democracy" refers to majority rule but also that majority rule is an end in itself—in fact, an all-important end; he firmly opposes the assumption he attributes to Spitz— that "a minority may set itself over the majority as final judge of what is right and good in the democratic polity" (ibid., pp. 51–52). The majority, Schaar seems to imply, must be the final judge of what is right and good regardless of levels of information and degrees of sensitivity; worse, he appears to say that what passes for majority choice in our polity, but in fact is choice by privileged minorities, must be the final judgment of right and wrong, prevailing over the individual's conscience.

Other political scientists have contributed research to the processes by which degrees of loyalty and democratic consent are brought about. Morton Grodzins ably demonstrated some of the psychological factors on which the loyalty of underprivileged or actually persecuted minority group members may hinge (1956). Others have studied the psychological processes by which average Americans develop their feelings and views, become committed or remain apathetic with respect to different political issues. Numerous researches on community power have established that there is no substantive majority rule in local communities either.

Overlooked by many writers in the liberal democratic tradition is the fact that people with political knowledge, with a sensitive social conscience, or with an inordinate moral commitment to whatever public cause, are always in a minority. Unless they appear at just the right historical moment they are doomed to a hopeless struggle against the privileged and the powerful, the makers of history and of legislation in democracies as well as other systems. Normally it is expedient to obey the laws even if one strongly disagrees with them and in fact can exert no effective influence toward changing them. But to say that a moral obligation to obey the law exists under such circumstances is to make a claim that needs more than a façade of formal democratic institutions to back it up. In the Locke tradition there is a right not only to commit civil disobedience but also to overthrow the government if it violates its trust; revolution, writes Joseph Tussman, "lurks at the outer fringes of political life" and "comes to life when the government weakens the moral and legal basis for its authority. It calls to the aid the moral revolutionist, the self-appointed agent of a body politic betrayed by its appointed agents" (1960, p. 46). Short of revolutionary activity, civil disobedience seems to be an essential corrective in democracies whose classical legitimation has been lost.

This assertion is especially true, perhaps, from the perspective of each young generation. Young people form a large minority group in terms of numbers but a very small one in terms of political influence; most laws as well as customs are shaped to suit middle-aged and especially older people, who have a disproportionate power in almost every society. Alert young people and student activists in particular are likely to become increasingly restless under the customary bombardment of admonitions to respect all laws, laws which they know they have had no effective share in bringing about. Paradoxically, even the formal niceties of democratic representation are ignored in the military draft legislation of several Western democracies, including the United States, which expects young men to go to war, if called on, before they have won the right to vote, much less to run for office. Similarly, campus unrest over the issues of university government, which is likely to keep increasing, also stems from the fact that young people are called on to respect rules which they have had no effective share in choosing.

The classical justification of democracy as a basis for political obligation having been undermined by modern political knowledge, democratic institutions will increasingly come to be valued as means rather than ends. The role of civil disobedience may be ambiguous if majority rule is an end in itself but it becomes vital if the ends of politics are sought in the realm of substantive values like justice, liberty, equality, or human rights.

While universal agreement on specific positive

ends of government is unlikely in any polity, there is in civilized societies an implicit agreement on negative ends: physical violence is to be minimized, as is persecution and oppression of underprivileged groups. One positive formulation of this widely shared attitude, which may claim a wide implicit acceptance, is the statement that governments exist for the purpose of establishing and defending human rights, with the most basic rights like protection against violence and starvation taking precedence over less basic rights. The common good, according to this view, hinges on the good of the least favored individuals, also taking into account the prospects for those not yet born.

This or any similar type of basis for political obligation directed to the ends of politics, which relegates not only democracy but also respect for the law in all its majesty to the status of means, takes the vestiges of the role of subject out of the role of citizen. It substitutes an ethics of individual responsibility for the probable results of one's political behavior, including law-abiding as well as legally obligated behavior, for an ethics of duty to subordinate conscience, knowledge, and individual judgment to existing legal norms, government directives, or a majority vote.

The judgments at Nuremberg and the wide attention given to the Eichmann trial in Jerusalem have increased acceptance for the view that the autonomy of the individual conscience is a vital resource in our modern technological and bureaucratized civilization [see HUMAN RIGHTS].

Thoreau, in his America, acted as if one could choose between morality and society; he dissociated himself from a government he could not recognize as his by withdrawing to his life in the forest. For modern metropolitan or cosmopolitan man this alternative does not exist. The problem of moral integrity for the dissenting citizen is to know when to obey and when to disobey unjust laws and policies. When is the violence and injustice of such magnitude that failure to commit civil disobedience would demean a morally sensitive and enlightened individual?

Thoreau would have no part of the usual democratic argument that unjust laws must be obeyed while we are working to change them. If the injustice is minor, let it go, he writes (1849); "but if it is of such a nature that it requires you to be the agent of injustice to another, then, I say, break the law. Let your life be a counter friction to stop the machine. What I have to do is to see, at any rate, that I do not lend myself to the wrong which I condemn."

In our complex society this is a difficult doctrine to apply. Every taxpayer lends himself to the wrongs committed by his government, yet few, if any, taxpayers, unless they stop earning, can effectively withhold their financial support to their government. There is uncomfortable truth in the slogan distributed by a New York anarchist group as a protest against American military policies: "Help stamp out human beings! Contribute to the war effort thru your local tax collector."

The conscientious dissenter's dilemma is complicated not only by the magnitude of evil that even democratic governments can inflict with modern technology but also by the usual lack of time to wait for evil policies to be changed and by the lack of effective ways of opting out from partnership with one's government. A further complication of the modern dissenter's dilemma is contributed by our expanding psychological knowledge. We are aware today of the wide extent to which government policies as well as public opinion are the outcome of neurotic anxieties and fears, which are difficult to diagnose with exactitude and are even more difficult to cure (Lewy 1961).

Modern social science has established in a general way how political opinions are developed to meet personality needs and how the individual's ability to cope with anxieties at various levels determines his capacity for rationality and a realistic long-term assessment of his own good as well as the common good. Most people are neurotic and conformist as well as rational, in varying mixtures; enlightened, civilized policies are unlikely to emanate from democratic processes except to the extent that influential leaders become capable of farsighted rationality. Yet democratic competition for office and power almost invariably strengthens the neurotic aspects and lessens the rational aspects of political behavior; most electoral appeals, especially in times of crises when cool rationality is most needed, are directed to anxieties and paranoid sentiments rather than to reason or enlightened hopes.

The conscientious dissenter who cannot opt out of this system has no easy guide available for determining when to obey and when to disobey the law. There is no general solution to his dilemma, except to recommend that he insist on protecting his own sanity and powers of reason, the autonomy of his own social conscience, and his own right to grow toward whatever moral stature or humanity he is capable of achieving. The criteria for concrete decisions to obey or disobey must depend on the nature of each situation, anticipating by careful inquiry and reflection the consequences of either obeying or disobeying; but they must also depend on each moral dissenter's personality and beliefs, especially his beliefs concerning priorities among evils or among good causes.

The open-endedness of the modern dilemma of civil disobedience fits well with Camus's theory of rebellion as an individual responsibility: while only an active and pressing social conscience can bring an individual to full life as a human being, the responsibility for action or inaction as a social being is strictly individual and lonesome. Others have made a strong case for the necessity of civil disobedience as a means of instructing the powerful about the strength of grievances and thus to push toward social justice and freedom for the underprivileged. Camus's most important contribution, which is in line with modern developments in psychology, is his stress on the necessity of resistance to injustice for the resisting individual's own health and welfare. He asserts that only by way of rebellion can we become human beings, or individuals conscious of our own humanness. A commitment to civil disobedience is as necessary for the full growth of the individual as a human being as the steady supply of individuals prepared to commit civil disobedience is necessary for the protection and development of a human rights-oriented society.

CHRISTIAN BAY

[See also AUTHORITY; CONSTITUTIONAL LAW; DUTY; FREEDOM; HUMAN RIGHTS; JUSTICE; PACIFISM. Other relevant material may be found in POLITICAL THEORY.]

BIBLIOGRAPHY

AQUINAS, THOMAS Summa theologica. 22 vols. Translated by the Fathers of the English Dominican Province. London: Oates & Washbourne, 1912–1925.

BEDAU, HUGO A. 1961 On Civil Disobedience. Journal of Philosophy 58:653–665.

BENTHAM, JEREMY (1776) 1951 A Fragment on Government. Edited by F. C. Montague. Oxford: Clarendon.

BONDURANT, JOAN V. (1958) 1965 Conquest of Violence: The Gandhian Philosophy of Conflict. Rev. ed. Berkeley: Univ. of California Press.

CAMUS, ALBERT (1951) 1954 The Rebel. New York: Knopf. → First published as L'homme révolté.

CATHOLIC CHURCH, POPE, 1958–1963 (JOANNES XXIII) 1963 Pacem in terris; Peace on Earth. Encyclical Letter of Pope John XXIII. New York: America Press.

COHEN, CARL 1964 Essence and Ethics of Civil Disobedience. Nation 198:257–262.

CORWIN, EDWARD S. 1948 Liberty Against Government: The Rise, Flowering and Decline of a Famous Juridical Concept. Baton Rouge: Louisiana State Univ. Press.

DOLCI, DANILO (1956) 1959 Report From Palermo. New York: Orion Press. → First published in Italian.

DRAPER, HAL 1965 Berkeley: The New Student Revolt. New York: Grove.

FISCHER, LOUIS 1954 Gandhi: His Life and Message for the World. New York: New American Library.

FREEMAN, HARROP A. et al. 1966 Civil Disobedience. Santa Barbara, Calif.: Center for the Study of Democratic Institutions. → See the essay on "Civil Disobedience," by Harrop A. Freeman.

GANDHI, MOHANDAS K. (1951) 1961 Non-violent Resistance (Satyagraha). New York: Schocken.

GODWIN, WILLIAM (1793) 1949 Political Justice. London: Allen & Unwin. → A reprint of Godwin's Essay on Property, from the original edition.

GREGG, RICHARD B. (1934) 1959 The Power of Nonviolence. 2d ed., rev. Nyack, N.Y.: Fellowship Publications.

GRODZINS, MORTON 1956 The Loyal and the Disloyal: Social Boundaries of Patriotism and Treason. Univ. of Chicago Press.

HOBBES, THOMAS (1651) 1950 Leviathan. With an introduction by A. D. Lindsay. New York: Dutton.

HOCHHUTH, ROLF (1963) 1964 The Deputy. New York: Grove. → First published in German as Der Stellvertreter.

HUME, DAVID (1739–1742) 1951 Theory of Politics. Contains A Treatise of Human Nature, book 3, parts 1–2, and 13 of the Essays, Moral, Political and Literary. Edited by Frederick Watkins. London: Nelson.

KING, MARTIN LUTHER JR. 1958 Stride Toward Freedom: The Montgomery Story. New York: Harper.

KUPER, LEO 1956 Passive Resistance in South Africa. London: Cape.

LEWY, GUENTER 1961 Superior Orders, Nuclear Warfare and the Dictates of Conscience: The Dilemma of Military Obedience in the Atomic Age. American Political Science Review 55:3–23.

LIPSET, SEYMOUR M.; and WOLIN, SHELDON S. (editors) 1965 The Berkeley Student Revolt: Facts and Interpretations. Garden City, N.Y.: Anchor.

LOCKE, JOHN (1690) 1964 The Second Treatise of Government: An Essay Concerning the True Original, Extent, and End of Civil Government. Pages 283–446 in John Locke, Two Treatises of Government. Cambridge Univ. Press.

LOMAX, LOUIS E. (1962) 1963 The Negro Revolt. New York: New American Library.

LUTHULI, ALBERT JOHN 1962 Let My People Go: An Autobiography. London: Collins.

MARITAIN, JACQUES (1938) 1940 Scholasticism and Politics. Translated by Mortimer J. Adler. New York: Macmillan. → Contains nine lectures given in the United States in 1938. A paperback edition was published in 1964 by Doubleday.

MAYER, MILTON S. 1964 What Can a Man Do? Univ. of Chicago Press.

MILL, JAMES 1825 Essays on Government, Jurisprudence, Liberty of the Press, Prisons and Prison Discipline, Colonies, Law of Nations, Education. London: Innes.

MILLER, WILLIAM R. (1964) 1966 Nonviolence, a Christian Interpretation. New York: Schocken.

NAESS, ARNE 1965 Gandhi and the Nuclear Age. Totowa, N.J.: Bedminster.

QUARLES, BENJAMIN 1964 The Negro in the Making of America. New York: Collier.

SCHAAR, JOHN H. 1957 Loyalty in America. Berkeley: Univ. of California Press.

SCHOLMER, JOSEPH 1954 Vorkuta. London: Wiedenfeld & Nicolson. → First published in the same year in German as Die Toten kehren zurück: Bericht eines Arztes aus Workuta.

SHARP, GENE 1960 Gandhi Wields the Weapon of Moral Power. Ahmedabad (India): Navajivan.

SIBLEY, MULFORD Q. (editor) 1963 *The Quiet Battle: Writings on the Theory and Practice of Non-violent Resistance.* Garden City, N.Y.: Doubleday.

SPITZ, DAVID 1954 Democracy and the Problem of Civil Disobedience. *American Political Science Review* 48: 386–403.

THOREAU, HENRY D. (1849) 1950 *Civil Disobedience.* Saugatuck, Conn.: The 5 x 8 Press. → First published in the *Aesthetic Papers* as "Resistance to Civil Government." A paperback edition was published in 1964 by Revell.

TOLSTOI, LEV N. (1888) 1961 *The Kingdom of God Is Within You: Or, Christianity Not as a Mystical Teaching but as a New Concept of Life.* New York: Noonday Press. → First published as *Tsarstvo boshie vnutri vas.*

TUSSMAN, JOSEPH 1960 *Obligation and the Body Politic.* New York: Oxford Univ. Press.

ZINN, HOWARD 1964 *SNCC: The New Abolitionists.* Boston: Beacon.

CIVIL LAW

See under LEGAL SYSTEMS.

CIVIL LIBERTIES

See under CONSTITUTIONAL LAW.

CIVIL–MILITARY RELATIONS

The term "civil–military relations" refers to the role of the armed forces in a society. It is not, perhaps, a happy phrase. It implies that the relations between the military and the civilian population are like labor–management relations, legislative–executive relations, or Soviet–American relations, where two concrete, organized groups with real conflicting interests contend and bargain with each other. It thus suggests a basic dichotomy and opposition between the civilian and the military viewpoints. This is a false opposition. First, in many societies little unity of interest, skill, or viewpoint exists among the military. Second, even where there is a distinct and identifiable military viewpoint, interest, and institution, in no society is there ever comparable unity among civilians. The word "civil" in the phrase civil–military relations simply means nonmilitary. Publicists and authors often talk about civil–military relations and, more especially, about civilian control as if there were a single civilian interest. In practice, they simply identify their own interest and viewpoint as *the* civilian interest and viewpoint in opposition to a hostile military interest and viewpoint. Any society, however, which is sufficiently well developed to have distinct military institutions also has a wide variety of civilian interests, institutions, and attitudes, the differences between any two of which may be much greater than the difference between any one of them and the military.

Thus, civil–military relations involve a multiplicity of relationships between military men, institutions, and interests, on the one hand, and diverse and often conflicting nonmilitary men, institutions, and interests, on the other. It is not a one-to-one relationship but a one-among-many relationship.

Military and nonmilitary groups

Civil–military relations in any society reflect the over-all nature and level of development of the society and its political system. The key question is the extent to which military men and interests are differentiated from nonmilitary men and interests. This differentiation may take place on three levels: (1) the relation between the armed forces as a whole and society as a whole; (2) the relation between the leadership of the armed forces (the officer corps) as an elite group and other elite groups; and (3) the relation between the commanders of the armed forces and the top political leaders of society. Thus, at the society level the military forces may be an integral part of society, reflecting and embodying its dominant social forces and ideologies. The military order, indeed, may be coextensive with society, with all members of society also performing military roles. At the opposite extreme the military order may be highly differentiated, its members playing no important roles except military ones. At the second level, connections between military officers and other leadership groups in society may be very close; the same people may be military, economic, and political leaders. At the other end of the continuum, military officership may be an exclusive professional career, incompatible with other roles. Finally, at the top level the same individuals may exercise both political and military leadership roles, or these roles may be quite distinct and their occupants recruited from different sources through different channels.

In general, high differentiation on one level tends to be associated with high differentiation on other levels, but this is by no means invariable. In the European armies of the seventeenth and eighteenth centuries, for instance, social, economic, political, and military leadership functions were all concentrated in the person of the monarch. Similarly, officership was, in general, a perquisite of the aristocracy; aristocrats acquired by ascription military as well as social, economic, and political leadership roles. The rank and file of the European armies, however, was recruited from the lower ranks of society for long periods of service, and their ties with any groups in civilian society were often tenuous at best.

In the nineteenth century these relations tended to be reversed. Political and military leadership roles became differentiated. Prime ministers and cabinets emerged from parliaments and party politics; commanding generals and chiefs of staff were the products of the military bureaucracy. Similarly, the military officership became professionalized; entry was usually at the lowest ranks and required specialized training. A career as a military officer became incompatible with other leadership careers. The relation of the enlisted personnel to society, however, tended to become closer. The core of modern armies remained the long-service soldier, but the rank and file was increasingly supplemented by large numbers of short-term "citizen-soldiers" initially recruited through conscription or universal military service and then organized into reserves, militia, territorial army, National Guard, or Landwehr.

At each level of civil–military relations military groups may differ from nonmilitary groups in terms of skills, values, and institutions. Military men may differ from nonmilitary men in their skill in the use of violence or in the management of violence. In a frontier society, such as eighteenth-century America, the differentiation was relatively small. The average farmer possessed most of the skills of the soldier; the social, economic, and political leaders of the society either possessed or could easily acquire most of the skills necessary to command armies. During the nineteenth century and the first part of the twentieth century military skills tended to become more sharply differentiated from civilian skills. In the mid-twentieth century in the advanced societies the difference between military and other skills may again be decreasing (Janowitz 1960).

Military men may also differ from civilian groups in terms of their attitudes and values. In most societies presumably the outlook of the military more closely resembles that of some civilian groups than it does that of other civilian groups. In the history of the West military values were often closely associated with aristocratic and conservative beliefs. In many of the modernizing countries in the second half of the twentieth century, the values of the dominant groups in the armed forces closely paralleled those of upward mobile, nationalistic, reformist middle-class civilians. The development of a professionalized officer corps generally stimulates distinctive attitudes and values (often referred to as "the military mind") that may differ significantly from the attitudes and values dominant within the society. The professional military ethic tends to be conservative in character. If the basic values of the society are liberal, fascist, or socialist, the tensions between the military and political leadership may be intense, particularly if the military leaders occupy a position of power or potential power in the political system or if the political leaders feel that they must insist upon a high degree of ideological uniformity on the part of all elements in the society, including the military. In these circumstances nationalism may furnish a common ground for the accommodation of the revolutionary ideology of the political leadership and the conservative outlook of the military.

Military institutions may also be differentiated in varying degrees from civilian institutions. The key questions here concern the extent to which the armed forces are made up of long-service career enlisted men and professional career officers; the extent to which men and officers are recruited from special segments of the population and trained in special educational institutions; the organizational position of the armed forces in the governmental structure; and the structure of authority relationships between the leaders of the armed forces and the political leadership of the society. At one extreme, military institutions may be so differentiated from other social institutions that they become virtually a "state within a state." In these circumstances they may become relatively impervious to control by the legislative and executive institutions of government. In societies with a tradition of hierarchy and executive leadership, such as Japan before 1945 and Germany before 1933, efforts by the legislature to exercise control over the military institutions may become futile in the face of opposition from both the military and the strongly entrenched and authoritative executive. In some societies, such as Burma and a few Latin American republics, the military may become not just a state within a state but a society within a society, performing many economic and social functions and achieving a high degree of economic self-sufficiency. At the other extreme, in societies with a "nation-in-arms" pattern of civil–military relations, the differentiation of military institutions from other institutions may be very slight, and the armed forces may be identical with society as a whole (see Rapaport 1962).

Traditional and modernizing societies

In general, the more primitive a society, the less differentiated are military skills, values, and institutions from those of other groups. In tribal systems the military forces typically consist of all adult males, and the tribal chiefs are the leaders in war as well as peace. In more highly organized fashion a somewhat similar system existed in the classical city-states of Greece and Rome. The military role was a responsibility of citizenship; the army was the citizen body organized for war. "The citizens of a free state," Aristotle remarked, "ought to consist of those only who bear arms." In feudal society military, political, and economic roles were all differentiated on a class rather than on a functional basis. The peasants or serfs occupied subordinate positions in all three capacities; the nobility and knights combined political authority, economic control of the land, and military leadership. In the centralized bureaucratic empires, such as those analyzed by Shmuel N. Eisenstadt (1963), the military was one component of the bureaucratic structure and usually did not reach a high level of differentiation in skills, values, or institutions. The military group was, however, more differentiated than it was in the city-state or feudal society, and at times military leaders played autonomous roles in the political struggle.

Civil–military relations in modern societies differ from those in these earlier societies because of the existence of an autonomous, professionalized officer corps. The emergence of such an officer corps is a key aspect of the process of modernization. In western Europe and the United States the professional officer corps was a product of the nineteenth century. From the breakdown of feudalism in Europe to the latter part of the seventeenth century, armies were usually led by mercenary officers who raised companies of men for hire to kings and princes. In consolidating their power in the seventeenth century, the national monarchs felt the need for permanent military forces to protect their dominions and support their rule. Consequently, they created standing armies and recruited the aristocrats they were subordinating to officer them. Thus, from the end of the seventeenth century to the French Revolution, officers, except in the artillery and engineer units, were usually aristocrats who assumed their posts with little regard to professional qualifications, experience, or talent.

The lead in developing a professional officer corps was taken by Prussia during the Napoleonic Wars. On August 6, 1808, a decree formally opened officer ranks to all in Prussian society on the basis of education, professional knowledge, valor, and perception (*Überblick*). During the subsequent century Prussia took the lead in introducing educational requirements for entry into the officer corps; prescribing a system of advancement within the corps on the basis of experience, ability, and achievements; creating a system of professional military education culminating in the Kriegsakademie; and developing a general staff system. The other continental European countries followed in the wake of Prussia, the professionalization of European officership being concentrated during two periods: during and immediately after the Napoleonic Wars and in the 1860s and 1870s, after the victories of the professional Prussian armies over the Danes, Austrians, and French. By the end of the nineteenth century most of the European countries had made military officership at least in theory a career open to all, although in practice a high proportion of the officers continued to be recruited from the aristocracy. They had also instituted requirements of general education and specialized training for entry into the officer corps; provided for advancement within the corps on the basis of examinations, achievement, and experience; created a hierarchy of military schools and colleges; brought into existence staff systems for the systematic analysis and planning of war; and through these devices created a distinct, autonomous social group with its own sense of corporate unity and responsibility. Similar developments also took place in Great Britain and the United States, although the insular position of these two countries caused them to lag behind the less secure countries on the European continent.

The pattern of military and political modernization in Europe and the United States contrasts with that in many of the countries of Asia, Africa, and Latin America. In Europe and the United States, political modernization usually preceded the development of a modern, professional officer corps. Only in those countries, such as France, where constitutional issues remained unresolved did military interventions play a critical role in politics. In other countries, such as Germany, the military played a significant but less overt role in politics as a result of the conflicting claims to legitimacy and authority on the part of monarchical and parliamentary institutions. In general, however, the professional officer corps developed within the framework of an established political order.

In the countries of Asia, Africa, and Latin America, by contrast, the military leaders have often also been the leaders in modernization. Countries that retained some degree of independence from European colonialism frequently felt compelled to engage in "defensive modernization" and to transform their traditional military institutions into modern ones that might offer some resistance to European penetration. As a result the army often became the most modern and effective institution in the society and its leaders the most ardent exponents of modernization, nationalism, and progressive reform. In these circumstances the military frequently possessed advantages over other groups and institutions because of its greater organizational coherence and discipline and hence its ability to get things done; its identification with society as a whole and its concern with national goals rather than with the parochial interests of class, party, ethnic, or communal group; and its technical expertise in terms of literacy, education, and engineering and mechanical skills. Thus, the Young Turks who seized power in the Ottoman Empire in 1908 came out of the Westernized military schools that the sultans had created in the latter part of the nineteenth century. Similarly, in the post-World War II era the military overthrew more traditional oligarchical regimes and seized the leadership in modernization in such countries as Egypt and Iraq.

In former colonies the military often seized power shortly after the achievement of independence, ousting what it held to be corrupt party regimes of civilian politicians and attempting to organize the society for more effective modernization (for example, in the Sudan, Pakistan, and Burma in 1958; in South Korea in 1961; and in South Vietnam in 1963).

In Latin America the relation of the military to modernization was somewhat more complex. During the nineteenth century neither effective political institutions nor professionalized officer corps existed in most Latin American countries. During the first part of the twentieth century the military officers became increasingly professionalized, increasingly middle class, and increasingly in favor of progress and reform. This led to a new period of military interventions in politics beginning in the 1930s. In Latin America, as in Asia and Africa, however, military interventions in politics may produce short-run gains in terms of modernization at the expense of continued long-term weakness of civilian political institutions. Only those countries that either have inherited strong political institutions (parties and civilian bureaucracies) from the colonial era (for example, India) or have been able to create effective modern political institutions through revolution (Mexico) or reform (Uruguay) have been able to minimize the military role in politics and to maintain nonpolitical professional military forces. [See MODERNIZATION.]

The modern state

"The great modern fact," Gaetano Mosca wrote in 1896, "is the huge standing army that is a severe custodian of the law, is obedient to the orders of a civil authority and has very little influence, exercising indirectly at best such influence as it has." This unique product of modern civilization, Mosca went on to note, is "a most fortunate exception, if it is not absolutely without parallel, in human history" ([1896] 1939, p. 229).

The phenomenon that amazed Mosca was the product of the emergence of constitutional consensus in the modern state and the increasing differentiation of the military from other social groups. In all societies military men differ from nonmilitary men by the possession of arms. In primitive tribes and in the nation in arms, this difference in theory is eliminated in fact by dispersing military functions among the citizens at large. In more advanced and differentiated systems only a portion of the population bears arms. Prior to the development of the professionalized officer corps in the nineteenth century, however, few inhibitions prevented such military forces from exploiting their monopoly of violence for their own advantage. The military could use its arms for purposes contrary to those of the acknowledged leaders of the polity or the dominant groups in the society. In traditional societies the problem of minimizing the role of force and violence and, hence, the dominance of the military in politics was the major continuing problem of civil–military relations. In the modern state, however, the line between politics and military affairs is much sharper, and the officer corps is a distinct professionalized body whose leaders devote their careers to the study and practice of the management of violence. The role of violence in the political order is latent; only during constitutional crisis and intense social conflict does force become the arbiter of politics. The more pervasive problem of civil–military relations concerns not the role of force in politics but the role of expertise in politics. The parallels to the modern problem of civil–military relations are to be found not in the Praetorian Guard but in the relations that exist in modern states between political leaders, on the one hand, and such specialists as diplomats, civil servants, scientists, and economists on the other.

Despite these similarities civil–military relations are an object of concern in the modern state in a way in which "civil–diplomacy" or "civil–science" relations are not. This concern may be attributed to a variety of factors. First, among many civilian groups there is a legacy of fear concerning past military participation in politics. Military officers and the armed forces are seen as alien and sinister in a way in which the other expert groups are not. Second, the organizational coherence and discipline of the armed forces contrast with the more egalitarian and voluntaristic organizational patterns characteristic of constitutional democracies. The military often seems to have a potential for disciplined political action not possessed by other groups. Third, in times of war and of prolonged international crisis the military may exercise control over a substantial portion of the resources of society. Forty per cent of the American gross national product during World War II and about 10 per cent during the cold war years from 1947 to 1964 was devoted to military purposes; the Soviet Union allocated about 18 per cent of its gross national product to military purposes in the latter period. Finally, the military is often identified with war and is viewed as the major protagonist of war. Actually, in most modern societies, including the United States, the officer corps and its leaders have played a moderating, restraining role in the conduct of foreign policy. Bellicosity has been far more typical of civilian groups and political movements than of the professional military. Nonetheless, the traditional identification of the military with war has lingered on and has manifested itself in the view that more political power for the military and the allocation of more resources to the military will increase the probability of war.

These traditional attitudes toward the military are found, in varying degrees, in most Western societies. In other ways, however, the image of the military has changed significantly. The creation of a professionalized officer corps has been generally accompanied by a long-term decline in the prestige and general status of the military. In eighteenth-century European society the military and the aristocracy were closely linked in fact and in image. Since then in most modern societies first upper-middle-class and then lower-middle-class elements have increasingly made their appearance in the officer corps. The result has been to break the identification of the military with the ruling class.

The decline in social status has been accompanied by increasing technical expertise. The aristocratic image of the officer has, in large measure, been replaced by the expert image. In many instances military leaders have elaborated upon and employed the complexities of modern military science to erect a defensive wall against pressures from civilian politicians and to invoke the authority of esoteric knowledge to buttress their policy recommendations. During periods of rapid change in warfare, however, military leaders, committed to the truths of another day, may lag behind civilians in adjusting military concepts and techniques to drastically changed conditions. In World War I, Lloyd George and other civilian politicians, not the Imperial General Staff, first appreciated the implications of total war. In the United States

after World War II civilian experts and intellectuals played a more important role than military officers in pointing out the implications of nuclear weapons for American strategy.

In the modern state the top military leaders have three general responsibilities: (1) to represent the needs of military security within the governmental framework, making claims on political leaders for the resources they believe necessary for security; (2) to advise the political leaders on the military implications of proposed courses of actions and to prepare plans for possible military contingencies; and (3) to implement in the military sphere the policy decisions of the political leaders. These responsibilities bring the higher military leaders into continuing conflicts with the political leaders and with the civilian branches of government. The military typically want more money, more weapons, and more men than the political leaders are prepared to allocate, their claims on resources conflicting with the demands of civilian agencies and other groups in society. The military also typically want political leaders to give them explicit and precise definitions of policy to use as the basis for their military plans. At the political level, however, policy inevitably has a tentative, ambiguous, and contingent quality, and the art of political leadership frequently lies in avoiding decision and blurring commitments. Generally, military leaders also want to have full control over the resources that may be necessary to the security of the state. They are, consequently, likely to place less confidence in treaties and alliances than do political leaders.

These differences in viewpoint give rise to the most typical controversies in civil–military relations in the modern state. At the bureaucratic level these controversies regularly involve the foreign office and the financial offices. The foreign office has general responsibility for external relations and consequently has the initiative in defining the circumstances in which military action may be necessary. The financial agencies (in the United States, the Treasury and the Bureau of the Budget; in the United Kingdom, the Exchequer) supervise the allocation of resources within the government and are usually the principal institutional interests attempting to reduce military spending. As a result, the military agencies often claim to be caught between a foreign office that is expanding their responsibilities and a financial office that is reducing their resources. These controversies, of course, are mediated and arbitrated by the political leaders of the state. To assist in this process, most constitutional states have created interagency committees (in the United States, the National Security Council; in the United Kingdom, the Defence and Oversea Policy Committee) composed of the interested parties and designed to serve as forums for consultation, bargaining, and advising the political leaders on the integration of foreign, financial, and military policies. These interagency conflicts and controversies reflect the functionally different roles of the military and other agencies in the modern state. They are thus a normal aspect of modern politics.

The organizational position of the military forces in the modern state varies with the nature of the political system. Both fascist and communist totalitarian states have taken extreme measures to ensure against undue military influence in government. In Germany and the Soviet Union the military were at one time deprived of their monopoly of violence, and large armed forces were created under the control of the secret police. In communist countries the party organization permeates the military forces, and often the military chain of command is paralleled by an independent or autonomous hierarchy of political commissars or political officers.

Constitutional systems do not rely on such methods of control. In parliamentary systems the chief of state usually is the titular commander in chief of the armed forces, but actual control is vested in the prime minister and cabinet. In the United States the president is both head of government and constitutional commander in chief. In constitutional democracies the minister in charge of the armed forces is usually a civilian, although practice varies from country to country and from time to time. The minister is normally assisted by a group of permanent civil servants. Modern states usually have at least three services, each with its military head. After World War II almost all modern states also had a superservice national military chief of staff or military commander who was the senior military officer in the country, who was assisted by a military general staff, and who exercised varying degrees of control or command over all the military services. In the United States, for instance, the position of chairman of the Joint Chiefs of Staff was created in 1949 and strengthened several times during the next 15 years. The service chiefs together with the national military chief were formed into a collegial organization, such as the Chiefs of Staff Committee (U.K.), Joint Chiefs of Staff (U.S.), or Military Council (U.S.S.R.). This committee usually had extensive authority over military planning, its actual powers varying inversely with the authority and influence of the national military chief. Before the increasing

complexity of modern war required continual close coordination among the air, sea, and land forces, each of these services, in Western democracies, was headed by a civilian minister. The integration of the armed forces and the emergence in almost all states of the position of minister of defense or minister of the armed forces have significantly reduced the stature and power of the service minister.

The degree of influence of the military and other groups in day-to-day politics is also affected by their degree of unity. The parliamentary–cabinet system, especially as it functions in Great Britain, unifies executive and legislative leadership and tends to maximize the authority of the political leaders in relation to the military. In the United States, on the other hand, control over military affairs is divided between the president and Congress. Top military leaders are thus compelled to be more political than they are in Great Britain. At times this may be awkward and embarrassing; at other times the leaders may be able to benefit from it. The military services often can generate support in Congress for particular projects; on the other hand, they may often find themselves used by the executive leaders to support projects which the executive leaders particularly favor. The definition of their lines of responsibility to the president and secretary of defense, on the one hand, and to the Congress, on the other, represents a continuing problem for American military leaders. In the 20 years after World War II the American Congress often appropriated more money to particular military services and programs than was requested by the president. In general, however, these 20 years saw a decline in the role of Congress in military affairs and an increasing centralization of power in the civilian leadership of the Defense Department.

Just as the unity of political leaders varies from country to country, so also does the unity of the military themselves. Particularly during peacetime the competition between military services for money and men may be extreme. Significantly, there seems to be some correlation between military unity and political unity. Interservice competition exists in all modern states, but there is little doubt that it achieved the most extreme forms in the United States, where the political leadership was also less unified than it is in most states. This interservice competition has major effects on civil–military relations. The inability of the military services to act together enhances the power of the political leaders and of the civilian bureaucratic agencies. In the United States after World War II, for instance, reductions in the military budget often exacerbated interservice relations much more than they did civil–military relations. Potential civil–military conflict was deflected into intramilitary conflict.

Military interventions in politics

The principal causes of military intervention in politics lie in politics, not in the military. In the absence of a professional officer corps, the line between military affairs and politics is never sharp. Even with a professionalized military establishment, however, military intervention may occur when the political institutions of society become weak and divided. Military intervention is encouraged by the absence of constitutional consensus and by intense conflict between classes, regions, and ethnic or communal groups.

In a modernizing country in which the traditional political institutions have been overthrown and modern ones have yet to achieve legitimacy, military intervention in politics is often continuous. In such societies civil–military relations assume a praetorian form with a recurring cycle of coups and countercoups (see Rapaport 1962). In those modern societies in which significant elements of the population deny legitimacy to the political system (such as in the Weimar Republic and the Third, Fourth, and Fifth French republics), the military are likely to play an active role in politics. Even in societies with a generally authoritative and legitimate political system, succession crises may enhance the role of the military. The intense struggle for power which followed the death of Stalin in the Soviet Union also strengthened the political position of the Soviet Army and enabled Marshal Zhukov to play a brief but important role in Soviet politics, a role which was quickly and decisively terminated once Khrushchev consolidated his political power.

Military intervention is also encouraged whenever the competence and decisiveness of a government are called into question. Defeat in war and blunders in diplomacy often provoke political action by the military. The most severe crisis in American civil–military relations after World War II occurred during the prolonged and frustrating Korean War, in which the government attempted to pursue political goals short of all-out military victory. In a more extreme case, military intervention triggered the end of the Fourth French Republic when its governments proved incapable of either maintaining or disposing of an empire.

Legitimate and effective political institutions are thus the first requirement for civilian control. The requirements on the military side of the equation have been a subject of controversy. The key issue has been the relation of civilian control to military professionalism and the differentiation of the military from other groups. Huntington (1957) argues that a high degree of civilian control can be achieved in the modern state only by a high degree of differentiation of military institutions from other social institutions and the creation of a thoroughly professional officer corps ("objective civilian control"). A professional officer corps, he argues, is jealous of its own limited sphere of competence but recognizes its incompetence in matters that lie outside the professional military sphere and hence is willing to accept its role as a subordinate instrument of the state. The less professionalized the officer corps, on the other hand, the less differentiation there is between military and political roles and therefore the less justification for military obedience to political authority.

Other authors have challenged Huntington's argument. Finer (1962) argues that professionalism alone does not prevent military intervention in politics. Military officers must also have an independent adherence to the principle of civilian control. They may also be deterred from intervention by fear for the fighting capacity of their forces, fear of dividing the military forces against themselves, and fear for the future of their institution if their intervention should fail. In addition, Finer argues that professionalism by itself may spur the military to political intervention because they may see themselves as the servants of the state rather than of the government in power, because they may become so obsessed with the needs of military security that they will act to override other values, and because they object to being used to maintain domestic order.

Civil–military relations in wartime differ somewhat from those which prevail in peace. The principal difference is simply quantitative. More resources are allocated to military purposes. Undoubtedly, war also tends to increase the power of the military, but the experience of the two world wars suggests that it is difficult to make any generalizations. The military played a key role in the conduct of the war in Germany in World War I and in Japan and in the United States during World War II. They rivaled the political leaders in France and Great Britain in World War I. They played distinctly subordinate roles in Britain and Germany in World War II and in Russia in both world wars. War does tend, however, to make generals, particularly successful ones, into popular heroes and hence to give them political influence, particularly in democracies. Hindenburg, Eisenhower, and de Gaulle became presidents of their countries largely as a result of their wartime reputations. Stalin was perhaps prudent to exile Zhukov to an obscure provincial command after World War II. In general, however, reputations made during a war can be politically exploited only after the war.

The continuing international tension which began in the late 1930s stimulated arguments that the modern polity was tending to become a "garrison state." The "trend of the time," in the words of Harold D. Lasswell, "is away from the dominance of the specialist on bargaining, who is the the businessman, and toward the supremacy of the specialist on violence, the soldier" (1941, p. 455). In the garrison state military values dominate, and all activities are subordinated to war and the preparation for war. Reviewing his concept in the early 1960s, Lasswell concluded that it was still relevant and that "the garrison hypothesis provides a probable image of the past and future of our epoch" (1962, p. 67). In *The Power Elite*, C. Wright Mills made a parallel analysis, arguing that in the United States power was becoming increasingly centralized in a national bureaucratic elite dominated by big businessmen and top military leaders. Similarly, in his farewell address, President Eisenhower warned that the United States "must guard against the acquisition of unwarranted influence, whether sought or unsought, by the military–industrial complex. The potential for the disastrous rise of misplaced power exists and will persist" (1961, p. 180).

These images of increasing military power in the United States were, however, at best only partially true. In actuality, military influence in the processes of government and in the formulation of military policy declined continuously after World War II. The growth of a large and permanent armaments industry, on the other hand, was a new phenomenon. The combined military, political, and economic pressures from this complex made it more difficult to reduce military spending. In addition, the emergence of vested economic and regional interests in certain types of military activity enormously complicated the problem of adapting the military machine to new requirements, eliminating old weapons and unneeded facilities, and securing the most efficient use of military resources. Instead of a division between military and civilian interests as a whole, top political and military leaders of the executive branch tended to favor rationalizing the military establishment, while subordinate military groups, local interests, defense businesses, and congressmen backed the continuation of particular military programs and facilities. The available evidence suggests that

Khrushchev and other Soviet political leaders have faced comparable problems in dealing with the vested interests of the heavy industry and military bureaucracies in their efforts to reduce and to rationalize Soviet military activities. In both countries, the "military–industrial complex" poses problems for military efficiency as well as for civilian control.

SAMUEL P. HUNTINGTON

[*See also* MILITARY; MILITARY POLICY.]

BIBLIOGRAPHY

ANDRZEJEWSKI, STANISLAW 1954 *Military Organization and Society.* London: Routledge.

CRAIG, GORDON A. 1955 *The Politics of the Prussian Army: 1640–1945.* New York: Oxford Univ. Press.

EISENHOWER, DWIGHT D. 1961 President Eisenhower's Farewell to the Nation. U.S. Department of State, *Department of State Bulletin* 44, no. 1128:179–182.

EISENSTADT, SHMUEL N. 1963 *The Political Systems of Empires.* New York: Free Press.

FINER, SAMUEL E. 1962 *The Man on Horseback: The Role of the Military in Politics.* New York: Praeger.

FISHER, SYDNEY N. (editor) 1963 *The Military in the Middle East: Problems in Society and Government.* Columbus: Ohio State Univ. Press.

GIRARDET, RAOUL 1953 *La société militaire dans la France contemporaine: 1815–1939.* Paris: Plon.

HOWARD, MICHAEL (editor) (1957) 1959 *Soldiers and Governments: Nine Studies in Civil–Military Relations.* Bloomington: Indiana Univ. Press.

HUNTINGTON, SAMUEL P. 1957 *The Soldier and the State: The Theory and Politics of Civil–Military Relations.* Cambridge, Mass.: Harvard Univ. Press.

HUNTINGTON, SAMUEL P. (editor) 1962 *Changing Patterns of Military Politics.* New York: Free Press.

JANOWITZ, MORRIS 1960 *The Professional Soldier: A Social and Political Portrait.* Glencoe, Ill.: Free Press. → A paperback edition was published in 1965.

JANOWITZ, MORRIS 1964 *The Military in the Political Development of New Nations: An Essay in Comparative Analysis.* Univ. of Chicago Press.

JOHNSON, JOHN J. (editor) 1962 *The Role of the Military in Underdeveloped Countries.* Princeton Univ. Press. → Papers of a conference sponsored by the Rand Corporation at Santa Monica, California, in August 1959.

JOHNSON, JOHN J. 1964 *The Military and Society in Latin America.* Stanford Univ. Press.

LASSWELL, HAROLD D. 1941 The Garrison State. *American Journal of Sociology* 46:455–468.

LASSWELL, HAROLD D. 1962 The Garrison-state Hypothesis Today. Pages 51–70 in Samuel P. Huntington (editor), *Changing Patterns of Military Politics.* New York: Free Press.

LIEUWEN, EDWIN (1960) 1961 *Arms and Politics in Latin America.* Rev. ed. Published for the Council on Foreign Relations. New York: Praeger.

MILLIS, WALTER; MANSFIELD, HARVEY C.; and STEIN, HAROLD 1958 *Arms and the State: Civil–Military Elements in National Policy.* New York: Twentieth Century Fund.

MOSCA, GAETANO (1896) 1939 *The Ruling Class.* New York: McGraw-Hill. → First published as *Elementi di scienza politica.*

Rapaport, David C. 1962 A Comparative Theory of Military and Political Types. Pages 71–101 in Samuel P. Huntington (editor), *Changing Patterns of Military Politics.* New York: Free Press.

Schilling, Warner R.; Hammond, P. Y.; and Snyder, G. H. 1962 *Strategy, Politics, and Defense Budgets.* New York: Columbia Univ. Press.

Stein, Harold (editor) 1963 *American Civil–Military Decisions: A Book of Case Studies.* University: Univ. of Alabama Press.

Vagts, Alfred (1937) 1960 *A History of Militarism: Civilian and Military.* Rev. ed. London: Hollis & Carter.

Vagts, Alfred 1956 *Defense and Diplomacy: The Soldier and the Conduct of Foreign Relations.* New York: King's Crown.

CIVIL RIGHTS

See under Constitutional law.

CIVIL SERVICE

Civil service is a relatively new term used to describe an old governmental feature that is becoming increasingly important in modern political systems. The phrase was first used in British administration in India and was popularized by Sir Charles Trevelyan a little more than a century ago. When the principle of open competitive examination was introduced in Great Britain in 1854, the phrase "civil service" was also carried over and was applied to the officials serving the state in a professional capacity, except for those in the military and judicial services. Of course, equivalent bodies of officials have served states throughout history, long before the term "civil service" was applied to them.

Civil service is not a precise concept. It is similar to, but not identical in meaning with, other terms, such as public service and public bureaucracy. Although it has the advantage of familiarity, there are several difficulties in its use. Perhaps the chief difficulty is the distinction built into the term between the civil and military segments of the public service. In some governments this dividing line is becoming blurred and the interrelationships between civil and military services are growing more intimate, especially in the newly independent nations.

The definition does place emphasis on the professional character of the service as against work performed for the state on a sporadic, voluntary, or forced basis. As used in Great Britain, and to a certain degree elsewhere, the term "civil service" refers to officials serving the central government or its agencies rather than local units of government. Even when "civil service" is considered to include officials in local units, it is customary to exclude teachers, despite the large number of people engaged in this government-supported profession. The term itself does not specify conditions as to professional preparation, methods of recruitment, social and economic origins, or other crucial matters, but it is now customarily associated with a merit system, as contrasted with a patronage system, and with a service open to all citizens on the basis of talent and proved capacity.

Despite the vagueness in accepted definition and variations in its usage, "civil service" does identify the expanding corps of trained manpower that must be maintained by every modern polity to carry out governmental functions. The trend is world-wide, despite differences in cultural, political, historical, geographic, and other factors, for the scope and range of these governmental functions appear to be increasing. The result is usually described by such terms as "welfare state," "administrative state," and "big government." Inevitably, the civil service plays a crucial role in the operation of modern governmental systems, whether in Western or non-Western states, in countries in the communist or noncommunist blocs, and in developed or developing nations. In all of them, the civil service is the core of modern government, growing in its power position vis-à-vis other political organs and therefore posing grave problems of control and accountability. At the same time that its contributions have become more essential, the question of the proper placement of the civil service in the governmental system has grown more difficult. While the external relationships of the civil service have been changing, its internal characteristics have also been modified in ways that transcend differences in the political systems generally. A consistent trend is that the proportion of the total work force that is encompassed by the civil service has been growing in most countries. Another is that the requirements of the civil service call for the services of a constantly expanding variety of occupational and technical specialists, representing all or most of those available in the society. These developments, in turn, have led to a trend toward professionalization among civil servants that affects their attitudes and behavior in ways that are significant both for the conduct of civil service activities and in the relationships of the civil service with other political groupings.

Common features

Certain requisites can be identified for the establishment and maintenance of any civil service system. Some kind of legal basis for the system must be provided. This may be largely customary and uncodified; it may take the form of ministerial regulations, as in Great Britain; or it may be set forth in considerable detail in a written constitution for the political jurisdiction, as is the case in Michigan and some other American states. More likely, it will have a statutory base, either in an elaborate civil service code, such as has existed in Germany for many years, or in a collection of civil service laws adopted at intervals and probably revealing some internal inconsistencies, as in the national civil service in the United States.

Another common feature is provision for a personnel agency or agencies charged with responsibility for maintenance of the system. The British practice, which has influenced arrangements in many other countries, is to divide this task between the Civil Service Commission, which is concerned solely with the selection of entrants into the service, and the Treasury, which is the central control agency in other personnel matters. Many countries with a British administrative tradition have adopted this bifurcated system, with selection functions assigned to a civil service or public service commission and other personnel functions usually allocated to the home or finance ministry. In the United States, the preference has been to set up a semiautonomous civil service commission with combined responsibility for supervision of all aspects of personnel management, although in recent years there has been some inclination to confine the independent commission to quasi-legislative and quasi-judicial functions and to assign most personnel functions to a staff agency responsible to the chief executive. The Continental tradition has been to avoid a full-fledged central personnel agency and rely upon each ministry or department to carry out its own personnel program within the framework of uniform civil service legislation. However, France abandoned this approach after World War II and created the Direction de la Fonction Publique, or Civil Service Directorate, to initiate reforms in civil service policy and exercise personnel controls over the various ministries. Whether or not there is a central personnel agency for the civil service system as a whole, the primary departments or ministries and their major subdivisions require specialized personnel units.

A developed civil service system calls for the installation of well-established procedures for the conduct of common personnel transactions, such as selection, promotion, compensation, performance evaluation, discipline, and separation. These standardized methods are intended to provide objectivity in the choice of entrants to the civil service from citizens who compete and to provide equity in treatment for those who already belong to the service.

The system must also provide status guaranties and establish canons of conduct for civil servants. Achievement of such qualities as competence and continuity in the civil service rests upon some assurances to the public servant that his status will be protected, provided he observes the standards of conduct that have been set for him. The social position of civil servants varies from country to country. The Continental tradition, as in Germany and France, is for the higher civil servant to consider himself as a representative of the sovereign state and to expect considerable deference and respect. In Great Britain and the United States, there is more of a tendency to regard the official as a servant of the public, with a consequent reluctance to confer special status or privileges. An imbalance in either direction can cause difficulties. In the first case, the civil servant may be tempted to take advantage of the situation by an elaboration of prerogatives and safeguards, which stresses bureaucratic self-interest rather than the public interest. In the second, the prestige of the civil service may be too low to attract sufficient talent.

Finally, the role of the civil service must be defined in the political system generally. The universal expectation is that the civil service should be neutral in the sense that it is loyal to the basic political order in the state but at the same time is amenable to shifts in political leadership from time to time. Devices for trying to achieve this vary a great deal from country to country, but responsiveness by the administrative staff to the directives of political leaders is an objective commonly sought, even among political regimes that differ greatly in other respects.

Civil service system patterns

Modern civil service systems are largely the products of developments in western Europe, with European patterns then being exported to, or copied by, nations in other parts of the world. In turn, European practices can be traced to historical antecedents in medieval and ancient times. China, Egypt, Greece, and Rome have all contributed something to present-day public administration, but Roman law and Roman administrative institutions have exerted by far the greatest influence. The Roman Empire provided legal principles and the rudiments of an administrative structure that have carried over into modern times.

The emergence of the civil service from ancient and medieval antecedents has been accurately described as a gradual transformation of the royal household into the public service. This occurred earliest and progressed furthest in Europe, particularly in Prussia and in France, where absolute monarchies laid the basis for centralized and professionalized bureaucracies. In Prussia, as early as the middle of the seventeenth century, Frederick William, the great elector of Brandenburg, had succeeded in uprooting feudal administration and creating an efficient administrative organization staffed by trained civil servants selected on a competitive basis. The eighteenth-century Prussian civil service is considered to be the first of the modern civil service systems, and the scientific study of government administration received much attention and formed the basis for training officials. In France, a parallel but weaker development of the administration under the monarchy gave way to the French Revolution and the Napoleonic administrative reforms, which replaced the king with the nation and converted the royal service into the public service. The Napoleonic administrative features of rationality, hierarchy, and competence became models for reform in other countries in Europe and later elsewhere. The Prussian and French systems of administration and civil service, despite their differences, can be grouped together as the European pattern, which continues to be one of the strongest and most influential. This pattern emphasizes the role of the civil servant as the agent of the state, the professionalized and career nature of membership in the civil service, the importance of safeguards to civil service status and tenure, and the crucial contribution of the civil service to continuity in the administration of state affairs.

Great Britain developed another influential pattern of civil service. Administrative evolution was slower, however, because political struggles turned more on issues of parliamentary versus royal ascendancy and of safeguarding individual liberties against the claims of political authority. Although the administrative apparatus became increasingly complex, it continued to be staffed primarily from the aristocracy on a patronage basis and without much regard to administrative efficiency, until the drastic reform measures that were taken in the middle of the nineteenth century. The Trevelyan–Northcote report of 1854 led the following year to the order-in-council that established the Civil Service Commission and laid the basis for civil service reform. The objectives were to abolish patronage, to admit candidates into the service at prescribed ages and through competitive examinations appropriate for the class of civil servant being recruited, and to stress the selection of out-standing Oxford and Cambridge graduates in the classics, history, science, and mathematics for appointment to the higher administrative class. The main features then adopted have been retained and have earned for the British civil service a deserved reputation for combining talent, integrity, and political responsiveness.

In the United States, civil service reform came later and took a somewhat different direction, although it was strongly influenced by the British experience. The patronage system was closely tied to political parties and resulted in frequent rotation in office as party control changed. The price of the "spoils system," in terms of administrative performance, was as a result higher than it had been in Great Britain. Following the Civil War, a civil service reform movement gathered momentum that led in 1883 to passage of the Pendleton Act at the national level and to subsequent reforms in state and local units of government, although substantial segments of the American civil service at these levels continue even today to be operated in the spoils system tradition. The United States civil service tends to reflect characteristics of the governmental system and social system generally. As a consequence, features include considerable mobility of personnel, recruitment on a position rather than a career basis, practical tests rather than examinations stressing broad cultural attainments, a relatively low prestige ranking for membership in the public service, and quasi independence for the central personnel agency. However, there are noticeable changes under way in all these areas, and the tendency seems to be for the American civil service to become more like the British, rather than for the differences between them to increase.

In the Soviet Union and other communist countries, the environment in which public employment exists is so markedly different that to make comparisons with other civil service systems is difficult. The scope of public administration is nearly all-inclusive, and the state has almost a monopoly on employment. The party is dominant in the operation of the administrative apparatus, and the line between party bureaucracy and state bureaucracy is hard to draw except in formal terms. Administration is carried on in a highly political context, and control agencies over administration have proliferated. For the ambitious young person, a choice between public and private employment is not possible since a career in the state service is the only career available.

Nevertheless, the Soviet civil service exhibits many operating characteristics common to bureaucracies everywhere, and methods have been developed in the Soviet Union as elsewhere for maintaining and controlling the personnel system. The main agency responsible for personnel policy and practices is the Central Establishments Administration in the U.S.S.R. Ministry of Finance, with subordinate agencies in the republics. These are not recruiting bodies, however. Employment is the responsibility of the various ministries and agencies. Each sector has its own schools and institutes, and recruitment and placement are closely tied in with the educational system, with graduates of the training schools obligated to serve for a prescribed period in assigned posts. Civil service examinations are not given, nor are panels of candidates provided for appointment. Job evaluation and description are apparently well developed, with wage scales attached to job categories but with variations according to the qualifications of the incumbents. The civil servant is protected from dismissal by a code similar to those in other countries, and an elaborate grievance procedure has been established by law. Within the strict limitations imposed by the political system on choice of career and job mobility, opportunities for advancement are provided for those who can demonstrate loyalty and talent, and the bureaucratic elite enjoys a privileged position in Soviet society.

Major problem areas

A number of recurrent issues have had to be dealt with by most civil service systems. These issues continue to be subject to controversy in regard to principle and subject to variation in practical operations. Some of the most important ones will be discussed briefly.

A central problem is that of selection of qualified personnel for the civil service. Even where competitive selection based on demonstrated competence is accepted as the proper approach, there are sharp differences as to how this should be done. The preference both on the Continent and in England has been to recruit graduates of educational institutions at an early age and on a career basis and, after a period of probation, arrange for the systematic advancement of those whose performance warrants promotion. The selection process is closely geared to the educational system, although there may be different views as to what kind of educational preparation is most appropriate for the future higher civil servant. The historical inclination in the United States, on the other hand, has been to keep opportunities open for entry into the service at all levels, rather than to require a career choice at the time of gradua-

tion, and to emphasize training that is closely related to the professional or technical specialty required on the job.

Nonmerit considerations continue to affect selection in numerous ways. In countries such as the United States, with its spoils background and a multiplicity of governmental jurisdictions, political party affiliation sometimes may still be decisive. In European countries, recruitment may be largely confined, as a matter of practice, to candidates from middle and upper social and economic groups rather than carried out on a basis that is more representative of the whole populace. All countries impose some standards of political loyalty. In communist countries, this identification with the ruling party becomes a primary consideration, although there is considerable evidence that professional qualifications receive increasing attention in choosing from among those meeting the political requirements. In developing countries where the supply of qualified manpower falls far short of existing and foreseeable needs, there is a tendency to overstress education as shown by degrees held and to relate placement in the civil service almost exclusively to this factor rather than to capacity to perform the work of the government.

Another common dilemma is how to make arrangements for status and for pay within the service. A complex modern bureaucracy must have a method for relating officials to one another in some systematic way. By far the most common system is one that utilizes a small number of broad classes within the service and then assigns ranks to the civil servants in each of these categories. Both Great Britain and France have four such general classes common to the ministries and departments, with the division based on clearly defined standards of education and training and with only limited movement upward from one category to another. The status of the civil servant is determined by his rank and the class to which he belongs, rather than by the particular assignment that he has at any given time. He is considered as primarily a member of a corps of career officials, rather than as the occupant of a particular position. There are indications that the rank system has advantages that make it more attractive to many of the newly independent states.

A contrasting approach is used in the United States, Canada, Brazil, and a few other countries influenced by American practice. Here the basic element in the civil service structure is the position, which is defined as a cluster of duties and responsibilities calling for the services of an individual. The position held determines status in such a duties classsification system, and similar positions are grouped into classes of positions, the occupants of which receive common treatment in matters of selection, pay, and so forth. These two systems are not mutually exclusive, however, and in many countries are employed together in various combinations.

Adequate compensation for civil servants, particularly in the higher categories, is essential to attract and hold qualified people. Only a few countries have succeeded in maintaining such pay levels and other perquisites. The best record has been made in the well-established and prestigious career services of western Europe. In the United States, compensation levels are competitive in the lower and middle levels but are grossly inadequate for the higher administrative, professional, and technical positions. In most of the developing countries, low salary scales are a major factor in explaining prevalent conditions of petty corruption, overstaffing, and low production.

The setting of suitable standards of conduct for civil servants is another common problem area in all systems. As an agent of the state, and in return for tenure and other guarantees, the civil servant is usually subjected to special regulations on matters such as the ethical standards he is expected to observe, the extent of permissible union activity, and participation in political life. Ethical norms in the civil service reflect, of course, the ethics of the society as a whole and vary widely from culture to culture [see ETHICS]. The general expectation is that the public servant should more than meet the standards prevalent in the community, and this is reflected in civil service regulations even where it is not achieved in practice. Integrity of behavior is part of the tradition in well-established civil service systems, such as the British system. In contrast, laxity in ethics often is a major problem in some developing countries, where temptation is great and administrative self-control is lower.

Organized activity by civil servants to negotiate with the state as employer is ordinarily accepted but frequently is restricted to a narrower compass than in the private sector. Officially sponsored machinery for joint consultation between management and staff has often been provided, the most successful example being the Whitley councils set up in Great Britain after World War I and copied elsewhere. But the usual channel is civil service unionism. In most countries, the right of association in unions has been established and with it the right of civil service unions to affiliate with the general trade union movement, but resort to the strike as a weapon by civil servants is not normally accepted, and in several countries, including the United States, it is expressly forbidden by law.

Policy concerning the political rights of civil servants is not uniform. Some European countries impose hardly any restrictions, even allowing the civil servant to serve in legislative bodies, including the national parliament, although with varying provisions concerning his civil service status while in office. Great Britain categorizes civil servants according to their policy-making functions and the public sensitivity of their duties and has a differential policy that frees a large proportion of civil servants for normal political activities and prohibits others only from membership in the House of Commons. The United States has a much more restrictive approach, with national legislation barring not only most civil servants in the national government but also state and local officials paid from federal funds from active participation in political management and in political campaigns. Most local governmental units with merit systems impose similar limitations on their civil servants.

The relationship of the civil service to other instrumentalities of government and to outside interest groups is a topic of concern in any political system. In the Western democracies, the role of the bureaucracy is fairly well defined and the problem is essentially one of maintaining an existing balance, which has been worked out over a long period of time. Despite apprehension in some quarters that the civil service has gained undue policy-making power, the principle that the career officials must be responsive to political leadership is clearly recognized. In the communist countries, the monolithic nature of the political system leaves no doubt as to the subservient position of the state bureaucracy, although as these polities mature, the bureaucracy may be able to build up a more influential role and protect it in competition with other power centers.

The most interesting current question has to do with the place of the career public service in the newly independent developing countries. Ordinarily in these nations the civil service has been the most fully matured governmental institution at the time of independence. Particularly in former British colonies such as India, Pakistan, and Nigeria, a strong civil service had already been built up, including native as well as expatriate officials. This undoubtedly has facilitated the transition to self-government, but it also has caused concern as to the long-run prospects for democratic development in the Western pattern. The reasons include an alleged carry-over from the colonial period of attitudes of superiority and disdain toward the public and a preoccupation with law and order considerations rather than with programs of economic development and social welfare. But the main argument is that the professionalization and expansion of the civil service has outpaced the growth of executive, legislative, and judicial organs of government, not to mention the development of interest groups in the private sector. This has led some to advocate a deliberate slowdown in further improvements of the public service until the rest of the political system has had a chance to catch up. Despite the superficial appeal of this thesis, it probably reflects an overoptimistic view of the adequacy of most transitional bureaucracies to meet the extraordinary demands pressed upon them, and it rests on what is still an unproved assumption that relatively weak bureaucratic institutions will give other political institutions a better chance to grow. At any rate, it is evident that the career civil service occupies a position of crucial importance in determining the political future of the non-Western developing countries.

Approaches and trends in writing and research

Both past and present literature on civil service reflects the stages through which contemporary civil service systems have evolved. Emphasis will be placed on American sources because they are most voluminous, as well as representative of what has been done in other countries.

After the middle of the nineteenth century, when systematic attention was first given to civil service issues, the initial concern was almost exclusively with a reform or "fight the spoilsmen" approach. The movement had the twin objectives of cleaning up politics and improving the quality of administration, and the British model was advocated with modifications to fit the American circumstances. The writings of those involved in the reform movement were highly significant in the accomplishment of civil service reforms.

After merit systems had been widely adopted, attention shifted to personnel management as a technical specialty, with concentration after the turn of the century on such subjects as examination techniques, position classification, promotion criteria, performance rating, employee relations, and organization for personnel administration. Personnel work became a professional field of specialization with its own standards and criteria for judging performance. A parallel development was the linkage between personnel administration

in public and private employment, with interchange of techniques based on the assumption that there were no fundamental differences between the two spheres.

In recent years a dominant theme, which began in the late 1920s and early 1930s and is usually associated with the "Hawthorne experiments" conducted at the Western Electric Company, has been to give special attention to human relations aspects of civil service operations and to apply findings from sociopsychological research to the relationships between productivity and motivation, small-group behavior, and supervisory practices. This led to a marked reorientation of personnel programs toward more emphasis on factors affecting work performance and relatively less emphasis on selection, status, and separation processes.

Notable current trends, which give every indication of continuing, include sociological studies of civil services as bureaucratic systems; reconsideration of public policies concerning such controversial matters as civil service unionism, political activity, and ethical standards; and increasing attention to problems of civil service contributions to the future development of the developing nations. All of these interests have encouraged the pursuit of comparative studies between public and private sectors of administration within nations and across national boundaries among civil service systems. These are healthy tendencies that should lead to a better understanding and to the future improvement of the civil service in diverse political settings.

FERREL HEADY

[*See also* ADMINISTRATION; BUREAUCRACY; MODERNIZATION; PUBLIC ADMINISTRATION.]

BIBLIOGRAPHY

AMERICAN ASSEMBLY (1954) 1965 *The Federal Government Service.* Englewood Cliffs, N.J.: Prentice-Hall.

BERGER, MORROE 1957 *Bureaucracy and Society in Modern Egypt: A Study of the Higher Civil Service.* Princeton Oriental Studies: Social Science, No. 1. Princeton Univ. Press.

CHAPMAN, BRIAN 1959 *The Profession of Government: The Public Service in Europe.* London: Allen & Unwin.

COLE, TAYLOR 1949 *The Canadian Bureaucracy: A Study of Canadian Civil Servants and Other Public Employees, 1939–1947.* Durham, N.C.: Duke Univ. Press.

EISENSTADT, SHMUEL N. 1963 *The Political Systems of Empires.* New York: Free Press.

FAINSOD, MERLE (1953) 1963 *How Russia Is Ruled.* Rev. ed. Russian Research Center Studies, No. 11. Cambridge, Mass.: Harvard Univ. Press.

FINER, HERMAN (1932) 1961 *Theory and Practice of Modern Government.* 4th ed. London: Methuen.

GRÉGOIRE, ROGER 1954 *La fonction publique.* Paris: Colin.

Grégoire, Roger 1956 The Civil Service in Western Europe. *Public Personnel Review* 17:288–294.

Hazard, John N. (1957) 1964 *The Soviet System of Government.* 3d ed., rev. & enl. Univ. of Chicago Press.

Heady, Ferrel 1966 *Public Administration: A Comparative Perspective.* Englewood Cliffs, N.J.: Prentice-Hall.

Kilpatrick, Franklin P.; Cummings, Milton C.; and Jennings, M. Kent 1964 *The Image of the Federal Service.* Washington: Brookings Institution.

LaPalombara, Joseph G. (editor) 1963 *Bureaucracy and Political Development.* Studies in Political Development, No. 2. Princeton Univ. Press.

Morstein Marx, Fritz 1957 *The Administrative State: An Introduction to Bureaucracy.* Univ. of Chicago Press.

Nigro, Felix A. 1959 *Public Personnel Administration.* New York: Holt.

Pigors, Paul; and Myers, Charles A. (1947) 1965 *Personnel Administration: A Point of View and a Method.* 5th ed. New York: McGraw-Hill.

Ribas, Jacques Jean 1956 *Les services de la fonction publique dans le monde.* Brussels: Institut International des Sciences Administratives.

Robson, William A. (editor) 1956 *The Civil Service in Britain and France.* New York: Macmillan; London: Hogarth.

Spero, Sterling D. 1948 *Government as Employer.* New York: Remsen Press.

Stahl, Oscar Glen (1936) 1962 *Public Personnel Administration.* 5th ed. New York: Harper → The authors of earlier editions were William E. Mosher and J. Donald Kingsley.

Van Riper, Paul P. 1958 *History of the United States Civil Service.* Evanston, Ill.: Row, Peterson.

CIVIL WAR

See Internal warfare.

CIVILIZATION

For a discussion of the concept of civilization, and a description of the early civilizations of the Old and New Worlds, see the articles under Urban revolution.

CLAN

See Kinship, *article on* descent groups.

CLAPARÈDE, ÉDOUARD

Édouard Claparède (1873–1940), Swiss psychologist, was born in Geneva. His choice of a career was decisively influenced by his cousin, Theodore Flournoy, also a psychologist, and his uncle, Édouard Claparède, a zoologist. After attending secondary school in Geneva, Claparède studied medicine in Leipzig and Geneva, concluding these studies with a thesis entitled *Du sens musculaire à propos de quelques cas d'hémiataxie posthémiplégique* (1897). He spent a year in Paris, where he worked with Joseph Déjerine in neurology and became acquainted with Alfred Binet.

Returning to Geneva, where he remained for the rest of his life, Claparède worked in Flournoy's psychological laboratory and as *Privatdozent* began giving a course on sensation. At the same time, he continued his work in neurology and became interested in animal psychology. Karl Groos's book, *The Play of Animals,* had a decisive influence on Claparède at that time, orienting him toward a functional point of view. In 1901, together with Flournoy, he founded the *Archives de psychologie,* of which he had charge until his death.

Claparède, in his book *L'association des idées* (1903), was one of the first to show the shortcomings of the associationism then dominant in the world of psychology. Two or three years before H. J. Watt and N. Ach wrote about the role of instructions and determining tendencies, Claparède realized that the problem of association cannot be solved without taking into account the entire set of attitudes of the subject to whom the inducing word is presented. This led him to consider the functional question of the value of an association for the subject's immediate situation or of the significance to the subject of the goal that may be attained by an association. He concluded that an "autonomous mechanism of the association of ideas" operates only in the case of fortuitous or purely mechanical associations; associations with relevance for the subject's situation are determined by the interest or meaning aroused by a particular connection and, hence, by an impelling quality that cannot be explained by association per se. [*See* Gestalt theory.]

Next, Claparède published his theory of sleep (1905a), the origin of which he described with some humor. In the course of an improvised lecture, he was rash enough to include sleep in the list of instinctive reactions and on his return home tried to discover whether he had, in fact, said something foolish. He quickly rejected the classical interpretation that sleep is a toxic reaction, suggesting instead that sleep is anticipatory protection against toxicity, or more general protection, as with hibernation. [*See* Sleep.]

In 1909, Claparède served as general secretary of the Sixth International Congress of Psychology, of which Flournoy was president; thereafter he attended all the international congresses of psychology, becoming permanent secretary and so insuring continuity between successive congresses. (Later the International Union of Scientific Psychology was founded, with a permanent secretary general.)

As early as 1906, Claparède had established a seminar in educational psychology, but it was met with hostility from the academic authorities. He also published his *Psychologie de l'enfant* (1905*b*), four editions of which were rapidly sold out (even though this was only an introductory volume and the further volumes were, unfortunately, never written). In 1912 he founded the Institut J. J. Rousseau, for the purpose of promoting child psychology and its application to pedagogy. The institute was highly successful, although it was initially organized on a private basis; eventually, in 1947, it became affiliated with the University of Geneva under the name Institut des Sciences de l'Éducation. Claparède had been appointed associate professor of psychology at the university in 1908, and in 1919 he succeeded Flournoy in the chair of experimental psychology.

In the last 25 years of his life Claparède published a whole series of experimental studies. One particularly interesting study, which appeared in 1918, dealt with the child's awareness of similarity and difference. In it, Claparède showed that although young children can much more readily describe differences between two objects (for example, a bee and a fly) than point out similarities, children do constantly generalize, which means making use of similarities. Accordingly, he formulated his "law of awareness," which states that the individual is not aware of mechanisms that work smoothly, awareness being aroused only by conflicts, problems, or maladjustments in general. [*See* LEARNING, *article on* DISCRIMINATION LEARNING; PERCEPTION, *article on* PERCEPTUAL DEVELOPMENT.]

Claparède devoted some attention to the field of the growth of intelligence. He maintained that a child's intelligence develops as he proceeds through a series of trials and errors (*tâtonne*) first to handle material objects and then to formulate hypotheses. In an article published in 1933, Claparède studied the formation of these hypotheses. Instead of announcing only the result of the reflections that led to the solution of a problem, his subjects had been trained to think out loud, to produce, as it were, a "spoken reflection." This procedure indicated that the subjects' tentative steps were guided, and sometimes preceded, by a kind of insight into "immediate implications"; Claparède gave a number of examples of such insights.

As early as 1929, at the closing session of the International Congress of Psychology at New Haven, Claparède spoke on the possible role that psychologists might play in international understanding, and he returned to this theme in 1937 in Paris, at the end of the Eleventh Congress. In 1928, he participated in the founding of the Bureau International de l'Éducation.

JEAN PIAGET

[*For discussion of the subsequent development of Claparède's ideas, see* CONCEPT FORMATION; DEVELOPMENTAL PSYCHOLOGY; INTELLECTUAL DEVELOPMENT; PROBLEM SOLVING.]

WORKS BY CLAPARÈDE

1897   *Du sens musculaire à propos de quelques cas d'hémiataxie posthémiplégique.* Geneva: Eggimann.
1903   *L'association des idées.* Paris: Doin.
1905a   Esquisse d'une théorie biologique du sommeil. *Archives de psychologie* 4:245–349.
(1905b) 1911   *Experimental Pedagogy and the Psychology of the Child.* New York: Longmans. → Translated from the 4th edition of *Psychologie de l'enfant et pédagogie expérimentale* by Mary Louch and Henry Holman.
1918   La conscience de la ressemblance et de la différence chez l'enfant. *Archives de psychologie* 17:67–78.
(1930) 1961   Autobiography. Volume 1, pages 63–97 in Carl Murchison (editor), *A History of Psychology in Autobiography.* New York: Russell. → Translated from the French by P. Beineman.
1933   La genèse de l'hypothèse: Étude expérimentale. *Archives de psychologie* 24:1–155.

CLAPHAM, JOHN HAROLD

John Harold Clapham (1873–1946), English economic historian, was born in Salford, Lancashire, of Wesleyan parents; his father was a jeweler and silversmith. Clapham's family was down-to-earth, disciplined, and unsentimental, and these qualities, coupled with integrity, characterized both the man and his scholarship. As a schoolboy he read Classics at the Leys School, Cambridge, and won a history scholarship to King's College, Cambridge, in 1892. Then, after a first class in the historical tripos, he won the Lightfoot scholarship in ecclesiastical history and the Prince Consort prize in 1898. Much of his early work lay in general European history, as did two of his first books, *The Causes of the War of 1792* (1899) and *The Abbé Sieyès* (1912), and several articles.

From 1898 to 1902 he resided as a fellow at King's College and worked under Lord Acton, Frederic W. Maitland, and Alfred Marshall. It was largely the influence of Marshall that induced Clapham to bend his energies to British economic history. Indeed, a letter from Marshall to Acton dated November 13, 1897, reveals Marshall's hopes: "I feel that the absence of any tolerable account of the economic development of England during the last century and a half," he wrote, "is a disgrace to the land, and a grievous hindrance to the right understanding of the economic problems of our time. . . . Clapham has more analytic faculty than any thorough historian whom I have ever taught; his future work is I think still uncertain. . . . If you could turn him towards XVIII and XIX century economic history economists would ever be grateful to you. . . ." (Sir John Clapham . . . 1946, p. 115). Marshall's influence was powerfully reinforced during the next formative period in Clapham's life when, in 1902, he went to Leeds, in Yorkshire, as professor of economics. He did much to shape the fortunes of the economics faculty in the new university and to establish close links with the local business community. His first important monograph in economic history was in an area appropriate for a Yorkshire professor: *The Woollen and Worsted Industries* (1907). During this period he also wrote many articles in economic history. Then, in 1908, Clapham returned to King's as dean and assistant tutor in history. From that date until his death in 1946, except during the two world wars, he lectured on English economic history, establishing this subject in the historical tripos for many generations of undergraduates.

He became increasingly burdened with office and dignities, conscious that he represented economic history perhaps more than any other scholar in the field in Britain. In King's College he was for 20 years senior tutor and, after 1936, vice-provost. The first chair of economic history in the university was established for him in 1928, and this constituted a major gesture of recognition on the part of that university. He became a hard-working president of the Economic History Society, president of the British Academy, a syndic of the Cambridge Press for 30 years, and founder and editor of the *Cambridge Studies in Economic History* and the *Cambridge Economic History of Europe*—grander designs than Marshall had envisaged. Clapham was knighted in 1943. His stature as a scholar did not diminish, however, as his administrative responsibilities accumulated. His own career gave a sort of institutional imprimatur to economic history as his own writings gave it scholastic probity. Characteristically, he took on two new lecture courses a few years before his death, one on the economic history of Europe, the other on France before the Revolution, and completed his major historical work *The Bank of England* (1944), at the same time fulfilling various wartime commitments. He was working to the last on volumes of the *Cambridge Economic History of Europe* and on his own general work, published posthumously as *A Concise Economic History of Britain From the Earliest Times to 1750.*

Clapham's greatest work was to lie not in the detailed working out of particular problems in monographs or articles but in the clearing of whole landscapes. First came *The Economic Development of France and Germany, 1815–1914* in 1921; then followed the three massive volumes of *An Economic History of Modern Britain* (1926–1938). He set his sights in the preface of the first volume, intending to work on a completely new scale, "to make the story more nearly quantitative than it has yet been made . . . to offer dimensions in place of blurred masses of unspecified size" ([1926] 1950, vol. 1, pp. vii–viii). Unsubstantiated assumptions as well as ignorance gave way before his steady accumulation and deployment of data. As his successor to the chair, M. M. Postan, acknowledged in 1938: "On the ground in which Dr. Clapham has worked and still works he found a mass of half-knowledge, overgrown with picturesque and stubborn weeds. This ground he not only cleared but in his own inimitable, lapidary way, has covered with a structure of facts as hard and certain as granite" (1939, p. 6).

Clapham did not believe that economic history should have its own methodology but that it should remain integral with human history. He was never imprisoned by hypotheses couched in purely economic or quantifiable terms. Indeed, his own view of economic history as a discipline was firm but modest: it was the most fundamental of all varieties of history, he wrote, not the most important. He marshaled his data not so much into statistical series upon which to forge theoretical tools of analysis as into a human record of change and achievement, and his landscape is not one of explanatory hypotheses but one of developing institutions, changes in the broad pattern of industrial and commercial organization, output, policy, trade, and agriculture.

This is not to say that Clapham worked in an analytical vacuum, isolated from theory. He was widely admired by the economists at the London School of Economics, agreeing with their advocacy of economic liberalism in current policy. Marshall was his mentor and A. C. Pigou and J. M. Keynes were his colleagues at King's College. Perhaps being so close to Keynes and the Cambridge economists in his everyday life made him aware that economic theory was changing so rapidly that historical investigation organized in terms of one set of assumptions would soon be overtaken by investigations organized in terms of others. He did not say this explicitly, but he did comment that much of the theoretical apparatus current in the social sciences was revealed as vacuous when put to the test of a concrete historical situation (1922). He thus became a man of periods rather than of problems, conscious that he was providing the groundwork upon which others might construct. Varying interpretations might come and go upon the winds of new theories, but the essential infrastructure (a word he would not have wished to use himself) would remain. The assumption that tested facts, firm in the light of critical historical research, stand somehow apart from and prior to ideas and hypotheses—that economic history can be built from them brick upon brick—raises problems of its own, of course. The result may be unchallengeable but largely tangential to problems and relationships that later generations see as crucial areas for analysis. In this sense, perhaps, Clapham's massive surveys have become dated more than his monographs. Certainly, Clapham's call for quantities has been answered by a deluge of figures: by national income accounts, with the intersectoral comparisons they make possible; by investment and output series; by growth-rate calculations; and by balances of payments, terms of trade, and cyclical and trend analysis tables. All these came after his death, as did the flood of economic history inspired by theoretical concepts of Keynesian or post-Keynesian economics and by the problems of economic growth facing the postwar world.

PETER MATHIAS

[*For the historical context of Clapham's work, see the biographies of* ACTON; MAITLAND; MARSHALL. *For discussion of the subsequent development of his ideas, see* HISTORY, *article on* ECONOMIC HISTORY.]

WORKS BY CLAPHAM

1899   *The Causes of the War of 1792.* Cambridge Historical Essays, No. 11. Cambridge Univ. Press.

1907   *The Woollen and Worsted Industries.* London: Methuen.

1912   *The Abbé Sieyès: An Essay in the Politics of the French Revolution.* London: King.

(1921) 1961   *The Economic Development of France and Germany, 1815–1914.* 4th ed. Cambridge Univ. Press.

1922   *Of Empty Economic Boxes. Economic Journal* 32: 305–314, 560–563.

(1926–1938) 1950–1952   *An Economic History of Modern Britain.* 3 vols. Cambridge Univ. Press. → Volume 1: *The Early Railway Age, 1820–1850.* Volume 2: *Free Trade and Steel, 1850–1886.* Volume 3: *Machines and National Rivalries (1887–1914) With an Epilogue (1914–1929).*

1944   *The Bank of England: A History.* 2 vols. Cambridge Univ. Press.

(1949) 1957   *A Concise Economic History of Britain From the Earliest Times to 1750.* Rev. ed. Cambridge Univ. Press. → A paperback edition was published in 1964 by Cambridge Univ. Press.

SUPPLEMENTARY BIBLIOGRAPHY

Bibliography of Sir John Clapham. 1946   *Cambridge Historical Journal* 8: 205–206.

CLARK, G. N. 1946   Sir John Harold Clapham, 1873–1946. British Academy, London, *Proceedings* 32: 339–352.

POSTAN, MICHAEL M. 1939   *The Historical Method in Social Science: An Inaugural Lecture.* Cambridge Univ. Press.

Sir John Clapham, 1873–1946. 1946   *Cambridge Historical Journal* 8: 115–116.

CLARK, JOHN BATES

John Bates Clark (1847–1938) was the leading creative economic theorist active in America during the period when Alfred Marshall and the great Austrian marginalists were active abroad. He developed a distinctive form of marginal utility–marginal productivity theory, which he presented not as a completed system, but as a first approximation and an approach to further analysis. His major theoretical work was cast in the form of comparative statics: he constructed the model of an imaginary "static state"—one of complete competitive equilibrium—following which he analyzed the general effects of hypothetical dynamic changes, including the "dynamic friction" encountered by adjustments to these changes. His work is permeated by a social–ethical perspective that is not always well integrated with the technical economic analysis.

Clark was descended from New England Puritans. In him the original rigorous and doctrinaire features of this heritage had been relaxed and humanized, but a powerful religious and moral conviction remained. He was a lifelong active church member. His ancestors included farmers and prosperous traders; all were moved by public duty. His father was a modestly successful retailer in Providence, Rhode Island, who became a trusted adviser in the Corliss Engine Works, later moved to Minnesota in search of health, and there engaged in a small plow business.

Clark attended Amherst College, twice interrupting his study to take charge of his father's firm when his father was incapacitated. After his father's death he disposed of the plow business. He was graduated from Amherst in 1872, more mature and experienced than most college graduates.

He had contemplated entering the ministry but was advised to pursue economics by Professor

Julius Seelye (later president of Amherst), who recognized Clark's promise in that field. He studied in Europe for three years, mainly at Heidelberg and Zurich, his chief professor being Karl Knies. From his exposure to the German historical school he absorbed chiefly what fitted his predisposition toward a social–ethical perspective, which also made him sympathetic with British Christian socialism.

Returning to the United States, he married Myra Smith, also of New England ancestry, and joined the faculty of Carleton College, but for two years he was prevented from teaching by a crippling illness. Compelled to husband his limited working strength, he saved the best hour of each day for writing and began in 1877 to publish in *The New Englander* magazine the essays that later became *The Philosophy of Wealth* (1886). His most brilliant student was Thorstein Veblen, whose quality he appreciated and whose difficulties with the college authorities he attempted to alleviate. Veblen's later writings had some kinship with the critical portions of Clark's *Philosophy of Wealth*, with the difference that Clark's criticism of social evils was always combined with a search for remedies.

In 1881 Clark went to Smith College, which was then six years old, where he taught until 1893, doing some part-time teaching at Amherst. He was active in forming the American Economic Association in 1885 and was its third president. During this time he formed a lifelong friendship with Franklin H. Giddings, then writing for a Springfield newspaper, and collaborated with him on economic writings. Having briefly presented his "social effective utility" theory of value in the *Philosophy of Wealth*, Clark staked out his marginal productivity theory of distribution in an early publication of the American Economic Association (1889). He presented his marginal productivity theory at the same session of the American Economic Association at which Stuart Wood presented his version. From 1893 to 1895 he taught full-time at Amherst; his students there included Calvin Coolidge, Lucius R. Eastman, Harlan F. Stone, and Dwight Morrow. Morrow spoke long afterward of the profound influence Clark had had upon him. Clark also lectured at Johns Hopkins, and in 1895 he joined the recently established faculty of political science at Columbia University. His more mature works appeared while he was at Columbia.

Becoming convinced that war was the greatest threat to human destiny, he took an increasingly active part in the peace movement, and after the Carnegie Endowment for International Peace was established he was chosen, in 1911, to head its division of economics and history. This post he held until his final retirement in 1923, continuing limited lecturing in economics at Columbia. He enlisted an international committee of distinguished scholars for a massive world-wide study of the economic effects of war. Work on the project was deferred by World War I, and it was later recast and completed under the editorship of Clark's successor, J. T. Shotwell.

Much of Clark's first book, *The Philosophy of Wealth*, consists of criticism of classical economics, and there is in it no constructive theory so completely worked out as that in his more famous *Distribution of Wealth*. In the earlier book Clark stressed the organic social character of economic processes and values. Although individual choices may be made marginally, they are nevertheless socially conditioned, since market forces are in fact integrated through social judgments embodied in the legal system. Instead of seeing self-centered interest alone as the key to human nature, Clark considered people to be motivated by a rational balance between different kinds of personal interests, self-centered and social.

He criticized classical economics for ignoring the importance of "inappropriable values," for example, those values created when an area is opened by railroads. He distinguished several forms of competition: competition in a framework of prevailing prices he characterized as rivalry in serving, whereas sharp bargaining for favorable departures from the market he classed as a form of plunder. When competition had already passed through both the conservative rivalry phase and the later destructive rivalry phase and had begun to move toward consolidation and monopoly, he looked favorably on a possible evolution based on producers' cooperation but thought it would succeed only under certain conditions.

He believed that workers need the protection of unions and that every man has the right to a living, particularly if socially generated adjustments prevent him from earning one. He deplored the economic "caste system" that prevails among certain Protestant denominations because it vitiates the spirit of fraternity so important to his religious beliefs. The ethical message of *The Philosophy of Wealth* elicited wide acclaim, as well as some criticism.

In Clark's next major work, *The Distribution of Wealth* (1899), he developed much more fully the marginalist theories for which he became known. His theories were published later than those of the great contemporary marginalists, but, so far as can be determined, they were independently arrived at.

Clark separated economic theory into statics and dynamics, presenting the statics first, as a first approximation and an approach to the greater complexities of dynamics. A dynamic analysis was his ultimate objective, but his "dynamics" were what we would now call comparative statics. Thus he depicted the forces acting toward equilibrium by means of an elaborate model of an imaginary society from which dynamic change and disturbance were eliminated, permitting the static forces to act in isolation and to bring processes to their "natural" (static) levels. The valid elements in the Ricardian type of deductive theory could thus be seen in properly limited perspective as unconscious statics (1899, pp. 68–69).

In this book Clark generalized the Ricardian marginal principle, applying it to both labor and capital (to which he assimilated land) and concluding that in the competitive static state the owners of all productive factors would get what each factor (marginally) produces. Although his conclusion was an important contribution to marginal analysis, the ethical approval he attached to his marginal productivity theory left many loose ends and is probably best construed as an emphatic rebuttal to the exploitation theories of Henry George and Karl Marx, in which rent and profits are, inherently, robbery.

Clark's *Distribution* contains a distinctive variant of utility theory. This is his idea that commodities represent "bundles of utilities"—that is, they have embodied in them diverse qualitative increments of utilities—and, further, that different purchasers are marginal for different items in such a "bundle" (1899, pp. 214, 220, 229–244). For example, a millionaire is a marginal buyer for the difference between a fine and a superfine watch, whereas poorer men determine the values of cruder grades of watches, for which the millionaire would be willing to pay much higher prices if he had to. E. R. A. Seligman called this "Clark's law." Its acceptance has suffered from its perhaps fortuitous alliance with the vulnerable doctrine of consumers' surplus, and its meaning seems currently submerged in the abstractions of indifference maps.

The concept of capital advanced in *The Distribution of Wealth* has become a part of the permanent legacy of economics. Clark distinguished capital goods from social capital, which is the permanent flow of resource services or future incomes, of which the capital goods are a temporary embodiment. It is the marginal productivity of social capital, not of specific capital goods, that determines the rate of interest.

This capital concept differs greatly from that of Clark's influential contemporary Böhm-Bawerk, and a lively controversy emerged between them. Clark (and, on different grounds, Irving Fisher) attacked Böhm-Bawerk's theory that capital constitutes advances to laborers and capitalists during the "period of production." Clark's thesis that production and consumption are "synchronous" was generally accepted by the theoretical tradition.

In his *Essentials of Economic Theory* (1907) Clark noted that the economic laws he analyzed apply only to economically developed regions in which factors are mobile and their response to market forces active (pp. 210–215). World-wide equilibrium between developed and underdeveloped areas he considered too long-term a matter for analysis; in actuality, a stable outcome would be heavily dependent on technical progress. Without considerable technical progress the developed economies would be forced down to the level of the underdeveloped (pp. 227–228).

After a condensed review of statics, Clark analyzed the impact of five major dynamic changes: growth of population, growth of capital, technical improvement, changes in market organization, and changes in consumers' wants, seeking to provide inductive dynamics with a deductive framework. Thus he made a heroic attempt to deduce the effect of each change by itself and then to combine them all (1907, esp. chapters 14–17). For the combined effects, he could cite observed tendencies and rationalize them. It is a tribute to his sense of reality that the bold attempt yielded meaningful results.

The proposition that a vigorously dynamic economy hovers closer to its temporary static norms than does a sluggish or stagnant one is convincing, even if it was not rigorously derived. Clark predicted that the increase of qualitative refinements of products will outstrip the increase in amount of materials consumed (1907, pp. 293 ff.) and declared that the displacement of one kind of machine tending by another inflicts less hardship on the worker than does the displacement of a skilled manual craft (1907, pp. 298–299). Machine tending is now being displaced by something harder to learn than another kind of machine tending, the enormous growth of professional and managerial services and departments of research and planning, but these could hardly have been foreseen in 1907. Clark recognized that dynamics includes relative time rates of change and reaction, but he did not fully treat this factor.

Of the five major dynamic changes he considered technical improvement the most important. Technical improvement is promoted by a judicious combination of competition and temporary monopoly or by delays in imitating successful innovations (1907, pp. 360–368). Ideally, the patent monopoly confers rights to something that would not have existed without the innovation, so that no one loses by the innovator's temporary tribute. Actually, rights could be made unduly broad; and an industry built on them could establish a monopoly power extending beyond the proper coverage of the patent. Meanwhile, competition between large corporations generates more rapid improvement than does monopoly, while their rivalry speeds the passing of the benefits on to the public.

In the concluding chapters of the *Essentials* Clark dealt with other specific problems, including principles of transportation and railroad problems, labor organization, wage arbitration and boycotts, protection in relation to monopoly, and money. In his analyses of current problems he always attempted to discover and apply general principles.

On the question of monopoly and competition he published two small but influential volumes, *The Control of Trusts* (1901) and *The Problem of Monopoly* (1904). In them he stressed the force of potential competition, the methods of unfair competition that had been used to handicap or extinguish small competitors, and the need to protect small competitors against such methods. His ideas were reflected in the part of the antitrust legislation of 1914 that included the prohibition of unfair competition and in the establishment of a Fair Trade Commission.

The contrast between the morally critical tone of *The Philosophy of Wealth* and the analytical emphasis and optimism of Clark's later theoretical works has suggested to many that his ethical views changed. On this difficult question the present writer is persuaded that the observed differences stem partly from a change in Clark's method of theoretical analysis, that is, his use of a model economy, and partly from his adaptation to new events. Enlightening evidence is afforded by his last economic utterance, a published lecture entitled *Social Justice Without Socialism* (1914). He no longer recommended producers' cooperation, with its merging of groups or classes; it had not fulfilled his optimistic expectations. Instead, he stressed collaboration between existing groups, in a prospective system of democratically disciplined economic activity amounting to a "welfare state." It seems that the author of *The Philosophy of Wealth* was responding to historical developments without changing his basic values.

Clark's concern with the preservation of peace persisted: his last publication, *A Tender of Peace* (1935), was a brief plea for a League of Nations with sufficient power and resolution to enforce peace. Clark died at 91 in March 1938, the year before world war again engulfed civilization.

JOHN M. CLARK

[*For the historical context of Clark's work, see* ECONOMIC THOUGHT, *articles on* THE AUSTRIAN SCHOOL *and* THE HISTORICAL SCHOOL; *and the biographies of* GEORGE; JEVONS; MARSHALL; MARX; MENGER; WIESER. *For discussion of the development of Clark's ideas both during and after his time, see* CAPITAL; UTILITY; WAGES, *article on* THEORY; *and the biographies of* BÖHM-BAWERK; FISHER, I.; VEBLEN.]

WORKS BY CLARK

1886   *The Philosophy of Wealth: Economic Principles Newly Formulated.* Boston: Ginn.

1888   *Capital and Its Earnings.* American Economic Association Monographs, Vol. 3, No. 2. Baltimore: American Economic Association.

1888   CLARK, JOHN BATES; and GIDDINGS, FRANKLIN H. *The Modern Distributive Process.* Boston: Ginn.

1889   *The Possibility of a Scientific Law of Wages.* Volume 4, pages 37–69 in American Economic Association, *Publications.* Baltimore: American Economic Association.

(1899) 1902   *The Distribution of Wealth: A Theory of Wages, Interest and Profits.* New York and London: Macmillan.

(1901) 1912   *The Control of Trusts.* 2d ed., enl. New York and London: Macmillan.

1904   *The Problem of Monopoly: A Study of a Grave Danger and of the Natural Mode of Averting It.* New York and London: Macmillan.

1907   *Essentials of Economic Theory as Applied to Modern Problems of Industry and Public Policy.* New York: Macmillan.

1914   *Social Justice Without Socialism.* Boston and New York: Houghton Mifflin.

1935   *A Tender of Peace: The Terms on Which Civilized Nations Can, If They Will, Avoid Warfare.* New York: Columbia Univ. Press.

WORKS ABOUT CLARK

[The Bibliography of] John Bates Clark. 1931 Pages 77–90 in Columbia University, Faculty of Political Science, *A Bibliography . . . 1880–1930.* New York: Columbia Univ. Press.

CLARK, A. H.; and CLARK, JOHN M. 1938 *John Bates Clark: A Memorial.* New York: Columbia Univ. Press.

CLARK, JOHN M. 1952 J. B. Clark. Pages 592–612 in Henry W. Spiegel (editor), *The Development of Economic Thought: Great Economists in Perspective.* New York: Wiley.

DORFMAN, JOSEPH 1949 John Bates Clark: The Conflict of Logic and Sentiment. Volume 3, pages 188–205 in Joseph Dorfman, *The Economic Mind in American Civilization.* New York: Viking.

HOLLANDER, JACOB H. (editor) 1927 *Economic Essays, Contributed in Honor of John Bates Clark.* Published on behalf of the American Economic Association. New York: Macmillan.

HOMAN, PAUL T. 1928 John Bates Clark. Pages 17–103 in Paul T. Homan, *Contemporary Economic Thought.* New York: Harper.

Shotwell, James T. 1938 John Bates Clark, 1847–1938: A Tribute. Pages 157–163 in Carnegie Endowment for International Peace, *Annual Report for 1937 of the Division of Economics and History*. New York: Carnegie Endowment.

Stigler, George J. (1941) 1948 John Bates Clark. Pages 296–319 in George J. Stigler, *Production and Distribution Theories*. New York: Macmillan.

CLARK, JOHN MAURICE

John Maurice Clark (1884–1963), thirty-seventh president of the American Economic Association, was born in Northampton, Massachusetts. After graduating from Amherst College with an A.B. degree in 1905, he pursued graduate studies in economics at Columbia University, where he received his M.A. in 1906 and his PH.D. in 1910. From the time he left Columbia in 1908 to accept an instructorship in economics and sociology at Colorado College until his retirement from Columbia in 1957, Clark devoted an uninterrupted half century to teaching and productive scholarship. In 1910 he returned as associate professor of economics to Amherst and stayed there until he joined the faculty of political economy of the University of Chicago in 1915. In 1926 he left Chicago to become professor of economics at Columbia University.

Clark has often been singled out as one of the few economists (John Maynard Keynes was another) born into the profession. He was the son of the famous American economist John Bates Clark, one of the founders and the third president of the American Economic Association. The father's influence on the son was pronounced in the latter's personal and professional life. The younger Clark's close colleagues at the University of Chicago and Columbia often felt that his esteem for his father and his economic works was so high that he was inclined to deprecate his own great contributions to economics. There is no doubt, of course, that his contributions to economics did owe much to his father. Clark wrote his PH.D. thesis, *Standards of Reasonableness in Local Freight Discriminations*, under his father's guidance; he stated in his preface: "The author cannot express sufficiently his indebtedness to his father . . . not only for his direct and invaluable assistance in preparing this monograph; but for the stimulus, guidance and instruction which have made possible whatever the author has achieved or may achieve" (1910, p. 5). He and his father coauthored a revision of *The Control of Trusts* (1914a). He dedicated his highly praised *Studies in the Economics of Overhead Costs* to his father and acknowledged in the preface that "[my] greatest debt of all is to my father, who started me in this field of inquiry as a graduate student . . ." (1923, pp. xi–xii). In his presidential address to the American Economic Association (1936a), he frequently referred to his father's publications, especially his two articles setting forth the marginal productivity theory of distribution, and two of his books, *The Philosophy of Wealth* and *The Distribution of Wealth*. And in the preface to his last major work published before his death, *Competition as a Dynamic Process*, he described his inquiry as one that ". . . goes back to my father's basic conception that the analysis of static equilibrium, for which he is chiefly known, is properly not an end, but an introduction to the study of dynamics, in which it should find its fulfilment" (1961, p. ix).

John Maurice Clark's major contribution to economics was, indeed, his grasp of the relationship between the study of static systems and of dynamics. Probably more than any of his contemporaries, and certainly more than anyone in the succeeding generation of economists, he concerned himself explicitly with bridging the enormous gap between the models of static theory and the dynamic realities of a market economy. Since the complexities of these dynamic realities could not be compressed into conventional geometric or algebraic models or clarified through modifications and adaptions of them, it is not surprising that Clark from the beginning of his career eschewed formal models as a means of presenting even his most rigorous theoretical concepts. In the *Handbook of the American Economic Association* he consistently listed microeconomic theory and industrial organization, in that order, as his areas of interest; yet his major works do not contain a single abstraction presented in a diagram or set of equations. (His thesis contained one such abstraction, an attempt to apply the doctrine of average value to the problem of local discrimination.) Clark digested and skillfully built upon the logic underlying the formal models of others, first of the marginalists and later of Edward H. Chamberlin and Joan Robinson, but he fashioned his own methodology from the written word. This feature of his work was in striking contrast with the heavy reliance his contemporary younger theorists placed on the mathematical formulation of theoretical problems. The contrast, however, was not attributable to Clark's lack of familiarity with mathematics: he often cited Cournot's *Researches Into the Mathematical Principles of the Theory of Wealth* and the works of other mathematical economists; he was a charter member of the Econometric Society and in 1947 was elected a fellow of the society. Rather, his abstinence from the use of abstract models followed from his having committed his intellectual energies to those economic complexities that did not lend themselves to such formulations. Referring in his above-mentioned presidential address to the recent founding of the Econometric Society, he said, "[The society] faces great and inherent difficulties in the framing of assumptions simple enough to lend themselves to mathematical formulas yet flexible enough to grapple effectively with the problems of dynamic economics" (1936a, p. 7).

Clark's concern with the dynamics of a complex market economy led him to explore many areas. His PH.D. thesis, *Standards of Reasonableness in Local Freight Discriminations*, anticipated a long list of his later publications concerned with the economics of costs and the logical relationships between costs and prices. By far the most important of his earlier publications was his *Studies in the Economics of Overhead Costs*, which was destined to be the standard reference on the subject throughout the remaining forty years of Clark's life. In this work Clark anticipated the distinctions between social and private costs so carefully drawn by welfare economists later on, elaborated the differences between genuine economies of scale and the private advantages of size ("bargaining power pure and simple" 1923, p. 127), and, most important, further developed the acceleration principle and its impact on business cycles that he had introduced in an earlier article, "Business Acceleration and the Law of Demand" (1917). This principle was later incorporated into post-Keynesian national income models as an important explanation of business cycles. Clark also worked out the differences between the accountants' and the economists' conceptions of costs, a line of inquiry he helped develop more fully in such later articles as "Valuation for the Balance-sheet and Profit" (1926a) and "Some Central Problems of Overhead Cost" (1927).

It was almost inevitable that Clark's concern with the dynamic aspects of a market economy would lead him to assess critically the implications of the postulates of perfect competition for welfare theory and public policy. While virtually all his works were in varying degrees concerned with this assessment, his article "Toward a Concept of Workable Competition" (1940) clearly had more influence on the subsequent development of the field of economics known as industrial organization than any other single publication, with the exception of Edward H. Chamberlin's *Theory of Monopolistic Competition*. Chamberlin's book transformed industrial organization from a descriptive study of institutions into a study in applied theory; Clark's article provided the framework and impetus for the search for more dynamic and more realistic theories and definitions of competition to apply to the market economy.

Clark's article on the concept of workable competition was a systematic elaboration of a central theme running through much of his work, the beginnings of which went back to his "Soundings in Non-Euclidean Economics" (1921) and *Studies in the Economies of Overhead Costs* (1923, especially chapter 21). The theory of perfect competition, argued Clark, applies to market conditions that are both theoretically and practically unattainable: theoretically unattainable because the theory is static, relating to an economy that in all its details constantly repeats itself, whereas the characteristic feature of the market economy is its dynamism and constant change; and practically unattainable simply because all the conditions prerequisite to such a state could not possibly exist simultaneously in a significant portion of the economy.

Since the theory of perfect competition, for these reasons, does not provide meaningful standards for assessing either the performance of the economy or the effectiveness of our public policies designed to maintain competition (the antitrust laws), there is a great need for new definitions of competition that can be applied to the dynamic realities of the marketplace. These new definitions should therefore focus on "workable," in contrast with "perfect," competition.

Clark did not attempt to set forth a complete and universally applicable definition of workable competition but proposed that such definitions reflect the following considerations:

Competition is rivalry in selling goods, in which each selling unit normally seeks maximum net revenue, under conditions such that the price or prices each seller can charge are effectively limited by the free option of the buyer to buy from a rival seller or sellers of what we think of as "the same" product, necessitating an effort by each seller to equal or exceed the attractiveness of the others' offerings to a sufficient number of buyers to accomplish the end in view. (1940, p. 243)

Characteristically, Clark provided price theory and industrial organization with a relevant framework for definitions and theories of competition rather than with formalized definitions and theories themselves. As he stated later in his article "Competition: Static Models and Dynamic Aspects" (1955a, p. 457), "A theory of competition as a dynamic process must be not a model but a framework within which many models may find their places, including equilibrium models as limiting hypothetical cases."

His concept of workable competition stimulated many graduate students to devote their theses to developing definitions and models of workable competition, an effort which significantly increased the number and enhanced the quality of case studies of industries and markets. For example, the Harvard University series on Competition in American Industry was a direct descendant of Clark's article.

Another and generally unrecognized contribution to economics contained in Clark's article on workable competition is the logic and form of the theory of "second best," expounded 16 years later by Kelvin Lancaster and Richard G. Lipsey (1956). In establishing the guideposts to definitions of workable competition, Clark argued that the conditions of competition were not additive but were rather interrelated in such a way that if one condition of a state of workable competition were absent, even the presence of all the other essential conditions might not make competition workable. The Lancaster and Lipsey article develops precisely the same argument with respect to conditions for a welfare optimum.

In his *Alternative to Serfdom* (1948), *The Ethical Basis of Economic Freedom* (1955b), and *Competition as a Dynamic Process* (1961), Clark disclosed the essential conclusions he had reached after nearly a half century of diligent research into the problems and prospects of competition within capitalism. The capitalistic system, he believed, would survive the communist threat because it was flexible and dynamic enough to provide economic abundance as well as individual freedom. This flexibility and dynamism derives from the presence in the system of a greater degree of beneficial competition than most students of industrial organization would attribute to it.

Clark's writings include treatises on virtually every economic problem that loomed large in his lifetime. Although he is chiefly recognized for his contributions designed to close the gap between the abstractions of statics and the realities of dynamics, he published works concerned with the business cycle, the economic costs of war, wartime controls and demobilization, public works, the labor market, education, and a host of other problems. He was a prolific writer, and his scholarly contributions earned the high praise of his peers and virtually every distinguished award conferred by his profession. John Kenneth Galbraith, in reviewing Clark's *Economic Institutions and Human Welfare* (1957), spoke for his fellow economists when he wrote:

More than any other economist of his generation . . . he has transcended controversy . . . he has dealt regularly with the most difficult and disputed questions of social policy. But his conclusions have been cast in a framework of patient and meticulous and reasonable argument which not only dissipates hostility but goes far to preclude argument.   (Galbraith 1957)

And Kenneth E. Boulding, reviewing the same volume, was equally eloquent in his praise:

There is something peculiarly American in the thought of J. M. Clark: it stems from the sweet reasonableness of Penn and of Emerson, from the pragmatism of William James, from what might be called the Gentle Tradition in American life. It stands over against the harshness and cruelty both of Manchester and of Marx, with their confident solutions and roughshod ideologies. To some extent too it stands over against the bright young world of the econometricians and operations researchers. . . .   (Boulding 1957, p. 1004)

Clark was awarded honorary degrees by Amherst College, Columbia University, the University of Paris, the New School for Social Research, and Yale University. In 1951 Columbia appointed him to the John Bates Clark chair, established in his father's honor. In 1952 the American Economic Association bestowed on him its highest honor by awarding him the Francis A. Walker medal for distinguished service to the field of economics.

It is true that Clark founded no special school of economic thought—there is no identifiable "Clarkian school"—but it is equally true that the appeal of his wisdom went far beyond the classroom.

JESSE W. MARKHAM

[*See also, in approximate order of relevance,* COMPETITION; OLIGOPOLY; MARKETS AND INDUSTRIES; COST; *and the biography of* CLARK, JOHN BATES.]

WORKS BY CLARK

1910 *Standards of Reasonableness in Local Freight Discriminations.* New York: Columbia Univ. Press.

1914a CLARK, JOHN BATES; and CLARK, JOHN MAURICE. *The Control of Trusts.* Rev. & enl. ed. New York: Macmillan. → John Bates Clark was sole author of the first edition, published in 1901.

1914b A Contribution to the Theory of Competitive Price. *Quarterly Journal of Economics* 28:747–771.

1917 Business Acceleration and the Law of Demand: A Technical Factor in Economic Cycles. *Journal of Political Economy* 25:217–235.

1921 Soundings in Non-Euclidean Economics. *American Economic Review* 11, no. 1:132–143.

(1923) 1962 *Studies in the Economics of Overhead Costs.* Univ. of Chicago Press.

1926a Valuation for the Balance-sheet and Profit. Pages 369–377 in International Congress of Accountants, Second, Amsterdam, 1926, *Proceedings.* Purmerend (Netherlands): Muusses.

(1926b) 1939 *Social Control of Business.* 2d ed. New York: McGraw-Hill; London: Whittlesey House.

1927 Some Central Problems of Overhead Cost. Taylor Society, New York, *Bulletin* 12:287–292.

1931   *The Costs of the World War to the American People.* New Haven: Yale Univ. Press.

1932   Business Cycles: The Problem of Diagnosis. *Journal of the American Statistical Association* 27 (Supplement): 212–217.

1934   *Strategic Factors in Business Cycles.* Publication No. 24. New York: National Bureau of Economic Research.

1936a   Past Accomplishments and Present Prospects of American Economics. *American Economic Review* 26:1–11.

1936b   *Preface to Social Economics: Essays on Economic Theory and Social Problems.* New York: Farrar & Rinehart.

1940   Toward a Concept of Workable Competition. *American Economic Review* 30:241–256.

1942   *How to Check Inflation.* New York: Public Affairs Committee.

1943   Imperfect Competition Theory and Basing-point Problems. *American Economic Review* 33:283–300.

1944   *Demobilization of Wartime Economic Controls.* New York: McGraw-Hill.

1946   Realism and Relevance in the Theory of Demand. *Journal of Political Economy* 54:347–353.

(1948) 1960   *Alternative to Serfdom.* 2d ed., rev. New York: Vintage.

1949a   *Guideposts in Time of Change: Some Essentials for a Sound American Economy.* New York: Harper.

1949b   Law and Economics of Basing Points. *American Economic Review* 39:430–447.

1950   The Orientation of Antitrust Policy. *American Economic Review* 40, no. 2:93–104. → Contains four pages of discussion.

1955a   Competition: Static Models and Dynamic Aspects. *American Economic Review* 45, no. 2:450–462.

1955b   *The Ethical Basis of Economic Freedom.* Westport, Conn.: Kazanjian Economics Foundation.

1957   *Economic Institutions and Human Welfare.* New York: Knopf.

1958   The Uses of Diversity: Competitive Bearings of Diversities in Cost and Demand Functions. *American Economic Review* 48, no. 2:474–482.

1960   *The Wage–Price Problem.* New York: American Bankers Association, Committee for Economic Growth Without Inflation.

1961   *Competition as a Dynamic Process.* Washington: Brookings Institution.

SUPPLEMENTARY BIBLIOGRAPHY

[The Bibliography of] John Maurice Clark. 1931   Pages 301–304 in Columbia University, Faculty of Political Science, *A Bibliography . . . 1880–1930.* New York: Columbia Univ. Press.

BOULDING, KENNETH E.   1957 [A Book Review of] *Economic Institutions and Human Welfare,* by John Maurice Clark. *American Economic Review* 47:1004–1005.

GALBRAITH, JOHN KENNETH   1957 [A Book Review of] *Economic Institutions and Human Welfare,* by John Maurice Clark. *New York Times* May 12, p. 3, col. 4.

LANCASTER, KELVIN; and LIPSEY, RICHARD G.   1956 The General Theory of Second Best. *Review of Economic Studies* 24:11–32.

CLASS, SOCIAL

See SOCIAL MOBILITY; STATUS, SOCIAL; STRATIFICATION, SOCIAL.

CLASSICAL CONDITIONING

See under LEARNING.

CLASSIFICATION

See CLUSTERING; INFORMATION STORAGE AND RETRIEVAL; MULTIVARIATE ANALYSIS, *article on* CLASSIFICATION AND DISCRIMINATION; TYPOLOGIES.

CLAUSEWITZ, KARL VON

Karl von Clausewitz, military theorist, was born in 1780 in Burg, Prussia, into a Protestant family of administrators and theologians. His father had assumed the particle of nobility and entered the Prussian Army. Like many other middle-class officers, he was dismissed after the Seven Years' War for being unable to substantiate his title; however, his military connections enabled three of his four sons to gain admittance to the service, in which they reached senior rank.

After joining an infantry regiment at the age of 12, Clausewitz took part in the campaigns against the French Republic and then served in a provincial garrison until he was sent to the Berlin War Academy (Allgemeine Kriegsschule) in 1801 —an event he later called the turning point of his life. There he studied military theory, philosophy, history, and literature, wrote his first essays, and gained the friendship of Scharnhorst, the leader of progressive thought in the army.

During the disastrous Prussian campaign against Napoleon in 1806, Clausewitz was captured and spent ten intellectually fruitful months in France and Switzerland before returning to Prussia. He soon became one of Scharnhorst's most trusted collaborators in the task of changing the class-ridden military establishment into a fighting force that tapped all sources of energy and enthusiasm in the nation. He contributed to the evolution of strategic and tactical doctrine through his lectures at the War Academy (Kriegsschule für Offiziere) on the functions of the general staff and on irregular warfare and through his work on the new infantry manual. His marriage to Countess Marie Brühl brought him in closer contact with the court, as did his appointment as teacher of military science to the crown prince. Nevertheless, when the Franco–Prussian alliance was concluded in the spring of 1812 he resigned his commission and joined the Russian Army, with which he served throughout the French invasion. At the end of the year he played a major role in the negotiations at Tauroggen, which detached the Prussian auxiliary corps from Napoleon's army, and during the following weeks he helped organize the East Prussian militia—two events with far-reaching political and military implications. Despite these achievements, conservative resentment of his readiness to subordinate monarchic loyalty to political convictions delayed his readmission to the Prussian Army until 1815 and continued to handicap him afterwards. In 1818 he was promoted to major general and appointed director of the War Academy (Allgemeine Kriegsschule, later known as Kriegs Akademie) a purely administrative post that allowed him no voice in the curriculum but did give him time to write. Dissatisfaction with routine duties prompted him several times to seek a place in the diplomatic service. In 1830 he was at last transferred to a more active position and the next year was appointed chief of staff of the observation forces mobilized at the outbreak of the Polish insurrection. On the verge of what appeared to be a new and promising stage in his career, he died of cholera in Breslau in 1831.

Clausewitz belonged to that sizable group of cultured officers that formed a distinctive part of the German classical movement. He wrote on education, aesthetics, and national character, as well as on professional topics, and occasionally attempted poetry. From Scharnhorst he learned the value of historical studies in the training of judgment, a lesson to which his admiration for Schiller's writings rendered him particularly receptive. The tenets of idealistic philosophy exerted a lasting influence on his thought from his twenties, when he acquired a sound knowledge of Kant's works and discussed Machiavelli with Fichte, to the years when he wrote *On War* and mustered his arguments in an almost Hegelian dialectic.

Where Clausewitz differed from other military intellectuals of his day was in combining the tools of logical analysis with a realistic appreciation of political and military affairs. He rejected the theorists who tried both to explain war and to provide keys for successful generalship in systems of universal rules, derived from mathematics, geography, ethics, and even technology. Force and the willingness to use it constituted in his mind the essential element of war, but he went beyond such writers as Jomini, who had grasped the Napoleonic technique of seeking decision by battle, in his stress on the political and psychological factors that were steadily increasing the intensity of war. No contemporary recognized so clearly as he that an adequate theory of conflict must accommodate both general propositions and the constant changes introduced by new weapons and new political forces. A solution to this fundamental problem was

suggested by his view of the past, which approached that of early historicism. Like Ranke, whom he resembled also in his distaste for moral judgments, he acknowledged the singularity of each period and each event: a particular campaign, therefore, can be understood only in its specific context. But in the varied history of warfare he discerned certain elements that are, in one way or another, present in every type of armed conflict: the force of accident; the role of the irrational, of emotions such as enthusiasm and patriotism; the power of numbers, both in regular units and in guerrilla bands; and, above all, the political nature and purpose of war. He reasoned that since war is basically political, its course should be determined by the political leadership. In his major but uncompleted work, *On War*, he attempted to develop his ideas into a comprehensive theory whose function was to guide inquiry and educate judgment, not to be an "algebraic formula" for victory.

Much of the criticism that has been leveled at Clausewitz stems from a failure to understand his purpose and methods. Readers have not always followed such distinctions as his differentiation between the ideal and the real: since violence is not in principle subject to limitations, the reciprocity of action and reaction escalates to the "ideal"—total war; but in real life considerations of policy, technology, and morality modify this absolute. Too often he has been misinterpreted as the prophet of brute force, perhaps because his dialectic does not lend itself easily to excerpting. Nevertheless, his writings have exerted great influence on the study of war, particularly among communist theorists from Engels and Lenin onward, enabling them to see significant concepts behind the operational speculations, which today are of largely historical interest. What is of lasting value in *On War* is its suggestive discussion of the relation between political and military power, its ability to delineate some basic problems of armed conflict between states, and its demonstration that these problems are amenable to logical analysis and empirical research.

PETER PARET

[See also MILITARY POWER POTENTIAL; STRATEGY; WAR.]

WORKS BY CLAUSEWITZ

Clausewitz published little during his lifetime. The bulk of his writings on the history and theory of war was brought out by his widow in ten volumes, 1832–1837, of which the first three constitute On War. *Other manuscripts and much of his correspondence have appeared since. Between the Franco–Prussian War and 1914, many of Clausewitz' writings were translated into French; several works have appeared in Russian; and Lenin's annotations to* On War *are in print. The only work available in English, aside from incidental pieces, excerpts, and some campaign histories, is* On War, *but even the 1943 translation is based upon corrupted texts.*

(1832–1834) 1943 *On War.* Translated by O. J. M. Jolles. New York: Modern Library. → First published in German as *Vom Kriege,* in three volumes.

1832–1837 *Hinterlassene Werke des Generals Carl von Clausewitz über Krieg und Kriegführung.* 10 vols. Berlin: Dümmler.

Politische Schriften und Briefe. Edited by Hans Rothfels. Munich: Drei Masken, 1922.

WORKS ABOUT CLAUSEWITZ

CROCE, BENEDETTO 1935 Action, succès et jugement dans le *Vom Kriege* de Clausewitz. *Revue de métaphysique et de morale* 42:247–258.

HAHLWEG, WERNER 1957 *Carl von Clausewitz: Soldat, Politiker, Denker.* Göttingen (Germany): Musterschmidt.

PARET, PETER 1965 Clausewitz: A Bibliographic Survey. *World Politics* 17:272–285.

PARET, PETER 1966 The Influence of Clausewitz on the Nineteenth Century. Chapter 2 in Michael Howard (editor), *The Theory and Practice of War: Essays Presented to Captain B. H. Liddell Hart.* London: Cassell.

ROTHFELS, HANS 1943 Clausewitz. Pages 93–113 in Edward Mead Earle (editor), *Makers of Modern Strategy: Military Thought From Machiavelli to Hitler.* Princeton Univ. Press.

SCHWARTZ, KARL 1878 *Leben des Generals Carl von Clausewitz und der Frau Marie von Clausewitz.* 2 vols. Berlin: Dümmler.

CLERGY
See RELIGIOUS SPECIALISTS.

CLIENT-CENTERED COUNSELING
See under MENTAL DISORDERS, TREATMENT OF.

CLINICAL PSYCHOLOGY

Clinical psychology, a branch of psychology, is that body of knowledge and skills which can be used to help persons with behavior disabilities or mental disorders to achieve better adjustment and self-expression. It encompasses the applied areas of diagnosis, treatment, and prevention, as well as the basic area of research. (In British countries the term "clinical psychology" is more or less interchangeable with "medical psychology.")

In function, clinical psychology overlaps a number of fields. The profession to which it is most closely related is psychiatry. Psychiatrists, although members of a medical specialty whose training includes medical school, general internship, and three years of psychiatric residency, have more in common with clinical psychologists than with other physicians. Because of their medical training, however, psychiatrists, unlike clinical psychologists, can use drugs. Psychotherapy as a major treatment technique and diagnosis are areas common to both clinical psychology and psychiatry, although the professions have somewhat different approaches. Psychiatry tends to use interviews and mental-status examinations, whereas psychology leans more to objective tests and projective devices. Both groups are increasingly directing attention to the rapidly expanding area of prevention. Clinical psychologists have generally been more active in research than psychiatrists, but a marked effort is being made to increase the number of psychiatrists participating in research activities. Clinical psychology also has much in common with social work, particularly in the area of treatment. Social workers are given excellent training in this function—perhaps better training than either of the other two major mental health professionals, clinical psychologists or psychiatrists. Social work has in recent years recognized the weakness of being a profession that has neither an underlying basic discipline nor a body of research, and it is attempting to remedy these difficulties. Clinical psychology borders on the fields of sociology, particularly in its social-psychological aspects, and the ministry, when the latter assumes the "helping" role. Clinical psychology's relation to anthropology is remote except for the analogies that may be drawn between patterns of collective behavior and forms of individual pathology.

The content of clinical psychology includes large portions of psychopathology, abnormal psychology, and similar areas. It is particularly dependent on personality theory and psychoanalysis for its theoretical underpinnings.

Origins. Clinical psychology is younger than many other branches of psychology. In an organized form it dates from 1896, when Lightner Witmer first established a psychological clinic at the University of Pennsylvania. (Witmer also coined the terms "clinical psychology," "psychological clinic," and "orthogenics.") From the beginning he called for the qualitative study of the *individual* patient, for therapeutic as well as diagnostic purposes. He acknowledged the need for the detailed consideration and prolonged observation of cases by establishing a children's hospital–school. Although in its early period the clinic was concerned almost entirely with the retarded child, in later years its major preoccupations were the problems of the superior child, vocational guidance, and speech disability. What has since become known as the "team" approach—coordinated work by representatives of a number of disciplines dealing with the same case—was, after a fashion, adopted at an early date by the clinic. Physicians, especially neurologists, and social workers collaborated on case studies. Witmer emphasized the need for professional training and developed a pattern of attack that included most of the elements of present-day clinics.

While Witmer's clinic was expanding its activities, the Binet movement in France was gathering force. Rumblings of it had been heard at the turn of the century, and with the publication of the Binet–Simon test in 1905 the potential of the intelligence test first became evident. The Vineland Training School, an institution for the mentally retarded, was among the first to adapt the test to American conditions. There, in 1906, H. H. Goddard started the first American psychological laboratory.

About 1910, a second university clinic, modeled on Witmer's was organized by Carl Seashore at the University of Iowa. During the same period, J. E. Wallace Wallin began to apply psychological techniques to school children. He started a psychoeducational clinic at the University of Pittsburgh in 1912. Emphasizing the educational, as opposed to the psychopathological significance of clinics, Wallin recommended that clinics be established in association with departments of education rather than with psychology departments.

In the latter part of the nineteenth century and through the early part of the twentieth, the activities of such men as J. M. Charcot and Pierre Janet —but most particularly Sigmund Freud, abroad, and Adolf Meyer in this country—brought prominence to the functional point of view. Their influence led to the development of perhaps the most important type of clinic in this country.

In 1909, in association with the Cook County Juvenile Court of Chicago, William Healy started a behavior clinic. It is from this event that the child-guidance movement dates its origin. Although impressed by Witmer's clinic, Healy, who was concerned mainly with social pathology, took a different approach. Despite Witmer's pioneering, Healy's approach was to have a greater and more lasting effect on clinical psychology specifically and on the field of mental hygiene in general.

Witmer versus Healy. Why this difference? Study of the programs of the two clinics shows Witmer's strikingly consistent concern with educational problems, primarily with those of the mentally retarded. His emphasis on the intellectual-cognitive aspects of personality naturally led to contact with educators in school settings or in institutions for the mentally retarded. When inter-

ested in a medical problem, Witmer focused on its physical or neurological aspects. Healy, on the other hand, emphasized the affective aspects of personality, looked at the psychiatric side of medical problems, and dealt with a variety of social agencies and institutions. Healy, it turns out, was wiser in his choice, for the study of the mentally retarded has remained relatively more narrow and distinctly less rewarding than the study of the personality differences associated with psychopathy, neurosis, or psychosis. Events such as those reflected in the mental health bills passed by Congress in 1963 may belie this statement, but professionals treating or doing research in mental disorder, with few exceptions, hold to it. [*See* MENTAL RETARDATION.]

The lack of organized information flowing from the Pennsylvania clinic also served to circumscribe the response to the Witmer approach. Witmer never published a systematic book on the clinical field; his major contributions were papers in his own journal. Holmes's book (1912) describing the clinic's procedure is rather anemic and unimaginative. In contrast, Healy's *The Individual Delinquent* (1915) is a rounded and challenging work.

The structure of the Pennsylvania clinic may have created additional obstacles to its influence. Because it was established in a university setting and was directed by a nonphysician, the clinic may have been effectively barred from social prominence. Association with student training may have limited its scope. Had the clinic been established in a medical school already recognized as a therapeutic center, or in a market place of social agencies (as Healy's clinic was), it might have had more general influence. Or perhaps Witmer was ahead of the times.

More important than the content of the programs, the way information was disseminated, or the characteristics of the clinics (or perhaps inextricably woven into all) were the outlooks of the respective leaders. Whereas Witmer's approach was essentially segmental and static, relatively uninspiring and plodding, Healy's was total, seminal, and stimulating. Whereas Healy was markedly influenced by the functional psychology of James and the dynamic views of Freud and Meyer, Witmer identified with the less imaginative Wundtian–Kraepelinian approach. A systematic skimming of *Psychological Clinic*, the journal Witmer founded, leaves one with the feeling that Witmer was burdened by a conservatism which led him to oppose dynamic psychology because it was "unscientific" and "radical." This attitude is paradoxical for a pioneer. Witmer's pioneering, however, was not really in new thinking but rather in new material to which old thinking was applied. Healy's perspective, in comparison, was to prove more suited to the developing field of clinical psychology.

Early developments.   Paralleling the growth of the clinics was the establishment of psychological laboratories in hospitals for the mentally disordered. The McLean Hospital, St. Elizabeth's Hospital, and the Boston Psychopathic Hospital were outstanding. In some respects the work in the hospital laboratories followed conservative academic–experimental lines. In other ways hospital activities promoted the liberal use of test devices.

Since the earliest days of clinical psychology, the American Psychological Association has made attempts to deal with problems related to the field (Fernberger 1932, pp. 42–53). Since 1895 it has taken an interest in the standardization of mental tests. In 1915 a study of the qualifications of mental examiners was initiated. In 1918 a committee appointed to explore the problem reported in favor of the certification of examiners by the association. A certifying committee was appointed in 1920, but by 1923 only 25 members had applied for certification, and in 1927 certification was discontinued. It was started again, however, in 1947.

During the 1930s various systematic efforts were made to deal with clinical psychological problems. Morrow (1946) has described the attempts of university, state, and national organizations to devise standards of training and experience.

In the early 1940s a considerable amount of clinical work was being done in communities and hospitals, as well as in universities (which had, however, taken a decidedly secondary role), by psychologists whose training was, with few exceptions, unsystematically acquired. Although there was wide concern with problems of training, few organized programs had been set up. Whatever background the clinical psychologist had was largely self-determined. His training was surprisingly uninfluenced by programs emanating from universities or other recognized psychological institutions.

Recent developments.   Since the 1940s there has been considerable preoccupation with the problems of clinical psychology. The play of a great variety of forces, both within and without psychology, has made clinical psychology into a field that calls upon its practitioners for competence in three major tasks: (1) *diagnosis*, or the acquisition of knowledge about the origin and nature of existing psychological conditions through the use of tests, measurements, standard interviews, and similar procedures; (2) *research*, or the advancement of knowledge by a systematic attack, in the laboratory or in the field setting, on specific problems capable of controlled, experimental resolution; and (3) *therapy*, or the intricate art and science of improving the condition of clients. Beyond these tasks lies always—implicitly at least, but increasingly at an explicit level—the important problem of prevention.

In the 1960s, doctoral training for these tasks calls for a minimum program of four years, one year of which (preferably the third) consists of an internship. Practica, clerkships, and internships are organized on a foundation of basic courses in theoretical, clinical, and dynamic psychology. The type of training program now generally accepted was initially proposed by the Committee on Training in Clinical Psychology of the American Psychological Association in its 1947 report and was further supported in conferences at Boulder (Conference . . . 1950), Stanford (Strother 1956), Miami (Conference. . . 1959), and Chicago (Hoch et al. 1966). The 1947 report recommended that clinical training be centered in existing university departments and that field-training units be integrated with university programs. Although proposals have been made for the establishment of special professional schools in clinical psychology, the solution still generally favored is the expansion of existing university psychology departments to meet the needs of clinical psychology. Such a plan underscores the model of the clinical psychologist as a scientist–professional and supports the motto "A clinical psychologist is a psychologist first and a clinician second."

As the professional consciousness of psychologists has developed, however, universities and field centers have come to recognize the importance of appropriate personality qualities and high intellectual abilities in clinical work. In the past, some professors had a tendency to direct their weaker students—those who did not have the makings of "scientists"—into clinical courses with the hope that they would then be able to find jobs in clinical settings. A number of poorly trained people, generally called "psychometricians," who presumably were nothing more than psychological technicians, thus entered the field. The present attention to selection and recruitment problems, however, has led to an increase in competently trained researchers and practitioners. Most have come from institutions in which standards have been maintained and a reasonably comfortable relationship exists between academic and clinical psychology. Some have also come from centers where the standards have not been of the highest level, but where exceptionally good people have managed, in one way or another, to educate themselves.

The American Psychological Association has, in recent years, taken an increasingly greater role in setting up standards for evaluating both training and practice in clinical psychology. The Committee on Graduate and Professional Training (American Psychological Association 1945) was followed by the Committees on Training in Clinical Psychology (American Psychological Association 1947; 1948; 1949) and more recently by the Education and Training Board (Conference . . . 1959). These committees have provided the criteria for approving universities and for recommending their participation in programs of the Veterans Administration and the Public Health Service (Ross 1964; 1965; Ross & Lockman 1964; Goodstein & Ross 1966).

To consolidate and advance standards, the American Board of Examiners in Professional Psychology was organized and, in April 1947, incorporated. It was modeled on the specialty boards in medicine and had similar standards. The board generally requires five years of acceptable experience, in addition to the doctoral degree, for admission to the examination for a diploma. A "grandfather clause," which expired December 31, 1949, allowed for certification of qualified persons on the basis of experience rather than actual examination.

With the protection of the public in mind, governmental bodies have made several attempts to set the standards for the certification of psychologists. The two types of legislation that have been under consideration by state agencies are exemplified, in their essentials, by the early laws of Connecticut and Virginia. The Connecticut law provides for the general certification of psychologists with a PH.D. degree plus one year of experience; the Virginia law entails the certification of specified kinds of psychologists with a PH.D. plus five years of experience. The consensus among psychologists is that state certification should follow the Connecticut pattern and that "expert" certification should be left to a professional agency, such as the American Board of Examiners in Professional Psychology.

Present picture. Since 1947, the growth of clinical psychology in the United States has been phenomenal. This is reflected, to a small degree, in the following statistics: (1) membership in the Division of Clinical Psychology of the American Psychological Association has risen from 787 in 1948 to 3,048 in 1966; (2) the number of schools fully approved by the Committee on Training in Clinical Psychology of the American Psychological Association has increased from 20 in 1948 to 67 in 1965; (3) there were an estimated 742 graduate students enrolled in doctoral-training programs in clinical psychology in the academic year 1947/1948 compared to 3,340 in 1962/1963; (4) the number of clinical psychologists certified by the American Board of Examiners in Professional Psychology has increased from 234 in 1948 to 1,793 in 1963 (of the total, 1,116 are "grandfathers"); (5) some form of statutory control has been established by 28 states and four Canadian provinces, and non-statutory control has been set up by 18 states.

But this unusual growth has not come about without much travail. An increasing number of questions have arisen which psychology and clinical psychology will have to answer in the coming years: (1) Can psychologists be trained who have both professional and scientific goals in mind? (2) How much application can there be in a field in which basic knowledge is still so meager? (3) Should clinical psychologists devote more time to research? (4) How can socially unprofitable trends toward private practice be curbed? (5) Should training for research and teaching be separated from training for the applications of psychology? (Shakow 1965).

Outside the United States there are signs of increasing interest in clinical psychology (David 1958). Growth rates for the countries differ, however, and the pace is decidedly less rapid outside the United States.

England and Canada. In Britain, the pattern has, in general, been less structured than in the United States. Formal programs, where they do exist, have been modeled on the Maudsley (University of London) pattern, which consists of one to two years of practical experience and a doctoral dissertation. The development of the National Health Service in 1948 led to an increase of clinical psychologists (Summerfield 1958). Whereas at the end of 1945 there were 77 professional psychologists in the British Psychological Society working in mental health, by 1958 the number had increased to some 400. University training facilities have been extended and the pursuit of higher degrees has been encouraged. In English-speaking Canadian universities, training has consisted of a combination of American and English patterns, generally calling for a diploma or special master's degree after one to two years of practical training, followed by two years of formal research leading to the PH.D. The report on the Conference on the Training of Professional Psychologists, held in May 1965 at the Couchiching Conference Center at Geneva Park, Ontario (Coons 1965), presents a detailed discussion of developments in Canada.

Western Europe. The situation in the western Continental countries is not as encouraging. A strong medical tradition still holds sway, limiting a good deal of the practice of clinical psychology (and particularly of psychotherapy) to physicians. In the last few years, however, these countries have made increasing inquiries about American training programs, and one can expect some growth of clinical training along American lines.

Eastern Europe. In eastern continental Europe, medical influence is even more pervasive. Particular emphasis is placed upon physiological functioning with a corresponding denigration of the place of psychological testing, objective or subjective, and of the study of individual differences generally. Rapid growth of clinical psychology appears less likely.

Japan. In Japan, noteworthy among Eastern countries, psychology is in an active ferment (McGinnies 1960). The field of clinical psychology is developing rapidly despite a number of handicaps—for instance, the rigidity of the university system and the overrepresentation of physicians in the field. Thus, at the 1958 meeting of the Japanese Psychological Association, of the 619 papers presented, representing 11 areas, clinical psychology ranked fourth in number, being preceded only by perception, education, and learning.

Problems and prospects. On the whole there has been a tremendous growth of clinical psychology in the United States and a moderate growth, along similar lines, in other countries. The hope is that countries will work out patterns suited to their own needs and not be guided too much by the patterns established in the United States—patterns that have brought with them problems of their own. A large number of major problems must be solved by both psychology and clinical psychology if clinical psychology is to make its proper contribution to the needs of society and to develop its potential as a profession. These include training both for old and new areas of endeavor, evaluation of both training institutions and individuals, and improvement of existing programs. Specifically, the following issues have to be faced.

Training for research. The role of the university, the role of the field center, and the relationship between the two types of institutions need elaboration. Concomitantly, the content of research needs redefinition so it will encompass the most rigorous laboratory research, systematic naturalistic observation, and a serious attitude of inquiry leading to deliberate efforts to answer questions that arise during clinical operations.

Application. The function of each of the training agencies and the way to integrate their work in institutional and community settings need clarification.

Areas for research and practice. Much imaginative thinking is demanded. New methods of therapy, new methods of diagnosis, and, particularly, preventive methods of education are becoming increasingly important. Clinical psychology must do everything it can to attract persons with the resourcefulness to meet problems in unconventional areas. It is clear that the personnel shortages in the area of mental health will be enormous. Much thought and experimentation must go into making use of a larger pool of persons, for example, younger persons with the ideals and resourcefulness represented in Peace Corps volunteers, older persons such as mothers whose children no longer need their attention (see the experiment by Margaret Rioch et al. 1963), and teachers whose effective use is crucial in the mental health area. In addition, new methods of therapy and prevention must be constantly invented for, and tested on, groups—especially the underprivileged—that have heretofore received little consideration in mental health projects.

University training programs. The proper university settings for training in clinical psychology should be described and the importance of programs coming from unified departments considered. The nature of the doctoral degree granted to clinical psychologists—whether strictly professional (say, a PS.D.) or a combined research degree (the PH.D.)—calls for special discussion. The place and nature of postdoctoral programs, especially such programs for psychotherapy training, should be given equal thought.

Evaluation and regulation. There should be a re-examination of the composition, responsibilities, and standards of those committees that evaluate the performance of institutions, both universities and field centers, and those that regulate the activities of individuals, such as the American Board of Examiners in Professional Psychology and state licensing and certification boards.

Upgrading research and practice. Periodic regional conferences to consider the details of existing and potential training programs would be an effort in the direction of upgrading research and practice. The kind of professional eclecticism proposed by Kubie (1954) or the intensive, integrated approach discussed in detail at the Gould House

Conference on an Ideal Program of Training for Psychotherapists (1963) may be possibilities. In addition, methods for making the private practice of psychology more effective and socially useful should be reviewed.

The major problems of clinical psychology continue to lie within the parent field, psychology. Clinical psychology, after a long period spent as part of an academic discipline, has been through the early stages of becoming a profession as well. It is going through the natural disturbances and difficulties that attend a growth process of this kind. These need not be of serious concern, however, if clinical psychology selects its students carefully, for personality as well as intellect; if it trains thoroughly, in spirit as well as letter; if it trains broadly, recognizing that narrowly educated specialists are not true clinical psychologists; if it remains flexible about its training and encourages experimentation; if it does not sacrifice more remote goals to the fulfillment of immediate needs; if it maintains its contact with its scientific background, remaining alert to the importance of theory as well as practice; if it keeps modest in the face of the complexity of its problems, rather than becoming pretentious—in short, if it finds good people and gives them good training its future in society and as a profession is then assured.

DAVID SHAKOW

[*Directly related are the entries* COUNSELING PSYCHOLOGY; MENTAL DISORDERS, TREATMENT OF, *article on* PSYCHOLOGICAL TREATMENT; PSYCHIATRY. *Other relevant material may be found in* MENTAL HEALTH; PSYCHOANALYSIS; SOCIAL WORK; *and in the biographies of* MEYER *and* SEASHORE.]

BIBLIOGRAPHY

AMERICAN PSYCHOLOGICAL ASSOCIATION, COMMITTEE ON TRAINING IN CLINICAL PSYCHOLOGY 1947 Recommended Graduate Training Program in Clinical Psychology. *American Psychologist* 2:539–558. → Reprinted in 1950 in Conference on Graduate Education in Clinical Psychology, University of Colorado, 1949, *Training in Clinical Psychology*.

AMERICAN PSYCHOLOGICAL ASSOCIATION, COMMITTEE ON TRAINING IN CLINICAL PSYCHOLOGY 1948 Clinical Training Facilities: 1948. *American Psychologist* 3: 317–318.

AMERICAN PSYCHOLOGICAL ASSOCIATION, COMMITTEE ON TRAINING IN CLINICAL PSYCHOLOGY 1949 Doctoral Training Programs in Clinical Psychology. *American Psychologist* 4:331–341.

AMERICAN PSYCHOLOGICAL ASSOCIATION–THE AMERICAN ASSOCIATION FOR APPLIED PSYCHOLOGY, COMMITTEES ON GRADUATE AND PROFESSIONAL TRAINING, SUBCOMMITTEE ON GRADUATE INTERNSHIP TRAINING 1945 Graduate Internship Training in Psychology. *Journal of Consulting Psychology* 9:243–266.

CONFERENCE ON AN IDEAL PROGRAM OF TRAINING FOR PSYCHOTHERAPISTS, GOULD HOUSE, ARDSLEY-ON-HUDSON, N.Y. 1963 Proceedings. Unpublished manuscript.

CONFERENCE ON GRADUATE EDUCATION IN CLINICAL PSYCHOLOGY, UNIVERSITY OF COLORADO, *1949* 1950 *Training in Clinical Psychology*. Edited by Victor Raimy. Englewood Cliffs, N.J.: Prentice-Hall.

CONFERENCE ON GRADUATE EDUCATION IN PSYCHOLOGY, MIAMI BEACH, *1958* 1959 *Graduate Education in Psychology: Report*. Washington: American Psychological Association.

COONS, W. H. 1965 The Conference on the Training of Professional Psychologists. *Canadian Psychologist* 6a: 155–156.

DAVID, HENRY P. 1958 Clinical Psychology in Other Lands. *Progress in Clinical Psychology* 3:235–247.

FERNBERGER, SAMUEL W. 1932 The American Psychological Association: A Historical Survey, 1892–1930. *Psychological Bulletin* 29:1–89.

GOODSTEIN, LEONARD D.; and ROSS, SHERMAN 1966 Accreditation of Graduate Programs in Psychology: An Analysis. *American Psychologist* 21:218–223.

HEALY, WILLIAM 1915 *The Individual Delinquent: A Text-book of Diagnosis and Prognosis for All Concerned in Understanding Offenders*. Boston: Little.

HOCH, ERASMUS L.; ROSS, ALAN O.; and WINDER, C. L. 1966 Conference on the Professional Preparation of Clinical Psychologists: A Summary. *American Psychologist* 21:42–51.

HOLMES, ARTHUR 1912 *The Conservation of the Child*. Philadelphia: Lippincott.

KUBIE, LAWRENCE S. 1954 The Pros and Cons of a New Profession: A Doctorate in Medical Psychology. *Texas Reports on Biology and Medicine* 12:692–737.

McGINNIES, ELLIOTT 1960 Psychology in Japan: 1960. *American Psychologist* 15:556–562.

MORROW, WILLIAM R. 1946 The Development of Psychological Internship Training. *Journal of Consulting Psychology* 10:165–183.

RIOCH, MARGARET J. et al. 1963 National Institute of Mental Health Pilot Study in Training Mental Health Counselors. *American Journal of Orthopsychiatry* 33: 678–689.

ROSS, SHERMAN 1964 Internships for Doctoral Training in Clinical Psychology Approved by the American Psychological Association. *American Psychologist* 19: 809–811.

ROSS, SHERMAN 1965 APA-approved Doctoral Programs in Clinical and in Counseling Psychology: 1965. *American Psychologist* 20:794–795.

ROSS, SHERMAN; and LOCKMAN, ROBERT F. 1964 Survey of Graduate Education in Psychology: Some Trends for the Last Decade. *American Psychologist* 19:623–628.

SHAKOW, DAVID 1965 Clinical Psychology in Light of the 1947 Committee on Training in Clinical Psychology Report. *American Psychologist* 20:353–362.

STROTHER, CHARLES (editor) 1956 *Psychology and Mental Health*. Washington: American Psychological Association.

SUMMERFIELD, ARTHUR 1958 Clinical Psychology in Britain. *American Psychologist* 13:171–176.

CLIQUES

See COALITIONS; FRIENDSHIP; GROUPS; SOCIOMETRY.

CLUBS

See POLITICAL CLUBS; VOLUNTARY ASSOCIATIONS.

CLUSTERING

A battery of psychological tests provides a profile of test scores for each subject. Can the subjects be grouped sensibly into a moderate number of classes or clusters so that the subjects in each class have similar profiles? Can the clustering process be made automatic and feasible while producing subjectively meaningful results?

These types of data and questions arise throughout the social and natural sciences. The "subjects" or units may be such things as census tracts, nations, tribes, legislators, plants, fossils, microorganisms, documents, languages, or corporations. The data consist of a vector or profile of measurements or observations for each unit, one measurement on each of a number of variables or characters. Both quantitative variables and binary characters, scored only "present" or "absent," are frequent and important.

Often, the profile of measurements on a unit may consist of some measure of interaction with each other unit. For example, the units might be importing nations and the variables the relative value of imports from each other (exporting) nation. Special attention must be given to any use of the interaction of the unit with itself. Social choices between individuals give other examples, and special techniques for analyzing such data have been developed [*see* SOCIOMETRY].

The role of units and variables may be interchanged. In the preceding example, if clustering on the basis of export pattern were desired, the old "variables" would become new "units." (The measurements would change, since relative value would be computed with respect to a different base.) Or, again, from the voting record of legislators on each of many issues, one might want to cluster legislators or to cluster issues.

Clustering methods form a loosely organized body of techniques for the analysis of such data. As with most methods of data analysis, the aim is to find, to describe, and, hopefully, to lead to an explanation of some simple structure in a complex mass of data. Clustering methods are distinguished by the type of structure that is sought.

Examples in two dimensions. Geometric notions motivate the terminology and methods of clustering, although only for one or two variables can the geometric representation be used directly.

For example, suppose the units are essays, putatively written by a single author, and that the variables are two quantitative indicators of style, say mean sentence length and the rate of occurrence of the word *of* in the essay.

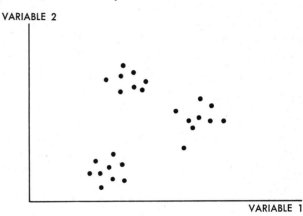

Figure 1 — Data exhibiting evident clustering

In Figure 1, each essay is represented by a point whose coordinates are the two measurements on the essay. Units are similar if their corresponding points are close together; clusters of units correspond to geometric clusters of points. In Figure 1, three clusters are visually evident and so clear-cut that a search for a theoretical explanation is natural. Might the essays have been written by three different authors?

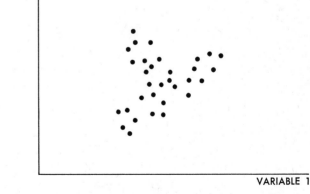

Figure 2 — Data exhibiting less clear-cut clustering

Figure 2 illustrates data in which the existence of two overlapping clusters is suggested, but the identification is incomplete. Further variables might permit better definition of clusters, but even the imperfect clustering may aid the description and understanding of the data.

Extensions to more than two dimensions. The aim of most clustering methods is to imitate and automate the process that can be done well visually in two dimensions and to extend it to any number of dimensions. The gain is the extension to many dimensions; that the process is in some ways inferior to visual inspection in two dimensions should be neither surprising nor disturbing.

If it is possible to group units into a moderate number of classes, within which the units have similar profiles, then a reduction of the data has been achieved that is easily described, that facilitates the analysis of further data, and that may be suggestive of theoretical structures underlying the data.

Each class can be described by a typical or average profile and, secondarily, by some measure of variability (shape and magnitude) within the class. Once the classes are well determined, future units can be placed in one of the classes through techniques of discriminant analysis [see MULTIVARIATE ANALYSIS, *article on* CLASSIFICATION AND DISCRIMINATION].

In some instances the clusters may correspond to underlying types explained by theory. In others they may represent only a convenient empirical reduction of the data. Interest may lie exclusively with the units included in the analysis or may extend to additional units.

The clustering process may be carried out on a finer scale, dividing a class into subclasses. More generally, an entire hierarchical classification or taxonomy can be obtained. It is in this latter form that clustering methods have been developed and applied in biology.

The technology of clustering is in an early and rapidly changing state. With a few exceptions, the development of clustering methods began only in the late 1950s, as large, high-speed computers became widely available. Many methods have been proposed and some have been tried and proved useful, but none is thoroughly understood or firmly established. The next few years should bring dramatic advances in the formulation of new methods, in techniques of computer execution, and in theoretical foundations. Most important, understanding of how and why procedures work or fail will be gained through experience and comparative experimentation.

Methods of clustering

Methods of clustering can usually be broken down into these steps: selection of units and of variables for inclusion in the data, determination of measures of similarity between pairs of units, grouping of units into clusters, interpretation and description of the results of grouping, possible iterations, and further analysis. Not all methods fit this decomposition, but each step has some counterpart in most methods.

Selection of units and variables. Specification of the data requires selection both of units and of variables and a choice of scale for each variable. The importance of selection of units is not yet fully understood. One effect is clear: including many units of one type will ensure that that type shows up as a cluster. Overrepresentation of a type has no strong effect on the clustering of the rest. Selection may be easy. In a study of voting behavior of a legislature, all legislators would be used. In a socioeconomic study of counties in the United States, a population of units is evident and a random or stratified sample might be included. Mostly, though, there is no clear universe of units, and those easily available are not a probability sample from any population. Understanding must await more experience with the results of clustering, especially in applications that go beyond a description of the original data.

Selection of variables and characters is more critical than selection of units and determines what aspects of behavior of units will be represented or emphasized in the clustering. Overrepresentation of variables in some area can strongly affect the entire outcome. Not only is there no natural universe of variables, but the notion of what constitutes an individual variable is not well defined. Variables can be refined, subdivided, and combined. Two variables that are functionally dependent or that are highly associated statistically can usually be recognized and avoided, but variables will inevitably have some statistical dependence over various groups of units. The choice of variables is a highly subjective, crucial element of the clustering process.

Scaling of variables. The data in any clustering process may be arranged in a rectangular array whose rows correspond to the units being clustered and whose columns correspond to the observed variables or characters. The entries in a row form the vector or profile of measurements of a unit on the respective variables. Most work has used variables that are measured on a numerical scale or else binary characters that can be so represented by denoting presence by a 1 and absence by a 0. Although the latter may be treated as a quantitative variable, there are substantial gains, primarily in computer technique, to be achieved by taking advantage of the 0-1 nature of binary characters. Much development has been restricted to binary variables. While any variable may be represented, at least approximately, by several binary variables, the representation introduces new arbitrariness and other difficulties.

With general quantitative variables, the problem of scaling or weighting is critical. If, for example, the first variable in Figure 2 were the median years of schooling (in a county, say) and the second were the median family income measured in thousands of dollars, to change to income measured in hundreds of dollars would expand the vertical scale by a factor of 10 and greatly distort the picture. While the eye may adjust for a bad choice, the numerical measures used in two and more dimensions are severely affected by a bad choice. Imposing an arbitrary, standard scaling by requiring each variable to have a standard deviation of 1 over the units included is a frequent choice. It is less subjective but no less arbitrary and often poorer than imposing a choice based on an external standard or on subjective judgment.

Choice of *nonlinear* scaling is even more difficult but offers potentially great benefits. [*See* STATISTICAL ANALYSIS, SPECIAL PROBLEMS OF, *article on* TRANSFORMATIONS OF DATA.]

Superficially, there is no scaling problem for binary variables that all take the same values, 0 and 1; but the difference between two variables, one about equally often 0 or 1 and another that takes the value 1 for about 2 per cent of the units, may indicate a need for some scaling of binary variables also.

Measures of similarity. The geometric representation of figures 1 and 2 can be extended conceptually to more than two variables. Generally, if the measurements of the first unit on k variables are denoted by $(x_{11}, \cdots, x_{1k})$, then the unit can be represented as a point in k-dimensional space with the measurements as coordinates. If the second unit has measurements $(x_{21}, \cdots, x_{2k})$, similarity of the two units corresponds to "closeness of the points" representing them. One natural measure of dissimilarity between points 1 and 2 is Euclidean squared distance,

$$(x_{11} - x_{21})^2 + (x_{12} - x_{22})^2 + \cdots + (x_{1k} - x_{2k})^2.$$

Unless the variables have been carefully scaled, a weighted distance,

$$w_1(x_{11} - x_{21})^2 + w_2(x_{12} - x_{22})^2 + \cdots + w_k(x_{1k} - x_{2k})^2,$$

is needed to make sense of the analysis. In order to allow for patterns of statistical dependence among the variables, a more complex weighting is required, such as

$$\sum_{i=1}^{k} \sum_{j=1}^{k} w_{ij} (x_{1i} - x_{2i})(x_{1j} - x_{2j}).$$

There is no uniquely correct choice of weights, but a careful subjective choice based on external knowledge of the variables, observed pattern of variability, and computational feasibility should be workable and will be preferable to an arbitrary but objective choice such as using the equally weighted Euclidean distance. New theory and methods— likely requiring lengthy and iterative computation —to make more effective use of internal patterns of variability to guide the choice and adjustment of weights will gradually be developed (see Ihm 1965).

For quantitative variables, the measures of similarity commonly used are equivalent to one of the weighted or unweighted squared distances. For binary variables, a greater variety of measures are in use. The equally weighted squared distance, when applied to variables taking only the values 0 and 1, yields the number of variables for which the items fail to match, a measure equivalent to the simple matching coefficient—the proportion of characters for which the two units have the same state. If a 1 represents possession of an attribute, a positive match, 1-1, may be more indicative of similarity than a negative match, 0-0, and numerous ways of taking account of the difference have been proposed (see Sokal & Sneath 1963, section 6.2).

Computation in grouping into clusters. Clustering methods require vast amounts of computation. Two examples illustrate some magnitudes and their relevance to methodology.

Suppose 100 units are to be clustered, so that there are 4,950 pairs of units. To compute unweighted distances for all pairs of units on the basis of, say, 50 variables requires sums of about 250,000 products. This is easily handled by currently available computers, although attention to computational technique, especially in the storage of data, will be critical as the number of units increases.

Consider next an operation that in principle is natural and attractive: Divide the 100 units into two groups in all possible ways, evaluate a criterion measuring the homogeneity of the groups for each partition, and choose the best one. With 100 units, there are $\frac{1}{2}(2^{100} - 2) \cong 6.3 \cdot 10^{29}$ groupings. Even if successive groupings could be generated and the criterion evaluated in a spectacularly efficient ten machine cycles, and using the fastest currently available machine cycle of 10^{-6} second, the process would require about 10^{17} years. Division into three and more groups is worse. Hence, many conceptually useful processes can never be realized in practice. Some modification or restriction is required to reduce drastically the possibilities to be considered, and even then results that only approximate conceptually optimum procedures must be accepted.

As an example of a possible extreme simplification, suppose that the units were dated and that time was an important variable. If the units in any cluster were required to be adjacent in the time sequence, then the number of partitions of 100 units into two groups is reduced to 99, into three groups to 4,851 (Fisher 1958).

A second possibility, based on the preceding one, is to require the grouping to be ordered on some variable, not prespecified but chosen to make the grouping best. When all variables are dichotomous, this procedure becomes remarkably simple and has been highly developed and used in plant classification with large numbers of units and variables. Lance and Williams (1965) survey these methods.

Hierarchical methods.   A third possibility is to reverse directions, building up clusters by combining one or more units at a time. Most of the procedures now used fall in this category. One commonly used version is built on repeated application of the following rule: Find the closest pair of clusters and combine them into a new, larger cluster and compute the distance between the new cluster and each of the remaining clusters. Initially, the clusters are the N units, treated as single-unit clusters. The first new cluster will be a two-unit cluster; the next may be a second two-unit cluster or it may be a three-unit cluster.

Since the process starts with N clusters and each stage reduces the number by one, the process terminates after exactly $N - 1$ steps, with all N items combined in one huge cluster. Of chief interest are the intermediate results, especially the last few, where the units are sorted into a moderate number of clusters. An interpretative phase is needed.

The output can be well presented in a linkage tree or dendrogram, as illustrated in Figure 3. The initial units are placed on a line in an order that is easily determined from the process. Vertical lines are dropped from each unit until it joins with another. If the distance measure is used as the vertical scale, then the vertical location of each joint shows how dissimilar the two groups joined were. Thus clusters formed near the top represent homogeneous groups, clusters formed farther down represent groups in which some units differ in larger ways, and clusters formed far down represent clusters formed only because the process goes to its logical end of one big group. The linkage tree generated by the process is a salient feature and potential advantage. A hierarchical nested structure is obtained upon choice of several horizontal slices of the tree. Slices may be made at standard vertical positions, or to give desired numbers of groups, or at natural breaks in the particular tree—where there are long vertical stretches without joints.

Another salient feature of this version is how little must be specified as part of the process. Once a distance measure is specified—between two clusters of any size, not just between two units—the process is completely determined. All judgment of how many clusters or how many levels of clustering is postponed to the next phase.

A major variation that gives up both salient features begins in the same way but proceeds by building up the first cluster until adding more units would make it too inhomogeneous. Then another cluster is constructed, etc. The process requires a rule for judging when to stop adding to a cluster (as well as the distance measure to determine which unit to add). As described, the process gives no hierarchy of clusters, but it could be reapplied to the clusters of the first round.

How should a measure of similarity between units be extended to a measure of similarity between clusters? Should it be based on the most similar units in the clusters? the least similar? an average? Should all units in a cluster be weighted equally, or should two joining stems be weighted equally? Methods based on these and many other possibilities have been tried. The choices matter—some favor large clusters, others smaller, equal-sized clusters—but no adequate basis for choice yet exists.

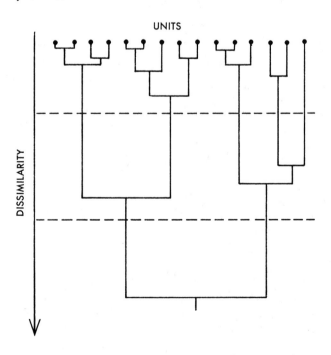

Figure 3 — Linkage tree of a stepwise clustering, showing two plausible slices

Where to stop clustering or how to cut the tree are open questions. The objectives of the analysis are essential to the decision, but perhaps some statistical models may be developed that would aid the choice.

Iteration. The possibility of treating clustering as an iterative process with the results of one clustering used to improve the next has just begun to be explored and will surely play an essential part in any thorough clustering procedure. Ihm (1965) illustrates one use of this idea to deal with the choice of weights. Ball (1965) describes a composite procedure that is highly iterative.

Relation to factor analysis. Factor analysis has frequently been used in lieu of direct clustering procedures. Both methods of analysis are attempts to discover and describe structure in an unstructured rectangular array of data. The methods seek different types of structure, although there is much overlap. Described in conventional statistical terms, factor analysis is an attempt to find a few "independent" variables such that regression on those variables fits the observed data. Geometrically, it is an attempt to locate a linear subspace that nearly contains the data [see FACTOR ANALYSIS].

In contrast, cluster analysis is an attempt to find an analysis of variance classification of the units (a one-way or nested design) that fits the observed data, that is, that reduces unexplained variation [see LINEAR HYPOTHESES, *article on* ANALYSIS OF VARIANCE].

Any cluster structure can be explained by a factor structure, although generally as many factors are needed as there are clusters. However, if two or three factors explain most of the variation, then by estimating factor scores for each unit, the units can be represented as points in two or three dimensions and clusters determined visually. This is one of the oldest routes for finding clusters.

Interchanging the role of units and variables in a factor analysis is common when clusters are sought. Then the process of rotation to "simple structure" may show directly the presence of clusters of units. These approaches permit the use of the older, better developed techniques of factor analysis.

Role of statistics. Clustering methodology has not yet advanced to the stage where sources of error and variation are considered formally; consequently, formal statistical methods play almost no role at present.

Unfortunately, even informal consideration of statistical variation has been neglected, in part because, typically, neither units nor variables are simple random samples, so conventional statistical theory is not *directly* applicable. Thus, although measures of similarity may be algebraically equivalent to correlation coefficients, conventional sampling theory and tests of hypotheses are not applicable or relevant.

Statistical variation. Several levels of statistical variation require consideration. At the lowest level are variation and error in the measurements. At this level there may be measurement error, as in determining the median income in a census tract, or there may be intraunit variability, as when units are Indian castes and tribes being clustered on the basis of physical measurements on individual members. Measurement error and intraunit variability, even on binary attributes, are present more often than is hoped or admitted, and they degrade the quality of clustering. Sometimes the variation must be accepted, but often it can be reduced by improved measurement technique or by inclusion of more than one instance of each unit.

A second level is variation of units within a cluster. This variation cannot be estimated until clusters are at least tentatively determined, but this is the important variability for determining statistical scales and weights, as would be used, for example, in classifying new units into established clusters.

Variation between clusters is the largest source and is the variation explainable by the clustering. Its magnitude depends heavily on the selection of units. Unfortunately, scaling variables according to over-all variability reflects largely this cluster-to-cluster variability.

Statistical models for variability in clustering are not yet highly developed. The fundamental paper by Rao (1948) and current work by Ihm (1965) are of note. One statistical model for clustering is very old. The distributions of observed data like those illustrated in figures 1 and 2 are naturally represented as mixtures whose component distributions correspond to the clusters. This formulation has greater conceptual than practical value; direct numerical use is troublesome even for a single variable [see DISTRIBUTIONS, STATISTICAL, *article on* MIXTURES OF DISTRIBUTIONS].

Development and applications. After a long, slow history in social science, notably in psychology and anthropology, numerical clustering methods underwent a rebirth of rapid, serious development —first through work in numerical taxonomy, both in conventional biology and in microbiology, and later in automatic classification and pattern recognition. These developments have spread throughout the social and natural sciences.

The book *Principles of Numerical Taxonomy* by

Sokal and Sneath (1963) provides the most comprehensive presentation of methods and principles and a thorough bibliography. Later developments in the biological area are represented in such periodicals as the *Journal of Ecology, Journal of Bacteriology, Journal of General Microbiology*, and the newsletter *Taxometrics*. The symposium of the Systematics Association (Heywood & McNeill 1964) is valuable.

The history of clustering in anthropology and linguistics has been surveyed by Driver (1965) in a detailed discussion of principles and results. [*Applications in geography are described in* GEOGRAPHY, *article on* STATISTICAL GEOGRAPHY.]

Clustering methods in psychology, often as an adjunct of factor analysis and often under the name "pattern analysis," have developed from Zubin (1938) and Tryon (1939). Many grouping ideas were introduced by McQuitty (1954; 1964) in a long series of papers.

Work on political districting is exemplified by Weaver and Hess (1963) and Kaiser (1966). Developments and applications in pattern recognition, information retrieval, and automatic classification are in large part not yet in the public literature (Needham 1965). Ball (1965) surveys approaches taken in many areas.

DAVID L. WALLACE

[*Other relevant material may be found in* MULTIVARIATE ANALYSIS, *article on* CLASSIFICATION AND DISCRIMINATION; TYPOLOGIES.]

BIBLIOGRAPHY

BALL, GEOFFREY H. 1965 Data Analysis in the Social Sciences. Volume 27, part 1, pages 533–560 in American Federation of Information Processing Societies Conference, *Proceedings*. Fall Joint Computer Conference. Washington: Spartan Books; London: Macmillan.

DRIVER, HAROLD E. 1965 Survey of Numerical Classification in Anthropology. Pages 301–344 in Dell Hymes (editor), *The Use of Computers in Anthropology*. The Hague: Mouton.

FISHER, WALTER D. 1958 On Grouping for Maximum Homogeneity. *Journal of the American Statistical Association* 53:789–798.

HEYWOOD, VERNON H.; and McNEILL, J. (editors) 1964 *Phenetic and Phylogenetic Classification*. London: Systematics Association.

IHM, PETER 1965 Automatic Classification in Anthropology. Pages 357–376 in Dell Hymes (editor), *The Use of Computers in Anthropology*. The Hague: Mouton.

KAISER, HENRY F. 1966 An Objective Method for Establishing Legislative Districts. *Midwest Journal of Political Science* 10, no. 2:200–213.

LANCE, G. N.; and WILLIAMS, W. T. 1965 Computer Programs for Monothetic Classification ("Association Analysis"). *Computer Journal* 8:246–249.

McQUITTY, LOUIS L. 1954 Pattern Analysis Illustrated in Classifying Patients and Normals. *Educational and Psychological Measurement* 14:598–604.

McQUITTY, LOUIS L. 1964 Capabilities and Improvements of Linkage Analysis as a Clustering Method. *Educational and Psychological Measurement* 24:441–456.

NEEDHAM, R. M. 1965 Computer Methods for Classification and Grouping. Pages 345–356 in Dell Hymes (editor), *The Use of Computers in Anthropology*. The Hague: Mouton.

RAO, C. RADHAKRISHNA 1948 The Utilization of Multiple Measurements in Problems of Biological Classification. *Journal of the Royal Statistical Society* Series B 10:159–193. → Pages 194–203 contain an especially interesting discussion of this paper.

SOKAL, ROBERT R.; and SNEATH, PETER H. A. 1963 *Principles of Numerical Taxonomy*. San Francisco: Freeman.

TRYON, ROBERT C. 1939 *Cluster Analysis: Correlation Profile and Orthometric (Factor) Analysis for the Isolation of Unities in Mind and Personality*. Ann Arbor, Mich.: Edwards.

WARD, JOE H. JR. 1963 Hierarchical Grouping to Optimize an Objective Function. *Journal of the American Statistical Association* 58:236–244.

WEAVER, JAMES B.; and HESS, SIDNEY W. 1963 A Procedure for Nonpartisan Districting: Development of Computer Techniques. *Yale Law Journal* 73:288–308.

ZUBIN, JOSEPH 1938 A Technique for Measuring Likemindedness. *Journal of Abnormal and Social Psychology* 33:508–516.

COALITIONS

I. THE STUDY OF COALITIONS .... *William H. Riker*
II. COALITION FORMATION .... *William A. Gamson*

I

THE STUDY OF COALITIONS

The word "coalition" has long been used in ordinary English to refer to a group of people who come together (usually on a temporary basis) to obtain some end. Typically, a coalition has been regarded as a parliamentary or political grouping less permanent than a party or a faction or an interest group [*see* PARLIAMENTARY GOVERNMENT]. Recently, however, the word has acquired a technical significance in social science theories with the elaboration (in the last two decades) of the theory of *n*-person games. The notion of coalition formation is central to this theory, since coalitions are the characteristic form of social organization by which the outcomes of such games are determined. To the degree that the theory provides a model for the study of national decision making in elections, parliaments, committees, cabinets, etc., or of international decision making in wars, diplomatic maneuvers, and international organizations, to that degree, coalitions are the characteristic form of social organization for political decision making generally.

The originators of the theory of *n*-person games,

John von Neumann and Oskar Morgenstern, observed a fundamental difference, with respect to discovering the best way to win, between two-person games and games involving more than two persons: In two-person games, the problem for each player is to select the best strategy against his opponent; but in three-person or larger games, the problem for each player is to select partner(s) who can collectively win. They called the artifact resulting from the mutual selection of partners a *coalition*, and they constructed the whole theory of *n*-person games about the process of forming coalitions. Since politics is often defined as the authoritative allocation of values and since, in all but dictatorial or duopolistic situations, allocation is a process of coalition formation (Riker 1962, chapter 1), it is apparent that a theory of coalitions is a central part of a theory of politics.

Main problems

Three main questions have been dealt with in the theory: (1) How should winnings be divided to ensure victory for a player or a coalition? (2) Given a particular set of rules, what chance does a particular player have to be in a crucial position in a winning coalition? (3) Which potential partners should come together in particular play? The theories relating to each of these questions will be summarized and then attempts at verification and use of the theories will be discussed.

The division of winnings. The Von Neumann–Morgenstern notion of a *solution* is the main contribution here. The substance of this notion is that, while it is not possible to specify a uniquely preferable coalition, it is possible to specify a set of preferable imputations, that is, a set of preferable ways to distribute gains and losses. To explain this notion the following vocabulary is required.

Let there be a set of players, I, where I is given by $\{1, 2, \cdots, n\}$, and let the subsets of I, which are *coalitions*, be designated by $S, T, \cdots$. Let the payment to each player at the end of the game be designated by x_i, where $i = 1, 2, \cdots, n$, so that the totality of payments, which is an *imputation* is a vector, $\boldsymbol{x} = (x_1, x_2, \cdots, x_n)$. Let the payment to a coalition, S, be designated by a function, v, which is a real valued set function with at least the following properties:

(1) $v(\phi) = 0$, where ϕ is the empty coalition; and (2) $v(S \cup T) \geqslant v(S) + v(T)$, where S and T are disjoint subsets of I.

The second property, superadditivity, records the fact that for at least some players in some games there is an increment in payoff from the very act of joining together. A coalition, S, is said to be *effective* for an imputation, $\boldsymbol{x}$, if

$$\sum_{i \text{ in } S} x_i \leqslant v(S).$$

That is, a coalition is effective if it can win as much or more than the sum of the payoffs to its members. An imputation, $\boldsymbol{x}$, is said to dominate an imputation, $\boldsymbol{y}$, if

(1) S is not empty
(2) S is effective for $\boldsymbol{x}$
(3) $x_i > y_i$, for all i in S.

A solution, $\boldsymbol{V}$, is a set of imputations such that (1) no $\boldsymbol{y}$ in $\boldsymbol{V}$ is dominated by an $\boldsymbol{x}$ in $\boldsymbol{V}$; and (2) every $\boldsymbol{y}$ not in $\boldsymbol{V}$ is dominated by an $\boldsymbol{x}$ in $\boldsymbol{V}$. To illustrate, for the zero-sum three-person game in normal form (for definitions of "zero-sum" and "normal form" see, e.g., Riker & Niemi 1964) the set $\boldsymbol{V}$ is $\{(\frac{1}{2}, \frac{1}{2}, -1), (\frac{1}{2}, -1, \frac{1}{2}), (-1, \frac{1}{2}, \frac{1}{2})\}$. The essence of this definition is that, regardless of which winning coalition forms [i.e., $(1, 2)$, $(1, 3)$, or $(2, 3)$], still any one that does form ought to adopt a split-the-winnings-equally kind of imputation. The heuristic rationale leading to this definition is the observation that a player, i, who seeks to obtain $x_i > \frac{1}{2}$ is creating a situation in which he may receive the worst possible payoff, i.e., $x_i = -1$. If, in the course of negotiations, a coalition of players 1 and 2 has arrived at a tentative imputation $\boldsymbol{y}$, where $\boldsymbol{y} = (\frac{3}{4}, \frac{1}{4}, -1)$, player 2 is likely to be especially receptive to offers from player 3 to form $(2, 3)$ with imputation $\boldsymbol{x} = (-1, \frac{1}{2}, \frac{1}{2})$ and where, of course, $\boldsymbol{y}$ is now dominated by $\boldsymbol{x}$. Thus player 1 is undone by his greed. On the other hand, none of the imputations in the solution are susceptible to that kind of renegotiation of coalitions, for no partner in a winning coalition is likely to feel disadvantaged by the imputation adopted. Hence, if an imputation in the solution is adopted, it is likely to be stable as are also the coalitions associated with it.

In short, a solution specifies a set of preferable imputations, but not preferable coalitions. Since, however, Von Neumann and Morgenstern had heuristically stated the problem of *n*-person games to be that of finding partners and since, in contrast, their mathematical "solution" specified not partners but rather the division of spoils among unspecified partners, much dissatisfaction has been expressed with the notion of a solution, and a number of alternatives have been offered (Von Neumann & Morgenstern 1944). The spirit of these alternatives, like the spirit of the Von Neumann–Morgenstern solution, is to pick out a limited number of acceptable imputations from the (usually) infinite number of imputations possible.

Ψ-stability: The most interesting of these alternatives is the notion of Ψ-stability, which can be explained with the following vocabulary: Let a partition of I into disjoint subsets be defined as a coalition structure, τ. For example, if $n = 3$, the partitions $(\{1, 2\}, \{3\})$ and $(\{1, 3\}, \{2\})$ are possible coalition structures. Let Ψ denote a rule of admissible changes from τ, and let Ψ(τ) denote the set of coalition structures resulting from the application of Ψ to τ. For example, if for $n = 3$, τ is the partition $(\{1, 2\}, \{3\})$, and if Ψ is a rule that permits any coalition formed by the addition of a single player to an existent coalition, then Ψ(τ) is the following set of alternative partitions:

$$[(\{1, 2, 3\}), (\{1, 3\}, \{2\}), (\{2, 3\}, \{1\})].$$

Since the point of this argument is to set some limit on possible imputations and coalitions, one wishes to find pairs, $(\boldsymbol{x}, \tau)$, of an imputation and a coalition structure such that players would not wish to depart from the pair (once they have reached it) by means of the changes permitted by Ψ. Such pairs, $(\boldsymbol{x}, \tau)$, are in a kind of equilibrium, which Luce called Ψ-stability (1954). Formally defined, a pair, $(\boldsymbol{x}, \tau)$, is Ψ-stable if:

(1) $v(S) \leqslant \sum_{i \text{ in } S} x_i$, for all S in Ψ(τ), and

(2) if $x_i = v(\{i\})$, then $\{i\}$ is in τ.

The first condition states that, for any coalition, S, that might be formed by the application of Ψ to τ, the players in this potential coalition cannot better themselves. The second condition states that if a player receives no more than he can get in the worst possible circumstances (i.e., when he is in a single-member coalition), then he must in fact be in such a condition in τ, that is to say for a member, i, of a multimember coalition in τ, $x_i > v(\{i\})$.

The advantage of this definition is that it permits some discussion of actual partners along with a discussion of imputations. Its disadvantage is that it requires a precise specification of Ψ for a particular game—and in social situations this is usually difficult to specify. Furthermore, there is an embarrassingly *ad hoc* flavor to the whole definition inasmuch as the specification of Ψ must be in terms of standards of behavior prevailing among particular players of a game.

Other alternatives to solution theory have also been offered, but they are no more satisfactory than what they purport to supplant; so instead of summarizing them here, the reader is referred to Luce and Raiffa, where Ψ-stability is also admirably discussed (1957, pp. 220–245).

The chance of obtaining a crucial position. Here the main contribution is Shapley's notion of a value for n-person games, which is an a priori method for estimating whether or not, for a particular player, a game is worth playing (Shapley 1953; Shapley & Shubik 1954). Suppose, in a game of n players, a coalition of k players, where $k \leqslant n$, is necessary to win. Let coalitions of k players be constructed by permuting the n players so that the first k players in any permutation are the minimally winning coalition, which is defined as a winning coalition that ceases to be winning if the kth player is subtracted. Let the kth position be designated as the *pivot* and let the number of times a player, i, occupies the pivot position be designated by p_i. Since there are $n!$ permutations of n, the chance, v, that a player, i, occupies the pivotal position is $v(i) = p_i/n!$.

Underlying this measure of value are two crucial sociological assumptions: (1) Since the notion of pivoting is defined with respect to minimal winning coalitions, one infers that membership of a coalition in excess of the minimally winning size is irrelevant. This is a version of the size principle to be discussed below. (2) The expectation about imputations is quite different from imputations prescribed in the Von Neumann–Morgenstern solution. In a solution, the division of winnings among equally weighted members is, regardless of their position in the coalition, equal. But in the sociological theory underlying Shapley's value, there is a time dimension to membership in a coalition so that the player in the pivotal position can expect to receive more than others. Over time, these advantages are expected to average out; but still the single imputation in the specific play is not an imputation in the solution. The difference is, of course, the assumption of the existence of a time dimension (and perhaps of a differentiation of roles in the coalition-formation process).

Which players should become partners. The main contributions here are those by Gamson (1961a; 1961b) and Riker (1962). Underlying these contributions is the *size principle,* which is the assertion that, with perfect and complete information, players should prefer minimally winning coalitions to larger winning ones. Using this principle, it is possible to show that if players have unequal weights then some possible coalitions are preferable to others, and indeed in some distributions of weights one possible coalition is uniquely preferable to others. Similarly, some players have unique advantages over others in the sense that the advantaged players can expect to be included in *any* preferable coalition. Since these two kinds of advantage are a function of the kind of ways in which the several weights can add up to k, which is the minimally winning size, it is not possible to specify in general these advantages for players and coalitions. Tables specifying these advantages for relevant variations in partitions of the total weight in the set of players are set forth in Gamson and in Riker for $n = 3$, 4, or 5. The most interesting result of such specifications is that *usually* the least weighty players ought to combine with each other, which leads to the somewhat paradoxical assertion that the weightiest player is *usually* the weakest in terms of combinatorial advantages. Note, however, that this conclusion follows from an argument in which perfect and complete information is assumed. Weakening the assumptions about information also weakens the force of this conclusion. As information is rendered less perfect and less complete, players may be expected to attempt to increase the size of winning coalitions above the minimum in order to guarantee victory.

Verification

Much more energy has been expended on the elaboration of the theory of coalitions than on the verification of it. The paucity of attempts at verification is explicable in terms of a theoretical difficulty: The whole theory is normative in the sense that it specifies what rational players should do to obtain the best possible payoff. It does not specify what real players will in fact do. To render the normative theory into a descriptive one, it must be assumed (1) that some players (that is, at least the winners) are rational, in the sense that they prefer to win rather than lose, and (2) that some political situations are sufficiently analogous to abstract games so that the theory of games is also a theory of political coalitions. Many social scientists are suspicious of both assumptions, and, given their reluctance to adopt them, the theory remains unverifiable just as all normative theories are unverifiable as truth-functional sentences. Nevertheless, some social scientists have been willing to assume that institutions that favor winners encourage the existence of rational political men and that political situations in which participants perceive their problem as one of winning are quite analogous to abstract games. Hence they have regarded the theory of coalitions as descriptive and have sought to verify it, hoping thereby to verify as well the assumption about rationality.

Verification and the "solution." Several experiments, most of which are well summarized by Rapoport and Orwant (1962) and Riker and Niemi (1964), have been conducted to test some features of the notion of a solution. In general, the results of these have not verified the Von Neumann–

Morgenstern theory, except when special precautions have been taken in the experimental design to encourage subjects to behave highly competitively. Usually the imputations arrived at have been of the sort $(1/n, 1/n, \cdots, 1/n)$, instead of the prescribed $\alpha_1, \alpha_2, \cdots, \alpha_k, \beta_1, \beta_2, \cdots, \beta_{n-k}$, where $\alpha_i = \alpha_j$ and $\alpha_i > 0 > \beta_i$. The latter imputation has been achieved with fair consistency only when, for example, stooges have been inserted among sophisticated subjects to insist upon imputations of the prescribed kind. Several explanations for the failure have been advanced, to wit, that the experimental design (1) failed to protect the outcome from the influence of variables in subjects' personalities (e.g., their attitudes toward gambling); (2) failed to provide stakes large enough to induce rational behavior; and (3) permitted subjects to perceive the experimenter as another player in an $(n + 1)$-player game, in which the imputation $(1/n, 1/n, \cdots, 1/n, -n)$ may be in the solution (provided the game is regarded as discriminatory). Further experiments with improved designs are necessary before any conclusion can be drawn on the truth or falsity of solution theory.

As for the notion of Ψ-stability, the one attempt to use it in analyzing a real situation (which attempt amounts indirectly to an attempt at verification) has produced interesting and intuitively plausible, but far from definitive, results. Luce and Rogow (1956) analyzed a simplified version of the three houses of the national legislature in the United States (i.e., the president, in his legislative capacity, the Senate, and the House of Representatives) in which there were assumed to exist two parties each with some members who always voted with the majority of the party (die-hards) and some who might on occasion vote with a majority of the other party (defectors). They examined the legislative branch according to variations in numbers of party members and numbers of die-hards and defectors in each party and produced two conclusions that do not otherwise seem immediately obvious: (1) a president is weak when *either* party has a more than two-thirds majority in Congress and (2) a president is strong when there is no party that can obtain a two-thirds majority even with the help of defectors from the other party. These nonobvious, but intuitively satisfying, conclusions suggest that much can be learned by further application of Ψ-stability theory to other situations.

Verification and use of value. It is hard to imagine how the notion of value might be verified, for it is a method to evaluate rather than predict or prescribe. Riker tried to determine by statistical analyses of roll calls in an assembly whether or not legislators seek to improve their chances of occupying the pivotal position; but his data and procedures were too crude to lead to any sure conclusions (1959). The notion of value has, however, been used to evaluate several real constitutions, treating them as games to be played: the Congress in the United States; the Security Council of the United Nations (Shapley & Shubik 1954); the Electoral College in the United States (Mann & Shapley 1960; 1962); and the federal relationship in the United States, Canada, and Australia (Riker & Schaps 1957).

Verification of prescriptions on partners. Vinacke and Arkoff (1957) and Gamson (1961b) have attempted to verify Caplow's predictions in experimental situations. Their results, with some reservations, tend to verify his specifications of preferable coalitions. Riker has offered historical evidence for the acceptance of the size principle by politicians in national and international political situations (1962, chapters 3, 7). Barth, assuming the size principle, has shown that Afghan chieftains conduct their intertribal diplomacy in terms of it (1959). Although far from satisfactorily verified, this feature of the theory of coalitions is closer to verification than any other.

Further developments

Considering the previous development of the theory of coalitions, it seems likely that future expansion of the theory can be expected only if additional sociological assumptions can be incorporated in the mathematical theory. The original theory of solutions to n-person games contained a bare minimum of assumptions about behavior, viz., (1) rational motives, i.e., participants' desire to win rather than to lose; (2) sets and subsets or the notion of coalitions itself; and (3) super additivity. Out of these minimal assumptions, Von Neumann and Morgenstern were able to arrive at the theory of solutions, which, however, seemed inadequate because it specified only the division of winnings and not the choice of partners. Luce's step toward the discussion of partners (i.e., Ψ-stability) involved the introduction of an additional sociological assumption, namely, the existence of a standard of behavior, Ψ, that admitted some kinds of bargaining about membership in coalitions but not others. Caplow's discussion of partners and Riker's elaboration of the size principle required the introduction of both the notion of differentials in weights (which is substantially equivalent to the introduction of the notion of "power") and the notion of a majority. Since these elaborations of the theory of coalitions depended upon the addition of

sociological premises, it can be expected that future elaborations will depend on future additions.

Dynamics of growth. One promising additional sociological assumption is the notion that coalitions go through a process of growth. Let the situation at the beginning of any decision-making or allocative process be such that participants are partitioned into n single-member subsets. Define *coalitions* as winning or losing subsets when a winning subset exists, and define *protocoalitions* as subsets when no winning coalition exists. Then the process of decision making is the transformation of some protocoalition into a winning coalition. If a winning coalition consists of k members, where $\frac{1}{2}n < k \leqslant n$, then the process of decision making or allocation is the development of a protocoalition from 1 member to 2 members, from 2 to 3 members, $\cdots$, from $(k-2)$ members to $(k-1)$ members, and from $(k-1)$ to k members. There are several crucial stages in this process, especially the movement from one-member to two-member protocoalitions and the movement from $(k-1)$ to k members (which latter may be called the "end-play"). Riker has set forth some of the strategic considerations of the end-play, but these have as yet to be developed in a general statement (1962, chapter 6). His conclusions can be summarized, however, as the assertion that the strategy of end-play is to find, for a given structure of protocoalitions, that coalition that most nearly approaches the minimally winning size. Doubtless many other strategic considerations enter into the growth process, although these are as yet unspecified.

Roles. Defining roles as positions specified by the rules of any particular process of coalition formation, Von Neumann and Morgenstern assumed that while roles of players may differ with respect to advantages in the rules, still the roles are identical with respect to the kind of behavior in bargaining. Furthermore, they assumed that players could rotate indiscriminately among roles. There is no reason to suppose that either assumption is appropriate for the description of the natural world. Indeed, it is likely that in reality there exists a variety of roles in the coalition-formation process: for example, *leader*, the role of initiating that bargaining by which protocoalitions are enlarged; *follower*, the role of moving, at the instigation of a leader, from a single-member protocoalition to a larger one; *pivot*, already defined as that follower who becomes the kth member of a minimally winning coalition; *reliable follower*, the role of irrevocably accepting membership in a multimember protocoalition; *defecting follower*, the role of accepting and subsequently rejecting membership in a multimember protocoalition; *wallflower*, a member of a single-member coalition who is not sought out for the role of follower; etc. Doubtless the theory of coalition formation may be rendered more appropriate for the study of nature by mathematizing the essential features of behavior in each of these roles. For example, with respect to the role of leader, it is likely, as Riker has argued, that his payments are different in kind from the payments to followers, that the leader (who quite possibly starts out as a wallflower) is willing to forgo material reward for the sake of obtaining the psychic reward of leadership and that the leader may, for the sake of retaining his leadership, pay out more material rewards than his prospective coalition can win. Assuming these possibilities do in fact prevail, then the notion of a solution must be modified. Solution theory requires a symmetric kind of imputation (although it allows for unequal rewards for roles with unequal advantages in the rules). But if differentials in behavior may affect imputations, then the notion of "equal rewards for equal advantages in the rules" must be abandoned for a notion of unequal rewards according to whether the participant plays the role of leader or follower, with the leader accepting the lesser material reward. (The sociological, but not the mathematical, consequences of accepting the notion of these differentials in roles is set forth in Riker 1962.)

In the beginning of this article, it was suggested that a theory of coalitions amounted to a theory of politics. The subsequent considerations, however, suggest that a theory of coalitions adequate to serve as a theory of politics has not yet been developed. The hope for the next generation is that it will be.

WILLIAM H. RIKER

[*Also relevant are the entries* DECISION MAKING; GAME THEORY; SIMULATION.]

BIBLIOGRAPHY

BARTH, FREDRIK 1959 Segmentary Opposition and the Theory of Games: A Study of Pathan Organization. *Journal of the Royal Anthropological Institute of Great Britain and Ireland* 89:5–21.

BUCHANAN, JAMES M.; and TULLOCK, GORDON 1962 *The Calculus of Consent: Logical Foundations of Constitutional Democracy.* Ann Arbor: Univ. of Michigan Press.

CAPLOW, THEODORE 1956 A Theory of Coalitions in the Triad. *American Sociological Review* 21:489–493.

GAMSON, WILLIAM A. 1961a A Theory of Coalition Formation. *American Sociological Review* 26:373–382.

GAMSON, WILLIAM A. 1961b An Experimental Test of a Theory of Coalition Formation. *American Sociological Review* 26:565–573.

LUCE, R. DUNCAN 1954 A Definition of Stability for *n*-Person Games. *Annals of Mathematics* 59:357–366.

LUCE, R. DUNCAN; and RAIFFA, HOWARD 1957 *Games and Decisions: Introduction and Critical Survey.* A Study of the Behavioral Models Project, Bureau of Applied Social Research, Columbia University. New York: Wiley. → First issued in 1954 as *A Survey of the Theory of Games*, Columbia University, Bureau of Applied Social Research, Technical Report No. 5.

LUCE, R. DUNCAN; and ROGOW, ARNOLD A. 1956 A Game Theoretic Analysis of Congressional Power Distributions for a Stable Two-party System. *Behavioral Science* 1:83–95.

MANN, IRWIN; and SHAPLEY, L. S. 1960 *Values of Large Games, IV: Evaluating the Electoral College by Monte-carlo Techniques.* U.S. Air Force Project, RAND, Memorandum RM-2651. Santa Monica, Calif.: RAND Corp.

MANN, IRWIN; and SHAPLEY, L. S. 1962 *Values of Large Games, VI: Evaluating the Electoral College Exactly.* Rand, Memorandum RM-3158-PR. Santa Monica, Calif.: RAND Corp.

RAPOPORT, ANATOL 1960 *Fights, Games, and Debates.* Ann Arbor: Univ. of Michigan Press.

RAPOPORT, ANATOL; and ORWANT, CAROL 1962 Experimental Games: A Review. *Behavioral Science* 7:1–37.

RIKER, WILLIAM H. 1959 A Test of the Adequacy of the Power Index. *Behavioral Science* 4:120–131.

RIKER, WILLIAM H. 1962 *The Theory of Political Coalitions.* New Haven: Yale Univ. Press.

RIKER, WILLIAM H.; and NIEMI, DONALD 1962 The Stability of Coalitions on Roll Calls in the House of Representatives. *American Political Science Review* 56:58–65.

RIKER, WILLIAM H.; and NIEMI, RICHARD G. 1964 Anonymity and Rationality in the Essential Three-person Game. *Human Relations* 17:131–141.

RIKER, WILLIAM H.; and SCHAPS, RONALD 1957 Disharmony in Federal Government. *Behavioral Science* 2:276–290.

SHAPLEY, L. S. 1953 A Value for *n*-Person Games. Volume 2, pages 307–317 in H. W. Kuhn and A. W. Tucker (editors), *Contributions to the Theory of Games.* Princeton Univ. Press.

SHAPLEY, L. S.; and SHUBIK, MARTIN 1954 A Method for Evaluating the Distribution of Power in a Committee System. *American Political Science Review* 48:787–792.

SHUBIK, MARTIN (editor) 1964 *Game Theory and Related Approaches to Social Behavior: Selections.* New York: Wiley.

VINACKE, W. E.; and ARKOFF, ABE 1957 An Experimental Study of Coalitions in the Triad. *American Sociological Review* 22:406–414.

VON NEUMANN, JOHN; and MORGENSTERN, OSKAR (1944) 1964 *Theory of Games and Economic Behavior.* 3d ed. New York: Wiley.

II
COALITION FORMATION

Few areas exhibit less external uniformity than the alliances of men. "Politics makes strange bedfellows," we say to express our bewilderment at some new coalition which belies our expectations from past knowledge of the participants. But this is not the only kind of surprise that the study of coalition formation has in store. "Strength is weakness" and "Playing to win is playing to lose" are only two examples of the lessons to be drawn from this area of human behavior. The fact that these lessons are not yet proverbial indicates only that the term "coalition" is in need of clarification, since the phenomena to which it should be applied are already sufficiently familiar.

As with many other terms, it is possible to use "coalition" in a manner that robs it of much of its meaning. Thus, it is sometimes used to mean no more than the kind of joint activity displayed by, say, two young children who hide in the same place when it is time for them to go to bed. A common extension of this usage is to denote the mutuality of affective support that often accompanies such activity; for instance, if the children agreed to tell their mother that they were fish and did not need to sleep, this little fantasy might be said to express a temporary coalition against the mother.

It is necessary to guard against such uses of "coalition" because the immense influence of Georg Simmel in this area has made them all too frequent. Simmel ([1902–1917] 1950, pp. 135–136) argued that in any closely knit group of three persons— a "triad," as he called it—situations were bound to arise in which two of the three would regard the third as an intruder. But Simmel's interest in triadic situations extended mainly to those in which there is *no* coalition of two against one, even in the sense of shared affective support. The situations to which he gave most attention are those in which two members of the triad are in conflict with each other and the third either mediates between them or acts as *tertius gaudens*— that is, as one who draws comfort and advantage from the conflict. Nevertheless, a number of social scientists have drawn on Simmel's formulation to support the proposition that any triad tends to split into a coalition of two and a third who is excluded.

The old proverb that when two is company, three is a crowd, undoubtedly has some truth in it and is worth investigating. But the truth of this proverb, or its scientific equivalent, is less at issue here than its relevance for the topic of coalition formation. If every clique within a larger group is to be called a coalition, then any partitioning of a group into subparts on whatever basis could be viewed as a "coalition structure," and the study of coalitions would be coextensive with the study of cliques or even with the entire field of sociometry. In order to avoid this kind of confusion, coalitions should be defined far more narrowly.

Defining a coalition

In this article, "coalition" will be used to mean the *joint use of resources to determine the outcome of a decision*, where a resource is some weight such that some critical quantity of it in the control of two or more parties to the decision is both necessary and sufficient to determine its outcome. Participants will be said to be using their resources jointly only if they coordinate their deployment of resources with respect to some decision. That is what is meant by saying that they have formed a coalition.

Some studies which have been cast in terms of coalition formation do not seem to meet the above criteria. For example, in Mills (1954) subjects were asked to decide (not necessarily on a group basis) what verdict they would have cast had they been present at the trial of Herman Melville's hero Billy Budd, and various indices of support between each pair of participants were calculated. But if such an experiment deals with coalition formation, it must be possible to say what kinds of resources are being deployed. To include the Mills study in our definition, we might consider "arguments" as the resource, so that persons who argued in favor of the same verdict would be coordinating their use of resources, and this would count as a coalition. But the fact that two people who argue for the same verdict have come to like or respect each other would still be only incidental to the coalition situation.

Not all situations in which resources are used to affect the outcome of a decision involve coalition formation. This can be made clearer for situations involving several parties by first examining the simpler two-person situation. Schelling (1958) classifies two-person games of strategy into "pure coordination" games, "pure conflict" (or "zero-sum") games, and "mixed-motive" games. One good example of a pure coordination game is the relation between two bridge partners, since they have the same interests and their only problem is one of coordinating their strategy. In contrast, the relation between two teams in bridge is one of pure conflict, since their interests are diametrically opposed. The classic example of a mixed-motive game is the situation known in game theory as the "prisoner's dilemma," in which neither of two prisoners accused of complicity in the same crime can be condemned if neither confesses; if only one prisoner confesses, the other will be condemned and the one who confessed set free; and if both confess, both will be condemned (Rapoport &

Chammah 1965; Rapoport & Orwant 1962). Thus the players are partly in conflict, because one prisoner can be set free only at the expense of the other, and partly in harmony, because both prisoners stand to gain if they agree not to confess, though this joint strategy will bring each of them less than the maximum he might have gained independently. The situation poses a dilemma because the prisoners are assumed to be held incommunicado, and each therefore has to make his decision in ignorance of what the other will do.

Schelling's classification can be adapted to cover situations involving more than two parties. Thus pure coordination games would be those in which there exists a solution that brings the greatest possible return to all parties at once, and there is no reason to exclude any participant, since in pursuing his own interests, each party is aiding the others to achieve theirs. The problem would then be one of achieving this goal as efficiently as possible by coordinating the use of all available resources. But to call this a coalition situation would be to dilute the meaning of the term, since any group in which there was no conflict of interest and which was pursuing some common goal could then be called a coalition. Much the same considerations apply to pure conflict situations; the issue of whether to form a coalition does not arise, since no player has anything to gain by forming one—indeed, the joint use of resources may be forbidden by the rules of the game. It should be noted that some n-person, zero-sum games are *not* pure conflict games, since they may allow some of the players to pool their resources and so gain at the expense of the other players. A pure conflict game, however, is one from which coalitions are excluded, either by definition or because there is no incentive for them.

It therefore seems necessary to conclude that coalitions can take place only within the context of mixed-motive, n-person games, in which both conflict and common interest are simultaneously present, and must govern the courses of action chosen. This is because in such games there is no outcome that brings the greatest possible return to all players at once, while there is always the possibility that at least two of the players may do better if they pool their resources.

The term "coalition" can now be defined with greater precision. It is the *joint use of resources to determine the outcome of a decision in a mixed-motive situation involving more than two units.* Many studies of three-person groups that have been cast in coalition terms have not studied coalition

formation under the above definition, though this does not mean that they lack relevance for the study of other aspects of group behavior.

Theories of coalition formation should predict who will combine with whom and how they will split the proceeds. Social scientists are not directly concerned with how people *should* behave in coalition situations, though obviously they can study normative prescriptions by treating them as statements about expected behavior. Each of the different theories of coalition formation that will be described depends on a different set of basic assumptions. In order to show how each type of theory can be applied, the following example of a coalition situation will be used. Suppose that successive polling at a political convention has reduced the list of candidates to three: candidate A, who controls 48 per cent of the votes; candidate B, who controls 30 per cent; and candidate C, who controls 22 per cent. Each of the three has absolute control over the votes of his supporters. The rules state that whoever obtains a simple majority is nominated.

Predicting coalitions

The first type of theory to be dealt with is minimum resource theory, which was first developed by Gamson (1961a) and Riker (1962), though some features of the theory were anticipated by Caplow (1956; 1959). The central hypothesis of the theory is that a coalition will form in which the total resources are as small as possible while still being sufficient. Thus, to use the convention example, since the coalition BC, with 52 per cent of the vote, is the smallest of three possible winning coalitions, it is clearly the one that will be formed. In this situation, strength, as defined by the amount of resources possessed before any coalition is formed, is really weakness, since the strongest candidate, with control over 48 per cent of the votes, is excluded from the winning coalition.

The cheapest coalition principle can be applied to groups of any size. It does not necessarily imply defeat for the strongest players; for example, if there had been a four-man game in which candidates A and B each controlled 24 per cent of the votes, with candidate C controlling 22 per cent and candidate D 30 per cent, candidate D would have been both the strongest player and a member of the cheapest winning coalition. Thus it is not true to say that initial strength never pays off in a coalition situation; strength is weakness only under certain conditions—conditions that can be clearly specified by minimum resource theory.

But what are the grounds on which the cheapest coalition prediction rests? One answer is that in many coalition situations the players believe that no one should gain proportionately more or less from a coalition than the amount of resources he is able to contribute to it. A convenient name for this belief is the *parity norm*. It should be noted that it *is* a belief about what the players feel in general that they deserve, not an empirical estimate of the distribution of power in any particular situation.

The parity norm is merely the ancient principle of distributive justice applied to coalitions. "A man in an exchange relation with another will expect that . . . the net rewards, or profits, of each man be proportional to his investments" (Homans 1961, p. 75). This norm discourages the formation of coalitions that are more powerful than necessary, because if a player gains from a coalition an amount proportional to the resources he brings to it, it is obviously to his advantage to join the coalition in which his resources will represent the largest possible share of the total resources pooled.

A second theory, the theory of *minimum power*, is based on an interpretation of L. S. Shapley's method for evaluating the worth of an *n*-person game for any player (Shapley 1953). This method is based on the number of times a player is the "pivotal" member who turns an insufficient coalition into a winning one. The method is, of course, part of mathematical game theory, and the descriptive application of it proposed here is in no sense intended as a contribution to that normative theory. One may interpret Shapley's measure of pivotal power as a measure of a player's initial bargaining power. This type of power is clearly distinct from the amount of a player's initial resources. In simple terms, a player's pivotal power is the proportion of times his resources can change a losing coalition into a winning one. It is expressed by the index P/N, where N is the total number of permutations among the players and P is the number of permutations in which his resources are pivotal (Shapley & Shubik 1954). Thus, in the three-man convention situation, since there are 3! or six permutations, each candidate will be pivotal twice. The relative power of the candidates is therefore equal, even though their initial resources are unequal.

One way of giving descriptive relevance to the concept of pivotal power is to assume that all players in a coalition situation will demand a share of the payoff proportional to their pivotal power. By deductions analogous to those in minimum resource theory, it follows that the winning coalition will be the smallest one possible in terms of the total pivotal power of its members. Thus, in the convention example, since each possible two-man coalition is the same "size," each is equally likely to occur. It also follows that, since partners have the same power, the rewards of coalition will be divided in equal shares.

A third theory of coalition formation known as *anti-competitive theory* is an outgrowth of a series of experiments by Vinacke (1959; Bond & Vinacke 1961), many of which involved female subjects. The basic assumption of anti-competitive theory is that players in the coalition situation do not want to compete with each other; on the contrary, they are concerned mainly with preserving social relationships within the group. It follows that coalitions in such a group will form along the lines of least resistance. This behavior is quite unlike that predicted by minimum resource theory, which assumes that players are trying to get as much as they feel is owed to them, or by minimum power theory, which assumes that players are trying to get as much they can. The "line of least resistance" in anti-competitive theory can be defined as the relation that exists between players who, if they combined, would have no problems about how to divide their gains. This would seem to be especially true of players who have equal amounts of initial resources, since both the parity norm and the principle of pivotal power would prescribe that, if they combined, they would share their gains equally.

Of course, if either the parity norm or the pivotal power principle were followed to the exclusion of any other principle, the players would not need to bargain even if their resources or power were unequal. But in actual coalition situations the possibility that one principle may be invoked against another can never be ruled out, and it therefore seems likely that, where resources are unequal, bargaining of some kind will take place.

Players who are interested in minimizing the disruptive effects of bargaining are likely to avoid the hard and skillful bargainer. It follows that, where the anti-competitive norm exists, playing to win is playing to lose, since the more openly a player seeks to get as much as he can, the less likely it is that he will find a partner who will help him to get it. This can lead to the ironic situation that those players who ultimately profit most from a coalition situation are those who have made least effort to do so.

In the convention example it is not clear what the outcome would be under the assumptions of anti-competitive theory, especially since initial resources are unequally divided between the candidates and the possibility of bargaining, as already explained, cannot be ruled out. If candidate A builds up his lead in voting strength by his known skill in bargaining, he may find himself without support from the other, initially weaker candidates if both the parity norm and the anti-competitive norm are at work in the situation. A player who looks for allies from a position of strength may find not only that playing to win is playing to lose but also that, in coalition situations, strength is weakness.

Coalitions and social organization

Coalition theory is relevant for understanding social organization in two ways: (1) in the rise of new forms of social organization and (2) in the operation of existing social systems.

The rise of social organization. Coalitions may be viewed as a nascent form of social organization. They may, of course, simply break up into their constituent parts, or they may become stable and institutionalized. In the latter case, the process of coalition formation is a social organizational process; it is an important mechanism for the creation of new social organizational forms.

In the primary group and *ad hoc* laboratory groups which have so frequently served as the object of empirical studies of coalition formation, individuals form coalitions and their coalitions are unlikely to be given any formal or permanent status. When, in more complex forms of social organization, the coordination of resources does become highly stable and enduring, are we still justified in calling them coalitions? The answer seems to depend on (1) the *degree* of institutionalization of the coalition and (2) the maintenance of the original boundaries of the units which form the coalition. For example, consider a situation in which a number of originally autonomous units join in an association that draws on the resources of the units to compete for the achievement of their collective goals. The new association might become so successful that its maintenance becomes more important for the members than the achievement of any advantage relative to each other. Finally, the autonomous nature of the original units may disappear completely.

The formation of a labor union, for example, does not seem too different from such a situation. Individuals who are seeking better working conditions, material benefits, and sometimes more general social changes are induced to join an association. This union comes to symbolize the collective interest of the members to such a degree that they are willing to forgo some short-run interest to themselves—for example, the kind of interest that would be served by "scabbing" or strikebreaking. Or they will be willing to risk personal injury and arrest to administer sanctions to those who do participate in such activities. Such forms of social organization are no longer nascent; they have arrived.

Coalitions in existing social systems. Coalition formation is important through its connection with cleavages and integration in a social system and through its impact on the content of decision. The constituent parts of a coalition do not always lose their separate identity. The Democratic party has a stable existence, but the diverse set of interests which constitute it have maintained their own boundaries. One faction of a political party may continue to act as an autonomous unit and to form coalitions on certain issues with other parties (Luce & Rogow 1956). Even when the original units disappear, coalitions may be quite relevant. New issues may create a new set of autonomous factions, perhaps quite different from the original units which formed the association. In either case, coalition formation is intimately connected with the structure of cleavages within a social system; such a structure provides the units from which coalitions are formed.

Since coalitions form around decisions or sets of decisions, the maintenance of a coalition will frequently require the tacit neutrality of the coalition on issues which divide the members. Lerner and Aron (1957) argue that the defeat of the European Defense Community (EDC) by the French National Assembly was particularly understandable in light of the coalition demands of the Mendès-France government. The MRP, chief supporters of EDC, were in opposition because of other issues (Indochina), while the Gaullists, who were part of the governing coalition, opposed EDC. Vigorous support on this issue by the Mendès-France government would have made salient a set of cleavages that crosscut the governing coalition.

A shifting coalition structure tends to reduce the severity of cleavage, since today's enemy may be needed tomorrow as an ally. On the other hand, a shifting coalition structure also reduces the degree of consensus required for action to occur; it need be based only on the temporary conjunction of interests. Coalition formation, then, involves one process by which cleavage and consensus are balanced in social organization.

WILLIAM A. GAMSON

[*See also* COHESION, SOCIAL; COOPERATION; GAME THEORY; GROUPS; PARTIES, POLITICAL; SOCIOMETRY; *and the biography of* SIMMEL.]

BIBLIOGRAPHY

BOND, JOHN R.; and VINACKE, W. EDGAR 1961 Coalitions in Mixed-sex Triads. *Sociometry* 24:61–75.

CAPLOW, THEODORE 1956 A Theory of Coalitions in the Triad. *American Sociological Review* 21:489–493.

CAPLOW, THEODORE 1959 Further Development of the Theory of Coalitions in the Triad. *American Journal of Sociology* 64:488–493.

GAMSON, WILLIAM A. 1961a A Theory of Coalition Formation. *American Sociological Review* 26:373–382.

GAMSON, WILLIAM A. 1961b An Experimental Test of a Theory of Coalition Formation. *American Sociological Review* 26:565–573.

GAMSON, WILLIAM A. 1962 Coalition Formation at Presidential Nominating Conventions. *American Journal of Sociology* 68:157–171.

GAMSON, WILLIAM A. 1964 Experimental Studies of Coalition Formation. Volume 1, pages 81–110 in Leonard Berkowitz (editor), *Advances in Experimental Social Psychology*. New York: Academic Press.

HOMANS, GEORGE C. 1961 *Social Behavior: Its Elementary Forms*. New York: Harcourt.

LERNER, DANIEL; and ARON, RAYMOND 1957 *France Defeats EDC*. New York: Praeger.

LIPSET, SEYMOUR M. (1959) 1962 Political Sociology. Pages 81–114 in American Sociological Society, *Sociology Today: Problems and Prospects*. Edited by Robert K. Merton, Leonard Broom, and Leonard S. Cottrell, Jr. New York: Basic Books.

LUCE, R. DUNCAN; and RAIFFA, HOWARD 1957 *Games and Decisions: Introduction and Critical Survey*. A study of the Behavioral Models Project, Bureau of Applied Social Research, Columbia University. New York: Wiley.

LUCE, R. DUNCAN; and ROGOW, ARNOLD A. 1956 A Game Theoretic Analysis of Congressional Power Distributions for a Stable Two-party System. *Behavioral Science* 1:83–95.

MILLS, THEODORE M. 1954 The Coalition Pattern in Three Person Groups. *American Sociological Review* 19:657–667.

RAPOPORT, ANATOL; and CHAMMAH, A. M. 1965 *Prisoner's Dilemma*. Ann Arbor: Univ. of Michigan Press.

RAPOPORT, ANATOL; and ORWANT, CAROL 1962 Experimental Games: A Review. *Behavioral Science* 7:1–37.

RIKER, WILLIAM H. 1962 *The Theory of Political Coalitions*. New Haven: Yale Univ. Press.

SCHELLING, THOMAS C. 1958 The Strategy of Conflict: Prospectus for a Reorientation of Game Theory. *Journal of Conflict Resolution* 2:203–264.

SHAPLEY, L. S. 1953 A Value for *n*-Person Games. Volume 2, pages 307–317 in H. W. Kuhn and A. W. Tucker (editors), *Contributions to the Theory of Games*. Princeton Univ. Press.

SHAPLEY, L. S.; and SHUBIK, MARTIN 1954 A Method for Evaluating the Distribution of Power in a Committee System. *American Political Science Review* 48:787–792.

SIMMEL, GEORG (1902–1917) 1950 *The Sociology of Georg Simmel*. Edited and translated by Kurt H. Wolff. Glencoe, Ill.: Free Press. → First published in German.

VINACKE, W. EDGAR 1959 Sex Roles in a Three-person Game. *Sociometry* 22:343–360.

VINACKE, W. EDGAR; and ARKOFF, ABE 1957 An Experimental Study of Coalitions in the Triad. *American Sociological Review* 22:406–414.

CODE LAW

See under LEGAL SYSTEMS.

CODETERMINATION

See LABOR UNIONS, *article on* LABOR MOVEMENTS AND COLLECTIVE BARGAINING IN EUROPE.

CODRINGTON, R. H.

The life of Robert Henry Codrington can best be summed up as: priest, Oxford don, missionary, and ethnographer. He was born in Wroughton, Wiltshire, England, in 1830, son of a Church of England priest, and was educated at Charterhouse public school and at Oxford, where in 1855 he became a fellow of Wadham College. He chose the church as a profession. Ordained in 1857, he emigrated to New Zealand and lived for a few years in Nelson. Then, in 1866, he joined the Melanesian (Church of England) mission, founded in 1849 to bring Christianity to the widely scattered islands of Melanesia. He worked as a missionary until 1877, acting as head of the mission from 1871 to 1877 but refusing a bishopric because he disliked prolonged travel at sea by whaleboat or schooner. Much of his mission work consisted in teaching in the mission school on Norfolk Island, but he also served from time to time as resident missionary on the more isolated Melanesian islands. Codrington returned to England in 1888, thereafter occupying various church offices and devoting himself to his ethnographic and linguistic studies. His theological colleagues thought of him as the saint and teacher of Melanesia. Social scientists can well regard him as the first systematic ethnographer of the area.

The Melanesians. Codrington's work on the social life and culture of those parts of Melanesia that he knew best—principally the Solomons, the New Hebrides, and the small islands lying between these two larger groups—remains a classic of ethnographic reporting. His chapters, always readable, contain a mass of firsthand data on such topics as kinship and marriage, status, property, secret societies, religion, ritual, magic, the life cycle, and folklore. Although the accounts tend heavily to emphasize aboriginal religious practices—the field in which Codrington was himself professionally interested—Codrington made a considerable effort to present a reasonably well-rounded picture of island life as it was before it was significantly changed by contact with such agents of European culture as missionaries, traders, blackbirders, administrators, and beachcombers. Elkin (1953, p. 8), in summarizing Codrington's ethnography, notes that although these accounts have many merits and flashes of insight, Codrington failed to depict a functioning community with discernible principles of cohesion or patterns of change. In extenuation, it must be remembered that Codrington studied and wrote about Melanesia long before contemporary anthropological theory about sociocultural processes was developed, and that inevitably he collected source material on those aspects of Melanesian life that most interested him as a missionary. It was left to Rivers to resurvey, in 1908, many of the islands earlier described by Codrington and, in the light of his own Torres Strait experiences, to go deeper in his investigations and to venture more firmly into theoretical waters (Rivers 1914; Elkin 1953, p. 115).

Concept of mana.   Codrington's work on the concept of mana ([1891] 1957, pp. 117–127, 191–217) is credited by Marett (1915) with being the classic source upon which the scientific study of the role of mana in comparative religion is based. It is doubtless true, as Lowie ([1924] 1948, pp. 75–76) and Marett both cogently argued, that somewhat similar concepts do exist in religious systems as far apart as the Crow and Iroquois of America and the Ekoi of Africa. Nonetheless, Codrington was the first to recognize and analyze the important details that make up the mana concept: the invisible power that explains for the preliterate many of those aspects of life that transcend what the European would now call the natural order of the world. With the idea of mana as the key, it is perfectly understandable how the Melanesians can explain those aspects of life that involve sickness, magic, dreams, prophecy, divination, and curses and that might otherwise be incomprehensible and therefore uncontrollable and frightening. By analyzing the mystique of mana Codrington paradoxically provided a significant clue to the rationality of the preliterate world view.

Secret societies.   Codrington devoted two long chapters ([1891] 1957, chapters 5, 6) to a vivid description of the general social structure and functions of secret societies and clubs, which are so characteristic a feature of Melanesian life. He was particularly concerned with what he regarded as two distinct classes of secret societies: the *sukwe*, or village club, and the *tamati*, or bush-meeting ghost society. He gave full accounts of the members' costumes and customs, their masks, badges, lodges (the *gamal*), dances and initiation ceremonies, and the characteristic ordering of statuses within the societies. Rivers (1914, chapters 3–5) later reconsidered the whole nature of this Melanesian institution, showing that a closer relationship existed between the two types of societies than Codrington had thought. Then, in a dramatic foreshadowing of functional anthropological theory, Rivers revised and amplified Codrington's views on the social functions of the secret society, emphasizing the role of the clubs in determining social rank and status (thus, in some respects, checking and muting the powers of the Oceanic hereditary chief), their role in redistributing native wealth (thus preventing establishment of a status system based on wealth alone), and their influence in protecting property rights and maintaining social order in the community. Far from being terrorist or reactionary secret societies, the Melanesian clubs encouraged and fostered the characteristic virtues that made the ideal Melanesian citizen. Codrington's contribution in this field, as enlarged by Rivers' field work, constitutes a significant step forward in the theory of social structure.

Melanesian languages.   One of the first tasks of the missionary, in Melanesia as elsewhere, is to study the indigenous language or languages. Some of the members of the Melanesian mission, like the able Bishop John Coleridge Patteson, were naturally gifted as linguists but wrote down no extended linguistic analyses. Others, like Codrington, produced, with painstaking labor, the definitive texts for those coming after to study and to use. Codrington's *Melanesian Languages* (1885), and his *Dictionary of the Language of Mota* (1896), written with J. Palmer, are a missioner's studies, not those of a trained linguist. The book on Melanesian languages is mostly concerned with the phonology, grammar, and vocabulary of the languages of the Banks Islands (twelve dialects, of which Mota became the approved vernacular mission language), the Torres Islands, Rotuma, the New Hebrides (seven dialects), the Loyalty Islands, Santa Cruz, and the Solomons. Codrington's erudition is both powerful and impressive: all who follow him in this field of study—the Malayo–Polynesian family of languages—will build to a large degree on the foundation he so painstakingly established. Capell (1962*a*; 1962*b*) makes many incidental references to Codrington's work that indicate its continuing relevance for the study of western Pacific languages.

Two contrasting pictures of Codrington serve to sum up the significance of his work and life for social scientists: first, the burly, bearded priest slowly and laboriously collecting data about Melanesian societies and languages as he worked as teacher and resident priest among lately converted cannibals; second, the retired priest, prebendary of Sidlesham and examining chaplain to the bishop of Winchester, writing his classic accounts of Melanesian life, yet finding time to enjoy the company and friendship of Victorian storytellers like Lewis Carroll and Hans Christian Andersen, eminent divines like Manning and Newman, as well as politicians and reformers like Gladstone and Wilberforce.

The master of Melanesian ethnography died suddenly—old in years, wise in theology, honored in scholarship—on September 11, 1922.

ERNEST BEAGLEHOLE

[*For further information about Melanesia, see* OCEANIAN SOCIETY. *See also* RELIGION; RELIGIOUS SPECIALISTS; *and the biography of* RIVERS.]

WORKS BY CODRINGTON

1885 *The Melanesian Languages.* Oxford Univ. Press.

(1891) 1957 *The Melanesians: Studies in Their Anthropology and Folklore.* New Haven: Human Relations Area Files Press.

1896 CODRINGTON, ROBERT HENRY; and PALMER, JOHN *A Dictionary of the Language of Mota, Sugarloaf Island, Banks' Islands; With a Short Grammar and Index.* London: Society for Promoting Christian Knowledge.

WORKS ABOUT CODRINGTON

ARMSTRONG, E. S. 1900 *The History of the Melanesian Mission.* London: Ibister.

CAPELL, ARTHUR 1962a *A Linguistic Survey of the South-western Pacific.* New & rev. ed. South Pacific Commission Technical Paper, No. 136. Nouméa (New Caledonia): The Commission.

CAPELL, ARTHUR 1962b *Oceanic Linguistics Today. Current Anthropology* 3:371–428.

CRANSTONE, BRYAN A. L. 1961 *Melanesia: A Short Ethnography.* London: British Museum.

ELKIN, ADOLPHUS P. 1953 *Social Anthropology in Melanesia.* Published under the auspices of the South Pacific Commission. Oxford Univ. Press.

FOX, CHARLES E. 1958 *Lord of the Southern Isles: Story of the Anglican Mission in Melanesia 1849–1949.* London: Mowbray.

LOWIE, ROBERT H. (1924) 1948 *Primitive Religion.* New York and London: Liveright.

MARETT, R. R. (1915) 1955 *Mana.* Volume 8, pages 375–380 in *Encyclopaedia of Religion and Ethics.* Edited by James Hastings. New York: Scribner.

RIVERS, WILLIAM H. R. 1914 *The History of Melanesian Society.* Vol. 1. Publication No. 1 of the Percy Sladen Trust Expedition to Melanesia. Cambridge Univ. Press.

COERCION

See POWER; SANCTIONS; WAR.

COGNITIVE DISSONANCE

See THINKING, *article on* COGNITIVE ORGANIZATION AND PROCESSES.

COGNITIVE THEORY

What do people perceive, think, and know? *How* do people perceive, think, and know? These questions are of interest to both anthropology and psychology, but whereas psychology emphasizes the second question, the cultural sciences are primarily concerned with the first question. [*See* THINKING.]

Cultural anthropology in particular has undertaken to describe and catalogue the cognitions typical of the various societies that make up mankind. An ethnography (the description of a culture) is very largely an account of *what* the people in a particular society perceive, think, and know. Thus, the large and growing archive of descriptive ethnographic materials is a repository of the information available about man's cognitions regarding the principal concerns of his existence: working, eating, sleeping, making love, treating illness, performing rituals, fabricating tools, fighting, raising children, and so on, through the outline of cultural categories. Traditional styles of ethnographic description have been humanistic rather than formal. But in recent years, as a result of the influence of linguistics on the one hand, and clinical and experimental psychology on the other, formal methods of field work, analysis, and description have been developed which provide more precise, economical, and cross-culturally comparable descriptions of the various kinds of cognition that constitute a culture. Furthermore, there is increased interest in the process of cognition at a level more general, and less conscious, than can be conveniently regarded as appropriate to an ethnographic description of the languages of people in various cultures. These new developments in the formal analysis of culture go beyond the two essential observations that all races or varieties of human beings can perform essentially the same cognitive operations and that what is actually perceived, thought, and known, even in response to the same physical stimuli, varies predictably with culture rather than with physical type.

Although language is conventionally and properly regarded as a fundamental aspect of "culture," it occupies an ambiguous position in cognitive studies and, as the development of the study of psycholinguistics may suggest, is probably more relevant to psychological than to cultural investigations. Language is employed in many, but by no means all, cognitive processes; there are, for instance, forms of thought in music, painting, and certain of the performing arts that are not linguistic. Language differences are in principle irrelevant to logical and mathematical thinking, which can be reduced from logical or mathematical symbols to linguistic ones in any of dozens of languages. And intraculturally, many of the most interesting individual differences in the cognitive process are observed in dialogues between speakers of the same language whose utterances are equally valid linguistically but not logically. A language provides a small and finite set of elementary signs and symbols, as well as rules for their permissible combination, which permit the construction of a very large number of utterances; but the rules of language do not "contain" the meaning of the utterances any more than the rules for attaching pieces of metal by nuts and bolts, screws, rivets, solder, pins, friction joints, clamps, etc., "contain" the design of an automobile engine. Therefore it would be a mistake to regard the structural description of a language as a description of cognitive process at anything more than a nuts-and-bolts level or for more than a portion of the cognitive operations of its speakers.

Culture as an ideal normative system. Ethnography, although it recognizes the existence of complementary individual variation in role and of individual deviancy from norm, initially describes a culture as an ideal structure that is generated by a group and is an attribute of that group. The formal, sometimes even mathematical, features of a culture thus are to be likened to the geometrical properties of a single object or to the interrelated statements of a highly organized body of knowledge, rather than to the multivariate statistical description of a population. The work of the ethnographer—describing the cognitive processes that have been culturally standardized in a given society—may perhaps best be made clear by an analogy. Let us suppose that a nonmathematician is given the task of describing a new mathematical calculus that is in active use by a group of people who have not formulated their system of calculation in a written text. It has, in other words, been developing informally over the years, is currently being used in its most matured form, and is being taught to new users by example and through oral instruction. The investigator is allowed to interview and observe—that is, he may ask questions during coffee breaks, watch people computing, save scraps of paper from wastebaskets, take photographs of the machines employed, talk a few times with the project director, listen to people teaching one another the right way to do things, and make other such minimally interfering kinds of observations and inquiries. He may even be permitted—and he will certainly be well advised—to join the group as a novice and learn to use the calculus himself.

Now, as he analyzes the data collected in these various ways, he does not merely tabulate the frequencies and intercorrelations of various classes of observed behavior in order to arrive at the calculus; if he did this, he would be giving equal weight to misunderstood jokes, learners' mistakes, slips of the pen, careless work, gibberish produced by broken computers, and competent professional operations. What he does, instead, is to infer the system of rules that these people are attempting to apply. He will gain the assurance that he is on the way to an adequate understanding of these rules from the logical completeness of the system he infers and from his ability, when using it, to produce behavior that an expert will reward by saying, in effect, "That's right; that's good; now you've got it." Of course, a sociologist or a psychologist might say, "But it is the behavior that is real, not this abstract system which no one actually applies perfectly and completely and which is merely the asymptote of the real curve of behaviors." The investigator replies that culture—conceived in this sense as a collection of formal calculi—is just as real as algebra, Euclidean geometry, and set theory, which are the asymptotes of the "real" behavior of fallible students, mathematicians, and machines. Indeed, he will point out, these other calculi *are* aspects of a culture, and their apparently greater tangibility stems from the incidental circumstance that they have been the object of more intensive study and explicit description than the calculus which he has been investigating.

Certain aspects of cultures that are understood as ideal normative systems have been subjected to formal analysis. The semantic analysis of kinship terminology and other taxonomic systems by such techniques as componential analysis, the reduction of prescriptive marriage and descent rules to the form of permutation matrices (Bush 1963; Kemeny et al. 1957; Weil 1949; White 1963), the treatment of certain status relationship systems as Guttman scales (Goodenough 1963), and the formalization of the Hindu purity–impurity transformation cycle as a product of Galois groups (Wallace 1966) are examples of this effort to delineate in the most economical form the essential structure of limited aspects of culture. To the extent that the cultural structures thus formally delineated require that some or all of the generating population entertain equivalent cognitive structures, these ideal normative systems give information about cognition.

But it would be naive to suppose that all members of a group maintain identical cognitive structures which are, in effect, the single normative structure revealed by ethnography and formal cultural analysis. Not only are there individuals with deviant or incomplete models but also the existence of complementary specialized roles in every human society requires that a model of the ideal normative system *not* be completely housed in the brain of every, or even any, single individual. Thus the question must be asked, What is the relationship of the ideal normative system to individual cognitions?

Culture as a cognitive system. Linguists, psychiatrists, philosophers, and social scientists have long been concerned with an issue which may be crudely but adequately stated as a pair of questions: Do all human beings, with more or less accuracy and complexity, follow one single neurologically founded logical calculus, the system that Boole called "the laws of thought" (i.e., the elementary logical calculus which is the root of all formal logical and mathematical reasoning), or are there many logics, mutually inconsistent, generated by differences in language (as the Sapir–Whorf hypothesis might suggest), by other aspects of culture, or by evolutionary level? The evidence to support the notion of logical pluralism has so far been unconvincing. Some "different" logics appear to be merely variants comparable to contrasts in emphasis on class products as opposed to relative products or preferences for probabilistic versus true–false truth values. And some appear to be based on mistaken assumptions about the primitiveness or irrationality of non-Western or ancient thinking. Although there are great differences in the degree of explicitness, the form, and the complexity of reasoning embedded in different linguistic and cultural traditions, and also differences in the determination of situations to which formal reasoning will be applied, it appears that such elementary rational procedures as syllogistic deduction and Mill's canons of inductive inference are universal. It is probable, furthermore, that the extent of the complexity of rational operations performed without mechanical aid or specialized training by the normal members of any society, regardless of their level of economic and political organization, has an upper limit which is roughly the same for all racial and cultural groups (see Wallace 1961*a*).

Social science studies of cognition tend to emphasize the description of those perceptions, beliefs, and thoughts which are standardized, repetitive, and conventional in a society. Where such cognitions seem to be shared by all mature persons in the society, there may be little need to consider the individual; but where cognitions are not shared by all, the individual becomes important as a unit of analysis. In the general case the individual may be conceived as the site of a large and complexly organized set of perceptions, thoughts, and knowledge. This assemblage has been variously denoted the "image," the "mazeway," and so on; the term refers to the entire structure of the individual's cognition about himself and the surrounding world, including memories, abstract knowledge, and rules of thought. Although the total description of any one person's mazeway would doubtless be an impracticably large task, portions of any one mazeway can be described as a set of propositions which, in symbolic form, will approximate an internally consistent system. When one considers the group of individuals who compose a community of any size, with regard to a given aspect of behavior, the sum of the propositions with regard to that aspect may or may not yield an approximation of a logically consistent system. If they do sum to a system, then that sum is referred to as an aspect of "their culture." In general, summing to culture will occur under two conditions: first, and obviously, if the individual mazeways are identical in content and internally consistent in structure; and second, if the individual mazeways, even if not all identical, sum to a consistent system. Anthropologists have traditionally drawn attention to the existence of identical (shared) structures and to a certain kind of sum (the equivalence structure) of nonshared structures. The two sorts of cultural summing of cognitions are represented schematically in Figure 1.

Examples of shared cultural cognitive elements in the United States, for instance, would be a speaking knowledge of basic English phonemes, vocabulary, and syntax; familiarity with the currency; and recognition of the American flag. Not all normal adult persons born and residing in the United States share even these minimal cognitions, but universality is closely approximated in most communities. Nonshared but complementary cognitions are just as readily discovered in division-of-labor systems: for instance, in household management, the wife's knowledge of how to buy, cook, and serve food is usually complementary to the husband's knowledge of how to secure enough money to provide the necessary transportation, cooking and sanitary appliances, and eating equip-

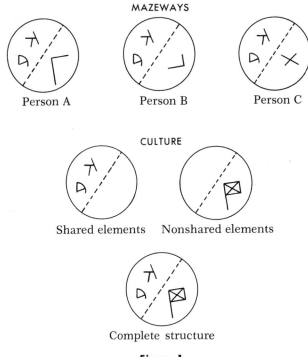

MAZEWAYS

Person A   Person B   Person C

CULTURE

Shared elements   Nonshared elements

Complete structure

Figure 1

ment; the professional pianist's skills are complementary to the skills of the piano manufacturer and the tuner; and so on. In some areas of behavior, it may be considered improper for complementary specialists to know each others' specialties, and in some situations (e.g., religious or military operations) it may be impious or illegal for persons with one role even to know, let alone practice, the role of the other. The analysis and classification of cultural structures in terms of the individual cognitive components of which they are the sum has not yet advanced very far.

At the present stage of research into these matters, however, there are technical and semantic difficulties in analyzing the relationship between individual cognitive structures and those cognitive sums that we have here called a "culture." Obviously, except in the special case of all members of the society sharing the same cognitive structure, culture cannot be considered to be embodied in any one individual even though it is a product of individual cognitions. Thus, ascribing the contents of ethnographic monographs to each and every, and sometimes even any, individual in the society cannot legitimately be done. Furthermore, even in the case of perfectly shared cognitions, the cultural sum may be ethnographically described in a logical transformation of individual cognitive contents and/or cultural sums which is empirically predictive of behavior and elegant in formulation but not descriptive of cognitive content in anybody at all.

In what sense are such logical transformations of the cultural sums themselves descriptive of cognitive content or structure of the individual mazeways from which the observed behavior was originally produced? The status of such transformations is precisely like that of newly formulated and proven theorems which were implicit in the axioms formulated by a mathematician but never anticipated by him. No doubt the possibility of performing such transformations has much to do with the generative power of culture; but it is necessary to keep firmly in mind that the actual cognitions of individuals may be different from these transformations and should be described in their own terms. Indeed, the possibility of understanding the dynamics of culture change would seem very largely to lie in the prospect of unraveling this relationship between individual cognition and unrealized summative implications.

ANTHONY F. C. WALLACE

[*Directly related are the entries* CULTURE, *article on* THE CONCEPT OF CULTURE; COMPONENTIAL ANALYSIS; ETHNOGRAPHY; LANGUAGE, *article on* LANGUAGE AND CULTURE; LINGUISTICS, *article on* THE FIELD; *and the biographies of* SAPIR *and* WHORF.]

BIBLIOGRAPHY

BUSH, ROBERT R. 1963 An Algebraic Treatment of Rules of Marriage and Descent. Pages 159–172 in Harrison C. White, *An Anatomy of Kinship: Mathematical Models for Structures of Cumulated Roles.* Englewood Cliffs, N.J.: Prentice-Hall.

COLBY, B. N. 1966 Ethnographic Semantics: A Preliminary Survey. *Current Anthropology* 7:3–32.

GOODENOUGH, WARD H. 1963 Some Applications of Guttman Scale Analysis to Ethnography and Culture Theory. *Southwestern Journal of Anthropology* 19:235–250.

HALLOWELL, A. IRVING 1955 *Culture and Experience.* Philadelphia: Univ. of Pennsylvania Press.

HAMMEL, E. A. (editor) 1965 Formal Semantic Analysis. *American Anthropologist* New Series 67, no. 5, part 2.

KEMENY, JOHN G. et al. (1957) 1962 *Introduction to Finite Mathematics.* Englewood Cliffs, N.J.: Prentice-Hall.

ROMNEY, A. KIMBALL; and D'ANDRADE, ROY G. (editors) 1964 Transcultural Studies in Cognition. *American Anthropologist* New Series 66, no. 3.

WALLACE, ANTHONY F. C. 1961a On Being Just Complicated Enough. National Academy of Sciences, *Proceedings* 47:458–464.

WALLACE, ANTHONY F. C. 1961b *Culture and Personality.* New York: Random House.

WALLACE, ANTHONY F. C. 1966 *Religion: An Anthropological Study.* New York: Random House.

WEIL, ANDRÉ (1949) 1963 On the Algebraic Study of Certain Types of Marriage Laws. Pages 151–157 in Harrison C. White, *An Anatomy of Kinship: Mathematical Models for Structures of Cumulated Roles.* Englewood Cliffs, N.J.: Prentice-Hall. → An analysis of the Murngin marriage structure. First published in

Claude Lévi-Strauss (editor), *Les structures élémentaires de la parenté.*

WHITE, HARRISON C. 1963 *An Anatomy of Kinship: Mathematical Models for Structures of Cumulated Roles.* Englewood Cliffs, N.J.: Prentice-Hall.

COHEN, MORRIS R.

Morris Raphael Cohen (1880–1947), American philosopher, was born in the ghetto of Minsk, Russia. In 1892 he was brought to New York City. At an early age he became a skeptic and agnostic, yet the traditional Judaic veneration for learning as well as a certain piety of spirit remained with him all his life. The hardships of life on New York's Lower East Side made him sympathetic to socialism. Inspired by Thomas Davidson, the Scottish scholar who lectured at the Educational Alliance settlement house, Cohen and fellow Davidsonians established the "Breadwinners' College" for the cultural education of the wage earner.

In 1900 Cohen received a B.S. from the College of the City of New York. From 1902 to 1904 he took graduate courses at Columbia University under Wilmon Sheldon, Charles A. Strong, Franklin H. Giddings, Henry R. Seager, and Frederick Woodbridge. He then studied at Harvard under William James, Josiah Royce, Hugo Münsterberg, and Crawford H. Toy, receiving his PH.D. in 1906. He wrote his thesis on Kant's doctrine of happiness.

In 1906 Cohen married Mary Ryshpan, who had also been a student of Davidson's. He taught mathematics at Townsend Harris Hall, the preparatory school to the College of the City of New York. From 1912 until his retirement in 1938 he was a professor at the college, where, besides teaching classes in logic, ethics, metaphysics, and the history of philosophy, he created courses in the philosophy of law, of science, and of civilization. From 1938 to 1941 he was professor of philosophy at the University of Chicago. He also taught or lectured at Columbia, Johns Hopkins, Yale, Stanford, Harvard, the New School for Social Research, and the law schools of Columbia, St. John's, Yale, Harvard, Cornell, the University of Buffalo, and others. After the advent of Hitler, he became the principal founder and president of the scholarly Conference on Jewish Relations. His strenuous activities on behalf of this organization, and his chairing of a Jewish research institute on peace and postwar studies, undermined his frail health. He died in Washington, D.C., in 1947, survived by three children: the late Dr. Felix S. Cohen who was principal editor of his father's posthumously published works, Dr. Leonora Cohen Rosenfield, and Dr. Victor William Cohen, a nuclear physicist.

Cohen's elaboration and use of scientific method lent unity to his philosophy, even though he never lived to finish its elucidation. The notion that abstract logical or mathematical relations are real, which he accepted after reading Bertrand Russell's *Principles of Mathematics* (1903), justified for him the procedure of science and served as his first guide for his independent work in philosophy.

The principle of polarity he called his second guide to systematic philosophy: opposing poles must be taken into account in explaining anything. For example, the world, which is the object of science, is a union of form and matter. Cohen made wide use of the concept of polarity, considering it both a heuristic and an ontological principle. His idea of polarity proved influential even outside of philosophy; John R. Commons, for example, applied it to economics.

Cohen envisaged further development of his idea of relationality when he discussed the theory of relativity with Einstein. He reasoned that if relations are real, then apparently polar assertions— for example, that something is both good and bad —may both be true when properly completed. He considered this a fruitful approach to problems in the natural and social sciences.

He accepted Charles Peirce's pragmatism to the extent of asserting that "the way to make our ideas clear is to examine . . . all their possible implications. [Logical pragmatism] is an attempt to extend the experimental method to the handling of ideas" (Rosenfield 1962, p. 326).

Scientific method, according to Cohen, is based on systematic doubt. We cannot begin with either pure facts or pure theory; both are necessary. Assumptions should be reduced to a minimum and always made explicit. Constant self-correction is important and is achieved by considering alternative hypotheses. Conclusions can be drawn only after observation, collection of evidence, measurement, experimentation, and testing of hypotheses. The hypothesis that is at the same time simplest, widest, and in best agreement with the facts is always favored. The ideal of scientific method is the interconnection of facts into a unitary system. This exposition by Cohen was widely acclaimed.

His social philosophy embodied the liberalism of a rationalist. It was based on the application of logic and scientific method to the social sciences. "Tolerance, the avoidance of fanaticism, and above all a wider and clearer view of the nature of our beliefs and their necessary consequences, is thus a goal or end which the development of logic serves. In this sense logic is a necessary element of any liberal civilization" (1944, p. 187). He considered logic to be the lifeblood of philosophy, the formal aspect of all being, in and out of space time. Appropriately, he called his intellectual autobiography "The Faith of a Logician" (1930).

He was the first North American philosopher to concern himself seriously with the law. He considered the law to be ever changing, with the sources of its growth or change lying in social facts, legal systems, and ethical ideals. A judge's decisions are influenced by his opinions on social and economic questions. When applied to legal problems, Cohen's use of logic, the scientific method, polarity, and pragmatism all seem to be particularly cogent. Legal thought, with its balance between the rational and the empirical, the theoretical and the practical, appealed to his underlying moral passion. Cohen's influence was felt perhaps most deeply in the field of law, not only because of the range, flexibility, and progressive character of the concepts he applied to it, but also because he had direct contact with the leading legal figures of his day, including Oliver Wendell Holmes, Jr., Felix Frankfurter, and many others.

The philosophy of history was considered by Cohen to be the focal point of all applications of history to life. At its best, history is more than a science that deals with evidence critically; as Cohen conceived of it in *The Meaning of Human History* (1947), it should also be artistic reconstruction. The historian makes value judgments, wittingly or unwittingly. The philosophy of history should then concern itself with the scientific and rational study of ethics.

For all his dedication to rationality and his belief in the reality of logical relations, Cohen considered the ultimate laws of nature to be contingent. In the preface of *Reason and Nature* (1931), he called himself a mystic—because he believed that words point to a realm of being deeper and wider than the words themselves—and an idealist in the Platonic sense—because he believed that abstract universals are real, not nominal. He admired Spinoza's *amor Dei intellectualis* and defined God, a word he rarely used, as an ideal of holiness. As a naturalist he did not believe in disembodied spirits, but he also rejected the materialist view that consciousness can be explained in purely physical terms. He considered consciousness to be a real addition to the phenomena of nature.

Like William James, Cohen thought that philosophy was for everyone, and he wrote accordingly. He was a prolific author, clear and pithy. Between 1914 and 1926 much of his writing appeared in the *New Republic*, which helped spread his influence in nonacademic circles.

He remained friendly to socialism but condemned communism. Despite his commitment to the contemplative life, he championed social causes and defended individuals subject to injustice or discrimination. Ernest Nagel called him a knight-errant in the cause of human enlightenment. He delighted in swimming against the currents of his time. According to John Dewey, his only fear was that someone might agree with him. He eschewed indoctrination and left no school of followers. Yet he was a famous teacher, and many distinguished philosophers, as well as leaders in other fields, were his students. For Huntington Cairns, he was, with John Dewey, the most influential of contemporary thinkers. Bertrand Russell was quoted by Harold Laski as saying that Cohen was the most significant philosopher in the United States.

A Socratic figure, an encyclopedic philosopher, an interdisciplinary pioneer and *animateur*, Cohen dedicated himself to his compelling sense of the exalted function of philosophy.

LEONORA COHEN ROSENFIELD

[See also JURISPRUDENCE; LEGAL REASONING; SCIENCE; and the biographies of COMMONS; HOLMES; JAMES; PEIRCE.]

WORKS BY COHEN

(1923) 1956 Introduction. In Charles S. Peirce, *Chance, Love and Logic: Philosophical Essays*. New York: Braziller.

(1930) 1959 The Faith of a Logician. Pages 3–32 in Morris R. Cohen, *Studies in Philosophy and Science*. New York: Ungar.

(1931) 1953 *Reason and Nature: An Essay on the Meaning of Scientific Method*. 2d ed. Glencoe, Ill.: Free Press. → A paperback edition was published in 1964.

1933 *Law and the Social Order: Essays in Legal Philosophy*. New York: Harcourt.

1934 COHEN, MORRIS R.; and NAGEL, ERNEST *An Introduction to Logic and Scientific Method*. New York: Harcourt.

1940 COHEN, MORRIS R. et al. Generalization in the Social Sciences. Pages 227–273 in Louis Wirth (editor), *Eleven Twenty-six: A Decade of Social Science Research*. Univ. of Chicago Press.

1944 *A Preface to Logic*. New York: Holt. → A paperback edition was published in 1956 by Meridian.

1946 *The Faith of a Liberal: Selected Essays*. New York: Holt.

(1947) 1961 *The Meaning of Human History*. 2d ed. La Salle, Ill.: Open Court.

(1948) 1958 COHEN, MORRIS R.; and DRABKIN, ISRAEL E. *A Source Book in Greek Science*. Cambridge, Mass.: Harvard Univ. Press.

1949a *A Dreamer's Journey: The Autobiography of Morris Raphael Cohen*. Boston: Beacon.

(1949b) 1959 *Studies in Philosophy and Science*. New York: Ungar.

1950 *Reason and Law: Studies in Juristic Philosophy*. Glencoe, Ill.: Free Press. → A paperback edition was published in 1961 by Collier.

SUPPLEMENTARY BIBLIOGRAPHY

CAIRNS, HUNTINGTON 1960 The Legal Philosophy of Morris R. Cohen. *Vanderbilt Law Review* 14:239–262.

Deregibus, Arturo 1960 *Il razionalismo di Morris R. Cohen nella filosofia americana d'oggi*. Turin (Italy): Giappichelli.

Konvitz, Milton R. 1951 The Life and Mind of Morris R. Cohen. Pages 11–31 in Salo W. Baron (editor), *Freedom and Reason: Studies in Philosophy and Jewish Culture, in Memory of Morris Raphael Cohen*. Glencoe, Ill.: Free Press.

Kuhn, Martin A. 1957 *Morris Raphael Cohen: A Bibliography*. New York: City College of New York Library.

Larsen, Robert E. 1959 Morris Cohen's Principle of Polarity. *Journal of the History of Ideas* 20:587–595.

Nagel, Ernest 1957 Morris R. Cohen in Retrospect. *Journal of the History of Ideas* 18:548–551.

Rosenfield, Leonora [Cohen] 1962 *Portrait of a Philosopher: Morris R. Cohen in Life and Letters*. New York: Harcourt.

Russell, Bertrand (1903) 1938 *Principles of Mathematics*. New York: Norton.

COHESION, SOCIAL

It is a commonplace observation that organisms cluster and seem to be drawn together. It is as if there were a sort of social cement drawing and binding individuals together into groups. The social forces that draw and keep men together may be called *cohesion*, or *cohesiveness*.

The formal study of this phenomenon of social clustering probably began with the conception of a "herd" instinct (Trotter 1916), or "gregarious" instinct (McDougall 1908). An attraction to other members of one's own species was presumed to be a biological given, somehow built into the nervous system. As this instinct mode of thought grew unfashionable, however, the study of cohesion switched to the investigation of the needs and functions satisfied in groups. On the purely biological level numerous studies (see Allee 1938 for an excellent survey) have demonstrated the biological and survival value of clustering to organisms extending through almost the full range of the phylogenetic scale.

Among social scientists an intensive concern with cohesiveness as a research topic developed during the 1940s, largely as an outgrowth of Kurt Lewin's work on human groups. In contrast to earlier approaches, modern work on cohesion has tended to treat cohesiveness as a variable and has concentrated on two broad classes of questions: What are the consequences of varying degrees of cohesiveness on group or social behavior? What factors determine the degree of cohesiveness of a group? In order to make studies concerned with these questions understandable, let us first consider some purely operational matters: how cohesiveness has been measured and how it has been manipulated.

Measuring cohesiveness. In an attempt to give an intuitive definition of the term, we have referred to cohesion as a sort of social cement binding together the members of a group. In probably the most widely accepted formal statement of the term, Leon Festinger (1950, p. 274) has defined cohesiveness as "the resultant of all the forces acting on the members to remain in the group." Whatever definition of the concept is favored, virtually all definitions have the clear implication that cohesiveness varies with the attractiveness of the group for its members. Most efforts to devise a measure or an index of the cohesiveness of a group have been guided by this implication and represent largely common-sense attempts to determine how much members of a group like one another or how highly they value their group membership.

The most popular technique for assessing cohesion has been the sociometric questionnaire designed to determine the pattern and intensity of friendships within a group. As an example of the use of this technique, Festinger, together with Stanley Schachter and Kurt Back (1950), in attempting to assess the relative cohesiveness of the several subdivisions of a housing project, asked all residents the question, What three people (in the housing project) do you see most of socially? From the answers to this question it was possible to construct various indices of subdivision cohesiveness, all of which were based on some variant of the assumption that the ratio of the number of choices made *within* a given subdivision of the housing project to the total number of choices made was an index of the cohesiveness of that subdivision. Obviously, it was assumed that the larger this proportion, the greater the cohesion.

In other research contexts, such questions have been asked as: How often do you think this group should meet? And how high would the dues of this club have to be to make you consider resigning? For this sort of question it is, of course, assumed that the more often the members would like to meet or the more they are willing to sacrifice to remain together, the greater the cohesiveness of the group. There have been exotic attempts (e.g., Libo 1953) to assess cohesiveness by such devices as group projective tests, but most studies have employed the common-sense sorts of measures described.

Manipulating cohesion. Although there have been occasional naturalistic field studies of the effects of cohesiveness on social behavior, most systematic studies of the subject have involved laboratory experimentation—a research format which requires that cohesion be experimentally manipulated. Just as the measures described have all focused on the determination of group attractiveness, so the techniques devised to manipulate cohesion have all involved an attempt to vary the attractiveness of experimentally created groups. Such manipulations have been executed by varying any of the following sources of group cohesiveness: the prestige of the group; the attractiveness of group activities; the attractiveness of the members of the group.

As an example of the sort of procedures used, one common technique is a latter-day adaptation of Shakespeare's device for enamoring Beatrice and Benedick in *Much Ado About Nothing*. In speeches for recruiting subjects the study is described as concerned with "people who really like one another." Potential subjects all answer pseudo personality tests ostensibly designed to select compatible people. When volunteer subjects show up for the experiment, they are told, in "high cohesive conditions," that they will be members of an extremely congenial group and that "there is every reason to expect that the other members of the group will like you and you will like them." In "low cohesive conditions" subjects are told that it had been impossible to put together a congenial group and that "there is no reason to think that you will like them or that they will care for you."

The reader who is unfamiliar with laboratory experimentation in social psychology may be somewhat doubtful that such a technique can be successful, but the disconcerting fact is that such techniques can be astonishingly effective. Study after study has demonstrated that these procedures do manipulate the extent to which subjects like one another, the degree to which they are eager to remain members of their groups, and so on.

These, then, are illustrations of the research techniques that have been used in studies of cohesion. Let us turn next to what is known about cohesion from such studies.

The effects of cohesiveness on social behavior

Of the many aspects of group behavior that interact with cohesiveness, the most thoroughly studied area is that of communication and social influence. Research in this area was stimulated by the finding of Festinger, Schachter, and Back (1950) that cohesiveness was directly related to the strength of group standards. In their study of a housing project, referred to above, it was found that the more cohesive (as determined by sociometric questionnaire) a subgroup, the fewer the deviates from a group norm. Theorizing about this finding led to a series of laboratory experiments that were guided by the line of thought discussed below, which was most fully developed by Festinger (1954).

Pressures to uniformity.   It is hypothesized, first,

that a drive exists in man to evaluate his opinions and abilities, that is, to determine the "rightness" or "wrongness" of an opinion and the "goodness" or "badness" of an ability. Second, it is hypothesized that when an objective, nonsocial means (e.g., a reality check or reference to an authoritative source) of evaluation is not available, evaluation will be made by comparison with the opinions and abilities of other people. Finally, it is hypothesized that stable and precise evaluation by social comparison is possible only when the opinions and abilities available for comparison are not too divergent from one's own; the tendency to compare oneself with others decreases as the discrepancy in opinion or ability increases.

From these several hypotheses it may be derived that when discrepancies of opinion or abilities exist among the members of a group, pressures will arise to reduce such discrepancies. In interpersonal settings such pressures to uniformity can be manifested in three ways. When discrepancies exist, tendencies will arise to change one's own opinion or ability in order to bring oneself closer to other group members; change others in the group so as to bring them closer to oneself; and cause one to reject deviates or at least to cease comparing oneself to those in the group who are extremely different from oneself.

Within this schema the reasonable assumption is made that within-group pressures to reduce discrepancy of opinion will be a direct function of the importance of the group to its members—that is, of the group's cohesiveness. It should be anticipated, then, that each of the postulated tendencies for restoring uniformity will be more strongly manifested in high than in low cohesive groups. And, indeed, experimental work has directly supported this expectation. In a series of laboratory experiments Back (1951) showed that in more cohesive groups there were stronger attempts to influence others than in less cohesive groups. These stronger influence attempts were accompanied by more change of opinion in the highly cohesive groups. Festinger, Harold Gerard, and others (1952) found that deviate members of highly cohesive groups changed their opinions more frequently than did deviate members of less attractive groups and, furthermore, that more influence attempts were made in high than in low cohesive groups. Schachter (1951) demonstrated that highly cohesive groups rejected deviate members significantly more than did less attractive groups.

These findings have all been replicated in a variety of studies, and there appears to be no question that cohesiveness is a major determiner of the expression and acceptance of influence and of tolerance for deviates. This line of thought and these basic findings on cohesiveness and influence processes have been extended and generalized to a large number of problem areas within social science, including group productivity, the formation and maintenance of political attitudes, voting behavior, social determinants of consumer preferences, and the like.

Other research findings. Unrelated to the influence area, other studies of cohesiveness and social behavior have demonstrated that members of highly cohesive groups feel more secure and at ease in group activities than do members of less cohesive groups. A related finding is that members of highly cohesive groups are freer in expressing hostility to an outside troublemaker than are members of less cohesive groups. Furthermore, highly attracted members of a group are more likely to take on responsibilities, to participate in meetings, and to persist in working toward difficult goals.

Clearly, the degree of cohesion has major effects on within-group behavior—a state of affairs that makes the analysis of the determinants and sources of cohesiveness a matter of practical as well as theoretical significance. Why are some groups highly attractive and others relatively unattractive to their members? What conditions will affect the cohesion of groups? A related set of questions is also important: What variables affect the social drives? When do people wish to be alone? and When do they wish to be with others?

Factors affecting cohesion

To understand the variables that will affect the degree of cohesion of a group, or the magnitude of the desire to affiliate with others, it is necessary to analyze the nature of the needs that can be satisfied in the company of others. Several such analyses have been attempted, most of which have been based on some version of the following somewhat truistic distinction.

People mediate goals for one another, and it may be necessary to associate with other people or belong to particular groups in order to attain specific individual goals. For example, to play bridge it may be necessary to join a bridge club, and to hold a job it may be necessary to join a union. Not surprisingly, a number of studies have demonstrated that the attractiveness of a group will vary with its promised or proven success in facilitating goal achievement (for a summary of such studies, see Cartwright & Zander [1953] 1960, pp. 69–94). Certainly a large, if not major, portion of our associational activities can be subsumed under this general class of affiliative behavior. It is a peculi-

arly asocial sort of affiliation, however, for people qua people may be considered as irrelevant. In these terms, a nonsocial means of goal attainment may be just as satisfactory and attractive as a social means.

More cogent in regard to present concerns is the substance of the following proposition: people, in and of themselves, represent goals for one another; that is, people have needs that can be satisfied only in interpersonal relations. Approval, support, prestige, and the like have been offered as examples of such needs. It is in the elaboration of this order of needs that one encounters some of the more intriguing, nonobvious speculations and findings on the sources of cohesiveness.

Individuating vs. deindividuating social needs. Leon Festinger, Albert Pepitone, and Theodore Newcomb (1952) suggest that there are two classes of needs that group membership satisfies: needs such as approval, status, and help, which require singling the individual out and necessarily involve high social visibility and individual identifiability; and needs whose satisfaction requires being "submerged in the group," a condition labeled "deindividuation" and described as a state of personal anonymity in which the individual does not feel singled out or identifiable. It is suggested in the same study that there are many kinds of behavior in which the individual would like to engage that he is prevented from engaging in by the existence of inner restraints. Instances of such behavior might be acting wildly and boisterously, "talking dirty," or expressing hostilities. The authors put forward the hypothesis that under conditions where the individual is not "individuated" in the group, such restraints will be reduced, and individuals will be able to satisfy needs that might otherwise remain unsatisfied. In an ingenious experiment, these authors demonstrate that the state of deindividuation in the group does occur and is accompanied by reduction of the inner restraints of the members of the group. Further, they demonstrate that groups in which such restraints are reduced are more attractive to their members than groups in which restraints are not reduced.

Evaluative needs as a source of cohesion. The formulation of social influence presented in the above discussion of the effects of cohesiveness on social behavior indicates another order of need that drives people to associate with one another and to seek membership in groups. Given the existence of a drive to evaluate one's opinions, feelings, and abilities and given the fact that an objective, nonsocial means of evaluation is not available, it should follow that individuals will choose to associate with one another as a means, via social comparison, of evaluating their feelings and ideas. From this line of thought, it should be expected that individuals in a state of uncertainty will choose to affiliate more than will individuals who are sure of their feelings and opinions.

This expectation has been indirectly tested in a series of studies initiated by Schachter (1959). The original experiments involved simply the manipulation of a state of anxiety or fear by informing subjects that they would receive a series of electric shocks. In one condition the shocks were described as intense and extremely painful, while in a comparison condition they were described as very mild and resembling "a tickle or a tingle." After manipulating fear in this fashion, the experimenter permitted the subjects to choose between being alone or being together with other subjects while they waited for the experiment to begin. The results of a number of such experiments have consistently indicated that the more anxious the subject, the more likely he is to choose to be with other subjects.

In attempting to interpret this finding, Schachter conducted a series of additional experiments, which led to the conclusion that "it appears theoretically rewarding to formulate this body of findings as a manifestation of needs for anxiety reduction and of the need for self-evaluation" (Schachter 1959, p. 132). Although in the original work it is impossible to partial out the independent operation of these two sets of needs, subsequent research by Harold Gerard and Jacob Rabbie (1961) and others indicates that these two sets of needs do operate independently as motivators of affiliative behavior. The more likely it is that a group can satisfy either of these needs, independently manipulated, the more attractive is the group to its members in a state of need arousal.

These studies of deindividuation and of evaluative needs as sources of cohesiveness represent the major systematic research attacks to date on the sources of cohesiveness. However, other studies that were not immediately directed to the subject have indicated other variables affecting the cohesion of a group.

Other factors affecting cohesion. Many of the studies of the relationships of *group structure* to group functioning have demonstrated that the pattern of within-group relationships can affect cohesiveness. In experimental studies of communication networks it has been repeatedly demonstrated (Glanzer & Glaser 1961) that morale and satisfaction are related to the average degree of centrality of the positions in a group's communication

network. In studies of leadership, Ralph White and Ronald Lippitt (1953) have demonstrated that groups in which leader–member relations are structured democratically have more "friendliness and group-mindedness" than do groups in which leaders play autocratic or laissez-faire roles. Finally, Morton Deutsch (1949) has shown that experimental groups structured so that the members are competitive have lower cohesiveness than groups structured so that the members are cooperative in pursuit of a goal. These are essentially fragmentary findings and by-products of the major interests of these studies, but they do illustrate the obvious fact: that the fashion in which a group is organized and the rules governing the pattern of interrelationships among group members can have profound effects on group cohesiveness.

There is also evidence that *initiation severity* can affect cohesion. It is a common observation that those who suffer to attain something will value it more highly than those who achieve the same thing easily. The implications of this observation for group cohesiveness have been directly tested in an experiment conducted by Elliot Aronson and Judson Mills (1959). In this study girl students who had indicated an interest in joining discussion groups on the psychology of sex underwent "initiation" before being permitted to join such groups. There were three experimental conditions: severely embarrassing initiation, mildly embarrassing initiation, and a control group that did not go through initiation. Following initiation, the subjects, under the impression that they were listening to an ongoing discussion group, listened to a prerecorded tape of a dreary, halting, worthless discussion of sex. They then rated the members of the group and the discussion proper on a variety of evaluative dimensions. Subjects in the severe initiation condition rated both the group members and the discussion as considerably more interesting and attractive than did subjects in either of the other conditions—a finding that suggests a rationale for fraternity-initiation excesses and for the punishing rites of passage of so many primitive tribes.

These, then, are the studies that have been most directly concerned with cohesion—its effects and its sources. Implicitly or explicitly, however, this topic pervades almost the entire social science enterprise, for the desires that draw men together furnish the substance of these sciences, which in large part are devoted to the study of the processes and products of human association.

STANLEY SCHACHTER

[*Directly related are the entries* FRIENDSHIP *and* SOCIOMETRY. *Other relevant material may be found in* COOPERATION; GROUPS; LEADERSHIP.]

BIBLIOGRAPHY

ALLEE, WARDER C. (1938) 1951 *Cooperation Among Animals, With Human Implications.* Rev. & enl. ed. New York: Schuman. → First published as *The Social Life of Animals.* A paperback edition was published in 1958 by Beacon.

ARONSON, ELLIOT; and MILLS, JUDSON 1959 The Effect of Severity of Initiation on Liking for a Group. *Journal of Abnormal and Social Psychology* 59:177–181.

BACK, KURT W. 1951 Influence Through Social Communication. *Journal of Abnormal and Social Psychology* 46:9–23.

CARTWRIGHT, DORWIN; and ZANDER, ALVIN (editors) (1953) 1960 *Group Dynamics: Research and Theory.* 2d ed. Evanston, Ill.: Row, Peterson.

DEUTSCH, MORTON 1949 An Experimental Study of the Effects of Co-operation and Competition Upon Group Process. *Human Relations* 2:199–231.

FESTINGER, LEON 1950 Informal Social Communication. *Psychological Review* 57:271–282.

FESTINGER, LEON 1954 A Theory of Social Comparison Processes. *Human Relations* 7:117–140.

FESTINGER, LEON; PEPITONE, A.; and NEWCOMB, T. 1952 Some Consequences of De-individuation in a Group. *Journal of Abnormal and Social Psychology* 47:382–389.

FESTINGER, LEON; SCHACHTER, STANLEY; and BACK, KURT W. (1950) 1963 *Social Pressures in Informal Groups: A Study of Human Factors in Housing.* Stanford (Calif.) Univ. Press.

FESTINGER, LEON et al. 1952 The Influence Process in the Presence of Extreme Deviates. *Human Relations* 5:327–346.

GERARD, HAROLD; and RABBIE, JACOB M. 1961 Fear and Social Comparison. *Journal of Abnormal and Social Psychology* 62:586–592.

GLANZER, MURRAY; and GLASER, ROBERT 1961 Techniques for the Study of Group Structure and Behavior. 2: Empirical Studies of the Effects of Structure in Small Groups. *Psychological Bulletin* 58:1–27.

LIBO, LESTER 1953 *Measuring Group Cohesiveness.* Ann Arbor: Univ. of Michigan, Institute for Social Research.

McDOUGALL, WILLIAM (1908) 1936 *An Introduction to Social Psychology.* 23d ed., enl. London: Methuen. → A paperback edition was published in 1960 by Barnes & Noble.

SCHACHTER, STANLEY 1951 Deviation, Rejection and Communication. *Journal of Abnormal and Social Psychology* 46:190–207.

SCHACHTER, STANLEY 1959 *The Psychology of Affiliation: Experimental Studies of the Sources of Gregariousness.* Stanford Studies in Psychology, No. 1. Stanford (Calif.) Univ. Press.

TROTTER, WILFRED (1916) 1953 *Instincts of the Herd in Peace and War: 1916–1919.* Edited by R. W. Chapman. New York: Macmillan.

WHITE, RALPH; and LIPPITT, RONALD (1953) 1960 Leader Behavior and Member Reaction in Three "Social Climates." Pages 527–553 in Dorwin Cartwright and Alvin Zander (editors), *Group Dynamics: Research and Theory.* 2d ed. Evanston, Ill.: Row, Peterson.

COHORT ANALYSIS

A cohort is an aggregate of individual elements, each of which experienced a significant event in its life history during the same chronological interval. Cohort analysis consists of the quantitative description of dated occurrences from the time a cohort is exposed to the risk of such occurrences. Since parameters of cohort aggregate behavior can be arranged in temporal sequence by reference to the date of the event defining and initiating cohort exposure, a time series of cohort parameters can be assembled for use as evidence in the study of temporal variations in the behavior on which attention is focused. This is the most important application of cohort analysis. If, in the life of an individual, event E_1 occurs at time T and event E_2, conditional upon E_1, occurs at time $t = T + i$, then cohort analysis is concerned with the characteristics of functions $E_2(i, T)$ for variations of i (intracohort) and T (intercohort) for the set of individuals in the class (E_1, T).

The idea of cohorts has long been familiar in historical and journalistic work, but under the name of "generations." This word has so many meanings that it is easily misconstrued. It may be an approximate length of time, an identification of an era, a biological term for the process of procreation, or a structural term derived from the parent–child relationship. It is recommended that the term "generation" be restricted to the last usage, where it signifies an important concept without competitive designation, and that the term "cohort" be used to identify or locate an aggregate in time [*see* GENERATIONS].

Cohort analysis has been developed and used most extensively in demography, particularly in the study of time series of fertility. Therefore, the focus of this article is on methods and results in that area and in analogous demographic inquiries [*see* FERTILITY].

Cohort and period time series of fertility. Because the probability of childbirth varies markedly with maternal age, it is almost mandatory in fertility analysis to examine the set of birth rates for each separate age. Given this orientation, time series analysis becomes the study of sections of the following fertility surface: if birth rates are given for each maternal age and for each year, then the horizontal axes are used to represent age and time and the birth rates are plotted vertically. Two time series of fertility indices are provided, the first characterizing vertical sections of the surface over all ages, one for each time period, and the second characterizing vertical sections of the surface over all ages, one for each particular difference between time and age. The former are *period* sections; the latter may be called *cohort* sections, because the members of a cohort age *pari passu* with time. In terms of the symbolic statement that was used in the first paragraph, each cohort section consists of some function of E_2 over i for a particular T and each period section consists of the same function of E_2 over i for a particular $t = T + i$, where E_1 is birth, E_2 is parenthood, and i is age (see Ryder 1964*b*).

Of the various ways of summarizing period or cohort fertility, two are particularly useful for relating the nature of the interdependence between cohort and period fertility. The first is the *total fertility rate*, obtained by summing the birth rates over all ages, and the second is the *mean age of fertility*, that is, the arithmetic mean of the age distribution of those birth rates. It can be shown that the time series of period and cohort total fertility rates diverge to the extent that there is temporal change in the cohort (or period) mean age of fertility, and that the time series of period and cohort mean ages of fertility diverge to the extent that there is temporal change in the cohort (or period) total fertility rate.

As a specific example, if the cohort mean age of fertility is declining, then the period total fertility rate is higher than the fertility rate for the cohort whose childbearing is centered in that period. This relationship may be visualized as follows: the fertility occurring in any year depends on the degree of overlap in the age spans of childbearing of the successive cohorts represented in that year. A progressively younger mean age of fertility implies an increase in the extent of this overlap, which is manifested in an apparent increase in the amount of fertility from period to period even in the absence of change in the cohort total fertility rate (Ryder 1960).

These formal propositions show why cohort and period time series of fertility parameters differ but provide no basis for choice between them in a given problem. The critical question is whether the more useful units of observation in time series analysis are period aggregates or cohort aggregates. To choose the former is the conventional practice; the latter is the essence of the proposal of cohort analysis. Let us examine the alternatives, first for short-run and then for long-run variations through time.

From 1935 to 1955 the period total fertility rate for the United States rose abruptly. Cohort analysis reveals that this was attributable to a small rise in the cohort total fertility rate combined with a drop in the cohort mean age of fertility. This decline had two aspects: postponement of births by the affected cohorts, because of the depression, and transition toward an earlier age of childbearing. The phenomenon of *postponement* refers to the transfer of a birth from an earlier to a later time in a cohort's history. Its direct observation requires cohort fertility records, since it is meaningless to posit recovery by one cohort of births postponed by another. Analysis of the fertility response to an economic fluctuation appears superficially to justify period-by-period aggregation of data, because all cohorts exposed to the events in question tend to react in the same direction. The difficulties with this view lie in the organic coherence and continuity of human behavior through time. Reproductive experience is not merely the sum of particular responses to the particular contexts of successive years; present behavior depends on past experience and on expectations of future experience. Cohorts at different stages of development show different degrees of reaction to the same external circumstances, and the response is not confined to the time the disturbance occurs. If it is granted that the fertility movements to be explained are transitory, then the problem of measurement is the discrimination between short-run and long-run change, i.e., between the behavior that is idiosyncratic to the period and the behavior that would have occurred in the absence of disturbance. Thus cohort analysis to establish the long-run path is analytically prior to period analysis of short-run deviations of cohorts from that long-run path.

Advantages of cohort analysis. Despite the cogency of the argument for the place of cohorts in short-run analysis, period aggregation has persisted because the synthetic formulation makes up in convenience what it lacks in accuracy, particularly if the focus of analytic interest is the contemporary situation. The cohorts whose behavior contributes most to current experience have completed an unknowable proportion of their eventual fertility. Changing distributions of cohort fertility through time cause difficulties in measuring not only the fertility in a period but also the fertility of an incomplete cohort. The optimal procedures for coping with these difficulties are still a matter of investigation. Cohort analysis has at least made explicit the inherent indeterminacy of current analysis and has not concealed it behind apparently comprehensive period aggregations of unknown accuracy. Patience is a luxury some kinds of analysis require.

Cohort analysis can make a contribution not

only to the study of fluctuations in the period total fertility rate, occasioned by temporary disturbance of the time pattern of childbearing, but also to the study of long-run distortions caused by permanent modification of that time pattern. For instance, from the time series of period total fertility rates for Sweden in the nineteenth century, it appears that fertility remained on a plateau until the 1870s, when decline began; the time series of cohort total fertility rates shows a decline that began in the 1830s. The discrepancy between these series is attributable to a rise and then a fall in the cohort mean age of fertility (Ryder 1956a).

Obviously the analyst attempting to trace the causation for this crucial phase in Swedish fertility history must have a basis for choice between the two temporal identifications. The implicit preference is for cohort analysis, judged by the terms used in verbal analyses of the determinants of long-run fertility change. Clearly, measurement techniques should be devised to provide observations corresponding to the concepts used in theoretical formulations. Yet the lone justification of this preference for cohort analysis, other than the assertion that it is only common sense to study consecutive human behavior when the data are available, is the observation that the time series of cohort total fertility rates tends to be much smoother than that for period total fertility rates.

The cohort in social change.   A social system is embodied in a population, and its duration exceeds the life of any member. Society, as a functioning collectivity, has inputs of birth and outputs of death but persists despite its ever-changing personnel. Each entering cohort poses a challenge to the society to reproduce itself. To preserve the system, socialization procedures are instituted to equip the entrants with the rational and normative apparatus needed for participation in group activities. The continual entry of new cohorts may be viewed as a stability problem, but it is also a continuing opportunity for modification of the social structure, since flexibility as well as stability is a requirement for survival in a changing environment (Ryder 1965). Socialization is the progressive confinement of behavior potentialities within a culturally acceptable range. Sanity and order are maintained by assimilating new experience so that it makes sense within the prevailing structure of ideas and norms. The faith in education rests on belief in premature plasticity and persistent influence. If man were molded into final form during his premature years, then the only opportunity for change would lie in the appearance of a new cohort each year.

An important role in social change is played by the changing content and agencies of socialization to which new cohorts are exposed. One institutional response of a society when it moves from comparative stability into persistent change is the transfer of authority for socialization from the family to the school. This tends to increase the temporal distance between child and parent and identifies the child's future with that of his contemporaries. The importance of this transition from an age-heterogeneous to an age-homogeneous context is increased by the growth of peer groups, subsets of the child's cohort. Cohorts are further differentiated by a lengthening of the period prior to commitment to adult roles and by the presence of alternative sources of normative direction, which by their very multiplicity encourage choice and innovation. The phase of cohort differentiation is gradually terminated by progressive commitments of the individual to his spouse and children and to the occupational hierarchy in which he earns his living. Resistance to change thus increases with the price of deviation implicit in acceptance of the rewards and responsibilities of successive roles within age-differentiated organizations. Some reservations to this discussion are necessary to obviate the implication that cohorts are the exclusive agents of social change. Socialization is a continuous process within any system. An individual moves through different systems during the course of his life, each with its own socialization procedure and opportunity for reorientation. The capacity of the individual for normative reformulations cannot be dogmatically ignored. Indeed the form of socialization may emphasize a flexible and contingent set of principles which tolerates or encourages subsequent modification.

Nevertheless, the prominence of young adults in the vanguard of social change is well recognized, particularly when the change is rapid and discontinuous—as in transitions from war to peace, from depression to prosperity, or from one culture to another. Youthful deviance may sometimes be anarchic and confined to small and unconnected groups, but it may also become an organized and self-conscious movement, dedicated to a radical pioneering ideology. Contemporary revolutionary movements throughout the world draw most of their support from young cohorts. The same phenomenon is recognized by the many historians of political, literary, and artistic movements who choose the cohort (which they call "generation") rather than the period as their unit of temporal analysis. With less drama but more fundamental significance, the cohorts of young adults have been central to the processes of urbanization and industrialization. The transformation from rural agriculture to urban industry has been accomplished primarily by the movement of cohorts of young adults from one sphere to the other. The continuing evolution of technological structure relies less on the retraining of older cohorts than on the recruitment of new ones. The annual entry of each new cohort provides one solution to the problem of transforming the distribution of personnel among roles as required by social change. In the process the cohort acquires a distinct shape which differentiates it from its predecessors. In fine, cohorts are differentiated from one another by the process of social change, and they are utilized to bring about social change. This is the core of the argument that the *measurement* of social change, as manifested in statistics of individual behavior, is most fruitfully accomplished by a temporal organization in cohort units.

Demographic applications. The approach described for fertility analysis was first used with the surface of mortality as a function of age and time. As before, the analytic justification for cohort analysis is the dependence of the behavior of the cohort at any age and time on its experience in previous ages and times. The practical difficulties associated with record keeping for a long-lived species have limited the employment of cohort analysis in mortality. Where such difficulties have been overcome, cohort analysis revealed some patterns of change that had been concealed by the synthetic construction implicit in conventional life tables, and these regularities have been exploited for projection purposes, *inter alia* [see LIFE TABLES].

For example, an important substantive contribution to the study of tuberculosis mortality was made possible by the cohort approach. An apparent rise in the modal age of tuberculosis mortality, which was difficult to explain, was revealed to be an artifact of cross-sectional analysis. When the surface of rates was re-examined as a succession of cohort mortality functions by age, it became apparent that the age pattern from cohort to cohort was relatively fixed and that the rise in the modal age for successive periods was a reflection of the steady decline in the level of tuberculosis mortality from cohort to cohort (Frost 1939).

Similar rewards have accrued from the extension of the cohort approach to the study of nuptiality. It has long been recognized that the number of marriages is prone to fluctuate from period to period with changing economic conditions, despite stability in the eventual likelihood of marriage. This is now interpretable in terms of cohorts as a contrast between a period and a cohort time series, generated by temporary modifications in the time pattern of cohort nuptiality (Ryder 1956b). Development of translation formulas for nuptiality and mortality functions has proved more difficult than for fertility because the required indices have a multiplicative rather than an additive construction. Beyond the realm of analysis, the concept of *birth cohort* has proved useful both as an accounting device to link together age-specific information of the same type in successive time periods and as a possible projection method [see NUPTIALITY].

The cohort approach has also been applied to the study of occupational careers by time of entry into the labor force, educational careers by time of entry into school, and morbidity histories by time of first exposure to the condition (Goldfarb 1960).

Thus the concept discussed, up to this point, in reference only to the group born in the same time period can be extended to the identification and surveillance of any group in terms of the time it enters any category of exposure to an event or behavior pattern of interest. For example, fertility analysis has progressed by measurement procedures having been brought into closer alignment with phases of the reproductive sequence. First births have been studied as occurrences to marriage cohorts at successive marital durations, second births as occurrences to first parity cohorts at successive birth intervals, and so forth. Each event is studied in terms of frequency and time distribution for aggregates that enter exposure to the event during the same time period.

The preponderance of references to birth cohorts, and to age as time interval, within cohort analysis is probably explained by the capacity of age to serve as a surrogate for other types of intervals, where there is only a small variance in age at entry into the particular population being investigated. But age is merely the most important of the general class of measurements of the length of time elapsing since the occurrence of cohort-defining events. This suggests a broad application of the cohort approach. Most social surveys, for instance, include the age of the respondent as a variable because all classes of behavior show variations with age. Interpretation of age-specific results requires consideration of the double meaning of age—as temporal location in terms of both personal career and history—because those whose ages differ at any time are members of different cohorts. This double meaning is particularly worth observing in the study of change, because its relevance varies directly with the extent of change (Ryder 1964a).

Relation to other approaches. This article has emphasized the importance of cohort analysis for the study of social change. The distinction between *social process* (the routinized patterning of behavior throughout the lives of individuals) and *social transformation* (the modification of processual parameters through time) can therefore be characterized as the differentiation of intracohort and intercohort variations.

The two cognate measurement procedures of cohort analysis are the study of aggregate life cycles of individuals from entry to exit with respect to any population and the study of parameters of these interval functions, arranged successively in time—in other words, intracohort measurement by age (or other interval) and intercohort measurement by time. Cohort analysis can therefore be seen as a blend of intensive small-scale studies that use a life-history format, with large-scale, extensive surveys of the population at one point of time. The organization of personal data in temporal sequence is the *raison d'être* of the case-history approach; records for individuals are collected on a longitudinal time axis simply because people live this way, aging year by year. But cohort analysis is distinct from longitudinal analysis in one important regard. Longitudinal analysis concerns the behavior of individual elements observed over successive times. Cohort analysis, on the contrary, concerns the changing characteristics of an aggregate through time; it is macrolongitudinal. The cohort analyst, in short, investigates the properties of populations rather than the behavior of individuals; he is concerned with specifying the net changes occurring to an aggregate rather than with identifying the changes particular to individual elements of that aggregate.

So long as extensive studies are framed within a period format of aggregation and index calculation, there will continue to be an unfortunate hiatus between two potentially complementary approaches to social analysis. Cross-sectional inquiries destroy individual sequences and thus imply that the past is irrelevant; they encourage static formulations because of the temptation to use age-*cum*-cohort as if it were age, thereby creating the illusion of unchanging structure. The cohort is a device for providing a macroanalytic link between movements of individuals from one to another status, category, or residence during their lives and movements of the population manifested in changes of distribution and composition from one time period to the next. In this way statistical measurements of the aggregate are equipped with the appropriate time dimension for linkage with the results of intensive and individual-oriented research. The cost of relative inconvenience implicit in cohort analysis is well justified by the research potentiality.

N. B. RYDER

[*See also* GENETICS, *article on* DEMOGRAPHY AND POPULATION GENETICS.]

BIBLIOGRAPHY

DAVIS, KINGSLEY 1940 The Sociology of Parent–Youth Conflict. *American Sociological Review* 5:523–535.

EISENSTADT, SHMUEL N. 1956 *From Generation to Generation: Age Groups and Social Structure.* Glencoe, Ill.: Free Press.

FROST, WADE H. (1939) 1940 The Age Selection of Mortality From Tuberculosis in Successive Decades. *Milbank Memorial Fund Quarterly* 18:61–66.

GOLDFARB, NATHAN 1960 *Introduction to Longitudinal Statistical Analysis: The Method of Repeated Observations From a Fixed Sample.* Glencoe, Ill.: Free Press.

MANNHEIM, KARL (1923–1929) 1952 *Essays on the Sociology of Knowledge.* Edited by Paul Kecskemeti. New York: Oxford Univ. Press. → First published in German. See especially pages 276–322 on "The Problem of Generations."

RENOUARD, YVES 1953 La notion de génération en histoire. *Revue historique* 209:1–23.

RYDER, N. B. 1956a Problems of Trend Determination During a Transition in Fertility. *Milbank Memorial Fund Quarterly* 34:5–21.

RYDER, N. B. 1956b La mesure des variations de la fécondité au cours du temps. *Population* (Paris) 11:29–46.

RYDER, N. B. 1960 The Structure and Tempo of Current Fertility. Pages 117–136 in Universities–National Bureau Committee for Economic Research, *Demographic and Economic Change in Developed Countries.* National Bureau of Economic Research, Special Conference Series, No. 11. Princeton Univ. Press.

RYDER, N. B. 1964a Notes on the Concept of a Population. *American Journal of Sociology* 69:447–463.

RYDER, N. B. 1964b The Process of Demographic Translation. *Demography* 1:74–82.

RYDER, N. B. 1965 The Cohort as a Concept in the Study of Social Change. *American Sociological Review* 30:843–861.

WHELPTON, PASCAL K. 1954 *Cohort Fertility: Native White Women in the United States.* Princeton Univ. Press.

COKE, EDWARD

Sir Edward Coke (1552–1634) was an English jurist who, as a judge and writer, significantly influenced the development of Anglo-American law. (His name was in his own time pronounced and often written "Cooke" and is still so pronounced.) After receiving his education at Trinity College, Cambridge, and at the Inner Temple, London, Coke was called to the bar in 1578; his rise in his profession was rapid. He soon became solicitor general, then speaker of the House of Commons, and in 1594 Queen Elizabeth I appointed him attorney general. As attorney general he was a forceful representative of the interests of the crown, and his harshness and brutality toward men accused of treason or sedition became notorious, shocking many of his contemporaries.

In 1606, King James I appointed Coke chief justice of the Court of Common Pleas, an appointment that caused an almost immediate change of attitude in Coke. The feared and relentless defender of royal power became an equally ardent champion of the supremacy of the common law. He led a vigorous attack against the Court of High Commission, which represented the royal prerogative in church matters, issuing many writs of prohibition against the exercise of jurisdiction by this court. Coke's position on the supremacy of common law brought him in direct conflict with King James. At a meeting between the king and the judges, held at Whitehall in 1608, King James stated that he could take any causes he pleased from the judges and determine them himself; Coke unequivocally denied this assertion and, quoting Henry de Bracton, declared that "the king should not be under any man, but under God and the law." In "Dr. Bonham's Case" (1610), Coke extended his views on the supremacy of the common law to the area of parliamentary legislation, holding that when an act of Parliament is against common right and reason, the common law will control such an act and adjudge it to be void.

In 1613, on the advice of Francis Bacon, Coke's great enemy, the king transferred Coke to the chief justiceship of the Court of King's Bench, an office higher in dignity but lower in salary. Bacon thought that Coke's capacity for doing harm to the royal interests would be diminished, since the main function of this court was the trial of pleas of the crown, i.e., criminal cases. But Coke soon started again to enforce his beliefs in the supremacy of common law, a system of law that he considered to be well-nigh perfect, and to fight those courts connected with the royal prerogative. When Lord Chancellor Ellesmere, as head of the Court of Chancery, granted an injunction against the execution of a judgment obtained fraudulently in the King's Bench, Coke declared interference by the Chancery to be a legal offense against the ancient statute of praemunire and secured an indictment both against the parties and against the master in chancery who had taken part in the proceedings. The jury, however, discarded the indictment. When the matter was brought before the king and his legal advisers, they held that the Chancery had been within its rights.

Shortly thereafter, in 1616, Coke was dismissed by the king. On the day following the dismissal, John Chamberlain summed up the reasons for this action correctly when he wrote: "fowre [four] P's have overthrown and put him down, that is Pride, Prohibitions, Premunire [*sic*], and Prerogative" ([1597–1626] 1939, vol. 2, p. 34).

In 1620, Coke was returned to the House of Commons and became a leader of the parliamentary opposition to the king. He was the chief architect of the Petition of Right, the great constitutional document designed to safeguard the basic liberties of the people. The document, published in 1628, declared that arbitrary imprisonment was unlawful, strengthened the writ of habeas corpus, forbade the billeting of soldiers without the householder's consent, and took a stand against the levying of loans or taxes without parliamentary approval. It was probably the crowning event in Coke's career that Charles I, who had succeeded James in 1625, had to accede to the demands made in this document.

Coke's writings belong to the classics of English legal literature. In his *Reports* (13 parts, 1600–1659) he set forth the pleadings, arguments, and rules of law as they arose in litigation before him and other judges. Each case contains a summary of authority upon the principle involved up to his own day. His *Institutes of the Laws of England*... consists of four parts: the first (1628) is a commentary on Littleton, who had published a book on tenures in the fifteenth century; the second (1642) deals with public and statutory law; the third (1644*a*), with criminal law; and the fourth (1644*b*), with the jurisdiction of courts.

It was chiefly because of Coke that the common law was able to preserve its continuity even during the revolutionary period of the seventeenth century and to become the dominant jurisdiction in England. He linked the law of the medieval period with that of the emerging modern world and thereby paved the way for a reform of the common law that did not abandon those of its values capable of being preserved in modern civilization. These attainments entitle Coke to a place among the great jurists of the world.

EDGAR BODENHEIMER

[*For the historical context of Coke's work, see* LEGAL SYSTEMS, *article on* COMMON LAW SYSTEMS; PARLIAMENTARY GOVERNMENT.]

WORKS BY COKE

(1600–1659) 1826   GREAT BRITAIN, COURTS *The Reports of Sir Edward Coke, knt.* [*1572–1617*]. In 13 parts, 6 vols., new ed. London: Butterworth.

(1610) 1826   Dr. Bonham's Case. Volume 4, part 8, pages 355–383 in Great Britain, Courts, *The Reports of Sir Edward Coke.* London: Butterworth.

(1628) 1853 *The First Part of the Institutes of the Laws of England, Or a Commentary Upon Littleton. . . .* 1st American ed. from the 19th London rev. & corrected ed. Philadelphia: Small.

(1642) 1817 *The Second Part of the Institutes of the Laws of England Containing the Exposition of Many Ancient and Other Statutes.* 2 vols. London: Clarke.

(1644a) 1817 *The Third Part of the Laws of England Concerning High Treason, and Other Pleas of the Crown and Criminal Causes. . . .* London: Clarke.

(1644b) 1817 *The Fourth Part of the Institute of the Laws of England Concerning the Jurisdiction of the Courts. . . .* London: Clarke.

SUPPLEMENTARY BIBLIOGRAPHY

BOWEN, CATHERINE DRINKER 1957 *The Lion and the Throne: The Life and Times of Sir Edward Coke (1552–1634).* Boston: Little.

CAMPBELL, JOHN C. (1849) 1874 Sir Edward Coke. Volume 1, pages 245–357 in John Campbell, *The Lives of the Chief Justices of England.* New York: Cockcroft.

CHAMBERLAIN, JOHN (1597–1626) 1939 *The Letters of John Chamberlain.* Edited and with an introduction by Norman E. McClure. 2 vols. Philadelphia: The American Philosophical Society. → See especially the "Letter to Sir Dudley Carleton, London, November 14, 1616."

HOLDSWORTH, WILLIAM E. 1924 Edward Coke and the Relations of the Common Law to Its Rivals. Volume 5, pages 423–493 in William Holdsworth, *History of English Law.* London: Methuen.

HOLDSWORTH, WILLIAM E. 1938 Sir Edward Coke. Pages 111–132 in William Holdsworth, *Some Makers of English Law: The Tagore Lectures, 1937–38.* Cambridge Univ. Press.

JOHNSON, CUTHBERT WILLIAM (1837) 1845 *The Life of Sir Edward Coke, Lord Chief Justice of England in the Reign of James I, With Memoirs of His Contemporaries.* 2 vols., 2d ed. London: Colburn.

LYON, WALTER HASTINGS; and BLOCK, HERMAN 1929 *Edward Coke, Oracle of the Law.* Boston: Houghton Mifflin.

McDONNELL, GEORGE P. (1887) 1921 Sir Edward Coke. Volume 4, pages 685–700 in *Dictionary of National Biography.* Oxford Univ. Press.

PLUCKNETT, THEODORE F. T. 1926 Bonham's Case and Judicial Review. *Harvard Law Review* 40:30–70.

COKER, FRANCIS W.

Born and reared in South Carolina, of an old and prominent Southern family, the political scientist Francis W. Coker (1878–1963) received his advanced education and lived and worked most of his adult life in the North. The statement of two colleagues on the occasion of his death, that he "blended the virtues of both regions," was not merely an encomium but is essential to an understanding of the man, his work, and his influence. In his personal relations and his professional writings he was simultaneously gentle and penetrating, kindly and candid, tolerant of what he regarded as error but firmly critical of it.

Coker received B.A. degrees from both the University of North Carolina and Harvard University. His advanced education and early teaching assignments covered a wide range, from the classics to biology, from philosophy to physics, all of which contributed to the breadth of understanding and depth of perspective in his later work. Settling finally on the emerging discipline of political science as his field of specialization, he took his doctorate, in 1910, at Columbia University, where he studied under such eminent figures of the times as John Bassett Moore, Franklin H. Giddings, E. R. A. Seligman, and James Harvey Robinson. He worked under William A. Dunning in the preparation of his dissertation, which was published under the title *Organismic Theories of the State: Nineteenth Century Interpretations of the State as Organism or as Person* (1910). This work, which established Coker's reputation as a scholar, was both a perceptive summary of the organismic theories and a critique thereof, which concluded that such theories were "invalid and superfluous . . . [throwing] no light upon the working of political institutions" (p. 204).

After a lengthy period at Ohio State University, Coker was appointed, in 1929, to the newly established Alfred Cowles professorship of government at Yale University. When a separate department of government and international relations was created at Yale in 1937, he was appointed its chairman, a position he held until two years before his retirement, in 1947. He was elected president of the American Political Science Association for 1935.

Coker's training and interests in political science were broad. Many of his early writings dealt with local government; his essay "Dogmas of Administrative Reform," in 1922, was a noted and influential dissent to the then prevailing formulas of political–administrative reform of state and local government, which may be briefly characterized as formulas of simplification and centralization. His main identification throughout his career and active retirement, however, was with that part of the political science spectrum identified as political theory. His *Recent Political Thought* (1934), combining enormous scholarship, lucid exposition, and critical interpretation, was his masterwork and, together with the two books of readings that he edited, *Readings in Political Philosophy* (1914) and *Democracy, Liberty, and Property: Readings in the American Political Tradition* (1942), became a "standard" work.

Coker's significance and influence, exerted through his teaching, personal example, and varied writings, was not so much in the formulation and dissemination of new doctrines or theories as in the firm support and intelligent application of the ideas and ideals of liberalism and democracy. Intellectually a master of all arguments against democracy and in favor of other schemes of government, and thoroughly knowledgeable about man's limitations and imperfections, nevertheless he took a firm stand upon the position that democracy is the "best" form of government, whether considered from the viewpoint of stability and efficiency or from the viewpoint of material well-being and individual fulfillment. He combined a loyalty to firmly held ideals with an experimental, pragmatic attitude respecting their realization. Rejecting both laissez-faire and any totalitarian approach, he sought a middle way through the complexities of modern life to the goals of humanism.

Coker's attitudes and influence may be seen reflected and exemplified in the works of two prominent political scientists who studied with him. David Fellman's works dealing with public law reflect Coker's lively concern for the protection of individual rights and the enlargement of the area of human liberties; and Robert A. Dahl's works dealing with such matters as majority rule and economic planning reflect Coker's concern to adapt governmental institutions to new conditions while simultaneously maximizing historically received democratic goals.

DWIGHT WALDO

WORKS BY COKER

1910   Organismic Theories of the State: Nineteenth Century Interpretations of the State as Organism or as Person. Columbia University Studies in History, Economics, and Public Law, Vol. 38, No. 2. New York: Columbia Univ. Press.

(1914) 1938   COKER, FRANCIS W. (editor) Readings in Political Philosophy. Rev. & enl. ed. New York: Macmillan.

1922   Dogmas of Administrative Reform as Exemplified in the Recent Reorganization in Ohio. American Political Science Review 16:399–411.

1934   Recent Political Thought. New York: Appleton.

1942   COKER, FRANCIS W. (editor) Democracy, Liberty, and Property: Readings in the American Political Tradition. New York: Macmillan.

COLE, FAY-COOPER

Fay-Cooper Cole (1881–1961) was born in Plainwell, Michigan. His family soon moved to California, where Cole spent his youth. He graduated from Northwestern University in 1903, and after a period of postgraduate work at the University of Chicago he joined the staff of the department of anthropology at the Field Museum of Natural History. The museum was then initiating an active program of exploration, and in preparation for his participation in this program Cole undertook formal graduate training in anthropology at Columbia and Berlin. On behalf of the museum, he then made two extended field trips to the Philippines, first working among the Tinguian of northern Luzon, 1907–1908, and then primarily in Mindanao, 1910–1912. His work among the Tinguian provided the material for his doctoral dissertation, and he received his PH.D. from Columbia in 1914.

In 1922/1923 Cole made a third trip for the museum to southeast Asia, spending much of this period in Indonesia. He returned to Chicago and in 1924 joined the faculty of the University of Chicago as assistant professor of sociology and anthropology. Through Cole's vigorous efforts, anthropology received separate departmental status in the university in 1929, and under his guidance the department developed as a widely recognized center for research and teaching in this field. Following his retirement in 1947, Cole established his home in Santa Barbara, California, but continued to be in great demand as a teacher. During this period he served in a visiting capacity at the University of Southern California, at Northwestern, Syracuse, Washington, Cornell, and Harvard.

Cole's published work made an original contribution to two distinct fields in anthropology. The first is Philippine ethnology. His monographs, The Tinguian (1922), Traditions of the Tinguian (1915a), The Wild Tribes of Davao District, Mindanao (1913), and The Bukidnon of Mindanao (1956), together with a number of shorter papers, form an important part of ethnological knowledge of the Philippines. The field studies on which these were based led to his more general book The Peoples of Malaysia (1945), which incorporated his accumulated knowledge and experience of this complex region. The second field in which Cole made a significant original contribution was North American archeology. At a time when administrative demands precluded extended field work away from the University of Chicago, he turned his efforts to the archeology of the American Middle West. Knowledge of the prehistory not only of the Middle West but of the entire eastern half of North America was at that time in a most immature state. Cole took an active role in stimulating systematic archeological excavations and in the development and application of refined techniques in the field and laboratory. Two volumes, *Rediscovering Illinois* (Cole & Deuel 1937) and *Kincaid: A Prehistoric Illinois Metropolis* (Cole et al. 1951), include the results of archeological surveys and excavations that he initiated and led.

In the United States Cole is perhaps best known as the founder of the department of anthropology at the University of Chicago. Despite the fact that the establishment of the department virtually coincided with the onset of economic depression and that during the following decade means were always very scarce, under Cole's direction the department grew and flourished. Edward Sapir, Radcliffe-Brown, and Redfield were among the distinguished men who joined the department faculty. The lectures of visiting scholars from abroad added distinction. The department attracted an able group of graduate students, who have continued Cole's work in anthropology at Chicago and at numerous other institutions in the United States.

Not so well known is Cole's contribution to museum development. The impressive and well-documented ethnographic collections from southeast Asia in the Field Museum of Natural History are to a large extent the result of his long effort. He was always sympathetic to the museum cause, and his service on the Illinois State Board of Museums greatly aided in developing a professional museum system.

Cole's career coincided with a period of unprecedented growth of professional scholarly societies in the United States and with a consequent expansion of their roles in the organization of teaching and of research and in public affairs. Particularly since World War II American professional societies have experienced recurring problems of growth, of accommodating special fields and interests, and of establishing working relations between the various branches of social science. To these problems Cole gave generously of his time and effort. He occupied numerous positions of responsibility—in the American Anthropological Association, the Social Science Research Council, and the National Research Council, to name but a few—but regarded his offices not merely as an honor but as a responsibility for contributing to the greater effectiveness of professional organizations in the advancement of knowledge.

Finally, Cole was devoted to education in the broadest sense. Here his interests ranged from teaching introductory undergraduate courses in anthropology to organizing the evidence for human evolution at the time of the Scopes trial in Tennessee. Much of his published writing was directed toward educated lay readers. He enjoyed presenting anthropology as an important approach to the understanding of man, and he gave his message with dignity and force.

ALEXANDER SPOEHR

[*Other relevant material may be found in* INDIANS, NORTH AMERICAN.]

WORKS BY COLE

1913   *The Wild Tribes of Davao District, Mindanao.* Field Museum of Natural History, Publication No. 170. Chicago: The Museum.

1915a   *Traditions of the Tinguian: A Study of Philippine Folk-lore.* Field Museum of Natural History, Publication No. 180. Chicago: The Museum.

1915b   A Study of Tinguian Folk-lore. Ph.D. dissertation, Columbia Univ.

1922   *The Tinguian: Social, Religious, and Economic Life of a Philippine Tribe.* Field Museum of Natural History, Publication No. 209. Chicago: The Museum.

1937   COLE, FAY-COOPER; and DEUEL, THORNE. *Rediscovering Illinois: Archaeological Explorations In and Around Fulton County.* Univ. of Chicago Press.

1945   *The Peoples of Malaysia.* Princeton, N.J.: Van Nostrand.

1951   COLE, FAY-COOPER et al. *Kincaid: A Prehistoric Illinois Metropolis.* Univ. of Chicago Press.

1956   *The Bukidnon of Mindanao.* Natural History Museum, Publication No. 792. Chicago: The Museum.

SUPPLEMENTARY BIBLIOGRAPHY

EGGAN, FRED 1963 Fay-Cooper Cole: 1881–1961. *American Anthropologist* New Series 65:641–645. → Contains a bibliography on pages 645–648.

COLE, G. D. H.

George Douglas Howard Cole (1889–1959), English historian, economist, and sociologist, was the son of a small builder in Ealing (West London). He had a brilliant career at Oxford, where he was known as a classical scholar and a minor poet, as well as an advanced social thinker. He became a fellow of Magdalen College, Oxford, in 1912; later a fellow of University College, All Souls, and Nuffield and first reader in economics; and, thereafter, Chichele professor of social and political theory. Throughout his life, which was divided between Oxford and London, his influence upon successive generations of students was immense; before his death a hostile periodical (the *Economist*) asserted with angry exaggeration that the majority of the leaders of the emergent states appeared to have been indoctrinated by Cole or Harold Laski. Unfortunately, only the briefest notes of Cole's lectures have survived.

His first book, which seemed to presage a new type of socialism, was *The World of Labour* (1913); it was a study of all labor movements—unions as well as political bodies—throughout the world and pointed to a method of reconciling the two main revolutionary theories of that time, syndicalism (or industrial unionism) and parliamentary, or state, socialism. The new program, worked out in conjunction with William Mellor, A. R. Orage, and others, basically called for public ownership of the main industries and democratic control of them by the unions; it took the name "guild socialism" in conscious memory of the Middle Ages, and its inspiration came more from William Morris than Karl Marx. Although guild socialism as an organization was disrupted by the Russian Revolution, its influence remained powerful especially through Cole's own expositions, of which *Self-government in Industry* (1917) was the first and the most influential.

After World War I, Cole attained a position of great influence as a teacher, political theorist, and adviser. He was the most complete polymath of his age and was widely consulted by every section of the labor, radical, and trade union movement, but he was less successful in direct political action. Although he was untiring in organizing committees, schools, societies, and journals, he frequently left them in an explosive manner. His enormous output of books and pamphlets (at one time he said he could easily write three thousand words a day) defies enumeration, but it falls into three main categories.

(1) Several of Cole's books were of a factual character, surveying the whole world economically and politically. They were long, detailed, clear, and at that time invaluable; they will almost certainly be turned to by students of history, but they are of course dated as reference books. The most important are *The Intelligent Man's Guide Through World Chaos* (1932), *The Intelligent Man's Review of Europe Today* (1933), and *The Intelligent Man's Guide to the Post-war World* (1947a), one-man encyclopedias of usually more than a thousand pages each. *The Condition of Britain* (1937) and *Local and Regional Government* (1947b) are examples of shorter but equally meticulous studies. In most of these and many other of his works, his coauthor was his wife, Margaret (née Postgate).

(2) Subsequent to the guild socialist books already mentioned, the most important of his works on economic theory are *Gold, Credit and Employment* (1930), *What Marx Really Meant* (1934), *Principles of Economic Planning* (1935), and *Money: Its Present and Future* (1944).

(3) Cole's historical books have, naturally, suffered far less from the passage of time than his economic works and in the 1960s were still widely studied as textbooks. His best biography is *Life of William Cobbett* (1924) and next to it *Life of Robert Owen* (1925); his *A Short History of the British Working-class Movement* (1925–1927) and *A Century of Co-operation* (1945) are classics in their sphere, but the most continuously successful book has been *The Common People, 1746–1946* (1938), written in collaboration with Raymond Postgate. Cole's monument, however, will probably prove to be his five-volume *History of Socialist Thought* (1953–1960). Four of these volumes were published at his death, and a last volume was completed by his widow. No other work of such comprehensiveness had ever before appeared, and no study either of modern social philosophy or of mass political or social movements can in the future be written without reference to it.

Between 1923 and 1945, Cole also wrote, as a parergon (as he would have said), a score of thrillers in collaboration with his wife. His style was clear and plain. When he wrote for political journals, it could sometimes carry emotional overtones but was usually detached and even aloof, as he often was himself; his main fault, stylistically, was excessive fluency.

He was thin, dark, fairly tall, and in his youth remarkably handsome. In his later years, partly because of diabetes, he became difficult in temper and indiscriminately censorious, but he was by nature kindly and generous. He is remembered with affection and respect not only by his many pupils but by almost all who worked with him.

RAYMOND POSTGATE

[*For the historical context of Cole's work, see* ECONOMIC THOUGHT, *article on* SOCIALIST THOUGHT.]

WORKS BY COLE

(1913) 1919 *The World of Labour: A Discussion of the Present and Future of Trade Unionism.* 4th ed. London: Bell.

(1917) 1920 *Self-government in Industry.* 5th ed., rev. London: Bell.

(1924) 1947 *Life of William Cobbett.* 3d ed., rev. London: Home & Van Thal.

(1925) 1930 *Life of Robert Owen.* 2d ed. London: Macmillan. → First published as *Robert Owen.* A reprint of the second edition was published in 1966 by Shoe String Press.

(1925–1927) 1948 *A Short History of the British Working-class Movement: 1789–1947.* Rev. ed. New York: Macmillan; London: Allen & Unwin.

1930 *Gold, Credit and Employment: Four Essays for Laymen.* New York: Macmillan.

1932 *The Intelligent Man's Guide Through World Chaos.* London: Gollancz. → The title of the American edition is *Guide Through World Chaos.*

1933 COLE, G. D. H.; and COLE, MARGARET I. *The Intelli-*

gent Man's Review of Europe Today. London: Gollancz.

(1934) 1937   *What Marx Really Meant.* New York: Knopf.

1935   *Principles of Economic Planning.* London: Macmillan. → Also published by Knopf in 1935 under the title *Economic Planning.*

1937   Cole, G. D. H.; and Cole, Margaret I. *The Condition of Britain.* London: Gollancz.

(1938) 1956   Cole, G. D. H.; and Postgate, Raymond *The Common People, 1746–1946.* 2d ed. London: Methuen. → A paperback edition was published by Methuen in 1961. The title of the American edition is *The British People, 1746–1946.*

(1944) 1947   *Money: Its Present and Future.* 3d ed., rev. London: Cassell.

1945   *A Century of Co-operation.* London: Allen & Unwin.

1947a   *The Intelligent Man's Guide to the Post-war World.* London: Gollancz.

1947b   *Local and Regional Government.* London: Cassell.

1953–1960   *A History of Socialist Thought.* 5 vols. New York: St. Martins; London: Macmillan. → Volume 1: *Socialist Thought: The Forerunners, 1789–1850,* 1953. Volume 2: *Marxism and Anarchism, 1850–1890,* 1954. Volume 3: *The Second International, 1889–1914,* 2 parts, 1956. Volume 4: *Communism and Social Democracy, 1914–1931,* 2 parts, 1958. Volume 5: *Socialism and Fascism, 1931–1939,* 1960.

SUPPLEMENTARY BIBLIOGRAPHY

Sweezy, Paul M.   1957   Professor Cole's *History of Socialist Thought. American Economic Review* 47:985–994.

COLLECTIVE BARGAINING

See under Labor relations *and under* Labor unions.

COLLECTIVE BEHAVIOR

Collective behavior is the field of sociology that focuses on the sequences and patterns of interaction that emerge in problematic situations. The phenomena studied range from responses to disaster, the disorderly street mob, or the radical social upheaval to the peaceful and comparatively trivial shifts in the orientations of individuals and small groups that, occurring en masse, can produce major changes in taste, fashion, or public opinion. Indeed, subtle shifts of sentiment and opinion, in themselves difficult to detect, are often the first signs of more explosive occurrences such as panics, booms, crazes, psychic epidemics, and revolutionary uprisings.

Problematic situations are defined here as those in which participants lack adequate guides to conduct. Whenever imagery that is conventionally accepted or officially sanctioned fails to take account of, or runs counter to, deeply felt sentiments or common perceptions of reality, people create currents of agitation by their actions. They are stirred from the planes along which they normally move and remain agitated until they settle back again into a pattern resistant to further change. What takes place during the interlude is *elementary* collective problem solving rather than structured social action.

What initially attracted much interest to collective behavior was the element of drama almost invariably present in certain "mass" phenomena, whether in the form of novelty, bizarre behavior, exaggerated emotionality, violence, extremist ideology, or some kind of oddity. But fascination with and criticism of these unusual and "irrational" aspects of collective behavior soon gave way to more basic sociological concerns. Collective problem solving, it was observed, occurred not only in the midst of widespread chaos, confusion, and uncertainty but also in the most highly institutionalized settings. Some elementary aspect is actually present in every social encounter, since the behavior of the participants is never completely determined by prior expectations associated with the positions they occupy in stable social structures. Therefore, in this more theoretical sense, collective behavior is in fact ubiquitous, and every analysis that focuses on the dynamic (and therefore problematic) aspects of interaction deals to that extent with collective behavior phenomena.

The nature of collective behavior. Every elementary collective behavior episode involves a partial derailment of social interaction from its normatively structured or expected course. The significance of the derailment is more evident when it affects a large number of people who are agitated and actively concerned over some condition that they are trying to alleviate or redress. Although normative standards continue to have some influence on the direction in which activities unfold, the interaction is characterized by relatively greater *spontaneity*, *volatility*, and *transitoriness* than it would be if the behavior of the participants were more securely anchored in recognized norms.

To say that elementary collective behavior occurs *spontaneously* is to point to the role played in its initiation by individuals who experience greater subjective freedom or psychological compulsion to express unconventional ideas, to engage in unconventional behavior, or otherwise to deviate from established standards. But a lowering of the threshold of inhibition does not imply a total loss of the capacity for critical self-appraisal, even in states of extreme agitation. Few participants even in a highly excited crowd are acting either randomly or blindly; fewer still are governed by an impulse irresistible in any absolute sense. In fact, collective behavior can be, and often is, the product of highly self-conscious individual actions; for instance, bizarre as a fad may appear to the outsider, faddists themselves often act deliberately and see nothing strange in their actions. Hence, what happens in collective behavior is spontaneous in that it is rarely the product of prior consensus or design.

Volatility refers to the explosive force with which intense affect, intemperate opinions, or clear misapprehensions of reality are sometimes communicated and acted out. It also refers to the instability of responses under these conditions. Once the situation is "unfrozen" and orientations are no longer firmly anchored in conventions, participants begin to pay more attention to cues directly inferred from the behavior of others. Leadership passes to individuals because their actions are congruent with the prevailing psychological atmosphere. As a collective mood develops, the responses to directives from established authorities become uncertain and participants can get caught up in a vicious cycle of self-validating definitions. Thus, the more widespread a rumor, the more acceptance it gains; or fashions, once adopted, can reach the height of absurdity—yet both may be abandoned and forgotten not long after.

The elementary and spontaneous phase of agitation or enthusiasm is always of *transitory* duration. Spontaneous acts of defiance can, to be sure, spark a movement of radical protest; a charismatic prophet can bring divine inspiration to his following. However, unless an organized nucleus or core group continues to arouse and provoke the participants, their interactions are not likely to become form-defining. The behavior, if satisfying and followed by desirable consequences, will quickly congeal into new conventions with their own supporting structure and legitimate basis, though the spirit will soon pass out of these initially spontaneous forms.

Collective redefinition

All social conduct rests on a fabric of common meanings, on an imagery shared by relevant persons. This represents the collective definition of the situation. The processes by which such a definition arises or changes to support new and disjunctive behavior are best observed in situations that are inherently unstable, namely, where the presence of an element of *choice, novelty, crisis, attrition, competitiveness,* or *conflict* creates a problem. The collective definitions that develop in these situations tend to be highly dependent upon what

participants themselves feel and directly experience at the given moment.

Choice implies the existence of alternatives and the freedom to select but no generally accepted criterion for making the selection. A *novel* situation is created by unfamiliar circumstances that have no precedents in the experience of participants. *Crisis* arises from extraordinary demands during an emergency that threaten to overtax the capacity of some organized group. *Attrition* develops when collective effort weakens as the result of a persistent and apparently irremediable difficulty. A *competitive* situation is one in which the reward structure, perceived as favoring an individual solution, interferes with a cooperative solution. Finally, *conflict* arises when one party attempts to enforce a dominant claim whose legitimacy is challenged by another.

When any of the above situations becomes problematic for many people, the conventionally accepted imagery will lose its authenticity. It may leave important areas of ambiguity, or it may be deliberately questioned and contradicted by some of those involved. The collective redefinition which then takes place provides the key to the new behavior likely to emerge. Though most problematic situations combine several elements—choice, novelty, etc.—each of these entails its own dynamic in generating a particular incident, episode, or movement clearly recognizable as collective behavior.

Choice. In the pure choice situation, the preference for one or the other of several alternatives reflects essentially subjective moods or tastes. Without an accepted utilitarian criterion to govern personal choice, people will orient themselves to the inferred appraisals of other persons, that is to say, to some transitory definition of what is "fitting" or in "good taste." Such a situation gives rise to fashion. Not only the choice of dress but also all kinds of consumption, conduct, and intellectual, artistic, and even political pursuits become subject to fashion to the extent that the selections are functionally irrelevant, passing fancies whose chief value lies in the image of up-to-dateness which they convey. Once the new standard has diffused, most others will feel compelled to conform.

Novelty. Novel situations brought about by changes in external life conditions or within the structure of the group also involve choices, but—in contrast with the pure choice situation—the selection among the alternatives is sought in terms of functionally relevant assessments. An innovation compatible with cultural definitions and social commitments can gain acceptance solely on the basis of its demonstrated effectiveness, because it requires only minor modifications in the collective image. Another innovation, whose acceptance would have far-reaching implications for several areas of behavior and belief, will need the support of prestigeful individuals to demonstrate its utility and thus to overcome resistance and inertia. This is all the more necessary where a collective decision is the only means of implementation. The propaganda and proselyting efforts by which images are manipulated to support an innovation are important attributes of social movements, which by their collective action seek to reconstitute the social order in some significant way.

Crisis. The problematic aspects of the crisis situation (and of attrition) involve not so much choice and decision as coordination and control. An emergency calls for quick and decisive action. Though there is always a risk that the initial response to a crisis will be based on less than a full and accurate assessment of what is happening and of what needs to be done, the element of novelty in a crisis caused by an unprecedented situation is likely to aggravate any confusion. Often communication channels break down from the overload; activities cannot be fully coordinated. Hence the interpretations people make will be based to an unusual degree on chance observations, hearsay, and other unofficial sources of information. The transmission of "rumors" should be viewed as an improvised effort to elicit responses that will contribute to a working definition of the situation, and not primarily as a product of cognitive error.

Attrition. The high level of activity demanded by a crisis cannot be sustained indefinitely. An attrition situation induces emotional adaptation of one kind or another to persisting and extreme demands. In the case of continuing threat, the inherent danger often comes to be minimized by a growing collective disbelief about its actual presence. The illusion that war is impossible ("unthinkable") because our weapons are too destructive is one form such adaptation can take. More often, the persistent problem that defies a solution promotes fatalism as a justification for apathy. Or the cumulative irritability aroused in these circumstances can be displaced against whatever targets are available. Likewise, it can be converted into hysterical beliefs and symptoms that interfere with effective collective action to deal with the source of the difficulty.

Competition and conflict. Individual responses to a competitive situation and collective responses to conflict have a special propensity for generating a vicious cycle of reciprocal reactions whereby the initial condition that the responses are intended to alleviate is instead aggravated. For example, competitive scare buying in anticipation of future shortages raises prices, thus confirming the expectation and justifying still more anticipatory purchases. Collectively these responses help produce the shortages individuals had anticipated. In like manner, reactive interaction between antagonists who feel threatened escalates whatever conflict already exists. The image of the opponents changes; they become transformed into enemies. Fear, hostility, and suspicion magnify the original source of dispute, often to the point where violence and treachery are condoned and an open test of strength must precede any serious negotiations.

In terms of social control, competition or conflict can lead either to a crisis or to an attrition situation. Unfettered competitive dumping on the stock market, for example, can drop prices and create a crisis of confidence; prolonged conflict to the point of stalemate is inevitably accompanied by signs of serious attrition on both sides, even to a point where continued exertion no longer seems worthwhile.

Collective processes and forms

Each of the problematic situations described above generates changes in the collective imagery (redefinitions) that legitimate changes in established social forms and lead to the emergence of new group properties. The problem-solving activity causes both temporary disruptions and permanent modifications of social structure. To understand the collective dynamics of these transformations, one must look not to the accidental attributes of the forms themselves but to the processes of transformation and the effects they have in different circumstances.

The first of these processes is *convergence*, either physical or behavioral. It results in a focalized response. Other collective responses develop from different processes, which may occur either concurrently or in temporal sequence. *Demoralization* culminates in an atomized response; *collective defense* in a solidary response; *polarization* in a reactive response; *mass conversion* in an apostate response; and *crystallization* in a schismatic response. To study processes is to depict the collective dynamics by which a particular incident, outburst, or movement develops.

Convergence. Some collective behavior is nothing but the outcome of convergence. In *physical* convergence, the actual movements of people who flock to the scene of an accident, rush to get on the same train, make a pilgrimage to the same shrine, or take their vacations at the same resort produce "crowds." *Behavioral* convergence refers to individual actions that coincide solely in being oriented toward the same object, as among those who purchase the same product, interest themselves in the same event, or adopt the same behavior, without all of the participants necessarily being in physical contact or even in communication with one another. Purely behavioral convergence by a sufficiently large number of individuals (or local groups) produces a "mass" rather than a crowd (Blumer 1939).

Sometimes convergence is the accidental product of independent but simultaneous actions by individuals (or local groups) that just happen to coincide; at other times, the convergence is largely imitative and occurs in stages. In either case, convergence is essentially an ecological phenomenon that does not depend on a cooperative response but merely on the exercise of individual (or unit) choices. Yet the convergence of choices can have serious implications. Accidental physical convergence, as in a traffic jam or during a disaster, creates bottlenecks, which constitute a problem and require special effort to resolve. At the same time, the density of any crowd and the difficulties in controlling it increase the likelihood that interaction will be derailed. Once such a multitude gets out of hand, new behavior often spreads by imitation, but accidental convergence, unless it becomes imitative, usually produces only the most transient forms of interaction. The spread of a fashion or fad, or the gradual acceptance of a new implement, technique, or policy, illustrates convergence that is both behavioral and imitative. Rapid diffusion of an innovation is usually made possible by a novel element that both attracts the attention of people and appeals to their hankering.

Demoralization. The simplest way to define demoralization is as the process by which morale is undermined. Morale is a condition or state that measures the capacity of members of a collectivity to pursue, despite disruptive influences, a socially legitimate objective. Groups, organizations, movements, and even whole societies have varying levels of morale. When morale is high, members of a collectivity individually or collectively confronted with a problematic situation will continue to exert themselves to cooperate. Demoralization sets in when changes in the perceived balance of rewards make cooperation no longer seem attractive or worth the effort. It leads to the atomization of responses.

By and large, the cohesiveness of a group, as well as the confidence its members have in the efficacy of any joint endeavor, will be adversely affected by prolonged and serious frustration, deprivation, threat, and other types of adversity. Moderate stress, however, promotes learning without causing loss of confidence in the collective enterprise. It gives the members an opportunity to rehearse and internalize the responses appropriate for overcoming specific difficulties they encounter. In general, when group morale is high, fear of failure ("letting the group down") will help counter fears of personal harm or injury, whose disruptive effects on performance are potentially greater. But the effects of severe or prolonged stress tend to become cumulative. They make focal to each individual the risks he personally faces, and ultimately weaken the group ties that can be invoked to counter the effects of harm anxiety. As studies of military groups and of communities in disaster have shown, the relationship between stress and demoralization is essentially curvilinear. Danger successfully weathered without serious loss or damage usually increases solidarity and the capacity to cope with similar situations.

Collective defense. The solidary response signifies the successful development of a collective defense against demoralization through the spontaneous coalescence of individual reactions. Most collective defenses are socially structured. All societies develop standard practices that function as mechanisms for containing anxieties, practices that are analogous and correspond to the characterological defenses of individual persons. Similarly, societies provide ritualistic occasions during which certain expressions in contradiction to moral standards are evoked. The latter function as safety valves for blocked emotions. In their ritual version such excesses tend to be explicitly condoned, but during an organized demonstration, a strike, or a celebration, behavior that is worrisome or even repugnant to authorities may simply be permitted to take its natural course. The process of collective defense represents the coalescence of behavior to serve as a spontaneously shared mechanism of defense against demoralization. Particularly in an emotionally charged group atmosphere, where there is considerable tension between the desires of individuals and the demands of group membership, any successful disguise or neutralization of this tension produces an elementary solidarity conducive to the acting out of impulses or to making demands whose open expression would not be tolerable.

Among the more common expressions of collective defense are bodily symptoms, convulsive laughter, and action based on hysterical beliefs. These can quickly become collective when the real source of anxiety, experienced by all, is poorly understood or cannot be acknowledged because of existing taboos. Disturbances that appear irrational —like witch hunts, nativist phenomena, violent mob action, and even some religious revivals—are typical of the forms collective defenses may take when institutional means for resolving tensions on the intrapersonal and interpersonal levels are lacking. The members of a mob typically refer to some norm of justice, personified by their particular heroes or violated by the villain against whom vengeance or redress is sought, which their action is intended to uphold.

Polarization. A solidary response achieved on the subgroup level at the expense of over-all consensus constitutes, in terms of the larger social system, a polarized or reactive response. The process of polarization develops from the reactive escalation of antagonisms that progressively harden divergent viewpoints into partisan commitments. Through mutual withdrawal, participation and communication gradually come to be confined within each sector, and mutually dependent but opposing definitions of the situation emerge.

Factional alignments that coincide with already existing social divisions have a high potential for polarization. The issues that emerge merely reinforce the cleavages already endemic within the collectivity, particularly if the effects of a persisting difficulty or of a disaster have very different effects on these segments. In such a case, the many issues that emerge will tend to coincide with the single dominant axis of polarization. Conversely, a highly pluralistic structure—whether in a society or in an organization—will tend to produce shifting coalitions that moderate the intensity of conflict on any single point. Only an issue with far-reaching moral ramifications can generate sufficient pressure to force all individuals to choose one of two sides and to disrupt all competing group allegiances that cut across the particular factional alignment.

Mass conversion. While polarization produces a strain toward consistency that sharpens endemic divisions and increases their salience, the process of mass conversion involves a drastic reorganization of experience through the assimilation of culturally and ideologically disjunctive attitudes and the development of new group affiliations to support them. In short, mass conversion culminates in collective apostasy.

Despite its evident historic significance, the dynamics of mass conversion and apostasy are poorly understood. The acceptance of a new ideology and of "culture change" seems to hinge on "critical" life experiences. Novelty, crisis, and attrition high-light inadequacies in prevailing imagery and weaken traditionally binding commitments. But the positive adherence to a new ideology by an individual involves a status change and the severance of existing interpersonal ties, or at least their redefinition. By the same token, collective apostasy entails parallel status movements, as when mass migrations, coercive acculturation, or structural change in the stratification system forces many people, more or less at the same time, to adapt to a new milieu.

The importance of status change is perhaps best documented by reference to ideological conversion ("brainwashing") fostered by techniques of coercive indoctrination in a controlled milieu. Here individuals are *isolated together* from their normal social relationships. But the crucial mechanism of conversion is to be found in the inevitable disruption of status relations by the succession of generations. Not only do unique "historical" experiences shared by members of one generation influence the way the present is viewed, but the "rising" generation is always under pressure to redefine its relation to the older generation, whose members are "on the way out." Disjunctive ideological changes are most likely to occur where the power monopoly of an older cohort prevents a younger one from asserting what it considers as its rightful claim. Sometimes, however, military defeat, economic depression, and other calamities bring status deprivation primarily to the old, who then transmit deviant ideological images to younger people whose status relations are not directly affected by the new conditions. [See GENERATIONS.]

Crystallization. The earliest articulation of diffuse unrest into ideologically deviant tendencies occurs within schismatic groups—gangs, sects, and other sectarian associations that usually recruit among alienated individuals disenchanted with culture-forming institutions. Such groups offer these individuals a fellowship and understanding they do not find elsewhere in the society. The nuclei of such groupings form by a process of crystallization that involves a conscious act of disaffiliation. Thus the activities and beliefs of sectarians do *not* naturally evolve from group relations linked to other statuses they occupy in society; rather, being a sectarian presupposes a willingness to subordinate all competing social relationships to the demands of the schismatic group.

As a consequence of their self-imposed insulation, the world of the radical sectarians is correspondingly narrowed. Common access to ecstatic experience and esoteric wisdom, not available to outsiders, promotes a mentality with low tolerance for dissent and invites frequent internal schisms to preserve the purity of the group from contamination. In the gang, the rejection of the dominant order is expressed in contempt for social constraints imposed by outsiders, but contempt may be coupled with a concern for reform or exploitation of the existing order. The rigoristic sect, by contrast, turns its attention away from a world defined as corrupt; its members seek a purer morality, sometimes realizable only in the hereafter. Sometimes the two forms exist together, as among the medieval Brethren of the Free Spirit, who, by virtue of their doctrine of immanence, believed that each of them incorporated the divine principle and hence was no longer subject to any law higher than himself. [*See* Sects and cults.]

In the schismatic group, one observes the direct influence of the deviant with charisma whose "inspired" message exerts a magnetic appeal to the culturally *déraciné,* to those suffering from marginality and downward mobility, and those who find in it a legitimized outlet for their intrapsychic conflicts. Thus, the schismatic group may offer a reliable source of support for pathological tendencies (for example, the adolescent gang leader's paranoid projections confirmed by gang codes). Schismatic groups are properly encompassed under collective behavior because (1) they form through the spontaneous sharing of sentiments expressed in fluid and transient patterns of interaction, whether or not these crystallize thereafter; (2) given the total commitment and fanaticism of their members, they provide the active cells and core groups of social movements, whose agitation and proselytizing efforts are directed, explicitly or unintentionally, toward the reconstitution of the social order in some significant way.

Crowd behavior as process

Crowd episodes are strategic research sites in which to observe collective problem-solving activity in its natural setting. Any large gathering of people at one place can properly be designated as a crowd; yet the behavior of such a gathering arouses interest primarily when participants, reacting to the presence of others, engage in some highly emotional, unusual, or disapproved activity or when this activity results in some significant harm or damage to persons or to property. Responsibility for this orientation can be traced to the nineteenth-century progenitors of the theory of the crowd— the collective psychologists, among whom Gustave Le Bon (1895) was the best-known, though certainly not the most systematic, thinker. Their speculations, spawned in decades of political distur-

bance, increasing industrial conflict, and rising patriotic fervor, dwelled on the "psychological crowd" and the "mass" as forms of collective behavior through which the lower orders exerted their will by sheer numbers. By metaphorical extension, these concepts then came to be applied not only to the actions of street mobs but to all traces of irrationality evident in even the most central institutions of bourgeois society, such as the parliament, the press, and the money markets. Caught up in the pathological contagion of the crowd, men were thought to be transformed and to be removed from the influence of society and culture, while all institutions responsive to the influence of large numbers (the "mass") were thereby corrupted. [*See* Mass society.]

The current theory of the crowd has only gradually freed itself from this mystique. Before it could do so, such diverse phenomena as riots, revolutionary crowds, lynch mobs, marauding mobs, collective revelry, solemn assemblies, excited audiences, noisy demonstrations, hysterical outbursts, panic flights, competitive stampedes, and so forth had to be viewed in their specific historical, social, and cultural settings instead of being attributed directly to the peculiar psychological forces inherent in large numbers. Although the images and collective definitions guiding participants may be changed, elaborated, and intensified within the crowd situation, they rarely spring full-blown from these interactions. The problem is to distinguish analytically between the ecological basis of crowd behavior, including the images and ideas that bring people to the scene, and the collective processes that account for its dynamic. Hence most crowds, far from being a simple antithesis to organized society, actually originate within some established group or express cleavages and divisions existing within the society at large.

Collective processes in crowd episodes.   Any unusual event occurring in a public place which many people traverse or where they congregate will quickly attract a large number of onlookers. By their physical convergence, those drawn to the scene collectively form a "crowd." Ordinarily their interactions will have no significance beyond momentary curiosity, which is satisfied once they have found out what is going on. There is some collective redefinition, but it does not culminate in what is usually thought of as crowd behavior.

When the physical convergence of a multitude results from individual actions of persons intent on gaining some highly valued object in scarce supply, the ecology of participation has significance beyond the mere focalization of responses. In an escape mob or a competitive stampede, for example, the efforts of individuals to attain their objectives are intensified as they become aware of the breakdown of social control. Their coincidental movements toward a narrow passageway to safety, toward some esteemed idol, or to gain some competitive advantage produce crowding that interferes with the movements of other individuals toward the same objective. While behavior on any individual's part can continue to be purposeful and adaptive, the interaction of all these individuals together results in chaos and disorder. It is because the individual responses remain atomized that the pattern, collectively, becomes one of demoralization. Collectively, these responses preclude concerted or cooperative action; the affective ties that may have united the participants before cease to be binding.

The *individualistic crowd* depicted here hardly provides an adequate model for the study of crowd behavior. First, its occurrence, like that of the crowd of onlookers, has a highly accidental character and hinges on very special ecological circumstances. Though the formation of an escape mob, for instance, is facilitated in situations where group ties are weak to begin with, such disengagement of individuals from their social obligations is more typically expressed in apathetic withdrawal, low personal *esprit,* violation of norms in private, psychiatric malaise, etc. Second, participants in other crowd episodes, as in a riot, a lynching, or a looting expedition, usually manifest some sense of common purpose. The psychic unity of the "crowd," no matter how rudimentary, signifies some degree of structuring that the individualistic crowd cannot develop unless the behavior of participants is reoriented and thereby ceases to be "individualistic." Third, many disorders treated as "crowds" involve behavioral rather than physical convergence. The collective pattern results as the behavior of a group in one area is repeated in other areas. A spate of racial incidents throughout a city adds up to a "race riot"; the cultivation of the paroxysms characteristic of *chorea minor* by many groups comes to be defined as an epidemic of "dancing mania."

Periods of special stress and tension have been marked by both a rise in crowd activity and an increased tendency toward demoralization. Thus, collective disturbances in custodial institutions, such as prison riots, tend to coincide with administrative changeover; outbreaks of the dancing mania in medieval Europe and Japan have been related to epidemic scourges and social dislocations; peaks of rioting in France, England, and Mexico have been shown to occur together with a sharp increase in the price of bread or a drop in wages; interethnic mob violence has its background in the competition for jobs, housing, or public facilities and benefits. The fact that the same precipitating conditions are associated with both a tendency toward demoralization and with outbursts of crowd activity points to a link between the two. Therefore, the physical suffering and status deprivations that contribute to demoralization appear to be necessary but not sufficient conditions for the increased activity of "crowds."

The second critical element is to be found in the adequacy of socially structured defenses for coping with stress. The activity developed by crowds can be understood as a spontaneously shared defense against demoralizing tendencies whenever acceptable modes for coping with anxiety generated within a situation are lacking. Through collective rather than individual action some of the stress experienced by individuals is transferred to the larger social system. This process whereby individuals and groups collectively defend themselves against demoralization can be observed en masse as well as among physical contact groups.

Three major elements involved in collective defense against the demoralizing effects of stress are *situationally sanctioned collective license, mass hysteria,* and the *coercive enforcement of norms by illicit and extralegal methods of intimidation.* A single episode or incident can involve all three elements, but the element predominating will vary according to the nature of the anxieties generated and the manner in which a collective response develops.

The licentious crowd. Collective license is usually triggered by the impulsiveness of some individuals who, lacking effective personal controls, are forever seeking opportunities for self-indulgence. Such personalities are exceedingly skillful in sizing up situations that permit them to violate norms while minimizing the risk of punishment or even having to face up to the full implications of antisocial acts. Large assemblages, especially after they have gotten a bit out of hand, attract persons with whose pathological dispositions these initial acts may coincide. Psychopaths, always found in prison populations, frequently touch off major disturbances; the probability of a disturbance can be inferred from the number of such psychopaths among the inmates of a prison.

Still, personality obviously represents only a condition that predisposes toward acting out. The effective neutralization of culpability and guilt constitutes an equally important condition: temporarily, at least, normative restraints must be perceived as having for practical purposes become inoperative. The failure of authorities to intervene decisively is of particular importance. It generates the impression that the acts of the "crowd" are at least tacitly condoned. Similarly, the image of authorities as hypocritical or corrupt negates the legitimacy of such intervention but gives tacit sanction to the contravention of norms.

The hysterical crowd.   Where hysteria is the predominant element, outbursts more likely involve persons who normally restrain their inclinations toward self-indulgence and impulsiveness but whose defenses are of such primitive character that they verge on panic when environmental pressures build up and habitual defenses are no longer adequate. The point is that the nature of the problem causing the anxiety is obscure to the participants. They feel in danger of being overwhelmed in ways that they cannot themselves accept and which they feel are equally unacceptable to other members of their group. In the classical form of the hysterical epidemic, the anxiety of persons, each of whom experiences inner conflict, is converted into a somatic disturbance, usually of a markedly stereotyped character. The behavioral symptom of the individual first or most shaken gives objective expression to the diffuse anxiety and hence becomes the catalyst around which the collective behavior crystallizes.

A highly repressive setting that offers few opportunities for individualized expression—a strictly supervised boarding school, or nunnery, or reformatory—is most conducive to outbreaks of epidemic hysteria. Many major social dislocations have been accompanied by the massive sharing of psychopathological symptoms. Convulsions, paroxysms, and other forms of hysteria are often deliberately elicited in religious revivals and by prophetic cults or nativist movements that arise as collective responses to stress. These first stammering attempts at collective problem solving are readily superseded by more effective forms of remedial action. The Welsh revival, for example, was replaced within a decade by militant trade unionism in the very areas in which it had its strongest hold. Similarly, the cargo cults of the southwest Pacific and the African prophet phenomena have been the precursors of political movements once new means for the articulation of grievances could be worked out. [*See* NATIVISM AND REVIVALISM.]

The acting crowd.   The character of crowd behavior as collective defense is most evident when an aggrieved population acts directly and coercively to assert its own norms against established authority or to impose its own conception of justice against deviants defined as a threat. Although such action often involves a deliberate defiance of authorities, the willful violation of laws, and savage acts of intimidation, violence, and destructiveness, it nevertheless represents a method of social control, however primitive the means employed. This type of acting crowd forms when institutional channels for the expression of grievances are ineffective or totally lacking. In such circumstances, crowds can usurp authority simply by virtue of the power that resides in superior numbers. The lynch mob sees that "justice" is done; the mass demonstration forces the recognition of its demands; and acts of destructiveness often succeed in drawing attention to social grievances (for instance, the Luddites destroyed machinery in order to intimidate the owners into complying with standards and practices by which handicraftsmen were trying to protect their interests). As Rudé (1964) in particular has pointed out, most crowds are far from indiscriminate in their selection of objects on which to heap vengeance. Their threats and destructiveness are confined to those who pose some direct or implied danger.

In its disposition to raise nondebatable demands, the acting crowd—much more than the licentious or hysterical crowd—underscores the breakdown of intergroup norms as a condition for its emergence. A rigidly stratified society without channels for airing protests or conducting negotiations to adjust grievances encourages the riot and the revolutionary demonstration as the only effective means of seeking redress. The typical race or ethnic riot is likewise indicative of a degree of polarization before mediating roles and accommodationist institutions have had a sufficient chance to emerge as a means of softening conflict. Each provocation, especially one involving direct action, arouses reactive responses that diminish the faith in orderly procedures and even-handed justice. Many incidents, in themselves of only minor significance, contribute to an atmosphere of suspiciousness in which violence becomes expected. In such an atmosphere, threats and response to threats are likely to reinforce each other, so that hostility on both sides is dramatically increased.

Explaining crowd behavior.   The fact that much direct action by crowds arises from the activity of groups leads to the temptation to attribute whatever course is pursued to the influence of instigators and agitators who seek to turn the anxieties and grievances of some susceptible population to their own advantage. Accordingly, a looting crowd is seen as a pillaging expedition led by a few daring individuals; a street brawl becomes a clash between groups led by paranoid leaders; or a political disturbance is denounced as the product of professional sectarian agitation. This class of explanations tends to overlook the internal dynamics by which a single crowd episode can pass through several mutations.

These mutations can be accounted for without recourse to uncanny psychological forces. The composition of a specific crowd supplies clues about the problems its activities mean to resolve. But most urban centers that contain dense populations also harbor many diverse elements who are likely to dilute the unity of purpose of any specific crowd. Thus, the confusion and disorder exploited by some persons as an opportunity for all kinds of license aggravates the anxieties of others and provides a focus for their hysterical fears. Mutations in behavior also occur as responses to the competitive efforts of *agents provocateurs* to gain the attention of and to influence those present. Most crowds contain not only participants—active and passive—but also victims and innocent bystanders, who respond to rumors and misapprehend the situation or who inadvertently find themselves swept up in the line of march. The involvement of these people in the crowd contributes to its unpredictability. Furthermore, the ecology of a crowd is such that persons experience it from different perspectives and no participant can have an overview of all that is going on. Physical crowding limits the view and confuses the picture. Under the cover of this confusion still other unanticipated acts of collective defense are committed by groups of persons who are reacting to what happens from their own particular perspective.

Finally, the experience in crowds can be related to the conversion process, since it may produce new images (ideological commitments) or new groupings out of which social ferment and social movements grow. It must be pointed out, however, that claims about the number of conversions effected during the crowd excitement of a mass revival have rarely withstood the objective scrutiny of the researcher. As a rule, such conversion experiences mark merely a *rite de passage* into a new status that the neophyte has eagerly sought; most others among the apparent converts backslide as soon as the excitement fades. On the other hand, crowd action that successfully defies authorities or brings governments tumbling down opens new spheres of participation that were never previously envisaged.

The special mystique with which the crowd has so often been invested—that of a pathological force compelling men to act contrary to their usual be-

havior—must finally be put to rest and be replaced by a sociological analysis. The main task for such analysis is to find links between the specific content of the impulses, fears, grievances, and demands that characterize the participants in any crowd episode and the conditions under which the crowd comes to form and the goals it pursues. The conceptualization of crowd episodes in terms of collective processes emphasizes the relationship of such apparently irrational outbursts to inadequacies and strains in the social structure. Crowd behavior needs to be studied as collective problem-solving activity within the larger context of social and organizational breakdown and change.

KURT LANG AND GLADYS ENGEL LANG

[*Directly related are the entries* FASHION; MASS PHENOMENA; SOCIAL MOVEMENTS. *Other relevant material may be found in* ATTITUDES, *article on* ATTITUDE CHANGE; BRAINWASHING; COHESION, SOCIAL; SOCIAL CONTROL; *and in the biography of* LE BON.]

BIBLIOGRAPHY

BLUMER, HERBERT (1939) 1951 *Collective Behavior.* Pages 167–222 in Alfred M. Lee (editor), *New Outline of the Principles of Sociology.* 2d ed., rev. New York: Barnes & Noble.

GLUCKMAN, MAX 1954 *Rituals of Rebellion in Southeast Africa.* Manchester Univ. Press.

GROSSER, GEORGE H. et al. (editors) 1964 *The Threat of Impending Disaster.* Cambridge, Mass.: M.I.T. Press. → On the process of demoralization.

JACQUES, ELLIOTT 1955 Social Systems as a Defense Against Persecutory and Depressive Anxiety. Pages 478–498 in Melanie Klein, Paula Heimann, and R. E. Money-Kyrle (editors), *New Directions in Psychoanalysis.* New York: Basic Books.

LANG, KURT; and LANG, GLADYS 1961 *Collective Dynamics.* New York: Crowell.

LE BON, GUSTAVE (1895) 1947 *The Crowd.* New York: Macmillan. → First published as *Psychologie des foules.* A paperback edition was published in 1960 by Viking.

McGILL UNIVERSITY, MONTREAL, DEPARTMENT OF SOCIOLOGY AND ANTHROPOLOGY 1956 *The Formation, Nature, and Control of Crowds,* by William A. Westley. Ottawa: Dept. of National Defense, Defense Research Board. → Contains a comprehensive bibliography.

PARK, ROBERT E. (1913–1944) 1950–1955 *Collected Papers of Robert Ezra Park.* 3 vols. Edited by Everett C. Hughes et al. Glencoe, Ill.: Free Press. → Volume 1: *Race and Culture,* 1913–1944. Volume 2: *Human Communities: The City and Human Ecology,* 1916–1939. Volume 3: *Society: Collective Behavior, News and Opinion, Sociology and Modern Society,* 1918–1942. → See especially Volume 3.

RUDÉ, GEORGE 1964 *The Crowd in History: 1730–1848.* New York: Wiley.

SMELSER, NEIL J. (1962) 1963 *Theory of Collective Behavior.* London: Routledge; New York: Free Press.

SWANSON, G. E. 1953 A Preliminary Laboratory Study of the Acting Crowd. *American Sociological Review* 18:522–533.

TURNER, RALPH H. 1964 *Collective Behavior.* Pages

382–425 in Robert E. L. Faris (editor), *Handbook of Modern Sociology*. Chicago: Rand McNally.

TURNER, RALPH H.; and KILLIAN, LEWIS M. 1957 *Collective Behavior*. Englewood Cliffs, N.J.: Prentice-Hall.

COLLECTIVE SECURITY

Collective security is a method of managing the power relations of nation states through a partially centralized system of security arrangements. While the ultimate power remains diffused among independent sovereign states, authority in the specifically defined spheres of maintenance and enforcement of peace is vested in an international body.

Collective security is not wholly novel in the history of statecraft. In the eighteenth and nineteenth centuries, nations sought to localize their neighbors' conflict and limit its spread. After World War I, however, it was widely recognized that the modern state system was entering a new era, in which not all warring powers were entitled to equally impartial and neutral treatment by the rest of society. U.S. Secretary of State Henry Stimson, for example, said in 1932 that in future conflicts one or more of the combatants must be designated as wrongdoer; he added that we no longer "draw a circle about them and treat them with the punctilios of the duelist's code. Instead we denounce them as lawbreakers" (Stimson & Bundy 1948, p. 259). This view—that nations may legally be held accountable for starting wars—became the cornerstone of the concept of collective security to which most statesmen have professed loyalty in the post-1945 period.

Development of the concept

Three far-reaching historical trends account for the rise of the new form of international relations and hence for the development of the concept of collective security. The first is the evolving sense of practical morality, according to which neither war nor poverty is any longer accepted as inevitable and foreordained. A succession of grand designs and peace plans originating in the philosophical concepts of the Enlightenment culminated in the League of Nations and the United Nations. The second far-reaching historical trend stems from a revolution in technology and in the world economy. Industrialization has caused the nations of the world to become interdependent. The activities and production of one region are increasingly required to gear and mesh with the functions of others. Industrialism has some of the qualities of a profound ecumenical movement drawing the world together. Third, the revolution in technology and the transformation of beliefs have accented the need for, and the trend toward, more rational and extensive international institutions. Organization and controls must be world-wide to manage world-wide relations and problems. A universalized system of collective security is intended to meet the demand for resistance to aggression and the maintenance of peace on a global scale.

The fundamental principle upon which collective security is founded provides that an attack on any one state will be regarded as an attack on all states. This principle was recognized by the League of Nations, whose Covenant implied that war anywhere is the concern of every state (art. 11). Neutral states are impartial when conflict breaks out, give their blessings to combatants to fight it out, and defer judgment regarding the justice or injustice of the cause involved.

This simple picture of the idea of collective security hardly furnishes a useful and realistic perspective on the way such a system operates in post-1945 practice. Nor are we helped by comparing the structure of the two historic experiments in collective security, the League of Nations and the United Nations. The formal agencies for collective security after World War I were, in several important respects, unimpressive. Article 16 of the Covenant of the League of Nations provided that any member resorting to war contrary to the Covenant had committed *ipso facto* an act of aggression against all other members. It was intended that first economic measures and then overt force be applied against any offender. But there was no clear provision for the organization or implementation of these measures by a central enforcement agency. Each nation had full freedom to provide what troops it saw fit. The Council of the League could then advise on additional measures. In contrast, article 39 of the Charter of the United Nations commissions the Security Council to determine the existence of a threat to the peace or an act of aggression, and articles 43–47 obligate the members, upon the completion of agreements, to supply troops to the Military Staff Committee. The agencies for partial collective security, as can be seen from the constitutional provisions of regional organizations like the North Atlantic Treaty Organization and the Warsaw Treaty Organization, are even more impressive and formidable.

From the beginning, however, the real issue concerning collective security has had little to do with charters or compacts. The real issue is the question of why the implementation of a system that is logically so flawless and enjoys such impressive official devotion and popular support should have been accompanied by a period of virtually unprecedented collective insecurity. It is a sobering fact that the nineteenth century, with its old-fashioned balance of power system, was perhaps the most peaceful in modern times; the twentieth, by contrast, has been an epoch of unparalleled bloodshed. There were only 18 months in the nineteenth century when France, Russia, Austria, Prussia, England, and Spain found themselves at war with one another (excluding the Crimean War, which was essentially a colonial struggle). Our experience thus far with the novel machinery of collective security has hardly warranted the unqualifiedly optimistic postwar belief that with the creation of a new international organization power politics and war are being left far behind in our progress toward utopia.

Basic problems

Four basic problems are responsible for the predicament of collective security: the problem of preconditions, the problem of conflicting national interests, the psychological problem, and the problem of peaceful change.

Preconditions.   The first problem is, from one standpoint, the most basic, for the preconditions of collective security, being frequently misunderstood, have presented the most stubborn obstacle to the maintenance of international peace. Collective enforcement assumes a *status quo,* or situation of peace, that the nations with predominant strength agree to maintain. In practical terms, the peace that a collective system must defend is the territorial *status quo* at the time the system is brought into being. There is nothing in past experience to indicate that all nations, or even a combination sufficiently powerful to defy the rest, will agree on the nature of a particular *status quo.* Following every war, the defeated powers, and even some of the victors, come to oppose the established *status quo.* No practical arrangement has been worked out that is acceptable to the major powers, the Soviet Union and the United States, and on which the post-World War II *status quo* can be founded. The unresolved conflict between East and West has prevented the establishment of peace. Consequently, the latest experiment in collective security presents us with the anomalous picture of a system created to defend a *status quo* that has not yet been brought into being.

Collective security also demands that nations subscribing to the *status quo* be willing and able at all times to muster overwhelming strength for collective defense at successive points of conflict. The supporters of the *status quo* might, in theory, be capable of mobilizing effective and decisive power against any single aggressor who sought to defy them. Or by a pooling of the resources of all the nations in a permanently organized international force, collective enforcement could be made automatic, instantaneous, and preponderant. The first condition, however, is practically impossible of fulfillment, inasmuch as the threat to the *status quo* comes historically from more than one dissatisfied power or aggressor. The second condition would call for the unprecedented practice of having international contingents operate under an international agency empowered to decide conclusively when and how they should be used.

The United Nations Charter seems to take a long step toward this objective by providing that all members "make available to the Security Council, on its call and in accordance with a special agreement or agreements, armed forces, assistance, and facilities" (art. 43, paragraph 1). Through this provision, the incurable weakness of decentralized enforcement, by which past international systems have been rendered impotent, is ostensibly overcome. In the earlier experiments separate nations retained the right to determine whether or not military forces would be made available to meet particular crises. Yet in practice the provision in article 43 has, with two exceptions, remained a dead letter. The stalemate in the Military Staff Committee is fundamentally a symptom of the struggles between the two great powers and between supporters and opponents of the undefined *status quo.* The realization of the second condition of overwhelming strength for collective enforcement has constantly run afoul of special national demands for military security and supremacy.

The final prerequisite of collective security in a world of unequal powers is that at least the major powers enjoy a minimum of political solidarity and moral community. Such solidarity has never been realized between the United States and the Soviet Union.

Conflicting national interests.   The chief practical obstacle to collective security is the political problem deriving from the conflict of independent national interests. The loyalties and interests of nations participating in international organizations and collective security systems are of a different order from those of individuals taking part in the more intimate communities of the family and the nation. There are institutions in integrated societies that provide common standards under which the individual can realize his aspirations. There need be no inherent conflict between an individual's private interests and his national loyalties, for the latter can often promote the realization of the former. On the other hand, conflicts are frequently inevitable between national and supranational loyalties.

The psychological problem. The third problem is psychological. Collective security sometimes breaks down because of collective resentments or hatreds and reactions that express certain features of a particular national character. In 1931 the Japanese spilled over into Manchuria. Why was it that more positive action was not taken? Economically, the world was deep in a painful depression; politically, Manchuria seemed far away and of little immediate interest to Western nations. There was, in addition, a psychological factor. Certain groups in the West harbored deep resentments against these victims of Japanese imperialism. In particular, certain elements within the British trading community remembered private scores that had not been settled and the recent ingratitude of the Chinese toward the West. This sector of Western public opinion took a kind of vicarious pleasure in the punishment the Japanese were inflicting upon China and viewed the Japanese action as a retaliation against the whole anti-European movement that was sweeping Asia.

Peaceful change. The fourth problem relates to international change. Peaceful change involves the whole of society, with its orderly machinery through which social groups seek support for their claims, which must be compatible with the society's fundamental values to be successful. It is the whole of domestic society, and not the legislature in isolation, that brings about social change. The role of legislatures is essentially to ratify the choices at which unorganized society has already arrived. This is made possible by the generally accepted framework of justice within which disputes can be settled.

It is obvious that the conditions and institutions that exist within domestic societies are not present or are greatly weakened in international society. Legislative bodies with lawmaking powers are conspicuously absent from the international scene. The United Nations General Assembly has the power to "make recommendations" on matters prescribed in the Charter; the Security Council may "decide" on measures to be taken and may "call upon" members to act. But although these powers appear to mark an advance, in practice they have not resulted in decisive steps toward international lawmaking or facilitated peaceful change.

Achievements

Yet, despite the inherent limitations, a relatively successful system of collective security evolved

after World War II. The United Nations has provided machinery—a United Nations "presence"—for preserving peace in areas threatened by possible aggression. An emergency force was formed, drawing on national contingents, to maintain a truce following the 1956 conflict over the Suez Canal. The most ambitious program of collective security was the one undertaken to preserve the peace and maintain order in the Congo.

These efforts are noteworthy because they serve to prevent direct confrontation between the two great powers on issues that are not primarily bilateral in character. When the area in dispute lies outside the authority of either great power, policing by the United Nations is sometimes accepted by both as the smallest evil among available alternatives. In the Congo, for example, a United Nations presence was more acceptable to the Soviets than a U.S. presence and more acceptable to the Americans than a Soviet presence.

Thus, collective security, as it affects the areas lying outside the immediate zones of interest of great powers, can be relatively effective. The new system applied pragmatically and with restraint may not function precisely as its architects intended, but it does serve in useful and constructive ways.

KENNETH W. THOMPSON

[*Directly related are the entries* BALANCE OF POWER; INTERNATIONAL CONFLICT RESOLUTION; NATIONAL SECURITY. *Other relevant material may be found in the articles* AGGRESSION; INTERNATIONAL ORGANIZATION.]

BIBLIOGRAPHY

BARTLETT, RUHL J. 1944 *The League to Enforce Peace.* Chapel Hill: Univ. of North Carolina Press.
CARR, EDWARD H. (1939) 1946 *The Twenty Years Crisis, 1919–1939: An Introduction to the Study of International Relations.* 2d ed. New York: Harper.
MITRANY, DAVID 1925 *The Problem of International Sanctions.* Oxford Univ. Press.
ROYAL INSTITUTE OF INTERNATIONAL AFFAIRS 1938 *International Sanctions: A Report by a Group of Members of the Royal Institute of International Affairs.* Oxford Univ. Press.
STIMSON, HENRY L.; and BUNDY, MCGEORGE 1948 *On Active Service in Peace and War.* 2 vols. New York: Harper.
THOMPSON, KENNETH W. 1960 *Political Realism and the Crisis of World Politics: An American Approach to Foreign Policy.* Princeton Univ. Press.
WOLFERS, ARNOLD (editor) 1959 *Alliance Policy in the Cold War.* Baltimore: Johns Hopkins Press.

COLLECTIVISM

See COMMUNISM; COMMUNISM, ECONOMIC ORGANIZATION OF; PLANNING, ECONOMIC, *article on* EASTERN EUROPE; SOCIALISM; UTOPIANISM.